ANTHOLOGIES
BY AND ABOUT
WOMEN

ANTHOLOGIES BY AND ABOUT WOMEN

An Analytical Index

Compiled by Susan Cardinale
With Jay Casey

GREENWOOD PRESS
WESTPORT, CONNECTICUT • LONDON, ENGLAND

Copyright Acknowledgments

Grateful acknowledgment is made to the following for permission to use copyrighted material.

Karyn Kay and Gerald Peary, eds., *Women and the Cinema: A Critical Anthology,* © 1977. Reprinted by permission of E. P. Dutton.

Richard C. Friedman, Ralph M. Richart, and Raymond L. Vande Weile, eds., *Sex Differences in Behavior,* © 1974. Reprinted by permission of John Wiley & Sons, Inc.

Alison Jaggar and Paula R. Struhl, eds., *Feminist Frameworks,* © 1977. Used with permission of McGraw-Hill Book Company.

Sandra S. Tangri, Martha T. S. Mednick, and Lois W. Hoffman, eds., *Women and Achievement,* © 1975. Reprinted by permission of Hemisphere Publishing Corporation.

Lois Beck and Nikki Keddie, eds., *Women in the Muslim World.* Reprinted by permission of Harvard University Press.

Bette Ann Stead, *Women in Management,* © 1978. Reprinted by permission of Prentice-Hall, Inc., Englewood Cliffs, New Jersey.

Lynne B. Iglitzin and Ruth Ross, eds., *Women in the World: A Comparative Study.* Reprinted by permission of ABC-Clio, Inc., Santa Barbara, California, © 1976.

Every reasonable effort has been made to trace the owners of copyright materials in this book, but in some instances this has proven impossible. The publisher will be glad to receive information leading to more complete acknowledgments in subsequent printings of the book, and in the meantime extend apologies for any omissions.

Library of Congress Cataloging in Publication Data

Cardinale, Susan.
Anthologies by and about women.

Bibliography: p.
Includes index.
1. Women—Indexes. I. Title.
HQ1111.C35 016.3054 81-13423
ISBN 0-313-22180-4 (lib. bdg.) AACR2

Library of Congress Catalog Card Number: 81-13423
ISBN: 0-313-22180-4

First published in 1982

Greenwood Press
A division of Congressional Information Service, Inc.
88 Post Road West
Westport, Connecticut 06881

Printed in the United States of America

10 9 8 7 6 5 4 3 2 1

CONTENTS

Acknowledgments *vii*
Introduction *ix*

1. ANTHOLOGIES: SUBJECT/GENRE INDEX 3

General and Interdisciplinary Collections 4
Feminism 5
Biography and Autobiography 6
General Literary Collections 6
Literary Criticism 7
Drama 7
Poetry 7
Fiction 7
Science Fiction 8
Art and Architecture 8
Film and Media 8
Philosophy 8
Religion 9
History: General Collections 9
Historical Source Collections 9
Work: Historical Collections 10
History and Area Studies 10
United States 10
Canada 11
Great Britain 12
Australia 12
Europe 12
Latin America 13
India 13

Middle East 13
Africa 14
Russia 14
China 14
Asia 14
Political Science, Public Policy, and Law 14
Sociology and Economics 15
Development 16
Anthropology, Folklore, and Cross-Cultural Studies 16
Work: Contemporary Studies 17
Sex Roles and Socialization 18
Language 19
Psychology and Biology 19
Psychoanalysis 20
Sex Differences 20
Health, Medicine, and Sexuality 21
Fertility and Contraception 21
Abortion 22
Education, General 22
Education, Higher 22
Women's Studies 23
Affirmative Action 23
Athletics 23
Black Women 23
Older Women 24
Children 24
Lesbianism 24
Crime 25

2. ANTHOLOGIES: TABLES OF CONTENTS 26

3. KEYWORD INDEX 184

4. CONTRIBUTOR INDEX 763

5. EDITOR INDEX 817

ACKNOWLEDGMENTS

A project of this magnitude necessarily depends on the indulgence, aid, and kindness of many people. Among those to whom I owe thanks are the students who enrolled in a women's studies course I taught in 1976. They encouraged me to take on the job and helped compile the list of anthologies which forms the core of this book. In addition, editors and publishers graciously offered prepublication information about forthcoming books or gave permission to reproduce the tables of contents of lengthy collections. Some sent review copies of volumes which were eventually included in the index. I am grateful to them all.

Other people helped in the tasks of typing and proofreading: Ellen Hursh, Lulu Hayman, Mary Biser, Bob Brunner, Karen Richardson, and Jim Mannerino are in this group. Thanks must go to Susan Grodsky, who helped design the subject index which was supplanted by the computerized Keyword Index. Frank Shulman offered valuable editorial suggestions for the introduction and, along with Barbara Levitz, helped improve the format. Hong-Jen Chen and Richard Oldakowski were central to the preparation of camera-ready copy.

Jay Casey created the computer programs for most of this book, collaborated with me on decisions about format, and guided me through the entire process. I thank him for the generous contribution of his time, for his tolerance of my efforts to comprehend the intricacies of his magical programs, and for his dogged insistence on perfection. His role in the shaping of this book cannot be overstated.

Finally, I wish to thank and dedicate this book to my husband Alan, who encouraged me when it loomed large, who facilitated the operation through his support, ingenuity, and wonderful humor, and who remains the inspiration for every task I undertake.

INTRODUCTION

SCOPE

One might ask, "Why compile an index to anthologies?" Those who have sought to verify or locate essays, short stories, or poetry in collections have discovered that, beyond the excellent *Essay and General Literature Index* (New York: Wilson, 1934-) and a few specialized subject indexes, the contents of most anthologies are fairly interred between their book covers. Because *Essay and General Literature Index* attempts to present material in several fields, its coverage is necessarily limited. And although the contents of anthologies are sometimes elaborated in notes on catalog cards, this practice is rare, and, in the case of lengthy collections, impractical. The Library of Congress has made subject subdivisions available for use in the cataloging of some collections (for example, Addresses, Essays, and Lectures; and Congresses, Collected Works, Literary Collections, and Sources). In cases where such a subdivision has been used, it has frequently been only as the tertiary heading under an often vague secondary heading such as Women—Social and Moral Questions. Finally, despite their inclusion in several fine women's studies bibliographies, the items within each collection are generally not accessible as separate pieces by subject and author. Thus the need for the present index—to serve as a guide to essays, stories, drama, and the like, which are not analyzed during the process of book cataloging, indexed in major reference tools, or listed as separate items in bibliographies.

All titles selected for inclusion in this index were published after the advent of the second great American "woman movement" which began in the early 1960s. Although most collections are new, several older volumes which were reissued during the 1960s and 1970s are also included. In addition, among the books analyzed are some historical collections which facilitated, for the first time, the wide dissemination of primary material. A complete listing of these titles appears in the Subject/Genre Index under the heading Historical Source Collections.

Most volumes in this index are obviously by or about women themselves; however, many address such issues of special concern to women as abortion, reproduction, sex roles, affirmative action, and the socialization of children. In addition, some peripheral collections are included because they contain a significant number of essays about women or about these issues, for example, *Philosophy and Sex* (1975) and *Perspectives on Human Sexuality* (1974).

Although there are fine collections about women which are based on special issues of journals like *Signs: Journal of Women in Culture and Society* and *Bucknell Review,* these titles are generally not included because their contents are accessible through periodical indexes. Because of space considerations, only works published in English or translated into English have been indexed.

The indexed anthologies vary in genre or type: poetry, fiction, drama, science fiction, biography, autobiography, reprint collections, literary criticism and other scholarly essays, primary historical material, and contemporary documents. They encompass a wide range of academic disciplines: history, psychology, political science, law, economics, sociology, literature, biology, anthropology, criminology, medicine and health, linguistics, art, architecture, education, folklore, philosophy, and religion. Within and across these fields, many subjects are covered in the collections—women's work, contemporary and historical; feminism, both theoretical and practical; sexuality from medical, academic, theological, and lay perspectives; religion, both from within and outside the formal institutional frameworks; sport, viewed by participants and observers; and cinema—the filmmakers, the actors, and the critics. The richness and scope of these subjects are evident in the initial broad index. This subject/genre listing supplements the Keyword Index discussed below.

ARRANGEMENT

This book provides access to anthologies in several ways. The first section, the Subject/Genre Index, is auxiliary to the Keyword Index. Book titles are listed here whenever several items in a collection pertain to a given subject or can be grouped according to genre: poetry, fiction, science fiction, and so on. Many titles appear under more than one category. This arrangement permits the location of book titles, as opposed to essay or short story titles, by subject or genre. Within these divisions, anthologies (including reprints) are grouped by date of publication.

The second section, Anthologies: Tables of Contents, reproduces the table of contents of each collection. Arrangement is alphabetical by book title. The reproduction of contents not only places the items within each anthology in context, but also enables researchers to identify individual

pieces when only a few words are known. Below the bibliographical information for each book, the abbreviated titles of essays, stories, or plays are listed with authors' surnames and first initials, as well as with inclusive pagination. Because of the large number of items indexed in this book, pagination has been inferred from the tables of contents. A few collections were examined while still in press when page numbers were temporary and, therefore, potentially inaccurate. The pagination of these books is omitted. In the case of fiction, complete titles, including articles, are listed. Nonfiction essays have been edited so that initial articles and extraneous phrases are omitted (except for well-known essays which are recognized by such phrases). Because both pagination and titles are approximate, this section should not be used for purposes of bibliographic citation, but rather for locating and identifying items within anthologies. Similarly, because it has not been possible to print in full the tables of contents of lengthy documentary and poetry collections, annotations instead describe their contents. Within each annotation, all contributors are listed. The names of these authors are included in the Contributor Index. Accent marks in contributors' names appear only in the Anthologies: Tables of Contents section and the Contributor Index.

The third section is the Keyword Index. Here important words from essay, short story, or play titles are first extracted, then placed in context with references to the anthologies in which they appear. Most articles, pronouns, and other commonly used words, for example, "women" and "female," are omitted from the Keyword Index; however, some terms which do appear often, like "sex," are included. These words are modified in order to obviate reading through an otherwise lengthy list of titles. For example, titles which contain the word "sex" are divided into several categories in order that finer distinctions can be specified, such as "sex—intelligence." This dyad indicates that the word "sex" and the word "intelligence" are coupled in an essay, story, or poem title. In addition, some multiword phrases are listed in this index: women's studies, affirmative action, and Equal Rights Amendment, for example. These entries typically appear as compound terms; their inclusion, therefore, should facilitate use of the index.

The fourth section lists contributors or authors of individual pieces. Beside the name of each author are numbers keyed to the titles of the books in which her or his work appears. When alternative names are known, cross-references are included, for example, from H.D. to Hilda Doolittle. There are also cross-references in the cases where authors' names are known to differ among various publications. Editors have been omitted in this section unless they have written particularly lengthy introductions (over twenty-five pages) or distinctively titled introductory essays. Unsigned bibliographies and other sorts of appendices are assumed to have been

compiled by the editors of the anthologies, and entries have not been made for these items. In general, the names of authors are listed as they appear in the tables of contents of the books. Whenever possible, alphabetization of author entries is based on common practice in the country of origin.

The final section lists the editors or compilers of the anthologies along with numbers keyed to the titles of the books for which they are responsible. Complete entries, with full first and middle names, comprise this index.

The remainder of this introduction will discuss the publication histories of the analyzed collections by topic. It is an attempt to record similarities among the anthologies, as well as to note trends in women's studies research during the past fifteen years. Short titles will be used throughout this discussion in order to minimize the awkwardness which is inevitable during the course of citing many bibliographical references. Complete book titles appear in the second section of this book.

BIOGRAPHY AND AUTOBIOGRAPHY

Biographical collections began to proliferate during the mid-seventies. In fact, seven of the thirteen indexed collections were published between 1974 and 1977. Of the thirteen, six present historical material, one is a collection of critical essays (*Women's Autobiography,* 1980), one contains biographical pieces by American women writers (*The Writer on Her Work*, 1980), one offers personal narratives by anthropologists (*Women in the Field,* 1970), one discusses Mormon women (*Sister Saints*, 1978), and one includes journals of literary women (*Revelations,* 1974). *These Modern Women* (1978), edited with commentary by Elaine Showalter, reproduces some of the documents originally reprinted in *Fragments of Autobiography* (1974). These pieces were solicited by the magazine *The Nation* during the 1920s from women who were asked to discuss how their feminist ideals had survived the pressures of their female role. This anthology is typical of most of the biographical material insofar as it focuses on the lives of exceptional women. There is considerable personal narrative by and about lesser-known women in some of the general collections listed. Additional accounts of this sort are available in anthologies which are not indexed in this book, for example, *Jewish Grandmothers* (Boston: Beacon Press, 1978) and *Middle Eastern Muslim Women Speak* (Austin: University of Texas Press, 1977). These collections demonstrate the importance of examining the lives of obscure women who have generally escaped the purview of traditional scholarship. Such an examination tends either to point to striking similarities in the patterns of women's lives across class and culture, or to balance distorted conclusions drawn from work primarily about the lives of "interesting," that is, upper class, women.

LITERATURE

Anthologies published early in the development of women's studies reflect concern with the literary curriculum (*A Case for Equity and Women's Liberation and Literature*, both 1971; and *Female Studies IX*, 1972), or they discuss the stereotypical portrayal of women in literature (*Images of Women in Fiction*, 1972). In fact, several of the collections are organized according to character type (*The Feminine Image in Literature*, 1973; *A House of Good Proportion*, 1973; and *Images of Women in Literature*, 1973, 1977). This approach is buttressed by a methodological rationale in a later anthology, *Who Am I This Time?* (1976), in which Carol Pearson and Katherine Pope employ a typology of female characters akin to literary critic Northrup Frye's classifications of myth and archetypal symbols.

Although Samuel Kostman uses the same principle of organization for *Women of Valor* (1978), his selections depict women only in positive ways—they are women of "courage," "devotion," and "principle." Likewise, *Women: An Affirmation*, published in 1979, offers strong female protagonists. Both of these anthologies present material from several literary genres—even the folktale, in the case of the latter book. Together they might be viewed as a natural development in the publication of women's studies literary collections. They are in the "character type" tradition, but they both emphasize admirable heroines. As Elaine Showalter has suggested, the study of female images in literature might well be appropriate "for the classroom where it raises consciousness."[1] Within this setting the positive portrayal of females permits the instructor to move beyond consciousness-raising to the presentation of female role models.

While the cataloging of character types may be appropriate as a pedagogical technique, it seems less useful as a methodology for the literary critic. Many critics have gone beyond this approach to the study of female characters as, for example, projections of male pathologies or participants in female cultures or communities. Although many other trends are evident in the critical collections indexed, perhaps three are salient: (1) nearly universal repudiation of the formalist tradition—the new critics are unabashedly looking at the social, historical, and psychological contexts of their subjects' creative activity; (2) increasing attention to work by, rather than about, women; and (3) greater, and more significant, participation by women in the criticism of women writers.

Most of the critical work included in these anthologies is concerned with English or American literature. Among the exceptions: *Contemporary French Women Poets* (1977), which presents and discusses work by Thérèse Plantier, Andrée Chedid, Annie Salager, Marie Françoise Prager, Yvonne Caroutch, and Denise Grappe; *Latin American Women Writers* (1977),

selected proceedings of a conference sponsored by the *Latin American Literary Review; Female Studies IX* (1975), prepared under the aegis of the Modern Language Association's Commission on the Status of Women, which examines work in German, French, Spanish, and Russian literatures; *Women Writing and Writing About Women* (1979), which contains work about nineteenth- and twentieth-century writers of several countries; and *Sturdy Black Bridges* (1979), which includes pieces by and about African, Latin American, and Caribbean writers. It should be noted that although most of the criticism is, in one way or another, feminist in its conception, some essays have been published together only because they are about women, for example, *Seven American Women Writers of the 20th Century* (1977).

Although stories about women are often included, most of the fiction collections concentrate on work by women. But fiction about both sexes comprises the basic content of two collections: *Women and Men, Men and Women* (1975) and *Women and Men Together* (1978). The publication of these anthologies in the latter half of the decade is not altogether surprising because a growing interest in the relationship between the sexes has recently been an active area of women's studies scholarship. The exploration of ways in which power exchanges occur between men and women is generally considered to be a fairly sophisticated stage in the study of women's roles in society. This approach might well be compared to an earlier one—the gathering of work by the "gentle sex" in several anthologies published by Lothrop, Lee, and Shepard beginning in the early 1970s. These collections, still in print at this writing, include fantasy, horror, and mystery stories. Their appearance reconfirms an antique idea that the woman writer's proper sphere is popular fiction. Only two collections in this series are included: *Ladies of the Gothics* (1975) and *Grande Dames of Detection* (1973).

The remaining anthologies do not collectively form a trend. One book presents stories by and about black women (*Black-Eyed Susans,* 1977); one is a collection of tales of women alone (*Solo,* 1977); one includes stories about work (*The World Outside,* 1978); one offers the work of Third World women (*Fragment of a Lost Diary,* 1973); one, *Women and Fiction 2* (1978), an international anthology, contains stories by nineteenth- and twentieth-century writers; and one is simply a collection of stories by modern English writers (*Women Writing,* 1979). Perhaps the most unusual of this group is an anthology which portrays women as the dominant sex in stories by authors as disparate as Herodotus and Booth Tarkington (*When Women Rule,* 1972).

Nearly all of the poetry anthologies included represent regional or national, rather than topical, divisions. Only *Tangled Vines* (1978) is

oriented to a subject, the mother-daughter relationship, while *The Other Voice* (1976) is directed to an appreciation of Third World women of many cultures. Three collections focus on the robust Anglo-American literary tradition—*The Women Poets in English* (1972), *The World Split Open* (1974), and *Salt and Bitter and Good* (1975). Seven reproduce the work of primarily American and Canadian poets: *Mountain Moving Day* (1973), *Psyche* (1973), *We Become New* (1975), *I Hear My Sisters Saying* (1976), *Tangled Vines* (1978), and *Women Poets of the West, 1850-1950* (1978). Two books edited by Kenneth Rexroth anthologize East Asian poets, namely, *The Burning Heart* (1977) (Japanese) and *The Orchid Boat* (1972) (Chinese). And the poetry of six French women is preserved in *Contemporary French Women Poets* (1977).

The three drama collections include plays by and about women (*Plays By and About Women,* 1973), plays in which women are protagonists (*Women in Drama,* 1975), and plays by contemporary American women (*The New Women's Theatre,* 1977). Again, as in other areas, there is a trend toward examining women as creators in addition to merely studying female characters. Of the playwrights represented in these books, the works of Ibsen and Shaw are most often excerpted in other women's studies collections. Of the new women dramatists, Myrna Lamb, Megan Terry, and Honor Moore continue to appear in the literature. And Alice Childress is becoming a major voice among contemporary black writers. Most striking perhaps is the versatility of the new female dramatists: many work in several genres—poetry, drama, and the short story. They are collectively worthy successors to Lillian Hellman and Doris Lessing, versatile writers whose dramatic works also appear in these anthologies.

Two of the four science fiction collections indexed were edited by Pamela Sargent (*Women of Wonder,* 1974 and *More Women of Wonder,* 1976). She is also responsible, together with Joanna Russ, for much of the feminist analysis of this genre which has been done thus far. Science fiction seems most propitious for women writers. As Sargent suggests in her introduction to *Women of Wonder,* "Science fiction provides women with possible scenarios for their own future development. It can explore what we might become if and when the present restrictions on our lives vanish, or show us new problems and restrictions that might arise."[2]

THE FINE ARTS

Two anthologies are concerned with women and art: *Woman as Sex Object* (1972) contains essays about women as depicted in erotic art by Ingres, Fuseli, Courbet, Manet, Montaut, Picasso, and other artists. *Art and Sexual Politics* (1973) focuses on women artists. It poses the

question, "Why have there been no great women artists?" Pieces by Elaine de Kooning, Louise Nevelson, Bridget Riley, and other women are included. Two anthologies are about women and architecture, *Women in American Architecture* (1977) and *New Space for Women* (1980). Among their contents are essays about the past contributions of female architects, the Woman's Building competition, architectural critics, domestic space, women in suburbia, and the status of women in the profession.

Two anthologies contain essays about women and film: *Women and the Cinema* (1977) and *Sexual Strategems* (1979). Although the earlier volume is subtitled "A Critical Anthology," it includes autobiographical pieces by Colette, Yoko Ono, and Greta Garbo, as well as interviews with Dorothy Arzner, Ida Lupino, Jane Fonda, Lina Wertmuller, and several British "cine-feminists." In addition, there are critical essays about actresses, female filmmakers, and cinematic art. *Sexual Strategems,* in turn, focuses on film images of women and on both male and female directors. Among the filmmakers discussed are Leni Riefenstahl, Mai Zetterling, Dorothy Arzner, Germaine Dulac, Alice Guy-Blaché, Lina Wertmuller, Jean Luc Godard, Ingmar Bergman, and Kenji Mizoguchi. A third volume, *Sexism and Youth* (1974), is not about the cinema but does include several essays about educational films and the television program "Sesame Street."

Hearth and Home (1978) presents a variety of essays about women in both print and nonprint media—television advertising and programming, journalism, and popular magazines. Its contributors discuss the status of women in media; the portrayal of females in movies, on TV, and in print, and the relationship of cultural values to dominant modes of communication.

HISTORY

A few of the historical anthologies are organized around particular time periods—*The Nineteenth-Century Woman* (1978), *Woman in the 18th Century* (1976), and *The Role of Women in the Middle Ages* (1975). Others are oriented to a population group. For example, *Damned Art* (1977) is concerned with witches in Europe, *Socialist Women* (1978) is about European socialist feminists, and *The Factory Girls* (1977) and *Women of Lowell* (1974) both present material about the Lowell, Massachusetts millworkers. Some collections are topical in their focus: *The Physician and Child Rearing* (1972) and *Abortion in Nineteenth-Century America* (1974). Nevertheless, most of the anthologies indexed in this book are fairly easily grouped by geographical area. They are combined with nonhistorical collections in the History/Area Studies sections in the Subject/Genre Index. Area Studies includes literary and general anthologies, as well as social science collections, so that persons interested in interdisciplinary research can readily locate material of like geographical orientation.

A large proportion of the historical material is documentary. These forty-odd collections are listed separately under Historical Source Collections. Arno Press issued some of these books as part of three series: Medicine and Society in America, Women in America from Colonial Times to the Twentieth Century, and Sex, Marriage, and Society. The Arno Press collections cited were published between 1972 and 1974. Like most of the source collections indexed, they are about issues in North American history.

Several collections contain documents relevant to the cross-cultural study of women's history. *Women From the Greeks to the French Revolution* (1973) contains selections primarily of European origin that are reflective of the cultural tradition of the West; *This Great Argument* (1972) excerpts both feminist and misogynic writings from Hesiod to Gunnar Myrdal; *Unsung Champions of Women* (1975) includes work by writers such as Bachofen, Plato, the Marquis de Condorcet, and Herbert Spencer; and *History of Ideas on Women* and *Toward Women* (both 1977) also reprint works primarily by noted male writers (see PHILOSOPHY below). *Philosophy of Woman* (1978) combines classical with modern, as well as primary with secondary, material; *Three Pamphlets on the Jacobean Antifeminist Controversy* (1978) contains three esoteric seventeenth-century tracts; and *Women in Latin American History* (1976) consists of writing by a diverse group of mostly twentieth-century Latin American women. The recent imprints of these collections indicate a salutary trend toward the publication of non-American primary material. (See also *Distaves and Dames: Renaissance Treatises For and About Women,* 1978, and *European Women: A Documentary History, 1789-1945*, as well as new essay collections entitled *Women, War, and Revolution; Beyond Their Sex: Learned Women of the European Past,* and *Affairs of the Mind,* all 1980.)

ANTHROPOLOGY, DEVELOPMENT, AND CROSS-CULTURAL STUDIES

In addition to the standard academic anthropological studies, there are three collections in this group which are unique: *Women in the Field* (1970), autobiograpical accounts of fieldwork by female anthropologists, and *Women and Folklore* (1975) and *Women in Ritual and Symbolic Roles* (1978), both of which report customs, tales, and behavior of women of several cultures. The other collections focus on a variety of issues including spheres of activity, status, the political participation of women, sex roles, and fertility. All told over thirty such anthologies are included in this index. Two collections have African women as their exclusive subject: *Women of Tropical Africa* (1963) and *Women in Africa* (1976). Others center on

North African, as well as Middle Eastern, women: *Women in the Muslim World* (1978) and *Women's Status and Fertility in the Muslim World* (1978). There are a number of nonfiction collections which address the position of women in many Third World countries, including Asian and aboriginal cultures. See, for example, *Women and Colonization* (1979) and *A World of Women, Women and Society,* and *Comparative Perspectives of Third World Women* (all 1980). Anthropologists are clearly producing a body of scholarship which is in the vanguard both with regard to methodology—women's historians are particularly interested in anthropological approaches—and subject: the structural bases of relationships between the sexes in society. Finally, anthropologists are actively investigating conditions in Third World countries—long a subject of vital concern to radical feminists, though, unfortunately, unexplored by many researchers in other disciplines.

SOCIOLOGY, ECONOMICS, AND SEX-ROLE SOCIALIZATION

A large proportion of the research on women asks questions about the social context of relations between the sexes. But some investigators instead seek information about how women function in society; under what conditions their status changes; how class, sex, and race interact to determine the roles which women assume; how societal attitudes and socioeconomic exigencies force women into low-status occupations; and how social institutions like marriage and the family change with changes in women's status and self-perceptions. Because the social and economic factors which contribute to change are so tightly interwoven, many anthologies include work by different sorts of social scientists—social psychologists, sociologists, economists, and anthropologists. Thus it seems appropriate to consider the interdisciplinary collections which explore women's socioeconomic status in one section.

Much of this work concerns the relation between the public and private lives of women. One link is the notion of sex role, a ubiquitous idea which provides a superstructure for familial, as well as occupational, division of labor. Nearly sixty books contain at least several essays about the socialization of women for sex roles or the effects of sex-role stereotypes. See PSYCHOLOGY and EDUCATION (below) for further discussion of this research.

Nearly fifty books are listed under Sociology and Economics. They have appeared with increasing frequency since the early 1960s. Among them are books which are geographically oriented—to China, Africa, the United States, India, Latin America, Canada, the Soviet Union and/or Russia, and the Third World. Some address issues of policy: employment, child

care, and development. Many contain essays about topics which have concerned social scientists for some time: social stratification, sex roles, labor force participation, and the impact of modernization on developing societies. The primary differences between current and traditional research are (1) a focus on women's problems in particular; (2) a recognition of the commonalities among women across cultures, races, and classes; and (3) a cognizance of the inadequacy of older theories and paradigms to account for women's position in society. The topics covered in these anthologies vary widely—minority-group characteristics of women, female ambivalence about career and family roles, sex segregation in the marketplace, changing notions of masculinity and femininity, myths about women workers, participation of married women in the labor force, characteristics of female-headed households, the relationship of women's fertility to education, work, and status, and the impact of capitalism on job segmentation.

PSYCHOLOGY

For some time feminist psychologists have been challenging what they consider to be an intransigent antifemale bias in psychological research. This bias has been noted not only in major psychological and psychoanalytical theories which have long been given credence by practitioners and experimentalists, but also in the selection of methodologies and subjects, topics of study, choice of research questions, and interpretation of results. Perhaps most significantly, feminist psychologists have suggested that insistence upon use of the experimental method, the bedrock of the discipline, may preclude legitimization of much important work on women.[3] Because this method usually requires the study of behavior in a laboratory setting, psychological processes are examined outside their social contexts. Research which takes into account the environments, attitudes, and social expectations that complicate these processes—in short, the sort of research which seems most revealing of bias toward females—is often viewed as less rigorous, and thus less important, than traditional experimentation.

Initially feminist psychologists countered traditional approaches by reevaluating classic articles, pointing out omissions and faults in experimental methods and analyses. In particular, critiques addressed research on women's sexuality, feminine personality, gender differences, and sex roles. Increasingly, revisionist work has been superseded by new research, both empirical and theoretical, which focuses on issues of special interest to women (for example, gender identity, biosocial aspects of reproduction, achievement motivation, role strain, adult female development, the relationship of communication styles to status, and factors which contribute to the maintenance of sex roles). There are over thirty anthologies listed under

Biology and Psychology in the Subject/Genre Index. Together they reflect these changes in focus and demonstrate the breadth of interest in gender issues. The large number of collections which are about sex differences (many published during the last five years) belie the contention of some feminist psychologists that this field is waning in popularity.

Finally, most of the collections which focus solely on psychoanalysis and therapy were published during the early 1970s. It is tempting to speculate that Juliet Mitchell's monumental *Psychoanalysis and Feminism* (1974), so controversial when it first appeared because of Mitchell's interpretation of Freudian psychology as descriptive rather than prescriptive, might have had the effect of discouraging discussion about women and psychoanalysis. To be sure, of the three indexed collections published after 1974, the psychoanalytically oriented essays are in two cases mostly reprinted material by Freud, Mead, Horney, Erikson, Deutsch, and Klein. Only *Female Psychology: Contemporary Psychoanalytic Views* (1977) presents entirely new work in the area.

SEXUALITY, MEDICINE, AND HEALTH

Complaints about women's health care in nineteenth-century and contemporary America bear striking resemblance. In both periods, women expressed a distrust of the predominantly male medical establishment. In addition, the conspicuous absence of women in the upper echelons of the medical hierarchy was, and continues to be, a source of consternation for women involved with health care. Women of both centuries complained of the paternalistic attitudes of many male physicians, and they regretted being isolated from other women during treatment and rehabilitation. Finally, there is some support for the contention that in both centuries, women have been victims of unnecessary surgery and medical experimentation.[4]

It is interesting to note how these similarities relate to the publication history of anthologies about women's health and sexuality. During the 1960s and early 1970s, authorities offered opinions about issues of female health from the perspectives of different disciplines. This type of essay prevailed particularly in the early literature about abortion: theologians, attorneys, psychiatrists, social scientists, and physicians (mostly male) expressed professional, and by implication, authoritative views of the abortion issue. By the mid-seventies, an interest in the historical antecedents of current health problems was reflected in the publication of several source collections, part of the Arno Press series, Medicine and Society in America.

Throughout the latter part of the decade, there was a gradual shift toward the publication of both lay and academic, rather than medical, views of professional health care (*Seizing Our Bodies,* 1977; *Women, Sexuality and*

Social Control, 1978; *Sexual and Reproductive Aspects of Women's Health Care,* 1978; *Women Look at Biology Looking at Women,* 1979; and *Psychology of Women: Selected Readings,* 1979). Many of these articles are distinctly critical of the medical profession. There has also been a clear tendency of late to attend to the uniquely female problems of certain populations: older women, mentally ill mothers, alcoholic women, working women, and anorexics. This progression from the domination of the literature by traditional professional opinion, to rediscovery of historical views of women's health issues, and to the partial co-opting of the literature by revisionist professionals and persons outside the medical establishment, is indeed remarkable. It seems to signal the impact of the popular women's health movement.

A change in theoretical orientation toward the subject matter is similarly striking. For example, in comparing two books by professionals about female sexuality, *Female Sexuality: New Psychoanalytic Views* (1970) and *Women: Body and Culture* (1976), one notes that in the former there is a preoccupation with phenomena like narcissism, the Oedipus complex, penis envy, and feminine guilt. In the latter collection, contributors either reach beyond traditional psychoanalytical explanations for female pathologies, or they address "new" issues like homosexuality in women, development of female gender identification, midlife sexual activity, clitoral eroticism, and female masturbation. These are the very issues upon which many activists in the women's health movement place emphasis. Along with other recent literature, these essays provide evidence of a willingness on the part of some professionals to regard female sexuality at last from the vantage of women. And they indicate the degree to which issues of health care are no longer solely the province of professional medical journals; indeed, they are also being discussed at length in the women's studies literature.

EDUCATION

Anthologies about education have been published with regularity during the last decade. There has been some interest in the history of women's education (*The Educated Woman in America*, 1965); however, most of the work published in anthologies concerns the problems of academic women (*Women in Academia,* 1975, *Women on Campus,* 1975, *Women and the Power to Change,* 1975, and *The Higher Education of Women,* 1978); sex role stereotypes in textbooks and bias in the school curriculum (*Sexism and Youth,* 1974, *Sex Bias in the Schools,* 1977, and *Perspectives on Non-Sexist Early Childhood Education,* 1978); and equality of opportunity (*A Case for Equity,* 1971, *Academic Women on the Move,* 1973, *Reverse Discrimination,* 1977, and *Women and Educational Leadership,* 1980). Among the other topics covered in these collections are the survival and desirability of

female colleges, the status of women educators, alternative methods of socializing both sexes in schools, the influence of television and toys in the learning process, bias in college admissions, educational testing, the pedagogy of women's studies, and special problems of black women in educational institutions.

PHILOSOPHY AND RELIGION

A surprising amount of work has been done by philosophers in the area of women's studies. Indeed, many scholars in other disciplines seem unaware that phenomenological philosophers are reconceptualizing moral categories and offering new ways of looking at the world which explain and often support feminist theory. These people are interested in systematically analyzing abstract notions like discrimination, sexual equality, and oppression, as well as current beliefs about sex, love, marriage, rape, and sex roles. In addition, philosophers are providing theoretical frameworks for understanding abortion and the preferential treatment of minorities. The premise upon which these scholars base their work is this: it is essential that we understand the deeper meanings of our ideas, and that we define precisely the injustices we perceive so that we can better resolve the problems inherent in the structure of our society. Clearly the gathering and analysis of data are important, but feminist philosophers go a step further—to the critical analysis of assumptions which underlie empirical enquiry. The collections which contain philosophical essays of this kind are *Philosophy and Sex* (1975), *Women and Philosophy* (1976), *Feminism and Philosophy* (1977), *Sex Equality* (1977), and *Philosophy and Women* (1979).

Another type of philosophical anthology has been published as well. It presents views of women—frequently misogynic and overwhelmingly male—written by prominent thinkers. The indexed books of this sort are *Toward Women* (1977), a collection of philosophical tracts by classical writers like Pythagoras, Plutarch, Epictetus, Galen, Lucian, and Cicero; *History of Ideas on Women* (1977), a book which includes the writings of Aristotle, Augustine, Rousseau, Schopenhauer, Nietzsche, and Freud, as well as works by Plato, Mill, Russell, de Beauvoir, and Marcuse; and *Philosophy of Woman* (1978), an anthology which combines pieces by such well-known philosophers as Hume, Kant, and Kierkegaard with contemporary feminist scholarship. While some might argue that the proper focus of women's studies is work by women, not antifeminist treatises by men, it is well to read such writings on occasion in order to appreciate the degree to which relations between the sexes have captured the philosophical imagination throughout history. Indeed, while most students have read standard texts of the great male thinkers, few are aware that most of them have felt impelled to devote some time to "the woman question."

The related area of religious studies has also received considerable attention during the past decade. Nine anthologies concern the allegedly endemic sexism of Western religious institutions, new possibilities for the participation of women in traditional religions, or cultural constructs born of religious dogma. Among the books listed are: *Sister Saints* (1978), biographical articles about Mormon women; *The Jewish Woman: New Perspectives* (1976), a motley collection of essays about the conflicting roles and images of women in Hebrew rituals and texts; and *Women of Spirit* (1979), a group of writings not only about individuals, but also about the participation of women in the development of religious institutions throughout history. Scholars in this area, as in other fields, seem to be moving from either a consideration of traditional female images or the oppression of women, to the discovery and analysis of women's substantive contributions, including new religious forms. (See *Womanspirit Rising,* 1979.)

SPECIAL POPULATIONS

Contemporary feminists have the curious distinction of being spokespeople for a majority population which has the earmarks of a minority group.[5] Traditionally they tend to empathize with groups who are unable to exercise certain rights because of popular bias or lack of power. Several anthologies have been compiled about these groups: black women, children, female victims of crime, older women, and lesbians.

Although a good deal of material by and about lesbians appears in these collections, only two are exclusively about homosexuals, *Lesbianism and the Women's Movement* (1975) and *After You're Out* (1976). They address the issues of "coming out," lesbian lifestyles, lesbianism vis-à-vis feminism, monogamy, bisexuality, acceptance by heterosexuals, homosexual parenthood, and the legal status of gays. *After You're Out* includes essays by homosexual men as well as lesbians.

The anthologies which are about children's issues generally discuss problems of socialization, care, and education. Considerable attention is given to the dilemma of working mothers, to society's responsibility for child care, and to the changing roles of parents (*Family Issues of Employed Women*, 1971; *Working Mothers*, 1974; *Women and Children in Contemporary Society*, 1976; *Child Care and Public Policy*, 1978; *Working Women and Families*, 1979; and *Women, Work and Family, 1978*). Some collections concern the perpetuation of traditional sex roles in the schools and in textbooks: *Sexism and Youth* (1974), *Sex Bias in the Schools* (1977), and *Perspectives on Non-Sexist Early Childhood Education* (1978). One reprints two guidebooks on child care for mothers written by nineteenth-century physicians (*The Physician and Child-Rearing,* 1971).

Four victimized groups are currently the focus of much public attention, due in large measure to feminist activity on their behalf: prostitutes, sexually abused children, battered women, and victims of rape. There are essays about one or more of these groups in *Forcible Rape* (1977), *The Victimization of Women* (1978), *The Prostitute and the Social Reformer* (1974), *Women, Sexuality and Social Control* (1978), and *The Criminology of Deviant Women* (1979).

A group which has been neglected, and disparaged in perhaps more subtle ways, is older women. Two collections discuss their situation, *No Longer Young* (1974) and *Looking Ahead* (1977). Among the topics covered in these volumes are: myths of aging, retirement dilemmas, self-concept, voluntarism, continuing education, sexuality, loneliness, friendship, and psychotherapy. *Psychology of Women: Selected Readings* (1979) also contains several articles about women and aging. Additional essays are included in many of the other anthologies.

Black women are said to be doubly disadvantaged—by their race and by their sex. It was not until the 1970s that the unique experience of this group was indirectly recognized through the publication of some of their creative work: *The Black Woman* (1970), an anthology of poetry, short stories, essays, and documents; *Keeping the Faith* (1974), a compilation of poetry, autobiography, and fiction; *Black-Eyed Susans* (1975), stories by and about black women written by prominent writers like Toni Morrison, Gwendolyn Brooks, and Alice Walker; and *Sturdy Black Bridges* (1979), a book which includes poetry, fiction, criticism, and interviews about and by African and Caribbean, as well as American, blacks.

During the 1970s two historical documentary collections also appeared, *Black Women in White America* (1973) and *Black Women in Nineteenth-Century American Life* (1976). They include the writings of figures like the Grimké sisters, Harriet Tubman, Mary McLeod Bethune, Nannie Burroughs, Frances Ellen Watkins Harper, and Frances Jackson Coppin. Several books about sexual/racial discrimination have also been published recently—*Social Justice and Preferential Treatment* (1977), *Women, Minorities and Employment Discrimination* (1977), *Conference on the Educational and Occupational Needs of Black Women (Proceedings)* (1978), and *Race, Sex and Policy Problems* (1979). The latter book is especially useful for its articles about the unique problems of contemporary black women in America. Although some historical research about black women appears in other anthologies, only one collection of secondary material is oriented solely to this group: *The Afro-American Woman* (1978). It contains articles about black female workers, blues singers, educators, politicians, and poetical images of black women. Work in this area should be forthcoming as researchers discover more primary material by and about black women.

POWER

Many feminists like Kate Millett have long held that the personal is political and that understanding power relationships between the sexes is principal to feminist analysis. Although many articles address these complex relationships, a few may be said to focus on power more directly. Anthologies discussed in this section are about power—physical power (athletics), the power of communication (language), power deriving from legislation and adjudication (law), and power which accrues formally to stronger, rather than weaker groups in the public sector (politics).

Four of these books published during the 1970s are about sport: *Women and Sport* (1972), *Women's Athletics* (1974), *Equality in Sport for Women* (1977), and *Out of the Bleachers* (1979). Essays deal with performance, body image, aggression, motivation, training, biomechanics, the Olympics, female spectators, equal opportunity, sex stereotyping, and sociology of sport. Researchers are exploring ways not only for encouraging women to compete in sports, but also for combatting institutionalized discrimination and popular bias against female fitness.

Both verbal and nonverbal communication are topics of interest to women's studies researchers in psychology, sociology, and communications. Four collections include essays about sexual differences in this area as well as in children's speech, sexism in language (including dictionaries and texts), English usage in different contexts, regional and ethnic differences in speech, fluency and pitch of women's speech, and prose styles of women writers. They are *Sexism and Language* (1977), *Language and Sex* (1978), *The Sociology of the Languages of American Women* (1978), and *Women's Language and Style* (1978). Although most of this work is basic research, there is little doubt that with information about how power is articulated through language, women can apply this knowledge and make changes to their advantage in personal styles of communication.

The largely political collections (apart from the many interdisciplinary ones listed under Feminism in the Subject/Genre Index) are typically theoretical, policy-oriented, or about the study of women's political participation. The theoretical anthologies are *Feminism and Socialism* (1972), *Feminism and Materialism* (1978), and *Capitalist Patriarchy* (1978, 1979). All three present Marxist-feminist perspectives toward issues such as matriarchy, the oppression of women and minorities, consumption, structures of capitalism, the division of labor, reproduction, modes of production, and revolutionary strategy. The policy-oriented books are *Economic Independence for Women* (1976), *Women Into Wives* (1977), *The Victimization of Women* (1978), and *Working Women and Families* (1979)—all four of which are volumes in the Sage Yearbooks in Women's Policy Studies series—also, *Women and the Workplace* (1976), *Women, Minorities and Employment Discrimination* (1977), *Child Care and Public*

Policy (1978), *Women Working* (1978), *Women, Work and Family* (1978), and *Race, Sex and Policy Problems* (1979). Finally, several books are about women's participation in the political system, notably, *Women in Politics* (1974), *A Portrait of Marginality* (1977), *The Role of Women in Conflict and Peace* (1977), *Women in the Labour Movement* (1977), *Women in the Courts* (1978), and *Women and Organizing* (1979).

CONCLUSION

In addition to the anthologies described above, more than forty are listed in the Work: Contemporary Studies category, while thirteen are historical studies of work or collections of primary documents about women workers, for example, *Women of Lowell* (1974) and *The Factory Girls* (1977). There are also nearly forty books listed under Feminism. Of course, it is inaccurate to conclude that the other volumes indexed in this book are not feminist in philosophy or spirit; rather, these collections are placed in this category because they are primarily about feminist theory or the history of feminism, or because they contain documents from the women's movements of the nineteenth or twentieth centuries. Like many other collections indexed in this book, they evidence a tendency toward material about women's contributions, rather than their past oppression; about the power relationships between the sexes; about suggestions for policy change which will ameliorate women's status; and about the unique ways in which women interact in female communities to preserve their special culture and reinforce their strong qualities. These complex themes are present in many of the anthologies indexed here. They seem to signal maturity in the formal discipline of women's studies, as well as a dovetailing of the interests of feminist scholars and political activists. This convergence is surely a healthy sign.

Susan Cardinale
College Park, Maryland

NOTES

1. Elaine Showalter, "Review Essay: Literary Criticism," *Signs* 2, no. 1 (Winter 1975): 452.

2. Pamela Sargent, ed., *Women of Wonder: Science Fiction Stories by Women About Women* (New York: Vintage Books, 1975).

3. Mary Brown Parlee, "Psychology and Women," *Signs* 5, no. 1 (Autumn 1979): 121-133.

4. For a discussion of women and nineteenth-century American medicine, *see* G. J. Barker-Benfield's *The Horrors of the Half-Known Life: Male Attitudes Toward Women and Sexuality in Nineteenth-Century America* (New York: Harper,

1976), Ann Douglas Wood's "The Fashionable Diseases: Women's Complaints and Their Treatment in Nineteenth-Century America," and Rita Morantz's "The Lady and Her Physician," both in *Clio's Consciousness Raised,* edited by Mary S. Hartman and Lois W. Banner (New York: Harper Torchbooks, 1974). *See also* Kathryn Kish Sklar's discussion of the communal atmosphere of the water cure establishments as a viable alternative to women's isolation during recuperation in "Protective Customs, 1855," in *Catherine Beecher: A Study in Domesticity* (New Haven: Yale University Press, 1973). In addition, Regina Morantz notes the opportunity to fraternize that the nineteenth-century health reform movement provided women in "Making Women Modern: Middle Class Women and Health Reform in 19th-Century America," *Journal of Social History* 10, no. 4 (Summer 1977): 490-507.

In *The Yellow Wallpaper* (New York: The Feminist Press, 1973, c1899), Charlotte Perkins Gilman presented a fictionalized account of physician S. Weir Mitchell's famous rest cure treatment, a technique which allegedly made temporary invalids of many women. (On occasion it was also used in treating men.) For opinions about the male medical establishment from female physicians, see Elizabeth Blackwell's *Pioneer Work in Opening the Medical Profession to Women* (New York: Longmans, Green, 1895) or Harriot K. Hunt's *Glances and Glimpses: Or, Fifty Years Social, Including Twenty Years Professional Life* (Boston: John P. Jewett, 1856).

Sheryl B. Ruzek offers a comprehensive account of the contemporary movement in *The Women's Health Movement: Feminist Alternatives to Medical Control* (New York: Praeger, 1978). Articles about the movement appear in *Seizing Our Bodies: The Politics of Women's Health,* edited by Claudia Dreifuss (New York: Vintage Books, 1978). In particular, note "A Case of Corporate Malpractice and the Dalkon Shield," by Mark Dowie and Tracey Johnson, about a successfully marketed, though dangerous, intrauterine device; "What Medical Students Learn About Women," by Kay Weiss, about medical views of women as masochistic children; and "The Epidemic of Unnecessary Hysterectomy," by Dorothy Larned, concerning a recent alarming increase in the number of these operations. In addition, several essays describe the influence of the current women's health movement on lay medical education, self-help, and preventive care programs—all presaged by the early health movement.

5. Helen Mayer Hacker, "Women as a Minority Group," *Social Forces* 30, no. 1 (October 1951): 60-69.

1
ANTHOLOGIES: SUBJECT/GENRE INDEX

This section lists short titles of anthologies under broad subjects and genres. Books may be entered under several different headings. The order of short titles in this section corresponds with the order in which they are discussed in the INTRODUCTION. To find a particular subject or genre, users should locate it in the alphabetical listing under SUBJECT/GENRE INDEX in the table of contents of this book. Full titles appear in ANTHOLOGIES: TABLES OF CONTENTS.

GENERAL AND INTERDISCIPLINARY COLLECTIONS

The Potential of Woman (1963)
The Woman in America (1965)
Women Around the World (1968)
Masculine-Feminine (1969)
The Black Woman (1970)
Voices of the New Feminism (1970)
The Other Half (1971)
Roles Women Play (1971)
Up Against the Wall, Mother (1971)
Woman in Sexist Society (1971)
Womankind (1971)
Women and Society (1972)
Women's Liberation (1972)
Female and Male in Latin America (1973)
Radical Feminism (1973)
A Sampler of Women's Studies (1973)
Sexism: Scientific Debates (1973)
Women in China (1973)
Women on the Move (1973)
Many Sisters (1974)
New Research on Women (1974)
Woman and Public Policy (1974)
Woman in the Year 2000 (1974)
Women and Religion (1974)
The Role of Women in the Middle Ages (1975)
The Roles and Images of Women in the Middle Ages and the Renaissance (1975)
We Become New (1975)
Woman: New Dimensions (1975, 1977)
Women: A Feminist Perspective (1975)
Women in a Changing World (1975)
Women in Chinese Society (1975)
Women in Contemporary India (1975)
Women in the Professions (1975)
Beyond Intellectual Sexism (1976)
New Research on Women and Sex Roles (1976)
The Rights and Wrongs of Women (1976)
Women: A PDI Reference Book (1976)
Women and Children in Contemporary Society (1976)
Women and Philosophy (1976)
Women and the Future (1976)
Women in Changing Japan (1976)
Women in the Canadian Mosaic (1976)
Women in the World (1976)
The Role of Women in Conflict and Peace (1977)
Sex Equality (1977)
Sexism and Language (1977)
Virtues in Conflict (1977)
Women and German Studies (1977)
Women and Men: Changing Roles, Relationships and Perceptions (1977)
Women and Men: The Consequences of Power (1977)
Women and Men: Traditions and Trends (1977)
Women into Wives (1977)

<u>Women's Lives</u> (1977)
<u>The Afro-American Woman</u> (1978)
<u>Capitalist Patriarchy</u> (1978, 1979)
<u>Feminist Frameworks</u> (1978)
<u>Tearing the Veil</u> (1978)
<u>Women: A Feminist Perspective</u> (2nd ed.) (1978)
<u>Women in the Muslim World</u> (1978)
<u>Women on Women</u> (1978)
<u>Women, Sexuality and Social Control</u> (1978)
<u>Women's Studies</u> (1978)
<u>Becoming Female: Perspectives on Development</u> (1979)
<u>Fit Work for Women</u> (1979)
<u>Philosophy and Women</u> (1979)
<u>The Future of Difference</u> (1980)

See also: FEMINISM

FEMINISM

<u>Up From the Pedestal</u> (1968)
<u>Masculine-Feminine</u> (1969, 1970)
<u>The Woman Movement</u> (1969, 1970)
<u>Essays on Sex Equality</u> (1970)
<u>The New Woman</u> (1970)
<u>Sisterhood is Powerful</u> (1970)
<u>Voices from Women's Liberation</u> (1970)
<u>Voices of the New Feminism</u> (1970)
<u>From Feminism to Liberation</u> (1971)
<u>Liberation Now!</u> (1971)
<u>The New Feminism</u> (1971)
<u>Roles Women Play</u> (1971)
<u>Up Against the Wall, Mother</u> (1971)
<u>Women in Sexist Society</u> (1971)
<u>Women's Liberation and Literature</u> (1971)
<u>The American Sisterhood</u> (1972)
<u>Female Liberation</u> (1972)
<u>Feminism and Socialism</u> (1972)
<u>Feminism: The Essential Historical Writings</u> (1972)
<u>This Great Argument</u> (1972)
<u>Women and Society</u> (1972)
<u>Women's Liberation</u> (1972)
<u>The Women's Movement</u> (1972)
<u>Our American Sisters</u> (1973)
<u>Radical Feminism</u> (1973) <u>Sex and Equality</u> (1974)
<u>Lesbianism and the Women's Movement</u> (1975)
<u>Women: A Feminist Perspective</u> (1975)
<u>Women on Campus</u> (1975)
<u>Women in a Changing World</u> (1975)
<u>Women and Philosophy</u> (1976)
<u>Feminism and Philosophy</u> (1977)
<u>Capitalist Patriarchy</u> (1978, 1979)
<u>Feminism and Materialism</u> (1978)
<u>Feminist Frameworks</u> (1978)
<u>Tearing the Veil</u> (1978)

Woman: A Feminist Perspective (2nd ed.) (1978)
Concise History of Woman Suffrage (1978)
Philosophy and Women (1979)
Flawed Liberation (in press)

See also: GENERAL AND INTERDISCIPLINARY COLLECTIONS; HISTORICAL SOURCE
COLLECTIONS

BIOGRAPHY AND AUTOBIOGRAPHY

Women in the Field (1970)
Growing Up Female in America (1971)
Fragments of Autobiography (1974)
Lives to Remember (1974)
Privilege of Sex (1974)
Revelations (1974)
Black Women in Nineteenth-Century American Life (1976)
Let Them Speak for Themselves (1977)
Working It Out (1977)
Sister Saints (1978)
These Modern Women (1978)
Women's Autobiography: Essays in Criticism (1980)
The Writer on Her Work (1980)

See also: HISTORICAL SOURCE COLLECTIONS

GENERAL LITERARY COLLECTIONS

Women's Liberation and Literature (1971)
About Woman (1973)
By a Woman Writt (1973, 1974)
The Feminine Image in Literature (1973)
A House of Good Proportion (1973)
Images of Women in Literature (1973)
Keeping the Faith (1974)
Revelations (1974)
Moving to Antarctica (1975)
By Women (1976)
Who Am I This Time? (1976)
Women in Canadian Literature (1976)
Women: Portraits (1976)
The Female Spectator (1977)
Images of Women in Literature (2nd ed.) (1977)
Woman as Writer (1978)
Women in Russian Modernism (1978)
Women of Valor (1978)
Women in Russian Modernism (1978)
Sturdy Black Bridges (1979)
Woman: An Affirmation (1979)
Women Working: An Anthology of Stories and Poems (1979)
The Writer on Her Work (1980)

LITERARY CRITICISM

A Case For Equity (1971)
Women's Liberation and Literature (1971)
Images of Women in Fiction (1972)
Female Studies IX (1975)
Feminist Literary Criticism (1975)
Woman in the 18th Century (1976)
The Authority of Experience (1977)
Contemporary French Women Poets (1977)
Contemporary Women Novelists (1977)
Fabian Feminist (1977)
Latin American Women Writers (1977)
Seven American Women Writers of the Twentieth Century (1977)
What Manner of Woman (1977)
Feminist Criticism (1978)
Shakespeare's Sisters (1979)
Sturdy Black Bridges (1979)
Women Writing and Writing About Women (1979)
Women's Autobiography: Essays in Criticism (1980)

DRAMA

Plays By and About Women (1973)
Women in Drama (1975)
The New Women's Theatre (1977)

POETRY

The Orchid Boat (1972)
The Women Poets in English (1972)
About Women (1973)
Mountain Moving Day (1973)
No More Masks (1973)
Psyche (1973)
The World Split Open (1974)
Salt and Bitter and Good (1975)
We Become New (1975)
I Hear My Sisters Saying (1976)
The Other Voice (1976)
The Burning Heart (1977)
Contemporary French Women Poets (1977)
Latin American Women Writers (1977)
Tangled Vines (1978)
Women Poets of the West, 1850-1950 (1978)

FICTION

Feminine Plural (1972)

Women Women Rule (1972)
Women: Feminist Stories by Nine New Authors (1972)
American Voices, American Women (1973)
By and About Women (1973)
Fragment of a Lost Diary (1973)
Grande Dames of Detection (1973)
Bitches and Sad Ladies (1975)
Black-Eyed Susans (1975)
Crime on Her Mind (1975)
Ladies of the Gothics (1975)
Women and Men, Men and Women (1975)
In the Looking Glass (1977)
Solo (1977)
Women and Fiction 2 (1978)
Women and Men Together (1978)
The World Outside (1978)
Women Writing (1979)

SCIENCE FICTION

Women of Wonder (1974, 1975)
Aurora (1976)
More Women of Wonder (1976)
Millennial Women (1978)

ART AND ARCHITECTURE

Women as Sex Object (1972)
Art and Sexual Politics (1973)
Women in American Architecture (1977)
New Space for Women (1980)

FILM AND MEDIA

Sexism and Youth (1974)
Women and the Cinema (1977)
Hearth and Home (1978)
Sexual Strategems (1979?)

PHILOSOPHY

Philosophy and Sex (1975)
Women and Philosophy (1976)
Feminism and Philosophy (1977)
History of Ideas on Women (1977)
Sex Equality (1977)
Toward Women (1977)
Philosophy of Woman (1978)
Philosophy and Women (1979)

See also: FEMINISM

RELIGION

RELIGION

Religion and Sexism (1974)
Sexist Religion and Women in the Church (1974)
Women and Religion (1974)
Woman: New Dimensions (1975, 1977)
The Jewish Woman (1976)
Sister Saints (1978)
Women in the Muslim World (1978)
Women of Spirit (1979)
Womanspirit Rising (1979)

HISTORY: GENERAL COLLECTIONS

Clio's Consciousness Raised (1974)
Liberating Women's History (1976)
The Rights and Wrongs of Women (1976)
Women, War and Revolution (1980)

HISTORICAL SOURCE COLLECTIONS

The Educated Woman in America (1965)
Up From the Pedestal (1968)
The Woman Movement (1969)
Essays on Sex Equality (1970)
Voices From Women's Liberation (1970)
The American Sisterhood (1972)
Female Liberation (1972)
Feminism: The Essential Historical Writings (1972)
The Oven Birds (1972)
The Physician and Child-Rearing (1972)
Root of Bitterness (1972)
This Great Argument (1972)
Woman's Rights. Woman's Wrongs. (1972)
Woman's Work in America (1972)
Black Women in White America (1973)
The Roots of American Feminist Thought (1973)
Women From the Greeks to the French Revolution (1973)
Abortion in Nineteenth-Century America (1974)
Fragments of Autoibiography (1974)
Liberating the Home (1974)
Lives to Remember (1974)
The Male Mid-Wife and the Female Doctor (1974)
Privilege of Sex (1974)
The Prostitute and the Social Reformer (1974)
Sex and Equality (1974)
Women of Lowell (1974)
Unsung Champions of Women (1975)
America's Working Women (1976)

Black Women in Nineteenth-Century American Life (1976)
Women in Latin American History (1976)
Women in the American Economy (1976)
The Female Experience (1977)
History of Ideas on Women (1977)
Let Them Speak for Themselves (1977)
Toward Women (1977)
Concise History of Woman Suffrage (1978)
Distaves and Dames (1978)
Philosophy of Woman (1978)
Three Pamphlets on the Jacobean Antifeminist
Controversy (1978)
European Women: A Documentary History 1789-1945 (1980)

WORK: HISTORICAL COLLECTIONS

Woman's Work in America (1972)
Women at Work: Ontario, 1850-1930 (1974)
Women of Lowell (1974)
America's Working Women (1976)
Women in the American Economy (1976)
Class, Sex and the Woman Worker (1977)
The Factory Girls (1977)
Women in the Labour Movement (1977)
Fit Work for Women (1979)

See also: WORK: CONTEMPORARY STUDIES

HISTORY AND AREA STUDIES: UNITED STATES

The Educated Woman in America (1965)
The Woman in America (1965)
Up From the Pedestal (1968)
The Woman Movement (1969, 1971)
Voices From Women's Liberation (1970)
Family Issues of Employed Women in Europe and
America (1971)
Growing Up Female in America (1971)
The New Feminism (1971)
The American Sisterhood (1972)
The Oven Birds (1972)
The Physician and Child-Rearing (1972)
Root of Bitterness (1972)
Woman's Rights. Woman's Wrongs. (1972)
Woman's Work in America (1891, 1972)
The Woman Poets in England (1972)
Black Women in White America (1973)
By a Woman Writt (1973, 1974)
Our American Sisters (1973)
Psyche (1973)
The Roots of American Feminist Thought (1973)
The Woman Question in American History (1973)

Women and Womanhood in America (1973)
Abortion in Nineteenth-Century America (1974)
The American Woman (1974)
And Jill Came Tumbling After (1974)
Fragments of Autobiography (1974)
Liberating the Home (19764)
Lives to Remember (1974)
The Male Midwife and the Female Doctor (1974)
The Prostitute and the Social Reformer (1974)
Sex and Equality (1974)
Women of Lowell (1974)
The World Split Open (1974)
"Remember the Ladies" (1975)
Salt and Bitter and Good (1975)
America's Working Women (1976)
Black Women in Nineteenth-Century American Life (1976)
Dialogue on Diversity (1976)
Who Am I This Time? (1976)
Women in the American Economy (1976)
Class, Sex and the Woman Worker (1977)
The Factory Girls (1977)
The Female Experience (1977)
Let Them Speak for Themselves (1977)
A Portrait of Marginality (1977)
Seven American Women Writers of the Twentieth Century (1977)
What Manner of Woman (1977)
Women in American Architecture (1977)
Capitalist Patriarchy (1978, 1979)
Concise History of Woman Suffrage (1978)
The Italian Immigrant Woman in North America (1978)
Sister Saints (1978)
The Sociology of the Languages of American Women (1978)
These Modern Women (1978)
Women in the Courts (1978)
Women Poets of the West, 1850-1950 (1978)
Sturdy Black Bridges (1979)
Women in the U.S. Labor Force (1979)
Women of America (1979)
Women of Spirit (1979)
Women's Experience in America (1979)
Affairs of the Mind (1980)
Women, War, and Revolution (1980)
Flawed Liberation (1981)

See also: POLITICAL SCIENCE, PUBLIC POLICY AND LAW; WORK: CONTEMPORARY STUDIES

HISTORY AND AREA STUDIES: CANADA

Privilege of Sex (1974)
Women at Work: Ontario, 1850-1930 (1974)
Women in Canadian Literature (1976)
Women in the Canadian Mosaic (1976)

The Neglected Majority (1977)
Women in Canada (1977)
The Italian Immigrant Woman in North America (1978)

HISTORY AND AREA STUDIES: GREAT BRITAIN

The Woman Movement (1969, 1971)
Suffer and Be Still (1972)
The Women Poets in English (1972)
By a Woman Writt (1973, 1974)
The World Split Open (1974)
Salt and Bitter and Good (1975)
Dependence and Exploitation in Work and Marriage (1976)
The Rights and Wrongs of Women (1976)
Who Am I This Time? (1976)
The Female Spectator (1977)
2080 What Manner of Woman (1977)
A Widening Sphere (1977)
Woman in the Labour Movement (1977)
The Nineteenth-Century Woman (1978)
Three Pamphlets on the Jacobean Antifeminist Controversy (1978)
Fit Work for Women (1979)
Women in Irish Society (1979)
The Women of England from Anglo-Saxon Times to the Present (1979)

See also: HISTORY AND AREA STUDIES: EUROPE

HISTORY AND AREA STUDIES: AUSTRALIA

Women's Role in Aboriginal Society (1974)

HISTORY AND AREA STUDIES: EUROPE

The Changing Roles of Men and Women (1967, 1971)
Family Issues of Employed Women in Europe and America (1971)
Popular Attitudes toward Birth Control in Pre-Industrial France and England (1972)
Women from the Greeks to the French Revolution (1973)
The Role of Women in the Middle Ages (1975)
The Roles and Images of Women in the Middle Ages and the Renaissance (1975)
Woman in the 18th Century (1976)
Women in Medieval Society (1976)
Becoming Visible (1977)
Contemporay French Women Poets (1977)
Damned Art (1977)
Women and German Studies (1977)

Demographic Aspects of the Changing Status of Women in Europe (1978)
Distaves and Dames (1978)
German Women Writers of the Twentieth Century (1978)
The Italian Immigrant Woman in North America (1978)
Socialist Women (1978)
Women of Spirit (1979)
Affairs of the Mind (1980)
Beyond Their Sex (1980)
European Women: A Documentary History 1789-1945 (1980)
Women, War, and Revolution (1980)

See also: HISTORY AND AREA STUDIES: GREAT BRITAIN

HISTORY AND AREA STUDIES: LATIN AMERICA

Female and Male in Latin America (1973)
Fragment from a Lost Diary (1973)
Sex and Class in Latin America (1976)
Women in Latin American History (1976)
Latin American Women Writers (1977)
Latin American Women (1978)
Sturdy Black Bridges (1979)
The Other Voice (1976)

HISTORY AND AREA STUDIES: INDIA

Indian Women (1975)
Women in Contemporary India (1975)
Indian Women from Purdah to Modernity (1976)

HISTORY AND AREA STUDIES: MIDDLE EAST

The Other Voice (1976)
Women in the Muslim World (1978)
Women's Status and Fertility in the Muslim World (1978)

See also: ANTHROPOLOGY, FOLKLORE AND CROSS-CULTURAL STUDIES; DEVELOPMENT, HISTORY AND AREA STUDIES: AFRICA

HISTORY AND AREA STUDIES: AFRICA

Women of Tropical Africa (1963)
Fragment of a Lost Diary (1973)
The Other Voice (1976)
Women in Africa (1976)
Women in the Muslim World (1978)
Women's Status and Fertility in the Muslim World (1978)
Sturdy Black Bridges (1979)

See also: ANTHROPOLOGY, FOLKLORE AND CROSS-CULTURAL STUDIES; DEVELOPMENT; HISTORY AND AREA STUDIES: CHINA; HISTORY AND AREA STUDIES: MIDDLE EAST

HISTORY AND AREA STUDIES: RUSSIA

The Role and Status of Women in the Soviet Union (1968)
Women in Russia (1977)
Women Writers in Russian Modernism (1978)

HISTORY AND AREA STUDIES: CHINA

The Orchid Boat (1972)
Women in China (1973)
Women in Chinese Society (1975)

HISTORY AND AREA STUDIES: ASIA

Southeast Asian Birth Customs (1965)
Fragment of a Lost Diary (1973)
The Other Voice (1976)
Women in Changing Japan (1976)
The Burning Heart (1977)
Virtues in Conflict (1977)

See also: ANTHROPOLOGY, FOLKLORE AND CROSS-CULTURAL STUDIES; HISTORY AND AREA STUDIES: CHINA

POLITICAL SCIENCE, PUBLIC POLICY, AND LAW

Feminism and Socialism (1972)
Women in Politics (1974)

Economic Independence for Women (1976)
Women and the Workplace (1976)
A Portrait of Marginality (1977)
The Role of Women in Conflict and Peace (1977)
Women in the Labour Movement (1977)
Women into Wives (1977)
Women, Minorities and Employment Discrimination (1977)
Child Care and Public Policy (1978)
Feminism and Materialism (1978)
The Victimization of Women (1978)
Women in the Courts (1978)
Women, Work and Family (1978)
Women Working (1978)
Capitalist Patriarchy (1978, 1979)
Race, Sex and Policy Problems (1979)
Women Organizing (1979)
Working Women and Families (1979)
Women, War, and Revolution (1980)

SOCIOLOGY AND ECONOMICS

Women of Tropical Africa (1963)
Women in the Modern World (1967)
The Role and Status of Women in the Soviet Union (1968)
The Professional Woman (1971)
Women in the Professions (1971)
Feminism and Socialism (1972)
Woman in a Man-Made World (1972)
Changing Women in a Changing Society (1973)
Women in China (1973)
Who Discriminates Against Women? (1974)
Women and Public Policy (1974)
Woman, Culture and Society (1974)
Another Voice (1975)
Sex, Discrimination and the Division of Labor (1975)
Women: A Feminist Perspective (1975)
Women in Contemporary India (1975)
Economic Independence for Women (1976)
Sex and Class in Latin America (1976)
Women and the American Economy (1976)
Women and the Workplace (1976)
Women Cross-Culturally (1976)
Women in Africa (1976)
Women in the American Economy (1976)
Women in the World (1976)
Sexual Stratification (1977)
Third World Women (1977)
Woman in a Man-Made World (2nd ed.) (1977)
Women and National Development (1977)
Women in Canada (1977)
Women in Russia (1977)
Women into Wives (1977)
Women, Minorities and Employment Discrimination (1977)
Women's Lives (1977)
Capitalist Patriarchy (1978, 1979)

Child Care and Public Policy (1978)
Demographic Aspects of the Changing Status of Women in Europe (1978)
Feminism and Materialism (1978)
Sex and Age as Principles of Social Differentiation (1978)
Socialist Women (1978)
Women: A Feminist Perspective (2nd ed.) (1978)
Women in the Muslim World (1978)
Women, Work and Family (1978)
Women Working: Theories and Facts in Perspective (1978)
Women's Status and Fertility in the Muslim World (1978)
Race, Sex and Policy Problems (1979)
Working Women and Families (1979)

See also: PSYCHOLOGY AND BIOLOGY; SEX ROLES AND SOCIALIZATION; POLITICAL SCIENCE, PUBLIC POLICY AND LAW

DEVELOPMENT

Women of Tropical Africa (1963)
Women in World Development (1976)
Women Cross-Culturally (1976)
Women in the World (1976)
Women Workers and Society (1976)
Third World Women (1977)
Women and National Development (1977)
Women in the Muslim World (1978)
Women's Status and Fertility in the Muslim World (1978)
Women United, Women Divided (1979)
Comparative Perspectives of Third World Women (1980)
Women and Colonization (1980)

See also: ANTHROPOLOGY, FOLKLORE AND CROSS-CULTURAL STUDIES

ANTHROPOLOGY, FOLKLORE, AND CROSS-CULTURAL STUDIES

Women of Tropical Africa (1963)
Southeast Asian Birth Customs (1965)
Women in the Modern World (1967)
Women Around the World (1968)
Sex Roles in Changing Society (1970)
Women in the Field (1970)
Bridewealth and Dowry (1973)
Many Sisters (1974)
Woman, Culture and Society (1974)
Women in Politics (1974)
Women's Role in Aboriginal Society (1974)
Being Female (1975)
Perceiving Women (1975)
Toward an Anthropology of Women (1975)

Women and Folklore (1975)
Women and World Development (1976)
Women Cross-Culturally (1976)
Women in Africa (1976)
Women in the World (1976)
Women Workers and Society (1976)
The Fertility of Working Women (1977)
Sexual Stratification (1977)
Third World Women (1977)
Women and National Development (1977)
Defining Females (1978)
Sex and Age as Principles of Social Differentiation (1978)
Tearing the Veil (1978)
Women in Ritual and Symbolic Roles (1978)
Women in the Muslim World (1978)
Women's Status and Fertility in the Muslim World (1978)
Women and Society (1979)
Women United, Women Divided (1979)
Comparative Perspectives of Third World Women (1980)
Women and Colonization (1980)
A World of Women (1980)

See also: DEVELOPMENT; HISTORY AND AREA STUDIES

WORK: CONTEMPORARY STUDIES

Family Issues of Employed Women in Europe and America (1971)
The Professional Woman (1971)
Women in the Professions (1971)
Woman in a Man-Made World (1972)
Academic Women on the Move (1973)
Affirmative Action for Women (1973)
Corporate Lib (1973)
Working Mothers (1974)
Emerging Woman (1975)
Sex, Discrimination and the Division of Labor (1975)
Women and Achievement (1975)
Women and the Power to Change (1975)
Women in the Professions (1975)
Dependence and Exploitation in Work and Marriage (1976)
Economic Independence for Women (1976)
Mothers in Employment (1976)
Women: A PDI Reference Work (1976)
Women and the American Economy (1976)
Women and the Workplace (1976)
Women in Changing Japan (1976)
Women Workers and Society (1976)
Changing Roles of Women in Industrial Societies (1977)
Equal Pay for Women (1977)
The Fertility of Working Women (1977)
Reverse Discrimination (1977)

Social Justice and Preferential Treatment (1977)
Woman in a Man-Made World (2nd ed.) (1977)
Women in National Development (1977)
Women in Industry (1977)
Women in the Labour Movement (1977)
Women, Minorities and Employment Discrimination (1977)
Working It Out (1977)
Capitalist Patriarchy (1978, 1979)
Conference on the Educational and Occupational Needs of Black Women (1978)
Covert Discrimination (1978)
Feminism and Materialism (1978)
Women in Management (1978)
Women, Work and Family (1978)
Women Working: Theories and Facts in Perspective (1978)
Women in the U.S. Labor Force (1979)
Working Women and Families (1979)

See also: WORK: HISTORICAL COLLECTIONS

SEX ROLES AND SOCIALIZATION

The Potential of Woman (1963)
The Changing Roles of Men and Women (1967, 1971)
Feminine Personality and Conflict (1970)
The New Woman (1970)
Sex Roles in Changing Society (1970)
Family Issues of Employed Women in Europe and America (1971)
Roles Women Play (1971)
Feminism and Socialism (1972)
Readings on the Psychology of Women (1972)
Woman in a Man-Made World (1972)
The Women's Movement (1972)
Changing Women in a Changing Society (1973)
The Female Experience (1973)
Sexism: Scientific Debates (1973)
The American Woman (1974)
Perspectives on Human Sexuality (1974)
Who Discriminates Against Women? (1974)
Women and Public Policy (1974)
Woman, Culture and Society (1974)
Woman in the Year 2000 (1974)
Working Mothers (1974)
Another Voice (1975)
Emerging Woman (1975)
Gender and Sex in Society (1975)
Language and Sex (1975)
Woman: Dependent or Independent Variable? (1975)
Women: A Feminist Perspective (1975)
Woman and Achievement (1975)
Women and Education (1975)
Beyond Intellectual Sexism (1976)
Beyond Sex-Role Stereotypes (1976)

Dependence and Exploitation in Work and Marriage (1976)
Dialogue on Diversity (1976)
Exploring Sex Differences (1976)
Female Psychology (1976)
Mothers in Employment (1976)
New Research on Women and Sex Roles (1976)
Sex Differences: Cultural and Developmental Dimensions (1976)
Sex Differences: Social and Biological Perspectives (1976)
Women: A PDI Reference Work (1976)
Women in the World (1976)
Changing Roles of Women in Industrial Societies (1977)
Sex Bias in the Schools (1977)
The Sex Role System (1977, 1978)
Woman in a Man-Made World (2nd ed.) (1977)
Women and Men: Changing Roles, Relationships and Perceptions (1977)
Women and Men: Tradition and Trends (1977)
Women into Wives (1977)
Women: A Feminist Perspective (2nd ed.) (1978)
Women in the Muslim World (1978)
Women, Work and Family (1978)
Psychology of Women: Selected Readings (1979)
Sex-Related Differences in Cognitive Functioning (1979)

See also: PSYCHOLOGY AND BIOLOGY; SEX DIFFERENCES

LANGUAGE

Language and Sex (1975)
Sexism and Language (1977)
The Sociology of the Languages of American Women (1978)
Woman's Language and Style (1978)

PSYCHOLOGY AND BIOLOGY

The Development of Sex Differences (1966)
Psychoanalysis and Female Sexuality (1966)
Feminine Personality and Conflict (1970)
Sex Differences in Personality (1971)
Readings on the Psychology of Women (1972)
The Women's Movement (1972)
The Female Experience (1973)
Psychoanalysis and Women (1973)
Perspectives on Human Sexuality (1974)
Sex Differences in Behavior (1974)
Who Discriminates Against Women? (1974)
Women and Analysis (1974)
Women in Therapy (1974)
Woman: Dependent or Independent Variable? (1975)
Women and Achievement (1975)

Beyond Sex-Role Stereotypes (1976)
Exploring Sex Differences (1976)
Female Psychology (1976)
Sex Differences: Cultural and Developmental Dimensions (1976)
Sex Differences: Social and Biological Perspectives (1976)
Women: A PDI Reference Work (1976)
Female Psychology (1977)
The Sex Role System (1977, 1978)
Genes and Gender: I (1978)
Becoming Female: Perspectives on Development (1979)
Gender and Disordered Behavior (1979)
Psychology and Women: In Transition (1979)
Psychology of Women: Selected Readings (1979)
Sex-Related Differences in Cognitive Functioning (1979)
Women Look at Biology Looking at Women (1979)
The Psychobiology of Sex Differences and Sex Roles (1980)

See also: PSYCHOANALYSIS; SEX DIFFERENCES; LANGUAGE; SEX ROLES AND SOCIALIZATION; HEALTH, MEDICINE AND SEXUALITY

PSYCHOANALYSIS

Psychoanalysis and Female Sexuality (1966)
Female Sexuality (1970)
Psychoanalysis and Women (1973)
Women and Analysis (1974)
Women in Therapy (1974)
Sex Differences: Cultural and Developmental Dimensions (1976)
Female Psychology (1977)
Psychology of Women: Selected Readings (1979)

SEX DIFFERENCES

The Development of Sex Differences (1966)
Sex Differences in Personality (1971)
Readings on the Psychology of Women (1972)
Sex Differences and Discrimination in Education (1972)
Sexism: Scientific Debates (1973)
Perspectives on Human Sexuality (1974)
Sex Differences in Behavior (1974)
Gender and Sex in Society (1975)
Language and Sex (1975)
Woman: Dependent or Independent Variable? (1975)
Exploring Sex Differences (1976)
Female Psychology (1976)
Sex Differences: Cultural and Developmental Dimensions (1976)
Sex Differences: Social and Biological

Perspectives (1976)
Genes and Gender: I (1978)
Gender and Disordered Behavior (1979)
Psychology and Women: In Transition (1979)
Psychology of Women: Selected Readings (1979)
Sex-Related Differences in Cognitive Functioning (1979)
The Future of Difference (1980)
The Psychobiology of Sex Differences and Sex Roles (1980)

HEALTH, MEDICINE, AND SEXUALITY

Psychoanalysis and Female Sexuality (1966)
The Emerging Woman (1970)
Female Sexuality (1970)
The Physician and Child-Rearing (1972)
Readings on the Psychology of Women (1972)
The Male Midwife and the Female Doctor (1974)
Perspectives on Human Sexuality (1974)
Sex Differences in Behavior (1974)
Gender and Sex in Society (1975)
Philosophy and Sex (1975)
Woman: Dependent or Independent Variable? (1975)
Women: Body and Culture (1975)
After You're Out (1976)
Women: A PDI Reference Work (1976)
Seizing Our Bodies (1977)
Women in Industry (1977)
Genes and Gender: I (1978)
The Nineteenth-Century Woman (1978)
Sexual and Reproductive Aspects of Women's Health Care (1978)
The Victimization of Women (1978)
Women, Sexuality and Social Control (1978)
Gender and Disordered Behavior (1979)
Psychology of Women: Selected Readings (1979)
Women Look at Biology Looking at Women (1979)

See also: ABORTION; FERTILITY AND CONTRACEPTION; LESBIANISM; CRIME

FERTILITY AND CONTRACEPTION

Southeast Asian Birth Customs (1965)
The Emerging Woman (1970)
Popular Attitudes Toward Birth Control in Pre-Industrial France and England (1972)
Being Female (1975)
Philosophy and Sex (1975)
Women: Body and Culture (1975)
The Fertility of Working Women (1977)
Demographic Aspects of the Changing Status of Women in Europe (1978)

Sexual and Reproductive Aspects of Women's
Health Care (1978)
Women's Status and Fertility in the Muslim World (1978)
Psychology of Women: Selected Readings (1979)

See also: ABORTION; HEALTH, MEDICINE AND SEXUALITY

ABORTION

Abortion in Nineteenth-Century America (1974)
Philosophy and Sex (1975)
Abortion: A New Direction for Policy Studies (1977)
Sexual and Reproductive Aspects of Women's
Health Care (1978)

See also: FERTILITY AND CONTRACEPTION; HEALTH, MEDICINE AND SEXUALITY

EDUCATION, GENERAL

The Educated Woman in America (1965)
Sex Differences and Discrimination in Education (1972)
And Jill Came Tumbling After (1974)
Sexism and Youth (1974)
Women and Education (1975)
Sex Bias in the Schools (1977)
Conference on the Educational and Occupational
Needs of Black Women (1978)
Perspectives on Non-Sexist Early
Childhood Education (1978)
Women and Educational Leadership (1980)

EDUCATION, HIGHER

A Case for Equity (1971)
Academic Women on the Move (1973)
Women and the Power to Change (1975)
Women in Academia (1975)
Women on Campus (1975)
Reverse Discrimination (1977)
Social Justice and Preferential Treatment (1977)
Covert Discrimination (1978)
The Higher Education of Women (1978)
Race, Sex and Policy Problems (1979)

WOMEN'S STUDIES

A Sampler of Women's Studies (1973)
Women on the Move (1973)
Female Studies IX (1975)
Women and Education (1975)
Women on Campus (1975)
Women's Studies (1978)

See also: GENERAL AND INTERDISCIPLINARY COLLECTIONS

AFFIRMATIVE ACTION

A Case for Equity (1971)
Academic Women on the Move (1973)
Affirmative Action for Women (1973)
Women in Academia (1975)
Reverse Discrimination (1977)
Social Justice and Preferential Treatment (1977)
Covert Discrimination (1978)
The Higher Education of Women (1978)
Women in Management (1978)
Race, Sex and Policy Problems (1979)

See also: POLITICAL SCIENCE, LAW AND PUBLIC POLICY; EDUCATION, HIGHER EDUCATION

ATHLETICS

Women and Sport (1972)
Women's Athletics (1974)
Equality in Sport for Women (1977)
Out of the Bleachers (1979)

BLACK WOMEN

The Black Woman (1970)
Black Matriarchy (1971)
Black Women in White America (1973)
Keeping the Faith (1974)
Black-Eyed Susans (1975)

Black Women in Nineteenth-Century American Life (1976)
Social Justice and Preferential Treatment (1977)
Women, Minorities and Employment Discrimination (1977)
The Afro-American Woman (1978)
Conference on the Educational and Occupational Needs of Black Women (1978)
Race, Sex and Policy Problems (1979)
Sturdy Black Bridges (1979)

See also: AFFIRMATIVE ACTION

OLDER WOMEN

No Longer Young (1974)
Looking Ahead (1977)
Psychology of Women: Selected Readings (1979)

CHILDREN

Family Issues of Employed Women in Europe and America (1971)
The Physician and Child-Rearing (1971)
Sexism and Youth (1974)
Working Mothers (1974)
Women and Children in Contemporary Society (1976)
Sex Bias in the Schools (1977)
Child Care and Public Policy (1978)
Perspectives on Non-Sexist Early Childhood Education (1978)
Women, Work and Family (1978)
Working Women and Families (1979)

See also: SEX ROLES AND SOCIALIZATION; EDUCATION, GENERAL; FERTILITY AND CONTRACEPTION

LESBIANISM

Lesbianism and the Women's Movement (1975)
After You're Out (1976)

See also: FEMINISM; HEALTH, MEDICINE AND SEXUALITY

CRIME

The Prostitute and the Social Reformer (1974)
The Female Offender (1975)
Forcible Rape (1977)
The Victimization of Women (1978)
Women, Sexuality and Social Control (1978)
The Criminology of Deviant Women (1979)

2

ANTHOLOGIES: TABLES OF CONTENTS

This section reproduces tables of contents of the 375 indexed anthologies. They are arranged in alphabetical order by book title. Because pagination has been inferred from the contents, and because extraneous phrases have been omitted, this section should not be used for purposes of bibliographic citation.

Annotations are substituted for tables of contents in the case of lengthy documentary and poetry collections. Contributors are listed in these annotations. Full names of contributors are printed in the CONTRIBUTOR INDEX.

Items are arranged in alphabetical sequence under each book title. If more than twenty-six items are listed, a second alphabetical sequence (indicated by double letters) or a third sequence (indicated by triple letters) may appear.

Because this section is computer-generated, some punctuation is of necessity slightly irregular. For example, book titles cited in essays are not underlined; rather, they are enclosed in quotation marks. Occurrences of unconventional punctuation are rare and do not change the sense of the phrases in which they appear.

References to this section appear in the SUBJECT/GENRE, EDITOR, CONTRIBUTOR and KEYWORD INDEXES.

American Association for the Advancement of Science. AAAS Seminar .on Women in Development, Mexico, 1975.
See: 293 WOMEN AND WORLD DEVELOPMENT

1 ABORTION IN NINETEENTH-CENTURY AMERICA. (Charles Rosenberg and Carroll Smith-Rosenberg, advisory eds.) (Sex, Marriage and Society) New York: Arno Press, 1974.

a) Foeticide, or Criminal Abortion (1869)(H.L. Hodge); b) Sermon on Ante-Natal Infanticide (1869)(E.F. Howe); c) Criminal Abortion (1870)(A. Nebinger); d) Is Man Too Prolific? (1891)(H.S. Pomeroy); e) Detection of Criminal Abortion (1872)(E. Van de Warker).

2 ABORTION: A NEW DIRECTION FOR POLICY STUDIES. Edward Manier, William Liu and David Solomon, eds. Notre Dame: University of Notre Dame Press, 1977.

a) Abortion and Public Policy in the U.S. (E. Manier), 1-30; b) Membership Decisions and the Limits of Moral Obligation (E.L. Pincoffs), 31-50; c) Abortion Decisions: Judicial Review and Public Opinion (J. Blake), 51-82; d) Abortion and the Constitution: The Cases of the United States and West Germany (D.P. Kommers), 83-116; e) Philosophy on Humanity (R. Wertheimer), 117-136; f) Abortion and the Social System (W.T. Liu), 137-158; g) Philosophers on Abortion (D. Solomon), 159-168; h) Conclusions (E. Manier, W. Liu, D. Solomon), 169-176; i) APPENDIX: Comments on the 1976 Supreme Court Decisions: "Planned Parenthood v. Danforth" and "Bellotti v. Baird" (E. Manier), 177-182.

3 ABOUT WOMEN: AN ANTHOLOGY OF CONTEMPORARY FICTION, POETRY AND ESSAYS. Stephen Berg and S.J. Marks, comps. Greenwich, Ct.: Fawcett Publications, 1973.

a) Growing Up Female (B. Bettelheim), 63-82; b) To All Black Women, From All Black Men (E. Cleaver), 83-88; c) Problem of Making Connections (J. Didion), 89-92; d) Inner and Outer Space: Reflections on Womanhood (E.H. Erikson), 93-126; e) FemLib Case Against Sigmund Freud (R. Gilman), 127-145; f) Stereotype (G. Greer), 146-156; g) An Unfinished Woman (L. Hellman), 157-188; h) The Three Pillars of Zen (Mrs. D.K.), 189-206; i) Cutting Loose (S. Kempton), 207-225; j) New Egalitarian Life Style (G. Steinem), 226-230; k) Sound of a Drunken Drummer (H.W. Blattner), 231-281; l) Mademoiselle from Kansas City (E.S. Connell, Jr.), 282-299; m) Bridgport Bus (M. Howard), 300-313; n) The Love Object (E. O'Brien), 314-342; o) What Is the Connection Between Men and Women? (J.C. Oates), 343-359; p) Alice Blaine (V. Randal), 360-394; q) Waiting for Daddy (H. Wolitzer), 395- ; Poets: S. Berg, S. Hochman, E. Jong, S. Kaufman, W. Kees, D. Levertov, P. Levine, S. Parker, S. Plath, A. Rich, M. Rukeyser, R. Schwartz,

A. Sexton, L. Simpson, G. Snyder, D. Wakoski.

4 ACADEMIC WOMEN ON THE MOVE. Alice S. Rossi and Ann Calderwood, eds. New York: Russell Sage Foundation, 1973.

a) Women on the Move: Roots of Revolt (J. Freeman), 1-36; b) Institutional Barriers to Women Students in Higher Education (P. Roby), 37-56; c) Women in the Male World of Higher Education (P. Schwartz, J. Lever), 57-78; d) Women Dropouts from Higher Education (M. Patterson, L. Sells), 79-92; e) Women Drop Back In: Educational Innovation in the Sixties (J.W. Campbell), 93-124; f) From Sugar to Spice to Professor (J. Huber), 125-138; g) Career Profiles of Women Doctorates (H.S. Astin), 139-162; h) Status Transitions of Women Students, Faculty, and Administrators (P.A. Graham), 163-172; i) Dilemma of the Black Woman in Higher Education (C.M. Carroll), 173-186; j) Faculty Wife: Her Academic Interests and Qualifications (M.M. Weissman, K. Nelson, J. Hackman, C. Pincus, B. Prusoff), 187-198; k) Institutional Variation in the Status of Academic Women (L.H. Robinson), 199-238; l) Representation, Performance and Status of Women on the Faculty at the Urbana-Champaign Campus of the University of Illinois (J.W. Loeb, M.A. Ferber), 239-254; m) Discipline Variation in the Status of Academic Women (L. Morlock), 255-312; n) Sex and Specialization in Academe and the Professions (M. Patterson), 313-332; o) Sex Discrimination in Academe (H.S. Astin, A.E. Bayer), 333- 358; p) Political Action by Academic Women (K. Klotzburger), 359-392; q) Women's Studies and Social Change (F. Howe, C. Ahlum), 393-424; r) Internal Remedies for Sex Discrimination in Colleges and Universities (M.L. Rumbarger), 425-438; s) W.E.A.L. and Contract Compliance (B. Sandler), 439-462; t) Affirmative Action Plans for Eliminating Sex Discrimination in Academe (L.J. Weitzman), 463-504; u) Summary and Prospects (A.S. Rossi), 505-530.

5 AFFAIRS OF THE MIND: THE SALON IN EUROPE AND AMERICA FROM THE 18TH TO THE 20TH CENTURY. Peter Quennell, ed. Washington, D.C.: New Republic Books, 1980.

a) Rahel Varnhagen (H. Spiel), 13-22; b) Lady Blessington (P. Hannay), 23-34; c) Lady Holland (P. Hannay), 35-46; d) Fanny Von Arnstein (H. Spiel), 47-56; e) Madame Recamier (C. Gladwyn), 57-70; f) Madame de Girardin (J. Richardson), 71-84; g) Madame de Lieven (P. Quennell), 85-100; h) Speranza (V. Glendinning), 101-116; i) Lady Desborough (M. Egremont), 117-130; j) Mabel Dodge (R.A. Rosenstone), 131-152; k) Salka Viertel (B. Cook), 153-166; l) Karel Capek (J. Wechsberg), 167-174; m) Lady Cunard (H. Acton), 175- .

6 AFFIRMATIVE ACTION FOR WOMEN: A PRACTICAL GUIDE. Dorothy Jongeward and Dru Scott, eds. Reading, Ma.: Addison-Wesley, 1973.

a) Organization Woman: Then and Now (D. Scott, D. Jongeward), 1-14; b) Women's Lack of Achievement: Then and Now (D. Scott, D. Jongeward), 15-37; c) Legislation and Litigation: Impact on Working Women (O.

Underwood), 39-70; d) Women in Government and Affirmative Action (J.B. Spain), 71-90; e) Women in Organized Religion (C.C. Wedel), 91-120; f) Working Black Women (S. Tolbert-Stroud), 121-138; g) Strategy for Change (P. King), 139-152; h) Obstacle to Women in Management (S. Daddio), 153-172; i) Bank of America's Affirmative Action Seminar (S. Cathey), 173-202; j) Seminars for Career Women: Combining Awareness Training with Transactional Analysis (D. Scott), 203-250; k) What Do I Want to do Next? (J.A. Kay), 251-286; l) Women in Psychotherapy (N.I. Moore), 287-306; m) How to Eliminate Sexist Language From Your Writing: Some Guidelines for the Manager and Supervisor (R.M. Wendlinger, L. Matthews), 307-320.

7 THE AFRO-AMERICAN WOMAN: STRUGGLES AND IMAGES. Sharon Harley and Rosalyn Terborg-Penn, eds. Port Washington, N.Y.: Kennikat Press, 1978.

a) Northern Black Female Workers: Jacksonian Era (S. Harley), 5-16; b) Discrimination Against Afro-American Women in the Woman's Movement, 1830-1920 (R. Terborg-Penn), 17-27; c) Black Male Perspectives on the Nineteenth Century Woman (R. Terborg-Penn), 28-42; d) Black Woman's Struggle for Equality in the South, 1895-1925 (C. Neverdon-Morton), 43-57; e) Black Women in the Blues Tradition (D.D. Harrison), 58-73; f) Images of Black Women in Afro-American Poetry (A.B. Rushing), 74-86; g) Anna J. Cooper: A Voice for Black Women (S. Harley), 87-96; h) Nannie Burroughs and the Education of Black Women (E.B. Barnett), 97-108; i) Win or Lose--We Win: The 1952 Vice-Presidential Campaign of Charlotta A. Bass (G.R. Gill), 109-118.

8 AFTER YOU'RE OUT: PERSONAL EXPERIENCES OF GAY MEN AND LESBIAN WOMEN. Karla Jay and Allen Young, (eds.) Westport, Ct.: Hyperion, 1976.

a) Lesbian Sexuality (N. Sabaroff), 5-15; b) What's a Dyke to Do? and What the Dyke Is Doing (J. Córdova), 16-21; c) With All Due Respect: In Defense of All Lesbian Lifestyles (J. Rule), 22-26; d) Human Identity and Gay Identity: A Liberationist Dilemma (A. Young), 27-34; e) Surviving Gay Coupledom (K. Jay), 35-43; f) Thoughts on Monogamy (J. Lee), 44-51; g) Living Alone (G. Whitmore), 52-61; h) Bi-Sexual Potential (L. Della-Rosa), 62-63; i) Bi-Sexual Offers Some Thoughts on Fences (Jem), 65-67; j) Butch or Fem?: The Third World Lesbian's Dilemma (Anon.), 68-69; k) Search for Words (K. Berlandt), 70-72; l) Entries in a Journal (G. Alinder), 73-84; m) How to Come Out Without Being Thrown Out (J. Córdova), 89-95; n) Thriving Decloseted in Rural Academe (L. Crew), 96-102; o) Out in the Workplace (D. Mager), 103-104; p) Bundles of Twigs in New Hampshire: A High School Teacher's Report (R. LaRiviere), 105-112; q) Hookers: Queer Fish (C. Nossa), 113-116; r) Hustler: A Boy for All Seasons (Anon.), 117-124; s) Lesbian Mother (J. Perreault), 125-127; t) Faggot Father (D. Mager), 128-134; u) Life and Death of a Gay Prisoner (E.E. Loftin, J. Hands), 135-144; v) Gay Couples and Straight Law (T. Hurley), 145-151; w) Lesbians and the Law (K. Dobinski),152-160; x) Pocket Legal Guide for Gay People (Chicago Gay People's Legal Committee), 161-170; y) Can Men and Women Work Together? (Forum), 173-194; z) Thoughts on How Gay Men

Relate to Women (A. Young), 195-204; aa) Oppression is Big Business: Scrutinizing Gay Therapy (K. Jay), 205-210; bb) Spirit is Liberationist but the Flesh is...or, You Can't Always Get Into Bed With Your Dogma (K. Jay), 211-214; cc) Aging (Riki), 215-217; dd) Nigger in the Woodpile (T. Dotton), 218-226; ee) We'd Better All Hang Together or Surely We'll All Hang Separately (R.M. Brown), 227-231; ff) Preserving the Past for the Future (J. Rook), 232-235; gg) Getting It Together Journalism: A View of FAG RAG (C. Shively), 236-247; hh) Power to Gay People: A Los Angeles Experiment in Community Action (R. Nash), 248-255; ii) Information on VD for Gay Women and Men (J. Bamford), 256-266; jj) Bottoms Up: An In-Depth Look at VD and Your Asshole (E. Guthmann), 267-276; kk) Alcohol Use and Abuse in the Gay Community (K.J. McGirr), 277-288.

9 THE AMERICAN SISTERHOOD: WRITINGS OF THE FEMINIST MOVEMENT FROM COLONIAL TIMES TO THE PRESENT. Wendy Martin, ed. New York: Harper and Row, 1972.

a) Trial of Anne Hutchinson, 15-32; b) Legal Disabilities of Women (S. Grimke), 33-41; c) Seneca Falls Convention: Declaration, 42-46; d) Speech: National Women's Rights Convention of 1855 (L. Stone), 47-50; e) Marriage Contract (L. Stone, H.B. Blackwell), 51-52; f) Discourse on Women (L. Mott), 53-60; g) Letters to Woman's Convention, 1851 (A. Bloomer), 61-66; h) Letter to Mrs. Janney, 1872 (A. Bloomer), 67-68; i) Speech: Legislature, 1860 (E.C. Stanton), 69-78; j) Letter on Marriage and Divorce, 1855 (E.C. Stanton), 79-81; k) Argument for Woman's Suffrage (M.J. Gage), 82-87; l) Social Purity (S.B. Anthony), 88-92; m) Demand for Party Recognition (S.B. Anthony), 93-100; n) Narrative (S. Truth), 101-105; o) Making Women into Men (A.S. Blackwell), 106-109; p) Statement: First Feminist Congress, 1919 (C. Eastman), 110-113; q) Why Women's Liberation? (M. Dixon), 114-127; r) Women--Terms of Liberation (A. Rossi), 128-143; s) 51% Minority (S. Chisholm), 144-151; t) Submissive Majority (F. Seidenberg); u) Modern Trends in the Law Concerning Women's Rights (F. Seidenberg), 152-161; v) Abortion Is No Man's Business (N. Shainess), 162-170; w) Why Women's Liberation Is Important to Black Women (M. Williams), 171-178; x) Take a Good Look at Our Problems (P. Newman), 179-182; y) What it Would be Like if Women Win (G. Steinem), 183-196; z) Free Enquiry (F. Wright), 197-202; aa) Woman in the Nineteenth Century and Kindred Papers (M. Fuller), 203-207; bb) Letter, 1881 (E. Blackwell), 208-210; cc) Filial Relations (J. Addams), 211-215; dd) As to Humanness (C.P. Gilman), 216-223; ee) Marriage and Love (E. Goldman), 224-233; ff) Birth Control--A Parent's Problem or a Woman's? (M. Sanger), 234-238; gg) My Life (I. Duncan), 239-242; hh) Cult of True Womanhood (B. Welter), 243-256; ii) Seduced and Abandoned in the New World: The Fallen Woman in American Fiction (W. Martin), 257-272; jj) Education of Women (F. Howe), 273-283; kk) Bright Woman Is Caught in a Double Bind (M. Horner), 284-291; ll) Woman as Nigger (N. Weisstein), 292-298; mm) Why Mothers Fail (D. Cyrus), 299-307; nn) Are You Hurting Your Daughter Without Knowing It? (A. Eliasburg), 308-312; oo) Effects of the Derogatory Attitude toward Female Sexuality (C. Thompson), 313-321; pp) Understanding Orgasm (S. Lydon), 322-328; qq) Sex Roles and Female Oppression (D. Densmore), 329-332; rr) Woman-Identified Woman (Radical Lesbians), 333-338; ss) Cutting Loose (S. Kempton); tt) Private View of the Woman's Uprising (S. Kempton),

339-352; uu) Love Is Just a Four-Letter Word (Lower East Side Women's Liberation Collective), 353-359; vv) Goodbye to All That (R. Morgan), 360-367.

10 AMERICAN VOICES, AMERICAN WOMEN. Lee R. Edwards and Arlyn Diamond, eds. New York: Avon Books, 1973.

a) The Amber Gods (H.P. Spofford), 21-64; b) The Story of Avis (E.S. Phelps), 65-150; c) A New England Nun (M.W. Freeman), 151-164; d) The Revolt of "Mother" (M.W. Freeman), 165-180; e) One Good Time (M.W. Freeman), 181-198; f) Old Woman Magoun (M.W. Freeman), 199-220; g) Lilacs (K.O. Chopin), 221-232; h) The Godmother (K.O. Chopin), 233-256; i) A Woman of Genius (M.H. Austin), 257-340; j) A Drop in the Bucket (D.C. Fisher), 341-358; k) A Jury of Her Peers (S.K. Glaspell), 359-384; l) Plum Bun "Home" (J.R. Fauset), 385-396; m) Plum Bun "Market" (J.R. Fauset), 397-422; n) Plum Bun "Plum Bun" (J.R. Fauset), 423- .

11 THE AMERICAN WOMAN: WHO WILL SHE BE? Mary Louise McBee and Kathryn A. Blake, eds. Beverly Hills: Glencoe Press, 1974.

a) Out of the Past and Present Controversies: Challenges for the Future (A.F. Scott), 7-20; b) Adjustment: New Approaches to Women's Mental Health (C.M. Nadelson), 21-36; c) Self-Actualized Woman (E.M. Lloyd-Jones), 37-48; d) Androgyny and Humanistic Goals (J.M. Bardwick), 49-66; e) Occupations: Wider Economic Opportunity (J.M. Kreps), 67-80; f) Women and the New Social Structures (J. Bernard), 81-94; g) Media: New Images of Women in Contemporary Society (J. Miller, L. Margulies), 95-106; h) Woman: The New Figure in American Politics (P.T. Mink), 107-120; i) Education of Women Today and Tomorrow (K.P. Cross), 121-138; j) American Woman: Who Will She Be? (K.A. Blake, M.L. McBee), 139-142.

12 AMERICA'S WORKING WOMEN. Rosalyn Baxandall, Linda Gordon, Susan Reverby, eds. and comps. New York: Vintage Books, 1976.

This documentary anthology focuses on the lives and contributions of working class women. Its editors suggest that this group, their history restored, can lead a socialist feminist revolution. Most selections are from the modern period of U.S. history. Arrangement is chronological, then topical, e.g., "The Depression," "The Feminine Mystique," "Homemaking." Contributors: R. Landes, A.M. Earle, E. Abbott, L. Salmon, R.B. Morris, E. Betts, J. Draper, E. Sparks, R. Starobin, H. Robinson, L. Larcom, E.R. Hemingway, H. Sumner, R. Ernst, J. Andrews, W.D.P. Bliss, Julianna, A. Kesselman, H.T. Upton, W. Sylvis, C. Dall, W. Sanger, L. Levine, S.B. Anthony, K. Mullany, E. Verdery, L. Barry, T. Powderly, E. Christman, R. Cristoforo, M.H. Vorse, F.S. Wright, R. Lynd, H. Lynd, H. Moscowitz, E. Packard, M. Byington, U.S. Dept. of Agriculture, M. Trueblood, M. Van Kleeck, N.Y. State Factory Investigating Committee, C. Eastman, E. O'Donnell, A. Henry, L. Matthews, A. Nestor, H. Marot, E.G. Flynn, S.A. Clark,

R. Schneiderman, U.S. Women's Bureau, T. Malkiel, M. Sanger, I. Goodman, L.A. Warner, M. Schepps, M. Hagood, M. Davies, W. Bakke, R. Shallcross, S.E. Ashford, A.W. Craton, S. Rozner, E.M. Wiggins, M. Le Sueur, S. Nowicki, R. Jefferson, A. Clawson, K. Blood, J. Colton, H.I. Safa, J. Cowley, E. Martin, S. Stupek, M. Hudson, M. Gubbay, S. Reverby, J. Tillmon, B. Baer, G. Matthews, H. Stanton, M. Wolfgang, G. Sellers, A. Tröger.

13 AND JILL CAME TUMBLING AFTER: SEXISM IN AMERICAN EDUCATION. Judith Stacey, Susan Beread, Joan Daniels, eds. New York: Dell, 1974.

a) Why Are There No Woman Geniuses? (A.G. Spencer), 33-36; b) Are Women Prejudiced Against Women? (P. Goldberg), 37-42; c) Achievement-Related Conflicts in Women (M.S. Horner), 43-63; d) Education of Women (F. Howe), 64-78; e) Male and Female (E.G. Pitcher), 79-90; f) As the Twig is Bent (C. Joffe), 91-109; g) Are Little Girls Being Harmed by "Sesame Street"? (J. Bergman), 110-115; h) Children's Books: The Second Sex, Junior Division (E. Fisher), 116-122; i) Report on Children's Toys (Ms. Magazine), 123-125; j) Impact of the Women's Liberation Movement on Child Development Texts (Z.S. Klapper), 126-136; k) Two Lives (C. Karkosza), 137-138; l) Schools Are Emasculating Our Boys (P.C. Sexton), 138-141; m) Do Schools Sell Girls Short? (B. Levy), 142-146; n) Teacher Interactions with Boys and with Girls (P.S. Sears, D.H. Feldman), 147-158; o) Look Jane Look. See Sex Stereotypes (Women on Words and Images), 159-177; p) Sex Problems of School Math Books (M. Federbush), 178-186; q) Sex-Role Pressures and the Socialization of the Male Child (R.E. Hartley), 185-198; r) Sex-Role Attitudes of Fifth-Grade Girls (G.K. Baruch), 199-212; s) High-School Women: Oppression and Liberation (J. Bull), 213-223; t) Down the Up Staircase (R. Rothstein), 224-235; u) Realistic Counseling for High-School Girls (I.M. Tiedt), 236-240; v) Use and Abuse of Vocational Tests (C. Tittle), 241-248; w) Women in U.S. History High-School Textbooks (J.L. Trecker), 249-268; x) High-School Sex(ist) Education (J. Albert), 269-274; y) Present Tendencies in Women's College and University Education (M.C. Thomas), 275-278; z) Our Failures Only Marry: Bryn Mawr and the Failure of Feminism (L. Schneider), 279-292; aa) Second Sex in Academe (A.S. Harris), 293-316; bb) Women and the Literary Curriculum (E. Showalter), 317-325; cc) Sexism in History (R. Rosen), 326-336; dd) Teaching is a Good Profession...for a Woman (A. Reich), 337-343; ee) Harvard Ed School (B. Useem), 344-347; ff) Women and the P.D.K.s (J. Askins), 348-350; gg) Para-Professional (C. Silvers), 351-352; hh) Portrait of a Teacher (F.G. Patten), 353-357; ii) Academic Women (M. Ellman), 358-365; jj) Discrimination and Demography Restrict Opportunities for Academic Women (A. Rossi), 366-376; kk) Feminist Experiment in Education (B. Harrison), 377-389; ll) Twelve and Turned-On (S. Wolfson), 390-393; mm) Jumping the Track (A.L. Di Rivera), 394-398; nn) It's Time for Equal Education (A. Scott), 399-409; oo) Feminist Studies: Frill or Necessity? (M. Webb), 410-422; pp) Equal Opportunity for Women: How Possible and How Quickly?

(F. Howe), 423- .

14 ANOTHER VOICE: FEMINIST PERSPECTIVES ON SOCIAL LIFE AND SOCIAL SCIENCE. Marcia Millman and Rosabeth Moss Kanter, eds. Garden City, New York: Anchor-Doubleday, 1975.

a) Nonsexist Perspective on Social and Political Change (T. McCormack), 1-33; b) Women and the Structure of Organizations: Explorations in Theory and Behavior (R.M. Kanter), 34-74; c) Women and Medical Sociology: Invisible Professionals and Ubiquitous Patients (J. Lorber), 75-105; d) Sociology of Education: Perspectives on Women (S.L. Lightfoot), 106-143; e) "Thereness" of Women: A Selective Review of Urban Sociology (L.H. Lofland), 144-170; f) Women and the Creation of Culture (G. Tuchman), 171-202; g) Sociology and Women in Working-class Jobs (P. Roby), 203-239; h) Black Women and Self-esteem (L.W. Myers), 240-250; i) Feminist Review of the Sociology of Deviance (M. Millman), 251-279; j) Sociology of Feeling and Emotion (A.R. Hochschild), k) Assumptions Made About Gender Roles (D. Tresemer), 308-339; l) Feminist Perspectives in Sociological Research (A.K. Daniels), 340-380.

15 ART AND SEXUAL POLITICS: WOMEN'S LIBERATION, WOMEN ARTISTS AND ART HISTORY. Thomas B. Hess and Elizabeth C. Baker, eds. New York: Macmillan, 1973.

a) Why Have There Been No Great Women Artists? (L. Nochlin), 1-43; b) Great Women Artists (T.B. Hess), 44-54;
WHY HAVE THERE BEEN NO GREAT WOMEN ARTISTS? TEN REPLIES: c) Dialogue (E. de Kooning, R. Drexler), 56-81; d) Hermaphrodite (B. Riley), 82-83; e) Do Your Work (L. Nevelson), 84-85; f) Women without Pathos (E. Antin), 86-87; g) Double-Bind (S. Gablik), 88-89; h) Healthy Self-Love (S. Stone), 90-92; i) Moving Out, Moving Up (M. Strider), 93-95; j) Social Conditions Can Change (L. Benglis), 96-97; k) Artists Transgress All Boundaries (R. Castoro), 98-107; l) Sexual Art-Politics (E.C. Baker), 108-129; m) In the University (L. Hall), 130- .

16 AURORA: BEYOND EQUALITY. Susan Janice Anderson and Vonda N. McIntyre, eds. New York: Fawcett, 1976.

a) Your Faces, O My Sisters! Your Faces Filled of Light! (R. Sheldon), 16-35; b) Houston, Houston, Do You Read? (J. Tiptree, Jr.), 36-98; c) The Mothers, the Mothers, How Eerily It Sounds (D. Skal), 99-106; d) The Antrim Hills (M.D. Broxon), 107-129; e) Is Gender Necessary? (U.K. Le Guin), 130-139; f) Corruption (J. Russ), 140-155; g) Here Be Dragons (P.J. Plauger), 156-174; h) Why Has the Virgin Mary Never Entered the Wigwam of Standing Bear? (C. Strete), 175-181; i) Woman on

the Edge of Time (M. Piercy), 182-218.

17 THE AUTHORITY OF EXPERIENCE: ESSAYS IN FEMINIST CRITICISM. Arlyn Diamond and Lee R. Edwards, eds. Amherst: The University of Massachusetts Press, 1977.

a) Female Criticism (A. Barnes), 1-15; b) Silent Woman: Towards a Feminist Critique (M. Landy), 16-27; c) Women and Fiction (L. Sukenick), 28-44; d) "Slydynge of Corage": Chaucer's Criseyde as Feminist and Victim (M. Fries), 45-59; e) Chaucer's Women and Women's Chaucer (A. Diamond), 60-83; f) "The Taming of the Shrew": Shakespeare's Mirror of Marriage (C. Kahn), 84-100; g) Moll Flanders: "A Woman on her own Account" (M. Lerenbaum), 101-117; h) Richardson's Empathy with Women (K. Rogers), 118-136; i) "Jane Eyre": Woman's Estate (M. Adams), 137-159; j) War and Roses: The Politics of "Mrs. Dalloway" (L.R. Edwards), 160-177; k) "Out of the chaos, a new kind of strength": Doris Lessing's "The Golden Notebook" (M. Cohen), 178-193; l) Eve Among the Indians (D. Lander), 194-211; m) What if Bartleby Were a Woman? (P. Barber), 212-223; n) Old Critics and New: The Treatment of Chopin's "The Awakening" (P. Allen), 224-238; o) Winning: Katherine Anne Porter's Women (B.H. Carson), 239-256; p) "A Farewell to Arms": Ernest Hemingway's "Resentful Cryptogram" (J. Fetterley), 257-302.

18 BECOMING FEMALE: PERSPECTIVES ON DEVELOPMENT. Claire B. Kopp, ed. (With Martha Kirkpatrick) New York: Plenum, 1979.

a) Development of Female Identity (P.A. Katz), 3-28; b) Growing Up Black and Female (G.J. Powell), 29-66; c) Growing Up with a Physical Handicap (S. Sargent), 67-88; d) Father-Daughter Relationship: Past, Present, and Future (M.E. Lamb, M.T. Owen, L. Chase-Lansdale), 89-112; e) Mothers and Daughters (P.R. Magrab), 113-132; f) Sex-Related Differences in Spatial Ability: A Developmental Psychological View (L.J. Harris), 133-182; g) Role of Laughter and Humor in Growing Up Female (P.E. McGhee), 183-206; h) Changing Nature of Female Delinquency (S. Balkan, R.J. Berger), 207-228; i) Play of Girls (B. Sutton-Smith), 229-258; j) Effects of Observed Violence on Females (S.H. Franzblau), 259-290; k) Where Are the Women Genuises? (M.F. Graham, B. Birns), 291-312; l) Cross-Cultural Perspectives on Becoming Female (T.S. Weisner), 313-332; m) Role Music Plays in Adolescent Development (J. Marks), 333-362; n) Portrait of a Female on Television: Some Possible Effects on Children (N.D. Feshbach, A.S. Dillman, T.S. Jordan), 363-386; o) Dressing Up (S. Adler), 387-400; p) Genetics of Sex and Its Consequences (K.K. Kidd), 401-426; q) Physical Growth of Adolescent Girls: Patterns and Sequence (M.S. Faust), 427-448; r) Nutrition and Women: Facts and Faddism (C. Neumann), 449-462.

19 BECOMING VISIBLE: WOMEN IN EUROPEAN HISTORY. Renate Bridenthal and Claudia Koonz, eds. Boston: Houghton Mifflin, 1977.

a) Women in Egalitarian Societies (E. Leacock), 11-35; b) Women in Transition: Crete and Sumer (R. Rohrlich-Leavitt), 36-59; c)

"Liberated" Women: The Classical Era (M. Arthur), 60-89; d) Sanctity and Power: The Dual Pursuit of Medieval Women (J. McNamara, S.F. Wemple), 90-118; e) Pedestal and the Stake: Courtly Love and Witchcraft (E.W. Monter), 119-136; f) Did Women Have a Renaissance? (J. Kelly-Gadol), 137-164; g) Women in the Reformation Era (S.M. Wyntjes), 165-191; h) Women in Preindustrial Capitalism (R.T. Vann), 192-216; i) Women in the Age of Light (A.R. Kleinbaum), 217-235; j) Loaves and Liberty: Women in the French Revolution (R. Graham), 236-254; k) Working-Class Women During the Industrial Revolution, 1780-1914 (M.L. McDougall), 255-279; l) Long Road Home: Women's Work and Industrialization (T.M. McBride), 280-295; m) Angels in the Devil's Workshop: Leisured and Charitable Women in Nineteenth-Century England and France (B.C. Pope), 296-324; n) International Sisterhood (E.F. Hurwitz), 325-345; o) Women as Revolutionaries: The Case of the Russian Populists (B. Engel), 346-369; p) Love on the Tractor: Women in the Russian Revolution and After (B.G. Rosenthal), 370-399; q) Other Scenarios: Women and Spanish Anarchism (T. Kaplan), 400-421; r) Something Old, Something New: Women Between the Two World Wars (R. Bridenthal), 422-444; s) Mothers in the Fatherland: Women in Nazi Germany (C. Koonz), 445-473; t) Family Models of the Future (A. Michel), 474-488.

20 BEING FEMALE: REPRODUCTION, POWER AND CHANGE. Dana Raphael, ed. Proceedings of the Ninth International Congress of Anthropological and Ethnological Sciences, Chicago. (World Anthropology Series) The Hague: Mouton, 1975.

a) Reproduction (L. Newman), 7-12; b) Socialization of Non-Human Primate Females (F.E. Poirier), 13-18; c) Prenatal Hormones and Human Behavior: Implications for the Status of Women (A.A. Ehrhardt), 19-24; d) Spontaneous and Induced Abortion in Human and Non-Human Primates (E. Nurge), 25-36; e) Birth Rituals in Cross-Cultural Perspective: Some Practical Applications (N. Newton), 37-42; f) Relevance of Nourishment to the Reproductive Cycle of the Female in India (J. Katona-Apte), 43-48; g) Nutrition and Pregnancy (J.R.K. Robson), 49-54; h) Defining Marriage Cross-Culturally (B.W. Dillingham, B.L. Isaac), 55-64; i) Matrescence, Becoming a Mother, a "New-Old" "Rite de Passage" (D. Raphael), 65-72; j) Matri-Patrilocality and the Birth of the First Child (S.F. Wilson), 73-86; k) Affectivity and Instrumentality in Friendship Patterns among American Women (Y.-Y. Yuan), 87-98; l) Explanation for Matrilocal Residence (W.T. Divale), 99-110; m) Women and Power (D. Raphael), 111-116; n) Women and Domestic Power: Political and Economic Strategies in Domestic Groups (L. Lamphere), 117-130; o) Feminine Factor in Cultural History (A. Lomax), 131-138; p) Non-Hierarchical, Hierarchical, and Masked Reciprocity in the Arab Village (H. Rosenfeld), 139-154; q) Bundu: Political Implications of Female Solidarity in a Secret Society (C.P. Hoffer), 155-164; r) Three Styles of Domestic Authority: A Cross-Cultural Study (A. Schlegel), 165-176; s) Women's Movement in the U.S. (B.S. Allen), 177-188; t) American Women in Politics: Culture, Structure, and Ideology (L. Garretson), 189-202; u) Social Trends (R. Jahan), 203-206; v) Eurogallegas: Female Spanish Migration (J.-M.H. Buechler), 207-214; w) Attitudes Towards Reproduction in a Rapidly Changing African Society (J.M. Namboze), 215-218; x) Concepts of "Femininity" and "Liberation" in the Context of Changing Sex-Roles: Women in Modern India and America

(M. Roy), 219-230; y) Vietnamese Women: Their Roles and Their Options (M.W. Hoskins), 231-248; z) Changing Roles of Women in Two African Muslim Cultures (E.E. Lord), 249-254; aa) Women and Social Customs within the Family: A Case Study of Attitudes in Kerala, India (G. Kurian, M. John), 255-266; bb) Legal Equality between Men and Women (O. Vidláková), 267-272.

21 BEYOND INTELLECTUAL SEXISM: A NEW WOMAN, A NEW REALITY. Joan I. Roberts, ed. New York: David Mckay, 1976.

a) Ramifications of the Study of Women (J.I. Roberts), 3-13; b) Pictures of Power and Powerlessness (J.I. Roberts), 14-62; c) Brain, Body and Behavior (R.H. Bleier), 63-73; d) Female Strategies: Animal Adaptations and Adaptive Significance (G. Kass-Simon), 74-84; e) Essential Emancipation: The Control of Reproduction (H.W. Ris), 85-112; f) Psychological "Facts" About Women (J.A. Sherman), 113-137; g) Feminine Self-Preservation in Groups (J.A. Piliavin), 138-159; h) Women Social Workers and Clients: Common Victims of Sexism (D.F. Kravetz), 160-174; i) New Feminist Criticisms: Exploring the History of the New Space (A.V. Pratt), 175-195; j) French Women Writers: A Problematic Perspective (G. Brée), 196-209; k) Images of Women in Contemporary Mexican Literature (V.J. Meyer), 210-230; l) Women in Legal Perspective (K.F. Clarenbach), 231-240; m) Power, Patriarchy, and "Political Primitives" (B.C. Freeman), 241-264; n) Women Who Work for Wages (A. Seidman), 265-276; o) Ideal and the Reality: Women in Sweden (I. Camerini), 277-285; p) Women in China: Problems of Sex Inequality and Socio-economic Change (K.A. Johnson), 286-319; q) Erosion of Sexual Equality in the Kibbutz: A Structural Interpretation (R.L. Blumberg), 320-342; r) Women and Girls in the Public Schools: Defeat or Liberation? (E. Fennema), 343-352; s) Women and Higher Education (K. Merritt), 353-364; t) Women in Physical Education (J.M. Brown), 365-380; u) Status of Home Economics and the Status of Women (E.A. Monts, L.J. Burger), 381- .

22 BEYOND SEX-ROLE STEREOTYPES: READINGS TOWARD A PSYCHOLOGY OF ANDROGYNY. Alexandra G. Kaplan and Joan P. Bean, eds. Boston: Little, Brown, 1976.

a) Sex Differences (J. Bernard), 9-26; b) Masculinity-Femininity: An Exception to a Famous Dictim? (A. Constantinople), 27-46; c) Probing the Promise of Androgyny (S.L. Bem), 47-62; d) Conceptions of Sex Role: Some Cross-Cultural and Longitudinal Perspectives (J.H. Block), 63-78; e) Sex Equality: The Beginnings of Ideology (A.S. Rossi), 79-88; f) Model of Sex-Role Transcendence (M. Rebecca, R. Hefner, B. Oleshansky), 89-97; g) Biologic Basis for Sex-Role Stereotypes (M. Rosenberg), 105-123; h) Premenstrual Syndrome (M.B. Parlee), 124-136; i) Men's Cycles (E. Ramey), 137-142; j) Aborting a Fetus: The Legal Right, The Personal Choice (S. Lessard), 143-152; k) Phallacy of Our Sexual Norm (K.F. Rotkin), 153-162; l) Woman Identified Woman (Radicalesbians), 163-167; m) Parents' Views on Sex of Newborns (J.Z. Rubin, F.J. Provenzano, Z. Luria), 178-186; n) Cross-Cultural Analysis of Sex Differences in the Behavior of Children Aged Three Through Eleven (B. Whiting, C.P. Edwards), 187-205; o) Sex-Role Concepts and Sex

Typing in Childhood as a Function of School and Home Environments (P. Minuchin), 206-222; p) Sexual Role Identification and Personality Functioning in Girls (J.H. Williams), 223-231; q) Sex-Role Stereotyping in Children's Television Programs (S.H. Sternglanz, L.A. Serbin), 232-238; r) Socialization of Achievement-Orientation in Females (A.H. Stein, M.M. Bailey), 239-261; s) Androgynous Themes Written to Sentence Cues by Sixth-, Eighth-, and Tenth-Grade Students (J.P. Bean, J.G. Levy), 262-271; t) Relationship Between Sex Roles, Marital Status, and Mental Illness (W.R. Gove), 281-292; u) Effects of Maternal Employment on the Child (L.W. Hoffman), 293-318; v) Attitudinal Barriers to Occupational Aspirations in Women (V.E. O'Leary), 319-337; w) Politics of Sexual Stereotypes (M.C. King), 338-351; x) Androgyny as a Model of Mental Health for Women: From Theory to Therapy (A.G. Kaplan), 352-362; y) Personality and Ideology: A Personological Study of Women's Liberation (C. Cherniss), 363-380.

23 BEYOND THEIR SEX: LEARNED WOMEN OF THE EUROPEAN PAST. Patricia H. Labalme, ed. New York: New York University Press, 1980.

a) Education of Women in the Middle Ages in Theory, Fact, and Fantasy (J.M. Ferrante), 9-42; b) Women, Learning, and Power: Eleonora of Aragon and the Court of Ferrara (W.L. Gundersheimer), 43-65; c) Book-Lined Cells: Women and Humanism in the Early Italian Renaissance (M.L. King), 66-90; d) Learned Women of Early Modern Italy: Humanists and University Scholars (P.O. Kristeller), 91-116; e) Learned Women in the Europe of the Sixteenth Century (R.H. Bainton), 117-128; f) Women's Roles in Early Modern Venice (P.H. Labalme), 129-152; g) Gender and Genre: Women as Historical Writers, 1400-1820 (N.Z. Davis), 153-182.

24 BITCHES AND SAD LADIES: AN ANTHOLOGY OF FICTION BY AND ABOUT WOMEN. Pat Rotter, ed. New York: Harper's Magazine Press, 1975.

a) Interstices (G. Godwin), 1-13; b) The Lady With the Pet Dog (J.C. Oates), 14-32; c) The Hollow Woman (G. Adams), 33-38; d) Flotsam and Jetsam (S. Claiborne), 39-48; e) The Sex Maniac (H. Wolitzer), 49-54; f) Good Housekeeping (R. Brown), 55-57; g) An Education (C. Ozick), 58-99; h) Joy In Our Cause (C. Emshwiller), 100-108; i) The Route (J. Williams), 109-119; j) The Hour of the Wolf (M. Karapanou), 120-128; k) Re: Femme (R. Brown), 129-152; l) Vision (G. Cravens), 151-161; m) Man in the Cellar (J. O'Faolain), 162-202; n) Food (S. Holahan), 203-212; o) Four Stories About Lovers (A. Beattie), 213-224; p) Mama's Turn (B. Lowry), 225-236; q) The Good Humor Man (R. Morris), 237-248; r) Still Life With Fruit (D. Betts), 249-266; s) The Enemy (J. Mayhall), 267-277; t) Bertha Schneiders' Existential Edge (A. Dworkin), 278-282; u) Wet (L. Colwin), 283-290; v) Over (E. O'Brien), 291-306; w) In Search of a Missing I.U.D. (A. Higgins), 307-323; x) Coming To (H. Wolitzer), 324-329; y) The Sisters (M.P. Battin), 330-339; z) Some Thoughts on the Question of Being a Separate Human Being (J. Rossner), 340-343; aa) The Letting Down of the Hair (A. Sexton), 344-351; bb) The Long-Distance Runner (G. Paley), 352-367; cc) My Man Bovanne (T.C. Bambara), 368-374; dd) The Day Before the Revolution (U.K. Le Guin), 375-389; ee) Why Was It? (E. Kraf), 390-393; ff) Tearing (M. Blumenthal), 394-402; gg) Dreamy

(S. Sonnett), 403-405; hh) The Rape (L. Schor), 406-416; ii) Notes on a Necessary Pact (M.F.K. Fisher), 417-423.

25 BLACK MATRIARCHY: MYTH OR REALITY? John H. Bracey, Jr., August Meier, and Elliott Rudwick, eds. (Explorations in the Black Experience Series) Belmont, Ca.: Wadsworth, 1971.

a) Negro Family in America (E.F. Frazier), 6-19; b) Matriarchate (E.F. Frazier), 20-32; c) West African Influences (M.J. Herskovits), 34-52; d) Family in the Plantation South (C.S. Johnson), 54-75; e) Crucible of Identity: The Negro Lower-Class Family (L. Rainwater), 76-111; f) Fathers without Children (E. Liebow), 112-124; g) Negro Family: The Case for National Action (D.P. Moynihan), 126-159; h) Family: Resources for Change (H. Lewis, E. Herzog), 160-184; i) "Black Matriarchy" Reconsidered: Evidence from Secondary Analysis of Sample Surveys (H.H. Hyman, J.S. Reed), 186-193; j) Family and Childhood in a Southern Negro Community (V.H. Young), 194-217.

26 THE BLACK WOMAN: AN ANTHOLOGY. Toni Cade, comp. New York: New American Library, 1970.

This collection includes poems, short stories, essays, and documents which help to clarify the issues of concern to black women. Many contributors are professional writers, although an attempt has been made to offer work by a cross-section of black women. Contributors: N. Giovanni, K. Lindsey, A. Lorde, P. Marshall, A. Walker, S. Williams, J. Grant, F. Sanders, F. Beale, T. Cade, J.C. Bond, P. Peery, V.M. Smart-Grosvenor, M.W. Katz, J. Green, G. Patton, A. Cook, H. Williams, A. Jones, G.L. Boggs, H.C. Brehon, C. Brown, F. Covington, P. Robinson, A. Lincoln.

27 BLACK WOMEN IN NINETEENTH-CENTURY AMERICAN LIFE: THEIR WORDS, THEIR FEELINGS. Bert James Loewenberg and Ruth Bogin, eds. University Park: The Pennsylvania State University Press, 1976.

Writing by twenty-four women born prior to the Civil War is included in this anthology. They were selected for their observations "stemming from personal events or from participation in organized social or political movements." Contributors: S. Dubois, "Cornelia," L. Picquet, E. Keckley, E. Eldridge, S.K. Taylor, A.L. Burton, E. Craft, "Elizabeth," J. Lee, A.B. Smith, A. Plato, M. Stewart, N. Prince, H. Tubman, S.P. Remond, S. Truth, F.E.W. Harper, I. Wells-Barnett, F.B. Williams, C.F. Grimke, L.C. Laney, F.J. Coppin, A.J. Cooper.

28 BLACK WOMEN IN WHITE AMERICA. Gerda Lerner, comp. New York: Vintage, 1973.

This collection reflects the editor's intention to "define the major themes in the history of black women as suggested by source material now

available." Many of the pieces are previously unknown or little-known documents. Material is also included which elucidates the contributions of leaders whose work was recognized as significant during their lifetimes. The documents date from the early nineteenth century through the 1970s. Contributors: M. Harrison, S.K. Taylor, J.T. White, M. Granson, H. Tubman, E. Craft, F.J.Coppin, C.F. Grimke, S.P. Clark, L. Laney, N. Burroughs, M.M. Bethune, F.E.W. Harper, J.C. Brown, E.L. Shields, E.R. Haynes, M.V. Lewis, S. Martinez, F. Rice, C.A. Jackson, F.A.J. Gaudet, M.L. Baldwin, E. Tarry, S. Tuck, Mrs. Weddington, D.L. Bates, L. Meriwether, H.H. Howard, M.A.S. Cary, E.D. Bowles, M.C. Terrell, E.P. Ensley, Mrs. R.M. Patterson, C. Bass, E. Baker, S. Chisholm, A. Spain, S.M. Douglass, S. Truth, C.H. Brown, M. Jackson, A. Moody, J.St.P. Ruffin, M.M. Washington, A.A. Hedgeman, M.W. Stewart, I.B.W. Barnett, A.S. Jemand, D. Abubakari, A.J. Cooper, A.-J. Garvey, R. Ferguson, P. Murray, P. Robinson, M. Wright, F.L. Hamer.

29 BLACK-EYED SUSANS: CLASSIC STORIES BY AND ABOUT BLACK WOMEN. Mary Helen Washington, ed. Garden City, New York: Doubleday-Anchor, 1975.

a) Frankie Mae (J.W. Smith), 3-22; b) The Coming of Maureen Peal (T. Morrison), 23-36; c) If You're Light and Have Long Hair (G. Brooks), 37-44; d) The Self-Solace (G. Brooks), 45-50; e) A Happening in Barbados (L. Meriwether), 51-68; f) My Man Bovanne (T.C. Bambara), 69-77; g) Everyday Use (A. Walker), 78-92; h) Seemothermotherisverynice (T. Morrison), 93-113; i) Reena (P. Marshall), 114-140; j) A Sudden Trip Home in the Spring (A. Walker), 141-154.

30 BRIDEWEALTH AND DOWRY. Jack Goody and S.J. Tambiah. (Cambridge Papers in Social Anthropology) Cambridge: Cambridge (England) University Press, 1973.

a) Bridewealth and Dowry in Africa and Eurasia (J. Goody), 1-58; b) Dowry and Bridewealth and the Property Rights of Women in South Asia (S.J. Tambiah), 59- .

31 THE BURNING HEART: WOMEN POETS OF JAPAN. Kenneth Rexroth, ed. and trans. New York: Seabury Press, 1977.

In addition to representative poetry by Japanese women, this collection includes biographical notes about each poet, a survey of women's poetry in Japan, anonymous geisha poetry, and a table of Japanese historical periods. Contributors: Princess Nukada, Empress Jitō, Otomo no Sakanoe no Iratsume, Yosami, Wife of Hitomaro; Lady Kii, Kasa no Iratsume, Ono no Komachi, Lady Ise, Shirome, Lady Ukon, Murasaki Shikibu, Abazome Emon, Sei Shōnagon, Mother of Michitsuna, Daini no Sanmi, Izumi Shikibu, Ise Tayū, Lady Sagami, Lady Suwo, Princess Shikishi, Kenrei Mon-in Ukyō no Daibu, Giō, Yokobue, Shizuka, Lady Horikawa, the Daughter of Minamoto no Toshitaka, Shunzei's Daughter, Abutsu-Ni, K. Chigetsu-Ni, D. Sute-Jo,

O. Shushiki, Chine-Jo, F. Chiyo-Ni, Ukihashi, E. Seifu-Jo, M. Koyū-Ni, I. Sogetsu-Ni, Tagami-Ni, Y. Akiko, Y. Tomiko, C. Masako, K. Takeko, O. Kanoko, G. Miyoko, H. Shizue, A. Suharu, B. Akiko, S. Hisajo, M. Takajo, H. Takajo, N. Teijo, H. Tatsuko, Y. Mikajo, F. Sumako, H. Fumiko, N. Kiyoko, N. Chio, T. Toshiko, T. Masako, M. Futabako, I. Rin, S. Chie, I. Noriko, F. Tomoko, F. Hisako, S. Kazue, I. Michiko, T. Chimako, S. Kazuko, Y. Sachiko, K. Rumuko, T. Taeko, Y. Rie, A. Ikuko, K. Mieko, N. Junko.

32 BY A WOMAN WRITT: LITERATURE FROM SIX CENTURIES BY AND ABOUT WOMEN. Joan Goulianos, ed. Baltimore: Penguin, 1974, c1973.

Selections are taken from journals, letters, autobiographies, and other poetic and narrative work by women. These previously neglected or undervalued writings concern the experience of being a woman. Later writers include only women whose contributions were substantial. Arrangement is largely chronological. Contributors: M. Kempe, J. Anger, A. Thornton, M. Cavendish, A. Finch, A. Behn, M. Manley, M.W. Montagu, M. Wollstonecraft, M. Shelley, H. Martineau, O. Schreiner, K. Chopin, M.E.W. Freeman, D. Richardson, A. Nin, D. Laing, M. Walker, S. Ashton-Warner, M. Rukeyser.

33 BY AND ABOUT WOMEN: AN ANTHOLOGY OF SHORT FICTION. Beth Schneiderman, ed. New York: Harcourt, Brace, Jovanovich, 1973.

a) The Waltz (D. Parker), 3-8; b) Helen (G. Brooks), 9-12; c) Girl Reading (E. Taylor), 13-30; d) Wunderkind (C. McCullers), 31-44; e) The Child's Day (J. West), 45-56; f) Lappin and Lapinova (V. Woolf), 57-64; g) Bliss (K. Mansfield), 65-78; h) Cruel and Barbarous Treatment (M. McCarthy), 79-92; i) Unmailed, Unwritten Letters (J.C. Oates), 93-112; j) A Man and Two Women (D. Lessing), 113-132; k) Birth (A. Nin), 133-138; l) Foothold (E. Bowen), 139-158; m) See How They Run (M.E. Vroman), 159-180; n) One Summer (M. Lavin), 181-216; o) Natural History (C. Urdang), 217-274; p) Revelation (F. O'Connor), 275-294; q) The Jilting of Granny Weatherall (K.A. Porter), 295-304; r) Island (S. Jackson), 305-316; s) A Worn Path (E. Welty), 317-326.

34 BY WOMEN: AN ANTHOLOGY OF LITERATURE. Marcia McClintock Folsom and Linda Heinlein Kirschner, eds. Boston: Houghton Mifflin, 1976.

These writings are representative of women's creative opus from Sappho to the present. Although most of the selections are by American women, work by women of other nationalities is included. Arrangement is by genre (short stories, poetry, drama) or topic ("Search for Self," "In a Role," "Breaking Free"). Review questions are appended to each chapter. Contributors: K. Chopin, W. Cather, K.A. Porter, E. Bowen, E. Welty, J.C. Oates, P. McGinley, N. Giovanni, A. Nin, A. Petry, D. Levertov, S. Plath, D. Laing, G. Paley, N. Gordimer, Sappho, S.O. Jewett, M. Rukeyser, K. Mansfield, S. Glaspell, L. Hansberry, B. Deutsch, E. St.V. Millay, T. Olsen, A. Sexton, C. Kizer, F. O'Connor, A. Rich, Colette, M. McCarthy, C. Carrier, C. McCullers, C. Mew, A. Bradstreet,

C.P. Gilman, A. Lowell, Teresa of Avila, M. Cavendish, A. Behn, J.I. de La Cruz, A. Finch, P. Wheatley, E.B. Browning, E. Bronte, C. Rossetti, E. Dickinson, E. Wylie, H. Doolitle, E.M. Roberts, E. Sitwell, A. Akhmatova, G. Mistral, M. Moore, M. Tsvetayeva, S.T. Warner, D. Parker, L. Bogan, P. Ludwig, M. Zaturenska, J. Miles, M. Sarton, G. Brooks, M. Swenson, M. Evans, M. Van Duyn, M. Kumin, P. Cumming, D. Chang, B. Akhmadulina, M. Atwood, M.W. Freeman, S. Teasdale, U. MacDougall, F. Kemble, J. West, I. Dinesen, M. Walker, D. Lessing, M. Moore, D. Wakoski, V. Woolf.

35 CAPITALIST PATRIARCHY AND THE CASE FOR SOCIALIST FEMINISM. Zillah R. Eisenstein, ed. New York: Monthly Review Press, 1979, c1978.

a) Developing a Theory of Capitalist Patriarchy and Socialist Feminism (Z. Eisenstein), 5-40; b) Relations of Capitalist Patriarchy (Z. Eisenstein), 41-55; c) Feminist Theory and the Development of Revolutionary Strategy (N. Hartsok), 56-82; d) Mothering, Male Dominance, and Capitalism (N. Chodorow), 83-106; e) Struggle for Reproductive Freedom: Three Stages of Feminism (L. Gordon), 107-136; f) Nineteenth-Century Woman Suffrage Movement and the Analysis of Women's Oppression (E. DuBois), 137-150; g) Femininity and Capitalism in Antebellum America (M.P. Ryan), 151-172; h) Women's Domestic Labor (J. Gardiner), 173-189; i) Monopoly Capital and the Structure of Consumption (B. Weinbaum, A. Bridges), 190-205; j) Capitalism, Patriarchy, and Job Segregation by Sex (H. Hartmann), 206-247; k) Feminization of the Clerical Labor Force (M. Davies), 248-270; l) Women and Work in Cuba (C. Bengelsdorf, A. Hageman), 271-295; m) Introducing the Family Code (M. Randall), 296-298; n) Significance of the Chinese Family Revolution for Feminist Theory (J. Stacey), 299-354; o) Berkeley-Oakland Women's Union Statement, 355-361; p) Black Feminist Statement (Combahee River Collective), 362-372; q) Report on Marxist-Feminist Groups 1-5 (R. Petchesky), 375-390.

36 A CASE FOR EQUITY: WOMEN IN ENGLISH DEPARTMENTS. Susan McAllester, comp. Urbana, Il.: National Council of Teachers of English, 1971.

a) Report on Women and the Profession (F. Howe), 1-8; b) Women and the Literary Curriculum (E. Showalter), 9-16; c) Identity and Expression: A Writing Course for Women (F. Howe), 17-25; d) New Feminist Criticism (A. Pratt), 26-32; e) Dwelling in Decencies: Radical Criticism and the Feminist Perspective (L.S. Robinson), 33-43; f) American Galatea (J.H. Montgomery), 44-53; g) Great American Bitch (D.B. Schmidt), 54-59; h) Emily Bronte in the Hands of Male Critics (C. Ohmann), 60-67; i) "Featureless Freedom" or Ironic Submission: Dorothy Richardson and May Sinclair (S. Kaplan), 68-71; j) Women in Children's Literature (A.P. Nilsen), 72-80; k) Job Market for Women: A Department Chairman's View (G. Gleason), 81-85; l) Response to Mr. Gleason (M.A. Ferguson), 86-88; m) University Women and the Law (S.P. Fuentes),

89-92; n) Twelfthmonth, or What You Get (A.L. Hopwood), 93- .

37 THE CHANGING ROLES OF MEN AND WOMEN. Edmund Dahlstrom, ed. Boston: Beacon Press, 1971, 1967.

a) Family and Married Women at Work (E. Dahlstrom, R. Liljestrom), 19-58; b) Sex Roles and the Socialization Process (S. Brun-Gulbrandsen), 59-78; c) Parental Role Division and the Child's Personality Development (P.O. Tiller), 79-104; d) Positions of Men and Women in the Labour Market (A. Baude, P. Holmberg), 105-134; e) Employer Attitudes to Female Employees (S. Thorsell), 135-169; f) Analysis of the Debate on Sex Roles (E. Dahlstrom), 170-206; g) APPENDIX: Status of Women in Sweden: Report to the United Nations, 1968, 209- .

38 CHANGING ROLES OF WOMEN IN INDUSTRIAL SOCIETIES. (Working Papers, The Rockefeller Foundation) New York: Rockefeller Foundation, 1977.

a) Social Trends and Women's Lives--1965-1985 (A.S. Rossi), 64-100; b) Evolving Relationships Between Women and Men (J. Katz), 101-117; c) Educating Women for Leadership (M. Rendel), 118-137; d) Projected Future Employment and Leadership Needs and Areas (A. Michel), 138- .

39 CHANGING WOMEN IN A CHANGING SOCIETY. Joan Huber, ed. Chicago: The University of Chicago Press, 1973.

a) Maid of All Work or Departmental Sister-in-Law? The Faculty Wife Employed on Campus (H.M. Hughes), 5-10; b) My Four Revolutions: An Autobiographical History of the A.S.A. (J. Bernard), 11-29; c) Origins of the Women's Liberation Movement (J. Freeman), 30-49; d) Adult Sex Roles and Mental Illness (W.R. Gove, J.F. Tudor), 50-73; e) Salon, Foyer, Bureau: Women and the Professions in France (C.B. Silver), 74-89; f) Men, Women, and Work: Reflections on the Two-Person Career (H. Papanek), 90-110; g) Cultural Contradictions and Sex Roles: The Masculine Case (M. Komarovsky), 111-122; h) Swinging: A Study of Decision Making in Marriage (A.-M. Henshel), 123-129; i) Changing Role of Women in the Armed Forces (N. Goldman), 130-149; j) Positive Effects of the Multiple Negative: Explaining the Success of Black Professional Women (C.F. Epstein), 150-173; k) Women and Social Stratification: A Case of Intellectual Sexism (J. Acker), 174-183; l) Demographic Influence on Female Employment and the Status of Women (V.K. Oppenheimer), 184-199; m) Income Differences between Men and Career Women (L.E. Suter, H.P. Miller), 200-212; n) Women, Work, and Wedlock: A Note on Female Marital Patterns in the U.S. (E.M. Havens), 213-219; o) Impediment or Stimulant? Marital Status and Graduate Education (S.D. Feldman), 220-232; p) Performance, Rewards, and Perceptions of Sex Discrimination among Male and Female Faculty (M.A. Ferber, J.W. Loeb), 233-230; q) Social Relations of Black and White Widowed Women in a Northern Metropolis (H.Z. Lopata), 241-248; r) Sex Role Research (A.R. Hochschild), 249-267; s) Woman Book Industry

35 CAPITALIST PATRIARCHY AND THE CASE FOR SOCIALIST FEMINISM. Zillah R. Eisenstein, ed. New York: Monthly Review Press, 1979, c1978.

36 A CASE FOR EQUITY: WOMEN IN ENGLISH DEPARTMENTS. Susan McAllester, comp. Urbana, Il.: National Council of Teachers of English, 1971.

89-92; n) Twelfthmonth, or What You Get (A.L. Hopwood), 93- .

37 THE CHANGING ROLES OF MEN AND WOMEN. Edmund Dahlstrom, ed. Boston: Beacon Press, 1971, 1967.

a) Family and Married Women at Work (E. Dahlstrom, R. Liljestrom), 19-58; b) Sex Roles and the Socialization Process (S. Brun-Gulbrandsen), 59-78; c) Parental Role Division and the Child's Personality Development (P.O. Tiller), 79-104; d) Positions of Men and Women in the Labour Market (A. Baude, P. Holmberg), 105-134; e) Employer Attitudes to Female Employees (S. Thorsell), 135-169; f) Analysis of the Debate on Sex Roles (E. Dahlstrom), 170-206; g) APPENDIX: Status of Women in Sweden: Report to the United Nations, 1968, 209- .

38 CHANGING ROLES OF WOMEN IN INDUSTRIAL SOCIETIES. (Working Papers, The Rockefeller Foundation) New York: Rockefeller Foundation, 1977.

a) Social Trends and Women's Lives--1965-1985 (A.S. Rossi), 64-100; b) Evolving Relationships Between Women and Men (J. Katz), 101-117; c) Educating Women for Leadership (M. Rendel), 118-137; d) Projected Future Employment and Leadership Needs and Areas (A. Michel), 138- .

39 CHANGING WOMEN IN A CHANGING SOCIETY. Joan Huber, ed. Chicago: The University of Chicago Press, 1973.

a) Maid of All Work or Departmental Sister-in-Law? The Faculty Wife Employed on Campus (H.M. Hughes), 5-10; b) My Four Revolutions: An Autobiographical History of the A.S.A. (J. Bernard), 11-29; c) Origins of the Women's Liberation Movement (J. Freeman), 30-49; d) Adult Sex Roles and Mental Illness (W.R. Gove, J.F. Tudor), 50-73; e) Salon, Foyer, Bureau: Women and the Professions in France (C.B. Silver), 74-89; f) Men, Women, and Work: Reflections on the Two-Person Career (H. Papanek), 90-110; g) Cultural Contradictions and Sex Roles: The Masculine Case (M. Komarovsky), 111-122; h) Swinging: A Study of Decision Making in Marriage (A.-M. Henshel), 123-129; i) Changing Role of Women in the Armed Forces (N. Goldman), 130-149; j) Positive Effects of the Multiple Negative: Explaining the Success of Black Professional Women (C.F. Epstein), 150-173; k) Women and Social Stratification: A Case of Intellectual Sexism (J. Acker), 174-183; l) Demographic Influence on Female Employment and the Status of Women (V.K. Oppenheimer), 184-199; m) Income Differences between Men and Career Women (L.E. Suter, H.P. Miller), 200-212; n) Women, Work, and Wedlock: A Note on Female Marital Patterns in the U.S. (E.M. Havens), 213-219; o) Impediment or Stimulant? Marital Status and Graduate Education (S.D. Feldman), 220-232; p) Performance, Rewards, and Perceptions of Sex Discrimination among Male and Female Faculty (M.A. Ferber, J.W. Loeb), 233-230; q) Social Relations of Black and White Widowed Women in a Northern Metropolis (H.Z. Lopata), 241-248; r) Sex Role Research (A.R. Hochschild), 249-267; s) Woman Book Industry

(C. Ehrlich), 268-282; t) Women in Gynecology Textbooks (D. Scully, P. Bart), 283-288; u) Introducing Students to Women's Place in Society (B.F. Kirschner), 289-292.

40 CHILD CARE AND PUBLIC POLICY: STUDIES OF THE ECONOMIC ISSUES. Philip K. Robins and Samuel Weiner, eds. Lexington, Ma.: Lexington Books, 1978.

a) Economic and Policy Issues of Child Care (P.K. Robins, S. Weiner), 1-16; b) Public Policy Toward Child Care in America: A Historical Perspective (J.D. Marver, M.A. Larson), 17-42; c) Child Care Market in Seattle and Denver (S. Weiner), 43-86; d) Substitution Among Child Care Modes and the Effect of a Child Care Subsidy Program (P.K. Robins, R.G. Spiegelman), 87-102; e) Quality of Day Care: Can It Be Measured (J. Stallings, M. Wilcox), 103-132; f) Vouchers for Child Care: The Santa Clara Child Care Pilot Study (S. Stoddard), 133-156; g) Estimating Cost Equations for Day Care (A. Hall), 157-186; h) Cost of Compliance with Federal Day Care Standards in Seattle and Denver (S. Weiner), 187-226.

41 CLASS, SEX AND THE WOMAN WORKER. Milton Cantor and Bruce Laurie, eds. Westport, Ct.: Greenwood Press, 1977.

a) Systematic Study of Urban Women (S.J. Kleinberg), 20-42; b) Women, Work and Protest in the Early Lowell Mills (T. Dublin), 43-63; c) New England Mill Women in the Early Nineteenth Century (L. Vogel), 64-82; d) Women Workers in a Mid-Nineteenth-Century New York City Community (C. Groneman), 83-100; e) Italian Women and Work: Experience and Perception (V. Yans-McLaughlin), 101-119; f) Italian-American Women in New York City, 1900-1950: Work and School (M. Cohen), 120-143; g) Organizing the Unorganizable: Three Jewish Women and Their Union (A. Kessler-Harris), 144-165; h) Imperfect Unions: Class and Gender in Cripple Creek, 1894- 1904 (E. Jameson), 166-202; i) Women's Trade Union League and American Feminism (R.M. Jacoby), 203-224; j) Creating a Feminist Alliance: Sisterhood and Class Conflict in the New York Women's Trade Union League, 1903- 1914 (N.S. Dye), 225-246.

42 CLIO'S CONSCIOUSNESS RAISED: NEW PERSPECTIVES ON THE HISTORY OF WOMEN. Mary S. Hartman and Lois W. Banner, eds. New York: Harper and Row, 1974.

a) "Fashionable Diseases": Women's Complaints and Their Treatment in Nineteenth-Century America (A.D. Wood), 1-22; b) Puberty to Menopause: The Cycle of Femininity in Nineteenth-Century America (C. Smith-Rosenberg), 23-37; c) Lady and Her Physician (R. Morantz), 38-53; d) Voluntary Motherhood: The Beginnings of Feminist Birth Control Ideas in the U.S. (L. Gordon), 54-71; e) Salon, Foyer, Bureau: Women and the Professions in France (C.B. Silver), 72-85; f) Sexual Politics of Victorian Social Anthropology (E. Fee), 86-102; g) Power of Women Through the Family in Medieval Europe: 500-1100 (J.A. McNamara, S. Wemple), 103-118; h) Family Limitation, Sexual Control, and Domestic

Feminism in Victorian America (D.S. Smith), 119-136; i) Feminization of American Religion: 1800-1860 (B. Welter), 137-157; j) Tender Technicians: Feminization of Public Librarianship, 1876-1905 (D. Garrison), 158-178; k) Image and Reality: The Myth of the Idle Victorian Woman (P. Branca), 179-191; l) Prostitution and the Poor in Plymouth and Southampton Under the Contagious Diseases Act (J.R. Walkowitz, D.J. Walkowitz), 192-225; m) Welfare of Women in Laboring Families: England, 1860-1950 (L. Oren), 226-244; n) Case Study of Technological and Social Change: The Washing Machine and the Working Wife (R.S. Cowan), 245- .

43 COMPARATIVE PERSPECTIVES OF THIRD WORLD WOMEN: THE IMPACT OF RACE, SEX, AND CLASS. Beverly Lindsay, ed. (Praeger Special Studies) New York: Praeger, 1980.

a) Perspectives and Introduction (B. Lindsay), 1-30; b) African Women and National Development (S. Lewis), 31-54; c) Women in Zaire: Disparate Status and Roles (L. Adams), 55-77; d) Issues Confronting Professional African Women: Illustrations from Kenya (B. Lindsay), 78-95; e) Chinese Women: The Relative Influences of Ideological Revolution, Economic Growth, and Cultural Change (B.L. Chan Wang), 96-122; f) Effects of Class and Sex on Political Life in Northern India (T.K. Devon), 123-142; g) Caribbean Women: The Impact of Race, Sex, and Class (G.I. Joseph), 143-161; h) Women in Cuba: The Revolution Within the Revolution (J.B. Cole), 162-178; i) Ancient Song, New Melody in Latin America: Women and Film (N.J. Weiser), 179-202; j) Native American Women: Twilight of a Long Maidenhood (L.W. Wittstock), 207-228; k) La Chicana: Guadalupe or Malinche (S.A. Gonzales), 229-250; l) Black Woman: Liberated or Oppressed? (G.R. Puryear), 251-275; m) Schooling of Vietnamese Immigrants: Internal Colonialism and its Impact on Women (G.P. Kelly), 276-296; n) Third World Women and Social Reality: Conclusion (B. Lindsay), 297-312.

44 CONCISE HISTORY OF WOMAN SUFFRAGE: SELECTIONS FROM THE CLASSIC WORK OF STANTON, ANTHONY, GAGE, AND HARPER. Mary Jo Buhle and Paul Buhle. Urbana: University of Illinois Press, 1978.

These excerpts are taken from the six-volume "History of Woman Suffrage," edited by Elizabeth Cady Stanton, Susan B. Anthony, Matilda Joslyn Gage, and Ida Husted Harper. The collection includes reports, reminiscences, speeches, and commentary about the American women's suffrage movement. Contributors: A. Kelley, M.J. Gage, S.T. Smith, A. Grimke, L. Mott, F.D. Gage, E. Rose, M.C. Vaughan, L. Stone, E.C. Stanton, A. Brown, S.B. Anthony, E. Jones, C. Sumner, H. Blackwell, S. Truth, V. Woodhull, O. Brown, C.C. Catt, B. Kearney, M.S. Howell, C.B. Colby, R.C.D. Havens, C.D. Wright, C.P. Gilman, A.G. Spencer, H.S. Blatch, F. Kelley, A. Barrows, J. Addams, L.J. Graddick, E.C. Phillips, C.A. Lowe, W. Wilson, A.H. Shaw.

CONFERENCE ON AGING, 26th, University of Michigan, 1973.
See: 146 NO LONGER YOUNG

CONFERENCE ON NONSEXIST EARLY CHILDHOOD EDUCATION.
See: 156 PERSPECTIVES ON NON-SEXIST EARLY CHILDHOOD EDUCATION

45 CONFERENCE ON THE EDUCATIONAL AND OCCUPATIONAL NEEDS OF BLACK WOMEN, December 16-17, 1975. Volume 2: Research Papers. Washington, D.C.: National Institute of Education, U.S. Department of Health, Education and Welfare, 1978.

a) Socialization and Education of Young Black Girls in Schools (S.L. Lightfoot), 3-32; b) Full Equality: More Job Education for Women (P.A. Roby), 33-70; c) Professional Schools and Their Impact on Black Women (E. Shaw), 71-86; d) Counseling Implications of Black Women's Market Position, Aspirations and Expectancies (P. Gurin, A. Pruitt), 87-154; e) Baseline Data on Mid-Career Change and Reentry for Black Women (B.A. Cossey, G.O. Toney), 155-168; f) Black Women Who Head Families: Economic Needs and Economic Resources (I.V. Sawhill), 169-182; g) Policy Issues on Day Care: The Special Needs of Black Working Women (B.S. Whaley, T.B. Lewis), 183-202; h) Health Issues Facing Black Women (I.S. Reid), 203-226; i) Media and Their Effect on Black Images (B. Rawles), 227-254; j) APPENDIX: Educational and Occupational Statistics on Black Women (E.C. Lee), 255- .

46 CONTEMPORARY FRENCH WOMEN POETS: A BILINGUAL CRITICAL ANTHOLOGY. Carl W. Hermey, ed. and trans. (Perivale Translation Series No. 4) Van Nuys, Ca: Perivale Press, 1977.

This bilingual anthology is intended to encourage critical discussion and recognition of the poetry of Thérèse Plantier, Andrée Chedid, Annie Salager, Marie Françoise Prager, Yvonne Caroutch and Denise Grappe. The poets were chosen because of their contribution to the shaping of a "contemporary poetic vision which goes beyond national and linguistic boundaries."

47 CONTEMPORARY WOMEN NOVELISTS: A COLLECTION OF CRITICAL ESSAYS. Patricia Meyer Spacks, ed. Englewood Cliffs, N.J.: Prentice-Hall, 1977.

a) Margaret Drabble: Novels of a Cautious Feminist (V.K. Beards), 18-29; b) Disorderly Company: From "The Golden Notebook" to "The Four-Gated City" (D. Barnouw), 30-54; c) Doris Lessing in the Sixties: The New Anatomy of Melancholy (F.R. Karl), 55-74; d) Case Against McCarthy: A Review of "The Group" (N. Mailer), 75-84; e) Mary McCarthy: Society's Demands (P.M. Spacks), 85-91; f) Iris Murdoch: The Novelist as Magician, The Magician as Artist (L. Kuehl), 92-107; g) Women in the Novels of Ann Petry (T.J. Shinn), 108-117; h) Character and Themes in the Novels of Jean Rhys (E.W. Mellown), 118-136; i) Muriel Spark's Fingernails (M. Bradbury), 137-149; j) "Delta Wedding" as Region and Symbol (J.E. Hardy), 150-166; k) Eudora's Web (J.C. Oates), 167-172;

l) APPENDIX: Chronology of Important Dates, 173-176.

48 CORPORATE LIB: WOMEN'S CHALLENGE TO MANAGEMENT. Eli Ginsberg and Alice M. Yohalem, eds. (Policy Studies in Employment and Welfare, No. 17) Baltimore: The Johns Hopkins University Press, 1973.

a) New Reality (E. Ginzberg, A.M. Yohalem), 1-8; b) Challenge to Management (E.A. Robie), 9-29; c) Sociologist's Skepticism (V.K. Oppenheimer), 30-38; d) Like Their Fathers Instead (R. Park), 39-57; e) Brainwashed Women (M.S. Fasenmyer), 58-62; f) Economist's View of Women's Work (J.W. Kuhn), 63-68; g) Sex Discrimination (P. Wallace), 69-84; h) Sources of Inequality (J. Kreps), 85-96; i) Family Life of the Successful Woman (W. Goode), 97-117; j) Family Life in Transition (E. Janeway), 118-124; k) Government in the Lead (M.H. Moskow), 125-132; l) Larger Stakes (C. De Carlo), 133-139; m) Challenge and Resolution (E. Ginzberg), 140- .

49 COVERT DISCRIMINATION AND WOMEN IN THE SCIENCES. Judith A. Ramaley, ed. (A.A.A.S. Selected Symposia Series, No. 14) Boulder, Co.: Westview Press, 1978.

a) Individual and the Institution (E.v.P. Smith), 7-36; b) Setting Up an Affirmative Action Program (L.J. Biermann), 37-44; c) Affirmative Action and the Continuing Majority: Women of All Races and Minority Men (C.A. Bonosaro), 45-64; d) Psychological Barriers for Women in Sciences: Internal and External (I.H. Frieze), 65-96; e) Male and Female Leadership Styles: The Double Bind (J.B. Chapman), 97-120.

50 CRIME ON HER MIND: FIFTEEN STORIES OF FEMALE SLEUTHS FROM THE VICTORIAN ERA TO THE FORTIES. Michelle B. Slung, ed. New York: Pantheon Books, 1975.

a) The Murder at Troyte's Hill (C.L. Pirkis), 3-33; b) The Man with the Wild Eyes (G.R. Sims), 34-61; c) The Stir Outside the Cafe Royal (C. Rook), 62-69; d) Mr. Bovey's Unexpected Will (L.T. Meade, R. Eustace), 70-89; e) The Fordwych Castle Mystery (Emmuska, Baroness Orczy), 90-111; f) The Man with Nine Lives (H.C. Weir), 112-151; g) The Golden Slipper (A.K. Green), 152-171; h) The Dope Fiends (A.B. Reeve), 172-191; i) The Murder at Fernhurst (H. Footner), 192-217; j) Too Many Dukes (E.P. Oppenheim), 218-242; k) The Calico Dog (M.G. Eberhart), 243-275; l) Angel Face (W. Irish), 276-307; m) The Mother of the Detective (G.D.H. Cole, M. Cole), 308-315; n) Daisy Bell (G. Mitchell), 316-333; o) Snafu Murder (S. Palmer), 334-356; p) APPENDIX: Women Detectives A Chronological Survey, 357-378.

51 THE CRIMINOLOGY OF DEVIANT WOMEN. Freda Adler and Rita James Simon, eds. Boston: Houghton Mifflin, 1979.

a) Look to the Future (R.J. Simon), 6-9; b) Criminals and Prostitutes (C. Lombroso, W. Ferrero), 10-13; c) Criminality of Women (W.A. Bonger), 14-21; d) Five Hundred Delinquent Women (E. Glueck, S. Glueck), 22-36; e) Masked Character of Female Crime (O. Pollack), 37-44; f) Sex Factor: Female Delinquency (H. Mannheim), 45-57; g) Etiology of Female Crime (D. Klein), 58-81; h) Any Woman's Blues (D. Klein, J. Kress), 82-90; i) Changing Patterns (F. Adler), 91-94; j) Arrest Statistics (R.J. Simon), 101-113; k) Crimes of Violence by Women (D.A. Ward, M. Jackson, R.E. Ward), 114-138; l) Race and Sex Differences (M. Wolfgang), 139-149; m) Woman as Terrorist (H.H.A. Cooper), 150-157; n) Shoplifting (M.O. Cameron), 158-166; o) Criminality in the Workplace: A Comparison of Male and Female Offenders (A. Franklin), 167-170; p) "Crime as Business" and the Female Offender (R.F. Sparks), 171-179; q) Women Criminals in Progressive New York (A. Block), 180-195; r) Prostitution: An Extreme Case of Sex Stratification (B. Heyl), 196-210; s) Prostitution Papers (K. Millett), 211-212; t) Oldest and Newest Profession (F. Adler), 213-222; u) Opiate Addiction Among Females in the United States Between 1850 and 1970 (W.R. Cuskey, T. Premkumar, L. Sigel), 223-248; v) Women in Court (R.J.Simon), 254-263; w) Women as Litigants (S.S. Nagel, L.J. Weitzman), 264-272; x) Discriminatory Sentencing of Women Offenders (C.E. Temin), 273-286; y) Sex Discrimination in the Criminal Law (L.J. Frankel), 287-306; z) Forgotten Offender: The Woman in Prison (R.J. Simon), 313-318; aa) Sexual Segregation of American Prisons (R.R. Arditi, F. Goldberg, Jr., M.M. Hartle, J.H. Peters, W.R. Phelps), 319-335; bb) Women and the Correctional Process (L.R. Singer), 336-343; cc) Competing Goals, Heterogeneity, and Classification (R. Giallombardo), 344-353; dd) Concrete Womb: "Gettin' In" (K.W. Burkhardt), 354-371; ee) Recidivism Among Women Parolees: A Long-Term Survey (C. Spencer, J.E. Berocochea), 372-379; ff) Parole System: How Women Fare (R.J. Simon), 380-386; gg) Women and Crime: Does the American Experience Generalize? (R.J. Simon, N. Sharma), 391-400; hh) Expansion and Distribution of Crime (M. Lopez-Rey), 401-406; ii) Interaction Between Women's Emancipation and Female Criminality: A Cross-Cultural Perspective (F. Adler), 407-418.

52 DAMNED ART: ESSAYS IN THE LITERATURE OF WITCHCRAFT. Sydney Anglo, ed. London: Routledge and Kegan Paul, 1977.

a) Evident Authority and Authoritative Evidence: the "Malleus Maleficarum" (S. Anglo), 1-31; b) Witchcraft and Magic in Renaissance Italy: Gianfrancesco Pico and his "Strix" (P. Burke), 32-52; c) Johann Weyer's "De Praetigiis Daemonum": Unsystematic Psychopathology (C. Baxter), 53-75; d) Jean Bodin's "De la Demonomanie des Sorciers": The Logic of Persecution (C. Baxter), 76-105; e) Reginald Scot's "Discoverie of Witchcraft": Scepticism and Sadduceeism (S. Anglo), 106-139; f) Tudor Anthropologist: George Gifford's "Discourse " and "Dialogue" (A. MacFarlane), 140-155; g) King James's "Daemonologie": Witchcraft and Kingship (S. Clark), 156-181; h) Pierre de Lancre's "Tableau de l'Inconstance des Mauvais Anges et Demons": The Sabbat Sensationalised (M.M. McGowan), 182-201; i) Cotton Mather's "Wonders of the Invisible World": Some Metamorphoses of Salem Witchcraft (M.W. Thomas), 202-226; j) Two Late Scottish Witchcraft Tracts: "Witch-Craft Proven" and "The Tryal of Witchcraft" (C. Larner),

227-245; k) Desiderata of Disbelief (S. Anglo), 246-248.

53 DEFINING FEMALES: THE NATURE OF WOMEN IN SOCIETY. Shirley Ardener, ed. New York: Wiley, 1978.

a) Nature of Women in Society (S. Ardener), 9-48; b) Semantics of Biology: Virginity (K. Hastrup), 49-65; c) Open Body, Closed Space: The Transformation of Female Sexuality (R. Hirschon), 66-88; d) Women, Taboo and the Supression of Attention (C. Humphrey), 89-108; e) Privileged, Schooled and Finished: Boarding Education for Girls (J. Okely), 109-139; f) Matrifocus on African Women (W. James), 140-162; g) "Most Essentially Female Function of All": Giving Birth (H. Callaway), 163-185; h) Female Brain: A Neuropsychological Viewpoint (F. Newcombe, G. Ratcliff), 186-199; i) Harems and Overlords: Biosocial Models and the Female (H. Callan), 200-219.

54 DEMOGRAPHIC ASPECTS OF THE CHANGING STATUS OF WOMEN IN EUROPE. Proceedings for the Second European Population Seminar. Marry Niphius-Nell, ed. (Publications of the Netherlands Interuniversity Demographic Institute and the Population and Family Study Centre, Vol. 7) Leiden: Martinus Nijhoff, 1978.

a) Population and the Status of Women: Results of the Bucharest and Mexico Conferences (Seminar Organizing Committee); b) Measurement of the Status of Women (R.W. Hommes); c) Divorce and the Status of Women (W.A. Dumon); d) Marriage and Marriage Dissolution and the Changing Status of Women: The Case of Poland (J. Piotrowski); e) Changes in Czechoslovak Marital Fertility (Z. Pavlik, J. Zborilova); f) Marital Fertility and the Changing Status of Women in Europe (A. Pinnelli); g) Extra-Marital Fertility and its Occurrence in Stable Unions: Recent Trends in Western Europe (P. Festy); h) Sociological and Demographic Aspects of the Changing Status of Migrant Women in Europe (H.-J. Hoffman-Nowotny); i) Report of the Symposium on Demographic Aspects of the Changing Status of Women in Europe (S. Vanistendael).

55 DEPENDENCE AND EXPLOITATION IN WORK AND MARRIAGE. Diane Leonard Barker and Sheila Allen, eds. London: Longman, 1976.

a) Women as Employees: Some Comments on Research in Industrial Sociology (R. Brown), 21-46; b) Sexual Divisions and the Dual Labour Market (R.D. Barron, G.M. Norris), 47-69; c) Sex and Occupational Role on Fleet Street (R. Smith), 70-87; d) Homeworkers in North London (E. Hope, M. Kennedy, A. De Winter), 88-108; e) Political Economy of Domestic Labour in Capitalist Society (J. Gardiner), 109-120; f) Rationalization of Housework (L. Davidoff), 121-151; g) Husbands and Wives: The Dynamics of the Deferential Dialectic (C. Bell, H. Newby), 152-168; h) Sexual Antagonism in Herefordshire (A. Whitehead), 169-203; i) Marriage, Role Division and Social Cohesion: The Case of Some French Upper-Middle Class Families (J. Marceau), 204-223; j)

Purdah in the British Situation (V. Saiffulah-Khan), 224-245.

56 THE DEVELOPMENT OF SEX DIFFERENCES. Eleanor E. Maccoby, ed. (Stanford Studies in Psychology, No. 5) Stanford: Stanford University Press, 1966.

a) Sex Hormones in the Development of Sex Differences in Human Behavior (D.A. Hamburg, D.T. Lunde), 1-24; b) Sex Differences in Intellectual Functioning (E.E. Maccoby), 25-55; c) Social-Learning View of Sex Differences in Behavior (W. Mischel), 56-81; d) Cognitive--Developmental Analysis of Children's Sex-Role Concepts and Attitudes (L. Kohlberg), 82-172; e) Sex Differences and Cultural Institutions (R.G. D'Andrade), 173-203; f) Afterword (S.M. Dornbusch), 204-222; g) Annotated Bibliography (R.M. Oetzel), 223-322; h) Classified Summary of Research in Sex Differences, 323- .

57 DIALOGUE ON DIVERSITY: A NEW AGENDA FOR AMERICAN WOMEN. Barbara Peters and Victoria Samuels, eds. New York: Institute on Pluralism and Group Identity, 1976.

a) Challenge of the "New Pluralism" (N. Seifer), 9-14; b) Brief Glimpses of Herstory (L. Lamphere), 15-21; c) Southern Woman (R. Hobson), 22-28; d) Black Woman (M. Russell), 29-34; e) White Ethnic Catholic Woman (B. Mikulski), 35-41; f) Jewish Woman (A. Wolfe), 42-50; g) Trade Union Woman (M. Albert), 51-58; h) Women's Movement Meets the Challenge of Diversity (C. Samuels), 59-68; i) APPENDIX: U.S. National Women's Agenda, 81- .

58 DISTAVES AND DAMES: RENAISSANCE TREATISES FOR AND ABOUT WOMEN. Diane Borstein, (ed.) Delmar, N.Y.: Scholars' Facsimiles and Reprints, 1978.

a) Gospelles of Dystaves (n.d.); b) Northren Mother's Blessing (1597); c) Boke of the Cyte of Ladyes (1521); d) Instruction of a Christen Woman (1529).

59 ECONOMIC INDEPENDENCE FOR WOMEN: THE FOUNDATION FOR EQUAL RIGHTS. Jane Roberts Chapman, ed. (Sage Yearbooks in Women's Policy Studies, Vol. 1) Beverly Hills: Sage, 1976.

a) How Much Is a Woman Worth? The American Public Policy (M.W. Griffiths), 23-38; b) Women's Roles in the Economy: Economic Investigation and Research Needs (H. Kahne), 39-76; c) Women in Industrial Society: An International Perspective (N.S. Barrett), 77-112; d) Women in Developing Societies: Economic Independence Is Not Enough (I. Tinker), 113-136; e) Poverty: Women and Children Last (H.L. Ross), 137-154; f) Condition of Women in Blue-Collar Jobs (P. Roby), 155-182; g) Search for a Partnership Role: Women in Labor Unions Today (B.M. Wertheimer), 183-210; h) Structural Change in the

Occupational Composition of the Female Labor Force (E.L. Vatter), 211-238; i) Working Wives and Family Income (C.S. Bell), 239-262; j) Sex Discrimination in Credit: The Backlash of Economic Dependency (J.R. Chapman), 263-282.

60 THE EDUCATED WOMAN IN AMERICA: SELECTED WRITINGS OF CATHARINE BEECHER, MARGARET FULLER AND M. CAREY THOMAS. Barbara M. Cross, ed. (Classics in Education, No. 25) New York: Teachers College Press, 1965.

a) Childhood (C. Beecher), 51-62; b) Hartford Female Seminary (C. Beecher), 63-66; c) Education of Female Teachers (C. Beecher), 67-75; d) Teachers to the West (C. Beecher), 76-80; e) Christian Family (C. Beecher), 81-93; f) Ministry of Women (C. Beecher), 94-104; g) Father (M. Fuller), 105-108; h) Schoolteaching (M. Fuller), 109-111; i) Conversations (M. Fuller), 112-122; j) Friendship (M. Fuller), 123-130; k) Maternity (M. Fuller), 131-138; l) "Bryn Mawr Woman" (M.C. Thomas), 139-144; m) Education for Women and for Men (M.C. Thomas), 145-154; n) Purpose of the College (M.C. Thomas), 155-157; o) Motives and Future of the Educated Woman (M.C. Thomas), 158-169; p) Marriage and the Woman Scholar (M.C. Thomas), 170- .

61 EMERGING WOMAN: CAREER ANALYSIS AND OUTLOOKS. Samuel H. Osipow, ed. (The Merrill Series in Career Programs) Columbus: Charles E. Merrill, 1975.

a) Demographic and Social Factors in Women's Work Lives (R.J. Schiffler), 10-22; b) Measuring the Vocational Interest of Women (V.Y. Peoples), 23-36; c) Parental Influences on Women's Career Development (J. Sorensen, C.J. Winters), 37-50; d) Individual Factors Related to Career Orientation in Women (C.J. Winters, J. Sorensen), 51-68; e) Marriage and the Employment of Women (S.D. Miyahira), 69-90; f) Sex Role Stereotypes and the Career Versus Homemaking Orientations of Women (R.E. Goldberg), 91-116; g) Barriers to the Career Development of Women (S.A. Mishler), 117-146; h) Perspective and Issues (S.H. Osipow), 147-158.

62 THE EMERGING WOMAN: THE IMPACT OF FAMILY PLANNING; AN INFORMAL SHARING OF INTERESTS, IDEAS AND CONCERNS. (Held at the University of Notre Dame) Martha Stuart, ed. with William T. Liu. Boston: Little, Brown, 1970.

a) What Is a Contraceptive Culture? (J.L. Thomas, C.S. Chilman), 1-24; b) Impact of Contraceptive Culture (W.T. Liu, R.H. Useem), 25-56; c) Unchanging Woman (E.F. Berman), 57-66; d) What Do Women Really Think and Feel About Themselves? (W.V. D'Antonio, M. Stuart), 67-84; e) Female Sexuality (W.H. Masters, V.E. Johnson), 85-124; f) Perspectives (H.W. Richardson), 125-142; g) Generation-Communication Gap (W.M. Lamers, Jr., S.M. Stone, J.P. Semmens), 143-182; h) How Can Men and Women Work Together? (C.P. Lecht, H.J. Gibbons, J. Grennan), 183-216; i) Anatomy of a Good Marriage (J.W. Bird, L.F. Bird),

217-254; j) Education for Real Living (M. Scriven, M. Gorman), 255-288; k) Where Are We Going Together? (K. Krantz, R.C. Cornuelle, M.A. Schaldenbrand, L.K. Dupre), 289-316.

63 EQUAL PAY FOR WOMEN: PROGRESS AND PROBLEMS IN SEVEN COUNTRIES. Barrie O. Pettman, ed. Washington: Hemisphere, 1977.

a) Equal Pay in Great Britain (B. Chiplin, P.J. Sloane), 9-34; b) Equal Pay in America (J.E. Buckley), 35-62; c) Equal Pay for Women in Australia and New Zealand (J. Nieuwenhuysen, J. Hicks), 63-98; d) Gleichberechtigung--The German Experience (J.T. Addison), 99-128; e) Equal Pay in Canada: History, Progress and Problems (M. Gunderson), 129-146; f) Equal Pay Question in Japan (E. Thurley,K. Thurley), 147-174.

64 EQUALITY IN SPORT FOR WOMEN. Patricia L. Geadelmann et al. Washington: National Association for Girls and Women in Sport, American Alliance for Health, Physical Education and Recreation, 1977.

a) What Does Equality Mean? (C. Grant), 1-25; b) How Can I Determine if Equality Exists? (P.L. Geadelmann), 26-32; c) What Does the Law Say? (P.L. Geadelmann), 33-55; d) Compliance Agencies (Y. Slatton), 56-66; e) Court Precedents (P.L. Geadelmann), 67-88; f) Sex Role Stereotyping (P.L. Geadelmann), 89-103; g) Effecting Change (C. Grant), 104-114; h) Remedial and Affirmative Action (N.P. Burke), 115-128; i) Gaining Support from Other Groups (N.P. Burke), 129-159.

65 ESSAYS ON SEX EQUALITY: JOHN STUART MILL, HARRIET TAYLOR MILL. Alice S. Rossi, ed. Chicago: The University of Chicago Press, 1970.

a) Sentiment and Intellect: The Story of John Stuart Mill and Harriet Taylor Mill (A.S. Rossi), 1-64; b) Early Essays on Marriage and Divorce (1832)(J.S. Mill, H. Taylor), 65-88; c) Enfranchisement of Women (1851)(H.T. Mill), 89-122; d) Subjection of Women (1869)(J.S. Mill), 123- .

66 EUROPEAN WOMEN: A DOCUMENTARY HISTORY 1789-1945. Eleanor S. Riemer and John C. Fout, eds. New York: Schocken Books, 1980.

The collection includes documents which were typical of women's experiences across classes in many parts of Europe from 1789 through 1945. It covers work, politics, family, health and sexuality. Most continental European selections have not been previously translated. Apart from anonymous documents, writing by the following contributors is included: A. Jameson, J. Heynrichs, O. de Gouges, D. Downright, H.G. Liddle, E. Pankhurst, French Union for Women's Suffrage, International Alliance of Women, L. Kautsky, F. Nurina, L. D'Aulnay, P. Kergomard, A. Popp, L. Otto, J. Sauget, E. Key, A. Kollontai,

F.W.S. Browne, A. Jacobs, and J. Butler.

67 EXPLORING SEX DIFFERENCES. Barbara Lloyd and John Archer, eds. New York: Academic Press, 1976.

a) Social Responsibility and Research on Sex Differences (B.B. Lloyd), 1-24; b) Development of Conceptions of Masculinity and Femininity (D.Z. Ullian), 25-48; c) Anthropological Perspective (M. Strathern), 49-70; d) Sex Differences in Cross-Cultural Perspective (P.C. Rosenblatt, M.R. Cunningham), 71-94; e) Intelligence, Occupational Status and Achievement Orientation (D.M. Kipnis), 95-122; f) Sex Differences in the Organization of Perception and Cognition (D. McGuinness), 123-156; g) Male Hormones and Behaviour (L. Rogers), 157-184; h) Female Hormones and Behaviour (P.R. Messent), 185-212; i) Sex Differences and Psychopathology (P. Mayo), 213-240; j) Biological Explanations of Psychological Sex Differences (J. Archer), 241-266.

68 FABIAN FEMINIST: BERNARD SHAW AND WOMAN. Rodelle Weintraub, ed. University Park: The Pennsylvania State University Press, 1977.

a) Shakespeare's "The Taming of the Shrew" vs. Shaw's "Pygmalion": Male Chauvinism vs. Women's Lib? (L. Pedersen), 14-22; b) Kipling on Women: A New Source for Shaw (J.C. McCauley), 23-29; c) Shavian Sphinx (R.B. Nathan), 30-38; d) Eliza's Choice: Transformation Myth and the Ending of "Pygmalion" (T.G. Vesonder), 39-47; e) Ann and Superman: Type and Archetype (S.P. Vogt), 48-67; f) Legal Climate of Shaw's Problem Plays (D. Kester), 68-83; g) "Press Cuttings": G.B.S. and Women's Suffrage (M. Weimer), 84-89; h) Mill, Marx and Bebel: Early Influences on Shaw's Characterizations of Women (N. Greiner), 90-98; i) "Unwomanly Woman" in Shaw's Drama (S. Lorichs), 99-113; j) New Woman and the New Comedy (B.B. Watson), 114-129; k) Whatever Happened to Shaw's Mother-Genius Portrait? (S.C. Stone), 130-142; l) Mr. Shaw's Many Mothers (A. Gilmartin), 143-155; m) Feminism and Female Stereotypes in Shaw (E. Adams), 156-162; n) Whore in Every Home (G. Greer), 163-167; o) Vivien Warren: A Psychological Study (M.P. Wasserman), 168-173; p) Shaw and Women's Lib (G.M. Crane), 174-184; q) Shaw's Lady Cicely and Mary Kingsley (S. Weintraub), 185-193; r) Shaw and Florence Farr (J. Johnson), 194-205; s) Interview with Clare Boothe Luce (R. Weintraub), 206-213; t) Interview with Megan Terry (R. Weintraub), 214-227; u) Torture by Forcible Feeding is Illegal (B. Shaw), 228-235; v) G.B.S. and a Suffragist (M.C. Braby), 236-242; w) Sir Almroth Wright's Case Against Woman Suffrage (B. Shaw), 243-247; x) Why All Women Are Peculiarly Fitted to Be Good Voters (B. Shaw), 248-254; y) Root of the White Slave Traffic (B. Shaw), 255-261; z) Bibliographical Checklist (L.K. Henderson), 262-272.

69 THE FACTORY GIRLS: A COLLECTION OF WRITINGS ON LIFE AND STRUGGLES IN THE NEW ENGLAND FACTORIES OF THE 1840s BY THE FACTORY GIRLS THEMSELVES, AND THE STORY, IN THEIR OWN WORDS, OF THE FIRST TRADE UNIONS OF WOMEN WORKERS IN THE UNITED STATES. Philip S. Foner, ed. Urbana: University of Illinois Press, 1977.

This collection includes some writings of "genteel" Lowell factory workers, but most selections are by militant female factory operatives. The pieces were published primarily during the 1830s and 1840s. Contributors: L. Larcom, M. Emerson, M. Hallingworth, J. Collins, J.A. Phillips, M. Hall, L.S. Hall, A.A. Goddard, A. Sargent, H. Tarlton, S. Rumrill, E. Kidder, P. Green, M. Eastman, W.F. Young, W. Schouler, H.E. Putnam, E. Munroe, H. Farley, S.G. Bagley, H.J. Stone, M. Eastman.

70 FAMILY ISSUES OF EMPLOYED WOMEN IN EUROPE AND AMERICA. Andree Michel, ed. Leiden: E.J. Brill, 1971.

a) Husband Provider Role: A Critical Appraisal (E. Grønseth), 11-31; b) Two Roles of Russian Working Women in an Urban Area (A. Kharchev, S. Golod), 32-42; c) Interaction and Goal Attainment in Parisian Working Wives' Families (A. Michel), 43-65; d) Problems Facing Czechoslovak Women Today (J. Prokopec), 66-72; e) Employment of Married Women and the Changing Sex Roles in Poland (J. Piotrowski), 73-90; f) Urban Working Woman in the U.S.S.R.: An Historical Overview (R. Somerville), 91-103; g) Effects of Children on the Family (H. Feldman), 104-125; h) Jobs or Careers: The Case of the Professionally Employed Married Woman (M.M. Poloma, T.N. Garland), 126-142; i) Historical Changes in How People Spend Their Time (J.B. Robinson), 143-153; j) Impact of Employment upon Fertility (R.H. Weller), 154- .

71 FEMALE AND MALE IN LATIN AMERICA: ESSAYS. Ann Pescatello, ed. Pittsburgh: University of Pittsburgh Press, 1973.

a) Literary Archetypes and Female Role Alternatives: The Woman and the Novel in Latin America (J.S. Jaquette), 3-28; b) "Brazileira": Images and Realities in Writings of Machado de Assis and Jorge Amado (A. Pescatello), 29-58; c) Passive Female and Social Change: A Cross-Cultural Comparison of Women's Magazine Fiction (C.B. Flora), 59-86; d) Marianismo: The Other Face of "Machismo" in Latin America (E.P. Stevens), 89-102; e) Women in Latin American Politics: The Case of Peru and Chile (E.M. Chaney), 103-140; f) Women: The Forgotten Half of Argentine History (N.C. Hollander), 141-158; g) Women Professionals in Buenos Aires (N.S. Kinzer), 159-190; h) Domestic Service as a Channel of Upward Mobility for the Lower Class Woman: The Lima Case (M.L. Smith), 191-208; i) "La Quisqueyana": The Dominican Woman, 1940-1970 (S.B. Tancer), 209-230; j) Pursuit of an Ideal: Migration, Social Class, and Women's Roles in Bogota, Colombia (S.J. Harkess), 231-254; k) Modernizing Women for a Modern Society: The Cuban Case (S.K. Purcell), 257-272; l) Honor, Shame, and Women's Liberation in Cuba: Views of Working-Class Emigre Men (G.E. Fox), 273-292.

72 THE FEMALE EXPERIENCE: AN AMERICAN DOCUMENTARY. Gerda Lerner, ed. Indianapolis: Bobbs-Merrill, 1977.

These primary documents reflect the experience of women in America from the seventeenth through the twentieth centuries. Items were chosen for

their rarity as well as their quality. Arrangement is by role or stage in life (old age, motherhood), by subject (education, work, politics), and by topics which represent feminist concerns (autonomy, sisterhood). Contributors: L.M. Alcott, M. Harrison, M.P. Jacobi, M.C. Wright, M.A. Livermore, F.E. Willard, R. Schneiderman, E.L. Pinckney, E.W. Garrison, R. Cohen, H.B. Stowe, M. Robinson, E. Robinson, J. Swisshelm, M. Dodd, F. Wright, Lucy Stone, F. Stone, W. Bowman, Luther Stone, S. Stone, S.M. Grimke, M. Sanger, C.M. Sedgwick, C.E. Beecher, L.M. Child, H.L. Snider, T. Malkiel, M. Inman, C.P. Gilman, E.C. Yarnall, S. Lincoln, M.A. Dennison, M.H. Everett, E.H. Willard, A.H. Shaw, S.B. Anthony, M.S. Battey, S.A. Allen, E.J. Wilson, R.R. Verduin, B. Sandler, C. Dall, L. Waight, R.C. Dorr, L.M. Barry, L. Chase, I.M. Van Etten, B. Tappan, L. Drake, V.C.Woodhull, F.E.W. Harper, C.M. Everhard, S.C. Stevens, L.M. Lewis, D. Sampson, H.K. Hunt, E. Blackwell, A. Preston, E.C. Stanton, B. Lockwood, E.G. Flynn, Radicalesbians, A. Koedt, A.L. Walters, R. Lichtman, A. Hutchinson, M. Dyer, M.L. Moore, S. Truth, L. Clifton, M. Rukeyser.

73 THE FEMALE EXPERIENCE. Editors of PSYCHOLOGY TODAY and Carol Tavris, eds. Del Mar, Ca.: Communications Research Machines, 1973.

a) In Praise of the Achieving Female Monkey (J. Beckman), 5-9; b) Her Body, the Battleground (J.M. Bardwick), 10-16; c) Women Learn to Sing the Menstrual Blues (K.E. Paige), 17-21; d) Trebly Sensuous Woman (N. Newton), 22-25; e) Natural Childbirth: Pain or Peak Experience (D. Tanner), 26-32; f) Sexual Fantasies of Women (E.B. Hariton), 33-38; g) New Look at Menopause (B.L. Neugarten), 39-45; h) There's No Unisex in the Nursery (M. Lewis), 46-49; i) Check One: Male (or) Female (J. Kagan), 50-53; j) Why Bright Women Fear Success (M. Horner), 54-57; k) Fear of Success: Popular, but Unproven (D. Tresemer), 58-62; l) Queen Bee Syndrome (G. Staines, C. Tavris, T.E. Jayaratne), 63-66; m) Woman as Nigger (N. Weisstein), 67-70; n) Woman is 58% of a Man (T.E. Levitin, R.T. Quinn, G. Staines), 71-75; o) Seven Deadly Half-Truths About Women (J.E. Crowley, T.E. Levitin, R.T. Quinn), 76-78; p) Men Drive Women Crazy (P. Chesler), 79-83; q) Women's Liberation: A Nice Idea, but It Won't Be Easy (J.M. Bardwick), 84-88; r) Conversation with Alice Rossi (G. Bermant), 89-98; s) Woman and Man: A Questionnaire and Survey Report (C. Tavris), 99- .

74 FEMALE LIBERATION: HISTORY AND CURRENT POLITICS. Roberta Salper, ed. New York: Alfred A. Knopf, 1972.

a) Rights of Woman (M. Wollstonecraft), 27-32; b) Enfranchisement of Women (H.T. Mill), 33-52; c) Woman's Bible (E.C. Stanton et al.), 53-67; d) Life and Writings (F. Douglass), 68-74; e) Narrative of a Life (S. Truth), 75-82; f) Marx and Engels on Women's Liberation (H. Draper), 83-107; g) Home: Its Work and Influence (C.P. Gilman), 108-118; h) Anarchism and Other Essays (E. Goldman), 119-135; i) We Are Many (E.R. Bloor), 136-148; j) Bread and Roses (K. McAfee, M. Wood), 153-168; k) Development of the American Women's Liberation Movement, 1967-1971 (R. Salper), 169-183; l) Why Women's Liberation--2? (M. Dixon), 184-199; m) The Trip (R. Dunbar), 200-202; n) Temptation to be a Beautiful Object (D. Densmore), 203-207; o) Double Jeopardy: To

Be Black and Female (F. Beal), 208-218; p) Politics of Day Care (K. Ellis), 219-227; q) Woman and Her Mind: The Story of Daily Life (M. Tax), 228-232; r) Fourth World Manifesto (B. Burris, K. Barry, T. Moon, J. DeLor, J. Parent, C. Stadelman), 233-242.

75 THE FEMALE OFFENDER. Annette M. Brodsky, ed. (Sage Contemporary Social Science Issues, No. 19) Beverly Hills: Sage, 1975.

a) Female Offender as an Object of Criminological Research (C.E. Rasche), 9-28; b) Physical Attractiveness of Female Offenders: Effects on Institutional Performance (H.E. Cavior, S.C. Hayes, N. Cavior), 29-39; c) Personality Differences Between Male and Female Prison Inmates: Measured by the M.M.P.I. (J.H. Panton), 40-47; d) Adult Female Offender: A Selected Bibliography (F. Goyer-Michaud), 48-64; e) Innovative Programs for Women in Jail and Prison: Trick or Treatment (V.E. Pendergrass), 67-76; f) Feminism and the "Fallen Woman" (W.S. Heide), 77-81; g) Current Status of Women in Prisons (M. Wheeler), 82-88; h) Remedies for Wrongs: Updating Programs for Delinquent Girls (E.N. Slack), 89-95; i) Ex-Offender Evaluates Correctional Programming for Women (F. Lawrence), 96-99; j) Planning for the Female Offender (A.M. Brodsky), 100- .

76 FEMALE PSYCHOLOGY: CONTEMPORARY PSYCHOANALYTIC VIEWS. Harold P. Blum, ed. New York: International Universities Press, 1977.

a) Freud's Views on Early Female Sexuality in the Light of Direct Child Observation (J.A. Kleeman), 3-28; b) Early Female Development (E. Galenson, H. Roiphe), 29-58; c) Primary Femininity (R.J. Stoller), 59-78; d) Girl's Entry into the Oedipus Complex (H. Parens, L. Pollock, J. Stern, S. Kramer), 79-108; e) Masturbation in Latency Girls (V.L. Clower), 109-126; f) Adolescent to Woman (S. Ritvo), 127-138; g) Female Autonomy and Young Adult Women (G.R. Ticho), 139-156; h) Masochism, the Ego Ideal, and the Psychology of Women (H.P. Blum), 157-192; i) Penis Envy: From Childhood Wish to Developmental Metaphor (W.I. Grossman, W.A. Stewart), 193-212; j) Regression and Reintegration in Pregnancy (J.S. Kestenberg), 213-250; k) Work Inhibitions in Women (A. Applegarth), 251-268; l) Parental Mislabeling of Female Genitals as a Determinant of Penis Envy and Learning Inhibitions in Women (H.F. Lerner), 269-284; m) Sleep Orgasm in Women (M. Heiman), 285-304; n) Psychic Representation and Female Orgasm (B.E. Moore), 305-330; o) Problems in Freud's Psychology of Women (R. Schafer), 331-360; p) Masculine Envy of Woman's Procreative Function (D.S. Jaffe), 361-392; q) New Female Psychology? (P. Barglow, M. Schaefer), 393-438.

77 FEMALE PSYCHOLOGY: THE EMERGING SELF. Sue Cox, ed. Chicago: Science Research Associates, 1976.

a) Sex Hormones and Executive Ability (E.R. Ramey), 20-30; b) Premenstrual Syndrome (M.B. Parlee), 31-45; c) Cross-Cultural Analysis of Sex Differences in the Behavior of Children Aged Three Through Eleven

(B. Whiting, C.P. Edwards), 50-62; d) Conclusion: "Sex and Temperament in Three Primitive Societies" (M. Mead), 63-71; e) Matriarchy: As Women See It (E. Newton, P. Webster), 72-87; f) Psychology Constructs the Female (N. Weisstein), 91-103; g) Summary and Commentary: "The Psychology of Sex Differences" (E.E. Maccoby, C.N. Jacklin), 104-121; h) Psychology of Women (M.T.S. Mednick, H.J. Weissman), 122-135; i) Social Construction of the Second Sex (J. Freeman), 136-151; j) Women as a Minority Group (H.M. Hacker), 156-170; k) Sexual Politics of Interpersonal Behavior (N. Henley, J. Freeman), 171-179; l) Case Study of a Nonconscious Ideology: Training the Woman to Know Her Place (S.L. Bem, D.J. Bem), 180-191; m) Who Has the Power? The Marital Struggle (D.L. Gillespie), 192-211; n) Black Movement and Women's Liberation (L. La Rue), 216-225; o) Heritage of La Hembra (A. Nieto-Gomez), 226-235; p) New Asian-American Woman (I. Fujitomi, D. Wong), 236-248; q) Native Women Today: Sexism and the Indian Woman (S.H. Witt), 249-259; r) Sexuality (A. Oakley), 264-277; s) Theory on Female Sexuality (M.J. Sherfey), 278-283; t) Myth of the Vaginal Orgasm (A. Koedt), 284-289; u) Rape: The All-American Crime (S. Griffin), 290-303; v) Woman Identified Woman (Radicalesbians), 304-308; w) Women's Sexuality: A Feminist View (E.K. Childs, E.A. Sachnoff, E.S. Stocker), 309-313; x) Patient and Patriarch: Women in the Psychotherapeutic Relationship (P. Chesler), 318-334; y) Masochistic Syndrome, Hysterical Personality, and the Illusion of a Healthy Woman (B. Belote), 335-348; z) Depression in Middle-Aged Women (P.B. Bart), 349-367; aa) Consciousness-Raising Group as a Model for Therapy with Women (A.M. Brodsky), 372-377; bb) What Happens in Feminist Therapy (H. Lerman), 378-384; cc) What Is a Healthy Woman? (M. Perlstein), 385-389; dd) Male Liberation (J. Sawyer), 390-392; ee) Manifesto (Berkeley Men's Center), 393; ff) Why Are Women So Hard on Women? (E. Walster, M.A. Pate), 394; gg) Male Power and the Women's Movement (B. Polk), 400-413; hh) APPENDIX: Chart of Basic Feminist Positions, 435- .

78 FEMALE SEXUALITY: NEW PSYCHOANALYTICAL VIEWS. Janine Chasseguet-Smirgel, (ed.) Ann Arbor, Mi: University of Michigan Press, 1970.

a) Masculine Mythology of Femininity (C. David), 47-67; b) Narcissism in Female Sexuality (B. Grunberger), 68-83; c) Change of Object (C. Luquet-Parat), 84-93; d) Feminine Guilt and the Oedipus Complex (J. Chasseguet- Smirgel), 94-134; e) Penis Envy in Women (M. Torok), 135-170; f) Homosexuality in Women (J. McDougall), 171-212.

79 THE FEMALE SPECTATOR: ENGLISH WOMEN WRITERS BEFORE 1800. Mary R. Mahl and Helene Koon, eds. Bloomington; Old Westbury, N.Y.: Indiana Univeristy Press and The Feminist Press, 1977.

a) XVI Revelations of Divine Love (Julian of Norwich), 15-20; b) Book of Margery Kempe (M. Kempe), 23-34; c) Lamentation of a Sinner (C. Parr), 38-42; d) Prayers or Meditations (C. Parr), 43; e) Speech to the Troops at Tilbury (Elizabeth, Queen of England), 48; f) Speech to the Parliament (Elizabeth, Queen of England), 49-51; g) Miscelanea: Prayers, Meditations, Memoratives (E. Grymeston), 55-61; h) To The

Thrice Sacred Queen Elizabeth (M.S. Herbert), 66-69; i) The Psalmes of David (M.S. Herbert), 70-72; j) Salve Deus Rex Judaeorum (A. Lanier), 75-87; k) Countess of Lincoln's Nurserie (E. Clinton), 90-98; l) Tragedie of Mariam, The Fair Queen of Jewry (E. Cary), 102-114; m) Malady and Remedy of Vexations and Unjust Arrests and Actions (B. Makin), 118-123; n) Upon the much lamented death of the Right Honourable the Lady Elizabeth Langham (B. Makin), 124-125; o) An Essay to Revive the Ancient Education of Gentlewomen (B. Makin), 126-135; p) Nature's Pictures, Drawn by Fancies Pencil to the Life (M. Cavendish), 140-153; q) To Rosania and Lucasia, Articles of Friendship (K. Philips), 157-158; r) Poems (K. Philips), 159-164; s) The Unfortunate Bride, or the Blind Lady a Beauty (A. Behn), 169-178; t) The Wife's Resentment (M.D. Manley), 182-208; u) Prefaces and Dedications (S. Centlivre), 212-222; v) Female Spectator (E. Haywood), 226-239; w) Letters to Elizabeth Robinson Montagu (F.G. Boscawen), 242-257; x) Works (A.L. Barbauld), 261-265; y) On Female Studies (A.L. Barbauld), 266-272; z) Letters to Elizabeth Robinson Montagu (H. More), 277-286; aa) Practical Use of Female Knowledge (H. More), 287-296; bb) Letters to Edward Jerningham (A. Seward), 300- .

80 FEMALE STUDIES IX: TEACHING ABOUT WOMEN IN THE FOREIGN LANGUAGES: FRENCH, SPANISH, GERMAN, RUSSIAN. Sidonie Cassirer, ed. Prepared for the Commission on the Status of Women of the Modern Language Association. Old Westbury, N.Y.: The Feminist Press, 1975.

a) "I am my own heroine": Some Thoughts about Women and Autobiography in France (E. Marks), 1-10; b) Women Writers in France: The "Initiators" (G. Brée), 11-18; c) Status of the Frenchwoman Today (A. Raitière), 19-34; d) Letter to Marguerite Durand from Paul and Victor Marguerite (F. Gontier), 35-36; e) Women in Contemporary French Society: Annotated Bibliography (J. Bragger), 37-44; f) "El casamiento enganoso": Marriage in the Novels of Maria Luisa Bombal, Silvina Bullrich, and Elisa Serrana (M. Welles), 121-130; g) "Protesta femenina" in Latin America (M.P. Stanley), 131-135; h) Three Peninsular Novelists Comment on the Spanish Woman (J. Cain), 136-137; i) Hispanic American Fiction and Drama Written by Women: (G. Mora), 138- ; j) Women in Germany (T. Sauter-Bailliet), 171-179; k) Virgins and Other Victims: Aspects of German Middle-Class Theatre (H. Tilton), 180-188; l) Inculcating a Slave Mentality: Women in German Popular Fiction of the Early Twentieth Century (R.K. Angress), 189-199; m) Women in the Third Reich (A. Leek), 200-201; n) Women and German Literature: A Bibliography (R.J. Horsley), 202-212; o) Metamorphosis of an Icon: Woman in Russian Literature (M. Banerjee), 228- .

81 THE FEMININE IMAGE IN LITERATURE. Barbara Warren, comp. (Hayden Humanities Series) Rochelle Park, N.J.: Hayden Book Company, 1973.

These selections, by both male and female writers, are arranged thematically or by literary type (the "Marble-Plastic Doll," the "Nun Syndrome," the "Androgynous Mind"). Questions follow each chapter. Contributors: J. Keats, T. Hardy, W. Wordsworth, E.A. Poe, C. Cullen,

W. Blake, W.B. Yeats, M.E. Harding, R. Wilbur, K. Vonnegut, Jr., A. Marvell, S. Anderson, J. Donne, Alfred, Lord Tennyson, E. Dowson, W. Shakespeare, E. Dickinson, E. Brontë, R. Jarrell, S. Coleridge, G. Brooks, S. Plath, V. Woolf, N. Hawthorne, Sappho, J. Swift, G. Gissing, W. Whitman, A. Sexton, J.A. Emanuel, J. Ciardi, B. Warren, S. Sutheim, J. Harriman, S. de Beauvoir, C. Jung.

82 FEMININE PERSONALITY AND CONFLICT. Judith M. Bardwick, (ed.) Belmont, Ca.: Brooks-Cole, 1970.

a) Psychological Conflict and the Reproductive System (J.M. Bardwick), 3-30; b) New Sources of Conflict in Females at Adolescence and Early Adulthood (E. Douvan), 31-44; c) Femininity and Successful Achievement: A Basic Inconsistency (M.S. Horner), 45-76; d) Female Ego Styles and Generational Conflict (D. Gutmann), 77-96.

83 FEMININE PLURAL: STORIES BY WOMEN ABOUT GROWING UP. Stephanie Spinner, ed. New York: Macmillan, 1972.

a) Wunderkind (C. McCullers), 1-18; b) Notes for a Case History (D. Lessing), 19-42; c) Green Sealing-Wax (Colette), 43-62; d) Miss Yellow Eyes (S.A. Grau), 63-105; e) Virgin Violeta (K.A. Porter), 106-120; f) My First Marriage (R.P. Jhabvala), 121-143; g) Irish Revel (E. O'Brien), 144-172; h) Your Body is a Jewel Box (K. Boyle), 173-194; i) O Yes (T. Olsen), 195-218; j) A Temple of the Holy Ghost (F. O'Connor), 219-236.

84 FEMINISM AND MATERIALISM: WOMEN AND MODES OF PRODUCTION. Annette Kuhn and AnnMarie Wolpe, eds. London, Boston: Routledge and Kegan Paul, 1978.

a) Feminism and Materialism (A. Kuhn, A. Wolpe), 1-10; b) Patriarchy and Relations of Production (R. McDonough, R. Harrison), 11-41; c) Structures of Patriarchy and Capital in the Family (A. Kuhn), 42-67; d) Church, State, and Family: The Women's Movement in Italy (L. Caldwell), 68-95; e) Sexual Division of Labour: The Case of Nursing (E. Gamarnikow), 96-123; f) Modes of Appropriation and the Sexual Division of Labour: A Case Study from Oaxaca, Mexico (K. Young), 124-154; g) Women and Production: A Critical Analysis of Some Sociological Theories of Women's Work (V. Beechey), 155-197; h) Domestic Labour and Marx's Theory of Value (P. Smith), 198-219; i) Women, Sex and Class (J. West), 220-253; j) State and the Oppression of Women (M. McIntosh), 254-289; k) Education and the Sexual Division of Labour (A. Wolpe), 290- .

85 FEMINISM AND PHILOSOPHY. Mary Vetterling-Braggin, Frederick A. Elliston, and Jane English, eds. Totowa, N.J.: Littlefield, Adams, 1977.

a) Political Philosophies of Women's Liberation (A. Jaggar), 5-21; b) Phenomenology of Feminist Consciousness (S.L. Bartky), 22-34; c) Androgyny As an Ideal for Human Development (A. Ferguson), 45-69; d) Two Forms of Androgynism (J. Trebilcot), 70-78; e) Feminine As a Universal (A. Dickason), 79-100; f) Sexism and Semantics (P. Grim), 109-116; g) Traits and Genderization (E.L. Beardsley), 117-123; h) Myth of the Neutral "Man" (J. Moulton), 124-137; i) Hidden Joke: Generic Uses of Masculine Terminology (C. Korsmeyer), 138-153; j) Linguistics and Feminism (V. Valian), 154-166; k) How Do We Know When Opportunities Are Equal? (O. O'Neill), 177-189; l) Preferential Treatment (L. Crocker), 190-209; m) Preferential Hiring (R.K. Fullinwider), 210-224; n) Limits to the Justification of Reverse Discrimination (A.H. Goldman), 225-241; o) Nature and Value of Marriage (L.H. O'Driscoll), 249-263; p) Liberalism and Marriage Law (S.A. Ketchum), 264-276; q) Myth of the Complete Person (J.E. Barnhart, M.A. Barnhart), 277-290; r) Separation of Marriage and Family (J. Margolis, C. Margolis), 291-301; s) Rape: The All-American Crime (S. Griffin), 313-332; t) Rape and Respect (C.M. Shafer, M. Frye), 333-346; u) What's Wrong with Rape (P. Foa), 347-359; v) Coercion and Rape: The State As a Male Protection Racket (S.R. Peterson), 360-371; w) Roman Catholic Doctrine of Therapeutic Abortion (S.T. Nicholson), 385-407; x) Abortion and Ethical Theory (E. Rapaport, P. Sagal), 408-416; y) Abortion and the Concept of a Person (J. English), 417-428; z) Abortion and the Quality of Life (H. Cohen), 429-440.

86 FEMINISM AND SOCIALISM. Linda Jenness, ed. New York: Pathfinder Press, 1972.

a) Female Liberation and Socialism, an Interview (C. Lund), 7-17; b) Are Feminism and Socialism Related? (M.-A. Waters), 18-26; c) Women and Political Power (B. Stone), 27-39; d) Why Women's Liberation is Important to Black Women (M. Williams), 40-47; e) Chicanas Speak Out--New Voice of La Raza (M. Vidal), 48-57; f) Issues Before the Abortion Movement (C. Jaquith), 58-62; g) Questions and Answers on the Equal Rights Amendment (B. Stone), 63-71; h) Family (D. Feeley), 72-86; i) Reply to Dr. Spock on Child Care (R. Miller), 87-90; j) Why Red-Baiting Hurts the Feminist Movement (C. Lipman), 91-103; k) Revolutionary Perspective on the Oppression of Women (K. Dawson), 104-107; l) In Defense of Engels on the Matriarchy (E. Reed), 108-112; m) Women and the Russian Revolution (D. Feeley), 113-118; n) Women's Oppression: the Literary Reflection (E. Chertov), 119-123; o) Answer to Norman Mailer's "Prisoner of Sex" (L. Jenness), 124-128; p) Mass Feminist Movement, 129- .

87 FEMINISM: THE ESSENTIAL HISTORICAL WRITINGS. Miriam Schneir, ed. New York: Random House, 1972.

The writings collected in this anthology cover the period from the Revolutionary period to the beginning of the Depression. Most of the material is American--a selection based on the editor's contention that the United States was the incubator of the "old feminism." The focus is on issues of concern to contemporary feminists. Arrangement is primarily chronological. Contributors: A. Adams, J. Addams,

M. Wollstonecraft, F. Wright, G. Sand, S.M. Grimke, H.H. Robinson, T. Hood, M. Fuller, F. Douglass, W.L. Garrison, S. Truth, L. Mott, L. Stone, E.L. Rose, S.B. Anthony, V. Woodhull, T. Claflin, J.S. Mill, H. Ibsen, F. Engels, A. Bebel, T. Veblen, C.P. Gilman, E.J. Putnam, A.G. Spencer, C.C. Catt, E. Pankhurst, Bread and Roses, E. Goldman, M. Sanger, C. Zetkin, V. Woolf, E.C. Stanton.

88 FEMINIST CRITICISM: ESSAYS ON THEORY, POETRY AND PROSE. Cheryl L. Brown and Karen Olson, eds. Metuchen, N.J.: The Scarecrow Press, 1978.

a) Feminism as a Criterion of the Literary Critic (M. Andersen), 1-10; b) New Feminist Criticism (A. Pratt), 11-20; c) Dwelling in Decencies: Radical Criticism and the Feminist Perspective (L.S. Robinson), 21-36; d) Defining a "Feminist Literary Criticism" (A. Kolodny), 37-58; e) Imperious Muse: Some Observations on Women, Nature and the Poetic Tradition (P. Di Pesa), 59-68; f) Room of Her Own: Emily Dickinson as Woman Artist (B.J. Williams), 69-91; g) Who Buried H.D.? A Poet, Her Critics, and Her Place in "The Literary Tradition" (S. Friedman), 92-110; h) "The Blood Jet": The Poetry of Sylvia Plath (S. Juhasz), 111-130; i) "I Dare to Live": The Transforming Art of Anne Sexton (R.B. Axelrod), 131-141; j) Moon and Contemporary Women's Poetry (D.F. Sadoff), 142-160; k) Feminist Poet: Alta and Adrienne Rich (S. Juhasz), 161-187; l) Poetry of Cynthia MacDonald (R.L. Widman), 188-197; m) Women and Feminism in the Works of Rosario Castellanos (B. Miller), 198-210; n) Female Faust (A. Ronald), 211-221; o) Pre-Feminism in Some Eighteenth-Century Novels (E.L. Steeves), 222-232; p) Constance Fenimore Woolson: First Novelist of Florida (E.T. Helmick), 233-243; q) Heroine as Her Author's Daughter (J.K. Gardiner), 244-253; r) Zora Neale Hurston (E.T. Helmick), 254-271; s) Humanbecoming: Form and Focus in the Neo-Feminist Novel (E. Morgan), 272-278; t) Definition of Literary Feminism (A.N. Krouse), 279-290; u) Jean Rhys' Recent Fiction: Humane Developments in "Wide Sargasso Sea" (C.L. Brown), 291-300; v) Alienation of the Woman Writer in "The Golden Notebook" (E. Morgan), 301-311; w) Anais Nin: A Critical Evaluation (E.C. Jelinek), 312-323; x) Promises Fulfilled: Positive Images of Women in Twentieth-Century Autobiography (L.Z. Bloom), 324-338; y) Need to Tell All: A Comparison of Historical and Modern Feminist "Confessional" Writing (K. Dehler), 339-352.

89 FEMINIST FRAMEWORKS: ALTERNATIVE THEORETICAL ACCOUNTS OF THE RELATIONS BETWEEN WOMEN AND MEN. Alison M. Jaggar and Paula Rothenberg Struhl, eds. New York: McGraw-Hill, 1978.

a) Homogenizing the American Woman: The Power of an Unconscious Ideology (S.L. Bem, D.J. Bem), 6-22; b) Women in the Work Force: Five Tables, 23-24; c) Black Women and the Market (M. Russell, M.J. Lupton), 25-27; d) Older Working Women (J.M. Berkeley), 28; e) Measuring Masculinity by the Size of a Paycheck (R.E. Gould), 29-32; f) Politics of Housework (P. Mainardi), 33-37; g) Liberation of Children (D. Babcox), 38-40; h) I Just Don't Know if I Can Make It (C. McNamara), 41-42; i) With an Eye to the Future (P. Adams), 43-44; j) Black Women in Revolt, 45-50; k) Mirror, Mirror (L. Phelps), 51-52; l) It Hurts to Be Alive and Obsolete

(Z. Moss), 53-56; m) Sexual Fantasies of Women (E.B. Hariton), 57-62; n) Socialized Penis (J. Litewka), 63-73; o) Facing Up to Breast Cancer (S.G. Radner), 74-76; p) Femininity (S. Freud), 86-92; q) Inevitability of Patriarchy (S. Goldberg), 93-98; r) Subjection of Women (J.S. Mill), 99-107; s) N.O.W. Bill of Rights, 108; t) Origin of the Family, Private Property, and the State (F. Engels), 109-118; u) Women: Caste, Class or Oppressed Sex? (E. Reed), 119-129; v) Dialectic of Sex (S. Firestone), 130-134; w) Lesbians in Revolt (C. Bunch), 135-139; x) View of Socialist Feminism (C.P. Gilman Chapter, New American Movement), 140-141; y) Woman's Estate (J. Mitchell), 142-153; z) Traffic in Women (G. Rubin), 154-166; aa) Give and Take (L. Tiger, R. Fox), 174-177; bb) In Support of the E.R.A. (M. Reagan), 178-181; cc) Workers (Female) Arise! (P.C. Sexton), 182-186; dd) Women and Society (V.I. Lenin), 187; ee) Political Economy of Women's Liberation (M. Benston), 188-195; ff) What's This about Feminist Businesses? (J. Woodul), 196-203; gg) Women as Workers under Capitalism (staff of WOMEN), 204-207; hh) Wages for Housework (G. Pompei), 208-210; ii) Women and Pay for Housework (C. Lopate), 211-216; jj) Mother-Child Bonding (L. Tiger, R. Fox), 226-230; kk) Fathers Shouldn't Try to Be Mothers (B. Bettelheim), 231-235; ll) Marriage Agreement (A.K. Shulman), 236-238; mm) Value of Housework (A.C. Scott), 239-243; nn) Family (F. Engels), 244; oo) Nuclear Family (Revolutionary Communist Party), 245; pp) Cuban Family Code, 246-251; qq) Marriage (S. Cronan), 252-256; rr) Living with Other Women (R.M. Brown), 257-259; ss) Building Extended Families (B. McKain, M. McKain), 260-262; tt) Capitalism, the Family, and Personal Life (E. Zaretsky), 263-270; uu) Aggression in the Relations between the Sexes (A. Storr), 278-279; vv) Price of Woman (D. Allen), 280-284; ww) Advanced Lovemaking (A. Comfort), 285-287; xx) Sexual Perversions (A. Ellis), 288-291; yy) Sexual Love (F. Engels), 292-297; zz) Lenin on Sexual Love (C. Zetkin), 298-300; aaa) Radical Feminism and Love (T.-G. Atkinson), 301-302; bbb) Coming Out (C. Reid), 303-309; ccc) Sex in a Capitalist Society (staff of WOMEN), 310-313; ddd) Imperialism and Sexuality (S. Rowbotham), 314-317.

90 FEMINIST LITERARY CRITICISM: EXPLORATIONS IN THEORY. Josephine Donovan, ed. Lexington: The University Press of Kentucky, 1975.

a) American Feminist Literary Criticism: A Bibliographical Introduction (C. Register), 1-28; b) Subjectives: A Theory of the Critical Process (D. Schumacher), 29-37; c) Consciousness and Authenticity: Toward a Feminist Aesthetic (M. Holly), 38-47; d) Virginia Woolf's Criticism: A Polemical Preface (B.C. Bell, C. Ohmann), 48-60; e) Theories of Feminist Criticism (C. Heilbrun, C. Stimpson), 61-73; f) Afterword: Critical Re-Vision (J. Donovan), 74-82.

91 THE FERTILITY OF WORKING WOMEN: A SYNTHESIS OF INTERNATIONAL RESEARCH. Stanley Kupinsky, ed. New York: Praeger, 1977.

a) Women's Work and Fertility in Africa (H. Ware), 1-34; b) Fertility, Women's Work, and Economic Class: A Case Study from Southeast Asia (V.J. Hull), 35-80; c) Chinese Women at Work: Work Commitment and Fertility in the Asian Setting (J.W. Salaff, A.K. Wong), 81-145; d)

Status of Women, Work and Fertility in India (R. Chahil), 146-171; e) Women, Employment, and Fertility Trends in the Arab Middle East and North Africa (M. Ahdab-Yehia), 172-187; f) Fertility of Working Women in the United States: Historical Trends and Theoretical Perspectives (S. Kupinsky), 188-249; g) Fertility and Women's Employment Outside the Home in Western Europe (V. Stolte-Heiskanen), 250-280; h) Fertility and Women's Employment in the Socialist Countries of Eastern Europe (E. Szabady), 281-316; i) Differential Fertility by Working Status of Women in Japan (K. Kobayashi), 317-341; j) Female Work Status and Fertility in Latin America (M. Davidson), 342-354; k) Relationship between Women's Work and Fertility: Some Methodological and Theoretical Issues (C. Safilios-Rothschild), 355-368; l) Overview and Policy Implications (S. Kupinsky), 369-380.

92 FIT WORK FOR WOMEN. Sandra Burman, ed. New York: St. Martin's Press, 1979.

a) Early Formation of Victorian Domestic Ideology (C. Hall), 15-32; b) Home From Home: Women's Philanthropic Work in the Nineteenth Century (A. Summers), 33-63; c) Separation of Home and Work? Landladies and Lodgers in Nineteenth-Century England (L. Davidoff), 64-97; d) Women Cotton Workers and the Suffrage Campaign: The Radical Suffragists in Lancashire, 1893-1914 (J. Liddington), 98-111; e) Militancy and Acquiescence Amongst Women Workers (K. Purcell), 112-133; f) Male Appendage: Legal Definitions of Women (K. O'Donovan), 134-152; g) Welfare State and the Needs of the Dependent Family (M. McIntosh), 153-172; h) Domestic Labor and the Household (M.M. Mackintosh), 173-191.

93 FLAWED LIBERATION: SOCIALISM AND FEMINISM. Sally M. Miller, ed. Westport, Ct.: Greenwood Press, in press.

a) Daniel Deleon and the Woman Question (L.G. Seretan); b) Women in the Party Bureaucracy: Subservient Functionaries (S.M. Miller); c) May Wood Simons: Party Theorist (G. Kreuter, K. Kreuter); d) Lena Morrow Lewis: Her Rise and Fall (M.J. Buhle); e) Jennie Higginses of the "New South in the West": A Regional Survey of Socialist Activities, Agitators, and Organizers, 1901-1917 (N.K. Basen); f) Politics of Mutual Frustration: Socialists and Suffragists in New York and Wisconsin (J.D. Buenker); g) Women Socialists and Their Male Comrades: The Reading Experience, 1927-1936 (W.C. Pratt); h) Commentary (S.M. Miller); i) APPENDIX: Woman and the Social Problem, (M.W. Simons).

94 FORCIBLE RAPE: THE CRIME, THE VICTIM, AND THE OFFENDER. Duncan Chappell, Robley Geis, and Gilbert Geis, eds. New York: Columbia University Press, 1977.

a) Forcible Rape (G. Geis), 1-46; b) Rape: The All-American Crime (S. Griffin), 47-66; c) Rape and Rape Law: Sexism in Society and Law (C.E. LeGrand), 67-86; d) Forcible Rape in the U.S.: A Statistical Profile (M.J. Hindeland, B.L. Davis), 87-114; e) Race, Rape, and the

Death Penalty (M.E. Wolfgang, M. Riedel), 115-128; f) Black Offender and White Victim: A Study of Forcible Rape in Oakland, Ca. (M.W. Agopian, D. Chappell, G. Geis), 129-141; g) Forcible Rape and the Problem of the Rights of the Accused (E. Sagarin), 142-160; h) Judicial Attitudes Toward Rape Victims (C. Bohmer), 161-169; i) Michigan's Criminal Sexual Assault Law (K.A. Cobb, N.R. Schauer), 170-188; j) Gusii Sex Offenses: A Study in Social Control (R.A. LeVine), 189-226; k) Comparative Study of Forcible Rape Offenses Known to the Police in Boston and Los Angeles (D. Chappell, G. Geis, S. Schafer, L. Siegel), 227-244; l) Rape in New York City: A Study of Material in the Police Files and Its Meaning (D. Chapell, S. Singer), 245-271; m) Hitchhike Victim of Rape (S. Nelson, M. Amir), 272-290; n) Psychology of Rapists (M.L. Cohen, R. Garofalo, R.B. Boucher, T. Seghorn), 291-314; o) Rape Trauma Syndrome (A.W. Burgess, L.L. Holmstrom), 315-328; p) Crisis Intervention with Victims of Rape (S. Sutherland, D.J. Scherl), 329-338; q) Philadelphia Rape Victim Project (J.J. Peters), 339-355; r) Selective Bibliography (F. Fogarty), 356-382.

95 FRAGMENT OF A LOST DIARY AND OTHER STORIES: WOMEN OF ASIA, AFRICA AND LATIN AMERICA. Naomi Katz and Nancy Milton, eds. New York: Pantheon, 1973.

a) Benediction (L. Hsun), 3-22; b) The Memorial Service on the Mountain (C. Zông-hûi), 23-43; c) Inem (P.A. Toer), 44-55; d) The Green Chrysanthemum (A. Su-gil), 56-71; e) Ah Ao (S. Hsi-chen), 72-83; f) Wedding Dance (A. Daguio), 84-92; g) Times Gone By (D. Alonso), 93-106; h) The Truly Married Woman (A. Nicol), 107-117; i) The Message (A.A. Aidoo), 118-126; j) On the Outskirts of the City (R. Sutiasumarga), 127-134; k) Song of Lawino, Song of Ocol (O. p'Bitek), 135-162; l) Who Cares? (S.R. Rau), 163-186; m) Order of the White Paulownia (T. Shûsei), 187-204; n) Cotton Candy (D. Alonso), 205-210; o) Fragment From a Lost Diary (S. Ming), 211-228; p) The Ivory Comb (N. Sang), 229-243; q) Coffee for the Road (A. La Guma), 244-253; r) A Woman's Life (M.J. Mbilinyi), 254-264; s) Resurrection (R. Rive), 265-274; t) Mrs. Plumb (E. Mphalele), 275-310.

96 FRAGMENTS OF AUTOBIOGRAPHY. Leon Stein, comp. (Women in America: From Colonial Times to the 20th Century) New York: Arno Press, 1974.

a) Memoir (1832)(H. Adams); b) Journey Across the Plains in 1836: Journal (N. Whitman); c) Female Prisoner: A Narrative of the Life and Singular Adventures of Josephine Amelia Perkins (1839)(J.A. Perkins); d) Demon in Female Apparel: Narrative of Josephine Amelia Perkins, the Notorious Female Horse Thief... (1842)(J.A. Perkins); e) Autobiography and Reminiscences of a Pioneer (1922)(P.J. Purcell); f) Impressions of an Indian Childhood (1900)(G. Bonnin); g) Schooldays of an Indian Girl (1900)(G. Bonnin); h) Indian Teacher Among Indians (1900)(G. Bonnin); i) Why I Am a Pagan (1902)(G. Bonnin); j) My Efforts to Become a Lawyer (1888)(B.A. Lockwood); k) How I Ran for the Presidency (1903)(B.A. Lockwood); l) Before Women Were Human Beings: Adventures of an American Fellow in German Universities of the '90s (1938)(I.H. Hyde); m) My Philadelphia (1926)(F. Kelley); n) When

Co-Education Was Young (1927)(F. Kelley); o) My Novitiate (1927)(F. Kelley); p) I Go To Work (1927)(F. Kelley); q) Race Problem--An Autobiography (1904)(Southern Colored Woman); r) Experiences of the Race Problem (1904)(Southern White Woman); s) Observations of the Southern Race Feeling (1904)(Northern Woman); t) Northern Negro's Autobiography (1904)(F.B. Williams); THESE MODERN WOMEN (AND) EXPLAINING WOMEN (1926-1927): u) Making of a Militant; v) Why I Earn My Own Living; w) Mother's Daughter; x) Peacock's Tale; y) Deflated Rebel; z) Poet Out of Pioneer; aa) Evolution of Disenchantment; bb) One Way to Freedom; cc) Woman Alone; dd) Mother-Worship; ee) Staying Free; ff) Lightning Speed Through Life; gg) Long Journey; hh) Free--For What?; ii) "Unpardonable"; jj) In Search of Adventure; kk) Hotbed of Feminists; ll) Why Feminism (B.M. Hinkle); mm) Weakness of Women (J.B. Watson); nn) Half-Confessed (J. Collins).

97 FROM FEMINISM TO LIBERATION. Edith Hoshino Altbach, comp. Cambridge: Schenkman, 1971.

a) Bread and Roses (K. McAfee, M. Wood), 21-38; b) Women's Liberation and the New Left (G.P. Kelly), 39-46; c) Where are We Going? (M. Dixon), 53-64; d) Women and the Socialist Party, 1901-1914 (M.J. Buhle), 65-86; e) Poems and Prose (Alta), 87-90; f) Women: The Longest Revolution (J. Mitchell), 93-124; g) Historical and Critical Essay for Black Women (P. Haden, D. Middleton, P. Robinson), 125-142; h) Psychology Constructs the Female, or the Fantasy Life of the Male Psychologist (N. Weisstein), 143-160; i) American Family: Decay and Rebirth (S. James), 163-198; j) Political Economy of Women's Liberation (M. Benston), 199-210; k) Woman's Work is Never Done (P. Morton), 211-228; l) Project Company Day-Care (H. Sander, E. Ekstein), 229-230; m) Project Company Kindergarten (H. Sander), 231-240; n) Abortion and Abortion Law (L. Cisler), 241-248; o) Abortion Warning 249-250; p) Like Bone to the Ground (L. Lifshin), 251-252.

98 THE FUTURE OF DIFFERENCE. Hester Eisenstein and Alice Jardine, eds. (The Scholar and the Feminist Conference Series, Vol. 1) Boston: G.K. Hall, 1980.

a) Gender, Relation, and Difference in Psychoanalytic Perspective (N. Chodorow), 3-19; b) Mother-Daughter Relationships: Psychodynamics, Politics, and Philosophy (J. Flax), 20-40; c) Bonds of Love: Rational Violence and Erotic Domination (J. Benjamin), 41-70; d) Language and Revolution: The Franco-American Dis-Connection (D.C. Stanton), 73-87; e) Powers of Difference (J. Féral), 88-94; f) To Be or Not to Be...A Feminist Speaker (C. Makward), 95-105; g) Psychoanalysis and Feminism in France (J. Gallop, C.G. Burke), 106-122; h) Poetry is Not a Luxury (A. Lorde), 125-127; i) For the Etruscans: Sexual Difference and Artistic Production--The Debate Over a Female Aesthetic (R.B. DuPlessis), 128-156; j) Difference and Language: A Linguist's Perspective (S. McConnell-Ginet), 157-166; k) For a Restricted Thematics: Writing, Speech, and Difference in Madame Bovary (N. Schor), 167-185; l) Separation and Survival: Mothers, Daughters, Sisters: The Women's Experimental Theatre (C. Coss, S. Segal, R. Sklar), 193-236; m)

Visibility and Difference: Black Women in History and Literature (Q.P. Stadler), 239-246; n) Black Women and Feminism (B. Omolade), 247-257; o) Androgyny and the Psychology of Sex Differences (C.G. Heilbrun), 258-266; p) Lesbianism and the Social Function of Taboo (P. Farley), 267-273; q) Women's Conceptions of Self and Morality (C. Gilligan), 274-317; r) Women in Power and Politics (R. Messinger), 319-326; s) Women and the Uses of Power (E. Janeway), 327-344.

99 GENDER AND DISORDERED BEHAVIOR: SEX DIFFERENCES IN PSYCHOPATHOLOGY. Edith S. Gomberg and Violet Franks, eds. New York: Brunner-Mazel, 1979.

a) Femaleness, Maleness and Behavior Disorders in Nonhumans (E. Tobach), 3-22; b) Sex Differences in the Epidemiology of Mental Disorder (W.R. Gove), 23-70; c) Problem Behavior in Adolescents (A. Locksley, E. Douvan), 71-100; d) Sex Differences in Divorce (P. Brown, H. Fox), 101-123; e) Sex Differences in Problems of Aging (L.E. Troll, B.F. Turner), 124-158; f) Crime and the Female Offender (R.C. Sarri), 159-203; g) Problems with Alcohol and Other Drugs (E.S. Gomberg), 204-240; h) Sex Differences in Obesity (R.B. Stuart, B. Jacobson), 241-256; i) Homosexuality in Females and Males (B.F. Riess, J.M. Safer), 257-286; j) Sex Differences in Suicidal Behavior (D. Lester), 287-300; k) Rape and Psychiatric Vocabularies of Motive (J.A. Marolla, D.H. Scully), 301-320; l) Gender and Schizophrenia (F. Schumer), 321-353; m) Politics of Hysteria: The Case of the Wandering Womb (P.B. Bart, D.H. Scully), 354-380; n) Sex Differences and the Epidemiology of Depression (M.M. Weissman, G.L. Klerman), 381-425; o) Gender Differences in Psychophysiological Illness (A.M. Seiden), 426-452; p) Gender and Psychotherapy (V. Franks), 453-485; q) Reflections (E.S. Gomberg, V.Franks), 486-504.

100 GENDER AND SEX IN SOCIETY. Lucile Duberman, ed. New York: Praeger, 1975.

a) Women Then and Now (L. Duberman), 3-22; b) Socialization, Sexuality, and Sex (L. Duberman), 23-57; c) Love Thine Enemy: Male-Female Relationships (L. Duberman), 58-82; d) Men and Women at Work (L. Duberman), 83-133; e) Class and Race Differences in Gender Roles (H.M. Hacker), 134-184; f) Gender Roles from a Cross-Cultural Perspective (H.M. Hacker), 185-215; g) Beyond Masculinity: Liberating Men and Their Relationships with Women (W.T. Farrell), 216-248.

101 GENES AND GENDER: I. Ethel Tobach and Betty Rosoff, eds. First in a Series on Hereditarianism and Women. (Gordian Science Series, No. 1) Staten Island, N.Y.: Gordian Press, 1978.

a) Pertinent Genetics for Understanding Gender (J. Probber, L. Ehrman), 13-30; b) Hormones and Gender (A.M. Briscoe), 31-50; c) Biology and Gender (D.C. Burnham), 51-60; d) Comments on "Science and Racism" (F.Y. Daly), 61-62; e) Psychology and Gender (H.B. Lewis), 63-74; f) Society and Gender (E. Leacock), 75-86; g) Epilogue (E. Tobach,

B. Rosoff), 87- .

102 GERMAN WOMEN WRITERS OF THE TWENTIETH CENTURY. E. Rutschi-Hermann and E. Huttenmaier Spitz, eds. Elmsford, N.Y.: Pergamon, 1978.

a) Love (R. Huch), 10-12; b) The Wife of Pilate (G. von le Fort), 15-31; c) In Hiding (E. Langgaesser), 34-36; d) The Excursion of the Dead Girls (A. Seghers), 39-52; e) Long Shadows (M.L. Kaschnitz), 54-57; f) Nina's Story (L. Rinser), 60-66; g) Doubts about Balconies (I. Aichinger), 69-71; h) Latencies (B. Koenig), 73-76; i) Barking (I. Bachmann), 78-86; j) Vocational Counselling (C. Reinig), 88-91; k) Change of Perspective (C. Wolf), 94-100; l) The Sisters (G. Wohmann), 102-105; m) Journey of a Woman Nihilist to Verona in Late Autumn (H. Novak), 108-114; n) The Initiation (G. Elsner), 116-124; o) The House (E. Meylan), 126-132; p) High-Rise Story (A. Mechtel), 134-139.

103 GRANDE DAMES OF DETECTION: TWO CENTURIES OF SLEUTHING STORIES BY THE GENTLE SEX. Seon Manley and Gogo Lewis, eds. New York: Lothrop, Lee and Shepard, 1973.

a) The Dublin Mystery (Baroness Orczy), 14-32; b) Christabel's Crystal (C. Wells), 33-49; c) The Plymouth Express (A. Christie), 50-68; d) The Learned Adventure of the Dragon's Head (D.L. Sayers), 69-95; e) Family Affair (M. Allingham), 96-110; f) A Memorable Murder (C. Thaxter), 111-140; g) Death on the Air (N. Marsh), 141-176; h) A Midsummer Night's Crime (P. Bentley), 177-212; i) Finger Prints Can't Lie (E. Johnson, G. Palmer), 213-220.

104 GROWING UP FEMALE IN AMERICA: TEN LIVES. Eve Merriam, ed. Garden City, N.Y.: Doubleday, 1971.

a) E. Southgate, 27-50; b) E.C. Stanton, 51-74; c) M. Mitchell, 75-92; d) M.A.W. Loughborough, 93-120; e) A.A. Cooper, 121-140; f) A.H. Shaw, 141-160; g) S.K. Taylor, 161-182; h) "Mother" M. Jones, 183-202; i) E.G. Stern, 203-226; j) Mountain Wolf Woman, 227-246.

105 HEARTH AND HOME: IMAGES OF WOMEN IN THE MASS MEDIA. Gaye Tuchman, Arlene Kaplan Daniels and James Benet, eds. New York: Oxford University Press, 1978.

a) Dynamics of Cultural Resistance (G. Gerbner), 46-50; b) Dominant or Dominated? Women on TV (J. Lemon), 51-68; c) Spot Messages within Saturday Morning TV Programs (S. Schuetz, J.N. Sprafkin), 69-77; d) Where are the Women in Public Broadcasting? (M.S. Cantor), 78-90; e) Imagery and Ideology: The Cover Photographs of Traditional Women's Magazines (M. Ferguson), 97-115; f) Magazine Heroines: Is MS. Just Another Member of the FAMILY CIRCLE? (B. Phillips), 116-129; g) Jackie! (C. Lopate), 130-140; h) Most Admired Woman: Image-Making in the News

(G.E. Lang), 147-160; i) Women's Page as a Window on the Ruling Class (G.W. Domhoff), 161-175; j) News of Women and the Work of Men (H.L. Molotch), 176-185; k) Newspaper as a Social Movement's Resource (G. Tuchman), 186-215; l) Women's Movement and the Women's Pages: Separate, Unequal and Unspectacular (C.F. Epstein), 216-222; m) Sex-typing and Children's Television Preferences (J.N. Sprafkin, R.M. Liebert), 228-239; n) Approaches to the Study of Media Effects (L. Gross, S. Jeffries-Fox), 240-265; o) Conclusion: Will Media Treatment of Women Improve? (J. Benet), 266-271; p) Image of Women in Television: An Annotated Bibliography (H. Franzwa), 272-300.

106 THE HIGHER EDUCATION OF WOMEN: ESSAYS IN HONOR OF ROSEMARY PARK. Helen S. Astin and Werner Z. Hirsch, eds. (Praeger Special Studies) New York: Praeger, 1978.

a) Higher Education of Women (R. Park), 3-28; b) Three Women: Creators of Change (E. Rauschenbush), 29-52; c) Women's Education: The Case for the Single-Sex College (S.R. Kaplan), 53-67; d) Liberal Arts Education and Women's Development (C.R. Pace), 68-79; e) Women's Studies: Its Origin, Organization, and Prospects (S. Tobias), 80-94; f) Undergraduate Woman (A.W. Astin), 95-112; g) University Behavior and Policies: Where Are the Women and Why? (M. Gordon, C. Kerr), 113-132; h) Factors Affecting Women's Scholarly Productivity (H.S. Astin), 133-161; i) Intellectual Quality: The Symbols and the Substance (H.E. Hirsch, W.Z. Hirsch), 162-165; j) Responsibility and Public Policy: Is It a Moral Question? (A. Pifer, A. Russell), 166-171; k) Civil Rights and the Women's Movement (T.M. Hesburgh), 172-180; l) Rosemary Park: Professional Activities, 181-182.

107 HISTORY OF IDEAS ON WOMEN: A SOURCE BOOK. Rosemary Agonito, ed. New York: G.P. Putnam, 1977.

a) Creation and Fall of Man and Woman (Bible), 19-24; b) Women as Equal to Men in the State (Plato), 25-42; c) Differences Between Men and Women (Aristotle), 43-56; d) Roles and Virtues of Men and Women (Plutarch), 57-68; e) Relationship of Men and Women (Paul), 69-74; f) Women as Auxiliary and Subject to Man (Augustine), 75-82; g) Woman as Derived Being (Thomas Aquinas), 83-92; h) Love and Marriage as Impediments to Man (F. Bacon), 93-96; i) Maternity and the Origin of Political Power (T. Hobbes), 97-104; j) Maternity, Paternity, and the Origin of Political Power (J. Locke), 105-116; k) Paternity and the Origin of Political Power (J.J. Rousseau), 117-122; l) Conventional Origin of Female Virtues (D. Hume), 123-128; m) Interrelations of the Two Sexes (I. Kant), 129-146; n) Effects of Discrimination Against Women (M. Wollstonecraft), 147-160; o) Marriage and the Family (G. Hegel), 161-172; p) Essence of Woman (S. Kierkegaard), 173-192; q) Weakness of Woman (A. Schopenhauer), 193-208; r) Woman's Suffrage (R.W. Emerson), 209-224; s) Subjection of Women (J.S. Mill), 225-250; t) Origin of Sexual Differences (C. Darwin), 251-266; u) Woman as Dangerous Plaything (F. Nietzsche), 267-272; v) Origin of the Oppression of Women (F. Engels), 273-290; w) Sexual Ethics and Women (B. Russell), 291-298; x) Woman as Castrated Man (S. Freud), 299-324; y) Response to Freud (K. Horney), 325-342; z) Existential Paralysis of

Women (S. de Beauvoir), 343- 362; aa) Intellectual and Bodily Superiority of Women (A. Montagu), 363-376; bb) Feminine Mystique (B. Friedan), 377-388; cc) Capitalism and Women's Liberation (H. Marcuse), 389-396; dd) Declaration of Women's Rights (United Nations), 397-402.

108 A HOUSE OF GOOD PROPORTION: IMAGES OF WOMEN IN LITERATURE. Michele Murray, ed. New York: Simon and Schuster, 1973.

a) Venus--Aghia Sophia (C. de Vinck), 37-40; b) White Mule (W.C. Williams), 41-47; c) The Threshold (D. Rutherford), 48-62; d) Olivia (D. Bussy), 63-73; e) Little Women (L.M. Alcott), 74-85; f) Clarissa (S. Richardson), 86-100; g) Sex (J. Valentine), 101-102; h) Another View into Love (C. Bergé), 103; i) "Ghazals: Homage to Ghalih" (A. Rich), 104; j) Love That I Bear (H. Doolittle), 105-106; k) Two poems (E. Dickinson), 107; l) Martha's Lady (S.O. Jewett), 108-124; m) The Awakening (K. Chopin), 125-137; n) Villette (C. Brontë), 138-150; o) The Bostonians (H. James), 151-164; p) Pilgrimage (D. Richardson), 165-173; q) Stepping Westward (D. Levertov), 174; r) On Barbara's Shore (D. Wakoski), 175-178; s) Family Happiness (L. Tolstoy), 179-190; t) Big Volodya and Little Volodya (A. Chekhov), 191-202; u) HUAN, or Dispersion (C. Bergé), 203-218; v) I Stand Here Ironing (T. Olsen), 219-226; w) My Mother's House: Where Are the Children? (S.G. Colette), 227-230; x) The Savage (S.G. Colette), 231-233; y) Jealousy (S.G. Colette), 234-238; z) Letter and poem (M. Tsvetaeva), 239-241; aa) Kindness (S. Plath), 242-244; bb) The Starless Air (D. Windham), 245-271; cc) Consorting with Angels (A. Sexton), 272; dd) Adam Bede (G. Eliot), 273-280; ee) Little Dorrit (C. Dickins), 281-289; ff) Nightwood: Night Watch (D. Barnes), 290-300; gg) On the Balcony (P. White), 301-313; hh) Two Women (T. Déry), 314-350; ii) The Birthmark (N. Hawthorne), 351-366; jj) The Woman Who Lives Inside the World (M. Murray), 367-370.

109 I HEAR MY SISTERS SAYING: POEMS BY TWENTIETH-CENTURY WOMEN. Carol Konek and Dorothy Walters, eds. New York: Crowell, 1976.

These poems, written primarily by contemporary American women, describe and are arranged by types of experience or stages of life--childhood, conception of children, the creative experience, life roles, madness. Contributors: B. Brigham, M. Walker, C. Maisel, D. Levertov, V.-M. D'Ambrosio, R. Whitman, N. Giovanni, G. Oden, V. Miller, S.M. Libera, A. Skeen, N. Willard, G. Ford, A. Rich, M. Atwood, M. Rukeyser, S. Plath, C. Konek, L. Hough, S. Sanchez, A. Sexton, B. Howes, P. Reingold, L. Mueller, L. Chester, M.N. Körte, A. Menebroker, A. Walker, L. Lifshin, M. Kumin, J.C. Oates, S. Juhasz, M. Angelou, J. Hathaway, D. Wakoski, L. Arnold, F. Kicknosway, V. Gilbert, P. Beauvais, E. Merriam, M. Swenson, N. Price, R.M. Brown, D. Munro, G. Brooks, J. Cooper, C. Urdang, K. Fraser, H. Chasin, C. Inez, M. Gordon, A. Hazelwood-Brady, E. Jong, Alta, D. Walters, E. Edelman, J. Vinograd, K. Walker, M.E. Evans, D. Di Prima, M. Fabilli, E. Pearce, L. Adler, C. Short, L. Lawner, P. Janik, B. Moraff, K. Norris, H. Sandburg, G. Hammond, H. Sorrells, J. Mils, A. Stanford, J. McCombs, H. Kahn, S. Youngblood, C. Kizer, L. Butler, M. Van Duyn,

S. Fromberg-Schaeffer, R. Morgan, L. Bogan, M. Piercy, E. Gidloo, V.W. Sykes, S. MacDonald, K. Spivack, J. Jordan, J. Lapidus, L. Strongin, J. Chambers, M. Himel, N.L. Madgett, G. Fox.

110 IMAGES OF WOMEN IN FICTION: FEMINIST PERSPECTIVES. Susan Koppelman Cornillon, ed. Bowling Green, Oh.: Bowling Green University Popular Press, 1972.

a) What Can a Heroine Do? Or Why Women Can't Write (J. Russ), 3-20; b) Popular Literature as Social Reinforcement: The Case of "Charlotte Temple" (K.C. McGrath), 21-27; c) Gentle Doubters: Images of Women in Englishwomen's Novels, 1840-1920 (S. Gorsky), 28-54; d) Servility of Dependence: The Dark Lady in Trollop (C. Blinderman), 55-67; e) Gentle Truths for Gentle Readers: The Fiction of Elizabeth Goudge (M. Marsden), 68-78; f) Image of Women in Science Fiction (J. Russ), 79-96; g) Silences: When Writers Don't Write (T. Olsen), 97-112; h) Fiction of Fiction (S.K. Cornillon), 113-130; i) Why Aren't We Writing About Ourselves? (C.Z. Yee), 131-134; j) Women of Cooper's "Leatherstocking Tales" (N. Baym), 135-154; k) Abuse of Eve by the New World Adam (L.R. Pratt), 155-174; l) Sex Roles in Three of Hermann Hesse's Novels (J. Leuchter), 175-182; m) Humanbecoming: Form and Focus in the Neo-Feminist Novel (E. Morgan), 183-205; n) Case for Violet Strange (J. Cornillon), 206-215; o) Fictional Feminists in "The Bostonians" and "The Odd Women" (N.B. Maglin), 216-236; p) Heroism in "To the Lighthouse" (J. Little), 237-242; q) May Sarton's Women (D.H. Anderson), 243-252; r) Feminism and Literature (F. Howe), 253-277; s) Modernism and History (L.S. Robinson, L. Vogel), 278-307; t) Value and Peril for Women of Reading Women Writers (N.B. Evans), 308-314; u) Other Criticism: Feminism vs. Formalism (F. Katz-Stoker), 315-327; v) Sexism and the Double Standard in Literature (M.R. Lieberman), 328-340; w) Feminist Style Criticism (J. Donovan), 341-354.

111 IMAGES OF WOMEN IN LITERATURE. Mary Anne Ferguson, ed. 2nd ed. Boston: Houghton Mifflin, 1977.

a) Little Woman (S. Benson), 40-44; b) The Darling (A. Chekhov), 45-54; c) The Other Two (E. Wharton), 55-69; d) Death in the Woods (S. Anderson), 70-79; e) Women (M. Swenson), 80; f) Cutting the Jewish Bride's Hair (R. Whitman), 81; g) On Being Told That Her Second Husband Has Taken His First Lover (T. Slesinger), 82-89; h) The Jailer (S. Plath), 90-92; i) The Sky Is Gray (E.J. Gaines), 96-118; j) His Idea of a Mother (K. Boyle), 119-124; k) Night-Pieces: For a Child (A. Rich), 125-126; l) At a Summer Hotel (I. Gardner), 127; m) SHE (C. Davis), 128-130; n) Hunting Season (J. Greenberg), 131-136; o) The Mother (G. Brooks), 137-138; p) Still Life with Fruit (D. Betts), 139-154; q) Before Breakfast (E. O'Neill), 159-165; r) The Ram in the Thicket (W. Morris), 166-179; s) The Short Happy Life of Francis Macomber (E. Hemingway), 180-203; t) Her Sweet Jerome (A. Walker), 204-210; u) Cassandra's Wedding Song (A. Stanford), 211-214; v) Fern (J. Toomer), 218-221; w) La Belle Dame sans Merci (J. Keats), 222-223; x) The Loreley (H. Heine), 224-225; y) The Pauper Witch of Grafton (R. Frost), 226-228; z) Rappaccini's Daughter (N. Hawthorne), 229-250;

aa) The Last of the Belles (F.S. Fitzgerald), 251-264; bb) Affair (H. Davis), 265-266; cc) The Girls in Their Summer Dresses (I. Shaw), 270-274; dd) Rima the Bird Girl (R. Jaffe), 275-294; ee) The Time of Her Time (N. Mailer), 295-315; ff) The Chase (A. Moravia), 316-320; gg) Belly Dancer (D. Wakoski), 321-322; hh) Barbie Doll (M. Piercy), 323; ii) At the Landing (E. Welty), 324-340; jj) Point of Departure (H. Calisher), 344-347; kk) Miss Gee (W.H. Auden), 348-351; ll) Miss Brill (K. Mansfield), 352-355; mm) A New England Nun (M.E.W. Freeman), 356-365; nn) Our Friend Judith (D. Lessing), 366-379; oo) The Other Wife (Colette), 380-382; pp) The Widow's Lament in Springtime (W.C. Williams), 383-384; qq) The Story of an Hour (K. Chopin), 385-388; rr) Tell Me a Riddle (T. Olsen), 392-420; ss) Trifles (S. Glaspell), 421-433; tt) Miss Rosie (L. Clifton), 434; uu) I Like to Think of Harriet Tubman (S. Griffin), 435-437; vv) Stepping Westward (D. Levertov), 438-439; ww) Homecoming (M. Collins), 440-442; xx) Wine in the Wilderness (A. Childress), 443-474.

112 IMAGES OF WOMEN IN LITERATURE. Mary Anne Ferguson, ed. Boston: Houghton Mifflin, 1973.

a) Little Woman (S. Benson), 33-37; b) The Darling (A. Chekhov), 38-47; c) The Other Two (E. Wharton), 48-62; d) Big Blonde (D. Parker), 63-78; e) Death in the Woods (S. Anderson), 79-88; f) Cutting the Jewish Bride's Hair (R. Whitman), 89; g) The Sky is Gray (E.J. Gaines), 93-114; h) His Idea of a Mother (K. Boyle), 115-120; i) Night Pieces for a Child: The Crib (A. Rich), 121; j) The Ram in the Thicket (W. Morris), 127-140; k) The Short Happy Life of Francis Macomber (E. Hemingway), 141-163; l) Her Sweet Jerome (A. Walker), 164-169; m) Fern (J. Toomer), 173-176; n) La Belle Dame sans Merci (J. Keats), 177-178; o) The Loreley (H. Heine), 179-180; p) The Pauper Witch of Grafton (R. Frost), 181-183; q) Rappaccini's Daughter (N. Hawthorne), 184-205; r) The Last of the Belles (F.S. Fitzgerald), 206-218; s) Editha (W.D. Howells), 219-229; t) Affair (H. Davis), 230-231; u) The Girls In Their Summer Dresses (I. Shaw), 235-239; v) The Patriarch (Colette), 240-244; w) At the Landing (E. Welty), 245-260; x) Rima the Bird Girl (R. Jaffe), 261-279; y) The Time of Her Time (N. Mailer), 280-299; z) The Chase (A. Moravia), 300-303; aa) Song (W. Blake), 304-308; bb) Miss Gee (W.H. Auden), 309-312; cc) Miss Brill (K. Mansfield), 313-316; dd) A New England Nun (M.E.W. Freeman), 317-325; ee) Tell Me a Riddle (T. Olsen), 331-357; ff) A Doll's House, 1970 (C.B. Luce), 358-369; gg) A Jury of Her Peers (S. Glaspell), 370-385; hh) Alraune (A. Nin), 386-390; ii) One Off the Short List (D. Lessing), 391-409; jj) See How They Run (M.E. Vroman), 410-426.

113 IN THE LOOKING GLASS: TWENTY-ONE MODERN SHORT STORIES BY WOMEN. Nancy Dean and Myra Stark, eds. New York: G.P. Putnam, 1977.

a) The Lady in the Looking Glass: A Reflection (V. Woolf), 3-8; b) In the Forests of Riga the Beasts Are Very Wild Indeed (M.F. Brown), 9-18; c) An Apple, an Orange (D. Johnson), 19-34; d) The Fifth Great Day of God (S. Boucher), 35-42; e) The Yellow Wallpaper (C.P. Gilman), 43-60; f) A Cup of Tea (K. Mansfield), 61-70; g) A Piece of News (E. Welty), 71-78; h) The De Wets Come to Kloof Grange (D. Lessing), 79-108; i)

The Fifteen-Dollar Eagle (S. Plath), 109-124; j) Dynastic Encounter (M. Piercy), 125-134; k) A Letter to Ismael in the Grave (R. Brown), 135-142; l) A Day in the Life of a Smiling Woman (M. Drabble), 143-166; m) A Sorrowful Woman (G. Godwin), 167-174; n) Downhill (A. Beattie), 175-182; o) Reclamation (G. Adams), 183-190; p) Asylum (J. Murray), 191-198; q) Red Dress--1946 (A. Munro), r) Where Are You Going, Where Have You Been? (J.C. Oates), 213-232; s) In the Basement of the House (J. Rule), 233-240; t) Pleasure (B. Barracks), 241-248; u) Raymond's Run (T.C. Bambara), 249-258.

114 INDIAN WOMEN. Devaki Jain, ed. New Delhi: Ministry of Information and Broadcasting, Government of India, 1975.

a) Looking Back in History (R. Thapar), 3-16; b) Women and the National Movement (L.N. Menon), 17-26; c) The Women's Movement--Then and Now (K. Chattopadhyay), 27-36; d) Cultural and Religious Influences (A. Rudra), 37-50; e) Panchakanya--An Age-old Benediction (M.A. Sreenivasan), 51-58; f) Position of Women in Indian Society (A. Beteille), 59-68; g) Marriage among the Hindus (V. Das), 69-86; h) Upbringing of a Girl (M. Kalakdina), 87-98; i) Women in the Labour Market (E. Boserup), 99-112; j) Legal Provisions (S. Pappu), 113-124; k) Demographic Profile of Indian Women (A. Bose), 125-186; l) Muslim Women of India (Q. Hyder), 187-202; m) Tribal Women (V. Elwin), 203-214; n) Women of Rural Bihar (O. Stokes), 215-228; o) Village Women of Rajasthan (G.M. Carstairs), 229-236; p) Slum Women of Bombay (S. Mody, S. Mhatra), 237-252; q) Nurses and Nuns of Kerala (G. Aravamudan), 253-262; r) Prostitutes--Notes from a Rescue Home (P. Aiyappan), 263-270; s) Chellamma--An Illustration of the Multiple Roles of Traditional Women (M. Swaminathan), 271-282; t) Girl Students: Between School and Marriage--a Delhi Sample (R. Jhabvala, P. Sinha), 283-290; u) Performing Arts (K. Vatsyayan), 291-300; v) Women in Politics (I. Ahmed), 301- .

115 INDIAN WOMEN FROM PURDAH TO MODERNITY. B.R. Nanda, ed. New Delhi: Vikas Publishing House, 1976.

a) Nehru and the Place of Women in Indian Society (B. Luthra), 1-15; b) Role of Women in the Indian Struggle for Freedom (A. Basu), 16-40; c) Social Reform Movement in India--From Ranade to Nehru (V. Mazumdar), 41-66; d) Hindu Woman at Home (T.N Madan), 67-86; e) Jawaharlal Nehru and the Hindu Code Bill (L. Sarkar), 87-98; f) Status of Muslim Women and Social Change (Z. Bhatty), 99-112; g) From Purdah to Modernity (R. Mehta), 113-128; h) Indian Women: Work, Power and Status (V. Das), 129-145; i) Woman Versus Womanliness: An Essay in Speculative Psychology (A. Nandy), 146-160.

116 THE ITALIAN IMMIGRANT WOMAN IN NORTH AMERICA. Betty Boyd Caroli, Robert F. Harney and Lydio F. Tomasi, eds. Proceedings of the Tenth Annual Conference of the American Italian Historical Association, October 28 and 29, 1977. Toronto: The Multicultural Historical Society of Ontario, 1978.

a) Silent Half: "Le Contadine del Sud" Before The First World War (E.P. Noether), 3-13; b) Civil Code of 1865 and the Origins of the Feminist Movement in Italy (J.J. Howard), 14-23; c) Prostitution and Feminism in Late Nineteenth-Century Italy (M. Gibson), 24-31; d) Women in the Canadian and Italian Trade Union Movements at the Turn of the Century (C. LaVigna), 32-43; e) Forging a Socialist Women's Movement: Angelica Balabanoff in Switzerland (N.G. Eshelman), 44-78; f) Men Without Women: Italian Migrants in Canada, 1885-1930 (R.F. Harney), 79-102; g) Settlement House and the Italian Family (R.N. Juliani), 103-123; h) Protestant Evangelism and the Italian Immigrant Woman (M.S. Seller), 124-137; i) Immigrants and Craft Arts: Scuola d'Industrie Italiane (G.E. Pozzetta), 138-153; j) Interaction Between Italian Immigrant Women and the Chicago Commons Settlement House, 1909-1944 (M.E.M. Batinich), 154-167; k) La Donna Italiana Durante Il Periodo Fascista in Toronto, 1930-1940 (L. Pautasso), 168-190; l) Italian American Women and Their Daughters in Rhode Island: The Adolescence of Two Generations, 1900-1950 (S.H. Strom), 191-205; m) Italian Mothers, American Daughters: Changes in Work and Family Roles (J.E. Smith), 206-221; n) Metonymic Definition of the Female and the Concept of Honour Among Italian Immigrant Families in Toronto (H. Perry), 222-233; o) Maternal Role in the Contemporary Italian-American Family (C.L. Johnson), 234-244; p) Italian-American Female College Students: A New Generation Connected to the Old (J. Krase), 246-251; q) Women, Ethnicity, and Mental Health: The Italian Woman, Impressions and Observations (F. Colecchia), 252-259; r) Oral History in Pittsburgh--Women, Ethnicity, and Mental Health: Rationale, Procedure, and Methodology (C.A. Krause), 260-272; s) Emigration, the Italian Family, and Changing Roles (L. Cellini), 273-287; t) Family and Kin Cohesion among South Italian Immigrants in Toronto (F. Sturino), 288-311; u) Women of Old Town (A. Mancuso), 312-323; v) Italian Immigrant Women in the Southwest (P.C. Martinelli), 324-340; w) Italian Immigrant Women in American Literature (R.B. Green), 341-349; x) Pasta or Paradigm: The Place of Italian-American Women in Popular Film (D. Golden), 350-357; y) Women in the Italian-American Theatre of the Nineteenth Century (E. Aleandri), 358-369; z) Selected Poems (P.G. Di Cicco, R. d'Agostino, M. Di Michele), 370- .

117 THE JEWISH WOMAN: NEW PERSPECTIVES. Elizabeth Koltun, ed. New York: Schocken Books, 1976.

a) Jewish Feminist: Conflict in Identities (J. Plaskow), 3-10; b) Women's Liberation and the Liberation of God: An Essay in Story Theology (C. Christ), 11-20; c) Birth of a Daughter (D.I. Leifer, M. Leifer), 21-30; d) Women and Jewish Education; A New Look at Bat Mitzvah (C. Koller-Fox), 31-42; e) Single and Jewish: Toward a New Definition of Completeness (L. Geller, E. Koltun), 43-49; f) Writing New KETUBOT (D.I. Leifer), 50-62; g) Tumah and Taharah; Ends and Beginnings (R. Adler), 63-71; h) Portnoy's Mother's Complaint: Depression in Middle-Aged Women (P. Bart), 72-83; i) This Month Is for You: Observing Rosh Hodesh as a Woman's Holiday (A. Agus), 84-93; j) Jewish Women's Haggadah (A.C. Zuckoff), 94-104; k) Other Half: Women in the Jewish Tradition (P. Hyman), 105-113; l) Status of Women in Halakhic Judaism (S. Berman), 114-128; m) Modest Beginning (E. Ticktin), 129-138; n) Bais Yaakov: A Historical Model for Jewish Feminists (D. Weissman),

139-148; o) Bertha Pappenheim: Founder of German-Jewish Feminism (M. Kaplan), 149-163; p) Henrietta Szold--Liberated Woman (S. Dworkin), 164-170; q) Stages (R. Janait), 171-178; r) Judaism and Feminism (B. Greenberg), 179-192; s) Changing(?)Role of Women in Jewish Communal Affairs: A Look into the U.J.A. (S.M. Cohen, S. Dessel, M. Pelavin), 193-201; t) Flight from Feminism: The Case of the Israeli Woman (C.N. Olapsaddle), 202-216; u) Depatriarchalizing in Biblical Interpretation (P. Trible), 217-240; v) Restoration of Vashti (M. Gendler), 241-247; w) Aggadic Approaches to Biblical Women (L. Kuzmack), 248-256; x) Women as Sources of Torah in the Rabbinic Tradition (A. Goldfeld), 257-271; y) Mothers and Daughters in American Jewish Literature: The Rotted Cord (S. Michel), 272-282.

118 KEEPING THE FAITH: WRITINGS BY CONTEMPORARY BLACK AMERICAN WOMEN. Pat Crutchfield Exum, ed. Greenwich, Ct.: Fawcett Publications , 1974.

This collection of poetry, autobiographical writings, and fiction is intended to show the concern of black women with racial unity and survival as well as their efforts to debunk racist myths. The selections also demonstrate the sensitivity and perceptiveness which characterize black female writing. Contributors: S.E. Wright, A. Lincoln, A. Childress, P. Marshall, C.F. Gerald, J. Adams, B. Banks, M. Bates, Sister Bernadine, G. Brooks, L. Clifton, J. Cortez, A. du Cille, M. Evans, P.C. Exum, J. Fields, N. Giovanni, B. Golden, S. Henderson, L. Hope, M. Jackson, G. Jones, M. Jones, J. Jordan, A. Lee, A. Lorde, E. Loftin, P. Nottingham, S. Sanchez, S.J. Skeeter, M. Walker, D.S. Williams, M. Angelou, L.-A. Henry, A. Moody, M. Wallace, T.C. Bambara, T. Morrison, A. Walker, S.A. Williams.

119 LADIES OF THE GOTHICS: TALES OF ROMANCE AND TERROR BY THE GENTLE SEX. (Selected and with introductions by Seon Manley and Gogo Lewis) New York: Lothrop, Lee and Shepard, 1975.

a) The Locked Room Upstairs (C. Fremlin), 13-28; b) The Long Corridor of Time (R. Rendell), 29-49; c) The Shadows on the Wall (M.W. Freeman), 50-70; d) The Haunted Palace (E.M. Roberts), 71-94; e) The Housekeeper's Story (E. Brontë), 95-124; f) The Haunted Chamber (A. Radcliffe), 125-147; g) Novels, Gothic Novels (J. Austen), 148-157; h) The Dream (M. Shelley), 158-176; i) The Mount of Sorrow (H.P. Spofford), 177-198; j) The Sailor Boy's Tales (I. Dinesen), 199-214.

120 LANGUAGE AND SEX: DIFFERENCE AND DOMINANCE. Barrie Thorne and Nancy Henley, eds. (Series in Sociolinguistics) Rowley, Ma.: Newbury House, 1975.

a) Difference and Dominance: An Overview of Language, Gender and Society (B. Thorne, N. Henley), 5-42; b) Women's Speech: Separate But Unequal? (C. Kramer), 43-56; c) Making of a Nonsexist Dictionary (A. Graham), 57-63; d) Semantic Derogation of Woman (M.R. Schulz), 64-75; e) Sex of

the Speaker as a Sociolinguistic Variable (M. Swacker), 76-83; f) Male-Female Intonation Patterns in American English (R.M. Brend), 84-87; g) Sex, Covert Prestige, and Linguistic Change in the Urban British English of Norwich (P. Trudgill), 88-104; h) Sex Roles, Interruptions and Silences (D.H. Zimmerman, C. West), 105-129; i) Sex Differentiation in Language (A. Boding), 130-151; j) Cues to the Identification of Sex in Children's Speech (J. Sachs), 152-171; k) Teacher-Child Verbal Interaction: An Approach to the Study of Sex Differences (L. Cherry), 172-183; l) Power, Sex, and Nonverbal Communication (N.M. Henley), 184-202; m) Sex Differences in Language, Speech, and Nonverbal Communication: An Annotated Bibliography, 205-306.

121 LATIN AMERICAN WOMEN: HISTORICAL PERSPECTIVES. Asunción Lavrin, ed. (Contributions in Women's Studies, No. 3) Westport, Ct.: Greenwood Press, 1978.

a) Colonial Women in Mexico: The Seventeenth and Eighteenth Centuries (A. Lavrin), 23-59; b) Female and Family in the Economy and Society of Colonial Brazil (A.J.R. Russell-Wood), 60-100; c) Indian Women and White Society: The Case of Sixteenth-Century Peru (E.C. Burkett), 101-128; d) Women in a Noble Family: The Mexican Counts of Regla, 1750-1830 (E. Couturier), 129-149; e) Indian Nuns of Mexico City's Monasterio of Corpus Christi, 1724-1821 (A.M. Gallagher), 150-172; f) Feminine Orders in Colonial Bahia, Brazil: Economic, Social, and Demographic Implications, 1677-1800 (S.A. Soeiro), 173-197; g) Feminine Press: The View of Women in the Colonial Journals of Spanish America, 1790-1810 (J.S.R. Mendelson), 198-218; h) Participation of Women in the Independence Movement in Gran Colombia, 1780-1830 (E. Cherpak), 219-234; i) Education, Philanthropy, and Feminism: Components of Argentine Womanhood, 1860-1926 (C.J. Little), 235-253; j) Nineteenth-Century Feminist Press and Women's Rights in Brazil (J.E. Hahner), 254-285; k) Felipe Carrillo Puerto and Women's Liberation in Mexico (A. Macías), 286-301; l) Trends and Issues in Latin American Women's History (A. Lavrin), 302-332.

122 LATIN AMERICAN WOMEN WRITERS: YESTERDAY AND TODAY. Selected Proceedings from the Conference on Women Writers from Latin America, March 15-16, 1975. Yvette E. Miller and Charles M. Tatum, eds. Pittsburgh: Latin American Literary Review, 1977.

a) Random Survey of the Ratio of Female Poets to Male in Anthologies: Less-Than-Tokenism as a Mexican Tradition (B. Miller), 11-17; b) Women Intellectuals in Chilean Society (M.C. Taylor), 18-24; c) Clorinda Matto de Turner and Mercedes Cabello de Carbonera: Societal Criticism and Morality (J.C. Miller), 25-32; d) Life and Early Literary Career of the Nineteenth-Century Colombian Writer, Coledad Acosta de Samper (H.E. Hinds, Jr.), 33-41; e) Teresa de la Parra, Venezuelan Novelist and Feminist (R.G. Stillman), 42-48; f) Elena Poniatowska's "Hasta no Verte, Jesus Mio" (C.M. Tatum), 49-58; g) Maria Angelica Bosco and Beatriz Guido: An Approach to Two Argentinian Novelists Between 1960 and 1970 (E.A. Azzario), 59-67; h) Argentine Women in the Novels of Silvina Bullrich (C.S. Mathieu), 68-74; i) Three Female Playwrights Explore

Contemporary Latin American Reality: Myrna Casas, Griselda Gambaro, Luisa Josefina Hernandez (G.F. Waldman), 75-84; j) Brechtian Aesthetics in Chile: Isidora Aguirre's "Los Papeleros" (E.M. Dial), 85-90; k) Thematic Exploration of the Works of Elena Garro (G. Mora), 91-97; l) Nellie Campobello: Romantic Revolutionary and Mexican Realist (D.E. Verlinger), 98-103; m) Feminine Symbolism in Gabriela Mistral's "Fruta" (C. Virgillo), 104-114; n) Two Poets of America: Juana de Asbaje and Sara de Ibanez (C. de Zapata), 115-127; o) Phenomenology of Nothingness in the Poetry of Julia de Burgos (E. Loguna-Diaz), 127-134; p) Love and Death: The Thematic Journey of Julia de Burgos (N.D. Santos), 134-147; q) Short Stories of Lydia Cabrera: Transpositions or Creations? (R. Valdes-Cruz), 148-154; r) Interview with Women Writers in Colombia (R.L. Williams), 155-164; POETS: S. Barros, A. de Hoyos, M. Islas, T. Pereria, M. Robles, O. Casanova-Sanchez, G. Zaldivar, I. Zavala.

123 LESBIANISM AND THE WOMEN'S MOVEMENT. Nancy Myron and Charlotte Bunch, eds. Baltimore: Diana Press, 1975.

a) Furies (G. Berson), 15-20; b) Such a Nice Girl (S. Deevey), 21-28; c) Lesbians in Revolt (C. Bunch), 29-38; d) Taking the Bullshit by the Horns (B. Soloman), 39-48; e) Lesbians and the Class Position of Women (M. Small), 49-62; f) Living with Other Women (R.M. Brown), 63-68; g) Shape of Things to Come (R.M. Brown), 69-78; h) Normative Status of Heterosexuality (PURPLE SEPTEMBER Staff), 79-84; i) Bisexuality (L. Ulmschneider), 85-90; j) Coming Out in the Women's Movement (C. Reid), 91- .

124 LET THEM SPEAK FOR THEMSELVES: WOMEN IN THE AMERICAN WEST, 1849-1900. Christiane Fischer, ed. Hamden, Ct.: Shoe String Press-Archon Books, 1977.

This collection presents accounts by women of American frontier life during the second half of the nineteenth century. Pieces are grouped according to affilation, vocation or situation, e.g., urban dwellers, travellers, army wives, farmers. Contributors: H.F. Behrins, M. Ballou, A. Mansur, R. Haskell, V.W. Ivins, H.P. Compton, Mrs. C.A. Teeples, M.A. Hafen, Mrs. O.B. Boyd, E.M. Biddle, M. Summerhaves, L.S. Wilson, C.N. Churchill, M.M. Matthews, H. Doyle, N.C. Larowe, M.E. Ackley, I. Saxon, S. Bixby-Smith, S.W. Hopkins, E. White, E.S. Kitt, Mrs. D.B. Bates, M.F. Leslie, E.H. Adams.

125 LIBERATING THE HOME. (Women in America: From Colonial Times to the 20th Century) New York: Arno Press, 1974.

a) Woman and Her Needs (1851)(E.O. Smith); b) Domestic Problem: Work

and Culture in the Household (1875)(A.M. Diaz).

126 LIBERATING WOMEN'S HISTORY: THEORETICAL AND CRITICAL ESSAYS. Berenice A. Carroll, ed. Urbana: University of Illinois Press, 1976.

a) Woman in Society: A Critique of Frederick Engels (A.J. Lane), 4-25; b) Mary Beard's "Woman As Force in History": A Critique (B.A. Carroll), 26-41; c) Invisible Woman: The Historian as Professional Magician (D.B. Schmidt, E.R. Schmidt), 42-54; d) Historical Phallacies: Sexism in American Historical Writing (L. Gordon, P. Hunt, E. Pleck, R.G. Ruthchild, M. Scott), 55-74; e) Problem of Women's History (A.D. Gordon, M.J. Buhle, N.S. Dye), 75-92; f) Gynecology and Ideology in Seventeenth-Century England (H. Smith), 97-114; g) Education and Ideology in Nineteenth-Century America: The Response of Educational Institutions to the Changing Role of Women (A. Simmons), 115-126; h) Feminism and Liberalism in Wilhelmine Germany, 1890-1918 (A. Hackett), 127-136; i) Feminism and Class Consciousness in the British and American Women's Trade Union Leagues, 1890-1925 (R.M. Jacoby), 137-160; j) Latina Liberation: Tradition, Ideology, and Social Change in Iberian and Latin American Cultures (A.M. Pescatello), 161-178; k) Racism and Tradition: Black Womanhood in Historical Perspective (J.A. Ladner), 179-193; l) Politics of Cultural Liberation: Male-Female Relations in Algeria (K. Boals), 194-212; m) Classical Scholar's Perspective on Matriarchy (S.B. Pomeroy), 217-223; n) Cheshire Cat: Reconstructing the Experience of Medieval Women (K. Casey), 224-249; o) Women in Convents: Their Economic and Social Role in Colonial Mexico (A. Lavrin), 250-277; p) Sex and Class in Colonial and Nineteenth-Century America (A.D. Gordon, M.J. Buhle), 278-300; q) Beyond "Kinder, Kuche, Kirche": Weimar Women in Politics and Work (R. Bridenthal, C. Koonz), 301-329; r) Women, Work and the Social Order (A. Kessler-Harris), 330-344; s) Study of Women in American History (G. Lerner), 349-356; t) Placing Women in History: A 1975 Perspective (G. Lerner), 357-368; u) Feminism and the Methodology of Women's History (H. Smith), 369-384; v) Four Structures in a Complex Unity (J. Mitchell), 385-399; w) "Herstory" As History: A New Field or Another Fad? (S.R. Johansson), 400-430.

127 LIBERATION NOW! WRITINGS FROM THE WOMEN'S LIBERATION MOVEMENT. (Deborah Babcox and Madeline Belkin, comps.) New York: Dell-Laurel, 1971.

a) Why Women's Liberation? (M. Dixon), 9-24; b) Next Great Moment in History is Ours (V. Gornick), 25-38; c) Cutting Loose (S. Kempton), 39-54; d) What It Would Be Like If Women Win (G. Steinem), 55-66; e) Job Discrimination and What Women Can Do About It (A.S. Rossi), 67-75; f) Metamorphosis into Bureaucrat (M. Piercy), 76; g) Drowning in the Steno Pool (M. Belkin), 77-81; h) Pie in the Sky (G. Reece), 82-87; i) Pages from a Shop Diary (O. Domanski), 88-93; j) Labor and Suffrage Movements: A View of Working-Class Women in the 20th Century (S. Reverby), 94-106; k) Where Is It Written? (J. Viorst), 107; l) Politics of Housework (Redstockings), 108-115; m) Liberation of Children (D. Babcox), 116-122; n) Day Care (L. Gross, P. Mac Ewan), 123-131; o) Women and Economics (C.P. Gilman), 132-138; p) Political

Economy of Women's Liberation (M. Benston), 139-144; q) Planned Obsolescence: The Middle-Aged Woman (R. Gladstone), 145-149; r) "In Trouble" (J. Harriman), 150-160; s) Marriage and Love (E. Goldman), 161-170; t) Storybook Lives: Growing Up Middle Class (E. Maslow), 171-176; u) To My White Working-Class Sisters (D. D'Amico), 177-181; v) "Freedom Is Something That All of Us Need" (M. Hobsen), 182-184; w) Double Jeopardy: To Be Black and Female (F.M. Beal), 185-196; x) Colonized Women: The Chicana (E. Sutherland), 197-208; y) A Work of Artifice (M. Piercy), 209; z) Conclusion, "Sex and Temperament in Three Primitive Societies" (M. Mead), 210-218; aa) "Second Sex" (S. de Beauvoir), 219-230; bb) "Sex and Semantics" (E. Merriam), 231-238; cc) "A Room of One's Own" (V. Woolf), 239-248; dd) Women: The Longest Revolution (J. Mitchell), 249-266; ee) Psychology Constructs the Female (N. Weisstein), 267-286; ff) Woman-Identified Woman (Radicalesbians), 287-292; gg) Education of Women (F. Howe), 293-310; hh) Myth of the Vaginal Orgasm (A. Koedt), 311-319; ii) Health Care May Be Hazardous to Your Health (A. Wolfson), 320-329; jj) Abortion Testimonial (B. Susan), 330-336; kk) Liberation Must Also Include the Women of Africa (S. Okoth), 337-342; ll) Asian Women in Revolution (C. Bunch-Weeks), 343-363; mm) Cuban Women (C. Camarano), 364-376.

128 LIVES TO REMEMBER. Leon Stein, comp. (Women in America: From Colonial Times to the 20th Century) New York: Arno Press, 1974.

a) Molly Brant--Loyalist (1953)(H.P. Gundy); b) Early Women Printers of America (1958)(E.M. Oldham); c) Prudence Crandall: Champion of Negro Education (1944)(E.W. Small, M.R. Small); d) Jane Grey Swisshelm: Agitator (1920)(L.B. Shippee); e) Original of Rebecca in "Ivanhoe" (1882)(G. Van Rensselaer); f) "Maria Del Occidente" (1926)(T.O. Mabbott); g) Reckless Lady: The Life Story of Adah Isaacs Menken (1941)(N. Fleischer); h) Amelia Bloomer and Bloomerism (1952)(P. Fatout); i) Four Sisters: Daughters of Joseph La Flesche (1964)(N.K. Green); j) Pamelia Mann: Texas Frontierswoman (1935)(W.R. Hogan); k) Women as Land-owners in the West (1886)(E. Haddock); l) Women in the Alliance Movement (1892)(A.L. Diggs); m) "Kate," the "Good Angel" of Oklahoma (1908)(A.J. McKelway); n) Julia Richman (1916)(A.R. Altman); o) "The Awakening" by Kate Chopin (1956)(R. Cantwell); p) Woman in Steel--Rebecca Lukens (1940)(R.W. Wolcott); q) Lady With the Hatchet (1926)(J.L. Dwyer); r) Poetess of Passion (1934)(M.A. de Ford); s) Laura Jean Libbey (1931)(L. Gold); t) Fannie Farmer and Her Cook Book (1944)(Z. Steele).

129 LOOKING AHEAD: A WOMAN'S GUIDE TO THE PROBLEMS AND JOYS OF GROWING OLDER. Lillian E. Troll, Joan Israel and Kenneth Israel, eds. Englewood Cliffs, N.J.: Prentice-Hall, 1977.

a) Poor, Dumb, and Ugly (L.E. Troll), 4-13; b) Way It Was (E. Foley), 14-20; c) More Than Wrinkles (R. Weg), 21-42; d) Sex and the Older Woman (M.H. Huyck), 43-58; e) Does Youthfulness Equal Attractiveness? (C.A. Nowak), 59-64; f) Confessions of a 45-Year-Old Feminist (J. Israel), 65-70; g) Penelope, Molly, Narcissus, and Susan (H. Feldman), 73-80; h) Coming Out of the Closet: Marriage and Other

Crises of Middle Age (F.B. Livson), 81-92; i) Meaning of Friendship in Widowhood (H.Z. Lopata), 93-105; j) What Do Women Use Friends For? (S.E.G. Candy), 106-112; k) Women and Leisure (J.A. Hendricks), 114-120; l) Older Women and Jobs (R.C. Atchley, S.L. Corbett), 121-125; m) Fostergrandparenting: A Unique Child-Care Service (R. Saltz), 126-132; n) Lifelong Learning (N.K. Schlossberg), 133-139; o) Education as Recreation (E.P. Carsman), 140-146; p) Older Black Women (J.J. Jackson), 149-156; q) Jewish-American Grandmothers (M. Seltzer), 157-161; r) Sexuality, Power, and Freedom Among "Older" Women (C. Safilios-Rothschild), 162-166; s) Mainstream Women (H. Fogel), 167-170; t) Nitty-Gritty of Survival (E. Kahana, A. Kiyak), 172-177; u) Is There a Psychiatrist in the House? (K. Israel), 178-183; v) Helping Each Other (E. Waters, B. White), 184-194; w) Those Endearing Young Charms: Fifty Years Later (R. Kastenbaum, D. Simonds), 196-206; x) Young Women, Old Women, and Power (J.D. Goodchilds), 207-209.

130 THE MALE MID-WIFE AND THE FEMALE DOCTOR: THE GYNECOLOGY CONTROVERSY IN NINETEENTH-CENTURY AMERICA. (Charles Rosenberg and Carroll Smith-Rosenberg, advisory eds.) (Sex, Marriage and Society) New York: Arno Press, 1974.

a) Employment of Females as Practitioners in Midwifery (1820)(W. Channing); b) Letters to Ladies in Favor of Female Physicians (1850)(S. Gregory); c) Man-Midwifery Exposed and Corrected (1848)(S. Gregory); d) Medical Morals (1853)(G. Gregory); e) Report of the Trial: The People versus Dr. Horatio N. Loomis, for Libel (1850).

131 MANY SISTERS: WOMEN IN CROSS-CULTURAL PERSPECTIVE. Carolyn J. Matthiasson, ed. New York: Free Press, 1974.

a) Marriages of Pacho: A Woman's Life among the Amahuaca (G.E. Dole), 3-36; b) Egyptian Woman: Between Modernity and Tradition (S.K. Mohsen), 37-58; c) Changing Frenchwoman: Her Challenged World (B.G. Anderson), 59-76; d) Guatemalan Women: Life under Two Types of Patriarchy (E. Maynard), 77-98; e) Women of North and Central India: Goddesses and Wives (D. Jacobson), 99-176; f) Lau, Malaita: "A Woman Is an Alien Spirit" (E.K. Maranda), 177-202; g) Women of Udu: Survival in a Harsh Land (A. Smedley), 205-228; h) Women in China: Past and Present (A.K. Wong), 229-260; i) Eskimo Women: Makers of Men (J.L. Briggs), 261-304; j) Khmer Village Women in Cambodia: A Happy Balance (M. Ebihara), 305-348; k) Women in Philippine Society: More Equal Than Many (H.E. Jacobson), 349-378; l) In Reality: Some Middle Eastern Women (L.E. Sweet), 379-398; m) Onondaga Women: Among the Liberated (C.E. Richards), 401-420; n) Conclusion (C.J. Matthiasson), 421-438.

132 MASCULINE-FEMININE: READINGS IN SEXUAL MYTHOLOGY AND THE LIBERATION OF WOMEN. Betty Roszak and Theodore Roszak, eds. New York: Harper and Row, 1970, c1969.

a) Woman De-Feminized (F. Nietzsche), 3-9; b) The Vampire Wife

(A. Strindberg), 10-18; c) Anatomy Is Destiny (S. Freud), 19-29; d) Real Women (R. Graves), 30-37; e) Why Men Need a Boys' Night Out (L. Tiger), 38-52; f) Womanly Woman (G.B. Shaw), 53-60; g) Love Rights of Women (H. Ellis), 61-67; h) Women, Servants, Mules, and Other Property (G. Myrdal), 68-75; i) Power Corrupts (R.V. Sampson), 76-86; j) Hard and the Soft: The Force of Feminism in Modern Times (T. Roszak), 87-106; k) Distrust Between the Sexes (K. Horney), 107-115; l) Human-Not-Quite-Human (D. Sayers), 116-121; m) Is Rape a Myth? (R. Herschberger), 122-129; n) Women as a Minority Group (H.M. Hacker), 130-147; o) Androgynous World (S. de Beauvoir), 148-159; p) Longest Revolution (J. Mitchell), 160-172; q) Sex Equality: The Beginning of Ideology (A. Rossi), 173-185; r) Rise of Women's Liberation (M. Dixon), 186-200; s) Understanding Orgasm (S. Lydon), 201-207; t) Poor Black Women (P. Robinson), u) Collective Statement, Black Sisters (P. Robinson), 208-212; v) Radical Women as Students (B. Jones), w) Female Liberation First, and Now (J.B. Brown), 213-229; x) Woman as Nigger (G. Rubin), 230-240; y) Goodbye to All That (R. Morgan), 241; z) Sisters, Brothers, Lovers...Listen (J. Bernstein, P. Morton, L. Seese, M. Wood), 251-253; aa) National Resolution on Women (S.D.S.), 254-258; bb) W.I.T.C.H. Manifesto, 259-261; cc) S.C.U.M. Manifesto (V. Solanas), 262-268; dd) Woman's Revolutionary Manifesto (Women's Liberation Collective), 269-271; ee) Manifesto (Redstockings), 272-274; ff) BITCH Manifesto (Joreen), 275-284; gg) Our Politics Begin with Our Feelings (San Francisco Redstockings), 285-290; hh) No "Chicks," "Broads," or "Niggers" for OLE MOLE, 291-296; ii) Human Continuum (B. Roszak), 297-306.

133 MILLENIAL WOMEN. Virginia Kidd, ed. New York: Dell, 1979.

a) No One Said Forever (C. Felice), 5-20; b) The Song of N'Sardi-El (D.L. Paxson), 21-39; c) Jubilee's Story (E.A. Lynn), 40-52; d) Mab Gallen Recalled (C. Wilder), 53-65; e) Phoenix in the Ashes (J.D. Vinge), 66-123; f) The Eye of the Heron (U.K. Le Guin), 124-302.

134 MORE WOMEN OF WONDER: SCIENCE FICTION NOVELETTES BY WOMEN ABOUT WOMEN. Pamela Sargent, ed. New York: Vintage Books, 1976.

a) Jirel Meets Magic (C.L. Moore), 3-52; b) The Lake of the Gone Forever (L. Brackett), 53-103; c) The Second Inquisition (J. Russ), 104-148; d) The Power of Time (J. Saxton), 149-174; e) The Funeral (K. Wilhelm), 175-213; f) Tin Soldier (J.D. Vinge), 214-278; g) The Day Before the Revolution (U.K. Le Guin), 279-302.

135 MOTHERS IN EMPLOYMENT. Nickie Fonda and Peter Moss, eds. Uxbridge, Middlesex: Management Programme, Brunel University, 1976.

a) Current Situation (P. Moss); b) Current Entitlements and Provisions (N. Fonda); c) Effects of Day Care on Young Children (J. Tizard); d) Women, Work and Conflict (S. Ginsberg); e) Employer's Attitude to Working Mothers (S. Green); f) Family, Employment and the Allocation of Time (D. LeCoultre); g) Next Five Years: Projections and Policy

Implications (P. Moss, N. Fonda).

136 MOUNTAIN MOVING DAY: POEMS BY WOMEN. Elaine Gill, comp. (The Crossing Press Series of Contemporary Anthologies) Trumansburg, N.Y.: Crossing Press, 1973.

This collection contains poems written by seventeen contemporary North American women. They evidence a wide range, both in theme and tone. Contributors: Alta, M. Atwood, C. Bergé, E. Brewster, C. Cox, S. Griffin, J.T. Hagedorn, M. Harris, E. Jong, L. Lifshin, P. Lowther, G. MacEwen, M. Piercy, C. Quirk, P. Webb, K. Wiegner, F. Winant.

137 MOVING TO ANTARCTICA: AN ANTHOLOGY OF WOMEN'S WRITING. Margaret Kaminski, ed. (The American Dust Series, No. 2) Paradise, Ca.: Dustbooks, 1975.

This collection of contemporary writings includes poetry, a novel excerpt, short stories, journal entries, brief dramatic pieces and articles. Contributors: L. Lifshin, B. Kelves, N. Nimnicht,

Contributors: L. Lifshin, B. Kelves, N. Nimnicht, A. Lorde, M. Piercy, M. Frank, G. Steslick, A. Rich, J. McCombs, W. Covintree, S. Fromberg-Schaeffer, H. Sorrells, L. Bita, J. Larkin, L.L. Vaughn, T.O. Zimmerman, F. Kicknosway, J. Goren, A.A. Chatelin, J. Gartland, R.T. Stainton, Alta, C. Matkovic, E. Meese, A. Peckenpaugh, R. Morgan, D. Richardson, B. Gravelle, G.L. House, P. Joan, A. DeWiel, M. Atwood, M. Kaminski, N.L.M. Petesch, B. Annis, L.C. Gottlieb, G. Rubin, A. Ingram, S.R. Quiroz, B. Drake, A. Nin, G. Dyc, J. Jensen, G. Smitherman, S. Shaw, D. Durkee, E. Bass.

138 THE NEGLECTED MAJORITY: ESSAYS IN CANADIAN WOMEN'S HISTORY. Susan Mann Trofimenkoff and Alison Prentice, eds. (Canadian Social History Series) Toronto: McClelland and Stewart, 1977.

a) Women of Three Rivers: 1651-63 (I. Foulché-Delbosc), 14-26; b) Impact of White Women on Fur Trade Society (S. Van Kirk), 27-48; c) Feminization of Teaching (A. Prentice), 49-65; d) Neglected Majority: The Changing Role of Women in 19th Century Montreal (D.S. Cross), 66-86; e) National Organization and the Women's Movement in the Late 19th Century (V. Strong-Boag), 87-103; f) Henri Bourassa and "the Woman Question" (S.M. Trofimenkoff), 104-115; g) Image of Women in Mass Circulation Magazines in the 1920s (M. Vipond), 116-124; h) Women's Emancipation and the Recruitment of Women into the Labour Force in World

War II (R. Pierson), 125-145.

139 THE NEW FEMINISM IN TWENTIETH-CENTURY AMERICA. June Sochen, ed. Lexington, Ma.: D.C. Heath, 1971.

a) Struggle for Woman's Suffrage (S.B. Anthony, I.H. Harper), 1-9; b) Two Suffrage Movements (M. Gruening), 10-13; c) Suffering Suffragettes (W.E.B. Du Bois), 14-16; d) Younger Suffragists (W.H. Cooley), 17-26; e) Stereotypes (F.G. Seabury), 27-32; f) Nature of Woman (F. Dell), 33-35; g) Waste of Private Housekeeping (C.P. Gilman), 36-41; h) Case for Birth Control (M. Sanger), 42-44; i) Revolutionary Birth Control (M. Eastman), 45-46; j) Henrietta Rodman: An Interview with a Feminist (G. MacAdam), 47-59; k) Women's Peace Party Organized (Survey Report) l) Now We Can Begin (C. Eastman), 64-72; m) Women Are Prisoners of Their Sex (B. Brophy), 73-78; n) Womanly Image (P. Stern), 79-86; o) Equality Between the Sexes: An Immodest Proposal (A.S. Rossi), 87-112; p) Politics of Housework (P. Mainardi), 113-119; q) Peace Ladies (M. Dector), 120-132; r) Woman as Nigger (N. Weisstein), 133-139; s) Myth of the Vaginal Orgasm (A. Koedt), 140-148; t) Revolution is Happening in Our Minds (J. Freeman), 149-160; u) Second Feminist Wave (M.W. Lear), 161-172; v) N.O.W. Organized (L. Hammel), 173-175; w) Editorial from N.O.W.'s President (A. Hernandez), 176-178; x) Female Liberation as the Basis for Social Revolution (R. Dunbar), 179-191; y) Political Economy of Women's Liberation (M. Benston), 192-202; z) Visions for the Future (A.S. Rossi), 203-205.

140 NEW RESEARCH ON WOMEN AND SEX ROLES AT THE UNIVERSITY OF MICHIGAN. Dorothy G. McGuigan, ed. (University of Michigan Papers and Reports) Ann Arbor: Center for Continuing Education of Women, University of Michigan, 1976.

a) Sex Roles in Transition: The Historical Perspective (E. Pleck), 6-24; b) Great Revolution (J.M. Bardwick), 25-34; c) Male Sex Role Behaviors in a Representative National Sample, 1973 (J.H. Pleck), 35-45; d) Change in U.S. Women's Sex-Role Attitudes, 1964-1974 (abstract)(K.O. Mason), 46; e) Female Employment and Family Organization in West Africa (N. Sudarkasa), 48-63; f) From Peasants to Proletarians: Black Women in the Cauca Valley, Colombia (A. Rubbo), 64-75; g) Domestic Servants in London and Paris, 1890 to 1914 (L.P. Moch), 76-89; h) Did Rosie the Riveter Give Up Her Job? Women War Workers During and After World War II (K. Hattaway), 90-102; i) Women's Roles in World Change: What About the Family? (J. Platt), 103-111; j) Women at Home and at Work (A. Campbell), 112-123; k) Role of Wife in the Black Extended Family: Perspectives from a Rural Community in Southern United States (B.A. Agbasegbe), 124-138; l) Women's Employment and Changing Sex Roles, 1900 to 1930 (research in progress)(L. Tentler), 139-143; m) Postwar Attitudes Toward Women and Work (abstract)(B. McGowan), 144-145; n) Stress, Primary Support Systems and Women's Employment Status (abstract)(R. Warren), 146-149; o) Italian-American Women in New York City, 1890 to 1940 (research in progress)(M. Cohen), 150-156; p) Women and Words in a Spanish Village (S. Harding), 158-182; q) Pollution and Power (E.C. Zelman), 183-194; r) Status of Women: Partial Summary of a Cross-Cultural Survey

(M.K. Whyte), 195-208; s) Rise of the Women's Movement: A Case Study in Political Development (E.D. Klein), 209-220; t) You Can Lead a Lady to Vote, But What Will She Do With It? The Problem of a Woman's Bloc Vote (V. Sapiro), 221-237; u) Climbing the Political Ladder: The Aspirations and Expectations of Partisan Elites (B.G. Farah), 238-250; v) Study of Women Coping with Divorce (P. Brown), 252-261; w) Assaulted Wife: "Catch 22" Revisited (abstract)(S.E. Eisenberg, P.L. Micklow), 262-263; x) Current Attitudes Toward Women and Men Who Never Marry (abstract)(J.M.F. Carl son), 265-266; y) Family Planning, Decision Making: Attitudes and Intentions of Mothers and Fathers (abstract)(D.K. Vinokur), 267-268; z) Perception of Parents by London Five-Year-Olds (abstract)(L. Nadelman), 269-271; aa) Fathering and Marital Separation (research in progress)(H. Finkelstein), 272-280; bb) Men and the Abortion Experience--Anxiety and Social Supports (research in progress)(R.B. Lees), 281-282; cc) Sex-Role Constraints: The College-Educated Black Woman (P. Gurin, C. Gaylord), 284-304; dd) Self-Concept and the Coping Process of Black Graduate and Undergraduate Women at a Predominantly White University (M. Wright), 305-313; ee) Promoting Creative Risk-Taking in Women (abstract)(M.A. Talburtt), 314-315; ff) Feminist Process in Learning (abstract)(S.A. Lincoln), 316-317; gg) Why Sex Discrimination? A Model of Sex-Role Transcendence (abstract)(M. Rebecca), 318; hh) Black Women in Higher Education: Research Literature (S.W. McAfee), 319-331; ii) Bibliography of Dissertations for and about Women in Administration in Colleges and Universities (P. Donisi), 332-340; jj) Women in English Literature (M.A. Lourie), 342-343; kk) Djuna Barnes' "Nightwood" (E.A. Meese), 344-352; ll) The End (P. Sharpe), 353-363; mm) Sexual Identity in the Early Fiction of V. Sackville-West (abstract)(M. Edwards), 364-365; nn) Victorian Pornography and Attitudes Reflected Toward Women (abstract)(G. Stavitsky), 366-368; oo) Sex-Role Media Research and Sources (L.J. Busby), 370-376; pp) Assembling Videotaped Materials for Instructional Purposes (B.M. Fodale), 377-380; qq) American Principles in Print: The Hero, The Harlot and the Glorified Horse (abstract)(C.J. Deming, B.J. Wahlstrom), 381-382; rr) Directions and Needs of Research on Women (E. Douvan), 383- .

141 NEW RESEARCH ON WOMEN AT THE UNIVERSITY OF MICHIGAN. (University of Michigan Papers and Reports) Dorothy G. McGuigan, ed. Ann Arbor: Center for Continuing Education of Women, University of Michigan, 1974.

a) Anthropology of Women (N. Diamond), 4-6; b) Four Levels of Women's History (K.K. Sklar), 7-10; c) Literary Women and the Masculated Sensibility (M. Lourie), 11-15; d) Psychology Looks at the Female (L.W. Hoffman), 16-18; e) Novel Women: Origins of the Feminist Literary Tradition in England and France (A.M. Fritz), 20-47; f) WOMEN IN HISTORY: Introduction (C. Lougee), 48-49; g) Influential Women in Anglo-Saxon England (E. Judd), 50-57; h) Feminist Culture from 1790 to 1850: A Trans-Atlantic Community (L.C. Schiller), 58-69; i) Feminism and Class Consciousness in the British and American Women's Trade Union Leagues, 1890-1925 (R.M. Jacoby), 70-76; j) Role of Women in the Organization of the Men's Garment Industry, Chicago, 1910 (M. Cohen), 77-84; k) Dynamics of Successful People (J. Bardwick), 86-104; l) Re-Examination of the Fear of Success (L.W. Hoffman), 105-111; m) Effects of Participation in Women's Consciousness-Raising Groups

(S. Riger), 112-116; n) WOMEN, FAMILY AND FERTILITY: Introduction (L.M. Verbrugge), 118-119; o) Adolescent Experience of Pregnancy and Abortion (S.L. Hatcher), 120-125; p) Fertility Motivations and Career Conflicts in Educated Women (J.D. Manis, L.W. Hoffman), 126-131; q) Men and Women in the Family: History of the Idea of Family in America's Depression Generation (R.L. Wolkoff), 132-135; r) Son Preference in Taiwan: Verbal Preference and Demographic Behavior (S. Danaraj), 136-137; s) Social Psychology of the "Decision" to Have or Not Have Children (S. Bram), 138-140; t) Welfare Careers, Low Wage Workers and Sexism (L.A. Ferman), 143-151; u) Woman is 58% of a Man (T.E. Levitin, R.F. Quinn, G.L. Staines), 152-158; v) Social Research on Women's Professional Careers (D.C. Herberg), 159-162; w) STATUS OF WOMEN IN THIS AND OTHER CULTURES: Introduction (M.F. Fox), 164; x) Chinese Women in the Early Communist Movement (S. Leith), 165-187; y) Cross-Cultural Study of the Relative Status of Women (M.K. Whyte), 188-190; z) Changing Status and Role of Women in Politics (B.G Farah, W.J. Hoag), 191-198; aa) Biological and Cultural Determinants of the Division of Labor by Sex (K. Weiss), 199-212; bb) Hrotsvitha of Gandersheim: The Playable Dramas of a Woman Playwright of the Tenth Century (M.M. Butler), 215-222; cc) Madame Vestris in America (L.S. Casey), 223-230; dd) Lillian Hellman: Dramatist of the Second Sex (V.M. Patraka), 231-235; ee) Historical and Theoretical Evolution of Viola Spolin's Theatre Games (B. Levitt), 236-242; ff) Women and Art (summary, panel discussion), 245-248; gg) Woman Artist and the Art Academy: A Case Study in Institutional Prejudice (M. Kamerick), 249-260; hh) From Social Fact to Social Action (R.L. Kahn), 262-272; ii) Recent and On-Going Research Projects at the University of Michigan, 274-285.

142 THE NEW WOMAN: A MOTIVE ANTHOLOGY ON WOMEN'S LIBERATION. Joanne Cooke, comp. (Robin Morgan, poetry editor) Indianapolis: Bobbs-Merrill, 1970.

a) Demise of the Dancing Dog (C. Ozick), 8-26; b) Revolutionary Letter #1 (D. Di Prima), 27; c) Inside Outside (J. Tepperman), 28-31; d) Restless Eagles: Women's Liberation 1969 (M. Dixon), 32-42; e) Metamorphosis into Bureaucrat (M. Piercy), 43; f) Double Jeopardy: To Be Black and Female (F.M. Beal), 44-57; g) Birthright (M. Magid), 58; h) Subversion of Betty Crocker (S. Sutheim), 64-74; i) The Playground (L. Fritz), 75-76; j) For a Brilliant Young Woman Who Lost Her Mind (R.M. Brown), 77; k) Realities of Lesbianism (D. Martin, P. Lyon), 78-88; l) To My Friend Miriam (M. Shelley), 89; m) Woman as Secretary, Sexpot, Spender, Sow, Civic Actor, Sickie (M.S. Webb), 94-117; n) My House in the Trees (J. Joesting), 118-119; o) Man's View (A. Hawley), 120-127; p) Witch Power (W.I.T.C.H.), 128-131; q) Kinder, Kuche, Kirche as Scientific Law: Psychology Constructs the Female (N. Weisstein), 132-146; r) The Pill--Radio News 2-24-70 (M.L. Fletcher), 153; s) You've Come a Long Way, Baby (L. Seese), 154-163; t) Broom of One's Own: Notes on the Women's Liberation Program

(C. Bunch-Weeks), 164-187.

143 NEW SPACE FOR WOMEN. Gerda R. Wekerle, Rebecca Peterson and David Morley, eds. Boulder: Westview, 1980.

a) Introduction (G.R. Wekerle, R. Peterson, D. Morley), 1-36; b) Home: A Critical Problem for Changing Sex Roles (S. Saegert, G. Winkel), 41-64; c) Household as Workplace: Wives, Husbands, and Children (S.F. Berk), 65-82; d) Appropriation of the House: Changes in House Design and Concepts of Domesticity (C. Rock, S. Torre, G. Wright), 83-100; e) Redesigning the Domestic Workplace (D. Hayden), 101-124; f) Women's Place in the New Suburbia (S.F. Fava), 129-150; g) Women's Travel Patterns in a Suburban Development (M.K. Cichocki), 151-164; h) Women in the Suburban Environment: A U.S.--Sweden Comparison (D. Popenoe), 165-174; i) Swedish Women in Single-Family Housing (K. Werner), 175-188; j) Toward Supportive Neighborhoods: Women's Role in Changing the Segregated City (J. Stamp), 189-200; k) Architecture: Toward a Feminist Critique (E.P. Berkeley), 205-218; l) Women in Planning: There's More to Affirmative Action than Gaining Access (J. Leavitt), 219-234; m) Unconscious Discrimination in Environmental Design Education, 235-254; n) From Kitchen to Storefront: Women in the Tenant Movement (R. Lawson, S. Barton, J.W. Joselit), 255-272; o) Women at City Hall (R.W. Butler, S. Phillips), 273-288; p) Los Angeles Women's Building: A Public Center for Woman's Culture (S.L. de Bretteville), 293-310; q) Emergency Shelter: The Development of an Innovative Women's Environment (A. Cools), 311-318; r) Housing for Single-Parent Families: A Women's Design (M. Soper), 319- .

144 THE NEW WOMEN'S THEATRE: TEN PLAYS BY CONTEMPORARY AMERICAN WOMEN. Honor Moore, ed. New York: Vintage, 1977.

a) Bits and Pieces (C. Jacker), 1-60; b) Window Dressing (J. Russ), 61-74; c) Breakfast Past Noon (U. Molinaro), 75-98; d) Birth and After Birth (T. Howe), 99-188; e) Mourning Pictures (H. Moore), 189-254; f) Wedding Band (A. Childress), 255-338; g) The Abdication (R. Wolff), 339-454; h) The Ice Wolf (J.H. Kraus), 455-496; i) I Lost a Pair of Gloves Yesterday (M. Lamb), 497-504; j) Out of Our Fathers' House (E. Merriam, P. Wagner, J. Hoffsiss), 505- .

145 THE NINETEENTH-CENTURY WOMAN: HER CULTURAL AND PHYSICAL WORLD. Sara Delamont and Lorna Duffin, eds. New York: Barnes and Noble, 1978.

a) Conspicuous Consumptive: Woman as an Invalid (L. Duffin), 26-56; b) Prisoners of Progress: Women and Evolution (L. Duffin), 57-91; c) Fitness, Feminism and Schooling (P. Atkinson), 92-133; d) Contradictions in Ladies' Education (S. Delamont), 134-163; e) Domestic Ideology and Women's Education (S. Delamont), 164-187; f) George Eliot

and Mary Wollstonecraft (N. McGuinn), 188-205.

146 NO LONGER YOUNG: WORK GROUP REPORTS FROM THE 26th ANNUAL CONFERENCE ON AGING. Ann Arbor: Institute of Gerontology, University of Michigan-Wayne State University, 1974.

a) Woman Alone (S.G. Jacobson), 1-4; b) Sexuality and Alternative Life Styles (P.J. Roeper), 5-8; c) Psychotherapy and Counseling (J. Sarnat), 9-14; d) Biological Realities and Myths (C. Ravenscroft), 15-22; e) Low Pay-Low Status (S.B. Haberkorn), 23-26; f) Political Importance of the Older Woman (A. Jones), 27-30; g) Life Span Behavior Patterns--Class and Ethnic Variations (S.T. Darrow), 31-36; h) Service Needs (A. King), 37-38; i) Literature and Myths (V.M. Patraka), 39-42; j) Self Image and Roles (C. Uits), 43-46; k) Family Relationships (M. Cameron), 47-52; l) Volunteerism (M.P. Westerman), 53-56; m) Economic and Legal Status (K. O'Neil), 57-62; n) Continuing Education and Second Careers (A. Wax), 63-68; o) Retirement: Career and Non-Career (D.S. Engel), 69-72; p) Media: Use and Misuse (I. Faure), 73-76; q) Gerontology Trends and Career Perspectives (J.L. Olah), 77-80.

147 NO MORE MASKS: AN ANTHOLOGY OF POEMS BY WOMEN . Florence Howe and Ellen Bass, eds. Garden City, N.Y.: Anchor Press, 1973.

This collection is both historical and contemporary, although most poems were written by Americans after 1960. Arrangement is primarily chronological. Contributors: A. Lowell, G. Stein, E. Wylie, H. Doolittle, M. Moore, E. St.V. Millay, L. Bogan, K. Boyle, P. McGinley, H. Adam, P. Murray, M. Rukeyser, R. Stone, M. Walker, E. Merriam, G. Brooks, N. Replansky, M. DeFrees, M. Swenson, M. Van Duyn, G. Paley, S. Kaufman, D. Levertov, J. Randall, J. Cooper, V. Miller, C. Kizer, M. Kumin, A. Halley, A. Sexton, A. Rich, R. Fainlight, C. Inez, C. Macdonald, S. Plath, A. Stevenson, A. Lorde, D. Di Prima, E.N. Sargent, L. Clifton, S. Hochman, J. Jordan, F. Kicknosway, R. Owens, M. Piercy, J. Stembridge, K. Fraser, J. Rechter, S. Sanchez, L. Sukenick, H. Chasin, K. Spivak, M. Atwood, L. Strongin, M. Evans, L. Kandel, W.G. Rickert, J. Grahn, P. Beauvais, C. Freeman, R. Morgan, Alta, C.M. Rodgers, S. Sutheim, E. Fenton, N. Giovanni, S. Griffin, S. McPherson, S. Axelrod, R.M. Brown, C. Quirk, S.B. Rioff, A. Walker, I. Wendt, C.G. Clemmons, N. Forman, J. Tepperman, A.Gottlieb, M. Palmer, A. Barrows, E. Bass, M. Magid, B. Walter, P. Henderson, M. Taft, W. Wieber, R.H. Crosby.

148 THE ORCHID BOAT: WOMEN POETS OF CHINA. (Translated and edited by Kenneth Rexroth and Ling Chung) New York: McGraw-Hill, 1972.

This collection includes poems by Chinese women written between c.300 B.C. and the twentieth century. The arrangement is primarily chronological. Three appendices offer notes, a survey of the participation of women in Chinese literary history, and a table of Chinese historical periods. Contributors: Lady Ho, Chuo Wen-Chün, Pan

Chieh-Yü, Ts'ai Yen, Mêng Chu, Tzu Yeh, Su Hsiao-Hsaio, Pao Ling-Hui, Wu Tsê-Tien, Kuan P'an-P'an, Yü Hsüan-Chi, Hsüeh T'ao, Hsüeh Ch'iung, Han Ts'ui-P'in, Chang Wên-Chi, Chao Luan-Luan, Lady Hua Jui, Ch'ien T'ao, Lady Wei, Li Ch'ing-Chao, Chu Shu-Chên, Nieh Sheng-Ch'iung, T'ang Wan, Sun Tao-Hsüan, Wang Ch'ing-Hui, Kuan Tao-Shêng, Chu Chung-Hsien, Huang O, Ma Hsiang-Lan, Shao Fei-Fei, Wang Wei, Ho Shuang-Ch'ing, Sun Yün-Feng, Wu Tsao, Yü Ch'in-Tsêng, Ch'iu Chin, Ping Hsin, Pai Wei, Cheng Min, Jung Tzu, Lin Ling, Tuo Ssu, Hsiung Hung, Lan Ling, Tan Ying, Chung Ling, Jên Jui, Li Chü, Li Yeh.

149 THE OTHER HALF: ROADS TO WOMEN'S EQUALITY. Cynthia Fuchs Epstein and William J. Goode, eds. and comps. Englewood Cliffs, N.J.: Prentice-Hall, 1971.

a) Status of Women in Modern Patterns of Culture (J. Bernard), 11-20; b) Civil and Social Rights of Women (W.J. Goode), 21-32; c) What Do You Mean "The Sexes"? (J. Bernard), 39-47; d) Sex Differences: Biological, Cultural, Societal Implications (F.A. Ruderman), 48-54; e) Possible Biological Origins of Sexual Discrimination (L. Tiger), 55-61; f) Down with Myth America (S. Shevey), 62-64; g) Sexual Politics (K. Millett), 65-72; h) Wife Problem (W.H. Whyte, Jr.), 79-86; i) Socio-Cultural Setting (F.I. Nye, L.W. Hoffman), 87-92; j) Declining Status of Women: Popular Myths and the Failure of Functionalist Thought (D.D. Knudsen), 93-109; k) Women in Science: Why So Few? (A.S. Rossi), 110-121; l) Women and the Professions (C.F. Epstein), 122-130; m) Leads on Old Questions from a New Revolution: Notes on Cuban Women, 1969 (V. Olesen), 134-142; n) Elements and Types in Soviet Marriage (K. Geiger), 143-154; o) Origins of American Feminism (W. O'Neill), 159-164; p) Women's Lib: The War on "Sexism" (H. Dudar), 165-176; q) Equality between the Sexes: An Immodest Proposal (A.S. Rossi), 180-192; r) Statement of Purpose (N.O.W.), 193-198; s) Manifesto (Redstockings), 199-202; t) Dangers in the Pro-woman Line and Consciousness-Raising (Feminists), 203- .

150 THE OTHER VOICE: TWENTIETH-CENTURY WOMEN'S POETRY IN TRANSLATION. Joanna Bankier et al., eds. New York: Norton, 1976.

The poetry in this anthology has been translated into English from thirty-one languages. The poets are mostly twentieth-century figures whose work has heretofore remained largely unavailable to Western readers. Foreword by Adrienne Rich. Contributors: A. Hébert, G. Fuertes, L. Goldberg, A. Rhydstedt-Dannstedt, S. de M.B. Andresen, J. de Burgos, K. Molodowsky, A. Margolin, A. Storni, F. Farrokhzād, V. Khoury, B. Dmitrova, I. Jonker, T. Ditlevsen, D. Ravikovitch, N. ní Dhomhnaill, N. Cassian, K. Boye, M. Mhac an tSaoi, A. Blandiana, C. Meireles, E. Lasker-Schüler, M. Tsvetayeva, A. Smith, N. Tuéni, M.T. Horta, M.L. Kaschnitz, B. Backberger, C. Dropkin, O. Aslan, E. Södergran, N. Gorbanevskaya, S. Kirsch, M. Banus, A. Pritam, S. Åkesson, M. n'Ait Attik, V. Parra, M. Clerbout, M.H. Tussman, A. Negri, T. Torres, M. Johansson, E. Warmond, E.-L. Manner, B. Akhmadulina, A. Pozzi, V. Porumbacu, I. Vukovic, Y. Akiko, Hsiung-hung, Ping-hsin, A. Akhmatova, Cheng Min, N. da Sousa, A. do Espírito Santo, F. Tuqan, C.N.M. Khaketla, G. Mistral, N. al-Malā'ikah,

L. Corpi, S. Sālih, E. Adnan, Hien Luong, Li Chü, S. Weil, N. Sachs, K. Anghelaki-Rooke, M. Szécsi, A. Károlyi, A.N. Nagy.

151 OUR AMERICAN SISTERS: WOMEN IN AMERICAN LIFE AND THOUGHT. Jean E. Friedman and William G. Shade, eds. Boston: Allyn and Bacon, 1973.

a) Puritans and Sex (E.S. Morgan), 16-29; b) Husbands and Wives (J. Demos), 30-44; c) Participation in Public Affairs (J.C. Spruill), 45-59; d) Dynamics of Interracial Sex in Colonial America (W.D. Jordan), 60-81; e) Lady and the Mill Girl: Changes in the Status of Women in the Age of Jackson (G. Lerner), 82-95; f) Cult of True Womanhood: 1820-1860 (B. Welter), 96-123; g) Reality and the Southern Lady (A.F. Scott), 124-136; h) Hagar and Her Children (E.F. Frazier), 137-151; i) Grimke Sisters: Women and the Abolition Movement (G. Lerner), 152-167; j) Woman as Alien (C. Lasch), 168-186; k) "New Woman" in the New South (A.F. Scott), 187-196; l) Charlotte Perkins Gilman on the Theory and Practice of Feminism (C.N. Degler), 197-218; m) Woman Suffrage in Perspective (A.S. Kraditor), 219-236; n) American Woman's Pre-World War I Freedom in Manners and Morals (J.R. McGovern), 237-259; o) Campaign for Women's Rights in the 1920's (C.A. Chambers), 260-283; p) Decline and Fall of the Double Standard (E.O. Smigel, R. Seiden), 284-300; q) Feminism as a Radical Ideology (W.L. O'Neill), 301-325; r) Liberation of Black Women (P. Murray), 326-339; s) Women's Liberation: Theory and Practice (J.E. Friedman), 340- .

152 OUT OF THE BLEACHERS: WOMEN AND SPORT. Stephanie L. Twin, ed. Old Westbury, N.Y.: The Feminist Press, 1979.

a) Woman as an Athlete (A. Kenaly), 27-37; b) Are Athletics Making Girls Masculine? (D.A. Sargent), 38-47; c) Physiological Considerations of the Female Participant (T.E. Shaffer), 48-58; d) Women Athletes (P. Weiss), 59-69; e) Being Female in Sport (M.M. Hart), 70-79; f) Closing the Muscle Gap (A.C. Scott), 80-84; g) Sweet Home (P. Jordan), 85-97; h) See Jane Run (L. Franks), 98-105; i) How I Learned to Ride the Bicycle (F.E. Willard), 106-115; j) Memoirs of a Would-Be Swim Champ (A. Geracimos), 116-125; k) I Always Wanted to Be Somebody (A. Gibson), 126-135; l) Gertrude Ederle (P. Gallico), 136-146; m) Confessions of an Ex-Cheerleader (L. Bernikow), 147-152; n) Giving Women a Sporting Chance (B.F. Fasteau), 153-159; o) Shedding Light on Title IX (C. Hogan), 160-167; p) Radical Ethic for Sports (J. Scott), 168-172; q) Desegregating Sexist Sport (H. Edwards), 173-177; r) Women in Motion (L. Franks), 178-189; s) Women's Sports in China (A. Gibbons), 190-193; t) Last Word (O. Connolly), 194- .

153 THE OVEN BIRDS: AMERICAN WOMEN ON WOMANHOOD, 1820-1920. Gail Parker, comp. Garden City, N.Y.: Doubleday-Anchor, 1972.

a) 'Twas But a Babe (L.H. Sigourney), 59-60; b) The Father (L.H. Sigourney), 61-70; c) The African Mother at Her Daughter's Grave (L.H. Sigourney), 71-72; d) Letters from New York (L.M. Child),

77-102; e) Appeal to the Christian Women of the South (A.G. Weld), 105-144; f) Address to the Christian Women of America (C. Beecher), 147-164; g) Statistics of Female Health (C. Beecher), 165-178; h) Lady Who Does Her Own Work (H.B. Stowe), 183-194; i) Servants (H.B. Stowe), 195-198; j) Dress, or Who Makes the Fashions (H.B. Stowe), 199-202; k) The Cathedral (H.B. Stowe), 203-214; l) The Courting of Sister Wisby (S.O. Jewett), 217-234; m) Reminiscences (E.C. Stanton), 237-254; n) Letters (E.C. Stanton), 255-266; o) Diary (E.C. Stanton), 267-276; p) Woman's Bible (E.C. Stanton), 277-286; q) Twenty Years at Hull-House (J. Addams), 289-304; r) Filial Relations (J. Addams), 305-314; s) The Yellow Wall-Paper (C.P. Gilman), 317-334; t) Two Callings (C.P. Gilman), 335-338; u) Domestic Mythology (C.P. Gilman), 339-352; v) Living of Charlotte Perkins Gilman (C.P. Gilman), 353- .

154 PERCEIVING WOMEN. Shirley Ardener, ed. New York: Wiley, 1975.

a) Belief and the Problem of Women (E. Ardener), 1-18; b) "Problem" Revisited (E. Ardener), 19-28; c) Sexual Insult and Female Militancy (S. Ardener), 29-54; d) Gypsy Women: Models in Conflict (J. Okely), 55-86; e) Premiss of Dedication: Notes towards an Ethnography of Diplomats' Wives (H. Callan), 87-104; f) Brides of Christ (D. Williams), 105-126; g) Female Militancy and Colonial Revolt: The Women's War of 1929, Eastern Nigeria (C. Ifeka-Moller), 127-158.

155 PERSPECTIVES ON HUMAN SEXUALITY: PSYCHOLOGICAL, SOCIAL AND CULTURAL RESEARCH FINDINGS. Nathaniel N. Wagner, ed. New York: Behavioral Publications, 1974.

a) Psychological Consequences of the Anatomical Distinction Between the Sexes (S. Freud), 6-19; b) Sex-Role Stereotypes and Clinical Judgments of Mental Health (I.K. Broverman, D.M. Broverman, F.E. Clarkson, P.S. Rosenkrantz, S.R. Vogel), 20-35; c) Are Women Prejudiced Against Women? (P. Goldberg), 36-41; d) Sexual Dimorphism and Homosexual Gender Identity (J. Money), 42-79; e) Self-Conceptions, Motivations and Interpersonal Attitudes of Early- and Late-Maturing Girls (M.C. Jones, P.H. Mussen), 80-95; f) Sex Differences in Responses to Psychosexual Stimulation by Films and Slides (G. Schmidt, V. Sigusch), 96-114; g) Differentiation of Male and Female Orgasm: An Experimental Study (E.B. Proctor, N.N. Wagner, J.C. Butler), 115-134; h) Aspects of Lower Class Sexual Behavior (L. Rainwater), 135-154; i) Premarital Sexual Permissiveness Among Negroes and Whites (I.L. Reiss), 155-177; j) Women's Sexual Responsiveness and the Duration and Quality of Their Marriages (A.L. Clark, P. Wallin), 178-199; k) Relationship of the Frequency of Masturbation to Several Aspects of Personality and Behavior (P.R. Abramson), 200-213; l) Mothers and Daughters: Perceived and Real Differences in Sexual Values (J. LoPiccolo), 214-223; m) Early Sexual Behavior in Adult Homosexual and Heterosexual Males (M. Manosevitz), 224-242; n) Comparison of Sexual Attitudes and Behavior in an International Sample (E.B. Luckey, G.D. Nass), 243-279; o) Changing Sex Norms in America and Scandinavia (H.T. Christensen, C.F. Gregg), 280-307; p) Gusii Sex Offenses: A Study in Social Control (R.A. LeVine), 308-352; q) Teenage Boys and Girls in West Germany (V. Sigusch, G. Schmidt), 353-370; r) Sex-Role Attitudes in Finland,

1966-1970 (E. Haavio-Mannila), 371-394; s) Sexual Behavior in Pregnancy (D.A. Solberg, J. Butler, N.N. Wagner), 395-411; t) Contraception and Pregnancy: Experience of Young Unmarried Women in the United States (J.F. Kantner, M. Zelnik), 412-466; u) Group Sex Among the Mid-Americans (G.D. Bartell), 467-489; v) Attribution of Fault to a Rape Victim as a Function of Respectability (C. Jones, E. Aronson), 490-500; w) Sexual Activities and Attitudes in Older Persons (G. Newman, C.R. Nichols), 501-508.

156 PERSPECTIVES ON NON-SEXIST EARLY CHILDHOOD EDUCATION. Barbara Sprung, ed. Conference on Non-Sexist Early Childhood Education, Airlie House, 1976. New York: Teachers College Press, 1978.

a) Sexism and Racism in Education (B.T. Bowman), 25-39; b) Preschool and the Politics of Sexism (S. Greenberg), 40-56; c) Teacher Education and Non-Sexist Early Childhood Education (L.G. Katz), 57-61; d) Liberating Toys: You Are What You Play (R. Queen), 62-70; e) Social Psychology of Sex-Role Intervention (M. Guttentag), 71-78; f) Teachers, Peers, and Play Preferences: An Environmental Approach to Sex Typing in the Preschool (L.A. Serbin), 79-93; g) Development of Psychological Androgyny: Early Childhood Socialization (J.P. Bean), 94-100; h) Sex Differences in the Use of Outdoor Space (R. Hart), 101-112; i) Non-Sexist Parenting at Home and at School (L.C. Pogrebin), 113-121; j) Problems and Priorities of Poor, Culturally Different Parents (H. Rodriguez-Trias), 122-127; k) Fathers are Parents Too (J. Levine), 128-136; l) Sex Role and Human Culture (P.C. Lee), 137-148; m) Epilogue (B. Sprung), 149-153; n) APPENDIX: Guidelines for the Development and Evaluation of Unbiased Educational Materials (F.R. George), 154-168; o) APPENDIX: Sources of Non-Sexist Materials, 169-182; p) APPENDIX: Non-Sexist Picture Books for Children, 188- .

157 PHILOSOPHY AND SEX. Robert Baker and Frederick Elliston, eds. Buffalo: Prometheus Books, 1975.

a) Four-Letter Words CAN Hurt You (B. Lawrence), 31-33; b) Sex and Reference (J. Moulton), 34-44; c) "Pricks" and "Chicks": A Plea for "Persons" (R. Baker), 45-64; d) Male Chauvinism: A Conceptual Analysis (M. Frye), 65-82; e) Better Sex (S. Ruddick), 83-104; f) Sexual Love and Moral Experience (D.P. Verene), 105-115; g) Sexual Immorality Delineated (B.H. Baumrin), 116-130; h) Humanae Vitae (Pope Paul VI), 131-149; i) Sex, Birth Control, and Human Life (C. Cohen), 150-165; j) Monogamy: A Critique (J. McMurtry), 166-177; k) Consolation of the Wedded (D. Palmer), 178-189; l) Marriage, Love, and Procreation (M.D. Bayles), 190-206; m) Is Adultery Immoral? (R. Wasserstrom), 207-221; n) In Defense of Promiscuity (F. Elliston), 222-246; o) Sexual Perversion (T. Nagel), 247-260; p) Inapplicable Concepts and Sexual Perversion (M. Slote), 261-267; q) Sex and Perversion (R. Solomon), 268-287; r) Question of Homosexuality (J. Margolis), 288-304; s) Defense of Abortion (J.J. Thomson), 305-323; t) Abortion and a Woman's Right to Decide (A. Jaggar), 324-337; u) Fetal Humanity and the Theory of Essentialism (B. Brody), 338-355; v) Abortion and the

Golden Rule (R.M. Hare), 356-376.

158 PHILOSOPHY AND WOMEN. Sharon Bishop and Marjorie Weinzweig, eds. Belmont, Ca.: Wadsworth, 1979.

a) Sexism as Inequality (J.S. Mill), 2-4; b) Racism and Sexism (R.A. Wasserstrom), 5-20; c) "Pricks" and "Chicks": A Plea for "Persons" (R. Baker), 21-25; d) Male Chauvinism: A Conceptual Analysis (M. Frye), 26-32; e) Psychological Oppression (S.L. Bartky), 33-41; f) Equality of Women (Plato), 42-44; g) Reply to Plato (Aristotle), 45-46; h) Femininity (S. Freud), 47-51; i) Nature of Women (J.S. Mill), 52-58; j) "Sex and Temperament in Three Primitive Societies" (M. Mead), 59-67; k) Self-Determination and Autonomy (S.B. Hill), 68-76; l) Sexual Equality (A. Jaggar), 77-87; m) Sexuality as a Metaphysical Dimension (K. Morgan), 88-95; n) Purpose of Sex (T. Aquinas), 97-99; o) Sex and Language (R. Baker), 100-102; p) Sex and Reference (J. Moulton), 103-108; q) Better Sex (S. Ruddick), 109-119; r) Is Adultery Immoral? (R.A. Wasserstrom), 120-127; s) Pornography and Respect for Women (A. Garry), 128-139; t) What's Wrong With Rape (P. Foa), 140-146; u) Love and Dependency (S. Bishop), 147-153; v) Love and Women's Oppression (S. Firestone), 154-158; w) Marx, Sex and the Transformation of Society (V. Held), 159-162; x) Separatism and Sexual Relationships (S.A. Ketchum, C. Pierce), 163-171; y) Origin of the Family, Private Property, and the State (F. Engels), 172-180; z) Ideology of the Family (J. Mitchell), 181-183; aa) Liberalism and Marriage Law (S.A. Ketchum), 184-189; bb) Altruism and Women's Oppression (L. Blum, M. Homiak, J. Housman, N. Scheman), 190-199; cc) Marriage and Its Alternatives (S. Firestone), 200-205; dd) Defense of Abortion (J.J. Thomson), 207-215; ee) Moral and Legal Status of Abortion (M.A. Warren), 216-226; ff) Preferential Hiring (J.J. Thomson), 227-236; gg) Secondary Sexism and Quota Hiring (M.A. Warren), 237-246; hh) Preferential Treatment (R.A. Wasserstrom), 247-250; ii) Phenomenology of Feminist Consciousness (S.L. Bartky), 252-257; jj) Political Philosophies of Women's Liberation (A. Jaggar), 258-265.

159 PHILOSOPHY OF WOMAN: CLASSICAL TO CURRENT CONCEPTS. Mary Briody Mahowald, ed. Indianapolis: Hackett, 1978.

a) Stereotype (G. Greer), 7-11; b) Our Revolution is Unique (B. Freidan), 12-19; c) Radical Feminism (T.-G. Atkinson), 20-29; d) What Is Woman? (E. Vilar), 30-33; e) Liberated Woman (M. Dector), 34-42; f) Republic V (Plato), 45-60; g) On the Generation of Animals (Aristotle), 61-65; h) Politics (Aristotle), 66-70; i) The Trinity (Augustine), 71-73; j) Treatises on Marriage and Other Subjects (Augustine), 74-75; k) Confessions (Augustine), 76; l) The City of God (Augustine), 76-78; m) On the First Man (T. Aquinas), 79-89; n) Of Love and Marriage (D. Hume), 92-94; o) Of Polygamy and Divorce (D. Hume), 95-102; p) Marriage (J.J. Rousseau), 103-115; q) Of the Distinction of the Beautiful and the Sublime in the Interrelations of the Two Sexes (I. Kant), 116-127; r) Vindication of the Rights of Woman (M. Wollstonecraft), 128-143; s) On Women (A. Schopenhauer), 144-155; t) Subjection of Women (J.S. Mill), 157-173; u) Diary of the Seducer

(S. Kierkegaard), 176-179; v) Of Womenkind, Old and Young (F. Nietzsche), 180-181; w) Of Child and Marriage (F. Nietzsche), 182; x) Our Virtues (F. Nietzsche), 183-189; y) Second Sex (S. de Beauvoir), 190-207; z) Origin of the Family (F. Engels), 210-225; aa) Emancipation of Women (V.I. Lenin), 226-236; bb) Marriage and Morals (B. Russell), 239-249; cc) Woman--A Philosophical Analysis (H. Hein), 250-260; dd) Contemporary Approach to Sex Identity (C.G. Allen), 261-275; ee) Natural Law Language and Women (C. Pierce), 276-287; ff) Sex Roles: The Argument from Nature (J. Trebilcot), 288-295; gg) Because You Are a Woman (J.R. Lucas), 296-304; hh) Woman's Place (T.R. Govier), 305-312; ii) Woman Question: Philosophy of Liberation and the Liberation of Philosophy (C.C. Gould), 313- .

160 THE PHYSICIAN AND CHILD-REARING: TWO GUIDES, 1809-1854. (Medicine and Society in America) New York: Arno Press, 1972.

a) Advice to Mothers, on the Subject of Their Own Health, and, of the Means of Promoting the Health, Strength and Beauty of Their Offspring (1809)(W. Buchan); b) Care and Feeding of Children: A Catechism for the Use of Mothers and Children's Nurses (1894)(L.E. Holt).

161 PLAYS BY AND ABOUT WOMEN: AN ANTHOLOGY. Victoria Sullivan and James Hatch, eds. New York: Random House, 1973.

a) Overtones (A. Gerstenberg), 1-18; b) The Children's Hour (L. Hellman), 19-96; c) The Women (C. Boothe), 97-200; d) Play with a Tiger (D. Lessing), 201-274; e) Calm Down Mother (M. Terry), 275-294; f) The Advertisement (N. Ginzburg), 295-344; g) Rites (M. Duffy), 345-378; h) Wine in the Wilderness (A. Childress), 379- .

162 POPULAR ATTITUDES TOWARD BIRTH CONTROL IN PRE-INDUSTRIAL FRANCE AND ENGLAND. Orest and Patricia Ranum, eds. (Basic Conditions of Life) New York: Harper and Row, 1972.

a) Origins of Contraception in France (P. Ariès), 10-20; b) Christianity and Population (M. Riquet), 21-44; c) Population of Crulai, a Norman Parish (E. Gautier, L. Henry), 45-52; d) Family Limitation in Pre-Industrial England (E.A. Wrigley), 53-99; e) Interpretation to Be Used for a History of Mentalities (P. Ariès), 100-126.

163 A PORTRAIT OF MARGINALITY: THE POLITICAL BEHAVIOR OF THE AMERICAN WOMAN. Marianne Githens and Jewel L. Prestage, eds. New York: D. McKay, 1977.

a) Sex, Socialization, and Politics (A.M. Orum, R.S. Cohen, S. Grasmuch, A.W. Orum), 17-37; b) Continuity and Change in Opinions about Sex Roles (B. Bozeman, S. Thornton, M. McKinney), 38-65; c) Sex Differences in Black Political Beliefs and Behavior (J.C. Pierce, W.P. Avery, A. Carey,

Jr.), 66-74; d) Working-Class Women's Political Participation: Its Potential in Developed Countries (C.B. Flora), 75-95; e) Case Study in Patriarchal Politics: Women on Welfare (L.B. Iglitzen), 96-112; f) Why Few Women Hold Public Office: Factors Affecting the Participation of Women in Local Politics (M.M. Lee), 118-138; g) Societal Punishment and Aspects of Female Political Participation: 1972 National Convention Delegates (N. Lynn, C.B. Flora), 139-149; h) Campaign Theory and Practice--The Gender Variable (V. Currey), 150-172; i) Comparative Study of Male-Female Political Attitudes at Citizen and Elite Levels (J.W. Soule, W.E. McGrath), 178-195; j) Spectators, Agitators, or Lawmakers: Women in State Legislatures (M. Githens), 196-209; k) Recruitment of Women for Congress (C.S. Bullock III, P.L. Findley Heys), 210-220; l) Women as Politicians: The Social Background, Personality, and Political Careers of Female Party Leaders (E. Costantini, K.H. Craik), 221-240; m) New Dimension in Political Participation: The Women's Political Caucus (B. Burrell), 241-258; n) Women as Voters: Their Maturation as Political Persons in American Society (J.J. Stucker), 264-283; o) Women in Iowa Legislative Politics (E.G. King), 284-303; p) Women Members of Congress: A Distinctive Role (F.L. Gehlen), 304-319; q) Wife and Politician: Role Strain Among Women in Public Office (E. Stoper), 320-338; r) Politics of Sexual Stereotypes (M.C. King), 346-365; s) Traditional Political Animals? A Loud No (I.S. Reid), 366-378; t) Voting Patterns of American Black Women (M. Lansing), 379-394; u) Black Women in Electoral Politics (H.J. Bryce, A.E. Warrick), 395-400; v) Black Women State Legislators: A Profile (J.L. Prestage), 401-418; w) Conclusion (M. Githens, J.L. Prestage), 421- .

164 THE POTENTIAL OF WOMAN. Seymour Farber and Roger L. Wilson, eds. New York: McGraw-Hill, 1963.

a) Female Primate (P.C. Jay), 3-12; b) Biological Make-Up of Woman (E.W. Overstreet), 13-23; c) Women's Intellect (E.E. Maccoby), 24-39; d) Developmental Differentiation of Femininity and Masculinity Compared (J. Money), 51-65; e) Women in the Field of Art (T.C. Howe), 66-78; f) Woman in Man (A. Watts), 79-86; g) Roles of Women: A Question of Values (E.M. Albert), 105-115; h) Problems of Creative Women (M. Mannes), 116-130; i) Interpretation of Roles (P. Koestenbaum), 131-150; j) Implication of Rivalry (B.B. Gunderson), 165-187; k) Impact of Education (E. Peterson), 188-198; l) Two Cheers for Equality (A. Koch), 199-215; m) One American Woman: A Speculation upon Disbelief (M. Harris), 231-240; n) Repository of Wealth (A.E. Schwabacher, Jr.), 241-254; o) Direction of Feminine Evolution (M.M. Hunt), 255-272.

165 PRIVILEGE OF SEX: A CENTURY OF CANADIAN WOMEN. Eve Zaremba, ed. Toronto: House of Anasi, 1974.

a) A. Langton, 9-30; b) F. Stewart, 31-35; c) A.B. Jameson, 36-50; d) T. Gowanlock, 55-91; e) N. Davenport, 92-126; f) N.L. McClung, 133-162; g) M. Cran, 163-166; h) M. Macmurch, 167-170; i) A.

MacPhail, 171-

166 THE PROFESSIONAL WOMAN. Athena Theodore, ed. Cambridge: Schenkman, 1971.

a) Professional Woman: Trends and Prospects (A. Theodore), 1-38; b) Plus Ca Change...? The Sexual Structure of Occupations Over Time (E. Gross), 39-51; c) Encountering the Male Establishment: Sex-Status Limits on Woman's Careers in the Professions (C.F. Epstein), 52-73; d) Male and Female: Differing Perceptions of the Teaching Experience (H. Ziegler), 74-92; e) Head Librarians: How Many Men? How Many Women? (W.C. Blankenship), 93-102; f) Predominance of Male Authors in Social Work Publications (A. Rosenblatt, E. Turner, A.R. Patterson, C.K. Rollesson), 103-118; g) Farmer's Daughter Effect: The Case of the Negro Female Professional (E.W. Bock), 119-134; h) Clash Between Beautiful Women and Science (D.P. Campbell), 135-141; i) Occupational Advice for Women in Magazines (P. Clark, V. Esposito), 142-155; j) Masculinity or Femininity? Differentiating Career-Oriented and Homemaking-Oriented College Freshman Women (L. Rand), 156-166; k) Are Women Prejudiced Against Women? (P. Goldberg), 167-172; l) Occupational Aspects of Social Work (R.M. Bucklew, V.J. Parenton), 173-181; m) Social Influence and the Social-Psychological Function of Deference: A Study of Psychiatric Nursing (W.A. Rushing), 182-194; n) Female Physician in Public Health: Conflict and Reconciliation of the Sex and Professional Roles (J. Kosa, R.E. Coker, Jr.), 195-206; o) Women in the Soviet Economy (N. Dodge), 207-226; p) Women's Ambition (R.H.Turner), 227-251; q) Fail: Bright Women (M. Horner), 252-259; r) Career of Marriage? A Longitudinal Study of Able Young Women (D.J. Watley), 260-274; s) Female Identity and Career Choice: The Nursing Case (R.F. White), 275-289; t) Career Choice Processes (F.E. Katz, H.M. Martin), 290-300; u) Role Model Influences on College Women's Career Aspirations (E.M. Almquist, S.S. Angrist), 301-323; v) Interest of High School Girls in Dental Auxiliary Careers (L.K. Cohen, E.M. Knott), 324-333; w) Career Dreams of Teachers (B.D. Wright, S.A. Tuska), 334-345; x) Academic Women (R.E. Eckert, J.E. Stecklein), 346-354; y) Differential Recruitment of Female Professionals: A Case Study of Clergywomen (A.R. Jones, L. Taylor), 355-364; z) Self-Concept, Occupational Role Expectations, and Occupational Choice in Nursing and Social Work (A.J. Davis), 365-376; aa) Women Preparing to Teach (F. Schab), 377-380; bb) Perspective of College Women (W.L. Wallace), 381-396; cc) Female in Engineering (S.S. Robin), 397-413; dd) Graduate Limbo for Women (D. Boroff), 414-426; ee) Career Expectations of Negro Women Graduates (J.H. Fichter), 427-440; ff) Participation of Women Doctorates in the Labor Force (H.S. Astin), 441-452; gg) Factors Influencing Married Women's Actual or Planned Work Participation (M.W. Weil), 453-466; hh) College Women Seven Years After Graduation (Women's Bureau), 467-493; ii) Marriage and Medicine (C. Lopate), 494-515; jj) Career Patterns of Married Couples (L.L. Holmstrom), 516-524; kk) Married Professional Social Worker (J.E. Tropman), 525-535; ll) Inactive Nurse (D.E. Reese, S.E. Siegel, A. Testoff), 536-544; mm) Career and Family Orientations of Husbands and Wives in Relation to Marital Happiness (L. Bailyn), 545-567; nn) Professional and Non-Professional Women as Mothers (F.H. Von Mering), 568-586; oo) Women as a Minority Group in Higher Academics (A.E. Davis), 587-598; pp) Female Clergy: A Case of Professional Marginality (E.W. Bock),

599-611; qq) Women in Science: Why So Few? (A. Rossi), 612-628; rr) Women in Architecture (B. Dinerman), 629-634; ss) What You Should Know About Women Engineers (H. Popper), 635-646; tt) Women in the Law (J.J. White), 647-659; uu) Vanguard Artist: Portrait and Self-Portrait (B. Rosenberg, N. Fliegel), 660-668; vv) Women Lawyers and Their Profession: Inconsistency of Social Controls and Their Consequences for Professional Performance (C.F. Epstein), 669-684; ww) Do "Bad Girls" Become Good Nurses? (C. Krueger), 685-696; xx) Employer Acceptance of the Mature Home Economist (L.A. Stedman, P.S. Anderson), 697-708; yy) Women and Medicine in a Changing World (J. Kosa), 709-719; zz) Women in Academe (P.A. Graham), 720-740; aaa) Myth of the Egalitarian Family: Familial Roles and the Professionally Employed Wife (M.M. Poloma, T.N. Garland), 741- .

167 THE PROSTITUTE AND THE SOCIAL REFORMER: COMMERCIAL VICE IN THE PROGRESSIVE ERA. (Sex, Marriage and Society) New York: Arno Press, 1974.

a) Report (1911)(Vice Commission of Minneapolis); b) Report on Existing Conditions with Recommendations (1913)(Vice Commission of Philadelphia).

168 PSYCHE: THE FEMININE POETIC CONSCIOUSNESS. AN ANTHOLOGY OF MODERN AMERICAN WOMEN POETS. Barbara Segnitz and Carol Rainey, eds. New York: Dial Press, 1973.

Poetry by contemporary American women explores the motifs and images of women's private lives in this collection. The work of ten major poets is emphasized: E. Dickinson, E. Wylie, M. Moore, G. Brooks, M. Swenson, D. Levertov, A. Sexton, A. Rich, S. Plath, and M. Atwood, a Canadian. Some poetry by newer poets is included as well: B. Brigham, M. Evans, C. Kizer, P. Goedicke, M. Piercy, R. Owens, D. Wakoski, L. Lifshin, E. Jong, and N. Giovanni.

169 PSYCHOANALYSIS AND FEMALE SEXUALITY. Hendrik M. Ruitenbeek, ed. New Haven: College and University Press, 1966.

a) Early Development of Female Sexuality (E. Jones), 21-35; b) Evolution of the Oedipus Complex in Women (J. Lampl-de-Groot), 36-50; c) Effects of the Derogatory Attitude Toward Female Sexuality (C. Thompson), 51-60; d) Masculinity Complex in Women (J.H.W. van Ophuijsen), 61-72; e) Denial of the Vagina (K. Horney), 73-87; f) Female Sexuality (S. Freud), 88-105; g) Female Homosexuality (H. Deutsch), 106-129; h) Passivity, Masochism and Femininity (M. Bonaparte), 130-139; i) Special Problems of Early Female Sexual Development (P. Greenacre), 140-160; j) Self-Esteem (Dominance-Feeling) and Sexuality in Women (A.H. Maslow), 161-197; k) Orgasm in the Female (J. Marmor), 198-208; l) Womanliness as a Masquerade (J. Riviere), 209-220; m) Women Who Hate Their Husbands (D.A. Freedman), 221-237; n) Problem of Vaginal Orgasm (S. Lorand), 238-245; o) "Penis Envy" in

Women (C. Thompson), 246- .

170 PSYCHOANALYSIS AND WOMEN. Jean Baker Miller, ed. New York: Brunner-Mazel, 1973.

a) Flight from Womanhood: The Masculinity Complex in Women as Viewed by Men and by Women (K. Horney), 5-20; b) Problem of Feminine Masochism (K. Horney), 21-38; c) Sex (A. Adler), 40-50; d) "Penis Envy" in Women (C. Thompson), 52-57; e) Effects of the Derogatory Attitude Toward Female Sexuality (C. Thompson), 58-68; f) Cultural Pressures in the Psychology of Women (C. Thompson), 69-84; g) Denial of Women's Sexual Pleasure: Discussion of Dr. Thompson's Paper (F. Fromm-Reichmann, V. Gunst), 86-94; h) Masculine and Feminine: Some Biological and Cultural Aspects (G. Zilboorg), 96-134; i) Nature of Female Sexuality (M.J. Sherfey), 136-154; j) Personal Identity and Sexual Identity (M.B. Cohen), 156-182; k) Feminine Psychology and Infantile Sexuality (P. Chodoff), 184-200; l) Psychology of the Female: A New Look (L. Salzman), 202-220; m) Changing Patterns of Femininity: Psychoanalytic Implications (J. Marmor), 222-238; n) Survey and Reevaluation of the Concept of Penis Envy (R. Moulton), 240-258; o) Sense of Femaleness (R.J. Stoller), 260-272; p) "Bedrock" of Masculinity and Femininity: Bisexuality (R.J. Stoller), 273-286; q) Phobias after Marriage: Women's Declaration of Dependence (A. Symonds), 288-304; r) Is Anatomy Destiny? (R. Seidenberg), 306-329; s) For the Future--Equity? (R. Seidenberg), 330-349; t) Trauma of Eventlessness (R. Seidenberg), 350-362; u) Masculinity-Femininity: A Study in Imposed Inequality (L.A. Galb), 364-374; v) Conclusion: New Issues, New Approaches 375-406.

171 THE PSYCHOBIOLOGY OF SEX DIFFERENCES AND SEX ROLES. Jacquelynne E. Parsons, ed. Washington: Hemisphere, 1980.

a) Psychosexual Neutrality: Is Anatomy Destiny? (J.E. Parsons), 3-30; b) Biospsychosocial Processes in the Development of Sex-related Differences (A.C. Petersen), 31-56; c) Gonadal Hormones and Cognitive Functioning (D.M. Broverman, E.L. Klaiber, W. Vogel), 57-80; d) Human Sex-Hormone Abnormalities Viewed from an Androgynous Perspective: A Reconsideration of the Work of John Money (A.G. Kaplan), 81-94; e) Biochemical and Neurophysiological Influences on Human Sexual Behavior (F. Ledwitz-Rigby), 95-104; f) Homosexual Orientation in Women and Men: A Hormonal Basis? (H.F.L. Meyer-Bahlburg), 105-130; g) Social Psychological Model of Human Sexuality (T. Falbo), 131-144; h) American Birth Practices (S.R. Hahn, K.E. Paige), 145-176; i) Maternal Stress in the Postpartum Period (E.M. Magnus), 177-208; j) Adult Life Cycles: Changing Roles and Changing Hormones (M. Notman), 209-226; k) Menstrual-related Psychological Changes (D.N. Ruble, J. Brooks-Gunn, A. Clarke), 227-244; l) Social Psychological Perspective on the Menstrual Cycle (C.W. Sherif), 245-268; m) Body Time and Social Time: Mood Patterns by Menstrual Cycle Phase and Day of Week (A.S. Rossi,

P.E. Rossi), 269-304.

172 PSYCHOLOGY AND WOMEN: IN TRANSITION. Jeanne E. Gullahorn, (ed.) (Scripta Series in Personality and Social Psychology) Washington, D.C.: V.H. Winston, 1979.

a) Sex-Related Behaviors: Historical and Psychobiological Perspectives (J.E. Gullahorn), 1-8; b) Sex-Related Factors in Cognition and in Brain Lateralization (J.E. Gullahorn), 9-36; c) Meaning of Sex-Related Variations in Maturation Rate (D.P. Waber), 37-62; d) Individuals and Families in Transition: Dilemmas and Coping (J.E. Gullahorn), 63-70; e) Dilemmas of Masculinity in a Changing World (M. Komarovsky), 71-82; f) American Family: A Twenty-Year View (E. Douvan, R. Kulka), 83-94; g) Stress and Coping in Divorce: A Focus on Women (E.M. Hetherington, M. Cox, R. Cox), 95-130; h) Psychology in Transition: Continuities, Critiques, and Perspectives (J.E. Gullahorn), 131-146; i) Woman's Sociobiological Heritage: Destiny or Free Choice? (E.E. Maccoby), 147-166; j) Traits, Roles, and the Concept of Androgyny (J.T. Spence), 167-188; k) New Psychology of Women: A Feminist Analysis (M.T.S. Mednick), 189-212.

173 PSYCHOLOGY OF WOMEN: SELECTED READINGS. Juanita H. Williams, ed. New York: W.W. Norton, 1979.

a) Psychology of Women (G.T.W. Patrick), 3-11; b) Functionalism, Darwinism, and the Psychology of Women (S.A. Shields), 12-34; c) Femininity (S. Freud), 40-52; d) Freud's View of Female Psychology (M. Mead), 53-61; e) Problem of Feminine Masochism (K. Horney), 62-70; f) Once More the Inner Space (E. Erikson), 71-84; g) Brain, Body, and Behavior (R.H. Bleier), 87-98; h) Premenstrual Syndrome (M.B. Parlee), 99-114; i) Symbolic Significance of Menstruation and the Menopause (V. Skultans), 115-128; j) Parents' Views on Sex of Newborns (J.Z. Rubin, F.J. Provenzano, Z. Luria), 134-141; k) Early Sex Differences in the Human: Studies of Socioemotional Development (M. Lewis), 142-148; l) Psychology (R.M. Vaughter), 149-171; m) Androgyny Reconsidered (K.E. Grady), 172-178; n) How Nursery Schools Teach Girls to Shut Up (L.A. Serbin, K.D. O'Leary), 183-187; o) Implications and Applications of Recent Research on Feminine Development (G.K. Baruch, R.C. Barnett), 188-199; p) Social Values, Femininity, and the Development of Female Competence (J.A. Sherman), 200-211; q) Growing Up Black (J.A. Ladner), 212-224; r) Women's Liberation and Human Sexual Relations (P.S. Faunce, S. Phipps-Yonas), 228-240; s) Social Dimensions of the Menstrual Taboo and the Effects on Female Sexuality (E.B. Breit, M.M. Ferrandino), 241-254; t) Realities of Lesbianism (D. Martin, P. Lyon), 255-262; u) Contraceptives for Males (W.J. Bremner, D.M. de Kretser), 266-274; v) Psychosocial Factors of the Abortion Experience (L.R. Shusterman), 275-297; w) !Kung Hunter-Gatherers: Feminism, Diet, and Birth Control (G.B. Kolata), 298-302; x) Sex Preferences, Sex Control, and the Status of Women (N.E. Williamson), 303-316; y) Childbirth in Crosscultural Perspective (N. Newton, M. Newton), 321-341; z) Breast Feeding (N. Newton), 342-350; aa) Maternal Attachment: Importance of the First Post-Partum Days (M.H. Klaus, R. Jerauld, N.C. Kreger, W. McAlpine, M. Steffa,

J.H. Kennell), 351-358; bb) Anger and Tenderness (A. Rich), 363-376; cc) Big-Time Careers for the Little Woman: A Dual-Role Dilemma (S.A. Darley), 377-387; dd) Role of Models in Women's Professional Development (E. Douvan), 388-400; ee) Male Sex Role: Definitions, Problems, and Sources of Change (J.H. Pleck), 401-408; ff) Nature of Female Criminality (D. Harrentsian), 413-428; gg) Sex Differences and Psychiatric Disorders (B.P. Dohrenwend, B.S. Dohrenwend), 429-435; hh) Cinderella's Stepsisters: A Feminist Perspective on Anorexia Nervosa and Bulimia (M. Boskind-Lodahl), 436-448; ii) Consciousness-Raising Group as a Model for Therapy with Women (A.M. Brodsky), 449-456; jj) Double Standard of Aging (S. Sontag), 462-478; kk) Women in the Middle Years: Conceptions and Misconceptions (R. Barnett, G. Baruch), 479-487; ll) Cross-Cultural Investigation of Behavioral Changes at Menopause (J. Griffen), 488-495; mm) Women in Widowhood (C.J. Barrett), 496- .

174 RACE, SEX, AND POLICY PROBLEMS. Marian Lief Palley and Michael B. Preston, eds. (Policy Studies Organization Series) Lexington, Ma.: Lexington Books, 1979.

a) Eliminating Sex Discrimination in Education: Lobbying for Implementation of Title IX (A.N. Costain), 3-12; b) Impact of Collective Bargaining on Minorities in the Public Sector: Some Policy Implications (M.B. Preston), 13-26; c) Black Women in the Continuing Struggle for Equality (T.-M.C. Travis), 27-38; d) Impact of Organizational Structure, Technology, and Professionalism on the Policy of Affirmative Action (C. Swanson, H.B. Milward), 41-56; e) Affirmative Action: Constraints and Policy Impact (K.J. Meier), 57-74; f) Discrimination and the Law: The Equal Credit Opportunity Act (M.M. Conway), 75-86; g) Minorities and Policy Problems: An Overview Seen by the U.S. Commission on Civil Rights (M.C. Woodard, E.R. Jackson), 87-100; h) Sex and the Burger Court: Recent Judicial Policy Making toward Women (L.F. Goldstein), 103-114; i) Incidence and Correlates of Second Generation Discrimination (C.S. Bullock III, J. Stewart, Jr.), 115-130; j) Abortion Policy since 1973: Political Cleavage and Its Impact on Policy Outputs (H.A. Palley), 131-144; k) Combatting Dual Discrimination: The Impact of Civil Rights Policies on the Income Status of Black Women (D.J. McCrone, R.J. Hardy), 147-160; l) Women's Educational Equity: Favorable Student Response (S.S. Schramm), 161-174; m) Policy Impacts on Hispanics and Women: A State Case Study (C. Clark, J. Clark, J.Z. Garcia), 177-192; n) Women and Public Policy: A Comparative Analysis (S. Welch, D.L. Gottheil), 193-206; o) Political Power and Policy Benefits: Voting Rights and Welfare Policy in Mississippi (G.T. Broach), 207-220; p) Styles and Priorities of Marginality: Women State Legislators (M. Githens, J.L. Prestage), 221-236; q) Abortion in Israel: Social Demands and Political Responses (Y. Yishai), 239-260.

175 RADICAL FEMINISM. Anne Koedt, Ellen Levine and Anita Rapone, eds. New York: Quadrangle Books, 1973.

a) First Feminists (J.Hole, E. Levine), 3-16; b) Trial of Susan B. Anthony, 17-22; c) Woman and Her Mind (M. Tax), 23-36; d) Getting Angry (S. Kaplow), 37-41; e) Woman in the Middle (F. Rush), 42-49; f)

Bitch Manifesto (Joreen), 50-59; g) Why I Want a Wife (J. Syfers), 60-62; h) Men and Violence (WBAI Consciousness Raising), 63-71; i) Speaking Out on Prostitution (S. Brownmiller), 72-77; j) Man-Hating (P. Kearon), 78-80; k) Black Feminism (C. Ware), 81-84; l) Loving Another Woman, 85-93; m) Feminist Look at Children's Books (Feminists on Children's Media), 94-106; n) Independence From the Sexual Revolution (D. Densmore), 107-118; o) Feminist Graffiti (E. Levine), 119-126; p) Building of the Gilded Cage (J. Freeman), 127-150; q) Abortion Law Repeal(sort of): A Warning to Women (L. Cisler), 151-164; r) Jane Crow and the Law (P. Murray, M. Eastwood), 165-177; s) Psychology Constructs the Female (N. Weisstein), 178-197; t) Myth of the Vaginal Orgasm (A. Koedt), 198-207; u) Housework: Slavery or Labor of Love (B. Warrior), 208-212; v) Marriage (S. Cronan), 213-221; w) A.D.C.: Marriage to the State (A. Leo), 222-227; x) Rape: An Act of Terror (B. Mehrhof, P. Kearon), 228-233; y) Radical Feminism 1 (B. Kreps), 234-239; z) Woman Identified Woman (Radicalesbians), 240-245; aa) Lesbianism and Feminism (A. Koedt), 246-258; bb) Spiritual Dimension of Women's Liberation (M. Daly), 259-270; cc) Free Space (P. Allen), 271-279; dd) Consciousness Raising, 280-281; ee) Consciousness Raising: A Dead End? (C.W. Payne), 282-285; ff) Tyranny of Structurelessness (Joreen), 285-299; gg) Notes From the Third Year, 300-301; hh) Congress to Unite Women (Report, 1969), 302-317; ii) Women and the Radical Movement (A. Koedt), 318-321; jj) Fourth World Manifesto (B. Burris), 322-357; kk) Selling of a Feminist (C. Dreifus), 358-364; ll) Sexual Politics: A Manifesto for Revolution (K. Millett), 365-367; mm) Feminists: A Political Organization to Annihilate Sex Roles, 368-378; nn) Politics of the Ego: A Manifesto for New York Radical Feminists, 379-383; oo) Westchester Radical Feminists, 384-390; pp) Women Writers and the Female Experience (E. Showalter), 391-406; qq) Body is the Role: Sylvia Plath (A. Rapone), 407-412; rr) Women's Private Writings: Anaïs Nin (A. Snitow), 413-418; ss) Woman's Place is in the Oven (S.S. Trumbo), 419- .

176 READINGS ON THE PSYCHOLOGY OF WOMEN. Judith M. Bardwick, ed. New York: Harper and Row, 1972.

a) Sexual Dimorphism and Homosexual Gender Identity (J. Money), 3-12; b) Sex Differences in the Incidence of Neonatal Abnormalities and Abnormal Performance in Early Childhood (J.E. Singer, M. Westphal, K.R. Niswander), 13-17; c) Attachment Differences in Male and Female Infant Monkeys (G.D. Mitchell), 18-21; d) Sex, Age, and State as Determinants of Mother-Infant Interaction (H.A. Moss), 22-29; e) Play Behavior in the Year-Old Infant: Early Sex Differences (S. Goldberg, M. Lewis), 30-33; f) Sex Differences in Intellectual Functioning (E.E. Maccoby), 34-43; g) Sex Differences in Adolescent Character Processes (E. Douvan), 44-48; h) Ambivalence: The Socialization of Women (J.M. Bardwick, E. Douvan), 52-57; i) Cultural Contradictions and Sex Roles (M. Komarovsky), 58-61; j) Motive to Avoid Success and Changing Aspirations of College Women (M. Horner), 62-67; k) Race, Social Class, and the Motive to Avoid Success in Women (P.J. Weston, M.T. Mednick), 68-71; l) Barriers to the Career Choice of Engineering, Medicine, or Science Among American Women (A.S. Rossi), 72-82; m) Woman Ph.D.: A Recent Profile (R.J. Simon, S.M. Clark, K. Galway), 83-92; n) Women Mathematicians and the Creative Personality (R. Helson), 93-100; o) Study of Sex Roles (S.S. Angrist), 101-106; p) Career and Family

Orientations of Husbands and Wives in Relation to Marital Happiness (L. Bailyn), 107-116; q) Implications of Current Changes in Sex Role Patterns (R.E. Hartley), 119-124; r) Roots of Ambivalence in American Women (A.S. Rossi), 125-127; s) Marriage and the Family (R.D. Cox), 128-130; t) Motherhood (J. Clark), 131-133; u) Depression in Middle-Aged Women (P.B. Bart), 134-142; v) First Year of Bereavement (C.M. Parkes), 143-155; w) Six Stations of Divorce (P. Bohannan), 156-164; x) Differences in Attitudinal Responses Under Conditions of Implicitly Manipulated Group Salience (R.W. Shomer, R. Centers), 167-169; y) Consciousness (V. Gornick), 170-177; z) Black Women 1970 (N. Hare, J. Hare), 178-180; aa) Middle-Class Mind of Kate Millett (I. Howe), 181-186; bb) Rise of Women's Liberation (M. Dixon), 187-192; cc) Pre-Industrial Patterns in the Colonial Family in America: A Content Analysis of Colonial Magazines (H.R. Lantz, M. Britton, R. Schmitt, E.C. Snyder), 196-204; dd) Cross-Cultural Survey of Some Sex Differences in Socialization (H. Barry III, M.K. Bacon, I.L. Child), 205-209; ee) Sex Differentiation in Role Expectations and Performance (E. Haavio-Mannila), 210-217; ff) Worker, Mother, Housewife: Soviet Women Today (M.G. Field, K.I. Flynn), 218-230; gg) Re-Evaluation of the Primary Role of the Communist Chinese Woman: The Homemaker or the Worker (L.J. Huang), 231-234; hh) Women in the Kibbutz: Changing Status and Concepts (M. Rosner), 235-242; ii) Psychobiology of Pregnancy (T. Benedek), 246-250; jj) Castration Anxiety and Phallus Envy: A Reformulation (B.C. Bosselman), 251-253; kk) Behavior Therapy Approaches to Modification of Sexual Preferences: Biological Perspective and Critique (G. Bermant), 254-258; ll) Predictive Study of Psychological and Psychosomatic Responses to Oral Contraceptives (J.M. Bardwick), 259-262; mm) Lower Class Sexual Behavior (L. Rainwater), 263-268; nn) Emotional Factors in Obstetric Complications (R.L. McDonald), 269-276; oo) Psychologic Aspects of Lactation (N. Newton, M. Newton), 277-283; pp) Postpartum Psychiatric Syndromes (F.T. Melges), 284-291; qq) Psychological Investigation of Habitual Abortion (E.R. Grimm), 292-298; rr) Sex Differences in Fantasy Patterns (R. May), 301-306; ss) Hysterical Character and Feminine Identity (H.W. Wolowitz), 307-313; tt) Women's Lib--Rational? Or Socially Pathological? (E.B. McNeil), 314-319; uu) Sex-Role Stereotypes and Clinical Judgements of Mental Health (I.K. Broverman, D.M. Broverman, F.E. Clarkson, P.S. Rosenkrantz, S.R. Vogel), 320-324.

177 RELIGION AND SEXISM: IMAGES OF WOMAN IN THE JEWISH AND CHRISTIAN TRADITIONS. Rosemary Radford Ruether, ed. New York: Simon and Schuster, 1974.

a) Women and Religion: Psychological and Cultural Implications (P.M. Doyle), 15-40; b) Images of Women in the Old Testament (P. Bird), 41-88; c) Woman: Seductive Siren and Source of Sin? (B.P. Prusak), 89-116; d) Theology and Leadership of Women in the New Testament (C.F. Parvey), 117-149; e) Misogynism and Virginal Feminism in the Fathers of the Church (R.R. Ruether), 150-183; f) Images of Women in the Talmud (J. Hauptman), 184-212; g) Equality of Souls, Inequality of Sexes: Woman in Medieval Theology (E.C. McLaughlin), 213-266; h) Canon Law and the Battle of the Sexes (C.M. Henning), 267-291; i) Women and the Continental Reformation (J.D. Douglass), 292-318; j) Protestant Principle: A Woman's Eye-View of Barth and Tillich (J.A. Romero),

319-340; k) Epilogue: The Coming of Lilith (J.P. Goldenberg), 341-344.

178 "REMEMBER THE LADIES": NEW PERSPECTIVES ON WOMEN IN AMERICAN HISTORY. ESSAYS IN HONOR OF NELSON MANFRED BLAKE. Carol V.R. George, ed. Syracuse: Syracuse University Press, 1975.

a) Anne Hutchinson and the "Revolution Which Never Happened" (C.V.R. George), 13-38; b) Eighteenth-Century Theorists of Women's Liberation (M. Fisher), 39-48; c) Puritan Ethic in the Revolutionary Era: Abigail Adams and Thomas Jefferson (R. Ketcham), 49-66; d) Women and the Nativist Movement (D.H. Bennett), 71-89; e) Man-Midwifery and the Delicacy of the Sexes (J.B. Donegan), 90-109; f) Meaning of Harriet Tubman (O. Scruggs), 110-122; g) Divorce as a Moral Issue: A Hundred Years of Controversy (W.L. O'Neill), 127-144; h) Flapper and Her Critics (G. Critoph), 145-160; i) Ume Tsuda and Motoko Hani: Echoes of American Cultural Feminism in Japan (N. Shimada, H. Takamura, M. Iino, H. Ito), 161-178; j) Role of Women in the Founding of the U.S. Children's Bureau (J. Johnson), 179-196.

179 REVELATIONS: DIARIES OF WOMEN. Mary Jane Moffat and Charlotte Painter, eds. New York: Random House, 1974.

a) M. Fleming, 21-27; b) L.M. Alcott, 28-33; c) A. Frank, 34-45; d) M. Bashkirtseff, 46-55; e) N. Ptaschkina, 56-66; f) H. Senesh, 67-74; g) S. Shonagon, 75-78; h) G. Sand, 79-85; i) A. Nin, 86-97; j) E. Scott, 98-108; k) F.K. Santamaria, 109-115; l) C. Painter, 116-130; m) A. Dostoevsky, 131-137; n) S. Tolstoy, 138-148; o) R. Benedict, 149-162; p) Unknown Japanese Woman, 163-177; q) D. Wordsworth, 178-191; r) A. James, 192-205; s) S. Ashton-Warner, 206-217; t) G. Eliot, 218-224; u) V. Woolf, 225-236; v) K. Kollwitz, 237-254; w) F.A. Kemble, 255-269; x) M.B. Chesnut, 270-287; y) C. Maria de Jesus, 288-300; z) M. Martin, 301-313; aa) S. Lagerlöf, 314-324; bb) K. Mansfield, 325-334; cc) L. Hurnscot, 335-346; dd) J. Field, 347-360; ee) F. Scott-Maxwell, 361-371; ff) E. Carr, 372-391; gg) "Psychic Bisexuality" (C. Painter), 392-404; hh) APPENDIX: Resources for Women's Diaries, 409- .

180 REVERSE DISCRIMINATION. Barry R. Gross, ed. Buffalo: Prometheus Books, 1977.

a) Discrimination in Higher Education: A Debate on Faculty Employment (M.M. Todorovich, H.A. Glickstein), 12-40; b) Drive Toward Equality (J.S. Pottinger), 41-49; c) Affirmative Action--A Liberal Program (L. Nisbet), 50-53; d) H.E.W., the University and Women (F.K. Barasch), 54-65; e) Case for Preferential Admissions (R.M. O'Neill), 66-83; f) Discrimination, Color Blindness, and the Quota System (S. Hook), 84-87; g) Bias in Anti-bias Regulations (S. Hook), 88-96; h) H.E.W. and the Universities (P. Seabury), 97-112; i) "Affirmative Action" Reconsidered (T. Sowell), 113-131; j) Emergence of an American Ethnic Pattern (N. Glazer), 132-158; k) Erosion of Legal Principles in the Creation of Legal Policies (V. Black), 163-183; l) Harvard College Amicus Curiae,

DeFunis v. Odegaard, Supreme Court of the U.S., 1973 (A. Cox), 184-197; m) DeFunis v. Odegaard, Dissenting Opinion (W.O. Douglas), 198-207; n) Constitutionality of Reverse Racial Discrimination (J.H. Ely), 208-216; o) Judicial Scrutiny of "Benign" Racial Preference in Law School Admissions (K. Greenawalt), 217-238; p) Racial Preferences in Higher Education: Political Responsibility and the Judicial Role (T. Sandalow), 239-266; q) Morality of Reparation (B. Boxhill), 270-278; r) Identifying the Beneficiaries (B. Bittker), 279-287; s) Discrimination and Morally Relevant Characteristics (J.W. Nickel), 288-290; t) Inverse Discrimination (L.J. Cowan), 291-293; u) Justification of Inverse Discrimination (P. Silvestri), 294-295; v) Reverse Discrimination and Compensatory Justice (P.W. Taylor), 296-302; w) Reparations to Wronged Groups (M.D. Bayles), 303-305; x) Reverse Discrimination (W.A. Nunn III), 306-309; y) Individuals, Groups, and Inverse Discrimination (R.A. Shiner), 310-313; z) Should Reparations be to Individuals or to Groups? (J.W.Nickel), 314-320; aa) Reparations to Individuals or Groups? (A.H. Goldman), 321-323; bb) Preferential Policies in Hiring and Admissions: A Jurisprudential Approach (J.W. Nickel), 324-347; cc) Justifiability of Reverse Discrimination (H.E. Jones), 348-357; dd) Justice, Merit, and the Good (R. Hoffman), 358-372; ee) Reverse Discrimination as Unjustified (L.H. Newton), 373-378; ff) Is Turn-About Fair Play? (B.R. Gross), 379-388.

181 THE RIGHTS AND WRONGS OF WOMEN. Juliet Mitchell and Ann Oakley, eds. Harmondsworth; New York: Penguin, 1976.

a) Wisewoman and Medicine Man: Changes in the Management of Childbirth (A. Oakley), 17-58; b) Women's Work in Nineteenth-Century London: A Study of the Years 1820-50 (S. Alexander), 59-111; c) Women and Nineteenth-Century Radical Politics: A Lost Dimension (D. Thompson), 112-138; d) Landscape with Figures: Home and Community in English Society (L. Davidoff, J. L'Esperance, H. Newby), 139-175; e) Femininity in the Classroom: An Account of Changing Attitudes (P. Marks), 176-198; f) Education of Girls Today (T. Blackstone), 199-216; g) Woman and the Literary Text (J. Goode), 217-255; h) Women in American Trade Unions: An Historical Analysis (R. Baxandall), 256-270; i) Looking Again at Engels' "Origin of the Family, Private Property and the State" (R. Delmar), 271-287; j) Women in Revolutionary China (D. Davin), 288-303; k) Rights and Wrongs of Women: Mary Wollstonecraft, Harriet Martineau, Simone de Beauvoir (M. Walters), 304-378; l) Women and Equality (J. Mitchell), 379-399.

182 THE ROLE AND STATUS OF WOMEN IN THE SOVIET UNION. Donald R. Brown, ed. New York: Teachers College Press, 1968.

a) Workers (and Mothers): Soviet Women Today (M.G. Field), 7-56; b) Woman Student in Russia (P. Carden), 57-59; c) Changing Image of Women in Soviet Literature (V.S. Dunham), 60-97; d) Changing Soviet Family (U. Bronfenbrenner), 98-124; e) Childbearing Functions of the Soviet Family (D.M. Heer), 125-129; f) Marriage and the Family (R.D. Cox),

130-136.

183 THE ROLE OF WOMEN IN CONFLICT AND PEACE: PAPERS. Dorothy McGuigan, ed. Ann Arbor: Center for the Continuing Education of Women, The University of Michigan, 1977.

a) Sex Differences in Aggression and Dominance (E. Douvan), 9-18; b) Men, Women and Violence: Some Reflections on Equality (N.Z. Davis), 19-30; c) Women and Collective Action in Europe (L.A. Tilly), 31-44; d) American Peace Party: New Departures and Old Arguments (B.J. Steinson), 45-54; e) Gender Imagery and Issues of War and Peace: The Case of the Draft Resistance Movement of the 1960's (B. Thorne), 55-60; f) Feminist Politics and Peace (B.A. Carroll), 61-70; g) Role of Women in Underdeveloped Countries: Some Sociological Issues Concerning Conflict and Peace (S.A. Nuss), 71-82; h) Attitudes of Men and Women Toward Violence: Report of a National Survey (T.E. Dielman), 83-86; i) Bibliography: Role of Women in Conflict and Peace (P.A. Kusnerz), 87- .

184 THE ROLE OF WOMEN IN THE MIDDLE AGES. Rosemarie Thee Morewedge, ed. Papers of the Sixth Annual Conference of the Center for Medieval and Renaissance Studies, State University of New York at Binghamton, 6-7 May, 1972. Albany: State University of New York Press, 1975.

a) Life Expectancies for Women in Medieval Society (D. Herlihy), 1-22; b) Transformations of the Heroine: From Epic Heard to Epic Read (F.H. Baũml), 23-40; c) Isolt and Guenevere: Two Twelfth-Century Views of Woman (G.J. Brault), 41-64; d) Petrarch's Laura: The Convolutions of a Humanistic Mind (A.S. Bernardo), 65-89; e) Fifteenth-Century View of Women's Role in Medieval Society: Christine de Pizan's "Livre des Trois Vertus" (C.C. Willard), 90-120; f) Woman in the Marginalia of Gothic Manuscripts and Related Works (P. Verdier), 121-160; g) ILLUSTRATIONS, 161-188.

185 THE ROLES AND IMAGES OF WOMEN IN THE MIDDLE AGES AND THE RENAISSANCE. Douglas Radcliffe-Umstead, ed. (University Of Pittsburgh Publications on the Middle Ages and Renaissance, Vol. 3) Pittsburgh: Center for Medieval and Renaissance Studies, Institute for the Human Sciences, 1975.

a) Sin and Salvation: The Dramatic Context of Hrotswitha's Women (S. Sticca), 3-22; b) Popular Image of Brunhilde (R.A. Boggs), 23-39; c) Saints and Witches (L. Koehler), 43-56; d) Nature is a Woman (P.A. Knapp), 59-71; e) Boccaccio's Idle Ladies (D. Radcliffe-Umstead), 75-103; f) Woman as Artist and Patron in the Middle Ages and the Renaissance (D. Wilkins), 107-121; g) Education of Women in the Middle Ages (S. Lehrman), 133-144; h) Roles of Medieval Women in the Healing

Arts (T.G. Benedek), 145-159.

186 ROLES WOMEN PLAY: READINGS TOWARD WOMEN'S LIBERATION. Michele Hoffnung Garskof, comp. (Contemporary Psychology Series) Belmont, Ca.: Brooks-Cole, 1971.

a) Woman as Secretary, Sexpot, Spender, Sow, Civic Actor, Sickie (M. Salzman-Webb), 7-24; b) Unmothered Woman (E. Albert), 25-38; c) Sex Map of the Work World.(C. Bird), 39-58; d) Politics of Orgasm (S. Lydon), 62-67; e) Psychology Constructs the Female, or the Fantasy Life of the Male Psychologist (N. Weisstein), 68-83; f) Training the Woman to Know Her Place: The Power of a Nonconscious Ideology (S.L. Bem, D.J. Bem), 84-96; g) Femininity and Successful Achievement: A Basic Inconsistency (M.S. Horner), 97-122; h) Social Construction of the Second Sex (J. Freeman), 123-142; i) Equality Between the Sexes: An Immodest Proposal (A.S. Rossi), 145-164; j) Why Women's Liberation (M. Dixon), 165-178; k) I Am Furious (Female) (E. Cantarow, E. Diggs, K. Ellis, J. Marx, L. Robinson, M. Schien), 179-193; l) Political Economy of Women's Liberation (M. Benston), 194- .

187 ROOT OF BITTERNESS: DOCUMENTS OF THE SOCIAL HISTORY OF AMERICAN WOMEN. Nancy F. Cott, ed. New York: E.P. Dutton, 1972.

This collection includes documents which demonstrate how the intimate experiences of American women have interfaced with cultural norms since the Colonial period. Seventeenth- and eighteenth- century items are arranged in chronological order. Later materials are grouped by topic: slavery and sex, sexuality and gynecology, work, pioneers and utopians, leisure and discontent. Contributors: G. Savile, S. Wister, A.H. Warder, E. Southgate, A. de Toqueville, S. Jennings, T.S. Arthur, E. Farnham, M.W. Ovington, G. Austin, L. Larcom, Mrs. A.J. Graves, C. Beecher, S. Grimke, A. Grimke, L. Brent, M.B. Chesnut, F. Wright, H. Noble, N. Whitman, E.D.S. Greer, V. Woodhull, Mrs. R.B. Gleason, W. Alcott, M.G. Nichols, M. Livermore, E. Blackwell, M.P. Jacobi, I. Van Etten, B.M. Herron, A.B. Blackwell, J. Addams, K. Chopin, C. Gilman.

188 THE ROOTS OF AMERICAN FEMINIST THOUGHT. James L. Cooper and Sheila McIsaac Cooper, eds. and comps. Boston: Allyn and Bacon, 1973.

a) Vindication of the Rights of Women (M. Wollstonecraft), 25-50; b) Letters on the Equality of the Sexes (S. Grimke), 65-90; c) Woman in the Nineteenth Century (M. Fuller), 107-130; d) Subjection of Women (J.S. Mill), 149-176; e) Women and Economics (C.P. Gilman), 193-218; f) Woman and the New Race (M. Sanger), 237-260; g) Concerning Women

(S. LaFollette), 277-

189 SALT AND BITTER AND GOOD: THREE CENTURIES OF ENGLISH AND AMERICAN WOMEN POETS. Cora Kaplan, ed. (Original portraits by Lisa Unger Baskin) New York: Paddington Press, 1975.

The work of twenty-four deceased poets is included in this anthology. Poems have been chosen for their quality, relative obscurity and theme--usually women or nature. Contributors: A. Bradstreet, K. Philips, A. Behn, A. Finch, C. Smith, P. Wheatley, F. Hemans, E.B. Browning, C. Rossetti, E. Dickinson, M. Blind, E. Lazarus, A. Meynell, C. Mew, A. Lowell, E. Wylie, H. Doolittle, M. Moore. E. St.V. Millay, V. Sackville-West, D. Parker, L. Bogan, S. Smith, S. Plath.

190 A SAMPLER OF WOMEN'S STUDIES. Dorothy G. McGuigan, ed. Ann Arbor: Center for Continuing Education of Women, University of Michigan, 1973.

a) Woman as Artistic Innovator: The Case of the Choreographer (S.J. Cohen), 5-16; b) City Women and Religious Change in Sixteenth-Century France (N.Z. Davis), 17-46; c) Women and the Jural Domain: An Evolutionary Perspective (N. Gonzales), 47-58; d) Women: The New Political Class (M. Lansing), 59-76; e) Classical Mythology and the Role of Women in Modern Literature (M. Lefkowitz), 77-84; f) Feminist History in Perspective: Sociological Contributions to Biographic Analysis (A. Rossi), 85-108; g) Educating Women for Leadership: A Program for the Future (S. Tobias), 109-114.

191 SEIZING OUR BODIES: THE POLITICS OF WOMEN'S HEALTH. Claudia Dreifus, ed. New York: Vintage Books, 1977.

a) Women's Health Movement: Past Roots (H. Marieskind), 3-12; b) Sexual Surgery in Late Nineteenth-Century America (G.J. Barker-Benfield), 13-42; c) Complaints and Disorders: The Sexual Politics of Sickness (B. Ehrenreich, D. English), 43-56; d) Birth Controllers (J. Sharpe), 57-74; e) Dangers of Oral Contraception (B. Seaman), 75-85; f) Case of Corporate Malpractice and the Dalkon Shield (M. Dowie, T. Johnston), 86-104; g) Sterilizing the Poor (C. Dreifus), 105-120; h) Have You Ever Wondered about the Male Pill? (R. Arditti), 121-130; i) Abortion: This Piece Is for Remembrance (C. Dreifus), 131-145; j) Theft of Childbirth (A. Rich), 146-166; k) Dangers of Sex Hormones (B. Seaman), 167-176; l) Pushers (A. Spake), 177-185; m) Politics of Breast Cancer (R. Kushner), 186-194; n) Epidemic in Unnecessary Hysterectomy (D. Larned), 195-208; o) What Doctors Won't Tell You about Menopause (R. Reitz), 209-211; p) What Medical Students Learn about Women (K. Weiss), 212-222; q) Class Factor: Mountain Women Speak Out on Women's Health (D. Baker), 223-234; r) Women Workers in the Health Service Industry (C.A. Brown), 235-250; s) Building a Hospital Workers' Union: Doris Turner, the Woman from 1199 (C. Dreifus), 251-262; t) Vaginal Politics (E. Frankfort), 263-270; u) Women's Health Movement:

Where Are We Now? (R.G. Fruchter, N. Fatt, P. Booth, D. Leidel), 271-278; v) Women and Health Care: A Comparison of Theories (E. Fee), 279-298.

192 SEVEN AMERICAN WOMEN WRITERS OF THE TWENTIETH CENTURY: AN INTRODUCTION. Maureen Howard, ed. (Minnesota Library on American Writers) Minneapolis: University of Minnesota Press, 1977.

a) E. Wharton and G. Stein (M. Howard), 28-34; b) Ellen Glasgow (L. Auchincloss), 35-78; c) Willa Cather (D. Van Ghent), 79-121; d) Katherine Anne Porter (R.B. West, Jr.), 122-165; e) Eudora Welty (J.A. Bryant, Jr.), 166-213; f) Mary McCarthy (I. Stock), 214-264; g) Carson McCullers (L. Graver), 265-310; h) Flannery O'Connor (S.E. Hyman), 311-358.

193 SEX AND AGE AS PRINCIPLES OF SOCIAL DIFFERENTIATION. J.S. La Fontaine, ed. (Association of Social Anthropologists Commonwealth Monograph Series, No. 17) New York: Academic Press, 1978.

a) Complementarity and Conflict: An Andean View of Men and Women (O. Harris), 21-40; b) Food for Thought--Patterns of Production and Consumption in Pira-Parana Society (C. Hugh-Jones), 41-66; c) Aspects of the Distinction Between the Sexes in the Nyamwezi and Some Other African Systems of Kinship and Marriage (R.G. Abrahams), 67-88; d) Sex, Age and Social Control in Mobs of the Darwin Hinterland (B. Sansom), 89-108; e) Roles of Children in Urban Kano (E. Schildkrout), 109-138; f) Gerontology, Polygyny and Scarce Resources (U. Almagor), 139-158; g) Observations about Generations (P.T. Baxter, U. Almagor), 159-182.

194 SEX AND CLASS IN LATIN AMERICA. June Nash and Helen Icken Safa, eds. (Praeger Special Studies in International Politics and Government) New York: Praeger, 1976.

a) Mythology About Women, With Special Reference to Chile (J.G. Bustos), 30-45; b) Women's Work and Fertility (M. del Carmen Elu de Lenero), 46-68; c) Class Consciousness Among Working-Class Women in Latin America: Puerto Rico (H.I. Safa), 69-85; d) Sexual Hierarchy Among the Yanomama (J. Shapiro), 86-104; e) Impact of Industrialization on Women's Work Roles in Northeast Brazil (N. Aguiar), 110-128; f) Bahiana in the Labor Force in Salvador, Brazil (E. Jelin), 129-146; g) Relationships of Sex and Social Class in Brazil (H.I.B. Saffioti), 147-159; h) Women and Modernization: Access to Tools (E.M. Chaney, M. Schmink), 160-182; i) Participation of Women in the Mexican Labor Force (G.G. Salazar), 183-201; j) History of Women's Struggle for Equality in Puerto Rico (I.P. Vidal), 202-216; k) Female Political Participation in Latin America (J. Jacquette)(sic), 221-244; l) Selective Omission and Theoretical Distortion in Studying the Political Activity of Women in Brazil (M.J. Blachman), 245-264; m) Politics and Feminism in the Dominican Republic: 1931-45 and 1966-74 (V.M. Mota), 265-278; n) Chile: The Feminine Version of the Coup d'Etat (M. Mattelart), 279-301; o) Emergence of a Mapuche Leader: Chile

(X. Bunster), 302-319.

195 SEX AND EQUALITY. (Women in America: From Colonial Times to the 20th Century) New York: Arno Press, 1974.

a) Observations on the Real Rights of Women (1818)(H.M. Crocker); b) Great Lawsuit: Man versus Men, Woman versus Women (1843)(M.F. Ossoli); c) Uncivil Liberty: An Essay to Show the Injustice and Impolicy of Ruling Woman Without Her Consent (1877)(E.H. Heywood); d) Cupid's Yokes; Or The Binding Forces of Conjugal Life (1887)(E.H. Heywood); e) Letter to a Prospective Bride (1897)(I.C. Craddock); f) Barbarian Status of Women (1899)(T. Veblen).

196 SEX BIAS IN THE SCHOOLS: THE RESEARCH EVIDENCE. Janice Potter and Andrew Fishel, eds. Rutherford, N.J.; London: Fairleigh Dickinson University Press and Associated University Presses, 1977.

a) Sex-Role Socialization and the Nursery School: As the Twig is Bent (C. Joffe), 25-39; b) Sex-Role Concepts Among Elementary-School Age Girls (R.E. Hartley, A. Klein), 40-47; c) Sex Differences in the Self-Concepts of Elementary-School Children (C.L. Reed, D.W. Felker, R.S. Kay, D.J. Stanwyck), 48-59; d) Girls--More Moral Than Boys or Just Sneakier? (R.L. Krebs), 60-66; e) Adolescent Culture (J. Coleman), 69-77; f) Sex-Typing in the High School (M.J. Gander), 78-91; g) Sex Bias in Secondary Schools: The Impact of Title IX (A. Fishel, J. Pottker), 92-104; h) Teachers' Perceptions of Ideal Male and Female Students: Male Chauvinism in the Schools (A.J.H. Gaite), 105-108; i) Psychological and Occupational Sex Stereotypes in Elementary School Readers (J. Pottker), 111-125; j) Sex Stereotyping in Elementary-School Mathematics Textbooks (W.T. Jay), 126-145; k) Women in U.S. History High-School Textbooks (J.L. Trecker), 146-162; l) Woman's Place: Children's Sex Stereotyping of Occupations (N.K. Schlossberg, J. Goodman), 167-172; m) Sex Differences in the Occupational Choices of Second Graders (C.L.F. Siegel), 173-177; n) Sex-Typing and Politicization in Children's Attitudes (L. Iglitzin), 178-199; o) Attitudes Toward Increased Social, Economic, and Political Participation by Women as Reported by Elementary and Secondary Students (S. Greenberg), 200-206; p) Adolescents' Views of Women's Work-Role (D.R. Entwisle, E. Greenberger), 207-216; q) Counselor Bias and the Female Occupational Role (J.J. Pietrofesa, N.K. Schlossberg), 221-229; r) Female-Role Perception as a Factor in Counseling (A. Steinmann), 230-238; s) Counselors View Women and Work: Accuracy of Information (W.C. Bingham, E.W. House), 239-246; t) Counselors' Attitudes Toward Women and Work (W.C. Bingham, E.W. House), 247-255; u) Women and Educational Testing (C.K. Tittle, K. McCarthy, J.F. Steckler), 256-274; v) Women Teachers and Teacher Power (A. Fishel, J. Pottker), 277-288; w) Performance of Women Principals: A Review of Behavioral and Attitudinal Studies (A. Fishel, J. Pottker), 289-299; x) Attitudes of Superintendents and Board of Education Members Toward the Employment and Effectiveness of Women as Public-School Administrators (S.S. Taylor), 300-310; y) School Boards and Sex Bias in American Education (A. Fishel, J. Pottker), 311-319; z) Sex Discrimination as Public Policy: The Case of Maternity-Leave Policies for Teachers (J. Pottker,

A. Fishel), 320-330; aa) Effect of Sex on College Admission, Work Evaluation, and Job Interviews (M.M. Clifford, E. Walster), 335-343; bb) Sex Bias in Selective College Admissions (G.R. Hanson, N.S. Cole, R.R. Lamb), 344-353; cc) Continuing Education for Women: Factors Influencing a Return to School and the School Experience (H. Markus), 354-379; dd) Overt and Covert Forms of Discrimination Against Academic Women (J. Pottker), 380-410; ee) Characteristics and Attitudes of Women Trustees (R.T. Harnett), 411-414; ff) Reports of the Women's Rights Committee (Dayton Public Schools), 417-463; gg) Task Force on Education Report, Governor's Commission on the Status of Women, Ma. (B. Fitzpatrick), 464-502; hh) Women in Educational Governance (A. Fishel, J. Pottker), 505-513; ii) Women in Academic Governance (R. Oltman), 514-524; jj) Equal Rights for Women (National Education Association), 527-528; kk) Schoolbook Sex Bias (NATION'S SCHOOLS), 529-530; ll) Participation in Sports by Girls (G.H. Gallup), 531; mm) What, If Anything, Impedes Women from Serving on School Boards? (National School Boards Association), 532-544; nn) Sex Differential in School Enrollment and Educational Attainment (C.E. Johnson, Jr., J.T. Jennings), 547-553; oo) Proportion of Doctorates Earned by Women, by Area and Field, 1960-1969 (Council for University Women's Progress, University of Mn.), 554-561.

197 SEX DIFFERENCES AND DISCRIMINATION IN EDUCATION. Scarvia B. Anderson, comp. (Series on Contemporary Educational Issues) Worthington, Oh.: Charles A. Jones, 1972.

a) What Kind of Difference Does Sex Make? (S. Messick), 2-8; b) Sex Differences in Intellectual Functioning (E.E. Maccoby), 9-27; c) He Only Does It To Annoy (M.P. Smith), 28-43; d) "Look, Jane, Look! See Dick Run and Jump! Admire Him!" (K. DeCrow), 44-49; e) Are Little Girls Being Harmed by "Sesame Street"? (J. Bergman), 50-53; f) Down the Up Staircase: Sex Roles, Professionalization, and the Status of Teachers (B. Heyns), 54-61; g) Dilemmas of Women's Education (D. Riesman), 62-73; h) Effect of Race and Sex on College Admission (E. Walster, T.A. Cleary, M.M. Clifford), 74-82; i) How Coeducation Fails Women (S. Tobias), 83-91; j) Myth is Better Than a Miss: Men Get the Edge in Academic Employment (L.A. Simpson), 92- .

198 SEX DIFFERENCES: CULTURAL AND DEVELOPMENTAL DIMENSIONS. Robert S. Stewart and Patrick Lee, eds. New York: Urizen Books, 1976.

a) Psychoanalysis and Sex Differences: Freud and Beyond Freud (R.S. Stewart), 35-44; b) Psychical Consequences of the Anatomical Distinction Between the Sexes (S. Freud), 45-56; c) Flight from Womanhood: The Masculinity-Complex in Women as Viewed by Men and by Women (K. Horney), 57-74; d) Early Stages of the Oedipus Conflict (M. Klein), 75-90; e) Motherhood and Sexuality (H. Deutsch), 91-104; f) Inner and Outer Space: Reflections on Womanhood (E.H. Erikson), 105-132; g) Woman and Her Discontents: A Reassessment of Freud's Views on Female Sexuality (W.H. Gillespie), 133-150; h) Anthropology and Sex Differences (P.C. Lee), 153-160; i) Family in Father-Right and Mother-Right: Complex of Mother-Right (B. Malinowski), 161-170; j) Status and Role: Raw Materials for Society, Marriage (R. Linton),

171-192; k) Standardization of Sex-Temperament (M. Mead), 193-202; l) Family Structure and the Socialization of the Child (T. Parsons), 203-216; m) Cross-Cultural Survey of Some Sex Differences in Socialization (H. Barry III, M.K. Bacon, I.L. Child), 217-230; n) Absent Father and Cross-Sex Identity (R.V. Burton, J.W.M. Whiting), 231-246; o) Women and Men (Y. Murphy, R.F. Murphy), 247-258; p) Ethology and Sex Differences (P.C. Lee), 261-268; q) Functions of the Sexual Companion (K. Lorenz), 269-296; r) Mating Behavior (N. Tinbergen), 297-312; s) Masculinity and Femininity as Display (R.L. Birdwhistell), 313-322; t) Fetal Hormones and the Brain: Effects on Sexual Dimorphism of Behavior (J. Money, A.A. Ehrhardt), 323-356; u) Psychology and Sex Differences (P.C. Lee), 359-370; v) Biological and Anthropological Differences between the Sexes (G.S. Hall), 371-380; w) Sex and Personality: Studies in Masculinity and Femininity (L.M. Terman, C.C. Miles), 381-394; x) Sex Differences in Personality Characteristics (L.E. Tyler), 395-410; y) Self and Sex (A. Gesell, F.L. Ilg), 411-422; z) Theories of Identification and Exposure to Multiple Models (A. Bandura, R.H. Walters), 423-434; aa) Physiological Development, Cognitive Development, and Socialization Antecedents of Children's Sex-Role Attitudes (L. Kohlberg, E. Zigler), 435-444; bb) Possible Causal Factors of Sex Differences in Intellectual Abilities (E.E. Maccoby), 445-462; cc) Sex, Age, and State as Determinants of Mother-Infant Interaction (H.A. Moss), 463- .

199 SEX DIFFERENCES IN BEHAVIOR. Richard C. Friedman, Ralph M. Richart, Raymond L. Vande Wiele, eds. Lenore O. Stern, ass't. ed. A Conference Sponsored by the International Institute for the Study of Human Reproduction. New York: Wiley, 1974.

a) Sexual Behavior Differentiation: Prenatal Hormonal and Environmental Control (I.L. Ward), 3-18; b) Prenatal Testosterone in the Nonhuman Primate and Its Consequences for Behavior (C.H. Phoenix), 19-32; c) Fetal Androgens, Human Central Nervous System Differentiation, and Behavior Sex Differences (A.A. Ehrhardt, S.W. Baker), 33-52; d) Prenatal Androgen, Intelligence and Cognitive Sex Differences (S.W. Baker, A.A. Ehrhardt), 53-76; e) Differential Response to Early Experiences as a Function of Sex Difference (S. Levine), 87-98; f) Sex Differences in Rhesus Monkeys Following Varied Rearing Experiences (G.P. Sackett), 99-122; g) Sex Differences in Mother-Infant Attachment in Monkeys (L.A. Rosenblum), 123-142; h) Early Sex Differences and Mother-Infant Interaction (H.A. Moss), 149-164; i) Sex of Parent x Sex of Child: Socioemotional Development (M. Lewis, M. Weinraub), 165-190; j) Methodological Considerations in Studying Sex Differences in the Behavioral Functioning of Newborns (A.F. Korner), 197-208; k) Stages in the Development of Psychosexual Concepts and Attitudes (L. Kohlberg, D.Z. Ullman), 209-222; l) Emergence of Genital Awareness During the Second Year of Life (E. Galenson, H. Roiphe), 223-232; m) Ethological Study of Children Approaching a Strange Adult: Sex Differences (D.N. Stern, E.P. Bender), 233-258; n) Sex Differences in Field Independence among Preschool Children (S. Coates), 259-274; o) Cryptorchidism, Development of Gender Identity, and Sex Behavior (H.F.L. Meyer-Bahlburg, E. McCauley, S. Schenck, T. Aceto, Jr., L. Pinch), 281-300; p) Behaviorally Feminine Male Child: Pretranssexual? Pretransvestite? Prehomosexual? Preheterosexual? (R. Green), 301-314; q) Psychodynamics of Male Transsexualism

(E.S. Person, L. Ovesey), 315-326; r) Sex Differences in Aggression (K.E. Moyer), 335-372; s) Psychobiology of Sex Differences: An Evolutionary Perspective (B.A. Hamburg), 373-392; t) Bisexual Behavior of Female Rhesus Monkeys (R.P. Michael, M.I. Wilson, D. Zumpe), 399-412; u) Plasma Testosterone Levels and Psychologic Measures in Men Over a 2-Month Period (C.H. Doering, H.K.H. Brodie, H. Kraemer, H. Becker, D.A. Hamburg), 413-432; v) Aggression, Androgens, and the XYY Syndrome (H.F.L. Meyer- Bahlburg), 433-454; w) Reproductive Hormones, Moods, and the Menstrual Cycle (H. Persky), 455-476; x) Sexual Differentiation: Models, Methods, and Mechanisms (R.E. Whalen), 477-482.

200 SEX DIFFERENCES IN PERSONALITY: READINGS. Dirk L. Schaeffer, comp. Belmont, Ca.: Brooks-Cole, 1971.

a) Psychological Consequences of the Anatomical Distinction between the Sexes (S. Freud), 11-21; b) Psychoanalytic Theory of Psychosexual Development (G.S. Blum), 22-40; c) Process of Learning Parental and Sex-Role Identification (D.B. Lynn), 41-49; d) Child's Sex-Role Classification of School Objects (J. Kagan), 50-55; e) Differences in Perception of the Opposite Sex by Males and Females (C.T. MacBrayer), 56-61; f) Are Women Prejudiced against Women? (P. Goldberg), 62-66; g) Sex Differences in the Play Configurations of Preadolescents (E.H. Erikson), 68-78; h) Modest Confirmation of Freud's Theory of a Distinction between the Superego of Men and Women (C. Hall), 79-82; i) Dreams: Sex Differences in Aggressive Content (A.F. Paolino), 83-94; j) Memory for Names and Faces: A Characteristic of Social Intelligence? (W.A. Kaess, S.L. Witryol), 95-103; k) Cognitive Conflict and Compromise between Males and Females (D.L. Schaeffer, J. Eisenberg), 104-115; l) Sex Differences in Job Values and Desires (S.L. Singer, B. Stefflre), 116-120; m) Sexual Behavior in the Human Female: Part II. Biological Data (J.E. Barmarck), 123-130; n) Self-Conceptions, Motivations and Interpersonal Attitudes of Early- and Late-Maturing Girls (M.C. Jones, P.H. Mussen), 131-141; o) Sex Differences in Dating Aspirations and Satisfaction with Computer-Selected Partners (R.H. Coombs, W.F. Kenkel), 142-151; p) Unacceptable Impulses, Anxiety, and the Appreciation of Cartoons (D. Spiegel, S.G. Brodkin, P. Keith-Spiegel), 152-159; q) Interview (W.H. Masters, V.E. Johnson), 160-170.

201 SEX DIFFERENCES: SOCIAL AND BIOLOGICAL PERSPECTIVES. Michael S. Teitelbaum, ed. Garden City, N.Y.: Doubleday-Anchor, 1976.

a) Sex Roles in Primate Societies (J.B. Lancaster), 22-61; b) Biological Influences on Sex Differences in Behavior (A. Barfield), 62-121; c) Anthropological Perspective on Sex Roles and Subsistence (J.K. Brown), 122-137; d) Social Influences on Sex Differences in Behavior (V. Stewart), 138-174; e) Science and the Woman Problem:

Historical Perspectives (E. Fee), 175-223.

202 SEX, DISCRIMINATION AND THE DIVISION OF LABOR. Cynthia B. Lloyd, comp. New York: Columbia University Press, 1975.

a) Division of Labor between the Sexes (C.B. Lloyd), 1-26; b) Participation of Married Women in the Labor Force (T.A. Finegan), 27-60; c) Geographic Immobility and Labor Force Mobility: A Study of Female Unemployment (B. Niemi), 61-89; d) Discontinuous Labor Force Participation and Its Effect on Women's Market Earnings (S.W. Polachek), 90-124; e) Determinants of Occupational Segregation (H. Zellner), 125-145; f) Discrimination--A Manifestation of Male Market Power? (J.F. Madden), 146-174; g) Relative Wages and Sex Segregation by Occupation (M.H. Stevenson), 175-200; h) Women and the Academic Labor Market (G.E. Johnson, F.P. Stafford), 201-222; i) Women's Work in the Home (A. Leibowitz), 223-243; j) Economics of Marital Status (F.P. Santos), 244-268; k) Child Investment and Women (M.R. Rosenzweig), 269-291; l) Nonmarket Returns to Women's Investment in Education (L. Benham), 292-312; m) Vicious Cycle of Welfare: Problems of the Female-Headed Household in N.Y.C. (E. Durbin), 313-345; n) Formal Extrafamily Child Care--Some Economic Observations (M.H. Strober), 346-378; o) Income and Employment Effects of Women's Liberation (E. James), 379-400; p) Impact of Women's Liberation on Marriage, Divorce, and Family Life-Style (S.B. Johnson), 401-426.

203 SEX EQUALITY. Jane English, ed. Englewood Cliffs, N.J.: Prentice-Hall, 1977.

a) Republic, Book V (Plato), 13-19; b) Politics, Book I (Aristotle), 20-30; c) Second Treatise of Government (J. Locke), 31-41; d) Emile (J.J. Rousseau), 42-47; e) Science of Rights (J.G. Fichte), 48-53; f) Subjection of Women (J.S. Mill), 54-65; g) Origin of the Family, Private Property and the State (F. Engels), 66-70; h) Second Sex (S. de Beauvoir), 71-78; i) Idea of Equality (B. Williams), 79-92; j) Sexual Equality (A. Jaggar), 93-109; k) "Because You Are a Woman" (J.R. Lucas), 110-120; l) Sex Roles: The Argument from Nature (J. Trebilcot), 121-129; m) Natural Law Language and Women (C. Pierce), 130-142; n) How Do We Know When Opportunities Are Equal? (O. O'Neill), 143-154; o) Reverse Discrimination as Unjustified (L. Newton), 155-160; p) Reverse Discrimination and the Future (I. Thalberg), 161-169; q) Servility and Self-Respect (T.E. Hill, Jr.), 170-182; r) Equal Rights Amendment (S. Ervin, Jr.), 183-187; s) Equal Opportunity, Free from Gender-Based Discrimination (R.B. Ginsburg), 188-195; t) Inevitability of Patriarchy (S. Goldberg), 196-204; u) Psychology Constructs the Female (N. Weisstein), 205-215; v) Vs. MS (M. Levin), 216-219; w) Language and Woman's Place (R. Lakoff), 220-230; x) Battle for Coed Teams (R. De Wolf), 231-238; y) Supermom! (M. Bedell),

239-247.

204 SEX-RELATED DIFFERENCES IN COGNITIVE FUNCTIONING: DEVELOPMENTAL ISSUES. Michele A. Wittig and Anne C. Petersen, eds. New York: Academic Press, 1979.

a) Sex-Related Differences in Cognitive Functioning: An Overview (A.C. Petersen, M.A. Wittig), 1-20; b) Genetic Influences on Sex-Related Differences in Intellectual Performance: Theoretical and Methodological Issues (M.A. Wittig), 21-66; c) Spatial Ability: A Critical Review of the Sex-Linked Major Gene Hypothesis (S.G. Vanderberg, A.R. Kuse), 67-96; d) Patterns of Cognitive Functioning in Relation to Handedness and Sex-Related Differences (L. Carter-Saltzman), 97-120; e) Evidence for Sex-Related Differences in Cerebral Organization (M.P. Bryden), 121-144; f) Sex-Related Differences in Cognition Among the Elderly (D. Cohen, F. Wilkie), 145-160; g) Cognitive Abilities and Sex-Related Variations in the Maturation of Cerebral Cortical Functions (D.P. Waber), 161-188; h) Hormones and Cognitive Functioning in Normal Development (A.C. Petersen), 189-214; i) Prenatal Influences on Cognitive Abilities: Data from Experimental Animals and Human and Endocrine Syndromes (J.M. Reinisch, R. Gandelman, F.S. Spiegel), 215-240; j) Menstrual Cycle and Sex-Related Differences in Cognitive Variability (A.J. Dan), 241-262; k) Sex Role as a Mediator of Intellectual Functioning (S.C. Nash), 263-302; l) Sex-Role Socialization and Achievement in Mathematics (L.H. Fox, D. Tobin, L. Brody), 303-334; m) Role of Tests and Their Construction in Producing Apparent Sex-Related Differences (C.A. Dwyer), 335-356; n) Epilogue (C.N. Jacklin), 335-356.

205 THE SEX ROLE SYSTEM: PSYCHOLOGICAL AND SOCIOLOGICAL PERSPECTIVES. Jane Chetwynd and Oonagh Hartnett, eds. London: Routledge and Kegan Paul, 1978, c1977.

a) Biological Explanations of Sex-Role Stereotypes (J. Archer), 4-17; b) Sex-Role Socialisation (H. Weinrich), 18-27; c) Sex-Role Stereotyping (J. Newson, E. Newson, D. Richardson, J. Scaife), 28-49; d) Influence of the School on Sex-Role Stereotyping (G. Lobban), 50-61; e) Sex-Role Stereotyping in Studies of Marriage and the Family (R. Rapoport), 62-75; f) Sex-Role Stereotyping at Work (O. Hartnett), 76-92; g) Women and Psychiatry (S. Lipshitz), 93-108; h) Clinical Aspects of Sex-Role Stereotyping (G.K. Litman), 109-126; i) Sex-Role Stereotyping in the Social Security and Income Tax Systems (H. Land), 127-142; j) Sex-Role Stereotyping and Social Science (M. Fuller), 143-157.

206 SEX ROLES IN CHANGING SOCIETY. Georgene H. Seward and Robert C. Williamson, eds. New York: Random House, 1970.

a) Primitive Societies (C.S. Ford), 25-43; b) Emergent Africa (E.E. Lord), 44-66; c) Sexual Identity Crises in the Life Cycle

(I.M. Josselyn), 67-92; d) Sex Identity Deviation and Inversion (F.J. Goldstein), 93-106; e) Sex Roles, Ancient to Modern (G.H. Seward), 109-125; f) American Core Culture: Changes and Continuities (R.E. Hartley), 126-149; g) Marriage Roles, American Style (R.C. Williamson), 150-176; h) Role Themes in Latin America (R.C. Williamson), 177-199; i) Swedish Model (R. Liljeström), 200-219; j) Male and Female in the German Federal Republic (U. Lehr, H. Rauh), 220-239; k) Male and Female in the German Democratic Republic (A. Katzenstein), 240-256; l) Worker, Mother, Housewife: Soviet Woman Today (M.G. Field, K.I. Flynn), 257-284; m) Sexes: Ideology and Reality in the Israeli Kibbutz (A.I. Rabin), 285-307; n) Milieu Development and Male-Female Roles in Contemporary Greece (C.D. Spinellis, V. Vassiliou, G. Vassiliou), 308-318; o) Men and Women of India Today (S.N. Sinha), 321-333; p) Status and Role Behavior in Changing Japan (G. De Vos, H. Wagatsuma), 334-370; q) Sex Roles in the Modern Fabric of China (S.L.M. Fong), 371-400; r) Generation Gap (M. Mead), 401-405.

207 SEXISM AND LANGUAGE. Alleen Pace Nilsen, Haig Bosmajian, H. Lee Gershuny, and Julia P. Stanley, eds. Urbana, Il.: National Council of Teachers of English, 1977.

a) Linguistic Sexism as a Social Issue (A.P. Nilsen), 1-26; b) Sexism as Shown through the English Vocabulary (A.P. Nilsen), 27-42; c) Gender-Marking in American English: Usage and Reference (J.P. Stanley), 43-76; d) Sexism in the Language of Legislatures and Courts (H. Bosmajian), 77-106; e) Sexism in the Language of Literature (H.L. Gershuny), 107-130; f) Sexism in the Language of Marriage (A.P. Nilsen), 131-142; g) Sexism in Dictionaries and Texts: Omissions and Commissions (H.L. Gershuny), 143-160; h) Sexism in Children's Books and Elementary Teaching Materials (A.P. Nilsen), 161-180; i) APPENDIX: N.C.T.E. Guidelines for Nonsexist Use of Language, , 181-192.

208 SEXISM AND YOUTH. Diane Gersoni (sic), comp. New York: R.R. Bowker, 1974.

a) Why I Won't Celebrate Brotherhood Week (A.M. Schmid), 3-5; b) Equality: Men's Lib (M.H. Freedman), 6-9; c) Training the Woman To Know Her Place: The Power of a Nonconscious Ideology (S.L. Bem, D.J. Bem), 10-22; d) Social Construction of the Second Sex (J. Freeman), 23-41; e) Men: Being a Boy (J. Lester), 42-48; f) School's Role in the Sex-Role Stereotyping of Girls: A Feminist Review of the Literature (B. Levy), 49-69; g) Schooling of Tomorrow's Women (P. Minuchin), 70-77; h) Diary 1972 of a Mad 12-Year-Old (S. Kitman), 78-82; i) Does Different Equal Less? A High School Woman Speaks Out (C. Williams), j) Segregated Academic and Vocational Schools: Separate But Not Equal (Commissioner's Task Force on the Impact of Office of Education Programs on Women), 88-89; k) Sex Bias in the Public Schools (N.O.W., Education Committee, N.Y.C.), 90-100; l) Expelling Pregnant Students (Commissioner's Task Force on the Impact of Office of Education Programs on Women), 101-102; m) Consciousness-Raising in the Classroom: Some Games, Projects, Discussion-Openers, Etc. (Emma Willard Task Force on Education), 103-106; n) "Let Brother Bake the Cake" (A.M. Schmid), 107-112; o) Changing the School Environment (D. Schumacher), 113-119;

p) Feminist Studies: The Schools and Sex-Role Stereotyping (C. Ahlum, J. Fralley), 120-122; q) Realistic Counseling for High School Girls (I.M. Tiedt), 123-126; r) Let Them Aspire! A Plea and Proposal for Equality of Opportunity for Males and Females in the Ann Arbor Public Schools (Committee to Eliminate Sexual Discrimination in the Public Schools), 127-162; s) Women in Children's Literature (A.P. Nilsen), 163-173; t) Sex-Role Socialization in Picture Books for Preschool Children (L.J. Weitzman, D. Eifler, E. Hokada, C. Ross), 174-195; u) Dick and Jane as Victims: Sex Stereotyping in Children's Readers (Women on Words and Images), 196-208; v) Run, Mama, Run: Women Workers in Elementary Readers (B. Stefflre), 209-213; w) Liberated Chinese Primers (F. Howe), 214-216; x) Negative Image of Women in Children's Literature (D. Donlan), 217-227; y) Female Acculturation Through the Fairy Tale (M.R. Lieberman), 228-243; z) Louisa May Alcott: The Author of "Little Women" as Feminist (K. Lindsey), 244-248; aa) Feminist Look at Children's Books (Feminists on Children's Media), 249-259; bb) Skirts in Fiction About Boys: A Maxi Mess (D. Gersoni), 260-271; cc) Feminists Look at the 100 Books: The Portrayal of Women in Children's Books on Puerto Rican Themes (D. Prida, S. Ribner et al.), 272-288; dd) Reducing the "Miss Muffet" Syndrome: An Annotated Bibliography (D. Gersoni), 289-298; ee) All Pregnant Girls Have Boy Babies (C.G. Heilbrun), 299-302; ff) Textbooks and Channeling (J.K. Frisof), 303-308; gg) Women in U.S. History High School Textbooks (J.L. Trecker), 309-325; hh) Guidelines for Equal Treatment of the Sexes in Social Studies Textbooks (E. Burr, S. Dunn, N. Farquhar), 326-338; ii) Lost Herstory: The Treatment of Women in Children's Encyclopedias (L. Kraft), 339-357; jj) Sexism in History or, Writing Women's History is a Tricky Business (R. Rosen), 358-363; kk) Secondary Level Language Arts Presentation (N.O.W., Education Task Force, Boulder, Co.), 364-366; ll) Sex Stereotypes in Mathematics and Science Textbooks for Elementary and Junior High Schools (J. Mlinar), 367-376; mm) Feminist Criticism (D. Gersoni), 377-386; nn) Wonder Woman Revisited (J. Edgar), 387-389; oo) Why Children's Films Are Not Rated "R" (H. Miller), 390-392; pp) Film Resources for Sex-Role Stereotyping (Resource Center on Sex Roles in Education), 393-394; qq) Sesame Street and Sex-Role Stereotypes (J.-A.E. Gardner), 395-397; rr) Sesame Street and Sex-Role Stereotypes (updated) (S. Vogel, I. Broverman, J.-A.E. Gardner), 398-403; ss) Children's Toys and Socialization to Sex Roles (N. Lyon), 404-406; tt) Toys for Free Children (L.C. Pogrebin), 407-428; uu) Movement Behavior (E.C. Umstead), 429-434.

209 SEXISM: SCIENTIFIC DEBATES. Clarice Stasz Stoll, comp. (Addison-Wesley Series in Dialogues in the Social Sciences) Reading, Ma.: Addison-Wesley, 1973.

a) Developmental Differentiation of Femininity and Masculinity Compared (J. Money), 13-27; b) Infant Sex Differences (J. Bardwick), 28-42; c) Sex and Politics (L. Tiger), 43-60; d) Feminized Male (P. Sexton), 61-73; e) Sex Differences in Game Strategy (C.S. Stoll, P.T. McFarlane), 74-86; f) Women in Labor (M. Suelzle), 87-106; g) Toward a Society of Neuters (C. Winick), 107-120; h) Adjusting the

Lives of Women to the Establishment (J. Bernard), 121- .

210 SEXIST RELIGION AND WOMEN IN THE CHURCH: NO MORE SILENCE! Alice L. Hageman, ed. (With the Women's Caucus of Harvard Divinity School) New York: Association Press, 1974.

a) Preaching the Word (N. Morton), 29-46; b) Women and Ministry (L.M. Russell), 47-62; c) Black Women and the Churches: Triple Jeopardy (T. Hoover), 63-76; d) Religious Socialization of Women Within U.S. Subcultures (G.K. Neville), 77-92; e) Judaeo-Christian Influences on Female Sexuality (D.D. Burlage), 93-116; f) Enrichment or Threat? When the Eves Come Marching In (K. Stendahl), 117-124; g) Theology After the Demise of God the Father: A Call for the Castration of Sexist Religion (M. Daly), 125-142; h) View From the Back of the Synagogue: Women in Judaism (G.B. Shulman), 143-166; i) Women and Missions: The Cost of Liberation (A.L. Hageman), 167-194; j) Sexism and the Contemporary Church: When Evasion Becomes Complicity (B.W. Harrison), 195-216.

211 SEXUAL AND REPRODUCTIVE ASPECTS OF WOMEN'S HEALTH CARE. Malkah T. Notman and Carol C. Nadelson, eds. (The Woman Patient: Medical and Psychological Interfaces, Vol. 1) New York: Plenum Press, 1978.

a) Woman Patient (M.T. Notman, C.C. Nadelson), 1-8; b) Feminism: Making a Difference in Our Health (W.S. Heide), 9-20; c) Prenatal Influences on Child Health and Development (E.G. Shore), 21-32; d) Decisions about Reproduction: Genetic Counseling (J.G. Davis), 33-54; e) Physiological Aspects of Pregnancy (E.A. Friedman), 55-72; f) "Normal" and "Special" Aspects of Pregnancy: A Psychological Approach (C.C. Nadelson), 73-86; g) Sense of Mastery in the Childbirth Experience (A.M. Seiden), 87-106; h) C.O.P.E. Story: A Service to Pregnant and Postpartum Women (M.F. Turner, M.H. Izzi), 107-122; i) Adolescent Sexuality and Pregnancy (C.C. Nadelson, M.T. Notman, J. Gillon), 23-130; j) Conflicts between Fertility and Infertility (R.W. Lidz), 131-136; k) Problem of Infertility (M.D. Mazor), 137-160; l) Historical Understanding of Contraception (P. Reich), 161-172; m) Emotional Impact of Abortion (C.C. Nadelson), 173-180; n) Medical Gynecology: Problems and Patients (G. Guzinski), 181-202; o) Surgical Gynecology (A.B. Barnes, C.B. Tinkham), 203-216; p) Hysterectomy and Other Gynecological Surgeries: A Psychological View (N.C.A. Roeske), 217-232; q) Breast Disorders (S.L. Tishler), 233-246; r) Psychological Consideration of Mastectomy (M.T. Notman), 247-256; s) "Difficult" Patient: Observations on the Staff-Patient Interaction (E.B. Kahan, E.B. Gaskill), 257-270; t) Woman and Esthetic Surgery (R.M. Goldwyn), 271-280; u) Problems in Sexual Functioning (C.C. Nadelson), 281-292; v) Female Sexual Dysfunctions: A Clinical Approach (M.-B. Rosenbaum), 293-302; w) Impact of Rape (E. Hilberman), 303-322; x) Gynecological Approach to Menopause (J.F. Perlmutter), 323-336; y) Menopause (P.B. Bart, M. Grossman),

337-354.

212 SEXUAL STRATEGEMS: THE WORLD OF WOMEN IN FILM. Patricia Erens, ed. New York: Horizon, 1979.

a) Popcorn Venus or How the Movies Have Made Women Smaller Than Life (M. Rosen), 19-30; b) Monster and the Victim (G. Lenne), 31-40; c) Image of Woman as Image: The Optical Politics of Dames (L. Fischer), 41-61; d) "Madame de": A Musical Passage (M. Haskell), 62-71; e) "Two or Three Things I Know About Her" (C. Kleinhans), 72-81; f) "Lucia" (A.M. Taylor), 82-90; g) Bergman's Portrait of Women: Sexism or Subjective Metaphor? (B. Steene), 91-107; h) Mizoguchi's Oppressed Women (D. Serceau), 108-114; i) Women's Cinema as Counter-Cinema (C. Johnston), 133-143; j) Feminist Film Criticism: Theory and Practice (J. Lesage), 144-155; k) Feminist Aesthetic: Reflection Revolution Ritual (P. Erens), 156-167; l) Out of Oblivion: Alice Guy-Blache (F. Lacassin), 168-178; m) Esther Schub (J. Leyda), 179-184; n) Maya Deren and Germaine Dulac: Activists of the Avant-Garde (R. Cornwell), 185-201; o) Leni Riefenstahl: The Deceptive Myth (B.R. Rich), 202-209; p) Mai Zetterling: Free Fall (D. Elley), 210-218; q) "Maedchen in Uniform" (N. Scholar), 219-223; r) Work of Dorothy Arzner (P. Cook), 224-235; s) "A Very Curious Girl" (K. Kay), 236-243; t) Lina Wertmuller: Swept Away on a Wave of Sexism (M. Haskell), 244-247; u) Reflections on "Jeanne Dielman" (M. Kinder), 248-257; v) Family Portraits: Filmmakers Explore Their Roots (E. Weis), 258-265; w) APPENDIX: Filmographies of Women Directors, 266- .

213 SEXUAL STRATIFICATION: A CROSS-CULTURAL VIEW. Alice Schlegel, ed. New York: Columbia University Press, 1977.

a) Theory of Sexual Stratification (A. Schlegel), 1-40; b) Bridging the Gap between the Sexes in Moroccan Legal Practice (D.H. Dwyer), 41-66; c) Illusion and Reality in Sicily (C. Cronin), 67-93; d) Caste Differences between Brahmin and Non-Brahmin Women in a South Indian Village (H.E. Ullrich), 94-108; e) Female Husbands in Southern Bantu Societies (D. O'Brien), 109-126; f) Agitation for Change in the Sudan (C. Fluehr-Lobban), 127-143; g) Iyalode in the Traditional Yoruba Political System (B. Awe), 144-160; h) Economic Activity and Marriage among Ivoirian Urban Women (B.C. Lewis), 161-191; i) Impact of Modernization on Women's Position in the Family in Ghana (A.C. Smock), 192-214; j) Women, Work, and Power in Modern Yugoslavia (B. Denich), 215-244; k) Male and Female in Hopi Thought and Action (A. Schlegel), 245-269; l) Mechanistic Cooperation and Sexual Equality among the Western Bontoc (A.S. Bacdayan), 270-291; m) Social Inequality and Sexual Status in Barbados (C. Sutton, S. Makiesky-Barrow), 292-325; n) Ecological Antecedents and Sex-Role Consequences in Traditional and Modern Israeli Subcultures (N. Datan), 326-343; o) Overview

(A. Schlegel), 344-358.

214 SHAKESPEARE'S SISTERS: FEMINIST ESSAYS ON WOMEN POETS. Sandra M. Gilbert and Susan Gubar, eds. Bloomington: Indiana University Press, 1979.

a) Gender, Creativity, and the Woman Poet (S.M. Gilbert, S. Gubar), xv-xxvi; b) Jane Lead: Mysticism and the Woman Cloathed with the Sun (C.F. Smith), 3-18; c) Anne Bradstreet's Poetry: A Study of Subversive Piety (W. Martin), 19-31; d) Anne Finch, Countess of Winchilsea: An Augustan Woman Poet (K. Rogers), 32-46; e) Emily Bronte's Anti-Romance (N. Auerbach), 49-64; f) Elizabeth Barrett Browning (H. Cooper), 65-81; g) Christina Rossetti: The Inward Pose (D. Rosenblum), 82-98; h) Power of Emily Dickinson (A. Rich), 99-121; i) Emily Dickinson and the Deerslayer: The Dilemma of the Woman Poet in America (A. Gelpi), 122-134; j) Dickinson, Whitman, and Their Successors (T. Diggory), 135-150; k) Art of Silence and the Forms of Women's Poetry (J. Kammer), 153-164; l) Afro-American Women Poets: A Bio-Critical Survey (G.T. Hull), 165-182; m) Edna St. Vincent Millay and the Language of Vulnerability (J. Stanbrough), 183-199; n) Echoing Spell of H.D.'s "Trilogy" (S. Gubar), 200-218; o) May Swenson and the Shapes of Speculation (A. Ostriker), 221-232; p) Gwendolyn the Terrible: Propositions on Eleven Poems (H.J. Spillers), 233-244; q) Life-Work of Sylvia Plath (S.M. Gilbert), 245-260; r) Poetry and Salvation in the Career of Anne Sexton (S. Juhasz), 261-268; s) Common Language: The American Woman Poet (B.C. Gelpi), 269-279; t) Critique of Consciousness and Myth in Levertov, Rich, and Rukeyser (R.B. Duplessis), 280-300.

215 SISTER SAINTS. Vicky Burgess-Olson, ed. (Series in Mormon History, Vol. 5) Provo, Ut.: Brigham Young University Press, 1978.

a) Life and Legend of Eliza R. Snow (M.U. Beecher), 1-20; b) Sarah Melissa Granger Kimball: The Liberal Shall Be Blessed (J.M. Derr), 21-42; c) Louisa Barnes Pratt: Missionary Wife, Missionary Mother, Missionary (A.G. Stone), 43-60; d) Susa Young Gates: The Thirteenth Apostle (R.F. Cornwall), 61-94; e) Amy Brown Lyman: Raising the Quality of Life for All (L.L. Hefner), 95-118; f) Susanna Goudin Cardon: An Italian Convert to Mormonism (L. Degn), 119-138; g) Lucinda Lee Dalton: A Tough Kind of Testimony (L.F. Anderson), 139-172; h) Jane Snyder Richards: The Blue-White Diamond (C.D. Cannon), 173-200; i) Bathsheba Bigler Smith: Woman of Faith and Courage (B.F. Watt), 201-222; j) Aurelia Read Spencer Rogers: Humble Heroine (E.K. Ritchie), 223-241; k) Two Miss Cooks: Pioneer Professionals for Utah's Schools (J.M. Derr), 242-260; l) Maud May Babcock: "Understand the Thought, Hold the Thought, Give the Thought" (A.G. Stone), 261-274; m) Alice Louise Reynolds: A Woman's Woman (R. Keele), 275-288; n) Stena Scorup: First Lady of Salina (V. Burgess-Olson), 289-302; o) Patty Bartlett Sessions: More Than a Midwife (S.S. Rugh), 303-324; p) Dr. Ellen Brooke Ferguson: Nineteenth-Century Renaissance Woman (A.G. Stone), 325-340; q) Dr. Romania Pratt Penrose: To Brave the World (C.C. Waters), 341-362; r) Dr. Ellis Reynolds Shipp: Pioneer Utah Physician (G.F. Casterline), 363-382; s) Dr. Martha Hughes Cannon: Doctor, Wife, Legislator, Exile (J.B. White), 383-398; t) Dr. Margaret Ann Freece: Entrepreneur of

Southern Utah (V. Burgess-Olson), 399-414; u) Sarah Elizabeth Carmichael: Poetic Genius of Pioneer Utah (M.B. Murphy), 415-432; v) Louisa Lula Greene Richards: "Remember the Women of Zion" (C.C. Madsen), 433-454; w) Emmeline Blanche Woodward Wells: "I Have Risen Triumphant" (P.R. Eaton-Gadsby, J.R. Dushku), 455-480; x) Augusta Joyce Crocheron: A Representative Woman (J.R. Dushku, P.R. Eaton-Gadsby), 481- .

216 SISTERHOOD IS POWERFUL: AN ANTHOLOGY OF WRITINGS FROM THE WOMEN'S LIBERATION MOVEMENT. Robin Morgan, comp. New York: Random House, 1970.

This anthology is a potpourri of articles, poems, manifestos and documents which were spawned by the American women's liberation movement. Arrangement is primarily by topic, e.g., professional women, sexual and psychological repression, minority women, feminist ideology. Contributors: C. Brown, J. Seitz, B. Jones, M. Gilbert, L. Furman, S.S. Hobson, S. Schnall, L. Van Gelder, J. Ann, Women's Caucus-Political Science Dept.-U. Chicago, C. Glassman, J. Tepperman, M. Daly, D.B. Schulder, Z. Moss, A. Embree, Florika, S. Lydon, Joreen, N. Weisstein, M.J. Sherfey, N. Shainess, L. Cisler, E. Strong, G. Damon, M. Shelley, K. Millett, I. Peslikis, F.M. Beal, E.H. Norton, Black Women's Liberation Group-Mt. Vernon, N.Y., C. Dvorkin, A. de Rivera, Women's Collective-N.Y. High School Students' Union, E. Sutherland, L. Fritz, M.A. Britton, R.M. Brown, J. West, M. Piercy, J. Russo, S. Plath, V. Solanis, N.Y. Radical Women, Women of the American Revolution, E. Longauex y Vasquez, C.B. Cohen, F. Kennedy, P. Mainardi, K. Sacks, S. Pascale, R. Moon, L.B. Tanner, R. Dunbar, S. Sutheim, Redstockings, K. Lindsey, M.L. Fletcher, L. Strongin, Media Women, Women's Majority Union-Seattle, Women Against Daddy Warbucks, Women's Caucus-Youth International Party, Feminists, Witches.

217 SOCIAL JUSTICE AND PREFERENTIAL TREATMENT: WOMEN AND RACIAL MINORITIES IN EDUCATION AND BUSINESS. William T. Blackstone and Robert D. Heslep, eds. Athens: University of Georgia Press, 1977.

a) University and the Case for Preferential Treatment (R. Wasserstrom), 16-32; b) Preferential Treatment in Admitting Racial Minority Students (R.D. Heslep), 33-51; c) Reverse Discrimination and Compensatory Justice (W.T. Blackstone), 52-83; d) Justification of Reverse Discrimination (T.L. Beauchamp), 84-110; e) Preferential Consideration and Justice (A. Edel), 111-134; f) Realizing the Equality Principle (R.B. Ginzburg), 135-153; g) Preferential Treatment (D. Rusk), 154-160; h) Discrimination against Blacks: A Historical Perspective (P.E. Wilson), 161-175; i) Equality and Inviolability: An Approach to Compensatory Justice (M. Greene), 176-198; j) Compensatory Justice and the Meaning of Equity (W.A. Banner), 199-209.

218 SOCIALIST WOMEN: EUROPEAN SOCIALIST FEMINISM IN THE 19th AND EARLY 20th CENTURIES. Marilyn J. Boxer and Jean H. Quataert, eds. New York: Elsevier North-Holland, 1978.

a) Class and Sex Connection (M.J. Boxer, J.H. Quataert), 1-18; b) Feminism and Socialism: The Utopian Synthesis of Flora Tristan (S.J. Moon), 19-50; c) From Separatism to Socialism: Women in the Russian Revolutionary Movement of the 1870s (B.A. Engel), 51-74; d) Socialism Faces Feminism: The Failure of Synthesis in France, 1879-1914 (M.J. Boxer), 75-111; e) Unequal Partners in an Uneasy Alliance: Women and the Working Class in Imperial Germany (J.H. Quataert), 112-145; f) Marxist Ambivalence Toward Women: Between Socialism and Feminism in the Italian Socialist Party (C. LaVigna), 146-181; g) Bolshevism, The Woman Question, and Aleksandra Kollontai (B. Farnsworth), 182-214; h) Five Socialist Women: Traditionalist Conflicts and Socialist Visions in Austria, 1893-1934 (I. Lafleur), 215-248.

219 THE SOCIOLOGY OF THE LANGUAGES OF AMERICAN WOMEN. Betty Lou Dubois and Isabel Crouch, eds. (Papers in Southwest English IV) Proceedings of the Conference on the Sociology of the Languages of American Women. San Antonio: Trinity University, 1978.

a) "What Do Women Sociolinguists Want?": Prospects For a Research Field (S. Ervin-Tripp), 3-16; b) Problem of Orientation in Sex-Language Research (C. Kramer), 17-32; c) Two Features of "Women's Speech"? (M. Baumann), 33-40; d) Male-Female Conversational Interaction Cues: Using Data From Dialect Surveys (B.K. Dumas), 41-52; e) Verbal Turn-Taking and Exchanges in Faculty Dialogue (B. Eakins, G. Eakins), 53-62; f) Sex, Color and Money: Who's Perceiving What? Or Men and Women: Where Did All the Differences Go (To)? (G.N. Garcia, S.F. Frosch), 63-72; g) Phonological Differences in the English of Adolescent Chicanas and Chicanos (B.S. Hartford), 73-80; h) Descriptive Study of the Language of Men and Women Born in Maine Around 1900 as It Reflects the Lakoff Hypotheses in "Language and Women's Place" (M. Hartman), 81-90; i) Women's Verbal Images and Associations (V. John-Steiner, P. Irvine), 91-102; j) Black Women In the Rural South: Conservative and Innovative (P.C. Nichols), 103-114; k) Difference Beyond Inherent Pitch (W. Von Raffler-Engel, J. Buckner), 115-118; l) Mothers' Speech to Children in Bilingual Mexican-American Homes (W. Redlinger), 119-130; m) Fluency of Women's Speech (E.-M. Silverman, C.H. Zimmer), 131-136; n) Sociocultural and Sociopsychological Factors in Differential Language Retentiveness by Sex (Y.R. Solé), 137-154; o) Women's Verbal Behavior at Learned and Professional Conferences (M. Swacker), 155-160; p) Effects of the Ethnicity of the Interviewer on Conversation: A Study of Chicana Women (Y. Tixier y Vigil, N. Elsasser), 161-170; q) Alignment Strategies in Verbal Accounts of Problematic Conduct: The Case of Abortion (M. Zimmerman), 171-186.

220 SOLO: WOMEN ON WOMAN ALONE. Linda Hamalian and Leo Hamalian, eds. New York: Dell, 1977.

a) Management (M. Lamb), 25-40; b) Nanette: An Aside (W. Cather), 41-47; c) 6:27 PM (J.C. Oates), 48-62; d) As We Have Learnt from Freud, There Are No Jokes (P. Gilliatt), 63-79; e) Go With Love, He Says (E. Gottlieb), 80-93; f) A Negative Balance (A. Wells), 94-100; g) Mending (S. Bingham), 101-112; h) The Love Object (E. O'Brien),

113-138; i) How Soon Can I Leave? (S. Hill), 139-151; j) A Stroke of Luck (K. Roe), 152-160; k) Sweets to the Sweet (J. Mayhall), 161-182; l) Dreamy (S. Sonnett), 183-185; m) I Love Someone (J. Stafford), 186-193; n) Success Is Not a Destination But the Road To It (K. Harding), 194-209; o) The Lover (J. Williams), 210-218; p) Secretive (J. Augustine), 219-223; q) World of Heroes (A. Kavan), 224-231; r) And the Soul Shall Dance (W. Yamauchi), 232-239; s) The Good Humor Man (R. Morris), 240-252; t) Lunch (R. Rass), 253-263; u) Reena (P. Marshall), 264-283; v) Let Them Call It Jazz (J. Rhys), 284-302; w) Dynastic Encounter (M. Piercy), 303-311; x) A Cold-Water Flat (E. Pollet), 312-331; y) An Old Woman and Her Cat (D. Lessing), 332-348; z) Tuesday Night (A. Beattie), 349-356; aa) Pure Will (H. Zinnes), 357-358.

221 SOUTHEAST ASIAN BIRTH CUSTOMS: THREE STUDIES IN HUMAN REPRODUCTION. (Donn Vorhis Hart, ed.) New Haven: Human Relations Area File Press, 1965.

a) From Pregnancy through Birth in a Bisayan Filipino Village (D.V. Hart), 1-114; b) Customs Connected with Birth and the Rearing of Children (P.A. Rajadhon), 115-204; c) Pregnancy and Birth in Vietnam (R.J. Coughlin), 205- .

222 STURDY BLACK BRIDGES: VISIONS OF BLACK WOMEN IN LITERATURE. Roseann P. Bell, Bettye J. Parker and Beverly Guy-Sheftall, eds. Garden City, N.Y.: Anchor-Doubleday, 1979.

a) Black Women In and Out of Fiction (B.J. Parker), xv-xxxi; b) Analytical Vision (R.P. Bell, B.J. Parker), 3-7; c) War on African Familyhood (I.E. Carruthers), 8-17; d) Images of Black Women in Modern African Poetry (A.B. Rushing), 18-24; e) Ama Ata Aidoo's "Dilemma of a Ghost" (K.C. Chapman), 25-38; f) African Heroine (M. Linton-Umeh), 39-51; g) Awakening of the Self in the Heroines of Ousmane Sembene (S. Lee), 52-60; h) Caribbean Woman as Writer (E. Apandaye), 61-68; i) Black Women Poets from Wheatley to Walker (G.T. Hull), 69-86; j) Politics of Intimacy (H. Spillers), 87-106; k) Images of Self and Race in the Autobiographies of Black Women (M. Burgher), 107-122; l) Black Eve or Madonna? Antithetical Views of the Mother in Black American Literature (D.C. Dance), 123-132; m) Alice Walker (M.H. Washington), 133-149; n) Alice Walker: "The Diary of an African Nun" and Du Bois' Double Consciousness (C.J. Fontenot), 150-156; o) Women of Bronzeville (B. Guy-Sheftall), 157-170; p) Influence of Voodoo on the Fiction of Zora Neale Hurston (E. Southerland), 171-183; q) Bridges and Deep Water (J.D. Ward), 184-192; r) Conversational Vision (R.P. Bell), 193-196; s) Ann Petry Talks About First Novel (J.W. Ivy), 197-200; t) Reflections: Arthenia Bates Millican (B.J. Parker), 201-208; u) Judgment: Addison Gayle (R.P. Bell), 209-216; v) Substance: George Kent (R.P. Bell), 217-229; w) Commitment: Toni Cade Bambara Speaks (B. Guy-Sheftall), 230-249; x) Complexity: Toni Morrison's Women--An Interview Essay (B.J. Parker), 250-257; y) Wisdom: An Interview with C.L.R. James (L. Anthony-Welch), 258-262; z) Mississippi Mothers: Roots (B.J. Parker), 263-281; aa) Gayl Jones Takes a Look at "Corregidora"--An Interview (R.P. Bell), 282-290; bb) Creative Vision

(B. Guy-Sheftall), 291-293; cc) The Collector of Treasures (B. Head), 294-312; dd) Return of the Native (P. Marshall), 314-321; ee) The Word Is Love (L.V. Williams), 322-327; ff) Cleaning Out the Closet (M. Jackson), 345-351; gg) The Neighborhood (B. De Ramus), 371-374; POETS: S. Otoo, J.F. Hunter, M. Williams, N. Guillén, M. Evans, M. Walker, N. Giovanni, S. Sanchez, N. Johnson, P.C. White, O. Loving, M. Danner, M.J. Boyd, K.A. McClane, G. Gayles, L. Suruma, R.A. Bell, H.R. Madhubuti, A. Lourde (sic), C. Rodgers.

223 SUFFER AND BE STILL: WOMEN IN THE VICTORIAN AGE. Martha Vicinus, ed. Bloomington: Indiana University Press, 1972.

a) Victorian Governess: Status Incongruence in Family and Society (M.J. Peterson), 3-19; b) From Dame to Woman: W.S. Gilbert and Theatrical Transvestism (J.W. Stedman), 20-37; c) Victorian Women and Menstruation (E. Showalter, E. Showalter), 38-44; d) Marriage, Redundancy or Sin: The Painter's View of Women in the First Twenty-Five Years of Victoria's Reign (H.E. Roberts), 45-76; e) Study of Victorian Prostitution and Venereal Disease (E.M. Sigsworth, T.J. Wyke), 77-99; f) Working-Class Women in Britain, 1890-1914? (P.N. Stearns), 100-120; g) Debate over Women : Ruskin vs. Mill (K. Millett), 121-139; h) Stereotypes of Femininity in a Theory of Sexual Evolution (J. Conway), 140-154; i) Innocent Femina Sensualis in Unconscious Conflict (P.T. Cominos), 155-172; j) Women of England in a Century of Social Change, 1815-1914: A Select Bibliography (S.B. Kanner), 173-206.

224 TANGLED VINES: A COLLECTION OF MOTHER AND DAUGHTER POEMS. Lyn Lifshin, ed. Boston: Beacon Press, 1978.

This collection explores and celebrates the relationship between mother and daughter. Manuscripts were solicited primarily from established poets. Contributors: L. Pastan, S. Plath, J. Hoffman, S. Hochmann, H. Chasin, G. Tod, J. Minty, B. Eve, A. Lorde, S. Kaufman, A. Sexton, S. Olds, P. Goedicke, M. Kumin, E. Wittlinger, K. Fraser, L. Ullmann, J. Hemschemeyer, J. McDaniel, L. Clifton, E. Bass, M. Piercy, D. Wakoski, E. Jong, K. Spivack, J. Sternburg, L. Lifshin, L.L. Zeiger, Yvonne, P. Traxler, A. Luttinger, D. Wier, S. Hoben, A. Waldman, S. Sanchez, N. Giovanni, S.C. Fox, H. Moore, A. Rich.

225 TEARING THE VEIL: ESSAYS ON FEMININITY. Susan Lipshitz, ed. Boston: Routledge and Kegan Paul, 1978.

a) Mother and the Hospital: An Unfortunate Fit Between the Woman's Internal World and Some Hospital Practices (D. Breen), 15-36; b) Witch and Her Devils: An Exploration of the Relationship Between Femininity and Illness (S. Lipshitz), 37-54; c) Whore in Peru: The Splitting of Women into Good and Bad and the Isolation of the Prostitute (K. Arnold), 55-72; d) Tess: The Making of a Pure Woman (M. Jacobus), 75-92; e) City's Achievements: The Patriotic Amazonomachy and Ancient Athens (M. Merck), 93-116; f) Woman-Power: Religious Heresy and Feminism in

Early English Socialism (B. Taylor), 117-144.

226 THESE MODERN WOMEN: AUTOBIOGRAPHICAL ESSAYS FROM THE TWENTIES. Elaine Showalter, ed. Old Westbury, N.Y.: The Feminist Press, 1978.

a) Making of a Militant (I.H. Irwin), 34-39; b) Why I Earn My Own Living (M.A. Hopkins), 41-44; c) Mother's Daughter (S.S. White), 46-51; d) Peacock's Tail (A.M. Kimball), 53-57; e) Deflated Rebel (R. Pickering), 58-61; f) Poet Out of Pioneer (G. Taggard), 63-67; g) Evolution of Disenchantment (L.L. Pruette), 69-72; h) One Way to Freedom (K.L. Gregg), 74-77; i) Woman Alone (M.H. Austin), 79-85; j) Mother Worship (C. Eastman), 87-91; k) Staying Free (E. Stuyvesant), 92-96; l) Lightning Speed Through Life (L. Rogers), 98-104; m) Long Journey (P. Blanchard), 105-108; n) Free--For What? (V. McAlmon), 110-114; o) Unpardonable Sin (G. Smith), 116-119; p) In Search of Adventure (C.B. Pinchot), 121-125; q) Hotbed of Feminists (W. Gág), 127-134; r) Why Feminism? (B.M. Hinkle), 137-140; s) Weakness of Women (J.B. Watson), 141-143; t) Half-Confessed (J. Collins), 144- .

227 THIRD WORLD WOMEN: FACTORS IN THEIR CHANGING STATUS. Jean O'Barr, ed. Durham, N.C.: Center for International Studies, Duke University, 1977.

a) Sexual Asymmetry and the Status of Women (J. O'Barr), 6-11; b) Control of Resources (J. O'Barr), 12-15; c) Indirect Access to Influence (J. O'Barr), 16-21; d) Social Change and the Roles of Women (J. O'Barr), 22-28; e) Women Under Communist and Socialist Regimes (J. O'Barr), 29-37; f) Women's Participation in Politics (J. O'Barr), 38-49; g) Ideology and Control (S. Lindenbaum), 50-63; h) Adverse Impact of Development (I. Tinker). 64-76; i) Bibliographies on Third World Women, 86-88.

228 THIS GREAT ARGUMENT: THE RIGHTS OF WOMEN. Hamida Bosmajian and Haig Bosmajian, eds. Reading, Ma.: Addison-Wesley, 1972.

The pieces in this collection are representative of writings, both feminist and misogynic, about women throughout history. They demonstrate the breadth and longevity of interest in the status of women and expose the foundations upon which contemporary arguments rest. Contributors: Hesiod, Plato, Petrarch, P. Sidney, W. Shakespeare, J. Donne, A. Finch, J. Swift, J. Milton, J.J. Rousseau, M. Wollstonecraft, J.S. Mill, H. Ibsen, L. Fiedler, B. Bettelheim, G. Myrdal, H.M. Hacker, D.D. Knudsen, E. Fisher, F.A. Seidenberg, N.O.W., J. Brown, P. Way, H. Fanninngs, M. Wood, K. McAfee.

229 THREE PAMPHLETS ON THE JACOBEAN ANTIFEMINIST CONTROVERSY. (B.J. Baines, comp.) Delmar, N.Y.: Scholars' Facsimiles and Reprints, 1978.

a) Hic Mulier (1620); b) Haec-Vir (1620); c) Mulde Sacke (1620).

230 TOWARD AN ANTHROPOLOGY OF WOMEN. Rayna R. Reiter, ed. New York: Monthly Review Press, 1975.

a) Perspectives on the Evolution of Sex Differences (L. Liebowitz), 20-35; b) Woman the Gatherer: Male Bias in Anthropology (S. Slocum), 36-50; c) Origin of the Family (K. Gough), 51-76; d) !Kung Women: Contrasts in Sexual Egalitarianism in Foraging and Sedentary Contexts (P. Draper), 77-109; e) Aboriginal Woman: Male and Female Anthropological Perspectives (R. Rohrlich-Leavitt, B. Sykes, E. Weatherford), 110-126; f) Concept of Pollution Among the Kafe of the Papua New Guinea Highlands (E. Faithorn), 127-140; g) Matriarchy: A Vision of Power (P. Webster), 141-156; h) Traffic in Women: Notes on the "Political Economy" of Sex (G. Rubin), 157-210; i) Engels Revisited: Women, the Organization of Production, and Private Property (K. Sacks), 211-234; j) Iroquois Women: An Ethnohistoric Note (J.K. Brown), 235-251; k) Men and Women in the South of France: Public and Private Domains (R.R. Reiter), 252-282; l) Women and Words in a Spanish Village (S. Harding), 283-308; m) Life Crisis as a Clue to Social Function: The Case of Italy (S.F. Silverman), 309-321; n) Love Unites Them and Hunger Separates Them: Poor Women in the Dominican Republic (S.E. Brown), 322-332; o) Spread of Capitalism in Rural Colombia: Effects on Poor Women (A. Rubbo), 333-357; p) Underdevelopment and the Experience of Women: A Nigerian Case Study (D. Remy), 358-371; q) Collectivization, Kinship, and the Status of Women in Rural China (N. Diamond), 372-395.

231 TOWARD WOMEN: A STUDY OF THE ORIGINS OF WESTERN ATTITUDES THROUGH GRECO-ROMAN PHILOSOPHY. Joseph P. Ghougassian, ed. San Diego: Lukas and Sons, 1977.

a) Moral Equality (Pythagoras), 12-17; b) Indulgent Woman (Theano), 18-21; c) Of the Harmony of the Woman (Perictione), 22-25; d) Female Sexuality and Embryo (Hippocrates), 26-30; e) Task of a Housewife (Socratics, Xenophon), 31-40; f) Community of Wives (Plato), 41-54; g) Different Virtues for Women (Aristotle), 55-59; h) Of the Relation Between Husband and Wife (Aristotle), 60-61; i) Procreation (Aristotle), 62-65; j) Epicurean Doctrine of Love (Lucretius), 66-72; k) Contra Women's Liberation Movement (Cato), 73-79; l) Social Aspects of the Woman in the "Res Publica" (Cicero), 80-88; m) Philosopher to His Mother (Seneca), 89-95; n) That Women Too Should Study Philosophy (Musonius Rufus), 96-101; o) On Adultery (Epictetus), 102-104; p) On Adornment (Epictetus), 105-106; q) The Cynic Should Not Marry (Epictetus), 107-109; r) Conjugal Precepts (Plutarch), 110-115; s) Female Genitals (Galen), 116-121; t) De-Feminized Lesbian (Lucian), 122-125; u) Initiation of a Courtesan (Lucian), 126-129; v) Letter to

the Wife (Porphyry), 130-134.

232 UNSUNG CHAMPIONS OF WOMEN. Mary Cohart, ed. Albuquerque: University of New Mexico Press, 1975.

a) Evolution of Woman (E.B. Gamble), 9-24; b) Gynaecocentric Theory (L.F. Ward), 25-60; c) Investigation of the Religious and Judicial Character of Matriarchy in the Ancient World (J.J. Bachofen), 63-84; d) God-Idea of the Ancients (E.B. Gamble), 85-104; e) Dominant Sex (M. Vaerting, M. Vaerting), 105-132; f) Brief History of the Condition of Women (L.M. Child), 135-150; g) Woman and Her Master (Lady S.Morgan), 151-164; h) Woman's Share in Primitive Culture (O.T. Mason), 165-180; i) Short History of Women's Rights (E.A. Heckler), 181-208; j) Dialogues (Plato), 211-217; k) First Essay on the Political Rights of Women (Marquis de Condorcet), 218-225; l) Principles of Ethics (H. Spencer), 226-234; m) Tyranny of Man (Stella), 237-249; n) Ancilla's Share (E. Robins), 250-265.

233 UP AGAINST THE WALL, MOTHER...ON WOMEN'S LIBERATION. Elsie Bonita Adams and Mary Louise Briscoe, eds. Beverly Hills, Ca.: Glencoe Press, 1971.

a) Genesis, 4-7; b) Jewish Prayer, 8; c) Leviticus, 9; d) Catholic Teaching on Women (W.B. Faherty), 10-14; e) Psychical Consequences of the Anatomical Distinction between the Sexes (S. Freud), 15-24; f) Womanly Image: Character Assassination through the Ages (P. Stern), 25-32; g) Woman in the Elizabethan Sonnet: Poems (E. Spenser, W. Shakespeare), 34-36; h) Victorian Woman (Anon.), 37; i) Playboys and Bunnies (H.M. Hefner), 38-39; j) In Memoriam: "Sex and the Single Girl", 40; k) Princess Grace Turns Forty (W.B. Arthur), 40-43; l) Achieving Womanhood (W.H. Grier, P.M. Cobbs), 44-53; m) Bride of Frankenstein (E. Field), 54-56; n) Tickets, Please (D.H. Lawrence), 58-68; o) Faustine (A.C. Swinburne), 69-73; p) "The Mill on the Floss" (G. Eliot), 74; q) S.C.U.M. Manifesto (V. Solanus), 75-77; r) Common Women (P. Wylie), 78-95; s) Lysistrata (Aristophanes), 96-102; t) The Golden Ass (Apuleius), 104-106; u) True Woman--Herself (D.G. Rossetti), 107; v) Riders to the Sea (J.M. Synge), 108-110; w) Three Poems (R. Graves), 111; x) Karintha (J. Toomer), 112-114; y) Subjection of Women (J.S. Mill), 118-132; z) Political and Civil Status of Women as of January 1, 1969 (U.S. Dept. of Labor), 133-143; aa) Matriarchal Myth (E. Merriam), 144-153; bb) "X" Doesn't Equal "Y" (A. Montagu), 154-160; cc) Three Sexual Myths Exploded (R. Brecher, E. Brecher), 161-166; dd) Myth of the Vaginal Orgasm (A. Koedt), 167-175; ee) Psychology Constructs the Female, or The Fantasy Life of the Male Psychologist (N. Weisstein), 176-192; ff) Monogamous Family (F. Engels), 196-206; gg) Problem that Has No Name (B. Friedan), 207-221; hh) Main Street (S. Lewis), 222-228; ii) To Room Nineteen (D. Lessing), 229-256; jj) The Mother (G. Brooks), 257-258; kk) Man and Wife (A. Sexton), 259; ll) Communes: A Footnote for the Future (M.L. Briscoe), 260-262; mm) Women in the Labor Force (U.S. Dept. of Labor), 263-267; nn) Day Care (L. Gross, P. Mac Ewan), 268-274; oo) The Morning Half-Life Blues (M. Piercy), 275-276; pp) Mrs. Warren's Profession (B. Shaw), 277-283; qq) Invisible Bar (C. Bird), 284-301;

rr) Fail: Bright Women (M. Horner), 302-308; ss) Her Story (N.L. Madgett), 309; tt) Room of One's Own (V. Woolf), 310-322; uu) Sojourner Truth: On Women's Rights (F.D. Gage), 325-327; vv) A Doll's House (H. Ibsen), 328-334; ww) Changing Women (S. Steiner), 335-347; xx) One Woman's Lib (J. Jones), 348-349; yy) Sisterhood (D. Densmore), 350-352; zz) Women of Lesbos (M. Shelley), 353-357; aaa) Celibacy (D. Densmore), 358-361; bbb) Abortion: Women, Men and the Law (W. Lafferty), 362-374; ccc) Man's Role in Women's Liberation (M.L. Briscoe, E. Adams), 375-384.

234 UP FROM THE PEDESTAL: SELECTED WRITINGS IN THE HISTORY OF AMERICAN FEMININISM. Aileen S. Kraditor, comp. and ed. Chicago: Quadrangle Books, 1968.

These documents represent the primary focus of each period of American feminist activity. Emphasis is on material unavailable in reprinted form at the time of selection. Although chronology is considered, items are arranged roughly by topic: the early feminist concern with "spheres," the arguments directed to women's status, roles and education; women and government, and recent political action. Contributors: A. Bradstreet, J. Winthrop, Constantia, H.M. Crocker, T.R. Dew, J.F. Stearns, S.M. Grimke, M.C. Thomas, A.E. Grimke, M. Fuller, L. Stone, E.H. Willard, C.E. Beecher, A.L. Kellogg, M.J. Gage, A.G. Spencer, H. Grew, H.T. Cutler, L. Mott, E.C. Stanton, W.L. Garrison, E.R. Coe, C.W. McCulloch, E.S. Miller, G. Smith, T.C. Claflin, T. Veblen, R.D. Owen, M. Robinson, H.B. Blackwell, L. Stone, A.B. Blackwell, S.B. Anthony, H.S. Blatch, C.P. Gilman, O.A. Brownson, G.G. Vest, G. Cleveland, C.C. Catt, F.P. Dunne, A.D. Miller, E. Rose, H.K. Hunt, O. Brown, B. Kearney, H.P. Jenkins, O.W. Bates, F. Kelley, J. Ashley, J. Addams, B.S. Matthews, A. Pollitzer, R. Schneiderman, F. Miller, Mrs. W.J. Carson, F.E. Willard, S. Kopald, E.N. Blair, E.M. Stern, M.I. Bunting.

235 THE VICTIMIZATION OF WOMEN. Jane Roberts Chapman and Margaret Gates, eds. (Sage Yearbooks in Women's Policy Studies, Vol. 3) Beverly Hills: Sage, 1978.

a) Men and the Victimization of Women (J.V. Becker, G.G. Abel), 29-52; b) Rape (D.D. Schram), 53-80; c) Sexual Abuse of Children (K. MacFarlane), 81-110; d) Battered Women: Society's Problem (D. Martin), 111-142; e) Treatment Alternatives for Battered Women (L.E. Walker), 143-174; f) Prostitute as Victim (J. James), 175-202; g) Sexual Harassment: Women's Hidden Occupational Hazard (L.J. Evans), 203-224; h) Women's Health: The Side Effects of Sex Bias (J.G. Lear), 225-250; i) Economics of Women's Victimization (J.R. Chapman), 251-268; j) Women and Victimization: The Aftermath (K. Saltzman), 269-278.

236 VIRTUES IN CONFLICT: TRADITION AND THE KOREAN WOMAN TODAY. Sandra Mattielli, ed. (Published for the Royal Asiatic Society, Korean Branch) Seoul: Samhwa Publishing Company, 1977.

a) Tradition: Women During the Yi Dynasty (M. Deuchler), 1-48; b) Korean Proverbs about Women (H.R. Tieszen), 49-66; c) Women Surviving: Palace Life in Seoul after the Annexation (E. Salem), 67-98; d) Women's Modernization Movement in Korea (P. Yong-Ock), 99-112; e) Boy Preference Reflected in Korean Folklore (C. Jae-Ho, C. Bom-Mo, L. Sung-Jin), 113-128; f) Psychological Problems among Korean Women (R. Bou-Yong), 129-146; g) Status of Korean Women Today (L. Hyo-Chae, K. Chu-Suk), 147-156; h) Role of Korean Women in National Development (S.Y.S. Yoon), 157-168; i) Interviews with Young Working Women in Seoul (B.R. Mintz), 169-190; j) Occupations, Male Housekeeper: Male-Female Roles on Cheju Island (S.Y.S. Yoon), 191-208.

237 VOICES FROM WOMEN'S LIBERATION. Leslie Barbara Tanner, comp. New York: New American Library, 1971, c1970.

Articles written by contemporary women involved in the women's liberation movement are published here with selected writings of earlier feminists. The introduction is reprinted from "The History of Woman Suffrage" (1881). Contributors: A. Adams, M. Wollstonecraft, S.M. Grimke, E.C. Stanton, S.B. Anthony, E. Blackwell, E. Collins, F. Wright, L. Mott, J.E. Jones, M.U. Ferrin, P.W. Davis, F.D. Gage, H. Martineau, M. Haskell, E. Rose, H.K. Hunt, E.O. Smith, M.J. Gage, M. Johnson, A. Preston, S. Truth, A.K. Foster, L. Stone, A.G. Weld, J.E. Smith, A.H. Smith, A.S. Duniway, A.S. Blackwell, L. Clay, C.C. Catt, L. Harris, G. Laughlin, E.S. Tillinghast, H.M. Mills, F. Kelley, E. Leo, C. Hanisch, K. Amatniek, S.M. Wood, K. Sarachild, A. Koedt, D.A. Pappas, E. Reed, L. Gordon, R. Van Lew, V. Pollard, L. Gross, P. MacEwan, C. Driscoll, A. Harris, N. Rainone, P. Charney, J. Stein, P. Marcus, J. Gardner, I. Peslikis, E. Leo, B. Susan, B. Warrior, R. Moon, L.B. Tanner, S. Pascale, D. Densmore, R. Morgan, M. Benston, B. Balogun (Jackson), N. Weisstein, M.A. Weathers, E. Willis, R. Dunbar, L. Leghorn, P. Haden, D. Middleton, P. Robinson, D. Narek, R. Gootblatt, P. Mainardi, S. Firestone, M. Shelley, L. Hart, B. Jones, J. Brown, K. McAfee, M. Wood.

238 VOICES OF THE NEW FEMINISM. Mary Lou Thompson, ed. Boston: Beacon Press, 1970.

a) Pioneers of Women's Liberation (J. Cowley), 3-28; b) Our Revolution Is Unique (B. Friedan), 31-43; c) Female Liberation as the Basis for Social Revolution (R. Dunbar), 44-58; d) Sex Equality: The Beginnings of Ideology (A.S. Rossi), 59-74; e) Women as a Minority Group (E.D. Koontz), 77-86; f) Liberation of Black Women (P. Murray), 87-102; g) Women and Legislation (M. Griffiths), 103-114; h) Educational Establishment: Wasted Women (D.L. Pullen), 115-135; i) Toward Partnership in the Church (M. Daly), 136-152; j) Status of Women in Sweden (U.N.), 155-177; k) Androgynous Life (C. Bird), 178-198; l) Forecast for Feminism (M.L. Thompson), 201-206; m) Women Must Rebel

(S. Chisholm), 207-216; n) Women: A Bibliography (L. Cisler), 217-

239 WE BECOME NEW: POEMS BY CONTEMPORARY AMERICAN WOMEN. Lucille Iverson and Kathryn Ruby, eds. New York: Bantam Books, 1975.

This anthology of poetry by forty-three women includes both established and little-known artists. Their work reflects "a range of feminist attitudes and feelings," supposedly indicative of a trend toward concern for the personal among contemporary American women. Contributors: M. Piercy, S. Sanchez, D. Gioseffi, J. McCombs, A. Sexton, A. Walker, H. Moore, C. Kizer, A.H. Brady, K. Fraser, L. Iverson, M. Kumin, F. Winant, J. Grahn, K. Swenson, D. Levertov, R. Daniell, R. Owens, A. Rich, R.M. Brown, R. Herschberger, K. Ruby, J. Jordan, M. Rukeyser, Yvonne, R. Ratner, A. Darr, C. Inez, B.A. Holland, M. Wallace, R. Morgan, M. Sanders, J. Mayhall, J. Braxton, O. Cabral, M. Shelley, J.J. Sherwin, A. Lorde, M. Bass, S.F. Schaeffer, E. Jong, E. Sargent, C. Macdonald.

240 WHAT MANNER OF WOMAN: ESSAYS ON ENGLISH AND AMERICAN LIFE AND LITERATURE. Marlene Springer, ed. (The Gotham Library) New York: New York University Press, 1977.

a) Portrayal of Women by Chaucer and His Age (A.S. Haskell), 1-14; b) Changing Image of Woman in Renaissance Society and Literature (C.M. Dunn), 15-38; c) Praising Virtuous Ladies: The Literary Image and Historical Reality of Women in Seventeenth-century England (D.J. Latt), 39-64; d) Portrayal of Women in Restoration and Eighteenth-century English Literature (J.J. Richetti), 65-97; e) Gender and Genre: Women in British Romantic Literature (I. Tayler, G. Luria), 98-123; f) Angels and Other Women in Victorian Literature (M. Springer), 124-159; g) Marriage Perceived: English Literature, 1873-1941 (C.G. Heilbrun), 160-184; h) Images of Women in Early American Literature (A. Stanford), 185-210; i) Portrayal of Women in American Literature, 1790-1870 (N. Baym), 211-234; j) They Shall Have Faces, Minds, and (One Day) Flesh: Women in Late Nineteenth-century and Early Twentieth-century American Literature (M. Banta), 235-270; k) "Combat in the Erogenous Zone": Women in the American Novel between the Two World Wars (J.W. Tuttleton), 271-296; l) Second-class Citizenship: The Status of Women in Contemporary American Fiction (M. Masinton, C.G. Masinton), 297-315; m) "Free in Fact and at Last": The Image of the Black Woman in Black American Literature (E. Schultz), 316- .

241 WHEN WOME RULE. Samuel Moskowitz, comp. New York: Walker, 1972.

a) When Women Rule (S. Moskowitz), 1-27; b) The Amazons (Herodotus), 28-30; c) The Queen of California (G. Ordonez de Mantalvo), 31-61; d) The Revolt of the ___ (R. Barr), 62-71; e) June 6, 2016 (G.A. England), 72-94; f) The Veiled Feminists of Atlantis (B. Tarkington), 95-103; g) The Last Man (W.G. West), 104-130; h) The Last Woman (T.S. Gardner), 131-148; i) The Feminine Metamorphosis (D.H. Keller), 149-197; j) The

Priestess Who Rebelled (N.S. Bond), 198- .

242 WHO AM I THIS TIME? FEMALE PORTRAITS IN BRITISH AND AMERICAN LITERATURE. Carol Pearson and Katherine Pope, eds. New York: McGraw-Hill, 1976.

This collection of British and American literature provides a basis for a typology of female literary characters. Such a scheme is meant to aid in understanding literature, myth and social roles. Both male and female writers are included. Arrangement is according to portrait type: Heroine (virgin, mistress and helpmate) and Hero (sage, artist and warrior). Contributors: P. Sidney, E. Spenser, A. Marvell, M. Cavendish, J. Dryden, J. Edwards, P. Wheatley, W. Blake, J. Keats, A. Brontë, M.E. Coleridge, W. Faulkner, A. Boleyn, W. Raleigh, W. Shakespeare, T. Campion, E. Waller, A. Behn, M.W. Montagu, A. Pope, J. Swift, O. Goldsmith, R. Burns, E.A. Poe, N. Hawthorne, E. Dickinson, D.G. Rossetti, O. Wilde, E.St.V. Millay, J. Toomer, T.S. Eliot, H. James, M. Rukeyser, G. Chaucer, J. Donne, E. Carey, J. Milton, A. Bradstreet, A. Finch, A. Barnard, R. Browning, G. Meredith, C.G. Rossetti, K. Chopin, A. Meynell, R. Frost, C. Mew, D. Laing, D. Levertov, Alurista, R. Speght, M. Lee, C.P. Gilman, T. Hardy, W.B. Yeats, D. West, P.B. Shelley, Alfred, Lord Tennyson, E.B. Browning, R.T. Cooke, A.C. Swinburne, M. Freeman, V. Woolf, W. Stevens, W. Congreve, W. Shenstone, B. Franklin, T. Gray, E. Bronte, T. Hood, M. Shelley, W. Whitman, M.W. Fordham, M. Twain, E. Welty, M. Walker, P. Roche, J. Tepperman.

243 WHO DISCRIMINATES AGAINST WOMEN? Florence Denmark, ed. Beverly Hills: Sage, 1974.

a) Prejudice of Parents (E. Mintz), 9-23; b) Women Who Discriminate Against Other Women: The Process of Denial (M.G. Keiffer, D.M. Cullen), 24-36; c) Male Attitudes Toward Women's Rights as a Function of Their Level of Self-Esteem (T.W. Miller), 37-46; d) Men Who Discriminate Against Women (B.B. Wolman), 47-54; e) Prejudice Toward Women: Some Personality Correlates (P.A. Goldberg), 55-66; f) Discrimination Against Aspiring Women (R. Starer, F. Denmark), 67-72; g) Are Women a "Minority" Group? Sometimes! (R.K. Unger, B.J. Raymond, S.M. Levine), 73-83; h) Institutional Discrimination: The Case of Achievement-Oriented Women in Higher Education (M. Groszko, R. Morgenstern), 84-94; i) Status of Women in Psychology: How Many and How Come? (R.M. Fields), 95-123; j) Women as a Minority Group: Twenty Years Later (H.M. Hacker), 124-134; k) Who Discriminates Against Women? (L. Marlowe), 135- .

244 A WIDENING SPHERE: CHANGING ROLES OF VICTORIAN WOMEN. Martha Vicinus, ed. Bloomington: Indiana University Press, 1977.

a) Victorian Wives and Property: Reform of the Married Women's Property Law, 1857-1882 (L. Holcombe), 3-28; b) Forgotten Woman of the Period: Penny Weekly Family Magazines of the 1840's and 1850's (S. Mitchell),

29-51; c) Feminism and Female Emigration, 1861-1886 (A.J. Hammerton), 52-71; d) Making of an Outcast Group: Prostitutes and Working Women in Nineteenth-Century Plymouth and Southampton (J. Walkowitz), 72-93; e) Image and Reality: The Actress and Society (C. Kent), 94-116; f) Women and Degrees at Cambridge University, 1862-1897 (R. McWilliams-Tulberg), 117-145; g) Victorian Masculinity and the Angel in the House (C. Christ), 146-162; h) Sex and Death in Victorian England: An Examination of Age- and Sex-Specific Death Rates, 1840-1910 (S.R. Johansson), 163-181; i) Sexuality in Britain, 1800-1900: Some Suggested Revisions (F.B. Smith), 182-198; j) Women of England in a Century of Social Change, 1815-1914: A Select Bibliography, Part II (B. Kanner), 199-270.

245 WOMAN: AN AFFIRMATION. Alice Fannin, Rebecca Lukens, Catherine Mann and Margaret Parish, eds. Lexington, Ma.: D.C. Heath, 1979.

Prose narratives, poetry, drama, folk tales and short stories are grouped thematically in this collection to depict women in positive ways. Contributors: S. Truth, L. Hellman, M. Angelou, J. Didion, F. Howe, G. Paley, V. Woolf, K.A. Porter, S.O. Jewett, J. Stafford, J. Reeves, J. Tepperman, A. Lorde, N. Giovanni, O. Cabral, M. Rukeyser, K. Fraser, S. Glaspell, I. Dinesen, W. Cather, D. Betts, N. Gordimer, A. Walker, G. Oden, E.St.V. Millay, B. Eve, A. Rich, L. Pastan, H. Sorrells, S. Griffin, E. Wylie, D. Wakoski, T. Hardy, E. Dickinson, H. Calisher, T.C. Bambara, M.W. Freeman, M. Lavin, D. Levertov, M. Kumin, L. Clifton, E. Jong, B. Deutsch, B. Spacks, A. Behn, M. Atwood, E.B. Browning, M. Evans, E. Bagnold, D. Lessing, J. Greenberg, Ting Ling, L. Lifshin, C. Fein, M. Moore, M. Johansson, A. Stanford, E. Glasgow, M. Laurence, Colette, J. Garrigue, T. Roethke, C. Short, U.K. Le Guin.

246 WOMAN AND PUBLIC POLICY: A HUMANISTIC PERSPECTIVE. Mildred H. Lavin and Clara H. Oleson, eds. Iowa City: Institute of Public Affairs, University of Iowa, 1974.

a) Radical and Conservative Trends in the Women's Rights Movement (L.R. Noun), 3-10; b) Changing Status of Women in the Law (C.H. Albright), 11-24; c) Socialization of Women in Educational Institutions: Resultant Effects (C.H. Foxley), 25-34; d) Myth America: Women in American Literature (panel) (P. Addis, L.S. Cannon, R. Cannon), 35-46; e) Female Dimension in the Image of God: A Christian Perspective (P. Wilson), 47-56; f) Place of Contemporary Women from a Psychological Perspective (M. Jeffers), 57-62; g) Psychotherapy for Women: Myths and Legacies (D.K. Carter), 63-74; h) Proposed Model for Examining Sex Discrimination in Education (J.W. McLure), 75-84; i) Women in the Economic Sphere: The Coming Struggle for Jobs (A. Costantino), 85-94; j) Women in History: Public Life and Historical Consciousness (S.H. Madden), 95-102; k) Language of Sexism (M.B. McDowell), 103-118; l) American Character vs. The Ideal Woman (V.M. Kouidis), 119-126; m) Images of Women and Men in American Popular Magazines (M.D. Frenier, 127-134; n) Sociological Examination of the Women's Movement

(G. Sehested), 135-142.

247 WOMAN AS SEX OBJECT: STUDIES IN EROTIC ART, 1730-1970. Thomas B. Hess and Linda Nochlin, eds. New York: Newsweek, 1972.

a) Eroticism and Female Imagery in Nineteenth-Century Art (L. Nochlin), 8-15; b) Ingres and the Erotic Intellect (J.L. Connolly, Jr.), 16-31; c) Henry Fuseli's "Nightmare": Eroticism or Pornography? (M. Allentuck), 32-41; d) Caritas Romana after 1760: Some Romantic Lactations (R. Rosenblum), 42-63; e) Courbet's "Baigneuses" and the Rhetorical Feminine Image (B. Farwell), 64-79; f) Manet, "Olympia" and Pornographic Photography (G. Needham), 80-89; g) Corset as Erotic Alchemy: From Rococo Galanterie to Montaut's Physiologies (D. Kunzle), 90-165; h) Renoir's Sensuous Women (B.E. White), 166-181; i) Femme Fatale and Her Sisters (M. Kingsbury), 182-205; j) Vampires, Virgins and Voyeurs in Imperial Vienna (A. Comini), 206-221; k) Pinup and Icon (T.B. Hess), 222-237; l) Picasso's Suite 347, or Painting as an Act of Love (G. Schiff), 238- .

248 WOMAN AS WRITER. Jeanettte Webber and Joan Grumman, eds. Boston: Houghton Mifflin, 1978.

This anthology is divided into two sections: commentary by women writers about their craft and selections from the work of the same authors. The design is intended to explore the creative process. Most authors are twentieth-century Americans. Contributors: V. Woolf, K. Mansfield, Z. Fitzgerald, E. Welty, A. Nin, M. McCarthy, M. Rukeyser, T. Olsen, C. McCullers, G. Brooks, D. Lessing, D. Levertov, C. Kizer, F. O'Connor, C. Ozick, A. Sexton, M. Angelou, A. Rich, M. Lamb, A. Kennedy, S. Plath, J. Didion, D. Johnson, J, Russ, D. Wakoski, J.C. Oates, M. Atwood, E. Jong, N. Giovanni, A. Walker, Marie-Elise.

249 WOMAN, CULTURE AND SOCIETY. Michelle Zimbalist Rosaldo and Louise Lamphere, eds. Stanford: Stanford University Press, 1974.

a) Woman, Culture, and Society: A Theoretical Overview (M.Z. Rosaldo), 17-42; b) Family Structure and Feminine Personality (N. Chodorow), 43-66; c) Is Female to Male as Nature Is to Culture? (S.B. Ortner), 67-88; d) Women in Politics (J.F. Collier), 89-96; e) Strategies, Cooperation, and Conflict Among Women in Domestic Groups (L. Lamphere), 97-112; f) Sex Roles and Survival Strategies in an Urban Black Community (C.B. Stack), 113-128; g) Matrifocality in Indonesia and Africa and Among Black Americans (N. Tanner), 129-156; h) Chinese Women: Old Skills in a New Context (M. Wolf), 157-172; i) Madam Yoko: Ruler of the Kpa Mende Confederacy (C.P. Hoffer), 173-188; j) Female Status in the Public Domain (P.R. Sanday), 189-206; k) Engels Revisited: Women, the Organization of Production, and Private Property (K. Sacks), 207-222; l) Women in Groups: Ijaw Women's Associations (N.B. Leis), 223-242; m) Sex and Power in the Balkans (B.S. Denich), 243-262; n) Myth of Matriarchy: Why Men Rule in Primitive Society (J. Bamberger), 263-280; o) Mastery of Work and the Mystery of Sex in a

Guatemalan Village (L. Paul), 281-300; p) Mediation of Contradiction: Why Mbum Women Do Not Eat Chicken (B. O'Laughlin), 301- .

250 WOMAN: DEPENDENT OR INDEPENDANT VARIABLE? Rhoda Kesler Unger and Florence L. Denmark, eds. New York: Psychological Dimensions, 1975.

a) Stereotype of Femininity (V. Klein), 19-30; b) Evaluation of the Performance of Women as a Function of Their Sex, Achievement, and Personal History (G.I. Phetersen, S.B. Kiesler, P.A. Goldberg), 31-40; c) Female Roles in Women's Magazine Fiction, 1940-1970 (H.H. Franzwa), 41-54; d) Male and Female in Children's Books (M.R. Key), 55-70; e) Male-Female Perception of the Female Sex Role in the United States (A. Steinmann, D.J. Fox), 71-84; f) Women as a Minority Group (H.M. Hacker), 85-102; g) Women as a Minority Group: Some Twenty Years Later (H.M. Hacker), 103-116; h) Psychological Consequences of the Anatomic Distinction Between the Sexes (S. Freud), 127-136; i) Women as Psychiatric and Psychotherapeutic Patients (P. Chessler), 137-162; j) Sex-Role Stereotypes and Clinical Judgments of Mental Health (I.K. Broverman, D.M. Broverman, F.E. Clarkson, P.S. Rosenkrantz, S.R. Vogel), 163-176; k) Between Men and Women (B.B. Wolman), 177-194; l) Women in Rage: A Psychological Look at the Helpless Heroine (J. Mundy), 195-216; m) Sex Differences in the Development of Masculine and Feminine Identification (D.B. Lynn), 231-246; n) Parents' Differential Reactions to Sons and Daughters (M.K. Rothbart, E.E. Maccoby), 247-262; o) Developmental Study of the Effects of Sex of the Dominant Parent on Sex-Role Preference, Identification, and Imitation in Children (E.M. Hetherington), 263-274; p) Woman's Role in Cross-Cultural Perspective (C.J. Weithorn), 275-296; q) Roles of Activation and Inhibition in Sex Differences in Cognitive Abilities (D.M. Broverman, E.L. Klaiber, Y. Kobayashi, W. Vogel), 311-354; r) Comments on "Roles of Activation and Inhibition in Sex Differences in Cognitive Abilities" (M.B. Parlee), 355-366; s) Parental Education, Sex Differences, and Performance on Cognitive Tasks Among Two-Year-Old Children (N.D. Reppucci), 367-378; t) Sex Differences in Space Perception and Aspects of Intellectual Functioning (J.A. Sherman), 379-394; u) Pattern Copying Under Three Conditions of an Expanded Spatial Field (B.K. Keogh), 395-408; v) Effects of Sex of Examiner and Subject on Children's Quantitative Test Performance (D.M. Pedersen, M.M. Shinedling, D.L. Johnson), 409-416; w) Social Factors Influencing Problem Solving in Women (L.R. Hoffman, N.R.F. Maier), 417-434; x) Early Hormonal Influences on the Development of Sexual and Sex- Related Behaviors (R.W. Goy), 447-472; y) Sexual Dimorphic Behavior, Normal and Abnormal (J. Money), 473-486; z) Attachment Differences in Male and Female Infant Monkeys (G.D. Mitchell), 487-500; aa) Hormonal Interaction, Menstruation, and the Oral Contraceptives (M. Garcia), 509-528; bb) Influences of Mother's Menstruation on Her Child (K. Dalton), 529- 536; cc) Patterns of Affective Fluctuation in the Menstrual Cycle (M.E. Ivey, J.M. Bardwick), 537-552; dd) Effects of Oral Contraceptives on Affective Fluctuations Associated with the Menstrual Cycle (K.E. Paige), 553-590; ee) Psychoendocrine Study of Pregnancy and Puerperium (C.R. Treadway, F.J. Kane, Jr., A. Jarrahi-Zadeh, M.A. Lipton), 591-604; ff) Postpartum Psychiatric Syndromes (F.T. Melges), 605-626; gg) Case for Human Cycles (R.K. Unger), 627-632; hh) Sex Differences in Expectancy of

Intellectual and Academic Reinforcement (V.C. Crandall), 649-686; ii) Experimental Arousal of Achievement Motivation in Adolescent Girls (G.S. Lesser, R.N. Krawitz, R. Packard), 687-702; jj) Achievement-Related Conflicts in Women (M.S. Horner), 703-722; kk) Early Childhood Experiences and Women's Achievement Motives (L.W. Hoffman), 723-750; ll) Encountering the Male Establishment: Sex Status Limits on Woman's Careers in the Professions (C.F. Epstein), 751-772; mm) Empirical Verification of Sex Discrimination in Hiring Practices in Psychology (L.S. Fidell), 773-786; nn) Female Sexual Behavior (F.L. Denmark), 787-795.

251 WOMAN IN A MAN-MADE WORLD: A SOCIOECONOMIC HANDBOOK. 2nd ed. Nona Glazer and Helen Youngelson Waehrer, eds. Chicago: Rand McNally, 1977.

a) Implications of a Sociology for Women (D.E. Smith), 15-29; b) Economics, Sex, and Gender (C.S. Bell), 30-38; c) Capitalism, the Family, and Personal Life (E. Zaretsky), 55-70; d) Capitalism, Patriarchy, and Job Segregation by Sex (H. Hartmann), 71-84; e) Changing Economic Role of Women (Manpower Rpt.), 85-98; f) Assumptions About Gender Role (D.E. Tresemer), 114-127; g) Division of Labor by Sex (J.K. Brown), 128-136; h) Woman (sic) as a Minority Group (H.M. Hacker), 137-147; i) Origins of the Status of Women (F. Engels), 148-155; j) Anthropologist Looks at Engels (K. Gough), 156-168; k) Women: The Longest Revolution (J. Mitchell), 169-179; l) Labor Force Participation of Married Women (J. Mincer), 189-193; m) Sex Segregation in the Labor Market (F.D. Blau, C.L. Jusenius), 194-207; n) Labor Market Segmentation (M. Reich, D.M. Gordon, R.C. Edwards), 208-215; o) Political Economy of Women's Liberation (M. Benston), 216-226; p) Sex Roles and Family Structure (T. Parsons), 234-238; q) Task and Emotional Behavior in the Marital Dyad (A.E. Craddock), 239-247; r) Sex Role Differentiation (J. Aronoff, W.D. Crano), 248-255; s) Marriage and the Construction of Reality (P. Berger, H. Kellner), 262-271; t) Family Life in an Antifamily Setting (R. Feldberg, J. Kohen), 272- 278; u) Myth of Black Matriarchy (K.T. Dietrich), 279-286; v) Legal Equality in Marriage (L.J. Weitzman), 287-301; w) Differences in Hourly Earnings Between Men and Women (V. Fuchs), 307-312; x) Differences in Return to Educational Investment (A. Niemi, Jr.), 313-319; y) Supply and Demand for Women Workers (R. Gubbels), 320-331; z) Sex Bias and Cyclical Unemployment (B.M. Gray), 332-334; aa) Disadvantaged Status of Black Women (E. Almquist), 335-344; bb) Social Situation of Divorced Mothers and Their Families (R.A. Brandwein, C.A. Brown, E.M. Fox), 350-359; cc) Housework (N. Glazer), 360-369; dd) Sex Discrimination in the Universities (L. Bienen, A. Ostriker, J.P. Ostriker), 370-377; ee) Women and Wealth (R. Lampman), 378-380; ff) Women's Contribution to Family Income (Women's Bureau), 381-386; gg) Have Swedish Women Achieved Equality? (N.S. Barrett), 394-399; hh) Chinese Family Revolution and Feminist Theory (J. Stacey), 400-414; ii) Family Structure and Communism (M. Vajda, A. Heller), 415-426.

252 WOMAN IN A MAN-MADE WORLD: A SOCIOECONOMIC HANDBOOK. Nona Glazer-Malbin and Helen Youngelson Waehrer, eds. (Rand McNally Sociology Series) Chicago: Rand McNally, 1972.

a) Family and Cultural Change (B.J. Stern), 13-16; b) Family Patterns and Human Rights (W.J. Goode), 17-22; c) Women Workers and the Industrial Revolution (I. Pinchbeck), 23-29; d) Changes in the Labor Force Activity of Women (E. Waldman), 30-38; e) Women as a Minority Group (H.M. Hacker), 39-44; f) Women: The Longest Revolution (J. Mitchell), 45-52; g) Psychology of Women: Biology as Destiny (S. Freud), 58-61; h) Female Sexuality and Psychoanalytic Theory (M.J. Sherfey), 62-67; i) Changing Patterns of Femininity and Masculinity (J. Marmor), 68-73; j) Dread of Woman (K. Horney), 74-78; k) Personal Identity and Sexual Identity (M.B. Cohen), 79-88; l) Sex Differences in Identification Development (D.B. Lynn), 89-95; m) Stigma and Social Identity (E. Goffman), 96-99; n) Origins of the Status of Women (F. Engels), 100-106; o) Anthropologist Looks at Engels (K. Gough), 107-118; p) Political Economy of Women's Liberation (M. Benston), 119-128; q) Sex-Role Differentiation in an Equalitarian Society (Y. Talmon), 142-156; r) Task and Social Behavior in Marriage (G. Levinger), 157-163; s) Durkheim on Women (B.D. Johnson), 164-167; t) Feminine Role and the Kinship System (T. Parsons), 168-173; u) Marriage and the Construction of Reality (P. Berger, H. Kellner), 174-182; v) Problems of Married Working Women as Presented by Three Popular Working Women's Magazines (M.G. Hatch, D.L. Hatch), 183-186; w) Monetary Value of a Housewife (Chong Soo Pyun), 187-193; x) Working Wives: Their Contribution to Family Income (U.S. Dept. of Labor), 194-197; y) Labor Participation of Married Women: A Study of Labor Supply (J. Mincer), 198-202; z) Marriage and Motherhood of Black Women Graduates (J.H. Fichter), 203-207; aa) Supply and Demand for Women Workers (R. Gubbels), 208-218; bb) Counselor Bias and the Female Occupational Role (J.J. Pietrofesa, N.K. Schlossberg), 219-221; cc) Differences in Hourly Earnings Between Men and Women (V.R. Fuchs), 222-227; dd) Social and Private Rates of Return to Investment in Schooling (F. Hines, L. Tweeten, M. Redfern), 228-234; ee) Sex Bias and Cyclical Unemployment (B.M. Gray), 235-237; ff) Reducing Discrimination: Role of the Equal Pay Act (R.D. Moran), 238-244; gg) Men and Women in Community Agencies: A Note on Power and Prestige (N. Babchuk, R. Massey, C.W. Gordon), 248-253; hh) Economic Status of Families Headed by Women (R.L. Stein), 254-264; ii) Women's Absenteeism and Labor Turnover (U.S. Dept. of Labor), 265- 271; jj) Women and Wealth (R.J. Lampman), 272-274; kk) Platform on Women's Rights (New Democratic Coalition), 280-286; ll) Sexual Politics: A Manifesto for Revolution (K. Millett), 287-288; mm) Politics of Housework (P. Mainardi), 289-291; nn) Family Structure and Communism (M. Vajda, A. Heller), 292-304.

253 THE WOMAN IN AMERICA. Robert Jay Lifton, ed. Boston: Houghton Mifflin, 1965.

a) Inner and Outer Space: Reflections on Womanhood (E.H. Erikson), 1-26; b) Woman as Knower: Some Psychohistorical Perspectives (R.J. Lifton), 27-51; c) Image of Women in Contemporary Literature (D. Trilling), 52-71; d) Two Generations (D. Riesman), 72-97; e) Equality Between the Sexes: An Immodest Proposal (A.S. Rossi), 98-143; f) Working Women (E. Peterson), 144-172; g) Wanted: A New Self-Image for Women (D.C. McClelland), 173-192; h) Revolution Without Ideology: The Changing Place of Women in America (C.N. Degler), 193-210; i) Conflict and Accommodation (E.G. Rostow), 211-235; j) Role of Choice in

the Psychology of Professional Women (L. Bailyn), 236-246; k) Jane Addams: An American Heroine (J. Conway), 247-266; l) Nothing to Fear: Notes on the Life of Eleanor Roosevelt (J.M. Erikson), 267-287.

254 WOMAN IN SEXIST SOCIETY: STUDIES IN POWER AND POWERLESSNESS. Vivan Gornick and Barbara K. Moran, eds. and comps. New York: Basic Books, 1971.

a) "Pretty" (Alta), 3; b) Two Plays on Love and Marriage (M. Lamb), 4-20; c) Prostitution: A Quartet for Female Voices (K. Millett), 21-69; d) Woman as Outsider (V. Gornick), 70-84; e) Paradox of the Happy Marriage (J. Bernard), 85-98; f) Depression in Middle-Aged Women (P.B. Bart), 99-117; g) Mask of Beauty (U. Stannard), 118-132; h) Psychology Constructs the Female (N. Weisstein), 133-146; i) Ambivalence: The Socialization of Women (J.M. Bardwick, E. Douvan), 147-159; j) Natural Law Language and Women (C. Pierce), 160-172; k) Being and Doing: A Cross-Cultural Examination of the Socialization of Males and Females (N. Chodorow), 173-197; l) Organs and Orgasms (A. Shulman), 198-206; m) Image of Woman in Advertising (L. Komisar), 207-217; n) Image of Woman in Textbooks (M.B. U'Ren), 218-225; o) Seduced and Abandoned in the New World: The Image of Woman In American Fiction (W. Martin), 226-239; p) Our Sexist Language (E. Strainchamps), 240-250; q) Patient and Patriarch: Women in the Psychotherapeutic Relationship (P. Chesler), 251-275; r) Women in Other Cultures (R.R. Leavitt), 276-306; s) Women and Creativity: The Demise of the Dancing Dog (C. Ozick), 307-322; t) Women Writers and the Double Standard (E. Showalter), 323-343; u) Why Are There No Great Women Artists? (L. Nochlin), 344-366; v) Working in "A Man's World": The Woman Executive (R.S. Willett), 367-383; w) Women and Voluntarism (D.B. Gold), 384-400; x) Compassion Trap (M. Adams), 401-418; y) Our Failures Only Marry: Bryn Mawr and the Failure of Feminism (L. Schneider), 419-435; z) Is Women's Liberation a Lesbian Plot? (S. Abbott, B. Love), 436-452; aa) Women's Liberation and Black Civil Rights (C. Stimpson), 453-479; bb) Consumerism and Women (Redstockings), 480-484; cc) American Feminism (S. Firestone), 485-502.

255 WOMAN IN THE 18th CENTURY AND OTHER ESSAYS. Paul Fritz and Richard Morton, eds. Toronto, Ontario: Samuel Stevens Hakkert, 1976.

a) Feminism of Daniel Defoe (K. Rogers), 3-24; b) Astraea's "Vacant Throne": The Successors of Aphra Behn (F.P. Lock), 25-36; c) Woman's Concept of Self in the Eighteenth Century (M.J. Benkovitz), 37-54; d) Women and Literature in Eighteenth Century England (R. Halsband), 55-72; e) Eighteenth-Century Englishwoman: According to the Gentleman's Magazine (J.E. Hunter), 73-88; f) "Treated Like Imbecile Children" (Diderot): The Enlightenment and the Status of Women (A.M. Wilson), 89-104; g) La Condition de la Femme Francaise au Dix-huitieme Siecle d'apres les Romans (M.L. Swiderski), 105-126; h) Rousseau's Sexism

Revolutionized (R. Graham), 127- .

256 WOMAN IN THE YEAR 2000. Maggie Tripp, ed. New York: Arbor House, 1974.

a) Whatever Will Become of Me? Glancing Backward, Looking at Today and Thinking About Tomorrow (M. Tripp), xiii- ; b) Born Free: A Feminist Fable (L.C. Pogrebin), 1-24; c) Female Facade: Fierce, Fragile and Fading (J. Trahey), 25-37; d) No More Sapphires or Black Pearls: Self-definition is Where It Starts (I. Turner, D. Robinson, D. Singletary, M. Jefferson), 38-49; e) Child Rearing: 2000 AD (G. Steinem), 50-51; f) Free Married Woman: A New Style of Living in an Old Institution (M. Tripp), 52-70; g) Fractured Family (A. Toffler), 71-88; h) Femininity: 2000 (C. Rinzler), 89-98; i) Wages of Wrath: Women's Relationships in the Working World (N. Sayre), 99-106; j) Impact of Mid-twentieth Century Movement for Sex Equality in Employment on Three Contemporary Economic Institutions (C. Bird), 107-127; k) Women in the Arts: Insights to the Cultural Impact of Women's Role in the Creative Arts (compendium), 128-140; l) Chief Justice Wore a Red Dress (D. Sassower), 141-154; m) What Women Will Do in Medicine and What Medicine Will Do for Women (R. Cherry) 155-163; n) Social Sex: The New Single Standard for Men and Women (R. Francoeur, A. Francoeur), 164-178; o) Degree in Enlightenment: When a Woman's Education Will No Longer Be an Academic Question (C. Rosenthal), 179-194; p) When The Veils Come Tumbling Down: "And Women Shall Leave Their Comfortable Pews to Give Birth to a New and Inclusive Religious Vision" (S. Collins), 195-221; q) Women in Motion: It's Not Who Wins Or Loses, But How Many Play the Game (L. Franks), 222-236; r) When Women in Politics Are Old Hat (B. Abzug interviewed by M. Kelber), 237-248; s) Genderless Sexuality: A Male-Female Psychological Exploration of the Future of Sexual Relationships (L. Karp, R. Mandis), 249-269; t) Changing Woman's Thinking and Lifestyle Through the Great Communication Revolution (D. Saperstein), 270-280; u) X: A Fabulous Child's Story (L. Gould), 281-290; v) Transhumans--2000 (F.M. Esfandiary), 291-298.

257 THE WOMAN MOVEMENT: FEMINISM IN THE UNITED STATES AND ENGLAND. William O'Neill, ed. Chicago: Quadrangle Books, 1971, c1969.

a) Introductory (W. O'Neill), 13-102; b) Duties of Women, 103-107; c) Declaration of Sentiments, Resolutions, Seneca Falls, 108-111; d) Marriage of Lucy Stone Under Protest, 112-113; e) Bloomer Costume (E.C. Stanton), 114-115; f) Who Are Our Friends? (E.C. Stanton), 116-118; g) Slave-Women of America (L.C. Bullard), 119-121; h) (Speech, National Woman's Suffrage Association, 1889) (O. Brown), 122-123; i) Patriotism and Chastity (E.C. Stanton), 124-128; j) Home (C.P. Gilman), 129-132; k) Declaration of Principles (Nat'l. American Woman Suffrage Association), 133-135; l) Strikes and Their Causes (H.M. Winslow), 136-141; m) Woman's Clubs from a Reporter's Point of View (J. Woodward), 142-147; n) Work of the Woman's Club (M.E.D. White), 148-157; o) Woman's Mission and Woman's Clubs (G. Cleveland), 158-163; p) Russia (M. Antin), 164-167; q) Present Tendencies in Women's College and University Education (M.C. Thomas), 168-171; r) Class-Consciousness (V. Scudder), 172-182; s) (Remarks,

National American Woman's Suffrage Association) A.H. Shaw, 183-184; t) Modern Industry and Morality (F. Kelley), 185-187; u) Editorial (General Federation of Women's Clubs. MAGAZINE), 188-189; v) John Hay, Mrs. Catt and Patriotism (C.C. Catt), 190-195; w) Meaning of Progress in the Woman Movement (E.P. Howes), 196-204.

258 WOMAN: NEW DIMENSIONS. Walter J. Burghardt, ed. New York: Paulist Press, 1977, c1975.

a) Current Status of Women Cross-Culturally: Changes and Persisting Barriers (C. Safilios-Rothschild), 1-28; b) Feminist Theology as a Critical Theory of Liberation (E.S. Fiorenza), 29-50; c) New Patterns of Relationship: Beginnings of a Moral Revolution (M.A. Farley), 51-70; d) Home and Work: Women's Roles and the Transformation of Values (R.R. Ruether), 71-83; e) Women and Ministry (E. Carroll), 84-111; f) Roles of Women in the Fourth Gospel (R.E. Brown), 112-123; g) Sexist Language in Theology? (G.H. Tavard), 124-148; h) Renewed Anthropology (M.A. O'Neill), 149-160; i) Women and Religion: A Survey of Significant Literature, 1965-1974 (A.E. Patrick), 161- .

THE WOMAN PATIENT: MEDICAL AND PSYCHOLOGICAL INTERFACES. See: 211 SEXUAL AND REPRODUCTIVE ASPECTS OF WOMEN'S HEALTH CARE

259 THE WOMAN QUESTION IN AMERICAN HISTORY. Barbara Welter, comp. Hinsdale, Il.: The Dryden Press, 1973.

a) American Indian Women (W. O'Meara), 13-21; b) Eighteenth Century Women (M.S. Benson), 22-34; c) Frontier Women (E.R. Groves), 35-43; d) Black Women in Bondage (E.F. Frazier), 44-57; e) Ante-Bellum Southern Women (W.R. Taylor), 58-64; f) Ladies, Not Women (A. Sinclair), 65-72; g) Rights of Women (A.F. Tyler), 75-82; h) Ideology of the Suffrage Movement (A.S. Kraditor), 83-92; i) Patterns of Nineteenth Century Feminism (R.E. Riegel), 93-105; j) Enemies of Suffrage (E. Flexner), 106-114; k) American Women and the American Character (D.M. Potter), 117-132; l) Changing Place of Women in America (C.N. Degler), 133-146; m) Woman as Alien (C. Lasch), 147-154; n) Liberally Educated Woman (P. McGinley), 155-161; o) Politics of Sex (K. Millett), 162-171.

260 WOMANKIND: BEYOND THE STEREOTYPES. Nancy Reeves, comp. Chicago: Aldine, Atherton, 1971.

a) ...How Ischomachus Trained His Wife (Xenophon), 156-159; b) Female Character (C. Butler), 160-162; c) Critique of Mill on Women (S. Freud), 163; d) Reflections on Womanhood (E.H. Erikson), 164-168; e) Woman and Labor (O. Schreiner), 170-176; f) New Woman (C. Bird), 177-182; g) Pecuniary Power (T. Veblen), 184-189; h) New Ways to Manliness (M. Brenton), 190-202; i) Marriage as a Trade (C. Hamilton), 204-211; j) Sex in the Social Structure (T. Parsons), 212-218; k) Married Women and the Law of Support (L. Kanowitz), 221-225; l) Marriage and Family Support (Task Force on Family Law Policy), 226-238;

m) Women as a "Social Problem" (M. Komarovsky), 240-242; n) Social Change and the Family (L.K. Frank), 243-252; o) Home and Community (President's Commission on the Status of Women), 253-254; p) Children of Mankind (Letter to the Editor), 255-256; q) Women and Labor (E. Flexner), 258-273; r) Women and Work (President's Commission on the Status of Women), 274-278; s) Title VII of the 1964 Civil Rights Act (L. Kanowitz), 279-287; t) Job Discrimination and the Black Woman (S.P. Fuentes), 288-294; u) Differences Between Men and Women (J.S. Mill), 297-299; v) Women and Education (C.P. Gilman), 300-302; w) Where Angels Fear to Tread (M. Komarovsky), 303-309; x) Modest Proposal for the Educating of Women (E.L. Cless), 310-317; y) Role of Women in the Political Organization of African Societies (A.M.D. Lebeuf), 319-332; z) Saint-Watching (P. McGinley), 333-343; aa) Roles of Women (E.M. Albert), 345-352; bb) Sexual Repression and the Family (L. Limpus), 353-363; cc) Sex and Psychology (V. Klein), 366-375; dd) Sex and Temperament (M. Mead), 376-392; ee) Early Sex-Role Development (P.H. Mussen), 393-418.

261 WOMAN'S RIGHTS. WOMAN'S WRONGS: A COUNTER-IRRITANT. (American Women: Images and Realities) New York: Arno Press, 1972.

a) Woman's Rights (1867)(J. Todd); b) Woman's Wrongs: A Counter-Irritant (1868)(M.A. Dodge, G. Hamilton, pseud.).

262 WOMAN'S WORK IN AMERICA. (American Women: Images and Realities) Annie Nathan Meyer, ed. New York: Arno Press, 1972, c1891.

a) Introduction (J.W. Howe), 1-2; b) Education of Woman in the Eastern States (M.F. Eastman), 3-53; c) Education of Woman in the Western States (M.W. Sewall), 54-88; d) Education of Woman in the Southern States (C.L. Franklin), 89-106; e) Woman in Literature (H.G. Cone), 107-127; f) Woman in Journalism (S.E. Dickinson), 128-138; g) Woman in Medicine (M.P. Jacobi), 139-205; h) Woman in the Ministry (A.C. Bowles), 206-217; i) Woman in Law (A.M. Bittenbender), 218-244; j) Woman in the State (M.A. Livermore), 245-275; k) Woman in Industry (A.H. Rhine), 276-322; l) Woman in Philanthropy--Charity (J.S. Lowell), 323-345; m) Woman in Philanthropy--Care of the Sick (E.D. Cheney), 346-358; n) Woman in Philanthropy--Care of the Criminal (S.H. Barney), 359-372; o) Woman in Philanthropy--Care of the Indian (A.S. Quinton), 373-391; p) Woman in Philanthropy--Work of Anti-Slavery Women (L.B.C. Wyman), 392-398; q) Woman in Philanthropy--Work of the W.C.T.U. (F.E. Willard), 399-410; r) Woman in Philanthropy--Work of the Red Cross Society (C. Barton), 411-420.

263 WOMANSPIRIT RISING: A FEMINIST READER IN RELIGION. Carol P. Christ and Judith Plaskow, eds. New York: Harper and Row, 1979.

a) Human Situation: A Feminine View (V. Saiving), 25-42; b) Motherearth and the Megamachine (R.R. Ruether), 43-52; c) After the Death of God the Father (M. Daly), 53-62; d) Reflections on the Meaning of Herstory

(S. Collins), 68-73; e) Eve and Adam: Genesis 2-3 Reread (P. Trible), 74-83; f) Women in the Early Christian Movement (E. Fiorenza), 84-92; g) Christian Past: Does It Hold a Future for Women? (E. McLaughlin), 93-106; h) What Became of God the Mother? (E. Pagels), 107-119; i) When God Was a Woman (M. Stone), 120-130; j) Feminist Spirituality, Christian Identity, and Catholic Vision (E. Fiorenza), 136-148; k) Theology in the Politics of Appalachian Women (S. Collins), 149-158; l) Dilemma of Celebration (N. Morton), 159-166; m) Female God Language in a Jewish Context (R. Gross), 167-173; n) Sabbath Prayers for Women (N. Janowitz, M. Wenig), 174-178; o) Bringing a Daughter into the Covenant (J. Plaskow), 179-184; p) Jewish Woman's Haggadah (A. Cantor), 185-192; q) Coming of Lilith: Toward a Feminist Theology (J. Plaskow), 198-209; r) Why Speak about God? (M. Daly), 210-218; s) Dreams and Fantasies as Sources of Revelation: Feminist Appropriation of Jung (N.R. Goldenberg), 219-227; t) Spiritual Quest and Women's Experience (C.P. Christ), 228-245; u) Becoming a Woman: Menstruation as Spiritual Experience (P. Washbourn), 246-258; v) Witchcraft and Women's Culture (Starhawk), 259-268; w) Self-Blessing Ritual (Z.E. Budapest), 269-272; x) Why Women Need the Goddess: Phenomenological, Psychological, and Political Reflections (C.P. Christ), 273- .

264 WOMEN: A FEMINIST PERSPECTIVE. 2nd ed. Jo Freeman, ed. Palo Alto, Ca.: Mayfield, 1978.

a) Woman's Biology--Mankind's Destiny: The Population Explosion and Women's Changing Roles (M. Bolt, A. Wilson, W. Larsen), 3-17; b) Female Sexual Alienation (L. Phelps), 18-26; c) Women, Health, and Medicine (B.K. Rothman), 27-40; d) Rape Culture (D. Herman), 41-63; e) Abortion: The Controversial Choice (N. Bishop), 64-82; f) Origin of the Family (K. Gough), 83-105; g) Power in Dating Relationships (L.A. Peplau), 106-121; h) Mother Role (J. Bernard), 122-133; i) History and Development of Day Care in the U.S. (R.F. Baxandall), 134-152; j) Sex-Role Socialization (L.J. Weitzman), 153-216; k) How to Discriminate Against Women Without Really Trying (J. Freeman), 217-232; l) Double Standard: Age (I.P. Bell), 233-244; m) Loneliness of the Long-Distance Mother (P. Bart), 245-264; n) Women in the Labor Force (F.D. Blau), 265-289; o) Women and Unemployment: Assessing the Biggest Myths (K.L. Schlozman), 290-338; p) Clerical Work: The Female Occupation (E.N. Glenn, R.L. Feldberg), 339-358; q) Women in the Professions: Psychological and Social Barriers to Women in Science (M.S. White), 359-370; r) Trust, Loyalty, and the Place of Women in the Informal Organization of Work (J. Lorber), 371-384; s) Feminism and the Law (M. Eastwood), 385-403; t) American Women and the Political Process (N.B. Lynn), 404-429; u) Black Women and the Pursuit of Equality (E.M. Almquist), 430-450; v) Why Witches Were Women (M. Nelson), 451-468; w) Violence: The Most Obscene Fantasy (L. Shapiro), 469-473; x) Sexual Politics of Interpersonal Behavior (N. Henley, J. Freeman), 474-486; y) Sexism and the English Language: The Linguistic Implications of Being a Woman (K.L. Adams, N.C. Ware), 487-504; z) Women as a Minority Group (H.M. Hacker), 505-522; aa) Historical Background (of Feminism) (V. Klein), 523-542; bb) First Feminists (J. Hole, E. Levine), 543-556; cc) Women's Liberation Movement: Its Origins, Organizations, Activities, and Ideas (J. Freeman), 557-574; dd) Feminist Consciousness and Black Women (P.T. Stone), 575-588; ee)

Male Power and the Women's Movement (B.B. Polk), 589-

265 WOMEN: A FEMINIST PERSPECTIVE. Jo Freeman, ed. Palo Alto, Ca.: Mayfield, 1975.

a) Woman's Biology--Mankind's Destiny: The Population Explosion and Women's Changing Roles (A. Wilson, M. Bolt, W. Larsen), 3-15; b) Female Sexual Alienation (L. Phelps), 16-23; c) Rape: The All-American Crime (S. Griffin), 24-40; d) Origin of the Family (K. Gough), 43-63; e) Who Has the Power? The Marital Struggle (D.L. Gillespie), 64-87; f) History and Development of Day Care in the U.S. (R.F. Baxandall), 88-102; g) Sex-Role Socialization (L.J. Weitzman), 105-144; h) Double Standard: Age (I.P. Bell), 145-155; i) Loneliness of the Long-Distance Mother (P. Bart), 156-170; j) Structural and Internalized Barriers to Women in Higher Education (P. Roby), 171-193; k) How to Discriminate Against Women Without Really Trying (J. Freeman), 194-208; l) Women in the Labor Force (F.D. Blau), 211-226; m) Women in the Professions: Psychological and Social Barriers to Women in Science (M.S. White), 227-237; n) Women's Economic Status: Some Cliches and Some Facts (S. Bernard), 238-241; o) Working Poor Women (K. Shortridge), 242-253; p) Sex Discrimination in the Trade Unions: Legal Resources for Change (G. Falk), 254-276; q) Women in the American Novel (K. Snow), 279-292; r) Images of American Woman in Popular Songs (K.F. Reinartz), 293-308; s) Sexism in Western Art (L.M. Brown), 309-322; t) Feminism and the Law (M. Eastwood), 325-334; u) Why Witches Were Women (M. Nelson), 335-350; v) Liberation of Black Women (P. Murray), 351-363; w) Women in American Politics (N. Lynn), 364-385; x) Marriage and Psychotherapy (P. Chesler), 386-390; y) Sexual Politics of Interpersonal Behavior (N. Henley, J. Freeman), 391-401; z) Women as a Minority Group (H.M. Hacker), 402-416; aa) Historical Background (of feminism) (V. Klein), 419-435; bb) First Feminists (J. Hole, E. Levine), 436-447; cc) Women's Liberation Movement: Its Origins, Structures, Impact, and Ideas (J. Freeman), 448-460.

266 WOMEN: A PDI REFERENCE WORK. Volume I. Florence L. Denmark and Robert W. Wesner, eds. New York: Psychological Dimensions, 1976.

a) Masculinity-Femininity: An Exception To a Famous Dictim (A. Constantinople), 5-24; b) Measurement of Psychological Androgyny (S.L. Bem), 25-32; c) Sexual Role Identification and Personality Functioning in Girls (J. Williams), 33-40; d) Premenstrual Syndrome (M.B. Parlee), 41-52; e) Heroic and Tender Modes in Women Authors of Fantasy (R. Helson), 53-76; f) Socialization of Achievement Orientation in Females (A.H. Stein, M.M. Bailey), 77-98; g) Relationship Between Role Orientation and Achievement Motivation in College Women (T.G. Alper), 99-122; h) Bringing Women In: Rewards, Punishments, And the Structure of Achievement (C.F. Epstein), 123-132; i) Future Goals of College Women (F.L. Denmark, B.K. Baxter, E.J. Shirk), 133-140; j) Fear of Success: Qualms and Queries (C.P. Smith), 141-160; k) Measuring the Vocational Interests of Women (N.S. Cole), 161-168; l) Female College Students' Scores On the Men's And Women's Strong Vocational Interest Blanks (P.H. Munley, et al.), 169-174; m) Effects of Career

Choices on Married Women (D.T. Hall, F.E. Gordon), 175-182; n) Positive Effects of the Multiple Negative: Explaining the Success of Black Professional Women (C.P. Epstein), 183-206; o) New Views of Rosie the Riveter (S. Tobias), 207-220; p) Tender Technicians: The Feminization of Public Librarianship, 1876-1905 (D. Garrison), 221-250; q) Changing Role of Women in the Armed Forces (N. Goldman), 251-270; r) Frontiero v. Richardson (R.B. Ginsberg), 271-274; s) Alternative Methods For Measuring Sex Discrimination in Occupational Incomes G. Staines, et al.), 275-300; t) Phyletic and Idiosyncratic Determinants of Gender Identity (J. Money), 301-316; u) Identification and Complementation in the Differentiation of Gender Identity (J.Money), 317-326; v) Effect of Contraceptive Pills on Sexual Activity in the Luteal Phase of the Human Menstrual Cycle (J.R. Udry, et al.), 327-336; w) Sexuality of Pregnant and Breastfeeding Women (J.A. Kenny), 337-352; x) Dimensions of Lesbian Sexual Experience (J.H. Hedblom), 353-370; y) Sex-Role Boundaries and Resistance to Sex-Role Change (D. Tresemer, J. Pleck), 371-388; z) Effects of Live Modelled Sex-Appropriate Play Behavior In a Naturalistic Setting (T.M. Wolf), 389-392; aa) Relationship Between Sex-Role Stereotypes And Requisite Management Characteristics (V.E. Schein), 393-398; bb) Adult Sex Roles and Mental Health (W.R. Gove), 399-422; cc) When Women Are More Deserving Than Men: Equity, Attribution, And Perceived Sex Differences (J. Taynor, K. Deaux), 423-430; dd) Are Women A "Minority" Group? Sometimes! (R.K. Unger, B.J. Raymond, S.M. Levine), 431-446; ee) Status of Women--Population--Development (B. Linner), 447-452; ff) Interrelationship of the Status of Women and Family Planning (U.N. Economic and Social Council, Commission on the Status of Women), 453-548; gg) Salon, Foyer, Bureau: Women And The Professions in France (C.B. Silver), 549-564; hh) Ancient and Contemporary Perspectives on The Women of Israel (N. Datan), 565-578; ii) Socio-Economic Context Of Sex And Power: A Study of Women, Work And Family Roles in Four Israeli Institutional Frameworks (H.M. Hacker), 579-600; jj) Life and Death of Ms. Solomon Grundy (THE ECONOMIST), 601-

267 WOMEN AND ACHIEVEMENT: SOCIAL AND MOTIVATIONAL ANALYSES. Martha Shuch Mednick, Sandra Schwartz Tangri, and Lois Wladis Hoffman. Washington, D.C.: Hemisphere, 1975.

a) Sex Roles and Social Change (H. Holter), 6-19; b) Understanding Women: Implications for Personality Theory and Research (R. Carlson), 20-31; c) Sex-Role Stereotypes: A Current Appraisal (I.K. Broverman, S.R. Vogel, D.M. Broverman, F.E. Clarkson, P.S. Rosenkrantz), 32-47; d) Cross-cultural Examination of Women's Marital, Educational and Occupational Options (C. Safilios-Rothschild), 48-70; e) Convergences between East and West: Tradition and Modernity in Sex Roles in Sweden, Finland, and the Soviet Union (E. Haavio-Mannila), 71-84; f) Social Change and Sex-Role Inertia: The Case of the Kibbutz (M.T.S. Mednick), 85-103; g) Employment of Women, Education, and Fertility (L.W. Hoffman), 104-122; h) Early Childhood Experiences and Women's Achievement Motives (L.W. Hoffman), 129-150; i) Socialization of Achievement Motivation in Females (A.H. Stein, M.M. Bailey), 151-157; j) Women's Expectations for and Causal Attributions of Success and Failure (I.H. Frieze), 158-171; k) Varieties of Achievement Motivation (J. Veroff, L. McClelland, D. Ruhland), 172-205; l) Achievement-Related Conflicts in Women (M.S. Horner), 206-220; m) Fear of Success in Males

and Females: 1965 and 1971 (L.W. Hoffman), 221-230; n) Race, Social Class, and the Motive to Avoid Success in Women (P.J. Weston, M.T.S. Mednick), 231-238; o) Implied Demand Character of the Wife's Future and Role Innovation: Patterns of Achievement Orientation Among College Women (S.S. Tangri), 239-254; p) Determinants of Occupational Role Innovation Among College Women (S.S. Tangri), 255-273; q) Sex-Role Attitudes and Psychological Well-Being (J.P. Gump), 274-284; r) Psychological Sex Differences (J.A. Sherman), 292-306; s) Sex-Labeling of Jobs (V.K. Oppenheimer), 307-325; t) Sex Discrimination Against the American Working Woman (T. Levitin, R.P. Quinn, G.L. Staines), 326-338; u) Women As New Students (K.P. Cross), 339-354; v) Woman Ph.D.: A Recent Profile (R.J. Simon, S.M. Clark, K. Galway), 355-371; w) Sex Discrimination in Academe (H.S. Astin, A.E. Bayer), 372-395; x) Life Patterns and Self-Esteem in Gifted Family Oriented and Career Committed Women (J.A. Birnbaum), 396-419; y) Changing Image of the Career Woman (R. Helson), 420-432.

268 WOMEN AND ANALYSIS: DIALOGUES ON PSYCHOANALYTIC VIEWS OF FEMININITY. Joan Strouse, comp. New York: Grossman, 1974.

a) Psychical Consequences of the Anatomical Distinction Between the Sexes (S. Freud), 17-26; b) Freud and the Distinction Between the Sexes (J. Mitchell), 27-38; c) Female Sexuality (S. Freud), 39-56; d) Female Sexuality (E. Janeway), 57-72; e) Femininity (S. Freud), 73-94; f) Freud's View of Female Psychology (M. Mead), 95-108; g) Manifestations of the Female Castration Complex (K. Abraham), 109-135; h) Castration Complex Reconsidered (J. Kovel), 136-146; i) Psychology of women in Relation to the Functions of Reproduction (H. Deutsch), 147-161; j) Since 1924: Toward a New Psychology of Women (M. Cavell), 162-170; k) Flight from Womanhood (K. Horney), 171-186; l) Karen Horney's Flight from Orthodoxy (R. Coles), 187-194; m) Nature of the Animus (E. Jung), 195-226; n) Androgyne (B.C. Gelpi), 227-240; o) Passivity, Masochism and Femininity (M. Bonaparte), 241-249; p) Origins of Femininity (E. Person), 250-264; q) Role of Women in This Culture (C.M. Thompson), 265-277; r) Role of Clara Thompson in the Psychoanalytic Study of Women (R. Moulton), 278-290; s) Womanhood and the Inner Space (E.H. Erikson), 291-319; t) Once More the Inner Space (E.H. Erikson), 320-342; u) Freud's Concept of Bisexuality (R.J. Stoller), 343-366.

269 WOMEN AND CHILDREN IN CONTEMPORARY SOCIETY. Nancy Hammond, ed. Proceedings of a Conference at Kellogg Center, Michigan State University, November 22, 1975. Lansing: Michigan Women's Commission, 1976.

a) Women and Religion (A.M. Cheek), 3-11; b) Women and Their Work Roles (D.W. Warshay), 12-16; c) Education and Socialization (L.E. Pettigrew), 17-23; d) Hunger in the U.S.: Women and Children First (J. Pope), 24-30; e) Cultural Production of Childbirth (B. Jordan), 33-43; f) Public Policy and Childbearing (J.E. Mulligan), 44-52; g) Learning Not To: It Takes a Long Time (E.A. Strommen), 55-61; h) Parent's Role in Values Education (J. McCue), 62-72; i) Parenting and Family Life Styles (D.R. Imig, G.L. Imig), 73-78; j) Modern Family: Sticky Myths, Diverse Realities, and the Problem of Isolation (B. Thorne), 81-89; k)

Community Organizations and Child-care Arrangements (L. Easley), 90-94; l) Women in Families and History (A.C. Meyering), 95-103.

270 WOMEN AND COLONIZATION: ANTHROPOLOGICAL PERSPECTIVES. Mona Etienne and Eleanor Leacock, eds. (Praeger Special Studies) New York: Praeger, 1980.

a) Montagnais Women and the Jesuit Program for Colonization (E. Leacock), 25-42; b) Sunksquaws, Shamans, and Tradeswomen: Middle Atlantic Coastal Algonkian Women During the Seventeenth and Eighteenth Centuries (R.S. Grumet), 43-62; c) Mothers of a Nation: Seneca Resistance to Quaker Intervention (D. Rothenberg), 63-87; d) Contending with Colonization: Tlingit Men and Women in Change (L.F. Klein), 88-108; e) Forced Transition from Egalitarianism to Male Dominance: The Bari of Colombia (E. Buenaventura-Posso, S.E. Brown), 109-133; f) Aztec Women: The Transition from Status to Class in Empire and Colony (J. Nash), 134-148; g) Andean Women Under Spanish Rule (I. Silverblatt), 149-185; h) Daughters of the Lakes and Rivers: Colonization and the Land Rights of Luo Women (A.P. Okeyo), 186-213; i) Women and Men, Cloth and Colonization: The Transformation of Production-Distribution Relations among the Baule (Ivory Coast) (M. Etienne), 214-238; j) Desert Politics: Choices in the "Marriage Market" (D. Bell), 239-269; k) Stability in Banana Leaves: Colonization and Women in Kiriwina, Trobriand Islands (A.B. Weiner), 270-293; l) Putting Down Sisters and Wives: Tongan Women and Colonization (C.W. Gailey), 294-322.

271 WOMEN AND EDUCATION. Elizabeth Steiner Maccia, ed. (With Martha Ann Coleman, Myrna Eopk, and Trudy Miller Shiel) Springfield, Il.: Charles C. Thomas, 1975.

a) Sexual Stereotypes Start Early (F. Howe), 8-21; b) Sugar'n Spice (S. Spinks), 22-36; c) How Ideology Shapes Women's Lives (J. Lipman-Blumen), 37-49; d) Why Can't Women Be More Like Men? (J. Prather), 50-59; e) From Each According to Her Ability (D. Baumrind), 60-96; f) Determinants of Intellectual Growth in Women (D.B. Lynn), 100-119; g) View From the Doll Corner (K. Barry), 120-123; h) Sex-Role Concepts and Sex Typing in Childhood as a Function of School and Home Environments (P. Minuchin), 124-142; i) Assessment of Teaching Practice: An "Attractive" Hypothesis (T. Hore), 143-145; j) Dilemmas of Women's Education (D. Riesman), 146-160; k) Second Sex in Academe (A.S. Harris), 161-194; l) Women in Children's Literature (A.P. Nilsen), 198-211; m) Feminist Look at Children's Books (Feminists on Children's Media), 212-225; n) Sex Roles in Early Reading Textbooks (R. Frasher, A. Walker), 226-238; o) Women Workers in Elementary Readers (B. Stefflre), 239-244; p) Textbooks and Channeling (J.K. Frisof), 245-251; q) Women in U.S. History High School Textbooks (J.L. Trecker), 252-271; r) Woman's Place Is in the Curriculum (J.L. Trecker), 272-281; s) Teaching Female Studies: Looking Back Over Three Years (S. Tobias), 282-292; t) Time Is Here for Women's Liberation (K.T. Romer, C. Secor), 296-312; u) Sex Equality: The Beginnings of Ideology (A.S. Rossi), 313-327; v) Feminism: The Sine Qua Non for a Just Society (W.S. Heide), 328-346; w) Schooling of

Tomorrow's Women (P. Minuchin), 347-356; x) Sex Roles and Education in Sweden (I. Fredriksson), 357-370; y) Education and Women's Liberation (E.S. Maccia), 371- .

272 WOMEN AND EDUCATIONAL LEADERSHIP. Sari Knopp Biklen and Marilyn B. Brannigan, eds. Lexington, Ma: Lexington Books, 1980.

a) Prophets, Chiefs, Commissioners, and Queens: The Moral and Institutional Context of Leadership (M. Freedman), 27-34; b) Psychology of Leadership: Implications for Women (J.C. Conoley), 35-46; c) Power and Opportunity in the Principalship: The Case of Two Women Leaders in Education (W. Greenfield, A. Beam), 47-62; d) Historical Perspectives on Women in Educational Leadership (J. Burstyn), 65-76; e) Feminism and the Woman School Administrator (M. Gribskov), 77-92; f) Single-Sex Education and Leadership: The Early Years of Simmons College (S.G. Kohlstedt), 93-112; g) Coeducation and the Development of Leadership Skills in Women: Historical Perspectives from Cornell University, 1868-1900 (P.F. Haines), 113-128; h) Sex Bias in School Administration (J. Clement), 131-138; i) Socialization and Education of Young Black Girls in School (S.L. Lightfoot), 139-164; j) Black Female Administrator: Woman in a Double Bind (R. Doughty), 165-174; k) How Real is Fear of Success? (M. Johnson), 175-182; l) Need for Female Role Models in Education (T. Antonucci), 185-196; m) Working and Parenting: The Male and Father Role (H.R. Keller), 197-208; n) Transition from Parenting to Working and Parenting (J. Bogdan), 209-222; o) Leadership Training for Increased Effectiveness among Women Educational Administrators (M.B. Winslow), 223-238; p) Changing Women's Representation in School Management: A Systems Perspective (P.A. Schmuck), 239-260.

273 WOMEN AND FICTION 2: SHORT STORIES BY AND ABOUT WOMEN. Susan Cahill, ed. New York: New American Library, 1978.

a) The Courting of Sister Wisby (S.O. Jewett), 1-16; b) The Eclipse (S. Lagerlöf), 17-22; c) Pilgrimage (selection) (D. Richardson), 23-32; d) The Bedquilt (D.C. Fisher), 33-43; e) Kristin Lavransdatter (selection) (S. Undset), 44-61; f) The Cooboo (K. Prichard), 62-66; g) Sorrow-Acre (I. Dinesen), 67-98; h) Outside the Machine (J. Rhys), 99-119; i) The Petrified Woman (C. Gordon), 120-134; j) Sunday Afternoon (E. Bowen), 135-144; k) The Gilded Six-Bits (Z.N. Hurston), 145-158; l) The Wind-Chill Factor or, A Problem of Mind and Matter (M.F.K. Fisher), 159-166; m) Miss MacIntosh, My Darling (selection) (M. Young), 167-176; n) The Tree (M.-L. Bombal), 177-187; o) Woman Driver (G. Fussenegger), 188-191; p) Girls Together (O. Manning), 192-212; q) The Mother (N. Ginsburg), 213-224; r) Camp Cataract (J. Bowles), 225-261; s) The First Year of My Life (M. Spark), 262-269; t) Pillar of Salt (S. Jackson), 270-285; u) Acceptance of Their Ways (M. Gallant), 286-295; v) The Train from Rhodesia (N. Gordimer), 296-302; w) A Bird in the House (M. Laurence), 303-321; x) The Englishwoman (R.P. Jhabvala), 322-335; y) Still Life with Fruit

(D. Betts), 336-354; z) Idioms (E. Cullinan), 355-366.

274 WOMEN AND FOLKLORE. Claire R. Farrer, ed. Austin: University of Texas Press, 1975.

a) Personal Narratives in Women's Rap Groups (S. Kalčik), 3-11; b) Games Mexican Girls Play (I. Cardozo-Freeman), 12-24; c) Image of the Frontier Woman (B.J. Stoeltje), 25-41; d) Things Walt Disney Never Told Us (K. Stone), 42-50; e) Native Costumes of the Oberwallis: Tourist Gimmick or Tradition? (A.F. Hostettler), 51-57; f) Negotiating Respect: Patterns of Presentation among Black Women (R.D. Abrahams), 58-80; g) Bormliza: Maltese Folksong Style and Women (N. McLeod, M. Herndon), 81- .

275 WOMEN AND GERMAN STUDIES: AN INTERDISCIPLINARY AND COMPARATIVE APPROACH. Kay Goodman and Ruth H. Sanders, eds. Proceedings of the Second Annual Women in German Symposium. Oxford, Oh.: Miami University, 1977.

a) Impact of German Thought and Culture on Madame de Stael's Thinking about Women (L. Morros), 5-24; b) Woman Question in the Early Work of Alfred Doblin (H. Tewarson), 25-46; c) Stereotype of the Emancipated Woman in the Weimar Republic (R. Harrigan), 47-79; d) More Than a Question of Numbers: Women Deputies in the German National Constituent Assembly and the Reichstag, 1919-1933 (P.K. Fessenden), 80-98; e) German Women University Students: National Socialism and the War, 1939-1945 (J.R. Pauwels), 99-113; f) Frau und Staatsburger in Volker Braun's Schauspiel "Tinka" (C. Cosentino), 114-120; g) Women and the Aesthetic of the Positive Hero in the G.D.R. (H. Fehervary), 121- .

276 WOMEN AND MEN: CHANGING ROLES, RELATIONSHIPS, AND PERCEPTIONS: REPORT OF A WORKSHOP. Libby A. Cater, Anne Firor Scott and Wendy Martyna, eds. New York: Praeger, 1977.

a) Family and Gender Roles in Historical Perspective (T.K. Haraven), 93-118; b) Women and Men in the World of Work: Present and Future (M.H. Strober), 119-152; c) Women, Men and Mental Health (M. Guttentag, S. Salasin), 153-180; d) Psychology of Sex Roles (J.H. Pleck), 181-200; e) Sex, Gender, and American Culture (C.R. Stimpson), 201-244; f) Equality Between Men and Women in Sweden (M.-B. Carlsson), 245-272.

277 WOMEN AND MEN, MEN AND WOMEN: AN ANTHOLOGY OF SHORT STORIES. William Smart, ed. New York: St. Martin's Press, 1975.

a) Araby (J. Joyce), 3-7; b) Debut (K. Hunter), 8-14; c) The Nightingales Sing (E. Parson), 15-26; d) Oh, the Wonder! (J. Larner), 27-42; e) The Old Chevalier (I. Dinesen), 43-60; f) The Magic Barrel (B. Malamud), 61-76; g) Reservations: A Love Story (P. Taylor), 77-97;

h) The White Stocking (D.H. Lawrence), 98-116; i) Rope (K.A. Porter), 117-122; j) A Man and Two Women (D. Lessing), 123-137; k) The Beach Umbrella (C. Colter), 138-155; l) An Interest in Life (G. Paley), 156-170; m) One off the Short List (D. Lessing), 171-190; n) The Five-forty-eight (J. Cheever), 191-201; o) Accomplished Desires (J.C. Oates), 202-216; p) The Short Happy Life of Francis Macomber (E. Hemingway), 217-241; q) The Dentist's Wife (W.M. Kelley), 242-256; r) A Good Investment (J. Cary), 257-270; s) A Dill Pickle (K. Mansfield), 271-276; t) Astronomer's Wife (K. Boyle), 277-281; u) Songs My Father Sang Me (E. Bowen), 282-292; v) Truant (C. McKay), 293-303; w) Samson and Delilah (D.H. Lawrence), 304-318; x) The Lady with the Dog (A. Chekhov), 319-332; y) Winter in July (D. Lessing), 333-362; z) A Country Love Story (J. Stafford), 363-373; aa) Brooklyn (P. Marshall), 374-388; bb) Odour of Chrysanthemums (D.H. Lawrence), 389- .

278 WOMEN AND MEN: THE CONSEQUENCES OF POWER. A COLLECTION OF NEW ESSAYS. Dana V. Hiller and Robin Ann Sheets, eds. Selected papers from the National Bicentennial Conference "Pioneers for Century III," April 22-25, 1976, Cincinnati, Ohio. Cincinnati: Office of Women's Studies, University of Cincinnati, 1977.

a) Men's Power with Women, Other Men and Society (J. Pleck), 12-23; b) Male Power Motivation and the Status of Women (D. Winter), 24-35; c) Entrails of Power: Bogus Manhood and the Language of Grief (C. Shatan), 36-46; d) Sexism, Patriarchy and Feminism (S. Ruth), 47-60; e) Sexism in American Naming Traditions (J. Carson), 64-73; f) Pope's Portraits of Women: The Tyranny of the Pictorial Eye (C. Fabricant), 74-91; g) Worship of Women in Courtly Love and Rock and Roll (L. Friedlander), 92-110; h) Power, Presentations and the Presentable (C.R. Stimpson), 111-131; i) Materfamilias: Power and Presumption (N. Auerbach), 132-139; j) Heroine as Her Author's Daughter (J. Gardiner), 140-148; k) Female Powerlessness: The Altruistic Other Orientation (J.J. Walstedt), 153-167; l) History of Married Women's Rights (M.J. Hamilton), 168-183; m) Work in the Lives of Married Women, 1900-1930 (L.W. Tentler), 184-195; n) Black Women in Urban Schools (J. Payne), 196-213; o) Women in a Man's World: The Female Engineers (P. Durchholz), 214-230; p) Women in the Professions and Semi-Professions: A Question of Power (D.A. Klegon), 231-238; q) Childbearing and the Woman's Role (L. Hoffman), 239-250; r) Black Women Respond to Slavery (M. Obitko), 256-269; s) Crisis in Coeducation, 1890-1920 (M.R. Walsh, F.R. Walsh), 270-286; t) Influential Alliances: Cincinnati Women in the Political Arena, 1920-1945 (P. Dubeck), 287-297; u) Damnation and Stereotyping in Joke Telling (C. Mitchell), 298-310; v) Androgynous Administration (S. Tucker, H. Gideonse), 311-332; w) Future of Parenthood: Implications of Declining Fertility (J. Huber), 333-351; x) Huck--An Androgynous Hero (B. Tenenbaum), 355-363; y) Before Androgyny: An Examination of the Stages Toward Neo-Masculinity (B.E.A. Liddell), 364-371; z) Poetry of Self-Definition (S.M. Gilbert), 372-385; aa) Mother, Maiden, and the Marriage of Death: Women Writers and an Ancient Myth (S. Gubar), 386-397; bb) Mysticism and Feminism: Jacob Boehme and Jane Lead (C. Smith), 398-408; cc)

Sexism and Godtalk (R.R. Ruether), 409-425.

279 WOMEN AND MEN TOGETHER: AN ANTHOLOGY OF SHORT FICTION. Dawson Gaillard and John Mosier, eds. Boston: Houghton Mifflin, 1978.

a) Ligeia (E.A. Poe), 5-18; b) The Birthmark (N. Hawthorne), 19-33; c) Veronika (T. Storm), 34-44; d) A New England Nun (M.E.W. Freeman), 45-56; e) Midnight Mass (J.M. de Machado de Assis), 57-64; f) The Storm (K. Chopin), 65-71; g) The Bride Comes to Yellow Sky (S. Crane), 72-82; h) The Darling (A. Chekhov), 83-94; i) Cicely's Dream (C.W. Chesnutt), 95-111; j) Simonsen (S. Undset), 112-135; k) Romance of a Fisherman's Wife (S. Lagerlöf), 136-143; l) A Painful Case (J. Joyce), 144-152; m) The Difference (E. Glasgow), 153-171; n) Cat in the Rain (E. Hemingway), 172-176; o) The Rocking-Horse Winner (D.H. Lawrence), 177-190; p) Dry September (W. Faulkner), 191-201; q) Permanent Wave (E. Wharton), 202-214; r) Psychology (K. Mansfield), 215-222; s) Long Black Song (R. Wright), 223-244; t) Old Mr. Marblehall (E. Welty), 245-252; u) Tears, Idle Tears (E. Bowen), 253-260; v) We're Very Poor (J. Rulfo), 261-265; w) Daydreams of a Drunk Woman (C. Lispector), 266-273; x) Wine (D. Lessing), 274-279; y) Tuesday Siesta (G. García Márquez), 280-286; z) The Fathers' Daughters (M. Spark), 287-297; aa) Giving Blood (J. Updike), 298-309; bb) Bodies (J.C. Oates), 310-328; cc) Beasts of the Southern Wild (D. Betts), 329-342; dd) Her Sweet Jerome (A. Walker), 343- .

280 WOMEN AND MEN: TRADITION AND TRENDS. Suzanne Fremon, ed. (The Reference Shelf, Vol. 49, No. 5) New York: H.W. Wilson, 1977.

a) Women in the American Culture (C. Thompson), 10-21; b) Why Men and Women Think Differently (K. Lamott), 22-27; c) Understanding the Difference (P. Schlafly), 28-37; d) Way We Were--1949 (B. Friedan), 38-46; e) Cultural Dilemma (M. Mead), 47-57; f) Early Stereotypes (B.G. Harrison), 59-69; g) Boys, Girls, and Sports (G. Williams, III), 70-76; h) Sex Bias in Schools (EDITORIALS ON FILE), 77-81; i) Unisex and the Public Schools (R. Kirk), 82-83; j) Unisex Pressures on Children (R.L. Lorand), 84-86; k) Test Scores and Unequal Education (U.S. NEWS & WORLD REPORT), 87-89; l) Changing the Stereotypes (R.J. Trotter), 90-95; m) Young Male Reacts (V. Packard), 97-104; n) New Choices, New Roles (C. Bird), 105-113; o) Matter of Identity (J. Klemesrud), 114-119; p) Choosing Equality (J. Stapleton, R. Bright), 120-128; q) Social Security and Equal Rights (EDITORIALS ON FILE), 130-132; r) Men and Emotional Problems (J.L. Collier), 133-136; s) Women and Jobs (R. Lindsey), 137-141; t) Fear of Success (SCIENCE DIGEST), 142-143; u) Women in Business Administration (B. Greiff), 144-156; v) Chauvinism--At Work and at Home (M. Korda), 157-163; w) Women in the Clergy (U.S. NEWS & WORLD REPORT), 164-166; x) Television and the Image of the Father (C. Christ), 167-172; y) Equal Rights Amendment: A Threat to Family Life? (EDITORIALS ON FILE), 173-176; z) Who Is Man? (C. Miller, K. Swift), 178-198; aa) Eliminating Bias in Publications 199-213; bb) Whole Human Being (S. Edmiston), 214-217;

cc) Reflections on the Changed World (E. Janeway), 218-230.

281 WOMEN AND NATIONAL DEVELOPMENT: THE COMPLEXITIES OF CHANGE. Wellesley Editorial Committee, eds. (Ximena Bunster B., Carolyn M. Elliott, Michelle McAlpin, Achola O. Pala, Hanna Papanek, Helen I. Safa, Catharine R. Stimpson, Niara Sudarkasa, Roxane Witke) Chicago: University of Chicago Press, 1977.

a) Theories of Development (C.M. Elliott), 1-8; b) Definitions of Women and Development: An African Perspective (A.O. Pala), 9-13; c) Development Planning for Women (H. Papanek), 14-21; d) Women in the Informal Labor Sector: The Case of Mexico City (L. Arizpe), 25-37; e) Industrialization, Monopoly, Capitalism, and Women's Work in Guatemala (N.S. Chinchilla), 38-56; f) Sex Roles and Social Change: A Comparative Appraisal of Turkey's Women (D. Kandiyoti), 57-73; g) Class Structures and Female Autonomy in Rural Java (A. Stoler), 74-89; h) Biological Events and Cultural Control (C.P. MacCormack), 93-100; i) Women, Saints, and Sanctuaries (F. Mernissi), 101-112; j) Women and the Hindu Tradition (S.S. Wadley), 113-125; k) Migration and Labor Force Participation of Latin American Women: The Domestic Servants in the Cities (E. Jelin), 129-141; l) Female Status, the Family, and Male Dominance in a West Indian Community (Y.T. Moses), 142-153; m) Women and Men, Power and Powerlessness in Lesotho (M. Mueller), 154-166; n) How African Women Cope with Migrant Labor in South Africa (H. Sibisi), 167-177; o) Women and Migration in Contemporary West Africa (N. Sudarkasa), 178-189; p) Raising the Status of Women through Law: The Case of Israel (P. Lahav), 193-209; q) Shaping of the Kaum Ibu (Women's Section) of the United Maylays National Organization (L. Manderson), 210-223; r) Case of Eva Peron (M. Navarro), 229-240; s) Social Change and Sexual Differentiation in the Cameroun and the Ivory Coast (R. Clignet), 244-260; t) Women's Labor Force Participation in a Developing Society: The Case of Brazil (G. Vasques de Miranda), 261-274; u) Talking Pictures: Field Method and Visual Mode (X. Bunster B.), 278-293; v) Sexuality and Birth Control Decisions among Lebanese Couples (M. Chamie), 294-312; w) Reflections on the Conference on Women and Development (M. McAlpin, B. Awe, L. Casals, E. Leacock, V. Mazumdar, M. Ahdab-Yehia), 313-329; x) Introductions: H.I. Safa, F.I. Ekejiuba, L. Peattie, J.S. Jaquette, C. Nelson, N.H. Youssef.

282 WOMEN AND PHILOSOPHY: TOWARD A THEORY OF LIBERATION. Carol C. Gould and Marx W. Wartofsky, eds. New York: G.P. Putnam, 1976.

a) Anatomy and Destiny: The Role of Biology in Plato's Views of Women (A. Dickason), 45-53; b) Theories of Sex Difference (C. Whitbeck), 54-80; c) Biology, Sex Hormones, and Sexism in the 1920's (D.L. Hall), 81-96; d) Reason and Morals in the Early Feminist Movement: Mary Wollstonecraft (C. Korsmeyer), 97-111; e) Holes and Slime: Sexism in Sartre's Psychoanalysis (M. Collins, C. Pierce), 112-127; f) There's Nobody Here But Us Persons (R.P. Wolff), 128-144; g) Women's Liberation and Human Emancipation (M. Marković), 145-167; h) Marx, Sex, and the Transformation of Society (V. Held), 168-184; i) Future of Love: Rousseau and the Radical Feminists (E. Rapaport), 185-205; j) Exploitation, Oppression, and Self-Sacrifice (J. Tormey), 206-221; k)

Altruism and Women's Oppression (L. Blum, M. Homiak, J. Housman, N. Scheman), 222-247; l) Reaction and the Women's Movement (H. Hein), 248-270; m) Feminism: Reform or Revolution (S. Harding), 271-284; n) Referential Genderization (E. Beardsley), 285-293; o) Reverse Discrimination and the Future (I. Thalberg), 294-308; p) In Defense of Preferential Hiring (M.G. Fried), 309-319; q) Preferential Hiring (M. Vetterling), 320-324; r) Pedagogical Arguments for Preferential Hiring and Tenuring of Women Teachers in the University (M. Martin), 325-333; s) How Do We Know When Opportunities are Equal? (O. Nell), 334-346; t) Abortion and a Woman's Right to Decide (A. Jaggar), 347-360.

283 WOMEN AND RELIGION. Rev. ed. Judith Plaskow, comp. (Papers of the Working Group on Women and Religion, 1972-73) Chambersburg, Pa.: American Academy of Religion, 1974.

a) Theology After the Demise of God the Father: A Call for the Castration of Sexist Religion (M. Daly); b) Feminine Imagery in an Analogue for God (P. Wilson); c) Explorations with Doris Lessing in Quest of The Four-Gated City (C. Christ); d) Karl Barth's Theology of the Word of God: Or, How to Keep Women Silent and in Their Place (J.A. Romero); e) Phallic Worship: The Ultimate Idolatry (E. Farians); f) Image of the Virgin Mother (B. Bruteau); g) Image of Woman in Old Buddhist Literature: The Daughters of Mara (N. Falk); h) Beyond Male Morality (J. Raymond); i) Differentiation and Difference--Reflections on the Ethical Implications of Women's Liberation (P. Washbourn); j) Feminist View of Abortion (M. MacRae); k) Methodological Remarks on the Study of Women in Religion (R. Gross); l) Is Sexism a Sign of Decadence in Religion? (L. Swidler); m) Counter-Ideology (G. Kimball); n) Patriarchy and Charismatic Community in "Paul" (W. Munro); o) Zoroastrian Menstruation Taboos: A Woman's Studies Perspective (E.E. Culpepper).

284 WOMEN AND SOCIETY. Diana L. Reische, comp. (The Reference Shelf, Vol. 43, No. 6) New York: H.W. Wilson, 1972.

a) What Is Women's Liberation Really All About? (M. Wiegers), 12-18; b) Man's Primer to Women's Liberation (M. Savoy), 19-23; c) Backlash Against Women's Lib (B. Rollin), 24-31; d) Women's Studies on the Campuses (B. Isenberg), 32-35; e) Women in the Churches (NEWSWEEK), 36-38; f) Abortion Law Reform (R.L. Worsnop), 39-47; g) Women's Status Fifty Years After the Vote (R. Girson), 48-53; h) Women in the Labor Force (F. Linden), 55-60; i) Trends in Educational Attainment of Women 61-65; j) Education and Jobs 66-67; k) Job Bias Against Women Easing Under Pressure (J.M. Flint), 68-73; l) Women's Job Rights Gain in Federal Court Rulings (E. Shanahan), 74-78; m) Status of Women (H.B. Shaffer), 79-87; n) U.N. Declaration on Women's Rights, 89-93; o) Still Inequalities in Socialist Society (CHRISTIAN SCIENCE MONITOR), 94-96; p) Where Did It All Go Wrong? (R. Gilman), 97-109; q) Decade of Widening Horizons (J. Rosenthal), 110-113; r) Social Construction of the Second Sex (J. Freeman), 116-136; s) There are Sex Differences in the Mind, Too (T. Alexander), 137-152; t) Question of Psychological Differences Between the Sexes (B. Spock), 153-161; u) Female Biology in

a Male Culture (D. Trilling), 162-171; v) Working Mother's Crises (M.L. Loper), 172-175; w) Raising a Bright and Happy Child (M. Blyth), 176-186; x) Children and Their Families (B. Spock), 187-194; y) Future of Marriage (M. Hunt), 195-217; z) What It Would Be Like If Women Win (G. Steinem), 218-224.

285 WOMEN AND SOCIETY: AN ANTHROPOLOGICAL READER. Sharon W. Tiffany, ed. St. Albans, Vt.: Eden Press Women's Publications, 1979.

a) Theoretical Issues in the Anthropological Study of Women (S.W. Tiffany), 1-35; b) Division of Labor by Sex (J.K. Brown), 36-47; c) Economic Organization and the Position of Women Among the Iroquois (J.K. Brown), 48-74; d) Role of Women in a Changing Navaho Society (L.S. Hamamsy), 75-92; e) Women in Modernizing Societies (L. Bossen), 93-119; f) Bargaining from Weakness: Spirit Possession on the South Kenya Coast (R. Gomm), 120-144; g) Jural Relations between the Sexes Among the Barabaig (G. Klima), 145-162; h) Colonialism and the Lost Political Institutions of Igbo Women (J. Van Allen), 163-187; i) Traditional Marriage among the Irigwe of Benue-Plateau State, Nigeria (W.H. Sangree), 188-207; j) Woman-Marriage, With Special Reference to the Lovedu--Its Significance for the Definition of Marriage (E.J. Krige), 208-237; k) Sex Differences in the Incidence of Susto in Two Zapotec Pueblos: An Analysis of the Relationships between Sex Role Expectations and a Folk Illness (C.W. O'Nell, H.A. Selby), 238-255; l) Sexual Antagonism in the New Guinea Highlands: A Bena Bena Example (L.L. Langness), 256-279; m) Male and Female in Tokelau Culture (J. Huntsman, A. Hooper), 280-303.

286 WOMEN AND SPORT: A NATIONAL RESEARCH CONFERENCE. Dorothy V. Harris, ed. Proceedings from the National Research Conference, Women and Sport, held at The Pennsylania State University, August 13-18, 1972, conducted by the College of Health, Physical Education and Recreation and the Division of Continuing Education. University Park: College of Health, Physical Education and Recreation, The Pennsylvania State University, 1972.

a) Dimensions of Physical Activity (D.V. Harris), 3-18; b) Psychological Aspects of Sport with Special Reference to the Female (J.E. Kane), 19-34; c) Self Concept and the Female Participant (D. Allen), 35-52; d) Kinesis and the Concept of Self in Sport (S. Kleinman), 53-60; e) Body Image and Performance (J. Strati), 61-70; f) Stress Seeking and Sport Involvement (D.V. Harris), 71-90; g) Aggression and the Female Athlete (M. Smith), 91-114; h) Females in the Competitive Process (C. Sherif), 115-140; i) Motivation and the Female Participant (J.E. Kane), 141-156; j) Masks of Identity (L. Kennicke), 157-168; k) Use of Hypnosis in Sport--Is It Legitimate? (G.T. Tait), 169-172; l) Needed Approaches for a Better Understanding of Behavior and Performance (D.V. Harris), 173-184; m) Sociological Considerations of the Female Participant (M. Phillips), 185-202; n) Femininity and Achievement in Sports (J. Zoble), 203-224; o) Influence of Birth Order and Sibling Sex on Sports Participation (E. Portz), 225-234; p) Socialization, Dialectics, and Sport (A. Ingham), 235-277;

q) American Business Values and Involvement in Sport (A. Sack), 278-292; r) Self-Perception of Athletes and Coaches (S. Zigler), 293-306; s) Female Spectator (W. Heinhold), 307-320;; t) Physiological Considerations of the Female Participant (T.E. Sheffer), 321-332; u) Training and Condition Techniques for the Female Athlete (K. Stoedefalke), 333-338; v) Nutritional Requirements for Women in Sport (E.R. Buskirk, E. Haymes), 339-374; w) Maximal Oxygen Uptake of Females (B. Drinkwater), 375-388; x) Sex Differences in Biomechanics (M. Adrian), 389-400.

287 WOMEN AND THE AMERICAN ECONOMY: A LOOK TO THE 1980s. Juanita M. Kreps, ed. Englewood Cliffs, N.J.: Prentice-Hall, 1976.

a) Looking Backward in Order to Look Forward: Women, Work and Social Values in America (W.H. Chafe), 6-30; b) Family and Work: The Social Life Cycle of Women (K.E. Taeuber, J.A. Sweet), 31-60; c) Home Work, Market Work, and the Allocation of Time (J.M. Kreps, R.J. Leaper), 61-81; d) Women in Work Occupations (H.T. Schrank, J.W. Riley, Jr.), 82-101; e) Implications of Women's Employment for Home and Family Life (K.A. Moore, I.V. Sawhill), 102-122; f) Impact of Equal Employment Opportunity Laws (P.A. Wallace), 123-145; g) Requisites for Equality (M.W. Griffiths), 146-154; h) Economy Ahead of Us: Will Women Have Different Roles? (N.S. Barrett), 155-172.

288 WOMEN AND THE CINEMA: A CRITICAL ANTHOLOGY. Karyn Kay and Gerald Peary, eds. New York: E.P. Dutton, 1977.

a) Short Manual for an Aspiring Scenario Writer (Colette), 3-8; b) Dorothy Arzner's "Dance, Girl, Dance" (K. Kay, G. Peary), 9-25; c) Divided Woman: Bree Daniels in "Klute" (D. Giddis), 26-36; d) "Belle de Jour" (K. Murphy), 37-43; e) Hollywood Heroines Under the Influence: Alice Still Lives Here (J. Maslin), 44-49; f) Twilight of Romanticism: "Adele H." (M. Klein), 50-55; g) "Swept Away" (R. McCormick), 56-60; h) Ten That Got Away (J. Basinger), 61-72; i) Making Pabst's Lulu (L. Brooks), 77-85; j) Why I'm Called a Recluse (G. Garbo), 86-89; k) What Maisie Knows: Mae West (S. Young), 90-92; l) Marlene Dietrich: At Heart a Gentleman (A. Walker), 93-98; m) Actress Archetypes in the 1950s: Doris Day, Marilyn Monroe, Elizabeth Taylor, Audrey Hepburn (J. Welsch), 99-111; n) Brigitte Bardot and the Lolita Syndrome (S. de Beauvoir), 112-116; o) Liv Ullmann: The Goddess as Ordinary Woman (M. Haskell), 117-133; p) Alice Guy Blache: Czarina of the Silent Screen (G. Peary), 139-145; q) Years Have Not Been Kind to Lois Weber (R. Koszarski), 146-152; r) Interview with Dorothy Arzner (K. Kay, G. Peary), 153-168; s) Interview with Ida Lupino (D. Weiner), 169-178; t) Stephanie Rothman: R-Rated Feminist (D. Peary), 179-192; u) Working with Hawks (L. Brackett), 193-198; v) Dede Allen (P. McGilligan), 199-207; w) Germaine Dulac: First Feminist Filmmaker (W. Van Wert), 213-223; x) Letter to James Card (M. Deren), 224-230; y) Conversation (S. de Hirsch, S. Clarke), 231-242; z) On Yoko Ono (Y. Ono), 243-245; aa) Interview with Joyce Wieland (K. Armatage), 246-261; bb) "Marilyn Times Five" (C. Kleinhans), 262-263; cc) Women at Work: Warners in the 1930s (S.E. Dalton), 267-282; dd) Women's Liberation Cinema (R. McCormick), 283-291; ee) Interview with Jane Fonda (D. Georgakas,

L. Rubenstein), 292-299; ff) Coup pour coup: Radical French Cinema (J. Lesage), 300-304; gg) "Sambizanga" (S. Maldoror), 305-310; hh) "Part-Time Work of a Domestic Slave," or Putting the Screws to Screwball Comedy (K. Kay), 311-323; ii) Interview with Lina Wertmuller (P. Biskind), 324-332; jj) Woman's Place in Photoplay Production (A.G. Blache), 337-340; kk) That's Not Brave, That's Just Stupid (B. Bernstein), 341-346; ll) Documenting the Patriarchy: "Chinatown" (B.H. Martineau), 347-351; mm) Fascinating Fascism (S. Sontag), 352-376; nn) Is Lina Wertmuller Just Once of the Boys? (E. Willis), 377-383; oo) Ladies' Auxiliary, 1976 (A. Sarris), 384-387; pp) Interview with British Cine-Feminists (E.A. Kaplan), 393-406; qq) Myths of Women in the Cinema (C. Johnston), 407-411; rr) Visual Pleasure and Narrative Cinema (L. Mulvey), 412-428; ss) Are Women Directors Different? (M. Haskell), 429-435.

289 WOMEN AND THE FUTURE. Guy Streatfeild, ed. Guildford, Surrey: IFC Science and Technology Press, 1976. Binghamton, N.Y.: Center for Integration Studies, 1976.

a) Women's Year and Beyond (G. Streatfeild), 362-363; b) Women and World Change (M. Cordell, J. McHale, G. Streatfeild), 364-384; c) Women's Time: Women in the Light of Contemporary Time-Budget Research (A. Szalai), 385-399; d) Tanzanian Women Confront the Past and the Future (M. Mbilinyi), 400-413; e) Technicalities and Fantasy About Men and Women (M. Jahoda), 414-419; f) Women's Roles and the Great World Transformation (J. Platt), 420-427; g) Women and the Future of Education (G. Keller), 428-433; h) Women in Science Fiction (P. Sargent), 434-441; i) Science Fiction Survey (D. Livingston), 442-443.

290 WOMEN AND THE POWER TO CHANGE. Florence Howe, ed. Sponsored by The Carnegie Commission on Higher Education. New York: McGraw-Hill, 1975.

a) Woman-Centered University (A. Rich), 15-46; b) Inside the Clockwork of Male Careers (A.R. Hochschild), 47-80; c) View from the Law School (A. Wallach), 81-126; d) Women and the Power to Change (F. Howe), 127-172.

291 WOMEN AND THE WORKPLACE: THE IMPLICATIONS OF OCCUPATIONAL SEGREGATION. Martha Blaxall and Barbara Reagan, eds. Chicago: University of Chicago Press, 1976.

a) Occupational Segregation in International Women's Year (B.B. Reagan, M. Blaxall), 1-6; b) Can We Still Afford Occupational Segregation? (M.W. Griffiths), 7-14; c) Homosocial Theory of Sex Roles: An Explanation of the Sex Segregation of Social Institutions (J. Lipman-Blumen), 15-32; d) Work Aspirations of Women: False Leads and New Starts (J.L. Laws), 33-50; e) Dual Linkages between the Occupational and Family Systems: A Macrosociological Analysis (C. Safilios-Rothschild), 51-60; f) Occupational Segregation and the

Law (M.J. Gates), 61-74; g) Historical and Structural Barriers to Occupational Desegregation (J. Bernard), 87-94; h) Familial Constraints on Women's Work Roles (E. Boulding), 95-118; i) Occupational Segregation and Public Policy: A Comparative Analysis of American and Soviet Patterns (G.W. Lapidus), 118-136; j) Capitalism, Patriarchy, and Job Segregation by Sex (H. Hartmann), 137-170; k) Economists' Approaches to Sex Segregation in the Labor Market: An Appraisal (F.D. Blau, C.L. Jusenius), 181-200; l) Discrimination and Poverty among Women Who Head Families (I. Sawhill), 201-212; m) Women: The New Reserve Army of the Unemployed (M.A. Ferber, H.M. Lowry), 213-232; n) Toward Dimorphics: A Summary Statement to the Conference on Occupational Segregation (M.H. Strober), 293-302; o) Sex Differences in Economists' Fields of Specialization (M.H. Strober, B.B. Reagan), 303-318.

292 WOMEN AND WOMANHOOD IN AMERICA. Ronald W. Hogeland, ed. (Problems in American Civilization) Lexington, Ma.: D.C. Heath, 1973.

a) Up From the Pedestal (A.S. Kraditor), 3-14; b) New Approaches to the Study of Women in American History (G. Lerner), 15-27; c) Ornaments for the Daughters of Zion (C. Mather), 28-31; d) Eighteenth-Century Womanhood (H. St.J. de Crèvecoeur), 32-33; e) Indian and Black Women (T. Jefferson), 34-36; f) Anne Bradstreet: Dogmatist and Rebel (A. Stanford), 37-46; g) Dynamics of Interracial Sex (W.D. Jordan), 47-56; h) Sex on the American Indian Frontier (W. O'Meara), 57-71; i) American Maidens and Wives (A. de Tocqueville), 72-76; j) Woman (H. Martineau), 77-85; k) Principles of Domestic Science (C. Beecher, H.B. Stowe), 86-89; l) Lady and the Mill Girl (G. Lerner), 90-102; m) Cult of True Womanhood, 1820-1860 (B. Welter), 103-113; n) Troubled Souls of Females (D.B. Meyer), 114-127; o) Home Life as a Profession (Mrs. B. Harrison), 128-132; p) Are Women Human Beings? (C.P. Gilman), 133-134; q) Problems of Sex and Sex Role (B. Spock), 135-137; r) Double Jeopardy: To Be Black and Female (F. Beal), 138-142; s) Nineteenth-Century Heritage: The Family, Feminism and Sex (D.M. Kennedy), 143-152; t) American Woman's Pre-World War I Freedom in Manners and Morals (J.R. McGovern), 153-162; u) Equality Between the Sexes: An Immodest Proposal (A.S. Rossi), 163-180.

293 WOMEN AND WORLD DEVELOPMENT. Irene Tinker and Michèle Bo Bramsen, eds. Prepared under the auspices of the American Association for the Advancement of Science. Washington, D.C.: Overseas Development Council, 1976.

a) Role of Women in Agriculture (M. Mead), 9-11; b) Economy, Family, Fertility, and the Female (R.L. Blumberg), 12-21; c) Adverse Impact of Development on Women (I. Tinker), 22-34; d) Moslem World: Women Excluded from Development (F. Mernissi), 35-44; e) Critical Analysis of Latin American Programs to Integrate Women in Development (T. Orrego de Figueroa), 45-53; f) Women in Cities: Problems and Perspectives (H. Papanek), 54-69; g) Women in Development: Urban Life and Labor (N.H. Youssef), 70-77; h) Women in African Towns South of the Sahara: The Urbanization Dilemma (K. Little), 78-87; i) Dilemma of Peasant Women: A View from a Village in Yucatan (M. Elmendorf), 88-94; j)

Toward Liberating Women: A Communications Perspective (M. Vajrathon), 95-104; k) Women as Co-Managers: The Family as a General Model of Human Social Organization (U. Olin), 105-128; l) Development Approach to Liberation: Suggestions for Planning (E. Childers), 129-140.

294 WOMEN AROUND THE WORLD. Althea Kratz Hottel, ed. Philadelphia: The American Academy of Political and Social Science, 1968.

a) Status of Women in Modern Patterns of Culture (J. Bernard), 3-14; b) Demographic Change and the Roles and Status of Women (J.C. Ridley), 15-25; c) Impact of the World Social Situation on Women (J.J. Henderson), 26-33; d) From Constitutional Recognition to Public Office (L.N. Menon), 34-43; e) Status of Women in Private Law (I.M. Pedersen), 44-51; f) Women and Politics in the U.S. and Canada (R.R. Boyd), 52-57; g) Women in Public Life in Peru (N. Festini), 58-60; h) Political Participation of Western European Women (M.S. Devaud), 61-66; i) Political Activity of Women in Eastern Europe (K. Chylińska), 67-71; j) Women in the Middle East and North Africa and Universal Suffrage (B.Z. Üngör), 72-81; k) Political Participation of Women in Africa South of the Sahara (A.E. Brooks), 82-85; l) Political Role of Southeast Asian Women (A. Raksasataya), 86-90; m) Women and Politics in Japan (T. Fujita), 91-95; n) Women's Political Participation in the South Pacific (A. Norris), 96-101; o) Women in Economic Life: Rights and Opportunities (E. Johnstone), 102-114; p) Women in the Rural Areas (A.R. Lanier), 115-123; q) Women and American Trade Unions (A.H. Cook), 124-132; r) Access to Education at All Levels (N.M. Friderich), 133-144; s) U.N.E.S.C.O. Long-Range Program for the Advancement of Women (J.H. Chaton), 145-153; t) Education Is the Key for Women (I.M. Beasley), 154-162; u) United Nations Action to Advance the Status of Women (M.K. Bruce), 163- .

295 WOMEN AT WORK: ONTARIO, 1850-1930. Janice Acton, Penny Goldsmith and Bonnie Shepard, eds. Toronto: Canadian Women's Educational Press, 1974.

a) Political Economy of Ontario Women in the Nineteenth Century (L. Johnson), 13-32; b) Toronto's Prostitute at the Turn of the Century (L. Rotenberg), 33-70; c) Domestic Service in Canada, 1880-1920 (G. Leslie), 71-126; d) Short History of Nursing in Ontario (J. Coburn), 127-164; e) Schoolmarms and Early Teaching in Ontario (E. Graham), 165-210; f) The "Problem" and Problems of Working Women--Toronto, 1896-1914 (A. Klein, W. Roberts), 211-260; g) Women during the Great War (C. Ramkhalawansingh), 261-308; h) Women in Production: The Toronto Dressmakers' Strike of 1931 (C. MacLeod), 309-330; i) Women's Organization: Learning from Yesterday (D. Kidd), 331-362; j) Research Guide (P. Schulz), 363- .

296 WOMEN: BODY AND CULTURE. ESSAYS ON THE SEXUALITY OF WOMEN IN A CHANGING SOCIETY. Signe Hammer, ed. New York: Harper and Row, 1975.

a) Denial of the Vagina (K. Horney), 19-30; b) Early Childhood Experiences and Women's Achievement Motives (L.W. Hoffman), 31-57; c) Feminism and Psychotherapy (B.J. Kronsky), 58-72; d) Homosexuality in Women (J. McDougall), 73-82; e) Fathers, Mothers and Sex Typing (E.G. Pitcher), 83-90; f) Psychosexual Differentiation (J. Money), 91-112; g) Authority and Masturbation (R.A. Spitz), 113-119; h) Masturbation (A.C. Kinsey, W.B. Pomeroy, C.E. Martin, P.H. Gebhard), 120-131; i) Clitoral Eroticism and the Sexual Response Cycle in Human Females (M.J. Sherfey), 132-139; j) Trebly Sensuous Woman (N. Newton), 139-147; k) Psychologic and Sociologic Factors of Orgasm (W.H. Masters, V.E. Johnson), 148-155; l) Multiple Factors in Frigidity (R. Moulton), 156-178; m) Feminine Fertility Cycles (C.S. Ford, F.A. Beach), 179-192; n) Effects of Oral Contraceptives on Affective Fluctuations Associated with the Menstrual Cycle (K.E. Paige), 193-204; o) Re-evaluation of Some Aspects of Femininity through a Study of Menstruation (N. Shainess), 205-210; p) Sex after Forty--And after Seventy (I. Rubin), 211-222; q) Middle Age (C. Thompson), 223-242; r) Pregnancy and Abortion: Implications for Career Development of Professional Women (M.T. Notman), 243-253; s) Specific Psychological Tasks in Pregnancy and Motherhood (G.L. Bibring), 254-261; t) Delivery (H. Deutsch), 262-276; u) Childbirth in America (A. Ostrum), 277-292; v) Acceptance of the Concept of the Maternal Role by Behavioral Scientists: Its Effects on Women (R.P. Wortis), 293-317; w) Cultural Anthropologist's Approach to Maternal Deprivation (M. Mead), 318-336.

297 WOMEN CROSS-CULTURALLY: CHANGE AND CHALLENGE. Ruby Rohrlich-Leavitt, ed. International Congress of Anthropological and Ethnological Sciences, 9th, Chicago, 1973. The Hague: Mouton, 1976.

a) Women in Bangladesh (R. Jahan), 5-30; b) Role of Women in the Development of Culture in Nigeria (K. Okonjo), 31-40; c) African Women: Identity Crisis? Some Observations on Education and the Changing Role of Women in Sierra Leone and Zaire (I.F. Rousseau), 41-54; d) Female Labor and Capitalism in the U.S. and Brazil (H.I.B. Saffioti), 59-94; e) Women in Mexico (A.G. Sánchez, A.E. Domínguez), 95-110; f) Mayan Woman and Change (M.L. Elmendorf), 111-128; g) Marital Status and Sexual Identity: The Position of Women in a Mexican Peasant Society (D.L. Slade), 129-148; h) Lower Economic Sector: Female Mating Patterns in the Dominican Republic (S.E. Brown), 149-162; i) Female Domestic Servant and Social Change: Lima, Peru (M.L. Smith), 163-180; j) Sociocultural Factors Mitigating Role Conflict of Buenos Aires Professional Women (N.S. Kinzer), 181-198; k) Life and Labor of the Woman Textile Worker in Mexico City (V. Piho), 199-246; l) Women as Workers: The Experience of the Puerto Rican Woman in the 1930's (B. Silvestrini-Pacheco), 247-260; m) Resistance as Protest: Women in the Struggle of Bolivian Tin-Mining Communities (J. Nash), 261-274; n) Economic Basis of the Status of Women (I. Larguia), 281-296; o) Evolutionism and the Place of Women in the U.S., 1855-1900 (C. Ehrlich), 297-326; p) Legislation: An Aid in Eliminating Sex Bias in Education in the U.S. (K.G. Heath), 327-360; q) Discrimination Against Women in the U.S.: Higher Education, Government Enforcement Agencies, and Unions (A.M. Babey-Brooke), 361-374; r) Women's Liberation Movement in the U.S. (J. Freeman), 375-388; s) Politics of Theory: Participant Observation in the U.S. (B.G. Schoepf, A.M. Mariotti), 389-422; t) Role

and Status of Women in the Soviet Union: 1917 to the Present (B.G. Rosenthal), 429-456; u) Women's Movement in the People's Republic of China (D. Davin), 457-470; v) Mobilization of Women: Three Societies (E.M. Chaney), 471-490; w) Image and Reality: Women's Status in Israel (D. Padan-Eisenstark), 491-506; x) Sources of the Matrilineal Family System in the Works of Carl J.L. Almqvist (K.W. Berg), 507-530; y) Women in the Anthropology Profession--1 (D. Barker), 537-546; z) Women in the Anthropology Profession--2 (P. Caplan), 547-550; aa) Women and Fieldwork (J. Bujra), 551-558; bb) Female Factor in Anthropology (C. Ifeka), 559-566; cc) Aboriginal Woman: Male and Female Anthropological Perspectives (R. Rohrlich-Leavitt, B. Sykes, E. Weatherford), 567-580; dd) Women, Knowledge, and Power (C. Sutton, S. Makiesky, B. Sykes, L. Klein), 581-600; ee) Class, Commodity, and the Status of Women (E. Leacock), 601-618; ff) Conclusions (R. Rohrlich-Leavitt), 619-642.

298 WOMEN: FEMINIST STORIES BY NINE NEW AUTHORS. New York: Eakins Press, 1972.

a) Management and Possession (M. Lamb), 1-35; b) My Sisters' Keeper (E. Fisher), 36-51; c) Pigeon Pie (M. Rouse), 52-61; d) The Grandmother (I. Nova), 62-68; e) Gypsies (Photographs) (M. Ollier), 69-80; f) The Power and the Danger (M. Swenson), 81-92; g) The Saffron Boat (S. Berkman), 93-104; h) The Dark Unfathomed Caves (H. Neville), 105-131; i) Payday (M. Barker), 132-141; j) The Sink (S. Griffin), 142- .

299 WOMEN FROM THE GREEKS TO THE FRENCH REVOLUTION. Susan G. Bell, ed. Belmont, Ca.: Wadsworth Publishing Company, 1973.

These selections constitute an interdisciplinary introduction to the historical position of women in Western civilization. Material includes older primary documents as well as recent scholarship. Contributors: Plato, Aristotle, W.K. Lacey, J.P.V.D. Balsdon, J. Carcopino, (Bible), C. Seltman, K.M. Rogers, St. Jerome, L. Eckenstein, Fortunatus, St. Thomas Aquinas, J. Rudel, Countess of Dia, A. Capellanus, G. Chaucer, A. Abram, E. Power, J.L. Vives, Erasmus, J. Burkhardt, W. Boulting, Margaret of Angoulême, R. Ascham, Elizabeth I, D. Stenton, K. Thomas, E. de Goncourt, J. de Goncourt, F. Nozière (E. Weyl), J.J. Rousseau, O. Hufton.

300 WOMEN IN A CHANGING WORLD. Uta West, ed. New York: McGraw-Hill, 1975.

a) Rough Times (M. Piercy), 3-4; b) Weak Are the Second Sex (E. Janeway), 5-24; c) Not a Very Nice Story (D. Lessing), 25-47; d) Sexual Chic, Sexual Fascism and Sexual Confusion (B.G. Harrison), 48-63; e) Diary of a Mad Househusband (M. Weiss), 64-67; f) What Feminists and Freudians Can Learn From Each Other (J. Lazarre), 68-87; g) The Used-Boy Raisers (G. Paley), 88-94; h) If Love is the Answer, What is the Question? (U. West), 95-114; i) In Favor of the Sensitive

Man (A. Nin), 115-122; j) The Bill (D. Barthelme), 123-125; k) Pornography for Women (L. Gould), 126-140; l) New Anxiety of Motherhood (C. Rivers), 141-152; m) God Is a Verb (M. Daly), 153- .

301 WOMEN IN ACADEMIA: EVOLVING POLICIES TOWARD EQUAL OPPORTUNITIES. Elga Wasserman, Arie Y. Lewin and Linda H. Bleiweis, eds. (Praeger Special Studies in U.S. Economic, Social, and Political Issues) New York: Praeger, 1975.

a) Affirmative Action Through Affirmative Attitudes (L.S. Hornig), 8-19; b) Sex Discrimination, Educational Institutions, and the Law: A New Issue on Campus (B. Sandler), 20-36; c) Race, Sex, and Jobs: The Drive Toward Equality (J.S. Pottinger), 37-44; d) Legal Requirements, Structures, and Strategies for Eliminating Sex Discrimination in Academe (L.J. Weitzman), 45-81; e) Developing Criteria and Measures of Equal Opportunities for Women (E.L. Scott), 82-114; f) Creating Opportunities for Women in Science (M.I. Bunting), 115-119; g) Sex Discrimination at Universities: An Ombudsman's View (A.H. Cook), 120-127; h) Case History of Affirmative Action (R. Beach), 128-138; i) Affirmative Action at Stanford University (A.S. Miner, et al.), 139-162; j) Conclusions, 163-164.

302 WOMEN IN AFRICA: STUDIES IN SOCIAL AND ECONOMIC CHANGE. Nancy J. Hafkin and Edna G. Bay, eds. Stanford: Stanford University Press, 1976.

a) Signares of Saint-Louis and Goree: Women Entrepreneurs in Eighteenth-Century Senegal (G.E. Brooks, Jr.), 19-44; b) Dual-Sex Political System in Operation: Igbo Women and Community Politics in Midwestern Nigeria (K. Okonjo), 45-58; c) "Aba Riots" or Igbo "Women's War"? Ideology, Stratification, and the Invisibility of Women (J. Van Allen), 59-86; d) Luo Women and Economic Change During the Colonial Period (M.J. Hay), 87-110; e) Ga Women and Socioeconomic Change in Accra, Ghana (C. Robertson), 111-134; f) Limitations of Group Action Among Entrepreneurs: The Market Women of Abidjan, Ivory Coast (B.C. Lewis), 135-156; g) Rebels or Status-Seekers? Women as Spirit Mediums in East Africa (I. Berger), 157-182; h) From Lelemama to Lobbying: Women's Associations in Mombasa, Kenya (M. Strobel), 183-213; i) Protestant Women's Associations in Freetown, Sierra Leone (F. Chiomasteady), 213-238; j) Women and Economic Change in Africa (L. Mullings), 239-264; k) Less Than Second-Class: Women in Rural Settlement Schemes in Tanzania (J.L. Brain), 265-284.

303 WOMEN IN AMERICAN ARCHITECTURE: A HISTORIC AND CONTEMPORARY PERSPECTIVE. Susanna Torre, ed. A publication and exhibition organized by The Architectural League of New York through its Archive of Women in Architecture. New York: Watson-Guptill Publications, 1977.

a) Model Domestic Environment: Icon or Option? (G. Wright), 18-31; b) Challenging the American Domestic Ideal (D. Hayden), 32-39; c)

Catharine Beecher and the Politics of Housework (D. Hayden), 40-50; d) Pioneer Women Architects (J. Paine), 54-69; e) Sophia Hayden and the Woman's Building Competition (J. Paine), 70-72; f) Report to the Board of Lady Managers (S. Hayden), 73-74; g) Marion Mahony Griffin (S.F. Berkon), 75-78; h) Julia Morgan (S. Boutelle), 79-87; i) Struggle for Place: Women in Architecture: 1920-1960 (M.O. Stevens), 88-102; j) Eleanor Raymond (D. Cole), 103-107; k) Lilian Rice (J. Paine), 108-111; l) Natalie de Blois (J. Paine), 112-114; m) New Professional Identities: Four Women in the Sixties (J. McGroarty, S. Torre), 115-132; n) Voices of Consequence: Four Architectural Critics (S. Stephens), 136-161; o) Women in Architecture and the New Feminism (S. Torre), 148-161; p) Current Portfolio of Projects and Ideas (S. Torre, et al.), 162-182; q) Centers and Fragments: Women's Spaces (L.R. Lippard), 186-197; r) Pyramid and the Labyrinth (S. Torre), 198-202; s) Historic Chart Relating Architectural Projects to General and Women's History in the U.S. (N. Leff), 203-208.

304 WOMEN IN CANADA. Rev. ed. Marylee Stephenson, ed. Don Mills, Ontario: General Publishing, 1977.

a) Women, the Family and Corporate Capitalism (D.E. Smith), 14-48; b) Women as Personal Dependents (M. Eichler), 49-70; c) Women and Success: A Basic Conflict? (M.M. Kimball), 73-89; d) Child-Free Alternative: Rejection of the Motherhood Mystique (J.E. Veevers), 90-108; e) Housewives in Women's Liberation: Social Change as Role-Making (M. Stephenson), 109-126; f) Women's Work in Montreal at the Beginning of the Century (M. Lavigne, J. Stoddart), 129-147; g) Canadian Labour Force: Jobs for Women (M.P. Marchak), 148-159; h) Sexual Division of Labour and Inequality: Labour and Leisure (M. Meissner), 160-180; i) Wages of Work: A Widening Gap Between Men and Women (L. McDonald), 181-192; j) Indian Women: An Historical Example and a Contemporary View (S. Cheda, G. Quijano), 195-208; k) Women in Prison (V. Rosenbluth), 209-227; l) Status of Immigrant Women in Canada (M. Boyd), 228-244; m) Guide to Historical Literature Pertaining to Canadian Women (V. Strong-Boag), 245-274; n) Bibliography of Materials on Canadian Women, 1950-1975 (Social Sciences) (M. Eichler, J. Newton, L. Primrose), 275- .

305 WOMEN IN CANADIAN LITERATURE. Myra G. Hesse, ed. Ottawa: Borealis Press, 1976.

Canadian men and women are contributors to this literary anthology of poetry, short stories and excerpts from longer fiction. Arrangement is topical. Contributors: J. LeMoyne, A. Munro, R. Souster, C. Martin, S.J. Duncan, M. Ostenso, I. Kiriak, H. MacLennan, E. Wilson, E. Buckler, G. Whalley, A. Hébert, P.K. Page, R.T. Allen, M. Callaghan, Y. Theriault, F.P. Grove, S. Ross, A. Henry, M. Engel, D. Helwig, G. Roy, S. Faessler, H. Garner, D. Livesay, B. Harvor, M.-C. Blais, I. Layton, I. Baird, M. Laurence, M. Atwood, C. Beresford-Howe,

R. Davies, P.B. Young, E. Brewster, N.L. McClung, J. LaMarsh.

306 WOMEN IN CHANGING JAPAN. Joyce Lebra, Joy Paulson and Elizabeth Powers, eds. (Westview Special Studies on China and East Asia) Boulder, Co.: Westview, 1976.

a) Evolution of the Feminine Ideal (J. Paulson), 1-24; b) Women in Rural Japan (G.L. Bernstein), 25-50; c) Women in Factories (S. Matsumoto), 51-74; d) "Office Ladies" (R. Carter, L. Dilatush), 75-88; e) Women in Family Businesses (M.L. Maxson), 89-106; f) Women in Service Industries (J. Lebra), 107-132; g) Bar Hostesses (L. Jackson), 133-156; h) Women in Teaching (E.K. Mouer), 157-190; i) Women in the Professions (L. Dilatush), 191-208; j) Women in Media (J. Paulson), 209-232; k) Women in the Political System (E. Carlberg), 233-254; l) Women in Sports (E. Powers), 255-262; m) Women and Suicide (R.M. Cecchini), 263-296; n) Conclusions (J. Lebra), 297-304.

307 WOMEN IN CHINA: STUDIES IN SOCIAL CHANGE AND FEMINISM. Marilyn B. Young, ed. (Michigan Papers in Chinese Studies, No.15) Ann Arbor: Center for Chinese Studies, The University of Michigan, 1973.

a) Mao Tse-tung, Women and Suicide (R. Witke), 7-32; b) Woman as Politician in China of the 1920s (R. Witke), 33-46; c) Chinese Women in the Early Communist Movement (S. Leith), 47-72; d) Women in the Liberated Areas (D. Davin), 73-92; e) Institutionalized Motivation for Fertility Limitation (J. Salaff), 93-144; f) Women and Revolution: The Lessons of the Soviet Union and China (J. Salaff, J. Merkle), 145-178; g) Response to "Women and Revolution" (N. Milton), 179-192; h) Women Hold Up Half the Sky (J. Barrett), 193-200; i) Women's Liberation (S. Ching-ling), 201-204; j) Liberation of Women (Lu Yu-lan), 205-210; k) Status of Women in Taiwan: One Step Forward, Two Steps Back (N. Diamond), 211-242.

308 WOMEN IN CHINESE SOCIETY. Margery Wolf and Roxane Witke, eds. Stanford: Stanford University Press, 1975.

a) Lu K'un's New Audience: The Influence of Women's Literacy on Sixteenth-Century Thought (J.F. Handlin), 13-38; b) Emergence of Women at the End of the Ch'ing: The Case of Ch'iu Chin (M.B. Rankin), 39-66; c) Marriage Resistance in Rural Kwangtung (M. Topley), 67-88; d) Women of Hai-shan: A Demographic Portrait (A.P. Wolf), 89-110; e) Women and Suicide in China (M. Wolf), 111-142; f) Women as Writers in the 1920's and 1930's (Yi-Tsi Feuerweker), 143-168; g) Chiang Ch'ing's Coming of Age (R. Witke), 169-192; h) Power and Pollution of Chinese Women (E.M. Ahern), 193-215; i) Women and Childbearing in Kwan Mun Hau Village: A Study of Social Change (E. Johnson), 215-242; j) Women in

the Countryside of China (D. Davin), 243-276.

309 WOMEN IN CONTEMPORARY INDIA: TRADITIONAL IMAGES AND CHANGING ROLES. Alfred de Souza, ed. Delhi: Manohar, 1975.

a) International Women's Year: Its Significance for Women in India (S. Chitnis), 1-24; b) Women in Uttar Pradesh: Social Mobility and Directions of Change (Z. Bhatty), 25-36; c) Employment and Family Change: A Study of Middle-Class Women in Urban Gujarat (M.R. Wood), 37-53; d) Etiquette among Women in Karnataka: Forms of Address in the Village and the Family (H.E. Ullrich), 54-72; e) Women in Kerala: Changing Socio-Economic Status and Self-Image (J. Murickan), 73-95; f) Women and the Law: Constitutional Rights and Continuing Inequalities (J. Minattur), 96-109; g) Women and Religion: The Status and Image of Women in Major Religious Traditions (U. King), 110-128; h) Family Status and Female Work Participation (V.S. d'Souza), 129-141; i) Aging Women in India: Self-Perceptions and Changing Roles (S. Vatuk), 142-163; j) Asian Women in Britain: Strategies of Adjustment of Indian and Pakistani Migrants (V.S. Khan), 164-188; k) Study of Women in India: Some Problems in Methodology (A.M. Singh), 189-218; l) Draft, International Plan of Action, 219-252.

310 WOMEN IN DRAMA: AN ANTHOLOGY. Harriet Kriegel, ed. New York: New American Library, 1975.

a) Medea (Euripides), 1-38; b) Lysistrata (Aristophanes), 39-78; c) Women Beware Women (T. Middleton), 79-162; d) The Lady From the Sea (H. Ibsen), 163-238; e) Miss Julie (A. Strindberg), 239-276; f) Mrs. Warren's Profession (G.B. Shaw), 277-338; g) Trifles (S. Glaspell), 339-356; h) Approaching Simone (M. Terry), 357- .

311 WOMEN IN INDUSTRY. Pasquale A. Carone, Sherman N. Kieffer, Leonard W. Krinsky, Stanley F. Yolles, eds. Stoneybrook, N.Y.: South Oaks Foundation and the Medical School of the State University of New York at Stoney Brook, 1977.

a) Women in Employment (M.A. Krupsak), 3-9; b) Woman in the Labor Organization (A.H. Nelson), 10-21; c) Health Professions--Opportunities and Limitations (J.R. Hott), 43-56; d) Financial Problems of Women (V. Moss), 77-84; e) Emotional Conflicts of the Career Woman (A. Symonds), 113-123; f) Unique Health Problems of Women in Industry (P.W. Budoff), 154-166; g) Career Choices Opportunities for Women h) Closing Remarks (S.F. Yolles), 220- .

312 WOMEN IN IRISH SOCIETY: THE HISTORICAL DIMENSION. Margaret Mac Curtain and Donncha O Corrain, eds. (Contributions in Women's Studies, No.11) Co-published with Arlen House, The Women's Press, Dublin. Westport, Ct.: Greenwood Press, 1979.

a) Women in Norman Ireland (K. Simms), 14-25; b) Role of Women in Ireland under the New English Order (G. O Tuathaigh), 26-36; c) Women and the Church since the Famine (J.J. Lee), 37-45; d) Women, the Vote and Revolution (M. Mac Curtain), 46-57; e) Women and the New Irish State (M.T.W. Robinson), 58-70; f) Women, Work and Trade Unionism (M.E. Daly), 71-81; g) Women and the Family (P. Redlich), 82-91; h) Women in Irish National and Local Politics, 1922-77 (M. Manning), 92-102; i) Women and Work in Ireland: The Present and Preparing for the Future (E. McCarthy), 103-117.

313 WOMEN IN LATIN AMERICAN HISTORY: THEIR LIVES AND VIEWS. June E. Hahner, ed. (UCLA Latin American Studies Series, Vol. 34) Los Angeles: UCLA Latin American Center Publications, University of California, 1976.

This collection presents selections written by Latin American women of different classes, periods and countries. Arrangement is chronological. Twentieth-century material comprises roughly two-thirds of the book. Contributors: I. de Guevara, S.J.I. de la Cruz, M. Bastidas Puyucahua, F. Calderon de la Barca, F.S. da Motta Diniz, A. Brant (H. Morley), A. Zamudio, C.C. Catt, M. Portal, E. Peron, T. Fabbri, T. Cari, M. Lopes, O. Uribe de Acosta, "Fernanda Fuentes," C.M. de Jesus, "Esperanza," V. Espin, A. Storni.

314 WOMEN IN MANAGEMENT. Bette Ann Stead, ed. Englewood Cliffs, N.J.: Prentice-Hall, 1978.

a) Women as Managers--Stereotypes and Realities (R.L. Dipboye), 2-10; b) Exploding Some Myths About Women Managers (W.E. Reif, J.W. Newstrom, R.M. Monczka), 11-24; c) Female Dimension: Barriers to Effective Utilization of Women in the World of Work (M. Fenn), 25-34; d) Sharon Kirkman: Mind Over Myth (J. Minahan), 35-41; e) Potential of Women (J.J. Durkin), 42-46; f) Myth and the Reality (Women's Bureau, U.S. Dept. of Labor), 47-50; g) Women in Work Force Post Better Records for Stability in Jobs (M. Tharp), 51-56; h) Real Equal Opportunity for Women Executives (B.A. Stead), 58-66; i) Patrons, Rabbis, Mentors--Whatever You Call Them, Women Need Them Too (J. Thompson), 67-74; j) New Work Patterns--for Better Use of Womanpower (F.N. Schwartz), 75-83; k) Assessment Center: Opportunities for Women (D.W. Bray), 84-89; l) Accountability--The Key to Successful Affirmative Action (R.B. Maddux), 90-93; m) Preparing for the Future: Commitment and Action (S. Ekberg-Jordan), 94-100; n) Guidelines for Interviewing and Hiring Women Candidates, 101-104; o) Struggle for Status (D.E. Alpert), 106-112; p) Humanizing the World of Work (S.B. Lord), 113-120; q) Businessman's Guide to Women's Liberation (G. Marine), 121-130; r) Everyday Dealings with Women (P.S. Meyer), 131-135; s) "Women Executives are Different" (P. Meyer), 136-141; t) What's It Like for Women Executives? (L. Smith), 142-148; u) Women in Management: How Is It Working Out? (M.M. Wood), 149-158; v) Semantics of Sex Discrimination (B.A. Stead), 160-167; w) Woman Is Not a Girl and Other Lessons in Corporate Speech (P. Hogan), 168-172; x) "He" and "She": Changing Language to Fit a Changing World (C.S. Johnson, I.K. Kelly), 173-178; y) Addendum to Style Guide for Authors (ACADEMY

OF MANAGEMENT REVIEW), 179-183; z) 52 Job Titles Revised to Eliminate Sex-Stereotyping (Women's Bureau, U.S. Dept. of Labor), 184-186; aa) Differential Recruitment and Control: The Sex Structuring of Organizations (J. Acker, D.R. Van Houten), 188-203; bb) Women and the Informal Organization (D.W. Zacharias), 204-208; cc) Informal Interaction Patterns of Professional Women (S. Albrecht), 209-215; dd) Women and Success in Organizations (M. Williams), 216-226; ee) Female Leadership Dilemma (B. Chapman, F. Luthans), 228-238; ff) Women in Management: Keys to Success or Failure (L.A. Koff, J.H. Handlon), 239-248; gg) Women in Management: The Fallacy of the Trait Approach (L. Putnam, J.S. Heinen), 249-260; hh) Women's Contributions to Management Thought (B.A. Stead), 263-270; ii) What Does it Take for a Woman to Make it in Management? (M.M. Wood), 271-281; jj) Keys to the Executive Powder Room (C. Donnelly), 282-288; kk) Educating Women for Administration (B.A. Stead), 289-297; ll) Consequences of Equal Opportunity for Women (J.W. Torrey), 298-312; mm) APPENDIX: Cases, 313-330.

315 WOMEN IN MEDIEVAL SOCIETY. Susan Mosher Stuard, ed. (The Middle Ages) Philadelphia: University of Pennsylvania Press, 1976.

a) Land, Family, and Women in Continental Europe, 701-1200 (D. Herlihy), 13-46; b) Infanticide in the Early Middle Ages (E. Coleman), 47-70; c) Women in Reconquest Castile: The Fueros of Sepulveda and Cuenca (H. Dillard), 71-94; d) Marriage and Divorce in the Frankish Kingdom (J.-A. McNamara, S.F. Wemple), 95-124; e) Female Felon in Fourteenth-Century England (B.A. Hanawalt), 125-140; f) Mulieres Sanctae (B.M. Bolton), 141-158; g) Widow and Ward: The Feudal Law of Child Custody in Medieval England (S.S. Walker), 159-172; h) Dowries and Kinsmen in Early Renaissance Venice (S. Chojnacki), 173-198; i) Women in Charter and Statute Law: Medieval Ragusa-Dubrovnik (S.M. Stuard), 199-208.

316 WOMEN IN POLITICS. Jane S. Jaquette, ed. New York: Wiley, 1974.

a) American Woman: Voter and Activist (M. Lansing), 5-24; b) Apolitical Woman: Femininity and Sex-Stereotyping in Girls (L.B. Iglitzin), 25-36; c) Women and Political Socialization: Considerations of the Impact of Motherhood (C.B. Flora, N.B. Lynn), 37-53; d) Women's Attitudes Toward Women in Politics: A Survey of Urban Registered Voters and Party Committeewomen (A.S. Wells, E.C. Smeal), 54-72; e) Personality Characteristics of Women in American Politics (E.E. Werner, L.M. Bachtold), 75-84; f) Role and Status of Women in the Daley Organization (M.C. Porter, A.B. Matasar), 85-108; g) Career Structures of Federal Executives: A Focus on Women (M.M. Lepper), 109-130; h) Ideology and the Law: Sexism and Supreme Court Decisions (S.K. Purcell), 131-154; i) Contemporary Feminism, Consciousness-Raising, and Changing Views of the Political (N. McWilliams), 157-170; j) Women's and Men's Liberation Groups: Political Power Within the System and Outside the System (W.T. Farrell), 171-201; k) Tyranny of Structurelessness (J. Freeman), 202-214; l) Women Under Communism (B. Jancar), 217-242; m) Modernization Theory and Sex Roles in Critical Perspective: The Case

of the Soviet Union (G.W. Lapidus), 243-256; n) Marxist Analysis of Women and Capitalism (T. Kaplan), 257-266; o) Mobilization of Women in Allende's Chile (E.M. Chaney), 267-280; p) Changing the Political Role of Women: A Costa Rican Case Study (J. Aviel), 281-303; q) Memsahib, Militante, Femme Libre: Political and Apolitical Styles of Modern African Women (J. Van Allen), 304-321; r) Politics of Cultural Liberation (K. Boals), 322-342; s) Bibliography (M.C. Porter), 343-360.

317 WOMEN IN RITUAL AND SYMBOLIC ROLES. Judith Hoch-Smith and Anita Spring, eds. New York: Plenum Press, 1978.

a) Bride of Christ Is Filled with His Spirit (D.N. Maltz), 27-44; b) Celibes, Mothers, and Church Cockroaches: Religious Participation of Women in a Mexican Village (M. Arnold), 45-54; c) Hats as a Symbol of Women's Position in Three Evangelical Churches in Edinburgh, Scotland (R. Borker), 55-74; d) Coming of Age in Kelton: The Constraints on Gender Symbolism in Jewish Ritual (R.-E. Prell-Foldes), 75-100; e) Misery of the Embodied: Representations of Women in Sinhalese Myth (L.R.A. Singham), 101-128; f) Careers of Midwives in a Mayan Community (L. Paul), 129-150; g) Southern Lay Midwives as Ritual Specialists (M.C. Dougherty), 151-164; h) Epidemiology of Spirit Possession among the Luvale of Zambia (A. Spring), 165-190; i) Convivial Sisterhood: Spirit Mediumship and Client-Core Network among Black South African Women (S. Middleton-Keirn), 191-206; j) Bobbes and Zeydes: Old and New Roles for Elderly Jews (B. Myerhoff), 207-244; k) Radical Yoruba Female Sexuality: The Witch and the Prostitute (J. Hoch-Smith), 245-268; l) Jive Dope Fiend Whoes: In the Street and in Rehabilitation (P. Cleckner), 269-286.

318 WOMEN IN RUSSIA. Dorothy Atkinson, Alexander Dallin and Gail Warshofsky Lapidus, eds. Stanford: Stanford University Press, 1977.

a) Society and the Sexes in the Russian Past (D. Atkinson), 3-38; b) Women and the Russian Intelligentsia: Three Perspectives (R. Stites), 39-62; c) Russian Factory Women, 1880-1914 (R.L. Glickman), 63-84; d) Marxism and the Women's Movement (A.C. Meyer), 85-114; e) Sexual Equality in Soviet Policy: A Developmental Perspective (G.W. Lapidus), 115-138; f) Bolshevik Alternatives and the Soviet Family: The 1926 Marriage Law Debate (B.B. Farnsworth), 139-166; g) Russian Rural Women (E. Dunn), 167-188; h) Women in the Industrial Labor Force (M.P. Sacks), 189-204; i) Women in the Professions (N.T. Dodge), 205-224; j) Equal Pay for Equal Work? (J.G. Chapman), 225-242; k) Women and Sex in Soviet Law (P.H. Juviler), 243-266; l) Educational Policies and Attainment (R.B. Dobson), 267-292; m) Images of Male and Female in Children's Readers (M.S. Rosenhan), 293-306; n) Social Services for Women: Problems and Priorities (B. Madison), 307-332; o) Women in Political Roles (J.C. Moses), 333-354; p) Women and Women's Issues in Soviet Policy Debates (J.F. Hough), 355-374; q) Individual and the Collective (C. Shulman), 375-384; r) Conclusions (A. Dallin),

385-400.

319 WOMEN IN THE AMERICAN ECONOMY: A DOCUMENTARY HISTORY, 1675 to 1929. W. Elliot Brownlee and Mary M. Brownlee, eds. New Haven: Yale University Press, 1976.

The pieces in this collection are meant to demonstrate the extent and diversity of women's contributions to the economic development of America. In addition, the selections aid in linking the working and social lives of women. Contributors: M. van Rensselaer, E.L. Pinckney, A.S. Adams, B. Franklin, M. Bradley, R. Williams, E.A. Pringle, M. Holley, E. Farnham, S.E. Beaulieu, B.A. Owens-Adair, M. Carey, L. Larcom, B. van Vorst, D. Richardson, T.V. Powderly, E. O'Donnell, M.D. Robins, F.M. Cohn, J. Matyas, M.H. "Mother" Jones, H. Mann, E. Blackwell, A. Hamilton, B. Lockwood, W.I. Bowditch, M. Nathan, E.H. Richards, E. Bok, H. Hoover.

320 WOMEN IN THE CANADIAN MOSAIC. Gwen Matheson, ed. Toronto: P. Martin Associates, 1976.

a) Nellie McClung: "Not a Nice Woman" (G. Matheson, V.E. Lang), 1-22; b) Canadian Suffragists (D. Gorham), 23-56; c) Women in Quebec (C. Pestieau), 57-70; d) Voice of Women: A History (K. Macpherson, M. Sears), 71-92; e) Changes in the Churches (C. Wallace), 93-130; f) Immigrant Woman (A. Alberro, G. Montero), 131-150; g) Farm Wife (N. Taylor), 151-166; h) Sex Stereotyping in Canadian Schools (F. Nelson), 167-182; i) Women's Studies (F. Wilson), 183-198; j) Women in the Universities (J. Vickers), 199-242; k) Women and the Unions (G. Hartman), 243-256; l) Paradoxes and Dilemmas: Woman as Writer (M. Atwood), 257-274; m) Breaking Out of the Female Mould (M. Kantaroff), 275-288; n) New Kind of Power (R. Brown), 289-300; o) Feminist Mosaic (L. Teather), 301-346; p) APPENDIX: Women's Centres, Women's Newspapers and Regional Contacts, 347-351.

321 WOMEN IN THE COURTS. Winifred L. Hepperle and Laura Crites, eds. Williamsburg, Va.: National Center for State Courts, 1978.

a) Female in the Trial Court (M. Oliver), 1-20; b) Women, Men, and The Constitution: Key Supreme Court Rulings (R.B. Ginsburg), 21-46; c) Burger Court and Women's Rights, 1971-1977 (B.B. Cook), 47-83; d) Women Judges: The End of Tokenism (B.B. Cook), 84-105; e) Women in Court Administration (W.L. Hepperle, J.L. Hendryx), 106-113; f) Sexism in Voir Dire: The Use of Sex Stereotypes in Jury Selection (A.R. Mahoney), 114-135; g) Changes in Domestic Relations Court (B. Hoffman), 136-159; h) Women in the Criminal Court (L. Crites), 160-175; i) Victims of Rape and Wife Abuse (M. Gates), 176-201; j) Justice: A Woman Blindfolded? (L. Nader, J. Collier), 202-221; k) Conclusion (W.L. Hepperle),

222-226.

322 WOMEN IN THE FIELD: ANTHROPOLOGICAL EXPERIENCES. Peggy J. Golde, comp. Chicago: Aldine Publishing Company, 1970.

a) Kapluna Daughter (J. Briggs), 19-46; b) Exploring American Indian Communities in Depth (L. Thompson), 47-66; c) Odyssey of Encounter (P. Golde), 67-96; d) From Anguish to Exultation (L. Nader), 97-118; e) Woman Anthropologist in Brazil (R. Landes), 119-142; f) Field Work in Rwanda, 1959-1960 (H. Codere), 143-166; g) World of Women: Field Work in a Yoruba Community (G. Marshall), 167-194; h) Field Work in a Greek Village (E. Friedl), 195-220; i) Studies in an Indian Town (C. Du Bois), 221-238; j) Ambivalence in the Field (H.H. Weidman), 239-266; k) Field Work in Five Cultures (A. Fischer), 267-292; l) Field Work in the Pacific Islands, 1925-1967 (M. Mead), 293-332.

323 WOMEN IN THE LABOUR MOVEMENT: THE BRITISH EXPERIENCE. Lucy Middletcn, ed. London: Croom Helm; Totawa, N.J.: Rowman and Littlefield, 1977.

a) Women in Labour Politics (L. Middleton), 22-37; b) Labour Women and the Social Services (S. Ferguson), 38-56; c) Contribution of the Women's Labour League to the Winning of the Franchise (M. Rendel), 57-83; d) Labour Women and Internationalism (M. Walker), 84-93; e) Early Years in the Trade Unions (A. Godwin), 94-112; f) Women and Cooperation (J. Gaffin), 113-143; g) Women in the Labour Party (O. McDonald), 144-160; h) Women in Trade Unions (M. McCarthy), 161-174; i) Women in Parliament and Government (M. Denby), 175-190.

324 WOMEN IN THE MODERN WORLD. Raphael Patai, ed. New York: Free Press, 1967.

a) India (V. Narain), 21-41; b) Pakistan (S.A. Ahmed), 42-58; c) Iran (L. Yarshater), 61-81; d) Turkey (N. Abadan), 82-105; e) Arab World (C.W. Churchill), 106-128; f) Greece (E. Psaltis), 131-152; g) Italy (T. Tentori), 153-175; h) Spain (M. Formica de Careaga), 176-191; i) Spanish America (R. Signorelli de Marti), 192-208; j) Brazil (L. Cruz), 209-226; k) France (A. Lehmann), 229-246; l) West Germany (H. Pross), 247-266; m) Israel (Z. Harman), 267-289; n) Japan (T. Koyama, H. Nakamura, M. Hiramatsu), 290-314; o) Sub-Saharan Africa (E.H. Wheeler), 317-345; p) Burma and South-East Asia (M.M. Khang), 346-360; q) Indonesia (C. Vreede-de Stuers), 361-384; r) Soviet Union (V. Alexandrova), 387-409; s) Mainland China (A.S. Chin), 410-434; t) Scandinavia (H. Holter), 437-462; u) Great Britain (V. Klein), 463-488; v) United States (M.G. Benz), 489-510.

325 WOMEN IN THE MUSLIM WORLD. Lois Beck and Nikki Keddie, eds. Cambridge, Ma.: Harvard University Press, 1978.

a) Women and Law Reform in Contemporary Islam (N. Coulson, D. Hinchcliffe), 37-51; b) Legal Reform as an Indicator of Women's Status in Muslim Nations (E.H. White), 52-68; c) Status and Fertility Patterns of Muslim Women (N.H. Youssef), 69-99; d) Women and Social Change in Morocco (V. Maher), 100-123; e) Women in Turkish Society (F.M. Coşar), 124-140; f) Women's Emancipation in Tunisia (M.A. Tessler, J. Rogers, D. Schneider), 141-158; g) Women in Algeria (J. Minces), 159-171; h) Education and Employment among Kuwaiti Women (K. Nath), 172-188; i) Changing the Concept and Position of Persian Women (M.M.J. Fischer), 189-215; j) Legal and Social Positions of Iranian Women (B. Pakizegi), 216-226; k) Turkish Women in the Ottoman Empire: The Classical Age (I.Ç. Dengler), 229-244; l) Women as Patrons of Architecture in Turkey (Ü.Ü. Bates), 245-260; m) Revolutionary Gentlewomen in Egypt (A.L. al-Sayyid Marsot), 261-276; n) Feminism and National Politics in Egypt (T. Philipp), 277-294; o) Women and Revolution in Iran, 1905-1911 (M. Bayat-Philipp), 295-308; p) Status of Women in Four Middle East Communities (E.L. Peters), 311-350; q) Women among Qashqa'i Nomadic Pastoralists in Iran (L. Beck), 351-373; r) Women's Subsociety among the Shahsevan Nomads of Iran (N. Tapper), 374-398; s) Changing Sex Roles in Bedouin Society in Syria and Lebanon (D. Chatty), 399-415; t) Working women in a Moroccan Village (S.S. Davis), 416-433; u) Status of Women and Property on a Baluchistan Oasis in Pakistan (C.McC. Pastner), 434-450; v) Iranian Women in Family Alliance and Sexual Politics (P. Vieille), 451-472; w) Women, Class, and Power: Examples from the Hatay, Turkey (B.C. Aswad), 473-481; x) Comparative Perspective on Women in Provincial Iran and Turkey (M.-J.D. Good), 482-500; y) Domestic Social Environment of Women and Girls in Isfahan, Iran (J. Gulick, M.E. Gulick), 501-521; z) Self-Images of Traditional Urban Women in Cairo (S. el-Messiri), 522-540; aa) Women and the Neighborhood Street in Borj Hammoud, Lebanon (S. Joseph), 541-558; bb) Negotiation of Reality: Male-Female Relations in Sefrou, Morocco (L. Rosen), 561-584; cc) Women, Sufism, and Decision-Making in Moroccan Islam (D.H. Dwyer), 585-598; dd) Sex Differences and Folk Illness in an Egyptian Village (S.A. Morsy), 599-616; ee) Theme of Sexual Oppression in the North African Novel (E. Accad), 617-628; ff) Women in Contemporary Persian Folktales (E. Friedl), 629-650; gg) Being Female in a Muslim Minority in China (B.L.K. Pillsbury), 651-676.

326 WOMEN IN THE PROFESSIONS. Laurily Keir Epstein, ed. Lexington, Ma.: Lexington Books, 1975.

a) Success Motivation and Social Structure: Comments on Women and Achievement (C.F. Epstein), 1-14; b) Women in Academia: Today is Different (J.M. Kreps), 15-24; c) Recent Trends in the Employment of American Women (J.A. Sweet), 25-66; d) Female Status: A New Population Policy (V. Gray), 67-80; e) Black Women Officeholders: The Case of State Legislators (J. Prestage), 81-96; f) Women as Voters: Their Maturation as Political Persons in American Society (J.J. Stucker), 97-114; g) Government Policy and the Legal Status of Women (R.B. Conlin), 115-122; h) Alternatives for Social Change: The Future

Status of Women (C.S. Bell), 123-136.

327 WOMEN IN THE PROFESSIONS: WHAT'S ALL THE FUSS ABOUT? Linda S. Fidell and John DeLamater, eds. (Sage Contemporary Social Science Issues, No. 8) Beverly Hills, Ca.: Sage, 1971.

a) Status of Women (J. DeLamater, L.S. Fidell), 5-13; b) Why Can't Women Be More Like Men: A Summary of the Sociopsychological Factors Hindering Women's Advancement in the Professions (J. Prather), 14-24; c) Regional Approach to Analyzing the Recruitment of Academic Women (J.M. Mitchell, R.R. Starr), 25-47; d) Nonacademic Professional Political Scientists (I. Tinker), 48-54; e) Analysis of Femininity in Nursing (V. Wilson), 55-62; f) Male Managers' Attitudes Toward Working Women (B.M. Bass, J. Krusell, R.A. Alexander), 63-78; g) Sex Discrimination Against the American Working Woman (T. Levitin, R.P. Quinn, G.L. Staines), 79-96; h) Soviet Women in the Work Force and Professions (W.M. Mandel), 97-122; i) Women in the Professional Caucuses (R.M. Oltman), 123- .

328 WOMEN IN THE U.S. LABOR FORCE. Ann Foote Cahn, ed. Edited for the Joint Economic Committee. New York: Praeger, 1979.

a) Women's Stake in Full Employment: Their Disadvantaged Role in the Economy--Challenges to Action (M.D. Keyserling), 25-39; b) Way to Full Equality (I.V. Sawhill), 40-60; c) Legal Road to Equal Employment Opportunity (M.C. Dunlap), 61-74; d) Legal Remedies beyond Title VII to Combat Sex Discrimination in Employment (M. Greenberger, D. Gutmann), 75-89; e) De Facto Job Segregation (B.R. Reagan), 90-102; f) Women Workers, Nontraditional Occupations and Full Employment (B.G. Reubens, E.P. Reubens), 103-126; g) Underemployment of Women: Policy Implications for a Full Employment Economy (G.P. Glyde), 127-141; h) Lifetime Participation in the Labor Force and Unemployment among Mature Women (S.H. Sandell), 142-154; i) Homemaker, the Family, and Employment (N. Glazer, L. Majka, J. Acker, C. Bose), 155-169; j) Economic Aspects of Child Care (M.H. Strober), 170-181; k) Part-Time Work (C.S. Greenwald), 182-194; l) Facilitating Full Employment of Women through Career Education (A.M. Mitchell), 195-202; m) Vocational Education (P.A. Roby), 203-224; n) Apprenticeship (N. Briggs), 225-236; o) Federal Income Tax and Social Security Law (G.G. Blumberg), 237-248; p) Impact of Mass-Media Stereotypes upon the Full Employment of Women (G. Tuchman), 249-270; q) Working Women: European Experience and American Need (A.H. Cook), 271-306.

329 WOMEN IN THE WORLD: A COMPARATIVE STUDY. Lynne B. Iglitzin and Ruth Ross, eds. (Studies in Comparative Politics, No. 6) Santa Barbara, Ca.: Clio Books, 1976.

a) Patriarchal Heritage (L.B. Iglitzin), 7-24; b) African Women, "Modernization," and National Liberation (J. Van Allen), 25-54; c) Female Political Participation in Latin America (J.S. Jaquette), 55-76; d) Catholicism and Women's Role in Italy and Ireland (M.C. Porter,

C. Venning), 81-104; e) Condition of Women in Italy (C. Bielli), 105-114; f) Women in France (J.R. Juillard), 115-128; g) Politics of Sex: West Germany (P.H. Merkl), 129-148; h) Female Labor Force in Western Europe (R. Gubbels), 149-162; i) Tradition and the Role of Women in Great Britain (R. Ross), 163-174; j) Political Change for the American Woman (M. Lansing), 175-184; k) Women in Ghana (B.J. Callaway), 189-202; l) Women in the Muslim World (N.H. Youssef), 203-218; m) Women in Iran (H. Sedghi), 219-228; n) Algerian Women: Honor, Survival, and Islamic Socialism (J. Stiehm), 229-242; o) Women's Changing Roles in Colombia (S.W. Schmidt), 243-256; p) Female Political Elites in Mexico: 1974 (A.S. Riddell), 257-268; q) Industrialization and Hong Kong Women (J. Salaff), 269-286; r) Yugoslav Women (B. Springer), 291-302; s) Changing Women's Roles in the U.S.S.R. (G.W. Lapidus), 303-318; t) Kibbutz Women: From the Fields of Revolution to the Laundries of Discontent (R.L. Blumberg), 319-344; u) Chinese Women on the Road to Complete Emancipation (Siu-Tsung Lin), 345-362; v) Marriage Law: Basis of Change for China's Women (A. Holly, C.T. Bransfield), 363-374; w) Scandinavian Women (I.N. Means), 375-390; x) Sweden: A Feminist Model? (S.R. Herman), 391-400; y) Conference Postscript (E.M. Borgese), 401-404; z) Afterword: New Research Directions (A. Myrdal), 405-412.

330 WOMEN IN THERAPY: NEW PSYCHOTHERAPIES FOR A CHANGING SOCIETY. Violet Franks and Vasanti Burtle, eds. New York: Brunner-Mazel, 1974.

a) Changing Views of Women and Therapeutic Approaches: Some Historical Considerations (H. Osmond, V. Franks, V. Burtle), 3-26; b) Sex Hormones, The Central Nervous System and Affect Variability in Humans (J.M. Bardwick), 27-50; c) Cultural Values, Female Role Expectancies and Therapeutic Goals: Research and Interpretation (A. Steinmann), 51-82; d) Psychotherapist and the Female Patient: Perceptions, Misperceptions and Change (B. Fabrikant), 83-112; e) Cognitive Therapy with Depressed Women (A.T. Beck, R.L. Greenberg), 113-131; f) Phobic Syndrome in Women: Implications for Treatment (I.G. Fodor), 132-168; g) Women and Alcoholism (E.S. Gomberg), 169-190; h) Female Homosexual (B.F. Riess), 191-216; i) Women in Behavior Therapy (A.A. Lazarus), 217-229; j) Therapy of Women in the Light of Psychoanalytic Theory and the Emergence of a New View (E. Menaker), 230-246; k) Women in Therapy--A Gestalt Therapist's View (M. Polster), 247-262; l) Anna O.--Patient or Therapist? An Eidetic View (A. Ahsen), 263-283; m) Treatment of Sex and Love Problems in Women (A. Ellis), 284-306; n) Creative Exits: Fight-Therapy for Divorcees (G.R. Bach), 307-325; o) Consciousness-Raising Groups as Therapy for Women (B. Kirsch), 326-356; p) Women in Institutions: Treatment in Prisons and Mental Hospitals (E.M. Howard, J.L. Howard), 357-382; q) Psychotherapy with Women and Men of Lower Classes (I. Siassi), 383-410; r) Female Role: Constants and Change (S. Keller), 411-434.

331 WOMEN INTO WIVES: THE LEGAL AND ECONOMIC IMPACT OF MARRIAGE. Jane Roberts Chapman and Margaret Gates, eds. (Sage Yearbooks in Women's Policy Studies, Vol. 2) Beverly Hills: Sage, 1977.

a) Girls into Wives (R. Best), 15-58; b) Sexual Inequality, Cultural Norms, and Wife-Beating (M.A. Straus), 59-78; c) Women's Dependency and Federal Programs (S. Kinsley), 79-92; d) Partnership Marriage: Legal Reforms Needed (J.M. Krauskopf), 93-122; e) Health and Fertility Issues and the Dependency of Wives (M.E. King, J.A. Lipshutz, A. Moore), 123-150; f) Black Women and the Family (D.H. Painter), 151-168; g) Child Care for the 1980s: Traditional Sex Roles or Androgyny? (M.P. Rowe), 169-194; h) Public Policy and the Family: A New Strategy for Women as Wives and Mothers (S.B. Kamerman), 195-214; i) Homemakers into Widows and Divorcees: Can the Law Provide Economic Protection? (M. Gates), 215-232; j) Crisis Perspective on Divorce and Role Change (J. Lipman-Blumen), 233-258; k) Women into Mothers: Experimental Family Life-Styles (M. Kornfein, T.S. Weisner, J.C. Martin), 259-292; l) Conclusions (J.R. Chapman), 293-298.

332 WOMEN LOOK AT BIOLOGY LOOKING AT WOMEN: A COLLECTION OF FEMINIST CRITIQUES. Ruth Hubbard, Mary Sue Henifin and Barbara Fried, eds. (With Vicki Druss and Susan Leigh Star) Boston: G.K. Hall; Cambridge: Schenkman, 1979.

a) Have Only Men Evolved? (R. Hubbard), 7-36; b) Language of Sex and Gender (B. Fried), 37-60; c) Sex Differences in Hemispheric Brain Asymmetry (S.L. Star), 61-76; d) Displaced--The Midwife by the Male Physician (D.C. Brack), 83-102; e) Quirls of a Woman's Brain (M.R. Walsh), 103-126; f) Why Are So Many Anorexics Women? (V. Druss, M.S. Henifin), 127-134; g) Exploring Menstrual Attitudes (E.E. Culpepper), 135-162; h) Taking the Men Out of Menopause (M. Grossman, P. Bart), 163-186; i) Adventures of a Woman in Science (N. Weisstein), 187-204; j) Epilogue 205-212; k) Bibliography: Women, Science, and Health (M.S. Henifin), 213- .

333 WOMEN, MINORITIES AND EMPLOYMENT DISCRIMINATION. Phyllis A. Wallace and Annette M. La Mond, eds. Lexington, Ma.: D.C. Heath, 1977.

a) Economic Theories of Employment Discrimination (A.M. La Mond), 1-12; b) Role of Worker Expectancies in the Study of Employment Discrimination (P. Gurin), 13-37; c) What Psychological Research on the Labor Force Participation of Women is Needed? (J.L. Laws), 45-52; d) More Useful Modes of Research on Discrimination in Employment and Pay (B.R. Bergmann), 53-56; e) Black Employment in the South (R. Marshall), 57-81; f) Modeling a Segmented Labor Market (C.C. Holt), 83-119; g) Differences in Expected Post-School Investment as a Determinant of Market Wage Differentials (S.W. Polachek), 127-148; h) Dynamic Theory of Racial Income Differences (G.C. Loury), 153-186; i) Recommendations from Research Workshops on Equal Employment Opportunity (P.A. Wallace), 189-198.

334 WOMEN OF AMERICA: A HISTORY. Carol Ruth Berkin and Mary Beth Norton, eds. Boston: Houghton Mifflin, 1979.

a) Women and American History (M.B. Norton, C.R. Berkin), 3-15; b) Women's Lives Transformed: Demographic and Family Patterns in America, 1600-1970 (R.V. Wells), 16-36; c) Myth of the Golden Age (M.B. Norton), 37-47; d) Cherished Spirit of Independence: The Life of an Eighteenth-Century Boston Businesswoman (M.B. Norton), 48-67; e) Young Ladies Academy of Philadelphia (A.D. Gordon), 68-91; f) Equality or Submersion? Feme (sic) Couvert Status in Early Pennsylvania (M. Salmon), 92-113; g) Women of Light (M.M. Dunn), 114-138; h) Paradox of "Women's Sphere" (M.B. Norton), 139-149; i) Private Woman, Public Woman: The Contradictions of Charlotte Perkins Gilman (C.R. Berkin), 150-176; j) Founding of Mount Holyoke College (K.K. Sklar), 177-201; k) Irish Working Women in Troy (C. Turbin), 202-222; l) Chinese Immigrant Women in Nineteenth-Century California (L.C. Hirata), 223-244; m) Origins of Legal Restrictions on Planned Parenthood in Nineteenth-Century America (J.P. Harper), 245-272; n) Not Separate, Not Equal (C.R. Berkin), 273-288; o) From Aide to Organizer: The Oral History of Lillian Roberts (S. Reverby), 289-317; p) Academic Prism: New View of American Women (R. Rosenberg), 318-341; q) Propaganda and Public Opinion in the United States and Germany, 1939-1945 (L.J. Rupp), 342-359; r) Women Against Lynching in the Twentieth-Century South (J.D. Hall), 360-388; s) Feminist Consciousness and the Future of Women (S.M. Evans), 389-417.

335 THE WOMEN OF ENGLAND FROM ANGLO-SAXON TIMES TO THE PRESENT: INTERPRETIVE BIBLIOGRAPHICAL ESSAYS. Barbara Kanner, ed. Hamden, Ct.: Shoestring Press-Archon Books, 1979.

a) Old and New Women's History (B. Kanner), 9-31; b) Women in Anglo-Saxon Society (c.600-1066) (S.C. Dietrich), 32-56; c) Land Charters and the Legal Position of Anglo-Saxon Women (M.A. Meyer), 57-82; d) Women in Norman and Plantagenet England (K. Casey), 83-123; e) Women Under the Law in Medieval England: 1066-1485 (R. Kittel), 124-137; f) Women in an Age of Transition: 1485-1714 (R. Masek), 138-182; g) Eighteenth-Century Englishwoman (B.B. Schnorrenberg, J.E. Hunter), 183-228; h) Discovery of Women in Eighteenth-Century English Political Life (K. von den Steinen), 229-258; i) Demographic Contributions to the History of Victorian Women (S.R. Johansson), 259-295; j) Women in the Mirror: Using Novels to Study Victorian Women (P.O. Klaus), 296-344; k) Women in Twentieth-Century England (N.A. Ferguson), 345-387; l) Survey of Primary Sources and Archives for the History of Early Twentieth-Century English Women (J. Weeks), 388-418.

336 WOMEN OF LOWELL. (Women in America From Colonial Times to the 20th Century) New York: Arno Press, 1974.

a) Loom and Spindle; or, Life Among the Early Mill Girls (1898)(H.H. Robinson); b) Vindication of the Character and Condition of the Females Employed in the Lowell Mills... (1841)(E. Bartlett); c) Corporations and Operatives, Being an Exposition of the Condition of Factory Operatives... (1843)(Anon.); d) Among Lowell Mill-Girls: A Reminiscence (1881)(L. Larcom); e) Early Factory Magazines in New England: The LOWELL OFFERING and its Contemporaries

(1930)(B.M. Stearns).

337 WOMEN OF SPIRIT: FEMALE LEADERSHIP IN THE JEWISH AND CHRISTIAN TRADITIONS. Rosemary Ruether and Eleanor McLaughlin, eds. New York: Simon and Schuster, 1979.

a) Women's Leadership in the Jewish and Christian Traditions: Continuity and Change (R. Ruether, E. McLaughlin), 15-28; b) Women in Early Christian Communities (E.S. Fiorenza), 29-70; c) Ascetic Women in the Late Patristic Age (R. Ruether), 71-98; d) Women, Power and the Pursuit of Holiness in Medieval Christianity (E. McLaughlin), 99-130; e) Dispute over an Active Apostolate for Women During the Counter-Reformation (R.P. Liebowitz), 131-152; f) Quaker Women in the English Left Wing (E.C. Huber), 153-182; g) Jane Lead: The Feminist Mind and Art of a Seventeenth-Century Protestant Mystic (C.F. Smith), 183-204; h) Feminist Thrust of Sectarian Christianity (B.B. Zikmund), 205-224; i) Feminism in the Evangelical Tradition (N. Hardesty, L.S. Dayton, D.W. Dayton), 225-254; j) Liberated American Nun (M. Ewens), 255-278; k) Women, Religion and Reform in Antebellum America (D.C. Bass), 279-300; l) American Women in Ministry: A History of Protestant Beginning Points (V.L. Brereton, C.R. Klein), 301-332; m) Women in Judaism: From the Reform Movement to Contemporary Jewish Religious Feminism (E.M. Umansky), 333-355; n) Episcopalian Story (N. Carter), 356-372; o) Roman Catholic Story (R. Ruether), 373-384.

338 WOMEN OF TROPICAL AFRICA. Denise Paulme, ed. Berkeley: University of California Press, 1963.

a) Coniagui Women (Guinea) (M. Gessain), 17-46; b) Position of Women in a Pastoral Society (Fulani WoDaaBe, Nomads of the Niger) (M. Dupire), 47-92; c) Role of Women in the Political Organization of African Societies (A.M.D. Lebeuf), 93-120; d) Nzakara Women (Central African Republic) (A. Laurentin), 121-178; e) Women of Burundi: A Study of Social Values (E.M. Albert), 179-216; f) Women of Dakar and the Surrounding Urban Area (S. Faladé), 217-230; g) Analytical Bibliography (M. Perlman, M.P. Moal), 231-294.

339 WOMEN OF VALOR. Samuel Kostman, comp. New York: Richards Rosen Press, 1978.

a) Madame Bovary (G. Flaubert), 5-22; b) Anna Karenina (L. Tolstoy), 23-32; c) Dirge Without Music (E.St.V. Millay), 33-35; d) Patterns (A. Lowell), 36-40; e) Consorting With Angels (A. Sexton), 41-46; f) Saint Joan (G.B. Shaw), 47-56; g) A Doll's House (H. Ibsen), 57-70; h) The Scarlet Letter (N. Hawthorne), 71-81; i) Riders to the Sea (J.M. Synge), 82-96; j) The Book of Ruth (Old Testament), 97-100; k) The Corn is Green (E. Williams), 101-126; l) Vierochka (A. Chekhov), 127-140; m) The Soul Selects Her Own Society (E. Dickinson), 141-143; n) An Unposted Love Letter (D. Lessing), 144-155; o) The Applicant (S. Plath), 156-162; p) Pride and Prejudice (J. Austen), 163-170; q)

Antigone (Sophocles), 171- .

340 WOMEN OF WONDER: SCIENCE FICTION STORIES BY AND ABOUT WOMEN. Pamela Sargent, ed. New York: Vintage Books, 1975, c1974.

a) Women and Science Fiction (P. Sargent), xiii- ; b) The Child Dreams (S. Dorman), 3-4; c) That Only a Mother (J. Merril), 5-17; d) Contagion (K. MacLean), 18-58; e) The Wind People (M.Z. Bradley), 59-81; f) The Ship Who Sang (A. McCaffrey), 82-107; g) When I Was Miss Dow (S. Dorman), 108-124; h) The Food Farm (K. Reed), 125-138; i) Baby, You Were Great (K. Wilhelm), 139-158; j) Sex and-or Mr. Morrison (C. Emschwiller), 159-170; k) Vaster Than Empires and More Slow (U.K. Le Guin), 171-213; l) False Dawn (C.Q. Yarbro), 214-234; m) Nobody's Home (J. Russ), 235-256; n) Of Mist, and Grass, and Sand (V.N. McIntyre), 257- .

341 WOMEN ON CAMPUS: THE UNFINISHED LIBERATION. Editors of CHANGE MAGAZINE. New Rochelle, N.Y.: CHANGE MAGAZINE, 1975.

a) Women on Campus: The Unfinished Liberation (E. Janeway), 10-27; b) Odds Against Women (R.R. Hawkins), 28-33; c) Wives of Academe (D. Martin), 34-43; d) Rhodes: Still Blocked (A. Stent), 44-52; e) Uncertain Progress of Affirmative Action (C.J. Sugnet), 53-68; f) New Feminism and Women's Studies (C.R. Stimpson), 69-84; g) Women's Revolt in the M.L.A. (V. Barber), 85-94; h) Women and History (B. Watkins), 95-101; i) Feminist Press (J. Collins), 102-109; j) Make Policy, Not Coffee (E. Klein), 110-115; k) Lesbians--The Doors Open (C. Secor), 116-124; l) Learning the Hard Way (C. Morris), 125-139; m) Unemployed! An Academic Woman's Saga (E.B. Hopkins), 140-151; n) Search for Talented Women (E. Tidball), 152-159; o) Black, Female--and Qualified (R. Fischer), 160-166; p) Jacquelyn Mattfeld of Brown (N. McCain), 167-173; q) Women at Bryn Mawr (C.R. Stimpson), 174-194; r) Women and War (K. Millett), 195-219; s) Women's Lib and the Women's Colleges (C. Bird), 220-235; t) Why Women Go Back to College (P. Durchholz, J. O'Connor), 236-241; u) "Second-Chance" Program for Women (E. Hansot), 242-248; v) Fair Return (D.R. Margolis), 249- .

342 WOMEN ON THE MOVE: A FEMINIST PERSPECTIVE. Jean Ramage Leppaluoto, et al., eds. Eugene: University of Oregon, 1973.

a) Women and Anger: Alternatives (C. Naffziger), 5-14; b) If You're Depressed, You're Probably Sub-Assertive (S.K. Gilmore), 15-20; c) Sexual Politics (J.E. Prather), 21-26; d) Alienation and the Contemporary American Housewife (F.W. Pozzuto), 27-38; e) Women and Aging: The Unforgivable Sin (A.J. Kethley), 39-46; f) Group Dynamics and Consciousness Raising (C.M. Porter), 47-50; g) Women's Studies (F. Howe), 53-62; h) Nuts and Bolts View of Women's Studies (N.M. Porter), 63-72; i) Women's Perspectives of Family Studies (C. Naffziger), 73-78; j) Women's Work is Never Done (A. Froines), 79-88; k) Liberation of Clio (R. Rosen), 89-94; l) Male Bias in Psychology (J. Silveira), 95-110; m) Study of Male Society (J. Acker),

111-116; n) Political Economy of Women's Oppression (J.M. Newton), 117-128; o) Equal Employment Opportunities in Oregon (L.A. Martin), 129-144; p) Ideology of Prostitution (M.S. Goldman), 145-152; q) Familism and Sex Roles: A Chicana Perspective (M.B. Zinn), 153-164; r) Women and Language (M. Farwell), 165-172; s) Gogol's Female Characters (G. Bonnett), 173-186; t) Sexism in the Schools: Focus on the Woman Teacher (J. Goldman, L. Zaretsky), 187-198; u) Human Potentiality (E.E. Matthews), 201-206; v) Feminist Perspectives on Female Sexuality (P. Schwartz), 207-216; w) AfroAmerican Woman's Perspective on Racist Barriers (M.B. Wright), 217-220; x) Racism and Sexism (J. Burcart), 221-224; y) Agism and the Women's Movement (C.L. Brown), 225-228; z) Women's Oppression and the War in Vietnam (A. Froines), 229-234; aa) Working Women's Association of Vancouver (A. Hogan), 235-240; bb) Women's Role in Organized Labor (N. Fox), 241-244; cc) Politics of the Equal Rights Amendment (M. Suelzle), 245-260; dd) Ending Discrimination Against Women in Education: How Uncle Sam Can Help (B. Sandler), 261-268; ee) Affirmative Action in Higher Education (K.J.H. Brown), 269-278; ff) Analyzing Affirmative Action Data on the Computer (C.M. Porter), 279-282; gg) Sex Discrimination in Higher Education and Attitude Change (J.R. Leppaluoto), 283-288; hh) Sexist Language and Attitudes (K.L. Falco), 289-296; ii) Persuasion in the Feminist Movement (M. Trew), 297-302; jj) Women's Conferences: Women On the Move (R. Hanna), 303- .

343 WOMEN ON WOMEN. Ann B. Shteir, ed. (The Gerstein Lecture Series) Toronto: York University, 1978.

a) Curse of Eve--Or, What I Learned in School (Women and Literature) (M. Atwood), 13-28; b) Women and Politics (L. Sabia), 29-44; c) Women Artists of the 19th and 20th Centuries (L. Nochlin), 45-64; d) Women and Learning (P.A. Graham), 65- .

344 WOMEN ORGANIZING: AN ANTHOLOGY. Bernice Cummings and Victoria Schuck, eds. Metuchen, NJ: The Scarecrow Press, 1979.

a) Feminism, Power and Change: A Theoretical Analysis (N.C.M. Hartsock), 2-24; b) How Powerful Is Powerful? The Women's Movement and the Four Black Congresswomen (I.S. Reid), 25-46; c) Notes from a Political Career (K. Burstein), 49-60; d) Local Officeholding and the Community: The Case of Women on New Jersey's School Boards (M. Johnson, K. Stanwick), 61-81; e) Lobbying for Equal Credit (A.N. Costain), 82-110; f) League of Women Voters and Political Power (R.C. Clusen), 112-132; g) W.E.A.L.: The Growth of a Feminist Organization (A. Daniels), 133-151; h) New Approaches to Collective Power: Four Working Women's Organizations (N. Seifer, B. Wertheimer), 152-183; i) Organizing for Political Power: The National Women's Political Caucus (R.F. Feit), 183-208; j) Economic Strength Is What Counts (Y.B. Burke), 210-220; k) Women's Incomes as Workers and Dependents (L. Mallan), 221-238; l) Exploring the Relationship Between Female Candidacies and the Women's Movement (I. Diamond), 241-252; m) Congressional Ambitions of Female Political Elites (M. Fielder), 253-288; n) Women as Voluntary Political Activists (M.M. Conway), 289-303; o) Republican Women and the Future of the Republican Party (S.F. Liebshutz), 304-318; p) God, But

We're Getting Smart (L. Carpenter), 321-328; q) Fight for Women Jurors (C.A. Schweber), 329-344; r) Crisis Perspective on Emerging Health Roles: A Paradigm for the Entry of Women into New Occupational Roles (J. Lipman-Blumen), 345-362; s) Individualism, Marriage and the Liberal State: Beyond the Equal Rights Amendment (M.L. Shanley), 363-388.

345 THE WOMEN POETS IN ENGLISH: AN ANTHOLOGY. Ann Stanford, ed. New York: McGraw-Hill, 1972.

From Anglo-Saxon culture to the present, women's writings are here represented. Only English language material is included, primarily by recognized or previously published poets. Contributors: Marie de France, Lady of the Arbour, Lady of the Assembly, J. Barnes, M. Brews, Elizabeth, Queen of York; Ann Boleyn, Queen of England; A. Askew, Elizabeth I, Queen of England; I. Whitney, A. Howard, M.S. Herbert, E. Malvill, L. Harington, E. Carey, M.S. Wroth, R. Speght, D. Primrose, A. Collins, M. Cavendish, K. Philips, A. Behn, J. Philips, A. Killigrew, M. Lee, A. Finch, J. Brereton, M.W. Montagu, C. Grierson, L. Pilkington, J. Elliot, A. Bradstreet, A. Murry,, P. Wheatley, A.G. Brown, C. Smith, H. Oneil, A. Lindsay, J. Baillie, C. Oliphant, A. Radcliffe, F. Hemans, H.S. Sheridan, F. Kemble, J. Scott (A.A. Spottiswood), C. Brontë, E. Brontë, A. Brontë, J.W. Howe, D. Greenwell, C. Rossetti, E. Dickinson, M. Blind, E. Lazarus, E. Carberry, M.E. Coleridge, M. Field (K. Bradley), E. Cooper, E.B. Browning, A. Meynell, M. Austin, R. Pitter, L. Bogan, L. Adams, H. Flanner, J. Lewis, M. Zaturenska, S. Smith, K. Boyle, P. McGinley, R. Hyde, E. Langley, C.T. Wright, K. Raine, H. Sorrells, C. Carrier, G. Derwood, M. Young, F.M. Howard, J. Jacobsen, J. Miles, A. Stanford, N. Cato, E.M. Shiffert, G. Brooks, R. Herschberger, M. Swenson, G. Harwood, M.L. Masters, J. Finnigan, B. Chamberlain, M. Sarton, A. Ridler, M. Rukeyser, J. Garrigue, J. Burden, B. Howes, I. Gardner, B. Guest, R. Stone, B. Ames, J. Wright, M. Van Duyn, D. Levertov, J. Randall, J. Frame, V. Miller, M. Kumin, C. Kizer, E. Jennings, A. Sexton, A. Rich, S. Plath, M. Piercy, L. Clifton, S. Kaufman, M. Atwood, M. Oliver.

346 WOMEN POETS OF THE WEST, 1850-1950: AN ANTHOLOGY. A. Thomas Trusky, ed. (Modern and Contemporary Poets of the West) Boise, Idaho: Ahsahta Press, 1978.

This volume includes poems written over some one-hundred-twenty years. Most writers participated in the great westward movement in America, and the selections reflect their interest in the land, in native peoples, and in the isolation of a sparsely inhabited plain. Contributors: E.R. Snow, I. Coolbrith, E. Higginson, S. Hall, A. Corbin, H. Hall, M. Austin, G. Taggard, H. Flanner, G. Haste, J. Lewis, P.P. Church, N.B. Miller, P.S. Curry.

347 WOMEN: PORTRAITS. James Hall, Nancy J. Jones and Janet R. Sutherland, eds. (Patterns in Literary Art, No. 16) New York: McGraw-Hill, 1976.

This introductory interdisciplinary text portrays women of various cultures. The selections are classed in a progressive sequence: work about young women, mature women, and, finally, women who have challenged female stereotypes. Contributors: A. Lorde, M. Bass, E. Merriam, N. Larrick, K. Koch, M. Swenson, V. Huang, P.A. Toer, J. Maynard, C. McCullers, R. Garden, A. Gibson, M. Sarton, I. Day, J. Baez, N. Giovanni, L.C. Schmidt, M. Walker, K. Tsui, L.K. Inaba, M.W. Freeman, M. Allen, A. Rich, N.O. Lurie, W.F. Walters, J.S. Mitchell, K. Chopin, T. Olsen, A. Walker, H. Arnow, M. Mead, M.L. Espinosa, J. Alilkatuktuk, F. Howe, S. Griffin, S.R. Rau, S. Faessler, L. Chester, J. Collins.

348 WOMEN, SEXUALITY AND SOCIAL CONTROL. Carol Smart and Barry Smart, eds. London, Boston: Routledge and Kegan Paul, 1978.

a) Coercion of Privacy: A Feminist Perspective (T.S. Dahl, A. Snare), 8-26; b) Myth of Male Protectiveness and the Legal Subordination of Women: An Historical Analysis (A. Sachs), 27-40; c) Doctors and Their Patients: The Social Control of Women in General Practice (M. Barrett, H. Roberts), 41-52; d) Who Needs Prostitutes? The Ideology of Male Sexual Needs (M. McIntosh), 53-64; e) Sexual Codes and Conduct: A Study of Teenage Girls (D. Wilson), 65-73; f) Sexist Assumptions and Female Delinquency (L.S. Smith), 74-86; g) Accounting for Rape: Reality and Myth in Press Reporting (C. Smart, B. Smart), 87-103; h) Studying Rape: Integrating Research and Social Change (J.R. Schwendinger, H. Schwendinger), 104-111.

349 WOMEN, WAR, AND REVOLUTION. Carol R. Berkin and Clara M. Lovett, eds. New York: Holmes and Meier, 1980.

a) Women of the Popular Classes in Revolutionary Paris, 1789-1795 (D.G. Levy, H.B. Applewhite), 9-36; b) Women, Class, and War in Nazi Germany (L.J. Rupp), 37-54; c) American Women in the Shipyards During World War II (K.B. Skold), 55-76; d) Legal Status of Women After the American Revolution (M. Salmon), 85-106; e) Institutional Changes for Women of the People During the French Revolution (M.D. Johnson), 107-144; f) Communist Feminism: Its Synthesis and Demise (B.B. Farnsworth), 145-164; g) Women in the Chinese Communist Revolution: The Question of Political Equality (J.M. Maloney), 165-182; h) Revolution and Conciencia: Women in Cuba (L. Casals), 183-206; i) Revolution and Retreat: Upper-Class French Women After 1789 (B.C. Pope), 215-236; j) Patriot Mothers in the Post-Risorgimento: Women After the Italian Revolution (J.J. Howard), 237-258; k) American Women in the Peace and Preparedness Movements in World War I (B.J. Steinson). 259-284.

350 WOMEN UNITED, WOMEN DIVIDED: COMPARATIVE STUDIES OF TEN CONTEMPORARY CULTURES. Patricia Caplan and Janet M. Bujra, eds. (Tavistock Women's Studies) Bloomington, London: Indiana University Press, 1979.

a) Female Solidarity and the Sexual Division of Labour (J.M. Bujra),

13-45; b) Rural China: Segregation to Solidarity (E. Croll), 46-76; c) "Women Must Help Each Other" (N. Nelson), 77-98; d) Women's Organizations in Madras City, India (P. Caplan), 99-128; e) Women's Solidarity and the Preservation of Privilege (G. Cohen), 129-156; f) Women and Their Kin (M. Stivens), 157-184; g) Women's Spirit Possession and Urban Adaptation (P. Constantinides), 185-205; h) Two Contexts of Solidarity (M. Llewelyn-Davies), 206-237; i) Desirade: A Negative Case (J. Naish), 238-258; j) Segregation and Its Consequences in India (U. Sharma), 259-282.

351 WOMEN, WORK, AND FAMILY: DIMENSIONS OF CHANGE IN AMERICAN SOCIETY. Frank L. Mott, et al. Lexington, Ma.: D.C. Heath, 1978.

a) Young Women's Decisions to Attend College: Desires, Expectations and Realizations (S.H. Sandell), 17-28; b) Pregnancy, Motherhood and Work Activity (F.L. Mott, D. Shapiro), 29-56; c) Sex Segregation in the Labor Market: An Analysis of Young College Women's Occupational Preferences (P.K. Brito, C.L. Jusenius), 57-76; d) Work Attachment, Investments in Human Capital and the Earnings of Young Women (D. Shapiro, T.J. Carr), 77-94; e) Migration of Young Families: An Economic Perspective (S.H. Sandell, P.K. Koenig), 95-112; f) Causes and Consequences of Marital Breakdown (F.L. Mott, S.F. Moore), 113-136; g) Highlights and Policy Implications (F.L. Mott), 137-142.

352 WOMEN WORKERS AND SOCIETY. Geneva: International Labour Office, 1976.

a) Women at a Standstill: The Need for Radical Change (E. Reid), 1-10; b) Suggestions for the Advancement of Working Women (E. Vogel), 11-26; c) Division of Labour and Sexual Inequality: The Role of Education (E. Aventurin), 27-42; d) Development and Mounting Famine: A Role for Women (R. Dumont), 43-50; e) Women Workers and the Courts (F. Morgenstern), 51-64; f) Social Security and Women: A Partisan View (S.M. Gelber), 65-78; g) Women's Rights and Widows' Pensions (P. Laroque), 79-88; h) Equality of Remuneration for Men and Women in the Member States of the E.E.C. (E. Sullerot), 89-110; i) Women's Wages in Japan and the Question of Equal Pay (N. Takahashi), 111-128; j) Participation of Women in the Labour Force of Latin America: Fertility and Other Factors (J.C. Elizaga), 129-148; k) Trends in Women's Employment in the U.S.S.R. (S. Turchaninova), 149-160; l) Sexual Equality in the Labour Market: Some Experiences and Views of the Nordic Countries (A.-G. Leijon), 161-176; m) Handicrafts: A Source of Employment for Women in Developing Rural Economies (J. Dhamija), 177-184; n) Women Workers and the Trade Unions in Austria (E. Krebs), 185-198; o) APPENDIX: Texts Concerning Women Workers Adopted by the 60th Session of the International Labour Conference, 4-25 June 1975, 199- .

353 WOMEN WORKING: AN ANTHOLOGY OF STORIES AND POEMS. Nancy Hoffman and Florence Howe, eds. Old Westbury, N.Y.: The Feminist Press, 1979.

This collection includes prose and poetry about women's work primarily by American writers. Contributors: N. Replansky, M.W. Freeman, C. Reznikoff, A. Yezierska, W. Cather, R.H. Crosby, N. Giovanni, M. Walker, S.O. Jewett, Z.N. Hurston, J. Higgins, T.C. Bambara, R. Lights, B. Smith, J. Pedrick, E.B. Voigt, P. Cummings, C. Tafolla, A.L. Marriott, W. Shore, T. Olsen, S. Ballantyne, A. Strindberg, R. Brown, E. Field, A. Walker, D.C. Fisher, S. Asch, M. Le Sueur, S. Davidson, A. Rich, M. Piercy.

354 WOMEN WORKING: THEORIES AND FACTS IN PERSPECTIVE. Ann H. Stromberg and Shirley Harkess, eds. Palo Alto: Mayfield, 1978.

a) Women and Work: An Economic Appraisal (C.S. Bell); b) Data on Women Workers, Past, Present, and Future (F.D. Blau); c) Doubly Disadvantaged: Minority Women in the Labor Force (E.M. Almquist, J.L. Wehrle-Einhorn); d) Wage Differences between Men and Women: Economic Theories (M.H. Stevenson); e) Legal Protection against Sex Discrimination (M. Eastwood); f) Issues in the Sociological Study of Women's Work (J. Acker), 134-161; g) Inequalities in the Labor Force: Three Sociological Explanations (M.B. Morris), 162-175; h) Girls' Socialization for Work (C. Ireson), 176-200; i) Implications of Women's Employment for Home and Family Life (K.A. Moore, I.V. Sawhill), 201-225; j) Women's Labor Force Participation and the Residential Mobility of Families (L.H. Long), 226-238; k) Working in Mid-Life (E.R. Rosenthal), 239-256; l) Women in Male-Dominated Professions (M. Patterson, L. Engelberg), 266-292; m) Women in Female-Dominated Professions (J.W. Grimm), 293-315; n) Urban Nomads: Women in Temporary Clerical Services (V.L. Olesen, F. Katsuranis), 316-338; o) Women in Blue-Collar and Service Occupations (S.H. Baker), 339- ; p) Domestic Service: Woman's Work (D.M. Katzman); q) Housewives as Workers (J. Vanek); r) Women and Work: Policy Implications and Prospects for the Future (C. Safilios-Rothschild).

355 WOMEN WRITERS IN RUSSIAN MODERNISM: AN ANTHOLOGY. Temira Pachmuss, ed. Urbana: University of Illinois Press, 1978.

a) Poems (Z. Hippius),16-84; b) Poems (M. Lokhvitskaya),92-113; c) Mirage (A. Verbitskaya), 120-174; d) Poems (P. Solovyova), 175-190; e) The Tragic Menagerie (stories) (L. Zinovyeva-Annibal), 191-242; f) Poems (C. de Gabriak), 243-260; g) Humorous Tales (stories) (N. Teffi), 261-290; h) All about Love (stories) (N. Teffi), 291-313; i) Poems (A. Gertsyk), 325- .

356 WOMEN WRITING: AN ANTHOLOGY. Denys Val Baker, ed. New York: St. Martin's, 1979.

a) Lilacs (M. Lavin), 10-31; b) A Romantic Hero (O. Manning), 32-47; c) Mice and Birds and Boy (E. Taylor), 48-59; d) Men With No Eyes (F. Weldon), 60-79; e) Each Other (D. Lessing), 80-88; f) Blue Lenses (D. du Maurier), 89-125; g) The House of My Dreams (E. O'Brien), 126-145; h) Here and There in the Wastes of Ocean A Swimmer Was Seen

(P. Mortimer), 146-160; i) A Member of the Family (M. Spark), 161-173; j) Another Survivor (R. Fainlight), 174-182; k) The Elephant Man (S. Hill), 183-197; l) Fixing Pixie Loveless (A.L. Barker), 198-

357 WOMEN WRITING AND WRITING ABOUT WOMEN. Mary Jacobus, ed. New York: Harper and Row, 1979. (In association with Oxford University Women's Studies Committee)

a) Towards a New Feminist Poetics (E. Showalter), 22-41; b) Buried Letter: Feminism and Romanticism in Villette (M. Jacobus), 42-60; c) Indefinite Disclosed: Christina Rossetti and Emily Dickinson (C. Kaplan), 61-79; d) Beyond Determinism: George Eliot and Virginia Woolf (G. Beer), 80-99; e) Sue Bridehead and the New Woman (J. Goode), 100-113; f) Ibsen and the Language of Women (I-S. Ewbank), 114-132; g) Poetry and Conscience: Russian Women Poets of the Twentieth Century (E. Feinstein), 133-158; h) Writing as a Woman (A. Stevenson), 159-176; i) Feminism, Film and the Avant-Garde (L. Mulvey), 177-195.

358 WOMEN'S ATHELTICS: COPING WITH CONTROVERSY. Barbara J. Hoepner, ed. Washington, D.C.: American Association for Health, Physical Education and Recreation, 1974.

a) Equal Opportunity for Women in Sports (M.C. Dunkle), 9-19; b) Women's Rights in Athletics (M. Helling), 20-25; c) Emergence of Women in Sport (B. Spears), 26-42; d) Century of American Women's Sport (R.A. Swanson), 43-54; e) Development of Programs (L. Magnusson), 55-58; f) Relationship of D.G.W.S. to A.I.A.W. (J. Thorpe), 59-63; g) Future Directions and Issues (C. Oglesby), 64-68; h) Reflective Thoughts (A. Aldrich), 69-72; i) Past Olympic Reflections (N.C. Jackson), 73-75; j) Looking Forward to Montreal (O. Connolly), 76-82; k) Masculine Obsession in Sports (J. Scott), 83-88; l) Full Court Press for Women in Athletics (J. Felshin), 89-92; m) Environmental Effect on the Woman in Athletics (C. West), 93-98; n) Anxiety Levels Experienced by Women in Competition (M.R. Griffin), 99-103; o) Sociological Aspects of Women in Sports (B. Menzie), 104-110; p) Women Athletic Trainers (H. Wilson), 111- .

359 WOMEN'S AUTOBIOGRAPHY: ESSAYS IN CRITICISM. Estelle C. Jelinek, ed. Bloomington: Indiana University Press, 1980.

a) Emergence of Women's Autobiography in England (C.S. Pomerleau), 21-38; b) Quest for Community: Spiritual Autobiographies of Eighteenth-Century Quaker and Puritan Women in America (C. Edkins), 39-52; c) Harriet Martineau's Autobiography: The Making of a Female Philosopher (M. Myers), 53-70; d) Paradox and Success of Elizabeth Cady Stanton (E.C. Jelinek), 71-92; e) Autobiographer and Her Readers: From Apology to Affirmation (E. Winston), 93-111; f) Selves in Hiding (P.M. Spacks), 112-132; g) African-American Women's Autobiographies and Ethnicity (R. Blackburn), 133-148; h) Gertrude Stein and the Problems of Autobiography (J.E. Breslin), 149-162; i) Lillian Hellman and the Strategy of the "Other" (M.K. Billson, S.A. Smith), 163-179; j)

Metaphysics of Matrilinearism in Women's Autobiography: Studies of Mead's "Blackberry Winter," Hellman's "Pentimento," Angelou's "I Know Why the Caged Bird Sings," and Kingston's "The Woman Warrior" (S.A. Demetrakopoulos), 180-205; k) Anais Nin's "Diary" in Context (L.Z. Bloom, O. Holder), 206-220; l) Towards a Theory of Form in Feminist Autobiography: Kate Millett's "Flying" and "Sita"; Maxine Hong Kingston's "The Woman Warrior" (S. Juhasz), 221-237; m) Kate Millett and the Critics (A. Kolodny), 238-260.

360 WOMEN'S EXPERIENCE IN AMERICA: AN HISTORICAL ANTHOLOGY. Esther Katz and Anita Rapone, eds. New Brunswick, N.J.: Transaction Books, 1979.

a) American Women and Domestic Culture: An Approach to Women's History (E. Katz, A. Rapone); b) Anne Hutchinson and Female Agitation During the Years of the Antinomian Turmoil, 1636-1640 (L.W. Koehler); c) Widowhood in Eighteenth-Century Massachusetts: A Problem in the History of the Family (A. Keyssar); d) Lady and the Mill Girl: Changes in the Status of Women in the Age of Jackson (G. Lerner); e) Organized Women's Benevolence in Early Nineteenth-Century America (K. Melder); f) Women Nurses in the Union Army (A.D. Wood); g) Spiritualist Medium: A Study of Female Professionalization in Victorian America (R.L. Moore); h) Cultural Hybrid in the Slums: The College Woman and the Settlement House, 1889-1894 (J.P. Rousmaniere); i) Cult of True Womanhood, 1820-1860 (B. Welter); j) Catharine Beecher and the Education of American Women (J. Burstyn); k) Family Limitation, Sexual Control, and Domestic Feminism in Victorian America (D.S. Smith); l) Female World of Love and Ritual: Relations Between Women in Nineteenth-Century America (C. Smith-Rosenberg); m) Women and Their Families on the Overland Trail, 1842-1867 (J. Faragher, C. Stansell); n) Hysterical Woman: Sex Roles and Role Conflict in Nineteenth-Century America (C. Smith-Rosenberg); o) American Woman's Pre-World War I Freedom in Manners and Morals (J.R. McGovern); p) Prosperity's Child: Some Thoughts on the Flapper (K.A. Yellis); q) Cookbooks and Law Books: The Hidden History of Career Women in Twentieth-Century America (F. Stricker).

361 WOMEN'S LANGUAGE AND STYLE. Douglas Butturff, ed. Akron, Oh.: L & S Books, Department of English, University of Akron, 1978?

a) What Do Couples Talk About When They're Alone? (P. Fishman); b) Psychology of Women's Language (R. Lakoff); c) Address Forms in Sexual Politics (S. McConnell-Ginet); d) Historical Survey of Women's Language: From Medieval Courtesy Books to Seventeen Magazine (D. Bornstein); e) How Fictional Women Talk (P. Treichler); f) New Voices in Feminine Discourse (M. Richman); g) Inlaws-Outlaws and the Language of Women (V. Tiger, G. Luria); h) Women's Language in America: Myth and Reality (F. Frank); i) Art of Silence and the Forms of Women's Poetry (J. Kammer); j) Women on the New World Languagescape (A. Kolodny); k) Feminist Aesthetic (J.P. Stanley, S.W. Robbins); l) Women's Prose Style: A Study of Contemporary Authors (M. Hiatt); m) Style of One's Own (M. Schulz); n) Katharine Mansfield's "Passion for Technique" (S.J. Kaplan); o) Style of Djuna Barnes' "Nightwood"

(C. Allen); p) Virginia Woolf and the Voices of Silence (C. Mendez); q) Feminist Criticism: What Difference Does It Make? (P. Rosenthal).

362 WOMEN'S LIBERATION. Michael E. Adelstein and Jean G. Pival, eds. New York: St. Martin's, 1972.

a) Problem that Has No Name (B. Freidan), 3-16; b) New Woman: Out to Finish What the Suffragette Started (C. Bird), 17-26; c) Female Eunuch (G. Greer), 27-36; d) Up Against the Wall, Male Chauvinist Pig (M. Hunt), 37-50; e) Genius of Woman as the Genius of Humanity (A. Montagu), 51-58; f) Motherhood: Who Needs It? (B. Rollin), 59-70; g) Nature of Women (J.S. Mill), 71-84; h) Men, Women--and Politics (L. Romney), 85-88; i) Politics and War (L. Tiger), 89-100; j) Feminine Mistake (H. Lawrenson), 101-108; k) Women in Labor (M. Suelzle), 109-128; l) Women: A House Divided (M. Mead), 129-134; m) From Adam's Rib to Women's Lib (K. Woodward), 135-142; n) What It Would Be Like If Women Win (G. Steinem), 143-148.

363 WOMEN'S LIBERATION AND LITERATURE. Elaine Showalter, ed. New York: Harcourt Brace Jovanovich, 1971.

a) Observations on the State of Degradation to Which Woman Is Reduced by Various Causes (M. Wollstonecraft), 10-31; b) Subjection of Women (J.S. Mill), 34-57; c) A Doll's House (H. Ibsen), 62-118; d) Aurora Leigh (E.B. Browning), 121-135; e) Poems, A. Sexton, 137-140; f) Lesbos (S. Plath), 144-145; g) Mr. Durant (D. Parker), 147-155; h) Cruel and Barbarous Treatment (M. McCarthy), 158-166; i) Lady Novelists (G.H. Lewes), 171-182; j) A Room of One's Own (V. Woolf), 186-198; k) Subjection of Women (E. Hardwick), 201-209; l) Phallic Criticism (M. Ellmann), 213-221; m) No Important Woman Writer (H. Calisher), 223-229; n) Woman's Psyche (M.F. Farnham, F. Lundberg), 234-247; o) Sexual Solipsism of Sigmund Freud (B. Friedan), 250-268; p) Psychology Constructs the Female, or the Fantasy Life of the Male Psychologist (N. Weisstein), 271-285; q) Sexual Politics (K. Millett), 289-325; r) How Now Kate? (E. Van Den Haag), 326-328; s) Women's Lib Gets Rough (J. Yardley), 329-331.

364 WOMEN'S LIVES: PERSPECTIVES ON PROGRESS AND CHANGE. Virginia Lee Lussier and Joyce Jennings Walstedt, eds. Newark: University of Delaware, 1977.

a) "Women's History" in Transition: The European Case (N.Z. Davis), 5-26; b) Submission, Masochism and Narcissism: Three Aspects of Women's Role as Reflected in Dress (H. Roberts), 27-66; c) Anger in Women Writers: Source of Inspiration or Inhibition? (A. Douglas), 67-84; d) Black Woman in American History (D.H. Painter), 85-92; e) American Woman from 1900 to the First World War: A Profile (L. Banner), 93-119; f) Myths and Stereotypes: My Challenge to Black Women Cultural Workers (T.C. Bambara), 123-128; g) Fashioning of a Congresswoman: One Individual's Experience (P. Schroeder), 129-138; h) Confessions of a Female Screenwriter (E. Perry), 139-150; i) Women School

Administrators: My Experience with Discrimination (B. Sizemore), 151-162; j) Confronting the Sports Establishment: A Plan for Honesty and Sanity (D. McKnight), 163-172; k) Women of the People's Republic of China (J.J. Walstedt), 177-190; l) Conversation with Audrey Topping: Chinese Women Today (J.J. Walstedt), 191-210; m) Cuban Women Today: Constancy and Change (V.L. Lussier), 211-224; n) Think About Our Government: Now Think About Sweden's Policy (C. Servan-Schreiber), 225-234; o) Current Equality Issues in Sweden (G. Häggblom-Khakee), 235-

365 THE WOMEN'S MOVEMENT: SOCIAL AND PSYCHOLOGICAL PERSPECTIVES. Helen Wortis and Clara Rabinowitz, eds. Edited for the American Orthopsychiatry Association. New York: Wiley, 1972.

a) Evolutionary Aspects of Human Gender (E. Tobach), 3-9; b) Changing the Role of Women (M.J. Pollock), 10-20; c) Impact of the Women's Liberation Movement on Child Development Books (Z.S. Klapper), 21-31; d) Acceptance of the Concept of the Maternal Role by Behavioral Scientists: Its Effects on Women (R.P. Wortis), 32-51; e) What Does Equality Between the Sexes Imply? (B. Linner), 52-64; f) Changes in the Modern Family: Their Impact on Sex Roles (J.Z. Giele), 65-77; g) Psychological Consequences of Sexual Inequality (J.B. Miller, I. Mothner), 78-88; h) Single Woman in Today's Society (M. Adams), 89-101; i) Recent Writings of the Women's Movement (T.T. Walker, C.K. Riessman), 102-110; j) Resource Bibliography (M.G. Keiffer, P.A. Warren), 111-148.

366 WOMEN'S ROLE IN ABORIGINAL SOCIETY. 3rd ed. Fay Gale, ed. Canberra City: Australian Institute of Aboriginal Studies, 1974.

a) Woman the Gatherer (B. Hiatt), 4-15; b) Importance of Women in Determining the Composition of Residential Groups in Aboriginal Australia (N. Peterson), 16-27; c) Role of Women in Aboriginal Marriage Arrangements (A. Hamilton), 28-35; d) Aboriginal Women's Status: A Paradox Resolved (I.M. White), 36-45; e) "And the Lubras Are Ladies Now" (D.E. Barwick), 51-63; f) Digging Sticks and Spears, Or the Two-Sex Model (C.H. Berndt), 64-80.

367 WOMEN'S STATUS AND FERTILITY IN THE MUSLIM WORLD. James Allman, ed. (Praeger Special Studies) New York: Praeger, 1978.

a) Family Life, Women's Status, and Fertility: Middle East and North African Perspectives (J. Allman), xxiv- ; b) Demographic Transition in the Middle East and North Africa (J. Allman), 3-32; c) Family Planning and Population Policies in the Middle East and North Africa (International Planned Parenthood Federation, Middle East and North Africa), 33-53; d) Socioeconomic Determinants of Differential Fertility in Turkey (S. Timur), 54-76; e) Rural-Urban Fertility Differences and Trends in Egypt, 1930-70 (A.M. Khalifa), 77-94; f) Fertility Trends and Differentials in Kuwait (A.G. Hill), 95-112; g) Fertility Trends and Differentials in Jordan (H. Rizk), 113-130; h) Fertility in Algeria:

Trends and Differentials (J. Vallin), 131-151; i) Fertility Declines in Tunisia: Factors Affecting Recent Trends (M. Ayad, Y. Jemai), 152-163.

368 WOMEN'S STUDIES: AN INTERDISCIPLINARY COLLECTION. Kathleen O'Connor Blumhagen and Walter D. Johnson, eds. (Contributions in Women's Studies, No. 2) Westport, Ct.: Greenwood Press, 1978.

a) Women's Studies: Its Focus, Idea Power, and Promise (S.S. Schramm), 3-12; b) Reeducation of Sophie (S. Hoagland), 13-20; c) Evaluating Women's Studies- Academic Theory and Practice (E. Boneparth), 21-30; d) Sociology of Birth: A Critical Assessment of Theory and Research (M. Stewart, P. Erickson), 31-46; e) Cross-Cultural Investigation of Behavioral Changes at Menopause (J. Griffen), 47-54; f) Women and Socialism: Case of Angelica Balabanoff (M.J. Slaughter), 55-64; g) White Feminist/Movement: The Chicana Perspective (S. Gonzales), 65-74; h) Sisterhood in the Courtroom: Sex of Judge and Defendent in Criminal Case Disposition (H.M. Kritzer, T.M. Uhlman), 75-86; i) Sex-Linked Values: Their Impacts on Women in Engineering (L.K. Olson), 87-100; j) Impacts of Local Government Tax Structures on Women: Inefficiencies and Inequalities (S.A. Macmanus, N.R. Van Hightower), 101-114; k) Future of Women's Studies 115-120.

369 WORKING IT OUT: 23 WOMEN WRITERS, ARTISTS, SCIENTISTS, AND SCHOLARS TALK ABOUT THEIR LIVES AND WORK. Sara Ruddick and Pamela Daniels, eds. New York: Pantheon, 1977.

a) Finding New Forms (K.K. Hamond), 3-24; b) Juxtapositions (A.A. Lyndon), 25-37; c) Dependency, Individuality, and Work (A.O. Rorty), 38-54; d) Birth of the Amateur (P. Daniels), 55-70; e) On Work (C.R. Stimpson), 71-76; f) Anomaly of a Woman in Physics (E.F. Keller), 77-91; g) In Search of Our Mothers' Gardens (A. Walker), 92-102; h) My Work and My Working-Class Father (M. Stevens), 103-116; i) Scenes (J. Green), 117-127; j) Work of One's Own (S. Ruddick), 128-146; k) Catching the Sun (D. Michener), 147-178; l) Notes from an Extra in the American Moving Picture Show (C.Y. Yu), 179-195; m) Writing in the Real World (A. Lasoff), 196-212; n) Contradictions (M. Young), 213-227; o) Plain Truth (N. Thornton), 228-240; p) Adventures of a Woman in Science (N. Weisstein), 241-250; q) What Counts as Work? (C.L. Sears), 251-269; r) Coming of Age the Long Way Around (N.V. Mengel), 270-282; s) Notes from a Conversation on Art, Feminism, and Work (M. Schapiro), 283-305; t) Sacred Fire (C. Gilbert), 306-322; u) One Out of Twelve: Women Who Are Writers in Our Century (T. Olsen), 323-340.

370 WORKING MOTHERS: AN EVALUATIVE REVIEW OF THE CONSEQUENCES FOR WIFE, HUSBAND AND CHILD. Lois Wladis Hoffman and F. Ivan Nye, eds. (The Jossey-Bass Behavioral Science Series) San Francisco: Jossey-Bass, 1974.

a) Sociocultural Context (F.I. Nye), 1-31; b) Psychological Factors (L.W. Hoffman), 32-62; c) Commitment to Work (M.G. Sobol), 63-80; d)

Employment of Women and Fertility (L.W. Hoffman), 81-100; e) Child-Care Arrangements (A.C. Emlen, J.B. Perry, Jr.), 101-125; f) Effects on Child (L.W. Hoffman), 126-166; g) Effects on Power and Division of Labor in the Family (S.J. Bahr), 167-185; h) Husband-Wife Relationship (F.I. Nye), 186-206; i) Effects on Mother (F.I. Nye), 207-225; j) Concluding Remarks (L.W. Hoffman, F.I. Nye), 226-232.

371 WORKING WOMEN AND FAMILIES. Karen Wolk Feinstein, ed. (Sage Yearbooks in Women's Policy Studies, Vol. 4) Beverly Hills: Sage, 1979.

a) Women Working: Toward a New Society (A. Pifer), 13-34; b) Women Working: Historical Trends (S.J. Hesse), 35-62; c) Occupational Values and Family Roles: Women in Blue-Collar and Service Occupations (M.L. Walshok), 63-84; d) Racial Differences in Female Labor-Force Participation: Trends and Implications for the Future (F.L. Mott), 85-102; e) Women, Work, and Welfare: The Feminization of Poverty (D. Pearce), 103-124; f) Husbands at Home: Organization of the Husband's Household Day (S.F. Berk), 125-158; g) Job-Sharing Couples (W. Arkin, L.R. Dobrofsky), 159-176; h) Directions for Day Care (K.W. Feinstein), 177-194; i) Nontraditional Work Schedules for Women (D.F. Polit), 195-210; j) Hours Rigidity: Effects on the Labor-Market Status of Women (R.E. Smith), 211-222; k) Employment Problems of Women: Federal Government Examples (N.V. Benokraitis), 223-246; l) Women's Retirement Income (W.D. Spector), 247-276; m) Family Wholeness: New Conceptions of Family Roles (E. Boulding), 277- .

372 A WORLD OF WOMEN: ANTHROPOLOGICAL STUDIES OF WOMEN IN THE SOCIETIES OF THE WORLD. Erika Bourguignon, ed. (Praeger Special Studies) New York: Praeger, 1980.

a) Contemporary Saudi Woman (S. Deaver), 19-42; b) Women of Brunei (L.A. Kimball), 43-56; c) Women's Role in a Muslim Hausa Town--Mirria, Republic of Niger (M.O. Saunders), 57-86; d) Dioula Women in Town: A View of Intra-Ethnic Variation - Ivory Coast (R.S. Ellovich), 87-104; e) Spirit Magic in the Social Relations between Men and Women--Sao Paulo, Brazil (E. Pressel), 107-128; f) Spirit Mediums in Umbanda Evangelizada of Porto Alegre, Brazil: Dimensions of Power and Authority (P.B. Lerch), 129-160; g) Sex and Status: Women in St. Vincent (J.H. Henney), 161-184; h) Adaptive Strategies and Social Networks of Women in St. Kitts (J.D. Gussler), 185-210; i) Women in Yucatan (F.D. Goodman), 213-234; j) Uses of Traditional Concepts in the Development of New Urban Roles: Cuban Women in the United States (M.S. Boone), 235-270; k) Life of Sarah Penfield, Rural Ohio Grandmother: Tradition Maintained, Tradition Threatened (R. Joyce), 271-305; l) Economic Role of Women in Alaskan Eskimo Society (L.P. Ager), 305-318; m) Comparisons and Implications (E. Bourguignon),

321-342.

373 THE WORLD OUTSIDE: COLLECTED SHORT FICTION ABOUT WOMEN AT WORK. (Selected by Ann Reit) Englewood Cliffs, N.J.: Four Winds Press, 1978.

a) Martha's Lady (S.O. Jewett), 1-26; b) The Office (A. Munro), 27-46; c) The Trimmed Lamp (O. Henry), 47-62; d) Frankie Mae (J.W. Smith), 63-80; e) The Tone of Time (H. James), 81-108; f) The Pocketbook Game (A. Childress), 109-112; g) Esther Kahn (A. Symonds), 113-132; h) Mannequin (J. Rhys), 133-142; i) The Singing Lesson (K. Mansfield), 143-152; j) Echo from Ithaca (G.B. Stern), 153-166; k) A Gourdful of Glory (M. Laurence), 167-188; l) A Gold Slipper (W. Cather), 189-211.

374 THE WORLD SPLIT OPEN: FOUR CENTURIES OF WOMEN POETS IN ENGLAND AND AMERICA, 1552-1950. Louise Bernikow, ed. New York: Vintage Books, 1974.

The editor intends these poems to be "texts for the study of consciousness in poetry." Women's poetry is viewed as inherently political, and the energy generated by women's historical struggle is held to be the link among these writers. Contributors: Elizabeth I, Queen of England; M.S. Herbert, K. Philips, A. Collins, A. Behn, A. Killigrew, A. Finch, M.W. Montagu, E. Brontë, E.B. Browning, C. Rossetti, M.E. Coleridge, A. Meynell, R.A. Taylor, S. Pankhurst, A. Wickham, C. Mew, E. Sitwell, D. Wellesley, V. Moore, E. Daryush, R. Pitter, L.B. Lyon, A. Boodson, K. Raine, A. Ridler, J. Peirse, M. Battcock, A. Bradstreet, P. Wheatley, L. Larcom, M.W. Lowell, E. Dickinson, H.H. Jackson, F.E.W. Harper, J.W. Howe, E. Lazarus, E.W. Wilcox, C.P. Gilman, L.W. Reese, C. Brontë, A. Lowell, G. Stein, A.H. Branch, A. Crapsey, L. Speyer, L. Ridge, M. Loy, A.D. Nelson, A.W. Grimké, G.D. Johnson, A. Spencer, G. "Ma" Rainey, B. Smith, I. Cox, Memphis Minnie, S. Teasdale, E. Wylie, E.St.V. Millay, G. Taggard, B. Deutsch, J. Lewis, M. Jackson, S.O. Gunning, E.M. Wiggins, M. Moore, J. Miles, D.B. Laing, M. Walker, G. Brooks, M. Rukeyser.

375 THE WRITER ON HER WORK. Janet Sternburg, ed. New York: Norton, 1980.

a) Still Just Writing (A. Tyler), 3-16; b) Why I Write (J. Didion), 17-26; c) Parable of the Cave or: In Praise of Watercolors (M. Gordon), 27-32; d) De Memoria (N. Milford), 33-44; e) My Grandmother Who Painted (H. Moore), 45-70; f) Creating Oneself from Scratch (M. Murray), 71-94; g) On Being Female, Black, and Free (M. Walker), 95-106; h) Thoughts on Writing (S. Griffin), 107-120; i) One Child of One's Own: A Meaningful Digression within the Work(s) (A. Walker), 121-140; j) Middle Period (I. Bengis), 141-152; k) What It is I Think I'm Doing Anyhow (T.C. Bambara), 153-168; l) Blood and Guts: The Tricky Problem of Being a Woman Writer in the Late Twentieth Century (E. Jong), 169-180; m) Coming Book (M.H. Kingston), 181-186; n) Opening Nights:

The Opening Days (J. Burroway), 187-216; o) Education of a Poet (M. Rukeyser), 217-230; p) Becoming a Writer (G. Godwin), 231-256.

3

KEYWORD INDEX

This section lists significant words in the titles of essays, short stories, plays or documents contained in the indexed anthologies. Under each keyword, these titles appear with alphanumeric references to the book contents section. For example, 268dd indicates entry dd in book title number 268.

Authors can select from a great variety of words when they assign titles to their works; thus, a keyword index which is generated from these titles also includes a variety of words. Cross-references suggest alternative and related keywords. In addition to these suggested keywords, users should consider synonyms, as well as antonyms, broader or narrower terms and variant endings. Commonly used abbreviations are also used by authors and may appear in the KEYWORD INDEX. In many cases, word equivalencies are established for ease of use. For example, under the keyword "suffrage," titles which include the words "suffragist," "suffragette," and "suffragettes" are listed.

Most articles, pronouns and other commonly used words like "women" are omitted from this section; however, some terms which do appear often are included. These words are modified so that titles which contain, say, the word "sex" are divided into several categories so that finer distinctions can be specified, *e.g.*, "sex--intelligence." This phrase indicates that the word "sex" and the word "intelligence" are coupled in an essay title. In addition, some multiple-word phrases are listed in this section: women's studies, affirmative action, Equal Rights Amendment, etc. These entries typically appear as compound terms; their inclusion should facilitate use of this KEYWORD INDEX. Alphabetization of compound terms should be noted: First, a single word will appear, then the word will be coupled in a two-word unhyphenated phrase, then the word will appear in a hyphenated phrase, and finally, the word will appear as it has been modified (social, then social work, then social-learning, then social--sex).

Because this section is computer-generated, some inconsistencies among entries are inevitable. These discrepancies result from conventions required by the practicalities of programming. They ar-

tolerated only when they do not change the sense of individual entries.

See also the SUBJECT/GENRE INDEX. which lists book titles, rather than essay, story, document or play titles, by broad headings.

A.D.C.

175w A.D.C.: Marriage to the State

A.I.A.W.

358f Relationship of D.G.W.S. to A.I.A.W.

A.S.A.

39b My Four Revolutions: An Autobiographical History of the A.S.A.

ABA

302c "Aba Riots" or Igbo "Women's War"? Ideology, Stratification, and the Invisibility of Women

ABANDONED

9ii Seduced and Abandoned in the New World: The Fallen Woman in American Fiction
254o Seduced and Abandoned in the New World: The Image of Woman In American Fiction

ABDICATION

144g The Abdication

ABIDJAN

302f Limitations of Group Action Among Entrepreneurs: The Market Women of Abidjan, Ivory Coast

ABIGAIL

178c Puritan Ethic in the Revolutionary Era: Abigail Adams and Thomas Jefferson

ABILITY

18f Sex-Related Differences in Spatial Ability: A Developmental Psychological View
77a Sex Hormones and Executive Ability
198bb Possible Causal Factors of Sex Differences in Intellectual Abilities
204c Spatial Ability: A Critical Review of the Sex-Linked Major Gene Hypothesis
204g Cognitive Abilities and Sex-Related Variations in the Maturation of Cerebral Cortical Functions
204i Prenatal Influences on Cognitive Abilities: Data from Experimental Animals and Human and Endocrine Syndromes
250q Roles of Activation and Inhibition in Sex Differences in Cognitive Abilities
250r Comments on "Roles of Activation and Inhibition in Sex Differences in Cognitive Abilities"
271e From Each According to Her Ability

ABNORMALITIES

171d Human Sex-Hormone Abnormalities Viewed from an Androgynous Perspective: A Reconsideration of the Work of John Money
176b Sex Differences in the Incidence of Neonatal Abnormalities and Abnormal Performance in Early Childhood
250y Sexual Dimorphic Behavior, Normal and Abnormal

ABOLITION

151i Grimke Sisters: Women and the Abolition Movement

ABORIGINAL

230e Aboriginal Woman: Male and Female Anthropological Perspectives
297cc Aboriginal Woman: Male and Female Anthropological Perspectives
366b Importance of Women in Determining the Composition of Residential Groups in Aboriginal Australia
366c Role of Women in Aboriginal Marriage Arrangements
366d Aboriginal Women's Status: A Paradox Resolved

ABORTION

1a Foeticide, or Criminal Abortion
1c Criminal Abortion
1e Detection of Criminal Abortion
2a Abortion and Public Policy in the U.S.
2c Abortion Decisions: Judicial Review and Public Opinion
2d Abortion and the Constitution: The Cases of the United States and West Germany
2f Abortion and the Social System
2g Philosophers on Abortion
9v Abortion Is No Man's Business
20d Spontaneous and Induced Abortion in Human and Non-Human Primates
22j Aborting a Fetus: The Legal Right, The Personal Choice
85w Roman Catholic Doctrine of Therapeutic Abortion
85x Abortion and Ethical Theory
85y Abortion and the Concept of a Person
85z Abortion and the Quality of Life
86f Issues Before the Abortion Movement
97n Abortion and Abortion Law
97o Abortion Warning
127jj Abortion Testimonial
140bb Men and the Abortion Experience--Anxiety and Social Supports
141o Adolescent Experience of Pregnancy and Abortion
157s Defense of Abortion
157t Abortion and a Woman's Right to Decide
157v Abortion and the Golden Rule
158dd Defense of Abortion
158ee Moral and Legal Status of Abortion
173v Psychosocial Factors of the Abortion Experience
174j Abortion Policy since 1973: Political Cleavage and Its Impact on Policy Outputs
174q Abortion in Israel: Social Demands and Political Responses
175q Abortion Law Repeal(sort of): A Warning to Women
176qq Psychological Investigation of Habitual Abortion
191i Abortion: This Piece Is for Remembrance

211m Emotional Impact of Abortion
219q Alignment Strategies in Verbal Accounts of Problematic Conduct: The Case of Abortion
233bbb Abortion: Women, Men and the Law
264e Abortion: The Controversial Choice
282t Abortion and a Woman's Right to Decide
283j Feminist View of Abortion
284f Abortion Law Reform
296r Pregnancy and Abortion: Implications for Career Development of Professional Women

ABSENT

198n Absent Father and Cross-Sex Identity
252ii Women's Absenteeism and Labor Turnover

ABUSE

8kk Alcohol Use and Abuse in the Gay Community
13v Use and Abuse of Vocational Tests
110k Abuse of Eve by the New World Adam
235c Sexual Abuse of Children
321i Victims of Rape and Wife Abuse

ACADEMIA

see also COLLEGE; UNIVERSITY; CAMPUS; COEDUCATION; STUDENT; FACULTY; HIGHER EDUCATION

4j Faculty Wife: Her Academic Interests and Qualifications
4k Institutional Variation in the Status of Academic Women
4m Discipline Variation in the Status of Academic Women
4n Sex and Specialization in Academe and the Professions
4o Sex Discrimination in Academe
4p Political Action by Academic Women
4t Affirmative Action Plans for Eliminating Sex Discrimination in Academe
8n Thriving Decloseted in Rural Academe
13aa Second Sex in Academe
13ii Academic Women
13jj Discrimination and Demography Restrict Opportunities for Academic Women
141gg Woman Artist and the Art Academy: A Case Study in Institutional Prejudice
166x Academic Women
166oo Women as a Minority Group in Higher Academics
166zz Women in Academe
196dd Overt and Covert Forms of Discrimination Against Academic Women
196ii Women in Academic Governance
197j Myth is Better Than a Miss: Men Get the Edge in Academic Employment
202h Women and the Academic Labor Market
208j Segregated Academic and Vocational Schools: Separate But Not Equal
250hh Sex Differences in Expectancy of Intellectual and Academic Reinforcement
256o Degree in Enlightenment: When a Woman's Education Will No Longer Be an Academic Question
267w Sex Discrimination in Academe

271k Second Sex in Academe
301d Legal Requirements, Structures, and Strategies for Eliminating Sex Discrimination in Academe
326b Women in Academia: Today is Different
327c Regional Approach to Analyzing the Recruitment of Academic Women
334e Young Ladies Academy of Philadelphia
334p Academic Prism: New View of American Women
341c Wives of Academe
341m Unemployed! An Academic Woman's Saga
368c Evaluating Women's Studies- Academic Theory and Practice

ACCEPTANCE

166xx Employer Acceptance of the Mature Home Economist
273u Acceptance of Their Ways
296v Acceptance of the Concept of the Maternal Role by Behavioral Scientists: Its Effects on Women
365d Acceptance of the Concept of the Maternal Role by Behavioral Scientists: Its Effects on Women

ACCESS

143l Women in Planning: There's More to Affirmative Action than Gaining Access
194h Women and Modernization: Access to Tools
227c Indirect Access to Influence
294r Access to Education at All Levels

ACCOMMODATION

253i Conflict and Accommodation

ACCOUNT

17g Moll Flanders: "A Woman on her own Account"
181e Femininity in the Classroom: An Account of Changing Attitudes
219q Alignment Strategies in Verbal Accounts of Problematic Conduct: The Case of Abortion
314l Accountability--The Key to Successful Affirmative Action
348g Accounting for Rape: Reality and Myth in Press Reporting

ACCRA

302e Ga Women and Socioeconomic Change in Accra, Ghana

ACCULTURATION

208y Female Acculturation Through the Fairy Tale

ACCURACY

196s Counselors View Women and Work: Accuracy of Information

ACHIEVEMENT

see also FEAR OF SUCCESS; FAILURE; SUCCESS

6b Women's Lack of Achievement: Then and Now
13c Achievement-Related Conflicts in Women
67e Intelligence, Occupational Status and Achievement Orientation
73a In Praise of the Achieving Female Monkey
82c Femininity and Successful Achievement: A Basic Inconsistency
186g Femininity and Successful Achievement: A Basic Inconsistency
204l Sex-Role Socialization and Achievement in Mathematics
225e City's Achievements: The Patriotic Amazonomachy and Ancient Athens
233l Achieving Womanhood
250b Evaluation of the Performance of Women as a Function of Their Sex, Achievement, and Personal History
250ii Experimental Arousal of Achievement Motivation in Adolescent Girls
250jj Achievement-Related Conflicts in Women
250kk Early Childhood Experiences and Women's Achievement Motives
251gg Have Swedish Women Achieved Equality?
266f Socialization of Achievement Orientation in Females
266g Relationship Between Role Orientation and Achievement Motivation in College Women
266h Bringing Women In: Rewards, Punishments, And the Structure of Achievement
267h Early Childhood Experiences and Women's Achievement Motives
267i Socialization of Achievement Motivation in Females
267k Varieties of Achievement Motivation
267l Achievement-Related Conflicts in Women
267o Implied Demand Character of the Wife's Future and Role Innovation: Patterns of Achievement Orientation Among College Women
286n Femininity and Achievement in Sports
296b Early Childhood Experiences and Women's Achievement Motives
326a Success Motivation and Social Structure: Comments on Women and Achievement

ACHIEVEMENT-ORIENTATION

22r Socialization of Achievement-Orientation in Females
243h Institutional Discrimination: The Case of Achievement-Oriented Women in Higher Education

ACOSTA

122d Life and Early Literary Career of the Nineteenth-Century Colombian Writer, Coledad Acosta de Samper

ACQUIESCENCE

92e Militancy and Acquiescence Amongst Women Workers

ACT

42l Prostitution and the Poor in Plymouth and Southampton Under the Contagious Diseases Act
174f Discrimination and the Law: The Equal Credit Opportunity Act
175x Rape: An Act of Terror
247l Picasso's Suite 347, or Painting as an Act of Love
260s Title VII of the 1964 Civil Rights Act

ACTION

see also AFFIRMATIVE ACTION

4p Political Action by Academic Women
8hh Power to Gay People: A Los Angeles Experiment in Community Action
25g Negro Family: The Case for National Action
79m Malady and Remedy of Vexations and Unjust Arrests and Actions
141hh From Social Fact to Social Action
183c Women and Collective Action in Europe
213k Male and Female in Hopi Thought and Action
294u United Nations Action to Advance the Status of Women
302f Limitations of Group Action Among Entrepreneurs: The Market Women of Abidjan, Ivory Coast
309l Draft, International Plan of Action
314m Preparing for the Future: Commitment and Action
328a Women's Stake in Full Employment: Their Disadvantaged Role in the Economy--Challenges to Action

ACTIVATION

250q Roles of Activation and Inhibition in Sex Differences in Cognitive Abilities
250r Comments on "Roles of Activation and Inhibition in Sex Differences in Cognitive Abilities"

ACTIVIST

212n Maya Deren and Germaine Dulac: Activists of the Avant-Garde
316a American Woman: Voter and Activist
344n Women as Voluntary Political Activists

ACTIVITY

93e Jennie Higginses of the "New South in the West": A Regional Survey of Socialist Activities, Agitators, and Organizers, 1901-1917
106l Rosemary Park: Professional Activities
155w Sexual Activities and Attitudes in Older Persons
194l Selective Omission and Theoretical Distortion in Studying the Political Activity of Women in Brazil
213h Economic Activity and Marriage among Ivoirian Urban Women
252d Changes in the Labor Force Activity of Women
264cc Women's Liberation Movement: Its Origins, Organizations, Activities, and Ideas
266v Effect of Contraceptive Pills on Sexual Activity in the Luteal Phase of the Human Menstrual Cycle
286a Dimensions of Physical Activity
294i Political Activity of Women in Eastern Europe
337e Dispute over an Active Apostolate for Women During the Counter-Reformation
351b Pregnancy, Motherhood and Work Activity

ACTRESS

see also FILM; individual actresses

244e Image and Reality: The Actress and Society

288m Actress Archetypes in the 1950s: Doris Day, Marilyn Monroe, Elizabeth Taylor, Audrey Hepburn

ADAH

128g Reckless Lady: The Life Story of Adah Isaacs Menken

ADAM

108dd Adam Bede
110k Abuse of Eve by the New World Adam
263e Eve and Adam: Genesis 2-3 Reread
362m From Adam's Rib to Women's Lib

ADAMS

178c Puritan Ethic in the Revolutionary Era: Abigail Adams and Thomas Jefferson

ADAPTATION

21d Female Strategies: Animal Adaptations and Adaptive Significance
350g Women's Spirit Possession and Urban Adaptation
372h Adaptive Strategies and Social Networks of Women in St. Kitts

ADDAMS

253k Jane Addams: An American Heroine

ADDICTION

51u Opiate Addiction Among Females in the United States Between 1850 and 1970

ADDISON

222u Judgment: Addison Gayle

ADDRESS

153f Address to the Christian Women of America
309d Etiquette among Women in Karnataka: Forms of Address in the Village and the Family
361c Address Forms in Sexual Politics

ADELE H.

288f Twilight of Romanticism: "Adele H."

ADJUSTMENT

11b Adjustment: New Approaches to Women's Mental Health
309j Asian Women in Britain: Strategies of Adjustment of Indian and Pakistani Migrants

ADMINISTRATION

4h Status Transitions of Women Students, Faculty, and Administrators
140ii Bibliography of Dissertations for and about Women in Administration in Colleges and Universities
196x Attitudes of Superintendents and Board of Education Members Toward the Employment and Effectiveness of Women as Public-School Administrators
272e Feminism and the Woman School Administrator
272h Sex Bias in School Administration
272j Black Female Administrator: Woman in a Double Bind
272o Leadership Training for Increased Effectiveness among Women Educational Administrators
278v Androgynous Administration
280u Women in Business Administration
314kk Educating Women for Administration
321e Women in Court Administration
364i Women School Administrators: My Experience with Discrimination

ADMIRE

105h Most Admired Woman: Image-Making in the News
197d "Look, Jane, Look! See Dick Run and Jump! Admire Him!"

ADMISSION

180e Case for Preferential Admissions
180o Judicial Scrutiny of "Benign" Racial Preference in Law School Admissions
180bb Preferential Policies in Hiring and Admissions: A Jurisprudential Approach
196aa Effect of Sex on College Admission, Work Evaluation, and Job Interviews
196bb Sex Bias in Selective College Admissions
197h Effect of Race and Sex on College Admission
217b Preferential Treatment in Admitting Racial Minority Students

ADOLESCENCE

18m Role Music Plays in Adolescent Development
18q Physical Growth of Adolescent Girls: Patterns and Sequence
76f Adolescent to Woman
82b New Sources of Conflict in Females at Adolescence and Early Adulthood
99c Problem Behavior in Adolescents
116l Italian American Women and Their Daughters in Rhode Island: The Adolescence of Two Generations, 1900-1950
141o Adolescent Experience of Pregnancy and Abortion
155q Teenage Boys and Girls in West Germany
176g Sex Differences in Adolescent Character Processes
196e Adolescent Culture
196p Adolescents' Views of Women's Work-Role
200g Sex Differences in the Play Configurations of Preadolescents
211i Adolescent Sexuality and Pregnancy
219g Phonological Differences in the English of Adolescent Chicanas and Chicanos
250ii Experimental Arousal of Achievement Motivation in Adolescent Girls

348e Sexual Codes and Conduct: A Study of Teenage Girls

ADOPTED

352o APPENDIX: Texts Concerning Women Workers Adopted by the 60th Session of the International Labour Conference, 4-25 June 1975

ADORNMENT

231p On Adornment

ADRIENNE

88k Feminist Poet: Alta and Adrienne Rich

ADULT

39d Adult Sex Roles and Mental Illness
75d Adult Female Offender: A Selected Bibliography
76g Female Autonomy and Young Adult Women
82b New Sources of Conflict in Females at Adolescence and Early Adulthood
155m Early Sexual Behavior in Adult Homosexual and Heterosexual Males
171j Adult Life Cycles: Changing Roles and Changing Hormones
199m Ethological Study of Children Approaching a Strange Adult: Sex Differences
266bb Adult Sex Roles and Mental Health

ADULTERY

157m Is Adultery Immoral?
158r Is Adultery Immoral?
231o On Adultery

ADVANCEMENT

294s U.N.E.S.C.O. Long-Range Program for the Advancement of Women
327b Why Can't Women Be More Like Men: A Summary of the Sociopsychological Factors Hindering Women's Advancement in the Professions
352b Suggestions for the Advancement of Working Women

ADVENTURE

96c Female Prisoner: A Narrative of the Life and Singular Adventures of Josephine Amelia Perkins
96l Before Women Were Human Beings: Adventures of an American Fellow in German Universities of the '90s
96jj In Search of Adventure
103d The Learned Adventure of the Dragon's Head
226p In Search of Adventure
332i Adventures of a Woman in Science
369p Adventures of a Woman in Science

ADVERSE

227h Adverse Impact of Development

293c Adverse Impact of Development on Women

ADVERTISEMENT

161f The Advertisement
254m Image of Woman in Advertising

ADVICE

160a Advice to Mothers, on the Subject of Their Own Health, and, of the Means of Promoting the Health, Strength and Beauty of Their Offspring
166i Occupational Advice for Women in Magazines

AESTHETICS

90c Consciousness and Authenticity: Toward a Feminist Aesthetic
98i For the Etruscans: Sexual Difference and Artistic Production--The Debate Over a Female Aesthetic
122j Brechtian Aesthetics in Chile: Isidora Aguirre's "Los Papeleros"
211t Woman and Esthetic Surgery
212k Feminist Aesthetic: Reflection Revolution Ritual
275g Women and the Aesthetic of the Positive Hero in the G.D.R.
361k Feminist Aesthetic

AFFAIR

103e Family Affair
111bb Affair
112t Affair
117s Changing(?)Role of Women in Jewish Communal Affairs: A Look into the U.J.A.
151c Participation in Public Affairs

AFFECT

20k Affectivity and Instrumentality in Friendship Patterns among American Women
250cc Patterns of Affective Fluctuation in the Menstrual Cycle
250dd Effects of Oral Contraceptives on Affective Fluctuations Associated with the Menstrual Cycle
296n Effects of Oral Contraceptives on Affective Fluctuations Associated with the Menstrual Cycle
330b Sex Hormones, The Central Nervous System and Affect Variability in Humans

AFFIRMATION

359e Autobiographer and Her Readers: From Apology to Affirmation

AFFIRMATIVE ACTION

see also REVERSE DISCRIMINATION; PREFERENTIAL HIRING; SEX DISCRIMINATION; TITLE IX; TITLE VII; BIAS; SEXISM; QUOTA

4t Affirmative Action Plans for Eliminating Sex Discrimination in Academe

6d Women in Government and Affirmative Action
6i Bank of America's Affirmative Action Seminar
49b Setting Up an Affirmative Action Program
49c Affirmative Action and the Continuing Majority: Women of All Races and Minority Men
64h Remedial and Affirmative Action
143l Women in Planning: There's More to Affirmative Action than Gaining Access
174d Impact of Organizational Structure, Technology, and Professionalism on the Policy of Affirmative Action
174e Affirmative Action: Constraints and Policy Impact
180c Affirmative Action--A Liberal Program
180i "Affirmative Action" Reconsidered
301a Affirmative Action Through Affirmative Attitudes
301a Affirmative Action Through Affirmative Attitudes
301h Case History of Affirmative Action
301i Affirmative Action at Stanford University
314l Accountability--The Key to Successful Affirmative Action
341e Uncertain Progress of Affirmative Action
342ee Affirmative Action in Higher Education
342ff Analyzing Affirmative Action Data on the Computer

AFRICA

see also individual countries

30a Bridewealth and Dowry in Africa and Eurasia
91a Women's Work and Fertility in Africa
91e Women, Employment, and Fertility Trends in the Arab Middle East and North Africa
127kk Liberation Must Also Include the Women of Africa
140e Female Employment and Family Organization in West Africa
206b Emergent Africa
249g Matrifocality in Indonesia and Africa and Among Black Americans
281n How African Women Cope with Migrant Labor in South Africa
281o Women and Migration in Contemporary West Africa
294j Women in the Middle East and North Africa and Universal Suffrage
294k Political Participation of Women in Africa South of the Sahara
302g Rebels or Status-Seekers? Women as Spirit Mediums in East Africa
302j Women and Economic Change in Africa
324o Sub-Saharan Africa
367b Demographic Transition in the Middle East and North Africa
367c Family Planning and Population Policies in the Middle East and North Africa

AFRICAN

20w Attitudes Towards Reproduction in a Rapidly Changing African Society
20z Changing Roles of Women in Two African Muslim Cultures
25c West African Influences
43b African Women and National Development
43d Issues Confronting Professional African Women: Illustrations from Kenya
53f Matrifocus on African Women
153c The African Mother at Her Daughter's Grave

193c Aspects of the Distinction Between the Sexes in the Nyamwezi and Some Other African Systems of Kinship and Marriage
222c War on African Familyhood
222d Images of Black Women in Modern African Poetry
222f African Heroine
222n Alice Walker: "The Diary of an African Nun" and Du Bois' Double Consciousness
260y Role of Women in the Political Organization of African Societies
281b Definitions of Women and Development: An African Perspective
281n How African Women Cope with Migrant Labor in South Africa
293h Women in African Towns South of the Sahara: The Urbanization Dilemma
297c African Women: Identity Crisis? Some Observations on Education and the Changing Role of Women in Sierra Leone and Zaire
316q Memsahib, Militante, Femme Libre: Political and Apolitical Styles of Modern African Women
317i Convivial Sisterhood: Spirit Mediumship and Client-Core Network among Black South African Women
325ee Theme of Sexual Oppression in the North African Novel
329b African Women, "Modernization," and National Liberation
338c Role of Women in the Political Organization of African Societies
338d Nzakara Women (Central African Republic)
367a Family Life, Women's Status, and Fertility: Middle East and North African Perspectives

AFRO-AMERICA

see also BLACK; MINORITY; NEGRO; RACE

7b Discrimination Against Afro-American Women in the Woman's Movement, 1830-1920
7f Images of Black Women in Afro-American Poetry
214l Afro-American Women Poets: A Bio-Critical Survey
342w AfroAmerican Woman's Perspective on Racist Barriers
359g African-American Women's Autobiographies and Ethnicity

AFTERMATH

235j Women and Victimization: The Aftermath

AFTERNOON

273j Sunday Afternoon

AGE

see also OLD

8cc Aging
19i Women in the Age of Light
22n Cross-Cultural Analysis of Sex Differences in the Behavior of Children Aged Three Through Eleven
77c Cross-Cultural Analysis of Sex Differences in the Behavior of Children Aged Three Through Eleven
99e Sex Differences in Problems of Aging
129h Coming Out of the Closet: Marriage and Other Crises of Middle Age

151e Lady and the Mill Girl: Changes in the Status of Women in the Age of Jackson
173jj Double Standard of Aging
176d Sex, Age, and State as Determinants of Mother-Infant Interaction
193d Sex, Age and Social Control in Mobs of the Darwin Hinterland
196b Sex-Role Concepts Among Elementary-School Age Girls
198cc Sex, Age, and State as Determinants of Mother-Infant Interaction
204f Sex-Related Differences in Cognition Among the Elderly
233f Womanly Image: Character Assassination through the Ages
240a Portrayal of Women by Chaucer and His Age
244h Sex and Death in Victorian England: An Examination of Age- and Sex-Specific Death Rates, 1840-1910
264l Double Standard: Age
265h Double Standard: Age
296q Middle Age
308g Chiang Ch'ing's Coming of Age
309i Aging Women in India: Self-Perceptions and Changing Roles
317d Coming of Age in Kelton: The Constraints on Gender Symbolism in Jewish Ritual
317j Bobbes and Zeydes: Old and New Roles for Elderly Jews
325k Turkish Women in the Ottoman Empire: The Classical Age
334c Myth of the Golden Age
335f Women in an Age of Transition: 1485-1714
337c Ascetic Women in the Late Patristic Age
342e Women and Aging: The Unforgivable Sin
342y Agism and the Women's Movement
360d Lady and the Mill Girl: Changes in the Status of Women in the Age of Jackson
369r Coming of Age the Long Way Around

AGE-OLD

114e Panchakanya--An Age-old Benediction

AGENCIES

64d Compliance Agencies
252gg Men and Women in Community Agencies: A Note on Power and Prestige
297q Discrimination Against Women in the U.S.: Higher Education, Government Enforcement Agencies, and Unions

AGENDA

57i APPENDIX: U.S. National Women's Agenda

AGGADIC

117w Aggadic Approaches to Biblical Women

AGGRESSION

89uu Aggression in the Relations between the Sexes
183a Sex Differences in Aggression and Dominance
199r Sex Differences in Aggression
199v Aggression, Androgens, and the XYY Syndrome
200i Dreams: Sex Differences in Aggressive Content
286g Aggression and the Female Athlete

AGHIA

108a Venus--Aghia Sophia

AGITATION

93e Jennie Higginses of the "New South in the West": A Regional Survey of Socialist Activities, Agitators, and Organizers, 1901-1917
128d Jane Grey Swisshelm: Agitator
163j Spectators, Agitators, or Lawmakers: Women in State Legislatures
213f Agitation for Change in the Sudan
360b Anne Hutchinson and Female Agitation During the Years of the Antinomian Turmoil, 1636-1640

AGREEMENT

89ll Marriage Agreement

AGRICULTURE

293a Role of Women in Agriculture

AGUIRRE

122j Brechtian Aesthetics in Chile: Isidora Aguirre's "Los Papeleros"

AID

297p Legislation: An Aid in Eliminating Sex Bias in Education in the U.S.

AIDE

334o From Aide to Organizer: The Oral History of Lillian Roberts

AIDOO

222e Ama Ata Aidoo's "Dilemma of a Ghost"

AIR

103g Death on the Air
108bb The Starless Air

ALASKAN

372l Economic Role of Women in Alaskan Eskimo Society

ALCHEMY

247g Corset as Erotic Alchemy: From Rococo Galanterie to Montaut's Physiologies

ALCOHOL

8kk Alcohol Use and Abuse in the Gay Community
99g Problems with Alcohol and Other Drugs

330g Women and Alcoholism

ALCOTT

179b L.M. Alcott
208z Louisa May Alcott: The Author of "Little Women" as Feminist

ALEKSANDRA

218g Bolshevism, The Woman Question, and Aleksandra Kollontai

ALFRED

275b Woman Question in the Early Work of Alfred Doblin

ALGERIA

126l Politics of Cultural Liberation: Male-Female Relations in Algeria
325g Women in Algeria
329n Algerian Women: Honor, Survival, and Islamic Socialism
367h Fertility in Algeria: Trends and Differentials

ALGONKIAN

270b Sunksquaws, Shamans, and Tradeswomen: Middle Atlantic Coastal Algonkian Women During the Seventeenth and Eighteenth Centuries

ALICE

3p Alice Blaine
73r Conversation with Alice Rossi
212l Out of Oblivion: Alice Guy-Blache
215m Alice Louise Reynolds: A Woman's Woman
222m Alice Walker
222n Alice Walker: "The Diary of an African Nun" and Du Bois' Double Consciousness
288e Hollywood Heroines Under the Influence: Alice Still Lives Here
288p Alice Guy Blache: Czarina of the Silent Screen

ALIEN

88v Alienation of the Woman Writer in "The Golden Notebook"
131f Lau, Malaita: "A Woman Is an Alien Spirit"
151j Woman as Alien
259m Woman as Alien
264b Female Sexual Alienation
265b Female Sexual Alienation
342d Alienation and the Contemporary American Housewife

ALIGNMENT

219q Alignment Strategies in Verbal Accounts of Problematic Conduct: The Case of Abortion

ALIVE

89l It Hurts to Be Alive and Obsolete

ALL-AMERICAN

77u Rape: The All-American Crime
85s Rape: The All-American Crime
94b Rape: The All-American Crime
265c Rape: The All-American Crime

ALLEN

288v Dede Allen

ALLENDE

316o Mobilization of Women in Allende's Chile

ALLIANCE

41j Creating a Feminist Alliance: Sisterhood and Class Conflict in the New York Women's Trade Union League, 1903- 1914
128l Women in the Alliance Movement
218e Unequal Partners in an Uneasy Alliance: Women and the Working Class in Imperial Germany
278t Influential Alliances: Cincinnati Women in the Political Arena, 1920-1945
325v Iranian Women in Family Alliance and Sexual Politics

ALLOCATION

135f Family, Employment and the Allocation of Time
287c Home Work, Market Work, and the Allocation of Time

ALMQVIST

297x Sources of the Matrilineal Family System in the Works of Carl J.L. Almqvist

ALMROTH

68w Sir Almroth Wright's Case Against Woman Suffrage

ALONE

8g Living Alone
96cc Woman Alone
146a Woman Alone
226i Woman Alone
361a What Do Couples Talk About When They're Alone?

ALRAUNE

112hh Alraune

ALTA

88k Feminist Poet: Alta and Adrienne Rich

ALTERNATIVE

71a Literary Archetypes and Female Role Alternatives: The Woman and the Novel in Latin America
146b Sexuality and Alternative Life Styles
158cc Marriage and Its Alternatives
235e Treatment Alternatives for Battered Women
266s Alternative Methods For Measuring Sex Discrimination in Occupational Incomes
304d Child-Free Alternative: Rejection of the Motherhood Mystique
318f Bolshevik Alternatives and the Soviet Family: The 1926 Marriage Law Debate
326h Alternatives for Social Change: The Future Status of Women
342a Women and Anger: Alternatives

ALTRUISM

158bb Altruism and Women's Oppression
278k Female Powerlessness: The Altruistic Other Orientation
282k Altruism and Women's Oppression

AMA

222e Ama Ata Aidoo's "Dilemma of a Ghost"

AMADO

71b "Brazileira": Images and Realities in Writings of Machado de Assis and Jorge Amado

AMAHUACA

131a Marriages of Pacho: A Woman's Life among the Amahuaca

AMATEUR

369d Birth of the Amateur

AMAZONS

225e City's Achievements: The Patriotic Amazonomachy and Ancient Athens
241b The Amazons

AMBER

10a The Amber Gods

AMBITION

166p Women's Ambition
344m Congressional Ambitions of Female Political Elites

AMBIVALENCE

176h Ambivalence: The Socialization of Women
176r Roots of Ambivalence in American Women

218f Marxist Ambivalence Toward Women: Between Socialism and Feminism in the Italian Socialist Party
254i Ambivalence: The Socialization of Women
322j Ambivalence in the Field

AMELIA

96c Female Prisoner: A Narrative of the Life and Singular Adventures of Josephine Amelia Perkins
96d Demon in Female Apparel: Narrative of Josephine Amelia Perkins, the Notorious Female Horse Thief...
128h Amelia Bloomer and Bloomerism

AMERICA

see also LATIN AMERICA; UNITED STATES; SPANISH AMERICA

6i Bank of America's Affirmative Action Seminar
20x Concepts of "Femininity" and "Liberation" in the Context of Changing Sex-Roles: Women in Modern India and America
25a Negro Family in America
35g Femininity and Capitalism in Antebellum America
40b Public Policy Toward Child Care in America: A Historical Perspective
42a "Fashionable Diseases": Women's Complaints and Their Treatment in Nineteenth-Century America
42b Puberty to Menopause: The Cycle of Femininity in Nineteenth-Century America
42h Family Limitation, Sexual Control, and Domestic Feminism in Victorian America
63b Equal Pay in America
122n Two Poets of America: Juana de Asbaje and Sara de Ibanez
126g Education and Ideology in Nineteenth-Century America: The Response of Educational Institutions to the Changing Role of Women
126p Sex and Class in Colonial and Nineteenth-Century America
128b Early Women Printers of America
141q Men and Women in the Family: History of the Idea of Family in America's Depression Generation
141cc Madame Vestris in America
149f Down with Myth America
151d Dynamics of Interracial Sex in Colonial America
153f Address to the Christian Women of America
155o Changing Sex Norms in America and Scandinavia
176cc Pre-Industrial Patterns in the Colonial Family in America: A Content Analysis of Colonial Magazines
191b Sexual Surgery in Late Nineteenth-Century America
214i Emily Dickinson and the Deerslayer: The Dilemma of the Woman Poet in America
246d Myth America: Women in American Literature (panel)
253h Revolution Without Ideology: The Changing Place of Women in America
257g Slave-Women of America
259l Changing Place of Women in America
287a Looking Backward in Order to Look Forward: Women, Work and Social Values in America
296u Childbirth in America

334b Women's Lives Transformed: Demographic and Family Patterns in America, 1600-1970
334m Origins of Legal Restrictions on Planned Parenthood in Nineteenth-Century America
337k Women, Religion and Reform in Antebellum America
359b Quest for Community: Spiritual Autobiographies of Eighteenth-Century Quaker and Puritan Women in America
360e Organized Women's Benevolence in Early Nineteenth-Century America
360g Spiritualist Medium: A Study of Female Professionalization in Victorian America
360k Family Limitation, Sexual Control, and Domestic Feminism in Victorian America
360l Female World of Love and Ritual: Relations Between Women in Nineteenth-Century America
360n Hysterical Woman: Sex Roles and Role Conflict in Nineteenth-Century America
360q Cookbooks and Law Books: The Hidden History of Career Women in Twentieth-Century America
361h Women's Language in America: Myth and Reality

AMERICAN

9ii Seduced and Abandoned in the New World: The Fallen Woman in American Fiction
11j American Woman: Who Will She Be?
20k Affectivity and Instrumentality in Friendship Patterns among American Women
36f American Galatea
36g Great American Bitch
42i Feminization of American Religion: 1800-1860
43j Native American Women: Twilight of a Long Maidenhood
51gg Women and Crime: Does the American Experience Generalize?
59a How Much Is a Woman Worth? The American Public Policy
74k Development of the American Women's Liberation Movement, 1967-1971
80i Hispanic American Fiction and Drama Written by Women:
89a Homogenizing the American Woman: The Power of an Unconscious Ideology
96l Before Women Were Human Beings: Adventures of an American Fellow in German Universities of the '90s
97i American Family: Decay and Rebirth
116l Italian American Women and Their Daughters in Rhode Island: The Adolescence of Two Generations, 1900-1950
116w Italian Immigrant Women in American Literature
117y Mothers and Daughters in American Jewish Literature: The Rotted Cord
120f Male-Female Intonation Patterns in American English
140qq American Principles in Print: The Hero, The Harlot and the Glorified Horse
163t Voting Patterns of American Black Women
164m One American Woman: A Speculation upon Disbelief
171h American Birth Practices
172f American Family: A Twenty-Year View
176r Roots of Ambivalence in American Women
180j Emergence of an American Ethnic Pattern
183d American Peace Party: New Departures and Old Arguments
196y School Boards and Sex Bias in American Education
206g Marriage Roles, American Style

207c Gender-Marking in American English: Usage and Reference
214s Common Language: The American Woman Poet
222l Black Eve or Madonna? Antithetical Views of the Mother in Black American Literature
240h Images of Women in Early American Literature
240i Portrayal of Women in American Literature, 1790-1870
240j They Shall Have Faces, Minds, and (One Day) Flesh: Women in Late Nineteenth-century and Early Twentieth-century American Literature
240l Second-class Citizenship: The Status of Women in Contemporary American Fiction
240m "Free in Fact and at Last": The Image of the Black Woman in Black American Literature
246d Myth America: Women in American Literature (panel)
246l American Character vs. The Ideal Woman
246m Images of Women and Men in American Popular Magazines
249g Matrifocality in Indonesia and Africa and Among Black Americans
253k Jane Addams: An American Heroine
254o Seduced and Abandoned in the New World: The Image of Woman In American Fiction
257s (Remarks, National American Woman's Suffrage Association)
259a American Indian Women
259k American Women and the American Character
265q Women in the American Novel
265r Images of American Woman in Popular Songs
278e Sexism in American Naming Traditions
286q American Business Values and Involvement in Sport
291i Occupational Segregation and Public Policy: A Comparative Analysis of American and Soviet Patterns
292i American Maidens and Wives
294q Women and American Trade Unions
303b Challenging the American Domestic Ideal
316a American Woman: Voter and Activist
322b Exploring American Indian Communities in Depth
334p Academic Prism: New View of American Women
337j Liberated American Nun
342d Alienation and the Contemporary American Housewife
349c American Women in the Shipyards During World War II
349d Legal Status of Women After the American Revolution
358d Century of American Women's Sport
360j Catharine Beecher and the Education of American Women
369l Notes from an Extra in the American Moving Picture Show

AMERICAN--CULTURE

20t American Women in Politics: Culture, Structure, and Ideology
178i Ume Tsuda and Motoko Hani: Echoes of American Cultural Feminism in Japan
206f American Core Culture: Changes and Continuities
276e Sex, Gender, and American Culture
280a Women in the American Culture
360a American Women and Domestic Culture: An Approach to Women's History

AMERICAN--FEMINISM

41i Women's Trade Union League and American Feminism
90a American Feminist Literary Criticism: A Bibliographical Introduction

126i Feminism and Class Consciousness in the British and American Women's Trade Union Leagues, 1890-1925
141i Feminism and Class Consciousness in the British and American Women's Trade Union Leagues, 1890-1925
149o Origins of American Feminism
178i Ume Tsuda and Motoko Hani: Echoes of American Cultural Feminism in Japan
254cc American Feminism

AMERICAN--HISTORY

126d Historical Phallacies: Sexism in American Historical Writing
126s Study of Women in American History
181h Women in American Trade Unions: An Historical Analysis
292b New Approaches to the Study of Women in American History
334a Women and American History
337l American Women in Ministry: A History of Protestant Beginning Points
364d Black Woman in American History

AMERICAN--POLITICS

11h Woman: The New Figure in American Politics
20t American Women in Politics: Culture, Structure, and Ideology
163n Women as Voters: Their Maturation as Political Persons in American Society
264t American Women and the Political Process
265w Women in American Politics
316e Personality Characteristics of Women in American Politics
326f Women as Voters: Their Maturation as Political Persons in American Society
329j Political Change for the American Woman

AMERICAN--SEX

51aa Sexual Segregation of American Prisons
155u Group Sex Among the Mid-Americans
276e Sex, Gender, and American Culture
292h Sex on the American Indian Frontier

AMERICAN--WAR

151n American Woman's Pre-World War I Freedom in Manners and Morals
240k "Combat in the Erogenous Zone": Women in the American Novel between the Two World Wars
292t American Woman's Pre-World War I Freedom in Manners and Morals
349k American Women in the Peace and Preparedness Movements in World War I
360o American Woman's Pre-World War I Freedom in Manners and Morals
364e American Woman from 1900 to the First World War: A Profile

AMERICAN--WORK

116m Italian Mothers, American Daughters: Changes in Work and Family Roles
176l Barriers to the Career Choice of Engineering, Medicine, or Science Among American Women

267t Sex Discrimination Against the American Working Woman
326c Recent Trends in the Employment of American Women
327g Sex Discrimination Against the American Working Woman
328q Working Women: European Experience and American Need

AMICUS CURIAE

180l Harvard College Amicus Curiae, DeFunis v. Odegaard, Supreme Court of the U.S., 1973

AMY

215e Amy Brown Lyman: Raising the Quality of Life for All

ANAIS

88w Anais Nin: A Critical Evaluation
175rr Women's Private Writings: Anais Nin
359k Anais Nin's "Diary" in Context

ANALYTICAL

222b Analytical Vision
338g Analytical Bibliography

ANARCHISM

19q Other Scenarios: Women and Spanish Anarchism
74h Anarchism and Other Essays

ANATOMY

47c Doris Lessing in the Sixties: The New Anatomy of Melancholy
62i Anatomy of a Good Marriage
132c Anatomy Is Destiny
155a Psychological Consequances of the Anatomical Distinction Between the Sexes
170r Is Anatomy Destiny?
171a Psychosexual Neutrality: Is Anatomy Destiny?
198b Psychical Consequences of the Anatomical Distinction Between the Sexes
200a Psychological Consequences of the Anatomical Distinction between the Sexes
233e Psychical Consequences of the Anatomical Distinction between the Sexes
250h Psychological Consequences of the Anatomic Distinction Between the Sexes
268a Psychical Consequences of the Anatomical Distinction Between the Sexes
282a Anatomy and Destiny: The Role of Biology in Plato's Views of Women

ANCIENT

43i Ancient Song, New Melody in Latin America: Women and Film
79o An Essay to Revive the Ancient Education of Gentlewomen
206e Sex Roles, Ancient to Modern
225e City's Achievements: The Patriotic Amazonomachy and Ancient Athens

232c Investigation of the Religious and Judicial Character of Matriarchy in the Ancient World
232d God-Idea of the Ancients
266hh Ancient and Contemporary Perspectives on The Women of Israel
278aa Mother, Maiden, and the Marriage of Death: Women Writers and an Ancient Myth

ANCILLA

232n Ancilla's Share

ANDEAN

193a Complementarity and Conflict: An Andean View of Men and Women
270g Andean Women Under Spanish Rule

ANDROGEN

199c Fetal Androgens, Human Central Nervous System Differentiation, and Behavior Sex Differences
199d Prenatal Androgen, Intelligence and Cognitive Sex Differences
199v Aggression, Androgens, and the XYY Syndrome

ANDROGYNY

see also SEX ROLE; GENDER; ROLE

11d Androgyny and Humanistic Goals
22c Probing the Promise of Androgyny
22s Androgynous Themes Written to Sentence Cues by Sixth-, Eighth-, and Tenth-Grade Students
22x Androgyny as a Model of Mental Health for Women: From Theory to Therapy
85c Androgyny As an Ideal for Human Development
85d Two Forms of Androgynism
98o Androgyny and the Psychology of Sex Differences
132o Androgynous World
156g Development of Psychological Androgyny: Early Childhood Socialization
171d Human Sex-Hormone Abnormalities Viewed from an Androgynous Perspective: A Reconsideration of the Work of John Money
172j Traits, Roles, and the Concept of Androgyny
173m Androgyny Reconsidered
238k Androgynous Life
266b Measurement of Psychological Androgyny
268n Androgyne
278v Androgynous Administration
278x Huck--An Androgynous Hero
278y Before Androgyny: An Examination of the Stages Toward Neo-Masculinity
331g Child Care for the 1980s: Traditional Sex Roles or Androgyny?

ANGEL

19m Angels in the Devil's Workshop: Leisured and Charitable Women in Nineteenth-Century England and France
50l Angel Face

52h Pierre de Lancre's "Tableau de l'Inconstance des Mauvais Anges et Demons": The Sabbat Sensationalised
108cc Consorting with Angels
128m "Kate," the "Good Angel" of Oklahoma
240f Angels and Other Women in Victorian Literature
244g Victorian Masculinity and the Angel in the House
260w Where Angels Fear to Tread
339e Consorting With Angels

ANGELICA

116e Forging a Socialist Women's Movement: Angelica Balabanoff in Switzerland
122g Maria Angelica Bosco and Beatriz Guido: An Approach to Two Argentinian Novelists Between 1960 and 1970
368f Women and Socialism: Case of Angelica Balabanoff

ANGELOU

359j Metaphysics of Matrilinearism in Women's Autobiography: Studies of Mead's "Blackberry Winter," Hellman's "Pentimento," Angelou's "I Know Why the Caged Bird Sings," and Kingston's "The Woman Warrior"

ANGER

173bb Anger and Tenderness
342a Women and Anger: Alternatives
364c Anger in Women Writers: Source of Inspiration or Inhibition?

ANGLO-SAXON

see also ENGLAND; BRITAIN; ENGLISH WOMEN

141g Influential Women in Anglo-Saxon England
335b Women in Anglo-Saxon Society (c.600-1066)
335c Land Charters and the Legal Position of Anglo-Saxon Women

ANGRY

175d Getting Angry

ANGUISH

322d From Anguish to Exultation

ANIMAL

21d Female Strategies: Animal Adaptations and Adaptive Significance
159g On the Generation of Animals
163s Traditional Political Animals? A Loud No
204i Prenatal Influences on Cognitive Abilities: Data from Experimental Animals and Human and Endocrine Syndromes

ANIMUS

268m Nature of the Animus

ANN

47g Women in the Novels of Ann Petry
68e Ann and Superman: Type and Archetype
215t Dr. Margaret Ann Freece: Entrepreneur of Southern Utah
222s Ann Petry Talks About First Novel

ANN ARBOR

208r Let Them Aspire! A Plea and Proposal for Equality of Opportunity for Males and Females in the Ann Arbor Public Schools

ANNA

7g Anna J. Cooper: A Voice for Black Women
330l Anna O.--Patient or Therapist? An Eidetic View
339b Anna Karenina

ANNE

9a Trial of Anne Hutchinson
17o Winning: Katherine Anne Porter's Women
88i "I Dare to Live": The Transforming Art of Anne Sexton
178a Anne Hutchinson and the "Revolution Which Never Happened"
192d Katherine Anne Porter
214c Anne Bradstreet's Poetry: A Study of Subversive Piety
214d Anne Finch, Countess of Winchilsea: An Augustan Woman Poet
214r Poetry and Salvation in the Career of Anne Sexton
292f Anne Bradstreet: Dogmatist and Rebel
360b Anne Hutchinson and Female Agitation During the Years of the Antinomian Turmoil, 1636-1640

ANNEXATION

236c Women Surviving: Palace Life in Seoul after the Annexation

ANNIHILATE

175mm Feminists: A Political Organization to Annihilate Sex Roles

ANNOTATED

56g Annotated Bibliography
80e Women in Contemporary French Society: Annotated Bibliography
105p Image of Women in Television: An Annotated Bibliography
120m Sex Differences in Language, Speech, and Nonverbal Communication: An Annotated Bibliography
208dd Reducing the "Miss Muffet" Syndrome: An Annotated Bibliography

ANNOY

197c He Only Does It To Annoy

ANOMALY

369f Anomaly of a Woman in Physics

ANOREXIA NERVOSA

173hh Cinderella's Stepsisters: A Feminist Perspective on Anorexia Nervosa and Bulimia
332f Why Are So Many Anorexics Women?

ANTAGONISM

55h Sexual Antagonism in Herefordshire
285l Sexual Antagonism in the New Guinea Highlands: A Bena Bena Example

ANTE-NATAL

1b Sermon on Ante-Natal Infanticide

ANTEBELLUM

35g Femininity and Capitalism in Antebellum America
259e Ante-Bellum Southern Women
337k Women, Religion and Reform in Antebellum America

ANTECEDENTS

198aa Physiological Development, Cognitive Development, and Socialization Antecedents of Children's Sex-Role Attitudes
213n Ecological Antecedents and Sex-Role Consequences in Traditional and Modern Israeli Subcultures

ANTHOLOGIES

122a Random Survey of the Ratio of Female Poets to Male in Anthologies: Less-Than-Tokenism as a Mexican Tradition

ANTHONY

175b Trial of Susan B. Anthony

ANTHROPOLOGY

see also FIELD WORK; PRIMITIVE; various cultures

42f Sexual Politics of Victorian Social Anthropology
52f Tudor Anthropologist: George Gifford's "Discourse " and "Dialogue"
67c Anthropological Perspective
141a Anthropology of Women
198h Anthropology and Sex Differences
198v Biological and Anthropological Differences between the Sexes
201c Anthropological Perspective on Sex Roles and Subsistence
230b Woman the Gatherer: Male Bias in Anthropology
230e Aboriginal Woman: Male and Female Anthropological Perspectives
251j Anthropologist Looks at Engels
252o Anthropologist Looks at Engels
258h Renewed Anthropology
285a Theoretical Issues in the Anthropological Study of Women
296w Cultural Anthropologist's Approach to Maternal Deprivation
297y Women in the Anthropology Profession--1
297z Women in the Anthropology Profession--2

297bb Female Factor in Anthropology
297cc Aboriginal Woman: Male and Female Anthropological Perspectives
322e Woman Anthropologist in Brazil

ANTI-ROMANCE

214e Emily Bronte's Anti-Romance

ANTIGONE

339q Antigone

ANTINOMIAN

360b Anne Hutchinson and Female Agitation During the Years of the Antinomian Turmoil, 1636-1640

ANTRIM

16d The Antrim Hills

ANXIETY

140bb Men and the Abortion Experience--Anxiety and Social Supports
176jj Castration Anxiety and Phallus Envy: A Reformulation
200p Unacceptable Impulses, Anxiety, and the Appreciation of Cartoons
300l New Anxiety of Motherhood
358n Anxiety Levels Experienced by Women in Competition

APHRA

255b Astraea's "Vacant Throne": The Successors of Aphra Behn

APOLOGY

359e Autobiographer and Her Readers: From Apology to Affirmation

APOSTLE

215d Susa Young Gates: The Thirteenth Apostle
337e Dispute over an Active Apostolate for Women During the Counter-Reformation

APPALACHIAN

263k Theology in the Politics of Appalachian Women

APPAREL

96d Demon in Female Apparel: Narrative of Josephine Amelia Perkins, the Notorious Female Horse Thief...

APPEAL

153e Appeal to the Christian Women of the South

APPENDAGE

92f Male Appendage: Legal Definitions of Women

APPLE

113c An Apple, an Orange

APPLICATIONS

20e Birth Rituals in Cross-Cultural Perspective: Some Practical Applications
173o Implications and Applications of Recent Research on Feminine Development
339o The Applicant

APPRAISAL

70a Husband Provider Role: A Critical Appraisal
267c Sex-Role Stereotypes: A Current Appraisal
281f Sex Roles and Social Change: A Comparative Appraisal of Turkey's Women
291k Economists' Approaches to Sex Segregation in the Labor Market: An Appraisal
354a Women and Work: An Economic Appraisal

APPRENTICESHIP

328n Apprenticeship

APPROPRIATION

84f Modes of Appropriation and the Sexual Division of Labour: A Case Study from Oaxaca, Mexico
143d Appropriation of the House: Changes in House Design and Concepts of Domesticity
263s Dreams and Fantasies as Sources of Revelation: Feminist Appropriation of Jung

ARAB

see also MUSLIM; MIDDLE EAST; AFRICA; various Arab countries

20p Non-Hierarchical, Hierarchical, and Masked Reciprocity in the Arab Village
91e Women, Employment, and Fertility Trends in the Arab Middle East and North Africa
324e Arab World

ARABY

277a Araby

ARAGON

23b Women, Learning, and Power: Eleonora of Aragon and the Court of Ferrara

ARCHETYPE

68e Ann and Superman: Type and Archetype
71a Literary Archetypes and Female Role Alternatives: The Woman and the Novel in Latin America
288m Actress Archetypes in the 1950s: Doris Day, Marilyn Monroe, Elizabeth Taylor, Audrey Hepburn

ARCHITECTURE

143k Architecture: Toward a Feminist Critique
166rr Women in Architecture
303d Pioneer Women Architects
303i Struggle for Place: Women in Architecture: 1920-1960
303n Voices of Consequence: Four Architectural Critics
303o Women in Architecture and the New Feminism
303s Historic Chart Relating Architectural Projects to General and Women's History in the U.S.
325l Women as Patrons of Architecture in Turkey

ARCHIVES

335l Survey of Primary Sources and Archives for the History of Early Twentieth-Century English Women

AREA

38d Projected Future Employment and Leadership Needs and Areas
70b Two Roles of Russian Working Women in an Urban Area
196oo Proportion of Doctorates Earned by Women, by Area and Field, 1960-1969
294p Women in the Rural Areas
307d Women in the Liberated Areas
338f Women of Dakar and the Surrounding Urban Area

ARENA

278t Influential Alliances: Cincinnati Women in the Political Arena, 1920-1945

ARGENTINE

71f Women: The Forgotten Half of Argentine History
121i Education, Philanthropy, and Feminism: Components of Argentine Womanhood, 1860-1926
122g Maria Angelica Bosco and Beatriz Guido: An Approach to Two Argentinian Novelists Between 1960 and 1970
122h Argentine Women in the Novels of Silvina Bullrich

ARGUMENT

9k Argument for Woman's Suffrage
159ff Sex Roles: The Argument from Nature
183d American Peace Party: New Departures and Old Arguments
203l Sex Roles: The Argument from Nature
282r Pedagogical Arguments for Preferential Hiring and Tenuring of Women Teachers in the University

ARMED FORCES

see also DRAFT; WAR; names of wars

39i Changing Role of Women in the Armed Forces
266q Changing Role of Women in the Armed Forces
291m Women: The New Reserve Army of the Unemployed
360f Women Nurses in the Union Army

ARMS

17p "A Farewell to Arms": Ernest Hemingway's "Resentful Cryptogram"

ARMY

see also REVOLUTION; WAR; DRAFT; ARMED FORCES

ARNSTEIN

5d Fanny Von Arnstein

AROUSAL

250ii Experimental Arousal of Achievement Motivation in Adolescent Girls

ARRANGEMENTS

269k Community Organizations and Child-care Arrangements
366c Role of Women in Aboriginal Marriage Arrangements
370e Child-Care Arrangements

ARREST

51j Arrest Statistics
79m Malady and Remedy of Vexations and Unjust Arrests and Actions

ART

15a Why Have There Been No Great Women Artists?
15b Great Women Artists
15k Artists Transgress All Boundaries
47f Iris Murdoch: The Novelist as Magician, The Magician as Artist
88f Room of Her Own: Emily Dickinson as Woman Artist
88i "I Dare to Live": The Transforming Art of Anne Sexton
98i For the Etruscans: Sexual Difference and Artistic Production--The Debate Over a Female Aesthetic
106d Liberal Arts Education and Women's Development
114u Performing Arts
116i Immigrants and Craft Arts: Scuola d'Industrie Italiane
141ff Women and Art (summary, panel discussion)
141gg Woman Artist and the Art Academy: A Case Study in Institutional Prejudice
164e Women in the Field of Art
166uu Vanguard Artist: Portrait and Self-Portrait
185f Woman as Artist and Patron in the Middle Ages and the Renaissance
185h Roles of Medieval Women in the Healing Arts
190a Woman as Artistic Innovator: The Case of the Choreographer

208kk Secondary Level Language Arts Presentation
214k Art of Silence and the Forms of Women's Poetry
247a Eroticism and Female Imagery in Nineteenth-Century Art
254u Why Are There No Great Women Artists?
256k Women in the Arts: Insights to the Cultural Impact of Women's Role in the Creative Arts
265s Sexism in Western Art
337g Jane Lead: The Feminist Mind and Art of a Seventeenth-Century Protestant Mystic
343c Women Artists of the 19th and 20th Centuries
361i Art of Silence and the Forms of Women's Poetry
369s Notes from a Conversation on Art, Feminism, and Work

ARTHENIA

222t Reflections: Arthenia Bates Millican

ARTICLES

79q To Rosania and Lucasia, Articles of Friendship

ARTIFICE

127y A Work of Artifice

ARZNER

212r Work of Dorothy Arzner
288b Dorothy Arzner's "Dance, Girl, Dance"
288r Interview with Dorothy Arzner

ASBAJE

122n Two Poets of America: Juana de Asbaje and Sara de Ibanez

ASCETIC

337c Ascetic Women in the Late Patristic Age

ASHES

133e Phoenix in the Ashes

ASHTON-WARNER

179s S. Ashton-Warner

ASIA

see also individual countries

30b Dowry and Bridewealth and the Property Rights of Women in South Asia
91b Fertility, Women's Work, and Economic Class: A Case Study from Southeast Asia
91c Chinese Women at Work: Work Commitment and Fertility in the Asian Setting

127ll Asian Women in Revolution
294l Political Role of Southeast Asian Women
309j Asian Women in Britain: Strategies of Adjustment of Indian and Pakistani Migrants
324p Burma and South-East Asia

ASIAN-AMERICAN

77p New Asian-American Woman

ASPIRATIONS

22v Attitudinal Barriers to Occupational Aspirations in Women
45d Counseling Implications of Black Women's Market Position, Aspirations and Expectancies
140u Climbing the Political Ladder: The Aspirations and Expectations of Partisan Elites
166u Role Model Influences on College Women's Career Aspirations
176j Motive to Avoid Success and Changing Aspirations of College Women
200o Sex Differences in Dating Aspirations and Satisfaction with Computer-Selected Partners
208r Let Them Aspire! A Plea and Proposal for Equality of Opportunity for Males and Females in the Ann Arbor Public Schools
243f Discrimination Against Aspiring Women
288a Short Manual for an Aspiring Scenario Writer
291d Work Aspirations of Women: False Leads and New Starts

ASS

233t The Golden Ass

ASSASSINATION

233f Womanly Image: Character Assassination through the Ages

ASSAULT

94i Michigan's Criminal Sexual Assault Law
140w Assaulted Wife: "Catch 22" Revisited

ASSEMBLY

275d More Than a Question of Numbers: Women Deputies in the German National Constituent Assembly and the Reichstag, 1919-1933

ASSHOLE

8jj Bottoms Up: An In-Depth Look at VD and Your Asshole

ASSIS

71b "Brazileira": Images and Realities in Writings of Machado de Assis and Jorge Amado

ASSOCIATION

219i Women's Verbal Images and Associations

249l Women in Groups: Ijaw Women's Associations
257h (Speech, National Woman's Suffrage Association, 1889)
257s (Remarks, National American Woman's Suffrage Association)
302h From Lelemama to Lobbying: Women's Associations in Mombasa, Kenya
302i Protestant Women's Associations in Freetown, Sierra Leone
342aa Working Women's Association of Vancouver

ASTRAEA

255b Astraea's "Vacant Throne": The Successors of Aphra Behn

ASTRONOMER

277t Astronomer's Wife

ASYLUM

113p Asylum

ASYMMETRY

227a Sexual Asymmetry and the Status of Women
332c Sex Differences in Hemispheric Brain Asymmetry

ATA

222e Ama Ata Aidoo's "Dilemma of a Ghost"

ATHENS

225e City's Achievements: The Patriotic Amazonomachy and Ancient Athens

ATHLETICS

see also SPORT; TEAMS; TITLE IX

152a Woman as an Athlete
152b Are Athletics Making Girls Masculine?
152d Women Athletes
286g Aggression and the Female Athlete
286r Self-Perception of Athletes and Coaches
286u Training and Condition Techniques for the Female Athlete
358b Women's Rights in Athletics
358l Full Court Press for Women in Athletics
358m Environmental Effect on the Woman in Athletics
358p Women Athletic Trainers

ATLANTIC

270b Sunksquaws, Shamans, and Tradeswomen: Middle Atlantic Coastal Algonkian Women During the Seventeenth and Eighteenth Centuries

ATLANTIS

241f The Veiled Feminists of Atlantis

ATTACHMENT

173aa Maternal Attachment: Importance of the First Post-Partum Days
176c Attachment Differences in Male and Female Infant Monkeys
199g Sex Differences in Mother-Infant Attachment in Monkeys
250z Attachment Differences in Male and Female Infant Monkeys
351d Work Attachment, Investments in Human Capital and the Earnings of Young Women

ATTAINMENT

70c Interaction and Goal Attainment in Parisian Working Wives' Families
196nn Sex Differential in School Enrollment and Educational Attainment
284i Trends in Educational Attainment of Women
318l Educational Policies and Attainment

ATTENTION

53d Women, Taboo and the Supression of Attention

ATTITUDE

9oo Effects of the Derogatory Attitude toward Female Sexuality
13r Sex-Role Attitudes of Fifth-Grade Girls
20w Attitudes Towards Reproduction in a Rapidly Changing African Society
20aa Women and Social Customs within the Family: A Case Study of Attitudes in Kerala, India
22v Attitudinal Barriers to Occupational Aspirations in Women
37e Employer Attitudes to Female Employees
56d Cognitive--Developmental Analysis of Children's Sex-Role Concepts and Attitudes
94h Judicial Attitudes Toward Rape Victims
135e Employer's Attitude to Working Mothers
140d Change in U.S. Women's Sex-Role Attitudes, 1964-1974
140m Postwar Attitudes Toward Women and Work
140x Current Attitudes Toward Women and Men Who Never Marry
140y Family Planning, Decision Making: Attitudes and Intentions of Mothers and Fathers
140nn Victorian Pornography and Attitudes Reflected Toward Women
155e Self-Conceptions, Motivations and Interpersonal Attitudes of Early- and Late-Maturing Girls
155n Comparison of Sexual Attitudes and Behavior in an International Sample
155r Sex-Role Attitudes in Finland, 1966-1970
155w Sexual Activities and Attitudes in Older Persons
163i Comparative Study of Male-Female Political Attitudes at Citizen and Elite Levels
169c Effects of the Derogatory Attitude Toward Female Sexuality
170e Effects of the Derogatory Attitude Toward Female Sexuality
176x Differences in Attitudinal Responses Under Conditions of Implicitly Manipulated Group Salience
181e Femininity in the Classroom: An Account of Changing Attitudes
183h Attitudes of Men and Women Toward Violence: Report of a National Survey
196n Sex-Typing and Politicization in Children's Attitudes

196o Attitudes Toward Increased Social, Economic, and Political Participation by Women as Reported by Elementary and Secondary Students
196t Counselors' Attitudes Toward Women and Work
196w Performance of Women Principals: A Review of Behavioral and Attitudinal Studies
196x Attitudes of Superintendents and Board of Education Members Toward the Employment and Effectiveness of Women as Public-School Administrators
196ee Characteristics and Attitudes of Women Trustees
198aa Physiological Development, Cognitive Development, and Socialization Antecedents of Children's Sex-Role Attitudes
199k Stages in the Development of Psychosexual Concepts and Attitudes
200n Self-Conceptions, Motivations and Interpersonal Attitudes of Early- and Late-Maturing Girls
243c Male Attitudes Toward Women's Rights as a Function of Their Level of Self-Esteem
267q Sex-Role Attitudes and Psychological Well-Being
301a Affirmative Action Through Affirmative Attitudes
316d Women's Attitudes Toward Women in Politics: A Survey of Urban Registered Voters and Party Committeewomen
327f Male Managers' Attitudes Toward Working Women
332g Exploring Menstrual Attitudes
342gg Sex Discrimination in Higher Education and Attitude Change
342hh Sexist Language and Attitudes

ATTORNEY

see LAWYER

ATTRACTIVENESS

75b Physical Attractiveness of Female Offenders: Effects on Institutional Performance
129e Does Youthfulness Equal Attractiveness?
271i Assessment of Teaching Practice: An "Attractive" Hypothesis

ATTRIBUTION

155v Attribution of Fault to a Rape Victim as a Function of Respectability
266cc When Women Are More Deserving Than Men: Equity, Attribution, And Perceived Sex Differences
267j Women's Expectations for and Causal Attributions of Success and Failure

AUDIENCE

308a Lu K'un's New Audience: The Influence of Women's Literacy on Sixteenth-Century Thought

AUDREY

288m Actress Archetypes in the 1950s: Doris Day, Marilyn Monroe, Elizabeth Taylor, Audrey Hepburn
364l Conversation with Audrey Topping: Chinese Women Today

AUGUSTA

215x Augusta Joyce Crocheron: A Representative Woman

AUGUSTAN

214d Anne Finch, Countess of Winchilsea: An Augustan Woman Poet

AURELIA

215j Aurelia Read Spencer Rogers: Humble Heroine

AURORA

363d Aurora Leigh

AUSTRALIA

see also ABORIGINAL

63c Equal Pay for Women in Australia and New Zealand
366b Importance of Women in Determining the Composition of Residential Groups in Aboriginal Australia

AUSTRIA

218h Five Socialist Women: Traditionalist Conflicts and Socialist Visions in Austria, 1893-1934
352n Women Workers and the Trade Unions in Austria

AUTHENTICITY

90c Consciousness and Authenticity: Toward a Feminist Aesthetic

AUTHOR

see also WRITER; LITERATURE; individual authors

88q Heroine as Her Author's Daughter
166f Predominance of Male Authors in Social Work Publications
208z Louisa May Alcott: The Author of "Little Women" as Feminist
266e Heroic and Tender Modes in Women Authors of Fantasy
278j Heroine as Her Author's Daughter
314y Addendum to Style Guide for Authors
361l Women's Prose Style: A Study of Contemporary Authors

AUTHORITY

20r Three Styles of Domestic Authority: A Cross-Cultural Study
52a Evident Authority and Authoritative Evidence: the "Malleus Maleficarum"
296g Authority and Masturbation
372f Spirit Mediums in Umbanda Evangelizada of Porto Alegre, Brazil: Dimensions of Power and Authority

AUTOBIOGRAPHY

39b My Four Revolutions: An Autobiographical History of the A.S.A.
80a "I am my own heroine": Some Thoughts about Women and Autobiography in France
88x Promises Fulfilled: Positive Images of Women in Twentieth-Century Autobiography
96e Autobiography and Reminiscences of a Pioneer
96q Race Problem--An Autobiography
96t Northern Negro's Autobiography
222k Images of Self and Race in the Autobiographies of Black Women
359a Emergence of Women's Autobiography in England
359b Quest for Community: Spiritual Autobiographies of Eighteenth-Century Quaker and Puritan Women in America
359c Harriet Martineau's Autobiography: The Making of a Female Philosopher
359e Autobiographer and Her Readers: From Apology to Affirmation
359g African-American Women's Autobiographies and Ethnicity
359h Gertrude Stein and the Problems of Autobiography
359j Metaphysics of Matrilinearism in Women's Autobiography: Studies of Mead's "Blackberry Winter," Hellman's "Pentimento," Angelou's "I Know Why the Caged Bird Sings," and Kingston's "The Woman Warrior"
359l Towards a Theory of Form in Feminist Autobiography: Kate Millett's "Flying" and "Sita"; Maxine Hong Kingston's "The Woman Warrior"

AUTONOMY

76g Female Autonomy and Young Adult Women
158k Self-Determination and Autonomy
281g Class Structures and Female Autonomy in Rural Java

AUTUMN

102m Journey of a Woman Nihilist to Verona in Late Autumn

AUXILIARY

107f Women as Auxiliary and Subject to Man
166v Interest of High School Girls in Dental Auxiliary Careers
288oo Ladies' Auxiliary, 1976

AVANT-GARDE

212n Maya Deren and Germaine Dulac: Activists of the Avant-Garde
357i Feminism, Film and the Avant-Garde

AVIS

10b The Story of Avis

AVOID

176j Motive to Avoid Success and Changing Aspirations of College Women
176k Race, Social Class, and the Motive to Avoid Success in Women
267n Race, Social Class, and the Motive to Avoid Success in Women

AWAKENING

17n Old Critics and New: The Treatment of Chopin's "The Awakening"
108m The Awakening
128o "The Awakening" by Kate Chopin
222g Awakening of the Self in the Heroines of Ousmane Sembene

AWARENESS

6j Seminars for Career Women: Combining Awareness Training with Transactional Analysis
199l Emergence of Genital Awareness During the Second Year of Life

AZTEC

270f Aztec Women: The Transition from Status to Class in Empire and Colony

BABCOCK

215l Maud May Babcock: "Understand the Thought, Hold the Thought, Give the Thought"

BABE

153a 'Twas But a Babe

BABY

142s You've Come a Long Way, Baby
208ee All Pregnant Girls Have Boy Babies
340i Baby, You Were Great

BACKGROUND

163l Women as Politicians: The Social Background, Personality, and Political Careers of Female Party Leaders
264aa Historical Background (of Feminism)
265aa Historical Background (of feminism)

BACKLASH

59j Sex Discrimination in Credit: The Backlash of Economic Dependency
284c Backlash Against Women's Lib

BAHIA

121f Feminine Orders in Colonial Bahia, Brazil: Economic, Social, and Demographic Implications, 1677-1800

BAHIANA

194f Bahiana in the Labor Force in Salvador, Brazil

BAIGNEUSES

247e Courbet's "Baigneuses" and the Rhetorical Feminine Image

BAIRD

2i APPENDIX: Comments on the 1976 Supreme Court Decisions: "Planned Parenthood v. Danforth" and "Bellotti v. Baird"

BAIS

117n Bais Yaakov: A Historical Model for Jewish Feminists

BAKE

208n "Let Brother Bake the Cake"

BALABANOFF

116e Forging a Socialist Women's Movement: Angelica Balabanoff in Switzerland
368f Women and Socialism: Case of Angelica Balabanoff

BALANCE

131j Khmer Village Women in Cambodia: A Happy Balance
220f A Negative Balance

BALCONY

102g Doubts about Balconies
108gg On the Balcony

BALKANS

249m Sex and Power in the Balkans

BALUCHISTAN

325u Status of Women and Property on a Baluchistan Oasis in Pakistan

BAMBARA

222w Commitment: Toni Cade Bambara Speaks

BANANA

270k Stability in Banana Leaves: Colonization and Women in Kiriwina, Trobriand Islands

BANGLADESH

297a Women in Bangladesh

BANK

6i Bank of America's Affirmative Action Seminar

BANTU

213e Female Husbands in Southern Bantu Societies

BAR

233qq Invisible Bar
306g Bar Hostesses

BARABAIG

285g Jural Relations between the Sexes Among the Barabaig

BARBADOS

29e A Happening in Barbados
213m Social Inequality and Sexual Status in Barbados

BARBARA

108r On Barbara's Shore

BARBARIAN

33h Cruel and Barbarous Treatment
195f Barbarian Status of Women
363h Cruel and Barbarous Treatment

BARBIE

111hh Barbie Doll

BARDOT

288n Brigitte Bardot and the Lolita Syndrome

BARGAINING

174b Impact of Collective Bargaining on Minorities in the Public Sector: Some Policy Implications
285f Bargaining from Weakness: Spirit Possession on the South Kenya Coast

BARI

270e Forced Transition from Egalitarianism to Male Dominance: The Bari of Colombia

BARKING

102i Barking

BARNES

140kk Djuna Barnes' "Nightwood"
215c Louisa Barnes Pratt: Missionary Wife, Missionary Mother, Missionary
361o Style of Djuna Barnes' "Nightwood"

BARREL

277f The Magic Barrel

BARRETT

214f Elizabeth Barrett Browning

BARRIERS

4b Institutional Barriers to Women Students in Higher Education
22v Attitudinal Barriers to Occupational Aspirations in Women
49d Psychological Barriers for Women in Sciences: Internal and External
61g Barriers to the Career Development of Women
176l Barriers to the Career Choice of Engineering, Medicine, or Science Among American Women
258a Current Status of Women Cross-Culturally: Changes and Persisting Barriers
264q Women in the Professions: Psychological and Social Barriers to Women in Science
265j Structural and Internalized Barriers to Women in Higher Education
265m Women in the Professions: Psychological and Social Barriers to Women in Science
291g Historical and Structural Barriers to Occupational Desegregation
314c Female Dimension: Barriers to Effective Utilization of Women in the World of Work
342w AfroAmerican Woman's Perspective on Racist Barriers

BARTH

177j Protestant Principle: A Woman's Eye-View of Barth and Tillich
283d Karl Barth's Theology of the Word of God: Or, How to Keep Women Silent and in Their Place

BARTLEBY

17m What if Bartleby Were a Woman?

BARTLETT

215o Patty Bartlett Sessions: More Than a Midwife

BASELINE

45e Baseline Data on Mid-Career Change and Reentry for Black Women

BASEMENT

113s In the Basement of the House

BASHKIRTSEFF

179d M. Bashkirtseff

BASIS

22g Biologic Basis for Sex-Role Stereotypes
139x Female Liberation as the Basis for Social Revolution
171f Homosexual Orientation in Women and Men: A Hormonal Basis?
238c Female Liberation as the Basis for Social Revolution
297n Economic Basis of the Status of Women

329v Marriage Law: Basis of Change for China's Women

BASS

7i Win or Lose--We Win: The 1952 Vice-Presidential Campaign of Charlotta A. Bass

BAT MITZVAH

117d Women and Jewish Education; A New Look at Bat Mitzvah

BATES

222t Reflections: Arthenia Bates Millican

BATHSHEBA

215i Bathsheba Bigler Smith: Woman of Faith and Courage

BATTERED

235d Battered Women: Society's Problem
235e Treatment Alternatives for Battered Women

BATTLE

177h Canon Law and the Battle of the Sexes
203x Battle for Coed Teams

BATTLEGROUND

73b Her Body, the Battleground

BAULE

270i Women and Men, Cloth and Colonization: The Transformation of Production-Distribution Relations among the Baule (Ivory Coast)

BEACH

277k The Beach Umbrella

BEAR

108j Love That I Bear

BEARD

126b Mary Beard's "Woman As Force in History": A Critique

BEASTS

113b In the Forests of Riga the Beasts Are Very Wild Indeed
279cc Beasts of the Southern Wild

BEATRIZ

122g Maria Angelica Bosco and Beatriz Guido: An Approach to Two Argentinian Novelists Between 1960 and 1970

BEAUTY

74n Temptation to be a Beautiful Object
79s The Unfortunate Bride, or the Blind Lady a Beauty
159q Of the Distinction of the Beautiful and the Sublime in the Interrelations of the Two Sexes
160a Advice to Mothers, on the Subject of Their Own Health, and, of the Means of Promoting the Health, Strength and Beauty of Their Offspring
166h Clash Between Beautiful Women and Science
254g Mask of Beauty

BEAUVOIR

181k Rights and Wrongs of Women: Mary Wollstonecraft, Harriet Martineau, Simone de Beauvoir

BEBEL

68h Mill, Marx and Bebel: Early Influences on Shaw's Characterizations of Women

BED

8bb Spirit is Liberationist but the Flesh is...or, You Can't Always Get Into Bed With Your Dogma

BEDE

108dd Adam Bede

BEDOUIN

325s Changing Sex Roles in Bedouin Society in Syria and Lebanon

BEDQUILT

273d The Bedquilt

BEDROCK

170p "Bedrock" of Masculinity and Femininity: Bisexuality

BEE

731 Queen Bee Syndrome

BEECHER

303c Catharine Beecher and the Politics of Housework
360j Catharine Beecher and the Education of American Women

BEGINNINGS

22e Sex Equality: The Beginnings of Ideology
42d Voluntary Motherhood: The Beginnings of Feminist Birth Control Ideas in the U.S.
117g Tumah and Taharah; Ends and Beginnings
238d Sex Equality: The Beginnings of Ideology
258c New Patterns of Relationship: Beginnings of a Moral Revolution
271u Sex Equality: The Beginnings of Ideology

BEHAVIOR

see also PSYCHOLOGY; various behavioral phenomena

14b Women and the Structure of Organizations: Explorations in Theory and Behavior
20c Prenatal Hormones and Human Behavior: Implications for the Status of Women
21c Brain, Body and Behavior
22n Cross-Cultural Analysis of Sex Differences in the Behavior of Children Aged Three Through Eleven
56a Sex Hormones in the Development of Sex Differences in Human Behavior
56c Social-Learning View of Sex Differences in Behavior
67g Male Hormones and Behaviour
67h Female Hormones and Behaviour
77c Cross-Cultural Analysis of Sex Differences in the Behavior of Children Aged Three Through Eleven
77k Sexual Politics of Interpersonal Behavior
99a Femaleness, Maleness and Behavior Disorders in Nonhumans
99c Problem Behavior in Adolescents
99j Sex Differences in Suicidal Behavior
106g University Behavior and Policies: Where Are the Women and Why?
140c Male Sex Role Behaviors in a Representative National Sample, 1973
141r Son Preference in Taiwan: Verbal Preference and Demographic Behavior
146g Life Span Behavior Patterns--Class and Ethnic Variations
155h Aspects of Lower Class Sexual Behavior
155k Relationship of the Frequency of Masturbation to Several Aspects of Personality and Behavior
155m Early Sexual Behavior in Adult Homosexual and Heterosexual Males
155n Comparison of Sexual Attitudes and Behavior in an International Sample
155s Sexual Behavior in Pregnancy
163c Sex Differences in Black Political Beliefs and Behavior
171e Biochemical and Neurophysiological Influences on Human Sexual Behavior
172a Sex-Related Behaviors: Historical and Psychobiological Perspectives
173g Brain, Body, and Behavior
173ll Cross-Cultural Investigation of Behavioral Changes at Menopause
176e Play Behavior in the Year-Old Infant: Early Sex Differences
176kk Behavior Therapy Approaches to Modification of Sexual Preferences: Biological Perspective and Critique
176mm Lower Class Sexual Behavior
196w Performance of Women Principals: A Review of Behavioral and Attitudinal Studies
198r Mating Behavior

198t Fetal Hormones and the Brain: Effects on Sexual Dimorphism of Behavior
199a Sexual Behavior Differentiation: Prenatal Hormonal and Environmental Control
199b Prenatal Testosterone in the Nonhuman Primate and Its Consequences for Behavior
199c Fetal Androgens, Human Central Nervous System Differentiation, and Behavior Sex Differences
199j Methodological Considerations in Studying Sex Differences in the Behavioral Functioning of Newborns
199o Cryptorchidism, Development of Gender Identity, and Sex Behavior
199p Behaviorally Feminine Male Child: Pretranssexual? Pretransvestite? Prehomosexual? Preheterosexual?
199t Bisexual Behavior of Female Rhesus Monkeys
200m Sexual Behavior in the Human Female: Part II. Biological Data
201b Biological Influences on Sex Differences in Behavior
201d Social Influences on Sex Differences in Behavior
206p Status and Role Behavior in Changing Japan
208uu Movement Behavior
219o Women's Verbal Behavior at Learned and Professional Conferences
250x Early Hormonal Influences on the Development of Sexual and Sex-Related Behaviors
250y Sexual Dimorphic Behavior, Normal and Abnormal
250nn Female Sexual Behavior
251q Task and Emotional Behavior in the Marital Dyad
252r Task and Social Behavior in Marriage
264x Sexual Politics of Interpersonal Behavior
265y Sexual Politics of Interpersonal Behavior
266z Effects of Live Modelled Sex-Appropriate Play Behavior In a Naturalistic Setting
286l Needed Approaches for a Better Understanding of Behavior and Performance
296v Acceptance of the Concept of the Maternal Role by Behavioral Scientists: Its Effects on Women
330i Women in Behavior Therapy
365d Acceptance of the Concept of the Maternal Role by Behavioral Scientists: Its Effects on Women
368e Cross-Cultural Investigation of Behavioral Changes at Menopause

BEHN

255b Astraea's "Vacant Throne": The Successors of Aphra Behn

BEINGS

96l Before Women Were Human Beings: Adventures of an American Fellow in German Universities of the '90s
292p Are Women Human Beings?

BELIEF

154a Belief and the Problem of Women
163c Sex Differences in Black Political Beliefs and Behavior

BELL

50n Daisy Bell

BELLE

111w La Belle Dame sans Merci
111aa The Last of the Belles
112n La Belle Dame sans Merci
112r The Last of the Belles
288d "Belle de Jour"

BELLOTTI

2i APPENDIX: Comments on the 1976 Supreme Court Decisions: "Planned Parenthood v. Danforth" and "Bellotti v. Baird"

BELLY

111gg Belly Dancer

BENA

285l Sexual Antagonism in the New Guinea Highlands: A Bena Bena Example

BENEDICT

179o R. Benedict

BENEDICTION

95a Benediction
114e Panchakanya--An Age-old Benediction

BENEFICIARIES

180r Identifying the Beneficiaries

BENEVOLENCE

360e Organized Women's Benevolence in Early Nineteenth-Century America

BENIGN

180o Judicial Scrutiny of "Benign" Racial Preference in Law School Admissions

BENT

13f As the Twig is Bent
196a Sex-Role Socialization and the Nursery School: As the Twig is Bent

BENUE-PLATEAU STATE

285i Traditional Marriage among the Irigwe of Benue-Plateau State, Nigeria

BEREAVEMENT

176v First Year of Bereavement

BERGMAN

212g Bergman's Portrait of Women: Sexism or Subjective Metaphor?

BERKELEY-OAKLAND

35o Berkeley-Oakland Women's Union Statement

BERTHA

24t Bertha Schneiders Existential Edge
117o Bertha Pappenheim: Founder of German-Jewish Feminism

BETTY

142h Subversion of Betty Crocker

BEWARE

310c Women Beware Women

BIAS

see also SEX DISCRIMINATION; DISCRIMINATION; SEXISM; SEX BIAS; AFFIRMATIVE ACTION; TITLE VII

156n APPENDIX: Guidelines for the Development and Evaluation of Unbiased Educational Materials
180g Bias in Anti-bias Regulations
196q Counselor Bias and the Female Occupational Role
230b Woman the Gatherer: Male Bias in Anthropology
252bb Counselor Bias and the Female Occupational Role
280aa Eliminating Bias in Publications
284k Job Bias Against Women Easing Under Pressure
342l Male Bias in Psychology

BIBLE

74c Woman's Bible
117u Depatriarchalizing in Biblical Interpretation
117w Aggadic Approaches to Biblical Women
153p Woman's Bible

BIBLIOGRAPHY

56g Annotated Bibliography
68z Bibliographical Checklist
75d Adult Female Offender: A Selected Bibliography
80e Women in Contemporary French Society: Annotated Bibliography
80n Women and German Literature: A Bibliography
90a American Feminist Literary Criticism: A Bibliographical Introduction
94r Selective Bibliography
105p Image of Women in Television: An Annotated Bibliography
120m Sex Differences in Language, Speech, and Nonverbal Communication: An Annotated Bibliography

140ii Bibliography of Dissertations for and about Women in Administration in Colleges and Universities
183i Bibliography: Role of Women in Conflict and Peace
208dd Reducing the "Miss Muffet" Syndrome: An Annotated Bibliography
223j Women of England in a Century of Social Change, 1815-1914: A Select Bibliography
227i Bibliographies on Third World Women
238n Women: A Bibliography
244j Women of England in a Century of Social Change, 1815-1914: A Select Bibliography, Part II
304n Bibliography of Materials on Canadian Women, 1950-1975 (Social Sciences)
316s Bibliography
332k Bibliography: Women, Science, and Health
338g Analytical Bibliography
365j Resource Bibliography

BICYCLE

152i How I Learned to Ride the Bicycle

BIG

8aa Oppression is Big Business: Scrutinizing Gay Therapy
108t Big Volodya and Little Volodya
112d Big Blonde
173cc Big-Time Careers for the Little Woman: A Dual-Role Dilemma
264o Women and Unemployment: Assessing the Biggest Myths

BIGLER

215i Bathsheba Bigler Smith: Woman of Faith and Courage

BIHAR

114n Women of Rural Bihar

BILINGUAL

219l Mothers' Speech to Children in Bilingual Mexican-American Homes

BILL

89s N.O.W. Bill of Rights
115e Jawaharlal Nehru and the Hindu Code Bill
300j The Bill

BIND

9kk Bright Woman Is Caught in a Double Bind
49e Male and Female Leadership Styles: The Double Bind
195d Cupid's Yokes; Or The Binding Forces of Conjugal Life
272j Black Female Administrator: Woman in a Double Bind

BIOCHEMICAL

171e Biochemical and Neurophysiological Influences on Human Sexual Behavior

BIOGRAPHIC

190f Feminist History in Perspective: Sociological Contributions to Biographic Analysis

BIOLOGY

22g Biologic Basis for Sex-Role Stereotypes
53b Semantics of Biology: Virginity
67j Biological Explanations of Psychological Sex Differences
101c Biology and Gender
141aa Biological and Cultural Determinants of the Division of Labor by Sex
146d Biological Realities and Myths
149d Sex Differences: Biological, Cultural, Societal Implications
149e Possible Biological Origins of Sexual Discrimination
164b Biological Make-Up of Woman
170h Masculine and Feminine: Some Biological and Cultural Aspects
176kk Behavior Therapy Approaches to Modification of Sexual Preferences: Biological Perspective and Critique
198v Biological and Anthropological Differences between the Sexes
200m Sexual Behavior in the Human Female: Part II. Biological Data
201b Biological Influences on Sex Differences in Behavior
205a Biological Explanations of Sex-Role Stereotypes
252g Psychology of Women: Biology as Destiny
264a Woman's Biology--Mankind's Destiny: The Population Explosion and Women's Changing Roles
265a Woman's Biology--Mankind's Destiny: The Population Explosion and Women's Changing Roles
281h Biological Events and Cultural Control
282a Anatomy and Destiny: The Role of Biology in Plato's Views of Women
282c Biology, Sex Hormones, and Sexism in the 1920's
284u Female Biology in a Male Culture

BIOMECHANICS

286x Sex Differences in Biomechanics

BIOSOCIAL

53i Harems and Overlords: Biosocial Models and the Female

BIOSPSYCHOSOCIAL

171b Biospsychosocial Processes in the Development of Sex-related Differences

BIRD

111dd Rima the Bird Girl
112x Rima the Bird Girl
273w A Bird in the House
356c Mice and Birds and Boy

359j Metaphysics of Matrilinearism in Women's Autobiography: Studies of Mead's "Blackberry Winter," Hellman's "Pentimento," Angelou's "I Know Why the Caged Bird Sings," and Kingston's "The Woman Warrior"

BIRTH

see also NEWBORNS; PRENATAL; PREGNANCY; MATERNITY; PROCREATION; REPRODUCTION; POSTPARTUM

20e Birth Rituals in Cross-Cultural Perspective: Some Practical Applications
20j Matri-Patrilocality and the Birth of the First Child
33k Birth
53g "Most Essentially Female Function of All": Giving Birth
73e Natural Childbirth: Pain or Peak Experience
117c Birth of a Daughter
144d Birth and After Birth
171h American Birth Practices
173y Childbirth in Crosscultural Perspective
176nn Emotional Factors in Obstetric Complications
181a Wisewoman and Medicine Man: Changes in the Management of Childbirth
182e Childbearing Functions of the Soviet Family
191d Birth Controllers
191j Theft of Childbirth
211g Sense of Mastery in the Childbirth Experience
219h Descriptive Study of the Language of Men and Women Born in Maine Around 1900 as It Reflects the Lakoff Hypotheses in "Language and Women's Place"
221a From Pregnancy through Birth in a Bisayan Filipino Village
221b Customs Connected with Birth and the Rearing of Children
221c Pregnancy and Birth in Vietnam
256b Born Free: A Feminist Fable
256p When The Veils Come Tumbling Down: "And Women Shall Leave Their Comfortable Pews to Give Birth to a New and Inclusive Religious Vision"
269e Cultural Production of Childbirth
269f Public Policy and Childbearing
278q Childbearing and the Woman's Role
286o Influence of Birth Order and Sibling Sex on Sports Participation
296u Childbirth in America
308i Women and Childbearing in Kwan Mun Hau Village: A Study of Social Change
368d Sociology of Birth: A Critical Assessment of Theory and Research
369d Birth of the Amateur

BIRTH CONTROL

see also CONTRACEPTION; I.U.D.; PILL

9ff Birth Control--A Parent's Problem or a Woman's?
42d Voluntary Motherhood: The Beginnings of Feminist Birth Control Ideas in the U.S.
139h Case for Birth Control
139i Revolutionary Birth Control
157i Sex, Birth Control, and Human Life
173w !Kung Hunter-Gatherers: Feminism, Diet, and Birth Control
281v Sexuality and Birth Control Decisions among Lebanese Couples

BIRTHMARK

108ii The Birthmark
279b The Birthmark

BIRTHRIGHT

142g Birthright

BISAYAN

221a From Pregnancy through Birth in a Bisayan Filipino Village

BISEXUALITY

8h Bi-Sexual Potential
8i Bi-Sexual Offers Some Thoughts on Fences
123i Bisexuality
170p "Bedrock" of Masculinity and Femininity: Bisexuality
179gg "Psychic Bisexuality"
199t Bisexual Behavior of Female Rhesus Monkeys
268u Freud's Concept of Bisexuality

BITCH

36g Great American Bitch
132ff BITCH Manifesto
175f Bitch Manifesto

BITS

144a Bits and Pieces

BLACHE

see GUY BLACHE

BLACK

see also AFRO-AMERICA; MINORITY; NEGRO; RACE

3b To All Black Women, From All Black Men
4i Dilemma of the Black Woman in Higher Education
6f Working Black Women
7a Northern Black Female Workers: Jacksonian Era
7c Black Male Perspectives on the Nineteenth Century Woman
7d Black Woman's Struggle for Equality in the South, 1895-1925
7e Black Women in the Blues Tradition
7g Anna J. Cooper: A Voice for Black Women
9w Why Women's Liberation Is Important to Black Women
14h Black Women and Self-esteem
18b Growing Up Black and Female
25i "Black Matriarchy" Reconsidered: Evidence from Secondary Analysis of Sample Surveys
35p Black Feminist Statement
39j Positive Effects of the Multiple Negative: Explaining the Success of Black Professional Women

39q Social Relations of Black and White Widowed Women in a Northern Metropolis
43l Black Woman: Liberated or Oppressed?
45c Professional Schools and Their Impact on Black Women
45d Counseling Implications of Black Women's Market Position, Aspirations and Expectancies
45e Baseline Data on Mid-Career Change and Reentry for Black Women
45f Black Women Who Head Families: Economic Needs and Economic Resources
45g Policy Issues on Day Care: The Special Needs of Black Working Women
45h Health Issues Facing Black Women
57d Black Woman
77n Black Movement and Women's Liberation
86d Why Women's Liberation is Important to Black Women
89c Black Women and the Market
89j Black Women in Revolt
94f Black Offender and White Victim: A Study of Forcible Rape in Oakland, Ca.
97g Historical and Critical Essay for Black Women
98m Visibility and Difference: Black Women in History and Literature
98n Black Women and Feminism
126k Racism and Tradition: Black Womanhood in Historical Perspective
129p Older Black Women
132t Poor Black Women
132u Collective Statement, Black Sisters
140f From Peasants to Proletarians: Black Women in the Cauca Valley, Colombia
140k Role of Wife in the Black Extended Family: Perspectives from a Rural Community in Southern United States
140cc Sex-Role Constraints: The College-Educated Black Woman
140dd Self-Concept and the Coping Process of Black Graduate and Undergraduate Women at a Predominantly White University
140hh Black Women in Higher Education: Research Literature
151r Liberation of Black Women
163c Sex Differences in Black Political Beliefs and Behavior
163u Black Women in Electoral Politics
163v Black Women State Legislators: A Profile
173q Growing Up Black
174c Black Women in the Continuing Struggle for Equality
174k Combatting Dual Discrimination: The Impact of Civil Rights Policies on the Income Status of Black Women
175k Black Feminism
176z Black Women 1970
217h Discrimination against Blacks: A Historical Perspective
219j Black Women In the Rural South: Conservative and Innovative
222a Black Women In and Out of Fiction
222i Black Women Poets from Wheatley to Walker
238f Liberation of Black Women
249f Sex Roles and Survival Strategies in an Urban Black Community
251u Myth of Black Matriarchy
251aa Disadvantaged Status of Black Women
252z Marriage and Motherhood of Black Women Graduates
254aa Women's Liberation and Black Civil Rights
256d No More Sapphires or Black Pearls: Self-definition is Where It Starts
259d Black Women in Bondage
260t Job Discrimination and the Black Woman

264u Black Women and the Pursuit of Equality
264dd Feminist Consciousness and Black Women
265v Liberation of Black Women
266n Positive Effects of the Multiple Negative: Explaining the Success of Black Professional Women
272j Black Female Administrator: Woman in a Double Bind
274f Negotiating Respect: Patterns of Presentation among Black Women
278n Black Women in Urban Schools
278r Black Women Respond to Slavery
279s Long Black Song
292e Indian and Black Women
317i Convivial Sisterhood: Spirit Mediumship and Client-Core Network among Black South African Women
326e Black Women Officeholders: The Case of State Legislators
331f Black Women and the Family
333e Black Employment in the South
341o Black, Female--and Qualified
344b How Powerful Is Powerful? The Women's Movement and the Four Black Congresswomen
364f Myths and Stereotypes: My Challenge to Black Women Cultural Workers
375g On Being Female, Black, and Free

BLACK--AMERICAN

163t Voting Patterns of American Black Women
222l Black Eve or Madonna? Antithetical Views of the Mother in Black American Literature
240m "Free in Fact and at Last": The Image of the Black Woman in Black American Literature
249g Matrifocality in Indonesia and Africa and Among Black Americans
364d Black Woman in American History

BLACK--EDUCATION

7h Nannie Burroughs and the Education of Black Women
45a Socialization and Education of Young Black Girls in Schools
45j APPENDIX: Educational and Occupational Statistics on Black Women
272i Socialization and Education of Young Black Girls in School

BLACK--IMAGE

7f Images of Black Women in Afro-American Poetry
45i Media and Their Effect on Black Images
222d Images of Black Women in Modern African Poetry
222k Images of Self and Race in the Autobiographies of Black Women
240m "Free in Fact and at Last": The Image of the Black Woman in Black American Literature

BLACK--JEOPARDY

74o Double Jeopardy: To Be Black and Female
127w Double Jeopardy: To Be Black and Female
142f Double Jeopardy: To Be Black and Female
210c Black Women and the Churches: Triple Jeopardy
292r Double Jeopardy: To Be Black and Female

BLACKBERRY

359j Metaphysics of Matrilinearism in Women's Autobiography: Studies of Mead's "Blackberry Winter," Hellman's "Pentimento," Angelou's "I Know Why the Caged Bird Sings," and Kingston's "The Woman Warrior"

BLAINE

3p Alice Blaine

BLANCHE

215w Emmeline Blanche Woodward Wells: "I Have Risen Triumphant"

BLANKS

266l Female College Students' Scores On the Men's And Women's Strong Vocational Interest Blanks

BLESSING

58b Northren Mother's Blessing

BLESSINGTON

5b Lady Blessington

BLIND

79s The Unfortunate Bride, or the Blind Lady a Beauty
180f Discrimination, Color Blindness, and the Quota System
321j Justice: A Woman Blindfolded?

BLISS

33g Bliss

BLOC

140t You Can Lead a Lady to Vote, But What Will She Do With It? The Problem of a Woman's Bloc Vote

BLOIS

303l Natalie de Blois

BLONDE

112d Big Blonde

BLOOD

88h "The Blood Jet": The Poetry of Sylvia Plath
279aa Giving Blood
375l Blood and Guts: The Tricky Problem of Being a Woman Writer in the Late Twentieth Century

BLOOMER

128h Amelia Bloomer and Bloomerism
257e Bloomer Costume

BLUE

7e Black Women in the Blues Tradition
51h Any Woman's Blues
59f Condition of Women in Blue-Collar Jobs
73c Women Learn to Sing the Menstrual Blues
215h Jane Snyder Richards: The Blue-White Diamond
233oo The Morning Half-Life Blues
354o Women in Blue-Collar and Service Occupations
356f Blue Lenses
371c Occupational Values and Family Roles: Women in Blue-Collar and Service Occupations

BOARD

53e Privileged, Schooled and Finished: Boarding Education for Girls
196x Attitudes of Superintendents and Board of Education Members Toward the Employment and Effectiveness of Women as Public-School Administrators
196y School Boards and Sex Bias in American Education
196mm What, If Anything, Impedes Women from Serving on School Boards?
303f Report to the Board of Lady Managers
344d Local Officeholding and the Community: The Case of Women on New Jersey's School Boards

BOAT

298g The Saffron Boat

BOBBES

317j Bobbes and Zeydes: Old and New Roles for Elderly Jews

BOCCACCIO

185e Boccaccio's Idle Ladies

BODIN

52d Jean Bodin's "De la Demonomanie des Sorciers": The Logic of Persecution

BODY

21c Brain, Body and Behavior
53c Open Body, Closed Space: The Transformation of Female Sexuality
73b Her Body, the Battleground
83h Your Body is a Jewel Box
107aa Intellectual and Bodily Superiority of Women
171m Body Time and Social Time: Mood Patterns by Menstrual Cycle Phase and Day of Week
173g Brain, Body, and Behavior

175qq Body is the Role: Sylvia Plath
279bb Bodies
286e Body Image and Performance

BOEHME

278bb Mysticism and Feminism: Jacob Boehme and Jane Lead

BOGOTA

71j Pursuit of an Ideal: Migration, Social Class, and Women's Roles in Bogota, Colombia

BOGUS

278c Entrails of Power: Bogus Manhood and the Language of Grief

BOIS

222n Alice Walker: "The Diary of an African Nun" and Du Bois' Double Consciousness

BOLIVIAN

297m Resistance as Protest: Women in the Struggle of Bolivian Tin-Mining Communities

BOLSHEVISM

218g Bolshevism, The Woman Question, and Aleksandra Kollontai
318f Bolshevik Alternatives and the Soviet Family: The 1926 Marriage Law Debate

BOLTS

342h Nuts and Bolts View of Women's Studies

BOMBAL

80f "El casamiento enganoso": Marriage in the Novels of Maria Luisa Bombal, Silvina Bullrich, and Elisa Serrana

BOMBAY

114p Slum Women of Bombay

BONDAGE

259d Black Women in Bondage

BONDS

89jj Mother-Child Bonding
98c Bonds of Love: Rational Violence and Erotic Domination

BONE

97p Like Bone to the Ground

BONTOC

2131 Mechanistic Cooperation and Sexual Equality among the Western Bontoc

BOOK

see also TEXTBOOKS; READ; READING

13h Children's Books: The Second Sex, Junior Division
13p Sex Problems of School Math Books
23c Book-Lined Cells: Women and Humanism in the Early Italian Renaissance
39s Woman Book Industry
53c Boke of the Cyte of Ladyes
79b Book of Margery Kempe
128t Fannie Farmer and Her Cook Book
156p APPENDIX: Non-Sexist Picture Books for Children
175m Feminist Look at Children's Books
196kk Schoolbook Sex Bias
203a Republic, Book V
203b Politics, Book I
207h Sexism in Children's Books and Elementary Teaching Materials
208t Sex-Role Socialization in Picture Books for Preschool Children
208aa Feminist Look at Children's Books
208cc Feminists Look at the 100 Books: The Portrayal of Women in Children's Books on Puerto Rican Themes
250d Male and Female in Children's Books
271m Feminist Look at Children's Books
339j The Book of Ruth
360q Cookbooks and Law Books: The Hidden History of Career Women in Twentieth-Century America
361d Historical Survey of Women's Language: From Medieval Courtesy Books to Seventeen Magazine
365c Impact of the Women's Liberation Movement on Child Development Books
375m Coming Book

BOOTHE

68s Interview with Clare Boothe Luce

BORJ

325aa Women and the Neighborhood Street in Borj Hammoud, Lebanon

BORMLIZA

274g Bormliza: Maltese Folksong Style and Women

BOSCO

122g Maria Angelica Bosco and Beatriz Guido: An Approach to Two Argentinian Novelists Between 1960 and 1970

BOSTON

94k Comparative Study of Forcible Rape Offenses Known to the Police in Boston and Los Angeles
108o The Bostonians
110o Fictional Feminists in "The Bostonians" and "The Odd Women"
334d Cherished Spirit of Independence: The Life of an Eighteenth-Century Boston Businesswoman

BOTTOMS

8jj Bottoms Up: An In-Depth Look at VD and Your Asshole

BOUNDARIES

15k Artists Transgress All Boundaries
266y Sex-Role Boundaries and Resistance to Sex-Role Change

BOURASSA

138f Henri Bourassa and "the Woman Question"

BOVANNE

24cc My Man Bovanne
29f My Man Bovanne

BOVARY

98k For a Restricted Thematics: Writing, Speech, and Difference in Madame Bovary
339a Madame Bovary

BOVEY

50d Mr. Bovey's Unexpected Will

BOX

83h Your Body is a Jewel Box

BOY

8r Hustler: A Boy for All Seasons
13l Schools Are Emasculating Our Boys
13n Teacher Interactions with Boys and with Girls
119j The Sailor Boy's Tales
132e Why Men Need a Boys' Night Out
155q Teenage Boys and Girls in West Germany
196d Girls--More Moral Than Boys or Just Sneakier?
208e Men: Being a Boy
208bb Skirts in Fiction About Boys: A Maxi Mess
208ee All Pregnant Girls Have Boy Babies
236e Boy Preference Reflected in Korean Folklore

280g Boys, Girls, and Sports
288nn Is Lina Wertmuller Just Once of the Boys?
356c Mice and Birds and Boy

BRADSTREET

214c Anne Bradstreet's Poetry: A Study of Subversive Piety
292f Anne Bradstreet: Dogmatist and Rebel

BRAHMIN

213d Caste Differences between Brahmin and Non-Brahmin Women in a South Indian Village

BRAIN

21c Brain, Body and Behavior
48e Brainwashed Women
53h Female Brain: A Neuropsychological Viewpoint
172b Sex-Related Factors in Cognition and in Brain Lateralization
173g Brain, Body, and Behavior
198t Fetal Hormones and the Brain: Effects on Sexual Dimorphism of Behavior
332c Sex Differences in Hemispheric Brain Asymmetry
332e Quirls of a Woman's Brain

BRANT

128a Molly Brant--Loyalist

BRAUN

275f Frau und Staatsburger in Volker Braun's Schauspiel "Tinka"

BRAVE

215q Dr. Romania Pratt Penrose: To Brave the World
288kk That's Not Brave, That's Just Stupid

BRAZIL

71b "Brazileira": Images and Realities in Writings of Machado de Assis and Jorge Amado
121b Female and Family in the Economy and Society of Colonial Brazil
121f Feminine Orders in Colonial Bahia, Brazil: Economic, Social, and Demographic Implications, 1677-1800
121j Nineteenth-Century Feminist Press and Women's Rights in Brazil
194e Impact of Industrialization on Women's Work Roles in Northeast Brazil
194f Bahiana in the Labor Force in Salvador, Brazil
194g Relationships of Sex and Social Class in Brazil
194l Selective Omission and Theoretical Distortion in Studying the Political Activity of Women in Brazil
281t Women's Labor Force Participation in a Developing Society: The Case of Brazil
297d Female Labor and Capitalism in the U.S. and Brazil
322e Woman Anthropologist in Brazil

324j Brazil
372e Spirit Magic in the Social Relations between Men and Women--Sao Paulo, Brazil
372f Spirit Mediums in Umbanda Evangelizada of Porto Alegre, Brazil: Dimensions of Power and Authority

BREAD

74j Bread and Roses
97a Bread and Roses

BREAKDOWN

351f Causes and Consequences of Marital Breakdown

BREAKFAST

111q Before Breakfast
144c Breakfast Past Noon

BREAST

89o Facing Up to Breast Cancer
173z Breast Feeding
191m Politics of Breast Cancer
211q Breast Disorders
266w Sexuality of Pregnant and Breastfeeding Women

BRECHTIAN

122j Brechtian Aesthetics in Chile: Isidora Aguirre's "Los Papeleros"

BREE

288c Divided Woman: Bree Daniels in "Klute"

BRIDE

see also DOWRY; WEDDING; MARRIAGE

30a Bridewealth and Dowry in Africa and Eurasia
30b Dowry and Bridewealth and the Property Rights of Women in South Asia
79s The Unfortunate Bride, or the Blind Lady a Beauty
111f Cutting the Jewish Bride's Hair
112f Cutting the Jewish Bride's Hair
154f Brides of Christ
195e Letter to a Prospective Bride
233m Bride of Frankenstein
279g The Bride Comes to Yellow Sky
317a Bride of Christ Is Filled with His Spirit

BRIDEHEAD

357e Sue Bridehead and the New Woman

BRIDGES

222q Bridges and Deep Water

BRIDGPORT

3m Bridgport Bus

BRIGHT

9kk Bright Woman Is Caught in a Double Bind
73j Why Bright Women Fear Success
166q Fail: Bright Women
233rr Fail: Bright Women
284w Raising a Bright and Happy Child

BRIGITTE

288n Brigitte Bardot and the Lolita Syndrome

BRILL

111ll Miss Brill
112cc Miss Brill

BRILLIANT

142j For a Brilliant Young Woman Who Lost Her Mind

BRITAIN

see also ANGLO-SAXON; ENGLAND; ENGLISH WOMEN

55j Purdah in the British Situation
63a Equal Pay in Great Britain
120g Sex, Covert Prestige, and Linguistic Change in the Urban British English of Norwich
126i Feminism and Class Consciousness in the British and American Women's Trade Union Leagues, 1890-1925
141i Feminism and Class Consciousness in the British and American Women's Trade Union Leagues, 1890-1925
223f Working-Class Women in Britain, 1890-1914?
240e Gender and Genre: Women in British Romantic Literature
244i Sexuality in Britain, 1800-1900: Some Suggested Revisions
288pp Interview with British Cine-Feminists
309j Asian Women in Britain: Strategies of Adjustment of Indian and Pakistani Migrants
324u Great Britain
329i Tradition and the Role of Women in Great Britain

BROADCASTING

105d Where are the Women in Public Broadcasting?

BROADS

132hh No "Chicks," "Broads," or "Niggers" for OLE MOLE

BRONTE

36h Emily Bronte in the Hands of Male Critics
214e Emily Bronte's Anti-Romance

BRONZEVILLE

222o Women of Bronzeville

BROOKE

215p Dr. Ellen Brooke Ferguson: Nineteenth-Century Renaissance Woman

BROOKLYN

277aa Brooklyn

BROOM

142t Broom of One's Own: Notes on the Women's Liberation Program

BROTHER

9cc Filial Relations
132z Sisters, Brothers, Lovers...Listen
153r Filial Relations
208a Why I Won't Celebrate Brotherhood Week
208n "Let Brother Bake the Cake"

BROWN

215e Amy Brown Lyman: Raising the Quality of Life for All
341p Jacquelyn Mattfeld of Brown

BROWNING

214f Elizabeth Barrett Browning

BRUNEI

372b Women of Brunei

BRUNHILDE

185b Popular Image of Brunhilde

BRYN MAWR

13z Our Failures Only Marry: Bryn Mawr and the Failure of Feminism
60l "Bryn Mawr Woman"
254y Our Failures Only Marry: Bryn Mawr and the Failure of Feminism
341q Women at Bryn Mawr

BUCHAREST

54a Population and the Status of Women: Results of the Bucharest and Mexico Conferences

BUCKET

10j A Drop in the Bucket

BUDDHIST

283g Image of Woman in Old Buddhist Literature: The Daughters of Mara

BUENOS AIRES

71g Women Professionals in Buenos Aires
297j Sociocultural Factors Mitigating Role Conflict of Buenos Aires Professional Women

BUILDING

89ss Building Extended Families
143p Los Angeles Women's Building: A Public Center for Woman's Culture
175p Building of the Gilded Cage
191s Building a Hospital Workers' Union: Doris Turner, the Woman from 1199
303e Sophia Hayden and the Woman's Building Competition

BULIMIA

173hh Cinderella's Stepsisters: A Feminist Perspective on Anorexia Nervosa and Bulimia

BULLRICH

80f "El casamiento enganoso": Marriage in the Novels of Maria Luisa Bombal, Silvina Bullrich, and Elisa Serrana
122h Argentine Women in the Novels of Silvina Bullrich

BULLSHIT

123d Taking the Bullshit by the Horns

BUN

10l Plum Bun "Home"
10m Plum Bun "Market"
10n Plum Bun "Plum Bun"

BUNDLES

8p Bundles of Twigs in New Hampshire: A High School Teacher's Report

BUNDU

20q Bundu: Political Implications of Female Solidarity in a Secret Society

BUNNIES

233i Playboys and Bunnies

BUREAU

39e Salon, Foyer, Bureau: Women and the Professions in France
42e Salon, Foyer, Bureau: Women and the Professions in France
178j Role of Women in the Founding of the U.S. Children's Bureau
266gg Salon, Foyer, Bureau: Women And The Professions in France

BUREAUCRACY

93b Women in the Party Bureaucracy: Subservient Functionaries
127f Metamorphosis into Bureaucrat
142e Metamorphosis into Bureaucrat

BURGER

174h Sex and the Burger Court: Recent Judicial Policy Making toward Women
321c Burger Court and Women's Rights, 1971-1977

BURGOS

122o Phenomenology of Nothingness in the Poetry of Julia de Burgos
122p Love and Death: The Thematic Journey of Julia de Burgos

BURIED

88g Who Buried H.D.? A Poet, Her Critics, and Her Place in "The Literary Tradition"
357b Buried Letter: Feminism and Romanticism in Villette

BURMA

324p Burma and South-East Asia

BURROUGHS

7h Nannie Burroughs and the Education of Black Women

BURUNDI

338e Women of Burundi: A Study of Social Values

BUS

3m Bridgport Bus

BUSINESS

see also MANAGEMENT; CORPORATIONS

8aa Oppression is Big Business: Scrutinizing Gay Therapy
9v Abortion Is No Man's Business
51p "Crime as Business" and the Female Offender
89ff What's This about Feminist Businesses?
208jj Sexism in History or, Writing Women's History is a Tricky Business
280u Women in Business Administration
286q American Business Values and Involvement in Sport

306e Women in Family Businesses
314q Businessman's Guide to Women's Liberation
334d Cherished Spirit of Independence: The Life of an Eighteenth-Century Boston Businesswoman

BUTCH

8j Butch or Fem?: The Third World Lesbian's Dilemma

C.O.P.E.

211h C.O.P.E. Story: A Service to Pregnant and Postpartum Women

CABELLO

122c Clorinda Matto de Turner and Mercedes Cabello de Carbonera: Societal Criticism and Morality

CABRERA

122q Short Stories of Lydia Cabrera: Transpositions or Creations?

CADE

222w Commitment: Toni Cade Bambara Speaks

CADY

359d Paradox and Success of Elizabeth Cady Stanton

CAFE

50c The Stir Outside the Cafe Royal

CAGE

175p Building of the Gilded Cage
359j Metaphysics of Matrilinearism in Women's Autobiography: Studies of Mead's "Blackberry Winter," Hellman's "Pentimento," Angelou's "I Know Why the Caged Bird Sings," and Kingston's "The Woman Warrior"

CAIRO

325z Self-Images of Traditional Urban Women in Cairo

CAKE

208n "Let Brother Bake the Cake"

CALICO

50k The Calico Dog

CALIFORNIA

241c The Queen of California
334l Chinese Immigrant Women in Nineteenth-Century California

CALLINGS

153t Two Callings

CALM

161e Calm Down Mother

CAMBODIA

131j Khmer Village Women in Cambodia: A Happy Balance

CAMBRIDGE

244f Women and Degrees at Cambridge University, 1862-1897

CAMEROUN

281s Social Change and Sexual Differentiation in the Cameroun and the Ivory Coast

CAMP

273r Camp Cataract

CAMPAIGN

7i Win or Lose--We Win: The 1952 Vice-Presidential Campaign of Charlotta A. Bass
92d Women Cotton Workers and the Suffrage Campaign: The Radical Suffragists in Lancashire, 1893-1914
151o Campaign for Women's Rights in the 1920's
163h Campaign Theory and Practice--The Gender Variable

CAMPOBELLO

122l Nellie Campobello: Romantic Revolutionary and Mexican Realist

CAMPUS

see also STUDENT; COLLEGE; UNIVERSITY

4l Representation, Performance and Status of Women on the Faculty at the Urbana-Champaign Campus of the University of Illinois
39a Maid of All Work or Departmental Sister-in-Law? The Faculty Wife Employed on Campus
284d Women's Studies on the Campuses
301b Sex Discrimination, Educational Institutions, and the Law: A New Issue on Campus
341a Women on Campus: The Unfinished Liberation

CANADA

63e Equal Pay in Canada: History, Progress and Problems
116d Women in the Canadian and Italian Trade Union Movements at the Turn of the Century
116f Men Without Women: Italian Migrants in Canada, 1885-1930

294f Women and Politics in the U.S. and Canada
295c Domestic Service in Canada, 1880-1920
304g Canadian Labour Force: Jobs for Women
304l Status of Immigrant Women in Canada
304m Guide to Historical Literature Pertaining to Canadian Women
304n Bibliography of Materials on Canadian Women, 1950-1975 (Social Sciences)
320b Canadian Suffragists
320h Sex Stereotyping in Canadian Schools

CANCER

89o Facing Up to Breast Cancer
191m Politics of Breast Cancer

CANDIDATES

314n Guidelines for Interviewing and Hiring Women Candidates
344l Exploring the Relationship Between Female Candidacies and the Women's Movement

CANDY

95n Cotton Candy

CANNON

215s Dr. Martha Hughes Cannon: Doctor, Wife, Legislator, Exile

CANON

177h Canon Law and the Battle of the Sexes

CAPEK

5l Karel Capek

CAPITALISM

see also INDUSTRIALIZATION

19h Women in Preindustrial Capitalism
35a Developing a Theory of Capitalist Patriarchy and Socialist Feminism
35b Relations of Capitalist Patriarchy
35d Mothering, Male Dominance, and Capitalism
35g Femininity and Capitalism in Antebellum America
35i Monopoly Capital and the Structure of Consumption
35j Capitalism, Patriarchy, and Job Segregation by Sex
55e Political Economy of Domestic Labour in Capitalist Society
84c Structures of Patriarchy and Capital in the Family
89gg Women as Workers under Capitalism
89tt Capitalism, the Family, and Personal Life
89ccc Sex in a Capitalist Society
107cc Capitalism and Women's Liberation
230o Spread of Capitalism in Rural Colombia: Effects on Poor Women
251c Capitalism, the Family, and Personal Life
251d Capitalism, Patriarchy, and Job Segregation by Sex

281e Industrialization, Monopoly, Capitalism, and Women's Work in Guatemala
291j Capitalism, Patriarchy, and Job Segregation by Sex
297d Female Labor and Capitalism in the U.S. and Brazil
304a Women, the Family and Corporate Capitalism
316n Marxist Analysis of Women and Capitalism
351d Work Attachment, Investments in Human Capital and the Earnings of Young Women

CARBONERA

122c Clorinda Matto de Turner and Mercedes Cabello de Carbonera: Societal Criticism and Morality

CARD

288x Letter to James Card

CARDON

215f Susanna Goudin Cardon: An Italian Convert to Mormonism

CARE

see also CHILD CARE; DAY CARE

95l Who Cares?
127ii Health Care May Be Hazardous to Your Health
160b Care and Feeding of Children: A Catechism for the Use of Mothers and Children's Nurses
191v Women and Health Care: A Comparison of Theories
262m Woman in Philanthropy--Care of the Sick
262n Woman in Philanthropy--Care of the Criminal
262o Woman in Philanthropy--Care of the Indian

CAREER

see also OCCUPATION; JOB; EMPLOYMENT; PROFESSION; LABOR; VOCATIONAL; various careers

4g Career Profiles of Women Doctorates
6j Seminars for Career Women: Combining Awareness Training with Transactional Analysis
39f Men, Women, and Work: Reflections on the Two-Person Career
39m Income Differences between Men and Career Women
45e Baseline Data on Mid-Career Change and Reentry for Black Women
61c Parental Influences on Women's Career Development
61d Individual Factors Related to Career Orientation in Women
61f Sex Role Stereotypes and the Career Versus Homemaking Orientations of Women
61g Barriers to the Career Development of Women
70h Jobs or Careers: The Case of the Professionally Employed Married Woman
122d Life and Early Literary Career of the Nineteenth-Century Colombian Writer, Coledad Acosta de Samper
141p Fertility Motivations and Career Conflicts in Educated Women
141t Welfare Careers, Low Wage Workers and Sexism

141v Social Research on Women's Professional Careers
146n Continuing Education and Second Careers
146o Retirement: Career and Non-Career
146q Gerontology Trends and Career Perspectives
163l Women as Politicians: The Social Background, Personality, and Political Careers of Female Party Leaders
166c Encountering the Male Establishment: Sex-Status Limits on Woman's Careers in the Professions
166j Masculinity or Femininity? Differentiating Career-Oriented and Homemaking-Oriented College Freshman Women
166r Career of Marriage? A Longitudinal Study of Able Young Women
166s Female Identity and Career Choice: The Nursing Case
166t Career Choice Processes
166u Role Model Influences on College Women's Career Aspirations
166v Interest of High School Girls in Dental Auxiliary Careers
166w Career Dreams of Teachers
166ee Career Expectations of Negro Women Graduates
166jj Career Patterns of Married Couples
166mm Career and Family Orientations of Husbands and Wives in Relation to Marital Happiness
173cc Big-Time Careers for the Little Woman: A Dual-Role Dilemma
176l Barriers to the Career Choice of Engineering, Medicine, or Science Among American Women
176p Career and Family Orientations of Husbands and Wives in Relation to Marital Happiness
214r Poetry and Salvation in the Career of Anne Sexton
250ll Encountering the Male Establishment: Sex Status Limits on Woman's Careers in the Professions
266m Effects of Career Choices on Married Women
267x Life Patterns and Self-Esteem in Gifted Family Oriented and Career Committed Women
267y Changing Image of the Career Woman
290b Inside the Clockwork of Male Careers
296r Pregnancy and Abortion: Implications for Career Development of Professional Women
311e Emotional Conflicts of the Career Woman
311g Career Choices
316g Career Structures of Federal Executives: A Focus on Women
317f Careers of Midwives in a Mayan Community
328l Facilitating Full Employment of Women through Career Education
344c Notes from a Political Career
360q Cookbooks and Law Books: The Hidden History of Career Women in Twentieth-Century America

CARIBBEAN

43g Caribbean Women: The Impact of Race, Sex, and Class
222h Caribbean Woman as Writer

CARITAS

247d Caritas Romana after 1760: Some Romantic Lactations

CARL

297x Sources of the Matrilineal Family System in the Works of Carl J.L. Almqvist

CARMICHAEL

215u Sarah Elizabeth Carmichael: Poetic Genius of Pioneer Utah

CARR

179ff E. Carr

CARRILLO

121k Felipe Carrillo Puerto and Women's Liberation in Mexico

CARSON

192g Carson McCullers

CARTOONS

200p Unacceptable Impulses, Anxiety, and the Appreciation of Cartoons

CASAMIENTO

80f "El casamiento enganoso": Marriage in the Novels of Maria Luisa Bombal, Silvina Bullrich, and Elisa Serrana

CASAS

122i Three Female Playwrights Explore Contemporary Latin American Reality: Myrna Casas, Griselda Gambaro, Luisa Josefina Hernandez

CASSANDRA

111u Cassandra's Wedding Song

CASTE

89u Women: Caste, Class or Oppressed Sex?
213d Caste Differences between Brahmin and Non-Brahmin Women in a South Indian Village

CASTELLANOS

88m Women and Feminism in the Works of Rosario Castellanos

CASTILE

315c Women in Reconquest Castile: The Fueros of Sepulveda and Cuenca

CASTLE

50e The Fordwych Castle Mystery

CASTRATION

107x Woman as Castrated Man
176jj Castration Anxiety and Phallus Envy: A Reformulation

210g Theology After the Demise of God the Father: A Call for the Castration of Sexist Religion
268g Manifestations of the Female Castration Complex
268h Castration Complex Reconsidered
283a Theology After the Demise of God the Father: A Call for the Castration of Sexist Religion

CAT

126n Cheshire Cat: Reconstructing the Experience of Medieval Women
220y An Old Woman and Her Cat
279n Cat in the Rain

CATARACT

273r Camp Cataract

CATECHISM

160b Care and Feeding of Children: A Catechism for the Use of Mothers and Children's Nurses

CATHARINE

303c Catharine Beecher and the Politics of Housework
360j Catharine Beecher and the Education of American Women

CATHEDRAL

153k The Cathedral

CATHER

192c Willa Cather

CATHOLICISM

57e White Ethnic Catholic Woman
85w Roman Catholic Doctrine of Therapeutic Abortion
233d Catholic Teaching on Women
263j Feminist Spirituality, Christian Identity, and Catholic Vision
329d Catholicism and Women's Role in Italy and Ireland
337o Roman Catholic Story

CATT

257v John Hay, Mrs. Catt and Patriotism

CAUCA

140f From Peasants to Proletarians: Black Women in the Cauca Valley, Colombia

CAUCUS

163m New Dimension in Political Participation: The Women's Political Caucus

327i Women in the Professional Caucuses
344i Organizing for Political Power: The National Women's Political Caucus

CAUSE

24h Joy In Our Cause
198bb Possible Causal Factors of Sex Differences in Intellectual Abilities
257l Strikes and Their Causes
267j Women's Expectations for and Causal Attributions of Success and Failure
351f Causes and Consequences of Marital Breakdown
363a Observations on the State of Degradation to Which Woman Is Reduced by Various Causes

CAUTIOUS

47a Margaret Drabble: Novels of a Cautious Feminist

CAVE

298h The Dark Unfathomed Caves
375c Parable of the Cave or: In Praise of Watercolors

CELEBRATION

208a Why I Won't Celebrate Brotherhood Week
263l Dilemma of Celebration

CELIBACY

233aaa Celibacy

CELIBES

317b Celibes, Mothers, and Church Cockroaches: Religious Participation of Women in a Mexican Village

CELLAR

24m Man in the Cellar

CELLS

23c Book-Lined Cells: Women and Humanism in the Early Italian Renaissance

CENTER

131e Women of North and Central India: Goddesses and Wives
143p Los Angeles Women's Building: A Public Center for Woman's Culture
199c Fetal Androgens, Human Central Nervous System Differentiation, and Behavior Sex Differences
303q Centers and Fragments: Women's Spaces
314k Assessment Center: Opportunities for Women
320p APPENDIX: Women's Centres, Women's Newspapers and Regional Contacts

330b Sex Hormones, The Central Nervous System and Affect Variability in Humans
338d Nzakara Women (Central African Republic)

CEREBRAL

204e Evidence for Sex-Related Differences in Cerebral Organization
204g Cognitive Abilities and Sex-Related Variations in the Maturation of Cerebral Cortical Functions

CH'ING

308b Emergence of Women at the End of the Ch'ing: The Case of Ch'iu Chin
308g Chiang Ch'ing's Coming of Age

CH'IU

308b Emergence of Women at the End of the Ch'ing: The Case of Ch'iu Chin

CHAIRMAN

36k Job Market for Women: A Department Chairman's View

CHALLENGE

11a Out of the Past and Present Controversies: Challenges for the Future
48b Challenge to Management
48m Challenge and Resolution
57a Challenge of the "New Pluralism"
57h Women's Movement Meets the Challenge of Diversity
131c Changing Frenchwoman: Her Challenged World
303b Challenging the American Domestic Ideal
328a Women's Stake in Full Employment: Their Disadvantaged Role in the Economy--Challenges to Action
364f Myths and Stereotypes: My Challenge to Black Women Cultural Workers

CHAMBER

119f The Haunted Chamber

CHAMPION

128c Prudence Crandall: Champion of Negro Education
152j Memoirs of a Would-Be Swim Champ

CHANCE

152n Giving Women a Sporting Chance

CHANNEL

71h Domestic Service as a Channel of Upward Mobility for the Lower Class Woman: The Lima Case
208ff Textbooks and Channeling
271p Textbooks and Channeling

CHAOS

17k "Out of the chaos, a new kind of strength": Doris Lessing's "The Golden Notebook"

CHARACTER

47h Character and Themes in the Novels of Jean Rhys
51e Masked Character of Female Crime
68h Mill, Marx and Bebel: Early Influences on Shaw's Characterizations of Women
176g Sex Differences in Adolescent Character Processes
176ss Hysterical Character and Feminine Identity
232c Investigation of the Religious and Judicial Character of Matriarchy in the Ancient World
233f Womanly Image: Character Assassination through the Ages
246l American Character vs. The Ideal Woman
259k American Women and the American Character
260b Female Character
267o Implied Demand Character of the Wife's Future and Role Innovation: Patterns of Achievement Orientation Among College Women
336b Vindication of the Character and Condition of the Females Employed in the Lowell Mills...
342s Gogol's Female Characters

CHARISMATIC

283n Patriarchy and Charismatic Community in "Paul"

CHARITY

19m Angels in the Devil's Workshop: Leisured and Charitable Women in Nineteenth-Century England and France
262l Woman in Philanthropy--Charity

CHARLOTTA

7i Win or Lose--We Win: The 1952 Vice-Presidential Campaign of Charlotta A. Bass

CHARLOTTE

110b Popular Literature as Social Reinforcement: The Case of "Charlotte Temple"
151l Charlotte Perkins Gilman on the Theory and Practice of Feminism
153v Living of Charlotte Perkins Gilman
334i Private Woman, Public Woman: The Contradictions of Charlotte Perkins Gilman

CHARMS

129w Those Endearing Young Charms: Fifty Years Later

CHART

77hh APPENDIX: Chart of Basic Feminist Positions

303s Historic Chart Relating Architectural Projects to General and Women's History in the U.S.

CHARTER

315i Women in Charter and Statute Law: Medieval Ragusa-Dubrovnik
335c Land Charters and the Legal Position of Anglo-Saxon Women

CHASE

111ff The Chase
112z The Chase

CHASTITY

257i Patriotism and Chastity

CHAUCER

17d "Slydynge of Corage": Chaucer's Criseyde as Feminist and Victim
17e Chaucer's Women and Women's Chaucer
240a Portrayal of Women by Chaucer and His Age

CHAUVINISM

see also SEXISM; SEX BIAS; DISCRIMINATION; BIAS

68a Shakespeare's "The Taming of the Shrew" vs. Shaw's "Pygmalion": Male Chauvinism vs. Women's Lib?
157d Male Chauvinism: A Conceptual Analysis
158d Male Chauvinism: A Conceptual Analysis
196h Teachers' Perceptions of Ideal Male and Female Students: Male Chauvinism in the Schools
280v Chauvinism--At Work and at Home
362d Up Against the Wall, Male Chauvinist Pig

CHECK

68z Bibliographical Checklist
73i Check One: Male (or) Female

CHEERS

164l Two Cheers for Equality

CHEJU

236j Occupations, Male Housekeeper: Male-Female Roles on Cheju Island

CHELLAMMA

114s Chellamma--An Illustration of the Multiple Roles of Traditional Women

CHESHIRE

126n Cheshire Cat: Reconstructing the Experience of Medieval Women

CHESNUT

179x M.B. Chesnut

CHEVALIER

277e The Old Chevalier

CHIANG

308g Chiang Ch'ing's Coming of Age

CHIC

300d Sexual Chic, Sexual Fascism and Sexual Confusion

CHICAGO

116j Interaction Between Italian Immigrant Women and the Chicago Commons Settlement House, 1909-1944
141j Role of Women in the Organization of the Men's Garment Industry, Chicago, 1910

CHICANA

43k La Chicana: Guadalupe or Malinche
86e Chicanas Speak Out--New Voice of La Raza
127x Colonized Women: The Chicana
219g Phonological Differences in the English of Adolescent Chicanas and Chicanos
219p Effects of the Ethnicity of the Interviewer on Conversation: A Study of Chicana Women
342q Familism and Sex Roles: A Chicana Perspective
368g White Feminist Movement: The Chicana Perspective

CHICANOS

219g Phonological Differences in the English of Adolescent Chicanas and Chicanos

CHICKEN

249p Mediation of Contradiction: Why Mbum Women Do Not Eat Chicken

CHICKS

132hh No "Chicks," "Broads," or "Niggers" for OLE MOLE
157c "Pricks" and "Chicks": A Plea for "Persons"
158c "Pricks" and "Chicks": A Plea for "Persons"

CHIEF

256l Chief Justice Wore a Red Dress
272a Prophets, Chiefs, Commissioners, and Queens: The Moral and Institutional Context of Leadership

CHILD

13j Impact of the Women's Liberation Movement on Child Development Texts
13q Sex-Role Pressures and the Socialization of the Male Child
20j Matri-Patrilocality and the Birth of the First Child
22u Effects of Maternal Employment on the Child
33e The Child's Day
37c Parental Role Division and the Child's Personality Development
76a Freud's Views on Early Female Sexuality in the Light of Direct Child Observation
111k Night-Pieces: For a Child
112i Night Pieces for a Child: The Crib
159w Of Child and Marriage
198l Family Structure and the Socialization of the Child
199i Sex of Parent x Sex of Child: Socioemotional Development
199p Behaviorally Feminine Male Child: Pretranssexual? Pretransvestite? Prehomosexual? Preheterosexual?
200d Child's Sex-Role Classification of School Objects
202k Child Investment and Women
211c Prenatal Influences on Child Health and Development
250bb Influences of Mother's Menstruation on Her Child
256e Child Rearing: 2000 AD
256u X: A Fabulous Child's Story
284w Raising a Bright and Happy Child
304d Child-Free Alternative: Rejection of the Motherhood Mystique
315g Widow and Ward: The Feudal Law of Child Custody in Medieval England
340b The Child Dreams
360p Prosperity's Child: Some Thoughts on the Flapper
365c Impact of the Women's Liberation Movement on Child Development Books
370f Effects on Child
375i One Child of One's Own: A Meaningful Digression within the Work(s)

CHILD CARE

see also DAY CARE

40a Economic and Policy Issues of Child Care
40b Public Policy Toward Child Care in America: A Historical Perspective
40c Child Care Market in Seattle and Denver
40d Substitution Among Child Care Modes and the Effect of a Child Care Subsidy Program
40f Vouchers for Child Care: The Santa Clara Child Care Pilot Study
86i Reply to Dr. Spock on Child Care
129m Fostergrandparenting: A Unique Child-Care Service
202n Formal Extrafamily Child Care--Some Economic Observations
269k Community Organizations and Child-care Arrangements
328j Economic Aspects of Child Care
331g Child Care for the 1980s: Traditional Sex Roles or Androgyny?
370e Child-Care Arrangements

CHILDHOOD

22o Sex-Role Concepts and Sex Typing in Childhood as a Function of School and Home Environments

25j Family and Childhood in a Southern Negro Community
60a Childhood
76i Penis Envy: From Childhood Wish to Developmental Metaphor
96f Impressions of an Indian Childhood
156c Teacher Education and Non-Sexist Early Childhood Education
156g Development of Psychological Androgyny: Early Childhood Socialization
176b Sex Differences in the Incidence of Neonatal Abnormalities and Abnormal Performance in Early Childhood
250kk Early Childhood Experiences and Women's Achievement Motives
267h Early Childhood Experiences and Women's Achievement Motives
271h Sex-Role Concepts and Sex Typing in Childhood as a Function of School and Home Environments
296b Early Childhood Experiences and Women's Achievement Motives

CHILDREN

13i Report on Children's Toys
18n Portrait of a Female on Television: Some Possible Effects on Children
22n Cross-Cultural Analysis of Sex Differences in the Behavior of Children Aged Three Through Eleven
22q Sex-Role Stereotyping in Children's Television Programs
25f Fathers without Children
56d Cognitive--Developmental Analysis of Children's Sex-Role Concepts and Attitudes
59e Poverty: Women and Children Last
70g Effects of Children on the Family
77c Cross-Cultural Analysis of Sex Differences in the Behavior of Children Aged Three Through Eleven
89g Liberation of Children
105m Sex-typing and Children's Television Preferences
127m Liberation of Children
135c Effects of Day Care on Young Children
141s Social Psychology of the "Decision" to Have or Not Have Children
143c Household as Workplace: Wives, Husbands, and Children
151h Hagar and Her Children
156p APPENDIX: Non-Sexist Picture Books for Children
161b The Children's Hour
175m Feminist Look at Children's Books
196c Sex Differences in the Self-Concepts of Elementary-School Children
196n Sex-Typing and Politicization in Children's Attitudes
198aa Physiological Development, Cognitive Development, and Socialization Antecedents of Children's Sex-Role Attitudes
199m Ethological Study of Children Approaching a Strange Adult: Sex Differences
199n Sex Differences in Field Independence among Preschool Children
207h Sexism in Children's Books and Elementary Teaching Materials
208t Sex-Role Socialization in Picture Books for Preschool Children
208aa Feminist Look at Children's Books
208cc Feminists Look at the 100 Books: The Portrayal of Women in Children's Books on Puerto Rican Themes
208ii Lost Herstory: The Treatment of Women in Children's Encyclopedias
208oo Why Children's Films Are Not Rated "R"
208ss Children's Toys and Socialization to Sex Roles
208tt Toys for Free Children
221b Customs Connected with Birth and the Rearing of Children

250d Male and Female in Children's Books
250s Parental Education, Sex Differences, and Performance on Cognitive Tasks Among Two-Year-Old Children
255f "Treated Like Imbecile Children" (Diderot): The Enlightenment and the Status of Women
260p Children of Mankind
269d Hunger in the U.S.: Women and Children First
271m Feminist Look at Children's Books
280j Unisex Pressures on Children
284x Children and Their Families
318m Images of Male and Female in Children's Readers

CHILDREN--LITERATURE

36j Women in Children's Literature
208s Women in Children's Literature
208x Negative Image of Women in Children's Literature
271l Women in Children's Literature

CHILDREN--MOTHER

108w My Mother's House: Where Are the Children?
160b Care and Feeding of Children: A Catechism for the Use of Mothers and Children's Nurses
219l Mothers' Speech to Children in Bilingual Mexican-American Homes

CHILDREN--ROLE

178j Role of Women in the Founding of the U.S. Children's Bureau
193e Roles of Children in Urban Kano

CHILDREN--SEX

13h Children's Books: The Second Sex, Junior Division
120j Cues to the Identification of Sex in Children's Speech
196l Woman's Place: Children's Sex Stereotyping of Occupations
208u Dick and Jane as Victims: Sex Stereotyping in Children's Readers
235c Sexual Abuse of Children
250o Developmental Study of the Effects of Sex of the Dominant Parent on Sex-Role Preference, Identification, and Imitation in Children
250v Effects of Sex of Examiner and Subject on Children's Quantitative Test Performance

CHILE

71e Women in Latin American Politics: The Case of Peru and Chile
122b Women Intellectuals in Chilean Society
122j Brechtian Aesthetics in Chile: Isidora Aguirre's "Los Papeleros"
194a Mythology About Women, With Special Reference to Chile
194n Chile: The Feminine Version of the Coup d'Etat
194o Emergence of a Mapuche Leader: Chile
316o Mobilization of Women in Allende's Chile

CHIN

308b Emergence of Women at the End of the Ch'ing: The Case of Ch'iu Chin

CHINA

see also PEOPLE'S REPUBLIC OF CHINA; ASIA

21p Women in China: Problems of Sex Inequality and Socio-economic Change
35n Significance of the Chinese Family Revolution for Feminist Theory
43e Chinese Women: The Relative Influences of Ideological Revolution, Economic Growth, and Cultural Change
91c Chinese Women at Work: Work Commitment and Fertility in the Asian Setting
131h Women in China: Past and Present
141x Chinese Women in the Early Communist Movement
152s Women's Sports in China
176gg Re-Evaluation of the Primary Role of the Communist Chinese Woman: The Homemaker or the Worker
181j Women in Revolutionary China
206q Sex Roles in the Modern Fabric of China
208w Liberated Chinese Primers
230q Collectivization, Kinship, and the Status of Women in Rural China
249h Chinese Women: Old Skills in a New Context
251hh Chinese Family Revolution and Feminist Theory
288ll Documenting the Patriarchy: "Chinatown"
307b Woman as Politician in China of the 1920s
307c Chinese Women in the Early Communist Movement
307f Women and Revolution: The Lessons of the Soviet Union and China
308e Women and Suicide in China
308h Power and Pollution of Chinese Women
308j Women in the Countryside of China
324s Mainland China
325gg Being Female in a Muslim Minority in China
329u Chinese Women on the Road to Complete Emancipation
329v Marriage Law: Basis of Change for China's Women
334l Chinese Immigrant Women in Nineteenth-Century California
349g Women in the Chinese Communist Revolution: The Question of Political Equality
350b Rural China: Segregation to Solidarity
364l Conversation with Audrey Topping: Chinese Women Today

CHOICE

22j Aborting a Fetus: The Legal Right, The Personal Choice
68d Eliza's Choice: Transformation Myth and the Ending of "Pygmalion"
166s Female Identity and Career Choice: The Nursing Case
166t Career Choice Processes
166z Self-Concept, Occupational Role Expectations, and Occupational Choice in Nursing and Social Work
172i Woman's Sociobiological Heritage: Destiny or Free Choice?
176l Barriers to the Career Choice of Engineering, Medicine, or Science Among American Women
196m Sex Differences in the Occupational Choices of Second Graders
253j Role of Choice in the Psychology of Professional Women
264e Abortion: The Controversial Choice
266m Effects of Career Choices on Married Women
270j Desert Politics: Choices in the "Marriage Market"
280n New Choices, New Roles
311g Career Choices

CHOPIN

17n Old Critics and New: The Treatment of Chopin's "The Awakening"
128o "The Awakening" by Kate Chopin

CHOREOGRAPHER

190a Woman as Artistic Innovator: The Case of the Choreographer

CHRIST

154f Brides of Christ
317a Bride of Christ Is Filled with His Spirit

CHRISTABEL

103b Christabel's Crystal

CHRISTI

121e Indian Nuns of Mexico City's Monasterio of Corpus Christi, 1724-1821

CHRISTIANITY

58d Instruction of a Christen Woman
60e Christian Family
153e Appeal to the Christian Women of the South
153f Address to the Christian Women of America
162b Christianity and Population
246e Female Dimension in the Image of God: A Christian Perspective
263f Women in the Early Christian Movement
263g Christian Past: Does It Hold a Future for Women?
263j Feminist Spirituality, Christian Identity, and Catholic Vision
337a Women's Leadership in the Jewish and Christian Traditions: Continuity and Change
337b Women in Early Christian Communities
337d Women, Power and the Pursuit of Holiness in Medieval Christianity
337h Feminist Thrust of Sectarian Christianity

CHRISTINA

214g Christina Rossetti: The Inward Pose
357c Indefinite Disclosed: Christina Rossetti and Emily Dickinson

CHRISTINE

184e Fifteenth-Century View of Women's Role in Medieval Society: Christine de Pizan's "Livre des Trois Vertus"

CHRONOLOGY

47l APPENDIX: Chronology of Important Dates
50p APPENDIX: Women Detectives A Chronological Survey

CHRYSANTHEMUM

95d The Green Chrysanthemum
277bb Odour of Chrysanthemums

CHURCH

see also BIBLE; THEOLOGY; RELIGION; various denominations

84d Church, State, and Family: The Women's Movement in Italy
177e Misogynism and Virginal Feminism in the Fathers of the Church
210c Black Women and the Churches: Triple Jeopardy
210j Sexism and the Contemporary Church: When Evasion Becomes Complicity
238i Toward Partnership in the Church
284e Women in the Churches
312c Women and the Church since the Famine
317b Celibes, Mothers, and Church Cockroaches: Religious Participation of Women in a Mexican Village
317c Hats as a Symbol of Women's Position in Three Evangelical Churches in Edinburgh, Scotland
320e Changes in the Churches

CICELY

68q Shaw's Lady Cicely and Mary Kingsley
279i Cicely's Dream

CINCINNATI

278t Influential Alliances: Cincinnati Women in the Political Arena, 1920-1945

CINDERELLA

173hh Cinderella's Stepsisters: A Feminist Perspective on Anorexia Nervosa and Bulimia

CINEMA

see FILM

CIRCLE

105f Magazine Heroines: Is MS. Just Another Member of the FAMILY CIRCLE?

CIRCULATION

138g Image of Women in Mass Circulation Magazines in the 1920s

CITIZEN

163i Comparative Study of Male-Female Political Attitudes at Citizen and Elite Levels
240l Second-class Citizenship: The Status of Women in Contemporary American Fiction

CITY

31 Mademoiselle from Kansas City
39q Social Relations of Black and White Widowed Women in a Northern Metropolis
41d Women Workers in a Mid-Nineteenth-Century New York City Community
41f Italian-American Women in New York City, 1900-1950: Work and School
47b Disorderly Company: From "The Golden Notebook" to "The Four-Gated City"
58c Boke of the Cyte of Ladyes
94l Rape in New York City: A Study of Material in the Police Files and Its Meaning
95j On the Outskirts of the City
121e Indian Nuns of Mexico City's Monasterio of Corpus Christi, 1724-1821
140o Italian-American Women in New York City, 1890 to 1940
143j Toward Supportive Neighborhoods: Women's Role in Changing the Segregated City
143o Women at City Hall
159l The City of God
190b City Women and Religious Change in Sixteenth-Century France
225e City's Achievements: The Patriotic Amazonomachy and Ancient Athens
281d Women in the Informal Labor Sector: The Case of Mexico City
281k Migration and Labor Force Participation of Latin American Women: The Domestic Servants in the Cities
283c Explorations with Doris Lessing in Quest of The Four-Gated City
293f Women in Cities: Problems and Perspectives
297k Life and Labor of the Woman Textile Worker in Mexico City
350d Women's Organizations in Madras City, India

CIVIC

142m Woman as Secretary, Sexpot, Spender, Sow, Civic Actor, Sickie
186a Woman as Secretary, Sexpot, Spender, Sow, Civic Actor, Sickie

CIVIL

106k Civil Rights and the Women's Movement
116b Civil Code of 1865 and the Origins of the Feminist Movement in Italy
149b Civil and Social Rights of Women
174g Minorities and Policy Problems: An Overview Seen by the U.S. Commission on Civil Rights
174k Combatting Dual Discrimination: The Impact of Civil Rights Policies on the Income Status of Black Women
233z Political and Civil Status of Women as of January 1, 1969
254aa Women's Liberation and Black Civil Rights
260s Title VII of the 1964 Civil Rights Act

CLARA

40f Vouchers for Child Care: The Santa Clara Child Care Pilot Study
268r Role of Clara Thompson in the Psychoanalytic Study of Women

CLARE

68s Interview with Clare Boothe Luce

CLARISSA

108f Clarissa

CLASH

166h Clash Between Beautiful Women and Science

CLASS

14g Sociology and Women in Working-class Jobs
19k Working-Class Women During the Industrial Revolution, 1780-1914
41h Imperfect Unions: Class and Gender in Cripple Creek, 1894- 1904
41j Creating a Feminist Alliance: Sisterhood and Class Conflict in the New York Women's Trade Union League, 1903- 1914
43f Effects of Class and Sex on Political Life in Northern India
43g Caribbean Women: The Impact of Race, Sex, and Class
55i Marriage, Role Division and Social Cohesion: The Case of Some French Upper-Middle Class Families
71h Domestic Service as a Channel of Upward Mobility for the Lower Class Woman: The Lima Case
71j Pursuit of an Ideal: Migration, Social Class, and Women's Roles in Bogota, Colombia
71l Honor, Shame, and Women's Liberation in Cuba: Views of Working-Class Emigre Men
84i Women, Sex and Class
89u Women: Caste, Class or Oppressed Sex?
91b Fertility, Women's Work, and Economic Class: A Case Study from Southeast Asia
100e Class and Race Differences in Gender Roles
105i Women's Page as a Window on the Ruling Class
123e Lesbians and the Class Position of Women
126i Feminism and Class Consciousness in the British and American Women's Trade Union Leagues, 1890-1925
126p Sex and Class in Colonial and Nineteenth-Century America
127j Labor and Suffrage Movements: A View of Working-Class Women in the 20th Century
127t Storybook Lives: Growing Up Middle Class
127u To My White Working-Class Sisters
141i Feminism and Class Consciousness in the British and American Women's Trade Union Leagues, 1890-1925
146g Life Span Behavior Patterns--Class and Ethnic Variations
155h Aspects of Lower Class Sexual Behavior
163d Working-Class Women's Political Participation: Its Potential in Developed Countries
176k Race, Social Class, and the Motive to Avoid Success in Women
176mm Lower Class Sexual Behavior
190d Women: The New Political Class
191q Class Factor: Mountain Women Speak Out on Women's Health
194c Class Consciousness Among Working-Class Women in Latin America: Puerto Rico
194g Relationships of Sex and Social Class in Brazil
218a Class and Sex Connection
218e Unequal Partners in an Uneasy Alliance: Women and the Working Class in Imperial Germany
223f Working-Class Women in Britain, 1890-1914?
257r Class-Consciousness

267n Race, Social Class, and the Motive to Avoid Success in Women
270f Aztec Women: The Transition from Status to Class in Empire and Colony
281g Class Structures and Female Autonomy in Rural Java
297ee Class, Commodity, and the Status of Women
325w Women, Class, and Power: Examples from the Hatay, Turkey
330q Psychotherapy with Women and Men of Lower Classes
349a Women of the Popular Classes in Revolutionary Paris, 1789-1795
349b Women, Class, and War in Nazi Germany
349i Revolution and Retreat: Upper-Class French Women After 1789
369h My Work and My Working-Class Father

CLASSICAL

19c "Liberated" Women: The Classical Era
126m Classical Scholar's Perspective on Matriarchy
190e Classical Mythology and the Role of Women in Modern Literature
325k Turkish Women in the Ottoman Empire: The Classical Age

CLASSIFICATION

51cc Competing Goals, Heterogeneity, and Classification
56h Classified Summary of Research in Sex Differences
200d Child's Sex-Role Classification of School Objects

CLASSROOM

181e Femininity in the Classroom: An Account of Changing Attitudes
208m Consciousness-Raising in the Classroom: Some Games, Projects, Discussion-Openers, Etc.

CLEANING

222ff Cleaning Out the Closet

CLEAVAGE

174j Abortion Policy since 1973: Political Cleavage and Its Impact on Policy Outputs

CLERGY

166y Differential Recruitment of Female Professionals: A Case Study of Clergywomen
166pp Female Clergy: A Case of Professional Marginality
280w Women in the Clergy

CLERICAL

35k Feminization of the Clerical Labor Force
264p Clerical Work: The Female Occupation
354n Urban Nomads: Women in Temporary Clerical Services

CLICHES

265n Women's Economic Status: Some Cliches and Some Facts

CLIENTS

21h Women Social Workers and Clients: Common Victims of Sexism
317i Convivial Sisterhood: Spirit Mediumship and Client-Core Network among Black South African Women

CLIMATE

68f Legal Climate of Shaw's Problem Plays

CLIMBING

140u Climbing the Political Ladder: The Aspirations and Expectations of Partisan Elites

CLINICAL

155b Sex-Role Stereotypes and Clinical Judgments of Mental Health
176uu Sex-Role Stereotypes and Clinical Judgements of Mental Health
205h Clinical Aspects of Sex-Role Stereotyping
211v Female Sexual Dysfunctions: A Clinical Approach
250j Sex-Role Stereotypes and Clinical Judgments of Mental Health

CLIO

342k Liberation of Clio

CLITORAL

296i Clitoral Eroticism and the Sexual Response Cycle in Human Females

CLOCKWORK

290b Inside the Clockwork of Male Careers

CLORINDA

122c Clorinda Matto de Turner and Mercedes Cabello de Carbonera: Societal Criticism and Morality

CLOSED

53c Open Body, Closed Space: The Transformation of Female Sexuality

CLOSET

8n Thriving Decloseted in Rural Academe
129h Coming Out of the Closet: Marriage and Other Crises of Middle Age
222ff Cleaning Out the Closet

CLOSING

152f Closing the Muscle Gap
311h Closing Remarks

CLOTH

214b Jane Lead: Mysticism and the Woman Cloathed with the Sun
270i Women and Men, Cloth and Colonization: The Transformation of Production-Distribution Relations among the Baule (Ivory Coast)

CLUB

257m Woman's Clubs from a Reporter's Point of View
257n Work of the Woman's Club
257o Woman's Mission and Woman's Clubs

CLUE

230m Life Crisis as a Clue to Social Function: The Case of Italy

COACHES

286r Self-Perception of Athletes and Coaches

COAST

270b Sunksquaws, Shamans, and Tradeswomen: Middle Atlantic Coastal Algonkian Women During the Seventeenth and Eighteenth Centuries
270i Women and Men, Cloth and Colonization: The Transformation of Production-Distribution Relations among the Baule (Ivory Coast)
281s Social Change and Sexual Differentiation in the Cameroun and the Ivory Coast
285f Bargaining from Weakness: Spirit Possession on the South Kenya Coast
302f Limitations of Group Action Among Entrepreneurs: The Market Women of Abidjan, Ivory Coast
372d Dioula Women in Town: A View of Intra-Ethnic Variation - Ivory Coast

COCKROACHES

317b Celibes, Mothers, and Church Cockroaches: Religious Participation of Women in a Mexican Village

CODE

35m Introducing the Family Code
89pp Cuban Family Code
115e Jawaharlal Nehru and the Hindu Code Bill
116b Civil Code of 1865 and the Origins of the Feminist Movement in Italy
348e Sexual Codes and Conduct: A Study of Teenage Girls

COEDUCATION

96n When Co-Education Was Young
197i How Coeducation Fails Women
203x Battle for Coed Teams
272g Coeducation and the Development of Leadership Skills in Women: Historical Perspectives from Cornell University, 1868-1900
278s Crisis in Coeducation, 1890-1920

COERCION

85v Coercion and Rape: The State As a Male Protection Racket
348a Coercion of Privacy: A Feminist Perspective

COFFEE

95q Coffee for the Road
341j Make Policy, Not Coffee

COGNITION

56d Cognitive--Developmental Analysis of Children's Sex-Role Concepts and Attitudes
67f Sex Differences in the Organization of Perception and Cognition
171c Gonadal Hormones and Cognitive Functioning
172b Sex-Related Factors in Cognition and in Brain Lateralization
198aa Physiological Development, Cognitive Development, and Socialization Antecedents of Children's Sex-Role Attitudes
199d Prenatal Androgen, Intelligence and Cognitive Sex Differences
200k Cognitive Conflict and Compromise between Males and Females
204a Sex-Related Differences in Cognitive Functioning: An Overview
204d Patterns of Cognitive Functioning in Relation to Handedness and Sex-Related Differences
204f Sex-Related Differences in Cognition Among the Elderly
204g Cognitive Abilities and Sex-Related Variations in the Maturation of Cerebral Cortical Functions
204h Hormones and Cognitive Functioning in Normal Development
204i Prenatal Influences on Cognitive Abilities: Data from Experimental Animals and Human and Endocrine Syndromes
204j Menstrual Cycle and Sex-Related Differences in Cognitive Variability
250q Roles of Activation and Inhibition in Sex Differences in Cognitive Abilities
250r Comments on "Roles of Activation and Inhibition in Sex Differences in Cognitive Abilities"
250s Parental Education, Sex Differences, and Performance on Cognitive Tasks Among Two-Year-Old Children
330e Cognitive Therapy with Depressed Women

COHESION

55i Marriage, Role Division and Social Cohesion: The Case of Some French Upper-Middle Class Families
116t Family and Kin Cohesion among South Italian Immigrants in Toronto

COLD-WATER

220x A Cold-Water Flat

COLEDAD

122d Life and Early Literary Career of the Nineteenth-Century Colombian Writer, Coledad Acosta de Samper

COLLECTIVE

132u Collective Statement, Black Sisters
174b Impact of Collective Bargaining on Minorities in the Public Sector: Some Policy Implications
183c Women and Collective Action in Europe
230q Collectivization, Kinship, and the Status of Women in Rural China
318q Individual and the Collective
344h New Approaches to Collective Power: Four Working Women's Organizations

COLLECTOR

222cc The Collector of Treasures

COLLEGE

see also UNIVERSITY; EDUCATION; HIGHER EDUCATION; COEDUCATION; ACADEMIA; STUDENT; FACULTY; CAMPUS

4r Internal Remedies for Sex Discrimination in Colleges and Universities
13y Present Tendencies in Women's College and University Education
60n Purpose of the College
106c Women's Education: The Case for the Single-Sex College
116p Italian-American Female College Students: A New Generation Connected to the Old
140cc Sex-Role Constraints: The College-Educated Black Woman
140ii Bibliography of Dissertations for and about Women in Administration in Colleges and Universities
166j Masculinity or Femininity? Differentiating Career-Oriented and Homemaking-Oriented College Freshman Women
166u Role Model Influences on College Women's Career Aspirations
166bb Perspective of College Women
166hh College Women Seven Years After Graduation
176j Motive to Avoid Success and Changing Aspirations of College Women
180l Harvard College Amicus Curiae, DeFunis v. Odegaard, Supreme Court of the U.S., 1973
196aa Effect of Sex on College Admission, Work Evaluation, and Job Interviews
196bb Sex Bias in Selective College Admissions
197h Effect of Race and Sex on College Admission
257q Present Tendencies in Women's College and University Education
266g Relationship Between Role Orientation and Achievement Motivation in College Women
266i Future Goals of College Women
266l Female College Students' Scores On the Men's And Women's Strong Vocational Interest Blanks
267o Implied Demand Character of the Wife's Future and Role Innovation: Patterns of Achievement Orientation Among College Women
267p Determinants of Occupational Role Innovation Among College Women
272f Single-Sex Education and Leadership: The Early Years of Simmons College
334j Founding of Mount Holyoke College
341s Women's Lib and the Women's Colleges
341t Why Women Go Back to College

351a Young Women's Decisions to Attend College: Desires, Expectations and Realizations
351c Sex Segregation in the Labor Market: An Analysis of Young College Women's Occupational Preferences
360h Cultural Hybrid in the Slums: The College Woman and the Settlement House, 1889-1894

COLOMBIA

71j Pursuit of an Ideal: Migration, Social Class, and Women's Roles in Bogota, Colombia
121h Participation of Women in the Independence Movement in Gran Colombia, 1780-1830
122d Life and Early Literary Career of the Nineteenth-Century Colombian Writer, Coledad Acosta de Samper
122r Interview with Women Writers in Colombia
140f From Peasants to Proletarians: Black Women in the Cauca Valley, Colombia
230o Spread of Capitalism in Rural Colombia: Effects on Poor Women
270e Forced Transition from Egalitarianism to Male Dominance: The Bari of Colombia
329o Women's Changing Roles in Colombia

COLONY

43m Schooling of Vietnamese Immigrants: Internal Colonialism and its Impact on Women
121a Colonial Women in Mexico: The Seventeenth and Eighteenth Centuries
121b Female and Family in the Economy and Society of Colonial Brazil
121f Feminine Orders in Colonial Bahia, Brazil: Economic, Social, and Demographic Implications, 1677-1800
121g Feminine Press: The View of Women in the Colonial Journals of Spanish America, 1790-1810
126o Women in Convents: Their Economic and Social Role in Colonial Mexico
126p Sex and Class in Colonial and Nineteenth-Century America
127x Colonized Women: The Chicana
151d Dynamics of Interracial Sex in Colonial America
154g Female Militancy and Colonial Revolt: The Women's War of 1929, Eastern Nigeria
176cc Pre-Industrial Patterns in the Colonial Family in America: A Content Analysis of Colonial Magazines
270a Montagnais Women and the Jesuit Program for Colonization
270d Contending with Colonization: Tlingit Men and Women in Change
270f Aztec Women: The Transition from Status to Class in Empire and Colony
270h Daughters of the Lakes and Rivers: Colonization and the Land Rights of Luo Women
270i Women and Men, Cloth and Colonization: The Transformation of Production-Distribution Relations among the Baule (Ivory Coast)
270k Stability in Banana Leaves: Colonization and Women in Kiriwina, Trobriand Islands
270l Putting Down Sisters and Wives: Tongan Women and Colonization
285h Colonialism and the Lost Political Institutions of Igbo Women
302d Luo Women and Economic Change During the Colonial Period

COLOR

180f Discrimination, Color Blindness, and the Quota System
219f Sex, Color and Money: Who's Perceiving What? Or Men and Women: Where Did All the Differences Go (To)?

COMB

95p The Ivory Comb

COMBAT

240k "Combat in the Erogenous Zone": Women in the American Novel between the Two World Wars
328d Legal Remedies beyond Title VII to Combat Sex Discrimination in Employment

COMEDY

68j New Woman and the New Comedy
288hh "Part-Time Work of a Domestic Slave," or Putting the Screws to Screwball Comedy

COMFORTABLE

256p When The Veils Come Tumbling Down: "And Women Shall Leave Their Comfortable Pews to Give Birth to a New and Inclusive Religious Vision"

COMMISSION

174g Minorities and Policy Problems: An Overview Seen by the U.S. Commission on Civil Rights
196gg Task Force on Education Report, Governor's Commission on the Status of Women, Ma.
207g Sexism in Dictionaries and Texts: Omissions and Commissions
272a Prophets, Chiefs, Commissioners, and Queens: The Moral and Institutional Context of Leadership

COMMITMENT

91c Chinese Women at Work: Work Commitment and Fertility in the Asian Setting
222w Commitment: Toni Cade Bambara Speaks
314m Preparing for the Future: Commitment and Action
370c Commitment to Work

COMMITTEE

196ff Reports of the Women's Rights Committee
316d Women's Attitudes Toward Women in Politics: A Survey of Urban Registered Voters and Party Committeewomen

COMMODITY

297ee Class, Commodity, and the Status of Women

COMMON

21h Women Social Workers and Clients: Common Victims of Sexism
116j Interaction Between Italian Immigrant Women and the Chicago Commons Settlement House, 1909-1944
214s Common Language: The American Woman Poet
233r Common Women

COMMUNES

233ll Communes: A Footnote for the Future

COMMUNICATION

120l Power, Sex, and Nonverbal Communication
120m Sex Differences in Language, Speech, and Nonverbal Communication: An Annotated Bibliography
256t Changing Woman's Thinking and Lifestyle Through the Great Communication Revolution
293j Toward Liberating Women: A Communications Perspective

COMMUNISM

141x Chinese Women in the Early Communist Movement
176gg Re-Evaluation of the Primary Role of the Communist Chinese Woman: The Homemaker or the Worker
227e Women Under Communist and Socialist Regimes
251ii Family Structure and Communism
252nn Family Structure and Communism
307c Chinese Women in the Early Communist Movement
316l Women Under Communism
349f Communist Feminism: Its Synthesis and Demise
349g Women in the Chinese Communist Revolution: The Question of Political Equality

COMMUNITY

8hh Power to Gay People: A Los Angeles Experiment in Community Action
8kk Alcohol Use and Abuse in the Gay Community
25j Family and Childhood in a Southern Negro Community
41d Women Workers in a Mid-Nineteenth-Century New York City Community
117s Changing(?)Role of Women in Jewish Communal Affairs: A Look into the U.J.A.
140k Role of Wife in the Black Extended Family: Perspectives from a Rural Community in Southern United States
141h Feminist Culture from 1790 to 1850: A Trans-Atlantic Community
181d Landscape with Figures: Home and Community in English Society
231f Community of Wives
249f Sex Roles and Survival Strategies in an Urban Black Community
252gg Men and Women in Community Agencies: A Note on Power and Prestige
260o Home and Community
269k Community Organizations and Child-care Arrangements
281l Female Status, the Family, and Male Dominance in a West Indian Community
283n Patriarchy and Charismatic Community in "Paul"
297m Resistance as Protest: Women in the Struggle of Bolivian Tin-Mining Communities

302b Dual-Sex Political System in Operation: Igbo Women and Community Politics in Midwestern Nigeria
317f Careers of Midwives in a Mayan Community
322b Exploring American Indian Communities in Depth
322g World of Women: Field Work in a Yoruba Community
325p Status of Women in Four Middle East Communities
337b Women in Early Christian Communities
344d Local Officeholding and the Community: The Case of Women on New Jersey's School Boards
359b Quest for Community: Spiritual Autobiographies of Eighteenth-Century Quaker and Puritan Women in America

COMPANION

198q Functions of the Sexual Companion

COMPANY

47b Disorderly Company: From "The Golden Notebook" to "The Four-Gated City"
97l Project Company Day-Care
97m Project Company Kindergarten

COMPARISON

51o Criminality in the Workplace: A Comparison of Male and Female Offenders
71c Passive Female and Social Change: A Cross-Cultural Comparison of Women's Magazine Fiction
88y Need to Tell All: A Comparison of Historical and Modern Feminist "Confessional" Writing
94k Comparative Study of Forcible Rape Offenses Known to the Police in Boston and Los Angeles
143h Women in the Suburban Environment: A U.S.--Sweden Comparison
155n Comparison of Sexual Attitudes and Behavior in an International Sample
163i Comparative Study of Male-Female Political Attitudes at Citizen and Elite Levels
174n Women and Public Policy: A Comparative Analysis
191v Women and Health Care: A Comparison of Theories
281f Sex Roles and Social Change: A Comparative Appraisal of Turkey's Women
291i Occupational Segregation and Public Policy: A Comparative Analysis of American and Soviet Patterns
325x Comparative Perspective on Women in Provincial Iran and Turkey
372m Comparisons and Implications

COMPASSION

254x Compassion Trap

COMPENSATORY

180v Reverse Discrimination and Compensatory Justice
217c Reverse Discrimination and Compensatory Justice
217i Equality and Inviolability: An Approach to Compensatory Justice
217j Compensatory Justice and the Meaning of Equity

COMPETENCE

173p Social Values, Femininity, and the Development of Female Competence

COMPETITION

51cc Competing Goals, Heterogeneity, and Classification
286h Females in the Competitive Process
303e Sophia Hayden and the Woman's Building Competition
358n Anxiety Levels Experienced by Women in Competition

COMPLAINT

42a "Fashionable Diseases": Women's Complaints and Their Treatment in Nineteenth-Century America
117h Portnoy's Mother's Complaint: Depression in Middle-Aged Women
191c Complaints and Disorders: The Sexual Politics of Sickness

COMPLEMENTARITY

193a Complementarity and Conflict: An Andean View of Men and Women

COMPLEMENTATION

266u Identification and Complementation in the Differentiation of Gender Identity

COMPLETENESS

85q Myth of the Complete Person
117e Single and Jewish: Toward a New Definition of Completeness
329u Chinese Women on the Road to Complete Emancipation

COMPLEXITY

76d Girl's Entry into the Oedipus Complex
78d Feminine Guilt and the Oedipus Complex
126v Four Structures in a Complex Unity
169b Evolution of the Oedipus Complex in Women
169d Masculinity Complex in Women
170a Flight from Womanhood: The Masculinity Complex in Women as Viewed by Men and by Women
198i Family in Father-Right and Mother-Right: Complex of Mother-Right
222x Complexity: Toni Morrison's Women--An Interview Essay
268g Manifestations of the Female Castration Complex
268h Castration Complex Reconsidered

COMPLIANCE

4s W.E.A.L. and Contract Compliance
40h Cost of Compliance with Federal Day Care Standards in Seattle and Denver
64d Compliance Agencies

COMPLICATIONS

176nn Emotional Factors in Obstetric Complications

COMPLICITY

210j Sexism and the Contemporary Church: When Evasion Becomes Complicity

COMPOSITION

59h Structural Change in the Occupational Composition of the Female Labor Force
366b Importance of Women in Determining the Composition of Residential Groups in Aboriginal Australia

COMPROMISE

200k Cognitive Conflict and Compromise between Males and Females

COMPUTER

200o Sex Differences in Dating Aspirations and Satisfaction with Computer-Selected Partners
342ff Analyzing Affirmative Action Data on the Computer

COMRADES

93g Women Socialists and Their Male Comrades: The Reading Experience, 1927-1936

CONCIENCIA

349h Revolution and Conciencia: Women in Cuba

CONCRETE

51dd Concrete Womb: "Gettin' In"

CONDITION

15j Social Conditions Can Change
59f Condition of Women in Blue-Collar Jobs
167b Report on Existing Conditions with Recommendations
176x Differences in Attitudinal Responses Under Conditions of Implicitly Manipulated Group Salience
232f Brief History of the Condition of Women
250u Pattern Copying Under Three Conditions of an Expanded Spatial Field
255g La Condition de la Femme Francaise au Dix-huitieme Siecle d'apres les Romans
286u Training and Condition Techniques for the Female Athlete
329e Condition of Women in Italy
336b Vindication of the Character and Condition of the Females Employed in the Lowell Mills...
336c Corporations and Operatives, Being an Exposition of the Condition of Factory Operatives...

CONDUCT

219q Alignment Strategies in Verbal Accounts of Problematic Conduct: The Case of Abortion
348e Sexual Codes and Conduct: A Study of Teenage Girls

CONFEDERACY

249i Madam Yoko: Ruler of the Kpa Mende Confederacy

CONFERENCE

54a Population and the Status of Women: Results of the Bucharest and Mexico Conferences
219o Women's Verbal Behavior at Learned and Professional Conferences
281w Reflections on the Conference on Women and Development
291n Toward Dimorphics: A Summary Statement to the Conference on Occupational Segregation
329y Conference Postscript
342jj Women's Conferences: Women On the Move
352o APPENDIX: Texts Concerning Women Workers Adopted by the 60th Session of the International Labour Conference, 4-25 June 1975

CONFESSIONS

88y Need to Tell All: A Comparison of Historical and Modern Feminist "Confessional" Writing
129f Confessions of a 45-Year-Old Feminist
152m Confessions of an Ex-Cheerleader
159k Confessions
364h Confessions of a Female Screenwriter

CONFLICT

13c Achievement-Related Conflicts in Women
41j Creating a Feminist Alliance: Sisterhood and Class Conflict in the New York Women's Trade Union League, 1903- 1914
82a Psychological Conflict and the Reproductive System
82b New Sources of Conflict in Females at Adolescence and Early Adulthood
82d Female Ego Styles and Generational Conflict
117a Jewish Feminist: Conflict in Identities
135d Women, Work and Conflict
141p Fertility Motivations and Career Conflicts in Educated Women
154d Gypsy Women: Models in Conflict
166n Female Physician in Public Health: Conflict and Reconciliation of the Sex and Professional Roles
183g Role of Women in Underdeveloped Countries: Some Sociological Issues Concerning Conflict and Peace
183i Bibliography: Role of Women in Conflict and Peace
193a Complementarity and Conflict: An Andean View of Men and Women
198d Early Stages of the Oedipus Conflict
200k Cognitive Conflict and Compromise between Males and Females
211j Conflicts between Fertility and Infertility
218h Five Socialist Women: Traditionalist Conflicts and Socialist Visions in Austria, 1893-1934
223i Innocent Femina Sensualis in Unconscious Conflict
249e Strategies, Cooperation, and Conflict Among Women in Domestic Groups
250jj Achievement-Related Conflicts in Women
253i Conflict and Accommodation
267l Achievement-Related Conflicts in Women

297j Sociocultural Factors Mitigating Role Conflict of Buenos Aires Professional Women
304c Women and Success: A Basic Conflict?
311e Emotional Conflicts of the Career Woman
360n Hysterical Woman: Sex Roles and Role Conflict in Nineteenth-Century America

CONFRONT

43d Issues Confronting Professional African Women: Illustrations from Kenya
289d Tanzanian Women Confront the Past and the Future
364j Confronting the Sports Establishment: A Plan for Honesty and Sanity

CONFUSION

300d Sexual Chic, Sexual Fascism and Sexual Confusion

CONGRESS

9p Statement: First Feminist Congress, 1919
163k Recruitment of Women for Congress
163p Women Members of Congress: A Distinctive Role
175hh Congress to Unite Women (Report, 1969)
344b How Powerful Is Powerful? The Women's Movement and the Four Black Congresswomen
344m Congressional Ambitions of Female Political Elites
364g Fashioning of a Congresswoman: One Individual's Experience

CONIAGUI

338a Coniagui Women (Guinea)

CONJUGAL

195d Cupid's Yokes; Or The Binding Forces of Conjugal Life
231r Conjugal Precepts

CONNECTION

3c Problem of Making Connections
3o What Is the Connection Between Men and Women?
98d Language and Revolution: The Franco-American Dis-Connection
218a Class and Sex Connection

CONSCIENCE

357g Poetry and Conscience: Russian Women Poets of the Twentieth Century

CONSCIOUSNESS

77aa Consciousness-Raising Group as a Model for Therapy with Women
85b Phenomenology of Feminist Consciousness
90c Consciousness and Authenticity: Toward a Feminist Aesthetic
126i Feminism and Class Consciousness in the British and American Women's Trade Union Leagues, 1890-1925

141i Feminism and Class Consciousness in the British and American Women's Trade Union Leagues, 1890-1925
141m Effects of Participation in Women's Consciousness-Raising Groups
149t Dangers in the Pro-woman Line and Consciousness-Raising
158ii Phenomenology of Feminist Consciousness
173ii Consciousness-Raising Group as a Model for Therapy with Women
176y Consciousness
194c Class Consciousness Among Working-Class Women in Latin America: Puerto Rico
208m Consciousness-Raising in the Classroom: Some Games, Projects, Discussion-Openers, Etc.
214t Critique of Consciousness and Myth in Levertov, Rich, and Rukeyser
222n Alice Walker: "The Diary of an African Nun" and Du Bois' Double Consciousness
246j Women in History: Public Life and Historical Consciousness
264dd Feminist Consciousness and Black Women
316i Contemporary Feminism, Consciousness-Raising, and Changing Views of the Political
330o Consciousness-Raising Groups as Therapy for Women
334s Feminist Consciousness and the Future of Women

CONSCIOUSNESS RAISING

175dd Consciousness Raising
175ee Consciousness Raising: A Dead End?
342f Group Dynamics and Consciousness Raising

CONSENT

195c Uncivil Liberty: An Essay to Show the Injustice and Impolicy of Ruling Woman Without Her Consent

CONSEQUENCE

18p Genetics of Sex and Its Consequences
155a Psychological Consequences of the Anatomical Distinction Between the Sexes
166vv Women Lawyers and Their Profession: Inconsistency of Social Controls and Their Consequences for Professional Performance
198b Psychical Consequences of the Anatomical Distinction Between the Sexes
199b Prenatal Testosterone in the Nonhuman Primate and Its Consequences for Behavior
200a Psychological Consequences of the Anatomical Distinction between the Sexes
213n Ecological Antècedents and Sex-Role Consequences in Traditional and Modern Israeli Subcultures
233e Psychical Consequences of the Anatomical Distinction between the Sexes
250h Psychological Consequences of the Anatomic Distinction Between the Sexes
268a Psychical Consequences of the Anatomical Distinction Between the Sexes
303n Voices of Consequence: Four Architectural Critics
314ll Consequences of Equal Opportunity for Women
350j Segregation and Its Consequences in India
351f Causes and Consequences of Marital Breakdown

365g Psychological Consequences of Sexual Inequality

CONSERVATIVE

219j Black Women In the Rural South: Conservative and Innovative
246a Radical and Conservative Trends in the Women's Rights Movement

CONSOLATION

157k Consolation of the Wedded

CONSORTING

108cc Consorting with Angels
339e Consorting With Angels

CONSPICUOUS

145a Conspicuous Consumptive: Woman as an Invalid

CONSTANCE

88p Constance Fenimore Woolson: First Novelist of Florida

CONSTANTS

330r Female Role: Constants and Change
364m Cuban Women Today: Constancy and Change

CONSTITUENT

275d More Than a Question of Numbers: Women Deputies in the German National Constituent Assembly and the Reichstag, 1919-1933

CONSTITUTION

2d Abortion and the Constitution: The Cases of the United States and West Germany
180n Constitutionality of Reverse Racial Discrimination
294d From Constitutional Recognition to Public Office
309f Women and the Law: Constitutional Rights and Continuing Inequalities
321b Women, Men, and The Constitution: Key Supreme Court Rulings

CONSTRAINTS

140cc Sex-Role Constraints: The College-Educated Black Woman
174e Affirmative Action: Constraints and Policy Impact
291h Familial Constraints on Women's Work Roles
317d Coming of Age in Kelton: The Constraints on Gender Symbolism in Jewish Ritual

CONSTRUCTION

77f Psychology Constructs the Female
77i Social Construction of the Second Sex

97h Psychology Constructs the Female, or the Fantasy Life of the Male Psychologist
127ee Psychology Constructs the Female
142q Kinder, Kuche, Kirche as Scientific Law: Psychology Constructs the Female
175s Psychology Constructs the Female
186e Psychology Constructs the Female, or the Fantasy Life of the Male Psychologist
186h Social Construction of the Second Sex
203u Psychology Constructs the Female
204m Role of Tests and Their Construction in Producing Apparent Sex-Related Differences
208d Social Construction of the Second Sex
233ee Psychology Constructs the Female, or The Fantasy Life of the Male Psychologist
251s Marriage and the Construction of Reality
252u Marriage and the Construction of Reality
254h Psychology Constructs the Female
284r Social Construction of the Second Sex
363p Psychology Constructs the Female, or the Fantasy Life of the Male Psychologist

CONSUMERISM

35i Monopoly Capital and the Structure of Consumption
193b Food for Thought--Patterns of Production and Consumption in Pira-Parana Society
254bb Consumerism and Women

CONSUMPTIVE

145a Conspicuous Consumptive: Woman as an Invalid

CONTADINE

116a Silent Half: "Le Contadine del Sud" Before The First World War

CONTAGION

42l Prostitution and the Poor in Plymouth and Southampton Under the Contagious Diseases Act
340d Contagion

CONTEMPORARY

11g Media: New Images of Women in Contemporary Society
21k Images of Women in Contemporary Mexican Literature
80e Women in Contemporary French Society: Annotated Bibliography
88j Moon and Contemporary Women's Poetry
116o Maternal Role in the Contemporary Italian-American Family
122i Three Female Playwrights Explore Contemporary Latin American Reality: Myrna Casas, Griselda Gambaro, Luisa Josefina Hernandez
159dd Contemporary Approach to Sex Identity
206n Milieu Development and Male-Female Roles in Contemporary Greece
210j Sexism and the Contemporary Church: When Evasion Becomes Complicity
240l Second-class Citizenship: The Status of Women in Contemporary American Fiction

246f Place of Contemporary Women from a Psychological Perspective
253c Image of Women in Contemporary Literature
256j Impact of Mid-twentieth Century Movement for Sex Equality in Employment on Three Contemporary Economic Institutions
266hh Ancient and Contemporary Perspectives on The Women of Israel
281o Women and Migration in Contemporary West Africa
289c Women's Time: Women in the Light of Contemporary Time-Budget Research
304j Indian Women: An Historical Example and a Contemporary View
316i Contemporary Feminism, Consciousness-Raising, and Changing Views of the Political
325a Women and Law Reform in Contemporary Islam
325ff Women in Contemporary Persian Folktales
336e Early Factory Magazines in New England: The LOWELL OFFERING and its Contemporaries
337m Women in Judaism: From the Reform Movement to Contemporary Jewish Religious Feminism
342d Alienation and the Contemporary American Housewife
361l Women's Prose Style: A Study of Contemporary Authors
372a Contemporary Saudi Woman

CONTENT

176cc Pre-Industrial Patterns in the Colonial Family in America: A Content Analysis of Colonial Magazines
200i Dreams: Sex Differences in Aggressive Content

CONTEXTS

230d !Kung Women: Contrasts in Sexual Egalitarianism in Foraging and Sedentary Contexts
350h Two Contexts of Solidarity

CONTINENTAL

177i Women and the Continental Reformation
315a Land, Family, and Women in Continental Europe, 701-1200

CONTINUING EDUCATION

146n Continuing Education and Second Careers
196cc Continuing Education for Women: Factors Influencing a Return to School and the School Experience

CONTINUITY

132ii Human Continuum
163b Continuity and Change in Opinions about Sex Roles
172h Psychology in Transition: Continuities, Critiques, and Perspectives
202d Discontinuous Labor Force Participation and Its Effect on Women's Market Earnings
206f American Core Culture: Changes and Continuities
337a Women's Leadership in the Jewish and Christian Traditions: Continuity and Change

CONTRACEPTION

see also BIRTH CONTROL; I.U.D.; PILL

155t Contraception and Pregnancy: Experience of Young Unmarried Women in the United States
162a Origins of Contraception in France
191e Dangers of Oral Contraception
211l Historical Understanding of Contraception

CONTRACEPTIVE

62a What Is a Contraceptive Culture?
62b Impact of Contraceptive Culture
173u Contraceptives for Males
176ll Predictive Study of Psychological and Psychosomatic Responses to Oral Contraceptives
250aa Hormonal Interaction, Menstruation, and the Oral Contraceptives
250dd Effects of Oral Contraceptives on Affective Fluctuations Associated with the Menstrual Cycle
266v Effect of Contraceptive Pills on Sexual Activity in the Luteal Phase of the Human Menstrual Cycle
296n Effects of Oral Contraceptives on Affective Fluctuations Associated with the Menstrual Cycle

CONTRACT

4s W.E.A.L. and Contract Compliance
9e Marriage Contract

CONTRADICTION

39g Cultural Contradictions and Sex Roles: The Masculine Case
145d Contradictions in Ladies' Education
176i Cultural Contradictions and Sex Roles
249p Mediation of Contradiction: Why Mbum Women Do Not Eat Chicken
334i Private Woman, Public Woman: The Contradictions of Charlotte Perkins Gilman
369n Contradictions

CONTRASTS

230d !Kung Women: Contrasts in Sexual Egalitarianism in Foraging and Sedentary Contexts

CONTRIBUTION

251ff Women's Contribution to Family Income
252x Working Wives: Their Contribution to Family Income
323c Contribution of the Women's Labour League to the Winning of the Franchise

CONTROL

21e Essential Emancipation: The Control of Reproduction
42h Family Limitation, Sexual Control, and Domestic Feminism in Victorian America

94j Gusii Sex Offenses: A Study in Social Control
155p Gusii Sex Offenses: A Study in Social Control
166vv Women Lawyers and Their Profession: Inconsistency of Social Controls and Their Consequences for Professional Performance
173x Sex Preferences, Sex Control, and the Status of Women
191d Birth Controllers
193d Sex, Age and Social Control in Mobs of the Darwin Hinterland
199a Sexual Behavior Differentiation: Prenatal Hormonal and Environmental Control
227b Control of Resources
227g Ideology and Control
281h Biological Events and Cultural Control
314aa Differential Recruitment and Control: The Sex Structuring of Organizations
348c Doctors and Their Patients: The Social Control of Women in General Practice
360k Family Limitation, Sexual Control, and Domestic Feminism in Victorian America

CONTROVERSY

11a Out of the Past and Present Controversies: Challenges for the Future
178g Divorce as a Moral Issue: A Hundred Years of Controversy
264e Abortion: The Controversial Choice

CONVENTION

9c Seneca Falls Convention: Declaration
9d Speech: National Women's Rights Convention of 1855
9g Letters to Woman's Convention, 1851
107l Conventional Origin of Female Virtues
163g Societal Punishment and Aspects of Female Political Participation: 1972 National Convention Delegates

CONVENTS

126o Women in Convents: Their Economic and Social Role in Colonial Mexico

CONVERGENCES

267e Convergences between East and West: Tradition and Modernity in Sex Roles in Sweden, Finland, and the Soviet Union

CONVERSATION

60i Conversations
73r Conversation with Alice Rossi
219d Male-Female Conversational Interaction Cues: Using Data From Dialect Surveys
219p Effects of the Ethnicity of the Interviewer on Conversation: A Study of Chicana Women
222r Conversational Vision
288y Conversation
364l Conversation with Audrey Topping: Chinese Women Today
369s Notes from a Conversation on Art, Feminism, and Work

CONVERT

215f Susanna Goudin Cardon: An Italian Convert to Mormonism

CONVIVIAL

317i Convivial Sisterhood: Spirit Mediumship and Client-Core Network among Black South African Women

CONVOLUTIONS

184d Petrarch's Laura: The Convolutions of a Humanistic Mind

COOBOO

273f The Cooboo

COOK

128t Fannie Farmer and Her Cook Book
215k Two Miss Cooks: Pioneer Professionals for Utah's Schools
360q Cookbooks and Law Books: The Hidden History of Career Women in Twentieth-Century America

COOPER

7g Anna J. Cooper: A Voice for Black Women
104e A.A. Cooper
110j Women of Cooper's "Leatherstocking Tales"

COOPERATION

213l Mechanistic Cooperation and Sexual Equality among the Western Bontoc
249e Strategies, Cooperation, and Conflict Among Women in Domestic Groups
323f Women and Cooperation

COPYING

250u Pattern Copying Under Three Conditions of an Expanded Spatial Field

CORAGE

17d "Slydynge of Corage": Chaucer's Criseyde as Feminist and Victim

CORD

117y Mothers and Daughters in American Jewish Literature: The Rotted Cord

CORE

206f American Core Culture: Changes and Continuities

CORN

339k The Corn is Green

CORNELL

272g Coeducation and the Development of Leadership Skills in Women: Historical Perspectives from Cornell University, 1868-1900

CORNER

271g View From the Doll Corner

CORPORATIONS

see also BUSINESS; MANAGEMENT

191f Case of Corporate Malpractice and the Dalkon Shield
304a Women, the Family and Corporate Capitalism
314w Woman Is Not a Girl and Other Lessons in Corporate Speech
336c Corporations and Operatives, Being an Exposition of the Condition of Factory Operatives...

CORPUS

121e Indian Nuns of Mexico City's Monasterio of Corpus Christi, 1724-1821

CORRECTIONAL

51bb Women and the Correctional Process
75i Ex-Offender Evaluates Correctional Programming for Women

CORREGIDORA

222aa Gayl Jones Takes a Look at "Corregidora"--An Interview

CORRELATES

174i Incidence and Correlates of Second Generation Discrimination
243e Prejudice Toward Women: Some Personality Correlates

CORRIDOR

119b The Long Corridor of Time

CORRUPTION

16f Corruption
132i Power Corrupts

CORSET

247g Corset as Erotic Alchemy: From Rococo Galanterie to Montaut's Physiologies

CORTICAL

204g Cognitive Abilities and Sex-Related Variations in the Maturation of Cerebral Cortical Functions

COST

40g Estimating Cost Equations for Day Care
40h Cost of Compliance with Federal Day Care Standards in Seattle and Denver
210i Women and Missions: The Cost of Liberation

COSTA RICAN

316p Changing the Political Role of Women: A Costa Rican Case Study

COSTUME

257e Bloomer Costume
274e Native Costumes of the Oberwallis: Tourist Gimmick or Tradition?

COTTON

52i Cotton Mather's "Wonders of the Invisible World": Some Metamorphoses of Salem Witchcraft
92d Women Cotton Workers and the Suffrage Campaign: The Radical Suffragists in Lancashire, 1893-1914
95n Cotton Candy

COUNSELING

13u Realistic Counseling for High-School Girls
45d Counseling Implications of Black Women's Market Position, Aspirations and Expectancies
102j Vocational Counselling
146c Psychotherapy and Counseling
196q Counselor Bias and the Female Occupational Role
196r Female-Role Perception as a Factor in Counseling
196s Counselors View Women and Work: Accuracy of Information
196t Counselors' Attitudes Toward Women and Work
208q Realistic Counseling for High School Girls
211d Decisions about Reproduction: Genetic Counseling
252bb Counselor Bias and the Female Occupational Role

COUNTER-IRRITANT

261b Woman's Wrongs: A Counter-Irritant

COUNTER-REFORMATION

337e Dispute over an Active Apostolate for Women During the Counter-Reformation

COUNTESS

79k Countess of Lincoln's Nurserie

214d Anne Finch, Countess of Winchilsea: An Augustan Woman Poet

COUNTRY

91h Fertility and Women's Employment in the Socialist Countries of Eastern Europe
163d Working-Class Women's Political Participation: Its Potential in Developed Countries
183g Role of Women in Underdeveloped Countries: Some Sociological Issues Concerning Conflict and Peace
277z A Country Love Story
308j Women in the Countryside of China
352l Sexual Equality in the Labour Market: Some Experiences and Views of the Nordic Countries

COUNTS

121d Women in a Noble Family: The Mexican Counts of Regla, 1750-1830
344j Economic Strength Is What Counts
369q What Counts as Work?

COUP

288ff Coup pour coup: Radical French Cinema

COUP D'ETAT

194n Chile: The Feminine Version of the Coup d'Etat

COUPLES

see also MARRIAGE; HUSBAND; WIFE; FAMILY; SEX ROLE

8e Surviving Gay Coupledom
8v Gay Couples and Straight Law
166jj Career Patterns of Married Couples
281v Sexuality and Birth Control Decisions among Lebanese Couples
361a What Do Couples Talk About When They're Alone?
371g Job-Sharing Couples

COURAGE

215i Bathsheba Bigler Smith: Woman of Faith and Courage

COURBET

247e Courbet's "Baigneuses" and the Rhetorical Feminine Image

COURSE

36c Identity and Expression: A Writing Course for Women

COURT

see also LAW; LEGALIZATION; SUPREME COURT; case names

23b Women, Learning, and Power: Eleonora of Aragon and the Court of Ferrara
51v Women in Court
64e Court Precedents
174h Sex and the Burger Court: Recent Judicial Policy Making toward Women
207d Sexism in the Language of Legislatures and Courts
284l Women's Job Rights Gain in Federal Court Rulings
321a Female in the Trial Court
321c Burger Court and Women's Rights, 1971-1977
321e Women in Court Administration
321g Changes in Domestic Relations Court
321h Women in the Criminal Court
352e Women Workers and the Courts
358l Full Court Press for Women in Athletics
368h Sisterhood in the Courtroom: Sex of Judge and Defendent in Criminal Case Disposition

COURTESAN

231u Initiation of a Courtesan

COURTESY

361d Historical Survey of Women's Language: From Medieval Courtesy Books to Seventeen Magazine

COURTING

153l The Courting of Sister Wisby
273a The Courting of Sister Wisby

COURTLY LOVE

19e Pedestal and the Stake: Courtly Love and Witchcraft
278g Worship of Women in Courtly Love and Rock and Roll

COUVERT

334f Equality or Submersion? Feme (sic) Couvert Status in Early Pennsylvania

COVENANT

263o Bringing a Daughter into the Covenant

COVER

105e Imagery and Ideology: The Cover Photographs of Traditional Women's Magazines

COVERT

120g Sex, Covert Prestige, and Linguistic Change in the Urban British English of Norwich
196dd Overt and Covert Forms of Discrimination Against Academic Women

CRAFT

116i Immigrants and Craft Arts: Scuola d'Industrie Italiane

CRAN

165g M. Cran

CRANDALL

128c Prudence Crandall: Champion of Negro Education

CRAZY

73p Men Drive Women Crazy

CREATION

14f Women and the Creation of Culture
41j Creating a Feminist Alliance: Sisterhood and Class Conflict in the New York Women's Trade Union League, 1903- 1914
106b Three Women: Creators of Change
107a Creation and Fall of Man and Woman
122q Short Stories of Lydia Cabrera: Transpositions or Creations?
140ee Promoting Creative Risk-Taking in Women
164h Problems of Creative Women
176n Women Mathematicians and the Creative Personality
180k Erosion of Legal Principles in the Creation of Legal Policies
214a Gender, Creativity, and the Woman Poet
222bb Creative Vision
254s Women and Creativity: The Demise of the Dancing Dog
256k Women in the Arts: Insights to the Cultural Impact of Women's Role in the Creative Arts
301f Creating Opportunities for Women in Science
330n Creative Exits: Fight-Therapy for Divorcees
375f Creating Oneself from Scratch

CREDIT

59j Sex Discrimination in Credit: The Backlash of Economic Dependency
174f Discrimination and the Law: The Equal Credit Opportunity Act
344e Lobbying for Equal Credit

CREEK

41h Imperfect Unions: Class and Gender in Cripple Creek, 1894- 1904

CRETE

19b Women in Transition: Crete and Sumer

CRIB

112i Night Pieces for a Child: The Crib

CRIME

see also PAROLE; PRISONER; OFFENDER; various types of crime

1a Foeticide, or Criminal Abortion
1c Criminal Abortion
1e Detection of Criminal Abortion
51b Criminals and Prostitutes
51c Criminality of Women
51e Masked Character of Female Crime
51g Etiology of Female Crime
51k Crimes of Violence by Women
51o Criminality in the Workplace: A Comparison of Male and Female Offenders
51p "Crime as Business" and the Female Offender
51q Women Criminals in Progressive New York
51y Sex Discrimination in the Criminal Law
51gg Women and Crime: Does the American Experience Generalize?
51hh Expansion and Distribution of Crime
51ii Interaction Between Women's Emancipation and Female Criminality: A Cross-Cultural Perspective
75a Female Offender as an Object of Criminological Research
77u Rape: The All-American Crime
85s Rape: The All-American Crime
94b Rape: The All-American Crime
94i Michigan's Criminal Sexual Assault Law
99f Crime and the Female Offender
103h A Midsummer Night's Crime
173ff Nature of Female Criminality
262n Woman in Philanthropy--Care of the Criminal
265c Rape: The All-American Crime
321h Women in the Criminal Court
368h Sisterhood in the Courtroom: Sex of Judge and Defendent in Criminal Case Disposition

CRIPPLE

41h Imperfect Unions: Class and Gender in Cripple Creek, 1894- 1904

CRISEYDE

17d "Slydynge of Corage": Chaucer's Criseyde as Feminist and Victim

CRISIS

94p Crisis Intervention with Victims of Rape
129h Coming Out of the Closet: Marriage and Other Crises of Middle Age
206c Sexual Identity Crises in the Life Cycle
230m Life Crisis as a Clue to Social Function: The Case of Italy
278s Crisis in Coeducation, 1890-1920
284v Working Mother's Crises
297c African Women: Identity Crisis? Some Observations on Education and the Changing Role of Women in Sierra Leone and Zaire
331j Crisis Perspective on Divorce and Role Change
344r Crisis Perspective on Emerging Health Roles: A Paradigm for the Entry of Women into New Occupational Roles

CRITICISM

see also FEMINIST CRITICISM

17a Female Criticism
17b Silent Woman: Towards a Feminist Critique
17n Old Critics and New: The Treatment of Chopin's "The Awakening"
21i New Feminist Criticisms: Exploring the History of the New Space
36e Dwelling in Decencies: Radical Criticism and the Feminist Perspective
36h Emily Bronte in the Hands of Male Critics
70a Husband Provider Role: A Critical Appraisal
84g Women and Production: A Critical Analysis of Some Sociological Theories of Women's Work
88a Feminism as a Criterion of the Literary Critic
88c Dwelling in Decencies: Radical Criticism and the Feminist Perspective
88d Defining a "Feminist Literary Criticism"
88g Who Buried H.D.? A Poet, Her Critics, and Her Place in "The Literary Tradition"
88w Anais Nin: A Critical Evaluation
90a American Feminist Literary Criticism: A Bibliographical Introduction
90b Subjectives: A Theory of the Critical Process
90d Virginia Woolf's Criticism: A Polemical Preface
90f Afterword: Critical Re-Vision
97g Historical and Critical Essay for Black Women
110u Other Criticism: Feminism vs. Formalism
110w Feminist Style Criticism
122c Clorinda Matto de Turner and Mercedes Cabello de Carbonera: Societal Criticism and Morality
126a Woman in Society: A Critique of Frederick Engels
126b Mary Beard's "Woman As Force in History": A Critique
143b Home: A Critical Problem for Changing Sex Roles
143k Architecture: Toward a Feminist Critique
157j Monogamy: A Critique
172h Psychology in Transition: Continuities, Critiques, and Perspectives
176kk Behavior Therapy Approaches to Modification of Sexual Preferences: Biological Perspective and Critique
178h Flapper and Her Critics
204c Spatial Ability: A Critical Review of the Sex-Linked Major Gene Hypothesis
212j Feminist Film Criticism: Theory and Practice
214l Afro-American Women Poets: A Bio-Critical Survey
214t Critique of Consciousness and Myth in Levertov, Rich, and Rukeyser
258b Feminist Theology as a Critical Theory of Liberation
260c Critique of Mill on Women
293e Critical Analysis of Latin American Programs to Integrate Women in Development
303n Voices of Consequence: Four Architectural Critics
316m Modernization Theory and Sex Roles in Critical Perspective: The Case of the Soviet Union
359m Kate Millett and the Critics
363l Phallic Criticism
368d Sociology of Birth: A Critical Assessment of Theory and Research

CROCHERON

215x Augusta Joyce Crocheron: A Representative Woman

CROCKER

142h Subversion of Betty Crocker

CROSS

262r Woman in Philanthropy--Work of the Red Cross Society

CROSS CULTURAL

18l Cross-Cultural Perspectives on Becoming Female
20e Birth Rituals in Cross-Cultural Perspective: Some Practical Applications
20h Defining Marriage Cross-Culturally
20r Three Styles of Domestic Authority: A Cross-Cultural Study
22d Conceptions of Sex Role: Some Cross-Cultural and Longitudinal Perspectives
22n Cross-Cultural Analysis of Sex Differences in the Behavior of Children Aged Three Through Eleven
51ii Interaction Between Women's Emancipation and Female Criminality: A Cross-Cultural Perspective
67d Sex Differences in Cross-Cultural Perspective
71c Passive Female and Social Change: A Cross-Cultural Comparison of Women's Magazine Fiction
77c Cross-Cultural Analysis of Sex Differences in the Behavior of Children Aged Three Through Eleven
100f Gender Roles from a Cross-Cultural Perspective
140r Status of Women: Partial Summary of a Cross-Cultural Survey
141y Cross-Cultural Study of the Relative Status of Women
173y Childbirth in Crosscultural Perspective
173ll Cross-Cultural Investigation of Behavioral Changes at Menopause
176dd Cross-Cultural Survey of Some Sex Differences in Socialization
193m Cross-Cultural Survey of Some Sex Differences in Socialization
250p Woman's Role in Cross-Cultural Perspective
254k Being and Doing: A Cross-Cultural Examination of the Socialization of Males and Females
258a Current Status of Women Cross-Culturally: Changes and Persisting Barriers
267d Cross-cultural Examination of Women's Marital, Educational and Occupational Options
368e Cross-Cultural Investigation of Behavioral Changes at Menopause

CROW

175r Jane Crow and the Law

CRUCIBLE

25e Crucible of Identity: The Negro Lower-Class Family

CRUEL

33h Cruel and Barbarous Treatment

363h Cruel and Barbarous Treatment

CRULAI

162c Population of Crulai, a Norman Parish

CRYPTOGRAM

17p "A Farewell to Arms": Ernest Hemingway's "Resentful Cryptogram"

CRYPTORCHIDISM

199o Cryptorchidism, Development of Gender Identity, and Sex Behavior

CRYSTAL

103b Christabel's Crystal

CUBA

35l Women and Work in Cuba
43h Women in Cuba: The Revolution Within the Revolution
71k Modernizing Women for a Modern Society: The Cuban Case
71l Honor, Shame, and Women's Liberation in Cuba: Views of Working-Class Emigre Men
89pp Cuban Family Code
127mm Cuban Women
149m Leads on Old Questions from a New Revolution: Notes on Cuban Women, 1969
349h Revolution and Conciencia: Women in Cuba
364m Cuban Women Today: Constancy and Change
372j Uses of Traditional Concepts in the Development of New Urban Roles: Cuban Women in the United States

CUENCA

315c Women in Reconquest Castile: The Fueros of Sepulveda and Cuenca

CUES

22s Androgynous Themes Written to Sentence Cues by Sixth-, Eighth-, and Tenth-Grade Students
120j Cues to the Identification of Sex in Children's Speech
219d Male-Female Conversational Interaction Cues: Using Data From Dialect Surveys

CULT

9hh Cult of True Womanhood
151f Cult of True Womanhood: 1820-1860
292m Cult of True Womanhood, 1820-1860
360i Cult of True Womanhood, 1820-1860

CULTURE

see also SOCIETY; SOCIALIZATION; SOCIAL

14f Women and the Creation of Culture
20o Feminine Factor in Cultural History
20t American Women in Politics: Culture, Structure, and Ideology
20z Changing Roles of Women in Two African Muslim Cultures
39g Cultural Contradictions and Sex Roles: The Masculine Case
43e Chinese Women: The Relative Influences of Ideological Revolution, Economic Growth, and Cultural Change
56e Sex Differences and Cultural Institutions
62a What Is a Contraceptive Culture?
62b Impact of Contraceptive Culture
105a Dynamics of Cultural Resistance
114d Cultural and Religious Influences
125b Domestic Problem: Work and Culture in the Household
126j Latina Liberation: Tradition, Ideology, and Social Change in Iberian and Latin American Cultures
126l Politics of Cultural Liberation: Male-Female Relations in Algeria
141h Feminist Culture from 1790 to 1850: A Trans-Atlantic Community
141w STATUS OF WOMEN IN THIS AND OTHER CULTURES: Introduction
141aa Biological and Cultural Determinants of the Division of Labor by Sex
143p Los Angeles Women's Building: A Public Center for Woman's Culture
149a Status of Women in Modern Patterns of Culture
149d Sex Differences: Biological, Cultural, Societal Implications
156j Problems and Priorities of Poor, Culturally Different Parents
156l Sex Role and Human Culture
170f Cultural Pressures in the Psychology of Women
170h Masculine and Feminine: Some Biological and Cultural Aspects
176i Cultural Contradictions and Sex Roles
177a Women and Religion: Psychological and Cultural Implications
178i Ume Tsuda and Motoko Hani: Echoes of American Cultural Feminism in Japan
196e Adolescent Culture
206f American Core Culture: Changes and Continuities
210d Religious Socialization of Women Within U.S. Subcultures
213n Ecological Antecedents and Sex-Role Consequences in Traditional and Modern Israeli Subcultures
232h Woman's Share in Primitive Culture
249a Woman, Culture, and Society: A Theoretical Overview
249c Is Female to Male as Nature Is to Culture?
252a Family and Cultural Change
254r Women in Other Cultures
256k Women in the Arts: Insights to the Cultural Impact of Women's Role in the Creative Arts
263v Witchcraft and Women's Culture
264d Rape Culture
268q Role of Women in This Culture
269e Cultural Production of Childbirth
275a Impact of German Thought and Culture on Madame de Stael's Thinking about Women
276e Sex, Gender, and American Culture
280a Women in the American Culture
280e Cultural Dilemma
281h Biological Events and Cultural Control
284u Female Biology in a Male Culture
285m Male and Female in Tokelau Culture
294a Status of Women in Modern Patterns of Culture
296w Cultural Anthropologist's Approach to Maternal Deprivation

297b Role of Women in the Development of Culture in Nigeria
316r Politics of Cultural Liberation
322k Field Work in Five Cultures
330c Cultural Values, Female Role Expectancies and Therapeutic Goals: Research and Interpretation
331b Sexual Inequality, Cultural Norms, and Wife-Beating
360a American Women and Domestic Culture: An Approach to Women's History
360h Cultural Hybrid in the Slums: The College Woman and the Settlement House, 1889-1894
364f Myths and Stereotypes: My Challenge to Black Women Cultural Workers

CUNARD

5m Lady Cunard

CUP

113f A Cup of Tea

CUPID

195d Cupid's Yokes; Or The Binding Forces of Conjugal Life

CURIOUS

212s "A Very Curious Girl"

CURRICULUM

13bb Women and the Literary Curriculum
36b Women and the Literary Curriculum
271r Woman's Place Is in the Curriculum

CURSE

343a Curse of Eve--Or, What I Learned in School (Women and Literature)

CUSTODY

315g Widow and Ward: The Feudal Law of Child Custody in Medieval England

CUSTOMS

20aa Women and Social Customs within the Family: A Case Study of Attitudes in Kerala, India
221b Customs Connected with Birth and the Rearing of Children

CUTTING

3i Cutting Loose
9ss Cutting Loose
68g "Press Cuttings": G.B.S. and Women's Suffrage
111f Cutting the Jewish Bride's Hair
112f Cutting the Jewish Bride's Hair
127c Cutting Loose

CYCLE

20f Relevance of Nourishment to the Reproductive Cycle of the Female in India
22i Men's Cycles
42b Puberty to Menopause: The Cycle of Femininity in Nineteenth-Century America
171j Adult Life Cycles: Changing Roles and Changing Hormones
171l Social Psychological Perspective on the Menstrual Cycle
171m Body Time and Social Time: Mood Patterns by Menstrual Cycle Phase and Day of Week
199w Reproductive Hormones, Moods, and the Menstrual Cycle
202m Vicious Cycle of Welfare: Problems of the Female-Headed Household in N.Y.C.
204j Menstrual Cycle and Sex-Related Differences in Cognitive Variability
206c Sexual Identity Crises in the Life Cycle
250cc Patterns of Affective Fluctuation in the Menstrual Cycle
250dd Effects of Oral Contraceptives on Affective Fluctuations Associated with the Menstrual Cycle
250gg Case for Human Cycles
251z Sex Bias and Cyclical Unemployment
252ee Sex Bias and Cyclical Unemployment
266v Effect of Contraceptive Pills on Sexual Activity in the Luteal Phase of the Human Menstrual Cycle
287b Family and Work: The Social Life Cycle of Women
296i Clitoral Eroticism and the Sexual Response Cycle in Human Females
296m Feminine Fertility Cycles
296n Effects of Oral Contraceptives on Affective Fluctuations Associated with the Menstrual Cycle

CYNIC

231q The Cynic Should Not Marry

CYNTHIA

88l Poetry of Cynthia MacDonald

CZARINA

288p Alice Guy Blache: Czarina of the Silent Screen

CZECHOSLOVAK

54e Changes in Czechoslovak Marital Fertility
70d Problems Facing Czechoslovak Women Today

D.G.W.S.

358f Relationship of D.G.W.S. to A.I.A.W.

DADDY

3q Waiting for Daddy

DAEMONOLOGIE

52g King James's "Daemonologie": Witchcraft and Kingship

DAEMONUM

52c Johann Weyer's "De Praetigiis Daemonum": Unsystematic Psychopathology

DAILY

74q Woman and Her Mind: The Story of Daily Life

DAISY

50n Daisy Bell

DAKAR

338f Women of Dakar and the Surrounding Urban Area

DALEY

316f Role and Status of Women in the Daley Organization

DALKON SHIELD

191f Case of Corporate Malpractice and the Dalkon Shield

DALLOWAY

17j War and Roses: The Politics of "Mrs. Dalloway"

DALTON

215g Lucinda Lee Dalton: A Tough Kind of Testimony

DAME

111w La Belle Dame sans Merci
112n La Belle Dame sans Merci
212c Image of Woman as Image: The Optical Politics of Dames
223b From Dame to Woman: W.S. Gilbert and Theatrical Transvestism

DAMNATION

278u Damnation and Stereotyping in Joke Telling

DANCE

95f Wedding Dance
111gg Belly Dancer
142a Demise of the Dancing Dog
220r And the Soul Shall Dance
254s Women and Creativity: The Demise of the Dancing Dog
288b Dorothy Arzner's "Dance, Girl, Dance"

DANFORTH

2i APPENDIX: Comments on the 1976 Supreme Court Decisions: "Planned Parenthood v. Danforth" and "Bellotti v. Baird"

DANGER

107u Woman as Dangerous Plaything
149t Dangers in the Pro-woman Line and Consciousness-Raising
191e Dangers of Oral Contraception
191k Dangers of Sex Hormones
298f The Power and the Danger

DANIEL

93a Daniel Deleon and the Woman Question
255a Feminism of Daniel Defoe

DANIELS

288c Divided Woman: Bree Daniels in "Klute"

DARE

88i "I Dare to Live": The Transforming Art of Anne Sexton

DARK

110d Servility of Dependence: The Dark Lady in Trollop
298h The Dark Unfathomed Caves

DARLING

111b The Darling
112b The Darling
273m Miss MacIntosh, My Darling (selection)
279h The Darling

DARWIN

173b Functionalism, Darwinism, and the Psychology of Women
193d Sex, Age and Social Control in Mobs of the Darwin Hinterland

DATES

471 APPENDIX: Chronology of Important Dates

DATING

200o Sex Differences in Dating Aspirations and Satisfaction with Computer-Selected Partners
264g Power in Dating Relationships

DAUGHTER

9nn Are You Hurting Your Daughter Without Knowing It?
18e Mothers and Daughters

88q Heroine as Her Author's Daughter
96w Mother's Daughter
98l Separation and Survival: Mothers, Daughters, Sisters: The Women's Experimental Theatre
111z Rappaccini's Daughter
112q Rappaccini's Daughter
116l Italian American Women and Their Daughters in Rhode Island: The Adolescence of Two Generations, 1900-1950
116m Italian Mothers, American Daughters: Changes in Work and Family Roles
117c Birth of a Daughter
117y Mothers and Daughters in American Jewish Literature: The Rotted Cord
128i Four Sisters: Daughters of Joseph La Flesche
153c The African Mother at Her Daughter's Grave
155l Mothers and Daughters: Perceived and Real Differences in Sexual Values
166g Farmer's Daughter Effect: The Case of the Negro Female Professional
226c Mother's Daughter
250n Parents' Differential Reactions to Sons and Daughters
263o Bringing a Daughter into the Covenant
270h Daughters of the Lakes and Rivers: Colonization and the Land Rights of Luo Women
278j Heroine as Her Author's Daughter
279z The Fathers' Daughters
283g Image of Woman in Old Buddhist Literature: The Daughters of Mara
292c Ornaments for the Daughters of Zion
322a Kapluna Daughter

DAVENPORT

165e N. Davenport

DAVID

79i The Psalmes of David

DAWN

340l False Dawn

DAY

24dd The Day Before the Revolution
33e The Child's Day
113d The Fifth Great Day of God
113l A Day in the Life of a Smiling Woman
134g The Day Before the Revolution
171m Body Time and Social Time: Mood Patterns by Menstrual Cycle Phase and Day of Week
173aa Maternal Attachment: Importance of the First Post-Partum Days
240j They Shall Have Faces, Minds, and (One Day) Flesh: Women in Late Nineteenth-century and Early Twentieth-century American Literature
288m Actress Archetypes in the 1950s: Doris Day, Marilyn Monroe, Elizabeth Taylor, Audrey Hepburn
371f Husbands at Home: Organization of the Husband's Household Day
375n Opening Nights: The Opening Days

DAY CARE

see also CHILD CARE

40e Quality of Day Care: Can It Be Measured
40g Estimating Cost Equations for Day Care
40h Cost of Compliance with Federal Day Care Standards in Seattle and Denver
45g Policy Issues on Day Care: The Special Needs of Black Working Women
74p Politics of Day Care
97l Project Company Day-Care
127n Day Care
135c Effects of Day Care on Young Children
233nn Day Care
264i History and Development of Day Care in the U.S.
265f History and Development of Day Care in the U.S.
371h Directions for Day Care

DAYDREAMS

279w Daydreams of a Drunk Woman

DEAD

73o Seven Deadly Half-Truths About Women
102d The Excursion of the Dead Girls
175ee Consciousness Raising: A Dead End?

DEALINGS

314r Everyday Dealings with Women

DEATH

8u Life and Death of a Gay Prisoner
79n Upon the much lamented death of the Right Honourable the Lady Elizabeth Langham
94e Race, Rape, and the Death Penalty
103g Death on the Air
111d Death in the Woods
112e Death in the Woods
122p Love and Death: The Thematic Journey of Julia de Burgos
244h Sex and Death in Victorian England: An Examination of Age- and Sex-Specific Death Rates, 1840-1910
263c After the Death of God the Father
266jj Life and Death of Ms. Solomon Grundy
278aa Mother, Maiden, and the Marriage of Death: Women Writers and an Ancient Myth

DEBATE

37f Analysis of the Debate on Sex Roles
98i For the Etruscans: Sexual Difference and Artistic Production--The Debate Over a Female Aesthetic
180a Discrimination in Higher Education: A Debate on Faculty Employment
223g Debate over Women : Ruskin vs. Mill

318f Bolshevik Alternatives and the Soviet Family: The 1926 Marriage Law Debate
318p Women and Women's Issues in Soviet Policy Debates

DEBUT

277b Debut

DECADE

284q Decade of Widening Horizons

DECADENCE

283l Is Sexism a Sign of Decadence in Religion?

DECAY

97i American Family: Decay and Rebirth

DECENCIES

36e Dwelling in Decencies: Radical Criticism and the Feminist Perspective
88c Dwelling in Decencies: Radical Criticism and the Feminist Perspective

DECEPTIVE

212o Leni Riefenstahl: The Deceptive Myth

DECISION

2b Membership Decisions and the Limits of Moral Obligation
2c Abortion Decisions: Judicial Review and Public Opinion
2i APPENDIX: Comments on the 1976 Supreme Court Decisions: "Planned Parenthood v. Danforth" and "Bellotti v. Baird"
39h Swinging: A Study of Decision Making in Marriage
140y Family Planning, Decision Making: Attitudes and Intentions of Mothers and Fathers
141s Social Psychology of the "Decision" to Have or Not Have Children
157t Abortion and a Woman's Right to Decide
211d Decisions about Reproduction: Genetic Counseling
281v Sexuality and Birth Control Decisions among Lebanese Couples
282t Abortion and a Woman's Right to Decide
316h Ideology and the Law: Sexism and Supreme Court Decisions
325cc Women, Sufism, and Decision-Making in Moroccan Islam
351a Young Women's Decisions to Attend College: Desires, Expectations and Realizations

DECLARATION

9c Seneca Falls Convention: Declaration
107dd Declaration of Women's Rights
170q Phobias after Marriage: Women's Declaration of Dependence
257c Declaration of Sentiments, Resolutions, Seneca Falls
257k Declaration of Principles

284n U.N. Declaration on Women's Rights

DECLINE

149j Declining Status of Women: Popular Myths and the Failure of Functionalist Thought
151p Decline and Fall of the Double Standard
278w Future of Parenthood: Implications of Declining Fertility
367i Fertility Declines in Tunisia: Factors Affecting Recent Trends

DEDE

288v Dede Allen

DEDICATION

79u Prefaces and Dedications
154e Premiss of Dedication: Notes towards an Ethnography of Diplomats' Wives

DEEP

222q Bridges and Deep Water

DEERSLAYER

214i Emily Dickinson and the Deerslayer: The Dilemma of the Woman Poet in America

DEFEAT

21r Women and Girls in the Public Schools: Defeat or Liberation?

DEFENSE

8c With All Due Respect: In Defense of All Lesbian Lifestyles
86l In Defense of Engels on the Matriarchy
157n In Defense of Promiscuity
157s Defense of Abortion
158dd Defense of Abortion
282p In Defense of Preferential Hiring
368h Sisterhood in the Courtroom: Sex of Judge and Defendent in Criminal Case Disposition

DEFERENCE

55g Husbands and Wives: The Dynamics of the Deferential Dialectic
166m Social Influence and the Social-Psychological Function of Deference: A Study of Psychiatric Nursing

DEFINITION

20h Defining Marriage Cross-Culturally
83d Defining a "Feminist Literary Criticism"
88t Definition of Literary Feminism
92f Male Appendage: Legal Definitions of Women

116n Metonymic Definition of the Female and the Concept of Honour Among Italian Immigrant Families in Toronto
117e Single and Jewish: Toward a New Definition of Completeness
173ee Male Sex Role: Definitions, Problems, and Sources of Change
281b Definitions of Women and Development: An African Perspective
285j Woman-Marriage, With Special Reference to the Lovedu--Its Significance for the Definition of Marriage

DEFLATED

96y Deflated Rebel
226e Deflated Rebel

DEFOE

255a Feminism of Daniel Defoe

DEFUNIS

180l Harvard College Amicus Curiae, DeFunis v. Odegaard, Supreme Court of the U.S., 1973
180m DeFunis v. Odegaard, Dissenting Opinion

DEGRADATION

363a Observations on the State of Degradation to Which Woman Is Reduced by Various Causes

DEGREE

244f Women and Degrees at Cambridge University, 1862-1897
256o Degree in Enlightenment: When a Woman's Education Will No Longer Be an Academic Question

DELEGATES

163g Societal Punishment and Aspects of Female Political Participation: 1972 National Convention Delegates

DELEON

93a Daniel Deleon and the Woman Question

DELHI

114t Girl Students: Between School and Marriage--a Delhi Sample

DELICACY

178e Man-Midwifery and the Delicacy of the Sexes

DELILAH

277w Samson and Delilah

DELINQUENCY

18h Changing Nature of Female Delinquency
51d Five Hundred Delinquent Women
51f Sex Factor: Female Delinquency
75h Remedies for Wrongs: Updating Programs for Delinquent Girls
348f Sexist Assumptions and Female Delinquency

DELIVERY

296t Delivery

DELTA

47j "Delta Wedding" as Region and Symbol

DEMAND

9m Demand for Party Recognition
47e Mary McCarthy: Society's Demands
174q Abortion in Israel: Social Demands and Political Responses
251y Supply and Demand for Women Workers
252aa Supply and Demand for Women Workers
267o Implied Demand Character of the Wife's Future and Role Innovation: Patterns of Achievement Orientation Among College Women

DEMISE

142a Demise of the Dancing Dog
210g Theology After the Demise of God the Father: A Call for the Castration of Sexist Religion
254s Women and Creativity: The Demise of the Dancing Dog
283a Theology After the Demise of God the Father: A Call for the Castration of Sexist Religion
349f Communist Feminism: Its Synthesis and Demise

DEMOCRATIC

206k Male and Female in the German Democratic Republic

DEMOGRAPHY

see also HOUSEHOLD; FERTILITY; POPULATION

13jj Discrimination and Demography Restrict Opportunities for Academic Women
39l Demographic Influence on Female Employment and the Status of Women
54h Sociological and Demographic Aspects of the Changing Status of Migrant Women in Europe
54i Report of the Symposium on Demographic Aspects of the Changing Status of Women in Europe
61a Demographic and Social Factors in Women's Work Lives
114k Demographic Profile of Indian Women
121f Feminine Orders in Colonial Bahia, Brazil: Economic, Social, and Demographic Implications, 1677-1800
141r Son Preference in Taiwan: Verbal Preference and Demographic Behavior

294b Demographic Change and the Roles and Status of Women
303d Women of Hai-shan: A Demographic Portrait
334b Women's Lives Transformed: Demographic and Family Patterns in America, 1600-1970
335i Demographic Contributions to the History of Victorian Women
367b Demographic Transition in the Middle East and North Africa

DEMON

52h Pierre de Lancre's "Tableau de l'Inconstance des Mauvais Anges et Demons": The Sabbat Sensationalised
96d Demon in Female Apparel: Narrative of Josephine Amelia Perkins, the Notorious Female Horse Thief...

DEMONOMANIE

52d Jean Bodin's "De la Demonomanie des Sorciers": The Logic of Persecution

DENIAL

169e Denial of the Vagina
170g Denial of Women's Sexual Pleasure: Discussion of Dr. Thompson's Paper
243b Women Who Discriminate Against Other Women: The Process of Denial
296a Denial of the Vagina

DENTIST

166v Interest of High School Girls in Dental Auxiliary Careers
277q The Dentist's Wife

DENVER

40c Child Care Market in Seattle and Denver
40h Cost of Compliance with Federal Day Care Standards in Seattle and Denver

DEPARTMENT

36k Job Market for Women: A Department Chairman's View
39a Maid of All Work or Departmental Sister-in-Law? The Faculty Wife Employed on Campus

DEPARTURE

111jj Point of Departure
183d American Peace Party: New Departures and Old Arguments

DEPENDENCY

59j Sex Discrimination in Credit: The Backlash of Economic Dependency
92g Welfare State and the Needs of the Dependent Family
110d Servility of Dependence: The Dark Lady in Trollop
158u Love and Dependency
170q Phobias after Marriage: Women's Declaration of Dependence
304b Women as Personal Dependents

331c Women's Dependency and Federal Programs
331e Health and Fertility Issues and the Dependency of Wives
344k Women's Incomes as Workers and Dependents
369c Dependency, Individuality, and Work

DEPRESSION

77z Depression in Middle-Aged Women
99n Sex Differences and the Epidemiology of Depression
117h Portnoy's Mother's Complaint: Depression in Middle-Aged Women
141q Men and Women in the Family: History of the Idea of Family in America's Depression Generation
176u Depression in Middle-Aged Women
254f Depression in Middle-Aged Women
330e Cognitive Therapy with Depressed Women
342b If You're Depressed, You're Probably Sub-Assertive

DEPRIVATION

296w Cultural Anthropologist's Approach to Maternal Deprivation

DEPUTIES

275d More Than a Question of Numbers: Women Deputies in the German National Constituent Assembly and the Reichstag, 1919-1933

DEREN

212n Maya Deren and Germaine Dulac: Activists of the Avant-Garde

DEROGATION

9oo Effects of the Derogatory Attitude toward Female Sexuality
120d Semantic Derogation of Woman
169c Effects of the Derogatory Attitude Toward Female Sexuality
170e Effects of the Derogatory Attitude Toward Female Sexuality

DESBOROUGH

5i Lady Desborough

DESERT

270j Desert Politics: Choices in the "Marriage Market"

DESIDERATA

52k Desiderata of Disbelief

DESIGN

143d Appropriation of the House: Changes in House Design and Concepts of Domesticity
143m Unconscious Discrimination in Environmental Design Education
143r Housing for Single-Parent Families: A Women's Design

DESIRADE

350i Desirade: A Negative Case

DESIRES

200l Sex Differences in Job Values and Desires
277o Accomplished Desires
351a Young Women's Decisions to Attend College: Desires, Expectations and Realizations

DESTINY

132c Anatomy Is Destiny
170r Is Anatomy Destiny?
171a Psychosexual Neutrality: Is Anatomy Destiny?
172i Woman's Sociobiological Heritage: Destiny or Free Choice?
220n Success Is Not a Destination But the Road To It
252g Psychology of Women: Biology as Destiny
264a Woman's Biology--Mankind's Destiny: The Population Explosion and Women's Changing Roles
265a Woman's Biology--Mankind's Destiny: The Population Explosion and Women's Changing Roles
282a Anatomy and Destiny: The Role of Biology in Plato's Views of Women

DETECTION

1e Detection of Criminal Abortion
50m The Mother of the Detective
50p APPENDIX: Women Detectives A Chronological Survey

DETERMINANT

76l Parental Mislabeling of Female Genitals as a Determinant of Penis Envy and Learning Inhibitions in Women
141aa Biological and Cultural Determinants of the Division of Labor by Sex
176d Sex, Age, and State as Determinants of Mother-Infant Interaction
198cc Sex, Age, and State as Determinants of Mother-Infant Interaction
202e Determinants of Occupational Segregation
266t Phyletic and Idiosyncratic Determinants of Gender Identity
267p Determinants of Occupational Role Innovation Among College Women
271f Determinants of Intellectual Growth in Women
333g Differences in Expected Post-School Investment as a Determinant of Market Wage Differentials
367d Socioeconomic Determinants of Differential Fertility in Turkey

DETERMINISM

357d Beyond Determinism: George Eliot and Virginia Woolf

DEUS

79j Salve Deus Rex Judaeorum

DEVELOPMENT

see also THIRD WORLD; individual countries

18a Development of Female Identity
18f Sex-Related Differences in Spatial Ability: A Developmental Psychological View
18m Role Music Plays in Adolescent Development
35a Developing a Theory of Capitalist Patriarchy and Socialist Feminism
35c Feminist Theory and the Development of Revolutionary Strategy
43b African Women and National Development
61c Parental Influences on Women's Career Development
61g Barriers to the Career Development of Women
74k Development of the American Women's Liberation Movement, 1967-1971
85c Androgyny As an Ideal for Human Development
88u Jean Rhys' Recent Fiction: Humane Developments in "Wide Sargasso Sea"
106d Liberal Arts Education and Women's Development
140s Rise of the Women's Movement: A Case Study in Political Development
143g Women's Travel Patterns in a Suburban Development
143q Emergency Shelter: The Development of an Innovative Women's Environment
156n APPENDIX: Guidelines for the Development and Evaluation of Unbiased Educational Materials
163d Working-Class Women's Political Participation: Its Potential in Developed Countries
171b Biospsychosocial Processes in the Development of Sex-related Differences
173dd Role of Models in Women's Professional Development
199k Stages in the Development of Psychosexual Concepts and Attitudes
200b Psychoanalytic Theory of Psychosexual Development
204h Hormones and Cognitive Functioning in Normal Development
227h Adverse Impact of Development
230p Underdevelopment and the Experience of Women: A Nigerian Case Study
236h Role of Korean Women in National Development
252l Sex Differences in Identification Development
264i History and Development of Day Care in the U.S.
265f History and Development of Day Care in the U.S.
266ee Status of Women--Population--Development
272g Coeducation and the Development of Leadership Skills in Women: Historical Perspectives from Cornell University, 1868-1900
281a Theories of Development
281b Definitions of Women and Development: An African Perspective
281c Development Planning for Women
281t Women's Labor Force Participation in a Developing Society: The Case of Brazil
281w Reflections on the Conference on Women and Development
293c Adverse Impact of Development on Women
293d Moslem World: Women Excluded from Development
293e Critical Analysis of Latin American Programs to Integrate Women in Development
293g Women in Development: Urban Life and Labor
293l Development Approach to Liberation: Suggestions for Planning
296r Pregnancy and Abortion: Implications for Career Development of Professional Women
297b Role of Women in the Development of Culture in Nigeria
301e Developing Criteria and Measures of Equal Opportunities for Women

358e Development of Programs

DEVELOPMENT--CHILD

13j Impact of the Women's Liberation Movement on Child Development Texts
37c Parental Role Division and the Child's Personality Development
56d Cognitive--Developmental Analysis of Children's Sex-Role Concepts and Attitudes
76i Penis Envy: From Childhood Wish to Developmental Metaphor
156g Development of Psychological Androgyny: Early Childhood Socialization
198aa Physiological Development, Cognitive Development, and Socialization Antecedents of Children's Sex-Role Attitudes
199i Sex of Parent x Sex of Child: Socioemotional Development
211c Prenatal Influences on Child Health and Development
250o Developmental Study of the Effects of Sex of the Dominant Parent on Sex-Role Preference, Identification, and Imitation in Children
365c Impact of the Women's Liberation Movement on Child Development Books

DEVELOPMENT--EARLY

76b Early Female Development
156g Development of Psychological Androgyny: Early Childhood Socialization
169a Early Development of Female Sexuality
169i Special Problems of Early Female Sexual Development
173k Early Sex Differences in the Human: Studies of Socioemotional Development
250x Early Hormonal Influences on the Development of Sexual and Sex-Related Behaviors
260ee Early Sex-Role Development

DEVELOPMENT--ECONOMY

59d Women in Developing Societies: Economic Independence Is Not Enough
352m Handicrafts: A Source of Employment for Women in Developing Rural Economies

DEVELOPMENT--FEMININITY

67b Development of Conceptions of Masculinity and Femininity
164d Developmental Differentiation of Femininity and Masculinity Compared
173o Implications and Applications of Recent Research on Feminine Development
173p Social Values, Femininity, and the Development of Female Competence
209a Developmental Differentiation of Femininity and Masculinity Compared
250m Sex Differences in the Development of Masculine and Feminine Identification

DEVELOPMENT--ROLE

206n Milieu Development and Male-Female Roles in Contemporary Greece
352d Development and Mounting Famine: A Role for Women

372j Uses of Traditional Concepts in the Development of New Urban Roles: Cuban Women in the United States

DEVELOPMENT--SEX

56a Sex Hormones in the Development of Sex Differences in Human Behavior
169i Special Problems of Early Female Sexual Development
199i Sex of Parent x Sex of Child: Socioemotional Development
199o Cryptorchidism, Development of Gender Identity, and Sex Behavior
250o Developmental Study of the Effects of Sex of the Dominant Parent on Sex-Role Preference, Identification, and Imitation in Children
250x Early Hormonal Influences on the Development of Sexual and Sex-Related Behaviors
318e Sexual Equality in Soviet Policy: A Developmental Perspective

DEVIANCE

14i Feminist Review of the Sociology of Deviance
206d Sex Identity Deviation and Inversion

DEVIL

19m Angels in the Devil's Workshop: Leisured and Charitable Women in Nineteenth-Century England and France
225b Witch and Her Devils: An Exploration of the Relationship Between Femininity and Illness

DIALECT

219d Male-Female Conversational Interaction Cues: Using Data From Dialect Surveys

DIALECTIC

55g Husbands and Wives: The Dynamics of the Deferential Dialectic
89v Dialectic of Sex
286p Socialization, Dialectics, and Sport

DIALOGUE

15c Dialogue
52f Tudor Anthropologist: George Gifford's "Discourse " and "Dialogue"
219e Verbal Turn-Taking and Exchanges in Faculty Dialogue
232j Dialogues

DIAMOND

215h Jane Snyder Richards: The Blue-White Diamond

DIARY

95o Fragment From a Lost Diary
127i Pages from a Shop Diary
153o Diary
159u Diary of the Seducer
179hh APPENDIX: Resources for Women's Diaries

208h Diary 1972 of a Mad 12-Year-Old
222n Alice Walker: "The Diary of an African Nun" and Du Bois' Double Consciousness
300e Diary of a Mad Househusband
359k Anais Nin's "Diary" in Context

DICK

197d "Look, Jane, Look! See Dick Run and Jump! Admire Him!"
208u Dick and Jane as Victims: Sex Stereotyping in Children's Readers

DICKINSON

88f Room of Her Own: Emily Dickinson as Woman Artist
214h Power of Emily Dickinson
214i Emily Dickinson and the Deerslayer: The Dilemma of the Woman Poet in America
214j Dickinson, Whitman, and Their Successors
357c Indefinite Disclosed: Christina Rossetti and Emily Dickinson

DICTIM

22b Masculinity-Femininity: An Exception to a Famous Dictim?
266a Masculinity-Femininity: An Exception To a Famous Dictim

DICTIONARY

120c Making of a Nonsexist Dictionary
207g Sexism in Dictionaries and Texts: Omissions and Commissions

DIDEROT

255f "Treated Like Imbecile Children" (Diderot): The Enlightenment and the Status of Women

DIELMAN

212u Reflections on "Jeanne Dielman"

DIET

173w !Kung Hunter-Gatherers: Feminism, Diet, and Birth Control

DIETRICH

288l Marlene Dietrich: At Heart a Gentleman

DIFFERENCE

98a Gender, Relation, and Difference in Psychoanalytic Perspective
98e Powers of Difference
98i For the Etruscans: Sexual Difference and Artistic Production--The Debate Over a Female Aesthetic
98j Difference and Language: A Linguist's Perspective
98k For a Restricted Thematics: Writing, Speech, and Difference in Madame Bovary
98m Visibility and Difference: Black Women in History and Literature

120a Difference and Dominance: An Overview of Language, Gender and Society
166d Male and Female: Differing Perceptions of the Teaching Experience
197a What Kind of Difference Does Sex Make?
199e Differential Response to Early Experiences as a Function of Sex Difference
211b Feminism: Making a Difference in Our Health
219k Difference Beyond Inherent Pitch
279m The Difference
280c Understanding the Difference
282b Theories of Sex Difference
283i Differentiation and Difference--Reflections on the Ethical Implications of Women's Liberation
361q Feminist Criticism: What Difference Does It Make?

DIFFERENCES

see also SEX DIFFERENCES

39m Income Differences between Men and Career Women
75c Personality Differences Between Male and Female Prison Inmates: Measured by the M.M.P.I.
99o Gender Differences in Psychophysiological Illness
100e Class and Race Differences in Gender Roles
107c Differences Between Men and Women
107t Origin of Sexual Differences
155l Mothers and Daughters: Perceived and Real Differences in Sexual Values
171b Biospsychosocial Processes in the Development of Sex-related Differences
176c Attachment Differences in Male and Female Infant Monkeys
176x Differences in Attitudinal Responses Under Conditions of Implicitly Manipulated Group Salience
198v Biological and Anthropological Differences between the Sexes
200e Differences in Perception of the Opposite Sex by Males and Females
204a Sex-Related Differences in Cognitive Functioning: An Overview
204b Genetic Influences on Sex-Related Differences in Intellectual Performance: Theoretical and Methodological Issues
204d Patterns of Cognitive Functioning in Relation to Handedness and Sex-Related Differences
204e Evidence for Sex-Related Differences in Cerebral Organization
204f Sex-Related Differences in Cognition Among the Elderly
204j Menstrual Cycle and Sex-Related Differences in Cognitive Variability
204m Role of Tests and Their Construction in Producing Apparent Sex-Related Differences
213d Caste Differences between Brahmin and Non-Brahmin Women in a South Indian Village
219f Sex, Color and Money: Who's Perceiving What? Or Men and Women: Where Did All the Differences Go (To)?
219g Phonological Differences in the English of Adolescent Chicanas and Chicanos
250z Attachment Differences in Male and Female Infant Monkeys
251w Differences in Hourly Earnings Between Men and Women
251x Differences in Return to Educational Investment
252cc Differences in Hourly Earnings Between Men and Women
260u Differences Between Men and Women

333g Differences in Expected Post-School Investment as a Determinant of Market Wage Differentials
333h Dynamic Theory of Racial Income Differences
354d Wage Differences between Men and Women: Economic Theories
367e Rural-Urban Fertility Differences and Trends in Egypt, 1930-70
371d Racial Differences in Female Labor-Force Participation: Trends and Implications for the Future

DIFFERENCES--PSYCHOLOGY

18f Sex-Related Differences in Spatial Ability: A Developmental Psychological View
284t Question of Psychological Differences Between the Sexes

DIFFERENT

156j Problems and Priorities of Poor, Culturally Different Parents
208i Does Different Equal Less? A High School Woman Speaks Out
231g Different Virtues for Women
287h Economy Ahead of Us: Will Women Have Different Roles?
288ss Are Women Directors Different?
314s "Women Executives are Different"
326b Women in Academia: Today is Different

DIFFERENTIAL

91i Differential Fertility by Working Status of Women in Japan
166y Differential Recruitment of Female Professionals: A Case Study of Clergywomen
196nn Sex Differential in School Enrollment and Educational Attainment
199e Differential Response to Early Experiences as a Function of Sex Difference
219n Sociocultural and Sociopsychological Factors in Differential Language Retentiveness by Sex
250n Parents' Differential Reactions to Sons and Daughters
314aa Differential Recruitment and Control: The Sex Structuring of Organizations
333g Differences in Expected Post-School Investment as a Determinant of Market Wage Differentials
367d Socioeconomic Determinants of Differential Fertility in Turkey
367f Fertility Trends and Differentials in Kuwait
367g Fertility Trends and Differentials in Jordan
367h Fertility in Algeria: Trends and Differentials

DIFFERENTIATION

120i Sex Differentiation in Language
155g Differentiation of Male and Female Orgasm: An Experimental Study
164d Developmental Differentiation of Femininity and Masculinity Compared
166j Masculinity or Femininity? Differentiating Career-Oriented and Homemaking-Oriented College Freshman Women
176ee Sex Differentiation in Role Expectations and Performance
199a Sexual Behavior Differentiation: Prenatal Hormonal and Environmental Control
199c Fetal Androgens, Human Central Nervous System Differentiation, and Behavior Sex Differences

199x Sexual Differentiation: Models, Methods, and Mechanisms
209a Developmental Differentiation of Femininity and Masculinity Compared
251r Sex Role Differentiation
252q Sex-Role Differentiation in an Equalitarian Society
266u Identification and Complementation in the Differentiation of Gender Identity
281s Social Change and Sexual Differentiation in the Cameroun and the Ivory Coast
283i Differentiation and Difference--Reflections on the Ethical Implications of Women's Liberation
296f Psychosexual Differentiation

DIFFICULT

211s "Difficult" Patient: Observations on the Staff-Patient Interaction

DIGGING

366f Digging Sticks and Spears, Or the Two-Sex Model

DIGRESSION

375i One Child of One's Own: A Meaningful Digression within the Work(s)

DILEMMA

4i Dilemma of the Black Woman in Higher Education
8d Human Identity and Gay Identity: A Liberationist Dilemma
8j Butch or Fem?: The Third World Lesbian's Dilemma
172d Individuals and Families in Transition: Dilemmas and Coping
172e Dilemmas of Masculinity in a Changing World
173cc Big-Time Careers for the Little Woman: A Dual-Role Dilemma
197g Dilemmas of Women's Education
214i Emily Dickinson and the Deerslayer: The Dilemma of the Woman Poet in America
222e Ama Ata Aidoo's "Dilemma of a Ghost"
263l Dilemma of Celebration
271j Dilemmas of Women's Education
280e Cultural Dilemma
293h Women in African Towns South of the Sahara: The Urbanization Dilemma
293i Dilemma of Peasant Women: A View from a Village in Yucatan
314ee Female Leadership Dilemma
320l Paradoxes and Dilemmas: Woman as Writer

DILL

277s A Dill Pickle

DIMORPHISM

155d Sexual Dimorphism and Homosexual Gender Identity
176a Sexual Dimorphism and Homosexual Gender Identity
198t Fetal Hormones and the Brain: Effects on Sexual Dimorphism of Behavior
250y Sexual Dimorphic Behavior, Normal and Abnormal

291n Toward Dimorphics: A Summary Statement to the Conference on Occupational Segregation

DIOULA

372d Dioula Women in Town: A View of Intra-Ethnic Variation - Ivory Coast

DIPLOMATS

154e Premiss of Dedication: Notes towards an Ethnography of Diplomats' Wives

DIRECTORS

see also FILMMAKER

212w APPENDIX: Filmographies of Women Directors
288ss Are Women Directors Different?

DIRGE

339c Dirge Without Music

DISABILITIES

9b Legal Disabilities of Women

DISADVANTAGED

251aa Disadvantaged Status of Black Women
328a Women's Stake in Full Employment: Their Disadvantaged Role in the Economy--Challenges to Action
354c Doubly Disadvantaged: Minority Women in the Labor Force

DISBELIEF

52k Desiderata of Disbelief
164m One American Woman: A Speculation upon Disbelief

DISCIPLINE

4m Discipline Variation in the Status of Academic Women

DISCONTENT

198g Woman and Her Discontents: A Reassessment of Freud's Views on Female Sexuality
329t Kibbutz Women: From the Fields of Revolution to the Laundries of Discontent

DISCOURSE

9f Discourse on Women
52f Tudor Anthropologist: George Gifford's "Discourse " and "Dialogue"
361f New Voices in Feminine Discourse

DISCOVERIE

52e Reginald Scot's "Discoverie of Witchcraft": Scepticism and Sadduceeism

DISCRIMINATION

see also SEX DISCRIMINATION; SEXISM; BIAS; AFFIRMATIVE ACTION; TITLE IX; QUOTA; SEX BIAS

7b Discrimination Against Afro-American Women in the Woman's Movement, 1830-1920
13jj Discrimination and Demography Restrict Opportunities for Academic Women
51x Discriminatory Sentencing of Women Offenders
107n Effects of Discrimination Against Women
127e Job Discrimination and What Women Can Do About It
143m Unconscious Discrimination in Environmental Design Education
149e Possible Biological Origins of Sexual Discrimination
174f Discrimination and the Law: The Equal Credit Opportunity Act
174i Incidence and Correlates of Second Generation Discrimination
174k Combatting Dual Discrimination: The Impact of Civil Rights Policies on the Income Status of Black Women
180a Discrimination in Higher Education: A Debate on Faculty Employment
180f Discrimination, Color Blindness, and the Quota System
180n Constitutionality of Reverse Racial Discrimination
180s Discrimination and Morally Relevant Characteristics
196dd Overt and Covert Forms of Discrimination Against Academic Women
202f Discrimination--A Manifestation of Male Market Power?
203s Equal Opportunity, Free from Gender-Based Discrimination
217h Discrimination against Blacks: A Historical Perspective
243b Women Who Discriminate Against Other Women: The Process of Denial
243d Men Who Discriminate Against Women
243f Discrimination Against Aspiring Women
243h Institutional Discrimination: The Case of Achievement-Oriented Women in Higher Education
243k Who Discriminates Against Women?
252ff Reducing Discrimination: Role of the Equal Pay Act
260t Job Discrimination and the Black Woman
264k How to Discriminate Against Women Without Really Trying
265k How to Discriminate Against Women Without Really Trying
291l Discrimination and Poverty among Women Who Head Families
297q Discrimination Against Women in the U.S.: Higher Education, Government Enforcement Agencies, and Unions
333a Economic Theories of Employment Discrimination
333b Role of Worker Expectancies in the Study of Employment Discrimination
333d More Useful Modes of Research on Discrimination in Employment and Pay
342dd Ending Discrimination Against Women in Education: How Uncle Sam Can Help
364i Women School Administrators: My Experience with Discrimination

DISCUSSION-OPENERS

208m Consciousness-Raising in the Classroom: Some Games, Projects, Discussion-Openers, Etc.

DISEASE

42a "Fashionable Diseases": Women's Complaints and Their Treatment in Nineteenth-Century America
421 Prostitution and the Poor in Plymouth and Southampton Under the Contagious Diseases Act
223e Study of Victorian Prostitution and Venereal Disease

DISENCHANTMENT

96aa Evolution of Disenchantment
226g Evolution of Disenchantment

DISNEY

274d Things Walt Disney Never Told Us

DISORDER

47b Disorderly Company: From "The Golden Notebook" to "The Four-Gated City"
99a Femaleness, Maleness and Behavior Disorders in Nonhumans
99b Sex Differences in the Epidemiology of Mental Disorder
173gg Sex Differences and Psychiatric Disorders
191c Complaints and Disorders: The Sexual Politics of Sickness
211q Breast Disorders

DISPERSION

108u HUAN, or Dispersion

DISPLACED

332d Displaced--The Midwife by the Male Physician

DISPLAY

198s Masculinity and Femininity as Display

DISSENTING

180m DeFunis v. Odegaard, Dissenting Opinion

DISSERTATIONS

140ii Bibliography of Dissertations for and about Women in Administration in Colleges and Universities

DISSOLUTION

54d Marriage and Marriage Dissolution and the Changing Status of Women: The Case of Poland

DISTINCTION

155a Psychological Consequences of the Anatomical Distinction Between the Sexes

159q Of the Distinction of the Beautiful and the Sublime in the Interrelations of the Two Sexes
193c Aspects of the Distinction Between the Sexes in the Nyamwezi and Some Other African Systems of Kinship and Marriage
198b Psychical Consequences of the Anatomical Distinction Between the Sexes
200a Psychological Consequences of the Anatomical Distinction between the Sexes
200h Modest Confirmation of Freud's Theory of a Distinction between the Superego of Men and Women
233e Psychical Consequences of the Anatomical Distinction between the Sexes
250h Psychological Consequences of the Anatomic Distinction Between the Sexes
268a Psychical Consequences of the Anatomical Distinction Between the Sexes
268b Freud and the Distinction Between the Sexes

DISTRUST

132k Distrust Between the Sexes

DIVERSITY

57h Women's Movement Meets the Challenge of Diversity
269j Modern Family: Sticky Myths, Diverse Realities, and the Problem of Isolation

DIVINE

79a XVI Revelations of Divine Love

DIVISION

13h Children's Books: The Second Sex, Junior Division
37c Parental Role Division and the Child's Personality Development
55b Sexual Divisions and the Dual Labour Market
55i Marriage, Role Division and Social Cohesion: The Case of Some French Upper-Middle Class Families
84e Sexual Division of Labour: The Case of Nursing
84f Modes of Appropriation and the Sexual Division of Labour: A Case Study from Oaxaca, Mexico
84k Education and the Sexual Division of Labour
141aa Biological and Cultural Determinants of the Division of Labor by Sex
202a Division of Labor between the Sexes
251g Division of Labor by Sex
285b Division of Labor by Sex
288c Divided Woman: Bree Daniels in "Klute"
304h Sexual Division of Labour and Inequality: Labour and Leisure
350a Female Solidarity and the Sexual Division of Labour
352c Division of Labour and Sexual Inequality: The Role of Education
362l Women: A House Divided
370g Effects on Power and Division of Labor in the Family

DIVORCE

9j Letter on Marriage and Divorce, 1855
54c Divorce and the Status of Women
65b Early Essays on Marriage and Divorce
99d Sex Differences in Divorce
140v Study of Women Coping with Divorce
159o Of Polygamy and Divorce
172g Stress and Coping in Divorce: A Focus on Women
176w Six Stations of Divorce
178g Divorce as a Moral Issue: A Hundred Years of Controversy
202p Impact of Women's Liberation on Marriage, Divorce, and Family Life-Style
251bb Social Situation of Divorced Mothers and Their Families
315d Marriage and Divorce in the Frankish Kingdom
330n Creative Exits: Fight-Therapy for Divorcees
331i Homemakers into Widows and Divorcees: Can the Law Provide Economic Protection?
331j Crisis Perspective on Divorce and Role Change

DJUNA

140kk Djuna Barnes' "Nightwood"
361o Style of Djuna Barnes' "Nightwood"

DOBLIN

275b Woman Question in the Early Work of Alfred Doblin

DOCTOR

see PHYSICIAN

DOCTORATE

4g Career Profiles of Women Doctorates
166ff Participation of Women Doctorates in the Labor Force
196oo Proportion of Doctorates Earned by Women, by Area and Field, 1960-1969

DOCTRINE

85w Roman Catholic Doctrine of Therapeutic Abortion
231j Epicurean Doctrine of Love

DODGE

5j Mabel Dodge

DOG

24b The Lady With the Pet Dog
50k The Calico Dog
142a Demise of the Dancing Dog
254s Women and Creativity: The Demise of the Dancing Dog
277x The Lady with the Dog

DOGMA

8bb Spirit is Liberationist but the Flesh is...or, You Can't Always Get Into Bed With Your Dogma
292f Anne Bradstreet: Dogmatist and Rebel

DOLL

111hh Barbie Doll
112ff A Doll's House, 1970
233vv A Doll's House
271g View From the Doll Corner
339g A Doll's House
363c A Doll's House

DOMAIN

190c Women and the Jural Domain: An Evolutionary Perspective
230k Men and Women in the South of France: Public and Private Domains
249j Female Status in the Public Domain

DOMESTICITY

see also HOUSEWORK; HOMEMAKER; HOUSEWIFE

20n Women and Domestic Power: Political and Economic Strategies in Domestic Groups
20r Three Styles of Domestic Authority: A Cross-Cultural Study
35h Women's Domestic Labor
42h Family Limitation, Sexual Control, and Domestic Feminism in Victorian America
55e Political Economy of Domestic Labour in Capitalist Society
71h Domestic Service as a Channel of Upward Mobility for the Lower Class Woman: The Lima Case
84h Domestic Labour and Marx's Theory of Value
92a Early Formation of Victorian Domestic Ideology
92h Domestic Labor and the Household
125b Domestic Problem: Work and Culture in the Household
140g Domestic Servants in London and Paris, 1890 to 1914
143d Appropriation of the House: Changes in House Design and Concepts of Domesticity
143e Redesigning the Domestic Workplace
145e Domestic Ideology and Women's Education
153u Domestic Mythology
249e Strategies, Cooperation, and Conflict Among Women in Domestic Groups
281k Migration and Labor Force Participation of Latin American Women: The Domestic Servants in the Cities
288hh "Part-Time Work of a Domestic Slave," or Putting the Screws to Screwball Comedy
292k Principles of Domestic Science
295c Domestic Service in Canada, 1880-1920
297i Female Domestic Servant and Social Change: Lima, Peru
303a Model Domestic Environment: Icon or Option?
303b Challenging the American Domestic Ideal
321g Changes in Domestic Relations Court
325y Domestic Social Environment of Women and Girls in Isfahan, Iran

354p Domestic Service: Woman's Work
360a American Women and Domestic Culture: An Approach to Women's History
360k Family Limitation, Sexual Control, and Domestic Feminism in Victorian America

DOMINANCE

35d Mothering, Male Dominance, and Capitalism
98c Bonds of Love: Rational Violence and Erotic Domination
105b Dominant or Dominated? Women on TV
120a Difference and Dominance: An Overview of Language, Gender and Society
169j Self-Esteem (Dominance-Feeling) and Sexuality in Women
183a Sex Differences in Aggression and Dominance
232e Dominant Sex
250o Developmental Study of the Effects of Sex of the Dominant Parent on Sex-Role Preference, Identification, and Imitation in Children
270e Forced Transition from Egalitarianism to Male Dominance: The Bari of Colombia
281l Female Status, the Family, and Male Dominance in a West Indian Community

DOMINICAN

71i "La Quisqueyana": The Dominican Woman, 1940-1970
194m Politics and Feminism in the Dominican Republic: 1931-45 and 1966-74
230n Love Unites Them and Hunger Separates Them: Poor Women in the Dominican Republic
297h Lower Economic Sector: Female Mating Patterns in the Dominican Republic

DONNA

116k La Donna Italiana Durante Il Periodo Fascista in Toronto, 1930-1940

DOPE

50h The Dope Fiends
317l Jive Dope Fiend Whoes: In the Street and in Rehabilitation

DORIS

17k "Out of the chaos, a new kind of strength": Doris Lessing's "The Golden Notebook"
47c Doris Lessing in the Sixties: The New Anatomy of Melancholy
191s Building a Hospital Workers' Union: Doris Turner, the Woman from 1199
283c Explorations with Doris Lessing in Quest of The Four-Gated City
288m Actress Archetypes in the 1950s: Doris Day, Marilyn Monroe, Elizabeth Taylor, Audrey Hepburn

DOROTHY

36i "Featureless Freedom" or Ironic Submission: Dorothy Richardson and May Sinclair
212r Work of Dorothy Arzner

288b Dorothy Arzner's "Dance, Girl, Dance"
288r Interview with Dorothy Arzner

DORRIT

108ee Little Dorrit

DOSTOEVSKY

179m A. Dostoevsky

DOUBLE

9kk Bright Woman Is Caught in a Double Bind
15g Double-Bind
49e Male and Female Leadership Styles: The Double Bind
74o Double Jeopardy: To Be Black and Female
110v Sexism and the Double Standard in Literature
127w Double Jeopardy: To Be Black and Female
142f Double Jeopardy: To Be Black and Female
151p Decline and Fall of the Double Standard
173jj Double Standard of Aging
222n Alice Walker: "The Diary of an African Nun" and Du Bois' Double Consciousness
254t Women Writers and the Double Standard
264l Double Standard: Age
265h Double Standard: Age
272j Black Female Administrator: Woman in a Double Bind
292r Double Jeopardy: To Be Black and Female
354c Doubly Disadvantaged: Minority Women in the Labor Force

DOUBTS

102g Doubts about Balconies
110c Gentle Doubters: Images of Women in Englishwomen's Novels, 1840-1920

DOW

340g When I Was Miss Dow

DOWNHILL

113n Downhill

DOWRY

see also BRIDE; BRIDEWEALTH; MARRIAGE; WEDDING

30a Bridewealth and Dowry in Africa and Eurasia
30b Dowry and Bridewealth and the Property Rights of Women in South Asia
315h Dowries and Kinsmen in Early Renaissance Venice

DRABBLE

47a Margaret Drabble: Novels of a Cautious Feminist

DRAFT

see also WAR; ARMED FORCES

183e Gender Imagery and Issues of War and Peace: The Case of the Draft Resistance Movement of the 1960's
309l Draft, International Plan of Action

DRAGON

16g Here Be Dragons
103d The Learned Adventure of the Dragon's Head

DRAMA

see also THEATRE; PLAY; PLAYWRIGHT; individual playwrights

68i "Unwomanly Woman" in Shaw's Drama
80i Hispanic American Fiction and Drama Written by Women:
141bb Hrotsvitha of Gandersheim: The Playable Dramas of a Woman Playwright of the Tenth Century
141dd Lillian Hellman: Dramatist of the Second Sex
185a Sin and Salvation: The Dramatic Context of Hrotswitha's Women

DREAD

252j Dread of Woman

DREAM

24gg Dreamy
119h The Dream
166w Career Dreams of Teachers
200i Dreams: Sex Differences in Aggressive Content
220l Dreamy
263s Dreams and Fantasies as Sources of Revelation: Feminist Appropriation of Jung
279i Cicely's Dream
340b The Child Dreams
356g The House of My Dreams

DRESS

18o Dressing Up
111cc The Girls in Their Summer Dresses
112u The Girls In Their Summer Dresses
113q Red Dress--1946
144b Window Dressing
153j Dress, or Who Makes the Fashions
256l Chief Justice Wore a Red Dress
295h Women in Production: The Toronto Dressmakers' Strike of 1931
364b Submission, Masochism and Narcissism: Three Aspects of Women's Role as Reflected in Dress

DRIVE

73p Men Drive Women Crazy

180b Drive Toward Equality
273o Woman Driver
301c Race, Sex, and Jobs: The Drive Toward Equality

DROP

4d Women Dropouts from Higher Education
4e Women Drop Back In: Educational Innovation in the Sixties
10j A Drop in the Bucket

DROWNING

127g Drowning in the Steno Pool

DRUGS

99g Problems with Alcohol and Other Drugs

DRUMMER

3k Sound of a Drunken Drummer

DRUNK

3k Sound of a Drunken Drummer
279w Daydreams of a Drunk Woman

DRY

279p Dry September

DUAL

19d Sanctity and Power: The Dual Pursuit of Medieval Women
55b Sexual Divisions and the Dual Labour Market
173cc Big-Time Careers for the Little Woman: A Dual-Role Dilemma
174k Combatting Dual Discrimination: The Impact of Civil Rights Policies on the Income Status of Black Women
291e Dual Linkages between the Occupational and Family Systems: A Macrosociological Analysis
302b Dual-Sex Political System in Operation: Igbo Women and Community Politics in Midwestern Nigeria

DUBLIN

103a The Dublin Mystery

DUKES

50j Too Many Dukes

DULAC

212n Maya Deren and Germaine Dulac: Activists of the Avant-Garde
288w Germaine Dulac: First Feminist Filmmaker

DUMB

129a Poor, Dumb, and Ugly

DURAND

80d Letter to Marguerite Durand from Paul and Victor Margueritte

DURANT

363g Mr. Durant

DURATION

155j Women's Sexual Responsiveness and the Duration and Quality of Their Marriages

DURKHEIM

252s Durkheim on Women

DUTIES

257b Duties of Women

DWELLING

36e Dwelling in Decencies: Radical Criticism and the Feminist Perspective
88c Dwelling in Decencies: Radical Criticism and the Feminist Perspective

DYAD

251q Task and Emotional Behavior in the Marital Dyad

DYNAMICS

55g Husbands and Wives: The Dynamics of the Deferential Dialectic
105a Dynamics of Cultural Resistance
141k Dynamics of Successful People
151d Dynamics of Interracial Sex in Colonial America
292g Dynamics of Interracial Sex
333h Dynamic Theory of Racial Income Differences
342f Group Dynamics and Consciousness Raising

DYNASTY

113j Dynastic Encounter
220w Dynastic Encounter
236a Tradition: Women During the Yi Dynasty

DYSFUNCTIONS

211v Female Sexual Dysfunctions: A Clinical Approach

DYSTAVES

58a Gospelles of Dystaves

E.E.C.

352h Equality of Remuneration for Men and Women in the Member States of the E.E.C.

E.R.A.

see EQUAL RIGHTS AMENDMENT

EAGLE

113i The Fifteen-Dollar Eagle
142d Restless Eagles: Women's Liberation 1969

EARLY

23c Book-Lined Cells: Women and Humanism in the Early Italian Renaissance
23d Learned Women of Early Modern Italy: Humanists and University Scholars
23f Women's Roles in Early Modern Venice
41b Women, Work and Protest in the Early Lowell Mills
41c New England Mill Women in the Early Nineteenth Century
65b Early Essays on Marriage and Divorce
68h Mill, Marx and Bebel: Early Influences on Shaw's Characterizations of Women
76a Freud's Views on Early Female Sexuality in the Light of Direct Child Observation
76b Early Female Development
80l Inculcating a Slave Mentality: Women in German Popular Fiction of the Early Twentieth Century
82b New Sources of Conflict in Females at Adolescence and Early Adulthood
92a Early Formation of Victorian Domestic Ideology
122d Life and Early Literary Career of the Nineteenth-Century Colombian Writer, Coledad Acosta de Samper
128b Early Women Printers of America
140mm Sexual Identity in the Early Fiction of V. Sackville-West
141x Chinese Women in the Early Communist Movement
155e Self-Conceptions, Motivations and Interpersonal Attitudes of Early- and Late-Maturing Girls
155m Early Sexual Behavior in Adult Homosexual and Heterosexual Males
156c Teacher Education and Non-Sexist Early Childhood Education
156g Development of Psychological Androgyny: Early Childhood Socialization
169a Early Development of Female Sexuality
169i Special Problems of Early Female Sexual Development
173k Early Sex Differences in the Human: Studies of Socioemotional Development
176b Sex Differences in the Incidence of Neonatal Abnormalities and Abnormal Performance in Early Childhood
176e Play Behavior in the Year-Old Infant: Early Sex Differences
198d Early Stages of the Oedipus Conflict

199e Differential Response to Early Experiences as a Function of Sex Difference
199h Early Sex Differences and Mother-Infant Interaction
200n Self-Conceptions, Motivations and Interpersonal Attitudes of Early- and Late-Maturing Girls
225f Woman-Power: Religious Heresy and Feminism in Early English Socialism
240h Images of Women in Early American Literature
240j They Shall Have Faces, Minds, and (One Day) Flesh: Women in Late Nineteenth-century and Early Twentieth-century American Literature
250x Early Hormonal Influences on the Development of Sexual and Sex-Related Behaviors
250kk Early Childhood Experiences and Women's Achievement Motives
260ee Early Sex-Role Development
263f Women in the Early Christian Movement
267h Early Childhood Experiences and Women's Achievement Motives
271a Sexual Stereotypes Start Early
271n Sex Roles in Early Reading Textbooks
272f Single-Sex Education and Leadership: The Early Years of Simmons College
275b Woman Question in the Early Work of Alfred Doblin
280f Early Stereotypes
282d Reason and Morals in the Early Feminist Movement: Mary Wollstonecraft
295e Schoolmarms and Early Teaching in Ontario
296b Early Childhood Experiences and Women's Achievement Motives
307c Chinese Women in the Early Communist Movement
315b Infanticide in the Early Middle Ages
315h Dowries and Kinsmen in Early Renaissance Venice
323e Early Years in the Trade Unions
334f Equality or Submersion? Feme (sic) Couvert Status in Early Pennsylvania
335l Survey of Primary Sources and Archives for the History of Early Twentieth-Century English Women
336a Loom and Spindle; or, Life Among the Early Mill Girls
336e Early Factory Magazines in New England: The LOWELL OFFERING and its Contemporaries
337b Women in Early Christian Communities
360e Organized Women's Benevolence in Early Nineteenth-Century America

EARNINGS

see also PAY; WAGE; INCOME

96v Why I Earn My Own Living
196oo Proportion of Doctorates Earned by Women, by Area and Field, 1960-1969
202d Discontinuous Labor Force Participation and Its Effect on Women's Market Earnings
226b Why I Earn My Own Living
251w Differences in Hourly Earnings Between Men and Women
252cc Differences in Hourly Earnings Between Men and Women
351d Work Attachment, Investments in Human Capital and the Earnings of Young Women

EAST

91h Fertility and Women's Employment in the Socialist Countries of Eastern Europe
131l In Reality: Some Middle Eastern Women
154g Female Militancy and Colonial Revolt: The Women's War of 1929, Eastern Nigeria
262b Education of Woman in the Eastern States
267e Convergences between East and West: Tradition and Modernity in Sex Roles in Sweden, Finland, and the Soviet Union
294i Political Activity of Women in Eastern Europe
302g Rebels or Status-Seekers? Women as Spirit Mediums in East Africa

ECHO

373j Echo from Ithaca

ECLIPSE

273b The Eclipse

ECOLOGICAL

213n Ecological Antecedents and Sex-Role Consequences in Traditional and Modern Israeli Subcultures

ECONOMICS

11e Occupations: Wider Economic Opportunity
20n Women and Domestic Power: Political and Economic Strategies in Domestic Groups
21u Status of Home Economics and the Status of Women
40a Economic and Policy Issues of Child Care
43e Chinese Women: The Relative Influences of Ideological Revolution, Economic Growth, and Cultural Change
45f Black Women Who Head Families: Economic Needs and Economic Resources
59b Women's Roles in the Economy: Economic Investigation and Research Needs
59d Women in Developing Societies: Economic Independence Is Not Enough
59j Sex Discrimination in Credit: The Backlash of Economic Dependency
91b Fertility, Women's Work, and Economic Class: A Case Study from Southeast Asia
121f Feminine Orders in Colonial Bahia, Brazil: Economic, Social, and Demographic Implications, 1677-1800
126o Women in Convents: Their Economic and Social Role in Colonial Mexico
127o Women and Economics
146m Economic and Legal Status
188e Women and Economics
196o Attitudes Toward Increased Social, Economic, and Political Participation by Women as Reported by Elementary and Secondary Students
202j Economics of Marital Status
202n Formal Extrafamily Child Care--Some Economic Observations
213h Economic Activity and Marriage among Ivoirian Urban Women
235i Economics of Women's Victimization

246i Women in the Economic Sphere: The Coming Struggle for Jobs
251b Economics, Sex, and Gender
251e Changing Economic Role of Women
252hh Economic Status of Families Headed by Women
256j Impact of Mid-twentieth Century Movement for Sex Equality in Employment on Three Contemporary Economic Institutions
265n Women's Economic Status: Some Cliches and Some Facts
285c Economic Organization and the Position of Women Among the Iroquois
294o Women in Economic Life: Rights and Opportunities
297h Lower Economic Sector: Female Mating Patterns in the Dominican Republic
297n Economic Basis of the Status of Women
302d Luo Women and Economic Change During the Colonial Period
302j Women and Economic Change in Africa
328j Economic Aspects of Child Care
331i Homemakers into Widows and Divorcees: Can the Law Provide Economic Protection?
333a Economic Theories of Employment Discrimination
344j Economic Strength Is What Counts
351e Migration of Young Families: An Economic Perspective
354a Women and Work: An Economic Appraisal
354d Wage Differences between Men and Women: Economic Theories
372l Economic Role of Women in Alaskan Eskimo Society

ECONOMIST

48f Economist's View of Women's Work
166xx Employer Acceptance of the Mature Home Economist
291k Economists' Approaches to Sex Segregation in the Labor Market: An Appraisal
291o Sex Differences in Economists' Fields of Specialization

ECONOMY

see also DEVELOPMENT; SOCIO ECONOMIC; LABOR

55e Political Economy of Domestic Labour in Capitalist Society
59b Women's Roles in the Economy: Economic Investigation and Research Needs
89ee Political Economy of Women's Liberation
97j Political Economy of Women's Liberation
121b Female and Family in the Economy and Society of Colonial Brazil
127p Political Economy of Women's Liberation
139y Political Economy of Women's Liberation
166o Women in the Soviet Economy
186l Political Economy of Women's Liberation
230h Traffic in Women: Notes on the "Political Economy" of Sex
251o Political Economy of Women's Liberation
252p Political Economy of Women's Liberation
287h Economy Ahead of Us: Will Women Have Different Roles?
293b Economy, Family, Fertility, and the Female
295a Political Economy of Ontario Women in the Nineteenth Century
328a Women's Stake in Full Employment: Their Disadvantaged Role in the Economy--Challenges to Action
328g Underemployment of Women: Policy Implications for a Full Employment Economy
342n Political Economy of Women's Oppression

352m Handicrafts: A Source of Employment for Women in Developing Rural Economies

EDERLE

152l Gertrude Ederle

EDGE

16i Woman on the Edge of Time
24t Bertha Schneiders Existential Edge
197j Myth is Better Than a Miss: Men Get the Edge in Academic Employment

EDINBURGH

317c Hats as a Symbol of Women's Position in Three Evangelical Churches in Edinburgh, Scotland

EDITHA

112s Editha

EDITORIAL

139w Editorial from N.O.W.'s President
257u Editorial

EDNA

214m Edna St. Vincent Millay and the Language of Vulnerability

EDUCATE

38c Educating Women for Leadership
60o Motives and Future of the Educated Woman
141p Fertility Motivations and Career Conflicts in Educated Women
190g Educating Women for Leadership: A Program for the Future
259n Liberally Educated Woman
260x Modest Proposal for the Educating of Women
314kk Educating Women for Administration

EDUCATION

see also SCHOOL; various types and levels of education

4e Women Drop Back In: Educational Innovation in the Sixties
7h Nannie Burroughs and the Education of Black Women
9jj Education of Women
11i Education of Women Today and Tomorrow
13d Education of Women
13x High-School Sex(ist) Education
13y Present Tendencies in Women's College and University Education
13ee Harvard Ed School
13kk Feminist Experiment in Education
13nn It's Time for Equal Education
14d Sociology of Education: Perspectives on Women
21t Women in Physical Education

23a Education of Women in the Middle Ages in Theory, Fact, and Fantasy
24g An Education
39o Impediment or Stimulant? Marital Status and Graduate Education
45a Socialization and Education of Young Black Girls in Schools
45b Full Equality: More Job Education for Women
45j APPENDIX: Educational and Occupational Statistics on Black Women
53e Privileged, Schooled and Finished: Boarding Education for Girls
60c Education of Female Teachers
60m Education for Women and for Men
62j Education for Real Living
79o An Essay to Revive the Ancient Education of Gentlewomen
84k Education and the Sexual Division of Labour
106c Women's Education: The Case for the Single-Sex College
106d Liberal Arts Education and Women's Development
117d Women and Jewish Education; A New Look at Bat Mitzvah
121i Education, Philanthropy, and Feminism: Components of Argentine Womanhood, 1860-1926
126g Education and Ideology in Nineteenth-Century America: The Response of Educational Institutions to the Changing Role of Women
127gg Education of Women
128c Prudence Crandall: Champion of Negro Education
129o Education as Recreation
143m Unconscious Discrimination in Environmental Design Education
145d Contradictions in Ladies' Education
145e Domestic Ideology and Women's Education
156a Sexism and Racism in Education
156c Teacher Education and Non-Sexist Early Childhood Education
156n APPENDIX: Guidelines for the Development and Evaluation of Unbiased Educational Materials
164k Impact of Education
174a Eliminating Sex Discrimination in Education: Lobbying for Implementation of Title IX
174l Women's Educational Equity: Favorable Student Response
181f Education of Girls Today
185g Education of Women in the Middle Ages
196u Women and Educational Testing
196x Attitudes of Superintendents and Board of Education Members Toward the Employment and Effectiveness of Women as Public-School Administrators
196y School Boards and Sex Bias in American Education
196gg Task Force on Education Report, Governor's Commission on the Status of Women, Ma.
196hh Women in Educational Governance
196nn Sex Differential in School Enrollment and Educational Attainment
197g Dilemmas of Women's Education
202l Nonmarket Returns to Women's Investment in Education
238h Educational Establishment: Wasted Women
246c Socialization of Women in Educational Institutions: Resultant Effects
246h Proposed Model for Examining Sex Discrimination in Education
250s Parental Education, Sex Differences, and Performance on Cognitive Tasks Among Two-Year-Old Children
251x Differences in Return to Educational Investment
256o Degree in Enlightenment: When a Woman's Education Will No Longer Be an Academic Question
257q Present Tendencies in Women's College and University Education
260v Women and Education

262b Education of Woman in the Eastern States
262c Education of Woman in the Western States
262d Education of Woman in the Southern States
267d Cross-cultural Examination of Women's Marital, Educational and Occupational Options
267g Employment of Women, Education, and Fertility
269c Education and Socialization
269h Parent's Role in Values Education
271j Dilemmas of Women's Education
271x Sex Roles and Education in Sweden
271y Education and Women's Liberation
272c Power and Opportunity in the Principalship: The Case of Two Women Leaders in Education
272d Historical Perspectives on Women in Educational Leadership
272f Single-Sex Education and Leadership: The Early Years of Simmons College
272i Socialization and Education of Young Black Girls in School
272l Need for Female Role Models in Education
272o Leadership Training for Increased Effectiveness among Women Educational Administrators
280k Test Scores and Unequal Education
284i Trends in Educational Attainment of Women
284j Education and Jobs
289g Women and the Future of Education
294r Access to Education at All Levels
294t Education Is the Key for Women
297c African Women: Identity Crisis? Some Observations on Education and the Changing Role of Women in Sierra Leone and Zaire
297p Legislation: An Aid in Eliminating Sex Bias in Education in the U.S.
301b Sex Discrimination, Educational Institutions, and the Law: A New Issue on Campus
318l Educational Policies and Attainment
325h Education and Employment among Kuwaiti Women
328l Facilitating Full Employment of Women through Career Education
328m Vocational Education
342dd Ending Discrimination Against Women in Education: How Uncle Sam Can Help
352c Division of Labour and Sexual Inequality: The Role of Education
360j Catharine Beecher and the Education of American Women
368b Reeducation of Sophie
375o Education of a Poet

EDWARD

79bb Letters to Edward Jerningham

EGALITARIANISM

3j New Egalitarian Life Style
19a Women in Egalitarian Societies
166aaa Myth of the Egalitarian Family: Familial Roles and the Professionally Employed Wife
230d !Kung Women: Contrasts in Sexual Egalitarianism in Foraging and Sedentary Contexts
270e Forced Transition from Egalitarianism to Male Dominance: The Bari of Colombia

EGO

76h Masochism, the Ego Ideal, and the Psychology of Women
82d Female Ego Styles and Generational Conflict
175nn Politics of the Ego: A Manifesto for New York Radical Feminists

EGYPT

131b Egyptian Woman: Between Modernity and Tradition
325m Revolutionary Gentlewomen in Egypt
325n Feminism and National Politics in Egypt
325dd Sex Differences and Folk Illness in an Egyptian Village
367e Rural-Urban Fertility Differences and Trends in Egypt, 1930-70

EIDETIC

330l Anna O.--Patient or Therapist? An Eidetic View

EIGHTEENTH

88o Pre-Feminism in Some Eighteenth-Century Novels
121a Colonial Women in Mexico: The Seventeenth and Eighteenth Centuries
178b Eighteenth-Century Theorists of Women's Liberation
240d Portrayal of Women in Restoration and Eighteenth-century English Literature
255c Woman's Concept of Self in the Eighteenth Century
255d Women and Literature in Eighteenth Century England
255e Eighteenth-Century Englishwoman: According to the Gentleman's Magazine
255g La Condition de la Femme Francaise au Dix-huitieme Siecle d'apres les Romans
259b Eighteenth Century Women
270b Sunksquaws, Shamans, and Tradeswomen: Middle Atlantic Coastal Algonkian Women During the Seventeenth and Eighteenth Centuries
292d Eighteenth-Century Womanhood
302a Signares of Saint-Louis and Goree: Women Entrepreneurs in Eighteenth-Century Senegal
334d Cherished Spirit of Independence: The Life of an Eighteenth-Century Boston Businesswoman
335g Eighteenth-Century Englishwoman
335h Discovery of Women in Eighteenth-Century English Political Life
359b Quest for Community: Spiritual Autobiographies of Eighteenth-Century Quaker and Puritan Women in America
360c Widowhood in Eighteenth-Century Massachusetts: A Problem in the History of the Family

EIGHTH-

22s Androgynous Themes Written to Sentence Cues by Sixth-, Eighth-, and Tenth-Grade Students

ELEANOR

253l Nothing to Fear: Notes on the Life of Eleanor Roosevelt
303j Eleanor Raymond

ELECTORAL

163u Black Women in Electoral Politics

ELEMENTARY

196i Psychological and Occupational Sex Stereotypes in Elementary School Readers
196o Attitudes Toward Increased Social, Economic, and Political Participation by Women as Reported by Elementary and Secondary Students
207h Sexism in Children's Books and Elementary Teaching Materials
208v Run, Mama, Run: Women Workers in Elementary Readers
208ll Sex Stereotypes in Mathematics and Science Textbooks for Elementary and Junior High Schools
271o Women Workers in Elementary Readers

ELEMENTARY-SCHOOL

196b Sex-Role Concepts Among Elementary-School Age Girls
196c Sex Differences in the Self-Concepts of Elementary-School Children
196j Sex Stereotyping in Elementary-School Mathematics Textbooks

ELENA

122f Elena Poniatowska's "Hasta no Verte, Jesus Mio"
122k Thematic Exploration of the Works of Elena Garro

ELEONORA

23b Women, Learning, and Power: Eleonora of Aragon and the Court of Ferrara

ELEPHANT

356k The Elephant Man

ELEVEN

22n Cross-Cultural Analysis of Sex Differences in the Behavior of Children Aged Three Through Eleven
77c Cross-Cultural Analysis of Sex Differences in the Behavior of Children Aged Three Through Eleven
214p Gwendolyn the Terrible: Propositions on Eleven Poems

ELIOT

145f George Eliot and Mary Wollstonecraft
179t G. Eliot
357d Beyond Determinism: George Eliot and Virginia Woolf

ELISA

80f "El casamiento enganoso": Marriage in the Novels of Maria Luisa Bombal, Silvina Bullrich, and Elisa Serrana

ELITE

140u Climbing the Political Ladder: The Aspirations and Expectations of Partisan Elites
163i Comparative Study of Male-Female Political Attitudes at Citizen and Elite Levels
329p Female Political Elites in Mexico: 1974
344m Congressional Ambitions of Female Political Elites

ELIZA

68d Eliza's Choice: Transformation Myth and the Ending of "Pygmalion"
215a Life and Legend of Eliza R. Snow

ELIZABETH

79h To The Thrice Sacred Queen Elizabeth
79n Upon the much lamented death of the Right Honourable the Lady Elizabeth Langham
79w Letters to Elizabeth Robinson Montagu
79z Letters to Elizabeth Robinson Montagu
110e Gentle Truths for Gentle Readers: The Fiction of Elizabeth Goudge
214f Elizabeth Barrett Browning
215u Sarah Elizabeth Carmichael: Poetic Genius of Pioneer Utah
288m Actress Archetypes in the 1950s: Doris Day, Marilyn Monroe, Elizabeth Taylor, Audrey Hepburn
359d Paradox and Success of Elizabeth Cady Stanton

ELIZABETHAN

233g Woman in the Elizabethan Sonnet: Poems

ELLEN

192b Ellen Glasgow
215p Dr. Ellen Brooke Ferguson: Nineteenth-Century Renaissance Woman

ELLIS

215r Dr. Ellis Reynolds Shipp: Pioneer Utah Physician

EMANCIPATION

21e Essential Emancipation: The Control of Reproduction
51ii Interaction Between Women's Emancipation and Female Criminality: A Cross-Cultural Perspective
138h Women's Emancipation and the Recruitment of Women into the Labour Force in World War II
159aa Emancipation of Women
275c Stereotype of the Emancipated Woman in the Weimar Republic
282g Women's Liberation and Human Emancipation
325f Women's Emancipation in Tunisia
329u Chinese Women on the Road to Complete Emancipation

EMASCULATING

131 Schools Are Emasculating Our Boys

EMBRYO

231d Female Sexuality and Embryo

EMERGENCE

180j Emergence of an American Ethnic Pattern
194o Emergence of a Mapuche Leader: Chile
199l Emergence of Genital Awareness During the Second Year of Life
206b Emergent Africa
308b Emergence of Women at the End of the Ch'ing: The Case of Ch'iu Chin
330j Therapy of Women in the Light of Psychoanalytic Theory and the Emergence of a New View
344r Crisis Perspective on Emerging Health Roles: A Paradigm for the Entry of Women into New Occupational Roles
358c Emergence of Women in Sport
359a Emergence of Women's Autobiography in England

EMERGENCY

143q Emergency Shelter: The Development of an Innovative Women's Environment

EMIGRATION

71l Honor, Shame, and Women's Liberation in Cuba: Views of Working-Class Emigre Men
116s Emigration, the Italian Family, and Changing Roles
244c Feminism and Female Emigration, 1861-1886

EMILE

203d Emile

EMILY

36h Emily Bronte in the Hands of Male Critics
88f Room of Her Own: Emily Dickinson as Woman Artist
214e Emily Bronte's Anti-Romance
214h Power of Emily Dickinson
214i Emily Dickinson and the Deerslayer: The Dilemma of the Woman Poet in America
357c Indefinite Disclosed: Christina Rossetti and Emily Dickinson

EMMELINE

215w Emmeline Blanche Woodward Wells: "I Have Risen Triumphant"

EMOTION

14j Sociology of Feeling and Emotion
62d What Do Women Really Think and Feel About Themselves?
96s Observations of the Southern Race Feeling
132gg Our Politics Begin with Our Feelings
176nn Emotional Factors in Obstetric Complications
211m Emotional Impact of Abortion
251q Task and Emotional Behavior in the Marital Dyad

280r Men and Emotional Problems
311e Emotional Conflicts of the Career Woman

EMPATHY

17h Richardson's Empathy with Women

EMPIRE

270f Aztec Women: The Transition from Status to Class in Empire and Colony
325k Turkish Women in the Ottoman Empire: The Classical Age
340k Vaster Than Empires and More Slow

EMPLOYMENT

see also LABOR; WORK; OCCUPATION; CAREER; PROFESSION

22u Effects of Maternal Employment on the Child
37e Employer Attitudes to Female Employees
38d Projected Future Employment and Leadership Needs and Areas
39a Maid of All Work or Departmental Sister-in-Law? The Faculty Wife Employed on Campus
39l Demographic Influence on Female Employment and the Status of Women
55a Women as Employees: Some Comments on Research in Industrial Sociology
61e Marriage and the Employment of Women
70e Employment of Married Women and the Changing Sex Roles in Poland
70h Jobs or Careers: The Case of the Professionally Employed Married Woman
70j Impact of Employment upon Fertility
91e Women, Employment, and Fertility Trends in the Arab Middle East and North Africa
91g Fertility and Women's Employment Outside the Home in Western Europe
91h Fertility and Women's Employment in the Socialist Countries of Eastern Europe
130a Employment of Females as Practitioners in Midwifery
135e Employer's Attitude to Working Mothers
135f Family, Employment and the Allocation of Time
140e Female Employment and Family Organization in West Africa
140l Women's Employment and Changing Sex Roles, 1900 to 1930
140n Stress, Primary Support Systems and Women's Employment Status
166xx Employer Acceptance of the Mature Home Economist
166aaa Myth of the Egalitarian Family: Familial Roles and the Professionally Employed Wife
180a Discrimination in Higher Education: A Debate on Faculty Employment
196x Attitudes of Superintendents and Board of Education Members Toward the Employment and Effectiveness of Women as Public-School Administrators
197j Myth is Better Than a Miss: Men Get the Edge in Academic Employment
202o Income and Employment Effects of Women's Liberation
256j Impact of Mid-twentieth Century Movement for Sex Equality in Employment on Three Contemporary Economic Institutions
267g Employment of Women, Education, and Fertility
287e Implications of Women's Employment for Home and Family Life
287f Impact of Equal Employment Opportunity Laws

309c Employment and Family Change: A Study of Middle-Class Women in Urban Gujarat
311a Women in Employment
325h Education and Employment among Kuwaiti Women
326c Recent Trends in the Employment of American Women
328a Women's Stake in Full Employment: Their Disadvantaged Role in the Economy--Challenges to Action
328c Legal Road to Equal Employment Opportunity
328d Legal Remedies beyond Title VII to Combat Sex Discrimination in Employment
328f Women Workers, Nontraditional Occupations and Full Employment
328g Underemployment of Women: Policy Implications for a Full Employment Economy
328i Homemaker, the Family, and Employment
328l Facilitating Full Employment of Women through Career Education
328p Impact of Mass-Media Stereotypes upon the Full Employment of Women
333a Economic Theories of Employment Discrimination
333b Role of Worker Expectancies in the Study of Employment Discrimination
333d More Useful Modes of Research on Discrimination in Employment and Pay
333e Black Employment in the South
333i Recommendations from Research Workshops on Equal Employment Opportunity
336b Vindication of the Character and Condition of the Females Employed in the Lowell Mills...
342o Equal Employment Opportunities in Oregon
352k Trends in Women's Employment in the U.S.S.R.
352m Handicrafts: A Source of Employment for Women in Developing Rural Economies
354i Implications of Women's Employment for Home and Family Life
370d Employment of Women and Fertility
371k Employment Problems of Women: Federal Government Examples

ENCOUNTER

113j Dynastic Encounter
166c Encountering the Male Establishment: Sex-Status Limits on Woman's Careers in the Professions
220w Dynastic Encounter
250ll Encountering the Male Establishment: Sex Status Limits on Woman's Careers in the Professions
322c Odyssey of Encounter

ENCYCLOPEDIAS

208ii Lost Herstory: The Treatment of Women in Children's Encyclopedias

ENDEARING

129w Those Endearing Young Charms: Fifty Years Later

ENDOCRINE

204i Prenatal Influences on Cognitive Abilities: Data from Experimental Animals and Human and Endocrine Syndromes

ENDS

117g Tumah and Taharah; Ends and Beginnings

ENEMY

24s The Enemy
100c Love Thine Enemy: Male-Female Relationships
259j Enemies of Suffrage

ENFORCEMENT

297q Discrimination Against Women in the U.S.: Higher Education, Government Enforcement Agencies, and Unions

ENGANOSO

80f "El casamiento enganoso": Marriage in the Novels of Maria Luisa Bombal, Silvina Bullrich, and Elisa Serrana

ENGELS

74f Marx and Engels on Women's Liberation
86l In Defense of Engels on the Matriarchy
126a Woman in Society: A Critique of Frederick Engels
181i Looking Again at Engels' "Origin of the Family, Private Property and the State"
230i Engels Revisited: Women, the Organization of Production, and Private Property
249k Engels Revisited: Women, the Organization of Production, and Private Property
251j Anthropologist Looks at Engels
252o Anthropologist Looks at Engels

ENGINEERING

166cc Female in Engineering
166ss What You Should Know About Women Engineers
176l Barriers to the Career Choice of Engineering, Medicine, or Science Among American Women
278o Women in a Man's World: The Female Engineers
368i Sex-Linked Values: Their Impacts on Women in Engineering

ENGLAND

see also ANGLO-SAXON; BRITAIN; ENGLISH WOMEN

10c A New England Nun
19m Angels in the Devil's Workshop: Leisured and Charitable Women in Nineteenth-Century England and France
41c New England Mill Women in the Early Nineteenth Century
42m Welfare of Women in Laboring Families: England, 1860-1950
92c Separation of Home and Work? Landladies and Lodgers in Nineteenth-Century England
111mm A New England Nun
112dd A New England Nun
126f Gynecology and Ideology in Seventeenth-Century England

141e Novel Women: Origins of the Feminist Literary Tradition in England and France
141g Influential Women in Anglo-Saxon England
162d Family Limitation in Pre-Industrial England
223j Women of England in a Century of Social Change, 1815-1914: A Select Bibliography
240c Praising Virtuous Ladies: The Literary Image and Historical Reality of Women in Seventeenth-century England
244h Sex and Death in Victorian England: An Examination of Age- and Sex-Specific Death Rates, 1840-1910
244j Women of England in a Century of Social Change, 1815-1914: A Select Bibliography, Part II
255d Women and Literature in Eighteenth Century England
279d A New England Nun
315e Female Felon in Fourteenth-Century England
315g Widow and Ward: The Feudal Law of Child Custody in Medieval England
335d Women in Norman and Plantagenet England
335e Women Under the Law in Medieval England: 1066-1485
335k Women in Twentieth-Century England
336e Early Factory Magazines in New England: The LOWELL OFFERING and its Contemporaries
359a Emergence of Women's Autobiography in England

ENGLISH

120f Male-Female Intonation Patterns in American English
120g Sex, Covert Prestige, and Linguistic Change in the Urban British English of Norwich
140jj Women in English Literature
181d Landscape with Figures: Home and Community in English Society
207b Sexism as Shown through the English Vocabulary
207c Gender-Marking in American English: Usage and Reference
219g Phonological Differences in the English of Adolescent Chicanas and Chicanos
225f Woman-Power: Religious Heresy and Feminism in Early English Socialism
240d Portrayal of Women in Restoration and Eighteenth-century English Literature
240g Marriage Perceived: English Literature, 1873-1941
264y Sexism and the English Language: The Linguistic Implications of Being a Woman
312b Role of Women in Ireland under the New English Order
335h Discovery of Women in Eighteenth-Century English Political Life
335l Survey of Primary Sources and Archives for the History of Early Twentieth-Century English Women
337f Quaker Women in the English Left Wing

ENGLISH WOMEN

110c Gentle Doubters: Images of Women in Englishwomen's Novels, 1840-1920
255e Eighteenth-Century Englishwoman: According to the Gentleman's Magazine
273x The Englishwoman
335g Eighteenth-Century Englishwoman

ENLIGHTENMENT

255f "Treated Like Imbecile Children" (Diderot): The Enlightenment and the Status of Women
256o Degree in Enlightenment: When a Woman's Education Will No Longer Be an Academic Question

ENQUIRY

9z Free Enquiry

ENRICHMENT

210f Enrichment or Threat? When the Eves Come Marching In

ENROLLMENT

196nn Sex Differential in School Enrollment and Educational Attainment

ENTITLEMENTS

135b Current Entitlements and Provisions

ENTRAILS

278c Entrails of Power: Bogus Manhood and the Language of Grief

ENTREPRENEUR

215t Dr. Margaret Ann Freece: Entrepreneur of Southern Utah
302a Signares of Saint-Louis and Goree: Women Entrepreneurs in Eighteenth-Century Senegal
302f Limitations of Group Action Among Entrepreneurs: The Market Women of Abidjan, Ivory Coast

ENTRY

81 Entries in a Journal
76d Girl's Entry into the Oedipus Complex
344r Crisis Perspective on Emerging Health Roles: A Paradigm for the Entry of Women into New Occupational Roles

ENVIRONMENT

22o Sex-Role Concepts and Sex Typing in Childhood as a Function of School and Home Environments
143h Women in the Suburban Environment: A U.S.--Sweden Comparison
143m Unconscious Discrimination in Environmental Design Education
143q Emergency Shelter: The Development of an Innovative Women's Environment
156f Teachers, Peers, and Play Preferences: An Environmental Approach to Sex Typing in the Preschool
199a Sexual Behavior Differentiation: Prenatal Hormonal and Environmental Control
208o Changing the School Environment
271h Sex-Role Concepts and Sex Typing in Childhood as a Function of School and Home Environments

303a Model Domestic Environment: Icon or Option?
325y Domestic Social Environment of Women and Girls in Isfahan, Iran
358m Environmental Effect on the Woman in Athletics

ENVY

76i Penis Envy: From Childhood Wish to Developmental Metaphor
76l Parental Mislabeling of Female Genitals as a Determinant of Penis Envy and Learning Inhibitions in Women
76p Masculine Envy of Woman's Procreative Function
78e Penis Envy in Women
169o "Penis Envy" in Women
170d "Penis Envy" in Women
170n Survey and Reevaluation of the Concept of Penis Envy
176jj Castration Anxiety and Phallus Envy: A Reformulation

EPIC

184b Transformations of the Heroine: From Epic Heard to Epic Read

EPICUREAN

231j Epicurean Doctrine of Love

EPIDEMIC

191n Epidemic in Unnecessary Hysterectomy

EPIDEMIOLOGY

99b Sex Differences in the Epidemiology of Mental Disorder
99n Sex Differences and the Epidemiology of Depression
317h Epidemiology of Spirit Possession among the Luvale of Zambia

EPISCOPALIAN

337n Episcopalian Story

EQUAL

13nn It's Time for Equal Education
13pp Equal Opportunity for Women: How Possible and How Quickly?
63a Equal Pay in Great Britain
63b Equal Pay in America
63c Equal Pay for Women in Australia and New Zealand
63e Equal Pay in Canada: History, Progress and Problems
63f Equal Pay Question in Japan
85k How Do We Know When Opportunities Are Equal?
105l Woman's Movement and the Women's Pages: Separate, Unequal and Unspectacular
107b Women as Equal to Men in the State
120b Women's Speech: Separate But Unequal?
129e Does Youthfulness Equal Attractiveness?
131k Women in Philippine Society: More Equal Than Many
174f Discrimination and the Law: The Equal Credit Opportunity Act
196jj Equal Rights for Women
203n How Do We Know When Opportunities Are Equal?

203s Equal Opportunity, Free from Gender-Based Discrimination
208i Does Different Equal Less? A High School Woman Speaks Out
208j Segregated Academic and Vocational Schools: Separate But Not Equal
208hh Guidelines for Equal Treatment of the Sexes in Social Studies Textbooks
218e Unequal Partners in an Uneasy Alliance: Women and the Working Class in Imperial Germany
233bb "X" Doesn't Equal "Y"
280k Test Scores and Unequal Education
280q Social Security and Equal Rights
282s How Do We Know When Opportunities are Equal?
287f Impact of Equal Employment Opportunity Laws
301e Developing Criteria and Measures of Equal Opportunities for Women
314h Real Equal Opportunity for Women Executives
314ll Consequences of Equal Opportunity for Women
318j Equal Pay for Equal Work?
328c Legal Road to Equal Employment Opportunity
333i Recommendations from Research Workshops on Equal Employment Opportunity
334n Not Separate, Not Equal
342o Equal Employment Opportunities in Oregon
344e Lobbying for Equal Credit
352i Women's Wages in Japan and the Question of Equal Pay
358a Equal Opportunity for Women in Sports

EQUAL PAY ACT

252ff Reducing Discrimination: Role of the Equal Pay Act

EQUAL RIGHTS AMENDMENT

see also EQUALITY; AFFIRMATIVE ACTION; EQUITY

86g Questions and Answers on the Equal Rights Amendment
89bb In Support of the E.R.A.
203r Equal Rights Amendment
280y Equal Rights Amendment: A Threat to Family Life?
342cc Politics of the Equal Rights Amendment
344s Individualism, Marriage and the Liberal State: Beyond the Equal Rights Amendment

EQUALITY

see also EQUITY; EQUAL RIGHTS AMENDMENT; AFFIRMATIVE ACTION

7d Black Woman's Struggle for Equality in the South, 1895-1925
20bb Legal Equality between Men and Women
21p Women in China: Problems of Sex Inequality and Socio-economic Change
21q Erosion of Sexual Equality in the Kibbutz: A Structural Interpretation
22e Sex Equality: The Beginnings of Ideology
45b Full Equality: More Job Education for Women
48h Sources of Inequality
64a What Does Equality Mean?
64b How Can I Determine if Equality Exists?
132q Sex Equality: The Beginning of Ideology

139o Equality Between the Sexes: An Immodest Proposal
149q Equality between the Sexes: An Immodest Proposal
158a Sexism as Inequality
158f Equality of Women
158l Sexual Equality
164l Two Cheers for Equality
170u Masculinity-Femininity: A Study in Imposed Inequality
174c Black Women in the Continuing Struggle for Equality
177g Equality of Souls, Inequality of Sexes: Woman in Medieval Theology
180b Drive Toward Equality
181l Women and Equality
183b Men, Women and Violence: Some Reflections on Equality
186i Equality Between the Sexes: An Immodest Proposal
188b Letters on the Equality of the Sexes
194j History of Women's Struggle for Equality in Puerto Rico
203i Idea of Equality
203j Sexual Equality
208b Equality: Men's Lib
208r Let Them Aspire! A Plea and Proposal for Equality of Opportunity for Males and Females in the Ann Arbor Public Schools
213l Mechanistic Cooperation and Sexual Equality among the Western Bontoc
213m Social Inequality and Sexual Status in Barbados
217f Realizing the Equality Principle
217i Equality and Inviolability: An Approach to Compensatory Justice
231a Moral Equality
238d Sex Equality: The Beginnings of Ideology
251v Legal Equality in Marriage
251gg Have Swedish Women Achieved Equality?
252q Sex-Role Differentiation in an Equalitarian Society
253e Equality Between the Sexes: An Immodest Proposal
256j Impact of Mid-twentieth Century Movement for Sex Equality in Employment on Three Contemporary Economic Institutions
264u Black Women and the Pursuit of Equality
271u Sex Equality: The Beginnings of Ideology
276f Equality Between Men and Women in Sweden
280p Choosing Equality
284o Still Inequalities in Socialist Society
287g Requisites for Equality
292u Equality Between the Sexes: An Immodest Proposal
301c Race, Sex, and Jobs: The Drive Toward Equality
304h Sexual Division of Labour and Inequality: Labour and Leisure
309f Women and the Law: Constitutional Rights and Continuing Inequalities
318e Sexual Equality in Soviet Policy: A Developmental Perspective
328b Way to Full Equality
331b Sexual Inequality, Cultural Norms, and Wife-Beating
334f Equality or Submersion? Feme (sic) Couvert Status in Early Pennsylvania
349g Women in the Chinese Communist Revolution: The Question of Political Equality
352c Division of Labour and Sexual Inequality: The Role of Education
352h Equality of Remuneration for Men and Women in the Member States of the E.E.C.
352l Sexual Equality in the Labour Market: Some Experiences and Views of the Nordic Countries
354g Inequalities in the Labor Force: Three Sociological Explanations

364o Current Equality Issues in Sweden
365e What Does Equality Between the Sexes Imply?
365g Psychological Consequences of Sexual Inequality
368j Impacts of Local Government Tax Structures on Women: Inefficiencies and Inequalities

EQUITY

170s For the Future--Equity?
174l Women's Educational Equity: Favorable Student Response
217j Compensatory Justice and the Meaning of Equity
266cc When Women Are More Deserving Than Men: Equity, Attribution, And Perceived Sex Differences

ERA

7a Northern Black Female Workers: Jacksonian Era
19c "Liberated" Women: The Classical Era
19g Women in the Reformation Era
178c Puritan Ethic in the Revolutionary Era: Abigail Adams and Thomas Jefferson

ERNEST

17p "A Farewell to Arms": Ernest Hemingway's "Resentful Cryptogram"

EROSION

21q Erosion of Sexual Equality in the Kibbutz: A Structural Interpretation
180k Erosion of Legal Principles in the Creation of Legal Policies

EROTICISM

98c Bonds of Love: Rational Violence and Erotic Domination
240k "Combat in the Erogenous Zone": Women in the American Novel between the Two World Wars
247a Eroticism and Female Imagery in Nineteenth-Century Art
247b Ingres and the Erotic Intellect
247c Henry Fuseli's "Nightmare": Eroticism or Pornography?
247g Corset as Erotic Alchemy: From Rococo Galanterie to Montaut's Physiologies
296i Clitoral Eroticism and the Sexual Response Cycle in Human Females

ESKIMO

131i Eskimo Women: Makers of Men
372l Economic Role of Women in Alaskan Eskimo Society

ESSAY

65b Early Essays on Marriage and Divorce
74h Anarchism and Other Essays
79o An Essay to Revive the Ancient Education of Gentlewomen
97g Historical and Critical Essay for Black Women
115i Woman Versus Womanliness: An Essay in Speculative Psychology

117b Women's Liberation and the Liberation of God: An Essay in Story Theology
195c Uncivil Liberty: An Essay to Show the Injustice and Impolicy of Ruling Woman Without Her Consent
222x Complexity: Toni Morrison's Women--An Interview Essay
232k First Essay on the Political Rights of Women

ESSENCE

107p Essence of Woman

ESSENTIALISM

157u Fetal Humanity and the Theory of Essentialism

ESTABLISHMENT

166c Encountering the Male Establishment: Sex-Status Limits on Woman's Careers in the Professions
209h Adjusting the Lives of Women to the Establishment
238h Educational Establishment: Wasted Women
250ll Encountering the Male Establishment: Sex Status Limits on Woman's Careers in the Professions
364j Confronting the Sports Establishment: A Plan for Honesty and Sanity

ESTATE

17i "Jane Eyre": Woman's Estate
89y Woman's Estate

ESTHER

212m Esther Schub
373g Esther Kahn

ETHICS

85x Abortion and Ethical Theory
107w Sexual Ethics and Women
152p Radical Ethic for Sports
178c Puritan Ethic in the Revolutionary Era: Abigail Adams and Thomas Jefferson
232l Principles of Ethics
283i Differentiation and Difference--Reflections on the Ethical Implications of Women's Liberation

ETHNICITY

57e White Ethnic Catholic Woman
116q Women, Ethnicity, and Mental Health: The Italian Woman, Impressions and Observations
116r Oral History in Pittsburgh--Women, Ethnicity, and Mental Health: Rationale, Procedure, and Methodology
146g Life Span Behavior Patterns--Class and Ethnic Variations
154e Premiss of Dedication: Notes towards an Ethnography of Diplomats' Wives
180j Emergence of an American Ethnic Pattern

219p Effects of the Ethnicity of the Interviewer on Conversation: A Study of Chicana Women
230j Iroquois Women: An Ethnohistoric Note
359g African-American Women's Autobiographies and Ethnicity

ETHOLOGY

198p Ethology and Sex Differences
199m Ethological Study of Children Approaching a Strange Adult: Sex Differences

ETIOLOGY

51g Etiology of Female Crime

ETIQUETTE

309d Etiquette among Women in Karnataka: Forms of Address in the Village and the Family

ETRUSCANS

98i For the Etruscans: Sexual Difference and Artistic Production--The Debate Over a Female Aesthetic

EUDORA

47k Eudora's Web
192e Eudora Welty

EUNUCH

362c Female Eunuch

EURASIA

30a Bridewealth and Dowry in Africa and Eurasia

EUROGALLEGAS

20v Eurogallegas: Female Spanish Migration

EUROPE

see also individual countries

23e Learned Women in the Europe of the Sixteenth Century
42g Power of Women Through the Family in Medieval Europe: 500-1100
54f Marital Fertility and the Changing Status of Women in Europe
54g Extra-Marital Fertility and its Occurrence in Stable Unions: Recent Trends in Western Europe
54h Sociological and Demographic Aspects of the Changing Status of Migrant Women in Europe
54i Report of the Symposium on Demographic Aspects of the Changing Status of Women in Europe
91g Fertility and Women's Employment Outside the Home in Western Europe

91h Fertility and Women's Employment in the Socialist Countries of Eastern Europe
183c Women and Collective Action in Europe
294h Political Participation of Western European Women
294i Political Activity of Women in Eastern Europe
315a Land, Family, and Women in Continental Europe, 701-1200
328q Working Women: European Experience and American Need
329h Female Labor Force in Western Europe
364a "Women's History" in Transition: The European Case

EVA

281r Case of Eva Peron

EVALUATION

75i Ex-Offender Evaluates Correctional Programming for Women
88w Anais Nin: A Critical Evaluation
156n APPENDIX: Guidelines for the Development and Evaluation of Unbiased Educational Materials
176gg Re-Evaluation of the Primary Role of the Communist Chinese Woman: The Homemaker or the Worker
196aa Effect of Sex on College Admission, Work Evaluation, and Job Interviews
250b Evaluation of the Performance of Women as a Function of Their Sex, Achievement, and Personal History
296o Re-evaluation of Some Aspects of Femininity through a Study of Menstruation
368c Evaluating Women's Studies- Academic Theory and Practice

EVANGELISM

116h Protestant Evangelism and the Italian Immigrant Woman
317c Hats as a Symbol of Women's Position in Three Evangelical Churches in Edinburgh, Scotland
337i Feminism in the Evangelical Tradition

EVANGELIZADA

372f Spirit Mediums in Umbanda Evangelizada of Porto Alegre, Brazil: Dimensions of Power and Authority

EVASION

210j Sexism and the Contemporary Church: When Evasion Becomes Complicity

EVE

17l Eve Among the Indians
110k Abuse of Eve by the New World Adam
210f Enrichment or Threat? When the Eves Come Marching In
222l Black Eve or Madonna? Antithetical Views of the Mother in Black American Literature
263e Eve and Adam: Genesis 2-3 Reread
343a Curse of Eve--Or, What I Learned in School (Women and Literature)

EVENTS

170t Trauma of Eventlessness
281h Biological Events and Cultural Control

EVERYDAY

29g Everyday Use
314r Everyday Dealings with Women

EVOLUTION

38b Evolving Relationships Between Women and Men
96aa Evolution of Disenchantment
141ee Historical and Theoretical Evolution of Viola Spolin's Theatre Games
145b Prisoners of Progress: Women and Evolution
164o Direction of Feminine Evolution
169b Evolution of the Oedipus Complex in Women
190c Women and the Jural Domain: An Evolutionary Perspective
199s Psychobiology of Sex Differences: An Evolutionary Perspective
223h Stereotypes of Femininity in a Theory of Sexual Evolution
226g Evolution of Disenchantment
230a Perspectives on the Evolution of Sex Differences
232a Evolution of Woman
297o Evolutionism and the Place of Women in the U.S., 1855-1900
306a Evolution of the Feminine Ideal
332a Have Only Men Evolved?
365a Evolutionary Aspects of Human Gender

EX-CHEERLEADER

152m Confessions of an Ex-Cheerleader

EXAMINATION

141l Re-Examination of the Fear of Success
244h Sex and Death in Victorian England: An Examination of Age- and Sex-Specific Death Rates, 1840-1910
246n Sociological Examination of the Women's Movement
250v Effects of Sex of Examiner and Subject on Children's Quantitative Test Performance
254k Being and Doing: A Cross-Cultural Examination of the Socialization of Males and Females
267d Cross-cultural Examination of Women's Marital, Educational and Occupational Options
278y Before Androgyny: An Examination of the Stages Toward Neo-Masculinity

EXCHANGES

219e Verbal Turn-Taking and Exchanges in Faculty Dialogue

EXCURSION

102d The Excursion of the Dead Girls

EXECUTIVE

77a Sex Hormones and Executive Ability
254v Working in "A Man's World": The Woman Executive
314h Real Equal Opportunity for Women Executives
314s "Women Executives are Different"
314t What's It Like for Women Executives?
314jj Keys to the Executive Powder Room
316g Career Structures of Federal Executives: A Focus on Women

EXILE

215s Dr. Martha Hughes Cannon: Doctor, Wife, Legislator, Exile

EXISTENTIAL

24t Bertha Schneiders Existential Edge
107z Existential Paralysis of Women

EXITS

330n Creative Exits: Fight-Therapy for Divorcees

EXPECTANCY

45d Counseling Implications of Black Women's Market Position, Aspirations and Expectancies
140u Climbing the Political Ladder: The Aspirations and Expectations of Partisan Elites
166z Self-Concept, Occupational Role Expectations, and Occupational Choice in Nursing and Social Work
166ee Career Expectations of Negro Women Graduates
176ee Sex Differentiation in Role Expectations and Performance
184a Life Expectancies for Women in Medieval Society
250hh Sex Differences in Expectancy of Intellectual and Academic Reinforcement
267j Women's Expectations for and Causal Attributions of Success and Failure
285k Sex Differences in the Incidence of Susto in Two Zapotec Pueblos: An Analysis of the Relationships between Sex Role Expectations and a Folk Illness
330c Cultural Values, Female Role Expectancies and Therapeutic Goals: Research and Interpretation
333b Role of Worker Expectancies in the Study of Employment Discrimination
351a Young Women's Decisions to Attend College: Desires, Expectations and Realizations

EXPELLING

208l Expelling Pregnant Students

EXPERIMENT

8hh Power to Gay People: A Los Angeles Experiment in Community Action
13kk Feminist Experiment in Education

98l Separation and Survival: Mothers, Daughters, Sisters: The Women's Experimental Theatre
155g Differentiation of Male and Female Orgasm: An Experimental Study
204i Prenatal Influences on Cognitive Abilities: Data from Experimental Animals and Human and Endocrine Syndromes
250ii Experimental Arousal of Achievement Motivation in Adolescent Girls
331k Women into Mothers: Experimental Family Life-Styles

EXPLANATIONS

67j Biological Explanations of Psychological Sex Differences
205a Biological Explanations of Sex-Role Stereotypes
354g Inequalities in the Labor Force: Three Sociological Explanations

EXPLOITATION

282j Exploitation, Oppression, and Self-Sacrifice

EXPLORATION

14b Women and the Structure of Organizations: Explorations in Theory and Behavior
122i Three Female Playwrights Explore Contemporary Latin American Reality: Myrna Casas, Griselda Gambaro, Luisa Josefina Hernandez
122k Thematic Exploration of the Works of Elena Garro
212v Family Portraits: Filmmakers Explore Their Roots
225b Witch and Her Devils: An Exploration of the Relationship Between Femininity and Illness
256s Genderless Sexuality: A Male-Female Psychological Exploration of the Future of Sexual Relationships
283c Explorations with Doris Lessing in Quest of The Four-Gated City

EXPLOSION

264a Woman's Biology--Mankind's Destiny: The Population Explosion and Women's Changing Roles
265a Woman's Biology--Mankind's Destiny: The Population Explosion and Women's Changing Roles
314b Exploding Some Myths About Women Managers

EXPOSITION

336c Corporations and Operatives, Being an Exposition of the Condition of Factory Operatives...

EXPOSURE

198z Theories of Identification and Exposure to Multiple Models

EXPRESS

103c The Plymouth Express

EXPRESSION

36c Identity and Expression: A Writing Course for Women

EXTENDED

89ss Building Extended Families
140k Role of Wife in the Black Extended Family: Perspectives from a Rural Community in Southern United States

EXTERNAL

49d Psychological Barriers for Women in Sciences: Internal and External

EXTRA

369l Notes from an Extra in the American Moving Picture Show

EXULTATION

322d From Anguish to Exultation

EYE

50b The Man with the Wild Eyes
83d Miss Yellow Eyes
89i With an Eye to the Future
133f The Eye of the Heron
177j Protestant Principle: A Woman's Eye-View of Barth and Tillich
278f Pope's Portraits of Women: The Tyranny of the Pictorial Eye
356d Men With No Eyes

EYRE

17i "Jane Eyre": Woman's Estate

FABLE

256b Born Free: A Feminist Fable

FABRIC

206q Sex Roles in the Modern Fabric of China

FACADE

256c Female Facade: Fierce, Fragile and Fading

FACE

16a Your Faces, O My Sisters! Your Faces Filled of Light!
50l Angel Face
71d Marianismo: The Other Face of "Machismo" in Latin America
200j Memory for Names and Faces: A Characteristic of Social Intelligence?
218d Socialism Faces Feminism: The Failure of Synthesis in France, 1879-1914
240j They Shall Have Faces, Minds, and (One Day) Flesh: Women in Late Nineteenth-century and Early Twentieth-century American Literature

FACTO

328e De Facto Job Segregation

FACTORY

306c Women in Factories
318c Russian Factory Women, 1880-1914
336c Corporations and Operatives, Being an Exposition of the Condition of Factory Operatives...
336e Early Factory Magazines in New England: The LOWELL OFFERING and its Contemporaries

FACULTY

see also HIGHER EDUCATION; COLLEGE; UNIVERSITY; CAMPUS; AFFIRMATIVE ACTION; ACADEMIA; SCHOLAR; TEACHER

4f From Sugar to Spice to Professor
4h Status Transitions of Women Students, Faculty, and Administrators
4j Faculty Wife: Her Academic Interests and Qualifications
4l Representation, Performance and Status of Women on the Faculty at the Urbana-Champaign Campus of the University of Illinois
39a Maid of All Work or Departmental Sister-in-Law? The Faculty Wife Employed on Campus
39p Performance, Rewards, and Perceptions of Sex Discrimination among Male and Female Faculty
180a Discrimination in Higher Education: A Debate on Faculty Employment
219e Verbal Turn-Taking and Exchanges in Faculty Dialogue

FAD

18r Nutrition and Women: Facts and Faddism
126w "Herstory" As History: A New Field or Another Fad?

FAG

8gg Getting It Together Journalism: A View of FAG RAG

FAILURE

9mm Why Mothers Fail
13z Our Failures Only Marry: Bryn Mawr and the Failure of Feminism
149j Declining Status of Women: Popular Myths and the Failure of Functionalist Thought
166q Fail: Bright Women
197i How Coeducation Fails Women
218d Socialism Faces Feminism: The Failure of Synthesis in France, 1879-1914
233rr Fail: Bright Women
254y Our Failures Only Marry: Bryn Mawr and the Failure of Feminism
267j Women's Expectations for and Causal Attributions of Success and Failure
314ff Women in Management: Keys to Success or Failure

FAIR

791 Tragedie of Mariam, The Fair Queen of Jewry
180ff Is Turn-About Fair Play?
341v Fair Return

FAIRY

208y Female Acculturation Through the Fairy Tale

FAITH

215i Bathsheba Bigler Smith: Woman of Faith and Courage

FALL

9c Seneca Falls Convention: Declaration
9ii Seduced and Abandoned in the New World: The Fallen Woman in American Fiction
75f Feminism and the "Fallen Woman"
93d Lena Morrow Lewis: Her Rise and Fall
107a Creation and Fall of Man and Woman
151p Decline and Fall of the Double Standard
212p Mai Zetterling: Free Fall
257c Declaration of Sentiments, Resolutions, Seneca Falls

FALLACY

314gg Women in Management: The Fallacy of the Trait Approach

FALSE

291d Work Aspirations of Women: False Leads and New Starts
340l False Dawn

FAMILIES

42m Welfare of Women in Laboring Families: England, 1860-1950
45f Black Women Who Head Families: Economic Needs and Economic Resources
55i Marriage, Role Division and Social Cohesion: The Case of Some French Upper-Middle Class Families
70c Interaction and Goal Attainment in Parisian Working Wives' Families
89ss Building Extended Families
116n Metonymic Definition of the Female and the Concept of Honour Among Italian Immigrant Families in Toronto
143r Housing for Single-Parent Families: A Women's Design
172d Individuals and Families in Transition: Dilemmas and Coping
251bb Social Situation of Divorced Mothers and Their Families
252hh Economic Status of Families Headed by Women
269l Women in Families and History
284x Children and Their Families
291l Discrimination and Poverty among Women Who Head Families
351e Migration of Young Families: An Economic Perspective
354j Women's Labor Force Participation and the Residential Mobility of Families
360m Women and Their Families on the Overland Trail, 1842-1867

FAMILY

19t Family Models of the Future
20aa Women and Social Customs within the Family: A Case Study of Attitudes in Kerala, India
25d Family in the Plantation South
25h Family: Resources for Change
35m Introducing the Family Code
35n Significance of the Chinese Family Revolution for Feminist Theory
42g Power of Women Through the Family in Medieval Europe: 500-1100
60e Christian Family
70g Effects of Children on the Family
84d Church, State, and Family: The Women's Movement in Italy
85r Separation of Marriage and Family
86h Family
89nn Family
89oo Nuclear Family
89pp Cuban Family Code
92g Welfare State and the Needs of the Dependent Family
97i American Family: Decay and Rebirth
103e Family Affair
105f Magazine Heroines: Is MS. Just Another Member of the FAMILY CIRCLE?
107o Marriage and the Family
108s Family Happiness
116g Settlement House and the Italian Family
116o Maternal Role in the Contemporary Italian-American Family
116t Family and Kin Cohesion among South Italian Immigrants in Toronto
121b Female and Family in the Economy and Society of Colonial Brazil
121d Women in a Noble Family: The Mexican Counts of Regla, 1750-1830
140y Family Planning, Decision Making: Attitudes and Intentions of Mothers and Fathers
141n WOMEN, FAMILY AND FERTILITY: Introduction
141q Men and Women in the Family: History of the Idea of Family in America's Depression Generation
146k Family Relationships
158z Ideology of the Family
162d Family Limitation in Pre-Industrial England
172f American Family: A Twenty-Year View
176s Marriage and the Family
176cc Pre-Industrial Patterns in the Colonial Family in America: A Content Analysis of Colonial Magazines
182d Changing Soviet Family
182e Childbearing Functions of the Soviet Family
182f Marriage and the Family
198i Family in Father-Right and Mother-Right: Complex of Mother-Right
202n Formal Extrafamily Child Care--Some Economic Observations
202p Impact of Women's Liberation on Marriage, Divorce, and Family Life-Style
205e Sex-Role Stereotyping in Studies of Marriage and the Family
212v Family Portraits: Filmmakers Explore Their Roots
213i Impact of Modernization on Women's Position in the Family in Ghana
222c War on African Familyhood
223a Victorian Governess: Status Incongruence in Family and Society
233ff Monogamous Family
244b Forgotten Woman of the Period: Penny Weekly Family Magazines of the 1840's and 1850's
251ff Women's Contribution to Family Income

251hh Chinese Family Revolution and Feminist Theory
252a Family and Cultural Change
252b Family Patterns and Human Rights
256g Fractured Family
260l Marriage and Family Support
260n Social Change and the Family
266ff Interrelationship of the Status of Women and Family Planning
269j Modern Family: Sticky Myths, Diverse Realities, and the Problem of Isolation
281l Female Status, the Family, and Male Dominance in a West Indian Community
291e Dual Linkages between the Occupational and Family Systems: A Macrosociological Analysis
293b Economy, Family, Fertility, and the Female
293k Women as Co-Managers: The Family as a General Model of Human Social Organization
304a Women, the Family and Corporate Capitalism
306e Women in Family Businesses
309d Etiquette among Women in Karnataka: Forms of Address in the Village and the Family
312g Women and the Family
315a Land, Family, and Women in Continental Europe, 701-1200
318f Bolshevik Alternatives and the Soviet Family: The 1926 Marriage Law Debate
325v Iranian Women in Family Alliance and Sexual Politics
331h Public Policy and the Family: A New Strategy for Women as Wives and Mothers
331k Women into Mothers: Experimental Family Life-Styles
334b Women's Lives Transformed: Demographic and Family Patterns in America, 1600-1970
342i Women's Perspectives of Family Studies
342q Familism and Sex Roles: A Chicana Perspective
356i A Member of the Family
360c Widowhood in Eighteenth-Century Massachusetts: A Problem in the History of the Family
365f Changes in the Modern Family: Their Impact on Sex Roles
367c Family Planning and Population Policies in the Middle East and North Africa
370g Effects on Power and Division of Labor in the Family

FAMILY--BLACK

25a Negro Family in America
25e Crucible of Identity: The Negro Lower-Class Family
25g Negro Family: The Case for National Action
25j Family and Childhood in a Southern Negro Community
140k Role of Wife in the Black Extended Family: Perspectives from a Rural Community in Southern United States
331f Black Women and the Family

FAMILY--LIFE

48i Family Life of the Successful Woman
48j Family Life in Transition
89tt Capitalism, the Family, and Personal Life
251c Capitalism, the Family, and Personal Life
251t Family Life in an Antifamily Setting

267x Life Patterns and Self-Esteem in Gifted Family Oriented and Career Commited Women
269i Parenting and Family Life Styles
280y Equal Rights Amendment: A Threat to Family Life?
287b Family and Work: The Social Life Cycle of Women
287e Implications of Women's Employment for Home and Family Life
354i Implications of Women's Employment for Home and Family Life
367a Family Life, Women's Status, and Fertility: Middle East and North African Perspectives

FAMILY--ORIGIN

89t Origin of the Family, Private Property, and the State
158y Origin of the Family, Private Property, and the State
159z Origin of the Family
181i Looking Again at Engels' "Origin of the Family, Private Property and the State"
203g Origin of the Family, Private Property and the State
230c Origin of the Family
264f Origin of the Family
265d Origin of the Family

FAMILY--ROLE

116m Italian Mothers, American Daughters: Changes in Work and Family Roles
116s Emigration, the Italian Family, and Changing Roles
140i Women's Roles in World Change: What About the Family?
166aaa Myth of the Egalitarian Family: Familial Roles and the Professionally Employed Wife
266ii Socio-Economic Context Of Sex And Power: A Study of Women, Work And Family Roles in Four Israeli Institutional Frameworks
276a Family and Gender Roles in Historical Perspective
291h Familial Constraints on Women's Work Roles
371c Occupational Values and Family Roles: Women in Blue-Collar and Service Occupations
371m Family Wholeness: New Conceptions of Family Roles

FAMILY--SEX

42h Family Limitation, Sexual Control, and Domestic Feminism in Victorian America
260bb Sexual Repression and the Family
266ii Socio-Economic Context Of Sex And Power: A Study of Women, Work And Family Roles in Four Israeli Institutional Frameworks
292s Nineteenth-Century Heritage: The Family, Feminism and Sex
360k Family Limitation, Sexual Control, and Domestic Feminism in Victorian America

FAMILY--STRUCTURE

84c Structures of Patriarchy and Capital in the Family
198l Family Structure and the Socialization of the Child
249b Family Structure and Feminine Personality
251p Sex Roles and Family Structure
251ii Family Structure and Communism
252nn Family Structure and Communism

FAMILY--WORK

37a Family and Married Women at Work
59i Working Wives and Family Income
135f Family, Employment and the Allocation of Time
140e Female Employment and Family Organization in West Africa
166mm Career and Family Orientations of Husbands and Wives in Relation to Marital Happiness
166aaa Myth of the Egalitarian Family: Familial Roles and the Professionally Employed Wife
176p Career and Family Orientations of Husbands and Wives in Relation to Marital Happiness
252x Working Wives: Their Contribution to Family Income
267x Life Patterns and Self-Esteem in Gifted Family Oriented and Career Committed Women
287b Family and Work: The Social Life Cycle of Women
287e Implications of Women's Employment for Home and Family Life
291h Familial Constraints on Women's Work Roles
297x Sources of the Matrilineal Family System in the Works of Carl J.L. Almqvist
309c Employment and Family Change: A Study of Middle-Class Women in Urban Gujarat
309h Family Status and Female Work Participation
328i Homemaker, the Family, and Employment
354i Implications of Women's Employment for Home and Family Life

FAMINE

312c Women and the Church since the Famine
352d Development and Mounting Famine: A Role for Women

FAMOUS

22b Masculinity-Femininity: An Exception to a Famous Dictim?
266a Masculinity-Femininity: An Exception To a Famous Dictim

FANCIES

79p Nature's Pictures, Drawn by Fancies Pencil to the Life

FANNIE

128t Fannie Farmer and Her Cook Book

FANNY

5d Fanny Von Arnstein

FANTASY

23a Education of Women in the Middle Ages in Theory, Fact, and Fantasy
73f Sexual Fantasies of Women
89m Sexual Fantasies of Women
97h Psychology Constructs the Female, or the Fantasy Life of the Male Psychologist
176rr Sex Differences in Fantasy Patterns

186e Psychology Constructs the Female, or the Fantasy Life of the Male Psychologist
233ee Psychology Constructs the Female, or The Fantasy Life of the Male Psychologist
263s Dreams and Fantasies as Sources of Revelation: Feminist Appropriation of Jung
264w Violence: The Most Obscene Fantasy
266e Heroic and Tender Modes in Women Authors of Fantasy
289e Technicalities and Fantasy About Men and Women
363p Psychology Constructs the Female, or the Fantasy Life of the Male Psychologist

FARE

51ff Parole System: How Women Fare

FAREWELL

17p "A Farewell to Arms": Ernest Hemingway's "Resentful Cryptogram"

FARM

128t Fannie Farmer and Her Cook Book
166g Farmer's Daughter Effect: The Case of the Negro Female Professional
320g Farm Wife
340h The Food Farm

FARR

68r Shaw and Florence Farr

FASCINATING

288mm Fascinating Fascism

FASCISM

116k La Donna Italiana Durante Il Periodo Fascista in Toronto, 1930-1940
288mm Fascinating Fascism
300d Sexual Chic, Sexual Fascism and Sexual Confusion

FASHIONS

42a "Fashionable Diseases": Women's Complaints and Their Treatment in Nineteenth-Century America
153j Dress, or Who Makes the Fashions

FATALE

247i Femme Fatale and Her Sisters

FATHER

8t Faggot Father
18d Father-Daughter Relationship: Past, Present, and Future
19s Mothers in the Fatherland: Women in Nazi Germany
25f Fathers without Children

48d Like Their Fathers Instead
60g Father
89kk Fathers Shouldn't Try to Be Mothers
140y Family Planning, Decision Making: Attitudes and Intentions of Mothers and Fathers
140aa Fathering and Marital Separation
144j Out of Our Fathers' House
153b The Father
156k Fathers are Parents Too
177e Misogynism and Virginal Feminism in the Fathers of the Church
198i Family in Father-Right and Mother-Right: Complex of Mother-Right
198n Absent Father and Cross-Sex Identity
210g Theology After the Demise of God the Father: A Call for the Castration of Sexist Religion
263c After the Death of God the Father
272m Working and Parenting: The Male and Father Role
277u Songs My Father Sang Me
279z The Fathers' Daughters
280x Television and the Image of the Father
283a Theology After the Demise of God the Father: A Call for the Castration of Sexist Religion
296e Fathers, Mothers and Sex Typing
369h My Work and My Working-Class Father

FAULT

155v Attribution of Fault to a Rape Victim as a Function of Respectability

FAUST

88n Female Faust

FAUSTINE

233o Faustine

FAVOR

130b Letters to Ladies in Favor of Female Physicians
300i In Favor of the Sensitive Man

FEAR

73j Why Bright Women Fear Success
253l Nothing to Fear: Notes on the Life of Eleanor Roosevelt
260w Where Angels Fear to Tread

FEAR OF SUCCESS

see also ACHIEVEMENT; FAILURE; SUCCESS

73k Fear of Success: Popular, but Unproven
141l Re-Examination of the Fear of Success
266j Fear of Success: Qualms and Queries
267m Fear of Success in Males and Females: 1965 and 1971
272k How Real is Fear of Success?

280t Fear of Success

FEATURES

36i "Featureless Freedom" or Ironic Submission: Dorothy Richardson and May Sinclair
219c Two Features of "Women's Speech"?

FEDERAL

40h Cost of Compliance with Federal Day Care Standards in Seattle and Denver
206j Male and Female in the German Federal Republic
284l Women's Job Rights Gain in Federal Court Rulings
316g Career Structures of Federal Executives: A Focus on Women
328o Federal Income Tax and Social Security Law
331c Women's Dependency and Federal Programs
371k Employment Problems of Women: Federal Government Examples

FEEDING

68u Torture by Forcible Feeding is Illegal
160b Care and Feeding of Children: A Catechism for the Use of Mothers and Children's Nurses
173z Breast Feeding

FEELING

see EMOTION

FELIPE

121k Felipe Carrillo Puerto and Women's Liberation in Mexico

FELLOW

96l Before Women Were Human Beings: Adventures of an American Fellow in German Universities of the '90s

FELON

315e Female Felon in Fourteenth-Century England

FEM

8j Butch or Fem?: The Third World Lesbian's Dilemma

FEMALE-DOMINATED

354m Women in Female-Dominated Professions

FEMALE-HEADED

202m Vicious Cycle of Welfare: Problems of the Female-Headed Household in N.Y.C.

FEMALE-ROLE

196r Female-Role Perception as a Factor in Counseling

FEMALENESS

99a Femaleness, Maleness and Behavior Disorders in Nonhumans
170o Sense of Femaleness

FEME

334f Equality or Submersion? Feme (sic) Couvert Status in Early Pennsylvania

FEMENINA

80g "Protesta femenina" in Latin America

FEMINA

223i Innocent Femina Sensualis in Unconscious Conflict

FEMININE

20o Feminine Factor in Cultural History
21g Feminine Self-Preservation in Groups
78d Feminine Guilt and the Oedipus Complex
85e Feminine As a Universal
107bb Feminine Mystique
121f Feminine Orders in Colonial Bahia, Brazil: Economic, Social, and Demographic Implications, 1677-1800
121g Feminine Press: The View of Women in the Colonial Journals of Spanish America, 1790-1810
122m Feminine Symbolism in Gabriela Mistral's "Fruta"
164o Direction of Feminine Evolution
170b Problem of Feminine Masochism
170h Masculine and Feminine: Some Biological and Cultural Aspects
170k Feminine Psychology and Infantile Sexuality
173e Problem of Feminine Masochism
173o Implications and Applications of Recent Research on Feminine Development
176ss Hysterical Character and Feminine Identity
194n Chile: The Feminine Version of the Coup d'Etat
199p Behaviorally Feminine Male Child: Pretranssexual? Pretransvestite? Prehomosexual? Preheterosexual?
241i The Feminine Metamorphosis
247e Courbet's "Baigneuses" and the Rhetorical Feminine Image
249b Family Structure and Feminine Personality
250m Sex Differences in the Development of Masculine and Feminine Identification
252t Feminine Role and the Kinship System
263a Human Situation: A Feminine View
283b Feminine Imagery in an Analogue for God
296m Feminine Fertility Cycles
306a Evolution of the Feminine Ideal
361f New Voices in Feminine Discourse
362j Feminine Mistake

FEMININITY

see also WOMANLINESS

20x Concepts of "Femininity" and "Liberation" in the Context of Changing Sex-Roles: Women in Modern India and America
35g Femininity and Capitalism in Antebellum America
42b Puberty to Menopause: The Cycle of Femininity in Nineteenth-Century America
67b Development of Conceptions of Masculinity and Femininity
76c Primary Femininity
78a Masculine Mythology of Femininity
82c Femininity and Successful Achievement: A Basic Inconsistency
89p Femininity
158h Femininity
164d Developmental Differentiation of Femininity and Masculinity Compared
166j Masculinity or Femininity? Differentiating Career-Oriented and Homemaking-Oriented College Freshman Women
169h Passivity, Masochism and Femininity
170m Changing Patterns of Femininity: Psychoanalytic Implications
170p "Bedrock" of Masculinity and Femininity: Bisexuality
173c Femininity
173p Social Values, Femininity, and the Development of Female Competence
181e Femininity in the Classroom: An Account of Changing Attitudes
186g Femininity and Successful Achievement: A Basic Inconsistency
198s Masculinity and Femininity as Display
198w Sex and Personality: Studies in Masculinity and Femininity
209a Developmental Differentiation of Femininity and Masculinity Compared
223h Stereotypes of Femininity in a Theory of Sexual Evolution
225b Witch and Her Devils: An Exploration of the Relationship Between Femininity and Illness
250a Stereotype of Femininity
252i Changing Patterns of Femininity and Masculinity
256h Femininity: 2000
268e Femininity
268o Passivity, Masochism and Femininity
268p Origins of Femininity
286n Femininity and Achievement in Sports
296o Re-evaluation of Some Aspects of Femininity through a Study of Menstruation
316b Apolitical Woman: Femininity and Sex-Stereotyping in Girls
327e Analysis of Femininity in Nursing

FEMINISM

see also WOMEN'S LIBERATION; SUFFRAGE; MOVEMENT; VOTE

13z Our Failures Only Marry: Bryn Mawr and the Failure of Feminism
35a Developing a Theory of Capitalist Patriarchy and Socialist Feminism
35e Struggle for Reproductive Freedom: Three Stages of Feminism
41i Women's Trade Union League and American Feminism
42h Family Limitation, Sexual Control, and Domestic Feminism in Victorian America
68m Feminism and Female Stereotypes in Shaw
75f Feminism and the "Fallen Woman"

84a Feminism and Materialism
85j Linguistics and Feminism
86b Are Feminism and Socialism Related?
88a Feminism as a Criterion of the Literary Critic
88m Women and Feminism in the Works of Rosario Castellanos
88o Pre-Feminism in Some Eighteenth-Century Novels
88t Definition of Literary Feminism
89x View of Socialist Feminism
89aaa Radical Feminism and Love
96ll Why Feminism
98g Psychoanalysis and Feminism in France
98n Black Women and Feminism
110r Feminism and Literature
110u Other Criticism: Feminism vs. Formalism
116c Prostitution and Feminism in Late Nineteenth-Century Italy
117o Bertha Pappenheim: Founder of German-Jewish Feminism
117r Judaism and Feminism
117t Flight from Feminism: The Case of the Israeli Woman
121i Education, Philanthropy, and Feminism: Components of Argentine Womanhood, 1860-1926
126h Feminism and Liberalism in Wilhelmine Germany, 1890-1918
126i Feminism and Class Consciousness in the British and American Women's Trade Union Leagues, 1890-1925
126u Feminism and the Methodology of Women's History
132j Hard and the Soft: The Force of Feminism in Modern Times
141i Feminism and Class Consciousness in the British and American Women's Trade Union Leagues, 1890-1925
145c Fitness, Feminism and Schooling
149o Origins of American Feminism
151l Charlotte Perkins Gilman on the Theory and Practice of Feminism
151q Feminism as a Radical Ideology
159c Radical Feminism
173w !Kung Hunter-Gatherers: Feminism, Diet, and Birth Control
175k Black Feminism
175y Radical Feminism 1
175aa Lesbianism and Feminism
177e Misogynism and Virginal Feminism in the Fathers of the Church
178i Ume Tsuda and Motoko Hani: Echoes of American Cultural Feminism in Japan
194m Politics and Feminism in the Dominican Republic: 1931-45 and 1966-74
211b Feminism: Making a Difference in Our Health
218b Feminism and Socialism: The Utopian Synthesis of Flora Tristan
218d Socialism Faces Feminism: The Failure of Synthesis in France, 1879-1914
218f Marxist Ambivalence Toward Women: Between Socialism and Feminism in the Italian Socialist Party
225f Woman-Power: Religious Heresy and Feminism in Early English Socialism
226r Why Feminism?
238l Forecast for Feminism
244c Feminism and Female Emigration, 1861-1886
254y Our Failures Only Marry: Bryn Mawr and the Failure of Feminism
254cc American Feminism
255a Feminism of Daniel Defoe
259i Patterns of Nineteenth Century Feminism
264s Feminism and the Law

264aa Historical Background (of Feminism)
265t Feminism and the Law
265aa Historical Background (of feminism)
271v Feminism: The Sine Qua Non for a Just Society
272e Feminism and the Woman School Administrator
278d Sexism, Patriarchy and Feminism
278bb Mysticism and Feminism: Jacob Boehme and Jane Lead
282m Feminism: Reform or Revolution
292s Nineteenth-Century Heritage: The Family, Feminism and Sex
296c Feminism and Psychotherapy
303o Women in Architecture and the New Feminism
316i Contemporary Feminism, Consciousness-Raising, and Changing Views of the Political
325n Feminism and National Politics in Egypt
337i Feminism in the Evangelical Tradition
337m Women in Judaism: From the Reform Movement to Contemporary Jewish Religious Feminism
341f New Feminism and Women's Studies
344a Feminism, Power and Change: A Theoretical Analysis
349f Communist Feminism: Its Synthesis and Demise
357b Buried Letter: Feminism and Romanticism in Villette
357i Feminism, Film and the Avant-Garde
360k Family Limitation, Sexual Control, and Domestic Feminism in Victorian America
369s Notes from a Conversation on Art, Feminism, and Work

FEMINIST

see also NEO-FEMINIST

9p Statement: First Feminist Congress, 1919
13kk Feminist Experiment in Education
13oo Feminist Studies: Frill or Necessity?
14i Feminist Review of the Sociology of Deviance
14l Feminist Perspectives in Sociological Research
17b Silent Woman: Towards a Feminist Critique
17d "Slydynge of Corage": Chaucer's Criseyde as Feminist and Victim
21i New Feminist Criticisms: Exploring the History of the New Space
35c Feminist Theory and the Development of Revolutionary Strategy
35n Significance of the Chinese Family Revolution for Feminist Theory
35p Black Feminist Statement
36e Dwelling in Decencies: Radical Criticism and the Feminist Perspective
41j Creating a Feminist Alliance: Sisterhood and Class Conflict in the New York Women's Trade Union League, 1903- 1914
42d Voluntary Motherhood: The Beginnings of Feminist Birth Control Ideas in the U.S.
47a Margaret Drabble: Novels of a Cautious Feminist
77w Women's Sexuality: A Feminist View
77bb What Happens in Feminist Therapy
77hh APPENDIX: Chart of Basic Feminist Positions
85b Phenomenology of Feminist Consciousness
86j Why Red-Baiting Hurts the Feminist Movement
86p Mass Feminist Movement
88c Dwelling in Decencies: Radical Criticism and the Feminist Perspective
88d Defining a "Feminist Literary Criticism"

88k Feminist Poet: Alta and Adrienne Rich
88y Need to Tell All: A Comparison of Historical and Modern Feminist "Confessional" Writing
89ff What's This about Feminist Businesses?
90a American Feminist Literary Criticism: A Bibliographical Introduction
90c Consciousness and Authenticity: Toward a Feminist Aesthetic
98f To Be or Not to Be...A Feminist Speaker
110w Feminist Style Criticism
116b Civil Code of 1865 and the Origins of the Feminist Movement in Italy
117a Jewish Feminist: Conflict in Identities
121j Nineteenth-Century Feminist Press and Women's Rights in Brazil
122e Teresa de la Parra, Venezuelan Novelist and Feminist
129f Confessions of a 45-Year-Old Feminist
139j Henrietta Rodman: An Interview with a Feminist
139u Second Feminist Wave
140ff Feminist Process in Learning
141e Novel Women: Origins of the Feminist Literary Tradition in England and France
141h Feminist Culture from 1790 to 1850: A Trans-Atlantic Community
143k Architecture: Toward a Feminist Critique
158ii Phenomenology of Feminist Consciousness
172k New Psychology of Women: A Feminist Analysis
173hh Cinderella's Stepsisters: A Feminist Perspective on Anorexia Nervosa and Bulimia
175m Feminist Look at Children's Books
175o Feminist Graffiti
175kk Selling of a Feminist
183f Feminist Politics and Peace
190f Feminist History in Perspective: Sociological Contributions to Biographic Analysis
208f School's Role in the Sex-Role Stereotyping of Girls: A Feminist Review of the Literature
208p Feminist Studies: The Schools and Sex-Role Stereotyping
208z Louisa May Alcott: The Author of "Little Women" as Feminist
208aa Feminist Look at Children's Books
212j Feminist Film Criticism: Theory and Practice
212k Feminist Aesthetic: Reflection Revolution Ritual
251hh Chinese Family Revolution and Feminist Theory
256b Born Free: A Feminist Fable
258b Feminist Theology as a Critical Theory of Liberation
263j Feminist Spirituality, Christian Identity, and Catholic Vision
263q Coming of Lilith: Toward a Feminist Theology
263s Dreams and Fantasies as Sources of Revelation: Feminist Appropriation of Jung
264dd Feminist Consciousness and Black Women
271m Feminist Look at Children's Books
282d Reason and Morals in the Early Feminist Movement: Mary Wollstonecraft
283j Feminist View of Abortion
288t Stephanie Rothman: R-Rated Feminist
288w Germaine Dulac: First Feminist Filmmaker
320o Feminist Mosaic
329x Sweden: A Feminist Model?
334s Feminist Consciousness and the Future of Women

337g Jane Lead: The Feminist Mind and Art of a Seventeenth-Century Protestant Mystic
337h Feminist Thrust of Sectarian Christianity
341i Feminist Press
342v Feminist Perspectives on Female Sexuality
342ii Persuasion in the Feminist Movement
344g W.E.A.L.: The Growth of a Feminist Organization
348a Coercion of Privacy: A Feminist Perspective
357a Towards a New Feminist Poetics
359l Towards a Theory of Form in Feminist Autobiography: Kate Millett's "Flying" and "Sita"; Maxine Hong Kingston's "The Woman Warrior"
361k Feminist Aesthetic
368g White Feminist Movement: The Chicana Perspective

FEMINIST CRITICISM

see also CRITICISM

36d New Feminist Criticism
88b New Feminist Criticism
90e Theories of Feminist Criticism
208mm Feminist Criticism
361q Feminist Criticism: What Difference Does It Make?

FEMINISTS

96kk Hotbed of Feminists
110o Fictional Feminists in "The Bostonians" and "The Odd Women"
117n Bais Yaakov: A Historical Model for Jewish Feminists
175a First Feminists
175mm Feminists: A Political Organization to Annihilate Sex Roles
175nn Politics of the Ego: A Manifesto for New York Radical Feminists
175oo Westchester Radical Feminists
208cc Feminists Look at the 100 Books: The Portrayal of Women in Children's Books on Puerto Rican Themes
226q Hotbed of Feminists
241f The Veiled Feminists of Atlantis
264bb First Feminists
265bb First Feminists
282i Future of Love: Rousseau and the Radical Feminists
300f What Feminists and Freudians Can Learn From Each Other

FEMINIZATION

35k Feminization of the Clerical Labor Force
42i Feminization of American Religion: 1800-1860
42j Tender Technicians: Feminization of Public Librarianship, 1876-1905
138c Feminization of Teaching
266p Tender Technicians: The Feminization of Public Librarianship, 1876-1905
371e Women, Work, and Welfare: The Feminization of Poverty

FEMINIZED

132a Woman De-Feminized
209d Feminized Male
231t De-Feminized Lesbian

FEMLIB

3e FemLib Case Against Sigmund Freud

FEMME

24k Re: Femme
247i Femme Fatale and Her Sisters
255g La Condition de la Femme Francaise au Dix-huitieme Siecle d'apres les Romans
316q Memsahib, Militante, Femme Libre: Political and Apolitical Styles of Modern African Women

FENCES

8i Bi-Sexual Offers Some Thoughts on Fences

FENIMORE

88p Constance Fenimore Woolson: First Novelist of Florida

FERGUSON

215p Dr. Ellen Brooke Ferguson: Nineteenth-Century Renaissance Woman

FERN

111v Fern
112m Fern

FERNHURST

50i The Murder at Fernhurst

FERRARA

23b Women, Learning, and Power: Eleonora of Aragon and the Court of Ferrara

FERTILITY

see also REPRODUCTION; BIRTH CONTROL; DEMOGRAPHY; HOUSEHOLD

54e Changes in Czechoslovak Marital Fertility
54f Marital Fertility and the Changing Status of Women in Europe
54g Extra-Marital Fertility and its Occurrence in Stable Unions: Recent Trends in Western Europe
70j Impact of Employment upon Fertility
91a Women's Work and Fertility in Africa
91b Fertility, Women's Work, and Economic Class: A Case Study from Southeast Asia
91c Chinese Women at Work: Work Commitment and Fertility in the Asian Setting
91d Status of Women, Work and Fertility in India
91e Women, Employment, and Fertility Trends in the Arab Middle East and North Africa

91f Fertility of Working Women in the United States: Historical Trends and Theoretical Perspectives
91g Fertility and Women's Employment Outside the Home in Western Europe
91h Fertility and Women's Employment in the Socialist Countries of Eastern Europe
91i Differential Fertility by Working Status of Women in Japan
91j Female Work Status and Fertility in Latin America
91k Relationship between Women's Work and Fertility: Some Methodological and Theoretical Issues
141n WOMEN, FAMILY AND FERTILITY: Introduction
141p Fertility Motivations and Career Conflicts in Educated Women
194b Women's Work and Fertility
211j Conflicts between Fertility and Infertility
211k Problem of Infertility
267g Employment of Women, Education, and Fertility
278w Future of Parenthood: Implications of Declining Fertility
293b Economy, Family, Fertility, and the Female
296m Feminine Fertility Cycles
307e Institutionalized Motivation for Fertility Limitation
325c Status and Fertility Patterns of Muslim Women
331e Health and Fertility Issues and the Dependency of Wives
352j Participation of Women in the Labour Force of Latin America: Fertility and Other Factors
367a Family Life, Women's Status, and Fertility: Middle East and North African Perspectives
367d Socioeconomic Determinants of Differential Fertility in Turkey
367e Rural-Urban Fertility Differences and Trends in Egypt, 1930-70
367f Fertility Trends and Differentials in Kuwait
367g Fertility Trends and Differentials in Jordan
367h Fertility in Algeria: Trends and Differentials
367i Fertility Declines in Tunisia: Factors Affecting Recent Trends
370d Employment of Women and Fertility

FETUS

22j Aborting a Fetus: The Legal Right, The Personal Choice
157u Fetal Humanity and the Theory of Essentialism
198t Fetal Hormones and the Brain: Effects on Sexual Dimorphism of Behavior
199c Fetal Androgens, Human Central Nervous System Differentiation, and Behavior Sex Differences

FEUDAL

315g Widow and Ward: The Feudal Law of Child Custody in Medieval England

FICTION

9ii Seduced and Abandoned in the New World: The Fallen Woman in American Fiction
17c Women and Fiction
71c Passive Female and Social Change: A Cross-Cultural Comparison of Women's Magazine Fiction
80i Hispanic American Fiction and Drama Written by Women:
80l Inculcating a Slave Mentality: Women in German Popular Fiction of the Early Twentieth Century

88u Jean Rhys' Recent Fiction: Humane Developments in "Wide Sargasso Sea"
110e Gentle Truths for Gentle Readers: The Fiction of Elizabeth Goudge
110f Image of Women in Science Fiction
110h Fiction of Fiction
110o Fictional Feminists in "The Bostonians" and "The Odd Women"
140mm Sexual Identity in the Early Fiction of V. Sackville-West
208bb Skirts in Fiction About Boys: A Maxi Mess
222a Black Women In and Out of Fiction
222p Influence of Voodoo on the Fiction of Zora Neale Hurston
240l Second-class Citizenship: The Status of Women in Contemporary American Fiction
250c Female Roles in Women's Magazine Fiction, 1940-1970
254o Seduced and Abandoned in the New World: The Image of Woman In American Fiction
289h Women in Science Fiction
289i Science Fiction Survey
340a Women and Science Fiction
361e How Fictional Women Talk

FIELD

126w "Herstory" As History: A New Field or Another Fad?
164e Women in the Field of Art
179dd J. Field
196oo Proportion of Doctorates Earned by Women, by Area and Field, 1960-1969
199n Sex Differences in Field Independence among Preschool Children
219a "What Do Women Sociolinguists Want?": Prospects For a Research Field
250u Pattern Copying Under Three Conditions of an Expanded Spatial Field
281u Talking Pictures: Field Method and Visual Mode
291o Sex Differences in Economists' Fields of Specialization
322j Ambivalence in the Field
329t Kibbutz Women: From the Fields of Revolution to the Laundries of Discontent

FIELD WORK

see also ANTHROPOLOGY; PRIMITIVE; various cultures

297aa Women and Fieldwork
322f Field Work in Rwanda, 1959-1960
322g World of Women: Field Work in a Yoruba Community
322h Field Work in a Greek Village
322k Field Work in Five Cultures
322l Field Work in the Pacific Islands, 1925-1967

FIEND

50h The Dope Fiends
317l Jive Dope Fiend Whoes: In the Street and in Rehabilitation

FIERCE

256c Female Facade: Fierce, Fragile and Fading

FIFTEEN-DOLLAR

113i The Fifteen-Dollar Eagle

FIFTEENTH-CENTURY

184e Fifteenth-Century View of Women's Role in Medieval Society: Christine de Pizan's "Livre des Trois Vertus"

FIFTH

113d The Fifth Great Day of God

FIFTH-GRADE

13r Sex-Role Attitudes of Fifth-Grade Girls

FIFTY

129w Those Endearing Young Charms: Fifty Years Later
284g Women's Status Fifty Years After the Vote

FIGHT

330n Creative Exits: Fight-Therapy for Divorcees
344q Fight for Women Jurors

FIGURE

11h Woman: The New Figure in American Politics
181d Landscape with Figures: Home and Community in English Society

FILES

94l Rape in New York City: A Study of Material in the Police Files and Its Meaning

FILIPINO

221a From Pregnancy through Birth in a Bisayan Filipino Village

FILM

see also ACTRESS; DIRECTORS; SCREENWRITER; individual films

43i Ancient Song, New Melody in Latin America: Women and Film
116x Pasta or Paradigm: The Place of Italian-American Women in Popular Film
155f Sex Differences in Responses to Psychosexual Stimulation by Films and Slides
208oo Why Children's Films Are Not Rated "R"
208pp Film Resources for Sex-Role Stereotyping
212a Popcorn Venus or How the Movies Have Made Women Smaller Than Life
212i Women's Cinema as Counter-Cinema
212j Feminist Film Criticism: Theory and Practice
288dd Women's Liberation Cinema
288ff Coup pour coup: Radical French Cinema

288qq Myths of Women in the Cinema
288rr Visual Pleasure and Narrative Cinema
357i Feminism, Film and the Avant-Garde

FILMMAKER

see also DIRECTORS

212v Family Portraits: Filmmakers Explore Their Roots
288w Germaine Dulac: First Feminist Filmmaker
288pp Interview with British Cine-Feminists

FILMOGRAPHIES

212w APPENDIX: Filmographies of Women Directors

FINANCIAL

311d Financial Problems of Women

FINCH

214d Anne Finch, Countess of Winchilsea: An Augustan Woman Poet

FINGER

103i Finger Prints Can't Lie

FINGERNAILS

47i Muriel Spark's Fingernails

FINLAND

155r Sex-Role Attitudes in Finland, 1966-1970
267e Convergences between East and West: Tradition and Modernity in Sex Roles in Sweden, Finland, and the Soviet Union

FIRE

369t Sacred Fire

FIRST

9p Statement: First Feminist Congress, 1919
20j Matri-Patrilocality and the Birth of the First Child
83f My First Marriage
88p Constance Fenimore Woolson: First Novelist of Florida
111g On Being Told That Her Second Husband Has Taken His First Lover
116a Silent Half: "Le Contadine del Sud" Before The First World War
132w Female Liberation First, and Now
159m On the First Man
173aa Maternal Attachment: Importance of the First Post-Partum Days
175a First Feminists
176v First Year of Bereavement
215n Stena Scorup: First Lady of Salina
222s Ann Petry Talks About First Novel

223d Marriage, Redundancy or Sin: The Painter's View of Women in the First Twenty-Five Years of Victoria's Reign
232k First Essay on the Political Rights of Women
264bb First Feminists
265bb First Feminists
269d Hunger in the U.S.: Women and Children First
273s The First Year of My Life
288w Germaine Dulac: First Feminist Filmmaker
364e American Woman from 1900 to the First World War: A Profile

FISH

8q Hookers: Queer Fish

FISHERMAN

279k Romance of a Fisherman's Wife

FITNESS

68x Why All Women Are Peculiarly Fitted to Be Good Voters
145c Fitness, Feminism and Schooling
225a Mother and the Hospital: An Unfortunate Fit Between the Woman's Internal World and Some Hospital Practices
314x "He" and "She": Changing Language to Fit a Changing World

FIVE

51d Five Hundred Delinquent Women
89b Women in the Work Force: Five Tables
135g Next Five Years: Projections and Policy Implications
218h Five Socialist Women: Traditionalist Conflicts and Socialist Visions in Austria, 1893-1934
288bb "Marilyn Times Five"
322k Field Work in Five Cultures

FIVE-FORTY-EIGHT

277n The Five-forty-eight

FIVE-YEAR-OLDS

140z Perception of Parents by London Five-Year-Olds

FIXING

356l Fixing Pixie Loveless

FLANDERS

17g Moll Flanders: "A Woman on her own Account"

FLANNERY

192h Flannery O'Connor

FLAPPER

178h Flapper and Her Critics
360p Prosperity's Child: Some Thoughts on the Flapper

FLAT

220x A Cold-Water Flat

FLEET

55c Sex and Occupational Role on Fleet Street

FLEMING

179a M. Fleming

FLESCHE

128i Four Sisters: Daughters of Joseph La Flesche

FLESH

8bb Spirit is Liberationist but the Flesh is...or, You Can't Always Get Into Bed With Your Dogma
240j They Shall Have Faces, Minds, and (One Day) Flesh: Women in Late Nineteenth-century and Early Twentieth-century American Literature

FLIGHT

117t Flight from Feminism: The Case of the Israeli Woman
170a Flight from Womanhood: The Masculinity Complex in Women as Viewed by Men and by Women
198c Flight from Womanhood: The Masculinity-Complex in Women as Viewed by Men and by Women
268k Flight from Womanhood
268l Karen Horney's Flight from Orthodoxy

FLORA

218b Feminism and Socialism: The Utopian Synthesis of Flora Tristan

FLORENCE

68r Shaw and Florence Farr

FLORIDA

88p Constance Fenimore Woolson: First Novelist of Florida

FLOSS

233p "The Mill on the Floss"

FLOTSAM

24d Flotsam and Jetsam

FLUCTUATION

250cc Patterns of Affective Fluctuation in the Menstrual Cycle
250dd Effects of Oral Contraceptives on Affective Fluctuations Associated with the Menstrual Cycle
296n Effects of Oral Contraceptives on Affective Fluctuations Associated with the Menstrual Cycle

FLUENCY

219m Fluency of Women's Speech

FLYING

359l Towards a Theory of Form in Feminist Autobiography: Kate Millett's "Flying" and "Sita"; Maxine Hong Kingston's "The Woman Warrior"

FOETICIDE

1a Foeticide, or Criminal Abortion

FOLK

285k Sex Differences in the Incidence of Susto in Two Zapotec Pueblos: An Analysis of the Relationships between Sex Role Expectations and a Folk Illness
325dd Sex Differences and Folk Illness in an Egyptian Village

FOLKLORE

236e Boy Preference Reflected in Korean Folklore

FOLKSONG

274g Bormliza: Maltese Folksong Style and Women

FOLKTALES

325ff Women in Contemporary Persian Folktales

FONDA

288ee Interview with Jane Fonda

FOOD

24n Food
193b Food for Thought--Patterns of Production and Consumption in Pira-Parana Society
340h The Food Farm

FOOTHOLD

331 Foothold

FOOTNOTE

23311 Communes: A Footnote for the Future

FORAGING

230d !Kung Women: Contrasts in Sexual Egalitarianism in Foraging and Sedentary Contexts

FORCE

68u Torture by Forcible Feeding is Illegal
89b Women in the Work Force: Five Tables
94a Forcible Rape
94d Forcible Rape in the U.S.: A Statistical Profile
94f Black Offender and White Victim: A Study of Forcible Rape in Oakland, Ca.
94g Forcible Rape and the Problem of the Rights of the Accused
94k Comparative Study of Forcible Rape Offenses Known to the Police in Boston and Los Angeles
126b Mary Beard's "Woman As Force in History": A Critique
132j Hard and the Soft: The Force of Feminism in Modern Times
138h Women's Emancipation and the Recruitment of Women into the Labour Force in World War II
195d Cupid's Yokes; Or The Binding Forces of Conjugal Life
196gg Task Force on Education Report, Governor's Commission on the Status of Women, Ma.
270e Forced Transition from Egalitarianism to Male Dominance: The Bari of Colombia
304g Canadian Labour Force: Jobs for Women
314g Women in Work Force Post Better Records for Stability in Jobs
327h Soviet Women in the Work Force and Professions
352j Participation of Women in the Labour Force of Latin America: Fertility and Other Factors

FORDWYCH

50e The Fordwych Castle Mystery

FORECAST

2381 Forecast for Feminism

FORESTS

113b In the Forests of Riga the Beasts Are Very Wild Indeed

FOREVER

133a No One Said Forever
134b The Lake of the Gone Forever

FORGING

116e Forging a Socialist Women's Movement: Angelica Balabanoff in Switzerland

FORGOTTEN

51z Forgotten Offender: The Woman in Prison
71f Women: The Forgotten Half of Argentine History
244b Forgotten Woman of the Period: Penny Weekly Family Magazines of the 1840's and 1850's

FORM

85d Two Forms of Androgynism
88s Humanbecoming: Form and Focus in the Neo-Feminist Novel
110m Humanbecoming: Form and Focus in the Neo-Feminist Novel
196dd Overt and Covert Forms of Discrimination Against Academic Women
214k Art of Silence and the Forms of Women's Poetry
309d Etiquette among Women in Karnataka: Forms of Address in the Village and the Family
359l Towards a Theory of Form in Feminist Autobiography: Kate Millett's "Flying" and "Sita"; Maxine Hong Kingston's "The Woman Warrior"
361c Address Forms in Sexual Politics
361i Art of Silence and the Forms of Women's Poetry
369a Finding New Forms

FORMALISM

110u Other Criticism: Feminism vs. Formalism
202n Formal Extrafamily Child Care--Some Economic Observations

FORMATION

92a Early Formation of Victorian Domestic Ideology

FORTY

233k Princess Grace Turns Forty
296p Sex after Forty--And after Seventy

FOSTERGRANDPARENTING

129m Fostergrandparenting: A Unique Child-Care Service

FOUND

117o Bertha Pappenheim: Founder of German-Jewish Feminism
178j Role of Women in the Founding of the U.S. Children's Bureau
334j Founding of Mount Holyoke College

FOUR-GATED

47b Disorderly Company: From "The Golden Notebook" to "The Four-Gated City"
283c Explorations with Doris Lessing in Quest of The Four-Gated City

FOUR-LETTER

9uu Love Is Just a Four-Letter Word
157a Four-Letter Words CAN Hurt You

FOURTEENTH-CENTURY

315e Female Felon in Fourteenth-Century England

FOURTH

74r Fourth World Manifesto
175jj Fourth World Manifesto
258f Roles of Women in the Fourth Gospel

FOYER

39e Salon, Foyer, Bureau: Women and the Professions in France
42e Salon, Foyer, Bureau: Women and the Professions in France
266gg Salon, Foyer, Bureau: Women And The Professions in France

FRACTURED

256g Fractured Family

FRAGILE

256c Female Facade: Fierce, Fragile and Fading

FRAGMENT

95o Fragment From a Lost Diary
303q Centers and Fragments: Women's Spaces

FRAMEWORKS

266ii Socio-Economic Context Of Sex And Power: A Study of Women, Work And Family Roles in Four Israeli Institutional Frameworks

FRANCE

19j Loaves and Liberty: Women in the French Revolution
19m Angels in the Devil's Workshop: Leisured and Charitable Women in Nineteenth-Century England and France
21j French Women Writers: A Problematic Perspective
39e Salon, Foyer, Bureau: Women and the Professions in France
42e Salon, Foyer, Bureau: Women and the Professions in France
55i Marriage, Role Division and Social Cohesion: The Case of Some French Upper-Middle Class Families
80a "I am my own heroine": Some Thoughts about Women and Autobiography in France
80b Women Writers in France: The "Initiators"
80c Status of the Frenchwoman Today
80e Women in Contemporary French Society: Annotated Bibliography
98g Psychoanalysis and Feminism in France
131c Changing Frenchwoman: Her Challenged World
141e Novel Women: Origins of the Feminist Literary Tradition in England and France
162a Origins of Contraception in France
190b City Women and Religious Change in Sixteenth-Century France
218d Socialism Faces Feminism: The Failure of Synthesis in France, 1879-1914

230k Men and Women in the South of France: Public and Private Domains
255g La Condition de la Femme Francaise au Dix-huitieme Siecle d'apres les Romans
266gg Salon, Foyer, Bureau: Women And The Professions in France
288ff Coup pour coup: Radical French Cinema
324k France
329f Women in France
349e Institutional Changes for Women of the People During the French Revolution
349i Revolution and Retreat: Upper-Class French Women After 1789

FRANCIS

111s The Short Happy Life of Francis Macomber
112k The Short Happy Life of Francis Macomber
277p The Short Happy Life of Francis Macomber

FRANCO-AMERICAN

98d Language and Revolution: The Franco-American Dis-Connection

FRANK

179c A. Frank

FRANKENSTEIN

233m Bride of Frankenstein

FRANKIE

29a Frankie Mae
373d Frankie Mae

FRANKISH

315d Marriage and Divorce in the Frankish Kingdom

FRAU

275f Frau und Staatsburger in Volker Braun's Schauspiel "Tinka"

FREDERICK

126a Woman in Society: A Critique of Frederick Engels

FREECE

215t Dr. Margaret Ann Freece: Entrepreneur of Southern Utah

FREEDOM

9z Free Enquiry
35e Struggle for Reproductive Freedom: Three Stages of Feminism
36i "Featureless Freedom" or Ironic Submission: Dorothy Richardson and May Sinclair
96bb One Way to Freedom

96ee Staying Free
96hh Free--For What?
115b Role of Women in the Indian Struggle for Freedom
127v "Freedom Is Something That All of Us Need"
129r Sexuality, Power, and Freedom Among "Older" Women
151n American Woman's Pre-World War I Freedom in Manners and Morals
172i Woman's Sociobiological Heritage: Destiny or Free Choice?
175cc Free Space
203s Equal Opportunity, Free from Gender-Based Discrimination
208tt Toys for Free Children
212p Mai Zetterling: Free Fall
226h One Way to Freedom
226k Staying Free
226n Free--For What?
240m "Free in Fact and at Last": The Image of the Black Woman in Black American Literature
256b Born Free: A Feminist Fable
256f Free Married Woman: A New Style of Living in an Old Institution
292t American Woman's Pre-World War I Freedom in Manners and Morals
360o American Woman's Pre-World War I Freedom in Manners and Morals
375g On Being Female, Black, and Free

FREETOWN

302i Protestant Women's Associations in Freetown, Sierra Leone

FREQUENCY

155k Relationship of the Frequency of Masturbation to Several Aspects of Personality and Behavior

FRESHMAN

166j Masculinity or Femininity? Differentiating Career-Oriented and Homemaking-Oriented College Freshman Women

FREUD

3e FemLib Case Against Sigmund Freud
76a Freud's Views on Early Female Sexuality in the Light of Direct Child Observation
76o Problems in Freud's Psychology of Women
107y Response to Freud
173d Freud's View of Female Psychology
198a Psychoanalysis and Sex Differences: Freud and Beyond Freud
198g Woman and Her Discontents: A Reassessment of Freud's Views on Female Sexuality
200h Modest Confirmation of Freud's Theory of a Distinction between the Superego of Men and Women
220d As We Have Learnt from Freud, There Are No Jokes
268b Freud and the Distinction Between the Sexes
268f Freud's View of Female Psychology
268u Freud's Concept of Bisexuality
300f What Feminists and Freudians Can Learn From Each Other
363o Sexual Solipsism of Sigmund Freud

FRIEND

20k Affectivity and Instrumentality in Friendship Patterns among American Women
60j Friendship
79q To Rosania and Lucasia, Articles of Friendship
111nn Our Friend Judith
129i Meaning of Friendship in Widowhood
129j What Do Women Use Friends For?
142l To My Friend Miriam
257f Who Are Our Friends?

FRIGIDITY

296l Multiple Factors in Frigidity

FRILL

13oo Feminist Studies: Frill or Necessity?

FRONTIER

96e Autobiography and Reminiscences of a Pioneer
96z Poet Out of Pioneer
128j Pamelia Mann: Texas Frontierswoman
215k Two Miss Cooks: Pioneer Professionals for Utah's Schools
215r Dr. Ellis Reynolds Shipp: Pioneer Utah Physician
215u Sarah Elizabeth Carmichael: Poetic Genius of Pioneer Utah
226f Poet Out of Pioneer
238a Pioneers of Women's Liberation
259c Frontier Women
274c Image of the Frontier Woman
292h Sex on the American Indian Frontier
303d Pioneer Women Architects

FRONTIERO

266r Frontiero v. Richardson

FRUIT

24r Still Life With Fruit
111p Still Life with Fruit
273y Still Life with Fruit

FRUSTRATION

93f Politics of Mutual Frustration: Socialists and Suffragists in New York and Wisconsin

FRUTA

122m Feminine Symbolism in Gabriela Mistral's "Fruta"

FUEROS

315c Women in Reconquest Castile: The Fueros of Sepulveda and Cuenca

FULANI

338b Position of Women in a Pastoral Society (Fulani WoDaaBe, Nomads of the Niger)

FULL

45b Full Equality: More Job Education for Women
328a Women's Stake in Full Employment: Their Disadvantaged Role in the Economy--Challenges to Action
328b Way to Full Equality
328f Women Workers, Nontraditional Occupations and Full Employment
328g Underemployment of Women: Policy Implications for a Full Employment Economy
328l Facilitating Full Employment of Women through Career Education
328p Impact of Mass-Media Stereotypes upon the Full Employment of Women
358l Full Court Press for Women in Athletics

FUNCTION

22o Sex-Role Concepts and Sex Typing in Childhood as a Function of School and Home Environments
53g "Most Essentially Female Function of All": Giving Birth
76p Masculine Envy of Woman's Procreative Function
93p Lesbianism and the Social Function of Taboo
149j Declining Status of Women: Popular Myths and the Failure of Functionalist Thought
155v Attribution of Fault to a Rape Victim as a Function of Respectability
166m Social Influence and the Social-Psychological Function of Deference: A Study of Psychiatric Nursing
173b Functionalism, Darwinism, and the Psychology of Women
182e Childbearing Functions of the Soviet Family
198q Functions of the Sexual Companion
199e Differential Response to Early Experiences as a Function of Sex Difference
204g Cognitive Abilities and Sex-Related Variations in the Maturation of Cerebral Cortical Functions
230m Life Crisis as a Clue to Social Function: The Case of Italy
243c Male Attitudes Toward Women's Rights as a Function of Their Level of Self-Esteem
250b Evaluation of the Performance of Women as a Function of Their Sex, Achievement, and Personal History
268i Psychology of women in Relation to the Functions of Reproduction
271h Sex-Role Concepts and Sex Typing in Childhood as a Function of School and Home Environments

FUNCTIONARIES

93b Women in the Party Bureaucracy: Subservient Functionaries

FUNERAL

134e The Funeral

FUR

138b Impact of White Women on Fur Trade Society

FURIES

123a Furies

FURIOUS

186k I Am Furious (Female)

FUSELI

247c Henry Fuseli's "Nightmare": Eroticism or Pornography?

FUTURE

8ff Preserving the Past for the Future
11a Out of the Past and Present Controversies: Challenges for the Future
18d Father-Daughter Relationship: Past, Present, and Future
19t Family Models of the Future
38d Projected Future Employment and Leadership Needs and Areas
51a Look to the Future
60o Motives and Future of the Educated Woman
89i With an Eye to the Future
139z Visions for the Future
170s For the Future--Equity?
190g Educating Women for Leadership: A Program for the Future
203p Reverse Discrimination and the Future
233ll Communes: A Footnote for the Future
256s Genderless Sexuality: A Male-Female Psychological Exploration of the Future of Sexual Relationships
263g Christian Past: Does It Hold a Future for Women?
266i Future Goals of College Women
267o Implied Demand Character of the Wife's Future and Role Innovation: Patterns of Achievement Orientation Among College Women
276b Women and Men in the World of Work: Present and Future
278w Future of Parenthood: Implications of Declining Fertility
282i Future of Love: Rousseau and the Radical Feminists
282o Reverse Discrimination and the Future
284y Future of Marriage
289d Tanzanian Women Confront the Past and the Future
289g Women and the Future of Education
312i Women and Work in Ireland: The Present and Preparing for the Future
314m Preparing for the Future: Commitment and Action
326h Alternatives for Social Change: The Future Status of Women
334s Feminist Consciousness and the Future of Women
344o Republican Women and the Future of the Republican Party
354b Data on Women Workers, Past, Present, and Future
354r Women and Work: Policy Implications and Prospects for the Future
358g Future Directions and Issues
363k Future of Women's Studies
371d Racial Differences in Female Labor-Force Participation: Trends and Implications for the Future

G.D.R.

275g Women and the Aesthetic of the Positive Hero in the G.D.R.

GABRIELA

122m Feminine Symbolism in Gabriela Mistral's "Fruta"

GAIN

64i Gaining Support from Other Groups
143l Women in Planning: There's More to Affirmative Action than Gaining Access
284l Women's Job Rights Gain in Federal Court Rulings

GALANTERIE

247g Corset as Erotic Alchemy: From Rococo Galanterie to Montaut's Physiologies

GALATEA

36f American Galatea

GALLEN

133d Mab Gallen Recalled

GAMBARO

122i Three Female Playwrights Explore Contemporary Latin American Reality: Myrna Casas, Griselda Gambaro, Luisa Josefina Hernandez

GAME

141ee Historical and Theoretical Evolution of Viola Spolin's Theatre Games
208m Consciousness-Raising in the Classroom: Some Games, Projects, Discussion-Openers, Etc.
209e Sex Differences in Game Strategy
256q Women in Motion: It's Not Who Wins Or Loses, But How Many Play the Game
274b Games Mexican Girls Play
373f The Pocketbook Game

GANDERSHEIM

141bb Hrotsvitha of Gandersheim: The Playable Dramas of a Woman Playwright of the Tenth Century

GAP

62g Generation-Communication Gap
152f Closing the Muscle Gap
206r Generation Gap
213b Bridging the Gap between the Sexes in Moroccan Legal Practice
304i Wages of Work: A Widening Gap Between Men and Women

GARDENS

369g In Search of Our Mothers' Gardens

GARMENT

141j Role of Women in the Organization of the Men's Garment Industry, Chicago, 1910

GARRO

122k Thematic Exploration of the Works of Elena Garro

GATES

215d Susa Young Gates: The Thirteenth Apostle

GATHERER

see HUNTER-GATHERER

GAY

see also HOMOSEXUALITY; LESBIAN

8d Human Identity and Gay Identity: A Liberationist Dilemma
8e Surviving Gay Coupledom
8u Life and Death of a Gay Prisoner
8v Gay Couples and Straight Law
8x Pocket Legal Guide for Gay People
8z Thoughts on How Gay Men Relate to Women
8aa Oppression is Big Business: Scrutinizing Gay Therapy
8hh Power to Gay People: A Los Angeles Experiment in Community Action
8ii Information on VD for Gay Women and Men
8kk Alcohol Use and Abuse in the Gay Community

GAYL

222aa Gayl Jones Takes a Look at "Corregidora"--An Interview

GAYLE

222u Judgment: Addison Gayle

GEE

111kk Miss Gee
112bb Miss Gee

GENDER

see also SEX; ROLE; SEX ROLE

14k Assumptions Made About Gender Roles
16e Is Gender Necessary?
23g Gender and Genre: Women as Historical Writers, 1400-1820
41h Imperfect Unions: Class and Gender in Cripple Creek, 1894- 1904

85g Traits and Genderization
98a Gender, Relation, and Difference in Psychoanalytic Perspective
99l Gender and Schizophrenia
99o Gender Differences in Psychophysiological Illness
99p Gender and Psychotherapy
100e Class and Race Differences in Gender Roles
100f Gender Roles from a Cross-Cultural Perspective
101a Pertinent Genetics for Understanding Gender
101b Hormones and Gender
101c Biology and Gender
101e Psychology and Gender
101f Society and Gender
120a Difference and Dominance: An Overview of Language, Gender and Society
155d Sexual Dimorphism and Homosexual Gender Identity
163h Campaign Theory and Practice--The Gender Variable
176a Sexual Dimorphism and Homosexual Gender Identity
183e Gender Imagery and Issues of War and Peace: The Case of the Draft Resistance Movement of the 1960's
199o Cryptorchidism, Development of Gender Identity, and Sex Behavior
203s Equal Opportunity, Free from Gender-Based Discrimination
207c Gender-Marking in American English: Usage and Reference
214a Gender, Creativity, and the Woman Poet
240e Gender and Genre: Women in British Romantic Literature
251b Economics, Sex, and Gender
251f Assumptions About Gender Role
256s Genderless Sexuality: A Male-Female Psychological Exploration of the Future of Sexual Relationships
266t Phyletic and Idiosyncratic Determinants of Gender Identity
266u Identification and Complementation in the Differentiation of Gender Identity
276a Family and Gender Roles in Historical Perspective
276e Sex, Gender, and American Culture
282n Referential Genderization
317d Coming of Age in Kelton: The Constraints on Gender Symbolism in Jewish Ritual
332b Language of Sex and Gender
365a Evolutionary Aspects of Human Gender

GENERATION

62g Generation-Communication Gap
82d Female Ego Styles and Generational Conflict
116l Italian American Women and Their Daughters in Rhode Island: The Adolescence of Two Generations, 1900-1950
116p Italian-American Female College Students: A New Generation Connected to the Old
141q Men and Women in the Family: History of the Idea of Family in America's Depression Generation
159g On the Generation of Animals
174i Incidence and Correlates of Second Generation Discrimination
193g Observations about Generations
206r Generation Gap
253d Two Generations

GENERIC

85i Hidden Joke: Generic Uses of Masculine Terminology

GENESIS

233a Genesis
263e Eve and Adam: Genesis 2-3 Reread

GENETICS

18p Genetics of Sex and Its Consequences
101a Pertinent Genetics for Understanding Gender
204b Genetic Influences on Sex-Related Differences in Intellectual Performance: Theoretical and Methodological Issues
204c Spatial Ability: A Critical Review of the Sex-Linked Major Gene Hypothesis
211d Decisions about Reproduction: Genetic Counseling

GENITALS

76l Parental Mislabeling of Female Genitals as a Determinant of Penis Envy and Learning Inhibitions in Women
199l Emergence of Genital Awareness During the Second Year of Life
231s Female Genitals

GENIUS

10i A Woman of Genius
13a Why Are There No Woman Geniuses?
215u Sarah Elizabeth Carmichael: Poetic Genius of Pioneer Utah
362e Genius of Woman as the Genius of Humanity

GENRE

23g Gender and Genre: Women as Historical Writers, 1400-1820
240e Gender and Genre: Women in British Romantic Literature

GENTLE

110c Gentle Doubters: Images of Women in Englishwomen's Novels, 1840-1920
110e Gentle Truths for Gentle Readers: The Fiction of Elizabeth Goudge

GENTLEMAN

255e Eighteenth-Century Englishwoman: According to the Gentleman's Magazine
288l Marlene Dietrich: At Heart a Gentleman

GENTLEWOMEN

79o An Essay to Revive the Ancient Education of Gentlewomen
325m Revolutionary Gentlewomen in Egypt

GENUISES

18k Where Are the Women Genuises?

GEOGRAPHIC

202c Geographic Immobility and Labor Force Mobility: A Study of Female Unemployment

GEORGE

52f Tudor Anthropologist: George Gifford's "Discourse " and "Dialogue"
145f George Eliot and Mary Wollstonecraft
222v Substance: George Kent
357d Beyond Determinism: George Eliot and Virginia Woolf

GERMAINE

212n Maya Deren and Germaine Dulac: Activists of the Avant-Garde
288w Germaine Dulac: First Feminist Filmmaker

GERMAN-JEWISH

117o Bertha Pappenheim: Founder of German-Jewish Feminism

GERMANY

2d Abortion and the Constitution: The Cases of the United States and West Germany
19s Mothers in the Fatherland: Women in Nazi Germany
63d Gleichberechtigung--The German Experience
80j Women in Germany
80k Virgins and Other Victims: Aspects of German Middle-Class Theatre
80l Inculcating a Slave Mentality: Women in German Popular Fiction of the Early Twentieth Century
80n Women and German Literature: A Bibliography
96l Before Women Were Human Beings: Adventures of an American Fellow in German Universities of the '90s
126h Feminism and Liberalism in Wilhelmine Germany, 1890-1918
155q Teenage Boys and Girls in West Germany
206j Male and Female in the German Federal Republic
206k Male and Female in the German Democratic Republic
218e Unequal Partners in an Uneasy Alliance: Women and the Working Class in Imperial Germany
275a Impact of German Thought and Culture on Madame de Stael's Thinking about Women
275d More Than a Question of Numbers: Women Deputies in the German National Constituent Assembly and the Reichstag, 1919-1933
275e German Women University Students: National Socialism and the War, 1939-1945
324l West Germany
329g Politics of Sex: West Germany
334q Propaganda and Public Opinion in the United States and Germany, 1939-1945
349b Women, Class, and War in Nazi Germany

GERONTOLOGY

146q Gerontology Trends and Career Perspectives
193f Gerontology, Polygyny and Scarce Resources

GERTRUDE

152l Gertrude Ederle
359h Gertrude Stein and the Problems of Autobiography

GESTALT

330k Women in Therapy--A Gestalt Therapist's View

GHALIH

108i "Ghazals: Homage to Ghalih"

GHANA

213i Impact of Modernization on Women's Position in the Family in Ghana
302e Ga Women and Socioeconomic Change in Accra, Ghana
329k Women in Ghana

GHAZALS

108i "Ghazals: Homage to Ghalih"

GHOST

83j A Temple of the Holy Ghost
222e Ama Ata Aidoo's "Dilemma of a Ghost"

GIANFRANCESCO

52b Witchcraft and Magic in Renaissance Italy: Gianfrancesco Pico and his "Strix"

GIFFORD

52f Tudor Anthropologist: George Gifford's "Discourse " and "Dialogue"

GIFTED

267x Life Patterns and Self-Esteem in Gifted Family Oriented and Career Committed Women

GILBERT

223b From Dame to Woman: W.S. Gilbert and Theatrical Transvestism

GILDED

175p Building of the Gilded Cage
273k The Gilded Six-Bits

GILMAN

151l Charlotte Perkins Gilman on the Theory and Practice of Feminism
153v Living of Charlotte Perkins Gilman
334i Private Woman, Public Woman: The Contradictions of Charlotte Perkins Gilman

GIMMICK

274e Native Costumes of the Oberwallis: Tourist Gimmick or Tradition?

GIRARDIN

5f Madame de Girardin

GIRL

33c Girl Reading
76d Girl's Entry into the Oedipus Complex
96g Schooldays of an Indian Girl
111dd Rima the Bird Girl
112x Rima the Bird Girl
114h Upbringing of a Girl
114t Girl Students: Between School and Marriage--a Delhi Sample
123b Such a Nice Girl
151e Lady and the Mill Girl: Changes in the Status of Women in the Age of Jackson
212s "A Very Curious Girl"
233j In Memoriam: "Sex and the Single Girl"
288b Dorothy Arzner's "Dance, Girl, Dance"
292l Lady and the Mill Girl
314w Woman Is Not a Girl and Other Lessons in Corporate Speech
360d Lady and the Mill Girl: Changes in the Status of Women in the Age of Jackson

GIRLS

13g Are Little Girls Being Harmed by "Sesame Street"?
13m Do Schools Sell Girls Short?
13n Teacher Interactions with Boys and with Girls
13r Sex-Role Attitudes of Fifth-Grade Girls
13u Realistic Counseling for High-School Girls
18i Play of Girls
18q Physical Growth of Adolescent Girls: Patterns and Sequence
21r Women and Girls in the Public Schools: Defeat or Liberation?
22p Sexual Role Identification and Personality Functioning in Girls
45a Socialization and Education of Young Black Girls in Schools
53e Privileged, Schooled and Finished: Boarding Education for Girls
75h Remedies for Wrongs: Updating Programs for Delinquent Girls
76e Masturbation in Latency Girls
102d The Excursion of the Dead Girls
111cc The Girls in Their Summer Dresses
112u The Girls In Their Summer Dresses
152b Are Athletics Making Girls Masculine?
155e Self-Conceptions, Motivations and Interpersonal Attitudes of Early- and Late-Maturing Girls

155q Teenage Boys and Girls in West Germany
166v Interest of High School Girls in Dental Auxiliary Careers
166ww Do "Bad Girls" Become Good Nurses?
173n How Nursery Schools Teach Girls to Shut Up
181f Education of Girls Today
196b Sex-Role Concepts Among Elementary-School Age Girls
196d Girls--More Moral Than Boys or Just Sneakier?
196ll Participation in Sports by Girls
197e Are Little Girls Being Harmed by "Sesame Street"?
200n Self-Conceptions, Motivations and Interpersonal Attitudes of Early- and Late-Maturing Girls
208f School's Role in the Sex-Role Stereotyping of Girls: A Feminist Review of the Literature
208q Realistic Counseling for High School Girls
208ee All Pregnant Girls Have Boy Babies
250ii Experimental Arousal of Achievement Motivation in Adolescent Girls
266c Sexual Role Identification and Personality Functioning in Girls
272i Socialization and Education of Young Black Girls in School
273p Girls Together
274b Games Mexican Girls Play
280g Boys, Girls, and Sports
316b Apolitical Woman: Femininity and Sex-Stereotyping in Girls
325y Domestic Social Environment of Women and Girls in Isfahan, Iran
331a Girls into Wives
336a Loom and Spindle; or, Life Among the Early Mill Girls
348e Sexual Codes and Conduct: A Study of Teenage Girls
354h Girls' Socialization for Work

GLASGOW

192b Ellen Glasgow

GLASS

113a The Lady in the Looking Glass: A Reflection

GLEASON

361 Response to Mr. Gleason

GLEICHBERECHTIGUNG

63d Gleichberechtigung--The German Experience

GLORY

140qq American Principles in Print: The Hero, The Harlot and the Glorified Horse
373k A Gourdful of Glory

GLOVES

144i I Lost a Pair of Gloves Yesterday

GOAL

11d Androgyny and Humanistic Goals

51cc Competing Goals, Heterogeneity, and Classification
70c Interaction and Goal Attainment in Parisian Working Wives' Families
266i Future Goals of College Women
330c Cultural Values, Female Role Expectancies and Therapeutic Goals: Research and Interpretation

GOD

10a The Amber Gods
113d The Fifth Great Day of God
117b Women's Liberation and the Liberation of God: An Essay in Story Theology
159l The City of God
210g Theology After the Demise of God the Father: A Call for the Castration of Sexist Religion
232d God-Idea of the Ancients
246e Female Dimension in the Image of God: A Christian Perspective
263c After the Death of God the Father
263h What Became of God the Mother?
263i When God Was a Woman
263m Female God Language in a Jewish Context
263r Why Speak about God?
278cc Sexism and Godtalk
283a Theology After the Demise of God the Father: A Call for the Castration of Sexist Religion
283b Feminine Imagery in an Analogue for God
283d Karl Barth's Theology of the Word of God: Or, How to Keep Women Silent and in Their Place
300m God Is a Verb
344p God, But We're Getting Smart

GODDESS

131e Women of North and Central India: Goddesses and Wives
263x Why Women Need the Goddess: Phenomenological, Psychological, and Political Reflections
288o Liv Ullmann: The Goddess as Ordinary Woman

GODMOTHER

10h The Godmother

GOGOL

342s Gogol's Female Characters

GOLD

17k "Out of the chaos, a new kind of strength": Doris Lessing's "The Golden Notebook"
47b Disorderly Company: From "The Golden Notebook" to "The Four-Gated City"
50g The Golden Slipper
88v Alienation of the Woman Writer in "The Golden Notebook"
157v Abortion and the Golden Rule
233t The Golden Ass
334c Myth of the Golden Age

373l A Gold Slipper

GONADAL

171c Gonadal Hormones and Cognitive Functioning

GOODBYE

9vv Goodbye to All That
132y Goodbye to All That

GOREE

302a Signares of Saint-Louis and Goree: Women Entrepreneurs in Eighteenth-Century Senegal

GOSPEL

58a Gospelles of Dystaves
258f Roles of Women in the Fourth Gospel

GOTHIC

119g Novels, Gothic Novels
184f Woman in the Marginalia of Gothic Manuscripts and Related Works

GOUDGE

110e Gentle Truths for Gentle Readers: The Fiction of Elizabeth Goudge

GOUDIN

215f Susanna Goudin Cardon: An Italian Convert to Mormonism

GOURDFUL

373k A Gourdful of Glory

GOVERNESS

223a Victorian Governess: Status Incongruence in Family and Society

GOVERNMENT

see also POLITICS; POWER; branches of government

6d Women in Government and Affirmative Action
48k Government in the Lead
196hh Women in Educational Governance
196ii Women in Academic Governance
203c Second Treatise of Government
297q Discrimination Against Women in the U.S.: Higher Education, Government Enforcement Agencies, and Unions
323i Women in Parliament and Government
326g Government Policy and the Legal Status of Women
364n Think About Our Government: Now Think About Sweden's Policy

368j Impacts of Local Government Tax Structures on Women: Inefficiencies and Inequalities
371k Employment Problems of Women: Federal Government Examples

GOVERNOR

196gg Task Force on Education Report, Governor's Commission on the Status of Women, Ma.

GOWANLOCK

165d T. Gowanlock

GRACE

233k Princess Grace Turns Forty

GRADUATE

39o Impediment or Stimulant? Marital Status and Graduate Education
140dd Self-Concept and the Coping Process of Black Graduate and Undergraduate Women at a Predominantly White University
166dd Graduate Limbo for Women
166ee Career Expectations of Negro Women Graduates
166hh College Women Seven Years After Graduation
252z Marriage and Motherhood of Black Women Graduates

GRAFFITI

175o Feminist Graffiti

GRAFTON

111y The Pauper Witch of Grafton
112p The Pauper Witch of Grafton

GRAN

121h Participation of Women in the Independence Movement in Gran Colombia, 1780-1830

GRANDMOTHER

33q The Jilting of Granny Weatherall
129q Jewish-American Grandmothers
298d The Grandmother
372k Life of Sarah Penfield, Rural Ohio Grandmother: Tradition Maintained, Tradition Threatened
375e My Grandmother Who Painted

GRANGE

113h The De Wets Come to Kloof Grange
215b Sarah Melissa Granger Kimball: The Liberal Shall Be Blessed

GRASS

340n Of Mist, and Grass, and Sand

GRAVE

113k A Letter to Ismael in the Grave
153c The African Mother at Her Daughter's Grave

GRAY

111i The Sky Is Gray
112g The Sky is Gray

GREAT BRITAIN

see BRITAIN

GREECE

206n Milieu Development and Male-Female Roles in Contemporary Greece
322h Field Work in a Greek Village
324f Greece

GREEN

83c Green Sealing-Wax
95d The Green Chrysanthemum
339k The Corn is Green

GREENE

215v Louisa Lula Greene Richards: "Remember the Women of Zion"

GREY

128d Jane Grey Swisshelm: Agitator

GRIEF

278c Entrails of Power: Bogus Manhood and the Language of Grief

GRIFFIN

303g Marion Mahony Griffin

GRIMKE

151i Grimke Sisters: Women and the Abolition Movement

GRISELDA

122i Three Female Playwrights Explore Contemporary Latin American Reality: Myrna Casas, Griselda Gambaro, Luisa Josefina Hernandez

GROUND

97p Like Bone to the Ground

GROUP

47d Case Against McCarthy: A Review of "The Group"
77j Women as a Minority Group
77aa Consciousness-Raising Group as a Model for Therapy with Women
132n Women as a Minority Group
155u Group Sex Among the Mid-Americans
166oo Women as a Minority Group in Higher Academics
173ii Consciousness-Raising Group as a Model for Therapy with Women
176x Differences in Attitudinal Responses Under Conditions of Implicitly Manipulated Group Salience
238e Women as a Minority Group
243g Are Women a "Minority" Group? Sometimes!
243j Women as a Minority Group: Twenty Years Later
244d Making of an Outcast Group: Prostitutes and Working Women in Nineteenth-Century Plymouth and Southampton
250f Women as a Minority Group
250g Women as a Minority Group: Some Twenty Years Later
251h Woman (sic) as a Minority Group
252e Women as a Minority Group
264z Women as a Minority Group
265z Women as a Minority Group
266dd Are Women A "Minority" Group? Sometimes!
302f Limitations of Group Action Among Entrepreneurs: The Market Women of Abidjan, Ivory Coast
342f Group Dynamics and Consciousness Raising

GROUPS

20n Women and Domestic Power: Political and Economic Strategies in Domestic Groups
21g Feminine Self-Preservation in Groups
35q Report on Marxist-Feminist Groups 1-5
64i Gaining Support from Other Groups
141m Effects of Participation in Women's Consciousness-Raising Groups
180w Reparations to Wronged Groups
180y Individuals, Groups, and Inverse Discrimination
180z Should Reparations be to Individuals or to Groups?
180aa Reparations to Individuals or Groups?
249e Strategies, Cooperation, and Conflict Among Women in Domestic Groups
249l Women in Groups: Ijaw Women's Associations
274a Personal Narratives in Women's Rap Groups
316j Women's and Men's Liberation Groups: Political Power Within the System and Outside the System
330o Consciousness-Raising Groups as Therapy for Women
366b Importance of Women in Determining the Composition of Residential Groups in Aboriginal Australia

GROWTH

18q Physical Growth of Adolescent Girls: Patterns and Sequence

43e Chinese Women: The Relative Influences of Ideological Revolution, Economic Growth, and Cultural Change
271f Determinants of Intellectual Growth in Women
344g W.E.A.L.: The Growth of a Feminist Organization

GRUNDY

266jj Life and Death of Ms. Solomon Grundy

GUADALUPE

43k La Chicana: Guadalupe or Malinche

GUATEMALA

131d Guatemalan Women: Life under Two Types of Patriarchy
249o Mastery of Work and the Mystery of Sex in a Guatemalan Village
281e Industrialization, Monopoly, Capitalism, and Women's Work in Guatemala

GUENEVERE

184c Isolt and Guenevere: Two Twelfth-Century Views of Woman

GUIDE

8x Pocket Legal Guide for Gay People
295j Research Guide
304m Guide to Historical Literature Pertaining to Canadian Women
314q Businessman's Guide to Women's Liberation
314y Addendum to Style Guide for Authors

GUIDELINES

6m How to Eliminate Sexist Language From Your Writing: Some Guidelines for the Manager and Supervisor
156n APPENDIX: Guidelines for the Development and Evaluation of Unbiased Educational Materials
207i APPENDIX: N.C.T.E. Guidelines for Nonsexist Use of Language
208hh Guidelines for Equal Treatment of the Sexes in Social Studies Textbooks
314n Guidelines for Interviewing and Hiring Women Candidates

GUIDO

122g Maria Angelica Bosco and Beatriz Guido: An Approach to Two Argentinian Novelists Between 1960 and 1970

GUILT

78d Feminine Guilt and the Oedipus Complex

GUINEA

230f Concept of Pollution Among the Kafe of the Papua New Guinea Highlands
285l Sexual Antagonism in the New Guinea Highlands: A Bena Bena Example

338a Coniagui Women (Guinea)

GUJARAT

309c Employment and Family Change: A Study of Middle-Class Women in Urban Gujarat

GUSII

94j Gusii Sex Offenses: A Study in Social Control
155p Gusii Sex Offenses: A Study in Social Control

GUTS

375l Blood and Guts: The Tricky Problem of Being a Woman Writer in the Late Twentieth Century

GUY BLACHE

212l Out of Oblivion: Alice Guy-Blache
238p Alice Guy Blache: Czarina of the Silent Screen

GWENDOLYN

214p Gwendolyn the Terrible: Propositions on Eleven Poems

GYNAECOCENTRIC

232b Gynaecocentric Theory

GYNECOLOGY

39t Women in Gynecology Textbooks
126f Gynecology and Ideology in Seventeenth-Century England
211n Medical Gynecology: Problems and Patients
211o Surgical Gynecology
211p Hysterectomy and Other Gynecological Surgeries: A Psychological View
211x Gynecological Approach to Menopause

GYPSY

154d Gypsy Women: Models in Conflict
298e Gypsies (Photographs)

H.D.

88g Who Buried H.D.? A Poet, Her Critics, and Her Place in "The Literary Tradition"
214n Echoing Spell of H.D.'s "Trilogy"

H.E.W.

180d H.E.W., the University and Women
180h H.E.W. and the Universities

HAEC-VIR

229b Haec-Vir

HAGAR

151h Hagar and Her Children

HAGGADAH

117j Jewish Women's Haggadah
263p Jewish Woman's Haggadah

HAI-SHAN

308d Women of Hai-shan: A Demographic Portrait

HAIR

24aa The Letting Down of the Hair
29c If You're Light and Have Long Hair
111f Cutting the Jewish Bride's Hair
112f Cutting the Jewish Bride's Hair

HALAKHIC

117l Status of Women in Halakhic Judaism

HALF

71f Women: The Forgotten Half of Argentine History
73o Seven Deadly Half-Truths About Women
96nn Half-Confessed
116a Silent Half: "Le Contadine del Sud" Before The First World War
117k Other Half: Women in the Jewish Tradition
226t Half-Confessed
233oo The Morning Half-Life Blues
307h Women Hold Up Half the Sky

HALL

143o Women at City Hall

HAMMOUD

325aa Women and the Neighborhood Street in Borj Hammoud, Lebanon

HAMPSHIRE

8p Bundles of Twigs in New Hampshire: A High School Teacher's Report

HANDEDNESS

204d Patterns of Cognitive Functioning in Relation to Handedness and Sex-Related Differences

HANDICAP

18c Growing Up with a Physical Handicap

HANDICRAFTS

352m Handicrafts: A Source of Employment for Women in Developing Rural Economies

HANDS

36h Emily Bronte in the Hands of Male Critics

HANG

8ee We'd Better All Hang Together or Surely We'll All Hang Separately

HANI

178i Ume Tsuda and Motoko Hani: Echoes of American Cultural Feminism in Japan

HAPPINESS

108s Family Happiness
111s The Short Happy Life of Francis Macomber
112k The Short Happy Life of Francis Macomber
131j Khmer Village Women in Cambodia: A Happy Balance
166mm Career and Family Orientations of Husbands and Wives in Relation to Marital Happiness
176p Career and Family Orientations of Husbands and Wives in Relation to Marital Happiness
254e Paradox of the Happy Marriage
277p The Short Happy Life of Francis Macomber
284w Raising a Bright and Happy Child

HARASSMENT

235g Sexual Harassment: Women's Hidden Occupational Hazard

HARD

77ff Why Are Women So Hard on Women?
132j Hard and the Soft: The Force of Feminism in Modern Times
341l Learning the Hard Way

HAREMS

53i Harems and Overlords: Biosocial Models and the Female

HARLOT

140qq American Principles in Print: The Hero, The Harlot and the Glorified Horse

HARMONY

231c Of the Harmony of the Woman

HARRIET

65a Sentiment and Intellect: The Story of John Stuart Mill and Harriet Taylor Mill
111uu I Like to Think of Harriet Tubman
178f Meaning of Harriet Tubman
181k Rights and Wrongs of Women: Mary Wollstonecraft, Harriet Martineau, Simone de Beauvoir
359c Harriet Martineau's Autobiography: The Making of a Female Philosopher

HARSH

131g Women of Udu: Survival in a Harsh Land

HARTFORD

60b Hartford Female Seminary

HARVARD

13ee Harvard Ed School
180l Harvard College Amicus Curiae, DeFunis v. Odegaard, Supreme Court of the U.S., 1973

HASTA

122f Elena Poniatowska's "Hasta no Verte, Jesus Mio"

HAT

256r When Women in Politics Are Old Hat
317c Hats as a Symbol of Women's Position in Three Evangelical Churches in Edinburgh, Scotland

HATAY

325w Women, Class, and Power: Examples from the Hatay, Turkey

HATCHET

128q Lady With the Hatchet

HATE

169m Women Who Hate Their Husbands

HAUNTED

119d The Haunted Palace
119f The Haunted Chamber

HAUSA

372c Women's Role in a Muslim Hausa Town--Mirria, Republic of Niger

HAWKS

288u Working with Hawks

HAY

257v John Hay, Mrs. Catt and Patriotism

HAYDEN

303e Sophia Hayden and the Woman's Building Competition

HAZARD

127ii Health Care May Be Hazardous to Your Health
235g Sexual Harassment: Women's Hidden Occupational Hazard

HEAD

45f Black Women Who Head Families: Economic Needs and Economic Resources
103d The Learned Adventure of the Dragon's Head
166e Head Librarians: How Many Men? How Many Women?
291l Discrimination and Poverty among Women Who Head Families

HEALING

185h Roles of Medieval Women in the Healing Arts

HEALTH

11b Adjustment: New Approaches to Women's Mental Health
15h Healthy Self-Love
22x Androgyny as a Model of Mental Health for Women: From Theory to Therapy
45h Health Issues Facing Black Women
77y Masochistic Syndrome, Hysterical Personality, and the Illusion of a Healthy Woman
77cc What Is a Healthy Woman?
116q Women, Ethnicity, and Mental Health: The Italian Woman, Impressions and Observations
116r Oral History in Pittsburgh--Women, Ethnicity, and Mental Health: Rationale, Procedure, and Methodology
127ii Health Care May Be Hazardous to Your Health
153g Statistics of Female Health
155b Sex-Role Stereotypes and Clinical Judgments of Mental Health
160a Advice to Mothers, on the Subject of Their Own Health, and, of the Means of Promoting the Health, Strength and Beauty of Their Offspring
166n Female Physician in Public Health: Conflict and Reconciliation of the Sex and Professional Roles
176uu Sex-Role Stereotypes and Clinical Judgements of Mental Health
191a Women's Health Movement: Past Roots

191q Class Factor: Mountain Women Speak Out on Women's Health
191r Women Workers in the Health Service Industry
191u Women's Health Movement: Where Are We Now?
191v Women and Health Care: A Comparison of Theories
211b Feminism: Making a Difference in Our Health
211c Prenatal Influences on Child Health and Development
235h Women's Health: The Side Effects of Sex Bias
250j Sex-Role Stereotypes and Clinical Judgments of Mental Health
264c Women, Health, and Medicine
266bb Adult Sex Roles and Mental Health
276c Women, Men and Mental Health
311c Health Professions--Opportunities and Limitations
311f Unique Health Problems of Women in Industry
331e Health and Fertility Issues and the Dependency of Wives
332k Bibliography: Women, Science, and Health
344r Crisis Perspective on Emerging Health Roles: A Paradigm for the Entry of Women into New Occupational Roles

HEART

288l Marlene Dietrich: At Heart a Gentleman

HELEN

33b Helen

HELLMAN

141dd Lillian Hellman: Dramatist of the Second Sex
359i Lillian Hellman and the Strategy of the "Other"
359j Metaphysics of Matrilinearism in Women's Autobiography: Studies of Mead's "Blackberry Winter," Hellman's "Pentimento," Angelou's "I Know Why the Caged Bird Sings," and Kingston's "The Woman Warrior"

HELP

129v Helping Each Other
250l Women in Rage: A Psychological Look at the Helpless Heroine
342dd Ending Discrimination Against Women in Education: How Uncle Sam Can Help
350c "Women Must Help Each Other"

HEMBRA

77o Heritage of La Hembra

HEMINGWAY

17p "A Farewell to Arms": Ernest Hemingway's "Resentful Cryptogram"

HEMISPHERIC

332c Sex Differences in Hemispheric Brain Asymmetry

HENRI

138f Henri Bourassa and "the Woman Question"

HENRIETTA

117p Henrietta Szold--Liberated Woman
139j Henrietta Rodman: An Interview with a Feminist

HENRY

247c Henry Fuseli's "Nightmare": Eroticism or Pornography?

HEPBURN

288m Actress Archetypes in the 1950s: Doris Day, Marilyn Monroe, Elizabeth Taylor, Audrey Hepburn

HEREFORDSHIRE

55h Sexual Antagonism in Herefordshire

HERESY

225f Woman-Power: Religious Heresy and Feminism in Early English Socialism

HERITAGE

77o Heritage of La Hembra
172i Woman's Sociobiological Heritage: Destiny or Free Choice?
292s Nineteenth-Century Heritage: The Family, Feminism and Sex
329a Patriarchal Heritage

HERMANN

110l Sex Roles in Three of Hermann Hesse's Novels

HERMAPHRODITE

15d Hermaphrodite

HERNANDEZ

122i Three Female Playwrights Explore Contemporary Latin American Reality: Myrna Casas, Griselda Gambaro, Luisa Josefina Hernandez

HERO

110p Heroism in "To the Lighthouse"
140qq American Principles in Print: The Hero, The Harlot and the Glorified Horse
220q World of Heroes
266e Heroic and Tender Modes in Women Authors of Fantasy
275g Women and the Aesthetic of the Positive Hero in the G.D.R.
278x Huck--An Androgynous Hero
356b A Romantic Hero

HEROINE

80a "I am my own heroine": Some Thoughts about Women and Autobiography in France
88q Heroine as Her Author's Daughter
105f Magazine Heroines: Is MS. Just Another Member of the FAMILY CIRCLE?
110a What Can a Heroine Do? Or Why Women Can't Write
184b Transformations of the Heroine: From Epic Heard to Epic Read
215j Aurelia Read Spencer Rogers: Humble Heroine
222f African Heroine
222g Awakening of the Self in the Heroines of Ousmane Sembene
250l Women in Rage: A Psychological Look at the Helpless Heroine
253k Jane Addams: An American Heroine
278j Heroine as Her Author's Daughter
288e Hollywood Heroines Under the Influence: Alice Still Lives Here

HERON

133f The Eye of the Heron

HERSTORY

57b Brief Glimpses of Herstory
126w "Herstory" As History: A New Field or Another Fad?
208ii Lost Herstory: The Treatment of Women in Children's Encyclopedias
263d Reflections on the Meaning of Herstory

HESSE

110l Sex Roles in Three of Hermann Hesse's Novels

HETEROGENEITY

51cc Competing Goals, Heterogeneity, and Classification

HETEROSEXUALITY

123h Normative Status of Heterosexuality
155m Early Sexual Behavior in Adult Homosexual and Heterosexual Males
199p Behaviorally Feminine Male Child: Pretranssexual? Pretransvestite? Prehomosexual? Preheterosexual?

HIC

229a Hic Mulier

HIDDEN

85i Hidden Joke: Generic Uses of Masculine Terminology
102c In Hiding
235g Sexual Harassment: Women's Hidden Occupational Hazard
359f Selves in Hiding
360q Cookbooks and Law Books: The Hidden History of Career Women in Twentieth-Century America

HIERARCHY

20p Non-Hierarchical, Hierarchical, and Masked Reciprocity in the Arab Village

194d Sexual Hierarchy Among the Yanomama

HIGGINSES

93e Jennie Higginses of the "New South in the West": A Regional Survey of Socialist Activities, Agitators, and Organizers, 1901-1917

HIGH SCHOOL

8p Bundles of Twigs in New Hampshire: A High School Teacher's Report
13s High-School Women: Oppression and Liberation
13u Realistic Counseling for High-School Girls
13w Women in U.S. History High-School Textbooks
13x High-School Sex(ist) Education
166v Interest of High School Girls in Dental Auxiliary Careers
196f Sex-Typing in the High School
196k Women in U.S. History High-School Textbooks
208i Does Different Equal Less? A High School Woman Speaks Out
208q Realistic Counseling for High School Girls
208gg Women in U.S. History High School Textbooks
271q Women in U.S. History High School Textbooks

HIGH SCHOOLS

208ll Sex Stereotypes in Mathematics and Science Textbooks for Elementary and Junior High Schools

HIGH-RISE

102p High-Rise Story

HIGHER

166oo Women as a Minority Group in Higher Academics

HIGHER EDUCATION

see also UNIVERSITY; COLLEGE; CAMPUS; COEDUCATION; FACULTY; STUDENT; ACADEMIA; EDUCATION; AFFIRMATIVE ACTION; PH-D.

4b Institutional Barriers to Women Students in Higher Education
4c Women in the Male World of Higher Education
4d Women Dropouts from Higher Education
4i Dilemma of the Black Woman in Higher Education
21s Women and Higher Education
106a Higher Education of Women
140hh Black Women in Higher Education: Research Literature
180a Discrimination in Higher Education: A Debate on Faculty Employment
180p Racial Preferences in Higher Education: Political Responsibility and the Judicial Role
243h Institutional Discrimination: The Case of Achievement-Oriented Women in Higher Education
265j Structural and Internalized Barriers to Women in Higher Education
297q Discrimination Against Women in the U.S.: Higher Education, Government Enforcement Agencies, and Unions
342ee Affirmative Action in Higher Education
342gg Sex Discrimination in Higher Education and Attitude Change

HIGHLANDS

230f Concept of Pollution Among the Kafe of the Papua New Guinea Highlands
285l Sexual Antagonism in the New Guinea Highlands: A Bena Bena Example

HILL

16d The Antrim Hills
50a The Murder at Troyte's Hill

HINDU

114g Marriage among the Hindus
115d Hindu Woman at Home
115e Jawaharlal Nehru and the Hindu Code Bill
281j Women and the Hindu Tradition

HINTERLAND

193d Sex, Age and Social Control in Mobs of the Darwin Hinterland

HIRING

158gg Secondary Sexism and Quota Hiring
180bb Preferential Policies in Hiring and Admissions: A Jurisprudential Approach
250mm Empirical Verification of Sex Discrimination in Hiring Practices in Psychology
314n Guidelines for Interviewing and Hiring Women Candidates

HISPANIC

80i Hispanic American Fiction and Drama Written by Women:
174m Policy Impacts on Hispanics and Women: A State Case Study

HISTORIAN

126c Invisible Woman: The Historian as Professional Magician

HISTORICAL

23g Gender and Genre: Women as Historical Writers, 1400-1820
40b Public Policy Toward Child Care in America: A Historical Perspective
70f Urban Working Woman in the U.S.S.R.: An Historical Overview
70i Historical Changes in How People Spend Their Time
88y Need to Tell All: A Comparison of Historical and Modern Feminist "Confessional" Writing
91f Fertility of Working Women in the United States: Historical Trends and Theoretical Perspectives
97g Historical and Critical Essay for Black Women
117n Bais Yaakov: A Historical Model for Jewish Feminists
126d Historical Phallacies: Sexism in American Historical Writing
126k Racism and Tradition: Black Womanhood in Historical Perspective
140a Sex Roles in Transition: The Historical Perspective

141ee Historical and Theoretical Evolution of Viola Spolin's Theatre Games
172a Sex-Related Behaviors: Historical and Psychobiological Perspectives
181h Women in American Trade Unions: An Historical Analysis
201e Science and the Woman Problem: Historical Perspectives
211l Historical Understanding of Contraception
217h Discrimination against Blacks: A Historical Perspective
240c Praising Virtuous Ladies: The Literary Image and Historical Reality of Women in Seventeenth-century England
246j Women in History: Public Life and Historical Consciousness
264aa Historical Background (of Feminism)
265aa Historical Background (of feminism)
272d Historical Perspectives on Women in Educational Leadership
272g Coeducation and the Development of Leadership Skills in Women: Historical Perspectives from Cornell University, 1868-1900
276a Family and Gender Roles in Historical Perspective
291g Historical and Structural Barriers to Occupational Desegregation
303s Historic Chart Relating Architectural Projects to General and Women's History in the U.S.
304j Indian Women: An Historical Example and a Contemporary View
304m Guide to Historical Literature Pertaining to Canadian Women
330a Changing Views of Women and Therapeutic Approaches: Some Historical Considerations
348b Myth of Male Protectiveness and the Legal Subordination of Women: An Historical Analysis
361d Historical Survey of Women's Language: From Medieval Courtesy Books to Seventeen Magazine
371b Women Working: Historical Trends

HISTORY

see also HERSTORY; WOMEN'S HISTORY

13w Women in U.S. History High-School Textbooks
13cc Sexism in History
20o Feminine Factor in Cultural History
21i New Feminist Criticisms: Exploring the History of the New Space
33o Natural History
39b My Four Revolutions: An Autobiographical History of the A.S.A.
63e Equal Pay in Canada: History, Progress and Problems
71f Women: The Forgotten Half of Argentine History
83b Notes for a Case History
98m Visibility and Difference: Black Women in History and Literature
110s Modernism and History
114a Looking Back in History
116r Oral History in Pittsburgh--Women, Ethnicity, and Mental Health: Rationale, Procedure, and Methodology
126b Mary Beard's "Woman As Force in History": A Critique
126s Study of Women in American History
126t Placing Women in History: A 1975 Perspective
126w "Herstory" As History: A New Field or Another Fad?
127b Next Great Moment in History is Ours
141f WOMEN IN HISTORY: Introduction
141q Men and Women in the Family: History of the Idea of Family in America's Depression Generation
162e Interpretation to Be Used for a History of Mentalities

190f Feminist History in Perspective: Sociological Contributions to Biographic Analysis
194j History of Women's Struggle for Equality in Puerto Rico
196k Women in U.S. History High-School Textbooks
208gg Women in U.S. History High School Textbooks
208jj Sexism in History or, Writing Women's History is a Tricky Business
232f Brief History of the Condition of Women
232i Short History of Women's Rights
246j Women in History: Public Life and Historical Consciousness
250b Evaluation of the Performance of Women as a Function of Their Sex, Achievement, and Personal History
264i History and Development of Day Care in the U.S.
265f History and Development of Day Care in the U.S.
269l Women in Families and History
271q Women in U.S. History High School Textbooks
278l History of Married Women's Rights
292b New Approaches to the Study of Women in American History
295d Short History of Nursing in Ontario
301h Case History of Affirmative Action
320d Voice of Women: A History
334a Women and American History
334o From Aide to Organizer: The Oral History of Lillian Roberts
335i Demographic Contributions to the History of Victorian Women
335l Survey of Primary Sources and Archives for the History of Early Twentieth-Century English Women
337l American Women in Ministry: A History of Protestant Beginning Points
341h Women and History
360c Widowhood in Eighteenth-Century Massachusetts: A Problem in the History of the Family
360q Cookbooks and Law Books: The Hidden History of Career Women in Twentieth-Century America
364d Black Woman in American History

HITCHHIKE

94m Hitchhike Victim of Rape

HODESH

117i This Month Is for You: Observing Rosh Hodesh as a Woman's Holiday

HOLES

282e Holes and Slime: Sexism in Sartre's Psychoanalysis

HOLIDAY

117i This Month Is for You: Observing Rosh Hodesh as a Woman's Holiday

HOLINESS

337d Women, Power and the Pursuit of Holiness in Medieval Christianity

HOLLAND

5c Lady Holland

HOLLOW

24c The Hollow Woman

HOLLYWOOD

288e Hollywood Heroines Under the Influence: Alice Still Lives Here

HOLY

83j A Temple of the Holy Ghost

HOLYOKE

334j Founding of Mount Holyoke College

HOMAGE

108i "Ghazals: Homage to Ghalib"

HOME

10l Plum Bun "Home"
19l Long Road Home: Women's Work and Industrialization
21u Status of Home Economics and the Status of Women
22o Sex-Role Concepts and Sex Typing in Childhood as a Function of School and Home Environments
29j A Sudden Trip Home in the Spring
68n Whore in Every Home
74g Home: Its Work and Influence
91g Fertility and Women's Employment Outside the Home in Western Europe
92b Home From Home: Women's Philanthropic Work in the Nineteenth Century
92c Separation of Home and Work? Landladies and Lodgers in Nineteenth-Century England
114r Prostitutes--Notes from a Rescue Home
115d Hindu Woman at Home
140j Women at Home and at Work
143b Home: A Critical Problem for Changing Sex Roles
152g Sweet Home
156i Non-Sexist Parenting at Home and at School
166xx Employer Acceptance of the Mature Home Economist
181d Landscape with Figures: Home and Community in English Society
202i Women's Work in the Home
219l Mothers' Speech to Children in Bilingual Mexican-American Homes
257j Home
258d Home and Work: Women's Roles and the Transformation of Values
260o Home and Community
271h Sex-Role Concepts and Sex Typing in Childhood as a Function of School and Home Environments
280v Chauvinism--At Work and at Home
287c Home Work, Market Work, and the Allocation of Time
287e Implications of Women's Employment for Home and Family Life
292o Home Life as a Profession
340m Nobody's Home
354i Implications of Women's Employment for Home and Family Life
371f Husbands at Home: Organization of the Husband's Household Day

HOMECOMING

111ww Homecoming

HOMEMAKER

61f Sex Role Stereotypes and the Career Versus Homemaking Orientations of Women
166j Masculinity or Femininity? Differentiating Career-Oriented and Homemaking-Oriented College Freshman Women
176gg Re-Evaluation of the Primary Role of the Communist Chinese Woman: The Homemaker or the Worker
328i Homemaker, the Family, and Employment
331i Homemakers into Widows and Divorcees: Can the Law Provide Economic Protection?

HOMEWORKERS

55d Homeworkers in North London

HOMOGENIZING

89a Homogenizing the American Woman: The Power of an Unconscious Ideology

HOMOSEXUALITY

see also GAY; LESBIAN

8t Faggot Father
78f Homosexuality in Women
99i Homosexuality in Females and Males
155d Sexual Dimorphism and Homosexual Gender Identity
155m Early Sexual Behavior in Adult Homosexual and Heterosexual Males
157r Question of Homosexuality
169g Female Homosexuality
171f Homosexual Orientation in Women and Men: A Hormonal Basis?
176a Sexual Dimorphism and Homosexual Gender Identity
199p Behaviorally Feminine Male Child: Pretranssexual? Pretransvestite? Prehomosexual? Preheterosexual?
296d Homosexuality in Women
330h Female Homosexual

HOMOSOCIAL

291c Homosocial Theory of Sex Roles: An Explanation of the Sex Segregation of Social Institutions

HONESTY

364j Confronting the Sports Establishment: A Plan for Honesty and Sanity

HONG

359l Towards a Theory of Form in Feminist Autobiography: Kate Millett's "Flying" and "Sita"; Maxine Hong Kingston's "The Woman Warrior"

HONG KONG

329q Industrialization and Hong Kong Women

HONOR

71l Honor, Shame, and Women's Liberation in Cuba: Views of Working-Class Emigre Men
79n Upon the much lamented death of the Right Honourable the Lady Elizabeth Langham
116n Metonymic Definition of the Female and the Concept of Honour Among Italian Immigrant Families in Toronto
329n Algerian Women: Honor, Survival, and Islamic Socialism

HOOKERS

8q Hookers: Queer Fish

HOPI

213k Male and Female in Hopi Thought and Action

HORATIO

130e Report of the Trial: The People versus Dr. Horatio N. Loomis, for Libel

HORIZONS

284q Decade of Widening Horizons

HORMONES

20c Prenatal Hormones and Human Behavior: Implications for the Status of Women
56a Sex Hormones in the Development of Sex Differences in Human Behavior
67g Male Hormones and Behaviour
67h Female Hormones and Behaviour
77a Sex Hormones and Executive Ability
101b Hormones and Gender
171c Gonadal Hormones and Cognitive Functioning
171f Homosexual Orientation in Women and Men: A Hormonal Basis?
171j Adult Life Cycles: Changing Roles and Changing Hormones
191k Dangers of Sex Hormones
198t Fetal Hormones and the Brain: Effects on Sexual Dimorphism of Behavior
199a Sexual Behavior Differentiation: Prenatal Hormonal and Environmental Control
199w Reproductive Hormones, Moods, and the Menstrual Cycle
204h Hormones and Cognitive Functioning in Normal Development
250x Early Hormonal Influences on the Development of Sexual and Sex-Related Behaviors
250aa Hormonal Interaction, Menstruation, and the Oral Contraceptives
282c Biology, Sex Hormones, and Sexism in the 1920's
330b Sex Hormones, The Central Nervous System and Affect Variability in Humans

HORNEY

268l Karen Horney's Flight from Orthodoxy

HORNS

123d Taking the Bullshit by the Horns

HORSE

96d Demon in Female Apparel: Narrative of Josephine Amelia Perkins, the Notorious Female Horse Thief...
140qq American Principles in Print: The Hero, The Harlot and the Glorified Horse

HOSPITAL

191s Building a Hospital Workers' Union: Doris Turner, the Woman from 1199
225a Mother and the Hospital: An Unfortunate Fit Between the Woman's Internal World and Some Hospital Practices
330p Women in Institutions: Treatment in Prisons and Mental Hospitals

HOSTESSES

306g Bar Hostesses

HOTBED

96kk Hotbed of Feminists
226q Hotbed of Feminists

HOTEL

111l At a Summer Hotel

HOUR

24j The Hour of the Wolf
111qq The Story of an Hour
161b The Children's Hour
251w Differences in Hourly Earnings Between Men and Women
252cc Differences in Hourly Earnings Between Men and Women
371j Hours Rigidity: Effects on the Labor-Market Status of Women

HOUSE

102o The House
108w My Mother's House: Where Are the Children?
112ff A Doll's House, 1970
113s In the Basement of the House
116g Settlement House and the Italian Family
116j Interaction Between Italian Immigrant Women and the Chicago Commons Settlement House, 1909-1944
129u Is There a Psychiatrist in the House?
142n My House in the Trees

143d Appropriation of the House: Changes in House Design and Concepts of Domesticity
143i Swedish Women in Single-Family Housing
143r Housing for Single-Parent Families: A Women's Design
144j Out of Our Fathers' House
233vv A Doll's House
244g Victorian Masculinity and the Angel in the House
273w A Bird in the House
339g A Doll's House
356g The House of My Dreams
360h Cultural Hybrid in the Slums: The College Woman and the Settlement House, 1889-1894
362l Women: A House Divided
363c A Doll's House

HOUSEHOLD

see also DEMOGRAPHY; FERTILITY

92h Domestic Labor and the Household
125b Domestic Problem: Work and Culture in the Household
143c Household as Workplace: Wives, Husbands, and Children
202m Vicious Cycle of Welfare: Problems of the Female-Headed Household in N.Y.C.
371f Husbands at Home: Organization of the Husband's Household Day

HOUSEHUSBAND

300e Diary of a Mad Househusband

HOUSEKEEPING

24f Good Housekeeping
119e The Housekeeper's Story
139g Waste of Private Housekeeping
236j Occupations, Male Housekeeper: Male-Female Roles on Cheju Island

HOUSEWIFE

176ff Worker, Mother, Housewife: Soviet Women Today
206l Worker, Mother, Housewife: Soviet Woman Today
231e Task of a Housewife
252w Monetary Value of a Housewife
304e Housewives in Women's Liberation: Social Change as Role-Making
342d Alienation and the Contemporary American Housewife
354q Housewives as Workers

HOUSEWORK

see also HOMEMAKER; HOUSEWIFE; DOMESTICITY; HOUSEKEEPING

55f Rationalization of Housework
89f Politics of Housework
89hh Wages for Housework
89ii Women and Pay for Housework
89mm Value of Housework
127l Politics of Housework

139p   Politics of Housework
175u   Housework: Slavery or Labor of Love
251cc Housework
252mm Politics of Housework
303c   Catharine Beecher and the Politics of Housework

HOUSTON

 16b   Houston, Houston, Do You Read?

HROTSWITHA

141bb Hrotsvitha of Gandersheim: The Playable Dramas of a Woman
       Playwright of the Tenth Century
185a   Sin and Salvation: The Dramatic Context of Hrotswitha's Women

HUAN

108u   HUAN, or Dispersion

HUCK

278x   Huck--An Androgynous Hero

HUGHES

215s   Dr. Martha Hughes Cannon: Doctor, Wife, Legislator, Exile

HULL-HOUSE

153q   Twenty Years at Hull-House

HUMAN

  2e   Philosophy on Humanity
  8d   Human Identity and Gay Identity: A Liberationist Dilemma
  9dd As to Humanness
 20c   Prenatal Hormones and Human Behavior: Implications for the Status
       of Women
 20d   Spontaneous and Induced Abortion in Human and Non-Human Primates
 24z   Some Thoughts on the Question of Being a Separate Human Being
 56a   Sex Hormones in the Development of Sex Differences in Human
       Behavior
 85c   Androgyny As an Ideal for Human Development
 88s   Humanbecoming: Form and Focus in the Neo-Feminist Novel
 88u   Jean Rhys' Recent Fiction: Humane Developments in "Wide Sargasso
       Sea"
 96l   Before Women Were Human Beings: Adventures of an American Fellow in
       German Universities of the '90s
110m   Humanbecoming: Form and Focus in the Neo-Feminist Novel
132ii Human Continuum
156l   Sex Role and Human Culture
157i   Sex, Birth Control, and Human Life
157u   Fetal Humanity and the Theory of Essentialism
171d   Human Sex-Hormone Abnormalities Viewed from an Androgynous
       Perspective: A Reconsideration of the Work of John Money

171e Biochemical and Neurophysiological Influences on Human Sexual Behavior
171g Social Psychological Model of Human Sexuality
173k Early Sex Differences in the Human: Studies of Socioemotional Development
173r Women's Liberation and Human Sexual Relations
199c Fetal Androgens, Human Central Nervous System Differentiation, and Behavior Sex Differences
200m Sexual Behavior in the Human Female: Part II. Biological Data
204i Prenatal Influences on Cognitive Abilities: Data from Experimental Animals and Human and Endocrine Syndromes
250gg Case for Human Cycles
252b Family Patterns and Human Rights
263a Human Situation: A Feminine View
266v Effect of Contraceptive Pills on Sexual Activity in the Luteal Phase of the Human Menstrual Cycle
280bb Whole Human Being
282g Women's Liberation and Human Emancipation
292p Are Women Human Beings?
293k Women as Co-Managers: The Family as a General Model of Human Social Organization
296i Clitoral Eroticism and the Sexual Response Cycle in Human Females
314p Humanizing the World of Work
330b Sex Hormones, The Central Nervous System and Affect Variability in Humans
342u Human Potentiality
351d Work Attachment, Investments in Human Capital and the Earnings of Young Women
362e Genius of Woman as the Genius of Humanity
365a Evolutionary Aspects of Human Gender

HUMAN-NOT-QUITE-HUMAN

132l Human-Not-Quite-Human

HUMANAE

157h Humanae Vitae

HUMANISM

11d Androgyny and Humanistic Goals
23c Book-Lined Cells: Women and Humanism in the Early Italian Renaissance
23d Learned Women of Early Modern Italy: Humanists and University Scholars
184d Petrarch's Laura: The Convolutions of a Humanistic Mind

HUMBLE

215j Aurelia Read Spencer Rogers: Humble Heroine

HUMOR

18g Role of Laughter and Humor in Growing Up Female
24q The Good Humor Man
220s The Good Humor Man

355g Humorous Tales (stories)

HUNDRED

51d Five Hundred Delinquent Women
178g Divorce as a Moral Issue: A Hundred Years of Controversy

HUNGER

230n Love Unites Them and Hunger Separates Them: Poor Women in the Dominican Republic
269d Hunger in the U.S.: Women and Children First

HUNTER-GATHER

173w !Kung Hunter-Gatherers: Feminism, Diet, and Birth Control
230b Woman the Gatherer: Male Bias in Anthropology
366a Woman the Gatherer

HUNTING

111n Hunting Season

HURNSCOT

179cc L. Hurnscot

HURSTON

88r Zora Neale Hurston
222p Influence of Voodoo on the Fiction of Zora Neale Hurston

HURT

9nn Are You Hurting Your Daughter Without Knowing It?
86j Why Red-Baiting Hurts the Feminist Movement
89l It Hurts to Be Alive and Obsolete
157a Four-Letter Words CAN Hurt You

HUSBAND

see also WIFE; MARRIAGE; SEX ROLE; PARENT; FAMILY

55g Husbands and Wives: The Dynamics of the Deferential Dialectic
70a Husband Provider Role: A Critical Appraisal
111g On Being Told That Her Second Husband Has Taken His First Lover
143c Household as Workplace: Wives, Husbands, and Children
151b Husbands and Wives
166mm Career and Family Orientations of Husbands and Wives in Relation to Marital Happiness
169m Women Who Hate Their Husbands
176p Career and Family Orientations of Husbands and Wives in Relation to Marital Happiness
213e Female Husbands in Southern Bantu Societies
231h Of the Relation Between Husband and Wife
370h Husband-Wife Relationship
371f Husbands at Home: Organization of the Husband's Household Day

HUSTLER

8r Hustler: A Boy for All Seasons

HUTCHINSON

9a Trial of Anne Hutchinson
178a Anne Hutchinson and the "Revolution Which Never Happened"
360b Anne Hutchinson and Female Agitation During the Years of the Antinomian Turmoil, 1636-1640

HYBRID

360h Cultural Hybrid in the Slums: The College Woman and the Settlement House, 1889-1894

HYPNOSIS

286k Use of Hypnosis in Sport--Is It Legitimate?

HYPOTHESIS

204c Spatial Ability: A Critical Review of the Sex-Linked Major Gene Hypothesis
219h Descriptive Study of the Language of Men and Women Born in Maine Around 1900 as It Reflects the Lakoff Hypotheses in "Language and Women's Place"
271i Assessment of Teaching Practice: An "Attractive" Hypothesis

HYSTERECTOMY

191n Epidemic in Unnecessary Hysterectomy
211p Hysterectomy and Other Gynecological Surgeries: A Psychological View

HYSTERIA

77y Masochistic Syndrome, Hysterical Personality, and the Illusion of a Healthy Woman
99m Politics of Hysteria: The Case of the Wandering Womb
176ss Hysterical Character and Feminine Identity
360n Hysterical Woman: Sex Roles and Role Conflict in Nineteenth-Century America

I.U.D.

24w In Search of a Missing I.U.D.

IBANEZ

122n Two Poets of America: Juana de Asbaje and Sara de Ibanez

IBERIAN

126j Latina Liberation: Tradition, Ideology, and Social Change in Iberian and Latin American Cultures

IBSEN

357f Ibsen and the Language of Women

IBU

281q Shaping of the Kaum Ibu (Women's Section) of the United Maylays National Organization

ICE

144h The Ice Wolf

ICON

80o Metamorphosis of an Icon: Woman in Russian Literature
247k Pinup and Icon
303a Model Domestic Environment: Icon or Option?

IDA

288s Interview with Ida Lupino

IDEAL

21o Ideal and the Reality: Women in Sweden
71j Pursuit of an Ideal: Migration, Social Class, and Women's Roles in Bogota, Colombia
76h Masochism, the Ego Ideal, and the Psychology of Women
85c Androgyny As an Ideal for Human Development
196h Teachers' Perceptions of Ideal Male and Female Students: Male Chauvinism in the Schools
246l American Character vs. The Ideal Woman
303b Challenging the American Domestic Ideal
306a Evolution of the Feminine Ideal

IDENTIFICATION

22l Woman Identified Woman
22p Sexual Role Identification and Personality Functioning in Girls
77v Woman Identified Woman
120j Cues to the Identification of Sex in Children's Speech
175z Woman Identified Woman
180r Identifying the Beneficiaries
198z Theories of Identification and Exposure to Multiple Models
200c Process of Learning Parental and Sex-Role Identification
250m Sex Differences in the Development of Masculine and Feminine Identification
250o Developmental Study of the Effects of Sex of the Dominant Parent on Sex-Role Preference, Identification, and Imitation in Children
252l Sex Differences in Identification Development
266c Sexual Role Identification and Personality Functioning in Girls
266u Identification and Complementation in the Differentiation of Gender Identity

IDENTITY

8d Human Identity and Gay Identity: A Liberationist Dilemma
18a Development of Female Identity
25e Crucible of Identity: The Negro Lower-Class Family
36c Identity and Expression: A Writing Course for Women
117a Jewish Feminist: Conflict in Identities
140mm Sexual Identity in the Early Fiction of V. Sackville-West
155d Sexual Dimorphism and Homosexual Gender Identity
159dd Contemporary Approach to Sex Identity
166s Female Identity and Career Choice: The Nursing Case
170j Personal Identity and Sexual Identity
176a Sexual Dimorphism and Homosexual Gender Identity
176ss Hysterical Character and Feminine Identity
198n Absent Father and Cross-Sex Identity
199o Cryptorchidism, Development of Gender Identity, and Sex Behavior
206c Sexual Identity Crises in the Life Cycle
206d Sex Identity Deviation and Inversion
252k Personal Identity and Sexual Identity
252m Stigma and Social Identity
263j Feminist Spirituality, Christian Identity, and Catholic Vision
266t Phyletic and Idiosyncratic Determinants of Gender Identity
266u Identification and Complementation in the Differentiation of Gender Identity
280o Matter of Identity
285j Masks of Identity
297c African Women: Identity Crisis? Some Observations on Education and the Changing Role of Women in Sierra Leone and Zaire
297g Marital Status and Sexual Identity: The Position of Women in a Mexican Peasant Society
303m New Professional Identities: Four Women in the Sixties

IDEOLOGY

20t American Women in Politics: Culture, Structure, and Ideology
22e Sex Equality: The Beginnings of Ideology
22y Personality and Ideology: A Personological Study of Women's Liberation
43e Chinese Women: The Relative Influences of Ideological Revolution, Economic Growth, and Cultural Change
77l Case Study of a Nonconscious Ideology: Training the Woman to Know Her Place
89a Homogenizing the American Woman: The Power of an Unconscious Ideology
92a Early Formation of Victorian Domestic Ideology
105e Imagery and Ideology: The Cover Photographs of Traditional Women's Magazines
126f Gynecology and Ideology in Seventeenth-Century England
126g Education and Ideology in Nineteenth-Century America: The Response of Educational Institutions to the Changing Role of Women
126j Latina Liberation: Tradition, Ideology, and Social Change in Iberian and Latin American Cultures
132q Sex Equality: The Beginning of Ideology
145e Domestic Ideology and Women's Education
151q Feminism as a Radical Ideology
158z Ideology of the Family

186f Training the Woman to Know Her Place: The Power of a Nonconscious Ideology
206m Sexes: Ideology and Reality in the Israeli Kibbutz
208c Training the Woman To Know Her Place: The Power of a Nonconscious Ideology
227g Ideology and Control
238d Sex Equality: The Beginnings of Ideology
253h Revolution Without Ideology: The Changing Place of Women in America
259h Ideology of the Suffrage Movement
271c How Ideology Shapes Women's Lives
271u Sex Equality: The Beginnings of Ideology
283m Counter-Ideology
302c "Aba Riots" or Igbo "Women's War"? Ideology, Stratification, and the Invisibility of Women
316h Ideology and the Law: Sexism and Supreme Court Decisions
342p Ideology of Prostitution
348d Who Needs Prostitutes? The Ideology of Male Sexual Needs

IDIOMS

273z Idioms

IDIOSYNCRATIC

266t Phyletic and Idiosyncratic Determinants of Gender Identity

IDLE

42k Image and Reality: The Myth of the Idle Victorian Woman
185e Boccaccio's Idle Ladies
279u Tears, Idle Tears

IDOLATRY

283e Phallic Worship: The Ultimate Idolatry

IGBO

285h Colonialism and the Lost Political Institutions of Igbo Women
302b Dual-Sex Political System in Operation: Igbo Women and Community Politics in Midwestern Nigeria
302c "Aba Riots" or Igbo "Women's War"? Ideology, Stratification, and the Invisibility of Women

IJAW

249l Women in Groups: Ijaw Women's Associations

ILLINOIS

41 Representation, Performance and Status of Women on the Faculty at the Urbana-Champaign Campus of the University of Illinois

ILLNESS

22t Relationship Between Sex Roles, Marital Status, and Mental Illness
39d Adult Sex Roles and Mental Illness

99o Gender Differences in Psychophysiological Illness
225b Witch and Her Devils: An Exploration of the Relationship Between Femininity and Illness
285k Sex Differences in the Incidence of Susto in Two Zapotec Pueblos: An Analysis of the Relationships between Sex Role Expectations and a Folk Illness
325dd Sex Differences and Folk Illness in an Egyptian Village

ILLUSION

77y Masochistic Syndrome, Hysterical Personality, and the Illusion of a Healthy Woman
213c Illusion and Reality in Sicily

ILLUSTRATION

43d Issues Confronting Professional African Women: Illustrations from Kenya
114s Chellamma--An Illustration of the Multiple Roles of Traditional Women
184g ILLUSTRATIONS

IMAGE

see also SELF IMAGE; SELF PERCEPTION; PERCEPTION

7f Images of Black Women in Afro-American Poetry
11g Media: New Images of Women in Contemporary Society
21k Images of Women in Contemporary Mexican Literature
42k Image and Reality: The Myth of the Idle Victorian Woman
45i Media and Their Effect on Black Images
71b "Brazileira": Images and Realities in Writings of Machado de Assis and Jorge Amado
88x Premises Fulfilled: Positive Images of Women in Twentieth-Century Autobiography
105e Imagery and Ideology: The Cover Photographs of Traditional Women's Magazines
105h Most Admired Woman: Image-Making in the News
105p Image of Women in Television: An Annotated Bibliography
110c Gentle Doubters: Images of Women in Englishwomen's Novels, 1840-1920
110f Image of Women in Science Fiction
138g Image of Women in Mass Circulation Magazines in the 1920s
139n Womanly Image
177b Images of Women in the Old Testament
177f Images of Women in the Talmud
182c Changing Image of Women in Soviet Literature
183e Gender Imagery and Issues of War and Peace: The Case of the Draft Resistance Movement of the 1960's
185b Popular Image of Brunhilde
208x Negative Image of Women in Children's Literature
212c Image of Woman as Image: The Optical Politics of Dames
219i Women's Verbal Images and Associations
222d Images of Black Women in Modern African Poetry
222k Images of Self and Race in the Autobiographies of Black Women
233f Womanly Image: Character Assassination through the Ages
240b Changing Image of Woman in Renaissance Society and Literature

240c Praising Virtuous Ladies: The Literary Image and Historical Reality of Women in Seventeenth-century England
240h Images of Women in Early American Literature
240m "Free in Fact and at Last": The Image of the Black Woman in Black American Literature
244e Image and Reality: The Actress and Society
246e Female Dimension in the Image of God: A Christian Perspective
246m Images of Women and Men in American Popular Magazines
247a Eroticism and Female Imagery in Nineteenth-Century Art
247e Courbet's "Baigneuses" and the Rhetorical Feminine Image
253c Image of Women in Contemporary Literature
254m Image of Woman in Advertising
254n Image of Woman in Textbooks
254o Seduced and Abandoned in the New World: The Image of Woman In American Fiction
265r Images of American Woman in Popular Songs
267y Changing Image of the Career Woman
274c Image of the Frontier Woman
280x Television and the Image of the Father
283b Feminine Imagery in an Analogue for God
283f Image of the Virgin Mother
283g Image of Woman in Old Buddhist Literature: The Daughters of Mara
286e Body Image and Performance
297w Image and Reality: Women's Status in Israel
309g Women and Religion: The Status and Image of Women in Major Religious Traditions
318m Images of Male and Female in Children's Readers

IMBECILE

255f "Treated Like Imbecile Children" (Diderot): The Enlightenment and the Status of Women

IMITATION

250o Developmental Study of the Effects of Sex of the Dominant Parent on Sex-Role Preference, Identification, and Imitation in Children

IMMIGRANT

43m Schooling of Vietnamese Immigrants: Internal Colonialism and its Impact on Women
116h Protestant Evangelism and the Italian Immigrant Woman
116i Immigrants and Craft Arts: Scuola d'Industrie Italiane
116j Interaction Between Italian Immigrant Women and the Chicago Commons Settlement House, 1909-1944
116n Metonymic Definition of the Female and the Concept of Honour Among Italian Immigrant Families in Toronto
116t Family and Kin Cohesion among South Italian Immigrants in Toronto
116v Italian Immigrant Women in the Southwest
116w Italian Immigrant Women in American Literature
304l Status of Immigrant Women in Canada
320f Immigrant Woman
334l Chinese Immigrant Women in Nineteenth-Century California

IMMOBILITY

202c Geographic Immobility and Labor Force Mobility: A Study of Female Unemployment

IMMODEST

139o Equality Between the Sexes: An Immodest Proposal
149q Equality between the Sexes: An Immodest Proposal
186i Equality Between the Sexes: An Immodest Proposal
253e Equality Between the Sexes: An Immodest Proposal
292u Equality Between the Sexes: An Immodest Proposal

IMPACT

6c Legislation and Litigation: Impact on Working Women
13j Impact of the Women's Liberation Movement on Child Development Texts
43g Caribbean Women: The Impact of Race, Sex, and Class
43m Schooling of Vietnamese Immigrants: Internal Colonialism and its Impact on Women
45c Professional Schools and Their Impact on Black Women
62b Impact of Contraceptive Culture
70j Impact of Employment upon Fertility
138b Impact of White Women on Fur Trade Society
164k Impact of Education
174b Impact of Collective Bargaining on Minorities in the Public Sector: Some Policy Implications
174d Impact of Organizational Structure, Technology, and Professionalism on the Policy of Affirmative Action
174e Affirmative Action: Constraints and Policy Impact
174j Abortion Policy since 1973: Political Cleavage and Its Impact on Policy Outputs
174k Combatting Dual Discrimination: The Impact of Civil Rights Policies on the Income Status of Black Women
174m Policy Impacts on Hispanics and Women: A State Case Study
194e Impact of Industrialization on Women's Work Roles in Northeast Brazil
196g Sex Bias in Secondary Schools: The Impact of Title IX
202p Impact of Women's Liberation on Marriage, Divorce, and Family Life-Style
211m Emotional Impact of Abortion
211w Impact of Rape
213i Impact of Modernization on Women's Position in the Family in Ghana
227h Adverse Impact of Development
256j Impact of Mid-twentieth Century Movement for Sex Equality in Employment on Three Contemporary Economic Institutions
256k Women in the Arts: Insights to the Cultural Impact of Women's Role in the Creative Arts
265cc Women's Liberation Movement: Its Origins, Structures, Impact, and Ideas
275a Impact of German Thought and Culture on Madame de Stael's Thinking about Women
287f Impact of Equal Employment Opportunity Laws
293c Adverse Impact of Development on Women
294c Impact of the World Social Situation on Women

316c Women and Political Socialization: Considerations of the Impact of Motherhood
328p Impact of Mass-Media Stereotypes upon the Full Employment of Women
365c Impact of the Women's Liberation Movement on Child Development Books
365f Changes in the Modern Family: Their Impact on Sex Roles
368i Sex-Linked Values: Their Impacts on Women in Engineering
368j Impacts of Local Government Tax Structures on Women: Inefficiencies and Inequalities

IMPEDIMENT

39o Impediment or Stimulant? Marital Status and Graduate Education
107h Love and Marriage as Impediments to Man

IMPERFECT

41h Imperfect Unions: Class and Gender in Cripple Creek, 1894- 1904

IMPERIALISM

89ddd Imperialism and Sexuality
218e Unequal Partners in an Uneasy Alliance: Women and the Working Class in Imperial Germany
247j Vampires, Virgins and Voyeurs in Imperial Vienna

IMPERIOUS

88e Imperious Muse: Some Observations on Women, Nature and the Poetic Tradition

IMPLEMENTATION

174a Eliminating Sex Discrimination in Education: Lobbying for Implementation of Title IX

IMPOLICY

195c Uncivil Liberty: An Essay to Show the Injustice and Impolicy of Ruling Woman Without Her Consent

IMPRESSIONS

96f Impressions of an Indian Childhood
116q Women, Ethnicity, and Mental Health: The Italian Woman, Impressions and Observations

IMPULSES

200p Unacceptable Impulses, Anxiety, and the Appreciation of Cartoons

INCOME

see also WAGE; PAY; EARNINGS

39m Income Differences between Men and Career Women
59i Working Wives and Family Income

174k Combatting Dual Discrimination: The Impact of Civil Rights Policies on the Income Status of Black Women
202o Income and Employment Effects of Women's Liberation
205i Sex-Role Stereotyping in the Social Security and Income Tax Systems
251ff Women's Contribution to Family Income
252x Working Wives: Their Contribution to Family Income
266s Alternative Methods For Measuring Sex Discrimination in Occupational Incomes
328o Federal Income Tax and Social Security Law
333h Dynamic Theory of Racial Income Differences
344k Women's Incomes as Workers and Dependents
371l Women's Retirement Income

INCONSISTENCY

82c Femininity and Successful Achievement: A Basic Inconsistency
166vv Women Lawyers and Their Profession: Inconsistency of Social Controls and Their Consequences for Professional Performance
186g Femininity and Successful Achievement: A Basic Inconsistency

INCULCATING

80l Inculcating a Slave Mentality: Women in German Popular Fiction of the Early Twentieth Century

INDEPENDENCE

59d Women in Developing Societies: Economic Independence Is Not Enough
121h Participation of Women in the Independence Movement in Gran Colombia, 1780-1830
175n Independence From the Sexual Revolution
199n Sex Differences in Field Independence among Preschool Children
334d Cherished Spirit of Independence: The Life of an Eighteenth-Century Boston Businesswoman

INDIA

20f Relevance of Nourishment to the Reproductive Cycle of the Female in India
20x Concepts of "Femininity" and "Liberation" in the Context of Changing Sex-Roles: Women in Modern India and America
20aa Women and Social Customs within the Family: A Case Study of Attitudes in Kerala, India
43f Effects of Class and Sex on Political Life in Northern India
91d Status of Women, Work and Fertility in India
114l Muslim Women of India
115c Social Reform Movement in India--From Ranade to Nehru
131e Women of North and Central India: Goddesses and Wives
206o Men and Women of India Today
309a International Women's Year: Its Significance for Women in India
309i Aging Women in India: Self-Perceptions and Changing Roles
309k Study of Women in India: Some Problems in Methodology
324a India
350d Women's Organizations in Madras City, India
350j Segregation and Its Consequences in India

INDIAN

171 Eve Among the Indians
77q Native Women Today: Sexism and the Indian Woman
96f Impressions of an Indian Childhood
96g Schooldays of an Indian Girl
96h Indian Teacher Among Indians
114f Position of Women in Indian Society
114k Demographic Profile of Indian Women
115a Nehru and the Place of Women in Indian Society
115b Role of Women in the Indian Struggle for Freedom
115h Indian Women: Work, Power and Status
121c Indian Women and White Society: The Case of Sixteenth-Century Peru
121e Indian Nuns of Mexico City's Monasterio of Corpus Christi, 1724-1821
213d Caste Differences between Brahmin and Non-Brahmin Women in a South Indian Village
259a American Indian Women
262o Woman in Philanthropy--Care of the Indian
281l Female Status, the Family, and Male Dominance in a West Indian Community
292e Indian and Black Women
292h Sex on the American Indian Frontier
304j Indian Women: An Historical Example and a Contemporary View
309j Asian Women in Britain: Strategies of Adjustment of Indian and Pakistani Migrants
322b Exploring American Indian Communities in Depth
322i Studies in an Indian Town

INDICATOR

325b Legal Reform as an Indicator of Women's Status in Muslim Nations

INDIRECT

227c Indirect Access to Influence

INDIVIDUAL

49a Individual and the Institution
61d Individual Factors Related to Career Orientation in Women
172d Individuals and Families in Transition: Dilemmas and Coping
180y Individuals, Groups, and Inverse Discrimination
180z Should Reparations be to Individuals or to Groups?
180aa Reparations to Individuals or Groups?
318q Individual and the Collective
344s Individualism, Marriage and the Liberal State: Beyond the Equal Rights Amendment
364g Fashioning of a Congresswoman: One Individual's Experience
369c Dependency, Individuality, and Work

INDONESIA

249g Matrifocality in Indonesia and Africa and Among Black Americans
324q Indonesia

INDULGENT

231b Indulgent Woman

INDUSTRIALIZATION

see also CAPITALISM

19h Women in Preindustrial Capitalism
19k Working-Class Women During the Industrial Revolution, 1780-1914
19l Long Road Home: Women's Work and Industrialization
55a Women as Employees: Some Comments on Research in Industrial Sociology
59c Women in Industrial Society: An International Perspective
162d Family Limitation in Pre-Industrial England
176cc Pre-Industrial Patterns in the Colonial Family in America: A Content Analysis of Colonial Magazines
194e Impact of Industrialization on Women's Work Roles in Northeast Brazil
252c Women Workers and the Industrial Revolution
281e Industrialization, Monopoly, Capitalism, and Women's Work in Guatemala
318h Women in the Industrial Labor Force
329q Industrialization and Hong Kong Women

INDUSTRY

39s Woman Book Industry
141j Role of Women in the Organization of the Men's Garment Industry, Chicago, 1910
191r Women Workers in the Health Service Industry
257t Modern Industry and Morality
262k Woman in Industry
306f Women in Service Industries
311f Unique Health Problems of Women in Industry

INEM

95c Inem

INERTIA

267f Social Change and Sex-Role Inertia: The Case of the Kibbutz

INEVITABILITY

89q Inevitability of Patriarchy
203t Inevitability of Patriarchy

INFANT

1b Sermon on Ante-Natal Infanticide
170k Feminine Psychology and Infantile Sexuality
176c Attachment Differences in Male and Female Infant Monkeys
176e Play Behavior in the Year-Old Infant: Early Sex Differences
209b Infant Sex Differences
250z Attachment Differences in Male and Female Infant Monkeys

315b Infanticide in the Early Middle Ages

INFLUENTIAL

141g Influential Women in Anglo-Saxon England
278t Influential Alliances: Cincinnati Women in the Political Arena, 1920-1945

INFORMAL

264r Trust, Loyalty, and the Place of Women in the Informal Organization of Work
281d Women in the Informal Labor Sector: The Case of Mexico City
314bb Women and the Informal Organization
314cc Informal Interaction Patterns of Professional Women

INGRES

247b Ingres and the Erotic Intellect

INHIBITION

76k Work Inhibitions in Women
76l Parental Mislabeling of Female Genitals as a Determinant of Penis Envy and Learning Inhibitions in Women
250q Roles of Activation and Inhibition in Sex Differences in Cognitive Abilities
250r Comments on "Roles of Activation and Inhibition in Sex Differences in Cognitive Abilities"
364c Anger in Women Writers: Source of Inspiration or Inhibition?

INITIATION

80b Women Writers in France: The "Initiators"
102n The Initiation
231u Initiation of a Courtesan

INLAWS-OUTLAWS

361g Inlaws-Outlaws and the Language of Women

INMATES

75c Personality Differences Between Male and Female Prison Inmates: Measured by the M.M.P.I.

INNER

3d Inner and Outer Space: Reflections on Womanhood
173f Once More the Inner Space
198f Inner and Outer Space: Reflections on Womanhood
253a Inner and Outer Space: Reflections on Womanhood
268s Womanhood and the Inner Space
268t Once More the Inner Space

INNOCENT

223i Innocent Femina Sensualis in Unconscious Conflict

INNOVATION

4a Women Drop Back In: Educational Innovation in the Sixties
75e Innovative Programs for Women in Jail and Prison: Trick or Treatment
143q Emergency Shelter: The Development of an Innovative Women's Environment
190a Woman as Artistic Innovator: The Case of the Choreographer
219j Black Women In the Rural South: Conservative and Innovative
267o Implied Demand Character of the Wife's Future and Role Innovation: Patterns of Achievement Orientation Among College Women
267p Determinants of Occupational Role Innovation Among College Women

INQUISITION

134c The Second Inquisition

INSPIRATION

364c Anger in Women Writers: Source of Inspiration or Inhibition?

INSTITUTION

4b Institutional Barriers to Women Students in Higher Education
4k Institutional Variation in the Status of Academic Women
49a Individual and the Institution
56e Sex Differences and Cultural Institutions
75b Physical Attractiveness of Female Offenders: Effects on Institutional Performance
126g Education and Ideology in Nineteenth-Century America: The Response of Educational Institutions to the Changing Role of Women
141gg Woman Artist and the Art Academy: A Case Study in Institutional Prejudice
243h Institutional Discrimination: The Case of Achievement-Oriented Women in Higher Education
246c Socialization of Women in Educational Institutions: Resultant Effects
256f Free Married Woman: A New Style of Living in an Old Institution
256j Impact of Mid-twentieth Century Movement for Sex Equality in Employment on Three Contemporary Economic Institutions
266ii Socio-Economic Context Of Sex And Power: A Study of Women, Work And Family Roles in Four Israeli Institutional Frameworks
272a Prophets, Chiefs, Commissioners, and Queens: The Moral and Institutional Context of Leadership
285h Colonialism and the Lost Political Institutions of Igbo Women
291c Homosocial Theory of Sex Roles: An Explanation of the Sex Segregation of Social Institutions
301b Sex Discrimination, Educational Institutions, and the Law: A New Issue on Campus
307e Institutionalized Motivation for Fertility Limitation
330p Women in Institutions: Treatment in Prisons and Mental Hospitals
349e Institutional Changes for Women of the People During the French Revolution

INSTRUCTION

58d Instruction of a Christen Woman
140pp Assembling Videotaped Materials for Instructional Purposes

INSTRUMENTALITY

20k Affectivity and Instrumentality in Friendship Patterns among American Women

INSULT

154c Sexual Insult and Female Militancy

INTEGRATE

293e Critical Analysis of Latin American Programs to Integrate Women in Development
348h Studying Rape: Integrating Research and Social Change

INTELLECTUALS

122b Women Intellectuals in Chilean Society

INTELLIGENCE

see also ACHIEVEMENT; BRIGHT; COMPETENCE; SUCCESS

39k Women and Social Stratification: A Case of Intellectual Sexism
56b Sex Differences in Intellectual Functioning
65a Sentiment and Intellect: The Story of John Stuart Mill and Harriet Taylor Mill
67e Intelligence, Occupational Status and Achievement Orientation
106i Intellectual Quality: The Symbols and the Substance
107aa Intellectual and Bodily Superiority of Women
164c Women's Intellect
176f Sex Differences in Intellectual Functioning
197b Sex Differences in Intellectual Functioning
198bb Possible Causal Factors of Sex Differences in Intellectual Abilities
199d Prenatal Androgen, Intelligence and Cognitive Sex Differences
200j Memory for Names and Faces: A Characteristic of Social Intelligence?
204b Genetic Influences on Sex-Related Differences in Intellectual Performance: Theoretical and Methodological Issues
204k Sex Role as a Mediator of Intellectual Functioning
247b Ingres and the Erotic Intellect
250t Sex Differences in Space Perception and Aspects of Intellectual Functioning
250hh Sex Differences in Expectancy of Intellectual and Academic Reinforcement
271f Determinants of Intellectual Growth in Women

INTELLIGENTSIA

318b Women and the Russian Intelligentsia: Three Perspectives

INTERACTION

13n Teacher Interactions with Boys and with Girls
51ii Interaction Between Women's Emancipation and Female Criminality: A Cross-Cultural Perspective
70c Interaction and Goal Attainment in Parisian Working Wives' Families
116j Interaction Between Italian Immigrant Women and the Chicago Commons Settlement House, 1909-1944
120k Teacher-Child Verbal Interaction: An Approach to the Study of Sex Differences
176d Sex, Age, and State as Determinants of Mother-Infant Interaction
198cc Sex, Age, and State as Determinants of Mother-Infant Interaction
199h Early Sex Differences and Mother-Infant Interaction
211s "Difficult" Patient: Observations on the Staff-Patient Interaction
219d Male-Female Conversational Interaction Cues: Using Data From Dialect Surveys
250aa Hormonal Interaction, Menstruation, and the Oral Contraceptives
314cc Informal Interaction Patterns of Professional Women

INTEREST

4j Faculty Wife: Her Academic Interests and Qualifications
61b Measuring the Vocational Interest of Women
166v Interest of High School Girls in Dental Auxiliary Careers
266k Measuring the Vocational Interests of Women
266l Female College Students' Scores On the Men's And Women's Strong Vocational Interest Blanks
277l An Interest in Life

INTERNAL

4r Internal Remedies for Sex Discrimination in Colleges and Universities
43m Schooling of Vietnamese Immigrants: Internal Colonialism and its Impact on Women
49d Psychological Barriers for Women in Sciences: Internal and External
225a Mother and the Hospital: An Unfortunate Fit Between the Woman's Internal World and Some Hospital Practices
265j Structural and Internalized Barriers to Women in Higher Education

INTERNATIONAL WOMEN'S YEAR

291a Occupational Segregation in International Women's Year
309a International Women's Year: Its Significance for Women in India

INTERNATIONALISM

19n International Sisterhood
59c Women in Industrial Society: An International Perspective
155n Comparison of Sexual Attitudes and Behavior in an International Sample
309l Draft, International Plan of Action
323d Labour Women and Internationalism
352o APPENDIX: Texts Concerning Women Workers Adopted by the 60th Session of the International Labour Conference, 4-25 June 1975

INTERPERSONAL

77k Sexual Politics of Interpersonal Behavior
155e Self-Conceptions, Motivations and Interpersonal Attitudes of Early- and Late-Maturing Girls
200n Self-Conceptions, Motivations and Interpersonal Attitudes of Early- and Late-Maturing Girls
264x Sexual Politics of Interpersonal Behavior
265y Sexual Politics of Interpersonal Behavior

INTERPRETATION

21q Erosion of Sexual Equality in the Kibbutz: A Structural Interpretation
117u Depatriarchalizing in Biblical Interpretation
162e Interpretation to Be Used for a History of Mentalities
164i Interpretation of Roles
330c Cultural Values, Female Role Expectancies and Therapeutic Goals: Research and Interpretation

INTERRACIAL

151d Dynamics of Interracial Sex in Colonial America
292g Dynamics of Interracial Sex

INTERRELATIONS

107m Interrelations of the Two Sexes
159q Of the Distinction of the Beautiful and the Sublime in the Interrelations of the Two Sexes
266ff Interrelationship of the Status of Women and Family Planning

INTERRUPTIONS

120h Sex Roles, Interruptions and Silences

INTERSTICES

24a Interstices

INTERVENTION

94p Crisis Intervention with Victims of Rape
156e Social Psychology of Sex-Role Intervention
270c Mothers of a Nation: Seneca Resistance to Quaker Intervention

INTERVIEW

68s Interview with Clare Boothe Luce
68t Interview with Megan Terry
86a Female Liberation and Socialism, an Interview
122r Interview with Women Writers in Colombia
139j Henrietta Rodman: An Interview with a Feminist
196aa Effect of Sex on College Admission, Work Evaluation, and Job Interviews
200q Interview

219p Effects of the Ethnicity of the Interviewer on Conversation: A Study of Chicana Women
222x Complexity: Toni Morrison's Women--An Interview Essay
222y Wisdom: An Interview with C.L.R. James
222aa Gayl Jones Takes a Look at "Corregidora"--An Interview
236i Interviews with Young Working Women in Seoul
288r Interview with Dorothy Arzner
288s Interview with Ida Lupino
288aa Interview with Joyce Wieland
288ee Interview with Jane Fonda
288ii Interview with Lina Wertmuller
288pp Interview with British Cine-Feminists
314n Guidelines for Interviewing and Hiring Women Candidates

INTIMACY

222j Politics of Intimacy

INTONATION

120f Male-Female Intonation Patterns in American English

INTRA-ETHNIC

372d Dioula Women in Town: A View of Intra-Ethnic Variation - Ivory Coast

INVALID

145a Conspicuous Consumptive: Woman as an Invalid

INVERSE DISCRIMINATION

180t Inverse Discrimination
180u Justification of Inverse Discrimination
180y Individuals, Groups, and Inverse Discrimination

INVERSION

206d Sex Identity Deviation and Inversion

INVESTIGATION

59b Women's Roles in the Economy: Economic Investigation and Research Needs
173ll Cross-Cultural Investigation of Behavioral Changes at Menopause
176qq Psychological Investigation of Habitual Abortion
232c Investigation of the Religious and Judicial Character of Matriarchy in the Ancient World
368e Cross-Cultural Investigation of Behavioral Changes at Menopause

INVESTMENT

202k Child Investment and Women
202l Nonmarket Returns to Women's Investment in Education
251x Differences in Return to Educational Investment
252dd Social and Private Rates of Return to Investment in Schooling

277r A Good Investment
333g Differences in Expected Post-School Investment as a Determinant of Market Wage Differentials
351d Work Attachment, Investments in Human Capital and the Earnings of Young Women

INVIOLABILITY

217i Equality and Inviolability: An Approach to Compensatory Justice

INVISIBILITY

14c Women and Medical Sociology: Invisible Professionals and Ubiquitous Patients
52i Cotton Mather's "Wonders of the Invisible World": Some Metamorphoses of Salem Witchcraft
126c Invisible Woman: The Historian as Professional Magician
233qq Invisible Bar
302c "Aba Riots" or Igbo "Women's War"? Ideology, Stratification, and the Invisibility of Women

INVOLVEMENT

286f Stress Seeking and Sport Involvement
286q American Business Values and Involvement in Sport

INWARD

214g Christina Rossetti: The Inward Pose

IOWA

163o Women in Iowa Legislative Politics

IRAN

see also PERSIAN

324c Iran
325j Legal and Social Positions of Iranian Women
325o Women and Revolution in Iran, 1905-1911
325q Women among Qashqa'i Nomadic Pastoralists in Iran
325r Woman's Subsociety among the Shahsevan Nomads of Iran
325v Iranian Women in Family Alliance and Sexual Politics
325x Comparative Perspective on Women in Provincial Iran and Turkey
325y Domestic Social Environment of Women and Girls in Isfahan, Iran
329m Women in Iran

IRELAND

83g Irish Revel
312a Women in Norman Ireland
312b Role of Women in Ireland under the New English Order
312e Women and the New Irish State
312h Women in Irish National and Local Politics, 1922-77
312i Women and Work in Ireland: The Present and Preparing for the Future
329d Catholicism and Women's Role in Italy and Ireland

334k Irish Working Women in Troy

IRIGWE

285i Traditional Marriage among the Irigwe of Benue-Plateau State, Nigeria

IRIS

47f Iris Murdoch: The Novelist as Magician, The Magician as Artist

IRONIC

36i "Featureless Freedom" or Ironic Submission: Dorothy Richardson and May Sinclair

IRONING

108v I Stand Here Ironing

IROQUOIS

230j Iroquois Women: An Ethnohistoric Note
285c Economic Organization and the Position of Women Among the Iroquois

ISAACS

128g Reckless Lady: The Life Story of Adah Isaacs Menken

ISCHOMACHUS

260a ...How Ischomachus Trained His Wife

ISFAHAN

325y Domestic Social Environment of Women and Girls in Isfahan, Iran

ISIDORA

122j Brechtian Aesthetics in Chile: Isidora Aguirre's "Los Papeleros"

ISLAM

see MUSLIM

ISLAND

33r Island
236j Occupations, Male Housekeeper: Male-Female Roles on Cheju Island
270k Stability in Banana Leaves: Colonization and Women in Kiriwina, Trobriand Islands
322l Field Work in the Pacific Islands, 1925-1967

ISMAEL

113k A Letter to Ismael in the Grave

ISOLATION

225c Whore in Peru: The Splitting of Women into Good and Bad and the Isolation of the Prostitute
269j Modern Family: Sticky Myths, Diverse Realities, and the Problem of Isolation

ISOLT

184c Isolt and Guenevere: Two Twelfth-Century Views of Woman

ISRAEL

see also KIBBUTZ; JUDAISM

117t Flight from Feminism: The Case of the Israeli Woman
174q Abortion in Israel: Social Demands and Political Responses
206m Sexes: Ideology and Reality in the Israeli Kibbutz
213n Ecological Antecedents and Sex-Role Consequences in Traditional and Modern Israeli Subcultures
266hh Ancient and Contemporary Perspectives on The Women of Israel
266ii Socio-Economic Context Of Sex And Power: A Study of Women, Work And Family Roles in Four Israeli Institutional Frameworks
281p Raising the Status of Women through Law: The Case of Israel
297w Image and Reality: Women's Status in Israel
324m Israel

ITALIAN-AMERICAN

41f Italian-American Women in New York City, 1900-1950: Work and School
116o Maternal Role in the Contemporary Italian-American Family
116p Italian-American Female College Students: A New Generation Connected to the Old
116x Pasta or Paradigm: The Place of Italian-American Women in Popular Film
116y Women in the Italian-American Theatre of the Nineteenth Century
140o Italian-American Women in New York City, 1890 to 1940

ITALY

23c Book-Lined Cells: Women and Humanism in the Early Italian Renaissance
23d Learned Women of Early Modern Italy: Humanists and University Scholars
41e Italian Women and Work: Experience and Perception
52b Witchcraft and Magic in Renaissance Italy: Gianfrancesco Pico and his "Strix"
84d Church, State, and Family: The Women's Movement in Italy
116b Civil Code of 1865 and the Origins of the Feminist Movement in Italy
116c Prostitution and Feminism in Late Nineteenth-Century Italy
116d Women in the Canadian and Italian Trade Union Movements at the Turn of the Century
116f Men Without Women: Italian Migrants in Canada, 1885-1930
116g Settlement House and the Italian Family
116h Protestant Evangelism and the Italian Immigrant Woman

116j Interaction Between Italian Immigrant Women and the Chicago Commons Settlement House, 1909-1944
116k La Donna Italiana Durante Il Periodo Fascista in Toronto, 1930-1940
116l Italian American Women and Their Daughters in Rhode Island: The Adolescence of Two Generations, 1900-1950
116m Italian Mothers, American Daughters: Changes in Work and Family Roles
116n Metonymic Definition of the Female and the Concept of Honour Among Italian Immigrant Families in Toronto
116q Women, Ethnicity, and Mental Health: The Italian Woman, Impressions and Observations
116s Emigration, the Italian Family, and Changing Roles
116t Family and Kin Cohesion among South Italian Immigrants in Toronto
116v Italian Immigrant Women in the Southwest
116w Italian Immigrant Women in American Literature
215f Susanna Goudin Cardon: An Italian Convert to Mormonism
218f Marxist Ambivalence Toward Women: Between Socialism and Feminism in the Italian Socialist Party
230m Life Crisis as a Clue to Social Function: The Case of Italy
324g Italy
329d Catholicism and Women's Role in Italy and Ireland
329e Condition of Women in Italy
349j Patriot Mothers in the Post-Risorgimento: Women After the Italian Revolution

ITHACA

373j Echo from Ithaca

IVANHOE

123e Original of Rebecca in "Ivanhoe"

IVOIRIAN

213h Economic Activity and Marriage among Ivoirian Urban Women

IVORY

95p The Ivory Comb
270i Women and Men, Cloth and Colonization: The Transformation of Production-Distribution Relations among the Baule (Ivory Coast)
281s Social Change and Sexual Differentiation in the Cameroun and the Ivory Coast
302f Limitations of Group Action Among Entrepreneurs: The Market Women of Abidjan, Ivory Coast
372d Dioula Women in Town: A View of Intra-Ethnic Variation - Ivory Coast

IYALODE

213g Iyalode in the Traditional Yoruba Political System

JACKIE

105g Jackie!

JACKSON

7a Northern Black Female Workers: Jacksonian Era
151e Lady and the Mill Girl: Changes in the Status of Women in the Age of Jackson
360d Lady and the Mill Girl: Changes in the Status of Women in the Age of Jackson

JACOB

278bb Mysticism and Feminism: Jacob Boehme and Jane Lead

JACQUELYN

341p Jacquelyn Mattfeld of Brown

JAIL

75e Innovative Programs for Women in Jail and Prison: Trick or Treatment
111h The Jailer

JAMES

52g King James's "Daemonologie": Witchcraft and Kingship
179r A. James
222y Wisdom: An Interview with C.L.R. James
288x Letter to James Card

JAMESON

165c A.B. Jameson

JANE

13o Look Jane Look. See Sex Stereotypes
17i "Jane Eyre": Woman's Estate
128d Jane Grey Swisshelm: Agitator
152h See Jane Run
175r Jane Crow and the Law
197d "Look, Jane, Look! See Dick Run and Jump! Admire Him!"
208u Dick and Jane as Victims: Sex Stereotyping in Children's Readers
214b Jane Lead: Mysticism and the Woman Cloathed with the Sun
215h Jane Snyder Richards: The Blue-White Diamond
253k Jane Addams: An American Heroine
278bb Mysticism and Feminism: Jacob Boehme and Jane Lead
288ee Interview with Jane Fonda
337g Jane Lead: The Feminist Mind and Art of a Seventeenth-Century Protestant Mystic

JANNEY

9h Letter to Mrs. Janney, 1872

JANUARY

233z Political and Civil Status of Women as of January 1, 1969

JAPAN

63f Equal Pay Question in Japan
91i Differential Fertility by Working Status of Women in Japan
178i Ume Tsuda and Motoko Hani: Echoes of American Cultural Feminism in Japan
179p Unknown Japanese Woman
206p Status and Role Behavior in Changing Japan
294m Women and Politics in Japan
306b Women in Rural Japan
324n Japan
352i Women's Wages in Japan and the Question of Equal Pay

JAVA

281g Class Structures and Female Autonomy in Rural Java

JAWAHARLAL

115e Jawaharlal Nehru and the Hindu Code Bill

JAZZ

220v Let Them Call It Jazz

JEALOUSY

108y Jealousy

JEAN

47h Character and Themes in the Novels of Jean Rhys
52d Jean Bodin's "De la Demonomanie des Sorciers": The Logic of Persecution
88u Jean Rhys' Recent Fiction: Humane Developments in "Wide Sargasso Sea"
128s Laura Jean Libbey

JEANNE

212u Reflections on "Jeanne Dielman"

JEFFERSON

178c Puritan Ethic in the Revolutionary Era: Abigail Adams and Thomas Jefferson

JENNIE

93e Jennie Higginses of the "New South in the West": A Regional Survey of Socialist Activities, Agitators, and Organizers, 1901-1917

JEOPARDY

74o Double Jeopardy: To Be Black and Female
127w Double Jeopardy: To Be Black and Female
142f Double Jeopardy: To Be Black and Female

210c Black Women and the Churches: Triple Jeopardy
292r Double Jeopardy: To Be Black and Female

JERNINGHAM

79bb Letters to Edward Jerningham

JEROME

111t Her Sweet Jerome
112l Her Sweet Jerome
279dd Her Sweet Jerome

JERSEY

344d Local Officeholding and the Community: The Case of Women on New Jersey's School Boards

JESUIT

270a Montagnais Women and the Jesuit Program for Colonization

JESUS

122f Elena Poniatowska's "Hasta no Verte, Jesus Mio"
179y C. Maria de Jesus

JET

88h "The Blood Jet": The Poetry of Sylvia Plath

JETSAM

24d Flotsam and Jetsam

JEWEL

83h Your Body is a Jewel Box

JEWISH

see JUDAISM

JILTING

33q The Jilting of Granny Weatherall

JIREL

134a Jirel Meets Magic

JIVE

317l Jive Dope Fiend Whoes: In the Street and in Rehabilitation

JOAN

339f Saint Joan

JOB

see also VOCATIONAL; OCCUPATION; EMPLOYMENT; WORK; PROFESSION; CAREER

14g Sociology and Women in Working-class Jobs
35j Capitalism, Patriarchy, and Job Segregation by Sex
36k Job Market for Women: A Department Chairman's View
45b Full Equality: More Job Education for Women
59f Condition of Women in Blue-Collar Jobs
70h Jobs or Careers: The Case of the Professionally Employed Married Woman
127e Job Discrimination and What Women Can Do About It
129l Older Women and Jobs
140h Did Rosie the Riveter Give Up Her Job? Women War Workers During and After World War II
196aa Effect of Sex on College Admission, Work Evaluation, and Job Interviews
200l Sex Differences in Job Values and Desires
246i Women in the Economic Sphere: The Coming Struggle for Jobs
251d Capitalism, Patriarchy, and Job Segregation by Sex
260t Job Discrimination and the Black Woman
267s Sex-Labeling of Jobs
280s Women and Jobs
284j Education and Jobs
284k Job Bias Against Women Easing Under Pressure
284l Women's Job Rights Gain in Federal Court Rulings
291j Capitalism, Patriarchy, and Job Segregation by Sex
301c Race, Sex, and Jobs: The Drive Toward Equality
304g Canadian Labour Force: Jobs for Women
314g Women in Work Force Post Better Records for Stability in Jobs
314z 52 Job Titles Revised to Eliminate Sex-Stereotyping
328e De Facto Job Segregation
371g Job-Sharing Couples

JOHANN

52c Johann Weyer's "De Praetigiis Daemonum": Unsystematic Psychopathology

JOHN

65a Sentiment and Intellect: The Story of John Stuart Mill and Harriet Taylor Mill
171d Human Sex-Hormone Abnormalities Viewed from an Androgynous Perspective: A Reconsideration of the Work of John Money
257v John Hay, Mrs. Catt and Patriotism

JOKE

85i Hidden Joke: Generic Uses of Masculine Terminology
220d As We Have Learnt from Freud, There Are No Jokes
278u Damnation and Stereotyping in Joke Telling

JONES

104h "Mother" M. Jones
222aa Gayl Jones Takes a Look at "Corregidora"--An Interview

JORDAN

367g Fertility Trends and Differentials in Jordan

JORGE

71b "Brazileira": Images and Realities in Writings of Machado de Assis and Jorge Amado

JOSEFINA

122i Three Female Playwrights Explore Contemporary Latin American Reality: Myrna Casas, Griselda Gambaro, Luisa Josefina Hernandez

JOSEPH

128i Four Sisters: Daughters of Joseph La Flesche

JOSEPHINE

96c Female Prisoner: A Narrative of the Life and Singular Adventures of Josephine Amelia Perkins
96d Demon in Female Apparel: Narrative of Josephine Amelia Perkins, the Notorious Female Horse Thief...

JOUR

288d "Belle de Jour"

JOURNAL

81 Entries in a Journal
96b Journey Across the Plains in 1836: Journal
121g Feminine Press: The View of Women in the Colonial Journals of Spanish America, 1790-1810

JOURNALISM

8gg Getting It Together Journalism: A View of FAG RAG
262f Woman in Journalism

JOURNEY

96b Journey Across the Plains in 1836: Journal
96gg Long Journey
102m Journey of a Woman Nihilist to Verona in Late Autumn
122p Love and Death: The Thematic Journey of Julia de Burgos
226m Long Journey

JOY

24h Joy In Our Cause

JOYCE

215x Augusta Joyce Crocheron: A Representative Woman
288aa Interview with Joyce Wieland

JUANA

122n Two Poets of America: Juana de Asbaje and Sara de Ibanez

JUBILEE

133c Jubilee's Story

JUDAEO-CHRISTIAN

210e Judaeo-Christian Influences on Female Sexuality

JUDAEORUM

79j Salve Deus Rex Judaeorum

JUDAISM

see also ISRAEL; KIBBUTZ

41g Organizing the Unorganizable: Three Jewish Women and Their Union
57f Jewish Woman
79l Tragedie of Mariam, The Fair Queen of Jewry
111f Cutting the Jewish Bride's Hair
112f Cutting the Jewish Bride's Hair
117a Jewish Feminist: Conflict in Identities
117d Women and Jewish Education; A New Look at Bat Mitzvah
117e Single and Jewish: Toward a New Definition of Completeness
117j Jewish Women's Haggadah
117k Other Half: Women in the Jewish Tradition
117l Status of Women in Halakhic Judaism
117n Bais Yaakov: A Historical Model for Jewish Feminists
117r Judaism and Feminism
117s Changing(?)Role of Women in Jewish Communal Affairs: A Look into the U.J.A.
117y Mothers and Daughters in American Jewish Literature: The Rotted Cord
129q Jewish-American Grandmothers
210h View From the Back of the Synagogue: Women in Judaism
233b Jewish Prayer
263m Female God Language in a Jewish Context
263p Jewish Woman's Haggadah
317d Coming of Age in Kelton: The Constraints on Gender Symbolism in Jewish Ritual
317j Bobbes and Zeydes: Old and New Roles for Elderly Jews
337a Women's Leadership in the Jewish and Christian Traditions: Continuity and Change
337m Women in Judaism: From the Reform Movement to Contemporary Jewish Religious Feminism

JUDGE

2c Abortion Decisions: Judicial Review and Public Opinion
94h Judicial Attitudes Toward Rape Victims
174h Sex and the Burger Court: Recent Judicial Policy Making toward Women
180o Judicial Scrutiny of "Benign" Racial Preference in Law School Admissions
180p Racial Preferences in Higher Education: Political Responsibility and the Judicial Role
180bb Preferential Policies in Hiring and Admissions: A Jurisprudential Approach
232c Investigation of the Religious and Judicial Character of Matriarchy in the Ancient World
321d Women Judges: The End of Tokenism
368h Sisterhood in the Courtroom: Sex of Judge and Defendent in Criminal Case Disposition

JUDGMENT

155b Sex-Role Stereotypes and Clinical Judgments of Mental Health
176uu Sex-Role Stereotypes and Clinical Judgements of Mental Health
222u Judgment: Addison Gayle
250j Sex-Role Stereotypes and Clinical Judgments of Mental Health

JUDITH

111nn Our Friend Judith

JULIA

122o Phenomenology of Nothingness in the Poetry of Julia de Burgos
122p Love and Death: The Thematic Journey of Julia de Burgos
123n Julia Richman
303h Julia Morgan

JULIE

310e Miss Julie

JULY

277y Winter in July

JUMP

13mm Jumping the Track
197d "Look, Jane, Look! See Dick Run and Jump! Admire Him!"

JUNE

241e June 6, 2016
352o APPENDIX: Texts Concerning Women Workers Adopted by the 60th Session of the International Labour Conference, 4-25 June 1975

JUNG

263s Dreams and Fantasies as Sources of Revelation: Feminist Appropriation of Jung

JUNIOR

13h Children's Books: The Second Sex, Junior Division
208ll Sex Stereotypes in Mathematics and Science Textbooks for Elementary and Junior High Schools

JURAL

190c Women and the Jural Domain: An Evolutionary Perspective
285g Jural Relations between the Sexes Among the Barabaig

JURY

10k A Jury of Her Peers
112gg A Jury of Her Peers
321f Sexism in Voir Dire: The Use of Sex Stereotypes in Jury Selection
344q Fight for Women Jurors

JUSTICE

79m Malady and Remedy of Vexations and Unjust Arrests and Actions
180v Reverse Discrimination and Compensatory Justice
180dd Justice, Merit, and the Good
195c Uncivil Liberty: An Essay to Show the Injustice and Impolicy of Ruling Woman Without Her Consent
217c Reverse Discrimination and Compensatory Justice
217e Preferential Consideration and Justice
217i Equality and Inviolability: An Approach to Compensatory Justice
217j Compensatory Justice and the Meaning of Equity
256l Chief Justice Wore a Red Dress
321j Justice: A Woman Blindfolded?

JUXTAPOSITIONS

369b Juxtapositions

K'UN

308a Lu K'un's New Audience: The Influence of Women's Literacy on Sixteenth-Century Thought

KAFE

230f Concept of Pollution Among the Kafe of the Papua New Guinea Highlands

KAHN

373g Esther Kahn

KANO

193e Roles of Children in Urban Kano

KANSAS

31 Mademoiselle from Kansas City

KAPLUNA

322a Kapluna Daughter

KAREL

51 Karel Capek

KAREN

268l Karen Horney's Flight from Orthodoxy

KARENINA

339b Anna Karenina

KARINTHA

233x Karintha

KARL

283d Karl Barth's Theology of the Word of God: Or, How to Keep Women Silent and in Their Place

KARNATAKA

309d Etiquette among Women in Karnataka: Forms of Address in the Village and the Family

KATE

128m "Kate," the "Good Angel" of Oklahoma
128o "The Awakening" by Kate Chopin
176aa Middle-Class Mind of Kate Millett
359l Towards a Theory of Form in Feminist Autobiography: Kate Millett's "Flying" and "Sita"; Maxine Hong Kingston's "The Woman Warrior"
359m Kate Millett and the Critics
363r How Now Kate?

KATHERINE

17o Winning: Katherine Anne Porter's Women
192d Katherine Anne Porter
361n Katherine Mansfield's "Passion for Technique"

KAUM

281q Shaping of the Kaum Ibu (Women's Section) of the United Maylays National Organization

KEEPER

298b My Sisters' Keeper

KELTON

317d Coming of Age in Kelton: The Constraints on Gender Symbolism in Jewish Ritual

KEMBLE

179w F.A. Kemble

KEMPE

79b Book of Margery Kempe

KENT

222v Substance: George Kent

KENYA

43d Issues Confronting Professional African Women: Illustrations from Kenya
285f Bargaining from Weakness: Spirit Possession on the South Kenya Coast
302h From Lelemama to Lobbying: Women's Associations in Mombasa, Kenya

KERALA

20aa Women and Social Customs within the Family: A Case Study of Attitudes in Kerala, India
114q Nurses and Nuns of Kerala
309e Women in Kerala: Changing Socio-Economic Status and Self-Image

KETUBOT

117f Writing New KETUBOT

KEY

294t Education Is the Key for Women
314l Accountability--The Key to Successful Affirmative Action
314ff Women in Management: Keys to Success or Failure
314jj Keys to the Executive Powder Room
321b Women, Men, and The Constitution: Key Supreme Court Rulings

KHMER

131j Khmer Village Women in Cambodia: A Happy Balance

KIBBUTZ

see also ISRAEL; JUDAISM

21q Erosion of Sexual Equality in the Kibbutz: A Structural Interpretation
176hh Women in the Kibbutz: Changing Status and Concepts
206m Sexes: Ideology and Reality in the Israeli Kibbutz
267f Social Change and Sex-Role Inertia: The Case of the Kibbutz
329t Kibbutz Women: From the Fields of Revolution to the Laundries of Discontent

KIMBALL

215b Sarah Melissa Granger Kimball: The Liberal Shall Be Blessed

KIN

116t Family and Kin Cohesion among South Italian Immigrants in Toronto
193c Aspects of the Distinction Between the Sexes in the Nyamwezi and Some Other African Systems of Kinship and Marriage
230q Collectivization, Kinship, and the Status of Women in Rural China
252t Feminine Role and the Kinship System
315h Dowries and Kinsmen in Early Renaissance Venice
350f Women and Their Kin

KINDER

126q Beyond "Kinder, Kuche, Kirche": Weimar Women in Politics and Work
142q Kinder, Kuche, Kirche as Scientific Law: Psychology Constructs the Female

KINDERGARTEN

97m Project Company Kindergarten

KINDNESS

108aa Kindness

KINDRED

9aa Woman in the Nineteenth Century and Kindred Papers

KINESIS

286d Kinesis and the Concept of Self in Sport

KING

52g King James's "Daemonologie": Witchcraft and Kingship
315d Marriage and Divorce in the Frankish Kingdom

KINGSLEY

68q Shaw's Lady Cicely and Mary Kingsley

KINGSTON

359j Metaphysics of Matrilinearism in Women's Autobiography: Studies of Mead's "Blackberry Winter," Hellman's "Pentimento," Angelou's "I Know Why the Caged Bird Sings," and Kingston's "The Woman Warrior"
359l Towards a Theory of Form in Feminist Autobiography: Kate Millett's "Flying" and "Sita"; Maxine Hong Kingston's "The Woman Warrior"

KIPLING

68b Kipling on Women: A New Source for Shaw

KIRCHE

126q Beyond "Kinder, Kuche, Kirche": Weimar Women in Politics and Work
142q Kinder, Kuche, Kirche as Scientific Law: Psychology Constructs the Female

KIRIWINA

270k Stability in Banana Leaves: Colonization and Women in Kiriwina, Trobriand Islands

KIRKMAN

314d Sharon Kirkman: Mind Over Myth

KITCHEN

143n From Kitchen to Storefront: Women in the Tenant Movement

KITTS

372h Adaptive Strategies and Social Networks of Women in St. Kitts

KLOOF

113h The De Wets Come to Kloof Grange

KLUTE

288c Divided Woman: Bree Daniels in "Klute"

KNOWLEDGE

79aa Practical Use of Female Knowledge
297dd Women, Knowledge, and Power

KOLLONTAI

218g Bolshevism, The Woman Question, and Aleksandra Kollontai

KOLLWITZ

179v K. Kollwitz

KOREA

236b Korean Proverbs about Women
236d Women's Modernization Movement in Korea
236e Boy Preference Reflected in Korean Folklore
236f Psychological Problems among Korean Women
236g Status of Korean Women Today
236h Role of Korean Women in National Development

KPA MENDE

249i Madam Yoko: Ruler of the Kpa Mende Confederacy

KRISTIN

273e Kristin Lavransdatter (selection)

KUCHE

126q Beyond "Kinder, Kuche, Kirche": Weimar Women in Politics and Work
142q Kinder, Kuche, Kirche as Scientific Law: Psychology Constructs the Female

KUNG

173w !Kung Hunter-Gatherers: Feminism, Diet, and Birth Control
230d !Kung Women: Contrasts in Sexual Egalitarianism in Foraging and Sedentary Contexts

KUWAIT

325h Education and Employment among Kuwaiti Women
367f Fertility Trends and Differentials in Kuwait

KWAN MUN HAU

308i Women and Childbearing in Kwan Mun Hau Village: A Study of Social Change

KWANGTUNG

308c Marriage Resistance in Rural Kwangtung

L'INCONSTANCE

52h Pierre de Lancre's "Tableau de l'Inconstance des Mauvais Anges et Demons": The Sabbat Sensationalised

LABOR

see also EMPLOYMENT; JOB; UNION; various occupations

35h Women's Domestic Labor
42m Welfare of Women in Laboring Families: England, 1860-1950
55e Political Economy of Domestic Labour in Capitalist Society
59g Search for a Partnership Role: Women in Labor Unions Today
84e Sexual Division of Labour: The Case of Nursing

84f Modes of Appropriation and the Sexual Division of Labour: A Case Study from Oaxaca, Mexico
84h Domestic Labour and Marx's Theory of Value
84k Education and the Sexual Division of Labour
92h Domestic Labor and the Household
127j Labor and Suffrage Movements: A View of Working-Class Women in the 20th Century
138h Women's Emancipation and the Recruitment of Women into the Labour Force in World War II
141aa Biological and Cultural Determinants of the Division of Labor by Sex
175u Housework: Slavery or Labor of Love
202a Division of Labor between the Sexes
209f Women in Labor
251g Division of Labor by Sex
252y Labor Participation of Married Women: A Study of Labor Supply
252ii Women's Absenteeism and Labor Turnover
260e Woman and Labor
260q Women and Labor
281d Women in the Informal Labor Sector: The Case of Mexico City
281n How African Women Cope with Migrant Labor in South Africa
285b Division of Labor by Sex
293g Women in Development: Urban Life and Labor
297d Female Labor and Capitalism in the U.S. and Brazil
297k Life and Labor of the Woman Textile Worker in Mexico City
304g Canadian Labour Force: Jobs for Women
304h Sexual Division of Labour and Inequality: Labour and Leisure
311b Woman in the Labor Organization
323a Women in Labour Politics
323b Labour Women and the Social Services
323c Contribution of the Women's Labour League to the Winning of the Franchise
323d Labour Women and Internationalism
323g Women in the Labour Party
342bb Women's Role in Organized Labor
350a Female Solidarity and the Sexual Division of Labour
352c Division of Labour and Sexual Inequality: The Role of Education
352j Participation of Women in the Labour Force of Latin America: Fertility and Other Factors
352o APPENDIX: Texts Concerning Women Workers Adopted by the 60th Session of the International Labour Conference, 4-25 June 1975
362k Women in Labor
370g Effects on Power and Division of Labor in the Family

LABOR FORCE

35k Feminization of the Clerical Labor Force
59h Structural Change in the Occupational Composition of the Female Labor Force
166ff Participation of Women Doctorates in the Labor Force
194f Bahiana in the Labor Force in Salvador, Brazil
194i Participation of Women in the Mexican Labor Force
202b Participation of Married Women in the Labor Force
202c Geographic Immobility and Labor Force Mobility: A Study of Female Unemployment
202d Discontinuous Labor Force Participation and Its Effect on Women's Market Earnings

233mm Women in the Labor Force
251l Labor Force Participation of Married Women
252d Changes in the Labor Force Activity of Women
264n Women in the Labor Force
265l Women in the Labor Force
281k Migration and Labor Force Participation of Latin American Women: The Domestic Servants in the Cities
281t Women's Labor Force Participation in a Developing Society: The Case of Brazil
284h Women in the Labor Force
318h Women in the Industrial Labor Force
328h Lifetime Participation in the Labor Force and Unemployment among Mature Women
329h Female Labor Force in Western Europe
333c What Psychological Research on the Labor Force Participation of Women is Needed?
354c Doubly Disadvantaged: Minority Women in the Labor Force
354g Inequalities in the Labor Force: Three Sociological Explanations
354j Women's Labor Force Participation and the Residential Mobility of Families
371d Racial Differences in Female Labor-Force Participation: Trends and Implications for the Future

LABOR MARKET

202h Women and the Academic Labor Market
251m Sex Segregation in the Labor Market
251n Labor Market Segmentation
291k Economists' Approaches to Sex Segregation in the Labor Market: An Appraisal
333f Modeling a Segmented Labor Market
351c Sex Segregation in the Labor Market: An Analysis of Young College Women's Occupational Preferences
371j Hours Rigidity: Effects on the Labor-Market Status of Women

LABOUR MARKET

37d Positions of Men and Women in the Labour Market
55b Sexual Divisions and the Dual Labour Market
114i Women in the Labour Market
352l Sexual Equality in the Labour Market: Some Experiences and Views of the Nordic Countries

LABYRINTH

303r Pyramid and the Labyrinth

LACTATION

176oo Psychologic Aspects of Lactation
247d Caritas Romana after 1760: Some Romantic Lactations

LADDER

140u Climbing the Political Ladder: The Aspirations and Expectations of Partisan Elites

LADY

5b Lady Blessington
5c Lady Holland
5i Lady Desborough
5m Lady Cunard
24b The Lady With the Pet Dog
42c Lady and Her Physician
58c Boke of the Cyte of Ladyes
68q Shaw's Lady Cicely and Mary Kingsley
79n Upon the much lamented death of the Right Honourable the Lady Elizabeth Langham
79s The Unfortunate Bride, or the Blind Lady a Beauty
108l Martha's Lady
110d Servility of Dependence: The Dark Lady in Trollop
113a The Lady in the Looking Glass: A Reflection
128g Reckless Lady: The Life Story of Adah Isaacs Menken
128q Lady With the Hatchet
130b Letters to Ladies in Favor of Female Physicians
139q Peace Ladies
140t You Can Lead a Lady to Vote, But What Will She Do With It? The Problem of a Woman's Bloc Vote
145d Contradictions in Ladies' Education
151e Lady and the Mill Girl: Changes in the Status of Women in the Age of Jackson
151g Reality and the Southern Lady
153h Lady Who Does Her Own Work
185e Boccaccio's Idle Ladies
215n Stena Scorup: First Lady of Salina
240c Praising Virtuous Ladies: The Literary Image and Historical Reality of Women in Seventeenth-century England
259f Ladies, Not Women
277x The Lady with the Dog
288oo Ladies' Auxiliary, 1976
292l Lady and the Mill Girl
303f Report to the Board of Lady Managers
306d "Office Ladies"
310d The Lady From the Sea
334e Young Ladies Academy of Philadelphia
360d Lady and the Mill Girl: Changes in the Status of Women in the Age of Jackson
363i Lady Novelists
366e "And the Lubras Are Ladies Now"
373a Martha's Lady

LAGERLOF

179aa S. Lagerlof

LAKE

134b The Lake of the Gone Forever
270h Daughters of the Lakes and Rivers: Colonization and the Land Rights of Luo Women

LAKOFF

219h Descriptive Study of the Language of Men and Women Born in Maine Around 1900 as It Reflects the Lakoff Hypotheses in "Language and Women's Place"

LAMENT

79c Lamentation of a Sinner
79n Upon the much lamented death of the Right Honourable the Lady Elizabeth Langham
111pp The Widow's Lament in Springtime

LAMP

373c The Trimmed Lamp

LANCASHIRE

92d Women Cotton Workers and the Suffrage Campaign: The Radical Suffragists in Lancashire, 1893-1914

LANCRE

52h Pierre de Lancre's "Tableau de l'Inconstance des Mauvais Anges et Demons": The Sabbat Sensationalised

LAND

128k Women as Land-owners in the West
131g Women of Udu: Survival in a Harsh Land
270h Daughters of the Lakes and Rivers: Colonization and the Land Rights of Luo Women
315a Land, Family, and Women in Continental Europe, 701-1200
335c Land Charters and the Legal Position of Anglo-Saxon Women

LANDING

111ii At the Landing
112w At the Landing

LANDLADIES

92c Separation of Home and Work? Landladies and Lodgers in Nineteenth-Century England

LANDSCAPE

181d Landscape with Figures: Home and Community in English Society

LANGHAM

79n Upon the much lamented death of the Right Honourable the Lady Elizabeth Langham

LANGTON

165a A. Langton

LANGUAGE

6m How to Eliminate Sexist Language From Your Writing: Some Guidelines for the Manager and Supervisor
98d Language and Revolution: The Franco-American Dis-Connection
98j Difference and Language: A Linguist's Perspective
120a Difference and Dominance: An Overview of Language, Gender and Society
120i Sex Differentiation in Language
120m Sex Differences in Language, Speech, and Nonverbal Communication: An Annotated Bibliography
158o Sex and Language
159ee Natural Law Language and Women
203m Natural Law Language and Women
203w Language and Woman's Place
207d Sexism in the Language of Legislatures and Courts
207e Sexism in the Language of Literature
207f Sexism in the Language of Marriage
207i APPENDIX: N.C.T.E. Guidelines for Nonsexist Use of Language
208kk Secondary Level Language Arts Presentation
214m Edna St. Vincent Millay and the Language of Vulnerability
214s Common Language: The American Woman Poet
219b Problem of Orientation in Sex-Language Research
219h Descriptive Study of the Language of Men and Women Born in Maine Around 1900 as It Reflects the Lakoff Hypotheses in "Language and Women's Place"
219n Sociocultural and Sociopsychological Factors in Differential Language Retentiveness by Sex
246k Language of Sexism
254j Natural Law Language and Women
254p Our Sexist Language
258g Sexist Language in Theology?
263m Female God Language in a Jewish Context
264y Sexism and the English Language: The Linguistic Implications of Being a Woman
278c Entrails of Power: Bogus Manhood and the Language of Grief
314x "He" and "She": Changing Language to Fit a Changing World
332b Language of Sex and Gender
342r Women and Language
342hh Sexist Language and Attitudes
357f Ibsen and the Language of Women
361b Psychology of Women's Language
361d Historical Survey of Women's Language: From Medieval Courtesy Books to Seventeen Magazine
361g Inlaws-Outlaws and the Language of Women
361h Women's Language in America: Myth and Reality
361j Women on the New World Languagescape

LAPINOVA

33f Lappin and Lapinova

LAPPIN

33f Lappin and Lapinova

LARGER

481 Larger Stakes

LATE

52j Two Late Scottish Witchcraft Tracts: "Witch-Craft Proven" and "The Tryal of Witchcraft"
102m Journey of a Woman Nihilist to Verona in Late Autumn
116c Prostitution and Feminism in Late Nineteenth-Century Italy
129w Those Endearing Young Charms: Fifty Years Later
138e National Organization and the Women's Movement in the Late 19th Century
155e Self-Conceptions, Motivations and Interpersonal Attitudes of Early- and Late-Maturing Girls
191b Sexual Surgery in Late Nineteenth-Century America
200n Self-Conceptions, Motivations and Interpersonal Attitudes of Early- and Late-Maturing Girls
240j They Shall Have Faces, Minds, and (One Day) Flesh: Women in Late Nineteenth-century and Early Twentieth-century American Literature
243j Women as a Minority Group: Twenty Years Later
250g Women as a Minority Group: Some Twenty Years Later
337c Ascetic Women in the Late Patristic Age
375l Blood and Guts: The Tricky Problem of Being a Woman Writer in the Late Twentieth Century

LATENCY

76e Masturbation in Latency Girls
102h Latencies

LATERALIZATION

172b Sex-Related Factors in Cognition and in Brain Lateralization

LATIN AMERICA

see also SPANISH AMERICA; individual countries

43i Ancient Song, New Melody in Latin America: Women and Film
71a Literary Archetypes and Female Role Alternatives: The Woman and the Novel in Latin America
71d Marianismo: The Other Face of "Machismo" in Latin America
80g "Protesta femenina" in Latin America
91j Female Work Status and Fertility in Latin America
194c Class Consciousness Among Working-Class Women in Latin America: Puerto Rico
194k Female Political Participation in Latin America
206h Role Themes in Latin America
329c Female Political Participation in Latin America
352j Participation of Women in the Labour Force of Latin America: Fertility and Other Factors

LATIN AMERICAN

71e Women in Latin American Politics: The Case of Peru and Chile
121l Trends and Issues in Latin American Women's History
122i Three Female Playwrights Explore Contemporary Latin American Reality: Myrna Casas, Griselda Gambaro, Luisa Josefina Hernandez
126j Latina Liberation: Tradition, Ideology, and Social Change in Iberian and Latin American Cultures
281k Migration and Labor Force Participation of Latin American Women: The Domestic Servants in the Cities
293e Critical Analysis of Latin American Programs to Integrate Women in Development

LATINA

126j Latina Liberation: Tradition, Ideology, and Social Change in Iberian and Latin American Cultures

LAU

131f Lau, Malaita: "A Woman Is an Alien Spirit"

LAUGHTER

18g Role of Laughter and Humor in Growing Up Female

LAUNDRIES

329t Kibbutz Women: From the Fields of Revolution to the Laundries of Discontent

LAURA

128s Laura Jean Libbey
184d Petrarch's Laura: The Convolutions of a Humanistic Mind

LAVRANSDATTER

273e Kristin Lavransdatter (selection)

LAW

see also COURT; LEGALIZATION; LITIGATION; case names

8v Gay Couples and Straight Law
8w Lesbians and the Law
9u Modern Trends in the Law Concerning Women's Rights
36m University Women and the Law
51y Sex Discrimination in the Criminal Law
64c What Does the Law Say?
85p Liberalism and Marriage Law
94c Rape and Rape Law: Sexism in Society and Law
94i Michigan's Criminal Sexual Assault Law
97n Abortion and Abortion Law
142q Kinder, Kuche, Kirche as Scientific Law: Psychology Constructs the Female
158aa Liberalism and Marriage Law

159ee Natural Law Language and Women
163j Spectators, Agitators, or Lawmakers: Women in State Legislatures
166tt Women in the Law
174f Discrimination and the Law: The Equal Credit Opportunity Act
175q Abortion Law Repeal(sort of): A Warning to Women
175r Jane Crow and the Law
177h Canon Law and the Battle of the Sexes
180o Judicial Scrutiny of "Benign" Racial Preference in Law School Admissions
195b Great Lawsuit: Man versus Men, Woman versus Women
203m Natural Law Language and Women
233bbb Abortion: Women, Men and the Law
244a Victorian Wives and Property: Reform of the Married Women's Property Law, 1857-1882
246b Changing Status of Women in the Law
254j Natural Law Language and Women
260k Married Women and the Law of Support
262i Woman in Law
264s Feminism and the Law
265t Feminism and the Law
281p Raising the Status of Women through Law: The Case of Israel
284f Abortion Law Reform
287f Impact of Equal Employment Opportunity Laws
290c View from the Law School
291f Occupational Segregation and the Law
294e Status of Women in Private Law
301b Sex Discrimination, Educational Institutions, and the Law: A New Issue on Campus
309f Women and the Law: Constitutional Rights and Continuing Inequalities
315g Widow and Ward: The Feudal Law of Child Custody in Medieval England
315i Women in Charter and Statute Law: Medieval Ragusa-Dubrovnik
316h Ideology and the Law: Sexism and Supreme Court Decisions
318f Bolshevik Alternatives and the Soviet Family: The 1926 Marriage Law Debate
318k Women and Sex in Soviet Law
325a Women and Law Reform in Contemporary Islam
328o Federal Income Tax and Social Security Law
329v Marriage Law: Basis of Change for China's Women
331i Homemakers into Widows and Divorcees: Can the Law Provide Economic Protection?
335e Women Under the Law in Medieval England: 1066-1485
360q Cookbooks and Law Books: The Hidden History of Career Women in Twentieth-Century America

LAWINO

95k Song of Lawino, Song of Ocol

LAWYER

96j My Efforts to Become a Lawyer
166vv Women Lawyers and Their Profession: Inconsistency of Social Controls and Their Consequences for Professional Performance

LAY

317g Southern Lay Midwives as Ritual Specialists

LEADERSHIP

38c Educating Women for Leadership
38d Projected Future Employment and Leadership Needs and Areas
48k Government in the Lead
49e Male and Female Leadership Styles: The Double Bind
140t You Can Lead a Lady to Vote, But What Will She Do With It? The Problem of a Woman's Bloc Vote
149m Leads on Old Questions from a New Revolution: Notes on Cuban Women, 1969
163l Women as Politicians: The Social Background, Personality, and Political Careers of Female Party Leaders
177d Theology and Leadership of Women in the New Testament
190g Educating Women for Leadership: A Program for the Future
194o Emergence of a Mapuche Leader: Chile
214b Jane Lead: Mysticism and the Woman Cloathed with the Sun
272a Prophets, Chiefs, Commissioners, and Queens: The Moral and Institutional Context of Leadership
272b Psychology of Leadership: Implications for Women
272c Power and Opportunity in the Principalship: The Case of Two Women Leaders in Education
272d Historical Perspectives on Women in Educational Leadership
272f Single-Sex Education and Leadership: The Early Years of Simmons College
272g Coeducation and the Development of Leadership Skills in Women: Historical Perspectives from Cornell University, 1868-1900
272o Leadership Training for Increased Effectiveness among Women Educational Administrators
278bb Mysticism and Feminism: Jacob Boehme and Jane Lead
291d Work Aspirations of Women: False Leads and New Starts
314ee Female Leadership Dilemma
337a Women's Leadership in the Jewish and Christian Traditions: Continuity and Change
337g Jane Lead: The Feminist Mind and Art of a Seventeenth-Century Protestant Mystic

LEAGUE

41i Women's Trade Union League and American Feminism
41j Creating a Feminist Alliance: Sisterhood and Class Conflict in the New York Women's Trade Union League, 1903- 1914
126i Feminism and Class Consciousness in the British and American Women's Trade Union Leagues, 1890-1925
141i Feminism and Class Consciousness in the British and American Women's Trade Union Leagues, 1890-1925
323c Contribution of the Women's Labour League to the Winning of the Franchise
344f League of Women Voters and Political Power

LEARN

23b Women, Learning, and Power: Eleonora of Aragon and the Court of Ferrara

23d Learned Women of Early Modern Italy: Humanists and University Scholars
23e Learned Women in the Europe of the Sixteenth Century
73c Women Learn to Sing the Menstrual Blues
76l Parental Mislabeling of Female Genitals as a Determinant of Penis Envy and Learning Inhibitions in Women
103d The Learned Adventure of the Dragon's Head
129n Lifelong Learning
140ff Feminist Process in Learning
152i How I Learned to Ride the Bicycle
191p What Medical Students Learn about Women
200c Process of Learning Parental and Sex-Role Identification
219o Women's Verbal Behavior at Learned and Professional Conferences
220d As We Have Learnt from Freud, There Are No Jokes
269g Learning Not To: It Takes a Long Time
295i Women's Organization: Learning from Yesterday
300f What Feminists and Freudians Can Learn From Each Other
341l Learning the Hard Way
343a Curse of Eve--Or, What I Learned in School (Women and Literature)
343d Women and Learning

LEATHERSTOCKING

110j Women of Cooper's "Leatherstocking Tales"

LEAVES

270k Stability in Banana Leaves: Colonization and Women in Kiriwina, Trobriand Islands

LEBANESE

281v Sexuality and Birth Control Decisions among Lebanese Couples

LEBANON

325s Changing Sex Roles in Bedouin Society in Syria and Lebanon
325aa Women and the Neighborhood Street in Borj Hammoud, Lebanon

LEE

215g Lucinda Lee Dalton: A Tough Kind of Testimony

LEFT

97b Women's Liberation and the New Left
337f Quaker Women in the English Left Wing

LEGACIES

246g Psychotherapy for Women: Myths and Legacies

LEGALIZATION

see also COURT; LAW; case names

8x Pocket Legal Guide for Gay People

9b Legal Disabilities of Women
20bb Legal Equality between Men and Women
211 Women in Legal Perspective
22j Aborting a Fetus: The Legal Right, The Personal Choice
68f Legal Climate of Shaw's Problem Plays
68u Torture by Forcible Feeding is Illegal
92f Male Appendage: Legal Definitions of Women
114j Legal Provisions
146m Economic and Legal Status
158ee Moral and Legal Status of Abortion
180k Erosion of Legal Principles in the Creation of Legal Policies
213b Bridging the Gap between the Sexes in Moroccan Legal Practice
251v Legal Equality in Marriage
265p Sex Discrimination in the Trade Unions: Legal Resources for Change
301d Legal Requirements, Structures, and Strategies for Eliminating Sex Discrimination in Academe
325b Legal Reform as an Indicator of Women's Status in Muslim Nations
325j Legal and Social Positions of Iranian Women
326g Government Policy and the Legal Status of Women
328c Legal Road to Equal Employment Opportunity
328d Legal Remedies beyond Title VII to Combat Sex Discrimination in Employment
331d Partnership Marriage: Legal Reforms Needed
334m Origins of Legal Restrictions on Planned Parenthood in Nineteenth-Century America
335c Land Charters and the Legal Position of Anglo-Saxon Women
348b Myth of Male Protectiveness and the Legal Subordination of Women: An Historical Analysis
349d Legal Status of Women After the American Revolution
354e Legal Protection against Sex Discrimination

LEGEND

215a Life and Legend of Eliza R. Snow

LEGISLATION

6c Legislation and Litigation: Impact on Working Women
163o Women in Iowa Legislative Politics
238g Women and Legislation
297p Legislation: An Aid in Eliminating Sex Bias in Education in the U.S.

LEGISLATOR

163v Black Women State Legislators: A Profile
174p Styles and Priorities of Marginality: Women State Legislators
215s Dr. Martha Hughes Cannon: Doctor, Wife, Legislator, Exile
326e Black Women Officeholders: The Case of State Legislators

LEGISLATURE

9i Speech: Legislature, 1860
163j Spectators, Agitators, or Lawmakers: Women in State Legislatures
207d Sexism in the Language of Legislatures and Courts

LEIGH

363d Aurora Leigh

LEISURE

19m Angels in the Devil's Workshop: Leisured and Charitable Women in Nineteenth-Century England and France
129k Women and Leisure
304h Sexual Division of Labour and Inequality: Labour and Leisure

LELEMAMA

302h From Lelemama to Lobbying: Women's Associations in Mombasa, Kenya

LENA

93d Lena Morrow Lewis: Her Rise and Fall

LENI

212o Leni Riefenstahl: The Deceptive Myth

LENIN

89zz Lenin on Sexual Love

LENSES

356f Blue Lenses

LEONE

297c African Women: Identity Crisis? Some Observations on Education and the Changing Role of Women in Sierra Leone and Zaire
302i Protestant Women's Associations in Freetown, Sierra Leone

LESBIAN

see also GAY; HOMOSEXUALITY

8a Lesbian Sexuality
8b What's a Dyke to Do? and What the Dyke Is Doing
8c With All Due Respect: In Defense of All Lesbian Lifestyles
8j Butch or Fem?: The Third World Lesbian's Dilemma
8s Lesbian Mother
8w Lesbians and the Law
89w Lesbians in Revolt
98p Lesbianism and the Social Function of Taboo
123c Lesbians in Revolt
123e Lesbians and the Class Position of Women
142k Realities of Lesbianism
173t Realities of Lesbianism
175aa Lesbianism and Feminism
231t De-Feminized Lesbian
254z Is Women's Liberation a Lesbian Plot?
266x Dimensions of Lesbian Sexual Experience

341k Lesbians--The Doors Open

LESBOS

233zz Women of Lesbos
363f Lesbos

LESOTHO

281m Women and Men, Power and Powerlessness in Lesotho

LESS-THAN-TOKENISM

122a Random Survey of the Ratio of Female Poets to Male in Anthologies: Less-Than-Tokenism as a Mexican Tradition

LESSING

17k "Out of the chaos, a new kind of strength": Doris Lessing's "The Golden Notebook"
47c Doris Lessing in the Sixties: The New Anatomy of Melancholy
283c Explorations with Doris Lessing in Quest of The Four-Gated City

LESSON

307f Women and Revolution: The Lessons of the Soviet Union and China
314w Woman Is Not a Girl and Other Lessons in Corporate Speech
373i The Singing Lesson

LETTER

9g Letters to Woman's Convention, 1851
9h Letter to Mrs. Janney, 1872
9j Letter on Marriage and Divorce, 1855
9bb Letter, 1881
33i Unmailed, Unwritten Letters
79w Letters to Elizabeth Robinson Montagu
79z Letters to Elizabeth Robinson Montagu
79bb Letters to Edward Jerningham
80d Letter to Marguerite Durand from Paul and Victor Margueritte
108z Letter and poem
113k A Letter to Ismael in the Grave
130b Letters to Ladies in Favor of Female Physicians
142b Revolutionary Letter #1
153d Letters from New York
153n Letters
188b Letters on the Equality of the Sexes
195e Letter to a Prospective Bride
231v Letter to the Wife
288x Letter to James Card
339h The Scarlet Letter
339n An Unposted Love Letter
357b Buried Letter: Feminism and Romanticism in Villette

LEVEL

141b Four Levels of Women's History

163i Comparative Study of Male-Female Political Attitudes at Citizen and Elite Levels
199u Plasma Testosterone Levels and Psychologic Measures in Men Over a 2-Month Period
208kk Secondary Level Language Arts Presentation
243c Male Attitudes Toward Women's Rights as a Function of Their Level of Self-Esteem
294r Access to Education at All Levels
358n Anxiety Levels Experienced by Women in Competition

LEVERTOV

214t Critique of Consciousness and Myth in Levertov, Rich, and Rukeyser

LEVITICUS

233c Leviticus

LEWIS

93d Lena Morrow Lewis: Her Rise and Fall

LIBBEY

128s Laura Jean Libbey

LIBEL

130e Report of the Trial: The People versus Dr. Horatio N. Loomis, for Libel

LIBERAL

85p Liberalism and Marriage Law
106d Liberal Arts Education and Women's Development
126h Feminism and Liberalism in Wilhelmine Germany, 1890-1918
158aa Liberalism and Marriage Law
180c Affirmative Action--A Liberal Program
215b Sarah Melissa Granger Kimball: The Liberal Shall Be Blessed
259n Liberally Educated Woman
344s Individualism, Marriage and the Liberal State: Beyond the Equal Rights Amendment

LIBERATION

see also FEMINISM; WOMEN'S LIBERATION; EMANCIPATION; various movements

8d Human Identity and Gay Identity: A Liberationist Dilemma
8bb Spirit is Liberationist but the Flesh is...or, You Can't Always Get Into Bed With Your Dogma
9r Women--Terms of Liberation
13s High-School Women: Oppression and Liberation
19c "Liberated" Women: The Classical Era
20x Concepts of "Femininity" and "Liberation" in the Context of Changing Sex-Roles: Women in Modern India and America
21r Women and Girls in the Public Schools: Defeat or Liberation?

68a Shakespeare's "The Taming of the Shrew" vs. Shaw's "Pygmalion": Male Chauvinism vs. Women's Lib?
68p Shaw and Women's Lib
77dd Male Liberation
86a Female Liberation and Socialism, an Interview
100g Beyond Masculinity: Liberating Men and Their Relationships with Women
117b Women's Liberation and the Liberation of God: An Essay in Story Theology
117p Henrietta Szold--Liberated Woman
126j Latina Liberation: Tradition, Ideology, and Social Change in Iberian and Latin American Cultures
127kk Liberation Must Also Include the Women of Africa
131m Onondaga Women: Among the Liberated
132w Female Liberation First, and Now
139x Female Liberation as the Basis for Social Revolution
149p Women's Lib: The War on "Sexism"
156d Liberating Toys: You Are What You Play
159e Liberated Woman
159ii Woman Question: Philosophy of Liberation and the Liberation of Philosophy
176tt Women's Lib--Rational? Or Socially Pathological?
208b Equality: Men's Lib
208w Liberated Chinese Primers
210i Women and Missions: The Cost of Liberation
233xx One Woman's Lib
238c Female Liberation as the Basis for Social Revolution
258b Feminist Theology as a Critical Theory of Liberation
284c Backlash Against Women's Lib
293j Toward Liberating Women: A Communications Perspective
293l Development Approach to Liberation: Suggestions for Planning
307d Women in the Liberated Areas
307j Liberation of Women
329b African Women, "Modernization," and National Liberation
337j Liberated American Nun
341a Women on Campus: The Unfinished Liberation
341s Women's Lib and the Women's Colleges
342k Liberation of Clio
362m From Adam's Rib to Women's Lib
363s Women's Lib Gets Rough

LIBERATION--BLACK

43l Black Woman: Liberated or Oppressed?
151r Liberation of Black Women
238f Liberation of Black Women
265v Liberation of Black Women

LIBERATION--CHILD

89g Liberation of Children
127m Liberation of Children

LIBERATION--POLITICS

126l Politics of Cultural Liberation: Male-Female Relations in Algeria

316j Women's and Men's Liberation Groups: Political Power Within the System and Outside the System
316r Politics of Cultural Liberation

LIBERTY

19j Loaves and Liberty: Women in the French Revolution
195c Uncivil Liberty: An Essay to Show the Injustice and Impolicy of Ruling Woman Without Her Consent

LIBRARIAN

42j Tender Technicians: Feminization of Public Librarianship, 1876-1905
166e Head Librarians: How Many Men? How Many Women?
266p Tender Technicians: The Feminization of Public Librarianship, 1876-1905

LIBRE

316q Memsahib, Militante, Femme Libre: Political and Apolitical Styles of Modern African Women

LIE

103i Finger Prints Can't Lie

LIEVEN

5g Madame de Lieven

LIFE

8u Life and Death of a Gay Prisoner
9gg My Life
24r Still Life With Fruit
43f Effects of Class and Sex on Political Life in Northern India
48i Family Life of the Successful Woman
48j Family Life in Transition
74d Life and Writings
74e Narrative of a Life
74q Woman and Her Mind: The Story of Daily Life
79p Nature's Pictures, Drawn by Fancies Pencil to the Life
85z Abortion and the Quality of Life
89tt Capitalism, the Family, and Personal Life
95r A Woman's Life
96c Female Prisoner: A Narrative of the Life and Singular Adventures of Josephine Amelia Perkins
96ff Lightning Speed Through Life
97h Psychology Constructs the Female, or the Fantasy Life of the Male Psychologist
111p Still Life with Fruit
111s The Short Happy Life of Francis Macomber
112k The Short Happy Life of Francis Macomber
113l A Day in the Life of a Smiling Woman
122d Life and Early Literary Career of the Nineteenth-Century Colombian Writer, Coledad Acosta de Samper
128g Reckless Lady: The Life Story of Adah Isaacs Menken

129n Lifelong Learning
131a Marriages of Pacho: A Woman's Life among the Amahuaca
131d Guatemalan Women: Life under Two Types of Patriarchy
146b Sexuality and Alternative Life Styles
146g Life Span Behavior Patterns--Class and Ethnic Variations
157i Sex, Birth Control, and Human Life
171j Adult Life Cycles: Changing Roles and Changing Hormones
184a Life Expectancies for Women in Medieval Society
186e Psychology Constructs the Female, or the Fantasy Life of the Male Psychologist
195d Cupid's Yokes; Or The Binding Forces of Conjugal Life
199l Emergence of Genital Awareness During the Second Year of Life
206c Sexual Identity Crises in the Life Cycle
212a Popcorn Venus or How the Movies Have Made Women Smaller Than Life
215a Life and Legend of Eliza R. Snow
215e Amy Brown Lyman: Raising the Quality of Life for All
226l Lightning Speed Through Life
230m Life Crisis as a Clue to Social Function: The Case of Italy
233ee Psychology Constructs the Female, or The Fantasy Life of the Male Psychologist
236c Women Surviving: Palace Life in Seoul after the Annexation
238k Androgynous Life
246j Women in History: Public Life and Historical Consciousness
251c Capitalism, the Family, and Personal Life
251t Family Life in an Antifamily Setting
253l Nothing to Fear: Notes on the Life of Eleanor Roosevelt
266jj Life and Death of Ms. Solomon Grundy
267x Life Patterns and Self-Esteem in Gifted Family Oriented and Career Committed Women
269i Parenting and Family Life Styles
273s The First Year of My Life
273y Still Life with Fruit
277l An Interest in Life
277p The Short Happy Life of Francis Macomber
280y Equal Rights Amendment: A Threat to Family Life?
287b Family and Work: The Social Life Cycle of Women
287e Implications of Women's Employment for Home and Family Life
292o Home Life as a Profession
293g Women in Development: Urban Life and Labor
294g Women in Public Life in Peru
294o Women in Economic Life: Rights and Opportunities
297k Life and Labor of the Woman Textile Worker in Mexico City
328h Lifetime Participation in the Labor Force and Unemployment among Mature Women
334d Cherished Spirit of Independence: The Life of an Eighteenth-Century Boston Businesswoman
335h Discovery of Women in Eighteenth-Century English Political Life
336a Loom and Spindle; or, Life Among the Early Mill Girls
354i Implications of Women's Employment for Home and Family Life
354k Working in Mid-Life
363p Psychology Constructs the Female, or the Fantasy Life of the Male Psychologist
367a Family Life, Women's Status, and Fertility: Middle East and North African Perspectives
372k Life of Sarah Penfield, Rural Ohio Grandmother: Tradition Maintained, Tradition Threatened

LIFE STYLE

3j New Egalitarian Life Style
8c With All Due Respect: In Defense of All Lesbian Lifestyles
202p Impact of Women's Liberation on Marriage, Divorce, and Family Life-Style
256t Changing Woman's Thinking and Lifestyle Through the Great Communication Revolution
331k Women into Mothers: Experimental Family Life-Styles

LIGEIA

279a Ligeia

LIGHT

16a Your Faces, O My Sisters! Your Faces Filled of Light!
19i Women in the Age of Light
29c If You're Light and Have Long Hair
76a Freud's Views on Early Female Sexuality in the Light of Direct Child Observation
152o Shedding Light on Title IX
289c Women's Time: Women in the Light of Contemporary Time-Budget Research
330j Therapy of Women in the Light of Psychoanalytic Theory and the Emergence of a New View
334g Women of Light

LIGHTHOUSE

110p Heroism in "To the Lighthouse"

LIGHTNING

96ff Lightning Speed Through Life
226l Lightning Speed Through Life

LILACS

10g Lilacs
356a Lilacs

LILIAN

303k Lilian Rice

LILITH

177k Epilogue: The Coming of Lilith
263q Coming of Lilith: Toward a Feminist Theology

LILLIAN

141dd Lillian Hellman: Dramatist of the Second Sex
334o From Aide to Organizer: The Oral History of Lillian Roberts
359i Lillian Hellman and the Strategy of the "Other"

LIMA

71h Domestic Service as a Channel of Upward Mobility for the Lower Class Woman: The Lima Case
297i Female Domestic Servant and Social Change: Lima, Peru

LIMBO

166dd Graduate Limbo for Women

LIMITATION

2b Membership Decisions and the Limits of Moral Obligation
42h Family Limitation, Sexual Control, and Domestic Feminism in Victorian America
85n Limits to the Justification of Reverse Discrimination
162d Family Limitation in Pre-Industrial England
166c Encountering the Male Establishment: Sex-Status Limits on Woman's Careers in the Professions
250ll Encountering the Male Establishment: Sex Status Limits on Woman's Careers in the Professions
302f Limitations of Group Action Among Entrepreneurs: The Market Women of Abidjan, Ivory Coast
307e Institutionalized Motivation for Fertility Limitation
311c Health Professions--Opportunities and Limitations
360k Family Limitation, Sexual Control, and Domestic Feminism in Victorian America

LINA

212t Lina Wertmuller: Swept Away on a Wave of Sexism
288ii Interview with Lina Wertmuller
288nn Is Lina Wertmuller Just Once of the Boys?

LINCOLN

79k Countess of Lincoln's Nurserie

LINGUISTICS

85j Linguistics and Feminism
98j Difference and Language: A Linguist's Perspective
120g Sex, Covert Prestige, and Linguistic Change in the Urban British English of Norwich
207a Linguistic Sexism as a Social Issue
264y Sexism and the English Language: The Linguistic Implications of Being a Woman

LINKAGES

291e Dual Linkages between the Occupational and Family Systems: A Macrosociological Analysis

LIST

112ii One Off the Short List
277m One off the Short List

LISTEN

132z Sisters, Brothers, Lovers...Listen

LITERACY

308a Lu K'un's New Audience: The Influence of Women's Literacy on Sixteenth-Century Thought

LITERARY

13bb Women and the Literary Curriculum
36b Women and the Literary Curriculum
71a Literary Archetypes and Female Role Alternatives: The Woman and the Novel in Latin America
86n Women's Oppression: the Literary Reflection
88a Feminism as a Criterion of the Literary Critic
88d Defining a "Feminist Literary Criticism"
88g Who Buried H.D.? A Poet, Her Critics, and Her Place in "The Literary Tradition"
88t Definition of Literary Feminism
90a American Feminist Literary Criticism: A Bibliographical Introduction
122d Life and Early Literary Career of the Nineteenth-Century Colombian Writer, Coledad Acosta de Samper
141c Literary Women and the Masculated Sensibility
141e Novel Women: Origins of the Feminist Literary Tradition in England and France
181g Woman and the Literary Text
240c Praising Virtuous Ladies: The Literary Image and Historical Reality of Women in Seventeenth-century England

LITERATURE

see also CRITICISM; FEMINIST CRITICISM;
AUTHOR; WRITER; names of writers; various genres

21k Images of Women in Contemporary Mexican Literature
36j Women in Children's Literature
80n Women and German Literature: A Bibliography
80o Metamorphosis of an Icon: Woman in Russian Literature
98m Visibility and Difference: Black Women in History and Literature
110b Popular Literature as Social Reinforcement: The Case of "Charlotte Temple"
110r Feminism and Literature
110v Sexism and the Double Standard in Literature
116w Italian Immigrant Women in American Literature
117y Mothers and Daughters in American Jewish Literature: The Rotted Cord
140hh Black Women in Higher Education: Research Literature
140jj Women in English Literature
146i Literature and Myths
182c Changing Image of Women in Soviet Literature
190e Classical Mythology and the Role of Women in Modern Literature
207e Sexism in the Language of Literature
208f School's Role in the Sex-Role Stereotyping of Girls: A Feminist Review of the Literature

208s Women in Children's Literature
208x Negative Image of Women in Children's Literature
222l Black Eve or Madonna? Antithetical Views of the Mother in Black American Literature
240b Changing Image of Woman in Renaissance Society and Literature
240d Portrayal of Women in Restoration and Eighteenth-century English Literature
240e Gender and Genre: Women in British Romantic Literature
240f Angels and Other Women in Victorian Literature
240g Marriage Perceived: English Literature, 1873-1941
240h Images of Women in Early American Literature
240i Portrayal of Women in American Literature, 1790-1870
240j They Shall Have Faces, Minds, and (One Day) Flesh: Women in Late Nineteenth-century and Early Twentieth-century American Literature
240m "Free in Fact and at Last": The Image of the Black Woman in Black American Literature
246d Myth America: Women in American Literature (panel)
253c Image of Women in Contemporary Literature
255d Women and Literature in Eighteenth Century England
258i Women and Religion: A Survey of Significant Literature, 1965-1974
262e Woman in Literature
271l Women in Children's Literature
283g Image of Woman in Old Buddhist Literature: The Daughters of Mara
304m Guide to Historical Literature Pertaining to Canadian Women
343a Curse of Eve--Or, What I Learned in School (Women and Literature)

LITIGATION

6c Legislation and Litigation: Impact on Working Women
51w Women as Litigants

LITTLE

13g Are Little Girls Being Harmed by "Sesame Street"?
108e Little Women
108t Big Volodya and Little Volodya
108ee Little Dorrit
111a Little Woman
112a Little Woman
173cc Big-Time Careers for the Little Woman: A Dual-Role Dilemma
197e Are Little Girls Being Harmed by "Sesame Street"?
208z Louisa May Alcott: The Author of "Little Women" as Feminist

LIV

288o Liv Ullmann: The Goddess as Ordinary Woman

LIVE

8g Living Alone
13k Two Lives
38a Social Trends and Women's Lives--1965-1985
50f The Man with Nine Lives
61a Demographic and Social Factors in Women's Work Lives
62j Education for Real Living
88i "I Dare to Live": The Transforming Art of Anne Sexton
89rr Living with Other Women

96v Why I Earn My Own Living
108jj The Woman Who Lives Inside the World
123f Living with Other Women
127t Storybook Lives: Growing Up Middle Class
153v Living of Charlotte Perkins Gilman
209h Adjusting the Lives of Women to the Establishment
226b Why I Earn My Own Living
256f Free Married Woman: A New Style of Living in an Old Institution
266z Effects of Live Modelled Sex-Appropriate Play Behavior In a Naturalistic Setting
271c How Ideology Shapes Women's Lives
278m Work in the Lives of Married Women, 1900-1930
288e Hollywood Heroines Under the Influence: Alice Still Lives Here
334b Women's Lives Transformed: Demographic and Family Patterns in America, 1600-1970

LIVRE

184e Fifteenth-Century View of Women's Role in Medieval Society: Christine de Pizan's "Livre des Trois Vertus"

LOAVES

19j Loaves and Liberty: Women in the French Revolution

LOBBYING

174a Eliminating Sex Discrimination in Education: Lobbying for Implementation of Title IX
302h From Lelemama to Lobbying: Women's Associations in Mombasa, Kenya
344e Lobbying for Equal Credit

LOCAL

163f Why Few Women Hold Public Office: Factors Affecting the Participation of Women in Local Politics
312h Women in Irish National and Local Politics, 1922-77
344d Local Officeholding and the Community: The Case of Women on New Jersey's School Boards
368j Impacts of Local Government Tax Structures on Women: Inefficiencies and Inequalities

LOCKED

119a The Locked Room Upstairs

LODGERS

92c Separation of Home and Work? Landladies and Lodgers in Nineteenth-Century England

LOGIC

52d Jean Bodin's "De la Demonomanie des Sorciers": The Logic of Persecution

LOIS

288q Years Have Not Been Kind to Lois Weber

LOLITA

288n Brigitte Bardot and the Lolita Syndrome

LONDON

55d Homeworkers in North London
140g Domestic Servants in London and Paris, 1890 to 1914
140z Perception of Parents by London Five-Year-Olds
181b Women's Work in Nineteenth-Century London: A Study of the Years 1820-50

LONELINESS

264m Loneliness of the Long-Distance Mother
265i Loneliness of the Long-Distance Mother

LONG

191 Long Road Home: Women's Work and Industrialization
24bb The Long-Distance Runner
29c If You're Light and Have Long Hair
43j Native American Women: Twilight of a Long Maidenhood
51ee Recidivism Among Women Parolees: A Long-Term Survey
96gg Long Journey
97f Women: The Longest Revolution
102e Long Shadows
119b The Long Corridor of Time
127dd Women: The Longest Revolution
132p Longest Revolution
142s You've Come a Long Way, Baby
226m Long Journey
251k Women: The Longest Revolution
252f Women: The Longest Revolution
256o Degree in Enlightenment: When a Woman's Education Will No Longer Be an Academic Question
264m Loneliness of the Long-Distance Mother
265i Loneliness of the Long-Distance Mother
269g Learning Not To: It Takes a Long Time
279s Long Black Song
294s U.N.E.S.C.O. Long-Range Program for the Advancement of Women
369r Coming of Age the Long Way Around

LONGITUDINAL

22d Conceptions of Sex Role: Some Cross-Cultural and Longitudinal Perspectives
166r Career of Marriage? A Longitudinal Study of Able Young Women

LOOM

336a Loom and Spindle; or, Life Among the Early Mill Girls

LOOMIS

130e Report of the Trial: The People versus Dr. Horatio N. Loomis, for Libel

LOOSE

3i Cutting Loose
9ss Cutting Loose
127c Cutting Loose

LORELEY

111x The Loreley
112o The Loreley

LOS

122j Brechtian Aesthetics in Chile: Isidora Aguirre's "Los Papeleros"

LOS ANGELES

8hh Power to Gay People: A Los Angeles Experiment in Community Action
94k Comparative Study of Forcible Rape Offenses Known to the Police in Boston and Los Angeles
143p Los Angeles Women's Building: A Public Center for Woman's Culture

LOST

95o Fragment From a Lost Diary
142j For a Brilliant Young Woman Who Lost Her Mind
144i I Lost a Pair of Gloves Yesterday
181c Women and Nineteenth-Century Radical Politics: A Lost Dimension
208ii Lost Herstory: The Treatment of Women in Children's Encyclopedias
285h Colonialism and the Lost Political Institutions of Igbo Women

LOUD

163s Traditional Political Animals? A Loud No

LOUGHBOROUGH

104d M.A.W. Loughborough

LOUISA

208z Louisa May Alcott: The Author of "Little Women" as Feminist
215c Louisa Barnes Pratt: Missionary Wife, Missionary Mother, Missionary
215v Louisa Lula Greene Richards: "Remember the Women of Zion"

LOUISE

215m Alice Louise Reynolds: A Woman's Woman

LOVE

3n The Love Object

9ee Marriage and Love
9uu Love Is Just a Four-Letter Word
19p Love on the Tractor: Women in the Russian Revolution and After
24o Four Stories About Lovers
79a XVI Revelations of Divine Love
89ww Advanced Lovemaking
89yy Sexual Love
89zz Lenin on Sexual Love
89aaa Radical Feminism and Love
98c Bonds of Love: Rational Violence and Erotic Domination
100c Love Thine Enemy: Male-Female Relationships
102a Love
107h Love and Marriage as Impediments to Man
108h Another View into Love
108j Love That I Bear
111g On Being Told That Her Second Husband Has Taken His First Lover
122p Love and Death: The Thematic Journey of Julia de Burgos
127s Marriage and Love
132g Love Rights of Women
132z Sisters, Brothers, Lovers...Listen
157f Sexual Love and Moral Experience
157l Marriage, Love, and Procreation
158u Love and Dependency
158v Love and Women's Oppression
159n Of Love and Marriage
175l Loving Another Woman
175u Housework: Slavery or Labor of Love
220e Go With Love, He Says
220h The Love Object
220m I Love Someone
220o The Lover
222ee The Word Is Love
230n Love Unites Them and Hunger Separates Them: Poor Women in the Dominican Republic
231j Epicurean Doctrine of Love
247l Picasso's Suite 347, or Painting as an Act of Love
254b Two Plays on Love and Marriage
277g Reservations: A Love Story
277z A Country Love Story
282i Future of Love: Rousseau and the Radical Feminists
300h If Love is the Answer, What is the Question?
330m Treatment of Sex and Love Problems in Women
339n An Unposted Love Letter
355h All about Love (stories)
356l Fixing Pixie Loveless
360l Female World of Love and Ritual: Relations Between Women in Nineteenth-Century America

LOVEDU

285j Woman-Marriage, With Special Reference to the Lovedu--Its Significance for the Definition of Marriage

LOW

25e Crucible of Identity: The Negro Lower-Class Family

71h Domestic Service as a Channel of Upward Mobility for the Lower Class Woman: The Lima Case
141t Welfare Careers, Low Wage Workers and Sexism
146e Low Pay-Low Status
155h Aspects of Lower Class Sexual Behavior
176mm Lower Class Sexual Behavior
297h Lower Economic Sector: Female Mating Patterns in the Dominican Republic
330q Psychotherapy with Women and Men of Lower Classes

LOWELL

41b Women, Work and Protest in the Early Lowell Mills
336b Vindication of the Character and Condition of the Females Employed in the Lowell Mills...
336d Among Lowell Mill-Girls: A Reminiscence
336e Early Factory Magazines in New England: The LOWELL OFFERING and its Contemporaries

LOYALIST

128a Molly Brant--Loyalist

LOYALTY

264r Trust, Loyalty, and the Place of Women in the Informal Organization of Work

LU

308a Lu K'un's New Audience: The Influence of Women's Literacy on Sixteenth-Century Thought

LUBRAS

366e "And the Lubras Are Ladies Now"

LUCASIA

79q To Rosania and Lucasia, Articles of Friendship

LUCE

68s Interview with Clare Boothe Luce

LUCIA

212f "Lucia"

LUCINDA

215g Lucinda Lee Dalton: A Tough Kind of Testimony

LUCK

220j A Stroke of Luck

LUCY

257d Marriage of Lucy Stone Under Protest

LUISA

80f "El casamiento enganoso": Marriage in the Novels of Maria Luisa Bombal, Silvina Bullrich, and Elisa Serrana
122i Three Female Playwrights Explore Contemporary Latin American Reality: Myrna Casas, Griselda Gambaro, Luisa Josefina Hernandez

LUKENS

128p Woman in Steel--Rebecca Lukens

LULA

215v Louisa Lula Greene Richards: "Remember the Women of Zion"

LULU

288i Making Pabst's Lulu

LUNCH

220t Lunch

LUO

270h Daughters of the Lakes and Rivers: Colonization and the Land Rights of Luo Women
302d Luo Women and Economic Change During the Colonial Period

LUPINO

288s Interview with Ida Lupino

LUTEAL

266v Effect of Contraceptive Pills on Sexual Activity in the Luteal Phase of the Human Menstrual Cycle

LUVALE

317h Epidemiology of Spirit Possession among the Luvale of Zambia

LUXURY

98h Poetry is Not a Luxury

LYDIA

122q Short Stories of Lydia Cabrera: Transpositions or Creations?

LYMAN

215e Amy Brown Lyman: Raising the Quality of Life for All

LYNCHING

334r Women Against Lynching in the Twentieth-Century South

LYSISTRATA

233s Lysistrata
310b Lysistrata

M.L.A.

341g Women's Revolt in the M.L.A.

M.M.P.I.

75c Personality Differences Between Male and Female Prison.Inmates: Measured by the M.M.P.I.

MAB

133d Mab Gallen Recalled

MABEL

5j Mabel Dodge

MACDONALD

88l Poetry of Cynthia MacDonald

MACHADO

71b "Brazileira": Images and Realities in Writings of Machado de Assis and Jorge Amado

MACHINE

273h Outside the Machine

MACHISMO

71d Marianismo: The Other Face of "Machismo" in Latin America

MACINTOSH

273m Miss MacIntosh, My Darling (selection)

MACMURCH

165h M. Macmurch

MACOMBER

111s The Short Happy Life of Francis Macomber
112k The Short Happy Life of Francis Macomber
277p The Short Happy Life of Francis Macomber

MACPHAIL

165i A. MacPhail

MAD

208h Diary 1972 of a Mad 12-Year-Old
300e Diary of a Mad Househusband

MADAME

5e Madame Recamier
5f Madame de Girardin
5g Madame de Lieven
98k For a Restricted Thematics: Writing, Speech, and Difference in Madame Bovary
141cc Madame Vestris in America
212d "Madame de": A Musical Passage
249i Madam Yoko: Ruler of the Kpa Mende Confederacy
275a Impact of German Thought and Culture on Madame de Stael's Thinking about Women
339a Madame Bovary

MADEMOISELLE

31 Mademoiselle from Kansas City

MADONNA

222l Black Eve or Madonna? Antithetical Views of the Mother in Black American Literature

MADRAS

350d Women's Organizations in Madras City, India

MAE

29a Frankie Mae
288k What Maisie Knows: Mae West
373d Frankie Mae

MAEDCHEN

212q "Maedchen in Uniform"

MAGAZINE

71c Passive Female and Social Change: A Cross-Cultural Comparison of Women's Magazine Fiction
105e Imagery and Ideology: The Cover Photographs of Traditional Women's Magazines
105f Magazine Heroines: Is MS. Just Another Member of the FAMILY CIRCLE?
138g Image of Women in Mass Circulation Magazines in the 1920s
166i Occupational Advice for Women in Magazines
176cc Pre-Industrial Patterns in the Colonial Family in America: A Content Analysis of Colonial Magazines

244b Forgotten Woman of the Period: Penny Weekly Family Magazines of the 1840's and 1850's
246m Images of Women and Men in American Popular Magazines
250c Female Roles in Women's Magazine Fiction, 1940-1970
252v Problems of Married Working Women as Presented by Three Popular Working Women's Magazines
255e Eighteenth-Century Englishwoman: According to the Gentleman's Magazine
336e Early Factory Magazines in New England: The LOWELL OFFERING and its Contemporaries
361d Historical Survey of Women's Language: From Medieval Courtesy Books to Seventeen Magazine

MAGIC

47f Iris Murdoch: The Novelist as Magician, The Magician as Artist
52b Witchcraft and Magic in Renaissance Italy: Gianfrancesco Pico and his "Strix"
126c Invisible Woman: The Historian as Professional Magician
134a Jirel Meets Magic
277f The Magic Barrel
372e Spirit Magic in the Social Relations between Men and Women--Sao Paulo, Brazil

MAGOUN

10f Old Woman Magoun

MAHONY

303g Marion Mahony Griffin

MAI

212p Mai Zetterling: Free Fall

MAID

39a Maid of All Work or Departmental Sister-in-Law? The Faculty Wife Employed on Campus
43j Native American Women: Twilight of a Long Maidenhood
278aa Mother, Maiden, and the Marriage of Death: Women Writers and an Ancient Myth
292i American Maidens and Wives

MAILER

86o Answer to Norman Mailer's "Prisoner of Sex"

MAIN

233hh Main Street

MAINE

219h Descriptive Study of the Language of Men and Women Born in Maine Around 1900 as It Reflects the Lakoff Hypotheses in "Language and Women's Place"

MAINSTREAM

129s Mainstream Women

MAISIE

238k What Maisie Knows: Mae West

MAJOR

204c Spatial Ability: A Critical Review of the Sex-Linked Major Gene Hypothesis
309g Women and Religion: The Status and Image of Women in Major Religious Traditions

MAJORITY

9t Submissive Majority
49c Affirmative Action and the Continuing Majority: Women of All Races and Minority Men
138d Neglected Majority: The Changing Role of Women in 19th Century Montreal

MAKE-UP

164b Biological Make-Up of Woman

MALADY

79m Malady and Remedy of Vexations and Unjust Arrests and Actions

MALAITA

131f Lau, Malaita: "A Woman Is an Alien Spirit"

MALE

see also MAN; MEN; MASCULINITY; BOY

4c Women in the Male World of Higher Education
7c Black Male Perspectives on the Nineteenth Century Woman
13e Male and Female
13q Sex-Role Pressures and the Socialization of the Male Child
35d Mothering, Male Dominance, and Capitalism
36h Emily Bronte in the Hands of Male Critics
39p Performance, Rewards, and Perceptions of Sex Discrimination among Male and Female Faculty
49e Male and Female Leadership Styles: The Double Bind
51o Criminality in the Workplace: A Comparison of Male and Female Offenders
67g Male Hormones and Behaviour
68a Shakespeare's "The Taming of the Shrew" vs. Shaw's "Pygmalion": Male Chauvinism vs. Women's Lib?

73i Check One: Male (or) Female
75c Personality Differences Between Male and Female Prison Inmates: Measured by the M.M.P.I.
77dd Male Liberation
77gg Male Power and the Women's Movement
85v Coercion and Rape: The State As a Male Protection Racket
92f Male Appendage: Legal Definitions of Women
93g Women Socialists and Their Male Comrades: The Reading Experience, 1927-1936
97h Psychology Constructs the Female, or the Fantasy Life of the Male Psychologist
99a Femaleness, Maleness and Behavior Disorders in Nonhumans
99i Homosexuality in Females and Males
122a Random Survey of the Ratio of Female Poets to Male in Anthologies: Less-Than-Tokenism as a Mexican Tradition
140c Male Sex Role Behaviors in a Representative National Sample, 1973
155g Differentiation of Male and Female Orgasm: An Experimental Study
155m Early Sexual Behavior in Adult Homosexual and Heterosexual Males
157d Male Chauvinism: A Conceptual Analysis
158d Male Chauvinism: A Conceptual Analysis
166c Encountering the Male Establishment: Sex-Status Limits on Woman's Careers in the Professions
166d Male and Female: Differing Perceptions of the Teaching Experience
166f Predominance of Male Authors in Social Work Publications
173u Contraceptives for Males
173ee Male Sex Role: Definitions, Problems, and Sources of Change
176c Attachment Differences in Male and Female Infant Monkeys
186e Psychology Constructs the Female, or the Fantasy Life of the Male Psychologist
191h Have You Ever Wondered about the Male Pill?
196h Teachers' Perceptions of Ideal Male and Female Students: Male Chauvinism in the Schools
199p Behaviorally Feminine Male Child: Pretranssexual? Pretransvestite? Prehomosexual? Preheterosexual?
199q Psychodynamics of Male Transsexualism
200e Differences in Perception of the Opposite Sex by Males and Females
200k Cognitive Conflict and Compromise between Males and Females
202f Discrimination--A Manifestation of Male Market Power?
206j Male and Female in the German Federal Republic
206k Male and Female in the German Democratic Republic
208r Let Them Aspire! A Plea and Proposal for Equality of Opportunity for Males and Females in the Ann Arbor Public Schools
209d Feminized Male
213k Male and Female in Hopi Thought and Action
230b Woman the Gatherer: Male Bias in Anthropology
230e Aboriginal Woman: Male and Female Anthropological Perspectives
233ee Psychology Constructs the Female, or The Fantasy Life of the Male Psychologist
236j Occupations, Male Housekeeper: Male-Female Roles on Cheju Island
243c Male Attitudes Toward Women's Rights as a Function of Their Level of Self-Esteem
249c Is Female to Male as Nature Is to Culture?
250d Male and Female in Children's Books
250z Attachment Differences in Male and Female Infant Monkeys
250ll Encountering the Male Establishment: Sex Status Limits on Woman's Careers in the Professions

254k Being and Doing: A Cross-Cultural Examination of the Socialization of Males and Females
264ee Male Power and the Women's Movement
267m Fear of Success in Males and Females: 1965 and 1971
270e Forced Transition from Egalitarianism to Male Dominance: The Bari of Colombia
272m Working and Parenting: The Male and Father Role
278b Male Power Motivation and the Status of Women
280m Young Male Reacts
281l Female Status, the Family, and Male Dominance in a West Indian Community
283h Beyond Male Morality
284u Female Biology in a Male Culture
285m Male and Female in Tokelau Culture
290b Inside the Clockwork of Male Careers
297cc Aboriginal Woman: Male and Female Anthropological Perspectives
318m Images of Male and Female in Children's Readers
327f Male Managers' Attitudes Toward Working Women
332d Displaced--The Midwife by the Male Physician
342l Male Bias in Psychology
342m Study of Male Society
348b Myth of Male Protectiveness and the Legal Subordination of Women: An Historical Analysis
348d Who Needs Prostitutes? The Ideology of Male Sexual Needs
362d Up Against the Wall, Male Chauvinist Pig
363p Psychology Constructs the Female, or the Fantasy Life of the Male Psychologist

MALE-DOMINATED

354l Women in Male-Dominated Professions

MALE-FEMALE

100c Love Thine Enemy: Male-Female Relationships
120f Male-Female Intonation Patterns in American English
126l Politics of Cultural Liberation: Male-Female Relations in Algeria
163i Comparative Study of Male-Female Political Attitudes at Citizen and Elite Levels
206n Milieu Development and Male-Female Roles in Contemporary Greece
219d Male-Female Conversational Interaction Cues: Using Data From Dialect Surveys
236j Occupations, Male Housekeeper: Male-Female Roles on Cheju Island
250e Male-Female Perception of the Female Sex Role in the United States
256s Genderless Sexuality: A Male-Female Psychological Exploration of the Future of Sexual Relationships
325bb Negotiation of Reality: Male-Female Relations in Sefrou, Morocco

MALINCHE

43k La Chicana: Guadalupe or Malinche

MALLEUS MALEFICARUM

52a Evident Authority and Authoritative Evidence: the "Malleus Maleficarum"

MALPRACTICE

191f Case of Corporate Malpractice and the Dalkon Shield

MALTESE

274g Bormliza: Maltese Folksong Style and Women

MAMA

24p Mama's Turn
208v Run, Mama, Run: Women Workers in Elementary Readers

MAN

see also MEN; MALE; MASCULINITY; BOY

1d Is Man Too Prolific?
9v Abortion Is No Man's Business
24m Man in the Cellar
24q The Good Humor Man
24cc My Man Bovanne
29f My Man Bovanne
33j A Man and Two Women
50b The Man with the Wild Eyes
50f The Man with Nine Lives
73n Woman is 58% of a Man
73s Woman and Man: A Questionnaire and Survey Report
85h Myth of the Neutral "Man"
107a Creation and Fall of Man and Woman
107f Women as Auxiliary and Subject to Man
107h Love and Marriage as Impediments to Man
107x Woman as Castrated Man
141u Woman is 58% of a Man
142o Man's View
159m On the First Man
164f Woman in Man
181a Wisewoman and Medicine Man: Changes in the Management of Childbirth
195b Great Lawsuit: Man versus Men, Woman versus Women
220s The Good Humor Man
232m Tyranny of Man
233kk Man and Wife
233ccc Man's Role in Women's Liberation
241g The Last Man
254v Working in "A Man's World": The Woman Executive
260h New Ways to Manliness
277j A Man and Two Women
278c Entrails of Power: Bogus Manhood and the Language of Grief
278o Women in a Man's World: The Female Engineers
280z Who Is Man?
284b Man's Primer to Women's Liberation
300i In Favor of the Sensitive Man
356k The Elephant Man

MAN-HATING

175j Man-Hating

MANAGEMENT

see also BUSINESS; CORPORATIONS

6h Obstacle to Women in Management
48b Challenge to Management
181a Wisewoman and Medicine Man: Changes in the Management of Childbirth
220a Management
266aa Relationship Between Sex-Role Stereotypes And Requisite Management Characteristics
272p Changing Women's Representation in School Management: A Systems Perspective
298a Management and Possession
314u Women in Management: How Is It Working Out?
314ff Women in Management: Keys to Success or Failure
314gg Women in Management: The Fallacy of the Trait Approach
314hh Women's Contributions to Management Thought
314ii What Does it Take for a Woman to Make it in Management?

MANAGER

6m How to Eliminate Sexist Language From Your Writing: Some Guidelines for the Manager and Supervisor
293k Women as Co-Managers: The Family as a General Model of Human Social Organization
303f Report to the Board of Lady Managers
314a Women as Managers--Stereotypes and Realities
314b Exploding Some Myths About Women Managers
327f Male Managers' Attitudes Toward Working Women

MANET

247f Manet, "Olympia" and Pornographic Photography

MANIAC

24e The Sex Maniac

MANIFESTO

74r Fourth World Manifesto
77ee Manifesto
132bb W.I.T.C.H. Manifesto
132cc S.C.U.M. Manifesto
132dd Woman's Revolutionary Manifesto
132ee Manifesto
132ff BITCH Manifesto
149s Manifesto
175f Bitch Manifesto
175jj Fourth World Manifesto
175ll Sexual Politics: A Manifesto for Revolution
175nn Politics of the Ego: A Manifesto for New York Radical Feminists
233q S.C.U.M. Manifesto
252ll Sexual Politics: A Manifesto for Revolution

MANIPULATED

176x Differences in Attitudinal Responses Under Conditions of Implicitly Manipulated Group Salience

MANKIND

260p Children of Mankind
264a Woman's Biology--Mankind's Destiny: The Population Explosion and Women's Changing Roles
265a Woman's Biology--Mankind's Destiny: The Population Explosion and Women's Changing Roles

MANN

128j Pamelia Mann: Texas Frontierswoman

MANNEQUIN

373h Mannequin

MANNERS

151n American Woman's Pre-World War I Freedom in Manners and Morals
292t American Woman's Pre-World War I Freedom in Manners and Morals
360o American Woman's Pre-World War I Freedom in Manners and Morals

MANSFIELD

179bb K. Mansfield
361n Katherine Mansfield's "Passion for Technique"

MANUAL

288a Short Manual for an Aspiring Scenario Writer

MANUSCRIPTS

184f Woman in the Marginalia of Gothic Manuscripts and Related Works

MAO

307a Mao Tse-tung, Women and Suicide

MAP

186c Sex Map of the Work World

MAPUCHE

194o Emergence of a Mapuche Leader: Chile

MARA

283g Image of Woman in Old Buddhist Literature: The Daughters of Mara

MARBLEHALL

279t Old Mr. Marblehall

MARCHING

210f Enrichment or Threat? When the Eves Come Marching In

MARGARET

47a Margaret Drabble: Novels of a Cautious Feminist
215t Dr. Margaret Ann Freece: Entrepreneur of Southern Utah

MARGERY

79b Book of Margery Kempe

MARGINALIA

184f Woman in the Marginalia of Gothic Manuscripts and Related Works

MARGINALITY

166pp Female Clergy: A Case of Professional Marginality
174p Styles and Priorities of Marginality: Women State Legislators

MARGUERITE

80d Letter to Marguerite Durand from Paul and Victor Margueritte

MARGUERITTE

80d Letter to Marguerite Durand from Paul and Victor Margueritte

MARIA

80f "El casamiento enganoso": Marriage in the Novels of Maria Luisa Bombal, Silvina Bullrich, and Elisa Serrana
122g Maria Angelica Bosco and Beatriz Guido: An Approach to Two Argentinian Novelists Between 1960 and 1970
128f "Maria Del Occidente"
179y C. Maria de Jesus

MARIAM

79l Tragedie of Mariam, The Fair Queen of Jewry

MARIANISMO

71d Marianismo: The Other Face of "Machismo" in Latin America

MARILYN

288m Actress Archetypes in the 1950s: Doris Day, Marilyn Monroe, Elizabeth Taylor, Audrey Hepburn
288bb "Marilyn Times Five"

MARION

303g Marion Mahony Griffin

MARKET

10m Plum Bun "Market"
36k Job Market for Women: A Department Chairman's View
40c Child Care Market in Seattle and Denver
45d Counseling Implications of Black Women's Market Position, Aspirations and Expectancies
89c Black Women and the Market
202d Discontinuous Labor Force Participation and Its Effect on Women's Market Earnings
202f Discrimination--A Manifestation of Male Market Power?
202l Nonmarket Returns to Women's Investment in Education
270j Desert Politics: Choices in the "Marriage Market"
287c Home Work, Market Work, and the Allocation of Time
302f Limitations of Group Action Among Entrepreneurs: The Market Women of Abidjan, Ivory Coast
333g Differences in Expected Post-School Investment as a Determinant of Market Wage Differentials

MARLENE

288l Marlene Dietrich: At Heart a Gentleman

MARRIAGE

see also HUSBAND; WIFE; WEDDING; WIDOW; FAMILY; PARENT; COUPLES; MARRY; MATING; MONOGAMY

9e Marriage Contract
17f "The Taming of the Shrew": Shakespeare's Mirror of Marriage
20h Defining Marriage Cross-Culturally
39h Swinging: A Study of Decision Making in Marriage
54d Marriage and Marriage Dissolution and the Changing Status of Women: The Case of Poland
60p Marriage and the Woman Scholar
61e Marriage and the Employment of Women
62i Anatomy of a Good Marriage
80f "El casamiento enganoso": Marriage in the Novels of Maria Luisa Bombal, Silvina Bullrich, and Elisa Serrana
83f My First Marriage
85o Nature and Value of Marriage
89ll Marriage Agreement
89qq Marriage
114g Marriage among the Hindus
114t Girl Students: Between School and Marriage--a Delhi Sample
129h Coming Out of the Closet: Marriage and Other Crises of Middle Age
131a Marriages of Pacho: A Woman's Life among the Amahuaca
149n Elements and Types in Soviet Marriage
155j Women's Sexual Responsiveness and the Duration and Quality of Their Marriages
158cc Marriage and Its Alternatives
159j Treatises on Marriage and Other Subjects
159p Marriage

159w Of Child and Marriage
159bb Marriage and Morals
166r Career of Marriage? A Longitudinal Study of Able Young Women
166ii Marriage and Medicine
170q Phobias after Marriage: Women's Declaration of Dependence
175v Marriage
175w A.D.C.: Marriage to the State
193c Aspects of the Distinction Between the Sexes in the Nyamwezi and Some Other African Systems of Kinship and Marriage
207f Sexism in the Language of Marriage
213h Economic Activity and Marriage among Ivoirian Urban Women
223d Marriage, Redundancy or Sin: The Painter's View of Women in the First Twenty-Five Years of Victoria's Reign
240g Marriage Perceived: English Literature, 1873-1941
251s Marriage and the Construction of Reality
251v Legal Equality in Marriage
252r Task and Social Behavior in Marriage
252u Marriage and the Construction of Reality
252z Marriage and Motherhood of Black Women Graduates
254e Paradox of the Happy Marriage
257d Marriage of Lucy Stone Under Protest
260i Marriage as a Trade
265x Marriage and Psychotherapy
270j Desert Politics: Choices in the "Marriage Market"
278aa Mother, Maiden, and the Marriage of Death: Women Writers and an Ancient Myth
284y Future of Marriage
285i Traditional Marriage among the Irigwe of Benue-Plateau State, Nigeria
285j Woman-Marriage, With Special Reference to the Lovedu--Its Significance for the Definition of Marriage
308c Marriage Resistance in Rural Kwangtung
331d Partnership Marriage: Legal Reforms Needed
344s Individualism, Marriage and the Liberal State: Beyond the Equal Rights Amendment

MARRIAGE--DIVORCE

9j Letter on Marriage and Divorce, 1855
65b Early Essays on Marriage and Divorce
202p Impact of Women's Liberation on Marriage, Divorce, and Family Life-Style
315d Marriage and Divorce in the Frankish Kingdom

MARRIAGE--FAMILY

55i Marriage, Role Division and Social Cohesion: The Case of Some French Upper-Middle Class Families
85r Separation of Marriage and Family
107o Marriage and the Family
176s Marriage and the Family
182f Marriage and the Family
202p Impact of Women's Liberation on Marriage, Divorce, and Family Life-Style
205e Sex-Role Stereotyping in Studies of Marriage and the Family
260l Marriage and Family Support

318f Bolshevik Alternatives and the Soviet Family: The 1926 Marriage Law Debate

MARRIAGE--LAW

85p Liberalism and Marriage Law
158aa Liberalism and Marriage Law
318f Bolshevik Alternatives and the Soviet Family: The 1926 Marriage Law Debate
329v Marriage Law: Basis of Change for China's Women

MARRIAGE--LOVE

9ee Marriage and Love
107h Love and Marriage as Impediments to Man
127s Marriage and Love
157l Marriage, Love, and Procreation
159n Of Love and Marriage
254b Two Plays on Love and Marriage

MARRIAGE--ROLE

55i Marriage, Role Division and Social Cohesion: The Case of Some French Upper-Middle Class Families
198j Status and Role: Raw Materials for Society, Marriage
206g Marriage Roles, American Style
366c Role of Women in Aboriginal Marriage Arrangements

MARRY

13z Our Failures Only Marry: Bryn Mawr and the Failure of Feminism
22t Relationship Between Sex Roles, Marital Status, and Mental Illness
37a Family and Married Women at Work
39n Women, Work, and Wedlock: A Note on Female Marital Patterns in the U.S.
39o Impediment or Stimulant? Marital Status and Graduate Education
54e Changes in Czechoslovak Marital Fertility
54f Marital Fertility and the Changing Status of Women in Europe
54g Extra-Marital Fertility and its Occurrence in Stable Unions: Recent Trends in Western Europe
70e Employment of Married Women and the Changing Sex Roles in Poland
70h Jobs or Careers: The Case of the Professionally Employed Married Woman
77m Who Has the Power? The Marital Struggle
95h The Truly Married Woman
140x Current Attitudes Toward Women and Men Who Never Marry
140aa Fathering and Marital Separation
166gg Factors Influencing Married Women's Actual or Planned Work Participation
166jj Career Patterns of Married Couples
166kk Married Professional Social Worker
166mm Career and Family Orientations of Husbands and Wives in Relation to Marital Happiness
176p Career and Family Orientations of Husbands and Wives in Relation to Marital Happiness
202b Participation of Married Women in the Labor Force
202j Economics of Marital Status

231q The Cynic Should Not Marry
244a Victorian Wives and Property: Reform of the Married Women's Property Law, 1857-1882
251l Labor Force Participation of Married Women
251q Task and Emotional Behavior in the Marital Dyad
252v Problems of Married Working Women as Presented by Three Popular Working Women's Magazines
252y Labor Participation of Married Women: A Study of Labor Supply
254y Our Failures Only Marry: Bryn Mawr and the Failure of Feminism
256f Free Married Woman: A New Style of Living in an Old Institution
260k Married Women and the Law of Support
265e Who Has the Power? The Marital Struggle
266m Effects of Career Choices on Married Women
267d Cross-cultural Examination of Women's Marital, Educational and Occupational Options
278l History of Married Women's Rights
278m Work in the Lives of Married Women, 1900-1930
297g Marital Status and Sexual Identity: The Position of Women in a Mexican Peasant Society
351f Causes and Consequences of Marital Breakdown

MARTHA

108l Martha's Lady
215s Dr. Martha Hughes Cannon: Doctor, Wife, Legislator, Exile
373a Martha's Lady

MARTIN

179z M. Martin

MARTINEAU

181k Rights and Wrongs of Women: Mary Wollstonecraft, Harriet Martineau, Simone de Beauvoir
359c Harriet Martineau's Autobiography: The Making of a Female Philosopher

MARX

35q Report on Marxist-Feminist Groups 1-5
68h Mill, Marx and Bebel: Early Influences on Shaw's Characterizations of Women
74f Marx and Engels on Women's Liberation
84h Domestic Labour and Marx's Theory of Value
158w Marx, Sex and the Transformation of Society
218f Marxist Ambivalence Toward Women: Between Socialism and Feminism in the Italian Socialist Party
282h Marx, Sex, and the Transformation of Society
316n Marxist Analysis of Women and Capitalism
318d Marxism and the Women's Movement

MARY

16h Why Has the Virgin Mary Never Entered the Wigwam of Standing Bear?
47e Mary McCarthy: Society's Demands
68q Shaw's Lady Cicely and Mary Kingsley

126b Mary Beard's "Woman As Force in History": A Critique
145f George Eliot and Mary Wollstonecraft
181k Rights and Wrongs of Women: Mary Wollstonecraft, Harriet Martineau, Simone de Beauvoir
192f Mary McCarthy
282d Reason and Morals in the Early Feminist Movement: Mary Wollstonecraft

MASCULINITY

see also MAN; MALE; MEN; BOY

22b Masculinity-Femininity: An Exception to a Famous Dictim?
39g Cultural Contradictions and Sex Roles: The Masculine Case
67b Development of Conceptions of Masculinity and Femininity
76p Masculine Envy of Woman's Procreative Function
78a Masculine Mythology of Femininity
85i Hidden Joke: Generic Uses of Masculine Terminology
89e Measuring Masculinity by the Size of a Paycheck
100g Beyond Masculinity: Liberating Men and Their Relationships with Women
141c Literary Women and the Masculated Sensibility
152b Are Athletics Making Girls Masculine?
164d Developmental Differentiation of Femininity and Masculinity Compared
166j Masculinity or Femininity? Differentiating Career-Oriented and Homemaking-Oriented College Freshman Women
169d Masculinity Complex in Women
170a Flight from Womanhood: The Masculinity Complex in Women as Viewed by Men and by Women
170h Masculine and Feminine: Some Biological and Cultural Aspects
170p "Bedrock" of Masculinity and Femininity: Bisexuality
170u Masculinity-Femininity: A Study in Imposed Inequality
172e Dilemmas of Masculinity in a Changing World
198c Flight from Womanhood: The Masculinity-Complex in Women as Viewed by Men and by Women
198s Masculinity and Femininity as Display
198w Sex and Personality: Studies in Masculinity and Femininity
209a Developmental Differentiation of Femininity and Masculinity Compared
244g Victorian Masculinity and the Angel in the House
250m Sex Differences in the Development of Masculine and Feminine Identification
252i Changing Patterns of Femininity and Masculinity
266a Masculinity-Femininity: An Exception To a Famous Dictim
358k Masculine Obsession in Sports

MASK

20p Non-Hierarchical, Hierarchical, and Masked Reciprocity in the Arab Village
51e Masked Character of Female Crime
254g Mask of Beauty
286j Masks of Identity

MASOCHISM

76h Masochism, the Ego Ideal, and the Psychology of Women
77y Masochistic Syndrome, Hysterical Personality, and the Illusion of a Healthy Woman
169h Passivity, Masochism and Femininity
170b Problem of Feminine Masochism
173e Problem of Feminine Masochism
268o Passivity, Masochism and Femininity
364b Submission, Masochism and Narcissism: Three Aspects of Women's Role as Reflected in Dress

MASQUERADE

169l Womanliness as a Masquerade

MASS

86p Mass Feminist Movement
138g Image of Women in Mass Circulation Magazines in the 1920s
279e Midnight Mass

MASS-MEDIA

328p Impact of Mass-Media Stereotypes upon the Full Employment of Women

MASSACHUSETTS

360c Widowhood in Eighteenth-Century Massachusetts: A Problem in the History of the Family

MASTECTOMY

211r Psychological Consideration of Mastectomy

MASTER

232g Woman and Her Master

MASTERY

211g Sense of Mastery in the Childbirth Experience
249o Mastery of Work and the Mystery of Sex in a Guatemalan Village

MASTURBATION

76e Masturbation in Latency Girls
155k Relationship of the Frequency of Masturbation to Several Aspects of Personality and Behavior
296g Authority and Masturbation
296h Masturbation

MATERFAMILIAS

278i Materfamilias: Power and Presumption

MATERIAL

84a Feminism and Materialism
94l Rape in New York City: A Study of Material in the Police Files and Its Meaning
140pp Assembling Videotaped Materials for Instructional Purposes
156n APPENDIX: Guidelines for the Development and Evaluation of Unbiased Educational Materials
156o APPENDIX: Sources of Non-Sexist Materials
198j Status and Role: Raw Materials for Society, Marriage
207h Sexism in Children's Books and Elementary Teaching Materials
304n Bibliography of Materials on Canadian Women, 1950-1975 (Social Sciences)

MATERNAL

22u Effects of Maternal Employment on the Child
116o Maternal Role in the Contemporary Italian-American Family
171i Maternal Stress in the Postpartum Period
173aa Maternal Attachment: Importance of the First Post-Partum Days
296v Acceptance of the Concept of the Maternal Role by Behavioral Scientists: Its Effects on Women
296w Cultural Anthropologist's Approach to Maternal Deprivation
365d Acceptance of the Concept of the Maternal Role by Behavioral Scientists: Its Effects on Women

MATERNITY

see also BIRTH; PRENATAL; NEWBORNS; PREGNANCY; POSTPARTUM

60k Maternity
107i Maternity and the Origin of Political Power
107j Maternity, Paternity, and the Origin of Political Power
196z Sex Discrimination as Public Policy: The Case of Maternity-Leave Policies for Teachers

MATHEMATICS

13p Sex Problems of School Math Books
176n Women Mathematicians and the Creative Personality
196j Sex Stereotyping in Elementary-School Mathematics Textbooks
204l Sex-Role Socialization and Achievement in Mathematics
208ll Sex Stereotypes in Mathematics and Science Textbooks for Elementary and Junior High Schools

MATHER

52i Cotton Mather's "Wonders of the Invisible World": Some Metamorphoses of Salem Witchcraft

MATING

198r Mating Behavior
297h Lower Economic Sector: Female Mating Patterns in the Dominican Republic

MATRESCENCE

20i Matrescence, Becoming a Mother, a 'New-Old' 'Rite de Passage'

MATRI-PATRILOCALITY

20j Matri-Patrilocality and the Birth of the First Child

MATRIARCHY

25b Matriarchate
25i "Black Matriarchy" Reconsidered: Evidence from Secondary Analysis of Sample Surveys
77e Matriarchy: As Women See It
86l In Defense of Engels on the Matriarchy
126m Classical Scholar's Perspective on Matriarchy
230g Matriarchy: A Vision of Power
232c Investigation of the Religious and Judicial Character of Matriarchy in the Ancient World
233aa Matriarchal Myth
249n Myth of Matriarchy: Why Men Rule in Primitive Society
251u Myth of Black Matriarchy

MATRIFOCALITY

53f Matrifocus on African Women
249g Matrifocality in Indonesia and Africa and Among Black Americans

MATRILINEARISM

20l Explanation for Matrilocal Residence
297x Sources of the Matrilineal Family System in the Works of Carl J.L. Almqvist
359j Metaphysics of Matrilinearism in Women's Autobiography: Studies of Mead's "Blackberry Winter," Hellman's "Pentimento," Angelou's "I Know Why the Caged Bird Sings," and Kingston's "The Woman Warrior"

MATTFELD

341p Jacquelyn Mattfeld of Brown

MATTO

122c Clorinda Matto de Turner and Mercedes Cabello de Carbonera: Societal Criticism and Morality

MATURATION

163n Women as Voters: Their Maturation as Political Persons in American Society
166xx Employer Acceptance of the Mature Home Economist
172c Meaning of Sex-Related Variations in Maturation Rate
204g Cognitive Abilities and Sex-Related Variations in the Maturation of Cerebral Cortical Functions
326f Women as Voters: Their Maturation as Political Persons in American Society

328h Lifetime Participation in the Labor Force and Unemployment among Mature Women

MAUD

2151 Maud May Babcock: "Understand the Thought, Hold the Thought, Give the Thought"

MAUREEN

29b The Coming of Maureen Peal

MAUVAIS

52h Pierre de Lancre's "Tableau de l'Inconstance des Mauvais Anges et Demons": The Sabbat Sensationalised

MAXI

208bb Skirts in Fiction About Boys: A Maxi Mess

MAXIMAL

286w Maximal Oxygen Uptake of Females

MAXINE

3591 Towards a Theory of Form in Feminist Autobiography: Kate Millett's "Flying" and "Sita"; Maxine Hong Kingston's "The Woman Warrior"

MAYA

212n Maya Deren and Germaine Dulac: Activists of the Avant-Garde
297f Mayan Woman and Change
317f Careers of Midwives in a Mayan Community

MAYLAYS

281q Shaping of the Kaum Ibu (Women's Section) of the United Maylays National Organization

MBUM

249p Mediation of Contradiction: Why Mbum Women Do Not Eat Chicken

MCCARTHY

47d Case Against McCarthy: A Review of "The Group"
47e Mary McCarthy: Society's Demands
192f Mary McCarthy

MCCLUNG

165f N.L. McClung
320a Nellie McClung: "Not a Nice Woman"

MCCULLERS

192g Carson McCullers

MEAD

359j Metaphysics of Matrilinearism in Women's Autobiography: Studies of Mead's "Blackberry Winter," Hellman's "Pentimento," Angelou's "I Know Why the Caged Bird Sings," and Kingston's "The Woman Warrior"

MEASURE

40e Quality of Day Care: Can It Be Measured
54b Measurement of the Status of Women
61b Measuring the Vocational Interest of Women
75c Personality Differences Between Male and Female Prison Inmates: Measured by the M.M.P.I.
89e Measuring Masculinity by the Size of a Paycheck
199u Plasma Testosterone Levels and Psychologic Measures in Men Over a 2-Month Period
266b Measurement of Psychological Androgyny
266k Measuring the Vocational Interests of Women
266s Alternative Methods For Measuring Sex Discrimination in Occupational Incomes
301e Developing Criteria and Measures of Equal Opportunities for Women

MECHANISTIC

213l Mechanistic Cooperation and Sexual Equality among the Western Bontoc

MEDEA

310a Medea

MEDIA

11g Media: New Images of Women in Contemporary Society
45i Media and Their Effect on Black Images
105n Approaches to the Study of Media Effects
105o Conclusion: Will Media Treatment of Women Improve?
140oo Sex-Role Media Research and Sources
146p Media: Use and Misuse
306j Women in Media

MEDIATION

204k Sex Role as a Mediator of Intellectual Functioning
249p Mediation of Contradiction: Why Mbum Women Do Not Eat Chicken

MEDICINE

see also PHYSICIAN; NURSE; HEALTH; PATIENT; MIDWIFE; types of medicine and disorder

14c Women and Medical Sociology: Invisible Professionals and Ubiquitous Patients

130d Medical Morals
166ii Marriage and Medicine
166yy Women and Medicine in a Changing World
176l Barriers to the Career Choice of Engineering, Medicine, or Science Among American Women
181a Wisewoman and Medicine Man: Changes in the Management of Childbirth
191p What Medical Students Learn about Women
211n Medical Gynecology: Problems and Patients
256m What Women Will Do in Medicine and What Medicine Will Do for Women
262g Woman in Medicine
264c Women, Health, and Medicine

MEDIEVAL

19d Sanctity and Power: The Dual Pursuit of Medieval Women
42g Power of Women Through the Family in Medieval Europe: 500-1100
126n Cheshire Cat: Reconstructing the Experience of Medieval Women
177g Equality of Souls, Inequality of Sexes: Woman in Medieval Theology
184a Life Expectancies for Women in Medieval Society
184e Fifteenth-Century View of Women's Role in Medieval Society: Christine de Pizan's "Livre des Trois Vertus"
185h Roles of Medieval Women in the Healing Arts
315g Widow and Ward: The Feudal Law of Child Custody in Medieval England
315i Women in Charter and Statute Law: Medieval Ragusa-Dubrovnik
335e Women Under the Law in Medieval England: 1066-1485
337d Women, Power and the Pursuit of Holiness in Medieval Christianity
361d Historical Survey of Women's Language: From Medieval Courtesy Books to Seventeen Magazine

MEDITATIONS

79d Prayers or Meditations
79g Miscelanea: Prayers, Meditations, Memoratives

MEDIUM

302g Rebels or Status-Seekers? Women as Spirit Mediums in East Africa
317i Convivial Sisterhood: Spirit Mediumship and Client-Core Network among Black South African Women
360g Spiritualist Medium: A Study of Female Professionalization in Victorian America
372f Spirit Mediums in Umbanda Evangelizada of Porto Alegre, Brazil: Dimensions of Power and Authority

MEGAMACHINE

263b Motherearth and the Megamachine

MEGAN

68t Interview with Megan Terry

MELANCHOLY

47c Doris Lessing in the Sixties: The New Anatomy of Melancholy

MELISSA

215b Sarah Melissa Granger Kimball: The Liberal Shall Be Blessed

MELODY

43i Ancient Song, New Melody in Latin America: Women and Film

MEMBER

2b Membership Decisions and the Limits of Moral Obligation
105f Magazine Heroines: Is MS. Just Another Member of the FAMILY CIRCLE?
163p Women Members of Congress: A Distinctive Role
196x Attitudes of Superintendents and Board of Education Members Toward the Employment and Effectiveness of Women as Public-School Administrators
352h Equality of Remuneration for Men and Women in the Member States of the E.E.C.
356i A Member of the Family

MEMOIR

96a Memoir
152j Memoirs of a Would-Be Swim Champ

MEMORIA

375d De Memoria

MEMORY

79g Miscelanea: Prayers, Meditations, Memoratives
95b The Memorial Service on the Mountain
103f A Memorable Murder
200j Memory for Names and Faces: A Characteristic of Social Intelligence?
233j In Memoriam: "Sex and the Single Girl"

MEMSAHIB

316q Memsahib, Militante, Femme Libre: Political and Apolitical Styles of Modern African Women

MEN

see also MASCULINITY; MAN; MALE; BOY

3b To All Black Women, From All Black Men
3o What Is the Connection Between Men and Women?
8y Can Men and Women Work Together?
8z Thoughts on How Gay Men Relate to Women
8ii Information on VD for Gay Women and Men
9o Making Women into Men
20bb Legal Equality between Men and Women
22i Men's Cycles
37d Positions of Men and Women in the Labour Market
38b Evolving Relationships Between Women and Men

39f Men, Women, and Work: Reflections on the Two-Person Career
39m Income Differences between Men and Career Women
49c Affirmative Action and the Continuing Majority: Women of All Races and Minority Men
60m Education for Women and for Men
62h How Can Men and Women Work Together?
71l Honor, Shame, and Women's Liberation in Cuba: Views of Working-Class Emigre Men
73p Men Drive Women Crazy
100d Men and Women at Work
100g Beyond Masculinity: Liberating Men and Their Relationships with Women
105j News of Women and the Work of Men
107b Women as Equal to Men in the State
107c Differences Between Men and Women
107d Roles and Virtues of Men and Women
107e Relationship of Men and Women
116f Men Without Women: Italian Migrants in Canada, 1885-1930
131i Eskimo Women: Makers of Men
132e Why Men Need a Boys' Night Out
140x Current Attitudes Toward Women and Men Who Never Marry
140bb Men and the Abortion Experience--Anxiety and Social Supports
141j Role of Women in the Organization of the Men's Garment Industry, Chicago, 1910
141q Men and Women in the Family: History of the Idea of Family in America's Depression Generation
166e Head Librarians: How Many Men? How Many Women?
170a Flight from Womanhood: The Masculinity Complex in Women as Viewed by Men and by Women
171f Homosexual Orientation in Women and Men: A Hormonal Basis?
175h Men and Violence
183b Men, Women and Violence: Some Reflections on Equality
183h Attitudes of Men and Women Toward Violence: Report of a National Survey
193a Complementarity and Conflict: An Andean View of Men and Women
195b Great Lawsuit: Man versus Men, Woman versus Women
197j Myth is Better Than a Miss: Men Get the Edge in Academic Employment
198c Flight from Womanhood: The Masculinity-Complex in Women as Viewed by Men and by Women
198o Women and Men
199u Plasma Testosterone Levels and Psychologic Measures in Men Over a 2-Month Period
200h Modest Confirmation of Freud's Theory of a Distinction between the Superego of Men and Women
206o Men and Women of India Today
208b Equality: Men's Lib
208e Men: Being a Boy
219f Sex, Color and Money: Who's Perceiving What? Or Men and Women: Where Did All the Differences Go (To)?
219h Descriptive Study of the Language of Men and Women Born in Maine Around 1900 as It Reflects the Lakoff Hypotheses in "Language and Women's Place"
230k Men and Women in the South of France: Public and Private Domains
233bbb Abortion: Women, Men and the Law
235a Men and the Victimization of Women
243d Men Who Discriminate Against Women
246m Images of Women and Men in American Popular Magazines

249n Myth of Matriarchy: Why Men Rule in Primitive Society
250k Between Men and Women
251w Differences in Hourly Earnings Between Men and Women
252cc Differences in Hourly Earnings Between Men and Women
252gg Men and Women in Community Agencies: A Note on Power and Prestige
256n Social Sex: The New Single Standard for Men and Women
260u Differences Between Men and Women
266l Female College Students' Scores On the Men's And Women's Strong Vocational Interest Blanks
266cc When Women Are More Deserving Than Men: Equity, Attribution, And Perceived Sex Differences
270d Contending with Colonization: Tlingit Men and Women in Change
270i Women and Men, Cloth and Colonization: The Transformation of Production-Distribution Relations among the Baule (Ivory Coast)
271d Why Can't Women Be More Like Men?
276b Women and Men in the World of Work: Present and Future
276c Women, Men and Mental Health
276f Equality Between Men and Women in Sweden
278a Men's Power with Women, Other Men and Society
280b Why Men and Women Think Differently
280r Men and Emotional Problems
281m Women and Men, Power and Powerlessness in Lesotho
289e Technicalities and Fantasy About Men and Women
304i Wages of Work: A Widening Gap Between Men and Women
316j Women's and Men's Liberation Groups: Political Power Within the System and Outside the System
321b Women, Men, and The Constitution: Key Supreme Court Rulings
327b Why Can't Women Be More Like Men: A Summary of the Sociopsychological Factors Hindering Women's Advancement in the Professions
330q Psychotherapy with Women and Men of Lower Classes
332a Have Only Men Evolved?
332h Taking the Men Out of Menopause
352h Equality of Remuneration for Men and Women in the Member States of the E.E.C.
354d Wage Differences between Men and Women: Economic Theories
356d Men With No Eyes
362h Men, Women--and Politics
372e Spirit Magic in the Social Relations between Men and Women--Sao Paulo, Brazil

MENAGERIE

355e The Tragic Menagerie (stories)

MENDING

220g Mending

MENKEN

128g Reckless Lady: The Life Story of Adah Isaacs Menken

MENOPAUSE

42b Puberty to Menopause: The Cycle of Femininity in Nineteenth-Century America

73g New Look at Menopause
173i Symbolic Significance of Menstruation and the Menopause
173ll Cross-Cultural Investigation of Behavioral Changes at Menopause
191o What Doctors Won't Tell You about Menopause
211x Gynecological Approach to Menopause
211y Menopause
332h Taking the Men Out of Menopause
368e Cross-Cultural Investigation of Behavioral Changes at Menopause

MENSTRUATION

22h Premenstrual Syndrome
73c Women Learn to Sing the Menstrual Blues
77b Premenstrual Syndrome
171k Menstrual-related Psychological Changes
171l Social Psychological Perspective on the Menstrual Cycle
171m Body Time and Social Time: Mood Patterns by Menstrual Cycle Phase and Day of Week
173h Premenstrual Syndrome
173i Symbolic Significance of Menstruation and the Menopause
173s Social Dimensions of the Menstrual Taboo and the Effects on Female Sexuality
199w Reproductive Hormones, Moods, and the Menstrual Cycle
204j Menstrual Cycle and Sex-Related Differences in Cognitive Variability
223c Victorian Women and Menstruation
250aa Hormonal Interaction, Menstruation, and the Oral Contraceptives
250bb Influences of Mother's Menstruation on Her Child
250cc Patterns of Affective Fluctuation in the Menstrual Cycle
250dd Effects of Oral Contraceptives on Affective Fluctuations Associated with the Menstrual Cycle
263u Becoming a Woman: Menstruation as Spiritual Experience
266d Premenstrual Syndrome
266v Effect of Contraceptive Pills on Sexual Activity in the Luteal Phase of the Human Menstrual Cycle
283o Zoroastrian Menstruation Taboos: A Woman's Studies Perspective
296n Effects of Oral Contraceptives on Affective Fluctuations Associated with the Menstrual Cycle
296o Re-evaluation of Some Aspects of Femininity through a Study of Menstruation
332g Exploring Menstrual Attitudes

MENTAL

11b Adjustment: New Approaches to Women's Mental Health
22t Relationship Between Sex Roles, Marital Status, and Mental Illness
22x Androgyny as a Model of Mental Health for Women: From Theory to Therapy
39d Adult Sex Roles and Mental Illness
99b Sex Differences in the Epidemiology of Mental Disorder
116q Women, Ethnicity, and Mental Health: The Italian Woman, Impressions and Observations
116r Oral History in Pittsburgh--Women, Ethnicity, and Mental Health: Rationale, Procedure, and Methodology
155b Sex-Role Stereotypes and Clinical Judgments of Mental Health
176uu Sex-Role Stereotypes and Clinical Judgements of Mental Health
250j Sex-Role Stereotypes and Clinical Judgments of Mental Health

266bb Adult Sex Roles and Mental Health
276c Women, Men and Mental Health
330p Women in Institutions: Treatment in Prisons and Mental Hospitals

MENTALITY

80l Inculcating a Slave Mentality: Women in German Popular Fiction of the Early Twentieth Century
162e Interpretation to Be Used for a History of Mentalities

MENTORS

314i Patrons, Rabbis, Mentors--Whatever You Call Them, Women Need Them Too

MERCEDES

122c Clorinda Matto de Turner and Mercedes Cabello de Carbonera: Societal Criticism and Morality

MERCI

111w La Belle Dame sans Merci
112n La Belle Dame sans Merci

MERIT

180dd Justice, Merit, and the Good

MESS

208bb Skirts in Fiction About Boys: A Maxi Mess

MESSAGE

95i The Message
105c Spot Messages within Saturday Morning TV Programs

METAMORPHOSIS

52i Cotton Mather's "Wonders of the Invisible World": Some Metamorphoses of Salem Witchcraft
80o Metamorphosis of an Icon: Woman in Russian Literature
127f Metamorphosis into Bureaucrat
142e Metamorphosis into Bureaucrat
241i The Feminine Metamorphosis

METAPHOR

76i Penis Envy: From Childhood Wish to Developmental Metaphor
212g Bergman's Portrait of Women: Sexism or Subjective Metaphor?

METAPHYSICS

158m Sexuality as a Metaphysical Dimension

359j Metaphysics of Matrilinearism in Women's Autobiography: Studies of Mead's "Blackberry Winter," Hellman's "Pentimento," Angelou's "I Know Why the Caged Bird Sings," and Kingston's "The Woman Warrior"

METHOD

199x Sexual Differentiation: Models, Methods, and Mechanisms
266s Alternative Methods For Measuring Sex Discrimination in Occupational Incomes
281u Talking Pictures: Field Method and Visual Mode

METHODOLOGY

91k Relationship between Women's Work and Fertility: Some Methodological and Theoretical Issues
116r Oral History in Pittsburgh--Women, Ethnicity, and Mental Health: Rationale, Procedure, and Methodology
126u Feminism and the Methodology of Women's History
199j Methodological Considerations in Studying Sex Differences in the Behavioral Functioning of Newborns
204b Genetic Influences on Sex-Related Differences in Intellectual Performance: Theoretical and Methodological Issues
283k Methodological Remarks on the Study of Women in Religion
309k Study of Women in India: Some Problems in Methodology

METONYMIC

116n Metonymic Definition of the Female and the Concept of Honour Among Italian Immigrant Families in Toronto

MEXICO

21k Images of Women in Contemporary Mexican Literature
54a Population and the Status of Women: Results of the Bucharest and Mexico Conferences
84f Modes of Appropriation and the Sexual Division of Labour: A Case Study from Oaxaca, Mexico
121a Colonial Women in Mexico: The Seventeenth and Eighteenth Centuries
121d Women in a Noble Family: The Mexican Counts of Regla, 1750-1830
121e Indian Nuns of Mexico City's Monasterio of Corpus Christi, 1724-1821
121k Felipe Carrillo Puerto and Women's Liberation in Mexico
122a Random Survey of the Ratio of Female Poets to Male in Anthologies: Less-Than-Tokenism as a Mexican Tradition
122l Nellie Campobello: Romantic Revolutionary and Mexican Realist
126o Women in Convents: Their Economic and Social Role in Colonial Mexico
194i Participation of Women in the Mexican Labor Force
219l Mothers' Speech to Children in Bilingual Mexican-American Homes
274b Games Mexican Girls Play
281d Women in the Informal Labor Sector: The Case of Mexico City
297e Women in Mexico
297g Marital Status and Sexual Identity: The Position of Women in a Mexican Peasant Society
297k Life and Labor of the Woman Textile Worker in Mexico City
317b Celibes, Mothers, and Church Cockroaches: Religious Participation of Women in a Mexican Village

329p Female Political Elites in Mexico: 1974

MICE

356c Mice and Birds and Boy

MICHIGAN

94i Michigan's Criminal Sexual Assault Law
141ii Recent and On-Going Research Projects at the University of Michigan

MIDDLE

55i Marriage, Role Division and Social Cohesion: The Case of Some French Upper-Middle Class Families
77z Depression in Middle-Aged Women
80k Virgins and Other Victims: Aspects of German Middle-Class Theatre
117h Portnoy's Mother's Complaint: Depression in Middle-Aged Women
127q Planned Obsolescence: The Middle-Aged Woman
127t Storybook Lives: Growing Up Middle Class
129h Coming Out of the Closet: Marriage and Other Crises of Middle Age
131l In Reality: Some Middle Eastern Women
173kk Women in the Middle Years: Conceptions and Misconceptions
175e Woman in the Middle
176u Depression in Middle-Aged Women
176aa Middle-Class Mind of Kate Millett
254f Depression in Middle-Aged Women
270b Sunksquaws, Shamans, and Tradeswomen: Middle Atlantic Coastal Algonkian Women During the Seventeenth and Eighteenth Centuries
296q Middle Age
309c Employment and Family Change: A Study of Middle-Class Women in Urban Gujarat
375j Middle Period

MIDDLE AGES

23a Education of Women in the Middle Ages in Theory, Fact, and Fantasy
185f Woman as Artist and Patron in the Middle Ages and the Renaissance
185g Education of Women in the Middle Ages
315b Infanticide in the Early Middle Ages

MIDDLE EAST

91e Women, Employment, and Fertility Trends in the Arab Middle East and North Africa
294j Women in the Middle East and North Africa and Universal Suffrage
325p Status of Women in Four Middle East Communities
367a Family Life, Women's Status, and Fertility: Middle East and North African Perspectives
367b Demographic Transition in the Middle East and North Africa
367c Family Planning and Population Policies in the Middle East and North Africa

MIDNIGHT

279e Midnight Mass

MIDSUMMER

103h A Midsummer Night's Crime

MIDWESTERN

302b Dual-Sex Political System in Operation: Igbo Women and Community Politics in Midwestern Nigeria

MIDWIFE

130a Employment of Females as Practitioners in Midwifery
130c Man-Midwifery Exposed and Corrected
178e Man-Midwifery and the Delicacy of the Sexes
215o Patty Bartlett Sessions: More Than a Midwife
317f Careers of Midwives in a Mayan Community
317g Southern Lay Midwives as Ritual Specialists
332d Displaced--The Midwife by the Male Physician

MIGRANT

20v Eurogallegas: Female Spanish Migration
54h Sociological and Demographic Aspects of the Changing Status of Migrant Women in Europe
71j Pursuit of an Ideal: Migration, Social Class, and Women's Roles in Bogota, Colombia
116f Men Without Women: Italian Migrants in Canada, 1885-1930
281k Migration and Labor Force Participation of Latin American Women: The Domestic Servants in the Cities
281n How African Women Cope with Migrant Labor in South Africa
281o Women and Migration in Contemporary West Africa
309j Asian Women in Britain: Strategies of Adjustment of Indian and Pakistani Migrants
351e Migration of Young Families: An Economic Perspective

MILIEU

206n Milieu Development and Male-Female Roles in Contemporary Greece

MILITANT

92e Militancy and Acquiescence Amongst Women Workers
96u Making of a Militant
154c Sexual Insult and Female Militancy
154g Female Militancy and Colonial Revolt: The Women's War of 1929, Eastern Nigeria
226a Making of a Militant
316q Memsahib, Militante, Femme Libre: Political and Apolitical Styles of Modern African Women

MILL

41b Women, Work and Protest in the Early Lowell Mills
41c New England Mill Women in the Early Nineteenth Century
65a Sentiment and Intellect: The Story of John Stuart Mill and Harriet Taylor Mill

68h Mill, Marx and Bebel: Early Influences on Shaw's Characterizations of Women
151e Lady and the Mill Girl: Changes in the Status of Women in the Age of Jackson
223g Debate over Women : Ruskin vs. Mill
233p "The Mill on the Floss"
260c Critique of Mill on Women
292l Lady and the Mill Girl
336a Loom and Spindle; or, Life Among the Early Mill Girls
336b Vindication of the Character and Condition of the Females Employed in the Lowell Mills...
336d Among Lowell Mill-Girls: A Reminiscence
360d Lady and the Mill Girl: Changes in the Status of Women in the Age of Jackson

MILLAY

214m Edna St. Vincent Millay and the Language of Vulnerability

MILLETT

176aa Middle-Class Mind of Kate Millett
359l Towards a Theory of Form in Feminist Autobiography: Kate Millett's "Flying" and "Sita"; Maxine Hong Kingston's "The Woman Warrior"
359m Kate Millett and the Critics

MILLICAN

222t Reflections: Arthenia Bates Millican

MIND

74q Woman and Her Mind: The Story of Daily Life
139t Revolution is Happening in Our Minds
142j For a Brilliant Young Woman Who Lost Her Mind
175c Woman and Her Mind
176aa Middle-Class Mind of Kate Millett
184d Petrarch's Laura: The Convolutions of a Humanistic Mind
240j They Shall Have Faces, Minds, and (One Day) Flesh: Women in Late Nineteenth-century and Early Twentieth-century American Literature
273l The Wind-Chill Factor or, A Problem of Mind and Matter
284s There are Sex Differences in the Mind, Too
314d Sharon Kirkman: Mind Over Myth
337g Jane Lead: The Feminist Mind and Art of a Seventeenth-Century Protestant Mystic

MINISTRY

60f Ministry of Women
210b Women and Ministry
258e Women and Ministry
262h Woman in the Ministry
337l American Women in Ministry: A History of Protestant Beginning Points

MINORITY

see also RACE; various minority groups

9s 51% Minority
49c Affirmative Action and the Continuing Majority: Women of All Races and Minority Men
77j Women as a Minority Group
132n Women as a Minority Group
166oo Women as a Minority Group in Higher Academics
174b Impact of Collective Bargaining on Minorities in the Public Sector: Some Policy Implications
174g Minorities and Policy Problems: An Overview Seen by the U.S. Commission on Civil Rights
217b Preferential Treatment in Admitting Racial Minority Students
238e Women as a Minority Group
243g Are Women a "Minority" Group? Sometimes!
243j Women as a Minority Group: Twenty Years Later
250f Women as a Minority Group
250g Women as a Minority Group: Some Twenty Years Later
251h Woman (sic) as a Minority Group
252e Women as a Minority Group
264z Women as a Minority Group
265z Women as a Minority Group
266dd Are Women A "Minority" Group? Sometimes!
325gg Being Female in a Muslim Minority in China
354c Doubly Disadvantaged: Minority Women in the Labor Force

MIO

122f Elena Poniatowska's "Hasta no Verte, Jesus Mio"

MIRAGE

355c Mirage

MIRIAM

142l To My Friend Miriam

MIRRIA

372c Women's Role in a Muslim Hausa Town--Mirria, Republic of Niger

MIRROR

17f "The Taming of the Shrew": Shakespeare's Mirror of Marriage
89k Mirror, Mirror
335j Women in the Mirror: Using Novels to Study Victorian Women

MISCELANEA

79g Miscelanea: Prayers, Meditations, Memoratives

MISERY

317e Misery of the Embodied: Representations of Women in Sinhalese Myth

MISLABELING

76l Parental Mislabeling of Female Genitals as a Determinant of Penis Envy and Learning Inhibitions in Women

MISOGYNISM

177e Misogynism and Virginal Feminism in the Fathers of the Church

MISSION

210i Women and Missions: The Cost of Liberation
215c Louisa Barnes Pratt: Missionary Wife, Missionary Mother, Missionary
257o Woman's Mission and Woman's Clubs

MISSISSIPPI

174o Political Power and Policy Benefits: Voting Rights and Welfare Policy in Mississippi
222z Mississippi Mothers: Roots

MIST

340n Of Mist, and Grass, and Sand

MISTAKE

362j Feminine Mistake

MISTRAL

122m Feminine Symbolism in Gabriela Mistral's "Fruta"

MISUSE

146p Media: Use and Misuse

MITCHELL

104c M. Mitchell

MIZOGUCHI

212h Mizoguchi's Oppressed Women

MOBILITY

71h Domestic Service as a Channel of Upward Mobility for the Lower Class Woman: The Lima Case
202c Geographic Immobility and Labor Force Mobility: A Study of Female Unemployment
309b Women in Uttar Pradesh: Social Mobility and Directions of Change
354j Women's Labor Force Participation and the Residential Mobility of Families

MOBILIZATION

297v Mobilization of Women: Three Societies
316o Mobilization of Women in Allende's Chile

MOBS

193d Sex, Age and Social Control in Mobs of the Darwin Hinterland

MODEL

19t Family Models of the Future
22f Model of Sex-Role Transcendence
22x Androgyny as a Model of Mental Health for Women: From Theory to Therapy
53i Harems and Overlords: Biosocial Models and the Female
77aa Consciousness-Raising Group as a Model for Therapy with Women
117n Bais Yaakov: A Historical Model for Jewish Feminists
140gg Why Sex Discrimination? A Model of Sex-Role Transcendence
154d Gypsy Women: Models in Conflict
166u Role Model Influences on College Women's Career Aspirations
171g Social Psychological Model of Human Sexuality
173dd Role of Models in Women's Professional Development
173ii Consciousness-Raising Group as a Model for Therapy with Women
198z Theories of Identification and Exposure to Multiple Models
199x Sexual Differentiation: Models, Methods, and Mechanisms
206i Swedish Model
246h Proposed Model for Examining Sex Discrimination in Education
266z Effects of Live Modelled Sex-Appropriate Play Behavior In a Naturalistic Setting
272l Need for Female Role Models in Education
293k Women as Co-Managers: The Family as a General Model of Human Social Organization
303a Model Domestic Environment: Icon or Option?
329x Sweden: A Feminist Model?
333f Modeling a Segmented Labor Market
366f Digging Sticks and Spears, Or the Two-Sex Model

MODERN

9u Modern Trends in the Law Concerning Women's Rights
20x Concepts of "Femininity" and "Liberation" in the Context of Changing Sex-Roles: Women in Modern India and America
23d Learned Women of Early Modern Italy: Humanists and University Scholars
23f Women's Roles in Early Modern Venice
71k Modernizing Women for a Modern Society: The Cuban Case
88y Need to Tell All: A Comparison of Historical and Modern Feminist "Confessional" Writing
110s Modernism and History
115g From Purdah to Modernity
131b Egyptian Woman: Between Modernity and Tradition
132j Hard and the Soft: The Force of Feminism in Modern Times
149a Status of Women in Modern Patterns of Culture
190e Classical Mythology and the Role of Women in Modern Literature
194h Women and Modernization: Access to Tools
206e Sex Roles, Ancient to Modern

206q Sex Roles in the Modern Fabric of China
213i Impact of Modernization on Women's Position in the Family in Ghana
213j Women, Work, and Power in Modern Yugoslavia
213n Ecological Antecedents and Sex-Role Consequences in Traditional and Modern Israeli Subcultures
222d Images of Black Women in Modern African Poetry
236d Women's Modernization Movement in Korea
257t Modern Industry and Morality
267e Convergences between East and West: Tradition and Modernity in Sex Roles in Sweden, Finland, and the Soviet Union
269j Modern Family: Sticky Myths, Diverse Realities, and the Problem of Isolation
285e Women in Modernizing Societies
294a Status of Women in Modern Patterns of Culture
316m Modernization Theory and Sex Roles in Critical Perspective: The Case of the Soviet Union
316q Memsahib, Militante, Femme Libre: Political and Apolitical Styles of Modern African Women
329b African Women, "Modernization," and National Liberation
365f Changes in the Modern Family: Their Impact on Sex Roles

MODEST

117m Modest Beginning
200h Modest Confirmation of Freud's Theory of a Distinction between the Superego of Men and Women
260x Modest Proposal for the Educating of Women

MOLE

132hh No "Chicks," "Broads," or "Niggers" for OLE MOLE

MOLL

17g Moll Flanders: "A Woman on her own Account"

MOLLY

128a Molly Brant--Loyalist
129g Penelope, Molly, Narcissus, and Susan

MOMBASA

302h From Lelemama to Lobbying: Women's Associations in Mombasa, Kenya

MOMENT

127b Next Great Moment in History is Ours

MONASTERIO

121e Indian Nuns of Mexico City's Monasterio of Corpus Christi, 1724-1821

MONETARY

252w Monetary Value of a Housewife

MONEY

171d Human Sex-Hormone Abnormalities Viewed from an Androgynous Perspective: A Reconsideration of the Work of John Money
219f Sex, Color and Money: Who's Perceiving What? Or Men and Women: Where Did All the Differences Go (To)?

MONKEY

73a In Praise of the Achieving Female Monkey
176c Attachment Differences in Male and Female Infant Monkeys
199g Sex Differences in Mother-Infant Attachment in Monkeys
250z Attachment Differences in Male and Female Infant Monkeys

MONOGAMY

8f Thoughts on Monogamy
157j Monogamy: A Critique
233ff Monogamous Family

MONOPOLY

35i Monopoly Capital and the Structure of Consumption
281e Industrialization, Monopoly, Capitalism, and Women's Work in Guatemala

MONROE

288m Actress Archetypes in the 1950s: Doris Day, Marilyn Monroe, Elizabeth Taylor, Audrey Hepburn

MONSTER

212b Monster and the Victim

MONTAGNAIS

270a Montagnais Women and the Jesuit Program for Colonization

MONTAGU

79w Letters to Elizabeth Robinson Montagu
79z Letters to Elizabeth Robinson Montagu

MONTAUT

247g Corset as Erotic Alchemy: From Rococo Galanterie to Montaut's Physiologies

MONTH

117i This Month Is for You: Observing Rosh Hodesh as a Woman's Holiday
199u Plasma Testosterone Levels and Psychologic Measures in Men Over a 2-Month Period

MONTREAL

138d Neglected Majority: The Changing Role of Women in 19th Century Montreal
304f Women's Work in Montreal at the Beginning of the Century
358j Looking Forward to Montreal

MOOD

171m Body Time and Social Time: Mood Patterns by Menstrual Cycle Phase and Day of Week
199w Reproductive Hormones, Moods, and the Menstrual Cycle

MOON

88j Moon and Contemporary Women's Poetry

MORALITY

2b Membership Decisions and the Limits of Moral Obligation
98q Women's Conceptions of Self and Morality
106j Responsibility and Public Policy: Is It a Moral Question?
122c Clorinda Matto de Turner and Mercedes Cabello de Carbonera: Societal Criticism and Morality
130d Medical Morals
151n American Woman's Pre-World War I Freedom in Manners and Morals
157f Sexual Love and Moral Experience
157g Sexual Immorality Delineated
157m Is Adultery Immoral?
158r Is Adultery Immoral?
158ee Moral and Legal Status of Abortion
159bb Marriage and Morals
178g Divorce as a Moral Issue: A Hundred Years of Controversy
180q Morality of Reparation
180s Discrimination and Morally Relevant Characteristics
196d Girls--More Moral Than Boys or Just Sneakier?
231a Moral Equality
257t Modern Industry and Morality
258c New Patterns of Relationship: Beginnings of a Moral Revolution
272a Prophets, Chiefs, Commissioners, and Queens: The Moral and Institutional Context of Leadership
282d Reason and Morals in the Early Feminist Movement: Mary Wollstonecraft
283h Beyond Male Morality
292t American Woman's Pre-World War I Freedom in Manners and Morals
360o American Woman's Pre-World War I Freedom in Manners and Morals

MORGAN

303h Julia Morgan

MORMONISM

215f Susanna Goudin Cardon: An Italian Convert to Mormonism

MORNING

105c Spot Messages within Saturday Morning TV Programs
233oo The Morning Half-Life Blues

MOROCCO

213b Bridging the Gap between the Sexes in Moroccan Legal Practice
325d Women and Social Change in Morocco
325t Working women in a Moroccan Village
325bb Negotiation of Reality: Male-Female Relations in Sefrou, Morocco
325cc Women, Sufism, and Decision-Making in Moroccan Islam

MORRISON

222x Complexity: Toni Morrison's Women--An Interview Essay
340j Sex and-or Mr. Morrison

MORROW

93d Lena Morrow Lewis: Her Rise and Fall

MOSAIC

320o Feminist Mosaic

MOTHER

8s Lesbian Mother
10d The Revolt of "Mother"
20i Matrescence, Becoming a Mother, a 'New-Old' 'Rite de Passage'
35d Mothering, Male Dominance, and Capitalism
42d Voluntary Motherhood: The Beginnings of Feminist Birth Control Ideas in the U.S.
50m The Mother of the Detective
58b Northren Mother's Blessing
96w Mother's Daughter
104h "Mother" M. Jones
108w My Mother's House: Where Are the Children?
111j His Idea of a Mother
111o The Mother
112h His Idea of a Mother
117h Portnoy's Mother's Complaint: Depression in Middle-Aged Women
153c The African Mother at Her Daughter's Grave
161e Calm Down Mother
176t Motherhood
176ff Worker, Mother, Housewife: Soviet Women Today
198e Motherhood and Sexuality
206l Worker, Mother, Housewife: Soviet Woman Today
215c Louisa Barnes Pratt: Missionary Wife, Missionary Mother, Missionary
222l Black Eve or Madonna? Antithetical Views of the Mother in Black American Literature
225a Mother and the Hospital: An Unfortunate Fit Between the Woman's Internal World and Some Hospital Practices
226c Mother's Daughter
226j Mother Worship
231m Philosopher to His Mother

233jj The Mother
250bb Influences of Mother's Menstruation on Her Child
252z Marriage and Motherhood of Black Women Graduates
263h What Became of God the Mother?
264h Mother Role
264m Loneliness of the Long-Distance Mother
265i Loneliness of the Long-Distance Mother
273q The Mother
278aa Mother, Maiden, and the Marriage of Death: Women Writers and an Ancient Myth
283f Image of the Virgin Mother
284v Working Mother's Crises
296s Specific Psychological Tasks in Pregnancy and Motherhood
300l New Anxiety of Motherhood
304d Child-Free Alternative: Rejection of the Motherhood Mystique
316c Women and Political Socialization: Considerations of the Impact of Motherhood
340c That Only a Mother
351b Pregnancy, Motherhood and Work Activity
362f Motherhood: Who Needs It?
370i Effects on Mother

MOTHER-CHILD

89jj Mother-Child Bonding
98b Mother-Daughter Relationships: Psychodynamics, Politics, and Philosophy
176d Sex, Age, and State as Determinants of Mother-Infant Interaction
198cc Sex, Age, and State as Determinants of Mother-Infant Interaction
199g Sex Differences in Mother-Infant Attachment in Monkeys
199h Early Sex Differences and Mother-Infant Interaction

MOTHER-GENIUS

68k Whatever Happened to Shaw's Mother-Genius Portrait?

MOTHER-RIGHT

198i Family in Father-Right and Mother-Right: Complex of Mother-Right

MOTHER-WORSHIP

96dd Mother-Worship

MOTHEREARTH

263b Motherearth and the Megamachine

MOTHERS

9mm Why Mothers Fail
16c The Mothers, the Mothers, How Eerily It Sounds
18e Mothers and Daughters
19s Mothers in the Fatherland: Women in Nazi Germany
68l Mr. Shaw's Many Mothers
89kk Fathers Shouldn't Try to Be Mothers

98l Separation and Survival: Mothers, Daughters, Sisters: The Women's Experimental Theatre
116m Italian Mothers, American Daughters: Changes in Work and Family Roles
117y Mothers and Daughters in American Jewish Literature: The Rotted Cord
135e Employer's Attitude to Working Mothers
140y Family Planning, Decision Making: Attitudes and Intentions of Mothers and Fathers
155l Mothers and Daughters: Perceived and Real Differences in Sexual Values
160a Advice to Mothers, on the Subject of Their Own Health, and, of the Means of Promoting the Health, Strength and Beauty of Their Offspring
160b Care and Feeding of Children: A Catechism for the Use of Mothers and Children's Nurses
166nn Professional and Non-Professional Women as Mothers
182a Workers (and Mothers): Soviet Women Today
219l Mothers' Speech to Children in Bilingual Mexican-American Homes
222z Mississippi Mothers: Roots
251bb Social Situation of Divorced Mothers and Their Families
270c Mothers of a Nation: Seneca Resistance to Quaker Intervention
296e Fathers, Mothers and Sex Typing
317b Celibes, Mothers, and Church Cockroaches: Religious Participation of Women in a Mexican Village
331h Public Policy and the Family: A New Strategy for Women as Wives and Mothers
331k Women into Mothers: Experimental Family Life-Styles
349j Patriot Mothers in the Post-Risorgimento: Women After the Italian Revolution
369g In Search of Our Mothers' Gardens

MOTION

152r Women in Motion
256q Women in Motion: It's Not Who Wins Or Loses, But How Many Play the Game

MOTIVATION

141p Fertility Motivations and Career Conflicts in Educated Women
155e Self-Conceptions, Motivations and Interpersonal Attitudes of Early- and Late-Maturing Girls
200n Self-Conceptions, Motivations and Interpersonal Attitudes of Early- and Late-Maturing Girls
250ii Experimental Arousal of Achievement Motivation in Adolescent Girls
266g Relationship Between Role Orientation and Achievement Motivation in College Women
267i Socialization of Achievement Motivation in Females
267k Varieties of Achievement Motivation
278b Male Power Motivation and the Status of Women
286i Motivation and the Female Participant
307e Institutionalized Motivation for Fertility Limitation
326a Success Motivation and Social Structure: Comments on Women and Achievement

MOTIVE

60o Motives and Future of the Educated Woman
99k Rape and Psychiatric Vocabularies of Motive
176j Motive to Avoid Success and Changing Aspirations of College Women
176k Race, Social Class, and the Motive to Avoid Success in Women
250kk Early Childhood Experiences and Women's Achievement Motives
267h Early Childhood Experiences and Women's Achievement Motives
267n Race, Social Class, and the Motive to Avoid Success in Women
296b Early Childhood Experiences and Women's Achievement Motives

MOTOKO

178i Ume Tsuda and Motoko Hani: Echoes of American Cultural Feminism in Japan

MOULD

320m Breaking Out of the Female Mould

MOUNT

119i The Mount of Sorrow
334j Founding of Mount Holyoke College

MOUNTAIN

95b The Memorial Service on the Mountain
104j Mountain Wolf Woman
191q Class Factor: Mountain Women Speak Out on Women's Health

MOURNING

144e Mourning Pictures

MOVEMENT

see also various movements

7b Discrimination Against Afro-American Women in the Woman's Movement, 1830-1920
13j Impact of the Women's Liberation Movement on Child Development Texts
20s Women's Movement in the U.S.
35f Nineteenth-Century Woman Suffrage Movement and the Analysis of Women's Oppression
39c Origins of the Women's Liberation Movement
57h Women's Movement Meets the Challenge of Diversity
74k Development of the American Women's Liberation Movement, 1967-1971
77n Black Movement and Women's Liberation
77gg Male Power and the Women's Movement
84d Church, State, and Family: The Women's Movement in Italy
86f Issues Before the Abortion Movement
86j Why Red-Baiting Hurts the Feminist Movement
86p Mass Feminist Movement
105k Newspaper as a Social Movement's Resource

105l Women's Movement and the Women's Pages: Separate, Unequal and Unspectacular
106k Civil Rights and the Women's Movement
114b Women and the National Movement
114c The Women's Movement--Then and Now
115c Social Reform Movement in India--From Ranade to Nehru
116b Civil Code of 1865 and the Origins of the Feminist Movement in Italy
116d Women in the Canadian and Italian Trade Union Movements at the Turn of the Century
116e Forging a Socialist Women's Movement: Angelica Balabanoff in Switzerland
121h Participation of Women in the Independence Movement in Gran Colombia, 1780-1830
123j Coming Out in the Women's Movement
127j Labor and Suffrage Movements: A View of Working-Class Women in the 20th Century
128l Women in the Alliance Movement
138e National Organization and the Women's Movement in the Late 19th Century
139b Two Suffrage Movements
140s Rise of the Women's Movement: A Case Study in Political Development
141x Chinese Women in the Early Communist Movement
143n From Kitchen to Storefront: Women in the Tenant Movement
151i Grimke Sisters: Women and the Abolition Movement
175ii Women and the Radical Movement
178d Women and the Nativist Movement
183e Gender Imagery and Issues of War and Peace: The Case of the Draft Resistance Movement of the 1960's
191a Women's Health Movement: Past Roots
191u Women's Health Movement: Where Are We Now?
208uu Movement Behavior
218c From Separatism to Socialism: Women in the Russian Revolutionary Movement of the 1870s
231k Contra Women's Liberation Movement
236d Women's Modernization Movement in Korea
246a Radical and Conservative Trends in the Women's Rights Movement
246n Sociological Examination of the Women's Movement
256j Impact of Mid-twentieth Century Movement for Sex Equality in Employment on Three Contemporary Economic Institutions
257w Meaning of Progress in the Woman Movement
259h Ideology of the Suffrage Movement
263f Women in the Early Christian Movement
264cc Women's Liberation Movement: Its Origins, Organizations, Activities, and Ideas
264ee Male Power and the Women's Movement
265cc Women's Liberation Movement: Its Origins, Structures, Impact, and Ideas
282d Reason and Morals in the Early Feminist Movement: Mary Wollstonecraft
282l Reaction and the Women's Movement
297r Women's Liberation Movement in the U.S.
297u Women's Movement in the People's Republic of China
307c Chinese Women in the Early Communist Movement
318d Marxism and the Women's Movement
337m Women in Judaism: From the Reform Movement to Contemporary Jewish Religious Feminism

342y Agism and the Women's Movement
342ii Persuasion in the Feminist Movement
344b How Powerful Is Powerful? The Women's Movement and the Four Black Congresswomen
344l Exploring the Relationship Between Female Candidacies and the Women's Movement
349k American Women in the Peace and Preparedness Movements in World War I
365c Impact of the Women's Liberation Movement on Child Development Books
365i Recent Writings of the Women's Movement
368g White Feminist Movement: The Chicana Perspective

MOVING

15i Moving Out, Moving Up

MOVING PICTURE

369l Notes from an Extra in the American Moving Picture Show

MS

105f Magazine Heroines: Is MS. Just Another Member of the FAMILY CIRCLE?
203v Vs. MS
266jj Life and Death of Ms. Solomon Grundy

MUFFET

208dd Reducing the "Miss Muffet" Syndrome: An Annotated Bibliography

MULDE

229c Mulde Sacke

MULE

108b White Mule
132h Women, Servants, Mules, and Other Property

MULIER

229a Hic Mulier
315f Mulieres Sanctae

MULTIPLE

39j Positive Effects of the Multiple Negative: Explaining the Success of Black Professional Women
114s Chellamma--An Illustration of the Multiple Roles of Traditional Women
198z Theories of Identification and Exposure to Multiple Models
266n Positive Effects of the Multiple Negative: Explaining the Success of Black Professional Women
296l Multiple Factors in Frigidity

MURDER

50a The Murder at Troyte's Hill
50i The Murder at Fernhurst
50o Snafu Murder
103f A Memorable Murder

MURDOCH

47f Iris Murdoch: The Novelist as Magician, The Magician as Artist

MURIEL

47i Muriel Spark's Fingernails

MUSCLE

152f Closing the Muscle Gap

MUSE

88e Imperious Muse: Some Observations on Women, Nature and the Poetic Tradition

MUSIC

18m Role Music Plays in Adolescent Development
212d "Madame de": A Musical Passage
339c Dirge Without Music

MUSLIM

see also ARAB; MIDDLE EAST; various Arab countries

20z Changing Roles of Women in Two African Muslim Cultures
114l Muslim Women of India
115f Status of Muslim Women and Social Change
293d Moslem World: Women Excluded from Development
325a Women and Law Reform in Contemporary Islam
325b Legal Reform as an Indicator of Women's Status in Muslim Nations
325c Status and Fertility Patterns of Muslim Women
325cc Women, Sufism, and Decision-Making in Moroccan Islam
325gg Being Female in a Muslim Minority in China
329l Women in the Muslim World
329n Algerian Women: Honor, Survival, and Islamic Socialism
372c Women's Role in a Muslim Hausa Town--Mirria, Republic of Niger

MUTUAL

93f Politics of Mutual Frustration: Socialists and Suffragists in New York and Wisconsin

MYRNA

122i Three Female Playwrights Explore Contemporary Latin American Reality: Myrna Casas, Griselda Gambaro, Luisa Josefina Hernandez

MYSTERY

50e The Fordwych Castle Mystery
103a The Dublin Mystery
249o Mastery of Work and the Mystery of Sex in a Guatemalan Village

MYSTIC

214b Jane Lead: Mysticism and the Woman Cloathed with the Sun
278bb Mysticism and Feminism: Jacob Boehme and Jane Lead
337g Jane Lead: The Feminist Mind and Art of a Seventeenth-Century Protestant Mystic

MYSTIQUE

107bb Feminine Mystique
304d Child-Free Alternative: Rejection of the Motherhood Mystique

MYTH

42k Image and Reality: The Myth of the Idle Victorian Woman
68d Eliza's Choice: Transformation Myth and the Ending of "Pygmalion"
77t Myth of the Vaginal Orgasm
78a Masculine Mythology of Femininity
85h Myth of the Neutral "Man"
85q Myth of the Complete Person
127hh Myth of the Vaginal Orgasm
132m Is Rape a Myth?
139s Myth of the Vaginal Orgasm
146d Biological Realities and Myths
146i Literature and Myths
149f Down with Myth America
149j Declining Status of Women: Popular Myths and the Failure of Functionalist Thought
153u Domestic Mythology
166aaa Myth of the Egalitarian Family: Familial Roles and the Professionally Employed Wife
175t Myth of the Vaginal Orgasm
190e Classical Mythology and the Role of Women in Modern Literature
194a Mythology About Women, With Special Reference to Chile
197j Myth is Better Than a Miss: Men Get the Edge in Academic Employment
212o Leni Riefenstahl: The Deceptive Myth
214t Critique of Consciousness and Myth in Levertov, Rich, and Rukeyser
233aa Matriarchal Myth
233cc Three Sexual Myths Exploded
233dd Myth of the Vaginal Orgasm
246d Myth America: Women in American Literature (panel)
246g Psychotherapy for Women: Myths and Legacies
249n Myth of Matriarchy: Why Men Rule in Primitive Society
251u Myth of Black Matriarchy
264o Women and Unemployment: Assessing the Biggest Myths
269j Modern Family: Sticky Myths, Diverse Realities, and the Problem of Isolation
278aa Mother, Maiden, and the Marriage of Death: Women Writers and an Ancient Myth
288qq Myths of Women in the Cinema
314b Exploding Some Myths About Women Managers

314d Sharon Kirkman: Mind Over Myth
314f Myth and the Reality
317e Misery of the Embodied: Representations of Women in Sinhalese Myth
334c Myth of the Golden Age
348b Myth of Male Protectiveness and the Legal Subordination of Women: An Historical Analysis
348g Accounting for Rape: Reality and Myth in Press Reporting
361h Women's Language in America: Myth and Reality
364f Myths and Stereotypes: My Challenge to Black Women Cultural Workers

N.C.T.E.

207i APPENDIX: N.C.T.E. Guidelines for Nonsexist Use of Language

N.O.W.

89s N.O.W. Bill of Rights
139v N.O.W. Organized
139w Editorial from N.O.W.'s President

N.Y.C.

202m Vicious Cycle of Welfare: Problems of the Female-Headed Household in N.Y.C.

N'SARDI-EL

133b The Song of N'Sardi-El

NAME

200j Memory for Names and Faces: A Characteristic of Social Intelligence?
233gg Problem that Has No Name
278e Sexism in American Naming Traditions
362a Problem that Has No Name

NANETTE

220b Nanette: An Aside

NANNIE

7h Nannie Burroughs and the Education of Black Women

NARCISSISM

78b Narcissism in Female Sexuality
364b Submission, Masochism and Narcissism: Three Aspects of Women's Role as Reflected in Dress

NARCISSUS

129g Penelope, Molly, Narcissus, and Susan

NARRATIVE

9n Narrative
74e Narrative of a Life
96c Female Prisoner: A Narrative of the Life and Singular Adventures of Josephine Amelia Perkins
96d Demon in Female Apparel: Narrative of Josephine Amelia Perkins, the Notorious Female Horse Thief...
274a Personal Narratives in Women's Rap Groups
288rr Visual Pleasure and Narrative Cinema

NATALIE

303l Natalie de Blois

NATION

9d Speech: National Women's Rights Convention of 1855
25g Negro Family: The Case for National Action
43b African Women and National Development
57i APPENDIX: U.S. National Women's Agenda
114b Women and the National Movement
132aa National Resolution on Women
138e National Organization and the Women's Movement in the Late 19th Century
140c Male Sex Role Behaviors in a Representative National Sample, 1973
163g Societal Punishment and Aspects of Female Political Participation: 1972 National Convention Delegates
183h Attitudes of Men and Women Toward Violence: Report of a National Survey
236h Role of Korean Women in National Development
257h (Speech, National Woman's Suffrage Association, 1889)
257s (Remarks, National American Woman's Suffrage Association)
270c Mothers of a Nation: Seneca Resistance to Quaker Intervention
275d More Than a Question of Numbers: Women Deputies in the German National Constituent Assembly and the Reichstag, 1919-1933
275e German Women University Students: National Socialism and the War, 1939-1945
281q Shaping of the Kaum Ibu (Women's Section) of the United Maylays National Organization
312h Women in Irish National and Local Politics, 1922-77
325b Legal Reform as an Indicator of Women's Status in Muslim Nations
325n Feminism and National Politics in Egypt
329b African Women, "Modernization," and National Liberation
344i Organizing for Political Power: The National Women's Political Caucus

NATIVE

43j Native American Women: Twilight of a Long Maidenhood
77q Native Women Today: Sexism and the Indian Woman
178d Women and the Nativist Movement
222dd Return of the Native
274e Native Costumes of the Oberwallis: Tourist Gimmick or Tradition?

NATURE

18h Changing Nature of Female Delinquency
33o Natural History
53a Nature of Women in Society
73e Natural Childbirth: Pain or Peak Experience
79p Nature's Pictures, Drawn by Fancies Pencil to the Life
85o Nature and Value of Marriage
88e Imperious Muse: Some Observations on Women, Nature and the Poetic Tradition
139f Nature of Woman
158i Nature of Women
159ee Natural Law Language and Women
159ff Sex Roles: The Argument from Nature
170i Nature of Female Sexuality
173ff Nature of Female Criminality
185d Nature is a Woman
203l Sex Roles: The Argument from Nature
203m Natural Law Language and Women
249c Is Female to Male as Nature Is to Culture?
254j Natural Law Language and Women
266z Effects of Live Modelled Sex-Appropriate Play Behavior In a Naturalistic Setting
268m Nature of the Animus
362g Nature of Women

NAVAHO

285d Role of Women in a Changing Navaho Society

NAZI

19s Mothers in the Fatherland: Women in Nazi Germany
349b Women, Class, and War in Nazi Germany

NEALE

88r Zora Neale Hurston
222p Influence of Voodoo on the Fiction of Zora Neale Hurston

NEED

13oo Feminist Studies: Frill or Necessity?
38d Projected Future Employment and Leadership Needs and Areas
45f Black Women Who Head Families: Economic Needs and Economic Resources
45g Policy Issues on Day Care: The Special Needs of Black Working Women
59b Women's Roles in the Economy: Economic Investigation and Research Needs
88y Need to Tell All: A Comparison of Historical and Modern Feminist "Confessional" Writing
92g Welfare State and the Needs of the Dependent Family
125a Woman and Her Needs
127v "Freedom Is Something That All of Us Need"
132e Why Men Need a Boys' Night Out
140rr Directions and Needs of Research on Women
146h Service Needs

263x Why Women Need the Goddess: Phenomenological, Psychological, and Political Reflections
272l Need for Female Role Models in Education
314i Patrons, Rabbis, Mentors--Whatever You Call Them, Women Need Them Too
328q Working Women: European Experience and American Need
348d Who Needs Prostitutes? The Ideology of Male Sexual Needs
352a Women at a Standstill: The Need for Radical Change
362f Motherhood: Who Needs It?

NEGATIVE

39j Positive Effects of the Multiple Negative: Explaining the Success of Black Professional Women
208x Negative Image of Women in Children's Literature
220f A Negative Balance
266n Positive Effects of the Multiple Negative: Explaining the Success of Black Professional Women
350i Desirade: A Negative Case

NEGLECTED

138d Neglected Majority: The Changing Role of Women in 19th Century Montreal

NEGOTIATION

274f Negotiating Respect: Patterns of Presentation among Black Women
325bb Negotiation of Reality: Male-Female Relations in Sefrou, Morocco

NEGRO

see also AFRO-AMERICA; BLACK; MINORITY; RACE

25a Negro Family in America
25e Crucible of Identity: The Negro Lower-Class Family
25g Negro Family: The Case for National Action
25j Family and Childhood in a Southern Negro Community
96t Northern Negro's Autobiography
128c Prudence Crandall: Champion of Negro Education
155i Premarital Sexual Permissiveness Among Negroes and Whites
166g Farmer's Daughter Effect: The Case of the Negro Female Professional
166ee Career Expectations of Negro Women Graduates

NEHRU

115a Nehru and the Place of Women in Indian Society
115c Social Reform Movement in India--From Ranade to Nehru
115e Jawaharlal Nehru and the Hindu Code Bill

NEIGHBORHOOD

143j Toward Supportive Neighborhoods: Women's Role in Changing the Segregated City
222gg The Neighborhood
325aa Women and the Neighborhood Street in Borj Hammoud, Lebanon

NELLIE

122l Nellie Campobello: Romantic Revolutionary and Mexican Realist
320a Nellie McClung: "Not a Nice Woman"

NEO-FEMINIST

88s Humanbecoming: Form and Focus in the Neo-Feminist Novel
110m Humanbecoming: Form and Focus in the Neo-Feminist Novel

NEO-MASCULINITY

278y Before Androgyny: An Examination of the Stages Toward Neo-Masculinity

NERVOUS

199c Fetal Androgens, Human Central Nervous System Differentiation, and Behavior Sex Differences
330b Sex Hormones, The Central Nervous System and Affect Variability in Humans

NETWORK

317i Convivial Sisterhood: Spirit Mediumship and Client-Core Network among Black South African Women
372h Adaptive Strategies and Social Networks of Women in St. Kitts

NEUROPHYSIOLOGICAL

171e Biochemical and Neurophysiological Influences on Human Sexual Behavior

NEUROPSYCHOLOGICAL

53h Female Brain: A Neuropsychological Viewpoint

NEUTERS

209g Toward a Society of Neuters

NEUTRALITY

85h Myth of the Neutral "Man"
171a Psychosexual Neutrality: Is Anatomy Destiny?

NEW YORK

41d Women Workers in a Mid-Nineteenth-Century New York City Community
41f Italian-American Women in New York City, 1900-1950: Work and School
41j Creating a Feminist Alliance: Sisterhood and Class Conflict in the New York Women's Trade Union League, 1903- 1914
51q Women Criminals in Progressive New York
93f Politics of Mutual Frustration: Socialists and Suffragists in New York and Wisconsin
94l Rape in New York City: A Study of Material in the Police Files and Its Meaning

140o Italian-American Women in New York City, 1890 to 1940
153d Letters from New York
175nn Politics of the Ego: A Manifesto for New York Radical Feminists

NEW-OLD'

20i Matrescence, Becoming a Mother, a 'New-Old' 'Rite de Passage'

NEWBORNS

see also BIRTH; PRENATAL; PREGNANCY; MATERNITY

22m Parents' Views on Sex of Newborns
173j Parents' Views on Sex of Newborns
176b Sex Differences in the Incidence of Neonatal Abnormalities and Abnormal Performance in Early Childhood
199j Methodological Considerations in Studying Sex Differences in the Behavioral Functioning of Newborns

NEWS

105h Most Admired Woman: Image-Making in the News
105j News of Women and the Work of Men
113g A Piece of News
142r The Pill--Radio News 2-24-70

NEWSPAPER

105k Newspaper as a Social Movement's Resource
320p APPENDIX: Women's Centres, Women's Newspapers and Regional Contacts

NICE

73q Women's Liberation: A Nice Idea, but It Won't Be Easy
123b Such a Nice Girl
300c Not a Very Nice Story
320a Nellie McClung: "Not a Nice Woman"

NIGER

338b Position of Women in a Pastoral Society (Fulani WoDaaBe, Nomads of the Niger)
372c Women's Role in a Muslim Hausa Town--Mirria, Republic of Niger

NIGERIA

154g Female Militancy and Colonial Revolt: The Women's War of 1929, Eastern Nigeria
230p Underdevelopment and the Experience of Women: A Nigerian Case Study
285i Traditional Marriage among the Irigwe of Benue-Plateau State, Nigeria
297b Role of Women in the Development of Culture in Nigeria
302b Dual-Sex Political System in Operation: Igbo Women and Community Politics in Midwestern Nigeria

NIGGER

8dd Nigger in the Woodpile
9ll Woman as Nigger
73m Woman as Nigger
132x Woman as Nigger
132hh No "Chicks," "Broads," or "Niggers" for OLE MOLE
139r Woman as Nigger

NIGHT

103h A Midsummer Night's Crime
108ff Nightwood: Night Watch
111k Night-Pieces: For a Child
112i Night Pieces for a Child: The Crib
132e Why Men Need a Boys' Night Out
220z Tuesday Night
375n Opening Nights: The Opening Days

NIGHTINGALES

277c The Nightingales Sing

NIGHTMARE

247c Henry Fuseli's "Nightmare": Eroticism or Pornography?

NIGHTWOOD

108ff Nightwood: Night Watch
140kk Djuna Barnes' "Nightwood"
361o Style of Djuna Barnes' "Nightwood"

NIHILIST

102m Journey of a Woman Nihilist to Verona in Late Autumn

NIN

88w Anais Nin: A Critical Evaluation
175rr Women's Private Writings: Anais Nin
179i A. Nin
359k Anais Nin's "Diary" in Context

NINA

102f Nina's Story

NINE

50f The Man with Nine Lives

NINETEEN

233ii To Room Nineteen

NINETEENTH

7c Black Male Perspectives on the Nineteenth Century Woman
9aa Woman in the Nineteenth Century and Kindred Papers
19m Angels in the Devil's Workshop: Leisured and Charitable Women in Nineteenth-Century England and France
35f Nineteenth-Century Woman Suffrage Movement and the Analysis of Women's Oppression
41c New England Mill Women in the Early Nineteenth Century
41d Women Workers in a Mid-Nineteenth-Century New York City Community
42a "Fashionable Diseases": Women's Complaints and Their Treatment in Nineteenth-Century America
42b Puberty to Menopause: The Cycle of Femininity in Nineteenth-Century America
92b Home From Home: Women's Philanthropic Work in the Nineteenth Century
92c Separation of Home and Work? Landladies and Lodgers in Nineteenth-Century England
116c Prostitution and Feminism in Late Nineteenth-Century Italy
116y Women in the Italian-American Theatre of the Nineteenth Century
121j Nineteenth-Century Feminist Press and Women's Rights in Brazil
122d Life and Early Literary Career of the Nineteenth-Century Colombian Writer, Coledad Acosta de Samper
126g Education and Ideology in Nineteenth-Century America: The Response of Educational Institútions to the Changing Role of Women
126p Sex and Class in Colonial and Nineteenth-Century America
181b Women's Work in Nineteenth-Century London: A Study of the Years 1820-50
181c Women and Nineteenth-Century Radical Politics: A Lost Dimension
188c Woman in the Nineteenth Century
191b Sexual Surgery in Late Nineteenth-Century America
215p Dr. Ellen Brooke Ferguson: Nineteenth-Century Renaissance Woman
240j They Shall Have Faces, Minds, and (One Day) Flesh: Women in Late Nineteenth-century and Early Twentieth-century American Literature
244d Making of an Outcast Group: Prostitutes and Working Women in Nineteenth-Century Plymouth and Southampton
247a Eroticism and Female Imagery in Nineteenth-Century Art
259i Patterns of Nineteenth Century Feminism
292s Nineteenth-Century Heritage: The Family, Feminism and Sex
295a Political Economy of Ontario Women in the Nineteenth Century
334l Chinese Immigrant Women in Nineteenth-Century California
334m Origins of Legal Restrictions on Planned Parenthood in Nineteenth-Century America
360e Organized Women's Benevolence in Early Nineteenth-Century America
360l Female World of Love and Ritual: Relations Between Women in Nineteenth-Century America
360n Hysterical Woman: Sex Roles and Role Conflict in Nineteenth-Century America

NITTY-GRITTY

129t Nitty-Gritty of Survival

NOBLE

121d Women in a Noble Family: The Mexican Counts of Regla, 1750-1830

NOMAD

325q Women among Qashqa'i Nomadic Pastoralists in Iran
325r Women's Subsociety among the Shahsevan Nomads of Iran
338b Position of Women in a Pastoral Society (Fulani WoDaaBe, Nomads of the Niger)
354n Urban Nomads: Women in Temporary Clerical Services

NON-BRAHMIN

213d Caste Differences between Brahmin and Non-Brahmin Women in a South Indian Village

NON-CAREER

146o Retirement: Career and Non-Career

NON-HIERARCHICAL

20p Non-Hierarchical, Hierarchical, and Masked Reciprocity in the Arab Village

NON-HUMAN

20b Socialization of Non-Human Primate Females
20d Spontaneous and Induced Abortion in Human and Non-Human Primates

NON-PROFESSIONAL

166nn Professional and Non-Professional Women as Mothers

NONACADEMIC

327d Nonacademic Professional Political Scientists

NONCONSCIOUS

77l Case Study of a Nonconscious Ideology: Training the Woman to Know Her Place
186f Training the Woman to Know Her Place: The Power of a Nonconscious Ideology
208c Training the Woman To Know Her Place: The Power of a Nonconscious Ideology

NONHUMAN

99a Femaleness, Maleness and Behavior Disorders in Nonhumans
199b Prenatal Testosterone in the Nonhuman Primate and Its Consequences for Behavior

NONSEXIST

14a Nonsexist Perspective on Social and Political Change
120c Making of a Nonsexist Dictionary
156c Teacher Education and Non-Sexist Early Childhood Education
156i Non-Sexist Parenting at Home and at School
156o APPENDIX: Sources of Non-Sexist Materials

156p APPENDIX: Non-Sexist Picture Books for Children
207i APPENDIX: N.C.T.E. Guidelines for Nonsexist Use of Language

NONTRADITIONAL

328f Women Workers, Nontraditional Occupations and Full Employment
371i Nontraditional Work Schedules for Women

NONVERBAL

120l Power, Sex, and Nonverbal Communication
120m Sex Differences in Language, Speech, and Nonverbal Communication: An Annotated Bibliography

NOON

144c Breakfast Past Noon

NORDIC

352l Sexual Equality in the Labour Market: Some Experiences and Views of the Nordic Countries

NORM

22k Phallacy of Our Sexual Norm
123h Normative Status of Heterosexuality
155o Changing Sex Norms in America and Scandinavia
204h Hormones and Cognitive Functioning in Normal Development
211f "Normal" and "Special" Aspects of Pregnancy: A Psychological Approach
250y Sexual Dimorphic Behavior, Normal and Abnormal
331b Sexual Inequality, Cultural Norms, and Wife-Beating

NORMAN

86o Answer to Norman Mailer's "Prisoner of Sex"
162c Population of Crulai, a Norman Parish
312a Women in Norman Ireland
335d Women in Norman and Plantagenet England

NORTH

7a Northern Black Female Workers: Jacksonian Era
39q Social Relations of Black and White Widowed Women in a Northern Metropolis
43f Effects of Class and Sex on Political Life in Northern India
55d Homeworkers in North London
58b Northren Mother's Blessing
91e Women, Employment, and Fertility Trends in the Arab Middle East and North Africa
96t Northern Negro's Autobiography
131e Women of North and Central India: Goddesses and Wives
294j Women in the Middle East and North Africa and Universal Suffrage
325ee Theme of Sexual Oppression in the North African Novel
367a Family Life, Women's Status, and Fertility: Middle East and North African Perspectives

367b Demographic Transition in the Middle East and North Africa
367c Family Planning and Population Policies in the Middle East and North Africa

NORTHEAST

194e Impact of Industrialization on Women's Work Roles in Northeast Brazil

NORWICH

120g Sex, Covert Prestige, and Linguistic Change in the Urban British English of Norwich

NOTEBOOK

17k "Out of the chaos, a new kind of strength": Doris Lessing's "The Golden Notebook"
47b Disorderly Company: From "The Golden Notebook" to "The Four-Gated City"
88v Alienation of the Woman Writer in "The Golden Notebook"

NOTHINGNESS

122o Phenomenology of Nothingness in the Poetry of Julia de Burgos

NOTORIOUS

96d Demon in Female Apparel: Narrative of Josephine Amelia Perkins, the Notorious Female Horse Thief...

NOURISHMENT

20f Relevance of Nourishment to the Reproductive Cycle of the Female in India

NOVEL

47a Margaret Drabble: Novels of a Cautious Feminist
47f Iris Murdoch: The Novelist as Magician, The Magician as Artist
47g Women in the Novels of Ann Petry
47h Character and Themes in the Novels of Jean Rhys
71a Literary Archetypes and Female Role Alternatives: The Woman and the Novel in Latin America
80f "El casamiento enganoso": Marriage in the Novels of Maria Luisa Bombal, Silvina Bullrich, and Elisa Serrana
80h Three Peninsular Novelists Comment on the Spanish Woman
88o Pre-Feminism in Some Eighteenth-Century Novels
88p Constance Fenimore Woolson: First Novelist of Florida
88s Humanbecoming: Form and Focus in the Neo-Feminist Novel
110c Gentle Doubters: Images of Women in Englishwomen's Novels, 1840-1920
110l Sex Roles in Three of Hermann Hesse's Novels
110m Humanbecoming: Form and Focus in the Neo-Feminist Novel
119g Novels, Gothic Novels
122e Teresa de la Parra, Venezuelan Novelist and Feminist

122g Maria Angelica Bosco and Beatriz Guido: An Approach to Two Argentinian Novelists Between 1960 and 1970
122h Argentine Women in the Novels of Silvina Bullrich
141e Novel Women: Origins of the Feminist Literary Tradition in England and France
222s Ann Petry Talks About First Novel
240k "Combat in the Erogenous Zone": Women in the American Novel between the Two World Wars
265q Women in the American Novel
325ee Theme of Sexual Oppression in the North African Novel
335j Women in the Mirror: Using Novels to Study Victorian Women
363i Lady Novelists

NOVITIATE

96o My Novitiate

NUCLEAR

89oo Nuclear Family

NUMBERS

275d More Than a Question of Numbers: Women Deputies in the German National Constituent Assembly and the Reichstag, 1919-1933

NUN

10c A New England Nun
111mm A New England Nun
112dd A New England Nun
114q Nurses and Nuns of Kerala
121e Indian Nuns of Mexico City's Monasterio of Corpus Christi, 1724-1821
222n Alice Walker: "The Diary of an African Nun" and Du Bois' Double Consciousness
279d A New England Nun
337j Liberated American Nun

NURSE

see also HEALTH; MEDICINE

84e Sexual Division of Labour: The Case of Nursing
114q Nurses and Nuns of Kerala
160b Care and Feeding of Children: A Catechism for the Use of Mothers and Children's Nurses
166m Social Influence and the Social-Psychological Function of Deference: A Study of Psychiatric Nursing
166s Female Identity and Career Choice: The Nursing Case
166z Self-Concept, Occupational Role Expectations, and Occupational Choice in Nursing and Social Work
166ll Inactive Nurse
166ww Do "Bad Girls" Become Good Nurses?
295d Short History of Nursing in Ontario
327e Analysis of Femininity in Nursing
360f Women Nurses in the Union Army

NURSERY

73h There's No Unisex in the Nursery
79k Countess of Lincoln's Nurserie
173n How Nursery Schools Teach Girls to Shut Up
196a Sex-Role Socialization and the Nursery School: As the Twig is Bent

NUTRITION

18r Nutrition and Women: Facts and Faddism
20g Nutrition and Pregnancy
286v Nutritional Requirements for Women in Sport

NUTS

342h Nuts and Bolts View of Women's Studies

NYAMWEZI

193c Aspects of the Distinction Between the Sexes in the Nyamwezi and Some Other African Systems of Kinship and Marriage

NZAKARA

338d Nzakara Women (Central African Republic)

O'CONNOR

192h Flannery O'Connor

OAKLAND

94f Black Offender and White Victim: A Study of Forcible Rape in Oakland, Ca.

OASIS

325u Status of Women and Property on a Baluchistan Oasis in Pakistan

OAXACA

84f Modes of Appropriation and the Sexual Division of Labour: A Case Study from Oaxaca, Mexico

OBERWALLIS

274e Native Costumes of the Oberwallis: Tourist Gimmick or Tradition?

OBESITY

99h Sex Differences in Obesity

OBJECT

3n The Love Object
74n Temptation to be a Beautiful Object

75a Female Offender as an Object of Criminological Research
78c Change of Object
200d Child's Sex-Role Classification of School Objects
220h The Love Object

OBLIGATION

2b Membership Decisions and the Limits of Moral Obligation

OBSCENE

264w Violence: The Most Obscene Fantasy

OBSESSION

358k Masculine Obsession in Sports

OBSOLESCENCE

89l It Hurts to Be Alive and Obsolete
127q Planned Obsolescence: The Middle-Aged Woman

OBSTACLE

6h Obstacle to Women in Management

OCCIDENTE

128f "Maria Del Occidente"

OCCUPATION

see also CAREER; PROFESSION; LABOR; JOB; EMPLOYMENT; VOCATIONAL; various occupations

11e Occupations: Wider Economic Opportunity
22v Attitudinal Barriers to Occupational Aspirations in Women
45j APPENDIX: Educational and Occupational Statistics on Black Women
55c Sex and Occupational Role on Fleet Street
59h Structural Change in the Occupational Composition of the Female Labor Force
67e Intelligence, Occupational Status and Achievement Orientation
166b Plus Ca Change...? The Sexual Structure of Occupations Over Time
166i Occupational Advice for Women in Magazines
166l Occupational Aspects of Social Work
166z Self-Concept, Occupational Role Expectations, and Occupational Choice in Nursing and Social Work
196i Psychological and Occupational Sex Stereotypes in Elementary School Readers
196l Woman's Place: Children's Sex Stereotyping of Occupations
196m Sex Differences in the Occupational Choices of Second Graders
196q Counselor Bias and the Female Occupational Role
202e Determinants of Occupational Segregation
202g Relative Wages and Sex Segregation by Occupation
235g Sexual Harassment: Women's Hidden Occupational Hazard
236j Occupations, Male Housekeeper: Male-Female Roles on Cheju Island
252bb Counselor Bias and the Female Occupational Role

264p Clerical Work: The Female Occupation
266s Alternative Methods For Measuring Sex Discrimination in Occupational Incomes
267d Cross-cultural Examination of Women's Marital, Educational and Occupational Options
267p Determinants of Occupational Role Innovation Among College Women
287d Women in Work Occupations
291a Occupational Segregation in International Women's Year
291b Can We Still Afford Occupational Segregation?
291e Dual Linkages between the Occupational and Family Systems: A Macrosociological Analysis
291f Occupational Segregation and the Law
291g Historical and Structural Barriers to Occupational Desegregation
291i Occupational Segregation and Public Policy: A Comparative Analysis of American and Soviet Patterns
291n Toward Dimorphics: A Summary Statement to the Conference on Occupational Segregation
328f Women Workers, Nontraditional Occupations and Full Employment
344r Crisis Perspective on Emerging Health Roles: A Paradigm for the Entry of Women into New Occupational Roles
351c Sex Segregation in the Labor Market: An Analysis of Young College Women's Occupational Preferences
354o Women in Blue-Collar and Service Occupations
371c Occupational Values and Family Roles: Women in Blue-Collar and Service Occupations

OCEAN

356h Here and There in the Wastes of Ocean A Swimmer Was Seen

OCOL

95k Song of Lawino, Song of Ocol

ODD

110o Fictional Feminists in "The Bostonians" and "The Odd Women"
341b Odds Against Women

ODEGAARD

180l Harvard College Amicus Curiae, DeFunis v. Odegaard, Supreme Court of the U.S., 1973
180m DeFunis v. Odegaard, Dissenting Opinion

ODOUR

277bb Odour of Chrysanthemums

ODYSSEY

322c Odyssey of Encounter

OEDIPUS

76d Girl's Entry into the Oedipus Complex
78d Feminine Guilt and the Oedipus Complex

169b Evolution of the Oedipus Complex in Women
198d Early Stages of the Oedipus Conflict

OFFENDER

see also CRIME; PRISONER

51o Criminality in the Workplace: A Comparison of Male and Female Offenders
51p "Crime as Business" and the Female Offender
51x Discriminatory Sentencing of Women Offenders
51z Forgotten Offender: The Woman in Prison
75a Female Offender as an Object of Criminological Research
75b Physical Attractiveness of Female Offenders: Effects on Institutional Performance
75d Adult Female Offender: A Selected Bibliography
75i Ex-Offender Evaluates Correctional Programming for Women
75j Planning for the Female Offender
94f Black Offender and White Victim: A Study of Forcible Rape in Oakland, Ca.
99f Crime and the Female Offender

OFFENSES

94j Gusii Sex Offenses: A Study in Social Control
94k Comparative Study of Forcible Rape Offenses Known to the Police in Boston and Los Angeles
155p Gusii Sex Offenses: A Study in Social Control

OFFERING

336e Early Factory Magazines in New England: The LOWELL OFFERING and its Contemporaries

OFFICE

163f Why Few Women Hold Public Office: Factors Affecting the Participation of Women in Local Politics
163q Wife and Politician: Role Strain Among Women in Public Office
294d From Constitutional Recognition to Public Office
306d "Office Ladies"
326e Black Women Officeholders: The Case of State Legislators
344d Local Officeholding and the Community: The Case of Women on New Jersey's School Boards
373b The Office

OFFSPRING

160a Advice to Mothers, on the Subject of Their Own Health, and, of the Means of Promoting the Health, Strength and Beauty of Their Offspring

OHIO

372k Life of Sarah Penfield, Rural Ohio Grandmother: Tradition Maintained, Tradition Threatened

OKLAHOMA

128m "Kate," the "Good Angel" of Oklahoma

OLD

see also AGE

10f Old Woman Magoun
17n Old Critics and New: The Treatment of Chopin's "The Awakening"
19r Something Old, Something New: Women Between the Two World Wars
51t Oldest and Newest Profession
89d Older Working Women
116p Italian-American Female College Students: A New Generation Connected to the Old
116u Women of Old Town
129d Sex and the Older Woman
129l Older Women and Jobs
129p Older Black Women
129r Sexuality, Power, and Freedom Among "Older" Women
129x Young Women, Old Women, and Power
146f Political Importance of the Older Woman
149m Leads on Old Questions from a New Revolution: Notes on Cuban Women, 1969
155w Sexual Activities and Attitudes in Older Persons
159v Of Womankind, Old and Young
177b Images of Women in the Old Testament
183d American Peace Party: New Departures and Old Arguments
220y An Old Woman and Her Cat
249h Chinese Women: Old Skills in a New Context
256f Free Married Woman: A New Style of Living in an Old Institution
256r When Women in Politics Are Old Hat
277e The Old Chevalier
279t Old Mr. Marblehall
283g Image of Woman in Old Buddhist Literature: The Daughters of Mara
317j Bobbes and Zeydes: Old and New Roles for Elderly Jews
335a Old and New Women's History

OLE

132hh No "Chicks," "Broads," or "Niggers" for OLE MOLE

OLIVIA

108d Olivia

OLYMPIA

247f Manet, "Olympia" and Pornographic Photography

OLYMPIC

358i Past Olympic Reflections

OMBUDSMAN

301g Sex Discrimination at Universities: An Ombudsman's View

OMISSION

194l Selective Omission and Theoretical Distortion in Studying the Political Activity of Women in Brazil
207g Sexism in Dictionaries and Texts: Omissions and Commissions

ONESELF

375f Creating Oneself from Scratch

ONO

288z On Yoko Ono

ONONDAGA

131m Onondaga Women: Among the Liberated

ONTARIO

295a Political Economy of Ontario Women in the Nineteenth Century
295d Short History of Nursing in Ontario
295e Schoolmarms and Early Teaching in Ontario

OPEN

53c Open Body, Closed Space: The Transformation of Female Sexuality
341k Lesbians--The Doors Open
375n Opening Nights: The Opening Days

OPERATION

302b Dual-Sex Political System in Operation: Igbo Women and Community Politics in Midwestern Nigeria

OPERATIVES

336c Corporations and Operatives, Being an Exposition of the Condition of Factory Operatives...

OPIATE

51u Opiate Addiction Among Females in the United States Between 1850 and 1970

OPINION

163b Continuity and Change in Opinions about Sex Roles
180m DeFunis v. Odegaard, Dissenting Opinion

OPPORTUNITY

11e Occupations: Wider Economic Opportunity
13jj Discrimination and Demography Restrict Opportunities for Academic Women
13pp Equal Opportunity for Women: How Possible and How Quickly?
85k How Do We Know When Opportunities Are Equal?

174f Discrimination and the Law: The Equal Credit Opportunity Act
203n How Do We Know When Opportunities Are Equal?
203s Equal Opportunity, Free from Gender-Based Discrimination
208r Let Them Aspire! A Plea and Proposal for Equality of Opportunity for Males and Females in the Ann Arbor Public Schools
272c Power and Opportunity in the Principalship: The Case of Two Women Leaders in Education
282s How Do We Know When Opportunities are Equal?
287f Impact of Equal Employment Opportunity Laws
294o Women in Economic Life: Rights and Opportunities
301e Developing Criteria and Measures of Equal Opportunities for Women
301f Creating Opportunities for Women in Science
311c Health Professions--Opportunities and Limitations
314h Real Equal Opportunity for Women Executives
314k Assessment Center: Opportunities for Women
314ll Consequences of Equal Opportunity for Women
328c Legal Road to Equal Employment Opportunity
333i Recommendations from Research Workshops on Equal Employment Opportunity
342o Equal Employment Opportunities in Oregon
358a Equal Opportunity for Women in Sports

OPPOSITE

200e Differences in Perception of the Opposite Sex by Males and Females

OPPRESSION

8aa Oppression is Big Business: Scrutinizing Gay Therapy
9qq Sex Roles and Female Oppression
13s High-School Women: Oppression and Liberation
35f Nineteenth-Century Woman Suffrage Movement and the Analysis of Women's Oppression
43l Black Woman: Liberated or Oppressed?
84j State and the Oppression of Women
86k Revolutionary Perspective on the Oppression of Women
86n Women's Oppression: the Literary Reflection
89u Women: Caste, Class or Oppressed Sex?
107v Origin of the Oppression of Women
158e Psychological Oppression
158v Love and Women's Oppression
153bb Altruism and Women's Oppression
212h Mizoguchi's Oppressed Women
282j Exploitation, Oppression, and Self-Sacrifice
282k Altruism and Women's Oppression
325ee Theme of Sexual Oppression in the North African Novel
342n Political Economy of Women's Oppression
342z Women's Oppression and the War in Vietnam

OPTICAL

212c Image of Woman as Image: The Optical Politics of Dames

OPTION

20y Vietnamese Women: Their Roles and Their Options

267d Cross-cultural Examination of Women's Marital, Educational and Occupational Options
303a Model Domestic Environment: Icon or Option?

ORAL

116r Oral History in Pittsburgh--Women, Ethnicity, and Mental Health: Rationale, Procedure, and Methodology
176ll Predictive Study of Psychological and Psychosomatic Responses to Oral Contraceptives
191e Dangers of Oral Contraception
250aa Hormonal Interaction, Menstruation, and the Oral Contraceptives
250dd Effects of Oral Contraceptives on Affective Fluctuations Associated with the Menstrual Cycle
296n Effects of Oral Contraceptives on Affective Fluctuations Associated with the Menstrual Cycle
334o From Aide to Organizer: The Oral History of Lillian Roberts

ORANGE

113c An Apple, an Orange

ORDER

95m Order of the White Paulownia
121f Feminine Orders in Colonial Bahia, Brazil: Economic, Social, and Demographic Implications, 1677-1800
126r Women, Work and the Social Order
286o Influence of Birth Order and Sibling Sex on Sports Participation
287a Looking Backward in Order to Look Forward: Women, Work and Social Values in America
312b Role of Women in Ireland under the New English Order

OREGON

342o Equal Employment Opportunities in Oregon

ORGANIZATION

see also individual organizations

6a Organization Woman: Then and Now
14b Women and the Structure of Organizations: Explorations in Theory and Behavior
67f Sex Differences in the Organization of Perception and Cognition
106e Women's Studies: Its Origin, Organization, and Prospects
138e National Organization and the Women's Movement in the Late 19th Century
140e Female Employment and Family Organization in West Africa
141j Role of Women in the Organization of the Men's Garment Industry, Chicago, 1910
174d Impact of Organizational Structure, Technology, and Professionalism on the Policy of Affirmative Action
175mm Feminists: A Political Organization to Annihilate Sex Roles
204e Evidence for Sex-Related Differences in Cerebral Organization
230i Engels Revisited: Women, the Organization of Production, and Private Property

249k Engels Revisited: Women, the Organization of Production, and Private Property
260y Role of Women in the Political Organization of African Societies
264r Trust, Loyalty, and the Place of Women in the Informal Organization of Work
264cc Women's Liberation Movement: Its Origins, Organizations, Activities, and Ideas
269k Community Organizations and Child-care Arrangements
281q Shaping of the Kaum Ibu (Women's Section) of the United Maylays National Organization
285c Economic Organization and the Position of Women Among the Iroquois
293k Women as Co-Managers: The Family as a General Model of Human Social Organization
295i Women's Organization: Learning from Yesterday
311b Woman in the Labor Organization
314aa Differential Recruitment and Control: The Sex Structuring of Organizations
314bb Women and the Informal Organization
314dd Women and Success in Organizations
316f Role and Status of Women in the Daley Organization
338c Role of Women in the Political Organization of African Societies
344g W.E.A.L.: The Growth of a Feminist Organization
344h New Approaches to Collective Power: Four Working Women's Organizations
350d Women's Organizations in Madras City, India
371f Husbands at Home: Organization of the Husband's Household Day

ORGANIZING

6e Women in Organized Religion
41g Organizing the Unorganizable: Three Jewish Women and Their Union
93e Jennie Higginses of the "New South in the West": A Regional Survey of Socialist Activities, Agitators, and Organizers, 1901-1917
139k Women's Peace Party Organized
139v N.O.W. Organized
334o From Aide to Organizer: The Oral History of Lillian Roberts
342bb Women's Role in Organized Labor
344i Organizing for Political Power: The National Women's Political Caucus
360e Organized Women's Benevolence in Early Nineteenth-Century America

ORGANS

254l Organs and Orgasms

ORGASM

see also VAGINAL ORGASM

9pp Understanding Orgasm
76m Sleep Orgasm in Women
76n Psychic Representation and Female Orgasm
132s Understanding Orgasm
155g Differentiation of Male and Female Orgasm: An Experimental Study
169k Orgasm in the Female
186d Politics of Orgasm
254l Organs and Orgasms

296k Psychologic and Sociologic Factors of Orgasm

ORIENTATION

61d Individual Factors Related to Career Orientation in Women
61f Sex Role Stereotypes and the Career Versus Homemaking Orientations of Women
67e Intelligence, Occupational Status and Achievement Orientation
166mm Career and Family Orientations of Husbands and Wives in Relation to Marital Happiness
171f Homosexual Orientation in Women and Men: A Hormonal Basis?
176p Career and Family Orientations of Husbands and Wives in Relation to Marital Happiness
219b Problem of Orientation in Sex-Language Research
266f Socialization of Achievement Orientation in Females
266g Relationship Between Role Orientation and Achievement Motivation in College Women
267o Implied Demand Character of the Wife's Future and Role Innovation: Patterns of Achievement Orientation Among College Women
267x Life Patterns and Self-Esteem in Gifted Family Oriented and Career Committed Women
278k Female Powerlessness: The Altruistic Other Orientation

ORIGIN

39c Origins of the Women's Liberation Movement
89t Origin of the Family, Private Property, and the State
106e Women's Studies: Its Origin, Organization, and Prospects
107i Maternity and the Origin of Political Power
107j Maternity, Paternity, and the Origin of Political Power
107k Paternity and the Origin of Political Power
107l Conventional Origin of Female Virtues
107t Origin of Sexual Differences
107v Origin of the Oppression of Women
116b Civil Code of 1865 and the Origins of the Feminist Movement in Italy
128e Original of Rebecca in "Ivanhoe"
141e Novel Women: Origins of the Feminist Literary Tradition in England and France
149e Possible Biological Origins of Sexual Discrimination
149o Origins of American Feminism
158y Origin of the Family, Private Property, and the State
159z Origin of the Family
162a Origins of Contraception in France
181i Looking Again at Engels' "Origin of the Family, Private Property and the State"
203g Origin of the Family, Private Property and the State
230c Origin of the Family
251i Origins of the Status of Women
252n Origins of the Status of Women
264f Origin of the Family
264cc Women's Liberation Movement: Its Origins, Organizations, Activities, and Ideas
265d Origin of the Family
265cc Women's Liberation Movement: Its Origins, Structures, Impact, and Ideas
268p Origins of Femininity

334m Origins of Legal Restrictions on Planned Parenthood in Nineteenth-Century America

ORNAMENTS

292c Ornaments for the Daughters of Zion

ORTHODOXY

268l Karen Horney's Flight from Orthodoxy

OTTOMAN

325k Turkish Women in the Ottoman Empire: The Classical Age

OURSELVES

110i Why Aren't We Writing About Ourselves?

OUSMANE

222g Awakening of the Self in the Heroines of Ousmane Sembene

OUTCAST

244d Making of an Outcast Group: Prostitutes and Working Women in Nineteenth-Century Plymouth and Southampton

OUTDOOR

156h Sex Differences in the Use of Outdoor Space

OUTER

3d Inner and Outer Space: Reflections on Womanhood
198f Inner and Outer Space: Reflections on Womanhood
253a Inner and Outer Space: Reflections on Womanhood

OUTPUTS

174j Abortion Policy since 1973: Political Cleavage and Its Impact on Policy Outputs

OUTSIDER

254d Woman as Outsider

OUTSKIRTS

95j On the Outskirts of the City

OVEN

175ss Woman's Place is in the Oven

OVERLAND TRAIL

360m Women and Their Families on the Overland Trail, 1842-1867

OVERLORDS

53i Harems and Overlords: Biosocial Models and the Female

OVERT

196dd Overt and Covert Forms of Discrimination Against Academic Women

OVERTONES

161a Overtones

OXYGEN

286w Maximal Oxygen Uptake of Females

PABST

288i Making Pabst's Lulu

PACHO

131a Marriages of Pacho: A Woman's Life among the Amahuaca

PACIFIC

294n Women's Political Participation in the South Pacific
322l Field Work in the Pacific Islands, 1925-1967

PACT

24ii Notes on a Necessary Pact

PAGAN

96i Why I Am a Pagan

PAGE

105i Women's Page as a Window on the Ruling Class
105l Women's Movement and the Women's Pages: Separate, Unequal and Unspectacular
127i Pages from a Shop Diary

PAIN

73e Natural Childbirth: Pain or Peak Experience
279l A Painful Case

PAINTER

179l C. Painter

223d Marriage, Redundancy or Sin: The Painter's View of Women in the First Twenty-Five Years of Victoria's Reign
247l Picasso's Suite 347, or Painting as an Act of Love
375e My Grandmother Who Painted

PAIR

144i I Lost a Pair of Gloves Yesterday

PAKISTAN

309j Asian Women in Britain: Strategies of Adjustment of Indian and Pakistani Migrants
324b Pakistan
325u Status of Women and Property on a Baluchistan Oasis in Pakistan

PALACE

119d The Haunted Palace
236c Women Surviving: Palace Life in Seoul after the Annexation

PAMELIA

128j Pamelia Mann: Texas Frontierswoman

PANCHAKANYA

114e Panchakanya--An Age-old Benediction

PANEL

141ff Women and Art (summary, panel discussion)
246d Myth America: Women in American Literature (panel)

PAPELEROS

122j Brechtian Aesthetics in Chile: Isidora Aguirre's "Los Papeleros"

PAPERS

9aa Woman in the Nineteenth Century and Kindred Papers
51s Prostitution Papers

PAPPENHEIM

117o Bertha Pappenheim: Founder of German-Jewish Feminism

PAPUA

230f Concept of Pollution Among the Kafe of the Papua New Guinea Highlands

PARA-PROFESSIONAL

13gg Para-Professional

PARABLE

375c Parable of the Cave or: In Praise of Watercolors

PARADIGM

116x Pasta or Paradigm: The Place of Italian-American Women in Popular Film
344r Crisis Perspective on Emerging Health Roles: A Paradigm for the Entry of Women into New Occupational Roles

PARADOX

254e Paradox of the Happy Marriage
320l Paradoxes and Dilemmas: Woman as Writer
334h Paradox of "Women's Sphere"
359d Paradox and Success of Elizabeth Cady Stanton
366d Aboriginal Women's Status: A Paradox Resolved

PARALYSIS

107z Existential Paralysis of Women

PARENT

see also FAMILY; MARRIAGE; SEX ROLE; CHILD

2i APPENDIX: Comments on the 1976 Supreme Court Decisions: "Planned Parenthood v. Danforth" and "Bellotti v. Baird"
9ff Birth Control--A Parent's Problem or a Woman's?
22m Parents' Views on Sex of Newborns
37c Parental Role Division and the Child's Personality Development
61c Parental Influences on Women's Career Development
76l Parental Mislabeling of Female Genitals as a Determinant of Penis Envy and Learning Inhibitions in Women
140z Perception of Parents by London Five-Year-Olds
156i Non-Sexist Parenting at Home and at School
156j Problems and Priorities of Poor, Culturally Different Parents
156k Fathers are Parents Too
173j Parents' Views on Sex of Newborns
199i Sex of Parent x Sex of Child: Socioemotional Development
200c Process of Learning Parental and Sex-Role Identification
243a Prejudice of Parents
250n Parents' Differential Reactions to Sons and Daughters
250o Developmental Study of the Effects of Sex of the Dominant Parent on Sex-Role Preference, Identification, and Imitation in Children
250s Parental Education, Sex Differences, and Performance on Cognitive Tasks Among Two-Year-Old Children
269h Parent's Role in Values Education
269i Parenting and Family Life Styles
272m Working and Parenting: The Male and Father Role
272n Transition from Parenting to Working and Parenting
278w Future of Parenthood: Implications of Declining Fertility
334m Origins of Legal Restrictions on Planned Parenthood in Nineteenth-Century America

PARIS

140g Domestic Servants in London and Paris, 1890 to 1914
349a Women of the Popular Classes in Revolutionary Paris, 1789-1795

PARISH

162c Population of Crulai, a Norman Parish

PARISIAN

70c Interaction and Goal Attainment in Parisian Working Wives' Families

PARK

106l Rosemary Park: Professional Activities

PARLIAMENT

79f Speech to the Parliament
323i Women in Parliament and Government

PAROLE

51ee Recidivism Among Women Parolees: A Long-Term Survey
51ff Parole System: How Women Fare

PARRA

122e Teresa de la Parra, Venezuelan Novelist and Feminist

PART

200m Sexual Behavior in the Human Female: Part II. Biological Data
244j Women of England in a Century of Social Change, 1815-1914: A Select Bibliography, Part II

PART-TIME

288hh "Part-Time Work of a Domestic Slave," or Putting the Screws to Screwball Comedy
328k Part-Time Work

PARTICIPATION

121h Participation of Women in the Independence Movement in Gran Colombia, 1780-1830
141m Effects of Participation in Women's Consciousness-Raising Groups
151c Participation in Public Affairs
152c Physiological Considerations of the Female Participant
163d Working-Class Women's Political Participation: Its Potential in Developed Countries
163f Why Few Women Hold Public Office: Factors Affecting the Participation of Women in Local Politics
163g Societal Punishment and Aspects of Female Political Participation: 1972 National Convention Delegates

163m New Dimension in Political Participation: The Women's Political Caucus
166ff Participation of Women Doctorates in the Labor Force
166gg Factors Influencing Married Women's Actual or Planned Work Participation
194i Participation of Women in the Mexican Labor Force
194k Female Political Participation in Latin America
196o Attitudes Toward Increased Social, Economic, and Political Participation by Women as Reported by Elementary and Secondary Students
196ll Participation in Sports by Girls
202b Participation of Married Women in the Labor Force
202d Discontinuous Labor Force Participation and Its Effect on Women's Market Earnings
227f Women's Participation in Politics
251l Labor Force Participation of Married Women
252y Labor Participation of Married Women: A Study of Labor Supply
281k Migration and Labor Force Participation of Latin American Women: The Domestic Servants in the Cities
281t Women's Labor Force Participation in a Developing Society: The Case of Brazil
286c Self Concept and the Female Participant
286i Motivation and the Female Participant
286m Sociological Considerations of the Female Participant
286o Influence of Birth Order and Sibling Sex on Sports Participation
286t Physiological Considerations of the Female Participant
294h Political Participation of Western European Women
294k Political Participation of Women in Africa South of the Sahara
294n Women's Political Participation in the South Pacific
297s Politics of Theory: Participant Observation in the U.S.
309h Family Status and Female Work Participation
317b Celibes, Mothers, and Church Cockroaches: Religious Participation of Women in a Mexican Village
328h Lifetime Participation in the Labor Force and Unemployment among Mature Women
329c Female Political Participation in Latin America
333c What Psychological Research on the Labor Force Participation of Women is Needed?
352j Participation of Women in the Labour Force of Latin America: Fertility and Other Factors
354j Women's Labor Force Participation and the Residential Mobility of Families
371d Racial Differences in Female Labor-Force Participation: Trends and Implications for the Future

PARTISAN

140u Climbing the Political Ladder: The Aspirations and Expectations of Partisan Elites
352f Social Security and Women: A Partisan View

PARTNERS

59g Search for a Partnership Role: Women in Labor Unions Today
200o Sex Differences in Dating Aspirations and Satisfaction with Computer-Selected Partners

218e Unequal Partners in an Uneasy Alliance: Women and the Working Class in Imperial Germany
238i Toward Partnership in the Church
331d Partnership Marriage: Legal Reforms Needed

PARTY

9m Demand for Party Recognition
93b Women in the Party Bureaucracy: Subservient Functionaries
93c May Wood Simons: Party Theorist
97d Women and the Socialist Party, 1901-1914
139k Women's Peace Party Organized
163l Women as Politicians: The Social Background, Personality, and Political Careers of Female Party Leaders
183d American Peace Party: New Departures and Old Arguments
218f Marxist Ambivalence Toward Women: Between Socialism and Feminism in the Italian Socialist Party
316d Women's Attitudes Toward Women in Politics: A Survey of Urban Registered Voters and Party Committeewomen
323g Women in the Labour Party
344o Republican Women and the Future of the Republican Party

PASSAGE

20i Matrescence, Becoming a Mother, a 'New-Old' 'Rite de Passage'
212d "Madame de": A Musical Passage

PASSION

128r Poetess of Passion
361n Katherine Mansfield's "Passion for Technique"

PASSIVITY

71c Passive Female and Social Change: A Cross-Cultural Comparison of Women's Magazine Fiction
169h Passivity, Masochism and Femininity
268o Passivity, Masochism and Femininity

PAST

8ff Preserving the Past for the Future
11a Out of the Past and Present Controversies: Challenges for the Future
18d Father-Daughter Relationship: Past, Present, and Future
131h Women in China: Past and Present
144c Breakfast Past Noon
191a Women's Health Movement: Past Roots
263g Christian Past: Does It Hold a Future for Women?
289d Tanzanian Women Confront the Past and the Future
318a Society and the Sexes in the Russian Past
354b Data on Women Workers, Past, Present, and Future
358i Past Olympic Reflections

PASTA

116x Pasta or Paradigm: The Place of Italian-American Women in Popular Film

PASTORALISTS

325q Women among Qashqa'i Nomadic Pastoralists in Iran
338b Position of Women in a Pastoral Society (Fulani WoDaaBe, Nomads of the Niger)

PATERNITY

107j Maternity, Paternity, and the Origin of Political Power
107k Paternity and the Origin of Political Power

PATH

33s A Worn Path

PATHOLOGICAL

176tt Women's Lib--Rational? Or Socially Pathological?

PATHOS

15f Women without Pathos

PATIENT

14c Women and Medical Sociology: Invisible Professionals and Ubiquitous Patients
77x Patient and Patriarch: Women in the Psychotherapeutic Relationship
211a Woman Patient
211n Medical Gynecology: Problems and Patients
211s "Difficult" Patient: Observations on the Staff-Patient Interaction
250i Women as Psychiatric and Psychotherapeutic Patients
254q Patient and Patriarch: Women in the Psychotherapeutic Relationship
330d Psychotherapist and the Female Patient: Perceptions, Misperceptions and Change
330l Anna O.--Patient or Therapist? An Eidetic View
348c Doctors and Their Patients: The Social Control of Women in General Practice

PATRIARCHY

21m Power, Patriarchy, and "Political Primitives"
35a Developing a Theory of Capitalist Patriarchy and Socialist Feminism
35b Relations of Capitalist Patriarchy
35j Capitalism, Patriarchy, and Job Segregation by Sex
77x Patient and Patriarch: Women in the Psychotherapeutic Relationship
84b Patriarchy and Relations of Production
84c Structures of Patriarchy and Capital in the Family
89q Inevitability of Patriarchy
112v The Patriarch
117u Depatriarchalizing in Biblical Interpretation
131d Guatemalan Women: Life under Two Types of Patriarchy
163e Case Study in Patriarchal Politics: Women on Welfare
203t Inevitability of Patriarchy

251d Capitalism, Patriarchy, and Job Segregation by Sex
254q Patient and Patriarch: Women in the Psychotherapeutic Relationship
278d Sexism, Patriarchy and Feminism
283n Patriarchy and Charismatic Community in "Paul"
288ll Documenting the Patriarchy: "Chinatown"
291j Capitalism, Patriarchy, and Job Segregation by Sex
329a Patriarchal Heritage

PATRIOT

225e City's Achievements: The Patriotic Amazonomachy and Ancient Athens
257i Patriotism and Chastity
257v John Hay, Mrs. Catt and Patriotism
349j Patriot Mothers in the Post-Risorgimento: Women After the Italian Revolution

PATRISTIC

337c Ascetic Women in the Late Patristic Age

PATRON

185f Woman as Artist and Patron in the Middle Ages and the Renaissance
314i Patrons, Rabbis, Mentors--Whatever You Call Them, Women Need Them Too
325l Women as Patrons of Architecture in Turkey

PATTERN

18q Physical Growth of Adolescent Girls: Patterns and Sequence
20k Affectivity and Instrumentality in Friendship Patterns among American Women
39n Women, Work, and Wedlock: A Note on Female Marital Patterns in the U.S.
51i Changing Patterns
120f Male-Female Intonation Patterns in American English
143g Women's Travel Patterns in a Suburban Development
146g Life Span Behavior Patterns--Class and Ethnic Variations
149a Status of Women in Modern Patterns of Culture
163t Voting Patterns of American Black Women
166jj Career Patterns of Married Couples
170m Changing Patterns of Femininity: Psychoanalytic Implications
171m Body Time and Social Time: Mood Patterns by Menstrual Cycle Phase and Day of Week
176q Implications of Current Changes in Sex Role Patterns
176cc Pre-Industrial Patterns in the Colonial Family in America: A Content Analysis of Colonial Magazines
176rr Sex Differences in Fantasy Patterns
180j Emergence of an American Ethnic Pattern
193b Food for Thought--Patterns of Production and Consumption in Pira-Parana Society
204d Patterns of Cognitive Functioning in Relation to Handedness and Sex-Related Differences
250u Pattern Copying Under Three Conditions of an Expanded Spatial Field
250cc Patterns of Affective Fluctuation in the Menstrual Cycle
252b Family Patterns and Human Rights
252i Changing Patterns of Femininity and Masculinity

258c New Patterns of Relationship: Beginnings of a Moral Revolution
259i Patterns of Nineteenth Century Feminism
267o Implied Demand Character of the Wife's Future and Role Innovation: Patterns of Achievement Orientation Among College Women
267x Life Patterns and Self-Esteem in Gifted Family Oriented and Career Committed Women
274f Negotiating Respect: Patterns of Presentation among Black Women
291i Occupational Segregation and Public Policy: A Comparative Analysis of American and Soviet Patterns
294a Status of Women in Modern Patterns of Culture
297h Lower Economic Sector: Female Mating Patterns in the Dominican Republic
314j New Work Patterns--for Better Use of Womanpower
314cc Informal Interaction Patterns of Professional Women
325c Status and Fertility Patterns of Muslim Women
334b Women's Lives Transformed: Demographic and Family Patterns in America, 1600-1970
339d Patterns

PATTY

215o Patty Bartlett Sessions: More Than a Midwife

PAUL

80d Letter to Marguerite Durand from Paul and Victor Margueritte
283n Patriarchy and Charismatic Community in "Paul"

PAULOWNIA

95m Order of the White Paulownia

PAUPER

111y The Pauper Witch of Grafton
112p The Pauper Witch of Grafton

PAY

see also WAGE; EARNINGS; INCOME

63a Equal Pay in Great Britain
63b Equal Pay in America
63c Equal Pay for Women in Australia and New Zealand
63e Equal Pay in Canada: History, Progress and Problems
63f Equal Pay Question in Japan
89e Measuring Masculinity by the Size of a Paycheck
89ii Women and Pay for Housework
146e Low Pay-Low Status
298i Payday
318j Equal Pay for Equal Work?
333d More Useful Modes of Research on Discrimination in Employment and Pay
352i Women's Wages in Japan and the Question of Equal Pay

PDKS

13ff Women and the PDKs

PEACE

139k Women's Peace Party Organized
139q Peace Ladies
183d American Peace Party: New Departures and Old Arguments
183e Gender Imagery and Issues of War and Peace: The Case of the Draft Resistance Movement of the 1960's
183f Feminist Politics and Peace
183g Role of Women in Underdeveloped Countries: Some Sociological Issues Concerning Conflict and Peace
183i Bibliography: Role of Women in Conflict and Peace
349k American Women in the Peace and Preparedness Movements in World War I

PEACOCK

96x Peacock's Tale
226d Peacock's Tail

PEAK

73e Natural Childbirth: Pain or Peak Experience

PEAL

29b The Coming of Maureen Peal

PEARLS

256d No More Sapphires or Black Pearls: Self-definition is Where It Starts

PEASANT

140f From Peasants to Proletarians: Black Women in the Cauca Valley, Colombia
293i Dilemma of Peasant Women: A View from a Village in Yucatan
297g Marital Status and Sexual Identity: The Position of Women in a Mexican Peasant Society

PECUNIARY

260g Pecuniary Power

PEDAGOGICAL

282r Pedagogical Arguments for Preferential Hiring and Tenuring of Women Teachers in the University

PEDESTAL

19e Pedestal and the Stake: Courtly Love and Witchcraft
292a Up From the Pedestal

PEERS

10k A Jury of Her Peers
112gg A Jury of Her Peers
156f Teachers, Peers, and Play Preferences: An Environmental Approach to Sex Typing in the Preschool

PENALTY

94e Race, Rape, and the Death Penalty

PENCIL

79p Nature's Pictures, Drawn by Fancies Pencil to the Life

PENELOPE

129g Penelope, Molly, Narcissus, and Susan

PENFIELD

372k Life of Sarah Penfield, Rural Ohio Grandmother: Tradition Maintained, Tradition Threatened

PENINSULAR

80h Three Peninsular Novelists Comment on the Spanish Woman

PENIS

76i Penis Envy: From Childhood Wish to Developmental Metaphor
76l Parental Mislabeling of Female Genitals as a Determinant of Penis Envy and Learning Inhibitions in Women
78e Penis Envy in Women
89n Socialized Penis
169o "Penis Envy" in Women
170d "Penis Envy" in Women
170n Survey and Reevaluation of the Concept of Penis Envy

PENNSYLVANIA

334f Equality or Submersion? Feme (sic) Couvert Status in Early Pennsylvania

PENNY

244b Forgotten Woman of the Period: Penny Weekly Family Magazines of the 1840's and 1850's

PENROSE

215q Dr. Romania Pratt Penrose: To Brave the World

PENSIONS

352g Women's Rights and Widows' Pensions

PENTIMENTO

359j Metaphysics of Matrilinearism in Women's Autobiography: Studies of Mead's "Blackberry Winter," Hellman's "Pentimento," Angelou's "I Know Why the Caged Bird Sings," and Kingston's "The Woman Warrior"

PEOPLE

8x Pocket Legal Guide for Gay People
8hh Power to Gay People: A Los Angeles Experiment in Community Action
70i Historical Changes in How People Spend Their Time
130e Report of the Trial: The People versus Dr. Horatio N. Loomis, for Libel
141k Dynamics of Successful People
340e The Wind People
349e Institutional Changes for Women of the People During the French Revolution

PEOPLE'S REPUBLIC OF CHINA

see also CHINA

297u Women's Movement in the People's Republic of China
364k Women of the People's Republic of China

PERCEPTION

see also SELF PERCEPTION

39p Performance, Rewards, and Perceptions of Sex Discrimination among Male and Female Faculty
41e Italian Women and Work: Experience and Perception
67f Sex Differences in the Organization of Perception and Cognition
140z Perception of Parents by London Five-Year-Olds
155l Mothers and Daughters: Perceived and Real Differences in Sexual Values
166d Male and Female: Differing Perceptions of the Teaching Experience
196h Teachers' Perceptions of Ideal Male and Female Students: Male Chauvinism in the Schools
196r Female-Role Perception as a Factor in Counseling
200e Differences in Perception of the Opposite Sex by Males and Females
219f Sex, Color and Money: Who's Perceiving What? Or Men and Women: Where Did All the Differences Go (To)?
240g Marriage Perceived: English Literature, 1873-1941
250e Male-Female Perception of the Female Sex Role in the United States
250t Sex Differences in Space Perception and Aspects of Intellectual Functioning
266cc When Women Are More Deserving Than Men: Equity, Attribution, And Perceived Sex Differences
330d Psychotherapist and the Female Patient: Perceptions, Misperceptions and Change

PERFORMANCE

41 Representation, Performance and Status of Women on the Faculty at the Urbana-Champaign Campus of the University of Illinois

39p Performance, Rewards, and Perceptions of Sex Discrimination among Male and Female Faculty
75b Physical Attractiveness of Female Offenders: Effects on Institutional Performance
114u Performing Arts
166vv Women Lawyers and Their Profession: Inconsistency of Social Controls and Their Consequences for Professional Performance
176b Sex Differences in the Incidence of Neonatal Abnormalities and Abnormal Performance in Early Childhood
176ee Sex Differentiation in Role Expectations and Performance
196w Performance of Women Principals: A Review of Behavioral and Attitudinal Studies
204b Genetic Influences on Sex-Related Differences in Intellectual Performance: Theoretical and Methodological Issues
250b Evaluation of the Performance of Women as a Function of Their Sex, Achievement, and Personal History
250s Parental Education, Sex Differences, and Performance on Cognitive Tasks Among Two-Year-Old Children
250v Effects of Sex of Examiner and Subject on Children's Quantitative Test Performance
286e Body Image and Performance
286l Needed Approaches for a Better Understanding of Behavior and Performance

PERIL

110t Value and Peril for Women of Reading Women Writers

PERKINS

96c Female Prisoner: A Narrative of the Life and Singular Adventures of Josephine Amelia Perkins
96d Demon in Female Apparel: Narrative of Josephine Amelia Perkins, the Notorious Female Horse Thief...
151l Charlotte Perkins Gilman on the Theory and Practice of Feminism
153v Living of Charlotte Perkins Gilman
334i Private Woman, Public Woman: The Contradictions of Charlotte Perkins Gilman

PERMANENT

279q Permanent Wave

PERMISSIVENESS

155i Premarital Sexual Permissiveness Among Negroes and Whites

PERON

281r Case of Eva Peron

PERSECUTION

52d Jean Bodin's "De la Demonomanie des Sorciers": The Logic of Persecution

PERSIAN

325i Changing the Concept and Position of Persian Women
325ff Women in Contemporary Persian Folktales

PERSONAL

22j Aborting a Fetus: The Legal Right, The Personal Choice
89tt Capitalism, the Family, and Personal Life
170j Personal Identity and Sexual Identity
250b Evaluation of the Performance of Women as a Function of Their Sex, Achievement, and Personal History
251c Capitalism, the Family, and Personal Life
252k Personal Identity and Sexual Identity
274a Personal Narratives in Women's Rap Groups
304b Women as Personal Dependents

PERSONALITY

22p Sexual Role Identification and Personality Functioning in Girls
22y Personality and Ideology: A Personological Study of Women's Liberation
37c Parental Role Division and the Child's Personality Development
75c Personality Differences Between Male and Female Prison Inmates: Measured by the M.M.P.I.
77y Masochistic Syndrome, Hysterical Personality, and the Illusion of a Healthy Woman
155k Relationship of the Frequency of Masturbation to Several Aspects of Personality and Behavior
163l Women as Politicians: The Social Background, Personality, and Political Careers of Female Party Leaders
176n Women Mathematicians and the Creative Personality
198w Sex and Personality: Studies in Masculinity and Femininity
198x Sex Differences in Personality Characteristics
243e Prejudice Toward Women: Some Personality Correlates
249b Family Structure and Feminine Personality
266c Sexual Role Identification and Personality Functioning in Girls
267b Understanding Women: Implications for Personality Theory and Research
316e Personality Characteristics of Women in American Politics

PERSONOLOGICAL

22y Personality and Ideology: A Personological Study of Women's Liberation

PERSUASION

342ii Persuasion in the Feminist Movement

PERU

71e Women in Latin American Politics: The Case of Peru and Chile
121c Indian Women and White Society: The Case of Sixteenth-Century Peru
225c Whore in Peru: The Splitting of Women into Good and Bad and the Isolation of the Prostitute
294g Women in Public Life in Peru

297i Female Domestic Servant and Social Change: Lima, Peru

PERVERSION

89xx Sexual Perversions
157o Sexual Perversion
157p Inapplicable Concepts and Sexual Perversion
157q Sex and Perversion

PET

24b The Lady With the Pet Dog

PETRARCH

184d Petrarch's Laura: The Convolutions of a Humanistic Mind

PETRIFIED

273i The Petrified Woman

PETRY

47g Women in the Novels of Ann Petry
222s Ann Petry Talks About First Novel

PEWS

256p When The Veils Come Tumbling Down: "And Women Shall Leave Their Comfortable Pews to Give Birth to a New and Inclusive Religious Vision"

PH-D.

176m Woman Ph-D.: A Recent Profile
267v Woman Ph-D.: A Recent Profile

PHALLACY

22k Phallacy of Our Sexual Norm
126d Historical Phallacies: Sexism in American Historical Writing

PHALLUS

176jj Castration Anxiety and Phallus Envy: A Reformulation
283e Phallic Worship: The Ultimate Idolatry
363l Phallic Criticism

PHASE

171m Body Time and Social Time: Mood Patterns by Menstrual Cycle Phase and Day of Week
266v Effect of Contraceptive Pills on Sexual Activity in the Luteal Phase of the Human Menstrual Cycle

PHENOMENOLOGY

85b Phenomenology of Feminist Consciousness
122o Phenomenology of Nothingness in the Poetry of Julia de Burgos
158ii Phenomenology of Feminist Consciousness
263x Why Women Need the Goddess: Phenomenological, Psychological, and Political Reflections

PHILADELPHIA

94q Philadelphia Rape Victim Project
96m My Philadelphia
334e Young Ladies Academy of Philadelphia

PHILANTHROPY

92b Home From Home: Women's Philanthropic Work in the Nineteenth Century
121i Education, Philanthropy, and Feminism: Components of Argentine Womanhood, 1860-1926
262l Woman in Philanthropy--Charity
262m Woman in Philanthropy--Care of the Sick
262n Woman in Philanthropy--Care of the Criminal
262o Woman in Philanthropy--Care of the Indian
262p Woman in Philanthropy--Work of Anti-Slavery Women
262q Woman in Philanthropy--Work of the W.C.T.U.
262r Woman in Philanthropy--Work of the Red Cross Society

PHILIPPINE

131k Women in Philippine Society: More Equal Than Many

PHILOSOPHY

2e Philosophy on Humanity
2g Philosophers on Abortion
85a Political Philosophies of Women's Liberation
98b Mother-Daughter Relationships: Psychodynamics, Politics, and Philosophy
158jj Political Philosophies of Women's Liberation
159cc Woman--A Philosophical Analysis
159ii Woman Question: Philosophy of Liberation and the Liberation of Philosophy
231m Philosopher to His Mother
231n That Women Too Should Study Philosophy
359c Harriet Martineau's Autobiography: The Making of a Female Philosopher

PHOBIAS

170q Phobias after Marriage: Women's Declaration of Dependence
330f Phobic Syndrome in Women: Implications for Treatment

PHOENIX

133e Phoenix in the Ashes

PHONOLOGICAL

219g Phonological Differences in the English of Adolescent Chicanas and Chicanos

PHOTOGRAPHY

105e Imagery and Ideology: The Cover Photographs of Traditional Women's Magazines
247f Manet, "Olympia" and Pornographic Photography
298e Gypsies (Photographs)

PHOTOPLAY

288jj Woman's Place in Photoplay Production

PHYLETIC

266t Phyletic and Idiosyncratic Determinants of Gender Identity

PHYSICAL

18c Growing Up with a Physical Handicap
18q Physical Growth of Adolescent Girls: Patterns and Sequence
21t Women in Physical Education
75b Physical Attractiveness of Female Offenders: Effects on Institutional Performance
286a Dimensions of Physical Activity

PHYSICIAN

see also HEALTH; MEDICINE

42c Lady and Her Physician
86i Reply to Dr. Spock on Child Care
130b Letters to Ladies in Favor of Female Physicians
130e Report of the Trial: The People versus Dr. Horatio N. Loomis, for Libel
166n Female Physician in Public Health: Conflict and Reconciliation of the Sex and Professional Roles
170g Denial of Women's Sexual Pleasure: Discussion of Dr. Thompson's Paper
191o What Doctors Won't Tell You about Menopause
215p Dr. Ellen Brooke Ferguson: Nineteenth-Century Renaissance Woman
215q Dr. Romania Pratt Penrose: To Brave the World
215r Dr. Ellis Reynolds Shipp: Pioneer Utah Physician
215s Dr. Martha Hughes Cannon: Doctor, Wife, Legislator, Exile
215t Dr. Margaret Ann Freece: Entrepreneur of Southern Utah
332d Displaced--The Midwife by the Male Physician
348c Doctors and Their Patients: The Social Control of Women in General Practice

PHYSICS

369f Anomaly of a Woman in Physics

PHYSIOLOGIES

152c Physiological Considerations of the Female Participant
198aa Physiological Development, Cognitive Development, and Socialization Antecedents of Children's Sex-Role Attitudes
211e Physiological Aspects of Pregnancy
247g Corset as Erotic Alchemy: From Rococo Galanterie to Montaut's Physiologies
286t Physiological Considerations of the Female Participant

PICASSO

247l Picasso's Suite 347, or Painting as an Act of Love

PICKLE

277s A Dill Pickle

PICO

52b Witchcraft and Magic in Renaissance Italy: Gianfrancesco Pico and his "Strix"

PICTURE

21b Pictures of Power and Powerlessness
79p Nature's Pictures, Drawn by Fancies Pencil to the Life
144e Mourning Pictures
156p APPENDIX: Non-Sexist Picture Books for Children
208t Sex-Role Socialization in Picture Books for Preschool Children
278f Pope's Portraits of Women: The Tyranny of the Pictorial Eye
281u Talking Pictures: Field Method and Visual Mode

PIE

127h Pie in the Sky
298c Pigeon Pie

PIECE

112i Night Pieces for a Child: The Crib
113g A Piece of News
144a Bits and Pieces
191i Abortion: This Piece Is for Remembrance

PIERRE

52h Pierre de Lancre's "Tableau de l'Inconstance des Mauvais Anges et Demons": The Sabbat Sensationalised

PIETY

214c Anne Bradstreet's Poetry: A Study of Subversive Piety

PIG

362d Up Against the Wall, Male Chauvinist Pig

PIGEON

298c Pigeon Pie

PILATE

102b The Wife of Pilate

PILGRIMAGE

108p Pilgrimage
273c Pilgrimage (selection)

PILL

see also BIRTH CONTROL; CONTRACEPTION

142r The Pill--Radio News 2-24-70
191h Have You Ever Wondered about the Male Pill?
266v Effect of Contraceptive Pills on Sexual Activity in the Luteal Phase of the Human Menstrual Cycle

PILLAR

3h The Three Pillars of Zen
273t Pillar of Salt

PILOT

40f Vouchers for Child Care: The Santa Clara Child Care Pilot Study

PINUP

247k Pinup and Icon

PIONEER

see FRONTIER

PIRA-PARANA

193b Food for Thought--Patterns of Production and Consumption in Pira-Parana Society

PITCH

219k Difference Beyond Inherent Pitch

PITTSBURGH

116r Oral History in Pittsburgh--Women, Ethnicity, and Mental Health: Rationale, Procedure, and Methodology

PIXIE

356l Fixing Pixie Loveless

PIZAN

184e Fifteenth-Century View of Women's Role in Medieval Society: Christine de Pizan's "Livre des Trois Vertus"

PLACE

39u Introducing Students to Women's Place in Society
77l Case Study of a Nonconscious Ideology: Training the Woman to Know Her Place
88g Who Buried H.D.? A Poet, Her Critics, and Her Place in "The Literary Tradition"
115a Nehru and the Place of Women in Indian Society
116x Pasta or Paradigm: The Place of Italian-American Women in Popular Film
143f Women's Place in the New Suburbia
159hh Woman's Place
175ss Woman's Place is in the Oven
186f Training the Woman to Know Her Place: The Power of a Nonconscious Ideology
196l Woman's Place: Children's Sex Stereotyping of Occupations
203w Language and Woman's Place
208c Training the Woman To Know Her Place: The Power of a Nonconscious Ideology
219h Descriptive Study of the Language of Men and Women Born in Maine Around 1900 as It Reflects the Lakoff Hypotheses in "Language and Women's Place"
246f Place of Contemporary Women from a Psychological Perspective
253h Revolution Without Ideology: The Changing Place of Women in America
259l Changing Place of Women in America
264r Trust, Loyalty, and the Place of Women in the Informal Organization of Work
271r Woman's Place Is in the Curriculum
283d Karl Barth's Theology of the Word of God: Or, How to Keep Women Silent and in Their Place
288jj Woman's Place in Photoplay Production
297o Evolutionism and the Place of Women in the U.S., 1855-1900
303i Struggle for Place: Women in Architecture: 1920-1960

PLAIN

369o Plain Truth

PLAINS

96b Journey Across the Plains in 1836: Journal

PLAN

4t Affirmative Action Plans for Eliminating Sex Discrimination in Academe
75j Planning for the Female Offender
140y Family Planning, Decision Making: Attitudes and Intentions of Mothers and Fathers
143l Women in Planning: There's More to Affirmative Action than Gaining Access
266ff Interrelationship of the Status of Women and Family Planning

281c Development Planning for Women
2931 Development Approach to Liberation: Suggestions for Planning
3091 Draft, International Plan of Action
364j Confronting the Sports Establishment: A Plan for Honesty and Sanity
367c Family Planning and Population Policies in the Middle East and North Africa

PLANNING

2i APPENDIX: Comments on the 1976 Supreme Court Decisions: "Planned Parenthood v. Danforth" and "Bellotti v. Baird"
127q Planned Obsolescence: The Middle-Aged Woman
166gg Factors Influencing Married Women's Actual or Planned Work Participation
334m Origins of Legal Restrictions on Planned Parenthood in Nineteenth-Century America

PLANTAGENET

335d Women in Norman and Plantagenet England

PLANTATION

25d Family in the Plantation South

PLASMA

199u Plasma Testosterone Levels and Psychologic Measures in Men Over a 2-Month Period

PLATFORM

252kk Platform on Women's Rights

PLATH

88h "The Blood Jet": The Poetry of Sylvia Plath
175qq Body is the Role: Sylvia Plath
214q Life-Work of Sylvia Plath

PLATO

158g Reply to Plato
282a Anatomy and Destiny: The Role of Biology in Plato's Views of Women

PLAY

see also THEATRE; PLAYWRIGHT; DRAMA; individual playwrights

18i Play of Girls
18m Role Music Plays in Adolescent Development
68f Legal Climate of Shaw's Problem Plays
141bb Hrotsvitha of Gandersheim: The Playable Dramas of a Woman Playwright of the Tenth Century
156d Liberating Toys: You Are What You Play
156f Teachers, Peers, and Play Preferences: An Environmental Approach to Sex Typing in the Preschool

161d Play with a Tiger
176e Play Behavior in the Year-Old Infant: Early Sex Differences
180ff Is Turn-About Fair Play?
200g Sex Differences in the Play Configurations of Preadolescents
254b Two Plays on Love and Marriage
256q Women in Motion: It's Not Who Wins Or Loses, But How Many Play the Game
266z Effects of Live Modelled Sex-Appropriate Play Behavior In a Naturalistic Setting
274b Games Mexican Girls Play

PLAYBOYS

233i Playboys and Bunnies

PLAYGROUND

142i The Playground

PLAYTHING

107u Woman as Dangerous Plaything

PLAYWRIGHT

122i Three Female Playwrights Explore Contemporary Latin American Reality: Myrna Casas, Griselda Gambaro, Luisa Josefina Hernandez
141bb Hrotsvitha of Gandersheim: The Playable Dramas of a Woman Playwright of the Tenth Century

PLEA

157c "Pricks" and "Chicks": A Plea for "Persons"
158c "Pricks" and "Chicks": A Plea for "Persons"
208r Let Them Aspire! A Plea and Proposal for Equality of Opportunity for Males and Females in the Ann Arbor Public Schools

PLEASURE

113t Pleasure
170g Denial of Women's Sexual Pleasure: Discussion of Dr. Thompson's Paper
288rr Visual Pleasure and Narrative Cinema

PLOT

254z Is Women's Liberation a Lesbian Plot?

PLUM

10l Plum Bun "Home"
10m Plum Bun "Market"
10n Plum Bun "Plum Bun"

PLUMB

95t Mrs. Plumb

PLURALISM

57a Challenge of the "New Pluralism"

PLUS

166b Plus Ca Change...? The Sexual Structure of Occupations Over Time

PLYMOUTH

42l Prostitution and the Poor in Plymouth and Southampton Under the Contagious Diseases Act
103c The Plymouth Express
244d Making of an Outcast Group: Prostitutes and Working Women in Nineteenth-Century Plymouth and Southampton

POCKET

8x Pocket Legal Guide for Gay People

POCKETBOOK

373f The Pocketbook Game

POET

see also individual poets

88g Who Buried H.D.? A Poet, Her Critics, and Her Place in "The Literary Tradition"
88k Feminist Poet: Alta and Adrienne Rich
96z Poet Out of Pioneer
122a Random Survey of the Ratio of Female Poets to Male in Anthologies: Less-Than-Tokenism as a Mexican Tradition
122n Two Poets of America: Juana de Asbaje and Sara de Ibanez
128r Poetess of Passion
214a Gender, Creativity, and the Woman Poet
214d Anne Finch, Countess of Winchilsea: An Augustan Woman Poet
214i Emily Dickinson and the Deerslayer: The Dilemma of the Woman Poet in America
214l Afro-American Women Poets: A Bio-Critical Survey
214s Common Language: The American Woman Poet
222i Black Women Poets from Wheatley to Walker
226f Poet Out of Pioneer
357g Poetry and Conscience: Russian Women Poets of the Twentieth Century
375o Education of a Poet

POETRY

7f Images of Black Women in Afro-American Poetry
79r Poems
88e Imperious Muse: Some Observations on Women, Nature and the Poetic Tradition
88h "The Blood Jet": The Poetry of Sylvia Plath
88j Moon and Contemporary Women's Poetry
88l Poetry of Cynthia MacDonald
97e Poems and Prose

98h Poetry is Not a Luxury
108k Two poems
108z Letter and poem
116z Selected Poems
122o Phenomenology of Nothingness in the Poetry of Julia de Burgos
214c Anne Bradstreet's Poetry: A Study of Subversive Piety
214k Art of Silence and the Forms of Women's Poetry
214p Gwendolyn the Terrible: Propositions on Eleven Poems
214r Poetry and Salvation in the Career of Anne Sexton
215u Sarah Elizabeth Carmichael: Poetic Genius of Pioneer Utah
222d Images of Black Women in Modern African Poetry
233g Woman in the Elizabethan Sonnet: Poems
233w Three Poems
278z Poetry of Self-Definition
355a Poems
355b Poems
355d Poems
355f Poems
355i Poems
357a Towards a New Feminist Poetics
357g Poetry and Conscience: Russian Women Poets of the Twentieth Century
361i Art of Silence and the Forms of Women's Poetry
363e Poems

POLAND

54d Marriage and Marriage Dissolution and the Changing Status of Women: The Case of Poland
70e Employment of Married Women and the Changing Sex Roles in Poland

POLEMICAL

90d Virginia Woolf's Criticism: A Polemical Preface

POLICE

94k Comparative Study of Forcible Rape Offenses Known to the Police in Boston and Los Angeles
94l Rape in New York City: A Study of Material in the Police Files and Its Meaning

POLICY

2a Abortion and Public Policy in the U.S.
40a Economic and Policy Issues of Child Care
40b Public Policy Toward Child Care in America: A Historical Perspective
45g Policy Issues on Day Care: The Special Needs of Black Working Women
59a How Much Is a Woman Worth? The American Public Policy
91l Overview and Policy Implications
106g University Behavior and Policies: Where Are the Women and Why?
106j Responsibility and Public Policy: Is It a Moral Question?
135g Next Five Years: Projections and Policy Implications
174b Impact of Collective Bargaining on Minorities in the Public Sector: Some Policy Implications
174d Impact of Organizational Structure, Technology, and Professionalism on the Policy of Affirmative Action

174e Affirmative Action: Constraints and Policy Impact
174g Minorities and Policy Problems: An Overview Seen by the U.S. Commission on Civil Rights
174h Sex and the Burger Court: Recent Judicial Policy Making toward Women
174j Abortion Policy since 1973: Political Cleavage and Its Impact on Policy Outputs
174k Combatting Dual Discrimination: The Impact of Civil Rights Policies on the Income Status of Black Women
174m Policy Impacts on Hispanics and Women: A State Case Study
174n Women and Public Policy: A Comparative Analysis
174o Political Power and Policy Benefits: Voting Rights and Welfare Policy in Mississippi
180k Erosion of Legal Principles in the Creation of Legal Policies
180bb Preferential Policies in Hiring and Admissions: A Jurisprudential Approach
196z Sex Discrimination as Public Policy: The Case of Maternity-Leave Policies for Teachers
269f Public Policy and Childbearing
291i Occupational Segregation and Public Policy: A Comparative Analysis of American and Soviet Patterns
318e Sexual Equality in Soviet Policy: A Developmental Perspective
318l Educational Policies and Attainment
318p Women and Women's Issues in Soviet Policy Debates
326d Female Status: A New Population Policy
326g Government Policy and the Legal Status of Women
328g Underemployment of Women: Policy Implications for a Full Employment Economy
331h Public Policy and the Family: A New Strategy for Women as Wives and Mothers
341j Make Policy, Not Coffee
351g Highlights and Policy Implications
354r Women and Work: Policy Implications and Prospects for the Future
364n Think About Our Government: Now Think About Sweden's Policy
367c Family Planning and Population Policies in the Middle East and North Africa

POLITICAL

4p Political Action by Academic Women
14a Nonsexist Perspective on Social and Political Change
20n Women and Domestic Power: Political and Economic Strategies in Domestic Groups
20q Bundu: Political Implications of Female Solidarity in a Secret Society
21m Power, Patriarchy, and "Political Primitives"
43f Effects of Class and Sex on Political Life in Northern India
55e Political Economy of Domestic Labour in Capitalist Society
85a Political Philosophies of Women's Liberation
86c Women and Political Power
89ee Political Economy of Women's Liberation
97j Political Economy of Women's Liberation
107i Maternity and the Origin of Political Power
107j Maternity, Paternity, and the Origin of Political Power
107k Paternity and the Origin of Political Power
127p Political Economy of Women's Liberation
139y Political Economy of Women's Liberation

140s Rise of the Women's Movement: A Case Study in Political Development
140u Climbing the Political Ladder: The Aspirations and Expectations of Partisan Elites
146f Political Importance of the Older Woman
158jj Political Philosophies of Women's Liberation
163c Sex Differences in Black Political Beliefs and Behavior
163d Working-Class Women's Political Participation: Its Potential in Developed Countries
163g Societal Punishment and Aspects of Female Political Participation: 1972 National Convention Delegates
163i Comparative Study of Male-Female Political Attitudes at Citizen and Elite Levels
163l Women as Politicians: The Social Background, Personality, and Political Careers of Female Party Leaders
163m New Dimension in Political Participation: The Women's Political Caucus
163n Women as Voters: Their Maturation as Political Persons in American Society
163s Traditional Political Animals? A Loud No
174j Abortion Policy since 1973: Political Cleavage and Its Impact on Policy Outputs
174o Political Power and Policy Benefits: Voting Rights and Welfare Policy in Mississippi
174q Abortion in Israel: Social Demands and Political Responses
175mm Feminists: A Political Organization to Annihilate Sex Roles
180p Racial Preferences in Higher Education: Political Responsibility and the Judicial Role
186l Political Economy of Women's Liberation
190d Women: The New Political Class
194k Female Political Participation in Latin America
194l Selective Omission and Theoretical Distortion in Studying the Political Activity of Women in Brazil
196n Sex-Typing and Politicization in Children's Attitudes
196o Attitudes Toward Increased Social, Economic, and Political Participation by Women as Reported by Elementary and Secondary Students
213g Iyalode in the Traditional Yoruba Political System
230h Traffic in Women: Notes on the "Political Economy" of Sex
232k First Essay on the Political Rights of Women
233z Political and Civil Status of Women as of January 1, 1969
251o Political Economy of Women's Liberation
252p Political Economy of Women's Liberation
260y Role of Women in the Political Organization of African Societies
263x Why Women Need the Goddess: Phenomenological, Psychological, and Political Reflections
264t American Women and the Political Process
278t Influential Alliances: Cincinnati Women in the Political Arena, 1920-1945
285h Colonialism and the Lost Political Institutions of Igbo Women
294h Political Participation of Western European Women
294i Political Activity of Women in Eastern Europe
294k Political Participation of Women in Africa South of the Sahara
294l Political Role of Southeast Asian Women
294n Women's Political Participation in the South Pacific
295a Political Economy of Ontario Women in the Nineteenth Century
302b Dual-Sex Political System in Operation: Igbo Women and Community Politics in Midwestern Nigeria

306k Women in the Political System
316b Apolitical Woman: Femininity and Sex-Stereotyping in Girls
316c Women and Political Socialization: Considerations of the Impact of Motherhood
316i Contemporary Feminism, Consciousness-Raising, and Changing Views of the Political
316j Women's and Men's Liberation Groups: Political Power Within the System and Outside the System
316p Changing the Political Role of Women: A Costa Rican Case Study
316q Memsahib, Militante, Femme Libre: Political and Apolitical Styles of Modern African Women
318o Women in Political Roles
326f Women as Voters: Their Maturation as Political Persons in American Society
327d Nonacademic Professional Political Scientists
329c Female Political Participation in Latin America
329j Political Change for the American Woman
329p Female Political Elites in Mexico: 1974
335h Discovery of Women in Eighteenth-Century English Political Life
338c Role of Women in the Political Organization of African Societies
342n Political Economy of Women's Oppression
344c Notes from a Political Career
344f League of Women Voters and Political Power
344i Organizing for Political Power: The National Women's Political Caucus
344m Congressional Ambitions of Female Political Elites
344n Women as Voluntary Political Activists
349g Women in the Chinese Communist Revolution: The Question of Political Equality

POLITICIAN

163l Women as Politicians: The Social Background, Personality, and Political Careers of Female Party Leaders
163q Wife and Politician: Role Strain Among Women in Public Office
307b Woman as Politician in China of the 1920s

POLITICS

see also SEXUAL POLITICS; GOVERNMENT; POWER; branches of government

11h Woman: The New Figure in American Politics
17j War and Roses: The Politics of "Mrs. Dalloway"
20t American Women in Politics: Culture, Structure, and Ideology
22w Politics of Sexual Stereotypes
71e Women in Latin American Politics: The Case of Peru and Chile
74p Politics of Day Care
89f Politics of Housework
93f Politics of Mutual Frustration: Socialists and Suffragists in New York and Wisconsin
98b Mother-Daughter Relationships: Psychodynamics, Politics, and Philosophy
98r Women in Power and Politics
99m Politics of Hysteria: The Case of the Wandering Womb
114v Women in Politics
126l Politics of Cultural Liberation: Male-Female Relations in Algeria

126q Beyond "Kinder, Kuche, Kirche": Weimar Women in Politics and Work
127l Politics of Housework
132gg Our Politics Begin with Our Feelings
139p Politics of Housework
141z Changing Status and Role of Women in Politics
156b Preschool and the Politics of Sexism
159h Politics
163a Sex, Socialization, and Politics
163e Case Study in Patriarchal Politics: Women on Welfare
163f Why Few Women Hold Public Office: Factors Affecting the Participation of Women in Local Politics
163o Women in Iowa Legislative Politics
163r Politics of Sexual Stereotypes
163u Black Women in Electoral Politics
175nn Politics of the Ego: A Manifesto for New York Radical Feminists
181c Women and Nineteenth-Century Radical Politics: A Lost Dimension
183f Feminist Politics and Peace
186d Politics of Orgasm
191m Politics of Breast Cancer
191t Vaginal Politics
194m Politics and Feminism in the Dominican Republic: 1931-45 and 1966-74
203b Politics, Book I
209c Sex and Politics
212c Image of Woman as Image: The Optical Politics of Dames
222j Politics of Intimacy
227f Women's Participation in Politics
249d Women in Politics
252mm Politics of Housework
256r When Women in Politics Are Old Hat
259o Politics of Sex
263k Theology in the Politics of Appalachian Women
265w Women in American Politics
270j Desert Politics: Choices in the "Marriage Market"
294f Women and Politics in the U.S. and Canada
294m Women and Politics in Japan
297s Politics of Theory: Participant Observation in the U.S.
302b Dual-Sex Political System in Operation: Igbo Women and Community Politics in Midwestern Nigeria
303c Catharine Beecher and the Politics of Housework
312h Women in Irish National and Local Politics, 1922-77
316d Women's Attitudes Toward Women in Politics: A Survey of Urban Registered Voters and Party Committeewomen
316e Personality Characteristics of Women in American Politics
316r Politics of Cultural Liberation
323a Women in Labour Politics
325n Feminism and National Politics in Egypt
329g Politics of Sex: West Germany
342cc Politics of the Equal Rights Amendment
343b Women and Politics
362h Men, Women--and Politics
362i Politics and War

POLLUTION

140q Pollution and Power

230f Concept of Pollution Among the Kafe of the Papua New Guinea Highlands
308h Power and Pollution of Chinese Women

POLYGAMY

159o Of Polygamy and Divorce

POLYGYNY

193f Gerontology, Polygyny and Scarce Resources

PONIATOWSKA

122f Elena Poniatowska's "Hasta no Verte, Jesus Mio"

POOL

127g Drowning in the Steno Pool

POOR

see POVERTY

POPCORN

212a Popcorn Venus or How the Movies Have Made Women Smaller Than Life

POPE

278f Pope's Portraits of Women: The Tyranny of the Pictorial Eye

POPULAR

73k Fear of Success: Popular, but Unproven
80l Inculcating a Slave Mentality: Women in German Popular Fiction of the Early Twentieth Century
110b Popular Literature as Social Reinforcement: The Case of "Charlotte Temple"
116x Pasta or Paradigm: The Place of Italian-American Women in Popular Film
149j Declining Status of Women: Popular Myths and the Failure of Functionalist Thought
185b Popular Image of Brunhilde
246m Images of Women and Men in American Popular Magazines
252v Problems of Married Working Women as Presented by Three Popular Working Women's Magazines
265r Images of American Woman in Popular Songs
349a Women of the Popular Classes in Revolutionary Paris, 1789-1795

POPULATION

54a Population and the Status of Women: Results of the Bucharest and Mexico Conferences
162b Christianity and Population
162c Population of Crulai, a Norman Parish

264a Woman's Biology--Mankind's Destiny: The Population Explosion and Women's Changing Roles
265a Woman's Biology--Mankind's Destiny: The Population Explosion and Women's Changing Roles
266ee Status of Women--Population--Development
326d Female Status: A New Population Policy
367c Family Planning and Population Policies in the Middle East and North Africa

POPULISTS

19o Women as Revolutionaries: The Case of the Russian Populists

PORNOGRAPHY

140nn Victorian Pornography and Attitudes Reflected Toward Women
158s Pornography and Respect for Women
247c Henry Fuseli's "Nightmare": Eroticism or Pornography?
247f Manet, "Olympia" and Pornographic Photography
300k Pornography for Women

PORTER

17o Winning: Katherine Anne Porter's Women
192d Katherine Anne Porter

PORTFOLIO

303p Current Portfolio of Projects and Ideas

PORTNOY

117h Portnoy's Mother's Complaint: Depression in Middle-Aged Women

PORTO ALEGRE

372f Spirit Mediums in Umbanda Evangelizada of Porto Alegre, Brazil: Dimensions of Power and Authority

PORTRAIT

13hh Portrait of a Teacher
18n Portrait of a Female on Television: Some Possible Effects on Children
68k Whatever Happened to Shaw's Mother-Genius Portrait?
166uu Vanguard Artist: Portrait and Self-Portrait
212g Bergman's Portrait of Women: Sexism or Subjective Metaphor?
212v Family Portraits: Filmmakers Explore Their Roots
278f Pope's Portraits of Women: The Tyranny of the Pictorial Eye
308d Women of Hai-shan: A Demographic Portrait

PORTRAYAL

208cc Feminists Look at the 100 Books: The Portrayal of Women in Children's Books on Puerto Rican Themes
240a Portrayal of Women by Chaucer and His Age

240d Portrayal of Women in Restoration and Eighteenth-century English Literature
240i Portrayal of Women in American Literature, 1790-1870

POSE

214g Christina Rossetti: The Inward Pose

POSITION

37d Positions of Men and Women in the Labour Market
45d Counseling Implications of Black Women's Market Position, Aspirations and Expectancies
77hh APPENDIX: Chart of Basic Feminist Positions
114f Position of Women in Indian Society
123e Lesbians and the Class Position of Women
213i Impact of Modernization on Women's Position in the Family in Ghana
285c Economic Organization and the Position of Women Among the Iroquois
297g Marital Status and Sexual Identity: The Position of Women in a Mexican Peasant Society
317c Hats as a Symbol of Women's Position in Three Evangelical Churches in Edinburgh, Scotland
325i Changing the Concept and Position of Persian Women
325j Legal and Social Positions of Iranian Women
335c Land Charters and the Legal Position of Anglo-Saxon Women
338b Position of Women in a Pastoral Society (Fulani WoDaaBe, Nomads of the Niger)

POSITIVE

39j Positive Effects of the Multiple Negative: Explaining the Success of Black Professional Women
88x Promises Fulfilled: Positive Images of Women in Twentieth-Century Autobiography
266n Positive Effects of the Multiple Negative: Explaining the Success of Black Professional Women
275g Women and the Aesthetic of the Positive Hero in the G.D.R.

POSSESSION

285f Bargaining from Weakness: Spirit Possession on the South Kenya Coast
298a Management and Possession
317h Epidemiology of Spirit Possession among the Luvale of Zambia
350g Women's Spirit Possession and Urban Adaptation

POST

314g Women in Work Force Post Better Records for Stability in Jobs

POST-RISORGIMENTO

349j Patriot Mothers in the Post-Risorgimento: Women After the Italian Revolution

POSTPARTUM

171i Maternal Stress in the Postpartum Period
173aa Maternal Attachment: Importance of the First Post-Partum Days
176pp Postpartum Psychiatric Syndromes
211h C.O.P.E. Story: A Service to Pregnant and Postpartum Women
250ff Postpartum Psychiatric Syndromes

POSTSCRIPT

329y Conference Postscript

POSTWAR

140m Postwar Attitudes Toward Women and Work

POTENTIAL

8h Bi-Sexual Potential
163d Working-Class Women's Political Participation: Its Potential in Developed Countries
314e Potential of Women
342u Human Potentiality

POVERTY

42l Prostitution and the Poor in Plymouth and Southampton Under the Contagious Diseases Act
59e Poverty: Women and Children Last
129a Poor, Dumb, and Ugly
132t Poor Black Women
156j Problems and Priorities of Poor, Culturally Different Parents
191g Sterilizing the Poor
230n Love Unites Them and Hunger Separates Them: Poor Women in the Dominican Republic
230o Spread of Capitalism in Rural Colombia: Effects on Poor Women
265o Working Poor Women
279v We're Very Poor
291l Discrimination and Poverty among Women Who Head Families
371e Women, Work, and Welfare: The Feminization of Poverty

POWDER

314jj Keys to the Executive Powder Room

POWER

8hh Power to Gay People: A Los Angeles Experiment in Community Action
19d Sanctity and Power: The Dual Pursuit of Medieval Women
20m Women and Power
20n Women and Domestic Power: Political and Economic Strategies in Domestic Groups
21b Pictures of Power and Powerlessness
21m Power, Patriarchy, and "Political Primitives"
23b Women, Learning, and Power: Eleonora of Aragon and the Court of Ferrara
42g Power of Women Through the Family in Medieval Europe: 500-1100

77m Who Has the Power? The Marital Struggle
77gg Male Power and the Women's Movement
86c Women and Political Power
89a Homogenizing the American Woman: The Power of an Unconscious Ideology
98e Powers of Difference
98r Women in Power and Politics
98s Women and the Uses of Power
107i Maternity and the Origin of Political Power
107j Maternity, Paternity, and the Origin of Political Power
107k Paternity and the Origin of Political Power
115h Indian Women: Work, Power and Status
120l Power, Sex, and Nonverbal Communication
129r Sexuality, Power, and Freedom Among "Older" Women
129x Young Women, Old Women, and Power
132i Power Corrupts
134d The Power of Time
140q Pollution and Power
142p Witch Power
174o Political Power and Policy Benefits: Voting Rights and Welfare Policy in Mississippi
186f Training the Woman to Know Her Place: The Power of a Nonconscious Ideology
196v Women Teachers and Teacher Power
202f Discrimination--A Manifestation of Male Market Power?
208c Training the Woman To Know Her Place: The Power of a Nonconscious Ideology
213j Women, Work, and Power in Modern Yugoslavia
214h Power of Emily Dickinson
230g Matriarchy: A Vision of Power
249m Sex and Power in the Balkans
252gg Men and Women in Community Agencies: A Note on Power and Prestige
260g Pecuniary Power
264g Power in Dating Relationships
264ee Male Power and the Women's Movement
265e Who Has the Power? The Marital Struggle
266ii Socio-Economic Context Of Sex And Power: A Study of Women, Work And Family Roles in Four Israeli Institutional Frameworks
272c Power and Opportunity in the Principalship: The Case of Two Women Leaders in Education
278a Men's Power with Women, Other Men and Society
278b Male Power Motivation and the Status of Women
278c Entrails of Power: Bogus Manhood and the Language of Grief
278h Power, Presentations and the Presentable
278i Materfamilias: Power and Presumption
278k Female Powerlessness: The Altruistic Other Orientation
278p Women in the Professions and Semi-Professions: A Question of Power
281m Women and Men, Power and Powerlessness in Lesotho
290d Women and the Power to Change
297dd Women, Knowledge, and Power
298f The Power and the Danger
308h Power and Pollution of Chinese Women
316j Women's and Men's Liberation Groups: Political Power Within the System and Outside the System
320n New Kind of Power
325w Women, Class, and Power: Examples from the Hatay, Turkey
337d Women, Power and the Pursuit of Holiness in Medieval Christianity

344a Feminism, Power and Change: A Theoretical Analysis
344b How Powerful Is Powerful? The Women's Movement and the Four Black Congresswomen
344f League of Women Voters and Political Power
344h New Approaches to Collective Power: Four Working Women's Organizations
344i Organizing for Political Power: The National Women's Political Caucus
368a Women's Studies: Its Focus, Idea Power, and Promise
370g Effects on Power and Division of Labor in the Family
372f Spirit Mediums in Umbanda Evangelizada of Porto Alegre, Brazil: Dimensions of Power and Authority

PRACTICE

130a Employment of Females as Practitioners in Midwifery
151l Charlotte Perkins Gilman on the Theory and Practice of Feminism
151s Women's Liberation: Theory and Practice
163h Campaign Theory and Practice--The Gender Variable
171h American Birth Practices
212j Feminist Film Criticism: Theory and Practice
213b Bridging the Gap between the Sexes in Moroccan Legal Practice
225a Mother and the Hospital: An Unfortunate Fit Between the Woman's Internal World and Some Hospital Practices
250mm Empirical Verification of Sex Discrimination in Hiring Practices in Psychology
271i Assessment of Teaching Practice: An "Attractive" Hypothesis
348c Doctors and Their Patients: The Social Control of Women in General Practice
368c Evaluating Women's Studies- Academic Theory and Practice

PRADESH

309b Women in Uttar Pradesh: Social Mobility and Directions of Change

PRAETIGIIS

52c Johann Weyer's "De Praetigiis Daemonum": Unsystematic Psychopathology

PRAISE

73a In Praise of the Achieving Female Monkey
240c Praising Virtuous Ladies: The Literary Image and Historical Reality of Women in Seventeenth-century England
375c Parable of the Cave or: In Praise of Watercolors

PRATT

215c Louisa Barnes Pratt: Missionary Wife, Missionary Mother, Missionary
215q Dr. Romania Pratt Penrose: To Brave the World

PRAYER

79d Prayers or Meditations
79g Miscelanea: Prayers, Meditations, Memoratives
233b Jewish Prayer

263n Sabbath Prayers for Women

PREACHING

210a Preaching the Word

PRECEDENTS

64e Court Precedents

PRECEPTS

231r Conjugal Precepts

PREFERENCE

85l Preferential Treatment
105m Sex-typing and Children's Television Preferences
141r Son Preference in Taiwan: Verbal Preference and Demographic Behavior
156f Teachers, Peers, and Play Preferences: An Environmental Approach to Sex Typing in the Preschool
158hh Preferential Treatment
173x Sex Preferences, Sex Control, and the Status of Women
176kk Behavior Therapy Approaches to Modification of Sexual Preferences: Biological Perspective and Critique
180e Case for Preferential Admissions
180o Judicial Scrutiny of "Benign" Racial Preference in Law School Admissions
180p Racial Preferences in Higher Education: Political Responsibility and the Judicial Role
180bb Preferential Policies in Hiring and Admissions: A Jurisprudential Approach
217a University and the Case for Preferential Treatment
217b Preferential Treatment in Admitting Racial Minority Students
217e Preferential Consideration and Justice
217g Preferential Treatment
236e Boy Preference Reflected in Korean Folklore
250o Developmental Study of the Effects of Sex of the Dominant Parent on Sex-Role Preference, Identification, and Imitation in Children
351c Sex Segregation in the Labor Market: An Analysis of Young College Women's Occupational Preferences

PREFERENTIAL HIRING

see also REVERSE DISCRIMINATION; AFFIRMATIVE ACTION

85m Preferential Hiring
158ff Preferential Hiring
282p In Defense of Preferential Hiring
282q Preferential Hiring
282r Pedagogical Arguments for Preferential Hiring and Tenuring of Women Teachers in the University

PREGNANCY

see also BIRTH; PRENATAL; NEWBORNS; MATERNITY; POSTPARTUM

20g Nutrition and Pregnancy
76j Regression and Reintegration in Pregnancy
141o Adolescent Experience of Pregnancy and Abortion
155s Sexual Behavior in Pregnancy
155t Contraception and Pregnancy: Experience of Young Unmarried Women in the United States
176ii Psychobiology of Pregnancy
208l Expelling Pregnant Students
208ee All Pregnant Girls Have Boy Babies
211e Physiological Aspects of Pregnancy
211f "Normal" and "Special" Aspects of Pregnancy: A Psychological Approach
211h C.O.P.E. Story: A Service to Pregnant and Postpartum Women
211i Adolescent Sexuality and Pregnancy
221a From Pregnancy through Birth in a Bisayan Filipino Village
221c Pregnancy and Birth in Vietnam
250ee Psychoendocrine Study of Pregnancy and Puerperium
266w Sexuality of Pregnant and Breastfeeding Women
296r Pregnancy and Abortion: Implications for Career Development of Professional Women
296s Specific Psychological Tasks in Pregnancy and Motherhood
351b Pregnancy, Motherhood and Work Activity

PREJUDICE

13b Are Women Prejudiced Against Women?
141gg Woman Artist and the Art Academy: A Case Study in Institutional Prejudice
155c Are Women Prejudiced Against Women?
166k Are Women Prejudiced Against Women?
200f Are Women Prejudiced against Women?
243a Prejudice of Parents
243e Prejudice Toward Women: Some Personality Correlates
339p Pride and Prejudice

PREMARITAL

155i Premarital Sexual Permissiveness Among Negroes and Whites

PRENATAL

20c Prenatal Hormones and Human Behavior: Implications for the Status of Women
199a Sexual Behavior Differentiation: Prenatal Hormonal and Environmental Control
199b Prenatal Testosterone in the Nonhuman Primate and Its Consequences for Behavior
199d Prenatal Androgen, Intelligence and Cognitive Sex Differences
204i Prenatal Influences on Cognitive Abilities: Data from Experimental Animals and Human and Endocrine Syndromes
211c Prenatal Influences on Child Health and Development

PREPAREDNESS

349k American Women in the Peace and Preparedness Movements in World War I

PRESCHOOL

156b Preschool and the Politics of Sexism
156f Teachers, Peers, and Play Preferences: An Environmental Approach to Sex Typing in the Preschool
199n Sex Differences in Field Independence among Preschool Children
208t Sex-Role Socialization in Picture Books for Preschool Children

PRESENTATION

208kk Secondary Level Language Arts Presentation
274f Negotiating Respect: Patterns of Presentation among Black Women
278h Power, Presentations and the Presentable

PRESERVATION

8ff Preserving the Past for the Future
350e Women's Solidarity and the Preservation of Privilege

PRESIDENT

96k How I Ran for the Presidency
139w Editorial from N.O.W.'s President

PRESS

68g "Press Cuttings": G.B.S. and Women's Suffrage
121g Feminine Press: The View of Women in the Colonial Journals of Spanish America, 1790-1810
121j Nineteenth-Century Feminist Press and Women's Rights in Brazil
341i Feminist Press
348g Accounting for Rape: Reality and Myth in Press Reporting
358l Full Court Press for Women in Athletics

PRESSURE

13q Sex-Role Pressures and the Socialization of the Male Child
170f Cultural Pressures in the Psychology of Women
280j Unisex Pressures on Children
284k Job Bias Against Women Easing Under Pressure

PRESTIGE

120g Sex, Covert Prestige, and Linguistic Change in the Urban British English of Norwich
252gg Men and Women in Community Agencies: A Note on Power and Prestige

PRESUMPTION

278i Materfamilias: Power and Presumption

PRETTY

254a "Pretty"

PRICE

89vv Price of Woman

PRICKS

157c "Pricks" and "Chicks": A Plea for "Persons"
158c "Pricks" and "Chicks": A Plea for "Persons"

PRIDE

339p Pride and Prejudice

PRIESTESS

241j The Priestess Who Rebelled

PRIMARY

76c Primary Femininity
140n Stress, Primary Support Systems and Women's Employment Status
176gg Re-Evaluation of the Primary Role of the Communist Chinese Woman: The Homemaker or the Worker
335l Survey of Primary Sources and Archives for the History of Early Twentieth-Century English Women

PRIMATE

see also RHESUS MONKEYS

20b Socialization of Non-Human Primate Females
20d Spontaneous and Induced Abortion in Human and Non-Human Primates
164a Female Primate
199b Prenatal Testosterone in the Nonhuman Primate and Its Consequences for Behavior
201a Sex Roles in Primate Societies

PRIMER

208w Liberated Chinese Primers
284b Man's Primer to Women's Liberation

PRIMITIVE

21m Power, Patriarchy, and "Political Primitives"
77d Conclusion: "Sex and Temperament in Three Primitive Societies"
127z Conclusion, "Sex and Temperament in Three Primitive Societies"
158j "Sex and Temperament in Three Primitive Societies"
206a Primitive Societies
232h Woman's Share in Primitive Culture
249n Myth of Matriarchy: Why Men Rule in Primitive Society

PRINCESS

233k Princess Grace Turns Forty

PRINCIPALS

196w Performance of Women Principals: A Review of Behavioral and Attitudinal Studies
272c Power and Opportunity in the Principalship: The Case of Two Women Leaders in Education

PRINCIPLE

140qq American Principles in Print: The Hero, The Harlot and the Glorified Horse
177j Protestant Principle: A Woman's Eye-View of Barth and Tillich
180k Erosion of Legal Principles in the Creation of Legal Policies
217f Realizing the Equality Principle
232l Principles of Ethics
257k Declaration of Principles
292k Principles of Domestic Science

PRINT

103i Finger Prints Can't Lie
128b Early Women Printers of America
140qq American Principles in Print: The Hero, The Harlot and the Glorified Horse

PRIORITIES

156j Problems and Priorities of Poor, Culturally Different Parents
174p Styles and Priorities of Marginality: Women State Legislators
318n Social Services for Women: Problems and Priorities

PRISM

334p Academic Prism: New View of American Women

PRISONER

see also CRIME; OFFENDER

8u Life and Death of a Gay Prisoner
51z Forgotten Offender: The Woman in Prison
51aa Sexual Segregation of American Prisons
75c Personality Differences Between Male and Female Prison Inmates: Measured by the M.M.P.I.
75e Innovative Programs for Women in Jail and Prison: Trick or Treatment
75g Current Status of Women in Prisons
86o Answer to Norman Mailer's "Prisoner of Sex"
96c Female Prisoner: A Narrative of the Life and Singular Adventures of Josephine Amelia Perkins
139m Women Are Prisoners of Their Sex
145b Prisoners of Progress: Women and Evolution
304k Women in Prison
330p Women in Institutions: Treatment in Prisons and Mental Hospitals

PRIVACY

9tt Private View of the Woman's Uprising
89t Origin of the Family, Private Property, and the State
139g Waste of Private Housekeeping
158y Origin of the Family, Private Property, and the State
175rr Women's Private Writings: Anais Nin
181i Looking Again at Engels' "Origin of the Family, Private Property and the State"
203g Origin of the Family, Private Property and the State
230i Engels Revisited: Women, the Organization of Production, and Private Property
230k Men and Women in the South of France: Public and Private Domains
249k Engels Revisited: Women, the Organization of Production, and Private Property
252dd Social and Private Rates of Return to Investment in Schooling
294e Status of Women in Private Law
334i Private Woman, Public Woman: The Contradictions of Charlotte Perkins Gilman
348a Coercion of Privacy: A Feminist Perspective

PRIVILEGE

53e Privileged, Schooled and Finished: Boarding Education for Girls
350e Women's Solidarity and the Preservation of Privilege

PRO-WOMAN

149t Dangers in the Pro-woman Line and Consciousness-Raising

PROCESS

37b Sex Roles and the Socialization Process
51bb Women and the Correctional Process
90b Subjectives: A Theory of the Critical Process
140dd Self-Concept and the Coping Process of Black Graduate and Undergraduate Women at a Predominantly White University
140ff Feminist Process in Learning
166t Career Choice Processes
171b Biospsychosocial Processes in the Development of Sex-related Differences
176g Sex Differences in Adolescent Character Processes
200c Process of Learning Parental and Sex-Role Identification
243b Women Who Discriminate Against Other Women: The Process of Denial
264t American Women and the Political Process
286h Females in the Competitive Process

PROCREATION

76p Masculine Envy of Woman's Procreative Function
157l Marriage, Love, and Procreation
231i Procreation

PRODUCTION

84b Patriarchy and Relations of Production

84g Women and Production: A Critical Analysis of Some Sociological Theories of Women's Work
98i For the Etruscans: Sexual Difference and Artistic Production--The Debate Over a Female Aesthetic
193b Food for Thought--Patterns of Production and Consumption in Pira-Parana Society
230i Engels Revisited: Women, the Organization of Production, and Private Property
249k Engels Revisited: Women, the Organization of Production, and Private Property
269e Cultural Production of Childbirth
270i Women and Men, Cloth and Colonization: The Transformation of Production-Distribution Relations among the Baule (Ivory Coast)
288jj Woman's Place in Photoplay Production
295h Women in Production: The Toronto Dressmakers' Strike of 1931

PRODUCTIVITY

106h Factors Affecting Women's Scholarly Productivity

PROFESSION

see also CAREER; OCCUPATION; JOB; EMPLOYMENT; LABOR; VOCATIONAL; various professions

4n Sex and Specialization in Academe and the Professions
13dd Teaching is a Good Profession...for a Woman
36a Report on Women and the Profession
39e Salon, Foyer, Bureau: Women and the Professions in France
42e Salon, Foyer, Bureau: Women and the Professions in France
51t Oldest and Newest Profession
149l Women and the Professions
166c Encountering the Male Establishment: Sex-Status Limits on Woman's Careers in the Professions
166vv Women Lawyers and Their Profession: Inconsistency of Social Controls and Their Consequences for Professional Performance
233pp Mrs. Warren's Profession
250ll Encountering the Male Establishment: Sex Status Limits on Woman's Careers in the Professions
264q Women in the Professions: Psychological and Social Barriers to Women in Science
265m Women in the Professions: Psychological and Social Barriers to Women in Science
266gg Salon, Foyer, Bureau: Women And The Professions in France
278p Women in the Professions and Semi-Professions: A Question of Power
292o Home Life as a Profession
297y Women in the Anthropology Profession--1
297z Women in the Anthropology Profession--2
306i Women in the Professions
310f Mrs. Warren's Profession
311c Health Professions--Opportunities and Limitations
318i Women in the Professions
327b Why Can't Women Be More Like Men: A Summary of the Sociopsychological Factors Hindering Women's Advancement in the Professions
327h Soviet Women in the Work Force and Professions
354l Women in Male-Dominated Professions

354m Women in Female-Dominated Professions

PROFESSIONAL

14c Women and Medical Sociology: Invisible Professionals and Ubiquitous Patients
39j Positive Effects of the Multiple Negative: Explaining the Success of Black Professional Women
43d Issues Confronting Professional African Women: Illustrations from Kenya
45c Professional Schools and Their Impact on Black Women
70h Jobs or Careers: The Case of the Professionally Employed Married Woman
71g Women Professionals in Buenos Aires
106l Rosemary Park: Professional Activities
126c Invisible Woman: The Historian as Professional Magician
141v Social Research on Women's Professional Careers
166a Professional Woman: Trends and Prospects
166g Farmer's Daughter Effect: The Case of the Negro Female Professional
166n Female Physician in Public Health: Conflict and Reconciliation of the Sex and Professional Roles
166y Differential Recruitment of Female Professionals: A Case Study of Clergywomen
166kk Married Professional Social Worker
166nn Professional and Non-Professional Women as Mothers
166pp Female Clergy: A Case of Professional Marginality
166vv Women Lawyers and Their Profession: Inconsistency of Social Controls and Their Consequences for Professional Performance
166aaa Myth of the Egalitarian Family: Familial Roles and the Professionally Employed Wife
173dd Role of Models in Women's Professional Development
174d Impact of Organizational Structure, Technology, and Professionalism on the Policy of Affirmative Action
197f Down the Up Staircase: Sex Roles, Professionalization, and the Status of Teachers
215k Two Miss Cooks: Pioneer Professionals for Utah's Schools
219o Women's Verbal Behavior at Learned and Professional Conferences
253j Role of Choice in the Psychology of Professional Women
266n Positive Effects of the Multiple Negative: Explaining the Success of Black Professional Women
296r Pregnancy and Abortion: Implications for Career Development of Professional Women
297j Sociocultural Factors Mitigating Role Conflict of Buenos Aires Professional Women
303m New Professional Identities: Four Women in the Sixties
314cc Informal Interaction Patterns of Professional Women
327d Nonacademic Professional Political Scientists
327i Women in the Professional Caucuses
360g Spiritualist Medium: A Study of Female Professionalization in Victorian America

PROFILE

94d Forcible Rape in the U.S.: A Statistical Profile
114k Demographic Profile of Indian Women
163v Black Women State Legislators: A Profile
176m Woman Ph-D.: A Recent Profile

267v Woman Ph-D.: A Recent Profile
364e American Woman from 1900 to the First World War: A Profile

PROGRAM

22q Sex-Role Stereotyping in Children's Television Programs
40d Substitution Among Child Care Modes and the Effect of a Child Care Subsidy Program
49b Setting Up an Affirmative Action Program
75e Innovative Programs for Women in Jail and Prison: Trick or Treatment
75h Remedies for Wrongs: Updating Programs for Delinquent Girls
75i Ex-Offender Evaluates Correctional Programming for Women
105c Spot Messages within Saturday Morning TV Programs
142t Broom of One's Own: Notes on the Women's Liberation Program
180c Affirmative Action--A Liberal Program
190g Educating Women for Leadership: A Program for the Future
270a Montagnais Women and the Jesuit Program for Colonization
293e Critical Analysis of Latin American Programs to Integrate Women in Development
294s U.N.E.S.C.O. Long-Range Program for the Advancement of Women
331c Women's Dependency and Federal Programs
341u "Second-Chance" Program for Women
358e Development of Programs

PROGRESS

63e Equal Pay in Canada: History, Progress and Problems
145b Prisoners of Progress: Women and Evolution
257w Meaning of Progress in the Woman Movement
341e Uncertain Progress of Affirmative Action

PROGRESSIVE

51q Women Criminals in Progressive New York

PROJECTIONS

38d Projected Future Employment and Leadership Needs and Areas
135g Next Five Years: Projections and Policy Implications

PROLETARIANS

140f From Peasants to Proletarians: Black Women in the Cauca Valley, Colombia

PROMISCUITY

157n In Defense of Promiscuity

PROMISE

22c Probing the Promise of Androgyny
88x Promises Fulfilled: Positive Images of Women in Twentieth-Century Autobiography
368a Women's Studies: Its Focus, Idea Power, and Promise

PROMOTING

140ee Promoting Creative Risk-Taking in Women
160a Advice to Mothers, on the Subject of Their Own Health, and, of the Means of Promoting the Health, Strength and Beauty of Their Offspring

PROPAGANDA

334q Propaganda and Public Opinion in the United States and Germany, 1939-1945

PROPERTY

30b Dowry and Bridewealth and the Property Rights of Women in South Asia
89t Origin of the Family, Private Property, and the State
132h Women, Servants, Mules, and Other Property
158y Origin of the Family, Private Property, and the State
181i Looking Again at Engels' "Origin of the Family, Private Property and the State"
203g Origin of the Family, Private Property and the State
230i Engels Revisited: Women, the Organization of Production, and Private Property
244a Victorian Wives and Property: Reform of the Married Women's Property Law, 1857-1882
249k Engels Revisited: Women, the Organization of Production, and Private Property
325u Status of Women and Property on a Baluchistan Oasis in Pakistan

PROPHETS

272a Prophets, Chiefs, Commissioners, and Queens: The Moral and Institutional Context of Leadership

PROPOSITIONS

214p Gwendolyn the Terrible: Propositions on Eleven Poems

PROSE

97e Poems and Prose
361l Women's Prose Style: A Study of Contemporary Authors

PROSPERITY

360p Prosperity's Child: Some Thoughts on the Flapper

PROSTITUTE

42l Prostitution and the Poor in Plymouth and Southampton Under the Contagious Diseases Act
51b Criminals and Prostitutes
51r Prostitution: An Extreme Case of Sex Stratification
51s Prostitution Papers
114r Prostitutes--Notes from a Rescue Home
116c Prostitution and Feminism in Late Nineteenth-Century Italy

175i Speaking Out on Prostitution
223e Study of Victorian Prostitution and Venereal Disease
225c Whore in Peru: The Splitting of Women into Good and Bad and the Isolation of the Prostitute
235f Prostitute as Victim
244d Making of an Outcast Group: Prostitutes and Working Women in Nineteenth-Century Plymouth and Southampton
254c Prostitution: A Quartet for Female Voices
295b Toronto's Prostitute at the Turn of the Century
317k Radical Yoruba Female Sexuality: The Witch and the Prostitute
342p Ideology of Prostitution
348d Who Needs Prostitutes? The Ideology of Male Sexual Needs

PROTECTION

85v Coercion and Rape: The State As a Male Protection Racket
331i Homemakers into Widows and Divorcees: Can the Law Provide Economic Protection?
348b Myth of Male Protectiveness and the Legal Subordination of Women: An Historical Analysis
354e Legal Protection against Sex Discrimination

PROTEST

41b Women, Work and Protest in the Early Lowell Mills
257d Marriage of Lucy Stone Under Protest
297m Resistance as Protest: Women in the Struggle of Bolivian Tin-Mining Communities

PROTESTA

80g "Protesta femenina" in Latin America

PROTESTANT

116h Protestant Evangelism and the Italian Immigrant Woman
177j Protestant Principle: A Woman's Eye-View of Barth and Tillich
302i Protestant Women's Associations in Freetown, Sierra Leone
337g Jane Lead: The Feminist Mind and Art of a Seventeenth-Century Protestant Mystic
337l American Women in Ministry: A History of Protestant Beginning Points

PROVERBS

236b Korean Proverbs about Women

PROVINCIAL

325x Comparative Perspective on Women in Provincial Iran and Turkey

PROVISIONS

70a Husband Provider Role: A Critical Appraisal
114j Legal Provisions
135b Current Entitlements and Provisions

PRUDENCE

128c Prudence Crandall: Champion of Negro Education

PSALMES

79i The Psalmes of David

PSYCHE

363n Woman's Psyche

PSYCHIATRY

99k Rape and Psychiatric Vocabularies of Motive
129u Is There a Psychiatrist in the House?
166m Social Influence and the Social-Psychological Function of Deference: A Study of Psychiatric Nursing
173gg Sex Differences and Psychiatric Disorders
176pp Postpartum Psychiatric Syndromes
205g Women and Psychiatry
250i Women as Psychiatric and Psychotherapeutic Patients
250ff Postpartum Psychiatric Syndromes

PSYCHIC

76n Psychic Representation and Female Orgasm
179gg "Psychic Bisexuality"
198b Psychical Consequences of the Anatomical Distinction Between the Sexes
233e Psychical Consequences of the Anatomical Distinction between the Sexes
268a Psychical Consequences of the Anatomical Distinction Between the Sexes

PSYCHOANALYSIS

see also THERAPY; PSYCHOTHERAPY

98a Gender, Relation, and Difference in Psychoanalytic Perspective
98g Psychoanalysis and Feminism in France
170m Changing Patterns of Femininity: Psychoanalytic Implications
198a Psychoanalysis and Sex Differences: Freud and Beyond Freud
200b Psychoanalytic Theory of Psychosexual Development
252h Female Sexuality and Psychoanalytic Theory
268r Role of Clara Thompson in the Psychoanalytic Study of Women
282e Holes and Slime: Sexism in Sartre's Psychoanalysis
330j Therapy of Women in the Light of Psychoanalytic Theory and the Emergence of a New View

PSYCHOBIOLOGY

172a Sex-Related Behaviors: Historical and Psychobiological Perspectives
176ii Psychobiology of Pregnancy
199s Psychobiology of Sex Differences: An Evolutionary Perspective

PSYCHODYNAMICS

98b Mother-Daughter Relationships: Psychodynamics, Politics, and Philosophy
199q Psychodynamics of Male Transsexualism

PSYCHOENDOCRINE

250ee Psychoendocrine Study of Pregnancy and Puerperium

PSYCHOHISTORICAL

253b Woman as Knower: Some Psychohistorical Perspectives

PSYCHOLOGICAL

18f Sex-Related Differences in Spatial Ability: A Developmental Psychological View
21f Psychological "Facts" About Women
49d Psychological Barriers for Women in Sciences: Internal and External
67j Biological Explanations of Psychological Sex Differences
68o Vivien Warren: A Psychological Study
82a Psychological Conflict and the Reproductive System
155a Psychological Consequences of the Anatomical Distinction Between the Sexes
156g Development of Psychological Androgyny: Early Childhood Socialization
158e Psychological Oppression
171g Social Psychological Model of Human Sexuality
171k Menstrual-related Psychological Changes
171l Social Psychological Perspective on the Menstrual Cycle
176ll Predictive Study of Psychological and Psychosomatic Responses to Oral Contraceptives
176oo Psychologic Aspects of Lactation
176qq Psychological Investigation of Habitual Abortion
177a Women and Religion: Psychological and Cultural Implications
196i Psychological and Occupational Sex Stereotypes in Elementary School Readers
199u Plasma Testosterone Levels and Psychologic Measures in Men Over a 2-Month Period
200a Psychological Consequences of the Anatomical Distinction between the Sexes
211f "Normal" and "Special" Aspects of Pregnancy: A Psychological Approach
211p Hysterectomy and Other Gynecological Surgeries: A Psychological View
211r Psychological Consideration of Mastectomy
236f Psychological Problems among Korean Women
246f Place of Contemporary Women from a Psychological Perspective
250h Psychological Consequences of the Anatomic Distinction Between the Sexes
250l Women in Rage: A Psychological Look at the Helpless Heroine
256s Genderless Sexuality: A Male-Female Psychological Exploration of the Future of Sexual Relationships
263x Why Women Need the Goddess: Phenomenological, Psychological, and Political Reflections

264q Women in the Professions: Psychological and Social Barriers to Women in Science
265m Women in the Professions: Psychological and Social Barriers to Women in Science
266b Measurement of Psychological Androgyny
267q Sex-Role Attitudes and Psychological Well-Being
267r Psychological Sex Differences
284t Question of Psychological Differences Between the Sexes
286b Psychological Aspects of Sport with Special Reference to the Female
296k Psychologic and Sociologic Factors of Orgasm
296s Specific Psychological Tasks in Pregnancy and Motherhood
333c What Psychological Research on the Labor Force Participation of Women is Needed?
365g Psychological Consequences of Sexual Inequality
370b Psychological Factors

PSYCHOLOGY

see also BEHAVIOR; various psychological topics

76h Masochism, the Ego Ideal, and the Psychology of Women
76o Problems in Freud's Psychology of Women
76q New Female Psychology?
77f Psychology Constructs the Female
77g Summary and Commentary: "The Psychology of Sex Differences"
77h Psychology of Women
94n Psychology of Rapists
97h Psychology Constructs the Female, or the Fantasy Life of the Male Psychologist
98o Androgyny and the Psychology of Sex Differences
101e Psychology and Gender
115i Woman Versus Womanliness: An Essay in Speculative Psychology
127ee Psychology Constructs the Female
141d Psychology Looks at the Female
141s Social Psychology of the "Decision" to Have or Not Have Children
142q Kinder, Kuche, Kirche as Scientific Law: Psychology Constructs the Female
156e Social Psychology of Sex-Role Intervention
170f Cultural Pressures in the Psychology of Women
170k Feminine Psychology and Infantile Sexuality
170l Psychology of the Female: A New Look
172h Psychology in Transition: Continuities, Critiques, and Perspectives
172k New Psychology of Women: A Feminist Analysis
173a Psychology of Women
173b Functionalism, Darwinism, and the Psychology of Women
173d Freud's View of Female Psychology
173l Psychology
175s Psychology Constructs the Female
186e Psychology Constructs the Female, or the Fantasy Life of the Male Psychologist
198u Psychology and Sex Differences
203u Psychology Constructs the Female
233ee Psychology Constructs the Female, or The Fantasy Life of the Male Psychologist
243i Status of Women in Psychology: How Many and How Come?
250mm Empirical Verification of Sex Discrimination in Hiring Practices in Psychology

252g Psychology of Women: Biology as Destiny
253j Role of Choice in the Psychology of Professional Women
254h Psychology Constructs the Female
260cc Sex and Psychology
268f Freud's View of Female Psychology
268i Psychology of women in Relation to the Functions of Reproduction
268j Since 1924: Toward a New Psychology of Women
272b Psychology of Leadership: Implications for Women
276d Psychology of Sex Roles
279r Psychology
342l Male Bias in Psychology
361b Psychology of Women's Language
363p Psychology Constructs the Female, or the Fantasy Life of the Male Psychologist

PSYCHOPATHOLOGY

52c Johann Weyer's "De Praetigiis Daemonum": Unsystematic Psychopathology
67i Sex Differences and Psychopathology

PSYCHOPHYSIOLOGICAL

99o Gender Differences in Psychophysiological Illness

PSYCHOSEXUAL

155f Sex Differences in Responses to Psychosexual Stimulation by Films and Slides
171a Psychosexual Neutrality: Is Anatomy Destiny?
199k Stages in the Development of Psychosexual Concepts and Attitudes
200b Psychoanalytic Theory of Psychosexual Development
296f Psychosexual Differentiation

PSYCHOSOCIAL

173v Psychosocial Factors of the Abortion Experience

PSYCHOSOMATIC

176ll Predictive Study of Psychological and Psychosomatic Responses to Oral Contraceptives

PSYCHOTHERAPY

see also THERAPY; PSYCHOANALYSIS

61 Women in Psychotherapy
77x Patient and Patriarch: Women in the Psychotherapeutic Relationship
99p Gender and Psychotherapy
146c Psychotherapy and Counseling
246g Psychotherapy for Women: Myths and Legacies
250i Women as Psychiatric and Psychotherapeutic Patients
254q Patient and Patriarch: Women in the Psychotherapeutic Relationship
265x Marriage and Psychotherapy
296c Feminism and Psychotherapy

330d Psychotherapist and the Female Patient: Perceptions, Misperceptions and Change
330q Psychotherapy with Women and Men of Lower Classes

PTASCHKINA

179e N. Ptaschkina

PUBERTY

42b Puberty to Menopause: The Cycle of Femininity in Nineteenth-Century America

PUBLIC

2a Abortion and Public Policy in the U.S.
21r Women and Girls in the Public Schools: Defeat or Liberation?
40b Public Policy Toward Child Care in America: A Historical Perspective
42j Tender Technicians: Feminization of Public Librarianship, 1876-1905
59a How Much Is a Woman Worth? The American Public Policy
105d Where are the Women in Public Broadcasting?
106j Responsibility and Public Policy: Is It a Moral Question?
143p Los Angeles Women's Building: A Public Center for Woman's Culture
151c Participation in Public Affairs
163f Why Few Women Hold Public Office: Factors Affecting the Participation of Women in Local Politics
163q Wife and Politician: Role Strain Among Women in Public Office
166n Female Physician in Public Health: Conflict and Reconciliation of the Sex and Professional Roles
174b Impact of Collective Bargaining on Minorities in the Public Sector: Some Policy Implications
174n Women and Public Policy: A Comparative Analysis
196z Sex Discrimination as Public Policy: The Case of Maternity-Leave Policies for Teachers
208k Sex Bias in the Public Schools
208r Let Them Aspire! A Plea and Proposal for Equality of Opportunity for Males and Females in the Ann Arbor Public Schools
230k Men and Women in the South of France: Public and Private Domains
246j Women in History: Public Life and Historical Consciousness
249j Female Status in the Public Domain
266p Tender Technicians: The Feminization of Public Librarianship, 1876-1905
269f Public Policy and Childbearing
280i Unisex and the Public Schools
291i Occupational Segregation and Public Policy: A Comparative Analysis of American and Soviet Patterns
294d From Constitutional Recognition to Public Office
294g Women in Public Life in Peru
331h Public Policy and the Family: A New Strategy for Women as Wives and Mothers
334i Private Woman, Public Woman: The Contradictions of Charlotte Perkins Gilman

PUBLIC OPINION

2c Abortion Decisions: Judicial Review and Public Opinion

334q Propaganda and Public Opinion in the United States and Germany, 1939-1945

PUBLICA

231l Social Aspects of the Woman in the "Res Publica"

PUBLICATIONS

166f Predominance of Male Authors in Social Work Publications
280aa Eliminating Bias in Publications

PUEBLOS

285k Sex Differences in the Incidence of Susto in Two Zapotec Pueblos: An Analysis of the Relationships between Sex Role Expectations and a Folk Illness

PUERPERIUM

250ee Psychoendocrine Study of Pregnancy and Puerperium

PUERTO

121k Felipe Carrillo Puerto and Women's Liberation in Mexico

PUERTO RICAN

208cc Feminists Look at the 100 Books: The Portrayal of Women in Children's Books on Puerto Rican Themes
297l Women as Workers: The Experience of the Puerto Rican Woman in the 1930's

PUERTO RICO

194c Class Consciousness Among Working-Class Women in Latin America: Puerto Rico
194j History of Women's Struggle for Equality in Puerto Rico

PUNISHMENT

163g Societal Punishment and Aspects of Female Political Participation: 1972 National Convention Delegates
266h Bringing Women In: Rewards, Punishments, And the Structure of Achievement

PURDAH

55j Purdah in the British Situation
115g From Purdah to Modernity

PURITAN

151a Puritans and Sex
178c Puritan Ethic in the Revolutionary Era: Abigail Adams and Thomas Jefferson

359b Quest for Community: Spiritual Autobiographies of Eighteenth-Century Quaker and Puritan Women in America

PURITY

91 Social Purity

PURPOSE

60n Purpose of the College
140pp Assembling Videotaped Materials for Instructional Purposes
149r Statement of Purpose
158n Purpose of Sex

PURSUIT

19d Sanctity and Power: The Dual Pursuit of Medieval Women
71j Pursuit of an Ideal: Migration, Social Class, and Women's Roles in Bogota, Colombia
264u Black Women and the Pursuit of Equality
337d Women, Power and the Pursuit of Holiness in Medieval Christianity

PUSHERS

191l Pushers

PYGMALION

68a Shakespeare's "The Taming of the Shrew" vs. Shaw's "Pygmalion": Male Chauvinism vs. Women's Lib?
68d Eliza's Choice: Transformation Myth and the Ending of "Pygmalion"

PYRAMID

303r Pyramid and the Labyrinth

QASHQA'I

325q Women among Qashqa'i Nomadic Pastoralists in Iran

QUAKER

270c Mothers of a Nation: Seneca Resistance to Quaker Intervention
337f Quaker Women in the English Left Wing
359b Quest for Community: Spiritual Autobiographies of Eighteenth-Century Quaker and Puritan Women in America

QUALIFICATION

4j Faculty Wife: Her Academic Interests and Qualifications
341o Black, Female--and Qualified

QUALITY

40e Quality of Day Care: Can It Be Measured
85z Abortion and the Quality of Life
106i Intellectual Quality: The Symbols and the Substance

155j Women's Sexual Responsiveness and the Duration and Quality of Their Marriages
215e Amy Brown Lyman: Raising the Quality of Life for All

QUALMS

266j Fear of Success: Qualms and Queries

QUANTITATIVE

250v Effects of Sex of Examiner and Subject on Children's Quantitative Test Performance

QUARTET

254c Prostitution: A Quartet for Female Voices

QUEBEC

320c Women in Quebec

QUEEN

73l Queen Bee Syndrome
79h To The Thrice Sacred Queen Elizabeth
79l Tragedie of Mariam, The Fair Queen of Jewry
241c The Queen of California
272a Prophets, Chiefs, Commissioners, and Queens: The Moral and Institutional Context of Leadership

QUEER

8q Hookers: Queer Fish

QUERIES

266j Fear of Success: Qualms and Queries

QUESTIONNAIRE

73s Woman and Man: A Questionnaire and Survey Report

QUIRLS

332e Quirls of a Woman's Brain

QUISQUEYANA

71i "La Quisqueyana": The Dominican Woman, 1940-1970

QUOTA

158gg Secondary Sexism and Quota Hiring
180f Discrimination, Color Blindness, and the Quota System

RABBIS

117x Women as Sources of Torah in the Rabbinic Tradition
314i Patrons, Rabbis, Mentors--Whatever You Call Them, Women Need Them Too

RACE

43g Caribbean Women: The Impact of Race, Sex, and Class
49c Affirmative Action and the Continuing Majority: Women of All Races and Minority Men
51l Race and Sex Differences
94e Race, Rape, and the Death Penalty
96q Race Problem--An Autobiography
96r Experiences of the Race Problem
96s Observations of the Southern Race Feeling
100e Class and Race Differences in Gender Roles
101d Comments on "Science and Racism"
126k Racism and Tradition: Black Womanhood in Historical Perspective
156a Sexism and Racism in Education
158b Racism and Sexism
176k Race, Social Class, and the Motive to Avoid Success in Women
180n Constitutionality of Reverse Racial Discrimination
180o Judicial Scrutiny of "Benign" Racial Preference in Law School Admissions
180p Racial Preferences in Higher Education: Political Responsibility and the Judicial Role
188f Woman and the New Race
197h Effect of Race and Sex on College Admission
217b Preferential Treatment in Admitting Racial Minority Students
222k Images of Self and Race in the Autobiographies of Black Women
267n Race, Social Class, and the Motive to Avoid Success in Women
301c Race, Sex, and Jobs: The Drive Toward Equality
333h Dynamic Theory of Racial Income Differences
342w AfroAmerican Woman's Perspective on Racist Barriers
342x Racism and Sexism
371d Racial Differences in Female Labor-Force Participation: Trends and Implications for the Future

RACKET

85v Coercion and Rape: The State As a Male Protection Racket

RADICAL

36e Dwelling in Decencies: Radical Criticism and the Feminist Perspective
88c Dwelling in Decencies: Radical Criticism and the Feminist Perspective
89aaa Radical Feminism and Love
92d Women Cotton Workers and the Suffrage Campaign: The Radical Suffragists in Lancashire, 1893-1914
132v Radical Women as Students
151q Feminism as a Radical Ideology
152p Radical Ethic for Sports
159c Radical Feminism
175y Radical Feminism 1

175ii Women and the Radical Movement
175nn Politics of the Ego: A Manifesto for New York Radical Feminists
175oo Westchester Radical Feminists
181c Women and Nineteenth-Century Radical Politics: A Lost Dimension
246a Radical and Conservative Trends in the Women's Rights Movement
282i Future of Love: Rousseau and the Radical Feminists
288ff Coup pour coup: Radical French Cinema
317k Radical Yoruba Female Sexuality: The Witch and the Prostitute
352a Women at a Standstill: The Need for Radical Change

RADIO

142r The Pill--Radio News 2-24-70

RAG

8gg Getting It Together Journalism: A View of FAG RAG

RAGE

250l Women in Rage: A Psychological Look at the Helpless Heroine

RAGUSA-DUBROVNIK

315i Women in Charter and Statute Law: Medieval Ragusa-Dubrovnik

RAHEL

5a Rahel Varnhagen

RAIN

279n Cat in the Rain

RAISERS

300g The Used-Boy Raisers

RAISING

215e Amy Brown Lyman: Raising the Quality of Life for All
281p Raising the Status of Women through Law: The Case of Israel
284w Raising a Bright and Happy Child

RAJASTHAN

114o Village Women of Rajasthan

RAM

111r The Ram in the Thicket
112j The Ram in the Thicket

RAMIFICATIONS

21a Ramifications of the Study of Women

RANADE

115c Social Reform Movement in India--From Ranade to Nehru

RAP

274a Personal Narratives in Women's Rap Groups

RAPE

24hh The Rape
77u Rape: The All-American Crime
85s Rape: The All-American Crime
85t Rape and Respect
85u What's Wrong with Rape
85v Coercion and Rape: The State As a Male Protection Racket
94a Forcible Rape
94b Rape: The All-American Crime
94c Rape and Rape Law: Sexism in Society and Law
94d Forcible Rape in the U.S.: A Statistical Profile
94e Race, Rape, and the Death Penalty
94g Forcible Rape and the Problem of the Rights of the Accused
94k Comparative Study of Forcible Rape Offenses Known to the Police in Boston and Los Angeles
94l Rape in New York City: A Study of Material in the Police Files and Its Meaning
94n Psychology of Rapists
94o Rape Trauma Syndrome
99k Rape and Psychiatric Vocabularies of Motive
132m Is Rape a Myth?
158t What's Wrong With Rape
175x Rape: An Act of Terror
211w Impact of Rape
235b Rape
264d Rape Culture
265c Rape: The All-American Crime
348g Accounting for Rape: Reality and Myth in Press Reporting
348h Studying Rape: Integrating Research and Social Change

RAPE--VICTIM

94f Black Offender and White Victim: A Study of Forcible Rape in Oakland, Ca.
94h Judicial Attitudes Toward Rape Victims
94m Hitchhike Victim of Rape
94p Crisis Intervention with Victims of Rape
94q Philadelphia Rape Victim Project
155v Attribution of Fault to a Rape Victim as a Function of Respectability
321i Victims of Rape and Wife Abuse

RAPPACCINI

111z Rappaccini's Daughter
112q Rappaccini's Daughter

RATE

172c Meaning of Sex-Related Variations in Maturation Rate
208oo Why Children's Films Are Not Rated "R"
244h Sex and Death in Victorian England: An Examination of Age- and Sex-Specific Death Rates, 1840-1910
252dd Social and Private Rates of Return to Investment in Schooling

RATIO

122a Random Survey of the Ratio of Female Poets to Male in Anthologies: Less-Than-Tokenism as a Mexican Tradition

RATIONAL

98c Bonds of Love: Rational Violence and Erotic Domination
176tt Women's Lib--Rational? Or Socially Pathological?

RATIONALE

116r Oral History in Pittsburgh--Women, Ethnicity, and Mental Health: Rationale, Procedure, and Methodology

RATIONALIZATION

55f Rationalization of Housework

RAW

198j Status and Role: Raw Materials for Society, Marriage

RAYMOND

113u Raymond's Run
303j Eleanor Raymond

RAZA

86e Chicanas Speak Out--New Voice of La Raza

REACTION

250n Parents' Differential Reactions to Sons and Daughters
282l Reaction and the Women's Movement

READ

see also PRIMER; BOOK; TEXTBOOKS; READING

16b Houston, Houston, Do You Read?
110e Gentle Truths for Gentle Readers: The Fiction of Elizabeth Goudge
184b Transformations of the Heroine: From Epic Heard to Epic Read
196i Psychological and Occupational Sex Stereotypes in Elementary School Readers
208u Dick and Jane as Victims: Sex Stereotyping in Children's Readers
208v Run, Mama, Run: Women Workers in Elementary Readers
215j Aurelia Read Spencer Rogers: Humble Heroine

263e Eve and Adam: Genesis 2-3 Reread
271o Women Workers in Elementary Readers
318m Images of Male and Female in Children's Readers
359e Autobiographer and Her Readers: From Apology to Affirmation

READING

33c Girl Reading
93g Women Socialists and Their Male Comrades: The Reading Experience, 1927-1936
110t Value and Peril for Women of Reading Women Writers
271n Sex Roles in Early Reading Textbooks

REALIST

13u Realistic Counseling for High-School Girls
122l Nellie Campobello: Romantic Revolutionary and Mexican Realist
208q Realistic Counseling for High School Girls

REALITIES

71b "Brazileira": Images and Realities in Writings of Machado de Assis and Jorge Amado
142k Realities of Lesbianism
146d Biological Realities and Myths
173t Realities of Lesbianism
269j Modern Family: Sticky Myths, Diverse Realities, and the Problem of Isolation
314a Women as Managers--Stereotypes and Realities

REALIZATIONS

351a Young Women's Decisions to Attend College: Desires, Expectations and Realizations

REARING

199f Sex Differences in Rhesus Monkeys Following Varied Rearing Experiences
221b Customs Connected with Birth and the Rearing of Children
256e Child Rearing: 2000 AD

REASON

282d Reason and Morals in the Early Feminist Movement: Mary Wollstonecraft

REBECCA

128e Original of Rebecca in "Ivanhoe"
128p Woman in Steel--Rebecca Lukens

REBEL

96y Deflated Rebel
226e Deflated Rebel
238m Women Must Rebel

241j The Priestess Who Rebelled
292f Anne Bradstreet: Dogmatist and Rebel
302g Rebels or Status-Seekers? Women as Spirit Mediums in East Africa

REBIRTH

97i American Family: Decay and Rebirth

RECAMIER

5e Madame Recamier

RECIDIVISM

51ee Recidivism Among Women Parolees: A Long-Term Survey

RECIPROCITY

20p Non-Hierarchical, Hierarchical, and Masked Reciprocity in the Arab Village

RECKLESS

128g Reckless Lady: The Life Story of Adah Isaacs Menken

RECLAMATION

113o Reclamation

RECLUSE

288j Why I'm Called a Recluse

RECOGNITION

9m Demand for Party Recognition
294d From Constitutional Recognition to Public Office

RECONQUEST

315c Women in Reconquest Castile: The Fueros of Sepulveda and Cuenca

RECORDS

314g Women in Work Force Post Better Records for Stability in Jobs

RECREATION

129o Education as Recreation

RECRUITMENT

138h Women's Emancipation and the Recruitment of Women into the Labour Force in World War II
163k Recruitment of Women for Congress
166y Differential Recruitment of Female Professionals: A Case Study of Clergywomen

314aa Differential Recruitment and Control: The Sex Structuring of Organizations
327c Regional Approach to Analyzing the Recruitment of Academic Women

RED

86j Why Red-Baiting Hurts the Feminist Movement
113q Red Dress--1946
256l Chief Justice Wore a Red Dress
262r Woman in Philanthropy--Work of the Red Cross Society

REDUNDANCY

223d Marriage, Redundancy or Sin: The Painter's View of Women in the First Twenty-Five Years of Victoria's Reign

REENA

29i Reena
220u Reena

REENTRY

45e Baseline Data on Mid-Career Change and Reentry for Black Women

REFERENCE

157b Sex and Reference
158p Sex and Reference
194a Mythology About Women, With Special Reference to Chile
207c Gender-Marking in American English: Usage and Reference
282n Referential Genderization
285j Woman-Marriage, With Special Reference to the Lovedu--Its Significance for the Definition of Marriage
286b Psychological Aspects of Sport with Special Reference to the Female

REFORM

115c Social Reform Movement in India--From Ranade to Nehru
244a Victorian Wives and Property: Reform of the Married Women's Property Law, 1857-1882
282m Feminism: Reform or Revolution
284f Abortion Law Reform
325a Women and Law Reform in Contemporary Islam
325b Legal Reform as an Indicator of Women's Status in Muslim Nations
331d Partnership Marriage: Legal Reforms Needed
337k Women, Religion and Reform in Antebellum America
337m Women in Judaism: From the Reform Movement to Contemporary Jewish Religious Feminism

REFORMATION

19g Women in the Reformation Era
177i Women and the Continental Reformation

REGIMES

227e Women Under Communist and Socialist Regimes

REGINALD

52e Reginald Scot's "Discoverie of Witchcraft": Scepticism and Sadduceeism

REGION

47j "Delta Wedding" as Region and Symbol
93e Jennie Higginses of the "New South in the West": A Regional Survey of Socialist Activities, Agitators, and Organizers, 1901-1917
320p APPENDIX: Women's Centres, Women's Newspapers and Regional Contacts
327c Regional Approach to Analyzing the Recruitment of Academic Women

REGLA

121d Women in a Noble Family: The Mexican Counts of Regla, 1750-1830

REGRESSION

76j Regression and Reintegration in Pregnancy

REGULATIONS

180g Bias in Anti-bias Regulations

REHABILITATION

317l Jive Dope Fiend Whoes: In the Street and in Rehabilitation

REICH

80m Women in the Third Reich
275d More Than a Question of Numbers: Women Deputies in the German National Constituent Assembly and the Reichstag, 1919-1933

REINFORCEMENT

110b Popular Literature as Social Reinforcement: The Case of "Charlotte Temple"
250hh Sex Differences in Expectancy of Intellectual and Academic Reinforcement

REINTEGRATION

76j Regression and Reintegration in Pregnancy

RELATION

9cc Filial Relations
35b Relations of Capitalist Patriarchy
39q Social Relations of Black and White Widowed Women in a Northern Metropolis
84b Patriarchy and Relations of Production

89uu Aggression in the Relations between the Sexes
98a Gender, Relation, and Difference in Psychoanalytic Perspective
126l Politics of Cultural Liberation: Male-Female Relations in Algeria
153r Filial Relations
166mm Career and Family Orientations of Husbands and Wives in Relation to Marital Happiness
173r Women's Liberation and Human Sexual Relations
176p Career and Family Orientations of Husbands and Wives in Relation to Marital Happiness
204d Patterns of Cognitive Functioning in Relation to Handedness and Sex-Related Differences
231h Of the Relation Between Husband and Wife
268i Psychology of women in Relation to the Functions of Reproduction
270i Women and Men, Cloth and Colonization: The Transformation of Production-Distribution Relations among the Baule (Ivory Coast)
285g Jural Relations between the Sexes Among the Barabaig
321g Changes in Domestic Relations Court
325bb Negotiation of Reality: Male-Female Relations in Sefrou, Morocco
360l Female World of Love and Ritual: Relations Between Women in Nineteenth-Century America
372e Spirit Magic in the Social Relations between Men and Women--Sao Paulo, Brazil

RELATIONSHIP

18d Father-Daughter Relationship: Past, Present, and Future
22t Relationship Between Sex Roles, Marital Status, and Mental Illness
38b Evolving Relationships Between Women and Men
77x Patient and Patriarch: Women in the Psychotherapeutic Relationship
91k Relationship between Women's Work and Fertility: Some Methodological and Theoretical Issues
98b Mother-Daughter Relationships: Psychodynamics, Politics, and Philosophy
100c Love Thine Enemy: Male-Female Relationships
100g Beyond Masculinity: Liberating Men and Their Relationships with Women
107e Relationship of Men and Women
146k Family Relationships
155k Relationship of the Frequency of Masturbation to Several Aspects of Personality and Behavior
158x Separatism and Sexual Relationships
194g Relationships of Sex and Social Class in Brazil
225b Witch and Her Devils: An Exploration of the Relationship Between Femininity and Illness
254q Patient and Patriarch: Women in the Psychotherapeutic Relationship
256i Wages of Wrath: Women's Relationships in the Working World
256s Genderless Sexuality: A Male-Female Psychological Exploration of the Future of Sexual Relationships
258c New Patterns of Relationship: Beginnings of a Moral Revolution
264g Power in Dating Relationships
266g Relationship Between Role Orientation and Achievement Motivation in College Women
266aa Relationship Between Sex-Role Stereotypes And Requisite Management Characteristics
285k Sex Differences in the Incidence of Susto in Two Zapotec Pueblos: An Analysis of the Relationships between Sex Role Expectations and a Folk Illness

344l Exploring the Relationship Between Female Candidacies and the Women's Movement
358f Relationship of D.G.W.S. to A.I.A.W.
370h Husband-Wife Relationship

RELIGION

see also BIBLE; THEOLOGY; CHURCH; various denominations

6e Women in Organized Religion
42i Feminization of American Religion: 1800-1860
114d Cultural and Religious Influences
177a Women and Religion: Psychological and Cultural Implications
190b City Women and Religious Change in Sixteenth-Century France
210d Religious Socialization of Women Within U.S. Subcultures
210g Theology After the Demise of God the Father: A Call for the Castration of Sexist Religion
225f Woman-Power: Religious Heresy and Feminism in Early English Socialism
232c Investigation of the Religious and Judicial Character of Matriarchy in the Ancient World
256p When The Veils Come Tumbling Down: "And Women Shall Leave Their Comfortable Pews to Give Birth to a New and Inclusive Religious Vision"
258i Women and Religion: A Survey of Significant Literature, 1965-1974
269a Women and Religion
283a Theology After the Demise of God the Father: A Call for the Castration of Sexist Religion
283k Methodological Remarks on the Study of Women in Religion
283l Is Sexism a Sign of Decadence in Religion?
309g Women and Religion: The Status and Image of Women in Major Religious Traditions
317b Celibes, Mothers, and Church Cockroaches: Religious Participation of Women in a Mexican Village
337k Women, Religion and Reform in Antebellum America
337m Women in Judaism: From the Reform Movement to Contemporary Jewish Religious Feminism

REMEDIAL

64h Remedial and Affirmative Action

REMEDY

4r Internal Remedies for Sex Discrimination in Colleges and Universities
75h Remedies for Wrongs: Updating Programs for Delinquent Girls
79m Malady and Remedy of Vexations and Unjust Arrests and Actions
328d Legal Remedies beyond Title VII to Combat Sex Discrimination in Employment

REMINISCENCE

96e Autobiography and Reminiscences of a Pioneer
153m Reminiscences
336d Among Lowell Mill-Girls: A Reminiscence

REMUNERATION

352h Equality of Remuneration for Men and Women in the Member States of the E.E.C.

RENAISSANCE

19f Did Women Have a Renaissance?
23c Book-Lined Cells: Women and Humanism in the Early Italian Renaissance
52b Witchcraft and Magic in Renaissance Italy: Gianfrancesco Pico and his "Strix"
185f Woman as Artist and Patron in the Middle Ages and the Renaissance
215p Dr. Ellen Brooke Ferguson: Nineteenth-Century Renaissance Woman
240b Changing Image of Woman in Renaissance Society and Literature
315h Dowries and Kinsmen in Early Renaissance Venice

RENOIR

247h Renoir's Sensuous Women

REPARATION

180q Morality of Reparation
180w Reparations to Wronged Groups
180z Should Reparations be to Individuals or to Groups?
180aa Reparations to Individuals or Groups?

REPORTER

257m Woman's Clubs from a Reporter's Point of View
348g Accounting for Rape: Reality and Myth in Press Reporting

REPOSITORY

164n Repository of Wealth

REPRESENTATION

41 Representation, Performance and Status of Women on the Faculty at the Urbana-Champaign Campus of the University of Illinois
76n Psychic Representation and Female Orgasm
140c Male Sex Role Behaviors in a Representative National Sample, 1973
215x Augusta Joyce Crocheron: A Representative Woman
272p Changing Women's Representation in School Management: A Systems Perspective
317e Misery of the Embodied: Representations of Women in Sinhalese Myth

REPRESSION

260bb Sexual Repression and the Family

REPRODUCTION

see also BIRTH; PROCREATION; MATERNITY; PREGNANCY

20a Reproduction

20f Relevance of Nourishment to the Reproductive Cycle of the Female in India
20w Attitudes Towards Reproduction in a Rapidly Changing African Society
21e Essential Emancipation: The Control of Reproduction
35e Struggle for Reproductive Freedom: Three Stages of Feminism
82a Psychological Conflict and the Reproductive System
199w Reproductive Hormones, Moods, and the Menstrual Cycle
211d Decisions about Reproduction: Genetic Counseling
268i Psychology of women in Relation to the Functions of Reproduction

REPUBLIC

159f Republic V
194m Politics and Feminism in the Dominican Republic: 1931-45 and 1966-74
203a Republic, Book V
206j Male and Female in the German Federal Republic
206k Male and Female in the German Democratic Republic
230n Love Unites Them and Hunger Separates Them: Poor Women in the Dominican Republic
275c Stereotype of the Emancipated Woman in the Weimar Republic
297h Lower Economic Sector: Female Mating Patterns in the Dominican Republic
338d Nzakara Women (Central African Republic)
344o Republican Women and the Future of the Republican Party
372c Women's Role in a Muslim Hausa Town--Mirria, Republic of Niger

REQUIREMENTS

286v Nutritional Requirements for Women in Sport
301d Legal Requirements, Structures, and Strategies for Eliminating Sex Discrimination in Academe

RESCUE

114r Prostitutes--Notes from a Rescue Home

RESENTMENT

17p "A Farewell to Arms": Ernest Hemingway's "Resentful Cryptogram"
79t The Wife's Resentment

RESERVATIONS

277g Reservations: A Love Story

RESERVE

291m Women: The New Reserve Army of the Unemployed

RESIDENCE

201 Explanation for Matrilocal Residence
354j Women's Labor Force Participation and the Residential Mobility of Families

366b Importance of Women in Determining the Composition of Residential Groups in Aboriginal Australia

RESISTANCE

105a Dynamics of Cultural Resistance
183e Gender Imagery and Issues of War and Peace: The Case of the Draft Resistance Movement of the 1960's
266y Sex-Role Boundaries and Resistance to Sex-Role Change
270c Mothers of a Nation: Seneca Resistance to Quaker Intervention
297m Resistance as Protest: Women in the Struggle of Bolivian Tin-Mining Communities
308c Marriage Resistance in Rural Kwangtung

RESOLUTION

48m Challenge and Resolution
132aa National Resolution on Women
257c Declaration of Sentiments, Resolutions, Seneca Falls

RESPECT

8c With All Due Respect: In Defense of All Lesbian Lifestyles
85t Rape and Respect
155v Attribution of Fault to a Rape Victim as a Function of Respectability
158s Pornography and Respect for Women
274f Negotiating Respect: Patterns of Presentation among Black Women

RESPONSIBILITY

67a Social Responsibility and Research on Sex Differences
106j Responsibility and Public Policy: Is It a Moral Question?
180p Racial Preferences in Higher Education: Political Responsibility and the Judicial Role

RESPONSIVENESS

155j Women's Sexual Responsiveness and the Duration and Quality of Their Marriages

RESTLESS

142d Restless Eagles: Women's Liberation 1969

RESTORATION

117v Restoration of Vashti
240d Portrayal of Women in Restoration and Eighteenth-century English Literature

RESTRICTIONS

13jj Discrimination and Demography Restrict Opportunities for Academic Women
98k For a Restricted Thematics: Writing, Speech, and Difference in Madame Bovary

334m Origins of Legal Restrictions on Planned Parenthood in Nineteenth-Century America

RESULTS

54a Population and the Status of Women: Results of the Bucharest and Mexico Conferences
246c Socialization of Women in Educational Institutions: Resultant Effects

RESURRECTION

95s Resurrection

RETENTIVENESS

219n Sociocultural and Sociopsychological Factors in Differential Language Retentiveness by Sex

RETIREMENT

146o Retirement: Career and Non-Career
371l Women's Retirement Income

RETREAT

349i Revolution and Retreat: Upper-Class French Women After 1789

RETURN

196cc Continuing Education for Women: Factors Influencing a Return to School and the School Experience
202l Nonmarket Returns to Women's Investment in Education
222dd Return of the Native
251x Differences in Return to Educational Investment
252dd Social and Private Rates of Return to Investment in Schooling
341v Fair Return

REVEL

83g Irish Revel

REVELATION

33p Revelation
79a XVI Revelations of Divine Love
263s Dreams and Fantasies as Sources of Revelation: Feminist Appropriation of Jung

REVERSE

180n Constitutionality of Reverse Racial Discrimination

REVERSE DISCRIMINATION

see also AFFIRMATIVE ACTION; PREFERENTIAL HIRING

85n Limits to the Justification of Reverse Discrimination
180v Reverse Discrimination and Compensatory Justice
180x Reverse Discrimination
180cc Justifiability of Reverse Discrimination
180ee Reverse Discrimination as Unjustified
203o Reverse Discrimination as Unjustified
203p Reverse Discrimination and the Future
217c Reverse Discrimination and Compensatory Justice
217d Justification of Reverse Discrimination
282o Reverse Discrimination and the Future

REVISIONS

90f Afterword: Critical Re-Vision
244i Sexuality in Britain, 1800-1900: Some Suggested Revisions
314z 52 Job Titles Revised to Eliminate Sex-Stereotyping

REVOLT

4a Women on the Move: Roots of Revolt
10d The Revolt of "Mother"
89j Black Women in Revolt
89w Lesbians in Revolt
123c Lesbians in Revolt
154g Female Militancy and Colonial Revolt: The Women's War of 1929, Eastern Nigeria
241d The Revolt of the ___
341g Women's Revolt in the M.L.A.

REVOLUTION

see also WAR; names of wars

19j Loaves and Liberty: Women in the French Revolution
19k Working-Class Women During the Industrial Revolution, 1780-1914
19o Women as Revolutionaries: The Case of the Russian Populists
19p Love on the Tractor: Women in the Russian Revolution and After
24dd The Day Before the Revolution
35n Significance of the Chinese Family Revolution for Feminist Theory
39b My Four Revolutions: An Autobiographical History of the A.S.A.
43e Chinese Women: The Relative Influences of Ideological Revolution, Economic Growth, and Cultural Change
43h Women in Cuba: The Revolution Within the Revolution
86m Women and the Russian Revolution
97f Women: The Longest Revolution
98d Language and Revolution: The Franco-American Dis-Connection
127dd Women: The Longest Revolution
127ll Asian Women in Revolution
132p Longest Revolution
134g The Day Before the Revolution
139t Revolution is Happening in Our Minds
139x Female Liberation as the Basis for Social Revolution
140b Great Revolution
149m Leads on Old Questions from a New Revolution: Notes on Cuban Women, 1969
159b Our Revolution is Unique
175n Independence From the Sexual Revolution

175ll Sexual Politics: A Manifesto for Revolution
178a Anne Hutchinson and the "Revolution Which Never Happened"
212k Feminist Aesthetic: Reflection Revolution Ritual
238b Our Revolution Is Unique
238c Female Liberation as the Basis for Social Revolution
251k Women: The Longest Revolution
251hh Chinese Family Revolution and Feminist Theory
252c Women Workers and the Industrial Revolution
252f Women: The Longest Revolution
252ll Sexual Politics: A Manifesto for Revolution
253h Revolution Without Ideology: The Changing Place of Women in America
255h Rousseau's Sexism Revolutionized
256t Changing Woman's Thinking and Lifestyle Through the Great Communication Revolution
258c New Patterns of Relationship: Beginnings of a Moral Revolution
282m Feminism: Reform or Revolution
307f Women and Revolution: The Lessons of the Soviet Union and China
307g Response to "Women and Revolution"
312d Women, the Vote and Revolution
325o Women and Revolution in Iran, 1905-1911
329t Kibbutz Women: From the Fields of Revolution to the Laundries of Discontent
349d Legal Status of Women After the American Revolution
349e Institutional Changes for Women of the People During the French Revolution
349g Women in the Chinese Communist Revolution: The Question of Political Equality
349h Revolution and Conciencia: Women in Cuba
349i Revolution and Retreat: Upper-Class French Women After 1789
349j Patriot Mothers in the Post-Risorgimento: Women After the Italian Revolution

REVOLUTIONARY

35c Feminist Theory and the Development of Revolutionary Strategy
86k Revolutionary Perspective on the Oppression of Women
122l Nellie Campobello: Romantic Revolutionary and Mexican Realist
132dd Woman's Revolutionary Manifesto
139i Revolutionary Birth Control
142b Revolutionary Letter #1
178c Puritan Ethic in the Revolutionary Era: Abigail Adams and Thomas Jefferson
181j Women in Revolutionary China
218c From Separatism to Socialism: Women in the Russian Revolutionary Movement of the 1870s
325m Revolutionary Gentlewomen in Egypt
349a Women of the Popular Classes in Revolutionary Paris, 1789-1795

REWARDS

39p Performance, Rewards, and Perceptions of Sex Discrimination among Male and Female Faculty
266h Bringing Women In: Rewards, Punishments, And the Structure of Achievement

REX

79j Salve Deus Rex Judaeorum

REYNOLDS

215m Alice Louise Reynolds: A Woman's Woman
215r Dr. Ellis Reynolds Shipp: Pioneer Utah Physician

RHESUS MONKEYS

199f Sex Differences in Rhesus Monkeys Following Varied Rearing Experiences
199t Bisexual Behavior of Female Rhesus Monkeys

RHODE ISLAND

116l Italian American Women and Their Daughters in Rhode Island: The Adolescence of Two Generations, 1900-1950

RHODES

341d Rhodes: Still Blocked

RHODESIA

273v The Train from Rhodesia

RHYS

47h Character and Themes in the Novels of Jean Rhys
88u Jean Rhys' Recent Fiction: Humane Developments in "Wide Sargasso Sea"

RIB

362m From Adam's Rib to Women's Lib

RICE

303k Lilian Rice

RICH

88k Feminist Poet: Alta and Adrienne Rich
214t Critique of Consciousness and Myth in Levertov, Rich, and Rukeyser

RICHARDS

215h Jane Snyder Richards: The Blue-White Diamond
215v Louisa Lula Greene Richards: "Remember the Women of Zion"

RICHARDSON

17h Richardson's Empathy with Women
36i "Featureless Freedom" or Ironic Submission: Dorothy Richardson and May Sinclair

266r Frontiero v. Richardson

RICHMAN

128n Julia Richman

RIDDLE

111rr Tell Me a Riddle
112ee Tell Me a Riddle

RIDERS

233v Riders to the Sea
339i Riders to the Sea

RIEFENSTAHL

212o Leni Riefenstahl: The Deceptive Myth

RIGA

113b In the Forests of Riga the Beasts Are Very Wild Indeed

RIGHT

see also EQUAL RIGHTS AMENDMENT; EQUALITY

9d Speech: National Women's Rights Convention of 1855
9u Modern Trends in the Law Concerning Women's Rights
22j Aborting a Fetus: The Legal Right, The Personal Choice
30b Dowry and Bridewealth and the Property Rights of Women in South Asia
74a Rights of Woman
79n Upon the much lamented death of the Right Honourable the Lady Elizabeth Langham
89s N.O.W. Bill of Rights
94g Forcible Rape and the Problem of the Rights of the Accused
106k Civil Rights and the Women's Movement
107dd Declaration of Women's Rights
121j Nineteenth-Century Feminist Press and Women's Rights in Brazil
132g Love Rights of Women
149b Civil and Social Rights of Women
151o Campaign for Women's Rights in the 1920's
157t Abortion and a Woman's Right to Decide
159r Vindication of the Rights of Woman
174g Minorities and Policy Problems: An Overview Seen by the U.S. Commission on Civil Rights
174k Combatting Dual Discrimination: The Impact of Civil Rights Policies on the Income Status of Black Women
174o Political Power and Policy Benefits: Voting Rights and Welfare Policy in Mississippi
181k Rights and Wrongs of Women: Mary Wollstonecraft, Harriet Martineau, Simone de Beauvoir
188a Vindication of the Rights of Women
195a Observations on the Real Rights of Women
196ff Reports of the Women's Rights Committee

196jj Equal Rights for Women
203e Science of Rights
232i Short History of Women's Rights
232k First Essay on the Political Rights of Women
233uu Sojourner Truth: On Women's Rights
243c Male Attitudes Toward Women's Rights as a Function of Their Level of Self-Esteem
246a Radical and Conservative Trends in the Women's Rights Movement
252b Family Patterns and Human Rights
252kk Platform on Women's Rights
254aa Women's Liberation and Black Civil Rights
259g Rights of Women
260s Title VII of the 1964 Civil Rights Act
261a Woman's Rights
270h Daughters of the Lakes and Rivers: Colonization and the Land Rights of Luo Women
278l History of Married Women's Rights
280q Social Security and Equal Rights
282t Abortion and a Woman's Right to Decide
284l Women's Job Rights Gain in Federal Court Rulings
284n U.N. Declaration on Women's Rights
294o Women in Economic Life: Rights and Opportunities
309f Women and the Law: Constitutional Rights and Continuing Inequalities
321c Burger Court and Women's Rights, 1971-1977
352g Women's Rights and Widows' Pensions
358b Women's Rights in Athletics

RIGIDITY

371j Hours Rigidity: Effects on the Labor-Market Status of Women

RIMA

111dd Rima the Bird Girl
112x Rima the Bird Girl

RIOTS

302c "Aba Riots" or Igbo "Women's War"? Ideology, Stratification, and the Invisibility of Women

RISE

93d Lena Morrow Lewis: Her Rise and Fall
132r Rise of Women's Liberation
140s Rise of the Women's Movement: A Case Study in Political Development
176bb Rise of Women's Liberation
215w Emmeline Blanche Woodward Wells: "I Have Risen Triumphant"

RISK-TAKING

140ee Promoting Creative Risk-Taking in Women

RITE

20i Matrescence, Becoming a Mother, a 'New-Old' 'Rite de Passage'

RITUAL

20e Birth Rituals in Cross-Cultural Perspective: Some Practical Applications
161g Rites
212k Feminist Aesthetic: Reflection Revolution Ritual
263w Self-Blessing Ritual
317d Coming of Age in Kelton: The Constraints on Gender Symbolism in Jewish Ritual
317g Southern Lay Midwives as Ritual Specialists
360l Female World of Love and Ritual: Relations Between Women in Nineteenth-Century America

RIVALRY

164j Implication of Rivalry

RIVERS

138a Women of Three Rivers: 1651-63
270h Daughters of the Lakes and Rivers: Colonization and the Land Rights of Luo Women

RIVETER

140h Did Rosie the Riveter Give Up Her Job? Women War Workers During and After World War II
266o New Views of Rosie the Riveter

ROAD

19l Long Road Home: Women's Work and Industrialization
95q Coffee for the Road
220n Success Is Not a Destination But the Road To It
328c Legal Road to Equal Employment Opportunity
329u Chinese Women on the Road to Complete Emancipation

ROBERTS

334o From Aide to Organizer: The Oral History of Lillian Roberts

ROBINSON

79w Letters to Elizabeth Robinson Montagu
79z Letters to Elizabeth Robinson Montagu

ROCK AND ROLL

278g Worship of Women in Courtly Love and Rock and Roll

ROCKING-HORSE

279o The Rocking-Horse Winner

ROCOCO

247g Corset as Erotic Alchemy: From Rococo Galanterie to Montaut's Physiologies

RODMAN

139j Henrietta Rodman: An Interview with a Feminist

ROGERS

215j Aurelia Read Spencer Rogers: Humble Heroine

ROLE

see also SEX ROLE; ROLES

18g Role of Laughter and Humor in Growing Up Female
22p Sexual Role Identification and Personality Functioning in Girls
39i Changing Role of Women in the Armed Forces
59g Search for a Partnership Role: Women in Labor Unions Today
70a Husband Provider Role: A Critical Appraisal
71a Literary Archetypes and Female Role Alternatives: The Woman and the Novel in Latin America
115b Role of Women in the Indian Struggle for Freedom
117s Changing(?)Role of Women in Jewish Communal Affairs: A Look into the U.J.A.
126g Education and Ideology in Nineteenth-Century America: The Response of Educational Institutions to the Changing Role of Women
138d Neglected Majority: The Changing Role of Women in 19th Century Montreal
141j Role of Women in the Organization of the Men's Garment Industry, Chicago, 1910
143j Toward Supportive Neighborhoods: Women's Role in Changing the Segregated City
163p Women Members of Congress: A Distinctive Role
163q Wife and Politician: Role Strain Among Women in Public Office
175qq Body is the Role: Sylvia Plath
176ee Sex Differentiation in Role Expectations and Performance
178j Role of Women in the Founding of the U.S. Children's Bureau
183g Role of Women in Underdeveloped Countries: Some Sociological Issues Concerning Conflict and Peace
183i Bibliography: Role of Women in Conflict and Peace
184e Fifteenth-Century View of Women's Role in Medieval Society: Christine de Pizan's "Livre des Trois Vertus"
190e Classical Mythology and the Role of Women in Modern Literature
198j Status and Role: Raw Materials for Society, Marriage
204m Role of Tests and Their Construction in Producing Apparent Sex-Related Differences
206h Role Themes in Latin America
206p Status and Role Behavior in Changing Japan
208f School's Role in the Sex-Role Stereotyping of Girls: A Feminist Review of the Literature
233ccc Man's Role in Women's Liberation
250p Woman's Role in Cross-Cultural Perspective
251f Assumptions About Gender Role
252t Feminine Role and the Kinship System
252ff Reducing Discrimination: Role of the Equal Pay Act
253j Role of Choice in the Psychology of Professional Women

264h Mother Role
266c Sexual Role Identification and Personality Functioning in Girls
266g Relationship Between Role Orientation and Achievement Motivation in College Women
266q Changing Role of Women in the Armed Forces
267o Implied Demand Character of the Wife's Future and Role Innovation: Patterns of Achievement Orientation Among College Women
268r Role of Clara Thompson in the Psychoanalytic Study of Women
269h Parent's Role in Values Education
272l Need for Female Role Models in Education
278q Childbearing and the Woman's Role
282a Anatomy and Destiny: The Role of Biology in Plato's Views of Women
285d Role of Women in a Changing Navaho Society
293a Role of Women in Agriculture
296v Acceptance of the Concept of the Maternal Role by Behavioral Scientists: Its Effects on Women
297c African Women: Identity Crisis? Some Observations on Education and the Changing Role of Women in Sierra Leone and Zaire
297j Sociocultural Factors Mitigating Role Conflict of Buenos Aires Professional Women
297t Role and Status of Women in the Soviet Union: 1917 to the Present
304e Housewives in Women's Liberation: Social Change as Role-Making
312b Role of Women in Ireland under the New English Order
316f Role and Status of Women in the Daley Organization
329d Catholicism and Women's Role in Italy and Ireland
329i Tradition and the Role of Women in Great Britain
330r Female Role: Constants and Change
331j Crisis Perspective on Divorce and Role Change
342bb Women's Role in Organized Labor
352c Division of Labour and Sexual Inequality: The Role of Education
352d Development and Mounting Famine: A Role for Women
360n Hysterical Woman: Sex Roles and Role Conflict in Nineteenth-Century America
364b Submission, Masochism and Narcissism: Three Aspects of Women's Role as Reflected in Dress
365b Changing the Role of Women
365d Acceptance of the Concept of the Maternal Role by Behavioral Scientists: Its Effects on Women
366c Role of Women in Aboriginal Marriage Arrangements
372c Women's Role in a Muslim Hausa Town--Mirria, Republic of Niger

ROLE--CULTURE

256k Women in the Arts: Insights to the Cultural Impact of Women's Role in the Creative Arts
268q Role of Women in This Culture
297b Role of Women in the Development of Culture in Nigeria
330c Cultural Values, Female Role Expectancies and Therapeutic Goals: Research and Interpretation

ROLE--DEVELOPMENT

18m Role Music Plays in Adolescent Development
37c Parental Role Division and the Child's Personality Development
173dd Role of Models in Women's Professional Development
236h Role of Korean Women in National Development
297b Role of Women in the Development of Culture in Nigeria

ROLE--ECONOMY

126o Women in Convents: Their Economic and Social Role in Colonial Mexico
251e Changing Economic Role of Women
328a Women's Stake in Full Employment: Their Disadvantaged Role in the Economy--Challenges to Action
372l Economic Role of Women in Alaskan Eskimo Society

ROLE--FAMILY

55i Marriage, Role Division and Social Cohesion: The Case of Some French Upper-Middle Class Families
116o Maternal Role in the Contemporary Italian-American Family
140k Role of Wife in the Black Extended Family: Perspectives from a Rural Community in Southern United States

ROLE--OCCUPATION

55c Sex and Occupational Role on Fleet Street
166z Self-Concept, Occupational Role Expectations, and Occupational Choice in Nursing and Social Work
196q Counselor Bias and the Female Occupational Role
252bb Counselor Bias and the Female Occupational Role
267p Determinants of Occupational Role Innovation Among College Women

ROLE--POLITICS

141z Changing Status and Role of Women in Politics
180p Racial Preferences in Higher Education: Political Responsibility and the Judicial Role
260y Role of Women in the Political Organization of African Societies
294l Political Role of Southeast Asian Women
316p Changing the Political Role of Women: A Costa Rican Case Study
338c Role of Women in the Political Organization of African Societies

ROLE--WORK

166u Role Model Influences on College Women's Career Aspirations
176gg Re-Evaluation of the Primary Role of the Communist Chinese Woman: The Homemaker or the Worker
272m Working and Parenting: The Male and Father Role
328a Women's Stake in Full Employment: Their Disadvantaged Role in the Economy--Challenges to Action
333b Role of Worker Expectancies in the Study of Employment Discrimination

ROLES

see also SEX ROLES; ROLE

14k Assumptions Made About Gender Roles
20y Vietnamese Women: Their Roles and Their Options
20z Changing Roles of Women in Two African Muslim Cultures
23f Women's Roles in Early Modern Venice
43c Women in Zaire: Disparate Status and Roles

59b Women's Roles in the Economy: Economic Investigation and Research Needs
70b Two Roles of Russian Working Women in an Urban Area
71j Pursuit of an Ideal: Migration, Social Class, and Women's Roles in Bogota, Colombia
100e Class and Race Differences in Gender Roles
100f Gender Roles from a Cross-Cultural Perspective
107d Roles and Virtues of Men and Women
114s Chellamma--An Illustration of the Multiple Roles of Traditional Women
116m Italian Mothers, American Daughters: Changes in Work and Family Roles
116s Emigration, the Italian Family, and Changing Roles
140i Women's Roles in World Change: What About the Family?
146j Self Image and Roles
164g Roles of Women: A Question of Values
164i Interpretation of Roles
166n Female Physician in Public Health: Conflict and Reconciliation of the Sex and Professional Roles
166aaa Myth of the Egalitarian Family: Familial Roles and the Professionally Employed Wife
171j Adult Life Cycles: Changing Roles and Changing Hormones
172j Traits, Roles, and the Concept of Androgyny
185h Roles of Medieval Women in the Healing Arts
193e Roles of Children in Urban Kano
194e Impact of Industrialization on Women's Work Roles in Northeast Brazil
206g Marriage Roles, American Style
206n Milieu Development and Male-Female Roles in Contemporary Greece
227d Social Change and the Roles of Women
236j Occupations, Male Housekeeper: Male-Female Roles on Cheju Island
250c Female Roles in Women's Magazine Fiction, 1940-1970
250q Roles of Activation and Inhibition in Sex Differences in Cognitive Abilities
250r Comments on "Roles of Activation and Inhibition in Sex Differences in Cognitive Abilities"
258d Home and Work: Women's Roles and the Transformation of Values
258f Roles of Women in the Fourth Gospel
260aa Roles of Women
264a Woman's Biology--Mankind's Destiny: The Population Explosion and Women's Changing Roles
265a Woman's Biology--Mankind's Destiny: The Population Explosion and Women's Changing Roles
266ii Socio-Economic Context Of Sex And Power: A Study of Women, Work And Family Roles in Four Israeli Institutional Frameworks
269b Women and Their Work Roles
276a Family and Gender Roles in Historical Perspective
280n New Choices, New Roles
287h Economy Ahead of Us: Will Women Have Different Roles?
289f Women's Roles and the Great World Transformation
291h Familial Constraints on Women's Work Roles
294b Demographic Change and the Roles and Status of Women
309i Aging Women in India: Self-Perceptions and Changing Roles
317j Bobbes and Zeydes: Old and New Roles for Elderly Jews
318o Women in Political Roles
329o Women's Changing Roles in Colombia
329s Changing Women's Roles in the U.S.S.R.

344r Crisis Perspective on Emerging Health Roles: A Paradigm for the Entry of Women into New Occupational Roles
371c Occupational Values and Family Roles: Women in Blue-Collar and Service Occupations
371m Family Wholeness: New Conceptions of Family Roles
372j Uses of Traditional Concepts in the Development of New Urban Roles: Cuban Women in the United States

ROMAN

85w Roman Catholic Doctrine of Therapeutic Abortion
337o Roman Catholic Story

ROMANA

247d Caritas Romana after 1760: Some Romantic Lactations

ROMANCE

122l Nellie Campobello: Romantic Revolutionary and Mexican Realist
240e Gender and Genre: Women in British Romantic Literature
247d Caritas Romana after 1760: Some Romantic Lactations
279k Romance of a Fisherman's Wife
288f Twilight of Romanticism: "Adele H."
356b A Romantic Hero
357b Buried Letter: Feminism and Romanticism in Villette

ROMANIA

215q Dr. Romania Pratt Penrose: To Brave the World

ROMANS

255g La Condition de la Femme Francaise au Dix-huitieme Siecle d'apres les Romans

ROOM

88f Room of Her Own: Emily Dickinson as Woman Artist
119a The Locked Room Upstairs
127cc "A Room of One's Own"
233ii To Room Nineteen
233tt Room of One's Own
314jj Keys to the Executive Powder Room
363j A Room of One's Own

ROOSEVELT

253l Nothing to Fear: Notes on the Life of Eleanor Roosevelt

ROOT

4a Women on the Move: Roots of Revolt
68y Root of the White Slave Traffic
176r Roots of Ambivalence in American Women
191a Women's Health Movement: Past Roots
212v Family Portraits: Filmmakers Explore Their Roots

222z Mississippi Mothers: Roots

ROPE

277i Rope

ROSANIA

79q To Rosania and Lucasia, Articles of Friendship

ROSARIO

88m Women and Feminism in the Works of Rosario Castellanos

ROSEMARY

106l Rosemary Park: Professional Activities

ROSES

17j War and Roses: The Politics of "Mrs. Dalloway"
74j Bread and Roses
97a Bread and Roses

ROSH

117i This Month Is for You: Observing Rosh Hodesh as a Woman's Holiday

ROSIE

111tt Miss Rosie
140h Did Rosie the Riveter Give Up Her Job? Women War Workers During and After World War II
266o New Views of Rosie the Riveter

ROSSETTI

214g Christina Rossetti: The Inward Pose
357c Indefinite Disclosed: Christina Rossetti and Emily Dickinson

ROSSI

73r Conversation with Alice Rossi

ROTHMAN

288t Stephanie Rothman: R-Rated Feminist

ROTTED

117y Mothers and Daughters in American Jewish Literature: The Rotted Cord

ROUGH

300a Rough Times
363s Women's Lib Gets Rough

ROUSSEAU

255h Rousseau's Sexism Revolutionized
282i Future of Love: Rousseau and the Radical Feminists

ROUTE

24i The Route

ROYAL

50c The Stir Outside the Cafe Royal

RUKEYSER

214t Critique of Consciousness and Myth in Levertov, Rich, and Rukeyser

RULE

105i Women's Page as a Window on the Ruling Class
157v Abortion and the Golden Rule
195c Uncivil Liberty: An Essay to Show the Injustice and Impolicy of Ruling Woman Without Her Consent
241a When Women Rule
249i Madam Yoko: Ruler of the Kpa Mende Confederacy
249n Myth of Matriarchy: Why Men Rule in Primitive Society
270g Andean Women Under Spanish Rule
284l Women's Job Rights Gain in Federal Court Rulings
321b Women, Men, and The Constitution: Key Supreme Court Rulings

RUN

24bb The Long-Distance Runner
33m See How They Run
112jj See How They Run
113u Raymond's Run
152h See Jane Run
197d "Look, Jane, Look! See Dick Run and Jump! Admire Him!"
208v Run, Mama, Run: Women Workers in Elementary Readers

RURAL

8n Thriving Decloseted in Rural Academe
114n Women of Rural Bihar
140k Role of Wife in the Black Extended Family: Perspectives from a Rural Community in Southern United States
219j Black Women In the Rural South: Conservative and Innovative
230o Spread of Capitalism in Rural Colombia: Effects on Poor Women
230q Collectivization, Kinship, and the Status of Women in Rural China
281g Class Structures and Female Autonomy in Rural Java
294p Women in the Rural Areas
302k Less Than Second-Class: Women in Rural Settlement Schemes in Tanzania
306b Women in Rural Japan
308c Marriage Resistance in Rural Kwangtung
318g Russian Rural Women
350b Rural China: Segregation to Solidarity

352m Handicrafts: A Source of Employment for Women in Developing Rural Economies
367e Rural-Urban Fertility Differences and Trends in Egypt, 1930-70
372k Life of Sarah Penfield, Rural Ohio Grandmother: Tradition Maintained, Tradition Threatened

RUSKIN

223g Debate over Women : Ruskin vs. Mill

RUSSIA

see also SOVIET

19o Women as Revolutionaries: The Case of the Russian Populists
19p Love on the Tractor: Women in the Russian Revolution and After
70b Two Roles of Russian Working Women in an Urban Area
80o Metamorphosis of an Icon: Woman in Russian Literature
86m Women and the Russian Revolution
182b Woman Student in Russia
218c From Separatism to Socialism: Women in the Russian Revolutionary Movement of the 1870s
257p Russia
318a Society and the Sexes in the Russian Past
318b Women and the Russian Intelligentsia: Three Perspectives
318c Russian Factory Women, 1880-1914
318g Russian Rural Women
357g Poetry and Conscience: Russian Women Poets of the Twentieth Century

RUTH

339j The Book of Ruth

RWANDA

322f Field Work in Rwanda, 1959-1960

S.C.U.M.

132cc S.C.U.M. Manifesto
233q S.C.U.M. Manifesto

SABBAT

52h Pierre de Lancre's "Tableau de l'Inconstance des Mauvais Anges et Demons": The Sabbat Sensationalised

SABBATH

263n Sabbath Prayers for Women

SACKE

229c Mulde Sacke

SACKVILLE-WEST

140mm Sexual Identity in the Early Fiction of V. Sackville-West

SACRED

79h To The Thrice Sacred Queen Elizabeth
369t Sacred Fire

SADDUCEEISM

52e Reginald Scot's "Discoverie of Witchcraft": Scepticism and Sadduceeism

SAFFRON

298g The Saffron Boat

SAGA

341m Unemployed! An Academic Woman's Saga

SAHARA

293h Women in African Towns South of the Sahara: The Urbanization Dilemma
294k Political Participation of Women in Africa South of the Sahara

SAILOR

119j The Sailor Boy's Tales

SAINT

185c Saints and Witches
260z Saint-Watching
281i Women, Saints, and Sanctuaries
302a Signares of Saint-Louis and Goree: Women Entrepreneurs in Eighteenth-Century Senegal
339f Saint Joan

SALEM

52i Cotton Mather's "Wonders of the Invisible World": Some Metamorphoses of Salem Witchcraft

SALIENCE

176x Differences in Attitudinal Responses Under Conditions of Implicitly Manipulated Group Salience

SALINA

215n Stena Scorup: First Lady of Salina

SALKA

5k Salka Viertel

SALON

39e Salon, Foyer, Bureau: Women and the Professions in France
42e Salon, Foyer, Bureau: Women and the Professions in France
266gg Salon, Foyer, Bureau: Women And The Professions in France

SALT

273t Pillar of Salt

SALVADOR

194f Bahiana in the Labor Force in Salvador, Brazil

SALVATION

185a Sin and Salvation: The Dramatic Context of Hrotswitha's Women
214r Poetry and Salvation in the Career of Anne Sexton

SALVE

79j Salve Deus Rex Judaeorum

SAMBIZANGA

288gg "Sambizanga"

SAMPER

122d Life and Early Literary Career of the Nineteenth-Century Colombian Writer, Coledad Acosta de Samper

SAMPLE

25i "Black Matriarchy" Reconsidered: Evidence from Secondary Analysis of Sample Surveys
114t Girl Students: Between School and Marriage--a Delhi Sample
140c Male Sex Role Behaviors in a Representative National Sample, 1973
155n Comparison of Sexual Attitudes and Behavior in an International Sample

SAMSON

277w Samson and Delilah

SANCTAE

315f Mulieres Sanctae

SANCTITY

19d Sanctity and Power: The Dual Pursuit of Medieval Women

SANCTUARIES

281i Women, Saints, and Sanctuaries

SAND

179h G. Sand
340n Of Mist, and Grass, and Sand

SANITY

364j Confronting the Sports Establishment: A Plan for Honesty and Sanity

SANTA

40f Vouchers for Child Care: The Santa Clara Child Care Pilot Study

SANTAMARIA

179k F.K. Santamaria

SAO PAULO

372e Spirit Magic in the Social Relations between Men and Women--Sao Paulo, Brazil

SAPPHIRES

256d No More Sapphires or Black Pearls: Self-definition is Where It Starts

SARA

122n Two Poets of America: Juana de Asbaje and Sara de Ibanez

SARAH

215b Sarah Melissa Granger Kimball: The Liberal Shall Be Blessed
215u Sarah Elizabeth Carmichael: Poetic Genius of Pioneer Utah
372k Life of Sarah Penfield, Rural Ohio Grandmother: Tradition Maintained, Tradition Threatened

SARGASSO

88u Jean Rhys' Recent Fiction: Humane Developments in "Wide Sargasso Sea"

SARTON

110q May Sarton's Women

SARTRE

282e Holes and Slime: Sexism in Sartre's Psychoanalysis

SATURDAY

105c Spot Messages within Saturday Morning TV Programs

SAUDI

372a Contemporary Saudi Woman

SAVAGE

108x The Savage

SCANDINAVIA

155o Changing Sex Norms in America and Scandinavia
324t Scandinavia
329w Scandinavian Women

SCARLET

339h The Scarlet Letter

SCENE

19q Other Scenarios: Women and Spanish Anarchism
288a Short Manual for an Aspiring Scenario Writer
369i Scenes

SCHAUSPIEL

275f Frau und Staatsburger in Volker Braun's Schauspiel "Tinka"

SCHEDULES

371i Nontraditional Work Schedules for Women

SCHIZOPHRENIA

99l Gender and Schizophrenia

SCHNEIDERS

24t Bertha Schneiders Existential Edge

SCHOLAR

23d Learned Women of Early Modern Italy: Humanists and University Scholars
60p Marriage and the Woman Scholar
106h Factors Affecting Women's Scholarly Productivity
126m Classical Scholar's Perspective on Matriarchy

SCHOOL

see also various educational levels

13l Schools Are Emasculating Our Boys

13m Do Schools Sell Girls Short?
13p Sex Problems of School Math Books
13ee Harvard Ed School
21r Women and Girls in the Public Schools: Defeat or Liberation?
22o Sex-Role Concepts and Sex Typing in Childhood as a Function of School and Home Environments
41f Italian-American Women in New York City, 1900-1950: Work and School
43m Schooling of Vietnamese Immigrants: Internal Colonialism and its Impact on Women
45a Socialization and Education of Young Black Girls in Schools
45c Professional Schools and Their Impact on Black Women
53e Privileged, Schooled and Finished: Boarding Education for Girls
96g Schooldays of an Indian Girl
114t Girl Students: Between School and Marriage--a Delhi Sample
145c Fitness, Feminism and Schooling
156i Non-Sexist Parenting at Home and at School
173n How Nursery Schools Teach Girls to Shut Up
180o Judicial Scrutiny of "Benign" Racial Preference in Law School Admissions
196a Sex-Role Socialization and the Nursery School: As the Twig is Bent
196g Sex Bias in Secondary Schools: The Impact of Title IX
196h Teachers' Perceptions of Ideal Male and Female Students: Male Chauvinism in the Schools
196x Attitudes of Superintendents and Board of Education Members Toward the Employment and Effectiveness of Women as Public-School Administrators
196y School Boards and Sex Bias in American Education
196cc Continuing Education for Women: Factors Influencing a Return to School and the School Experience
196mm What, If Anything, Impedes Women from Serving on School Boards?
196nn Sex Differential in School Enrollment and Educational Attainment
200d Child's Sex-Role Classification of School Objects
208g Schooling of Tomorrow's Women
208j Segregated Academic and Vocational Schools: Separate But Not Equal
208k Sex Bias in the Public Schools
208o Changing the School Environment
208r Let Them Aspire! A Plea and Proposal for Equality of Opportunity for Males and Females in the Ann Arbor Public Schools
215k Two Miss Cooks: Pioneer Professionals for Utah's Schools
252dd Social and Private Rates of Return to Investment in Schooling
271h Sex-Role Concepts and Sex Typing in Childhood as a Function of School and Home Environments
271w Schooling of Tomorrow's Women
272e Feminism and the Woman School Administrator
272h Sex Bias in School Administration
272i Socialization and Education of Young Black Girls in School
272p Changing Women's Representation in School Management: A Systems Perspective
278n Black Women in Urban Schools
280h Sex Bias in Schools
280i Unisex and the Public Schools
290c View from the Law School
333g Differences in Expected Post-School Investment as a Determinant of Market Wage Differentials
342t Sexism in the Schools: Focus on the Woman Teacher
343a Curse of Eve--Or, What I Learned in School (Women and Literature)

344d Local Officeholding and the Community: The Case of Women on New Jersey's School Boards
364i Women School Administrators: My Experience with Discrimination

SCHOOL--STEREOTYPE

196i Psychological and Occupational Sex Stereotypes in Elementary School Readers
205d Influence of the School on Sex-Role Stereotyping
208f School's Role in the Sex-Role Stereotyping of Girls: A Feminist Review of the Literature
208p Feminist Studies: The Schools and Sex-Role Stereotyping
320h Sex Stereotyping in Canadian Schools

SCHOOLMARMS

295e Schoolmarms and Early Teaching in Ontario

SCHUB

212m Esther Schub

SCIENCE

49d Psychological Barriers for Women in Sciences: Internal and External
101d Comments on "Science and Racism"
110f Image of Women in Science Fiction
142q Kinder, Kuche, Kirche as Scientific Law: Psychology Constructs the Female
149k Women in Science: Why So Few?
166h Clash Between Beautiful Women and Science
166qq Women in Science: Why So Few?
176l Barriers to the Career Choice of Engineering, Medicine, or Science Among American Women
201e Science and the Woman Problem: Historical Perspectives
203e Science of Rights
205j Sex-Role Stereotyping and Social Science
208ll Sex Stereotypes in Mathematics and Science Textbooks for Elementary and Junior High Schools
264q Women in the Professions: Psychological and Social Barriers to Women in Science
265m Women in the Professions: Psychological and Social Barriers to Women in Science
289h Women in Science Fiction
289i Science Fiction Survey
292k Principles of Domestic Science
296v Acceptance of the Concept of the Maternal Role by Behavioral Scientists: Its Effects on Women
301f Creating Opportunities for Women in Science
304n Bibliography of Materials on Canadian Women, 1950-1975 (Social Sciences)
327d Nonacademic Professional Political Scientists
332i Adventures of a Woman in Science
332k Bibliography: Women, Science, and Health
340a Women and Science Fiction
365d Acceptance of the Concept of the Maternal Role by Behavioral Scientists: Its Effects on Women

369p Adventures of a Woman in Science

SCORES

266l Female College Students' Scores On the Men's And Women's Strong Vocational Interest Blanks
280k Test Scores and Unequal Education

SCORUP

215n Stena Scorup: First Lady of Salina

SCOT

52e Reginald Scot's "Discoverie of Witchcraft": Scepticism and Sadduceeism

SCOTLAND

52j Two Late Scottish Witchcraft Tracts: "Witch-Craft Proven" and "The Tryal of Witchcraft"
317c Hats as a Symbol of Women's Position in Three Evangelical Churches in Edinburgh, Scotland

SCOTT

179j E. Scott

SCOTT-MAXWELL

179ee F. Scott-Maxwell

SCRATCH

375f Creating Oneself from Scratch

SCREEN

288p Alice Guy Blache: Czarina of the Silent Screen

SCREENWRITER

364h Confessions of a Female Screenwriter

SCREWBALL

288hh "Part-Time Work of a Domestic Slave," or Putting the Screws to Screwball Comedy

SCRUTINY

8aa Oppression is Big Business: Scrutinizing Gay Therapy
180o Judicial Scrutiny of "Benign" Racial Preference in Law School Admissions

SCUOLA D'INDUSTRIE ITALIANE

116i Immigrants and Craft Arts: Scuola d'Industrie Italiane

SEA

88u Jean Rhys' Recent Fiction: Humane Developments in "Wide Sargasso Sea"
233v Riders to the Sea
310d The Lady From the Sea
339i Riders to the Sea

SEALING-WAX

83c Green Sealing-Wax

SEARCH

8k Search for Words
24w In Search of a Missing I.U.D.
59g Search for a Partnership Role: Women in Labor Unions Today
96jj In Search of Adventure
226p In Search of Adventure
341n Search for Talented Women
369g In Search of Our Mothers' Gardens

SEASON

8r Hustler: A Boy for All Seasons
111n Hunting Season

SEATTLE

40c Child Care Market in Seattle and Denver
40h Cost of Compliance with Federal Day Care Standards in Seattle and Denver

SECOND

13h Children's Books: The Second Sex, Junior Division
13aa Second Sex in Academe
77i Social Construction of the Second Sex
111g On Being Told That Her Second Husband Has Taken His First Lover
127aa "Second Sex"
134c The Second Inquisition
139u Second Feminist Wave
141dd Lillian Hellman: Dramatist of the Second Sex
146n Continuing Education and Second Careers
159y Second Sex
174i Incidence and Correlates of Second Generation Discrimination
186h Social Construction of the Second Sex
196m Sex Differences in the Occupational Choices of Second Graders
199l Emergence of Genital Awareness During the Second Year of Life
203c Second Treatise of Government
203h Second Sex
208d Social Construction of the Second Sex

240l Second-class Citizenship: The Status of Women in Contemporary American Fiction
271k Second Sex in Academe
284r Social Construction of the Second Sex
300b Weak Are the Second Sex
302k Less Than Second-Class: Women in Rural Settlement Schemes in Tanzania
341u "Second-Chance" Program for Women

SECONDARY

25i "Black Matriarchy" Reconsidered: Evidence from Secondary Analysis of Sample Surveys
158gg Secondary Sexism and Quota Hiring
196g Sex Bias in Secondary Schools: The Impact of Title IX
196o Attitudes Toward Increased Social, Economic, and Political Participation by Women as Reported by Elementary and Secondary Students
208kk Secondary Level Language Arts Presentation

SECRET

20q Bundu: Political Implications of Female Solidarity in a Secret Society
220p Secretive

SECRETARY

142m Woman as Secretary, Sexpot, Spender, Sow, Civic Actor, Sickie
186a Woman as Secretary, Sexpot, Spender, Sow, Civic Actor, Sickie

SECTARIAN

337h Feminist Thrust of Sectarian Christianity

SECTOR

174b Impact of Collective Bargaining on Minorities in the Public Sector: Some Policy Implications
281d Women in the Informal Labor Sector: The Case of Mexico City
297h Lower Economic Sector: Female Mating Patterns in the Dominican Republic

SEDENTARY

230d !Kung Women: Contrasts in Sexual Egalitarianism in Foraging and Sedentary Contexts

SEDUCER

9ii Seduced and Abandoned in the New World: The Fallen Woman in American Fiction
159u Diary of the Seducer
177c Woman: Seductive Siren and Source of Sin?
254o Seduced and Abandoned in the New World: The Image of Woman In American Fiction

SEEMOTHERMOTHERISVERYNICE

29h Seemothermotherisverynice

SEFROU

325bb Negotiation of Reality: Male-Female Relations in Sefrou, Morocco

SEGMENTATION

251n Labor Market Segmentation
333f Modeling a Segmented Labor Market

SEGREGATION

35j Capitalism, Patriarchy, and Job Segregation by Sex
51aa Sexual Segregation of American Prisons
143j Toward Supportive Neighborhoods: Women's Role in Changing the Segregated City
152q Desegregating Sexist Sport
202e Determinants of Occupational Segregation
202g Relative Wages and Sex Segregation by Occupation
208j Segregated Academic and Vocational Schools: Separate But Not Equal
251d Capitalism, Patriarchy, and Job Segregation by Sex
251m Sex Segregation in the Labor Market
291a Occupational Segregation in International Women's Year
291b Can We Still Afford Occupational Segregation?
291c Homosocial Theory of Sex Roles: An Explanation of the Sex Segregation of Social Institutions
291f Occupational Segregation and the Law
291g Historical and Structural Barriers to Occupational Desegregation
291i Occupational Segregation and Public Policy: A Comparative Analysis of American and Soviet Patterns
291j Capitalism, Patriarchy, and Job Segregation by Sex
291k Economists' Approaches to Sex Segregation in the Labor Market: An Appraisal
291n Toward Dimorphics: A Summary Statement to the Conference on Occupational Segregation
328e De Facto Job Segregation
350b Rural China: Segregation to Solidarity
350j Segregation and Its Consequences in India
351c Sex Segregation in the Labor Market: An Analysis of Young College Women's Occupational Preferences

SELF

98q Women's Conceptions of Self and Morality
198y Self and Sex
222g Awakening of the Self in the Heroines of Ousmane Sembene
222k Images of Self and Race in the Autobiographies of Black Women
255c Woman's Concept of Self in the Eighteenth Century
286d Kinesis and the Concept of Self in Sport
359f Selves in Hiding

SELF CONCEPT

140dd Self-Concept and the Coping Process of Black Graduate and Undergraduate Women at a Predominantly White University
155e Self-Conceptions, Motivations and Interpersonal Attitudes of Early- and Late-Maturing Girls
166z Self-Concept, Occupational Role Expectations, and Occupational Choice in Nursing and Social Work
196c Sex Differences in the Self-Concepts of Elementary-School Children
200n Self-Conceptions, Motivations and Interpersonal Attitudes of Early- and Late-Maturing Girls
286c Self Concept and the Female Participant

SELF IMAGE

see also IMAGE; SELF PERCEPTION; PERCEPTION

146j Self Image and Roles
253g Wanted: A New Self-Image for Women
309e Women in Kerala: Changing Socio-Economic Status and Self-Image
325z Self-Images of Traditional Urban Women in Cairo

SELF-ACTUALIZED

11c Self-Actualized Woman

SELF-BLESSING

263w Self-Blessing Ritual

SELF-DEFINITION

256d No More Sapphires or Black Pearls: Self-definition is Where It Starts
278z Poetry of Self-Definition

SELF-DETERMINATION

158k Self-Determination and Autonomy

SELF-ESTEEM

14h Black Women and Self-esteem
169j Self-Esteem (Dominance-Feeling) and Sexuality in Women
243c Male Attitudes Toward Women's Rights as a Function of Their Level of Self-Esteem
267x Life Patterns and Self-Esteem in Gifted Family Oriented and Career Committed Women

SELF-LOVE

15h Healthy Self-Love

SELF-PERCEPTION

286r Self-Perception of Athletes and Coaches
309i Aging Women in India: Self-Perceptions and Changing Roles

SELF-PORTRAIT

166uu Vanguard Artist: Portrait and Self-Portrait

SELF-PRESERVATION

21g Feminine Self-Preservation in Groups

SELF-RESPECT

203q Servility and Self-Respect

SELF-SACRIFICE

282j Exploitation, Oppression, and Self-Sacrifice

SELF-SOLACE

29d The Self-Solace

SELL

13m Do Schools Sell Girls Short?
175kk Selling of a Feminist

SEMANTICS

53b Semantics of Biology: Virginity
85f Sexism and Semantics
120d Semantic Derogation of Woman
127bb "Sex and Semantics"
314v Semantics of Sex Discrimination

SEMBENE

222g Awakening of the Self in the Heroines of Ousmane Sembene

SEMI-PROFESSIONS

278p Women in the Professions and Semi-Professions: A Question of Power

SEMINARS

6j Seminars for Career Women: Combining Awareness Training with Transactional Analysis

SEMINARY

60b Hartford Female Seminary

SENECA

9c Seneca Falls Convention: Declaration
257c Declaration of Sentiments, Resolutions, Seneca Falls
270c Mothers of a Nation: Seneca Resistance to Quaker Intervention

SENEGAL

302a Signares of Saint-Louis and Goree: Women Entrepreneurs in Eighteenth-Century Senegal

SENESH

179f H. Senesh

SENSE

170o Sense of Femaleness
211g Sense of Mastery in the Childbirth Experience

SENSIBILITY

141c Literary Women and the Masculated Sensibility

SENSITIVE

300i In Favor of the Sensitive Man

SENSUALIS

223i Innocent Femina Sensualis in Unconscious Conflict

SENSUOUS

73d Trebly Sensuous Woman
247h Renoir's Sensuous Women
296j Trebly Sensuous Woman

SENTENCE

22s Androgynous Themes Written to Sentence Cues by Sixth-, Eighth-, and Tenth-Grade Students
51x Discriminatory Sentencing of Women Offenders

SENTIMENT

65a Sentiment and Intellect: The Story of John Stuart Mill and Harriet Taylor Mill
257c Declaration of Sentiments, Resolutions, Seneca Falls

SEOUL

236c Women Surviving: Palace Life in Seoul after the Annexation
236i Interviews with Young Working Women in Seoul

SEPARATION

8ee We'd Better All Hang Together or Surely We'll All Hang Separately
24z Some Thoughts on the Question of Being a Separate Human Being
85r Separation of Marriage and Family
92c Separation of Home and Work? Landladies and Lodgers in Nineteenth-Century England

98l Separation and Survival: Mothers, Daughters, Sisters: The Women's Experimental Theatre
105l Women's Movement and the Women's Pages: Separate, Unequal and Unspectacular
120b Women's Speech: Separate But Unequal?
140aa Fathering and Marital Separation
158x Separatism and Sexual Relationships
208j Segregated Academic and Vocational Schools: Separate But Not Equal
218c From Separatism to Socialism: Women in the Russian Revolutionary Movement of the 1870s
230n Love Unites Them and Hunger Separates Them: Poor Women in the Dominican Republic
334n Not Separate, Not Equal

SEPTEMBER

279p Dry September

SEPULVEDA

315c Women in Reconquest Castile: The Fueros of Sepulveda and Cuenca

SERMON

1b Sermon on Ante-Natal Infanticide

SERRANA

80f "El casamiento enganoso": Marriage in the Novels of Maria Luisa Bombal, Silvina Bullrich, and Elisa Serrana

SERVANT

132h Women, Servants, Mules, and Other Property
140g Domestic Servants in London and Paris, 1890 to 1914
153i Servants
281k Migration and Labor Force Participation of Latin American Women: The Domestic Servants in the Cities
297i Female Domestic Servant and Social Change: Lima, Peru

SERVICE

71h Domestic Service as a Channel of Upward Mobility for the Lower Class Woman: The Lima Case
95b The Memorial Service on the Mountain
129m Fostergrandparenting: A Unique Child-Care Service
146h Service Needs
191r Women Workers in the Health Service Industry
211h C.O.P.E. Story: A Service to Pregnant and Postpartum Women
295c Domestic Service in Canada, 1880-1920
306f Women in Service Industries
318n Social Services for Women: Problems and Priorities
323b Labour Women and the Social Services
354n Urban Nomads: Women in Temporary Clerical Services
354o Women in Blue-Collar and Service Occupations
354p Domestic Service: Woman's Work

371c Occupational Values and Family Roles: Women in Blue-Collar and Service Occupations

SERVILITY

110d Servility of Dependence: The Dark Lady in Trollop
203q Servility and Self-Respect

SESAME STREET

13g Are Little Girls Being Harmed by "Sesame Street"?
197e Are Little Girls Being Harmed by "Sesame Street"?
208qq Sesame Street and Sex-Role Stereotypes
208rr Sesame Street and Sex-Role Stereotypes (updated)

SESSIONS

215o Patty Bartlett Sessions: More Than a Midwife

SETTLEMENT

116g Settlement House and the Italian Family
116j Interaction Between Italian Immigrant Women and the Chicago Commons Settlement House, 1909-1944
302k Less Than Second-Class: Women in Rural Settlement Schemes in Tanzania
360h Cultural Hybrid in the Slums: The College Woman and the Settlement House, 1889-1894

SEVEN

73o Seven Deadly Half-Truths About Women
166hh College Women Seven Years After Graduation

SEVENTEEN

121a Colonial Women in Mexico: The Seventeenth and Eighteenth Centuries
126f Gynecology and Ideology in Seventeenth-Century England
240c Praising Virtuous Ladies: The Literary Image and Historical Reality of Women in Seventeenth-century England
270b Sunksquaws, Shamans, and Tradeswomen: Middle Atlantic Coastal Algonkian Women During the Seventeenth and Eighteenth Centuries
337g Jane Lead: The Feminist Mind and Art of a Seventeenth-Century Protestant Mystic
361d Historical Survey of Women's Language: From Medieval Courtesy Books to Seventeen Magazine

SEVENTY

296p Sex after Forty--And after Seventy

SEX

see also SEX-RELATED; SEX-LINKED; SEXES; SEXUAL; SEXUALITY; GENDER; SEX DIFFERENCES; SEX ROLE; SEX DISCRIMINATION

4n Sex and Specialization in Academe and the Professions

13h Children's Books: The Second Sex, Junior Division
13o Look Jane Look. See Sex Stereotypes
13p Sex Problems of School Math Books
13x High-School Sex(ist) Education
13aa Second Sex in Academe
18p Genetics of Sex and Its Consequences
21p Women in China: Problems of Sex Inequality and Socio-economic Change
22e Sex Equality: The Beginnings of Ideology
22m Parents' Views on Sex of Newborns
22o Sex-Role Concepts and Sex Typing in Childhood as a Function of School and Home Environments
24e The Sex Maniac
35j Capitalism, Patriarchy, and Job Segregation by Sex
43f Effects of Class and Sex on Political Life in Northern India
43g Caribbean Women: The Impact of Race, Sex, and Class
51f Sex Factor: Female Delinquency
51r Prostitution: An Extreme Case of Sex Stratification
55c Sex and Occupational Role on Fleet Street
56a Sex Hormones in the Development of Sex Differences in Human Behavior
77a Sex Hormones and Executive Ability
77d Conclusion: "Sex and Temperament in Three Primitive Societies"
77i Social Construction of the Second Sex
84i Women, Sex and Class
86o Answer to Norman Mailer's "Prisoner of Sex"
89u Women: Caste, Class or Oppressed Sex?
89v Dialectic of Sex
89ccc Sex in a Capitalist Society
94j Gusii Sex Offenses: A Study in Social Control
100b Socialization, Sexuality, and Sex
108g Sex
120e Sex of the Speaker as a Sociolinguistic Variable
120g Sex, Covert Prestige, and Linguistic Change in the Urban British English of Norwich
120i Sex Differentiation in Language
120j Cues to the Identification of Sex in Children's Speech
120l Power, Sex, and Nonverbal Communication
126p Sex and Class in Colonial and Nineteenth-Century America
127z Conclusion, "Sex and Temperament in Three Primitive Societies"
127aa "Second Sex"
127bb "Sex and Semantics"
129d Sex and the Older Woman
132q Sex Equality: The Beginning of Ideology
139m Women Are Prisoners of Their Sex
141aa Biological and Cultural Determinants of the Division of Labor by Sex
141dd Lillian Hellman: Dramatist of the Second Sex
151a Puritans and Sex
151d Dynamics of Interracial Sex in Colonial America
155o Changing Sex Norms in America and Scandinavia
155p Gusii Sex Offenses: A Study in Social Control
155u Group Sex Among the Mid-Americans
156f Teachers, Peers, and Play Preferences: An Environmental Approach to Sex Typing in the Preschool
157b Sex and Reference
157e Better Sex

157i Sex, Birth Control, and Human Life
157q Sex and Perversion
158j "Sex and Temperament in Three Primitive Societies"
158n Purpose of Sex
158o Sex and Language
158p Sex and Reference
158q Better Sex
158w Marx, Sex and the Transformation of Society
159y Second Sex
159dd Contemporary Approach to Sex Identity
163a Sex, Socialization, and Politics
166n Female Physician in Public Health: Conflict and Reconciliation of the Sex and Professional Roles
170c Sex
173j Parents' Views on Sex of Newborns
173x Sex Preferences, Sex Control, and the Status of Women
174h Sex and the Burger Court: Recent Judicial Policy Making toward Women
176d Sex, Age, and State as Determinants of Mother-Infant Interaction
176ee Sex Differentiation in Role Expectations and Performance
186c Sex Map of the Work World
186h Social Construction of the Second Sex
191k Dangers of Sex Hormones
193d Sex, Age and Social Control in Mobs of the Darwin Hinterland
194g Relationships of Sex and Social Class in Brazil
196i Psychological and Occupational Sex Stereotypes in Elementary School Readers
196j Sex Stereotyping in Elementary-School Mathematics Textbooks
196l Woman's Place: Children's Sex Stereotyping of Occupations
196aa Effect of Sex on College Admission, Work Evaluation, and Job Interviews
196nn Sex Differential in School Enrollment and Educational Attainment
197a What Kind of Difference Does Sex Make?
197h Effect of Race and Sex on College Admission
198n Absent Father and Cross-Sex Identity
198w Sex and Personality: Studies in Masculinity and Femininity
198y Self and Sex
198cc Sex, Age, and State as Determinants of Mother-Infant Interaction
199e Differential Response to Early Experiences as a Function of Sex Difference
199i Sex of Parent x Sex of Child: Socioemotional Development
199o Cryptorchidism, Development of Gender Identity, and Sex Behavior
200e Differences in Perception of the Opposite Sex by Males and Females
202g Relative Wages and Sex Segregation by Occupation
203h Second Sex
206d Sex Identity Deviation and Inversion
208d Social Construction of the Second Sex
208u Dick and Jane as Victims: Sex Stereotyping in Children's Readers
208ll Sex Stereotypes in Mathematics and Science Textbooks for Elementary and Junior High Schools
209c Sex and Politics
218a Class and Sex Connection
219f Sex, Color and Money: Who's Perceiving What? Or Men and Women: Where Did All the Differences Go (To)?
219n Sociocultural and Sociopsychological Factors in Differential Language Retentiveness by Sex
230h Traffic in Women: Notes on the "Political Economy" of Sex

232e Dominant Sex
233j In Memoriam: "Sex and the Single Girl"
238d Sex Equality: The Beginnings of Ideology
244h Sex and Death in Victorian England: An Examination of Age- and Sex-Specific Death Rates, 1840-1910
249m Sex and Power in the Balkans
249o Mastery of Work and the Mystery of Sex in a Guatemalan Village
250b Evaluation of the Performance of Women as a Function of Their Sex, Achievement, and Personal History
250o Developmental Study of the Effects of Sex of the Dominant Parent on Sex-Role Preference, Identification, and Imitation in Children
250v Effects of Sex of Examiner and Subject on Children's Quantitative Test Performance
250x Early Hormonal Influences on the Development of Sexual and Sex-Related Behaviors
250ll Encountering the Male Establishment: Sex Status Limits on Woman's Careers in the Professions
251b Economics, Sex, and Gender
251d Capitalism, Patriarchy, and Job Segregation by Sex
251g Division of Labor by Sex
251m Sex Segregation in the Labor Market
256j Impact of Mid-twentieth Century Movement for Sex Equality in Employment on Three Contemporary Economic Institutions
256n Social Sex: The New Single Standard for Men and Women
259o Politics of Sex
260j Sex in the Social Structure
260cc Sex and Psychology
260dd Sex and Temperament
266ii Socio-Economic Context Of Sex And Power: A Study of Women, Work And Family Roles in Four Israeli Institutional Frameworks
271h Sex-Role Concepts and Sex Typing in Childhood as a Function of School and Home Environments
271k Second Sex in Academe
271u Sex Equality: The Beginnings of Ideology
276e Sex, Gender, and American Culture
282b Theories of Sex Difference
282c Biology, Sex Hormones, and Sexism in the 1920's
282h Marx, Sex, and the Transformation of Society
284r Social Construction of the Second Sex
285b Division of Labor by Sex
286o Influence of Birth Order and Sibling Sex on Sports Participation
291c Homosocial Theory of Sex Roles: An Explanation of the Sex Segregation of Social Institutions
291j Capitalism, Patriarchy, and Job Segregation by Sex
291k Economists' Approaches to Sex Segregation in the Labor Market: An Appraisal
292g Dynamics of Interracial Sex
292h Sex on the American Indian Frontier
292q Problems of Sex and Sex Role
292s Nineteenth-Century Heritage: The Family, Feminism and Sex
296e Fathers, Mothers and Sex Typing
296p Sex after Forty--And after Seventy
300b Weak Are the Second Sex
301c Race, Sex, and Jobs: The Drive Toward Equality
314aa Differential Recruitment and Control: The Sex Structuring of Organizations
318k Women and Sex in Soviet Law

320h Sex Stereotyping in Canadian Schools
321f Sexism in Voir Dire: The Use of Sex Stereotypes in Jury Selection
329g Politics of Sex: West Germany
330b Sex Hormones, The Central Nervous System and Affect Variability in Humans
330m Treatment of Sex and Love Problems in Women
332b Language of Sex and Gender
340j Sex and-or Mr. Morrison
351c Sex Segregation in the Labor Market: An Analysis of Young College Women's Occupational Preferences
368h Sisterhood in the Courtroom: Sex of Judge and Defendent in Criminal Case Disposition
372g Sex and Status: Women in St. Vincent

SEX BIAS

see also BIAS; DISCRIMINATION; SEXISM; SEX DISCRIMINATION

196g Sex Bias in Secondary Schools: The Impact of Title IX
196y School Boards and Sex Bias in American Education
196bb Sex Bias in Selective College Admissions
196kk Schoolbook Sex Bias
208k Sex Bias in the Public Schools
235h Women's Health: The Side Effects of Sex Bias
251z Sex Bias and Cyclical Unemployment
252ee Sex Bias and Cyclical Unemployment
272h Sex Bias in School Administration
280h Sex Bias in Schools
297p Legislation: An Aid in Eliminating Sex Bias in Education in the U.S.

SEX DIFFERENCES

see also DIFFERENCES

22a Sex Differences
22n Cross-Cultural Analysis of Sex Differences in the Behavior of Children Aged Three Through Eleven
51l Race and Sex Differences
56a Sex Hormones in the Development of Sex Differences in Human Behavior
56b Sex Differences in Intellectual Functioning
56c Social-Learning View of Sex Differences in Behavior
56e Sex Differences and Cultural Institutions
56h Classified Summary of Research in Sex Differences
67a Social Responsibility and Research on Sex Differences
67d Sex Differences in Cross-Cultural Perspective
67f Sex Differences in the Organization of Perception and Cognition
67i Sex Differences and Psychopathology
67j Biological Explanations of Psychological Sex Differences
77c Cross-Cultural Analysis of Sex Differences in the Behavior of Children Aged Three Through Eleven
77g Summary and Commentary: "The Psychology of Sex Differences"
98o Androgyny and the Psychology of Sex Differences
99b Sex Differences in the Epidemiology of Mental Disorder
99d Sex Differences in Divorce
99e Sex Differences in Problems of Aging

99h Sex Differences in Obesity
99j Sex Differences in Suicidal Behavior
99n Sex Differences and the Epidemiology of Depression
120k Teacher-Child Verbal Interaction: An Approach to the Study of Sex Differences
120m Sex Differences in Language, Speech, and Nonverbal Communication: An Annotated Bibliography
149d Sex Differences: Biological, Cultural, Societal Implications
155f Sex Differences in Responses to Psychosexual Stimulation by Films and Slides
156h Sex Differences in the Use of Outdoor Space
163c Sex Differences in Black Political Beliefs and Behavior
173k Early Sex Differences in the Human: Studies of Socioemotional Development
173gg Sex Differences and Psychiatric Disorders
176b Sex Differences in the Incidence of Neonatal Abnormalities and Abnormal Performance in Early Childhood
176e Play Behavior in the Year-Old Infant: Early Sex Differences
176f Sex Differences in Intellectual Functioning
176g Sex Differences in Adolescent Character Processes
176dd Cross-Cultural Survey of Some Sex Differences in Socialization
176rr Sex Differences in Fantasy Patterns
183a Sex Differences in Aggression and Dominance
196c Sex Differences in the Self-Concepts of Elementary-School Children
196m Sex Differences in the Occupational Choices of Second Graders
197b Sex Differences in Intellectual Functioning
198a Psychoanalysis and Sex Differences: Freud and Beyond Freud
198h Anthropology and Sex Differences
198m Cross-Cultural Survey of Some Sex Differences in Socialization
198p Ethology and Sex Differences
198u Psychology and Sex Differences
198x Sex Differences in Personality Characteristics
198bb Possible Causal Factors of Sex Differences in Intellectual Abilities
199c Fetal Androgens, Human Central Nervous System Differentiation, and Behavior Sex Differences
199d Prenatal Androgen, Intelligence and Cognitive Sex Differences
199f Sex Differences in Rhesus Monkeys Following Varied Rearing Experiences
199g Sex Differences in Mother-Infant Attachment in Monkeys
199h Early Sex Differences and Mother-Infant Interaction
199j Methodological Considerations in Studying Sex Differences in the Behavioral Functioning of Newborns
199m Ethological Study of Children Approaching a Strange Adult: Sex Differences
199n Sex Differences in Field Independence among Preschool Children
199r Sex Differences in Aggression
199s Psychobiology of Sex Differences: An Evolutionary Perspective
200g Sex Differences in the Play Configurations of Preadolescents
200i Dreams: Sex Differences in Aggressive Content
200l Sex Differences in Job Values and Desires
200o Sex Differences in Dating Aspirations and Satisfaction with Computer-Selected Partners
201b Biological Influences on Sex Differences in Behavior
201d Social Influences on Sex Differences in Behavior
209b Infant Sex Differences
209e Sex Differences in Game Strategy

230a Perspectives on the Evolution of Sex Differences
250m Sex Differences in the Development of Masculine and Feminine Identification
250q Roles of Activation and Inhibition in Sex Differences in Cognitive Abilities
250r Comments on "Roles of Activation and Inhibition in Sex Differences in Cognitive Abilities"
250s Parental Education, Sex Differences, and Performance on Cognitive Tasks Among Two-Year-Old Children
250t Sex Differences in Space Perception and Aspects of Intellectual Functioning
250hh Sex Differences in Expectancy of Intellectual and Academic Reinforcement
252l Sex Differences in Identification Development
266cc When Women Are More Deserving Than Men: Equity, Attribution, And Perceived Sex Differences
267r Psychological Sex Differences
284s There are Sex Differences in the Mind, Too
285k Sex Differences in the Incidence of Susto in Two Zapotec Pueblos: An Analysis of the Relationships between Sex Role Expectations and a Folk Illness
286x Sex Differences in Biomechanics
291o Sex Differences in Economists' Fields of Specialization
325dd Sex Differences and Folk Illness in an Egyptian Village
332c Sex Differences in Hemispheric Brain Asymmetry

SEX DISCRIMINATION

see also DISCRIMINATION; SEXISM; BIAS; SEX BIAS

4o Sex Discrimination in Academe
4r Internal Remedies for Sex Discrimination in Colleges and Universities
4t Affirmative Action Plans for Eliminating Sex Discrimination in Academe
39p Performance, Rewards, and Perceptions of Sex Discrimination among Male and Female Faculty
48g Sex Discrimination
51y Sex Discrimination in the Criminal Law
59j Sex Discrimination in Credit: The Backlash of Economic Dependency
140gg Why Sex Discrimination? A Model of Sex-Role Transcendence
174a Eliminating Sex Discrimination in Education: Lobbying for Implementation of Title IX
196z Sex Discrimination as Public Policy: The Case of Maternity-Leave Policies for Teachers
246h Proposed Model for Examining Sex Discrimination in Education
250mm Empirical Verification of Sex Discrimination in Hiring Practices in Psychology
251dd Sex Discrimination in the Universities
265p Sex Discrimination in the Trade Unions: Legal Resources for Change
266s Alternative Methods For Measuring Sex Discrimination in Occupational Incomes
267t Sex Discrimination Against the American Working Woman
267w Sex Discrimination in Academe
301b Sex Discrimination, Educational Institutions, and the Law: A New Issue on Campus

301d Legal Requirements, Structures, and Strategies for Eliminating Sex Discrimination in Academe
301g Sex Discrimination at Universities: An Ombudsman's View
314v Semantics of Sex Discrimination
327g Sex Discrimination Against the American Working Woman
328d Legal Remedies beyond Title VII to Combat Sex Discrimination in Employment
342gg Sex Discrimination in Higher Education and Attitude Change
354e Legal Protection against Sex Discrimination

SEX ROLE

see also SEX ROLES; ROLE; ANDROGYNY; STEREOTYPES

13q Sex-Role Pressures and the Socialization of the Male Child
13r Sex-Role Attitudes of Fifth-Grade Girls
22d Conceptions of Sex Role: Some Cross-Cultural and Longitudinal Perspectives
22f Model of Sex-Role Transcendence
22g Biologic Basis for Sex-Role Stereotypes
22o Sex-Role Concepts and Sex Typing in Childhood as a Function of School and Home Environments
22q Sex-Role Stereotyping in Children's Television Programs
39r Sex Role Research
56d Cognitive--Developmental Analysis of Children's Sex-Role Concepts and Attitudes
61f Sex Role Stereotypes and the Career Versus Homemaking Orientations of Women
64f Sex Role Stereotyping
140c Male Sex Role Behaviors in a Representative National Sample, 1973
140d Change in U.S. Women's Sex-Role Attitudes, 1964-1974
140cc Sex-Role Constraints: The College-Educated Black Woman
140gg Why Sex Discrimination? A Model of Sex-Role Transcendence
140oo Sex-Role Media Research and Sources
155b Sex-Role Stereotypes and Clinical Judgments of Mental Health
155r Sex-Role Attitudes in Finland, 1966-1970
156e Social Psychology of Sex-Role Intervention
156l Sex Role and Human Culture
173ee Male Sex Role: Definitions, Problems, and Sources of Change
176q Implications of Current Changes in Sex Role Patterns
176uu Sex-Role Stereotypes and Clinical Judgements of Mental Health
196a Sex-Role Socialization and the Nursery School: As the Twig is Bent
196b Sex-Role Concepts Among Elementary-School Age Girls
198aa Physiological Development, Cognitive Development, and Socialization Antecedents of Children's Sex-Role Attitudes
200c Process of Learning Parental and Sex-Role Identification
200d Child's Sex-Role Classification of School Objects
204k Sex Role as a Mediator of Intellectual Functioning
204l Sex-Role Socialization and Achievement in Mathematics
205a Biological Explanations of Sex-Role Stereotypes
205b Sex-Role Socialisation
205c Sex-Role Stereotyping
205d Influence of the School on Sex-Role Stereotyping
205e Sex-Role Stereotyping in Studies of Marriage and the Family
205f Sex-Role Stereotyping at Work
205h Clinical Aspects of Sex-Role Stereotyping
205i Sex-Role Stereotyping in the Social Security and Income Tax Systems

205j Sex-Role Stereotyping and Social Science
208f School's Role in the Sex-Role Stereotyping of Girls: A Feminist Review of the Literature
208p Feminist Studies: The Schools and Sex-Role Stereotyping
208t Sex-Role Socialization in Picture Books for Preschool Children
208pp Film Resources for Sex-Role Stereotyping
208qq Sesame Street and Sex-Role Stereotypes
208rr Sesame Street and Sex-Role Stereotypes (updated)
213n Ecological Antecedents and Sex-Role Consequences in Traditional and Modern Israeli Subcultures
250e Male-Female Perception of the Female Sex Role in the United States
250j Sex-Role Stereotypes and Clinical Judgments of Mental Health
250o Developmental Study of the Effects of Sex of the Dominant Parent on Sex-Role Preference, Identification, and Imitation in Children
251r Sex Role Differentiation
252q Sex-Role Differentiation in an Equalitarian Society
260ee Early Sex-Role Development
264j Sex-Role Socialization
265g Sex-Role Socialization
266y Sex-Role Boundaries and Resistance to Sex-Role Change
266aa Relationship Between Sex-Role Stereotypes And Requisite Management Characteristics
267c Sex-Role Stereotypes: A Current Appraisal
267f Social Change and Sex-Role Inertia: The Case of the Kibbutz
267q Sex-Role Attitudes and Psychological Well-Being
271h Sex-Role Concepts and Sex Typing in Childhood as a Function of School and Home Environments
285k Sex Differences in the Incidence of Susto in Two Zapotec Pueblos: An Analysis of the Relationships between Sex Role Expectations and a Folk Illness
292q Problems of Sex and Sex Role

SEX ROLES

see also ANDROGYNY; ROLES; SEX ROLE; STEREOTYPES

9qq Sex Roles and Female Oppression
20x Concepts of "Femininity" and "Liberation" in the Context of Changing Sex-Roles: Women in Modern India and America
22t Relationship Between Sex Roles, Marital Status, and Mental Illness
37b Sex Roles and the Socialization Process
37f Analysis of the Debate on Sex Roles
39d Adult Sex Roles and Mental Illness
39g Cultural Contradictions and Sex Roles: The Masculine Case
70e Employment of Married Women and the Changing Sex Roles in Poland
110l Sex Roles in Three of Hermann Hesse's Novels
120h Sex Roles, Interruptions and Silences
140a Sex Roles in Transition: The Historical Perspective
140l Women's Employment and Changing Sex Roles, 1900 to 1930
143b Home: A Critical Problem for Changing Sex Roles
159ff Sex Roles: The Argument from Nature
163b Continuity and Change in Opinions about Sex Roles
175mm Feminists: A Political Organization to Annihilate Sex Roles
176i Cultural Contradictions and Sex Roles
176o Study of Sex Roles
197f Down the Up Staircase: Sex Roles, Professionalization, and the Status of Teachers

201a Sex Roles in Primate Societies
201c Anthropological Perspective on Sex Roles and Subsistence
2031 Sex Roles: The Argument from Nature
206e Sex Roles, Ancient to Modern
206q Sex Roles in the Modern Fabric of China
203ss Children's Toys and Socialization to Sex Roles
249f Sex Roles and Survival Strategies in an Urban Black Community
251p Sex Roles and Family Structure
266bb Adult Sex Roles and Mental Health
267a Sex Roles and Social Change
267e Convergences between East and West: Tradition and Modernity in Sex Roles in Sweden, Finland, and the Soviet Union
271n Sex Roles in Early Reading Textbooks
271x Sex Roles and Education in Sweden
276d Psychology of Sex Roles
281f Sex Roles and Social Change: A Comparative Appraisal of Turkey's Women
291c Homosocial Theory of Sex Roles: An Explanation of the Sex Segregation of Social Institutions
316m Modernization Theory and Sex Roles in Critical Perspective: The Case of the Soviet Union
325s Changing Sex Roles in Bedouin Society in Syria and Lebanon
331g Child Care for the 1980s: Traditional Sex Roles or Androgyny?
342q Familism and Sex Roles: A Chicana Perspective
360n Hysterical Woman: Sex Roles and Role Conflict in Nineteenth-Century America
365f Changes in the Modern Family: Their Impact on Sex Roles

SEX-APPROPRIATE

266z Effects of Live Modelled Sex-Appropriate Play Behavior In a Naturalistic Setting

SEX-HORMONE

171d Human Sex-Hormone Abnormalities Viewed from an Androgynous Perspective: A Reconsideration of the Work of John Money

SEX-LABELING

267s Sex-Labeling of Jobs

SEX-LINKED

204c Spatial Ability: A Critical Review of the Sex-Linked Major Gene Hypothesis
368i Sex-Linked Values: Their Impacts on Women in Engineering

SEX-RELATED

18f Sex-Related Differences in Spatial Ability: A Developmental Psychological View
171b Biospsychosocial Processes in the Development of Sex-related Differences
172a Sex-Related Behaviors: Historical and Psychobiological Perspectives
172b Sex-Related Factors in Cognition and in Brain Lateralization
172c Meaning of Sex-Related Variations in Maturation Rate

204a Sex-Related Differences in Cognitive Functioning: An Overview
204b Genetic Influences on Sex-Related Differences in Intellectual Performance: Theoretical and Methodological Issues
204d Patterns of Cognitive Functioning in Relation to Handedness and Sex-Related Differences
204e Evidence for Sex-Related Differences in Cerebral Organization
204f Sex-Related Differences in Cognition Among the Elderly
204g Cognitive Abilities and Sex-Related Variations in the Maturation of Cerebral Cortical Functions
204j Menstrual Cycle and Sex-Related Differences in Cognitive Variability
204m Role of Tests and Their Construction in Producing Apparent Sex-Related Differences

SEX-SPECIFIC

244h Sex and Death in Victorian England: An Examination of Age- and Sex-Specific Death Rates, 1840-1910

SEX-STATUS

166c Encountering the Male Establishment: Sex-Status Limits on Woman's Careers in the Professions

SEX-TEMPERAMENT

198k Standardization of Sex-Temperament

SEX-TYPING

105m Sex-typing and Children's Television Preferences
196f Sex-Typing in the High School
196n Sex-Typing and Politicization in Children's Attitudes

SEXES

see also SEX; SEXUAL; SEXUALITY; GENDER

89uu Aggression in the Relations between the Sexes
107m Interrelations of the Two Sexes
132k Distrust Between the Sexes
139o Equality Between the Sexes: An Immodest Proposal
149c What Do You Mean "The Sexes"?
149q Equality between the Sexes: An Immodest Proposal
155a Psychological Consequences of the Anatomical Distinction Between the Sexes
159q Of the Distinction of the Beautiful and the Sublime in the Interrelations of the Two Sexes
177g Equality of Souls, Inequality of Sexes: Woman in Medieval Theology
177h Canon Law and the Battle of the Sexes
178e Man-Midwifery and the Delicacy of the Sexes
186i Equality Between the Sexes: An Immodest Proposal
188b Letters on the Equality of the Sexes
193c Aspects of the Distinction Between the Sexes in the Nyamwezi and Some Other African Systems of Kinship and Marriage
198b Psychical Consequences of the Anatomical Distinction Between the Sexes

198v Biological and Anthropological Differences between the Sexes
200a Psychological Consequences of the Anatomical Distinction between the Sexes
202a Division of Labor between the Sexes
206m Sexes: Ideology and Reality in the Israeli Kibbutz
208hh Guidelines for Equal Treatment of the Sexes in Social Studies Textbooks
213b Bridging the Gap between the Sexes in Moroccan Legal Practice
233e Psychical Consequences of the Anatomical Distinction between the Sexes
250h Psychological Consequences of the Anatomic Distinction Between the Sexes
253e Equality Between the Sexes: An Immodest Proposal
268a Psychical Consequences of the Anatomical Distinction Between the Sexes
268b Freud and the Distinction Between the Sexes
284t Question of Psychological Differences Between the Sexes
285g Jural Relations between the Sexes Among the Barabaig
292u Equality Between the Sexes: An Immodest Proposal
318a Society and the Sexes in the Russian Past
365e What Does Equality Between the Sexes Imply?

SEXISM

see also CHAUVINISM; HARASSMENT; DISCRIMINATION; BIAS; SEX BIAS; SEX DISCRIMINATION

6m How to Eliminate Sexist Language From Your Writing: Some Guidelines for the Manager and Supervisor
13cc Sexism in History
21h Women Social Workers and Clients: Common Victims of Sexism
39k Women and Social Stratification: A Case of Intellectual Sexism
77q Native Women Today: Sexism and the Indian Woman
85f Sexism and Semantics
94c Rape and Rape Law: Sexism in Society and Law
110v Sexism and the Double Standard in Literature
126d Historical Phallacies: Sexism in American Historical Writing
141t Welfare Careers, Low Wage Workers and Sexism
149p Women's Lib: The War on "Sexism"
152q Desegregating Sexist Sport
156a Sexism and Racism in Education
156b Preschool and the Politics of Sexism
158a Sexism as Inequality
158b Racism and Sexism
158gg Secondary Sexism and Quota Hiring
207a Linguistic Sexism as a Social Issue
207b Sexism as Shown through the English Vocabulary
207d Sexism in the Language of Legislatures and Courts
207e Sexism in the Language of Literature
207f Sexism in the Language of Marriage
207g Sexism in Dictionaries and Texts: Omissions and Commissions
207h Sexism in Children's Books and Elementary Teaching Materials
208jj Sexism in History or, Writing Women's History is a Tricky Business
210g Theology After the Demise of God the Father: A Call for the Castration of Sexist Religion
210j Sexism and the Contemporary Church: When Evasion Becomes Complicity
212g Bergman's Portrait of Women: Sexism or Subjective Metaphor?

212t Lina Wertmuller: Swept Away on a Wave of Sexism
246k Language of Sexism
254p Our Sexist Language
255h Rousseau's Sexism Revolutionized
258g Sexist Language in Theology?
264y Sexism and the English Language: The Linguistic Implications of Being a Woman
265s Sexism in Western Art
278d Sexism, Patriarchy and Feminism
278e Sexism in American Naming Traditions
278cc Sexism and Godtalk
282c Biology, Sex Hormones, and Sexism in the 1920's
282e Holes and Slime: Sexism in Sartre's Psychoanalysis
283a Theology After the Demise of God the Father: A Call for the Castration of Sexist Religion
283l Is Sexism a Sign of Decadence in Religion?
316h Ideology and the Law: Sexism and Supreme Court Decisions
321f Sexism in Voir Dire: The Use of Sex Stereotypes in Jury Selection
342t Sexism in the Schools: Focus on the Woman Teacher
342x Racism and Sexism
342hh Sexist Language and Attitudes
348f Sexist Assumptions and Female Delinquency

SEXPOT

142m Woman as Secretary, Sexpot, Spender, Sow, Civic Actor, Sickie
186a Woman as Secretary, Sexpot, Spender, Sow, Civic Actor, Sickie

SEXTON

88i "I Dare to Live": The Transforming Art of Anne Sexton
214r Poetry and Salvation in the Career of Anne Sexton

SEXUAL

15l Sexual Art-Politics
21q Erosion of Sexual Equality in the Kibbutz: A Structural Interpretation
22k Phallacy of Our Sexual Norm
22p Sexual Role Identification and Personality Functioning in Girls
22w Politics of Sexual Stereotypes
42h Family Limitation, Sexual Control, and Domestic Feminism in Victorian America
51aa Sexual Segregation of American Prisons
55b Sexual Divisions and the Dual Labour Market
55h Sexual Antagonism in Herefordshire
73f Sexual Fantasies of Women
84e Sexual Division of Labour: The Case of Nursing
84f Modes of Appropriation and the Sexual Division of Labour: A Case Study from Oaxaca, Mexico
84k Education and the Sexual Division of Labour
89m Sexual Fantasies of Women
89xx Sexual Perversions
89yy Sexual Love
89zz Lenin on Sexual Love
94i Michigan's Criminal Sexual Assault Law

98i For the Etruscans: Sexual Difference and Artistic Production--The Debate Over a Female Aesthetic
107t Origin of Sexual Differences
107w Sexual Ethics and Women
140mm Sexual Identity in the Early Fiction of V. Sackville-West
149e Possible Biological Origins of Sexual Discrimination
154c Sexual Insult and Female Militancy
155d Sexual Dimorphism and Homosexual Gender Identity
155h Aspects of Lower Class Sexual Behavior
155i Premarital Sexual Permissiveness Among Negroes and Whites
155j Women's Sexual Responsiveness and the Duration and Quality of Their Marriages
155l Mothers and Daughters: Perceived and Real Differences in Sexual Values
155m Early Sexual Behavior in Adult Homosexual and Heterosexual Males
155n Comparison of Sexual Attitudes and Behavior in an International Sample
155s Sexual Behavior in Pregnancy
155w Sexual Activities and Attitudes in Older Persons
157f Sexual Love and Moral Experience
157g Sexual Immorality Delineated
157o Sexual Perversion
157p Inapplicable Concepts and Sexual Perversion
158l Sexual Equality
158x Separatism and Sexual Relationships
163r Politics of Sexual Stereotypes
166b Plus Ca Change...? The Sexual Structure of Occupations Over Time
169i Special Problems of Early Female Sexual Development
170g Denial of Women's Sexual Pleasure: Discussion of Dr. Thompson's Paper
170j Personal Identity and Sexual Identity
171e Biochemical and Neurophysiological Influences on Human Sexual Behavior
173r Women's Liberation and Human Sexual Relations
175n Independence From the Sexual Revolution
176a Sexual Dimorphism and Homosexual Gender Identity
176kk Behavior Therapy Approaches to Modification of Sexual Preferences: Biological Perspective and Critique
176mm Lower Class Sexual Behavior
191b Sexual Surgery in Late Nineteenth-Century America
194d Sexual Hierarchy Among the Yanomama
198q Functions of the Sexual Companion
198t Fetal Hormones and the Brain: Effects on Sexual Dimorphism of Behavior
199a Sexual Behavior Differentiation: Prenatal Hormonal and Environmental Control
199x Sexual Differentiation: Models, Methods, and Mechanisms
200m Sexual Behavior in the Human Female: Part II. Biological Data
203j Sexual Equality
206c Sexual Identity Crises in the Life Cycle
211u Problems in Sexual Functioning
211v Female Sexual Dysfunctions: A Clinical Approach
213a Theory of Sexual Stratification
213l Mechanistic Cooperation and Sexual Equality among the Western Bontoc
213m Social Inequality and Sexual Status in Barbados
223h Stereotypes of Femininity in a Theory of Sexual Evolution

227a Sexual Asymmetry and the Status of Women
230d !Kung Women: Contrasts in Sexual Egalitarianism in Foraging and Sedentary Contexts
233cc Three Sexual Myths Exploded
235c Sexual Abuse of Children
235g Sexual Harassment: Women's Hidden Occupational Hazard
250x Early Hormonal Influences on the Development of Sexual and Sex-Related Behaviors
250y Sexual Dimorphic Behavior, Normal and Abnormal
250nn Female Sexual Behavior
252k Personal Identity and Sexual Identity
256s Genderless Sexuality: A Male-Female Psychological Exploration of the Future of Sexual Relationships
260bb Sexual Repression and the Family
264b Female Sexual Alienation
265b Female Sexual Alienation
266c Sexual Role Identification and Personality Functioning in Girls
266v Effect of Contraceptive Pills on Sexual Activity in the Luteal Phase of the Human Menstrual Cycle
266x Dimensions of Lesbian Sexual Experience
271a Sexual Stereotypes Start Early
281s Social Change and Sexual Differentiation in the Cameroun and the Ivory Coast
285l Sexual Antagonism in the New Guinea Highlands: A Bena Bena Example
296i Clitoral Eroticism and the Sexual Response Cycle in Human Females
297g Marital Status and Sexual Identity: The Position of Women in a Mexican Peasant Society
300d Sexual Chic, Sexual Fascism and Sexual Confusion
304h Sexual Division of Labour and Inequality: Labour and Leisure
318e Sexual Equality in Soviet Policy: A Developmental Perspective
325ee Theme of Sexual Oppression in the North African Novel
331b Sexual Inequality, Cultural Norms, and Wife-Beating
348d Who Needs Prostitutes? The Ideology of Male Sexual Needs
348e Sexual Codes and Conduct: A Study of Teenage Girls
350a Female Solidarity and the Sexual Division of Labour
352c Division of Labour and Sexual Inequality: The Role of Education
352l Sexual Equality in the Labour Market: Some Experiences and Views of the Nordic Countries
360k Family Limitation, Sexual Control, and Domestic Feminism in Victorian America
363o Sexual Solipsism of Sigmund Freud
365g Psychological Consequences of Sexual Inequality

SEXUAL POLITICS

see also POLITICS

42f Sexual Politics of Victorian Social Anthropology
77k Sexual Politics of Interpersonal Behavior
149g Sexual Politics
175ll Sexual Politics: A Manifesto for Revolution
191c Complaints and Disorders: The Sexual Politics of Sickness
252ll Sexual Politics: A Manifesto for Revolution
264x Sexual Politics of Interpersonal Behavior
265y Sexual Politics of Interpersonal Behavior
325v Iranian Women in Family Alliance and Sexual Politics
342c Sexual Politics

361c Address Forms in Sexual Politics
363q Sexual Politics

SEXUALITY

see also BISEXUALITY; GENITALS; MASTURBATION; MENSTRUATION; ORGASM; SEX

8a Lesbian Sexuality
9oo Effects of the Derogatory Attitude toward Female Sexuality
53c Open Body, Closed Space: The Transformation of Female Sexuality
62e Female Sexuality
76a Freud's Views on Early Female Sexuality in the Light of Direct Child Observation
77r Sexuality
77s Theory on Female Sexuality
77w Women's Sexuality: A Feminist View
78b Narcissism in Female Sexuality
89ddd Imperialism and Sexuality
100b Socialization, Sexuality, and Sex
129r Sexuality, Power, and Freedom Among "Older" Women
146b Sexuality and Alternative Life Styles
158m Sexuality as a Metaphysical Dimension
169a Early Development of Female Sexuality
169c Effects of the Derogatory Attitude Toward Female Sexuality
169f Female Sexuality
169j Self-Esteem (Dominance-Feeling) and Sexuality in Women
170e Effects of the Derogatory Attitude Toward Female Sexuality
170i Nature of Female Sexuality
170k Feminine Psychology and Infantile Sexuality
171g Social Psychological Model of Human Sexuality
173s Social Dimensions of the Menstrual Taboo and the Effects on Female Sexuality
198e Motherhood and Sexuality
198g Woman and Her Discontents: A Reassessment of Freud's Views on Female Sexuality
210e Judaeo-Christian Influences on Female Sexuality
211i Adolescent Sexuality and Pregnancy
231d Female Sexuality and Embryo
244i Sexuality in Britain, 1800-1900: Some Suggested Revisions
252h Female Sexuality and Psychoanalytic Theory
256s Genderless Sexuality: A Male-Female Psychological Exploration of the Future of Sexual Relationships
266w Sexuality of Pregnant and Breastfeeding Women
268c Female Sexuality
268d Female Sexuality
281v Sexuality and Birth Control Decisions among Lebanese Couples
317k Radical Yoruba Female Sexuality: The Witch and the Prostitute
342v Feminist Perspectives on Female Sexuality

SHADOWS

102e Long Shadows
119c The Shadows on the Wall

SHAHSEVAN

325r Women's Subsociety among the Shahsevan Nomads of Iran

SHAKESPEARE

17f "The Taming of the Shrew": Shakespeare's Mirror of Marriage
68a Shakespeare's "The Taming of the Shrew" vs. Shaw's "Pygmalion": Male Chauvinism vs. Women's Lib?

SHAMANS

270b Sunksquaws, Shamans, and Tradeswomen: Middle Atlantic Coastal Algonkian Women During the Seventeenth and Eighteenth Centuries

SHAME

71l Honor, Shame, and Women's Liberation in Cuba: Views of Working-Class Emigre Men

SHAPE

123g Shape of Things to Come
281q Shaping of the Kaum Ibu (Women's Section) of the United Maylays National Organization

SHARE

232h Woman's Share in Primitive Culture
232n Ancilla's Share

SHARON

314d Sharon Kirkman: Mind Over Myth

SHAW

68a Shakespeare's "The Taming of the Shrew" vs. Shaw's "Pygmalion": Male Chauvinism vs. Women's Lib?
68b Kipling on Women: A New Source for Shaw
68c Shavian Sphinx
68f Legal Climate of Shaw's Problem Plays
68h Mill, Marx and Bebel: Early Influences on Shaw's Characterizations of Women
68i "Unwomanly Woman" in Shaw's Drama
68k Whatever Happened to Shaw's Mother-Genius Portrait?
68l Mr. Shaw's Many Mothers
68m Feminism and Female Stereotypes in Shaw
68p Shaw and Women's Lib
68q Shaw's Lady Cicely and Mary Kingsley
68r Shaw and Florence Farr
104f A.H. Shaw

SHELTER

143q Emergency Shelter: The Development of an Innovative Women's Environment

SHIP

340f The Ship Who Sang
349c American Women in the Shipyards During World War II

SHIPP

215r Dr. Ellis Reynolds Shipp: Pioneer Utah Physician

SHONAGON

179g S. Shonagon

SHOP

127i Pages from a Shop Diary

SHOPLIFTING

51n Shoplifting

SHORE

108r On Barbara's Shore

SHORT

13m Do Schools Sell Girls Short?
111s The Short Happy Life of Francis Macomber
112k The Short Happy Life of Francis Macomber
112ii One Off the Short List
122q Short Stories of Lydia Cabrera: Transpositions or Creations?
232i Short History of Women's Rights
277m One off the Short List
277p The Short Happy Life of Francis Macomber
283a Short Manual for an Aspiring Scenario Writer
295d Short History of Nursing in Ontario

SHREW

17f "The Taming of the Shrew": Shakespeare's Mirror of Marriage
68a Shakespeare's "The Taming of the Shrew" vs. Shaw's "Pygmalion": Male Chauvinism vs. Women's Lib?

SHUT

173n How Nursery Schools Teach Girls to Shut Up

SIBLING

286o Influence of Birth Order and Sibling Sex on Sports Participation

SICILY

213c Illusion and Reality in Sicily

SICKNESS

142m Woman as Secretary, Sexpot, Spender, Sow, Civic Actor, Sickie
186a Woman as Secretary, Sexpot, Spender, Sow, Civic Actor, Sickie
191c Complaints and Disorders: The Sexual Politics of Sickness
262m Woman in Philanthropy--Care of the Sick

SIERRA

297c African Women: Identity Crisis? Some Observations on Education and the Changing Role of Women in Sierra Leone and Zaire
302i Protestant Women's Associations in Freetown, Sierra Leone

SIESTA

279y Tuesday Siesta

SIGNARES

302a Signares of Saint-Louis and Goree: Women Entrepreneurs in Eighteenth-Century Senegal

SILENCE

17b Silent Woman: Towards a Feminist Critique
110g Silences: When Writers Don't Write
116a Silent Half: "Le Contadine del Sud" Before The First World War
120h Sex Roles, Interruptions and Silences
214k Art of Silence and the Forms of Women's Poetry
283d Karl Barth's Theology of the Word of God: Or, How to Keep Women Silent and in Their Place
288p Alice Guy Blache: Czarina of the Silent Screen
361i Art of Silence and the Forms of Women's Poetry
361p Virginia Woolf and the Voices of Silence

SILVINA

80f "El casamiento enganoso": Marriage in the Novels of Maria Luisa Bombal, Silvina Bullrich, and Elisa Serrana
122h Argentine Women in the Novels of Silvina Bullrich

SIMMONS

272f Single-Sex Education and Leadership: The Early Years of Simmons College

SIMONE

181k Rights and Wrongs of Women: Mary Wollstonecraft, Harriet Martineau, Simone de Beauvoir
310h Approaching Simone

SIMONS

93c May Wood Simons: Party Theorist

SIMONSEN

279j Simonsen

SIN

177c Woman: Seductive Siren and Source of Sin?
185a Sin and Salvation: The Dramatic Context of Hrotswitha's Women
223d Marriage, Redundancy or Sin: The Painter's View of Women in the First Twenty-Five Years of Victoria's Reign
226o Unpardonable Sin
342e Women and Aging: The Unforgivable Sin

SINCLAIR

36i "Featureless Freedom" or Ironic Submission: Dorothy Richardson and May Sinclair

SINE QUA NON

271v Feminism: The Sine Qua Non for a Just Society

SING

see SONG

SINGLE

106c Women's Education: The Case for the Single-Sex College
117e Single and Jewish: Toward a New Definition of Completeness
143i Swedish Women in Single-Family Housing
143r Housing for Single-Parent Families: A Women's Design
233j In Memoriam: "Sex and the Single Girl"
256n Social Sex: The New Single Standard for Men and Women
272f Single-Sex Education and Leadership: The Early Years of Simmons College
365h Single Woman in Today's Society

SINHALESE

317e Misery of the Embodied: Representations of Women in Sinhalese Myth

SINK

298j The Sink

SINNER

79c Lamentation of a Sinner

SIREN

177c Woman: Seductive Siren and Source of Sin?

SISTER

16a Your Faces, O My Sisters! Your Faces Filled of Light!

19n International Sisterhood
24y The Sisters
39a Maid of All Work or Departmental Sister-in-Law? The Faculty Wife Employed on Campus
41j Creating a Feminist Alliance: Sisterhood and Class Conflict in the New York Women's Trade Union League, 1903- 1914
98l Separation and Survival: Mothers, Daughters, Sisters: The Women's Experimental Theatre
102l The Sisters
127u To My White Working-Class Sisters
128i Four Sisters: Daughters of Joseph La Flesche
132u Collective Statement, Black Sisters
132z Sisters, Brothers, Lovers...Listen
151i Grimke Sisters: Women and the Abolition Movement
153l The Courting of Sister Wisby
233yy Sisterhood
247i Femme Fatale and Her Sisters
270l Putting Down Sisters and Wives: Tongan Women and Colonization
273a The Courting of Sister Wisby
298b My Sisters' Keeper
317i Convivial Sisterhood: Spirit Mediumship and Client-Core Network among Black South African Women
368h Sisterhood in the Courtroom: Sex of Judge and Defendent in Criminal Case Disposition

SITA

359l Towards a Theory of Form in Feminist Autobiography: Kate Millett's "Flying" and "Sita"; Maxine Hong Kingston's "The Woman Warrior"

SIX

22s Androgynous Themes Written to Sentence Cues by Sixth-, Eighth-, and Tenth-Grade Students
176w Six Stations of Divorce
273k The Gilded Six-Bits

SIXTEEN

23e Learned Women in the Europe of the Sixteenth Century
121c Indian Women and White Society: The Case of Sixteenth-Century Peru
190b City Women and Religious Change in Sixteenth-Century France
308a Lu K'un's New Audience: The Influence of Women's Literacy on Sixteenth-Century Thought

SIXTIES

4e Women Drop Back In: Educational Innovation in the Sixties
47c Doris Lessing in the Sixties: The New Anatomy of Melancholy
303m New Professional Identities: Four Women in the Sixties

SKEPTICISM

48c Sociologist's Skepticism
52e Reginald Scot's "Discoverie of Witchcraft": Scepticism and Sadduceeism

SKILLS

249h Chinese Women: Old Skills in a New Context
272g Coeducation and the Development of Leadership Skills in Women: Historical Perspectives from Cornell University, 1868-1900

SKIRTS

208bb Skirts in Fiction About Boys: A Maxi Mess

SKY

111i The Sky Is Gray
112g The Sky is Gray
127h Pie in the Sky
279g The Bride Comes to Yellow Sky
307h Women Hold Up Half the Sky

SLAVE

68y Root of the White Slave Traffic
80l Inculcating a Slave Mentality: Women in German Popular Fiction of the Early Twentieth Century
175u Housework: Slavery or Labor of Love
257g Slave-Women of America
262p Woman in Philanthropy--Work of Anti-Slavery Women
278r Black Women Respond to Slavery
288hh "Part-Time Work of a Domestic Slave," or Putting the Screws to Screwball Comedy

SLEEP

76m Sleep Orgasm in Women

SLIDES

155f Sex Differences in Responses to Psychosexual Stimulation by Films and Slides

SLIME

282e Holes and Slime: Sexism in Sartre's Psychoanalysis

SLIPPER

50g The Golden Slipper
373l A Gold Slipper

SLUM

114p Slum Women of Bombay
360h Cultural Hybrid in the Slums: The College Woman and the Settlement House, 1889-1894

SLYDYNGE

17d "Slydynge of Corage": Chaucer's Criseyde as Feminist and Victim

SMALLER

212a Popcorn Venus or How the Movies Have Made Women Smaller Than Life

SMART

344p God, But We're Getting Smart

SMILING

1131 A Day in the Life of a Smiling Woman

SMITH

215i Bathsheba Bigler Smith: Woman of Faith and Courage

SNAFU

50o Snafu Murder

SNEAKIER

196d Girls--More Moral Than Boys or Just Sneakier?

SNOW

215a Life and Legend of Eliza R. Snow

SNYDER

215h Jane Snyder Richards: The Blue-White Diamond

SOCIAL

see also SOCIAL WORK; SOCIAL WELFARE; SOCIAL SECURITY; SOCIETY; SOCIALIZATION; CULTURE

2f Abortion and the Social System
4q Women's Studies and Social Change
9l Social Purity
11f Women and the New Social Structures
14a Nonsexist Perspective on Social and Political Change
15j Social Conditions Can Change
20u Social Trends
20aa Women and Social Customs within the Family: A Case Study of Attitudes in Kerala, India
38a Social Trends and Women's Lives--1965-1985
39k Women and Social Stratification: A Case of Intellectual Sexism
39q Social Relations of Black and White Widowed Women in a Northern Metropolis
42f Sexual Politics of Victorian Social Anthropology
42n Case Study of Technological and Social Change: The Washing Machine and the Working Wife
43n Third World Women and Social Reality: Conclusion
55i Marriage, Role Division and Social Cohesion: The Case of Some French Upper-Middle Class Families
61a Demographic and Social Factors in Women's Work Lives

67a Social Responsibility and Research on Sex Differences
71c Passive Female and Social Change: A Cross-Cultural Comparison of Women's Magazine Fiction
93i APPENDIX: Woman and the Social Problem
98p Lesbianism and the Social Function of Taboo
105k Newspaper as a Social Movement's Resource
110b Popular Literature as Social Reinforcement: The Case of "Charlotte Temple"
115c Social Reform Movement in India--From Ranade to Nehru
115f Status of Muslim Women and Social Change
121f Feminine Orders in Colonial Bahia, Brazil: Economic, Social, and Demographic Implications, 1677-1800
126j Latina Liberation: Tradition, Ideology, and Social Change in Iberian and Latin American Cultures
126r Women, Work and the Social Order
139x Female Liberation as the Basis for Social Revolution
140bb Men and the Abortion Experience--Anxiety and Social Supports
141s Social Psychology of the "Decision" to Have or Not Have Children
141v Social Research on Women's Professional Careers
141hh From Social Fact to Social Action
149b Civil and Social Rights of Women
156e Social Psychology of Sex-Role Intervention
163l Women as Politicians: The Social Background, Personality, and Political Careers of Female Party Leaders
166m Social Influence and the Social-Psychological Function of Deference: A Study of Psychiatric Nursing
166kk Married Professional Social Worker
166vv Women Lawyers and Their Profession: Inconsistency of Social Controls and Their Consequences for Professional Performance
171g Social Psychological Model of Human Sexuality
171l Social Psychological Perspective on the Menstrual Cycle
171m Body Time and Social Time: Mood Patterns by Menstrual Cycle Phase and Day of Week
173p Social Values, Femininity, and the Development of Female Competence
173s Social Dimensions of the Menstrual Taboo and the Effects on Female Sexuality
174q Abortion in Israel: Social Demands and Political Responses
176k Race, Social Class, and the Motive to Avoid Success in Women
176tt Women's Lib--Rational? Or Socially Pathological?
196o Attitudes Toward Increased Social, Economic, and Political Participation by Women as Reported by Elementary and Secondary Students
200j Memory for Names and Faces: A Characteristic of Social Intelligence?
201d Social Influences on Sex Differences in Behavior
205j Sex-Role Stereotyping and Social Science
207a Linguistic Sexism as a Social Issue
223j Women of England in a Century of Social Change, 1815-1914: A Select Bibliography
230m Life Crisis as a Clue to Social Function: The Case of Italy
231l Social Aspects of the Woman in the "Res Publica"
238c Female Liberation as the Basis for Social Revolution
244j Women of England in a Century of Social Change, 1815-1914: A Select Bibliography, Part II
250w Social Factors Influencing Problem Solving in Women
251bb Social Situation of Divorced Mothers and Their Families
252m Stigma and Social Identity

252r Task and Social Behavior in Marriage
252dd Social and Private Rates of Return to Investment in Schooling
260m Women as a "Social Problem"
260n Social Change and the Family
264q Women in the Professions: Psychological and Social Barriers to Women in Science
265m Women in the Professions: Psychological and Social Barriers to Women in Science
267a Sex Roles and Social Change
267f Social Change and Sex-Role Inertia: The Case of the Kibbutz
267n Race, Social Class, and the Motive to Avoid Success in Women
281f Sex Roles and Social Change: A Comparative Appraisal of Turkey's Women
287a Looking Backward in Order to Look Forward: Women, Work and Social Values in America
287b Family and Work: The Social Life Cycle of Women
293k Women as Co-Managers: The Family as a General Model of Human Social Organization
294c Impact of the World Social Situation on Women
297i Female Domestic Servant and Social Change: Lima, Peru
304n Bibliography of Materials on Canadian Women, 1950-1975 (Social Sciences)
308i Women and Childbearing in Kwan Mun Hau Village: A Study of Social Change
309b Women in Uttar Pradesh: Social Mobility and Directions of Change
318n Social Services for Women: Problems and Priorities
323b Labour Women and the Social Services
325d Women and Social Change in Morocco
325j Legal and Social Positions of Iranian Women
325y Domestic Social Environment of Women and Girls in Isfahan, Iran
326a Success Motivation and Social Structure: Comments on Women and Achievement
326h Alternatives for Social Change: The Future Status of Women
338e Women of Burundi: A Study of Social Values
348c Doctors and Their Patients: The Social Control of Women in General Practice
348h Studying Rape: Integrating Research and Social Change
372e Spirit Magic in the Social Relations between Men and Women--Sao Paulo, Brazil
372h Adaptive Strategies and Social Networks of Women in St. Kitts

SOCIAL SECURITY

205i Sex-Role Stereotyping in the Social Security and Income Tax Systems
280q Social Security and Equal Rights
328o Federal Income Tax and Social Security Law
352f Social Security and Women: A Partisan View

SOCIAL WORK

166f Predominance of Male Authors in Social Work Publications
166l Occupational Aspects of Social Work
166z Self-Concept, Occupational Role Expectations, and Occupational Choice in Nursing and Social Work

SOCIAL WORKERS

21h Women Social Workers and Clients: Common Victims of Sexism

SOCIAL-LEARNING

56c Social-Learning View of Sex Differences in Behavior

SOCIAL-PSYCHOLOGICAL

see also SOCIAL; SOCIOPSYCHOLOGICAL

166m Social Influence and the Social-Psychological Function of Deference: A Study of Psychiatric Nursing

SOCIAL--ROLE

71j Pursuit of an Ideal: Migration, Social Class, and Women's Roles in Bogota, Colombia
126o Women in Convents: Their Economic and Social Role in Colonial Mexico
227d Social Change and the Roles of Women
304e Housewives in Women's Liberation: Social Change as Role-Making

SOCIAL--SEX

77i Social Construction of the Second Sex
94j Gusii Sex Offenses: A Study in Social Control
155p Gusii Sex Offenses: A Study in Social Control
186h Social Construction of the Second Sex
193d Sex, Age and Social Control in Mobs of the Darwin Hinterland
194g Relationships of Sex and Social Class in Brazil
208d Social Construction of the Second Sex
208hh Guidelines for Equal Treatment of the Sexes in Social Studies Textbooks
213m Social Inequality and Sexual Status in Barbados
256n Social Sex: The New Single Standard for Men and Women
260j Sex in the Social Structure
281s Social Change and Sexual Differentiation in the Cameroun and the Ivory Coast
284r Social Construction of the Second Sex
291c Homosocial Theory of Sex Roles: An Explanation of the Sex Segregation of Social Institutions

SOCIALISM

35a Developing a Theory of Capitalist Patriarchy and Socialist Feminism
86a Female Liberation and Socialism, an Interview
86b Are Feminism and Socialism Related?
89x View of Socialist Feminism
91h Fertility and Women's Employment in the Socialist Countries of Eastern Europe
93e Jennie Higginses of the "New South in the West": A Regional Survey of Socialist Activities, Agitators, and Organizers, 1901-1917
93f Politics of Mutual Frustration: Socialists and Suffragists in New York and Wisconsin

93g Women Socialists and Their Male Comrades: The Reading Experience, 1927-1936
97d Women and the Socialist Party, 1901-1914
116e Forging a Socialist Women's Movement: Angelica Balabanoff in Switzerland
218b Feminism and Socialism: The Utopian Synthesis of Flora Tristan
218c From Separatism to Socialism: Women in the Russian Revolutionary Movement of the 1870s
218d Socialism Faces Feminism: The Failure of Synthesis in France, 1879-1914
218f Marxist Ambivalence Toward Women: Between Socialism and Feminism in the Italian Socialist Party
218h Five Socialist Women: Traditionalist Conflicts and Socialist Visions in Austria, 1893-1934
225f Woman-Power: Religious Heresy and Feminism in Early English Socialism
227e Women Under Communist and Socialist Regimes
275e German Women University Students: National Socialism and the War, 1939-1945
284o Still Inequalities in Socialist Society
329n Algerian Women: Honor, Survival, and Islamic Socialism
368f Women and Socialism: Case of Angelica Balabanoff

SOCIALIZATION

see also SOCIAL; SOCIETY; CULTURE; SEX ROLE

13q Sex-Role Pressures and the Socialization of the Male Child
20b Socialization of Non-Human Primate Females
22r Socialization of Achievement-Orientation in Females
37b Sex Roles and the Socialization Process
45a Socialization and Education of Young Black Girls in Schools
89n Socialized Penis
100b Socialization, Sexuality, and Sex
156g Development of Psychological Androgyny: Early Childhood Socialization
163a Sex, Socialization, and Politics
176h Ambivalence: The Socialization of Women
176dd Cross-Cultural Survey of Some Sex Differences in Socialization
196a Sex-Role Socialization and the Nursery School: As the Twig is Bent
198l Family Structure and the Socialization of the Child
198m Cross-Cultural Survey of Some Sex Differences in Socialization
198aa Physiological Development, Cognitive Development, and Socialization Antecedents of Children's Sex-Role Attitudes
204l Sex-Role Socialization and Achievement in Mathematics
205b Sex-Role Socialisation
208t Sex-Role Socialization in Picture Books for Preschool Children
208ss Children's Toys and Socialization to Sex Roles
210d Religious Socialization of Women Within U.S. Subcultures
246c Socialization of Women in Educational Institutions: Resultant Effects
254i Ambivalence: The Socialization of Women
254k Being and Doing: A Cross-Cultural Examination of the Socialization of Males and Females
264j Sex-Role Socialization
265g Sex-Role Socialization
266f Socialization of Achievement Orientation in Females

267i Socialization of Achievement Motivation in Females
269c Education and Socialization
272i Socialization and Education of Young Black Girls in School
286p Socialization, Dialectics, and Sport
316c Women and Political Socialization: Considerations of the Impact of Motherhood
354h Girls' Socialization for Work

SOCIETY

see also SOCIAL; SOCIALIZATION; CULTURE

11g Media: New Images of Women in Contemporary Society
19a Women in Egalitarian Societies
20q Bundu: Political Implications of Female Solidarity in a Secret Society
20w Attitudes Towards Reproduction in a Rapidly Changing African Society
39u Introducing Students to Women's Place in Society
47e Mary McCarthy: Society's Demands
53a Nature of Women in Society
55e Political Economy of Domestic Labour in Capitalist Society
59c Women in Industrial Society: An International Perspective
59d Women in Developing Societies: Economic Independence Is Not Enough
71k Modernizing Women for a Modern Society: The Cuban Case
77d Conclusion: "Sex and Temperament in Three Primitive Societies"
80e Women in Contemporary French Society: Annotated Bibliography
89dd Women and Society
89ccc Sex in a Capitalist Society
94c Rape and Rape Law: Sexism in Society and Law
101f Society and Gender
114f Position of Women in Indian Society
115a Nehru and the Place of Women in Indian Society
120a Difference and Dominance: An Overview of Language, Gender and Society
121b Female and Family in the Economy and Society of Colonial Brazil
121c Indian Women and White Society: The Case of Sixteenth-Century Peru
122b Women Intellectuals in Chilean Society
122c Clorinda Matto de Turner and Mercedes Cabello de Carbonera: Societal Criticism and Morality
126a Woman in Society: A Critique of Frederick Engels
127z Conclusion, "Sex and Temperament in Three Primitive Societies"
131k Women in Philippine Society: More Equal Than Many
138b Impact of White Women on Fur Trade Society
149d Sex Differences: Biological, Cultural, Societal Implications
158j "Sex and Temperament in Three Primitive Societies"
158w Marx, Sex and the Transformation of Society
163g Societal Punishment and Aspects of Female Political Participation: 1972 National Convention Delegates
181d Landscape with Figures: Home and Community in English Society
184a Life Expectancies for Women in Medieval Society
184e Fifteenth-Century View of Women's Role in Medieval Society: Christine de Pizan's "Livre des Trois Vertus"
193b Food for Thought--Patterns of Production and Consumption in Pira-Parana Society
193j Status and Role: Raw Materials for Society, Marriage
201a Sex Roles in Primate Societies

206a Primitive Societies
209g Toward a Society of Neuters
213e Female Husbands in Southern Bantu Societies
223a Victorian Governess: Status Incongruence in Family and Society
235d Battered Women: Society's Problem
240b Changing Image of Woman in Renaissance Society and Literature
244e Image and Reality: The Actress and Society
249a Woman, Culture, and Society: A Theoretical Overview
249n Myth of Matriarchy: Why Men Rule in Primitive Society
252q Sex-Role Differentiation in an Equalitarian Society
260y Role of Women in the Political Organization of African Societies
262r Woman in Philanthropy--Work of the Red Cross Society
271v Feminism: The Sine Qua Non for a Just Society
278a Men's Power with Women, Other Men and Society
281t Women's Labor Force Participation in a Developing Society: The Case of Brazil
282h Marx, Sex, and the Transformation of Society
284o Still Inequalities in Socialist Society
285d Role of Women in a Changing Navaho Society
285e Women in Modernizing Societies
297g Marital Status and Sexual Identity: The Position of Women in a Mexican Peasant Society
297v Mobilization of Women: Three Societies
318a Society and the Sexes in the Russian Past
325e Women in Turkish Society
325s Changing Sex Roles in Bedouin Society in Syria and Lebanon
335b Women in Anglo-Saxon Society (c.600-1066)
338b Position of Women in a Pastoral Society (Fulani WoDaaBe, Nomads of the Niger)
338c Role of Women in the Political Organization of African Societies
339m The Soul Selects Her Own Society
342m Study of Male Society
365h Single Woman in Today's Society
371a Women Working: Toward a New Society
372l Economic Role of Women in Alaskan Eskimo Society

SOCIETY--AMERICA

163n Women as Voters: Their Maturation as Political Persons in American Society
326f Women as Voters: Their Maturation as Political Persons in American Society

SOCIO ECONOMIC

see also ECONOMY; DEVELOPMENT; LABOR; SOCIOLOGY; STATUS

21p Women in China: Problems of Sex Inequality and Socio-economic Change
266ii Socio-Economic Context Of Sex And Power: A Study of Women, Work And Family Roles in Four Israeli Institutional Frameworks
302e Ga Women and Socioeconomic Change in Accra, Ghana
309e Women in Kerala: Changing Socio-Economic Status and Self-Image
367d Socioeconomic Determinants of Differential Fertility in Turkey

SOCIOBIOLOGICAL

172i Woman's Sociobiological Heritage: Destiny or Free Choice?

SOCIOCULTURAL

149i Socio-Cultural Setting
219n Sociocultural and Sociopsychological Factors in Differential Language Retentiveness by Sex
297j Sociocultural Factors Mitigating Role Conflict of Buenos Aires Professional Women
370a Sociocultural Context

SOCIOEMOTIONAL

173k Early Sex Differences in the Human: Studies of Socioemotional Development
199i Sex of Parent x Sex of Child: Socioemotional Development

SOCIOLINGUISTS

120e Sex of the Speaker as a Sociolinguistic Variable
219a "What Do Women Sociolinguists Want?": Prospects For a Research Field

SOCIOLOGY

see also SOCIETY; SOCIAL; CULTURE; SOCIO ECONOMIC; STATUS

14c Women and Medical Sociology: Invisible Professionals and Ubiquitous Patients
14d Sociology of Education: Perspectives on Women
14e "Thereness" of Women: A Selective Review of Urban Sociology
14g Sociology and Women in Working-class Jobs
14i Feminist Review of the Sociology of Deviance
14j Sociology of Feeling and Emotion
14l Feminist Perspectives in Sociological Research
48c Sociologist's Skepticism
54h Sociological and Demographic Aspects of the Changing Status of Migrant Women in Europe
55a Women as Employees: Some Comments on Research in Industrial Sociology
84g Women and Production: A Critical Analysis of Some Sociological Theories of Women's Work
183g Role of Women in Underdeveloped Countries: Some Sociological Issues Concerning Conflict and Peace
190f Feminist History in Perspective: Sociological Contributions to Biographic Analysis
246n Sociological Examination of the Women's Movement
251a Implications of a Sociology for Women
286m Sociological Considerations of the Female Participant
291e Dual Linkages between the Occupational and Family Systems: A Macrosociological Analysis
296k Psychologic and Sociologic Factors of Orgasm
354f Issues in the Sociological Study of Women's Work
354g Inequalities in the Labor Force: Three Sociological Explanations
358o Sociological Aspects of Women in Sports

368d Sociology of Birth: A Critical Assessment of Theory and Research

SOCIOPSYCHOLOGICAL

219n Sociocultural and Sociopsychological Factors in Differential Language Retentiveness by Sex
327b Why Can't Women Be More Like Men: A Summary of the Sociopsychological Factors Hindering Women's Advancement in the Professions

SOFT

132j Hard and the Soft: The Force of Feminism in Modern Times

SOJOURNER

233uu Sojourner Truth: On Women's Rights

SOLDIER

134f Tin Soldier

SOLIDARITY

20q Bundu: Political Implications of Female Solidarity in a Secret Society
350a Female Solidarity and the Sexual Division of Labour
350b Rural China: Segregation to Solidarity
350e Women's Solidarity and the Preservation of Privilege
350h Two Contexts of Solidarity

SOLIPSISM

363o Sexual Solipsism of Sigmund Freud

SOLOMON

266jj Life and Death of Ms. Solomon Grundy

SOLVING

250w Social Factors Influencing Problem Solving in Women

SON

141r Son Preference in Taiwan: Verbal Preference and Demographic Behavior
250n Parents' Differential Reactions to Sons and Daughters

SONG

43i Ancient Song, New Melody in Latin America: Women and Film
73c Women Learn to Sing the Menstrual Blues
95k Song of Lawino, Song of Ocol
111u Cassandra's Wedding Song
112aa Song
133b The Song of N'Sardi-El

265r Images of American Woman in Popular Songs
277c The Nightingales Sing
277u Songs My Father Sang Me
279s Long Black Song
340f The Ship Who Sang
359j Metaphysics of Matrilinearism in Women's Autobiography: Studies of Mead's "Blackberry Winter," Hellman's "Pentimento," Angelou's "I Know Why the Caged Bird Sings," and Kingston's "The Woman Warrior"
373i The Singing Lesson

SONNET

233g Woman in the Elizabethan Sonnet: Poems

SOPHIA

108a Venus--Aghia Sophia
303e Sophia Hayden and the Woman's Building Competition

SOPHIE

368b Reeducation of Sophie

SORCIERS

52d Jean Bodin's "De la Demonomanie des Sorciers": The Logic of Persecution

SORROW

113m A Sorrowful Woman
119i The Mount of Sorrow
273g Sorrow-Acre

SOUL

177g Equality of Souls, Inequality of Sexes: Woman in Medieval Theology
220r And the Soul Shall Dance
292n Troubled Souls of Females
339m The Soul Selects Her Own Society

SOUND

3k Sound of a Drunken Drummer
16c The Mothers, the Mothers, How Eerily It Sounds

SOUTH

7d Black Woman's Struggle for Equality in the South, 1895-1925
25d Family in the Plantation South
25j Family and Childhood in a Southern Negro Community
30b Dowry and Bridewealth and the Property Rights of Women in South Asia
57c Southern Woman
93e Jennie Higginses of the "New South in the West": A Regional Survey of Socialist Activities, Agitators, and Organizers, 1901-1917
96s Observations of the Southern Race Feeling

116t Family and Kin Cohesion among South Italian Immigrants in Toronto
140k Role of Wife in the Black Extended Family: Perspectives from a Rural Community in Southern United States
151g Reality and the Southern Lady
151k "New Woman" in the New South
153e Appeal to the Christian Women of the South
213d Caste Differences between Brahmin and Non-Brahmin Women in a South Indian Village
213e Female Husbands in Southern Bantu Societies
215t Dr. Margaret Ann Freece: Entrepreneur of Southern Utah
219j Black Women In the Rural South: Conservative and Innovative
230k Men and Women in the South of France: Public and Private Domains
259e Ante-Bellum Southern Women
262d Education of Woman in the Southern States
279cc Beasts of the Southern Wild
281n How African Women Cope with Migrant Labor in South Africa
285f Bargaining from Weakness: Spirit Possession on the South Kenya Coast
293h Women in African Towns South of the Sahara: The Urbanization Dilemma
294k Political Participation of Women in Africa South of the Sahara
294n Women's Political Participation in the South Pacific
317g Southern Lay Midwives as Ritual Specialists
317i Convivial Sisterhood: Spirit Mediumship and Client-Core Network among Black South African Women
333e Black Employment in the South
334r Women Against Lynching in the Twentieth-Century South

SOUTH ASIA

see ASIA; individual countries

SOUTHAMPTON

42l Prostitution and the Poor in Plymouth and Southampton Under the Contagious Diseases Act
244d Making of an Outcast Group: Prostitutes and Working Women in Nineteenth-Century Plymouth and Southampton

SOUTHEAST

91b Fertility, Women's Work, and Economic Class: A Case Study from Southeast Asia
294l Political Role of Southeast Asian Women
324p Burma and South-East Asia

SOUTHEAST ASIA

see ASIA; individual countries

SOUTHGATE

104a E. Southgate

SOUTHWEST

116v Italian Immigrant Women in the Southwest

SOVIET

see also RUSSIA

70f Urban Working Woman in the U.S.S.R.: An Historical Overview
149n Elements and Types in Soviet Marriage
166o Women in the Soviet Economy
176ff Worker, Mother, Housewife: Soviet Women Today
182a Workers (and Mothers): Soviet Women Today
182c Changing Image of Women in Soviet Literature
182d Changing Soviet Family
182e Childbearing Functions of the Soviet Family
206l Worker, Mother, Housewife: Soviet Woman Today
267e Convergences between East and West: Tradition and Modernity in Sex Roles in Sweden, Finland, and the Soviet Union
291i Occupational Segregation and Public Policy: A Comparative Analysis of American and Soviet Patterns
297t Role and Status of Women in the Soviet Union: 1917 to the Present
307f Women and Revolution: The Lessons of the Soviet Union and China
316m Modernization Theory and Sex Roles in Critical Perspective: The Case of the Soviet Union
318e Sexual Equality in Soviet Policy: A Developmental Perspective
318f Bolshevik Alternatives and the Soviet Family: The 1926 Marriage Law Debate
318k Women and Sex in Soviet Law
318p Women and Women's Issues in Soviet Policy Debates
324r Soviet Union
327h Soviet Women in the Work Force and Professions
329s Changing Women's Roles in the U.S.S.R.
352k Trends in Women's Employment in the U.S.S.R.

SOW

142m Woman as Secretary, Sexpot, Spender, Sow, Civic Actor, Sickie
186a Woman as Secretary, Sexpot, Spender, Sow, Civic Actor, Sickie

SPACE

3d Inner and Outer Space: Reflections on Womanhood
18f Sex-Related Differences in Spatial Ability: A Developmental Psychological View
21i New Feminist Criticisms: Exploring the History of the New Space
53c Open Body, Closed Space: The Transformation of Female Sexuality
156h Sex Differences in the Use of Outdoor Space
173f Once More the Inner Space
175cc Free Space
198f Inner and Outer Space: Reflections on Womanhood
204c Spatial Ability: A Critical Review of the Sex-Linked Major Gene Hypothesis
250t Sex Differences in Space Perception and Aspects of Intellectual Functioning
250u Pattern Copying Under Three Conditions of an Expanded Spatial Field
253a Inner and Outer Space: Reflections on Womanhood
268s Womanhood and the Inner Space
268t Once More the Inner Space
303q Centers and Fragments: Women's Spaces

SPAIN

see also IBERIAN

19q Other Scenarios: Women and Spanish Anarchism
20v Eurogallegas: Female Spanish Migration
80h Three Peninsular Novelists Comment on the Spanish Woman
140p Women and Words in a Spanish Village
230l Women and Words in a Spanish Village
270g Andean Women Under Spanish Rule
324h Spain

SPANISH AMERICA

see also LATIN AMERICA; individual countries

121g Feminine Press: The View of Women in the Colonial Journals of Spanish America, 1790-1810
324i Spanish America

SPARK

47i Muriel Spark's Fingernails

SPEAK

98f To Be or Not to Be...A Feminist Speaker
120e Sex of the Speaker as a Sociolinguistic Variable
175i Speaking Out on Prostitution

SPEARS

366f Digging Sticks and Spears, Or the Two-Sex Model

SPECIALIZATION

4n Sex and Specialization in Academe and the Professions
291o Sex Differences in Economists' Fields of Specialization
317g Southern Lay Midwives as Ritual Specialists

SPECTATOR

79v Female Spectator
163j Spectators, Agitators, or Lawmakers: Women in State Legislatures
286s Female Spectator

SPECULATION

115i Woman Versus Womanliness: An Essay in Speculative Psychology
164m One American Woman: A Speculation upon Disbelief
214o May Swenson and the Shapes of Speculation

SPEECH

9d Speech: National Women's Rights Convention of 1855
9i Speech: Legislature, 1860

79e Speech to the Troops at Tilbury
79f Speech to the Parliament
98k For a Restricted Thematics: Writing, Speech, and Difference in Madame Bovary
120b Women's Speech: Separate But Unequal?
120j Cues to the Identification of Sex in Children's Speech
120m Sex Differences in Language, Speech, and Nonverbal Communication: An Annotated Bibliography
219c Two Features of "Women's Speech"?
219l Mothers' Speech to Children in Bilingual Mexican-American Homes
219m Fluency of Women's Speech
257h (Speech, National Woman's Suffrage Association, 1889)
314w Woman Is Not a Girl and Other Lessons in Corporate Speech

SPEED

96ff Lightning Speed Through Life
226l Lightning Speed Through Life

SPELL

214n Echoing Spell of H.D.'s "Trilogy"

SPENCER

215j Aurelia Read Spencer Rogers: Humble Heroine

SPEND

70i Historical Changes in How People Spend Their Time
142m Woman as Secretary, Sexpot, Spender, Sow, Civic Actor, Sickie
186a Woman as Secretary, Sexpot, Spender, Sow, Civic Actor, Sickie

SPERANZA

5h Speranza

SPHERE

246i Women in the Economic Sphere: The Coming Struggle for Jobs
334h Paradox of "Women's Sphere"

SPHINX

68c Shavian Sphinx

SPICE

4f From Sugar to Spice to Professor
271b Sugar'n Spice

SPINDLE

336a Loom and Spindle; or, Life Among the Early Mill Girls

SPIRIT

8bb Spirit is Liberationist but the Flesh is...or, You Can't Always Get Into Bed With Your Dogma
131f Lau, Malaita: "A Woman Is an Alien Spirit"
175bb Spiritual Dimension of Women's Liberation
263j Feminist Spirituality, Christian Identity, and Catholic Vision
263t Spiritual Quest and Women's Experience
263u Becoming a Woman: Menstruation as Spiritual Experience
285f Bargaining from Weakness: Spirit Possession on the South Kenya Coast
302g Rebels or Status-Seekers? Women as Spirit Mediums in East Africa
317a Bride of Christ Is Filled with His Spirit
317h Epidemiology of Spirit Possession among the Luvale of Zambia
317i Convivial Sisterhood: Spirit Mediumship and Client-Core Network among Black South African Women
334d Cherished Spirit of Independence: The Life of an Eighteenth-Century Boston Businesswoman
350g Women's Spirit Possession and Urban Adaptation
359b Quest for Community: Spiritual Autobiographies of Eighteenth-Century Quaker and Puritan Women in America
360g Spiritualist Medium: A Study of Female Professionalization in Victorian America
372e Spirit Magic in the Social Relations between Men and Women--Sao Paulo, Brazil
372f Spirit Mediums in Umbanda Evangelizada of Porto Alegre, Brazil: Dimensions of Power and Authority

SPOCK

86i Reply to Dr. Spock on Child Care

SPOLIN

141ee Historical and Theoretical Evolution of Viola Spolin's Theatre Games

SPORT

see also ATHLETICS; TITLE IX; TEAMS

152e Being Female in Sport
152n Giving Women a Sporting Chance
152p Radical Ethic for Sports
152q Desegregating Sexist Sport
152s Women's Sports in China
196ll Participation in Sports by Girls
280g Boys, Girls, and Sports
286b Psychological Aspects of Sport with Special Reference to the Female
286d Kinesis and the Concept of Self in Sport
286f Stress Seeking and Sport Involvement
286k Use of Hypnosis in Sport--Is It Legitimate?
286n Femininity and Achievement in Sports
286o Influence of Birth Order and Sibling Sex on Sports Participation
286p Socialization, Dialectics, and Sport
286q American Business Values and Involvement in Sport
286v Nutritional Requirements for Women in Sport

306l Women in Sports
358a Equal Opportunity for Women in Sports
358c Emergence of Women in Sport
358d Century of American Women's Sport
358k Masculine Obsession in Sports
358o Sociological Aspects of Women in Sports
364j Confronting the Sports Establishment: A Plan for Honesty and Sanity

SPRING

29j A Sudden Trip Home in the Spring
111pp The Widow's Lament in Springtime

STAATSBURGER

275f Frau und Staatsburger in Volker Braun's Schauspiel "Tinka"

STABILITY

54g Extra-Marital Fertility and its Occurrence in Stable Unions: Recent Trends in Western Europe
270k Stability in Banana Leaves: Colonization and Women in Kiriwina, Trobriand Islands
314g Women in Work Force Post Better Records for Stability in Jobs

STAEL

275a Impact of German Thought and Culture on Madame de Stael's Thinking about Women

STAFF-PATIENT

211s "Difficult" Patient: Observations on the Staff-Patient Interaction

STAGES

35e Struggle for Reproductive Freedom: Three Stages of Feminism
117q Stages
198d Early Stages of the Oedipus Conflict
199k Stages in the Development of Psychosexual Concepts and Attitudes
278y Before Androgyny: An Examination of the Stages Toward Neo-Masculinity

STAIRCASE

13t Down the Up Staircase
197f Down the Up Staircase: Sex Roles, Professionalization, and the Status of Teachers

STAKE

19e Pedestal and the Stake: Courtly Love and Witchcraft
48l Larger Stakes
328a Women's Stake in Full Employment: Their Disadvantaged Role in the Economy--Challenges to Action

STANDARD

40h Cost of Compliance with Federal Day Care Standards in Seattle and Denver
110v Sexism and the Double Standard in Literature
151p Decline and Fall of the Double Standard
173jj Double Standard of Aging
198k Standardization of Sex-Temperament
254t Women Writers and the Double Standard
256n Social Sex: The New Single Standard for Men and Women
264l Double Standard: Age
265h Double Standard: Age

STANDING BEAR

16h Why Has the Virgin Mary Never Entered the Wigwam of Standing Bear?

STANDSTILL

352a Women at a Standstill: The Need for Radical Change

STANFORD

301i Affirmative Action at Stanford University

STANTON

104b E.C. Stanton
359d Paradox and Success of Elizabeth Cady Stanton

STARLESS

108bb The Starless Air

STATE

84d Church, State, and Family: The Women's Movement in Italy
84j State and the Oppression of Women
85v Coercion and Rape: The State As a Male Protection Racket
89t Origin of the Family, Private Property, and the State
92g Welfare State and the Needs of the Dependent Family
107b Women as Equal to Men in the State
158y Origin of the Family, Private Property, and the State
163j Spectators, Agitators, or Lawmakers: Women in State Legislatures
163v Black Women State Legislators: A Profile
174m Policy Impacts on Hispanics and Women: A State Case Study
174p Styles and Priorities of Marginality: Women State Legislators
175w A.D.C.: Marriage to the State
176d Sex, Age, and State as Determinants of Mother-Infant Interaction
181i Looking Again at Engels' "Origin of the Family, Private Property and the State"
198cc Sex, Age, and State as Determinants of Mother-Infant Interaction
203g Origin of the Family, Private Property and the State
262b Education of Woman in the Eastern States
262c Education of Woman in the Western States
262d Education of Woman in the Southern States
262j Woman in the State

312e Women and the New Irish State
326e Black Women Officeholders: The Case of State Legislators
344s Individualism, Marriage and the Liberal State: Beyond the Equal Rights Amendment
352h Equality of Remuneration for Men and Women in the Member States of the E.E.C.
363a Observations on the State of Degradation to Which Woman Is Reduced by Various Causes

STATEMENT

9p Statement: First Feminist Congress, 1919
35o Berkeley-Oakland Women's Union Statement
35p Black Feminist Statement
132u Collective Statement, Black Sisters
149r Statement of Purpose
291n Toward Dimorphics: A Summary Statement to the Conference on Occupational Segregation

STATISTICS

45j APPENDIX: Educational and Occupational Statistics on Black Women
51j Arrest Statistics
94d Forcible Rape in the U.S.: A Statistical Profile
153g Statistics of Female Health

STATUS

4h Status Transitions of Women Students, Faculty, and Administrators
4k Institutional Variation in the Status of Academic Women
4l Representation, Performance and Status of Women on the Faculty at the Urbana-Champaign Campus of the University of Illinois
4m Discipline Variation in the Status of Academic Women
20c Prenatal Hormones and Human Behavior: Implications for the Status of Women
22t Relationship Between Sex Roles, Marital Status, and Mental Illness
37g APPENDIX: Status of Women in Sweden: Report to the United Nations, 1968
39l Demographic Influence on Female Employment and the Status of Women
39o Impediment or Stimulant? Marital Status and Graduate Education
54a Population and the Status of Women: Results of the Bucharest and Mexico Conferences
54b Measurement of the Status of Women
54c Divorce and the Status of Women
54d Marriage and Marriage Dissolution and the Changing Status of Women: The Case of Poland
54f Marital Fertility and the Changing Status of Women in Europe
54h Sociological and Demographic Aspects of the Changing Status of Migrant Women in Europe
54i Report of the Symposium on Demographic Aspects of the Changing Status of Women in Europe
67e Intelligence, Occupational Status and Achievement Orientation
75g Current Status of Women in Prisons
80c Status of the Frenchwoman Today
91d Status of Women, Work and Fertility in India
91i Differential Fertility by Working Status of Women in Japan
91j Female Work Status and Fertility in Latin America

115f Status of Muslim Women and Social Change
115h Indian Women: Work, Power and Status
117l Status of Women in Halakhic Judaism
123h Normative Status of Heterosexuality
140n Stress, Primary Support Systems and Women's Employment Status
140r Status of Women: Partial Summary of a Cross-Cultural Survey
141w STATUS OF WOMEN IN THIS AND OTHER CULTURES: Introduction
141y Cross-Cultural Study of the Relative Status of Women
146e Low Pay-Low Status
149a Status of Women in Modern Patterns of Culture
149j Declining Status of Women: Popular Myths and the Failure of Functionalist Thought
151e Lady and the Mill Girl: Changes in the Status of Women in the Age of Jackson
158ee Moral and Legal Status of Abortion
174k Combatting Dual Discrimination: The Impact of Civil Rights Policies on the Income Status of Black Women
176hh Women in the Kibbutz: Changing Status and Concepts
195f Barbarian Status of Women
196gg Task Force on Education Report, Governor's Commission on the Status of Women, Ma.
197f Down the Up Staircase: Sex Roles, Professionalization, and the Status of Teachers
230q Collectivization, Kinship, and the Status of Women in Rural China
233z Political and Civil Status of Women as of January 1, 1969
236g Status of Korean Women Today
238j Status of Women in Sweden
240l Second-class Citizenship: The Status of Women in Contemporary American Fiction
243i Status of Women in Psychology: How Many and How Come?
249j Female Status in the Public Domain
251i Origins of the Status of Women
251aa Disadvantaged Status of Black Women
252n Origins of the Status of Women
255f "Treated Like Imbecile Children" (Diderot): The Enlightenment and the Status of Women
258a Current Status of Women Cross-Culturally: Changes and Persisting Barriers
266ee Status of Women--Population--Development
270f Aztec Women: The Transition from Status to Class in Empire and Colony
278b Male Power Motivation and the Status of Women
284g Women's Status Fifty Years After the Vote
284m Status of Women
294a Status of Women in Modern Patterns of Culture
294u United Nations Action to Advance the Status of Women
297w Image and Reality: Women's Status in Israel
297ee Class, Commodity, and the Status of Women
302g Rebels or Status-Seekers? Women as Spirit Mediums in East Africa
304l Status of Immigrant Women in Canada
307k Status of Women in Taiwan: One Step Forward, Two Steps Back
309e Women in Kerala: Changing Socio-Economic Status and Self-Image
309g Women and Religion: The Status and Image of Women in Major Religious Traditions
309h Family Status and Female Work Participation
314o Struggle for Status
325b Legal Reform as an Indicator of Women's Status in Muslim Nations

325c Status and Fertility Patterns of Muslim Women
325p Status of Women in Four Middle East Communities
325u Status of Women and Property on a Baluchistan Oasis in Pakistan
326d Female Status: A New Population Policy
326g Government Policy and the Legal Status of Women
326h Alternatives for Social Change: The Future Status of Women
327a Status of Women
334f Equality or Submersion? Feme (sic) Couvert Status in Early Pennsylvania
349d Legal Status of Women After the American Revolution
360d Lady and the Mill Girl: Changes in the Status of Women in the Age of Jackson
366d Aboriginal Women's Status: A Paradox Resolved
367a Family Life, Women's Status, and Fertility: Middle East and North African Perspectives
371j Hours Rigidity: Effects on the Labor-Market Status of Women

STATUS--ECONOMY

21u Status of Home Economics and the Status of Women
146m Economic and Legal Status
202j Economics of Marital Status
252hh Economic Status of Families Headed by Women
265n Women's Economic Status: Some Cliches and Some Facts
297n Economic Basis of the Status of Women

STATUS--FAMILY

223a Victorian Governess: Status Incongruence in Family and Society
252hh Economic Status of Families Headed by Women
266ff Interrelationship of the Status of Women and Family Planning
281l Female Status, the Family, and Male Dominance in a West Indian Community

STATUS--LAW

246b Changing Status of Women in the Law
281p Raising the Status of Women through Law: The Case of Israel
294e Status of Women in Private Law

STATUS--ROLE

43c Women in Zaire: Disparate Status and Roles
141z Changing Status and Role of Women in Politics
198j Status and Role: Raw Materials for Society, Marriage
206p Status and Role Behavior in Changing Japan
294b Demographic Change and the Roles and Status of Women
297t Role and Status of Women in the Soviet Union: 1917 to the Present
316f Role and Status of Women in the Daley Organization

STATUS--SEX

173x Sex Preferences, Sex Control, and the Status of Women
213m Social Inequality and Sexual Status in Barbados
227a Sexual Asymmetry and the Status of Women
250ll Encountering the Male Establishment: Sex Status Limits on Woman's Careers in the Professions

297g Marital Status and Sexual Identity: The Position of Women in a Mexican Peasant Society
372g Sex and Status: Women in St. Vincent

STATUTE

315i Women in Charter and Statute Law: Medieval Ragusa-Dubrovnik

STEEL

128p Woman in Steel--Rebecca Lukens

STEIN

192a E. Wharton and G. Stein
359h Gertrude Stein and the Problems of Autobiography

STENA

215n Stena Scorup: First Lady of Salina

STENO

127g Drowning in the Steno Pool

STEPHANIE

288t Stephanie Rothman: R-Rated Feminist

STEPSISTERS

173hh Cinderella's Stepsisters: A Feminist Perspective on Anorexia Nervosa and Bulimia

STEREOTYPE

3f Stereotype
13o Look Jane Look. See Sex Stereotypes
22g Biologic Basis for Sex-Role Stereotypes
22q Sex-Role Stereotyping in Children's Television Programs
22w Politics of Sexual Stereotypes
61f Sex Role Stereotypes and the Career Versus Homemaking Orientations of Women
64f Sex Role Stereotyping
68m Feminism and Female Stereotypes in Shaw
139e Stereotypes
155b Sex-Role Stereotypes and Clinical Judgments of Mental Health
159a Stereotype
163r Politics of Sexual Stereotypes
176uu Sex-Role Stereotypes and Clinical Judgements of Mental Health
196i Psychological and Occupational Sex Stereotypes in Elementary School Readers
196j Sex Stereotyping in Elementary-School Mathematics Textbooks
196l Woman's Place: Children's Sex Stereotyping of Occupations
205a Biological Explanations of Sex-Role Stereotypes
205c Sex-Role Stereotyping
205d Influence of the School on Sex-Role Stereotyping

205e Sex-Role Stereotyping in Studies of Marriage and the Family
205f Sex-Role Stereotyping at Work
205h Clinical Aspects of Sex-Role Stereotyping
205i Sex-Role Stereotyping in the Social Security and Income Tax Systems
205j Sex-Role Stereotyping and Social Science
208f School's Role in the Sex-Role Stereotyping of Girls: A Feminist Review of the Literature
208p Feminist Studies: The Schools and Sex-Role Stereotyping
208u Dick and Jane as Victims: Sex Stereotyping in Children's Readers
208ll Sex Stereotypes in Mathematics and Science Textbooks for Elementary and Junior High Schools
208pp Film Resources for Sex-Role Stereotyping
208qq Sesame Street and Sex-Role Stereotypes
208rr Sesame Street and Sex-Role Stereotypes (updated)
223h Stereotypes of Femininity in a Theory of Sexual Evolution
250a Stereotype of Femininity
250j Sex-Role Stereotypes and Clinical Judgments of Mental Health
266aa Relationship Between Sex-Role Stereotypes And Requisite Management Characteristics
267c Sex-Role Stereotypes: A Current Appraisal
271a Sexual Stereotypes Start Early
275c Stereotype of the Emancipated Woman in the Weimar Republic
278u Damnation and Stereotyping in Joke Telling
280f Early Stereotypes
280l Changing the Stereotypes
314a Women as Managers--Stereotypes and Realities
314z 52 Job Titles Revised to Eliminate Sex-Stereotyping
316b Apolitical Woman: Femininity and Sex-Stereotyping in Girls
320h Sex Stereotyping in Canadian Schools
321f Sexism in Voir Dire: The Use of Sex Stereotypes in Jury Selection
328p Impact of Mass-Media Stereotypes upon the Full Employment of Women
364f Myths and Stereotypes: My Challenge to Black Women Cultural Workers

STERILIZING

191g Sterilizing the Poor

STERN

104i E.G. Stern

STEWART

165b F. Stewart

STICKS

366f Digging Sticks and Spears, Or the Two-Sex Model

STICKY

269j Modern Family: Sticky Myths, Diverse Realities, and the Problem of Isolation

STIGMA

252m Stigma and Social Identity

STIMULATION

39o Impediment or Stimulant? Marital Status and Graduate Education
155f Sex Differences in Responses to Psychosexual Stimulation by Films and Slides

STIR

50c The Stir Outside the Cafe Royal

STOCKING

277h The White Stocking

STONE

257d Marriage of Lucy Stone Under Protest

STOREFRONT

143n From Kitchen to Storefront: Women in the Tenant Movement

STORM

279f The Storm

STORY

10b The Story of Avis
24o Four Stories About Lovers
65a Sentiment and Intellect: The Story of John Stuart Mill and Harriet Taylor Mill
74q Woman and Her Mind: The Story of Daily Life
102f Nina's Story
102p High-Rise Story
111qq The Story of an Hour
117b Women's Liberation and the Liberation of God: An Essay in Story Theology
119e The Housekeeper's Story
122q Short Stories of Lydia Cabrera: Transpositions or Creations?
127t Storybook Lives: Growing Up Middle Class
128g Reckless Lady: The Life Story of Adah Isaacs Menken
133c Jubilee's Story
211h C.O.P.E. Story: A Service to Pregnant and Postpartum Women
233ss Her Story
256u X: A Fabulous Child's Story
277g Reservations: A Love Story
277z A Country Love Story
300c Not a Very Nice Story
337n Episcopalian Story
337o Roman Catholic Story
355e The Tragic Menagerie (stories)
355g Humorous Tales (stories)
355h All about Love (stories)

STRAIGHT

8v Gay Couples and Straight Law

STRAIN

163q Wife and Politician: Role Strain Among Women in Public Office

STRANGE

110n Case for Violet Strange
199m Ethological Study of Children Approaching a Strange Adult: Sex Differences

STRATEGY

6g Strategy for Change
20n Women and Domestic Power: Political and Economic Strategies in Domestic Groups
21d Female Strategies: Animal Adaptations and Adaptive Significance
35c Feminist Theory and the Development of Revolutionary Strategy
209e Sex Differences in Game Strategy
219q Alignment Strategies in Verbal Accounts of Problematic Conduct: The Case of Abortion
249e Strategies, Cooperation, and Conflict Among Women in Domestic Groups
249f Sex Roles and Survival Strategies in an Urban Black Community
301d Legal Requirements, Structures, and Strategies for Eliminating Sex Discrimination in Academe
309j Asian Women in Britain: Strategies of Adjustment of Indian and Pakistani Migrants
331h Public Policy and the Family: A New Strategy for Women as Wives and Mothers
359i Lillian Hellman and the Strategy of the "Other"
372h Adaptive Strategies and Social Networks of Women in St. Kitts

STRATIFICATION

39k Women and Social Stratification: A Case of Intellectual Sexism
51r Prostitution: An Extreme Case of Sex Stratification
213a Theory of Sexual Stratification
302c "Aba Riots" or Igbo "Women's War"? Ideology, Stratification, and the Invisibility of Women

STREET

55c Sex and Occupational Role on Fleet Street
233hh Main Street
317l Jive Dope Fiend Whoes: In the Street and in Rehabilitation
325aa Women and the Neighborhood Street in Borj Hammoud, Lebanon

STRENGTH

17k "Out of the chaos, a new kind of strength": Doris Lessing's "The Golden Notebook"

160a Advice to Mothers, on the Subject of Their Own Health, and, of the Means of Promoting the Health, Strength and Beauty of Their Offspring
344j Economic Strength Is What Counts

STRESS

140n Stress, Primary Support Systems and Women's Employment Status
171i Maternal Stress in the Postpartum Period
172g Stress and Coping in Divorce: A Focus on Women
286f Stress Seeking and Sport Involvement

STRIKE

257l Strikes and Their Causes
295h Women in Production: The Toronto Dressmakers' Strike of 1931

STRIX

52b Witchcraft and Magic in Renaissance Italy: Gianfrancesco Pico and his "Strix"

STROKE

220j A Stroke of Luck

STRUCTURE

11f Women and the New Social Structures
14b Women and the Structure of Organizations: Explorations in Theory and Behavior
20t American Women in Politics: Culture, Structure, and Ideology
21q Erosion of Sexual Equality in the Kibbutz: A Structural Interpretation
35i Monopoly Capital and the Structure of Consumption
59h Structural Change in the Occupational Composition of the Female Labor Force
84c Structures of Patriarchy and Capital in the Family
126v Four Structures in a Complex Unity
166b Plus Ca Change...? The Sexual Structure of Occupations Over Time
174d Impact of Organizational Structure, Technology, and Professionalism on the Policy of Affirmative Action
175ff Tyranny of Structurelessness
198l Family Structure and the Socialization of the Child
249b Family Structure and Feminine Personality
251p Sex Roles and Family Structure
251ii Family Structure and Communism
252nn Family Structure and Communism
260j Sex in the Social Structure
265j Structural and Internalized Barriers to Women in Higher Education
265cc Women's Liberation Movement: Its Origins, Structures, Impact, and Ideas
266h Bringing Women In: Rewards, Punishments, And the Structure of Achievement
281g Class Structures and Female Autonomy in Rural Java
291g Historical and Structural Barriers to Occupational Desegregation

301d Legal Requirements, Structures, and Strategies for Eliminating Sex Discrimination in Academe
314aa Differential Recruitment and Control: The Sex Structuring of Organizations
316g Career Structures of Federal Executives: A Focus on Women
316k Tyranny of Structurelessness
326a Success Motivation and Social Structure: Comments on Women and Achievement
368j Impacts of Local Government Tax Structures on Women: Inefficiencies and Inequalities

STRUGGLE

7d Black Woman's Struggle for Equality in the South, 1895-1925
35e Struggle for Reproductive Freedom: Three Stages of Feminism
77m Who Has the Power? The Marital Struggle
115b Role of Women in the Indian Struggle for Freedom
139a Struggle for Woman's Suffrage
174c Black Women in the Continuing Struggle for Equality
194j History of Women's Struggle for Equality in Puerto Rico
246i Women in the Economic Sphere: The Coming Struggle for Jobs
265e Who Has the Power? The Marital Struggle
297m Resistance as Protest: Women in the Struggle of Bolivian Tin-Mining Communities
303i Struggle for Place: Women in Architecture: 1920-1960
314o Struggle for Status

STUART

65a Sentiment and Intellect: The Story of John Stuart Mill and Harriet Taylor Mill

STUDENT

4b Institutional Barriers to Women Students in Higher Education
4h Status Transitions of Women Students, Faculty, and Administrators
22s Androgynous Themes Written to Sentence Cues by Sixth-, Eighth-, and Tenth-Grade Students
39u Introducing Students to Women's Place in Society
114t Girl Students: Between School and Marriage--a Delhi Sample
116p Italian-American Female College Students: A New Generation Connected to the Old
132v Radical Women as Students
174l Women's Educational Equity: Favorable Student Response
182b Woman Student in Russia
191p What Medical Students Learn about Women
196h Teachers' Perceptions of Ideal Male and Female Students: Male Chauvinism in the Schools
196o Attitudes Toward Increased Social, Economic, and Political Participation by Women as Reported by Elementary and Secondary Students
203l Expelling Pregnant Students
217b Preferential Treatment in Admitting Racial Minority Students
266l Female College Students' Scores On the Men's And Women's Strong Vocational Interest Blanks
267u Women As New Students

275e German Women University Students: National Socialism and the War, 1939-1945

STUPID

288kk That's Not Brave, That's Just Stupid

STYLE

20r Three Styles of Domestic Authority: A Cross-Cultural Study
49e Male and Female Leadership Styles: The Double Bind
82d Female Ego Styles and Generational Conflict
110w Feminist Style Criticism
146b Sexuality and Alternative Life Styles
174p Styles and Priorities of Marginality: Women State Legislators
206g Marriage Roles, American Style
256f Free Married Woman: A New Style of Living in an Old Institution
269i Parenting and Family Life Styles
274g Bormliza: Maltese Folksong Style and Women
314y Addendum to Style Guide for Authors
316q Memsahib, Militante, Femme Libre: Political and Apolitical Styles of Modern African Women
361l Women's Prose Style: A Study of Contemporary Authors
361m Style of One's Own
361o Style of Djuna Barnes' "Nightwood"

SUB-ASSERTIVE

342b If You're Depressed, You're Probably Sub-Assertive

SUB-SAHARAN

324o Sub-Saharan Africa

SUBJECT

107f Women as Auxiliary and Subject to Man
159j Treatises on Marriage and Other Subjects
160a Advice to Mothers, on the Subject of Their Own Health, and, of the Means of Promoting the Health, Strength and Beauty of Their Offspring
250v Effects of Sex of Examiner and Subject on Children's Quantitative Test Performance

SUBJECTION

65d Subjection of Women
89r Subjection of Women
107s Subjection of Women
159t Subjection of Women
188d Subjection of Women
203f Subjection of Women
233y Subjection of Women
363b Subjection of Women
363k Subjection of Women

SUBJECTIVES

90b Subjectives: A Theory of the Critical Process
212g Bergman's Portrait of Women: Sexism or Subjective Metaphor?

SUBLIME

159q Of the Distinction of the Beautiful and the Sublime in the Interrelations of the Two Sexes

SUBMERSION

334f Equality or Submersion? Feme (sic) Couvert Status in Early Pennsylvania

SUBMISSION

9t Submissive Majority
36i "Featureless Freedom" or Ironic Submission: Dorothy Richardson and May Sinclair
364b Submission, Masochism and Narcissism: Three Aspects of Women's Role as Reflected in Dress

SUBORDINATION

348b Myth of Male Protectiveness and the Legal Subordination of Women: An Historical Analysis

SUBSERVIENT

93b Women in the Party Bureaucracy: Subservient Functionaries

SUBSIDY

40d Substitution Among Child Care Modes and the Effect of a Child Care Subsidy Program

SUBSISTENCE

201c Anthropological Perspective on Sex Roles and Subsistence

SUBSOCIETY

325r Women's Subsociety among the Shahsevan Nomads of Iran

SUBSTANCE

106i Intellectual Quality: The Symbols and the Substance
222v Substance: George Kent

SUBSTITUTION

40d Substitution Among Child Care Modes and the Effect of a Child Care Subsidy Program

SUBURBIA

143f Women's Place in the New Suburbia
143g Women's Travel Patterns in a Suburban Development
143h Women in the Suburban Environment: A U.S.--Sweden Comparison

SUBVERSION

142h Subversion of Betty Crocker

SUBVERSIVE

214c Anne Bradstreet's Poetry: A Study of Subversive Piety

SUCCESS

see also FEAR OF SUCCESS; ACHIEVEMENT; FAILURE

39j Positive Effects of the Multiple Negative: Explaining the Success of Black Professional Women
48i Family Life of the Successful Woman
73j Why Bright Women Fear Success
82c Femininity and Successful Achievement: A Basic Inconsistency
141k Dynamics of Successful People
176j Motive to Avoid Success and Changing Aspirations of College Women
176k Race, Social Class, and the Motive to Avoid Success in Women
186g Femininity and Successful Achievement: A Basic Inconsistency
220n Success Is Not a Destination But the Road To It
266n Positive Effects of the Multiple Negative: Explaining the Success of Black Professional Women
267j Women's Expectations for and Causal Attributions of Success and Failure
267n Race, Social Class, and the Motive to Avoid Success in Women
304c Women and Success: A Basic Conflict?
314l Accountability--The Key to Successful Affirmative Action
314dd Women and Success in Organizations
314ff Women in Management: Keys to Success or Failure
326a Success Motivation and Social Structure: Comments on Women and Achievement
359d Paradox and Success of Elizabeth Cady Stanton

SUCCESSORS

214j Dickinson, Whitman, and Their Successors
255b Astraea's "Vacant Throne": The Successors of Aphra Behn

SUD

116a Silent Half: "Le Contadine del Sud" Before The First World War

SUDAN

213f Agitation for Change in the Sudan

SUE

357e Sue Bridehead and the New Woman

SUFFERING

139c Suffering Suffragettes

SUFFRAGE

see also VOTE; FEMINISM

9k Argument for Woman's Suffrage
35f Nineteenth-Century Woman Suffrage Movement and the Analysis of Women's Oppression
68g "Press Cuttings": G.B.S. and Women's Suffrage
68v G.B.S. and a Suffragist
68w Sir Almroth Wright's Case Against Woman Suffrage
92d Women Cotton Workers and the Suffrage Campaign: The Radical Suffragists in Lancashire, 1893-1914
93f Politics of Mutual Frustration: Socialists and Suffragists in New York and Wisconsin
107r Woman's Suffrage
127j Labor and Suffrage Movements: A View of Working-Class Women in the 20th Century
139a Struggle for Woman's Suffrage
139b Two Suffrage Movements
139c Suffering Suffragettes
139d Younger Suffragists
151m Woman Suffrage in Perspective
257h (Speech, National Woman's Suffrage Association, 1889)
257s (Remarks, National American Woman's Suffrage Association)
259h Ideology of the Suffrage Movement
259j Enemies of Suffrage
294j Women in the Middle East and North Africa and Universal Suffrage
320b Canadian Suffragists
362b New Woman: Out to Finish What the Suffragette Started

SUFISM

325cc Women, Sufism, and Decision-Making in Moroccan Islam

SUGAR

4f From Sugar to Spice to Professor
271b Sugar'n Spice

SUICIDE

99j Sex Differences in Suicidal Behavior
306m Women and Suicide
307a Mao Tse-tung, Women and Suicide
308e Women and Suicide in China

SUITE

247l Picasso's Suite 347, or Painting as an Act of Love

SUMER

19b Women in Transition: Crete and Sumer

SUMMER

33n One Summer
111l At a Summer Hotel
111cc The Girls in Their Summer Dresses
112u The Girls In Their Summer Dresses

SUN

214b Jane Lead: Mysticism and the Woman Cloathed with the Sun
369k Catching the Sun

SUNDAY

273j Sunday Afternoon

SUNKSQUAWS

270b Sunksquaws, Shamans, and Tradeswomen: Middle Atlantic Coastal Algonkian Women During the Seventeenth and Eighteenth Centuries

SUPEREGO

200h Modest Confirmation of Freud's Theory of a Distinction between the Superego of Men and Women

SUPERINTENDENTS

196x Attitudes of Superintendents and Board of Education Members Toward the Employment and Effectiveness of Women as Public-School Administrators

SUPERIORITY

107aa Intellectual and Bodily Superiority of Women

SUPERMAN

68e Ann and Superman: Type and Archetype

SUPERMOM

203y Supermom!

SUPERVISOR

6m How to Eliminate Sexist Language From Your Writing: Some Guidelines for the Manager and Supervisor

SUPPLY

251y Supply and Demand for Women Workers
252y Labor Participation of Married Women: A Study of Labor Supply
252aa Supply and Demand for Women Workers

SUPPORT

64i Gaining Support from Other Groups
89bb In Support of the E.R.A.
140n Stress, Primary Support Systems and Women's Employment Status
140bb Men and the Abortion Experience--Anxiety and Social Supports
143j Toward Supportive Neighborhoods: Women's Role in Changing the Segregated City
260k Married Women and the Law of Support
260l Marriage and Family Support

SUPREME COURT

2i APPENDIX: Comments on the 1976 Supreme Court Decisions: "Planned Parenthood v. Danforth" and "Bellotti v. Baird"
180l Harvard College Amicus Curiae, DeFunis v. Odegaard, Supreme Court of the U.S., 1973
316h Ideology and the Law: Sexism and Supreme Court Decisions
321b Women, Men, and The Constitution: Key Supreme Court Rulings

SUPRESSION

53d Women, Taboo and the Supression of Attention

SURGERY

191b Sexual Surgery in Late Nineteenth-Century America
211o Surgical Gynecology
211p Hysterectomy and Other Gynecological Surgeries: A Psychological View
211t Woman and Esthetic Surgery

SURVEY

25i "Black Matriarchy" Reconsidered: Evidence from Secondary Analysis of Sample Surveys
50p APPENDIX: Women Detectives A Chronological Survey
51ee Recidivism Among Women Parolees: A Long-Term Survey
73s Woman and Man: A Questionnaire and Survey Report
93e Jennie Higginses of the "New South in the West": A Regional Survey of Socialist Activities, Agitators, and Organizers, 1901-1917
122a Random Survey of the Ratio of Female Poets to Male in Anthologies: Less-Than-Tokenism as a Mexican Tradition
140r Status of Women: Partial Summary of a Cross-Cultural Survey
170n Survey and Reevaluation of the Concept of Penis Envy
176dd Cross-Cultural Survey of Some Sex Differences in Socialization
183h Attitudes of Men and Women Toward Violence: Report of a National Survey
198m Cross-Cultural Survey of Some Sex Differences in Socialization
214l Afro-American Women Poets: A Bio-Critical Survey
219d Male-Female Conversational Interaction Cues: Using Data From Dialect Surveys
258i Women and Religion: A Survey of Significant Literature, 1965-1974
289i Science Fiction Survey
316d Women's Attitudes Toward Women in Politics: A Survey of Urban Registered Voters and Party Committeewomen

335l Survey of Primary Sources and Archives for the History of Early Twentieth-Century English Women
361d Historical Survey of Women's Language: From Medieval Courtesy Books to Seventeen Magazine

SURVIVAL

8e Surviving Gay Coupledom
98l Separation and Survival: Mothers, Daughters, Sisters: The Women's Experimental Theatre
129t Nitty-Gritty of Survival
131g Women of Udu: Survival in a Harsh Land
236c Women Surviving: Palace Life in Seoul after the Annexation
249f Sex Roles and Survival Strategies in an Urban Black Community
329n Algerian Women: Honor, Survival, and Islamic Socialism
356j Another Survivor

SUSA

215d Susa Young Gates: The Thirteenth Apostle

SUSAN

129g Penelope, Molly, Narcissus, and Susan
175b Trial of Susan B. Anthony

SUSANNA

215f Susanna Goudin Cardon: An Italian Convert to Mormonism

SUSTO

285k Sex Differences in the Incidence of Susto in Two Zapotec Pueblos: An Analysis of the Relationships between Sex Role Expectations and a Folk Illness

SWEDEN

21o Ideal and the Reality: Women in Sweden
37g APPENDIX: Status of Women in Sweden: Report to the United Nations, 1968
143i Swedish Women in Single-Family Housing
206i Swedish Model
238j Status of Women in Sweden
251gg Have Swedish Women Achieved Equality?
267e Convergences between East and West: Tradition and Modernity in Sex Roles in Sweden, Finland, and the Soviet Union
271x Sex Roles and Education in Sweden
276f Equality Between Men and Women in Sweden
329x Sweden: A Feminist Model?
364n Think About Our Government: Now Think About Sweden's Policy
364o Current Equality Issues in Sweden

SWEET

111t Her Sweet Jerome
112l Her Sweet Jerome

152g Sweet Home
220k Sweets to the Sweet
279dd Her Sweet Jerome

SWENSON

214o May Swenson and the Shapes of Speculation

SWEPT AWAY

212t Lina Wertmuller: Swept Away on a Wave of Sexism
288g "Swept Away"

SWIM

152j Memoirs of a Would-Be Swim Champ
356h Here and There in the Wastes of Ocean A Swimmer Was Seen

SWINGING

39h Swinging: A Study of Decision Making in Marriage

SWISSHELM

128d Jane Grey Swisshelm: Agitator

SWITZERLAND

116e Forging a Socialist Women's Movement: Angelica Balabanoff in Switzerland

SYLVIA

88h "The Blood Jet": The Poetry of Sylvia Plath
175qq Body is the Role: Sylvia Plath
214q Life-Work of Sylvia Plath

SYMBOL

47j "Delta Wedding" as Region and Symbol
106i Intellectual Quality: The Symbols and the Substance
122m Feminine Symbolism in Gabriela Mistral's "Fruta"
173i Symbolic Significance of Menstruation and the Menopause
317c Hats as a Symbol of Women's Position in Three Evangelical Churches in Edinburgh, Scotland
317d Coming of Age in Kelton: The Constraints on Gender Symbolism in Jewish Ritual

SYMPOSIUM

54i Report of the Symposium on Demographic Aspects of the Changing Status of Women in Europe

SYNAGOGUE

210h View From the Back of the Synagogue: Women in Judaism

SYNDROME

22h Premenstrual Syndrome
73l Queen Bee Syndrome
77b Premenstrual Syndrome
77y Masochistic Syndrome, Hysterical Personality, and the Illusion of a Healthy Woman
94o Rape Trauma Syndrome
173h Premenstrual Syndrome
176pp Postpartum Psychiatric Syndromes
199v Aggression, Androgens, and the XYY Syndrome
204i Prenatal Influences on Cognitive Abilities: Data from Experimental Animals and Human and Endocrine Syndromes
208dd Reducing the "Miss Muffet" Syndrome: An Annotated Bibliography
250ff Postpartum Psychiatric Syndromes
266d Premenstrual Syndrome
288n Brigitte Bardot and the Lolita Syndrome
330f Phobic Syndrome in Women: Implications for Treatment

SYNTHESIS

218b Feminism and Socialism: The Utopian Synthesis of Flora Tristan
218d Socialism Faces Feminism: The Failure of Synthesis in France, 1879-1914
349f Communist Feminism: Its Synthesis and Demise

SYRIA

325s Changing Sex Roles in Bedouin Society in Syria and Lebanon

SYSTEM

2f Abortion and the Social System
41a Systematic Study of Urban Women
51ff Parole System: How Women Fare
52c Johann Weyer's "De Praetigiis Daemonum": Unsystematic Psychopathology
82a Psychological Conflict and the Reproductive System
140n Stress, Primary Support Systems and Women's Employment Status
180f Discrimination, Color Blindness, and the Quota System
193c Aspects of the Distinction Between the Sexes in the Nyamwezi and Some Other African Systems of Kinship and Marriage
199c Fetal Androgens, Human Central Nervous System Differentiation, and Behavior Sex Differences
205i Sex-Role Stereotyping in the Social Security and Income Tax Systems
213g Iyalode in the Traditional Yoruba Political System
252t Feminine Role and the Kinship System
272p Changing Women's Representation in School Management: A Systems Perspective
291e Dual Linkages between the Occupational and Family Systems: A Macrosociological Analysis
297x Sources of the Matrilineal Family System in the Works of Carl J.L. Almqvist
302b Dual-Sex Political System in Operation: Igbo Women and Community Politics in Midwestern Nigeria
306k Women in the Political System

316j Women's and Men's Liberation Groups: Political Power Within the System and Outside the System
330b Sex Hormones, The Central Nervous System and Affect Variability in Humans

SZOLD

117p Henrietta Szold--Liberated Woman

TABLEAU

52h Pierre de Lancre's "Tableau de l'Inconstance des Mauvais Anges et Demons": The Sabbat Sensationalised

TABLES

89b Women in the Work Force: Five Tables

TABOO

53d Women, Taboo and the Supression of Attention
98p Lesbianism and the Social Function of Taboo
173s Social Dimensions of the Menstrual Taboo and the Effects on Female Sexuality
283o Zoroastrian Menstruation Taboos: A Woman's Studies Perspective

TAHARAH

117g Tumah and Taharah; Ends and Beginnings

TAIL

226d Peacock's Tail

TAIWAN

141r Son Preference in Taiwan: Verbal Preference and Demographic Behavior
307k Status of Women in Taiwan: One Step Forward, Two Steps Back

TALE

96x Peacock's Tale
110j Women of Cooper's "Leatherstocking Tales"
119j The Sailor Boy's Tales
208y Female Acculturation Through the Fairy Tale
355g Humorous Tales (stories)

TALENTED

341n Search for Talented Women

TALMUD

177f Images of Women in the Talmud

TAMING

17f "The Taming of the Shrew": Shakespeare's Mirror of Marriage
68a Shakespeare's "The Taming of the Shrew" vs. Shaw's "Pygmalion": Male Chauvinism vs. Women's Lib?

TANZANIA

289d Tanzanian Women Confront the Past and the Future
302k Less Than Second-Class: Women in Rural Settlement Schemes in Tanzania

TASK

196gg Task Force on Education Report, Governor's Commission on the Status of Women, Ma.
231e Task of a Housewife
250s Parental Education, Sex Differences, and Performance on Cognitive Tasks Among Two-Year-Old Children
251q Task and Emotional Behavior in the Marital Dyad
252r Task and Social Behavior in Marriage
296s Specific Psychological Tasks in Pregnancy and Motherhood

TAX

205i Sex-Role Stereotyping in the Social Security and Income Tax Systems
328o Federal Income Tax and Social Security Law
368j Impacts of Local Government Tax Structures on Women: Inefficiencies and Inequalities

TAYLOR

65a Sentiment and Intellect: The Story of John Stuart Mill and Harriet Taylor Mill
104g S.K. Taylor
288m Actress Archetypes in the 1950s: Doris Day, Marilyn Monroe, Elizabeth Taylor, Audrey Hepburn

TEA

113f A Cup of Tea

TEACH

13dd Teaching is a Good Profession...for a Woman
60h Schoolteaching
138c Feminization of Teaching
166d Male and Female: Differing Perceptions of the Teaching Experience
166aa Women Preparing to Teach
173n How Nursery Schools Teach Girls to Shut Up
207h Sexism in Children's Books and Elementary Teaching Materials
233d Catholic Teaching on Women
271i Assessment of Teaching Practice: An "Attractive" Hypothesis
271s Teaching Female Studies: Looking Back Over Three Years
295e Schoolmarms and Early Teaching in Ontario
306h Women in Teaching

TEACHER

see also FACULTY

8p Bundles of Twigs in New Hampshire: A High School Teacher's Report
13n Teacher Interactions with Boys and with Girls
13hh Portrait of a Teacher
60c Education of Female Teachers
60d Teachers to the West
96h Indian Teacher Among Indians
120k Teacher-Child Verbal Interaction: An Approach to the Study of Sex Differences
156c Teacher Education and Non-Sexist Early Childhood Education
156f Teachers, Peers, and Play Preferences: An Environmental Approach to Sex Typing in the Preschool
166w Career Dreams of Teachers
196h Teachers' Perceptions of Ideal Male and Female Students: Male Chauvinism in the Schools
196v Women Teachers and Teacher Power
196z Sex Discrimination as Public Policy: The Case of Maternity-Leave Policies for Teachers
197f Down the Up Staircase: Sex Roles, Professionalization, and the Status of Teachers
282r Pedagogical Arguments for Preferential Hiring and Tenuring of Women Teachers in the University
342t Sexism in the Schools: Focus on the Woman Teacher

TEAMS

203x Battle for Coed Teams

TEARING

24ff Tearing

TEARS

279u Tears, Idle Tears

TECHNICALITIES

289e Technicalities and Fantasy About Men and Women

TECHNIQUE

286u Training and Condition Techniques for the Female Athlete
361n Katherine Mansfield's "Passion for Technique"

TECHNOLOGY

42j Tender Technicians: Feminization of Public Librarianship, 1876-1905
42n Case Study of Technological and Social Change: The Washing Machine and the Working Wife
174d Impact of Organizational Structure, Technology, and Professionalism on the Policy of Affirmative Action
266p Tender Technicians: The Feminization of Public Librarianship, 1876-1905

TEENAGER

see ADOLESCENCE

TELEVISION

18n Portrait of a Female on Television: Some Possible Effects on Children
22q Sex-Role Stereotyping in Children's Television Programs
105b Dominant or Dominated? Women on TV
105c Spot Messages within Saturday Morning TV Programs
105m Sex-typing and Children's Television Preferences
105p Image of Women in Television: An Annotated Bibliography
280x Television and the Image of the Father

TEMPERAMENT

77d Conclusion: "Sex and Temperament in Three Primitive Societies"
127z Conclusion, "Sex and Temperament in Three Primitive Societies"
158j "Sex and Temperament in Three Primitive Societies"
260dd Sex and Temperament

TEMPLE

83j A Temple of the Holy Ghost
110b Popular Literature as Social Reinforcement: The Case of "Charlotte Temple"

TEMPTATION

74n Temptation to be a Beautiful Object

TEN

288h Ten That Got Away

TENANT

143n From Kitchen to Storefront: Women in the Tenant Movement

TENDERNESS

42j Tender Technicians: Feminization of Public Librarianship, 1876-1905
173bb Anger and Tenderness
266e Heroic and Tender Modes in Women Authors of Fantasy
266p Tender Technicians: The Feminization of Public Librarianship, 1876-1905

TENTH

22s Androgynous Themes Written to Sentence Cues by Sixth-, Eighth-, and Tenth-Grade Students
141bb Hrotsvitha of Gandersheim: The Playable Dramas of a Woman Playwright of the Tenth Century

TENURING

282r Pedagogical Arguments for Preferential Hiring and Tenuring of Women Teachers in the University

TERESA

122e Teresa de la Parra, Venezuelan Novelist and Feminist

TERMS

9r Women--Terms of Liberation
85i Hidden Joke: Generic Uses of Masculine Terminology

TERRIBLE

214p Gwendolyn the Terrible: Propositions on Eleven Poems

TERROR

51m Woman as Terrorist
175x Rape: An Act of Terror

TERRY

68t Interview with Megan Terry

TESS

225d Tess: The Making of a Pure Woman

TEST

13v Use and Abuse of Vocational Tests
196u Women and Educational Testing
204m Role of Tests and Their Construction in Producing Apparent Sex-Related Differences
250v Effects of Sex of Examiner and Subject on Children's Quantitative Test Performance
280k Test Scores and Unequal Education

TESTAMENT

177b Images of Women in the Old Testament
177d Theology and Leadership of Women in the New Testament

TESTIMONY

127jj Abortion Testimonial
215g Lucinda Lee Dalton: A Tough Kind of Testimony

TESTOSTERONE

199b Prenatal Testosterone in the Nonhuman Primate and Its Consequences for Behavior
199u Plasma Testosterone Levels and Psychologic Measures in Men Over a 2-Month Period

TEXAS

128j Pamelia Mann: Texas Frontierswoman

TEXTBOOKS

see also READ; READING; BOOK

13w Women in U.S. History High-School Textbooks
39t Women in Gynecology Textbooks
196j Sex Stereotyping in Elementary-School Mathematics Textbooks
196k Women in U.S. History High-School Textbooks
208ff Textbooks and Channeling
208gg Women in U.S. History High School Textbooks
208hh Guidelines for Equal Treatment of the Sexes in Social Studies Textbooks
208ll Sex Stereotypes in Mathematics and Science Textbooks for Elementary and Junior High Schools
254n Image of Woman in Textbooks
271n Sex Roles in Early Reading Textbooks
271p Textbooks and Channeling
271q Women in U.S. History High School Textbooks

TEXTILE

297k Life and Labor of the Woman Textile Worker in Mexico City

THEATRE

see also DRAMA; PLAY; PLAYWRIGHT; individual playwrights

80k Virgins and Other Victims: Aspects of German Middle-Class Theatre
98l Separation and Survival: Mothers, Daughters, Sisters: The Women's Experimental Theatre
116y Women in the Italian-American Theatre of the Nineteenth Century
141ee Historical and Theoretical Evolution of Viola Spolin's Theatre Games
223b From Dame to Woman: W.S. Gilbert and Theatrical Transvestism

THEFT

96d Demon in Female Apparel: Narrative of Josephine Amelia Perkins, the Notorious Female Horse Thief...
191j Theft of Childbirth

THEME

22s Androgynous Themes Written to Sentence Cues by Sixth-, Eighth-, and Tenth-Grade Students
47h Character and Themes in the Novels of Jean Rhys
98k For a Restricted Thematics: Writing, Speech, and Difference in Madame Bovary
122k Thematic Exploration of the Works of Elena Garro
122p Love and Death: The Thematic Journey of Julia de Burgos
206h Role Themes in Latin America
208cc Feminists Look at the 100 Books: The Portrayal of Women in Children's Books on Puerto Rican Themes

325ee Theme of Sexual Oppression in the North African Novel

THEOLOGY

see also BIBLE; CHURCH; RELIGION; various denominations

117b Women's Liberation and the Liberation of God: An Essay in Story Theology
177d Theology and Leadership of Women in the New Testament
177g Equality of Souls, Inequality of Sexes: Woman in Medieval Theology
210g Theology After the Demise of God the Father: A Call for the Castration of Sexist Religion
258b Feminist Theology as a Critical Theory of Liberation
258g Sexist Language in Theology?
263k Theology in the Politics of Appalachian Women
263q Coming of Lilith: Toward a Feminist Theology
283a Theology After the Demise of God the Father: A Call for the Castration of Sexist Religion
283d Karl Barth's Theology of the Word of God: Or, How to Keep Women Silent and in Their Place

THEORIST

91f Fertility of Working Women in the United States: Historical Trends and Theoretical Perspectives
91k Relationship between Women's Work and Fertility: Some Methodological and Theoretical Issues
93c May Wood Simons: Party Theorist
141ee Historical and Theoretical Evolution of Viola Spolin's Theatre Games
178b Eighteenth-Century Theorists of Women's Liberation
194l Selective Omission and Theoretical Distortion in Studying the Political Activity of Women in Brazil
204b Genetic Influences on Sex-Related Differences in Intellectual Performance: Theoretical and Methodological Issues
249a Woman, Culture, and Society: A Theoretical Overview
285a Theoretical Issues in the Anthropological Study of Women
344a Feminism, Power and Change: A Theoretical Analysis

THERAPY

see also PSYCHOANALYSIS; PSYCHOTHERAPY

8aa Oppression is Big Business: Scrutinizing Gay Therapy
22x Androgyny as a Model of Mental Health for Women: From Theory to Therapy
77aa Consciousness-Raising Group as a Model for Therapy with Women
77bb What Happens in Feminist Therapy
85w Roman Catholic Doctrine of Therapeutic Abortion
173ii Consciousness-Raising Group as a Model for Therapy with Women
176kk Behavior Therapy Approaches to Modification of Sexual Preferences: Biological Perspective and Critique
330a Changing Views of Women and Therapeutic Approaches: Some Historical Considerations
330c Cultural Values, Female Role Expectancies and Therapeutic Goals: Research and Interpretation
330e Cognitive Therapy with Depressed Women

330i Women in Behavior Therapy
330j Therapy of Women in the Light of Psychoanalytic Theory and the Emergence of a New View
330k Women in Therapy--A Gestalt Therapist's View
330l Anna O.--Patient or Therapist? An Eidetic View
330o Consciousness-Raising Groups as Therapy for Women

THERENESS

14e "Thereness" of Women: A Selective Review of Urban Sociology

THICKET

111r The Ram in the Thicket
112j The Ram in the Thicket

THINKING

256a Whatever Will Become of Me? Glancing Backward, Looking at Today and Thinking About Tomorrow
256t Changing Woman's Thinking and Lifestyle Through the Great Communication Revolution
275a Impact of German Thought and Culture on Madame de Stael's Thinking about Women

THIRD

80m Women in the Third Reich
175gg Notes From the Third Year

THIRD WORLD

see also DEVELOPMENT; individual countries

8j Butch or Fem?: The Third World Lesbian's Dilemma
43n Third World Women and Social Reality: Conclusion
227i Bibliographies on Third World Women

THIRTEENTH

215d Susa Young Gates: The Thirteenth Apostle

THOMAS

178c Puritan Ethic in the Revolutionary Era: Abigail Adams and Thomas Jefferson

THOMPSON

170g Denial of Women's Sexual Pleasure: Discussion of Dr. Thompson's Paper
268r Role of Clara Thompson in the Psychoanalytic Study of Women

THREAT

210f Enrichment or Threat? When the Eves Come Marching In
280y Equal Rights Amendment: A Threat to Family Life?

372k Life of Sarah Penfield, Rural Ohio Grandmother: Tradition Maintained, Tradition Threatened

THRESHOLD

108c The Threshold

THRICE

79h To The Thrice Sacred Queen Elizabeth

THRONE

255b Astraea's "Vacant Throne": The Successors of Aphra Behn

TICKETS

233n Tickets, Please

TIGER

161d Play with a Tiger

TILBURY

79e Speech to the Troops at Tilbury

TILLICH

177j Protestant Principle: A Woman's Eye-View of Barth and Tillich

TIME

10e One Good Time
13nn It's Time for Equal Education
16i Woman on the Edge of Time
70i Historical Changes in How People Spend Their Time
95g Times Gone By
111ee The Time of Her Time
112y The Time of Her Time
119b The Long Corridor of Time
132j Hard and the Soft: The Force of Feminism in Modern Times
134d The Power of Time
135f Family, Employment and the Allocation of Time
166b Plus Ca Change...? The Sexual Structure of Occupations Over Time
171m Body Time and Social Time: Mood Patterns by Menstrual Cycle Phase and Day of Week
269g Learning Not To: It Takes a Long Time
271t Time Is Here for Women's Liberation
287c Home Work, Market Work, and the Allocation of Time
288bb "Marilyn Times Five"
289c Women's Time: Women in the Light of Contemporary Time-Budget Research
300a Rough Times
373e The Tone of Time

TIN

134f Tin Soldier
297m Resistance as Protest: Women in the Struggle of Bolivian Tin-Mining Communities

TINKA

275f Frau und Staatsburger in Volker Braun's Schauspiel "Tinka"

TITLE

314z 52 Job Titles Revised to Eliminate Sex-Stereotyping

TITLE IX

152o Shedding Light on Title IX
174a Eliminating Sex Discrimination in Education: Lobbying for Implementation of Title IX
196g Sex Bias in Secondary Schools: The Impact of Title IX

TITLE VII

260s Title VII of the 1964 Civil Rights Act
328d Legal Remedies beyond Title VII to Combat Sex Discrimination in Employment

TLINGIT

270d Contending with Colonization: Tlingit Men and Women in Change

TOKELAU

285m Male and Female in Tokelau Culture

TOKENISM

321d Women Judges: The End of Tokenism

TOLSTOY

179n S. Tolstoy

TOMORROW

11i Education of Women Today and Tomorrow
208g Schooling of Tomorrow's Women
256a Whatever Will Become of Me? Glancing Backward, Looking at Today and Thinking About Tomorrow
271w Schooling of Tomorrow's Women

TONE

373e The Tone of Time

TONGAN

2701 Putting Down Sisters and Wives: Tongan Women and Colonization

TONI

222w Commitment: Toni Cade Bambara Speaks
222x Complexity: Toni Morrison's Women--An Interview Essay

TOOLS

194h Women and Modernization: Access to Tools

TOPPING

3641 Conversation with Audrey Topping: Chinese Women Today

TORAH

117x Women as Sources of Torah in the Rabbinic Tradition

TORONTO

116k La Donna Italiana Durante Il Periodo Fascista in Toronto, 1930-1940
116n Metonymic Definition of the Female and the Concept of Honour Among Italian Immigrant Families in Toronto
116t Family and Kin Cohesion among South Italian Immigrants in Toronto
295b Toronto's Prostitute at the Turn of the Century
295f The "Problem" and Problems of Working Women-- Toronto, 1896-1914
295h Women in Production: The Toronto Dressmakers' Strike of 1931

TORTURE

68u Torture by Forcible Feeding is Illegal

TOURIST

274e Native Costumes of the Oberwallis: Tourist Gimmick or Tradition?

TOWN

116u Women of Old Town
293h Women in African Towns South of the Sahara: The Urbanization Dilemma
322i Studies in an Indian Town
372c Women's Role in a Muslim Hausa Town--Mirria, Republic of Niger
372d Dioula Women in Town: A View of Intra-Ethnic Variation - Ivory Coast

TOYS

13i Report on Children's Toys
156d Liberating Toys: You Are What You Play
208ss Children's Toys and Socialization to Sex Roles
208tt Toys for Free Children

TRACK

13mm Jumping the Track

TRACTOR

19p Love on the Tractor: Women in the Russian Revolution and After

TRADE

41i Women's Trade Union League and American Feminism
41j Creating a Feminist Alliance: Sisterhood and Class Conflict in the New York Women's Trade Union League, 1903- 1914
57g Trade Union Woman
116d Women in the Canadian and Italian Trade Union Movements at the Turn of the Century
126i Feminism and Class Consciousness in the British and American Women's Trade Union Leagues, 1890-1925
138b Impact of White Women on Fur Trade Society
141i Feminism and Class Consciousness in the British and American Women's Trade Union Leagues, 1890-1925
181h Women in American Trade Unions: An Historical Analysis
260i Marriage as a Trade
265p Sex Discrimination in the Trade Unions: Legal Resources for Change
270b Sunksquaws, Shamans, and Tradeswomen: Middle Atlantic Coastal Algonkian Women During the Seventeenth and Eighteenth Centuries
294q Women and American Trade Unions
312f Women, Work and Trade Unionism
323e Early Years in the Trade Unions
323h Women in Trade Unions
352n Women Workers and the Trade Unions in Austria

TRADITION

7e Black Women in the Blues Tradition
88e Imperious Muse: Some Observations on Women, Nature and the Poetic Tradition
88g Who Buried H.D.? A Poet, Her Critics, and Her Place in "The Literary Tradition"
105e Imagery and Ideology: The Cover Photographs of Traditional Women's Magazines
114s Chellamma--An Illustration of the Multiple Roles of Traditional Women
117k Other Half: Women in the Jewish Tradition
117x Women as Sources of Torah in the Rabbinic Tradition
122a Random Survey of the Ratio of Female Poets to Male in Anthologies: Less-Than-Tokenism as a Mexican Tradition
126j Latina Liberation: Tradition, Ideology, and Social Change in Iberian and Latin American Cultures
126k Racism and Tradition: Black Womanhood in Historical Perspective
131b Egyptian Woman: Between Modernity and Tradition
141e Novel Women: Origins of the Feminist Literary Tradition in England and France
163s Traditional Political Animals? A Loud No
213g Iyalode in the Traditional Yoruba Political System
213n Ecological Antecedents and Sex-Role Consequences in Traditional and Modern Israeli Subcultures

218h Five Socialist Women: Traditionalist Conflicts and Socialist Visions in Austria, 1893-1934
236a Tradition: Women During the Yi Dynasty
267e Convergences between East and West: Tradition and Modernity in Sex Roles in Sweden, Finland, and the Soviet Union
274e Native Costumes of the Oberwallis: Tourist Gimmick or Tradition?

278e Sexism in American Naming Traditions
281j Women and the Hindu Tradition
285i Traditional Marriage among the Irigwe of Benue-Plateau State, Nigeria
309g Women and Religion: The Status and Image of Women in Major Religious Traditions
325z Self-Images of Traditional Urban Women in Cairo
329i Tradition and the Role of Women in Great Britain
331g Child Care for the 1980s: Traditional Sex Roles or Androgyny?
337a Women's Leadership in the Jewish and Christian Traditions: Continuity and Change
337i Feminism in the Evangelical Tradition
372j Uses of Traditional Concepts in the Development of New Urban Roles: Cuban Women in the United States
372k Life of Sarah Penfield, Rural Ohio Grandmother: Tradition Maintained, Tradition Threatened

TRAFFIC

68y Root of the White Slave Traffic
89z Traffic in Women
230h Traffic in Women: Notes on the "Political Economy" of Sex

TRAGEDIE

79l Tragedie of Mariam, The Fair Queen of Jewry
355e The Tragic Menagerie (stories)

TRAIN

6j Seminars for Career Women: Combining Awareness Training with Transactional Analysis
77l Case Study of a Nonconscious Ideology: Training the Woman to Know Her Place
186f Training the Woman to Know Her Place: The Power of a Nonconscious Ideology
208c Training the Woman To Know Her Place: The Power of a Nonconscious Ideology
260a ...How Ischomachus Trained His Wife
272o Leadership Training for Increased Effectiveness among Women Educational Administrators
273v The Train from Rhodesia
286u Training and Condition Techniques for the Female Athlete
358p Women Athletic Trainers

TRAIT

85g Traits and Genderization
172j Traits, Roles, and the Concept of Androgyny
314gg Women in Management: The Fallacy of the Trait Approach

TRANS-ATLANTIC

141h Feminist Culture from 1790 to 1850: A Trans-Atlantic Community

TRANSACTIONAL

6j Seminars for Career Women: Combining Awareness Training with Transactional Analysis

TRANSCENDENCE

22f Model of Sex-Role Transcendence
140gg Why Sex Discrimination? A Model of Sex-Role Transcendence

TRANSFORMATION

53c Open Body, Closed Space: The Transformation of Female Sexuality
68d Eliza's Choice: Transformation Myth and the Ending of "Pygmalion"
88i "I Dare to Live": The Transforming Art of Anne Sexton
158w Marx, Sex and the Transformation of Society
184b Transformations of the Heroine: From Epic Heard to Epic Read
258d Home and Work: Women's Roles and the Transformation of Values
270i Women and Men, Cloth and Colonization: The Transformation of Production-Distribution Relations among the Baule (Ivory Coast)
282h Marx, Sex, and the Transformation of Society
289f Women's Roles and the Great World Transformation

TRANSGRESS

15k Artists Transgress All Boundaries

TRANSHUMANS

256v Transhumans--2000

TRANSITION

4h Status Transitions of Women Students, Faculty, and Administrators
19b Women in Transition: Crete and Sumer
48j Family Life in Transition
140a Sex Roles in Transition: The Historical Perspective
172d Individuals and Families in Transition: Dilemmas and Coping
172h Psychology in Transition: Continuities, Critiques, and Perspectives
270e Forced Transition from Egalitarianism to Male Dominance: The Bari of Colombia
270f Aztec Women: The Transition from Status to Class in Empire and Colony
272n Transition from Parenting to Working and Parenting
335f Women in an Age of Transition: 1485-1714
364a "Women's History" in Transition: The European Case
367b Demographic Transition in the Middle East and North Africa

TRANSPOSITIONS

122q Short Stories of Lydia Cabrera: Transpositions or Creations?

TRANSSEXUALISM

199p Behaviorally Feminine Male Child: Pretranssexual? Pretransvestite? Prehomosexual? Preheterosexual?
199q Psychodynamics of Male Transsexualism

TRANSVESTISM

199p Behaviorally Feminine Male Child: Pretranssexual? Pretransvestite? Prehomosexual? Preheterosexual?
223b From Dame to Woman: W.S. Gilbert and Theatrical Transvestism

TRAP

254x Compassion Trap

TRAUMA

94o Rape Trauma Syndrome
170t Trauma of Eventlessness

TRAVEL

143g Women's Travel Patterns in a Suburban Development

TREASURES

222cc The Collector of Treasures

TREATISE

159j Treatises on Marriage and Other Subjects
203c Second Treatise of Government

TREATMENT

17n Old Critics and New: The Treatment of Chopin's "The Awakening"
33h Cruel and Barbarous Treatment
42a "Fashionable Diseases": Women's Complaints and Their Treatment in Nineteenth-Century America
75e Innovative Programs for Women in Jail and Prison: Trick or Treatment
85l Preferential Treatment
105o Conclusion: Will Media Treatment of Women Improve?
158hh Preferential Treatment
208hh Guidelines for Equal Treatment of the Sexes in Social Studies Textbooks
208ii Lost Herstory: The Treatment of Women in Children's Encyclopedias
217a University and the Case for Preferential Treatment
217b Preferential Treatment in Admitting Racial Minority Students
217g Preferential Treatment
235e Treatment Alternatives for Battered Women
255f "Treated Like Imbecile Children" (Diderot): The Enlightenment and the Status of Women
330f Phobic Syndrome in Women: Implications for Treatment
330m Treatment of Sex and Love Problems in Women
330p Women in Institutions: Treatment in Prisons and Mental Hospitals

363h Cruel and Barbarous Treatment

TREBLY

73d Trebly Sensuous Woman
296j Trebly Sensuous Woman

TREE

142n My House in the Trees
273n The Tree

TRENDS

9u Modern Trends in the Law Concerning Women's Rights
20u Social Trends
38a Social Trends and Women's Lives--1965-1985
54g Extra-Marital Fertility and its Occurrence in Stable Unions: Recent Trends in Western Europe
91e Women, Employment, and Fertility Trends in the Arab Middle East and North Africa
91f Fertility of Working Women in the United States: Historical Trends and Theoretical Perspectives
121l Trends and Issues in Latin American Women's History
146q Gerontology Trends and Career Perspectives
166a Professional Woman: Trends and Prospects
246a Radical and Conservative Trends in the Women's Rights Movement
284i Trends in Educational Attainment of Women
326c Recent Trends in the Employment of American Women
352k Trends in Women's Employment in the U.S.S.R.
367e Rural-Urban Fertility Differences and Trends in Egypt, 1930-70
367f Fertility Trends and Differentials in Kuwait
367g Fertility Trends and Differentials in Jordan
367h Fertility in Algeria: Trends and Differentials
367i Fertility Declines in Tunisia: Factors Affecting Recent Trends
371b Women Working: Historical Trends
371d Racial Differences in Female Labor-Force Participation: Trends and Implications for the Future

TRIAL

9a Trial of Anne Hutchinson
130e Report of the Trial: The People versus Dr. Horatio N. Loomis, for Libel
175b Trial of Susan B. Anthony
321a Female in the Trial Court

TRIBAL

114m Tribal Women

TRICK

75e Innovative Programs for Women in Jail and Prison: Trick or Treatment
208jj Sexism in History or, Writing Women's History is a Tricky Business

375l Blood and Guts: The Tricky Problem of Being a Woman Writer in the Late Twentieth Century

TRIFLES

111ss Trifles
310g Trifles

TRILOGY

214n Echoing Spell of H.D.'s "Trilogy"

TRINITY

159i The Trinity

TRIP

29j A Sudden Trip Home in the Spring
74m The Trip

TRIPLE

210c Black Women and the Churches: Triple Jeopardy

TRISTAN

218b Feminism and Socialism: The Utopian Synthesis of Flora Tristan

TROBRIAND

270k Stability in Banana Leaves: Colonization and Women in Kiriwina, Trobriand Islands

TROIS

184e Fifteenth-Century View of Women's Role in Medieval Society: Christine de Pizan's "Livre des Trois Vertus"

TROLLOP

110d Servility of Dependence: The Dark Lady in Trollop

TROOPS

79e Speech to the Troops at Tilbury

TROUBLE

127r "In Trouble"
292n Troubled Souls of Females

TROY

334k Irish Working Women in Troy

TROYTE

50a The Murder at Troyte's Hill

TRUANT

277v Truant

TRUE

9hh Cult of True Womanhood
151f Cult of True Womanhood: 1820-1860
233u True Woman--Herself
292m Cult of True Womanhood, 1820-1860
360i Cult of True Womanhood, 1820-1860

TRUST

264r Trust, Loyalty, and the Place of Women in the Informal Organization of Work

TRUSTEES

196ee Characteristics and Attitudes of Women Trustees

TRUTH

110e Gentle Truths for Gentle Readers: The Fiction of Elizabeth Goudge
233uu Sojourner Truth: On Women's Rights
369o Plain Truth

TRYAL

52j Two Late Scottish Witchcraft Tracts: "Witch-Craft Proven" and "The Tryal of Witchcraft"

TSE-TUNG

307a Mao Tse-tung, Women and Suicide

TSUDA

178i Ume Tsuda and Motoko Hani: Echoes of American Cultural Feminism in Japan

TUBMAN

111uu I Like to Think of Harriet Tubman
178f Meaning of Harriet Tubman

TUDOR

52f Tudor Anthropologist: George Gifford's "Discourse " and "Dialogue"

TUESDAY

220z Tuesday Night

279y Tuesday Siesta

TUMAH

117g Tumah and Taharah; Ends and Beginnings

TUNISIA

325f Women's Emancipation in Tunisia
367i Fertility Declines in Tunisia: Factors Affecting Recent Trends

TURKEY

281f Sex Roles and Social Change: A Comparative Appraisal of Turkey's Women
324d Turkey
325e Women in Turkish Society
325k Turkish Women in the Ottoman Empire: The Classical Age
325l Women as Patrons of Architecture in Turkey
325w Women, Class, and Power: Examples from the Hatay, Turkey
325x Comparative Perspective on Women in Provincial Iran and Turkey
367d Socioeconomic Determinants of Differential Fertility in Turkey

TURMOIL

360b Anne Hutchinson and Female Agitation During the Years of the Antinomian Turmoil, 1636-1640

TURN

131l Twelve and Turned-On
24p Mama's Turn
116d Women in the Canadian and Italian Trade Union Movements at the Turn of the Century
180ff Is Turn-About Fair Play?
219e Verbal Turn-Taking and Exchanges in Faculty Dialogue
233k Princess Grace Turns Forty
252ii Women's Absenteeism and Labor Turnover
295b Toronto's Prostitute at the Turn of the Century

TURNER

122c Clorinda Matto de Turner and Mercedes Cabello de Carbonera: Societal Criticism and Morality
191s Building a Hospital Workers' Union: Doris Turner, the Woman from 1199

TWELVE

131l Twelve and Turned-On
36n Twelfthmonth, or What You Get
184c Isolt and Guenevere: Two Twelfth-Century Views of Woman
369u One Out of Twelve: Women Who Are Writers in Our Century

TWENTY

801 Inculcating a Slave Mentality: Women in German Popular Fiction of the Early Twentieth Century
88x Promises Fulfilled: Positive Images of Women in Twentieth-Century Autobiography
153q Twenty Years at Hull-House
172f American Family: A Twenty-Year View
223d Marriage, Redundancy or Sin: The Painter's View of Women in the First Twenty-Five Years of Victoria's Reign
240j They Shall Have Faces, Minds, and (One Day) Flesh: Women in Late Nineteenth-century and Early Twentieth-century American Literature
243j Women as a Minority Group: Twenty Years Later
250g Women as a Minority Group: Some Twenty Years Later
256j Impact of Mid-twentieth Century Movement for Sex Equality in Employment on Three Contemporary Economic Institutions
334r Women Against Lynching in the Twentieth-Century South
335k Women in Twentieth-Century England
335l Survey of Primary Sources and Archives for the History of Early Twentieth-Century English Women
357g Poetry and Conscience: Russian Women Poets of the Twentieth Century
360q Cookbooks and Law Books: The Hidden History of Career Women in Twentieth-Century America
375l Blood and Guts: The Tricky Problem of Being a Woman Writer in the Late Twentieth Century

TWIG

8p Bundles of Twigs in New Hampshire: A High School Teacher's Report
13f As the Twig is Bent
196a Sex-Role Socialization and the Nursery School: As the Twig is Bent

TWILIGHT

43j Native American Women: Twilight of a Long Maidenhood
288f Twilight of Romanticism: "Adele H."

TWO-PERSON

39f Men, Women, and Work: Reflections on the Two-Person Career

TWO-SEX

366f Digging Sticks and Spears, Or the Two-Sex Model

TWO-YEAR-OLD

250s Parental Education, Sex Differences, and Performance on Cognitive Tasks Among Two-Year-Old Children

TYPE

22o Sex-Role Concepts and Sex Typing in Childhood as a Function of School and Home Environments
68e Ann and Superman: Type and Archetype
131d Guatemalan Women: Life under Two Types of Patriarchy
149n Elements and Types in Soviet Marriage
156f Teachers, Peers, and Play Preferences: An Environmental Approach to Sex Typing in the Preschool

271h Sex-Role Concepts and Sex Typing in Childhood as a Function of School and Home Environments
296e Fathers, Mothers and Sex Typing

TYRANNY

175ff Tyranny of Structurelessness
232m Tyranny of Man
278f Pope's Portraits of Women: The Tyranny of the Pictorial Eye
316k Tyranny of Structurelessness

U.J.A.

117s Changing(?)Role of Women in Jewish Communal Affairs: A Look into the U.J.A.

U.N.E.S.C.O.

294s U.N.E.S.C.O. Long-Range Program for the Advancement of Women

U.S.

see UNITED STATES; AMERICA

UDU

131g Women of Udu: Survival in a Harsh Land

UGLY

129a Poor, Dumb, and Ugly

ULLMANN

288o Liv Ullmann: The Goddess as Ordinary Woman

UMBANDA

372f Spirit Mediums in Umbanda Evangelizada of Porto Alegre, Brazil: Dimensions of Power and Authority

UMBRELLA

277k The Beach Umbrella

UME

178i Ume Tsuda and Motoko Hani: Echoes of American Cultural Feminism in Japan

UNCERTAIN

341e Uncertain Progress of Affirmative Action

UNCHANGING

62c Unchanging Woman

UNCIVIL

195c Uncivil Liberty: An Essay to Show the Injustice and Impolicy of Ruling Woman Without Her Consent

UNCLE SAM

342dd Ending Discrimination Against Women in Education: How Uncle Sam Can Help

UNCONSCIOUS

89a Homogenizing the American Woman: The Power of an Unconscious Ideology
143m Unconscious Discrimination in Environmental Design Education
223i Innocent Femina Sensualis in Unconscious Conflict

UNDERDEVELOPED

183g Role of Women in Underdeveloped Countries: Some Sociological Issues Concerning Conflict and Peace

UNDERGRADUATE

106f Undergraduate Woman
140dd Self-Concept and the Coping Process of Black Graduate and Undergraduate Women at a Predominantly White University

UNEASY

218e Unequal Partners in an Uneasy Alliance: Women and the Working Class in Imperial Germany

UNEMPLOYMENT

202c Geographic Immobility and Labor Force Mobility: A Study of Female Unemployment
251z Sex Bias and Cyclical Unemployment
252ee Sex Bias and Cyclical Unemployment
264o Women and Unemployment: Assessing the Biggest Myths
291m Women: The New Reserve Army of the Unemployed
328g Underemployment of Women: Policy Implications for a Full Employment Economy
328h Lifetime Participation in the Labor Force and Unemployment among Mature Women
341m Unemployed! An Academic Woman's Saga

UNFATHOMED

298h The Dark Unfathomed Caves

UNFINISHED

3g An Unfinished Woman
341a Women on Campus: The Unfinished Liberation

UNFORGIVABLE

342e Women and Aging: The Unforgivable Sin

UNFORTUNATE

79s The Unfortunate Bride, or the Blind Lady a Beauty
225a Mother and the Hospital: An Unfortunate Fit Between the Woman's Internal World and Some Hospital Practices

UNIFORM

212q "Maedchen in Uniform"

UNION

see also LABOR; WORK; EMPLOYMENT

35o Berkeley-Oakland Women's Union Statement
41g Organizing the Unorganizable: Three Jewish Women and Their Union
41h Imperfect Unions: Class and Gender in Cripple Creek, 1894- 1904
41i Women's Trade Union League and American Feminism
41j Creating a Feminist Alliance: Sisterhood and Class Conflict in the New York Women's Trade Union League, 1903- 1914
54g Extra-Marital Fertility and its Occurrence in Stable Unions: Recent Trends in Western Europe
57g Trade Union Woman
59g Search for a Partnership Role: Women in Labor Unions Today
116d Women in the Canadian and Italian Trade Union Movements at the Turn of the Century
126i Feminism and Class Consciousness in the British and American Women's Trade Union Leagues, 1890-1925
141i Feminism and Class Consciousness in the British and American Women's Trade Union Leagues, 1890-1925
181h Women in American Trade Unions: An Historical Analysis
191s Building a Hospital Workers' Union: Doris Turner, the Woman from 1199
265p Sex Discrimination in the Trade Unions: Legal Resources for Change
267e Convergences between East and West: Tradition and Modernity in Sex Roles in Sweden, Finland, and the Soviet Union
294q Women and American Trade Unions
297q Discrimination Against Women in the U.S.: Higher Education, Government Enforcement Agencies, and Unions
297t Role and Status of Women in the Soviet Union: 1917 to the Present
307f Women and Revolution: The Lessons of the Soviet Union and China
312f Women, Work and Trade Unionism
316m Modernization Theory and Sex Roles in Critical Perspective: The Case of the Soviet Union
320k Women and the Unions
323e Early Years in the Trade Unions
323h Women in Trade Unions
324r Soviet Union
352n Women Workers and the Trade Unions in Austria
360f Women Nurses in the Union Army

UNIQUE

129m Fostergrandparenting: A Unique Child-Care Service
159b Our Revolution is Unique
238b Our Revolution Is Unique
311f Unique Health Problems of Women in Industry

UNISEX

73h There's No Unisex in the Nursery
280i Unisex and the Public Schools
280j Unisex Pressures on Children

UNITED NATIONS

37g APPENDIX: Status of Women in Sweden: Report to the United Nations, 1968
284n U.N. Declaration on Women's Rights
294u United Nations Action to Advance the Status of Women

UNITED STATES

see also AMERICA

2a Abortion and Public Policy in the U.S.
2d Abortion and the Constitution: The Cases of the United States and West Germany
13w Women in U.S. History High-School Textbooks
20s Women's Movement in the U.S.
39n Women, Work, and Wedlock: A Note on Female Marital Patterns in the U.S.
42d Voluntary Motherhood: The Beginnings of Feminist Birth Control Ideas in the U.S.
51u Opiate Addiction Among Females in the United States Between 1850 and 1970
57i APPENDIX: U.S. National Women's Agenda
91f Fertility of Working Women in the United States: Historical Trends and Theoretical Perspectives
94d Forcible Rape in the U.S.: A Statistical Profile
140d Change in U.S. Women's Sex-Role Attitudes, 1964-1974
140k Role of Wife in the Black Extended Family: Perspectives from a Rural Community in Southern United States
155t Contraception and Pregnancy: Experience of Young Unmarried Women in the United States
174g Minorities and Policy Problems: An Overview Seen by the U.S. Commission on Civil Rights
178j Role of Women in the Founding of the U.S. Children's Bureau
180l Harvard College Amicus Curiae, DeFunis v. Odegaard, Supreme Court of the U.S., 1973
196k Women in U.S. History High-School Textbooks
208gg Women in U.S. History High School Textbooks
210d Religious Socialization of Women Within U.S. Subcultures
250e Male-Female Perception of the Female Sex Role in the United States
264i History and Development of Day Care in the U.S.
265f History and Development of Day Care in the U.S.
269d Hunger in the U.S.: Women and Children First
271q Women in U.S. History High School Textbooks

294f Women and Politics in the U.S. and Canada
297d Female Labor and Capitalism in the U.S. and Brazil
297o Evolutionism and the Place of Women in the U.S., 1855-1900
297p Legislation: An Aid in Eliminating Sex Bias in Education in the U.S.
297q Discrimination Against Women in the U.S.: Higher Education, Government Enforcement Agencies, and Unions
297r Women's Liberation Movement in the U.S.
297s Politics of Theory: Participant Observation in the U.S.
303s Historic Chart Relating Architectural Projects to General and Women's History in the U.S.
324v United States
334q Propaganda and Public Opinion in the United States and Germany, 1939-1945
372j Uses of Traditional Concepts in the Development of New Urban Roles: Cuban Women in the United States

UNITY

126v Four Structures in a Complex Unity
175hh Congress to Unite Women (Report, 1969)
230n Love Unites Them and Hunger Separates Them: Poor Women in the Dominican Republic
281q Shaping of the Kaum Ibu (Women's Section) of the United Maylays National Organization

UNIVERSAL

85e Feminine As a Universal
294j Women in the Middle East and North Africa and Universal Suffrage

UNIVERSITY

see also COLLEGE; EDUCATION; HIGHER EDUCATION; COEDUCATION; ACADEMIA; STUDENT; FACULTY; CAMPUS

4l Representation, Performance and Status of Women on the Faculty at the Urbana-Champaign Campus of the University of Illinois
4r Internal Remedies for Sex Discrimination in Colleges and Universities
13y Present Tendencies in Women's College and University Education
15m In the University
23d Learned Women of Early Modern Italy: Humanists and University Scholars
36m University Women and the Law
96l Before Women Were Human Beings: Adventures of an American Fellow in German Universities of the '90s
106g University Behavior and Policies: Where Are the Women and Why?
140dd Self-Concept and the Coping Process of Black Graduate and Undergraduate Women at a Predominantly White University
140ii Bibliography of Dissertations for and about Women in Administration in Colleges and Universities
141ii Recent and On-Going Research Projects at the University of Michigan
180d H.E.W., the University and Women
180h H.E.W. and the Universities
217a University and the Case for Preferential Treatment

244f Women and Degrees at Cambridge University, 1862-1897
251dd Sex Discrimination in the Universities
257q Present Tendencies in Women's College and University Education
272g Coeducation and the Development of Leadership Skills in Women: Historical Perspectives from Cornell University, 1868-1900
275e German Women University Students: National Socialism and the War, 1939-1945
282r Pedagogical Arguments for Preferential Hiring and Tenuring of Women Teachers in the University
290a Woman-Centered University
301g Sex Discrimination at Universities: An Ombudsman's View
301i Affirmative Action at Stanford University
320j Women in the Universities

UNMAILED

33i Unmailed, Unwritten Letters

UNMARRIED

155t Contraception and Pregnancy: Experience of Young Unmarried Women in the United States

UNMOTHERED

186h Unmothered Woman

UNPARDONABLE

96ii "Unpardonable"
226o Unpardonable Sin

UNPOSTED

339n An Unposted Love Letter

UNWOMANLY

68i "Unwomanly Woman" in Shaw's Drama

UPBRINGING

114h Upbringing of a Girl

UPRISING

9tt Private View of the Woman's Uprising

UPSTAIRS

119a The Locked Room Upstairs

UPTAKE

286w Maximal Oxygen Uptake of Females

UPWARD

71h Domestic Service as a Channel of Upward Mobility for the Lower Class Woman: The Lima Case

URBANA-CHAMPAIGN

41 Representation, Performance and Status of Women on the Faculty at the Urbana-Champaign Campus of the University of Illinois

URBANIZATION

14e "Thereness" of Women: A Selective Review of Urban Sociology
41a Systematic Study of Urban Women
70b Two Roles of Russian Working Women in an Urban Area
70f Urban Working Woman in the U.S.S.R.: An Historical Overview
120g Sex, Covert Prestige, and Linguistic Change in the Urban British English of Norwich
193e Roles of Children in Urban Kano
213h Economic Activity and Marriage among Ivoirian Urban Women
249f Sex Roles and Survival Strategies in an Urban Black Community
278n Black Women in Urban Schools
293g Women in Development: Urban Life and Labor
293h Women in African Towns South of the Sahara: The Urbanization Dilemma
309c Employment and Family Change: A Study of Middle-Class Women in Urban Gujarat
316d Women's Attitudes Toward Women in Politics: A Survey of Urban Registered Voters and Party Committeewomen
325z Self-Images of Traditional Urban Women in Cairo
338f Women of Dakar and the Surrounding Urban Area
350g Women's Spirit Possession and Urban Adaptation
354n Urban Nomads: Women in Temporary Clerical Services
372j Uses of Traditional Concepts in the Development of New Urban Roles: Cuban Women in the United States

US

127v "Freedom Is Something That All of Us Need"
274d Things Walt Disney Never Told Us
282f There's Nobody Here But Us Persons
287h Economy Ahead of Us: Will Women Have Different Roles?

UTAH

215k Two Miss Cooks: Pioneer Professionals for Utah's Schools
215r Dr. Ellis Reynolds Shipp: Pioneer Utah Physician
215t Dr. Margaret Ann Freece: Entrepreneur of Southern Utah
215u Sarah Elizabeth Carmichael: Poetic Genius of Pioneer Utah

UTOPIAN

218b Feminism and Socialism: The Utopian Synthesis of Flora Tristan

UTTAR

309b Women in Uttar Pradesh: Social Mobility and Directions of Change

VACANT

255b Astraea's "Vacant Throne": The Successors of Aphra Behn

VAGINA

169e Denial of the Vagina
191t Vaginal Politics
296a Denial of the Vagina

VAGINAL ORGASM

see also ORGASM

77t Myth of the Vaginal Orgasm
127hh Myth of the Vaginal Orgasm
139s Myth of the Vaginal Orgasm
169n Problem of Vaginal Orgasm
175t Myth of the Vaginal Orgasm
233dd Myth of the Vaginal Orgasm

VALLEY

140f From Peasants to Proletarians: Black Women in the Cauca Valley, Colombia

VALUE

84h Domestic Labour and Marx's Theory of Value
85o Nature and Value of Marriage
89mm Value of Housework
110t Value and Peril for Women of Reading Women Writers
155l Mothers and Daughters: Perceived and Real Differences in Sexual Values
164g Roles of Women: A Question of Values
173p Social Values, Femininity, and the Development of Female Competence
200l Sex Differences in Job Values and Desires
252w Monetary Value of a Housewife
258d Home and Work: Women's Roles and the Transformation of Values
269h Parent's Role in Values Education
286q American Business Values and Involvement in Sport
287a Looking Backward in Order to Look Forward: Women, Work and Social Values in America
330c Cultural Values, Female Role Expectancies and Therapeutic Goals: Research and Interpretation
338e Women of Burundi: A Study of Social Values
368i Sex-Linked Values: Their Impacts on Women in Engineering
371c Occupational Values and Family Roles: Women in Blue-Collar and Service Occupations

VAMPIRE

132b The Vampire Wife
247j Vampires, Virgins and Voyeurs in Imperial Vienna

VANCOUVER

342aa Working Women's Association of Vancouver

VANGUARD

166uu Vanguard Artist: Portrait and Self-Portrait

VARIABILITY

120e Sex of the Speaker as a Sociolinguistic Variable
163h Campaign Theory and Practice--The Gender Variable
204j Menstrual Cycle and Sex-Related Differences in Cognitive Variability
330b Sex Hormones, The Central Nervous System and Affect Variability in Humans

VARIATION

4k Institutional Variation in the Status of Academic Women
4m Discipline Variation in the Status of Academic Women
146g Life Span Behavior Patterns--Class and Ethnic Variations
172c Meaning of Sex-Related Variations in Maturation Rate
204g Cognitive Abilities and Sex-Related Variations in the Maturation of Cerebral Cortical Functions
372d Dioula Women in Town: A View of Intra-Ethnic Variation - Ivory Coast

VARNHAGEN

5a Rahel Varnhagen

VASHTI

117v Restoration of Vashti

VASTER

340k Vaster Than Empires and More Slow

VEILS

241f The Veiled Feminists of Atlantis
256p When The Veils Come Tumbling Down: "And Women Shall Leave Their Comfortable Pews to Give Birth to a New and Inclusive Religious Vision"

VENEREAL

8ii Information on VD for Gay Women and Men
8jj Bottoms Up: An In-Depth Look at VD and Your Asshole
223e Study of Victorian Prostitution and Venereal Disease

VENEZUELAN

122e Teresa de la Parra, Venezuelan Novelist and Feminist

VENICE

23f Women's Roles in Early Modern Venice
315h Dowries and Kinsmen in Early Renaissance Venice

VENUS

108a Venus--Aghia Sophia
212a Popcorn Venus or How the Movies Have Made Women Smaller Than Life

VERB

120k Teacher-Child Verbal Interaction: An Approach to the Study of Sex Differences
141r Son Preference in Taiwan: Verbal Preference and Demographic Behavior
219e Verbal Turn-Taking and Exchanges in Faculty Dialogue
219i Women's Verbal Images and Associations
219o Women's Verbal Behavior at Learned and Professional Conferences
219q Alignment Strategies in Verbal Accounts of Problematic Conduct: The Case of Abortion
300m God Is a Verb

VERONA

102m Journey of a Woman Nihilist to Verona in Late Autumn

VERONIKA

279c Veronika

VERTE

122f Elena Poniatowska's "Hasta no Verte, Jesus Mio"

VERTUS

184e Fifteenth-Century View of Women's Role in Medieval Society: Christine de Pizan's "Livre des Trois Vertus"

VESTRIS

141cc Madame Vestris in America

VEXATIONS

79m Malady and Remedy of Vexations and Unjust Arrests and Actions

VICE-PRESIDENTIAL

7i Win or Lose--We Win: The 1952 Vice-Presidential Campaign of Charlotta A. Bass

VICTIM

17d "Slydynge of Corage": Chaucer's Criseyde as Feminist and Victim
21h Women Social Workers and Clients: Common Victims of Sexism

80k Virgins and Other Victims: Aspects of German Middle-Class Theatre
94f Black Offender and White Victim: A Study of Forcible Rape in Oakland, Ca.
94h Judicial Attitudes Toward Rape Victims
94m Hitchhike Victim of Rape
94p Crisis Intervention with Victims of Rape
94q Philadelphia Rape Victim Project
155v Attribution of Fault to a Rape Victim as a Function of Respectability
208u Dick and Jane as Victims: Sex Stereotyping in Children's Readers
212b Monster and the Victim
235a Men and the Victimization of Women
235f Prostitute as Victim
235i Economics of Women's Victimization
235j Women and Victimization: The Aftermath
321i Victims of Rape and Wife Abuse

VICTOR

80d Letter to Marguerite Durand from Paul and Victor Margueritte

VICTORIAN

42f Sexual Politics of Victorian Social Anthropology
42h Family Limitation, Sexual Control, and Domestic Feminism in Victorian America
42k Image and Reality: The Myth of the Idle Victorian Woman
92a Early Formation of Victorian Domestic Ideology
140nn Victorian Pornography and Attitudes Reflected Toward Women
223a Victorian Governess: Status Incongruence in Family and Society
223c Victorian Women and Menstruation
223d Marriage, Redundancy or Sin: The Painter's View of Women in the First Twenty-Five Years of Victoria's Reign
223e Study of Victorian Prostitution and Venereal Disease
233h Victorian Woman
240f Angels and Other Women in Victorian Literature
244a Victorian Wives and Property: Reform of the Married Women's Property Law, 1857-1882
244g Victorian Masculinity and the Angel in the House
244h Sex and Death in Victorian England: An Examination of Age- and Sex-Specific Death Rates, 1840-1910
335i Demographic Contributions to the History of Victorian Women
335j Women in the Mirror: Using Novels to Study Victorian Women
360g Spiritualist Medium: A Study of Female Professionalization in Victorian America
360k Family Limitation, Sexual Control, and Domestic Feminism in Victorian America

VIDEOTAPED

140pp Assembling Videotaped Materials for Instructional Purposes

VIENNA

247j Vampires, Virgins and Voyeurs in Imperial Vienna

VIEROCHKA

3391 Vierochka

VIERTEL

5k Salka Viertel

VIETNAM

20y Vietnamese Women: Their Roles and Their Options
43m Schooling of Vietnamese Immigrants: Internal Colonialism and its Impact on Women
221c Pregnancy and Birth in Vietnam
342z Women's Oppression and the War in Vietnam

VILLAGE

20p Non-Hierarchical, Hierarchical, and Masked Reciprocity in the Arab Village
114o Village Women of Rajasthan
131j Khmer Village Women in Cambodia: A Happy Balance
140p Women and Words in a Spanish Village
213d Caste Differences between Brahmin and Non-Brahmin Women in a South Indian Village
221a From Pregnancy through Birth in a Bisayan Filipino Village
230l Women and Words in a Spanish Village
249o Mastery of Work and the Mystery of Sex in a Guatemalan Village
293i Dilemma of Peasant Women: A View from a Village in Yucatan
308i Women and Childbearing in Kwan Mun Hau Village: A Study of Social Change
309d Etiquette among Women in Karnataka: Forms of Address in the Village and the Family
317b Celibes, Mothers, and Church Cockroaches: Religious Participation of Women in a Mexican Village
322h Field Work in a Greek Village
325t Working women in a Moroccan Village
325dd Sex Differences and Folk Illness in an Egyptian Village

VILLETTE

108n Villette
357b Buried Letter: Feminism and Romanticism in Villette

VINCENT

214m Edna St. Vincent Millay and the Language of Vulnerability
372g Sex and Status: Women in St. Vincent

VINDICATION

159r Vindication of the Rights of Woman
188a Vindication of the Rights of Women
336b Vindication of the Character and Condition of the Females Employed in the Lowell Mills...

VIOLA

141ee Historical and Theoretical Evolution of Viola Spolin's Theatre Games

VIOLENCE

18j Effects of Observed Violence on Females
51k Crimes of Violence by Women
98c Bonds of Love: Rational Violence and Erotic Domination
175h Men and Violence
183b Men, Women and Violence: Some Reflections on Equality
183h Attitudes of Men and Women Toward Violence: Report of a National Survey
264w Violence: The Most Obscene Fantasy

VIOLET

110n Case for Violet Strange

VIOLETA

83e Virgin Violeta

VIRGIN

16h Why Has the Virgin Mary Never Entered the Wigwam of Standing Bear?
53b Semantics of Biology: Virginity
80k Virgins and Other Victims: Aspects of German Middle-Class Theatre
83e Virgin Violeta
177e Misogynism and Virginal Feminism in the Fathers of the Church
247j Vampires, Virgins and Voyeurs in Imperial Vienna
283f Image of the Virgin Mother

VIRGINIA

90d Virginia Woolf's Criticism: A Polemical Preface
357d Beyond Determinism: George Eliot and Virginia Woolf
361p Virginia Woolf and the Voices of Silence

VIRTUES

107d Roles and Virtues of Men and Women
107l Conventional Origin of Female Virtues
159x Our Virtues
231g Different Virtues for Women
240c Praising Virtuous Ladies: The Literary Image and Historical Reality of Women in Seventeenth-century England

VISIBILITY

98m Visibility and Difference: Black Women in History and Literature

VISION

241 Vision
139z Visions for the Future

218h Five Socialist Women: Traditionalist Conflicts and Socialist Visions in Austria, 1893-1934
222b Analytical Vision
222r Conversational Vision
222bb Creative Vision
230g Matriarchy: A Vision of Power
256p When The Veils Come Tumbling Down: "And Women Shall Leave Their Comfortable Pews to Give Birth to a New and Inclusive Religious Vision"
263j Feminist Spirituality, Christian Identity, and Catholic Vision
281u Talking Pictures: Field Method and Visual Mode
288rr Visual Pleasure and Narrative Cinema

VITAE

157h Humanae Vitae

VIVIEN

68o Vivien Warren: A Psychological Study

VOCABULARY

99k Rape and Psychiatric Vocabularies of Motive
207b Sexism as Shown through the English Vocabulary

VOCATIONAL

see also JOB; EMPLOYMENT; OCCUPATION

13v Use and Abuse of Vocational Tests
61b Measuring the Vocational Interest of Women
102j Vocational Counselling
208j Segregated Academic and Vocational Schools: Separate But Not Equal
266k Measuring the Vocational Interests of Women
266l Female College Students' Scores On the Men's And Women's Strong Vocational Interest Blanks
328m Vocational Education

VOICE

7g Anna J. Cooper: A Voice for Black Women
86e Chicanas Speak Out--New Voice of La Raza
254c Prostitution: A Quartet for Female Voices
303n Voices of Consequence: Four Architectural Critics
320d Voice of Women: A History
361f New Voices in Feminine Discourse
361p Virginia Woolf and the Voices of Silence

VOIR DIRE

321f Sexism in Voir Dire: The Use of Sex Stereotypes in Jury Selection

VOLKER

275f Frau und Staatsburger in Volker Braun's Schauspiel "Tinka"

VOLODYA

108t Big Volodya and Little Volodya

VOLUNTEERISM

42d Voluntary Motherhood: The Beginnings of Feminist Birth Control Ideas in the U.S.
146l Volunteerism
254w Women and Voluntarism
344n Women as Voluntary Political Activists

VOODOO

222p Influence of Voodoo on the Fiction of Zora Neale Hurston

VOTE

see also SUFFRAGE; FEMINISM

65c Enfranchisement of Women
68x Why All Women Are Peculiarly Fitted to Be Good Voters
74b Enfranchisement of Women
140t You Can Lead a Lady to Vote, But What Will She Do With It? The Problem of a Woman's Bloc Vote
163n Women as Voters: Their Maturation as Political Persons in American Society
163t Voting Patterns of American Black Women
174o Political Power and Policy Benefits: Voting Rights and Welfare Policy in Mississippi
284g Women's Status Fifty Years After the Vote
312d Women, the Vote and Revolution
316a American Woman: Voter and Activist
316d Women's Attitudes Toward Women in Politics: A Survey of Urban Registered Voters and Party Committeewomen
323c Contribution of the Women's Labour League to the Winning of the Franchise
326f Women as Voters: Their Maturation as Political Persons in American Society
344f League of Women Voters and Political Power

VOUCHERS

40f Vouchers for Child Care: The Santa Clara Child Care Pilot Study

VOYEURS

247j Vampires, Virgins and Voyeurs in Imperial Vienna

VULNERABILITY

214m Edna St. Vincent Millay and the Language of Vulnerability

W.C.T.U.

262q Woman in Philanthropy--Work of the W.C.T.U.

W.E.A.L.

4s W.E.A.L. and Contract Compliance
344g W.E.A.L.: The Growth of a Feminist Organization

W.I.T.C.H.

132bb W.I.T.C.H. Manifesto

WAGE

see also PAY; INCOME; EARNINGS

21n Women Who Work for Wages
89hh Wages for Housework
141t Welfare Careers, Low Wage Workers and Sexism
202g Relative Wages and Sex Segregation by Occupation
256i Wages of Wrath: Women's Relationships in the Working World
304i Wages of Work: A Widening Gap Between Men and Women
333g Differences in Expected Post-School Investment as a Determinant of Market Wage Differentials
352i Women's Wages in Japan and the Question of Equal Pay
354d Wage Differences between Men and Women: Economic Theories

WAITING

3q Waiting for Daddy

WALKER

222i Black Women Poets from Wheatley to Walker
222m Alice Walker
222n Alice Walker: "The Diary of an African Nun" and Du Bois' Double Consciousness

WALL

119c The Shadows on the Wall
362d Up Against the Wall, Male Chauvinist Pig

WALLPAPER

113e The Yellow Wallpaper
153s The Yellow Wall-Paper

WALT

274d Things Walt Disney Never Told Us

WALTZ

33a The Waltz

WANDERING

99m Politics of Hysteria: The Case of the Wandering Womb

WAR

see also REVOLUTION; ARMED FORCES; DRAFT; names of wars

17j War and Roses: The Politics of "Mrs. Dalloway"
19r Something Old, Something New: Women Between the Two World Wars
116a Silent Half: "Le Contadine del Sud" Before The First World War
140h Did Rosie the Riveter Give Up Her Job? Women War Workers During and After World War II
149p Women's Lib: The War on "Sexism"
151n American Woman's Pre-World War I Freedom in Manners and Morals
154g Female Militancy and Colonial Revolt: The Women's War of 1929, Eastern Nigeria
183e Gender Imagery and Issues of War and Peace: The Case of the Draft Resistance Movement of the 1960's
222c War on African Familyhood
240k "Combat in the Erogenous Zone": Women in the American Novel between the Two World Wars
275e German Women University Students: National Socialism and the War, 1939-1945
292t American Woman's Pre-World War I Freedom in Manners and Morals
295g Women during the Great War
302c "Aba Riots" or Igbo "Women's War"? Ideology, Stratification, and the Invisibility of Women
341r Women and War
342z Women's Oppression and the War in Vietnam
349b Women, Class, and War in Nazi Germany
349k American Women in the Peace and Preparedness Movements in World War I
360o American Woman's Pre-World War I Freedom in Manners and Morals
362i Politics and War
364e American Woman from 1900 to the First World War: A Profile

WARD

315g Widow and Ward: The Feudal Law of Child Custody in Medieval England

WARNERS

288cc Women at Work: Warners in the 1930s

WARREN

68o Vivien Warren: A Psychological Study
233pp Mrs. Warren's Profession
310f Mrs. Warren's Profession

WARRIOR

359j Metaphysics of Matrilinearism in Women's Autobiography: Studies of Mead's "Blackberry Winter," Hellman's "Pentimento," Angelou's "I Know Why the Caged Bird Sings," and Kingston's "The Woman Warrior"
359l Towards a Theory of Form in Feminist Autobiography: Kate Millett's "Flying" and "Sita"; Maxine Hong Kingston's "The Woman Warrior"

WASHING MACHINE

42n Case Study of Technological and Social Change: The Washing Machine and the Working Wife

WASTE

139g Waste of Private Housekeeping
238h Educational Establishment: Wasted Women
356h Here and There in the Wastes of Ocean A Swimmer Was Seen

WATCH

108ff Nightwood: Night Watch

WATER

222q Bridges and Deep Water

WATERCOLORS

375c Parable of the Cave or: In Praise of Watercolors

WAVE

139u Second Feminist Wave
212t Lina Wertmuller: Swept Away on a Wave of Sexism
279q Permanent Wave

WEAKNESS

96mm Weakness of Women
107q Weakness of Woman
226s Weakness of Women
235f Bargaining from Weakness: Spirit Possession on the South Kenya Coast
300b Weak Are the Second Sex

WEALTH

164n Repository of Wealth
251ee Women and Wealth
252jj Women and Wealth

WEATHERALL

33q The Jilting of Granny Weatherall

WEB

47k Eudora's Web

WEBER

288q Years Have Not Been Kind to Lois Weber

WEDDING

see also MARRIAGE; BRIDE; DOWRY

39n Women, Work, and Wedlock: A Note on Female Marital Patterns in the U.S.
47j "Delta Wedding" as Region and Symbol
95f Wedding Dance
111u Cassandra's Wedding Song
157k Consolation of the Wedded

WEDDING BAND

144f Wedding Band

WEEK

171m Body Time and Social Time: Mood Patterns by Menstrual Cycle Phase and Day of Week
208a Why I Won't Celebrate Brotherhood Week
244b Forgotten Woman of the Period: Penny Weekly Family Magazines of the 1840's and 1850's

WEIMAR

126q Beyond "Kinder, Kuche, Kirche": Weimar Women in Politics and Work
275c Stereotype of the Emancipated Woman in the Weimar Republic

WELFARE

42m Welfare of Women in Laboring Families: England, 1860-1950
92g Welfare State and the Needs of the Dependent Family
141t Welfare Careers, Low Wage Workers and Sexism
163e Case Study in Patriarchal Politics: Women on Welfare
174o Political Power and Policy Benefits: Voting Rights and Welfare Policy in Mississippi
202m Vicious Cycle of Welfare: Problems of the Female-Headed Household in N.Y.C.
371e Women, Work, and Welfare: The Feminization of Poverty

WELL-BEING

267q Sex-Role Attitudes and Psychological Well-Being

WELLS

215w Emmeline Blanche Woodward Wells: "I Have Risen Triumphant"

WELTY

192e Eudora Welty

WERTMULLER

212t Lina Wertmuller: Swept Away on a Wave of Sexism
288ii Interview with Lina Wertmuller
288nn Is Lina Wertmuller Just Once of the Boys?

WEST

2d Abortion and the Constitution: The Cases of the United States and West Germany
25c West African Influences
54g Extra-Marital Fertility and its Occurrence in Stable Unions: Recent Trends in Western Europe
60d Teachers to the West
91g Fertility and Women's Employment Outside the Home in Western Europe
93e Jennie Higginses of the "New South in the West": A Regional Survey of Socialist Activities, Agitators, and Organizers, 1901-1917
108q Stepping Westward
111vv Stepping Westward
128k Women as Land-owners in the West
140e Female Employment and Family Organization in West Africa
155q Teenage Boys and Girls in West Germany
213l Mechanistic Cooperation and Sexual Equality among the Western Bontoc
262c Education of Woman in the Western States
265s Sexism in Western Art
267e Convergences between East and West: Tradition and Modernity in Sex Roles in Sweden, Finland, and the Soviet Union
281l Female Status, the Family, and Male Dominance in a West Indian Community
281o Women and Migration in Contemporary West Africa
288k What Maisie Knows: Mae West
294h Political Participation of Western European Women
324l West Germany
329g Politics of Sex: West Germany
329h Female Labor Force in Western Europe

WESTCHESTER

175oo Westchester Radical Feminists

WET

24u Wet
113h The De Wets Come to Kloof Grange

WEYER

52c Johann Weyer's "De Praetigiis Daemonum": Unsystematic Psychopathology

WHARTON

192a E. Wharton and G. Stein

WHEATLEY

222i Black Women Poets from Wheatley to Walker

WHITE

39q Social Relations of Black and White Widowed Women in a Northern Metropolis

57e White Ethnic Catholic Woman
68y Root of the White Slave Traffic
94f Black Offender and White Victim: A Study of Forcible Rape in Oakland, Ca.
95m Order of the White Paulownia
108b White Mule
121c Indian Women and White Society: The Case of Sixteenth-Century Peru
127u To My White Working-Class Sisters
138b Impact of White Women on Fur Trade Society
140dd Self-Concept and the Coping Process of Black Graduate and Undergraduate Women at a Predominantly White University
155i Premarital Sexual Permissiveness Among Negroes and Whites
277h The White Stocking
368g White Feminist Movement: The Chicana Perspective

WHITMAN

214j Dickinson, Whitman, and Their Successors

WHOLENESS

280bb Whole Human Being
371m Family Wholeness: New Conceptions of Family Roles

WHORE

68n Whore in Every Home
225c Whore in Peru: The Splitting of Women into Good and Bad and the Isolation of the Prostitute
317l Jive Dope Fiend Whoes: In the Street and in Rehabilitation

WIDE

88u Jean Rhys' Recent Fiction: Humane Developments in "Wide Sargasso Sea"

WIDENING

284q Decade of Widening Horizons
304i Wages of Work: A Widening Gap Between Men and Women

WIDOW

see also BEREAVEMENT; AGE; OLD; MARRIAGE

39q Social Relations of Black and White Widowed Women in a Northern Metropolis
111pp The Widow's Lament in Springtime
129i Meaning of Friendship in Widowhood
173mm Women in Widowhood
315g Widow and Ward: The Feudal Law of Child Custody in Medieval England
331i Homemakers into Widows and Divorcees: Can the Law Provide Economic Protection?
352g Women's Rights and Widows' Pensions
360c Widowhood in Eighteenth-Century Massachusetts: A Problem in the History of the Family

WIELAND

288aa Interview with Joyce Wieland

WIFE

see also HUSBAND; MARRIAGE; WIDOW; PARENT; SEX ROLE; MARRY

4j Faculty Wife: Her Academic Interests and Qualifications
39a Maid of All Work or Departmental Sister-in-Law? The Faculty Wife Employed on Campus
42n Case Study of Technological and Social Change: The Washing Machine and the Working Wife
55g Husbands and Wives: The Dynamics of the Deferential Dialectic
59i Working Wives and Family Income
70c Interaction and Goal Attainment in Parisian Working Wives' Families
79t The Wife's Resentment
102b The Wife of Pilate
111oo The Other Wife
131e Women of North and Central India: Goddesses and Wives
132b The Vampire Wife
140k Role of Wife in the Black Extended Family: Perspectives from a Rural Community in Southern United States
140w Assaulted Wife: "Catch 22" Revisited
143c Household as Workplace: Wives, Husbands, and Children
149h Wife Problem
151b Husbands and Wives
154e Premiss of Dedication: Notes towards an Ethnography of Diplomats' Wives
163q Wife and Politician: Role Strain Among Women in Public Office
166mm Career and Family Orientations of Husbands and Wives in Relation to Marital Happiness
166aaa Myth of the Egalitarian Family: Familial Roles and the Professionally Employed Wife
175g Why I Want a Wife
176p Career and Family Orientations of Husbands and Wives in Relation to Marital Happiness
215c Louisa Barnes Pratt: Missionary Wife, Missionary Mother, Missionary
215s Dr. Martha Hughes Cannon: Doctor, Wife, Legislator, Exile
231f Community of Wives
231h Of the Relation Between Husband and Wife
231v Letter to the Wife
233kk Man and Wife
244a Victorian Wives and Property: Reform of the Married Women's Property Law, 1857-1882
252x Working Wives: Their Contribution to Family Income
260a ...How Ischomachus Trained His Wife
267o Implied Demand Character of the Wife's Future and Role Innovation: Patterns of Achievement Orientation Among College Women
270l Putting Down Sisters and Wives: Tongan Women and Colonization
277q The Dentist's Wife
277t Astronomer's Wife
279k Romance of a Fisherman's Wife
292i American Maidens and Wives
320g Farm Wife
321i Victims of Rape and Wife Abuse
331a Girls into Wives

331b Sexual Inequality, Cultural Norms, and Wife-Beating
331e Health and Fertility Issues and the Dependency of Wives
331h Public Policy and the Family: A New Strategy for Women as Wives and Mothers
341c Wives of Academe

WIGWAM

16h Why Has the Virgin Mary Never Entered the Wigwam of Standing Bear?

WILD

50b The Man with the Wild Eyes
111xx Wine in the Wilderness
113b In the Forests of Riga the Beasts Are Very Wild Indeed
161h Wine in the Wilderness
279cc Beasts of the Southern Wild

WILHELMINE

126h Feminism and Liberalism in Wilhelmine Germany, 1890-1918

WILLA

192c Willa Cather

WIN

7i Win or Lose--We Win: The 1952 Vice-Presidential Campaign of Charlotta A. Bass
9y What it Would be Like if Women Win
17o Winning: Katherine Anne Porter's Women
127d What It Would Be Like If Women Win
256q Women in Motion: It's Not Who Wins Or Loses, But How Many Play the Game
279o The Rocking-Horse Winner
284z What It Would Be Like If Women Win
323c Contribution of the Women's Labour League to the Winning of the Franchise
362n What It Would Be Like If Women Win

WINCHILSEA

214d Anne Finch, Countess of Winchilsea: An Augustan Woman Poet

WIND

273l The Wind-Chill Factor or, A Problem of Mind and Matter
340e The Wind People

WINDOW

105i Women's Page as a Window on the Ruling Class
144b Window Dressing

WINE

111xx Wine in the Wilderness
161h Wine in the Wilderness
279x Wine

WING

337f Quaker Women in the English Left Wing

WINTER

277y Winter in July
359j Metaphysics of Matrilinearism in Women's Autobiography: Studies of Mead's "Blackberry Winter," Hellman's "Pentimento," Angelou's "I Know Why the Caged Bird Sings," and Kingston's "The Woman Warrior"

WISBY

153l The Courting of Sister Wisby
273a The Courting of Sister Wisby

WISCONSIN

93f Politics of Mutual Frustration: Socialists and Suffragists in New York and Wisconsin

WISDOM

181a Wisewoman and Medicine Man: Changes in the Management of Childbirth
222y Wisdom: An Interview with C.L.R. James

WISH

76i Penis Envy: From Childhood Wish to Developmental Metaphor

WITCH

111y The Pauper Witch of Grafton
112p The Pauper Witch of Grafton
142p Witch Power
185c Saints and Witches
225b Witch and Her Devils: An Exploration of the Relationship Between Femininity and Illness
264v Why Witches Were Women
265u Why Witches Were Women
317k Radical Yoruba Female Sexuality: The Witch and the Prostitute

WITCHCRAFT

19e Pedestal and the Stake: Courtly Love and Witchcraft
52b Witchcraft and Magic in Renaissance Italy: Gianfrancesco Pico and his "Strix"
52e Reginald Scot's "Discoverie of Witchcraft": Scepticism and Sadduceeism
52g King James's "Daemonologie": Witchcraft and Kingship

52i Cotton Mather's "Wonders of the Invisible World": Some Metamorphoses of Salem Witchcraft
52j Two Late Scottish Witchcraft Tracts: "Witch-Craft Proven" and "The Tryal of Witchcraft"
263v Witchcraft and Women's Culture

WODAABE

338b Position of Women in a Pastoral Society (Fulani WoDaaBe, Nomads of the Niger)

WOLF

24j The Hour of the Wolf
104j Mountain Wolf Woman
144h The Ice Wolf

WOLLSTONECRAFT

145f George Eliot and Mary Wollstonecraft
181k Rights and Wrongs of Women: Mary Wollstonecraft, Harriet Martineau, Simone de Beauvoir
282d Reason and Morals in the Early Feminist Movement: Mary Wollstonecraft

WOMAN-CENTERED

290a Woman-Centered University

WOMAN-IDENTIFIED

9rr Woman-Identified Woman
127ff Woman-Identified Woman

WOMAN-MARRIAGE

285j Woman-Marriage, With Special Reference to the Lovedu--Its Significance for the Definition of Marriage

WOMANHOOD

3d Inner and Outer Space: Reflections on Womanhood
9hh Cult of True Womanhood
121i Education, Philanthropy, and Feminism: Components of Argentine Womanhood, 1860-1926
126k Racism and Tradition: Black Womanhood in Historical Perspective
151f Cult of True Womanhood: 1820-1860
159v Of Womenkind, Old and Young
170a Flight from Womanhood: The Masculinity Complex in Women as Viewed by Men and by Women
198c Flight from Womanhood: The Masculinity-Complex in Women as Viewed by Men and by Women
198f Inner and Outer Space: Reflections on Womanhood
233l Achieving Womanhood
253a Inner and Outer Space: Reflections on Womanhood
260d Reflections on Womanhood
268k Flight from Womanhood

268s Womanhood and the Inner Space
292d Eighteenth-Century Womanhood
292m Cult of True Womanhood, 1820-1860
360i Cult of True Womanhood, 1820-1860

WOMANLINESS

see also FEMININITY

115i Woman Versus Womanliness: An Essay in Speculative Psychology
132f Womanly Woman
139n Womanly Image
169l Womanliness as a Masquerade
233f Womanly Image: Character Assassination through the Ages

WOMANPOWER

225f Woman-Power: Religious Heresy and Feminism in Early English Socialism
314j New Work Patterns--for Better Use of Womanpower

WOMB

51dd Concrete Womb: "Gettin' In"
99m Politics of Hysteria: The Case of the Wandering Womb

WOMEN'S HISTORY

121l Trends and Issues in Latin American Women's History
126e Problem of Women's History
126u Feminism and the Methodology of Women's History
141b Four Levels of Women's History
208jj Sexism in History or, Writing Women's History is a Tricky Business
303s Historic Chart Relating Architectural Projects to General and Women's History in the U.S.
335a Old and New Women's History
360a American Women and Domestic Culture: An Approach to Women's History
364a "Women's History" in Transition: The European Case

WOMEN'S LIBERATION

see also FEMINISM; MOVEMENT

9q Why Women's Liberation?
9w Why Women's Liberation Is Important to Black Women
13j Impact of the Women's Liberation Movement on Child Development Texts
22y Personality and Ideology: A Personological Study of Women's Liberation
39c Origins of the Women's Liberation Movement
71l Honor, Shame, and Women's Liberation in Cuba: Views of Working-Class Emigre Men
73q Women's Liberation: A Nice Idea, but It Won't Be Easy
74f Marx and Engels on Women's Liberation
74k Development of the American Women's Liberation Movement, 1967-1971
74l Why Women's Liberation--2?
77n Black Movement and Women's Liberation

85a Political Philosophies of Women's Liberation
86d Why Women's Liberation is Important to Black Women
89ee Political Economy of Women's Liberation
97b Women's Liberation and the New Left
97j Political Economy of Women's Liberation
107cc Capitalism and Women's Liberation
117b Women's Liberation and the Liberation of God: An Essay in Story Theology
121k Felipe Carrillo Puerto and Women's Liberation in Mexico
127a Why Women's Liberation?
127p Political Economy of Women's Liberation
132r Rise of Women's Liberation
139y Political Economy of Women's Liberation
142d Restless Eagles: Women's Liberation 1969
142t Broom of One's Own: Notes on the Women's Liberation Program
151s Women's Liberation: Theory and Practice
158jj Political Philosophies of Women's Liberation
173r Women's Liberation and Human Sexual Relations
175bb Spiritual Dimension of Women's Liberation
176bb Rise of Women's Liberation
178b Eighteenth-Century Theorists of Women's Liberation
186j Why Women's Liberation
186l Political Economy of Women's Liberation
202o Income and Employment Effects of Women's Liberation
202p Impact of Women's Liberation on Marriage, Divorce, and Family Life-Style
231k Contra Women's Liberation Movement
233ccc Man's Role in Women's Liberation
238a Pioneers of Women's Liberation
251o Political Economy of Women's Liberation
252p Political Economy of Women's Liberation
254z Is Women's Liberation a Lesbian Plot?
254aa Women's Liberation and Black Civil Rights
264cc Women's Liberation Movement: Its Origins, Organizations, Activities, and Ideas
265cc Women's Liberation Movement: Its Origins, Structures, Impact, and Ideas
271t Time Is Here for Women's Liberation
271y Education and Women's Liberation
282g Women's Liberation and Human Emancipation
283i Differentiation and Difference--Reflections on the Ethical Implications of Women's Liberation
284a What Is Women's Liberation Really All About?
284b Man's Primer to Women's Liberation
288dd Women's Liberation Cinema
297r Women's Liberation Movement in the U.S.
304e Housewives in Women's Liberation: Social Change as Role-Making
307i Women's Liberation
314q Businessman's Guide to Women's Liberation
365c Impact of the Women's Liberation Movement on Child Development Books

WOMEN'S STUDIES

4q Women's Studies and Social Change
106e Women's Studies: Its Origin, Organization, and Prospects
284d Women's Studies on the Campuses

320i Women's Studies
341f New Feminism and Women's Studies
342g Women's Studies
342h Nuts and Bolts View of Women's Studies
368a Women's Studies: Its Focus, Idea Power, and Promise
368c Evaluating Women's Studies- Academic Theory and Practice
368k Future of Women's Studies

WONDER

52i Cotton Mather's "Wonders of the Invisible World": Some Metamorphoses of Salem Witchcraft
208nn Wonder Woman Revisited
277d Oh, the Wonder!

WOOD

8dd Nigger in the Woodpile
93c May Wood Simons: Party Theorist
111d Death in the Woods
112e Death in the Woods

WOODWARD

215w Emmeline Blanche Woodward Wells: "I Have Risen Triumphant"

WOOLF

90d Virginia Woolf's Criticism: A Polemical Preface
179u V. Woolf
357d Beyond Determinism: George Eliot and Virginia Woolf
361p Virginia Woolf and the Voices of Silence

WOOLSON

88p Constance Fenimore Woolson: First Novelist of Florida

WORD

8k Search for Words
9uu Love Is Just a Four-Letter Word
140p Women and Words in a Spanish Village
152t Last Word
157a Four-Letter Words CAN Hurt You
210a Preaching the Word
222ee The Word Is Love
230l Women and Words in a Spanish Village
283d Karl Barth's Theology of the Word of God: Or, How to Keep Women Silent and in Their Place

WORDSWORTH

179q D. Wordsworth

WORK

see also SOCIAL WORK; LABOR; EMPLOYMENT; JOB; CAREER; OCCUPATION

8y Can Men and Women Work Together?
15e Do Your Work
19l Long Road Home: Women's Work and Industrialization
21n Women Who Work for Wages
35l Women and Work in Cuba
37a Family and Married Women at Work
39a Maid of All Work or Departmental Sister-in-Law? The Faculty Wife Employed on Campus
39f Men, Women, and Work: Reflections on the Two-Person Career
39n Women, Work, and Wedlock: A Note on Female Marital Patterns in the U.S.
41b Women, Work and Protest in the Early Lowell Mills
41e Italian Women and Work: Experience and Perception
41f Italian-American Women in New York City, 1900-1950: Work and School
48f Economist's View of Women's Work
61a Demographic and Social Factors in Women's Work Lives
62h How Can Men and Women Work Together?
74g Home: Its Work and Influence
76k Work Inhibitions in Women
79x Works
84g Women and Production: A Critical Analysis of Some Sociological Theories of Women's Work
88m Women and Feminism in the Works of Rosario Castellanos
89b Women in the Work Force: Five Tables
92b Home From Home: Women's Philanthropic Work in the Nineteenth Century
92c Separation of Home and Work? Landladies and Lodgers in Nineteenth-Century England
96p I Go To Work
97k Woman's Work is Never Done
100d Men and Women at Work
105j News of Women and the Work of Men
115h Indian Women: Work, Power and Status
122k Thematic Exploration of the Works of Elena Garro
125b Domestic Problem: Work and Culture in the Household
126q Beyond "Kinder, Kuche, Kirche": Weimar Women in Politics and Work
126r Women, Work and the Social Order
127y A Work of Artifice
135d Women, Work and Conflict
140j Women at Home and at Work
140m Postwar Attitudes Toward Women and Work
153h Lady Who Does Her Own Work
166gg Factors Influencing Married Women's Actual or Planned Work Participation
171d Human Sex-Hormone Abnormalities Viewed from an Androgynous Perspective: A Reconsideration of the Work of John Money
181b Women's Work in Nineteenth-Century London: A Study of the Years 1820-50
184f Woman in the Marginalia of Gothic Manuscripts and Related Works
186c Sex Map of the Work World
194e Impact of Industrialization on Women's Work Roles in Northeast Brazil
196p Adolescents' Views of Women's Work-Role
196s Counselors View Women and Work: Accuracy of Information
196t Counselors' Attitudes Toward Women and Work

196aa Effect of Sex on College Admission, Work Evaluation, and Job Interviews
202i Women's Work in the Home
205f Sex-Role Stereotyping at Work
212r Work of Dorothy Arzner
213j Women, Work, and Power in Modern Yugoslavia
214q Life-Work of Sylvia Plath
249o Mastery of Work and the Mystery of Sex in a Guatemalan Village
257n Work of the Woman's Club
258d Home and Work: Women's Roles and the Transformation of Values
260r Women and Work
262p Woman in Philanthropy--Work of Anti-Slavery Women
262q Woman in Philanthropy--Work of the W.C.T.U.
262r Woman in Philanthropy--Work of the Red Cross Society
264p Clerical Work: The Female Occupation
264r Trust, Loyalty, and the Place of Women in the Informal Organization of Work
269b Women and Their Work Roles
275b Woman Question in the Early Work of Alfred Doblin
276b Women and Men in the World of Work: Present and Future
278m Work in the Lives of Married Women, 1900-1930
280v Chauvinism--At Work and at Home
281e Industrialization, Monopoly, Capitalism, and Women's Work in Guatemala
287a Looking Backward in Order to Look Forward: Women, Work and Social Values in America
287b Family and Work: The Social Life Cycle of Women
287c Home Work, Market Work, and the Allocation of Time
287d Women in Work Occupations
288cc Women at Work: Warners in the 1930s
288hh "Part-Time Work of a Domestic Slave," or Putting the Screws to Screwball Comedy
291d Work Aspirations of Women: False Leads and New Starts
291h Familial Constraints on Women's Work Roles
297x Sources of the Matrilineal Family System in the Works of Carl J.L. Almqvist
304f Women's Work in Montreal at the Beginning of the Century
304i Wages of Work: A Widening Gap Between Men and Women
309h Family Status and Female Work Participation
312f Women, Work and Trade Unionism
312i Women and Work in Ireland: The Present and Preparing for the Future
314c Female Dimension: Barriers to Effective Utilization of Women in the World of Work
314g Women in Work Force Post Better Records for Stability in Jobs
314j New Work Patterns--for Better Use of Womanpower
314p Humanizing the World of Work
318j Equal Pay for Equal Work?
327h Soviet Women in the Work Force and Professions
328k Part-Time Work
342j Women's Work is Never Done
351b Pregnancy, Motherhood and Work Activity
351d Work Attachment, Investments in Human Capital and the Earnings of Young Women
354a Women and Work: An Economic Appraisal
354f Issues in the Sociological Study of Women's Work
354h Girls' Socialization for Work
354p Domestic Service: Woman's Work

354r Women and Work: Policy Implications and Prospects for the Future
369c Dependency, Individuality, and Work
369e On Work
369h My Work and My Working-Class Father
369j Work of One's Own
369q What Counts as Work?
369s Notes from a Conversation on Art, Feminism, and Work
370c Commitment to Work
371e Women, Work, and Welfare: The Feminization of Poverty
371i Nontraditional Work Schedules for Women
375i One Child of One's Own: A Meaningful Digression within the Work(s)

WORK--FAMILY

116m Italian Mothers, American Daughters: Changes in Work and Family Roles
266ii Socio-Economic Context Of Sex And Power: A Study of Women, Work And Family Roles in Four Israeli Institutional Frameworks

WORK--FERTILITY

91a Women's Work and Fertility in Africa
91b Fertility, Women's Work, and Economic Class: A Case Study from Southeast Asia
91c Chinese Women at Work: Work Commitment and Fertility in the Asian Setting
91d Status of Women, Work and Fertility in India
91j Female Work Status and Fertility in Latin America
91k Relationship between Women's Work and Fertility: Some Methodological and Theoretical Issues
194b Women's Work and Fertility

WORKER

7a Northern Black Female Workers: Jacksonian Era
41d Women Workers in a Mid-Nineteenth-Century New York City Community
89cc Workers (Female) Arise!
89gg Women as Workers under Capitalism
92d Women Cotton Workers and the Suffrage Campaign: The Radical Suffragists in Lancashire, 1893-1914
92e Militancy and Acquiescence Amongst Women Workers
140h Did Rosie the Riveter Give Up Her Job? Women War Workers During and After World War II
141t Welfare Careers, Low Wage Workers and Sexism
166kk Married Professional Social Worker
176ff Worker, Mother, Housewife: Soviet Women Today
176gg Re-Evaluation of the Primary Role of the Communist Chinese Woman: The Homemaker or the Worker
182a Workers (and Mothers): Soviet Women Today
191r Women Workers in the Health Service Industry
191s Building a Hospital Workers' Union: Doris Turner, the Woman from 1199
206l Worker, Mother, Housewife: Soviet Woman Today
208v Run, Mama, Run: Women Workers in Elementary Readers
251y Supply and Demand for Women Workers
252c Women Workers and the Industrial Revolution
252aa Supply and Demand for Women Workers

271o Women Workers in Elementary Readers
297k Life and Labor of the Woman Textile Worker in Mexico City
297l Women as Workers: The Experience of the Puerto Rican Woman in the 1930's
328f Women Workers, Nontraditional Occupations and Full Employment
333b Role of Worker Expectancies in the Study of Employment Discrimination
344k Women's Incomes as Workers and Dependents
352e Women Workers and the Courts
352n Women Workers and the Trade Unions in Austria
352o APPENDIX: Texts Concerning Women Workers Adopted by the 60th Session of the International Labour Conference, 4-25 June 1975
354b Data on Women Workers, Past, Present, and Future
354q Housewives as Workers
364f Myths and Stereotypes: My Challenge to Black Women Cultural Workers

WORKING

6c Legislation and Litigation: Impact on Working Women
6f Working Black Women
42n Case Study of Technological and Social Change: The Washing Machine and the Working Wife
45g Policy Issues on Day Care: The Special Needs of Black Working Women
59i Working Wives and Family Income
70b Two Roles of Russian Working Women in an Urban Area
70c Interaction and Goal Attainment in Parisian Working Wives' Families
70f Urban Working Woman in the U.S.S.R.: An Historical Overview
89d Older Working Women
91f Fertility of Working Women in the United States: Historical Trends and Theoretical Perspectives
91i Differential Fertility by Working Status of Women in Japan
135e Employer's Attitude to Working Mothers
218e Unequal Partners in an Uneasy Alliance: Women and the Working Class in Imperial Germany
236i Interviews with Young Working Women in Seoul
244d Making of an Outcast Group: Prostitutes and Working Women in Nineteenth-Century Plymouth and Southampton
252v Problems of Married Working Women as Presented by Three Popular Working Women's Magazines
252x Working Wives: Their Contribution to Family Income
253f Working Women
254v Working in "A Man's World": The Woman Executive
256i Wages of Wrath: Women's Relationships in the Working World
265o Working Poor Women
267t Sex Discrimination Against the American Working Woman
272m Working and Parenting: The Male and Father Role
272n Transition from Parenting to Working and Parenting
284v Working Mother's Crises
288u Working with Hawks
295f The "Problem" and Problems of Working Women-- Toronto, 1896-1914
314u Women in Management: How Is It Working Out?
325t Working women in a Moroccan Village
327f Male Managers' Attitudes Toward Working Women
327g Sex Discrimination Against the American Working Woman
328q Working Women: European Experience and American Need
334k Irish Working Women in Troy
342aa Working Women's Association of Vancouver

344h New Approaches to Collective Power: Four Working Women's Organizations
352b Suggestions for the Advancement of Working Women
354k Working in Mid-Life
371a Women Working: Toward a New Society
371b Women Working: Historical Trends

WORKPLACE

8o Out in the Workplace
51o Criminality in the Workplace: A Comparison of Male and Female Offenders
143c Household as Workplace: Wives, Husbands, and Children
143e Redesigning the Domestic Workplace

WORLD

see also THIRD WORLD

4c Women in the Male World of Higher Education
9ii Seduced and Abandoned in the New World: The Fallen Woman in American Fiction
19r Something Old, Something New: Women Between the Two World Wars
52i Cotton Mather's "Wonders of the Invisible World": Some Metamorphoses of Salem Witchcraft
74r Fourth World Manifesto
108jj The Woman Who Lives Inside the World
110k Abuse of Eve by the New World Adam
116a Silent Half: "Le Contadine del Sud" Before The First World War
131c Changing Frenchwoman: Her Challenged World
132o Androgynous World
140i Women's Roles in World Change: What About the Family?
151n American Woman's Pre-World War I Freedom in Manners and Morals
166yy Women and Medicine in a Changing World
172e Dilemmas of Masculinity in a Changing World
175jj Fourth World Manifesto
186c Sex Map of the Work World
215q Dr. Romania Pratt Penrose: To Brave the World
220q World of Heroes
225a Mother and the Hospital: An Unfortunate Fit Between the Woman's Internal World and Some Hospital Practices
232c Investigation of the Religious and Judicial Character of Matriarchy in the Ancient World
240k "Combat in the Erogenous Zone": Women in the American Novel between the Two World Wars
254o Seduced and Abandoned in the New World: The Image of Woman In American Fiction
254v Working in "A Man's World": The Woman Executive
256i Wages of Wrath: Women's Relationships in the Working World
276b Women and Men in the World of Work: Present and Future
278o Women in a Man's World: The Female Engineers
280cc Reflections on the Changed World
289b Women and World Change
289f Women's Roles and the Great World Transformation
292t American Woman's Pre-World War I Freedom in Manners and Morals
293d Moslem World: Women Excluded from Development
294c Impact of the World Social Situation on Women

314c Female Dimension: Barriers to Effective Utilization of Women in the World of Work
314p Humanizing the World of Work
314x "He" and "She": Changing Language to Fit a Changing World
322g World of Women: Field Work in a Yoruba Community
324e Arab World
329l Women in the Muslim World
349k American Women in the Peace and Preparedness Movements in World War I
360l Female World of Love and Ritual: Relations Between Women in Nineteenth-Century America
360o American Woman's Pre-World War I Freedom in Manners and Morals
361j Women on the New World Languagescape
364e American Woman from 1900 to the First World War: A Profile
369m Writing in the Real World

WORLD WAR II

138h Women's Emancipation and the Recruitment of Women into the Labour Force in World War II
140h Did Rosie the Riveter Give Up Her Job? Women War Workers During and After World War II
349c American Women in the Shipyards During World War II

WORN

33s A Worn Path

WORSHIP

226j Mother Worship
278g Worship of Women in Courtly Love and Rock and Roll
283e Phallic Worship: The Ultimate Idolatry

WRATH

256i Wages of Wrath: Women's Relationships in the Working World

WRIGHT

68w Sir Almroth Wright's Case Against Woman Suffrage

WRINKLES

129c More Than Wrinkles

WRITER

see also AUTHOR; LITERATURE; individual writers

21j French Women Writers: A Problematic Perspective
23g Gender and Genre: Women as Historical Writers, 1400-1820
80b Women Writers in France: The "Initiators"
88v Alienation of the Woman Writer in "The Golden Notebook"
110g Silences: When Writers Don't Write
110t Value and Peril for Women of Reading Women Writers

122d Life and Early Literary Career of the Nineteenth-Century Colombian
      Writer, Coledad Acosta de Samper
122r Interview with Women Writers in Colombia
175pp Women Writers and the Female Experience
222h Caribbean Woman as Writer
254t Women Writers and the Double Standard
278aa Mother, Maiden, and the Marriage of Death: Women Writers and an
      Ancient Myth
288a Short Manual for an Aspiring Scenario Writer
308f Women as Writers in the 1920's and 1930's
320l Paradoxes and Dilemmas: Woman as Writer
363m No Important Woman Writer
364c Anger in Women Writers: Source of Inspiration or Inhibition?
369u One Out of Twelve: Women Who Are Writers in Our Century
375l Blood and Guts: The Tricky Problem of Being a Woman Writer in the
      Late Twentieth Century
375p Becoming a Writer

WRITING

  6m How to Eliminate Sexist Language From Your Writing: Some Guidelines
      for the Manager and Supervisor
 33i Unmailed, Unwritten Letters
 36c Identity and Expression: A Writing Course for Women
 71b "Brazileira": Images and Realities in Writings of Machado de Assis
      and Jorge Amado
 74d Life and Writings
 88y Need to Tell All: A Comparison of Historical and Modern Feminist
      "Confessional" Writing
 98k For a Restricted Thematics: Writing, Speech, and Difference in
      Madame Bovary
110a What Can a Heroine Do? Or Why Women Can't Write
110g Silences: When Writers Don't Write
110i Why Aren't We Writing About Ourselves?
117f Writing New KETUBOT
126d Historical Phallacies: Sexism in American Historical Writing
175rr Women's Private Writings: Anais Nin
208jj Sexism in History or, Writing Women's History is a Tricky Business
357h Writing as a Woman
365i Recent Writings of the Women's Movement
369m Writing in the Real World
375a Still Just Writing
375b Why I Write
375h Thoughts on Writing

WRONG

 75h Remedies for Wrongs: Updating Programs for Delinquent Girls
 85u What's Wrong with Rape
158t What's Wrong With Rape
180w Reparations to Wronged Groups
181k Rights and Wrongs of Women: Mary Wollstonecraft, Harriet Martineau,
      Simone de Beauvoir
261b Woman's Wrongs: A Counter-Irritant
284p Where Did It All Go Wrong?

WUNDERKIND

33d Wunderkind
83a Wunderkind

XYY

199v Aggression, Androgens, and the XYY Syndrome

YAAKOV

117n Bais Yaakov: A Historical Model for Jewish Feminists

YANOMAMA

194d Sexual Hierarchy Among the Yanomama

YEAR

see also INTERNATIONAL WOMEN'S YEAR

129w Those Endearing Young Charms: Fifty Years Later
135g Next Five Years: Projections and Policy Implications
153q Twenty Years at Hull-House
166hh College Women Seven Years After Graduation
173kk Women in the Middle Years: Conceptions and Misconceptions
175gg Notes From the Third Year
176v First Year of Bereavement
178g Divorce as a Moral Issue: A Hundred Years of Controversy
181b Women's Work in Nineteenth-Century London: A Study of the Years 1820-50
199l Emergence of Genital Awareness During the Second Year of Life
223d Marriage, Redundancy or Sin: The Painter's View of Women in the First Twenty-Five Years of Victoria's Reign
243j Women as a Minority Group: Twenty Years Later
250g Women as a Minority Group: Some Twenty Years Later
271s Teaching Female Studies: Looking Back Over Three Years
272f Single-Sex Education and Leadership: The Early Years of Simmons College
273s The First Year of My Life
284g Women's Status Fifty Years After the Vote
288q Years Have Not Been Kind to Lois Weber
289a Women's Year and Beyond
323e Early Years in the Trade Unions
360b Anne Hutchinson and Female Agitation During the Years of the Antinomian Turmoil, 1636-1640

YELLOW

83d Miss Yellow Eyes
113e The Yellow Wallpaper
153s The Yellow Wall-Paper
279g The Bride Comes to Yellow Sky

YI

236a Tradition: Women During the Yi Dynasty

YOKES

195d Cupid's Yokes; Or The Binding Forces of Conjugal Life

YOKO

249i Madam Yoko: Ruler of the Kpa Mende Confederacy
288z On Yoko Ono

YORUBA

213g Iyalode in the Traditional Yoruba Political System
317k Radical Yoruba Female Sexuality: The Witch and the Prostitute
322g World of Women: Field Work in a Yoruba Community

YOUTHFULNESS

45a Socialization and Education of Young Black Girls in Schools
76g Female Autonomy and Young Adult Women
96n When Co-Education Was Young
129e Does Youthfulness Equal Attractiveness?
129w Those Endearing Young Charms: Fifty Years Later
129x Young Women, Old Women, and Power
135c Effects of Day Care on Young Children
139d Younger Suffragists
142j For a Brilliant Young Woman Who Lost Her Mind
155t Contraception and Pregnancy: Experience of Young Unmarried Women in the United States
159v Of Womenkind, Old and Young
166r Career of Marriage? A Longitudinal Study of Able Young Women
215d Susa Young Gates: The Thirteenth Apostle
236i Interviews with Young Working Women in Seoul
272i Socialization and Education of Young Black Girls in School
280m Young Male Reacts
334e Young Ladies Academy of Philadelphia
351a Young Women's Decisions to Attend College: Desires, Expectations and Realizations
351c Sex Segregation in the Labor Market: An Analysis of Young College Women's Occupational Preferences
351d Work Attachment, Investments in Human Capital and the Earnings of Young Women
351e Migration of Young Families: An Economic Perspective

YUCATAN

293i Dilemma of Peasant Women: A View from a Village in Yucatan
372i Women in Yucatan

YUGOSLAVIA

213j Women, Work, and Power in Modern Yugoslavia
329r Yugoslav Women

ZAIRE

43c Women in Zaire: Disparate Status and Roles

297c African Women: Identity Crisis? Some Observations on Education and the Changing Role of Women in Sierra Leone and Zaire

ZAMBIA

317h Epidemiology of Spirit Possession among the Luvale of Zambia

ZAPOTEC

285k Sex Differences in the Incidence of Susto in Two Zapotec Pueblos: An Analysis of the Relationships between Sex Role Expectations and a Folk Illness

ZEALAND

63c Equal Pay for Women in Australia and New Zealand

ZEN

3h The Three Pillars of Zen

ZETTERLING

212p Mai Zetterling: Free Fall

ZEYDES

317j Bobbes and Zeydes: Old and New Roles for Elderly Jews

ZION

215v Louisa Lula Greene Richards: "Remember the Women of Zion"
292c Ornaments for the Daughters of Zion

ZONE

240k "Combat in the Erogenous Zone": Women in the American Novel between the Two World Wars

ZORA

88r Zora Neale Hurston
222p Influence of Voodoo on the Fiction of Zora Neale Hurston

ZOROASTRIAN

283o Zoroastrian Menstruation Taboos: A Woman's Studies Perspective

(none)

2h Conclusions
3a Growing Up Female
4u Summary and Prospects
6k What Do I Want to do Next?
8m How to Come Out Without Being Thrown Out
9x Take a Good Look at Our Problems
24v Over

24x Coming To
24ee Why Was It?
43a Perspectives and Introduction
48a New Reality
56f Afterword
61h Perspective and Issues
62f Perspectives
62k Where Are We Going Together?
64g Effecting Change
74i We Are Many
79y On Female Studies
83i O Yes
89h I Just Don't Know if I Can Make It
89aa Give and Take
89bbb Coming Out
93h Commentary
95e Ah Ao
97c Where are We Going?
99q Reflections
100a Women Then and Now
101g Epilogue
102k Change of Perspective
107g Woman as Derived Being
108hh Two Women
111c The Other Two
111e Women
111m SHE
112c The Other Two
113r Where Are You Going, Where Have You Been?
127k Where Is It Written?
129b Way It Was
131n Conclusion
132d Real Women
135a Current Situation
139l Now We Can Begin
140ll The End
142c Inside Outside
143a Introduction
152k I Always Wanted to Be Somebody
154b "Problem" Revisited
156m Epilogue
159d What Is Woman?
159s On Women
159gg Because You Are a Woman
161c The Women
163w Conclusion
167a Report
170v Conclusion: New Issues, New Approaches
188g Concerning Women
203k "Because You Are a Woman"
204n Epilogue
212e "Two or Three Things I Know About Her"
213o Overview
220c 6:27 PM
220i How Soon Can I Leave?
220aa Pure Will
233ww Changing Women

241h The Last Woman
257a Introductory
260f New Woman
262a Introduction
280d Way We Were--1949
281x
292j Woman
297ff Conclusions
301j Conclusions
306n Conclusions
314mm APPENDIX: Cases
318r Conclusions
321k Conclusion
329z Afterword: New Research Directions
331l Conclusions
332j Epilogue
356e Each Other
358h Reflective Thoughts
370j Concluding Remarks
375k What It is I Think I'm Doing Anyhow

4

CONTRIBUTOR INDEX

This section lists contributors to the indexed anthologies. Numbers refer to the book titles in ANTHOLOGIES: TABLES OF CONTENTS.

Abadan, Nermin 324
Abbott, Edith 12
Abbott, Sidney 254
Abel, Gene G. 235
Abraham, Karl 268
Abrahams, R.G. 193
Abrahams, Roger D. 274
Abram, A. 299
Abramson, Paul R. 155
Abubakari, Dara 28
Abutsu-Ni 31
Academy of Management Review 314
Accad, Evelyne 325
Aceto, T., Jr. 199
Acker, Joan 39 314 328 342 354
Ackley, Mary E. 124
Acosta, Ofelia Uribe de, see Uribe de Acosta, Ofelia
Acton, Harold 5
Adam, Helen 147
Adams, Abigail 87 237 319
Adams, Elsie 68 233
Adams, Emma Hildreth 124
Adams, Glenda 24 113
Adams, Hannah 96
Adams, Jeanette 118
Adams, Karen L. 264
Adams, Léonie 345
Adams, Lois 43
Adams, Margaret 254 365
Adams, Maurianne 17
Adams, Phyllis 89
Addams, Jane 9 44 87 153 187 234
Addis, Patricia 246
Addison, J.T. 63
Adler, Alfred 170
Adler, Freda 51
Adler, Lucile 109
Adler, Rachel 117
Adler, Shane 18
Adnan, Etel 150
Adrian, Marlene 286
Agbasegbe, Bamidele Ade 140
Ager, Lynn Price 372
Agopian, Michael W. 94
Aguiar, Neuma 194
Agus, Arlene 117
Ahdab-Yehia, May 91 281
Ahern, Emily M. 308
Ahlum, Carol 4 208
Ahmed, Imtiaz 114
Ahmed, Shereen Aziz 324
Ahsen, Akhter 330
Aichinger, Ilse 102
Aidoo, Ama Ata 95
Aiyappan, Parvathi 114
Akazome Emon 31
Åkesson, Sonja 150
Akhmadulina, Bella 34 150
Akhmatova, Anna 34 150
Akiko, Baba 31
Akiko, Yosano 31
al-Malā'ikah, Nāzik 150
al-Sayyid, Marsot Afaf Lutfi, see Marsot, Afaf Lutfi al-Sayyid
Alberro, Ana 320
Albert, Ethel M. 164 186 260 338
Albert, Janice 13
Albert, Marge 57
Albrecht, Sandy 314
Albright, Cynthia Hovden 246
Alcott, Louisa May 72 108 179
Alcott, William 187
Aldrich, Anita 358
Aleandri, Emilese 116
Alexander, Ralph A. 327
Alexander, Sally 181
Alexander, Tom 284
Alexandrova, Vera 324
Alilkatuktuk, Jeela 347
Alinder, Gary 8
Allen, Bettie Scott 20
Allen, Carolyn 361
Allen, Christine Garside 159
Allen, David 89
Allen, Dorothy 286
Allen, Judith Van, see Van Allen, Judith
Allen, Minerva 347
Allen, Pamela 175
Allen, Priscilla 17
Allen, Robert Thomas 305
Allen, Sarah A. 72
Allentuck, Marcia 247
Allingham, M. 103
Allman, James 367
Almagor, U. 193
Almquist, Elizabeth M. 166 251 264 354
Alonso, Dora 95
Alper, Thelma G. 266
Alpert, Dee Estelle 314
Alta 97 109 136 137 147 254
Altman, Addie R. 128
Alurista 242
Amatniek, Kathie 237
Ames, Bernice 345
Amir, Menachem 94
Anderson, Barbara Gallatin 131
Anderson, Dawn Holt 110
Anderson, Lavina Fielding 215
Anderson, Margaret 88
Anderson, Paul S. 166
Anderson, Scarvia B. 197

Anderson, Sherwood 81 111 112
Anderson, Susan Janice 16
Andresen, Sophia de Mello Breyner, see Mello Breyner Andreson, Sophia de
Andrews, John 12
Angelou, Maya 109 118 245 248
Anger, Jane 32
Anghelaki-Rooke, Katerina 150
Anglo, Sydney 52
Angoulême, Marguerite of, see Marguerite of Angoulême
Angress, Ruth K. 80
Angrist, Shirley S. 166 176
Annable, James E., Jr. 333
Anthony-Welch, L. 222
Anthony, Susan B. 9 44 72 87 139 234 237
Antin, Eleanor 15
Antin, Mary 257
Antonucci, Toni 272
Apandaye, Eintou 222
Applegarth, Adrienne 76
Applewhite, Harriet Branson 349
Apuleius 233
Aquinas, Thomas 107 158 159 299
Aravamudan, Gita 114
Archer, John 67 205
Ardener, Edwin 154
Ardener, Shirley 53 154
Arditi, R.R. 51
Arditti, Rita 191
Ariès, Philippe 162
Aristophanes 233 310
Aristotle 107 158 159 203 231 299
Arizpe, Lourdes 281
Arkin, William 371
Armitage, Kay 288
Arnold, Katherine 225
Arnold, Lila 109
Arnold, Marigene 317
Arnow, Harriette 347
Aronoff, Joel 251
Aronson, Elliot 155
Arrow, Kenneth 291
Arthur, Marilyn 19
Arthur, T.S. 187
Arthur, William B. 233
Asch, Sholem 353
Ascham, Roger 299
Ashford, Serena Elizabeth 12
Ashley, Jessie 234
Ashton-Warner, Sylvia 32 179
Askew, Anne 345
Askins, John 13
Aslan, Odette 150
Assis, J.M. de Machado de, see Machado de Assis, J.M. de
Astin, Alexander W. 106
Astin, Helen S. 4 106 166 267
Aswad, Barbara C. 325
Atchley, Robert C. 129
Atkinson, Dorothy 318
Atkinson, Paul 145
Atkinson, Ti-Grace 89 159
Attik, Mririda n'Ait 150
Atwood, Margaret 34 109 136 147 168 245 248 305 320 343 345
Auchincloss, Louis 192
Auden, W.H. 111 112
Auerbach, Nina 214 278
Augustine 107 159
Augustine, Jane 220
Austen, Jane 119 339
Austin, George 187
Austin, Mary 345 346
Austin, Mary Hunter 10 226
Aventurin, Elzéa 352
Avery, William P. 163
Aviel, JoAnn 316
Awe, Bolanle 213 281
Axelrod, Rise B. 88
Axelrod, Susan 147
Ayad, Mohamed 367
Azzario, Esther A. 122
Babchuk, Nicholas 252
Babcox, Deborah 89 127
Babey-Brooke, Anna M. 297
Bacdayan, Albert S. 213
Bach, George R. 330
Bachmann, Ingeborg 102
Bachofen, Johann Jakob 232
Bachtold, Louise M. 316
Backberger, Barbro 150
Bacon, Francis 107
Bacon, Margaret K. 176 198
Baer, Barbara 12
Baez, Joan 347
Bagley, Sarah G. 69
Bagnold, Enid 245
Bahr, Stephen J. 370
Bailey, Margaret M. 22 266 267
Baillie, Joanna 345
Bailyn, Lotte 166 176 253 333
Baines, Barbara 229
Bainton, Roland H. 23
Baird, Irene 305
Baker, Deborah 191
Baker, Elizabeth C. 15
Baker, Ella 28
Baker, Robert 157 158
Baker, Sally Hillsman 354
Baker, Susan W. 199

Bakke, Wight 12
Baldwin, Maria L. 28
Balkan, Sheila 18
Ballantyne, Sheila 353
Ballou, Mary 124
Balogun, Barbra (Jackson) 237
Balsdon, J.P.V.D. 299
Bambara, Toni Cade 24 29 113 118 245 353 364 375
Bambara, Toni Cade, see also Cade, Toni
Bamberger, Joan 249
Bamford, Julian 8
Bandura, Albert 198
Banerjee, Maria 80
Banks, Barbara 118 118
Banner, Lois 364
Banner, William A. 217
Banta, Martha 240
Banus, Maria 150
Baracks, Barbara 113
Barasch, F.K. 180
Barbauld, Anna Laetitia 79
Barber, Patricia 17
Barber, Virginia 341
Barca, Fanny Calderon de la, see Calderon de la Barca, Fanny
Bardwick, Judith M. 11 73 82 140 141 176 209 250 254 330
Barfield, Ashton 201
Barglow, Peter 76
Barker-Benfield, G.J. 191
Barker, A.L. 356
Barker, Diana 297
Barker, Mildred 298
Barmack, Joseph E. 200
Barnard, Lady Ann 242
Barnes, Ann B. 211
Barnes, Annette 17
Barnes, Djuna 108
Barnes, Julians 345
Barnett, Evelyn Brooks 7
Barnett, Ida B. Wells 28
Barnett, Rosalind C. 173
Barney, Susan Hammond 262
Barnhart, Joseph E. 85
Barnhart, Mary Ann 85
Barnouw, Dagmar 47
Barr, R. 241
Barrett, Carol J. 173
Barrett, Jane 307
Barrett, Michèle 348
Barrett, Nancy Smith 251 59 287
Barron, R.D. 55
Barros, Silvia 122
Barrows, Anita 147
Barrows, Anna 44
Barry, Herbert 176 198
Barry, Kathleen 271
Barry, Kathy 74
Barry, Leonora 12 72
Bart, Pauline 39 77 117 176 211 254 264 264 332 99
Bartell, Gilbert D. 155
Barthelme, Donald 300
Bartky, Sandra Lee 85 158
Bartlett, Elisha 336
Barton, Clara 262
Barton, Stephen 143
Baruch, Grace K. 13 173 173
Barwick, Diane E. 366
Basen, Neil K. 93
Bashkirtseff, Marie 179
Basinger, Jeanine 288
Bass, Bernard M. 327
Bass, Charlotta 28
Bass, Dorothy C. 337
Bass, Ellen 137 147 224
Bass, Madeline 239 347
Bastidas Pyucahua, Micaela 313
Basu, Aparna 115
Bates, Daisy 28
Bates, Mrs. D.B. 124
Bates, Myrtle 118
Bates, Octavia W. 234
Bates, Ülkü Ü. 325
Batinich, Mary Ellen Mancina 116
Battcock, Marjorie 374
Battey, Mary S. 72
Battin, M. Pabst 24
Baude, Annika 37
Baumann, Marie 219
Baũml, Franz H. 184
Baumrin, Bernard H. 157
Baumrind, Diana 271
Baxandall, Rosalyn F. 181 264 265
Baxter, Bernice K. 266
Baxter, Christopher 52
Baxter, P.T. 193
Bayat-Philipp, Mangol 325
Bayer, Alan E. 4 267
Bayles, Michael D. 157 180
Baym, Nina 110 240
Beach, Frank A. 296
Beach, Ruth 301
Beal, Frances M. 74 127 142 216 292 26
Beam, Amy 272
Bean, Joan P. 22 156
Beards, Virginia K. 47
Beardsley, Elizabeth 85 282
Beasley, Ina M. 294
Beattie, Ann 24 113 220
Beauchamp, Tom L. 217

Beaulieu, Sarah E. 319
Beauvais, Phyllis 109 147
Beauvoir, Simone de 81 107 127 132 159 203 288
Bebel, August 87
Beck, Aaron T. 330
Beck, Lois 325
Becker, H. 199
Becker, Judith V. 235
Bedell, Madelon 203
Beecher, Catharine 60 72 153 187 292 234
Beecher, Maureen Ursenbach 215
Beechey, Veronica 84
Beer, Gillian 357
Behn, Aphra 32 34 79 189 242 245 345 374
Behrins, Harriet F. 124
Belkin, Madeline 127
Bell, Barbara Currier 90
Bell, Carolyn Shaw 59 251 326 333 354
Bell, Colin 55
Bell, Diane 270
Bell, Inge Powell 264 264
Bell, Robert Alvin 222
Bell, Roseann P. 222
Belote, Betsy 77
Bem, Daryl J. 77 89 186 208
Bem, Sandra L. 22 77 89 186 208 266
Bender, Estelle P. 199
Benedek, Therese 176
Benedek, Thomas G. 185
Benedict, Ruth 179 179
Benet, James 105
Bengelsdorf, Carollee 35
Bengis, Ingrid 375
Benglis, Lynda 15
Benham, Lee 202
Benjamin, Jessica 98
Benkovitz, Miriam J. 255
Bennett, David H. 178
Benokraitis, Nijole V. 371
Benson, Mary Sumner 259
Benson, Sally 111 112
Benston, Margaret 89 97 127 139 186 237 252
Bentley, P. 103
Benz, Margaret G. 324
Beresford-Howe, Constance 305
Berg, Karin Westman 297
Berg, Stephen 3
Bergé, Carol 108 136
Berger, Iris 302
Berger, Peter 251 252
Berger, Ronald J. 18
Bergman, Jane 13 197
Bergmann, Barbara R. 333
Berk, Sarah Fenstermaker 143 371
Berkeley Men's Center 77
Berkeley-Oakland Women's Union 35
Berkeley, Ellen Perry 143
Berkeley, Joyce Maupin 89
Berkin, Carol Ruth 334
Berkman, Sylvia 298
Berkon, Susan Fondiler 303
Berlandt, Konstantin 8
Berman, Edgar F. 62
Berman, Saul 117
Bermant, Gordon 73 176
Bernadine, Sister 118
Bernard, Jessie 11 22 39 149 209 254 264 291 294
Bernard, Shirley 265
Bernardo, Aldo S. 184
Berndt, Catherine H. 366
Bernikow, Louise 152
Bernstein, Barbara 288
Bernstein, Gail Lee 306
Bernstein, Judi 132
Berocochea, John E. 51
Berson, Ginny 123
Best, Raphaela 331
Beteille, Andre 114
Bethune, Mary McLeod 28
Bettelheim, Bruno 3 89 228
Betts, Doris 24 111 245 273 279
Betts, Ellen 12
Bhatty, Zarina 115 309
Bibring, Grete L. 296
Biddle, Ellen McGowan 124
Bielli, Carla 329
Bienen, Lee 251
Biermann, Leonard J. 49
Billson, Marcus K. 359
Bingham, Sallie 220
Bingham, William C. 196
Bird, Caroline 186 233 238 256 260 280 341 362
Bird, Joseph W. 62
Bird, Lois F. 62
Bird, Phyllis 177
Birdwhistell, Ray L. 198
Birnbaum, Judith Abelew 267
Birns, Beverly 18
Bishop, Nadean 264
Bishop, Sharon 158
Biskind, Peter 288
Bita, Lili 137
Bittenbender, Ada M. 262
Bittker, Boris 180
Bixby-Smith, Sarah 124
Blaché, Alice Guy 288

Blachman, Morris J. 194
Black Women's Liberation Group, Mt. Vernon, N.Y. 216
Black, Virginia 180
Blackburn, Regina 359
Blackstone, Tessa 181
Blackstone, William T. 217
Blackwell, Alice Stone 9 234 237
Blackwell, Antoinette Brown 187 234
Blackwell, Elizabeth 9 72 187 237 319
Blackwell, Henry B. 9 44 234 257
Blair, Emily Newell 234
Blais, Marie-Claire 305
Blake, Judith 2
Blake, Kathryn A. 11
Blake, William 81 112 242
Blanchard, Phyllis 226
Blandiana, Ana 150
Blankenship, W.C. 166
Blatch, Harriot Stanton 44 234
Blattner, H.W. 3
Blau, Francine D. 264 265 291 354
Blaxall, Martha 291
Bleier, Ruth H. 21 173
Blind, Mathilde 189 345
Blinderman, Charles 110
Bliss, W.D.P. 12
Block, Alan 51
Block, Jeanne Humphrey 22
Blood, Kathryn 12
Bloom, Lynn Z. 88 359
Bloomer, Amelia 9
Bloor, Ella Reeve 74
Blum, Gerald S. 200
Blum, Harold P. 76
Blum, Larry 158 279
Blumberg, Grace Ganz 328
Blumberg, Rae Lesser 21 293 329
Blumenthal, Marcia 24
Blyth, Myrna 284
Boals, Kay 126 316
Bock, E. Wilbur 166 166
Bodine, Ann 120 219
Bogan, Louise 34 109 147 189 345
Bogdan, Janet 272
Boggs, Grace Lee 26
Boggs, Roy A. 185
Bogin, Ruth 27
Bohannan, Paul 176
Bohmer, Carol 94 94
Bok, Edward 319
Bolden, Dorothy 28
Boleyn, Anne, Queen of England 242 345
Bolt, Merry 264 264
Bolton, Brenda M. 315
Bombal, Maria-Luisa 273
Bonaparte, Marie 268 169
Bond, Jean Carey 26
Bond, N.S. 241
Boneparth, Ellen 368
Bonger, William A. 51
Bonnett, Gail 342
Bonnin, Gertrude 96
Bonosaro, Carol A. 49
Boodson, Alison 374
Boone, Margaret S. 372
Booth, Pamela 191
Borgese, Elisabeth Mann 329
Borker, Ruth 317
Bornstein, Diane 361
Boroff, David 166
Boscawen, Frances Glanville 79
Bose, Ashish 114
Bose, Christine 328
Boserup, Ester 114
Boskind-Lodahl, Marlene 173
Bosmajian, Haig 207
Bosselman, Beulah Chamberlain 176
Bossen, Laurel 285
Boucher, Richard B. 94
Boucher, Sandy 113
Boulding, Elise 291 371
Boulding, Kenneth 291
Boulting, William 299
Bourguignon, Erika 372
Boutelle, Sara 303
Bowditch, William I. 319
Bowen, Elizabeth 33 34 273 277 279
Bowles, Ada C. 262
Bowles, Eva D. 28 28
Bowles, Jane 273
Bowman, Barbara T. 156
Bowman, William 72
Boxer, Marilyn J. 218
Boxhill, Bernard 180
Boyd, Melba Joyce 222
Boyd, Mrs. Orsemus Bronson 124
Boyd, Rosamonde Ramsay 294
Boye, Karin 150
Boyle, Kay 83 111 112 147 277 345
Bozeman, Barry 163
Braby, Maud Churton 68
Brack, Datha Clapper 332
Brackett, Leigh 134 288
Bradbury, Malcolm 47
Bradley, Katharine, see Field, Michael
Bradley, Marion Zimmer 340
Bradley, Martha 319

Bradstreet, Anne 34 189 234 242 345 374
Brady, Anne Hazlewood 239
Bragger, Jeannette 80
Braggin, Mary, see Vetterling-Braggin, Mary
Brain, James L. 302
Bram, Susan 141
Bramsen, Michèle Bo 293
Branca, Patricia 42
Branch, Anna Hempstead 374
Brandwein, Ruth A. 251
Bransfield, Christine Towne 329
Brant, Alice 313
Brault, Gerard J. 184
Braxton, Jodi 239
Bray, Douglas W. 314
Bread and Roses 87
Brecher, Edward 233
Brecher, Ruth 233
Brée, Germaine 21 80
Breen, Dana 225
Brehon, Helen Cade 26
Breit, Etta Bender 173
Bremmer, William J. 173
Brend, Ruth M. 120
Brent, Linda 187
Brenton, Myron 260
Brereton, Jane 345
Brereton, Virginia Lieson 337
Breslin, James E. 359
Bretteville, Sheila Levrant de, see Levrant de Bretteville, Sheila
Brews, Margery 345
Brewster, Elizabeth 136 305
Bridenthal, Renate 19 126
Bridges, Amy 35
Briggs, Jean 131 322
Briggs, Norma 328
Brigham, Besmilr 109 168
Bright, Richard 280
Briscoe, Anne M. 101
Briscoe, Mary Louise 233
Brito, Patricia K. 351
Britton, Margaret 176
Britton, Maria Ann 216
Broach, Glen T. 174
Brodie, H.K.H. 199
Brodsky, Annette M. 75 77 173
Brody, Baruch A. 157
Brody, Linda 204
Bronfenbrenner, Urie 182
Brontë, Anne 345
Brontë, Charlotte 108 345 374
Brontë, Emily 81 119 242 345 374
Brooks-Gunn, Jeanne 171
Brooks, Angie E. 294
Brooks, George E. Jr. 302
Brooks, Gwendolyn 29 33 34 81 109 111 118 147 168 233 248 345 374
Brooks, Louise 288
Brophy, Brigid 139
Broverman, Donald M. 155 171 176 250 267
Broverman, Inge K. 155 176 208 250 267
Brown, Anna Gordon 345
Brown, Antoinette 44
Brown, Camie Lou 342
Brown, Carol A. 191 251
Brown, Carole 26
Brown, Charlotte Hawkins 28
Brown, Cheryl L. 88
Brown, Jean Collier 28
Brown, Joan 228
Brown, Judith K. 201 230 237 251 285
Brown, Julia M. 21
Brown, Karla J.H. 342
Brown, Lyvia Morgan 265
Brown, Margery Finn 113
Brown, Olympia 44 234 257
Brown, Prudence 99 140
Brown, Raymond E. 258
Brown, Richard 55
Brown, Rita Mae 8 89 109 123 142 147 216 239
Brown, Rosellen 24 113 353
Brown, Rosemary 320
Brown, Susan E. 230 270 297
Browne, F.W. Stella 66
Browning, Elizabeth Barrett 34 189 242 245 345 363 374
Browning, Robert 242
Brownmiller, Susan 175
Broxon, Mildred Downey 16
Bruce, Margaret K. 294
Brun-Gulbrandsen, Sverre 37
Bruteau, Beatrice 283
Bryant, J.A., Jr. 192
Bryce, Herrington J. 163
Bryden, M.P. 204
Buchan, William 160
Buckler, Ernest 305
Bucklew, Reba M. 166
Buckley, J.E. 63
Buckner, Janis 219
Budapest, Zsuzsanna E. 263
Budoff, Penny W. 311
Buechler, Judith-Maria Hess 20
Buenaventura-Posso, Elisa 270
Buenker, John D. 93
Buhle, Mari Jo 93 97 126

Bujra, Janet M. 297 350
Bull, Jenny 13
Bullard, Laura Curtis 257
Bullock, Charles S., III 163 174
Bunch-Weeks, Charlotte, see Bunch, Charlotte
Bunch, Charlotte 89 123 127 142
Bunster, Ximena 194 281
Bunting, Mary I. 234 301
Burcart, Janet 342
Burden, Jean 345
Burger, Laura A. 21
Burgess-Olsen, Vicky 215
Burgess, Ann Wolbert 94
Burgher, Mary 222
Burgos, Julia de 150
Burke, Carolyn G. 98
Burke, N. Peggy 64
Burke, Peter 52
Burke, Yvonne Braithwaite 344
Burkett, Elinor C. 121
Burkhardt, Jacob 299
Burkhardt, Karthryn Watterson 51
Burlage, Dorothy D. 210
Burnham, Dorothy C. 101
Burns, Robert 242
Burr, Elizabeth 208
Burrell, Barbara 163
Burris, Barbara 74 175
Burroughs, Nannie 28
Burroway, Janet 375
Burstein, Karen 344
Burstyn, Joan 360 272
Burtle, Vasanti 330
Burton, Annie Louise 27
Burton, Roger V. 198
Busby, Linda J. 140
Buskirk, E.R. 286
Bussy, Dorothy 108
Bustos, Joyce Gissi 194
Butler, Charles 260
Butler, Josephine 66
Butler, Julius C. 155 155
Butler, Lynne 109
Butler, Richard W. 143
Butler, Sister Mary Marguerite 141
Byington, Margaret 12
Cabral, Olga 239 245
Cade, Toni 26
Cade, Toni, see also Bambara, Toni Cade
Cain, Joan 80
Calderon de la Barca, Fanny 313
Caldwell, Lesley 84
California State Senate Committee 12
Calisher, Hortense 111 245
Callaghan, James 323
Callaghan, Morley 305
Callan, Hilary 53 154
Callaway, Barbara J. 329
Callaway, Helen 53
Callisher, Hortense 363
Camarano, Chris 127
Cameron, Marcia 146
Cameron, Mary Owen 51
Campbell, Angus 140
Campbell, David P. 166
Campbell, Jean W. 4
Campion, Thomas 242
Candy, Sandra E. Gibbs 129
Cannon, Connie Duncan 215
Cannon, Lori Shpunt 246
Cannon, Rick 246
Cantarow, Ellen 186
Cantor, Aviva 263
Cantor, Muriel S. 105
Cantwell, Robert 128
Caplan, Pat 297
Caplan, Patricia 350
Cappellanus, Andreas 299
Carberry, Ethna 345
Carcopino, Jerome 299
Carden, Patricia 182
Cardozo-Freeman, Inez 274
Careaga, Formica de 324
Carey, Addison, Jr. 163
Carey, Lady Elizabeth 242 345
Carey, Mathew 319
Cari, Teresa 313
Carlberg, Eileen 306
Carlson, Jean Marie Furniss 140
Carlson, Rae 267
Carlsson, May-Britt 276
Caroutch, Yvonne 46
Carpenter, Liz 344
Carr, Emily 179
Carr, Timothy J. 351
Carrier, Constance 34 345
Carroll, Anne Ella 237
Carroll, Berenice A. 126 183
Carroll, Constance M. 4
Carroll, Elizabeth 258
Carruthers, Iva E. 222
Carsman, Evaline P. 129
Carson, Barbara Harrell 17 17
Carson, Julie 278
Carson, Mrs. William J. 234
Carstairs, G. Morris 114
Carter-Saltzman, Louise 204
Carter, Dianne K. 246
Carter, Norene 337
Carter, Rose 306

Cary, Elizabeth, Viscountess Falkland 79
Cary, Joyce 277
Cary, Mary Ann Shadd 28
Casals, Lourdes 349 281
Casanova-Sanchez, Olga 122
Casey, Kathleen 126 335
Casey, Lillian S. 141
Casterline, Gail Farr 215
Castoro, Rosemarie 15
Cater, Libby A. 276
Cather, Willa 34 220 245 353 373
Cathey, Suki 6
Cato 231
Cato, Nancy 345
Catt, Carrie Chapman 44 87 234 237 257 313
Cavell, Marcia 268
Cavendish, Margaret, Duchess of Newcastle 34 345 79
Cavior, Helene Enid 75
Cavior, Norman 75
Cecchini, Rose Marie 306
Celler, Emanuel 228
Cellini, Leo 116
Centers, Richard 176
Centlivre, Susannah 79
Ch'ien, T'ao 148
Ch'iu, Chin 148
Cha, Jae-Ho 236
Chafe, William H. 287
Chahil, Renu 91
Chamberlain, Brenda 345
Chambers, Clarke A. 151
Chambers, Jane 109
Chamie, Mary 281
Chan Wang, Bee-Lan, see Wang, Bee-Lan Chan
Chaney, Elsa M. 71 194 297 316
Chang, Diana 34
Chang, Wên-Chi 148
Channing, Walter 130
Chao, Luan-Luan 148
Chapman, J. Brad 49 314
Chapman, Jane Roberts 59 235 331
Chapman, Janet G. 318
Chapman, Karen C. 222
Chappell, Duncan 94 94
Charney, Pam 237
Chase-Lansdale, Lindsay 18
Chase, Lucy 72
Chasin, Helen 109 147 224
Chasseguet-Smirgel, Janine 78
Chatelin, Adele A. 137
Chaton, Jeanne Henriette 294
Chattopadhyay, Kamaladevi 114
Chatty, Dawn 325
Chaucer, Geoffrey 242 299
Cheda, Sherrill 304
Chedid, Andrée 46
Cheek, Alison M. 269
Cheever, John 277
Chekhov, Anton 108 111 112 277 279 339
Cheney, Ednah Dow 262
Cheng, Min 148 150
Cherniss, Cary 22
Cherpak, Evelyn 121
Cherry, Louise 120
Cherry, Rona 256
Chertov, Eva 86
Chesler, Phyllis 73 77 250 254 265
Chesnut, Mary Boykin 179 187
Chesnutt, Charles Waddell 279
Chester, Laura 109 347
Chicago Gay People's Legal Committee 8
Chie, Shindō 31
Chigetsu-Ni, Kawai 31
Child, Irvin L. 176 198
Child, Lydia Maria 72 153 232
Childers, Erskine 293
Childress, Alice 111 118 144 161 373
Childs, E.K. 77
Chilman, Catherine S. 62
Chimako, Tada 31
Chin, Ai-li S. 324
Chinchilla, Norma S. 281
Chine-Jo 31
Chio, Nakamura 31
Chiplin, B. 63
Chisholm, Shirley 9 28 228 238
Chitnis, Suma 309
Chiyo-Ni, Fukuda 31
Chodoff, Paul 170
Chodorow, Nancy 35 98 249 254
Chojnacki, Stanley 315
Chong, Soo-Pyun 252
Chopin, Kate 10 32 34 108 111 187 242 279 347
Christ, Carol 117 244 280 283 263
Christensen, Harold T. 155
Christian Science Monitor 284
Christie, Agatha 103
Christman, Elizabeth 12
Chu, Chung-Hsien 148
Chu, Shu-Chên 148
Chudleigh, Lady Mary Lee 242
Chung, Bom-Mo 236
Chung, Ling 148
Chuo, Wen-Chün 148
Church, Peggy Pond 346

Churchill, Caroline N. 124
Churchill, Charles W. 324
Chylińska, Kamila 294
Ciardi, John 81
Cicco, Pier Giorgio Di, see Di Cicco, Pier Giorgio 231
Cichocki, Mary K. 143
Cille, Ann du 118
Cisler, Lucinda 97 175 216 238
Claflin, Tennessee 87 234
Claiborne, Sybil 24
Clapsaddle, Carol N. 117
Clarenbach, Kathryn F. 21
Clark, Alexander L. 155
Clark, Cal 174
Clark, Janet 174
Clark, Joanna 26 176
Clark, Septima Poinsetta 28
Clark, Shirley Merritt 176 267
Clark, Stuart 52
Clark, Sue Ainslie 12
Clarke, Anne 171
Clarke, Peter 166
Clarke, Shirley 288
Clarkson, Frank E. 155 176 250 267
Clawson, Augusta 12
Clay, Laura 237
Cleary, T.A. 197
Cleaver, Eldridge 3
Cleckner, Patricia 317
Cleinhans, Chuck 212
Clement, Jacqueline 272
Clemmons, Carole Gregory 147
Clerbout, Marguerite 150
Cless, Elizabeth L. 260
Cleveland, Grover 234 257
Clifford, Margaret M. 196 197
Clifton, Lucille 72 111 118 147 245 345
Clignet, Remi 281
Clinton, Elizabeth, Countess of Lincoln 79
Clower, Virginia L. 76
Clusen, Ruth C. 344
Coates, Susan 199
Cobb, Kenneth A. 94 94
Cobbs, Price M. 233
Coburn, Judi 295
Codere, Helen 322
Coe, Emma R. 234
Cohen, Carl 157
Cohen, Charlotte Bonny 216
Cohen, Donna 204
Cohen, Gaynor 350
Cohen, Howard 85
Cohen, Lois K. 166
Cohen, Mabel Blake 170 252
Cohen, Mary 17
Cohen, Miriam 41 140 141
Cohen, Murray L. 94
Cohen, Roberta S. 163
Cohen, Rose 72
Cohen, Selma Jeanne 190
Cohen, Stephen M. 117
Cohn, Fannia M. 319
Coker, Robert E., Jr. 166
Colby, Clara Bewick 44
Cole, Doris 303
Cole, G.D.H. 50
Cole, Johnnetta B. 43
Cole, M. 50
Cole, Nancy S. 196 266
Colecchia, Francesca 116
Coleman, Emily 315
Coleman, James 196
Coleridge, Mary Elizabeth 242 345 374
Coleridge, Samuel 81
Coles, Robert 268
Colette 34 83 108 111 112 245 288
Collier, James Lincoln 280
Collier, Jane Fishburne 249 321
Collins, Anne 345 374
Collins, Emily 237
Collins, Jean 341
Collins, Jennie 69
Collins, Joseph 96 226
Collins, Judy 347
Collins, Margery 282
Collins, Martha 111
Collins, Sheila 256 263
Collins, Virginia E.Y., see Abubakari, Dara
Colter, Cyrus 277
Colton, Jennifer 12
Colwin, Laurie 24
Combahee River Collective 35
Comfort, Alex 89
Comini, Alessandra 247
Cominos, Peter T. 223
Commissioner's Task Force on the Impact of Office of Education Programs on Women 208
Committee to Eliminate Sexual Discrimination in the Public Schools 208
Compton, Henria Packer 124
Condorcet, Marquis de 232
Cone, Helen Grey 262
Congreve, William 242
Conlin, Roxanne Barton 326
Connell, Evan S., Jr. 3
Connolly, John L., Jr. 247

Connolly, Olga 152 358
Conoley, Jane Close 272
Constantia, see Murray, Judith
Constantinides, Pamela 350
Constantinople, Anne 22 266
Conway, Jill 223 253
Conway, M. Margaret 174 344
Cook, Alice H. 294 301 328
Cook, Ann 26
Cook, Beverly Blair 321
Cook, Bruce 5
Cook, Pam 212
Cooke, Joanne 142
Cooke, Rose Terry 242
Coolbrith, Ina 346
Cooley, Winnifred Harper 139
Cools, Anne 143
Coombs, Robert H. 200
Cooper, Anna Julia 27 28
Cooper, Arvazine Angeline 104
Cooper, Edith 345
Cooper, H.H.A. 51
Cooper, Helen 214
Cooper, Jane 109 147
Coppin, Frances Jackson 27 28
Corbett, Sherry L. 129
Corbin, Alice 346
Córdova, Jeanne 8
Cornelia 27
Cornell, Magda 289
Cornillon, John 110
Cornillon, Susan Koppelman 110
Cornuelle, Richard C. 62
Cornwall, Rebecca Foster 215
Cornwell, Regina 212
Corpi, Lucha 150
Corrain, Donncha Ò, see Ò Corrain, Donncha
Cortez, Jayne 118
Coşar, Fatma Mansur 325
Cosentino, Christine 275
Coss, Clare 98
Cossey, Beatrice Abel 45 45
Costain, Anne N. 174 344
Costantini, Edmond 163
Costantino, Anthony 246
Coughlin, R.J. 221
Coulson, Noel 325
Council for University Women's Progress at the University of Minnesota 196
Couturiér, Edith 121
Covington, Francee 26
Covintree, Winifred 137
Cowan, L.J. 180
Cowan, Ruth Schwartz 42
Cowley, Joyce 12 238
Cox, Archibald 180
Cox, Carol 136
Cox, Ida 374
Cox, Martha 172
Cox, Rachel Dunaway 176 182
Cox, Roger 172
Craddock, Alan E. 251
Craddock, Ida C. 195
Craft, Ellen 27 28
Craik, Kenneth H. 163
Crain, Irving J. 170
Cran, Marion 165
Crandell, Virginia C. 250
Crane, Gladys M. 68
Crane, Stephen 279
Crano, William D. 251
Crapsey, Adelaide 374
Cravens, Gwyneth 24
Crèvecoeur, Hector St. John de 292
Crew, Louie 8
Cristoforo, Rosa 12
Crites, Laura 321
Critoph, Gerald 178
Crocker, Hannah Mather 195 234
Crocker, Lawrence 85
Croll, Elisabeth 350
Cronan, Sheila 89 175
Cronin, Constance 213
Crosby, Ranice Henderson 147 353
Cross, D. Suzanne 138
Cross, K. Patricia 11 267
Crowley, Joan E. 73
Cruz, Juana Ines de la 313 34
Cruz, Levy 324
Cullen, Countee 81
Cullen, Dallas M. 243
Cullinan, Elizabeth 273
Culpepper, Emily E. 283 332
Cumming, Patricia 34 353
Cunningham, Michael R. 67
Currey, Virginia 163
Curry, Peggy Simson 346
Curtain, Margaret Mac, see Mac Curtain, Margaret
Cuskey, Walter R. 51
Cutler, Hannah Tracy 234
Cyrus, Della 9
D'Ambrosio, Vinnie-Marie 109
D'Amico, Debby 127
D'Andrade, Roy G. 56
D'Antonio, William V. 62
D'Aulnay, Louise 66
da Sousa, Noémia 150
Daddio, Saundra 6
Daguio, Amador 95
Dahl, Tove Stang 348

Dahlström, Edmund 37
Daini no Sanmi 31
Dall, Caroline 12 72
Dallin, Alexander 318
Dalton, Katharina 250
Dalton, Susan Elizabeth 288
Daly, Frederica Y. 101
Daly, Mary 175 210 216 238 263 283 300
Daly, Mary E. 312
Damon, Gene 216
Dan, Alice J. 204
Danaraj, Shanta 141
Dance, Daryl C. 222
Daniell, Rosemary 239
Daniels, Arlene Kaplan 344 14
Daniels, Pamela 369
Danner, Margaret 222
Darley, Susan A. 173
Darr, Ann 239
Darrow, Susan T. 146
Darwin, Charles 107
Daryush, Elizabeth 374
Das, Veena 114 115
Datan, Nancy 213 266
Davenport, N. 165
David, C. 78
Davidoff, Leonore 55 92 181
Davidson, Maria 91
Davidson, Sue 353
Davies, Margery 12 35
Davies, Robertson 305
Davin, Delia 181 297 307 308
Davis, Ann E. 166
Davis, Anne J. 166
Davis, Bruce L. 94 94
Davis, Catherine 111
Davis, Helene 111 112
Davis, Jessica G. 211
Davis, Natalie Zemon 23 183 190 364
Davis, Paulina Wright 237
Davis, Susan Schaefer 325
Dawson, Kipp 86
Day, Ingeborg 347
Dayton Public Schools 196
Dayton, Donald W. 337
Dayton, Lucille Sider 337
De Bretteville, Sheila Levrant, see Levrant de Bretteville, Sheila
De Carlo, Charles 48
De Gabriak, Cherubina, see Gabriak, Cherubina de
de Gouges, Olympe, see Gouges, Olympe de
de Hoyos, Angela, see Hoyos, Angela de
de Kooning, Elaine 15
de Kretser, David M. 173
de Marti, Rosa Signorelli, see Signorelli de Marti, Rosa
De Ramus, Betty 222
De Sousa, Victor S. 309
De Vos, George 206
De Warker, Ely Van, see Van De Warker, Ely
De Winter, Anne 55
de Wolf, Rose 203
de Zapata, Celia, see Zapata, Celia de
Deaux, Kay 266
Deaver, Sherri 372
Decter, Midge 139 159
Deevey, Sharon 123
Degler, Carl N. 151 253 259 291
Degn, Louise 215
Dehler, Kathleen 88
Delamont, Sara 145
Dell, Floyd 139
Della Rosa, Laura 8
Delmar, Rosalind 181
Demetrakopoulous, Stephanie A. 359
Deming, Caren J. 140
Demos, John 151
Den Haag, Ernest Van, see Van Den Haag, Ernest
Denby, Maeve 323
Dengler, Ian C. 325
Denich, Bette S. 213 249
Denmark, Florence L. 243 250 266
Dennison, Mary A. 72
Densmore, Dana 9 74 175 233 237
Department of Agriculture 12
Department of Labor 233 252
Deren, Maya 288
Derr, Jill Mulvay 215
Derwood, Gene 345
Déry, Tibor 108
Dessel, Susan 117
Deuchler, Martina 236
Deutsch, Babette 34 245 374
Deutsch, Helene 169 198 268 296
Devaud, Marcelle Stanislas 294
Devon, Tonia K. 43
Dew, Thomas R. 234
DeCrow, Karen 197
deFord, Miriam Allen 128
DeFrees, Madeline 147
DeLamater, John 327
DeLor, Joann 74
Dhamija, Jasleen 352

Dhomhnaill, Nuala ní 150
Di Cicco, Pier Giorgio 116
Di Pesa, Pamela 88
Di Prima, Diane 142 147
Dia, Countess of 299
Dial, Eleanore Maxwell 122
Diamond, Arlyn 17
Diamond, Irene 344
Diamond, Norma 141 230 307
Diaz, Abby M. 125
Dickason, Anne 85 282
Dickins, Charles 108
Dickinson, Emily 34 81 108 168 189 242 245 339 345 374
Dickinson, Susan E. 262
Didion, Joan 3 242 245 375
Dielman, T.E. 183
Dietrich, Kathryn Thomas 251
Dietrich, Sheila C. 335
Diggory, Terence 214
Diggs, Annie L. 128
Diggs, Elizabeth 186
Dilatush, Lois 306
Dillard, Heath 315
Dillingham, Beth W. 20
Dillman, Arline S. 18
Dinerman, Beatrice 166
Dinesen, Isak 34 119 245 273 277
Diniz, Francisca de Motta 313
Dipboye, Robert L. 314
Ditlevsen, Tove 150
Divale, William Tulio 20
Dixon, Marlene 9 74 97 127 132 142 176 186
DiPrima, Diane 109
Dmitrova, Blaga 150
Dobinski, Karla 8
Dobrofsky, Lynne R. 371
Dobson, Richard B. 318
Dodd, Mary 72
Dodge, Mary A. 261
Dodge, Norton T. 166 318
Doering, Charles H. 199
Dohrenwend, Barbara Snell 173
Dohrenwend, Bruce P. 173
Dole, Gertrude E. 131
Domanski, Olga 127
Domhoff, G. William 105
Domínguez, Ana E. 297
Donceel, Joseph F. 62
Donegan, Jane B. 178
Donisi, Patricia 140
Donlan, Dan 208
Donne, John 81 228 242
Donnelly, Caroline 314
Donovan, Josephine 90 110
Doolittle, Hilda 34 108 147 189 374
Dorman, Sonya 340
Dornbusch, Sanford 56
Dorr, Rheta Childe 72
Dostoevsky, Anna 179
Dotton, Thomas 8
Dougherty, Molly C. 317
Doughty, Rosie 272
Douglas, Ann 364
Douglas, Ann, see also Wood, Ann Douglas
Douglas, Justice William O. 180
Douglass, Frederick 74 87
Douglass, Jane Dempsey 177
Douglass, Sarah Mapps 28
Douvan, Elizabeth 82 99 140 172 173 176 183 254
Dowie, Mark 191
Downright, Dora 66
Dowson, Ernest 81
Doyle, Helen 124
Doyle, Patricia Martin 177
Drabble, Margaret 113
Drake, Lydia 72
Draper, Hal 74
Draper, Joanna 12
Draper, Patricia 230
Dreifus, Claudia 175 191
Drexler, Rosalyn 15
Drinkwater, Barbara 286
Driscoll, Carol 237
Dropkin, Celia 150
Druss, Vicki 332
Dryden, John 242
Du Bois, Cora 322
Du Bois, W.E.B. 139
du Cille, Ann , see Cille, Ann du
du Maurier, Daphne 356
Dubeck, Paula 278
Duberman, Lucile 100
Dublin, Thomas 41
Dubois, Silvia 27
Dudar, Helen 149
Duffin, Lorna 145
Duffy, Maureen 161
Dumas, Bethany K. 219
Dumon, Wilfried A. 54
Dumont, Renée 352
Dunbar, Roxanne 74 139 216 237 238
Duncan, Isadora 9
Duncan, Sara Jeanette 305
Dunham, Vera S. 182
Duniway, Abigail Scott 237
Dunkle, Margaret C. 358
Dunlap, Mary C. 328

Dunn, Catherine M. 240
Dunn, Ethel 318
Dunn, Mary Maples 334
Dunn, Susan 208
Dunne, Finley Peter 234
Dupire, Marguerite 338
Duplessis, Rachel Blau 214
Dupré, Louis K. 62
Durbin, Elizabeth 202
Durchholz, Pat 278 341
Durkin, Jon J. 314
Dushku, Judith Rasmussen 215
Duyn, Mona Van, see Van Duyn, Mona
DuBois, Ellen 35
DuPlessis, Rachel Blau 98
Dvorkin, Connie 216
Dwight Manufacturing Co. 12
Dworkin, Andrea 24
Dworkin, Susan 117
Dwyer, Carol A. 204
Dwyer, Daisy Hilse 213 297 325
Dwyer, James L. 128
Dye, Nancy Schrom 41 126
Dyer, Mary 72
Eakins, Barbara 219
Eakins, Gene 219
Earle, Alice Morse 12
Easley, Linda 269
Eastman, Crystal 9 12 139 226
Eastman, Mary F. 262
Eastman, Max 139
Eastman, Mehitabel 69
Eastwood, Mary 175 264 265 354
Eaton-Gadsby, Patricia Rasmussen 215
Eberhart, Mignon G. 50
Ebihara, May 131
Eckenstein, Lina 299
Economist, The 266
Edel, Abraham 217
Edelman, Elaine 109
Edgar, Joanne 208
Edkins, Carol 359
Edmiston, Susan 280
Edwards, Carolyn Pope 22 77
Edwards, Harry 152
Edwards, Jonathan 242
Edwards, Lee R. 17
Edwards, Mary 140
Egremont, Max 5
Ehrenreich, Barbara 191
Ehrhardt, Anke A. 20 199
Ehrlich, Carol 39 297
Ehrman, Lee 101
Eichler, Margrit 304
Eifler, Deborah 208
Eisenberg, Joseph 200
Eisenberg, Sue E. 140
Eisenstein, Zillah 35
Ekberg-Jordan, Sandra 314
Ekejiuba, Felicia Ifeoma 281
Ekstein, Enid 97
el-Messiri, Sawsan 325
Elasser, Nan 219
Eldridge, Elleanor 27
Eliasberg, Ann 9
Eliot, George 108 179 233
Eliot, T.S. 242
Elizabeth I, Queen of England 79 299 345 374
Elizabeth, Queen of York 345
Elizaga, Jean C. 352
Elley, Derek 212
Elliot, Jane 345
Elliott, Carolyn M. 281
Ellis, Albert 89 330
Ellis, Havelock 132
Ellis, Katherine 74 186
Elliston, Frederick 157
Ellman, Mary 13 363
Ellovich, Risa S. 372
Elmendorf, M.L. 297
Elmendorf, Mary 293
Elsner, Gisela 102
Elu de Lenero, Maria de Carmen, see Lenero, Maria de Carmen Elu de
Elwin, Verrier 114
Ely, John Hart 130
Emanuel, James A. 81
Embree, Alice 216
Emerson, Mary 69
Emerson, Ralph Waldo 107
Emlen, Arthur C. 370
Emma Willard Task Force on Education 208
Emmanska, Baroness Orczy 50 103
Emshwiller, Carol 24 340
Engel, Barbara Alpern 19 218
Engel, Dorothy S. 146
Engel, Marian 305
Engelberg, Laurie 354
Engels, Friedrich 87 89 107 158 159 203 233 251 252
England, G.A. 241
English, Deirdre 191
English, Jane 85
Ensley, Elizabeth Piper 28
Entwisle, Doris 196
Ephelia, see Philips, Joan
Epictetus 231
Epstein, Cynthia Fuchs 39 105 149 166 250 266 326
Erasmus, Desiderius 299

Erens, Patricia 212
Erickson, Pat 368
Erikson, Erik H. 3 173 198 200 253 260 268
Erikson, Joan M. 253
Ernst, Robert 12
Ervin-Tripp, Susan 219
Ervin, Sam, Jr. 203
Esfandiary, F.M. 256
Eshelman, Nancy G. 116
Esperanza 313
Espin, Vilma 313
Espinosa, Mary Lou 347
Espírito Santo, Alda do 150
Esposito, Virginia 166
Etienne, Mona 270
Etten, Ida M. Van, see Van Etten, Ida M.
Euripides 310
Eustace, Robert 50
Evans, Laura J. 235
Evans, Mari 34 109 118 147 168 222 245
Evans, Nancy Burr 110
Evans, Sara M. 334
Eve, Barbara 224 245
Everett, Mary Holywell 72
Everhard, Caroline McCullough 72
Ewbank, Inga-Stina 357
Ewens, Mary 337
Exum, Pat Crutchfield 118
Fabbri, Tecla 313
Fabilli, Mary 109
Fabricant, Carole 278
Fabrikant, Benjamin 330
Faessler, Shirley 305 347
Faherty, W.B. 233
Fainlight, Ruth 147 356
Faithorn, Elizabeth 230
Faladé, Solange 338
Falbo, Toni 171
Falco, Kristine L. 342
Falk, Gail 265
Falk, Nancy 283
Fannings, Helen 228
Faragher, Johnny 360
Farah, Barbara G. 140 141
Farians, Elizabeth 283
Farley, Harriet 69
Farley, Margaret A. 258
Farley, Pamela 98
Farnham, Eliza 187
Farnham, Elizabeth 319
Farnham, Marynia F. 363
Farnsworth, Beatrice Brodsky 218 318 349
Farquhar, Norma 208
Farrell, Warren T. 100 316
Farrokhzād, Forūgh 150
Farwell, Beatrice 247
Farwell, Marilyn 342
Fasenmyer, Mary Sarah 48
Fasteau, Brenda Feigen 152
Fatout, Paul 128
Fatt, Naomi 191
Faulkner, William 242 279
Faunce, Patricia Spencer 173
Faure, Iris 146
Fauset, Jessie Redmon 10
Faust, Margaret S. 18
Fava, Sylvia F. 143
Federbush, Marsha 13
Fee, Elizabeth 42 191 201
Feeley, Dianne 86
Fehervary, Helen 275
Fein, Cheri 245
Feinstein, Elaine 357
Feinstein, Karen Wolk 371
Feit, Rona F. 344
Feldberg, Roslyn L. 251 264
Feldman, David H. 13
Feldman, Harold 70 129
Feldman, Saul D. 39
Felice, Cynthia 133
Felker, Donald W. 196
Felshin, Jan 358
Feminists 149 175 216
Feminists on Children's Media 175 208 271
Fenn, Margaret 314
Fennema, Elizabeth 21
Fenton, Elizabeth 147
Féral, Josette 98
Ferber, Marianne A. 4 39 291
Ferguson, Ann 85
Ferguson, Marjorie 105
Ferguson, Mary Anne 36 111 112
Ferguson, Neal A. 335
Ferguson, Renee 28
Ferguson, Sheila 323
Ferman, Louis A. 141
Ferrandino, Marilyn Myerson 173
Ferrante, Joan M. 23
Ferrero, William 51
Ferrin, Mary Upton 237
Feshbach, Norma D. 18
Fessenden, Patricia 275
Festini, Nelly 294
Festy, Patrick 54
Fetterley, Judith 17
Feuerwerker, Yi-tsi 308
Fichte, J.G. 203
Fichter, Joseph H. 166 252
Fidell, Linda S. 250 327

Fiedler, Leslie 228
Fiedler, Maureen 344
Field, Edward 233 353
Field, Joanna 179
Field, Mark G. 176 206
Field, Mary G. 182
Field, Michael 345
Fields, Julia 118
Fields, Rona M. 243
Figueroa, Teresa Orrego de, see Orrego de Figueroa, Teresa
Finch, Anne, Countess of Winchilsea 32 34 189 228 242 345 374
Finegan, T. Aldrich 202
Finkelstein, Harry 140
Finnigan, Joan 345
Fiorenza, Elisabeth 263
Fiorenza, Elisabeth Schussler 258 337
Firestone, Shulamith 89 158 237 254
Fischer, Ann 322
Fischer, Lucy 212
Fischer, Michael M.J. 325
Fischer, Ruth 341
Fishel, Andrew 196
Fisher, Dorothy Canfield 10 273 353
Fisher, Elizabeth 13 228 298
Fisher, M.F.K. 24 273
Fisher, Marguerite 178
Fishman, Pamela 361
Fitzgerald, F. Scott 111 112
Fitzgerald, Zelda 248
Fitzpatrick, Blanche 196
Flanner, Hildegarde 345 346
Flaubert, Gustave 339
Flax, Jane 98
Fleischer, Nat 128
Fleming, Marjory 179
Fletcher, Marilyn Lowen 142 216
Flexner, Eleanor 259 260
Fliegel, Norris 166
Flint, Jerry M. 284
Flora, Cornelia Butler 71 163 316
Fluehr-Lobban, Carolyn 213
Flynn, Elizabeth Gurley 12 72
Flynn, Karin I. 176 206
Foa, Pamela 85 158
Fodale, Barbara M. 140
Fodor, Iris E. Goldstein 330
Fogarty, Faith 94
Fogel, Helen 129
Foley, Eileen 129
Fonda, Nickie 135
Fong, Stanley L.M. 206
Fontenot, Chester J. 222
Footner, Hulbert 50
Ford, Clellan S. 206 296
Ford, Gena 109
Fordham, Mary Weston 242
Forman, Nicole 147
Fort, Gertrud von le, see le Fort, Gertrud von
Fortunatus 299
Foster, Abby Kelly 237
Foulché-Delbosc, Isabel 138
Fox, David J. 250
Fox, Elizabeth M. 251
Fox, Gail 109
Fox, Geoffrey E. 71
Fox, Hanna 99
Fox, Lynn H. 204
Fox, Mary Frank 141
Fox, Robin 89
Fox, Siv Cedering 224
Foxley, Cecelia H. 246
Fralley, Jackie 208
Frame, Janet 345
France, Marie de 345
Francoeur, Anna 256
Francoeur, Robert 256
Frank, Anne 179
Frank, Francine 361
Frank, Lawrence K. 260
Frank, Miriam 137
Frankel, Lois J. 51
Frankfort, Ellen 191
Franklin, Alice 51
Franklin, Benjamin 242 319
Franklin, Christine Ladd 262
Franks, Lucinda 152 256
Franks, Violet 99 330
Franzblau, Susan H. 18
Franzwa, Helen H. 105 250
Fraser, Kathleen 109 147 224 239 245
Frasher, Ramona 271
Frazier, E. Franklin 25 151 259
Frederiksson, Ingrid 271
Freedman, David A. 169
Freedman, Michael 272
Freedman, Monroe H. 208
Freeman, Bonnie Cook 21
Freeman, Carole 147
Freeman, Jo 4 39 77 139 175 186 208 264 265 284 297 316
Freeman, Mary 242
Freeman, Mary E. Wilkins 10 32 34 111 112 119 245 279 347 353
Fremlin, Celia 119
French Union for Women's Suffrage 66

Frenier, Miriam Darce 246
Freud, Sigmund 89 107 132 155 158 169 173 198 200 233 250 252 260 268
Friderich, Nicole M. 294
Fried, Barbara 332
Fried, Marlene Gerber 282
Friedan, Betty 107 159 238 280 362 363
Friedl, Erika 325
Friedl, Ernestine 322
Friedlander, Lynn 278
Friedman, Emanuel A. 211
Friedman, Jean E. 151
Friedman, Susan 88
Fries, Maureen 17
Frieze, Irene Hanson 49 267
Frisof, Jamie Kelem 208 271
Fritz, Angela McCourt 141
Fritz, Leah 142 216
Froines, Ann 342
Fromberg-Schaeffer, Susan 137
Fromm-Reichmann, Frieda 170
Frosch, Susa F. 219
Frost, Robert 111 112 242
Fruchter, Rachel Gillett 191
Frye, Marilyn 85 157 158
Fuchs, Victor R. 251 252
Fuentes, Fernanda 313
Fuentes, Sonia Pressman 36 260
Fuertes, Gloria 150
Fujita, Taki 294
Fuller, Margaret 9 60 87 188 195 234
Fuller, Mary 205
Fullinwider, Robert K. 85
Fumiko, Hayashi 31
Furay, Mortimer 228
Furman, Laura 216
Fussenegger, Gertrud 273
Futabako, Mitsui 31
Gablik, Suzi 15
Gabriak, Cherubina de 355
Gaffin, Jean 323
Gág, Wanda 226
Gage, Frances D. 44 233 237
Gage, Matilda Joslyn 9 44 234 237
Gailey, Christine Ward 270
Gaines, Ernest J. 111 112
Gaite, A.J.H. 196
Galen 231
Galenson, Eleanor 76 199
Gallagher, Ann Miriam 121
Gallant, Mavis 273
Gallico, Paul 152
Gallop, Jane 98
Gallup, George H. 196
Galway, Kathleen 176 267
Gamarnikow, Eva 84
Gamble, Eliza Burt 232
Gandelman, Ronald 204
Gander, Mary Jean 196
Garbo, Greta 288
García Márquez, Gabriel 279
Garçia, Gilbert Narro 219
Garcia, Jose Z. 174
Garcia, Margarita 250
Garden, Ramona 347
Gardiner, Jean 35 55
Gardiner, Judith 278
Gardiner, Judith Kegan 88
Gardner, Isabella 111 345
Gardner, Jennifer 237
Gardner, Jo-Ann Evans 208
Gardner, T.S. 241
Garland, T. Neal 70 166
Garner, Hugh 305
Garofalo, Ralph 94
Garretson, Lucy 20
Garrigue, Jean 245 345
Garrison, Dee 42 266
Garrison, Ellen Wright 72
Garrison, William Lloyd 87 234
Garry, Ann 158
Gartland, Joan 137
Garvey, Amy-Jacques 28
Gaskill, Elizabeth B. 211
Gates, Margaret 235 291 321 331
Gaudet, Frances A. Joseph 28
Gautier, Étiènne 162
Gayles, Gloria 222
Gaylord, Carolyn 140
Geadelmann, Patricia L. 64
Gebhard, Paul H. 296
Geer, Elizabeth Dixon Smith 187
Gehlen, Frieda L. 163
Geiger, Kent 149
Geis, Gilbert 94 94
Gelb, Lester A. 170
Gelber, Sylva M. 352
Gelder, Susan Van 216
Geller, Laura 117
Gelpi, Albert 214
Gelpi, Barbara Charlesworth 214 268
Gendler, Mary 117
General Federation of Women's Clubs Magazine 257
Georgakas, Dan 288
George, Carol V.R. 178
George, Felicia R. 156
Geracimos, Ann 152
Gerald, Carolyn F. 118
Gerbner, George 105

Gershuny, H. Lee 207
Gersoni, Diane 208
Gerstenberg, Alice 161
Gertsyk, Adelaida 355
Gesell, Arnold 198
Gessain, Monique 338
Ghent, Dorothy Van, see Van Ghent, Dorothy
Giallombardo, Rose 51
Gibbons, Anne 152
Gibbons, Harold J. 62
Gibson, Althea 152 347
Gibson, Graeme 305
Gibson, Mary 116
Giddis, Diane 212 288
Gideonse, Hendrik 278
Gidlow, Elsa 109
Giele, Janet Zollinger 365
Gilbert, Celia 369
Gilbert, Miriam 216
Gilbert, Sandra M. 214 278
Gilbert, Virginia 109
Gill, Gerald R. 7
Gillespie, Dair L. 77 265
Gillespie, William 198
Gilliatt, Penelope 220
Gilligan, Carol 98
Gillon, Jean 211
Gilman, Charlotte Perkins 9 34 44 72 74 87 113 127 139 153 187 188 234 242 257 260 292 374
Gilman, Richard 3 284
Gilmartin, Andrina 68
Gilmore, Susan K. 342
Ginsberg, Susannah 135
Ginsburg, Natalia 273
Ginsburg, Ruth Bader 203 217 266 321
Ginzberg, Eli 48
Ginzburg, Natalia 161
Glō 31
Gioseffi, Daniela 239
Giovanni, Nikki 26 34 109 118 147 168 222 224 245 248 347 353
Girson, Rochelle 284
Gissing, George 81
Githens, Marianne 163 174
Gladstone, Rose 127
Gladwyn, Cynthia 5
Glasgow, Ellen 245 279
Glaspell, Susan 10 34 111 112 245 310
Glassman, Carol 216
Glazer, Nathan 180
Glazer, Nona 251 328
Gleason, George 36
Gleason, Mrs. R.B. 187
Glendinning, Victoria 5
Glenn, Evelyn Nakano 264
Glickman, Rose L. 318
Glickstein, Howard A. 180
Glueck, Eleanor 51
Glueck, Sheldon 51
Glyde, Gerald P. 328
Goddard, Abba A. 69
Godwin, Anne 323
Godwin, Gail 24 113 375
Goedicke, Patricia 168 224
Goffman, Erving 252
Gold, Doris B. 254
Gold, Louis 128
Goldberg, F., Jr. 51
Goldberg, Leah 150
Goldberg, Philip 13 155 166 200 243 250
Goldberg, Ruth E. 61
Goldberg, Steven 89 203
Goldberg, Susan 176
Golde, Peggy 322
Golden, Bernette 118
Golden, Daniel 116
Goldenberg, Judith Plaskow 177
Goldenberg, Judith Plaskow, see also Plaskow, Judith
Goldenberg, Naomi R. 263
Goldfeld, Anne 117
Goldman, Alan H. 85 180
Goldman, Emma 9 74 87 127
Goldman, Jane 342
Goldman, Marion Sherman 342
Goldman, Nancy 39 266
Goldsmith, Oliver 242
Goldstein, Fred J. 206
Goldstein, Leslie Friedman 174
Goldwyn, Robert M. 211
Golod, Serge 70
Gomberg, Edith S. 99 330
Gomm, Roger 285
Goncourt, Edmond de 299
Goncourt, Jules de 299
Gontier, Fernande 80
Gonzales, Sylvia 368 43
Gonzalez, Nancie 190
Good, Mary-Jo DelVecchio 325
Goodchilds, Jacqueline D. 129
Goode, John 181 357
Goode, William J. 48 149 252
Goodman, Felicitas D. 372
Goodman, Inez 12
Goodman, Jane 196
Goody, Jack 30
Goot-Blatt, Roberta 237
Gorbanevskaya, Natalya 150
Gordimer, Nadine 34 245 273

Gordon, Ann D. 126 334
Gordon, C. Wayne 252
Gordon, Caroline 273
Gordon, David M. 291
Gordon, Francine E. 266
Gordon, Linda 35 42 126 237
Gordon, Margaret 106
Gordon, Mary 109 375
Goren, Judith 137
Gorham, Deborah 320
Gorman, Margaret 62
Gornick, Vivian 127 176 254
Gorsky, Susan 110
Gottheil, Diane Levitt 174
Gottlieb, Ann 147
Gottlieb, Elaine 220
Gouges, Olympe de 66
Gough, Kathleen 230 251 252 264 264
Gould, Carol C. 159 282
Gould, Lois 256 300
Gould, Robert E. 89
Gove, Walter R. 22 39 99 266
Govier, Trudy R. 159
Gowanlock, Theresa 165
Goy, Robert W. 250
Goyer-Michaud, Francyne 75
Graddick, Laura J. 44
Grady, Kathleen E. 173
Graham, Elizabeth 295
Graham, Alma 120
Graham, Marilyn F. 18
Graham, Patricia A. 4 166 343
Graham, Ruth 19 255
Grahn, Judy 147 239
Granson, Milla 28
Grant, Christine 64
Grant, Joanne 26
Grappe, Denise 46
Grasmuck, Sherri 163
Grau, S.A. 83
Graver, Lawrence 192
Graves, Mrs. A.J. 187
Graves, Robert 132 233
Gray, Betty MacMorran 251 252
Gray, Thomas 242
Gray, Virginia 326
Green, Anna Katherine 50
Green, Edith 228
Green, Joann 369
Green, Joyce 26
Green, Norma Kidd 128
Green, Peggy 69
Green, Richard 199
Green, Rose Basile 116
Green, Sheila 135
Greenacre, Phyllis 169
Greenawalt, Kent 180
Greenberg, Blu 117
Greenberg, Joanne 111 245
Greenberg, Ruth L. 330
Greenberg, Selma 156 196
Greenberger, Ellen 196
Greenberger, Marcia 328
Greene, Maxine 217
Greenfield, William 272
Greenglass, Esther 304
Greenwald, Carol S. 328
Greenwell, Dora 345
Greer, Germaine 3 68 159 362
Gregg, Christina F. 155
Gregg, Kate L. 226
Gregory, George 130
Gregory, Samuel 130
Greiff, Barrie 280
Greiner, Norbert 68
Grennan, Jacqueline 62
Grew, Henry 234
Gribskov, Margaret 272
Grier, William H. 233
Grierson, Constantia 345
Griffen, Joyce 173 368
Griffin, Mary Roland 358
Griffin, Susan 77 85 94 94 111 136 147 245 265 298 347 375
Griffiths, Martha W. 59 228 238 287 291
Grim, Patrick 85
Grimké, Angelina 44 153 187 234 237 374
Grimké, Charlotte 27 28
Grimké, Sarah 9 72 87 187 188 234 237 257
Grimm, Elaine R. 40 176
Grimm, James W. 354
Groneman, Carol 41
Grønseth, Erik 70
Groot, Lampl-de, Jeanne, see Lampl-de Groot, Jeanne
Gross, Barry R. 180
Gross, Edward 166
Gross, Larry 105
Gross, Louise 233 237
Gross, Rita 263 283
Grossman, Marlyn 211 332
Grossman, William I. 76
Groszko, Marie 243
Grove, Frederick P. 305
Groves, Ernest R. 259
Gruenberg, Ernest M. 40
Gruening, Martha 139
Grumet, Robert Steven 270
Grunberger, B. 78
Grymeston, Elizabeth 79

Gubar, Susan 214 278
Gubbay, Michele 12
Gubbels, Robert 251 252 329
Guest, Barbara 345
Guevara, Isabel de 313
Guillén, Nicholás 222
Gujitomi, Irene 77
Gulick, John 325
Gulick, Margaret E. 325
Gullahorn, Jeanne E. 172
Gump, Janice Porter 267
Gundersheimer, Werner L. 23
Gunderson, Barbara B. 164
Gunderson, Morley 63
Gundy, H. Pearson 128
Gunning, Sarah Ogan 374
Gunst, Virginia 170
Gurin, Patricia 45 140 333
Gussler, Judith D. 372
Guthmann, Edward 8
Gutmann, David 82
Gutmann, Diane 328
Guttentag, Marcia 156 276
Guy-Sheftall, Beverly 222
Guyen, Sang 95
Guzinski, Gay 211
H.D., see Doolittle, Hilda
Haag, Ernest Van Den, see Van Den Haag, Ernest
Haavio-Mannila, Elina 155 176 267
Haberkorn, Susan B. 146
Hacker, Helen Mayer 77 100 132 228 243 250 251 252 264 266
Hackett, Amy 126
Hackman, Judith 4
Haddock, Emma 128
Haden, Patricia 97 237
Hafen, Mary Ann 124
Hagedorn, Jessica Tarahata 136
Hageman, Alice L. 35 210
Häggblom-Khakee, Gunilla 364
Hagood, Margaret 12
Hahn, Susan Reed 171
Hahner, June E. 121
Haines, Patricia Foster 272
Hall, Arden 40
Hall, Calvin 200
Hall, Catherine 92
Hall, Diana Long 282
Hall, Douglas T. 266
Hall, G. Stanley 198
Hall, Hazel 346
Hall, Jacquelyn Dowd 334
Hall, Lee 15
Hall, Lydia S. 69
Hall, Mary 69
Hall, Sharlot 346
Halley, Anne 147
Hallingworth, Martha 69
Halsband, Robert 255
Hamamsy, Laila Shukry 285
Hamburg, Beatrix A. 199
Hamburg, David A. 56 199
Hamer, Fannie Lou 28
Hamilton, Alice 319
Hamilton, Annette 366
Hamilton, Cicely 260
Hamilton, Gail, see Dodge, Mary A.
Hamilton, Mary Jane 278
Hammel, Lisa 139
Hammerton, A. James 244
Hammond, Geraldine 109
Hamod, K. Keeshan 369
Han, Ts'ui-P'in 148
Hanawalt, Barbara A. 315
Handlin, Joanna F. 308
Handlon, Joseph H. 314
Hands, Join 8
Hanisch, Carol 237
Hanna, Roberta 342
Hannay, Prudence 5
Hansberry, Lorraine 34
Hanson, Gary R. 196
Hansot, Elizabeth 341
Hardesty, Nancy 337
Harding, Katherine 220
Harding, M. Esther 81
Harding, Sandra 282
Harding, Susan 230
Hardwick, Elizabeth 363
Hardy, John Edward 47
Hardy, Richard J. 174
Hardy, Thomas 81 242 245
Hare, Julia 176
Hare, Nathan 176
Hare, R.M. 157
Hareven, Tamara K. 276
Harington, Lucy 345
Hariton, E. Barbara 73 89
Harkess, Shirley J. 71
Harley, Sharon 7
Harman, Zena 324
Harnett, Rodney T. 196
Harney, Robert F. 116
Harper, Frances Ellen Watkins 27 28 72 374
Harper, Ida Husted 139
Harper, John Paul 334
Harrentsian, Dale 173
Harrigan, Renny 275
Harriman, Jane 81 127
Harris, A-neeta 237
Harris, Ann Sutherland 13 271
Harris, Dorothy V. 286

Harris, Lauren Julius 18
Harris, Marie 136
Harris, Mark 164
Harris, O. 193
Harrison, Barbara Grizzuti 13 280 300
Harrison, Bennett 333
Harrison, Beverly Wildung 210
Harrison, Daphne Duval 7
Harrison, Martha 28 72
Harrison, Mrs. Burton 292
Harrison, Rachel 84
Hart, Donn Vorhis 221
Hart, Lois 237
Hart, M. Marie 152
Hart, Roger 156
Hartford, Beverly S. 219
Hartle, M.M. 51
Hartley, Ruth E. 13 176 196 206
Hartman, Grace 320
Hartman, Maryann 219
Hartmann, Heidi 35 251 291
Hartnett, Oonagh 205
Hartsock, Nancy 35 344
Harvor, Beth 305
Harwood, Gwen 345
Haskell, Ann S. 240
Haskell, Mehitabel 237
Haskell, Molly 212 288
Haskell, Rachell 124
Haste, Gwendolen 346
Hastrup, Kirsten 53
Hatch, David L. 252
Hatch, Mary G. 252
Hatcher, Sherry Lynn 141
Hathaway, Jeanine 109
Hattaway, Kymberly 140
Hauptman, Judith 177
Havens, Elizabeth M. 39
Havens, Ruth C.D. 44
Hawkins, Ruth R. 341 341
Hawley, Andy 142
Hawthorne, Nathaniel 81 108 111 112 242 279 339
Hay, Margaret Jean 302
Hayden, Dolores 143 303
Hayden, Sophia 303
Hayes, Steven C. 75
Haynes, Elizabeth Ross 28
Haywood, Eliza 79
Hazlewood-Brady, Anne 109
Head, Bessie 222
Heath, Kathryn G. 297
Hébert, Anne 150 305
Hecker, Eugene A. 232
Hedblom, Jack H. 266
Hedgeman, Anna Arnold 28
Heer, David M. 182
Hefner, Hugh M. 233
Hefner, Loretta L. 215
Hefner, Robert 22
Hegel, Georg 107
Heide, Wilma Scott 75 211 271
Heilbrun, Carolyn G. 90 98 208 240
Heiman, Marcel 76
Hein, Hilde 159 282
Heine, Heinrich 111 112
Heinen, J. Stephen 314
Heinhold, William 286
Held, Virginia 158 282
Heller, Agnes 251 252
Helling, Marvin 358
Hellman, Lillian 3 161 245
Helmick, Evelyn Thomas 88
Helson, Ravenna 176 266 267
Helwig, David 305
Hemans, Felicia 189 345
Hemingway, Eliza R. 12
Hemingway, Ernest 111 112 277 279
Hemschemeyer, Judith 224
Henderson, Julia J. 294
Henderson, Lucile Kelling 68
Henderson, Peggy 147
Henderson, Sharon 118
Hendricks, Jon A. 129
Hendryx, Janice L. 321
Henifin, Mary Sue 332
Henley, Nancy 77 120 264 265
Henney, Jeannette H. 372
Henning, Clara Maria 177
Henry, Alice 12
Henry, Ann 305
Henry, Lois-Allison 118
Henry, Louis 162
Henry, O. 373
Henshel, Anne-Marie 39
Hepperle, Winifred L. 321
Herberg, Dorothy Chave 141
Herbert, Mary Sidney, Countess of Pembroke 345 32 242 79 374
Herlihy, David 184 315
Herman, Dianne 264
Herman, Sondra R. 329
Hernandez, Aileen 139
Herndon, Marcia 274
Herodotus 241
Herron, Belva Mary 187
Herschberger, Ruth 132 345 239
Herskovits, Melville J. 25
Herzog, Elizabeth 25
Hesburgh, Theodore M. 106
Hesiod 228
Heslep, Robert D. 217

Hess, Thomas B. 247
Hesse, Sharlene J. 371
Hetherington, E. Mavis 172 250
Heyl, Barbara 51
Heynrichs, Jenny 66
Heyns, Barbara 197
Heys, Patricia Lee Findley 163
Heywood, Ezra H. 195
Hiatt, Betty 366
Hiatt, Mary 361
Hicks, J. 63
Hien, Luong 150
Higgins, Anne 24
Higgins, Judith 353
Higginson, Ella 346
Hightower, Nikki R. Van, see Van Hightower, Nikki R.
Higier, Faye 166
Hilberman, Elaine 211
Hill, Allan G. 367
Hill, Sandra Bishop 158
Hill, Susan 220 356
Hill, Thomas E., Jr. 203
Hiller, Dana V. 278
Himel, Margery 109
Hinchcliffe, Doreen 325
Hindelang, Michael J. 94 94
Hinds, Harold E., Jr. 122
Hines, Fred 252
Hinkle, Beatrice M. 96 226
Hippius, Zinaida 355
Hippocrates 231
Hiramatsu, Masako 324
Hirata, Lucie Cheng 334
Hirsch, Hilde E. 106
Hirsch, Storm de 288
Hirsch, Werner Z. 106
Hirschon, Renée 53
Hisajo, Sugita 31
Hisako, Fukui 31
Ho, Lady 148
Ho, Shuang-Ch'ing 148
Hoag, Wendy J. 141
Hoagland, Sarah 368
Hobart, Charles 304
Hobbes, Thomas 107
Hoben, Sandra 224
Hobsen, Mabel 127
Hobson, Roxie 57
Hobson, Sheila Smith 216
Hoch-Smith, Judith 317
Hochman, Sandra 3 147 224
Hochschild, Arlie Russell 14 39 290
Hodge, Hugh L. 1
Hoffer, Carol P. 20 249
Hoffman-Nowotny, Hans-Joachim 54
Hoffman, Beatrice 321
Hoffman, Jill 224
Hoffman, L. Richard 250
Hoffman, Lois Wladis 22 141 149 250 267 278 296 370
Hoffman, Robert 180
Hogan, Anne 342
Hogan, Candace 152
Hogan, Patricia 314
Hogan, William Ransom 128
Hokada, Elizabeth 208
Holahan, Susan 24
Holcombe, Lee 244
Holder, Orlee 359
Hole, Judith 175 264 265
Holland, Barbara A. 239
Hollander, Nancy Caro 71
Holley, Marietta 319
Holly, Aleen 329
Holly, Marcia 90
Holmberg, Per 37
Holmstrom, Lynda Lytle 94 166
Holt, Charles C. 333
Holt, L. Emmett 160
Holter, Harriet 267 324
Homiak, Marcia 158 279
Hommes, Regina W. 54
Hood, Thomas 87 242
Hook, Sidney 180
Hooper, Antony 285
Hoover, Herbert 319
Hoover, Theressa 210
Hope, Emily 55
Hope, Lezli 118
Hopkins, Elaine B. 341
Hopkins, Mary Alden 226
Hopkins, Sarah Winnemucca 124
Hopwood, Alison L. 36
Hore, T. 271
Horikawa, Lady 31
Horner, Matina S. 9 13 73 82 166 176 186 233 250 267
Horney, Karen 107 132 169 170 173 198 252 268 296
Hornig, Lilli S. 301
Horsley, Ritta Jo 80
Horta, Maria Teresa 150
Hoskins, Marilyn W. 20
Hostettler, Agnes Freudenberg 274
Hott, Jacqueline Rose 311
Hough, Jerry F. 318
Hough, Lindy 109
House, Elaine W. 196
Housman, Judy 158 279
Houten, Donald R. Van, see Van Houten, Donald R.
How, Tina 144

Howard, Anne, Duchess of Arundel 345
Howard, Ephraim M. 330
Howard, Frances Minturn 345
Howard, Helen 28
Howard, Joyce L. 330
Howard, Judith Jeffrey 116 349
Howard, Maureen 3 192
Howe, Florence 4 9 13 36 110 127 208 245 271 290 342 347
Howe, Frank E. 1
Howe, Irving 176
Howe, Julia Ward 262 345 374
Howe, Thomas Carr 164
Howell, Mary Seymour 44
Howells, William Dean 112
Howes, Barbara 109 109 345
Howes, Ethel Puffer 257
Hoyos, Angela de 122
Hsi-chen, Sun 95
Hsiung, Hung 148 150
Hsüeh, Ch'iung 148
Hsüeh, T'ao 148
Hua, Lady Jui 148
Huang, Lucy Jen 176
Huang, O 148
Huang, Veronica 347
Hubbard, Ruth 332
Huber, Elaine C. 337
Huber, Joan 4 278
Huch, Ricarda 102 102
Hudson, Marion 12
Hufton, Olwen 299
Hugh-Jones, C. 193
Hughes, Helen MacGill 39
Hui, Czoe Zong 95
Hull, Gloria T. 214 222
Hull, Valerie J. 91
Hume, David 107 159
Humphrey, Caroline 53
Hunt, Harriot K. 72 234 237
Hunt, Morton 164 284 362
Hunt, Persis 126
Hunter, Jacquelyn Furgus 222
Hunter, Jean E. 255 335
Hunter, Kristin 277
Huntsman, Judith 285
Hurley, Tom 8
Hurnscot, Loran 179
Hurston, Zora Neale 273 353
Hurwitz, Edith F. 19
Hutchinson, Anne 72
Huyck, Margaret Hellie 129
Hyde, Ida H. 96
Hyde, Robin 345
Hyder, Qurratulain 114
Hyman, Herbert H. 25
Hyman, Paula 117
Hyman, Stanley Edgar 192
Ibsen, Henrik 87 228 233 310 339 363
Ifeka-Moller, Caroline 154 297
Iglitzin, Lynne B. 163 196 316 329
Iino, Masako 178
Ikuko, Atsumi 31
Ilg, Frances L. 198
Illsley, Raymond 40
Imig, David R. 269
Imig, Gail L. 269
Inaba, Leslie Kimiko 347
Inez, Colette 109 147 239
Ingham, Allen 286
Inman, Mary 72
International Alliance of Women 66
International Planned Parenthood Federation 367
Ireson, Carol 354
Irish, William 50
Irvine, Patricia 219
Irwin, Inez Haynes 226
Isaac, Barry L. 20
Ise Tayū 31
Ise, Lady 31
Isenberg, Barbara 284
Islas, Maya 122
Israel, Joan 129
Israel, Kenneth 129
Ito, Hisako 178
Iverson, Lucille 239
Ivey, Melville E. 250
Ivins, Virginia Wilcox 124
Ivy, James W. 222
Izumi Shikibu 31
Izzi, Martha H. 211
Jacker, Corinne 144
Jacklin, Carol Nagy 77 204
Jackson, Aunt Molly 374
Jackson, Barbra Balogun, see Balogun, Barbra (Jackson)
Jackson, Charlotte Ann 28
Jackson, Edward R. 174
Jackson, Helen Hunt 374
Jackson, Jacquelyne Johnson 129
Jackson, Laura 306
Jackson, Mae 118 222
Jackson, Mahalia 28
Jackson, Maurice 51
Jackson, Nell C. 358
Jackson, Shirley 33 273
Jacobi, Mary Putnam 72 187 262
Jacobs, Aletta 66
Jacobsen, Josephine 345

Jacobson, Barbara 99
Jacobson, Doranne 131
Jacobson, Helga E. 131
Jacobson, Solomon G. 146
Jacobus, Mary 225 357
Jacoby, Robin Miller 41 126 141
Jacoby, Susan 12
Jaffe, Daniel S. 76
Jaffe, Rona 111 112
Jaggar, Alison 85 157 158 203 282
Jahan, Rounaq 20 297
Jahoda, Marie 289
James, Alice 179
James, Estelle 202
James, Henry 108 242 373
James, Jennifer 235
James, Selma 97
James, Wendy 53
Jameson, Anna 66
Jameson, Anna Brownell 165
Jameson, Elizabeth 41
Janait, Rachel 117
Jancar, Barbara 316
Janeway, Elizabeth 48 98 268 278 280 300
Janik, Phyllis 109
Janowitz, Naomi 263
Jaquette, Jane S. 71 194 281 329
Jaquith, Cindy 86
Jarrahi-Zadeh, Ali 250
Jarrell, Randall 81
Jay, Karla 8
Jay, Phyllis C. 164
Jay, Winifred Tom 196
Jayaratne, Toby Epstein 73
Jbabvala, R.P. 83
Jeffers, Marlin 246
Jefferson, Margo 256
Jefferson, Richard 12
Jefferson, Thomas 292
Jeffries-Fox, Suzanne 105
Jelin, Elizabeth 194 281
Jelinek, Estelle C. 88 359
Jem 8
Jemai, Yolande 367
Jemand, Amanda Smith 28
Jên, Jui 148
Jenkins, Helen Philleo 234
Jenness, Linda 86
Jennings, Elizabeth 345
Jennings, Jerry T. 196
Jennings, Samuel 187
Jerauld, Richard 173
Jerome (Saint) 299
Jesus, Carolina Maria de 179 313
Jewett, Sarah Orne 34 108 153 245 273 353 373
Jhabvala, Renana 114
Jhabvala, Ruth Prawer 273
Jitō, Empress 31
Joesting, Joan 142
Joffe, Carole 13 196
Johansson, Majken 150 245
Johansson, Sheila Ryan 126 244 335
John-Steiner, Vera 219
John, Mariam 20
Johnson, Barclay D. 252
Johnson, Carole Schulte 314
Johnson, Carolyn 303
Johnson, Charles E., Jr. 196
Johnson, Charles S. 25
Johnson, Colleen L. 116
Johnson, Dee L. 250
Johnson, Diane 113 248
Johnson, E. 103
Johnson, Elizabeth 308
Johnson, George E. 202
Johnson, Georgia Douglas 374
Johnson, James 178
Johnson, Josephine 68
Johnson, Kay Ann 21
Johnson, Leo 295
Johnson, Mariana 237
Johnson, Marilyn 272 344
Johnson, Mary Durham 349
Johnson, Nathaniel 222
Johnson, Shirley B. 202
Johnson, Virginia E. 62 200 296
Johnston, Claire 212 288
Johnston, Tracy 191
Johnstone, Elizabeth 294
Jones, "Mother" Mary, see Jones, Mary Harris
Jones, Adele 26
Jones, Ann 146
Jones, Arthur R. 166
Jones, Beverly 132 216 237
Jones, Cathaleene 155
Jones, Elizabeth 44
Jones, Ernest 169
Jones, Gayl 118
Jones, Hardy E. 180
Jones, Jane Elizabeth 237
Jones, Joan 233
Jones, Marté 118
Jones, Mary C. 155 200
Jones, Mary Harris 104 319
Jong, Emma 268
Jong, Erica 3 109 136 168 224 239 245 248 375
Jongeward, Dorothy 6
Jonker, Ingrid 150
Jordan, Brigitte 269

Jordan, June 109 118 147 239
Jordan, Pat 152
Jordan, Tricia S. 18
Jordan, Winthrop D. 151 292
Joreen 132 175 216
Joselit, Jenna Weissman 143
Joseph, Gloria I. 43
Joseph, Suad 325
Josselyn, Irene M. 206
Joyce, James 277 279
Joyce, Rosemary 372
Judd, Elizabeth 141
Juhasz, Suzanne 88 109 214 359
Juillard, Joelle Rutherford 329
Juliani, Richard N. 116
Jung, Carl 81
Jung, Tzu 148
Junko, Nishi 31
Jusenius, Carol L. 291 351
Juviler, Peter H. 318
Kaess, Walter A. 200
Kagan, Jerome 73 200
Kahan, Eileen B. 211
Kahana, Eva 129
Kahn, Coppélia 17
Kahn, Hannah 109
Kahn, Robert L. 141
Kahne, Hilda 59
Kalakdina, Margaret 114
Kalčik, Susan 274
Kamerick, Maureen 141
Kamerman, Sheila B. 331
Kammer, Jeanne 214 361
Kandel, Lenore 147
Kandiyoti, Deniz 281
Kane, Francis J., Jr. 250
Kane, John E. 286
Kanner, Barbara 223 244 335 335
Kanoko, Okamoto 31
Kanowitz, Leo 260
Kant, Immanuel 107 159
Kantaroff, Maryon 320
Kanter, Rosabeth Moss 14 291
Kantner, John F. 155
Kaplan, Alexandra G. 22 171
Kaplan, Cora 357
Kaplan, E. Ann 288
Kaplan, Marion 117
Kaplan, Susan Romer 106
Kaplan, Sydney Janet 36 361
Kaplan, Temma 19 316
Kaplow, Susi 175
Karapanou, Margarita 24
Karkosza, Carolyn 13
Karl, Frederick R. 47
Károlyi, Amy 150
Karp, Lila 256
Kasa no Iratsume 31
Kaschnitz, Marie Luise 102 150
Kass-Simon, G. 21
Kastenbaum, Robert 129
Katona-Apte, Judit 20
Katsuranis, Frances 354
Katz-Stoker, Fraya 110
Katz, Fred E. 166
Katz, Joseph 38
Katz, Lilian G. 156
Katz, Maude White 26
Katz, Phyllis A. 18
Katzenstein, Alfred 206
Katzman, David M. 354
Kaufman, Shirley 3 147 224 345
Kautsky, Louise 66
Kavan, Anna 220
Kay, Janice A. 6
Kay, Karyn 212 288
Kay, Richard S. 196
Kazue, Shinkawa 31
Kazuko, Shiraishi 31
Kearney, Belle 44 234
Kearon, Pamela 175
Keats, John 81 111 112 242
Keckley, Elizabeth 27
Keddie, Nikki 325
Keele, Reba 215
Kees, Weldon 3
Keiffer, Miriam G. 243 365
Kelber, Mim 256
Keller, D.H. 241
Keller, Evelyn Fox 369
Keller, George 289
Keller, Harold R. 272
Keller, Suzanne 330
Kelley, Abby 44
Kelley, Florence 44 234 237
Kelley, William Melvin 277
Kellner, Hansfried 251 252
Kellogg, Abraham L. 234
Kelly-Gadol, Joan 19
Kelly, Florence 96 257
Kelly, Gail P. 43 97
Kelly, Inga Kromann 314
Kelves, Barbara 137
Kemble, Frances Anne 34 179 345
Kempe, Dame Margery 32 79
Kempton, Sally 3 9 127
Kenealy, Arabella 152
Kenicke, Lee 286
Kenkel, William F. 200
Kennedy, Adrienne 248
Kennedy, David M. 292
Kennedy, Florynce 216
Kennedy, Mary 55
Kennell, John H. 173

Kenny, James A. 266
Kenrei Mon-in Ukyō no Daibu 31
Kent, Christopher 244
Keogh, Barbara K. 250
Kergomard, Pauline 66
Kerr, Clark 106
Kessleman, Amy 12
Kessler-Harris, Alice 41 126
Kestenberg, Judith S. 76
Kester, Dolores 68
Ketcham, Ralph 178
Ketchum, Sara Ann 85 158
Kethley, Alice J. 342
Key, Ellen 66
Key, Mary Ritchie 250
Keyserling, Mary Dublin 328
Keyssar, Alexander 360
Khaing, Mi Mi 324
Khaketla, Caroline N.M. 150
Khalifa, Atef M. 367
Khan, Verity Saifullah 309
Kharchev, Anatole 70
Khoury, Venus 150
Kicknosway, Faye 109 137 147
Kidd, Dorothy 295
Kidd, Kenneth K. 18
Kidder, E. 69
Kierkegaard, Søren 107 159
Kiesler, Sara B. 250
Kii, Lady 31
Kikusha-Ni, Tagami 31
Killigrew, Anne 345 374
Kim, Chu-Suk 236
Kimball, Alice Mary 226
Kimball, Gayle 283
Kimball, Linda A. 372
Kimball, Meredith 304
Kinder, Marsha 212
King, Ardith 146
King, Elizabeth G. 163
King, Maa C. 22 163
King, Margaret L. 23
King, Mary E. 331
King, Pat 6
King, Ursula 309
Kingbury, Martha 247
Kingston, Maxine Hong 375
Kinsey, Alfred C. 296
Kinsley, Susan 331
Kinzer, Nora Scott 71 297
Kipnis, Dorothy McBride 67
Kiriak, Illia 305
Kirk, Russell 280
Kirk, Sylvia Van 138
Kirsch, Sarah 150
Kirschner, Betty Frankle 39
Kirsh, Barbara 330
Kitman, Suzy 208
Kitt, Edith Stratton 124
Kittel, Ruth 335
Kiyak, Asuman 129
Kiyoko, Nagase 31
Kizer, Carolyn 34 109 147 168 239 248 345
Klaiber, Edward L. 171 250
Klapper, Zelda S. 13 365
Klaus, Marshall H. 173
Klaus, Patricia Otto 335
Kleeck, Mary Van, see Van Kleeck, Mary
Kleeman, James A. 76
Klegon, Douglas A. 278
Klein, Alice 295
Klein, Armin 196
Klein, Christa Ressmeyer 337
Klein, Dorie 51
Klein, Easy 341
Klein, Ethel D. 140
Klein, Laura 297 270
Klein, Melanie 198
Klein, Michael 288
Klein, Viola 250 260 264 265 324
Kleinbaum, Abby R. 19
Kleinberg, Susan J. 41
Kleinhans, Chuck 288
Kleinman, Seymour 286
Klemesrud, Judy 280
Klerman, Gerald L. 99
Klima, George 285
Klotzburger, Kay 4
Knapp, Peggy Ann 185
Knott, Edward M. 166
Knudsen, Dean D. 149 228
Kobayashi, Kazumasa 91
Kobayashi, Yutaka 250
Koch, Adrienne 164
Koch, Kenneth 347
Koedt, Anne 72 77 127 139 175 233 237
Koehler, Ludmilla 185
Koehler, Lyle W. 360
Koenig, Barbara 102
Koenig, Peter K. 351
Koestenbaum, Peter 164
Koff, Lois Ann 314
Kohen, Janet 251
Kohlberg, Lawrence 56 198 199
Kohlstedt, Sally Gregory 272
Kolata, Gina Bari 173
Koller-Fox, Cherie 117
Kollontai, Alexandra 66
Kollwitz, Käthe 179
Kolodny, Annette 88 359 361
Koltun, Elizabeth 117

Komarovsky, Mirra 39 172 176 260
Komisar, Lucy 254
Kommers, Donald P. 2
Konek, Carol 109
Kooning, Elaine de, see de Kooning, Elaine
Koontz, Elizabeth Duncan 238
Koonz, Claudia 19 126
Kopald, Sylvia 234
Korda, Michael 280
Korner, Anneliese 199
Kornfein, Madeleine 331
Korsmeyer, Carolyn 85 282
Körte, Mary Norbert 109
Kosa, John 166
Koszarski, Richard 288
Kouidis, Virginia M. 246
Kovel, Joel 268
Koyama, Takashi 324
Koyū-Ni, Matsumoto 31
Kraditor, Aileen S. 151 259 292
Kraemer, H. 199
Kraf, Elaine 24
Kraft, Linda 208
Kramer, Cheris 120 219
Kramer, Selma 76
Krantz, Kermit 62
Krase, Jerome 116
Kraton, Ann Washington 12
Kraus, Joanna Halpert 144
Krause, Corinne Azen 116
Krauskopf, Joan M. 331
Kravetz, Diane F. 21
Krawitz, Rhoda N. 250
Krebs, Edith 352
Krebs, Richard L. 196
Kreger, Nancy C. 173
Kreps, Bonnie 175
Kreps, Juanita M. 11 48 287 326
Kress, June 51
Kretser, David M. de, see de Kretser, David M.
Kreuter, Gretchen 93
Kreuter, Kent 93
Krige, Eileen Jensen 285
Kristeller, Oskar Paul 23
Kritzer, Herbert M. 368
Kronsky, Betty J. 296
Krouse, Agate N. 88
Krueger, Cynthia 166
Krupsak, Mary Anne 311
Krusell, Judith 327
Kuan, P'an-P'an 148
Kuan, Tao-Shêng 148
Kuehl, Linda 47
Kuhn, Annette 84
Kuhn, James W. 48
Kulka, Richard 172
Kumin, Maxine 34 109 147 224 239 245 345
Kunzle, David 247
Kupinsky, Stanley 91
Kurian, George 20
Kuse, Alan R. 204
Kushner, Rose 191
Kuzmack, Linda 117
L'Esperance, Jean 181
La Guma, Alex 95
La Mond, Annette M. 333
La Rue, Linda 77
Labalme, Patricia H. 23
Lacassin, Francis 212
Lacey, W.K. 299
Ladner, Joyce A. 126 173
Lady of the Arbour 345
Lady of the Assembly 345
Lafferty, William 233
Lafleur, Ingrun 218
Lagerlöf, Selma 179 273 279
Lahav, Pnina 281
Laing, Dilys 32 34 242 374
Lakoff, Robin 203 361
Lamb, Margaret 220 298
Lamb, Michael E. 18
Lamb, Myrna 144 248 254
Lamb, Richard R. 196
Lamers, William M., Jr. 62
Lamott, Kenneth 280
Lamphere, Louise 20 57 249
Lampl-de Groot, Jeanne 169
Lampman, Robert J. 251 252
Lan, Ling 148
Lancaster, Jane Beckman 73 201
Land, Hilary 205
Lander, Dawn 17
Landes, Ruth 12 322
Landy, Marcia 17
Lane, Ann J. 126
Laney, Lucy Craft 27 28
Lang, Gladys Engel 105
Lang, V.E. 320
Langgaesser, Elisabeth 102
Langley, Eve 345
Langness, L.L. 285
Langton, Anne 165
Lanier, Aemelia 79
Lanier, Alison Raymond 294
Lansing, Marjorie 163 190 316 329
Lantz, Herman R. 176
Lapidus, Gail Warshofsky 291 316 318 329
Lapidus, Jacqueline 109
Larcom, Lucy 12 69 187 319 336 374

Larguia, Isabel 297
Larkin, Joan 137
Larned, Deborah 191
Larner, Christina 52
Larner, Jeremy 277
Laroque, Pierre 352
Larowe, Nina Churchman 124
Larrick, Nancy 347
Larsen, Wendy 264 264
Larson, Meredith A. 40
Lasch, Christopher 151 259
Lasker-Schüler, Else 150
Lasoff, Anne 369
Latt, David J. 240
Laughlin, Gail 237
Laurence, Margaret 245 273 305 373
Laurentin, Anne 338
Lavin, Mary 33 245 356
Lavrin, Asunción 121 126
Lawner, Lynne 109
Lawrence, Barbara 157
Lawrence, D.H. 233 277 279
Lawrence, Farris 75
Lawrenson, Helen 362
Laws, Judith Long 291 333
Lawson, Ronald 143
Layton, Irving 305
Lazarre, Jane 300
Lazarus, Arnold A. 330
Lazarus, Emma 189 345 374
LaFollette, Suzanne 188
LaMarsh, Judy 305
LaRiviere, Robert 8
LaVigna, Claire 116 218
le Fort, Gertrud von 102
Le Guin, Ursula K. 16 24 133 134 245 340
Le Sueur, Meridel 12 353
Leacock, Eleanor 19 101 270 281 297
Leaper, R. John 287
Lear, Julia Graham 235
Lear, Martha Weinman 139
Leavitt, Harold J. 291
Leavitt, Jacqueline 143
Leavitt, Ruby R. 254
Leavitt, Ruby R., see also Rohrlich-Leavitt, Ruby R.
Lebeuf, Annie M.D. 260 338
Lebra, Joyce 306
Lecht, Charles P. 62
Ledwitz-Rigby, Florence 171
Lee, Audrey 118
Lee, Edmina C. 45
Lee, Edmina C. 45
Lee, Joseph J. 312
Lee, Julia 8
Lee, Marcia M. 163
Lee, Mary, Lady Chudleigh 345
Lee, Patrick C. 156 198
Lee, Sonia 222
Lee, Sung-Jin 236
Leek, Ann 80
Lees, Robert B. 140
Leff, Naomi 303
Lefkowitz, Mary 190
Leghorn, Lisa 237
Lehmann, Andrée 324
Lehr, Ursula 206
Lehrman, Sara 185
Leibowitz, Arleen 202
Leibowitz, Lila 230
Leidel, Diana 191
Leifer, Daniel I. 117
Leifer, Myra 117
Leijon, Anna-Greta 352
Leis, Nancy B. 249
Leith, Suzette 141 307
Lemon, Judith 105
Lenero, Maria de Carmen Elu de 194
Lenglet, Marcia Smith 304
Lenin, V.I. 89 159
Lenne, Gérard 212
Leo, André 175
Leo, Evelyn 237
Leppaluoto, Jean R. 342
Lepper, Mary M. 316
Lerch, Patricia Barker 372
Lerenbaum, Miriam 17
Lerman, Hannah 77
Lerner, Gerda 126 151 292 360
Lerner, Harriet F. 76
Lesage, Julia 212 288
Leslie, Genevieve 295
Leslie, Myriam F. 124
Lessard, Suzannah 22
Lesser, Gerald S. 250
Lessing, Doris 33 34 83 111 112 113 161 220 233 245 248 277 279 300 339 356
Lester, David 99
Lester, Julius 208
Leuchter, Johanna 110
Lever, Janet 4
Levertov, Denise 3 34 108 109 111 147 168 239 242 245 248 345
Levin, Michael 203
Levine, Ellen 175 264 265
Levine, James 156
Levine, Louis 12
Levine, Philip 3
Levine, Seymour 199

Levine, Stephen M. 243 266
Levinger, George 252
Levitin, Teresa 73 141 267 327
Levitt, Bruce 141
Levrant de Bretteville, Sheila 143
Levy, Betty 13 208
Levy, Darline Gay 349
Levy, Judith G. 22
Lew, Rita Van, see Van Lew, Rita
Lewes, George Henry 363
Lewis, Barbara C. 213 302
Lewis, Helen Block 101
Lewis, Hylan 25
Lewis, Janet 345 346 374
Lewis, Lena Morrow 72
Lewis, Michael 73 173 176 199
Lewis, Mollie V. 28
Lewis, Shelby 43
Lewis, Sinclair 233
Lewis, Toye B. 45
Leyda, Jay 212
LeCoultre, Denise 135
LeGrand, Camille E. 94 94
LeMoyne, Jean 305
LeVine, Robert A. 94 155
LeVine, Rovebert A. 94
Li, Ch'ing-Chao 148
Li, Chü 148 150
Li, Yeh 148
Libera, Sharon Mayer 109
Lichtman, Ronnie 72
Liddell, Brendan E.A. 278
Liddington, Jill 92
Liddle, Helen Gordon 66
Lidz, Ruth W. 211
Lieberman, Marcia R. 110 208
Liebert, Robert M. 105
Liebow, Elliot 25
Liebowitz, Ruth P. 337
Liebschutz, Sarah F. 344
Lifshin, Lyn 97 109 136 137 168 224 245
Lifton, Robert J. 253
Lightfoot, Sara Lawrence 14 45 272
Lights, Rikki 353
Liljeström, Rita 37 206
Limpus, Laurel 260
Lin, Ling 148
Lin, Siu-Tsung 329
Lincoln, Abbey 26 118
Lincoln, Salome 72
Lincoln, Sarah Ann 140
Linden, Fabian 284
Lindenbau, Shirley 227
Lindsay, Beverly 43
Lindsay, Lady Anne 345
Lindsey, Karen 208 216
Lindsey, Kay 26 26
Lindsey, Robert 280
Linner, Birgitta 266 365
Linton-Umeh, Marie 222
Linton, Ralph 198
Lipman-Blumen, Jean 271 291 331 344
Lipman, Carol 86
Lippard, Lucy R. 303
Lipshitz, Susan 205 225
Lipshutz, Judith Ann 331
Lipton, Morris A. 250
Lispector, Clarice 279
Litewka, Jack 89
Litman, Gloria K. 205
Little, Cynthia Jeffress 121
Little, Judith 110
Little, Kenneth 293
Liu, William T. 2 62
Livermore, Mary A. 72 187 262
Livesay, Dorothy 305
Livson, Florine B. 129
Llewelyn-Davies, Melissa 350
Lloyd-Jones, Esther M. 11
Lloyd, Barbara B. 67
Lobban, Glenys 205
Lock, F.P. 255
Locke, John 107 203
Locksley, Anne 99
Lockwood, Belva 72 96 319
Loeb, Jane W. 4 39
Loewenberg, Bert James 27
Lofland, Lyn H. 14
Loftin, Edward E. 8
Loftin, Elouise 118
Loguna-Diaz, Elpidio 122
Lokhvitskaya, Mirra 355
Lomax, Alan 20
Lombroso, Caesar 51
Long, Larry H. 354
Long, Nira 291
Longauex y Vasquez, Enriqueta 216
Lopata, Helena Znaniecki 39 129
Lopate, Carol 89 105 166
Loper, Mary Lou 284
Lopes, Maria 313
Lopez-Rey, Manuel 51
Lorand, Rhoda L. 280
Lorand, Sandor 169
Lorber, Judith 14 264
Lord, Edith Elizabeth 20 206
Lord, Sharon B. 314
Lorde, Audré 26 98 118 137 147 222 224 239 245 347
Lorenz, Konrad 198

Lorichs, Sonja 68
Lougee, Carolyn 141
Loughborough, Mary Ann Webster 104
Lourie, Margaret A. 140 141
Loury, Glenn C. 333
Love, Barbara 254
Loving, Oyoko 222
Lowe, Caroline A. 44
Lowell Manufacturing Co. 12
Lowell, Amy 34 147 189 339 374
Lowell, Josephine Shaw 262
Lowell, Maria White 374
Lower East Side Women's Liberation Collective 9
Lowry, Beverly 24
Lowry, Helen M. 291
Lowther, Pat 136
Loy, Mina 374
LoPicolo, Joseph 155
Lu, Hsun 95
Lu, Yu-Lan 307
Lucas, Joseph R. 159 203
Luce, Clare Boothe 112 161
Lucian 231
Luckey, Eleanore B. 155
Lucretius 231
Ludwig, Paula 34
Lund, Caroline 86
Lundberg, Ferdinand 363
Lunde, Donald T. 56
Lupton, Mary Jane 89
Luquet-Parat, C. 78
Luria, Gina 240 361
Luria, Zella 22 173
Lurie, Nancy Oestrich 347
Lussier, Virginia Lee 364
Lutfi, al-Sayyid Marsot, Afaf, see Marsot, Afaf Lutfi al-Sayyid
Luthans, Fred 314
Luthra, Bimla 115
Luttinger, Abigail 224
Lydon, Susan 9 132 186 216
Lynd, Helen 12
Lynd, Robert 12
lyndon, alice atkinson 369
Lynn, David B. 200 250 252 271
Lynn, Elizabeth A. 133
Lynn, Naomi 163 264 265 316
Lyon, Lilian Bowes 374
Lyon, Nancy 208
Lyon, Phyllis 142 173
Ma, Hsiang-Lan 148
Mabbott, Thomas Ollive 128
Mac Curtain, Margaret 312
Maccia, Elizabeth Steiner 271
Maccoby, Eleanor E. 56 77 164 172 176 197 198 250
Macdonald, Cynthia 147
Machado de Assis, J.M. de 279
Macías, Anna 121
Mackintosh, Maureeen M. 92
Macleod, Catherine 295
Macmurchy, Marjory 165
Macpherson, Kay 320
MacAdam, George 139
MacBrayer, Caroline T. 200
MacCormack, Carol P. 281
MacDonald, Cynthia 239
MacDonald, Lynn 304
MacDonald, Susan 109
MacDougall, Ursula 34
MacEwan, Phyllis 127 233 237
MacEwen, Gwendolyn 136
MacFarlane, Alan 52
MacFarlane, Kee 235
MacFarlane, Paul T. 209
MacLean, Katherine 340
MacLennan, Hugh 305
MacManus, Anna Johnston, see Carberry, Ethna
MacManus, Susan A. 368
MacPhail, Agnes 165
MacRae, Jean 283
Madan, T.N. 115
Madden, Janice Fanning 202 291
Madden, Sarah Hanley 246
Maddux, R.B. 314
Madgett, Naomi Long 109 233
Madhubuti, Haki R. 222
Madison, Bernice 318
Madsen, Carol Cornwall 215
Mager, Don 8
Magid, Margo 142 147
Maglin, Nan Bauer 110
Magnus, Elizabeth M. 171
Magnusson, Lucille 358
Magrab, Phyllis R. 18
Maher, Vanessa 325
Mahoney, Anne Rankin 321
Maier, Norman R.F. 250
Mailer, Norman 47 111 112
Mainardi, Pat 89 139 216 237 252
Maisel, Carolyn 109
Majka, Linda 328
Makiesky-Barrow, Susan 213 297
Makin, Bathsua 79
Makward, Christiane 98
Malamud, Bernard 277
Maldoror, Sarah 288
Malinowski, Bronislaw 198
Malkiel, Theresa 12 72
Mallan, Lucy 344

Maloney, Joan M. 349
Maltz, Daniel N. 317
Mancuso, Arlene 116
Mandel, William M. 327
Manderson, Leonore 281
Mandis, Renos 256
Manier, Edward 2
Manis, Jean Denby 141
Manley, (Mary) Delariviere 32 79
Mann, Horace 319
Manner, Eeva-Liisa 150
Mannes, Marya 164
Mannheim, Hermann 51
Manning, Maurice 312
Manning, Olivia 273 356
Manosevitz, Martin 155
Mansfield, Katherine 33 34 111 112 113 179 248 277 279 373
Mansur, Abby 124
Maranda, Elli Köngäs 131
Marceau, Jane 55
Marchak, M. Patricia 304
Marcus, Paula 237
Marcuse, Herbert 107
Margolin, Anna 150
Margolis, Clorinda 85
Margolis, Diane Rothbard 341
Margolis, Joseph 85 157
Marguerite of Angoulême 299
Margulies, Leah 11
Marie-Ellse 248
Marieskind, Helen 191
Marine, Gene 314
Mariotti, Amelia M. 297
Marković, Mihailo 282
Marks, Elaine 80
Marks, Julie 18
Marks, Pauline 181
Markus, Hazel 196
Marlowe, Leigh 243
Marmor, Judd 169 170 252
Marolla, Joseph A. 99
Marot, Helen 12
Marquez, Gabriel Garçia, see Garçia Marquez, Gabriel
Marriott, Alice Lee 353
Marsden, Madonna 110
Marsh, N. 103
Marshall, Gloria 322
Marshall, Paule 26 29 118 220 222 277
Marshall, Ray 333
Marsot, Afaf Lutfi al-Sayyid 325
Marti, Rosa Signorelli de, see Signorelli de Marti, Rosa
Martin, Claire 305
Martin, Clyde E. 296
Martin, Del 142 173
Martin, Donna 341 341
Martin, Edna 12
Martin, Harry M. 166
Martin, Joan C. 331
Martin, Lois Ann 342
Martin, Martha 179
Martin, Michael 282
Martin, Wendy 9 214 254
Martineau, Barbara Halpern 288
Martineau, Harriet 32 237 292
Martinelli, Phylis Cancilla 116
Martinez, Sabina 28
Marvell, Andrew 81 242
Marver, James D. 40
Marx, Janet 186
Masako, Chino 31
Masako, Takiguchi 31
Masek, Rosemary 335
Masinton, Charles G. 240
Masinton, Martha 240
Maslin, Janet 288
Maslow, A.H. 169
Maslow, Ellen 127
Mason, Karen Oppenheim 140 291
Mason, Otis Tufton 232
Massey, Ruth 252
Masters, Marcia Lee 345
Masters, William H. 62 200 296
Matasar, Ann B. 316
Mather, Cotton 292
Matheson, Gwen 320
Mathews, Mary McNair 124
Mathieu, Corina S. 122
Matkovic, Charlotte 137
Matsumoto, Sheila 306
Mattelart, Michele 194
Matthews, Burnita Shelton 234
Matthews, Esther E. 342
Matthews, Glenna 12
Matthews, Lillian 12
Matthews, Lucille 6
Matthiasson, Carolyn J. 131
Matyas, Jennie 319
Maurier, Daphne du, see du Maurier, Daphne
Maxson, Mary Lou 306
May, Robert 176
Mayhall, Jane 24 220 239
Maynard, Eileen 131
Maynard, Joyce 347
Mayo, Peter 67
Mazor, Miriam D. 211
Mazumdar, Vina 115 281
Mbilinyi, Marjorie 95 289
McAfee, Kathy 74 97 228 237
McAfee, Sandra Wray 140

McAlmon, Victoria 226
McAlpin, Michelle 281
McAlpine, Willie 173
McBee, Mary Louise 11
McBride, Theresa 19
McCaffrey, Anne 340
McCain, Nina 341
McCarthy, Eunice 312
McCarthy, Karen 196
McCarthy, Margaret 323
McCarthy, Mary 33 34 248 363
McCauley, Elizabeth 199
McCauley, Janie Caves 68
McClane, Kenneth A. 222
McClelland, David C. 253
McClelland, Lou 267
McClung, Nellie L. 165 305
McCombs, Judith 109 137 239
McConnell-Ginet, Sally 98 219 361
McCormack, Thelma 14
McCormick, Ruth 288 288
McCrone, Donald J. 174
McCue, James 269
McCullers, Carson 33 34 83 248 347
McCulloch, Catharine Waugh 234
McDaniel, Judith 224
McDonald, Oonagh 323
McDonald, Robert L. 176
McDonough, Roisin 84
McDougald, Elsie Johnson 28
McDougall, J. 78
McDougall, Joyce 296
McDougall, Mary Lynn 19
McDowell, Margaret B. 246
McGhee, Paul E. 18
McGilligan, Patrick 288
McGinley, Phyllis 34 147 259 260 345
McGirr, Kevin J. 8
McGovern, James R. 151 292 360
McGowan, Barbara 140
McGowan, Margaret M. 52
McGrath, Kathleen Conway 110
McGrath, Wilma E. 163
McGroarty, Jane 303
McGuinn, Nicholas 145
McGuinness, Diane 67
McHale, John 289
McIntosh, Mary 84 92 348
McIntyre, Vonda 340
McKain, Barbara 89
McKain, Michael 89
McKay, Claude 277
McKelway, A.J. 128
McKinney, Michael 163
McKnight, Dorothy 364
McLaughlin, Eleanor Commo 263 177 337
McLeod, Norma 274
McLure, John W. 246
McMurtry, John 157
McNamara, Colleen 89
McNamara, Jo Ann 19 42 315
McNeil, Elton B. 176
McPherson, Sandra 147
McWilliams-Tullberg, Rita 244
McWilliams, Nancy 316
Mead, Margaret 268 11 40 77 127 158 173 198 206 260 280 293 296 322 347 362 365
Meade, L.T. 50
Means, Ingunn Norderval 329
Mechtel, Angelika 102
Media Women 216
Mednick, Martha T. Shuch 77 172 176 267
Meese, Elizabeth A. 137 140
Mehrhof, Barbara 175
Mehta, Rama 115
Meier, Kenneth J. 174
Meireles, Cecília 150
Melder, Keith 360
Melges, Frederick T. 176 250
Mello Breyner Andresen, Sophia de 150
Mellown, Elgin W. 47
Melvill, Elizabeth, Lady Culross 345
Memphis Minnie 374
Menaker, Esther 330
Mendelson, Johanna S.R. 121
Mendez, Charlotte 361
Menebroker, Ann 109
Mêng, Chu 148
Mengel, Nanette Vonnegut 369
Menon, Lakshmi N. 114 294
Menzie, Betty 358
Merck, Mandy 225
Meredith, George 242
Mering, Von 166
Meriwether, Louise 28 29
Merkl, Peter H. 329
Merkle, Judith 307
Mernissi, Fatima 281 293
Merriam, Eve 109 127 147 233 347
Merril, Judith 340
Merritt, Karen 21
Messent, Peter R. 67
Messick, Samuel 197
Messinger, Ruth 98
Mew, Charlotte 34 189 242 374
Meyer-Bahlburg, Heino F.L. 171 199

Meyer, Alfred G. 318
Meyer, Donald B. 292
Meyer, Marc A. 335
Meyer, Pearl 314
Meyer, Priscilla S. 314
Meyer, Victoria Junco 21
Meyering, Anne C. 269
Meylan, Elisabeth 102
Meynell, Alice 189 242 345 374
Mhac an tSaoi, Máire 150
Mhatra, Sharayu 114
Michael, Richard P. 199
Michel, Andrée 19 38 70
Michel, Sonya 117
Michener, Diana 369
Michiko, Inoue 31
Michitsuna, Mother of 31
Micklow, Patricia L. 140
Middleton-Keirn, Susan 317
Middleton, Donna 97 237
Middleton, Lucy 323
Middleton, Thomas 310
Mieko, Kanai 31
Mikajo, Yagi 31
Mikulski, Barbara 57
Miles, Catherine Cox 198
Miles, Josephine 34 109 345 374
Milford, Nancy 375
Mill, Harriet Taylor 65 74
Mill, John Stuart 65 87 89 107 158 159 188 203 228 233 260 362 363
Millay, Edna St. Vincent 34 147 189 242 245 339 374
Miller, Alice Duer 234
Miller, Beth 88 122
Miller, Casey 280
Miller, Elizabeth Smith 234
Miller, Frieda 234
Miller, Hannah 208
Miller, Herman P. 39
Miller, Jean Baker 365
Miller, John C. 122
Miller, Judith 11
Miller, Nellie Burget 346
Miller, Ruthann 86
Miller, Sally M. 93
Miller, Thomas W. 243
Miller, Vassar 109 147 345
Millett, Kate 51 149 175 216 223 252 254 259 341 363
Millman, Marcia 14
Mills, Harriet May 237
Milton, John 228 242
Milton, Nancy 307
Milward, H. Brinton 174
Minahan, John 314
Minamoto no Toshitaka, Daughter of 31
Minattur, Joseph 309
Mincer, Jacob 252
Minces, Juliette 325
Miner, Anne S. 301
Mink, Patsy T. 11
Minnie, Memphis, see Memphis Minnie
Minor, Virginia 72
Minty, Judith 224
Mintz, Barbara R. 236
Mintz, Ellen 243
Minuchin, Patricia 22 208 271
Miranda, Glaura Vasques de, see Vasques de Miranda, Glaura
Mischel, Walter 56
Mishler, Susan Anzivino 61
Mistral, Gabriela 34 150
Mitchell, Anita M. 328
Mitchell, Carol 278
Mitchell, Gary D. 176 250
Mitchell, Gladys 50
Mitchell, Joyce M. 327
Mitchell, Joyce S. 347
Mitchell, Juliet 89 97 126 127 132 158 181 251 252 268
Mitchell, Maria 104
Mitchell, Sally 244
Miyahira, Sarah D. 61
Miyoko, Gotō 31
Mlinar, Josephine 208
Moal, M.P. 338
Moch, Leslie Page 140
Mody, Susan 114
Mohsen, Safia K. 131
Molinaro, Ursule 144
Molodowsky, Kadia 150
Molotch, Harvey L. 105
Monczka, Robert M. 314
Mond, Frank 232
Money, John 155 164 176 198 209 250 266 296
Montagu, Ashley 107 233 362
Montagu, Lady Mary Wortley 32 242 345 374
Montalvo, G. Ordonez de, see Ordonez de Montalvo, G.
Monter, E. William 19
Montero, Gloria 320
Montgomery, Judith H. 36
Monts, Elizabeth A. 21
Moody, Anne 28 118
Moon, Rachel 216
Moon, Rebecca 237
Moon, Terry 74
Moore, Audry 331

Moore, Burness E. 76
Moore, C.L. 134
Moore, Honor 144 224 239 375
Moore, Kristin A. 287 354
Moore, Marian Louise 72 72
Moore, Marianne 34 147 168 189 245 374
Moore, Nanci I. 6
Moore, R. Laurence 360
Moore, Sylvia F 351
Moore, Viginia 374
Mora, Gabriela 80 122
Moraff, Barbara 109
Moran, Robert D. 252
Morantz, Regina 42
Moravia, Alberto 111 112
More, Hannah 79
Moreaux, Colette 304
Morgan, Edmund S. 151
Morgan, Ellen 88 110
Morgan, Kathryn 158
Morgan, Lady Sydney 232
Morgan, Robin 9 109 132 137 147 237 239
Morgenstern, Felice 352
Morgenstern, Richard 243
Morley, Helena, see Brant, Alice
Morlock, Laura 4
Morris, Celia 341
Morris, Monica B. 354
Morris, Rebecca 24 220
Morris, Richard B. 12
Morris, Wright 111 112
Morrison, Toni 29 118
Morros, Lucy 275
Morsy, Soheir A. 325
Mortimer, Penelope 356
Morton, Nelle 210 263
Morton, Peggy 97 132
Moscowitz, Henry 12
Moses, Joel C. 318
Moses, Yolanda T. 281
Moskow, Michael H. 48
Moss, Howard A. 176 198 199
Moss, Peter 135
Moss, Vicki 311
Moss, Zoe 89 216
Mota, Vivian M. 194
Mother Jones, see Jones, Mary Harris
Mothner, Ira 365
Mott, Frank L. 351 371
Mott, Lucretia 9 44 87 234 237
Motta Diniz, Francisca de, see Diniz, Francisca de Motta
Mouer, Elizabeth Knipe 306
Moulton, Janice 85 157 158
Moulton, Ruth 170 268 296
Mountain Wolf Woman 104
Moyer, Kenneth E. 199
Moynihan, Daniel P. 25
Mphalele, Ezekiel 95
Ms. Magazine 13
Mueller, Lisel 109
Mueller, Martha 281
Mullany, Kate 12
Mulligan, Joan E. 269
Mullings, Leith 302
Mulvey, Laura 288 357
Mundy, J. 243
Mundy, Jean 250
Munley, Patrick H. 266
Munro, Alice 113 305 373
Munro, Deborah 109
Munro, Winsome 283
Munroe, Ellen 69
Murasaki Shikibu 31
Murickan, J. 309
Murphy, Kathleen 288
Murphy, Miriam Brinton 215
Murphy, Robert F. 198
Murphy, Yolanda 198
Murray, Joan 113
Murray, Judith 234
Murray, Michele 108 375
Murray, Pauli 28 147 151 175 238 265
Murry, Ann 345
Musonius, Rufus 231
Mussen, Paul H. 155 200 260
Myerhoff, Barbara 317
Myers, Lena Wright 14
Myers, Mitzi 359
Myrdal, Alva 329
Myrdal, Gunnar 132 228
n'Ait Attik, Mririda, see Attik, Mririda n'Ait
Nadelman, Lorraine 140
Nadelson, Carol 211 11
Nader, Laura 321 322
Naffziger, Claudeen 342
Nagel, Stuart S. 51
Nagel, Thomas 157
Nagy, Ágnes Nemes 150
Naish, Julia 350
Nakamura, Hachiro 324
Namboze, Josephine M. 20
Nandy, Ashis 115
Narain, Vatsala 324
Narek, Diane 237
Nash, June 270 297
Nash, Richard 8
Nash, Sharon Churnin 204
Nass, Gilbert D. 155

Parker, Gail 153
Parker, Stephen 3
Parkes, Colin Murray 176
Parlee, Mary B. 22 77 173 250 266
Parr, Catharine, Queen of England 79
Parra, Violeta 150
Parsons, Elizabeth 277
Parsons, Jacquelynne E. 171
Parsons, Talcott 198 251 252 260
Parvey, Constance F. 177
Pascale, Susan 216 237
Pastan, Linda 224 245
Pastner, Carroll McC. 325
Pate, Mary Anne 77
Paterson, Michelle 354
Patraka, Vivian M. 141 146
Patrick, Anne E. 258
Patrick, G.T.W. 173
Patten, Frances Gray 13
Patterson, Adalene R. 166
Patterson, Michelle 4
Patterson, Mrs. Robert M. 28
Patton, Gwen 26
Paul of Tarsus 107
Paul VI, Pope 157
Paul, Lois 249 317
Paulson, Joy 306
Pautasso, Luigi 116
Pauwels, Jacques R. 275
Pavlik, Zdenek 54
Paxson, Diana L. 133
Payne, Carol Williams 175
Payne, Joyce 278
Pearce, Diana 371
Pearce, Ellen 109
Peary, Gerald 288
Peattie, Lisa 281
Peckenpaugh, Angela 137
Pedersen, Darhl M. 250
Pedersen, Lisë 68
Pederson, Inger Magrete 294
Pedrick, Jean 353
Peery, Pat 26
Peirse, Juanita 374
Pelavin, Michael 117
Pendergrass, Virginia E. 75
Peoples, Vickie Y. 61
Peplau, Letitia Anne 264
Pereira, Teresinha 122
Perictione 231
Perkins, Elizabeth 72
Perkins, Josephine Amelia 96
Perlman, M. 338
Perlmutter, Johanna F. 211
Perlstein, Marcia 77
Perón, Eva 313
Perreault, Jeanne 8
Perry, Dannis 288
Perry, Eleanor 364
Perry, Harriet 116
Perry, Joseph B., Jr. 370
Persky, Harold 199
Person, Ethel S. 199 268
Pesa, Pamela Di, see Di Pesa, Pamela
Pescatello, Ann M. 71 126
Peslikis, Irene 216 237
Pestieau, Caroline 320
Petchesky, Rosalind 35
Peters, Emrys L. 325
Peters, J.H. 51
Peters, Joseph J. 94
Petersen, Anne C. 171 204
Peterson, Esther 253
Peterson, M. Jeanne 223
Peterson, Nicolas 366
Peterson, Susan Rae 85
Petrarch 228
Petry, Ann 34
Pettigrew, L. Eudora 269
Phelps, Elizabeth Stuart 10
Phelps, Linda 89 264 264
Phelps, W.R. 51
Phetersen, Gail I. 250
Philipp, Thomas 325
Philips, Joan 345
Philips, Katherine 79 189 345 374
Phillips, Barbara 105
Phillips, Elsie Cole 44
Phillips, J.A. 69
Phillips, Madge 286
Phillips, Susan 143
Phipps-Yonas, Susan 173
Phoenix, Charles H. 199
Pickering, Ruth 226
Picquet, Louisa 27
Pierce, Christine 158 159 203 254 282
Pierce, John C. 163
Piercy, Marge 16 109 111 113 127 136 137 142 147 168 216 220 220 224 233 239 300 345 353
Pierson, Ruth 138
Pietrofesa, John J. 196 252
Pifer, Alan 106 371
Piho, Virve 297
Piliavin, Jane Allyn 21
Pilkington, Laetitia 345
Pillsbury, Barbara L.K. 325
Pinch, L. 199
Pinchbeck, Ivy 252
Pinchot, Cornelia Bryce 226
Pinckney, Eliza Lucas 72 319

Pincoffs, Edmund L. 2
Pincus, Cynthia 4
Ping, Hsin 148 150
Pinneli, Antonella 54
Piore, Michael 333
Piotrowski, Jerzy 54 70
Pirkis, C.L. 50
Pitcher, Evelyn Goodenough 13 296
Pitter, Ruth 345 374
Plantier, Thérèse 46
Plaskow, Judith 117 263
Plaskow, Judith, see also Goldenberg, Judith Plaskow
Plath, Sylvia 3 34 81 108 109 111 113 147 168 189 216 224 248 339 345 363
Plato 107 158 159 203 228 231 232 299
Platt, John 140 289
Plauger, P.J. 16
Pleck, Elizabeth 126 140
Pleck, Joseph H. 140 173 266 276 278
Plutarch 107 231
Poe, Edgar Allan 81 242 279
Pogrebin, Letty Cottin 156 256
Poirier, Frank E. 20
Polachek, Solomon W. 202 333
Polit, Denise F. 371
Polk, Barbara Bovee 77 264
Pollak, Otto 51
Pollard, Vicki 237
Pollet, Elizabeth 220
Pollitzer, Anita 234
Pollock, Leafy 76
Pollock, Mordeca Jane 365
Poloma, Margaret M. 70 166
Polster, Miriam 330
Pomerleau, Cynthia S. 359
Pomeroy, H.S. 1
Pomeroy, Sarah B. 126
Pomeroy, Wardell B. 296
Pompei, Giuliana 89
Pope, Alexander 242
Pope, Barbara Corrado 19 349
Pope, Jackie 269
Popenoe, David 143
Popp, Adelheid 66
Popper, Herbert 166
Porphyry 231
Portal, Magda 313
Porter, Catherine M. 342 342
Porter, Katherine Anne 33 34 83 245 277
Porter, Mary Cornelia 316 329
Porter, Nancy M. 342
Porter, William Sydney, see Henry, O.
Portz, Eileen 286
Porumbacu, Veronica 150
Potter, David M. 259
Pottinger, J. Stanley 180 301
Pottker, Janice 196
Powderly, Terence V. 12 319
Powell, Gloria Johnson 18
Power, Eileen 299
Powers, Elizabeth 306
Pozzetta, George E. 116
Pozzi, Antonia 150
Pozzuto, Frances H. 342
Prager, Marie Françoise 46
Prather, Jane 271 327 342
Pratt, Annis 21 36 88
Pratt, Linda Ray 110
Pratt, William C. 93
Prell-Foldes, Riv-Ellen 317
Premkumar, T. 51
Prentice, Alison 138
President's Commission on the Status of Women 228 234 260
Presidential Task Force on Women's Rights and Responsibilities 228
Pressel, Esther 372
Prestage, Jewel L. 163 174 326
Preston, Ann 72 237
Preston, Michael B. 174
Price, Nancy 109
Prichard, Katharine 273
Prida, Dolores 208
Prima, Diane Di, see Di Prima, Diane
Primrose, Lady Diana 345
Primrose, Lynn 304
Prince, Nancy 27
Pringle, Elizabeth Allston 319
Pritam, Amrita 150
Probber, Joan 101
Proctor, E.B. 155
Prokopec, Jiří 70
Pross, Helge 324
Provenzano, Frank J. 22 173
Pruette, Lorine Livingston 226
Pruitt, Anne 45
Prusak, Bernard P. 177
Prusoff, Brigitte 4
Psaltis, Egly 324
Ptaschkina, Nelly 179
Pullen, Doris L. 238
Purcell, Kate 92
Purcell, Polly Jane 96
Purcell, Susan Kaufman 71 316
Purple September, staff of 123
Puryear, Gwendolyn Randall 43

Putnam, Emily James 87
Putnam, Harriet E. 69
Putnam, Linda 314
Pythagoras 231
Quataert, Jean 218
Queen, Renee 156
Quennell, Peter 5
Quinn, Robert P. 73 141 267 327
Quinton, Amelia Stone 262
Quirk, Cathleen 136 147
Rabin, A.I. 206
Radcliffe-Umstead, Douglas 185
Radcliffe, Ann 119 345
Radical Feminists 175
Radicalesbians 9 22 72 77 127 175
Radner, Susan G. 89
Raffler-Engel, Walburga von 219
Raine, Kathleen 345 374
Rainey, Gertrude "Ma" 374
Rainone, Nanette 237
Rainwater, Lee 25 155 176
Raitièr, Anna 80
Rajadhom, P. Anuman 221
Raksasataya, Amara 294
Raleigh, Sir Walter 242
Ramey, Estelle R. 22 77
Ramkhalawansingh, Ceta 295
Rand, Lorraine 166
Randal, Vera 3
Randall, Julia 147 345
Randall, Margaret 35
Rankin, Mary Backus 308
Rapaport, Elizabeth 85 282
Raphael, Dana 20
Rapone, Anita 175
Rapoport, Rhona 205
Rasche, Christine E. 75
Rass, Rebecca 220
Ratcliff , Graham 53
Ratner, Rochelle 239
Rau, Santha Rama 95 347
Rauh, Hellgard 206
Raushenbush, Esther 106
Ravenscroft, Catherine 146
Ravikovitch, Dahlia 150
Rawles, Beth 45
Raymond, Beth J. 243 266
Raymond, Janice 283
Reagan, Barbara B. 291 328
Reagan, Maureen 89
Rebecca, Meda 22 140
Rechter, Judith 147
Redfern, Martin 252
Redlich, Patricia 312
Redlinger, Wendy 219
Redstockings 127 132 149 237
Reece, Gene 127
Reed, Cheryl L. 196
Reed, Evelyn 86 89 237
Reed, John Shelton 25
Reed, Kit 340
Reese, Dorothy E. 166
Reese, Lizette Woodworth 374
Reeve, Arthur B. 50
Reeves, James 245
Reeves, Nancy 260
Register, Sheri 90
Reich, Adria 13
Reich, Peter 211
Reid, Coletta 89 123
Reid, Elizabeth 352
Reid, Inez Smith 45 45 163 344
Reif, William E. 314
Reinartz, K.F. 265
Reingold, Paula 109
Reinig, Christa 102
Reinisch, June Machover 204
Reiss, Ira L. 155
Reiter, Rayna R. 230
Reitz, Rosetta 191
Remond, Sarah Parker 27
Remy, Dorothy 230
Rendel, Margherita 38 323
Rendell, Ruth 119
Rensselaer, Gratz Van, see Van Rensselaer, Gratz
Rensselaer, Maria van 319
Replansky, Naomi 147 353
Reppucci, N. Dickon 250
Resource Center on Sex Roles in Education 208
Reubens, Beatrice G. 328
Reubens, Edwin P. 328
Reverby, Susan 12 127 334
Revolutionary Communist Party 89
Reznikoff, Charles 353
Rhi, Bou-Yong 236
Rhine, Alice Hyneman 262
Rhys, Jean 220 273 373
Ribner, Susan 208
Rice, Florence 28
Rich, Adrienne 3 34 108 109 111 112 137 147 168 173 191 214 224 239 245 245 248 290 345 347 353
Rich, B. Ruby 212
Richards, Cara E. 131
Richards, Ellen H. 319
Richardson, Diane 205
Richardson, Dorothy 32 108 273 319
Richardson, Herbert W. 62
Richardson, Joanna 5
Richardson, Samuel 108
Richetti, John J. 240

Richman, Michele 361
Rickert, Wendy G. 147
Riddell, Adaljiza Sosa 329
Ridge, Lola 374
Ridler, Anne 345 374
Ridley, Jeanne Claire 294
Rie, Yoshiyuki 31
Riedel, Marc 94
Riegel, Robert E. 259
Riesman, David 197 253 271
Riess, Bernard F. 99 330
Riessman, Catherine Kohler 365
Riger, Stephanie 141
Riki 8
Riley, Bridget 15
Riley, John W., Jr. 287
Rin, Ishigaki 31
Rinser, Luise 102
Rinzler, Carol 256
Rioff, Suzanne Berger 147
Riquet, Michel 162
Ris, Hania W. 21
Ritchie, Elizabeth Kohler 215
Ritvo, Samuel 76
Rive, Richard 95
Rivera, Alice Leland de (sic) 216
Rivera, Alice Leland di (sic) 13
Rivers, Caryl 300
Riviere, Joan 169
Rizk, Hanna 367
Robbins, Susan W. 361
Roberts, Elizabeth Madox 34 119
Roberts, Helene E. 223 348 364
Roberts, Joan 21
Roberts, Wayne 295
Robertson, Claire 302
Robie, Edward A. 48
Robin, Stanley S. 166
Robins, Elizabeth 232
Robins, Mary Dreier 319
Robins, Philip K. 40
Robinson, Dorothy 256
Robinson, Emily 72
Robinson, Harriet H. 12 87 336
Robinson, John B. 70
Robinson, Lillian S. 36 88 110 186
Robinson, Lora H. 4
Robinson, Marius 72
Robinson, Mary 234
Robinson, Mary T.W. 312
Robinson, Patricia 26 28 97 132 237
Robles, Mireya 122
Robson, John R.K. 20
Roby, Pamela Ann 4 14 45 45 59 265 328
Roche, Paul 242
Rock, Cynthia 143
Rodgers, Carolyn M. 147 222
Rodriquez-Trias, Helen 156
Roe, Kathy 220
Roeper, Peter J. 146
Roeske, Nancy C.A. 211
Roethke, Theodore 245
Rogers, Janet 325
Rogers, Katharine M. 214 255 299 17
Rogers, Lesley 67
Rogers, Lou 226
Rohrlich-Leavitt, Ruby 19 230 297
Rohrlich-Leavitt, Ruby, see also Leavitt, Ruby R.
Roiphe, Herman 76 199
Rollesson, Clare K. 166
Rollin, Betty 284 362
Romer, Karen T. 271
Romero, Joan Arnold 177 283
Romney, Lenore 362
Ronald, Ann 88
Rook, Clarence 50
Rook, June 8
Rorty, Amelie Oksenberg 369
Rosa, Laura Della, see Della Rosa, Laura
Rosaldo, Michelle Zimbalist 249
Rose, Ernestine L. 44 87 234 237
Rosen, Lawrence 325
Rosen, Marjorie 212
Rosen, Ruth 13 208 342
Rosenbaum, Maj-Britt 211
Rosenberg, Bernard 166
Rosenberg, Miriam 22
Rosenberg, Rosalind 334
Rosenblatt, Aaron 166
Rosenblatt, Jay S. 40
Rosenblatt, Paul C. 67
Rosenblum, Dolores 214
Rosenblum, Leonard A. 199
Rosenblum, Robert 247
Rosenbluth, Vera 304
Rosenfeld, Henry 20
Rosenhan, Mollie Schwartz 318
Rosenkrantz, Paul S. 155 176 250 267
Rosenstone, Robert A. 5
Rosenthal, Bernice Glatzer 19 297
Rosenthal, Carole 256
Rosenthal, Evelyn R. 354
Rosenthal, Jack 284
Rosenthal, Peggy 361
Rosenzweig, Mark R. 202
Rosner, Menahem 176
Ross, Catherine 208

Ross, Heather L. 59
Ross, Ruth 329
Ross, Sinclair 305
Rossetti, Christina 34 189 242 345 374
Rossetti, Dante Gabriel 233 242
Rossi, Alice S. 4 9 13 22 38 65 127 132 139 149 166 171 176 186 190 238 253 271 292
Rossi, Peter E. 171
Rossner, Judith 24
Rostow, Edna 253
Roszak, Betty 132
Roszak, Theodore 132
Rotenberg, Lori 295
Rothbart, Mary K. 250
Rothenberg, Diane 270
Rothman, Barbara Katz 264
Rothstein, Richard 13
Rotkin, Karen F. 22
Rouse, Mary 298
Rousmaniere, John P. 360
Rousseau, Ida Faye 297
Rousseau, Jean Jacques 107 159 203 228 299
Rowbotham, Sheila 89
Rowe, Mary Potter 331
Roy, Gabrielle 305
Roy, Manisha 20
Rozner, Sarah 12
Rubbo, Anna 140 230
Rubenstein, Lenny 288
Rubin, Gayle 89 132 230
Rubin, Isadore 296
Rubin, Jeffrey Z. 22 173
Ruble, Diane N. 171
Ruby, Kathryn 239
Ruddick, Sara 157 158 369
Rudel, Jaufré 299
Ruderman, Florence A. 149
Rudra, Ashok 114
Ruether, Rosemary Radford 177 258 263 278 337
Ruffin, Josephine St. Pierre 28
Rugh, Susan Sessions 215
Ruhland, David 267
Rukeyser, Muriel 3 32 34 72 109 147 239 242 245 248 345 374 375
Rule, Jane 8 113
Rulfo, Juan 279
Rumbarger, Margaret L. 4
Rumiko, Kōra 31
Rumrill, Sarah 69
Rupp, Leila J. 334 349
Rush, Florence 175
Rushing, Andrea B. 222
Rushing, Andrea Benton 7
Rushing, William A. 166
Rusk, Dean 217
Russ, Joanna 16 110 134 144 248 340
Russell-Wood, A.J.R. 121
Russell, Avery 106
Russell, Bertrand 107 159
Russell, Letty M. 210
Russell, Michelle 57 89
Russo, Janet 216
Ruth, Carol 334
Ruth, Sheila 278
Ruthchild, Rochelle Goldberg 126
Rutherford, Dorothea 108
Ryan, Mary P. 35
Rydstedt-Dannstedt, Anna 150
Sabaroff, Nina 8
Sabia, Laura 343
Sachiko, Yoshihara 31
Sachnoff, E.A. 77
Sachs, Albie 348
Sachs, Jacqueline 120
Sachs, Nelly 150
Sack, Allen 286
Sackett, Gene P. 199
Sacks, Karen 216 230 249
Sacks, Michael Paul 318
Sackville-West, Vita 189
Sadoff, Dianne F. 88
Saegert, Susan 143
Safa, Helen Icken 12 194 281
Safer, Jeanne M. 99
Saffioti, Heleieth Iara Bongiovani 194 297
Safilios-Rothschild, Constantina 91 129 258 267 291 354
Sagal, Paul 85
Sagami, Lady 31
Sagarin, Edward 94
Saifullah-Khan, Verity 55
Saiving, Valerie 263
Salaff, Janet 91 307 329
Salager, Annie 46
Salasin, Susan 276
Salazar, Gloria Gonzalez 194
Salem, Ellen 236
Sālih, Saniya 150
Salmon, Lucy 12
Salmon, Marylynn 334 349
Salper, Roberta 74
Saltz, Roslyn 129
Saltzman, Katherine A. 235
Salzman-Webb, Marilyn 186
Salzman, Leon 170
Sampson, Deborah 72
Sampson, Ronald V. 132
Samuels, Catherine 57

Samuels, Victoria 57
Sánchez, Aurelia Guadalupé 297
Sanchez, Sonia 109 109 118 147 222 224 239
Sand, George 87 179
Sandalow, Terrance 180
Sanday, Peggy R. 249
Sandburg, Helga 109
Sandell, Steven H. 328 351
Sander, Helke 97
Sanders, Fran 26
Sanders, Morgan 239
Sandler, Bernice 4 72 291 301 342
Sanger, Margaret 9 12 72 87 139 188
Sanger, William 12
Sangree, Walter H. 285
Sansom, B. 193
Santamaria, Frances Karlen 179
Santos, Fredricka Pickford 202
Santos, Nelly D. 122
Saperstein, David 256
Sapiro, Virginia 140
Sappho 34 81
Sarachild, Kathie 237
Sargent, Amelia 69
Sargent, Dudley A. 152
Sargent, E.N. 147
Sargent, Elizabeth 239
Sargent, Pamela 289 340
Sargent, Shirley 18
Sarkar, Lotika 115
Sarnat, Joan 146
Sarri, Rosemary C. 99
Sarris, Andrew 288
Sarton, May 34 345 347
Sassower, Doris 256
Sauget, Julliette 66
Saunders, Margaret O. 372
Sauter-Bailliet, Theresia 80
Savile, George 187
Savoy, Maggie 284
Sawhill, Isabel V. 45 45 287 291 328 354
Sawyer, Jack 77
Saxon, Isabelle 124
Saxton, Josephine 134
Sayers, Dorothy 103 132
Sayre, Nora 256
Scaife, Joyce 205
Schab, Fred 166
Schaefer, Margaret 76
Schaeffer, Dirk L. 200
Schaeffer, Susan Fromberg 109 239
Schafer, Roy 76
Schafer, Stephen 94 94
Schaldenbrand, Mary Aloysius 62
Schapiro, Miriam 369
Schauer, Nancy R. 94 94
Schein, Virginia Ellen 266
Schemain, Naomi 279
Scheman, Naomi 158
Schenck, C. 199
Schepps, Mollie 12
Scherl, Donald J. 94
Schien, Muriel 186
Schiff, Gert 247
Schiffler, Richard J. 61
Schildkrout, E. 193
Schiller, Lee Chambers 141
Schlafly, Phyllis 280
Schlegel, Alice 20 213
Schlossberg, Nancy K. 129 196 252
Schlozman, Kay Lehman 264
Schmid, Anne McEvoy 208
Schmidt, Dolores Barracano 36 126
Schmidt, Earl Robert 126
Schmidt, Gunter 155
Schmidt, Lorenza Calvillo 347
Schmidt, Steffen W. 329
Schmink, Marianne 194
Schmitt, Raymond 176
Schmuck, Patricia A. 272
Schnall, Susan 216
Schneider, Daniel 325
Schneider, Liz 13 254
Schneiderman, Rose 12 72 234
Schnorrenberg, Barbara B. 335
Schoepf, Brooke Grundfest 297
Scholar, Nancy 212
School Students Union 216
Schopenhauer, Arthur 107 159
Schor, Lynda 24
Schor, Naomi 98
Schouler, William 69
Schram, Donna D. 235
Schramm, Sarah Slavin 174 368
Schrank, Harris T. 287
Schreiner, Olive 32 260
Schroeder, Patricia 364
Schuetz, Stephen 105
Schulder, Diane B. 216
Schultz, Elizabeth 240
Schulz, Muriel 361
Schulz, Patricia 295
Schumacher, Dorin 90 208
Schumer, Florence 99
Schwabacher, Albert E., Jr. 164
Schwartz, Felice N. 314
Schwartz, Pepper 4 342
Schwartz, Rhoda 3
Schweber, Claudine A. 344
Schwendinger, Herman 348
Schwendinger, Julia R. 348

Scott-Maxwell, Florida 179
Scott, Ann 13
Scott, Ann Crittenden 89 152
Scott, Anne Firor 11 151 276
Scott, Dru 6
Scott, Elizabeth L. 301
Scott, Evelyn 179
Scott, Jack 152 358
Scott, Lady John 345
Scott, Marcia 126
Scriven, Michael 62
Scruggs, Otey 178
Scudder, Vida 257
Scully, Diana 39 99
S.C.U.M., see Society to Cut Up Men
Seabury, Florence Guy 139
Seabury, Paul 180
Seaman, Barbara 191
Sears, Cynthia Lovelace 369
Sears, Meg 320
Sears, Pauline S. 13
Secor, Cynthia 271 341
Sedghi, Hamideh 329
Sedgwick, Catharine M. 72
Seese, Linda 132 142
Segal, Sondra 98
Seghers, Anna 102
Seghorn, Theoharis 94
Sehested, Glenda 246
Sei Shōnagon 31
Seiden, Anne M. 99 211
Seiden, Rita 151
Seidenberg, Faith A. 9 228
Seidenberg, Robert 170
Seidman, Ann 21
Seifer, Nancy 57 344
Seifu-Jo, Enomoto 31
Selby, Henry A. 285
Seller, Maxine S. 116
Sellers, Georgianna 12
Sells, Lucy 4
Seltman, Charles 299
Seltzer, Mildred 129
Semmens, James P. 62
Seneca 231
Senesh, Hannah 179
Serbin, Lisa A. 22 156 173
Serceau, Daniel 212
Seretan, L. Glen 93
Servan-Schreiber, Claude 364
Sewall, May Wright 262
Seward, Anna 79
Seward, Georgene H. 206
Sexton, Anne 3 24 34 81 108 109 147 168 224 233 239 248 339 345 363
Sexton, Patricia Cayo 13 89 209
Shaeffer, Ruth G. 291
Shafer, Carolyn M. 85
Shaffer, Helen B. 284
Shaffer, Thomas E. 152 286
Shainess, Natalie 9 216 296
Shakespeare, William 81 228 242
Shallcross, Ruth 12
Shanahan, Eileen 284
Shanley, Mary Lyndon 344
Shao, Fei-Fei 148
Shapiro, David 351
Shapiro, Judith 194
Shapiro, Laura 264
Sharma, Navin 51
Sharma, Ursula 350
Sharpe, Jean 191
Sharpe, Patricia 140
Shatan, Chaim 278
Shaw, Anna Howard 44 72 104 257
Shaw, Ethelrine 45 45
Shaw, George Bernard 68 132 233 310 339
Shaw, Irwin 111 112
Sheets, Robin 278
Sheldon, Raccoona 16
Shelley, Martha 142 216 216 233 237 239
Shelley, Mary 32 119 242
Shelley, Percy Bysshe 242
Shenstone, William 242
Sherfey, Mary Jane 77 170 216 252 296
Sheridan, Helen Selina, Lady Dufferin 345
Sherif, Carolyn Wood 286 171
Sherman, Julia A. 21 173 250 267
Sherwin, Judith Johnson 239
Shevey, Sandra 149
Shields, Emma L. 28
Shields, Stephanie A. 173
Shiffert, Edith Marcombe 345
Shih, Ming 95
Shikishi, Princess 31
Shimada, Noriko 178
Shinedling, Martin M. 250
Shiner, Roger A. 180
Shinn, Thelma J. 47
Shippee, Lester Burrell 128
Shirk, Ethel Jackson 266
Shirome 31
Shively, Charley 8
Shizue, Hatsui 31
Shizuka 31
Shomer, Robert W. 176
Shonagon, Sei 179
Shore, Eleanor G. 211

Shore, Meg 303
Shore, Wilma 353
Short, Clarice 109 245
Shortridge, Kathleen 265
Showalter, Elaine 13 36 175 223 254 357
Showalter, English 223
Shteir, Ann B. 343
Shulman, Alix Kates 89 254
Shulman, Colette 318
Shulman, Gail B. 210
Shultz, Muriel R. 120
Shunzei, Daughter of 31
Shūsei, Tokuda 95
Shushiki, Ōme 31
Shusterman, Lisa Roseman 173
Siassi, Iradj 330
Sibisi, Harriet 281
Sidney, Sir Philip 228 242
Siegel, Claire Lynn Fleet 196
Siegel, Larry 94 94
Siegel, Stanley E. 166
Sigel, Lois 51
Signorelli de Marti, Rosa 324
Sigourney, Lydia Huntley 153
Sigsworth, E.M. 223
Sigusch, Volkmar 155
Silveira, Jeanette 342
Silver, Catherine Bodard 39 42 266
Silverblatt, Irene 270
Silverman, Ellen-Marie 219
Silverman, Sydel F. 230
Silvers, Cleo 13
Silvestri, Philip 180
Silvestrini-Pacheco, Blanca 297
Simmons, Adele 126
Simms, Katherine 312
Simon, Rita James 51 176 267
Simonds, Deborah 129
Simpson, Lawrence A. 197
Simpson, Louis 3
Sims, George R. 50
Sinclair, Andrew 259
Singer, Judith E. 176
Singer, Linda R. 51
Singer, Stanley L. 200
Singer, Susan 94 94
Singh, Andrea Menefee 309
Singham, Lorna Rhodes Amara 316
Singletary, Deborah 256
Sinha, Pratima 114
Sinha, S.N. 206
Sipila, Helvi 352
Sitwell, Edith 34 374
Sizemore, Barbara 364
Skal, Dave 16
Skeen, Anita 109
Skeeter, Sharyn Jeanne 118
Sklar, Kathryn Kish 141 334
Sklar, Roberta 98
Skold, Karen Beck 349
Skultans, Vieda 173
Slack, Eileen N. 75
Slade, Doren L. 297
Slater, J.E. 276
Slatton, Yvonne 64
Slaughter, M. Jane 368
Slesinger, Tess 111
Sloane, P.J. 63
Slocum, Sally 230
Slote, Michael 157
Slotkin, Fran 311
Small, Edwin W. 128
Small, Margaret 123
Small, Miriam R. 128
Smart-Grosvenor, Verta Mae 26
Smart, Barry 348
Smart, Carol 348
Smeal, Eleanor Cutri 316
Smedley, Audrey 131
Smigel, Erwin O. 151
Smith-Rosenberg, Carroll 42 360
Smith, Abby H. 237
Smith, Amanda Berry 27
Smith, Ann 150
Smith, Barbara 353
Smith, Bessie 374
Smith, Catherine F. 214 278 337
Smith, Charles P. 266
Smith, Charlotte 189 345
Smith, Daniel Scott 42 360
Smith, Dorothy E. 251 304
Smith, Elizabeth Oakes 125 237
Smith, Elske V.P. 49
Smith, F. Barry 244
Smith, Garland 226
Smith, Gerrit 234
Smith, Hilda 126
Smith, Jean Wheeler 29 373
Smith, Judith E. 116
Smith, Julia E. 237
Smith, Lee 314
Smith, Lesley Shacklady 348
Smith, Margo L. 71 297
Smith, Marshall P. 197
Smith, Michael 286
Smith, Paul 84
Smith, Ralph E. 371
Smith, Roger 55
Smith, Sarah T. 44
Smith, Sidonie A. 359
Smith, Stevie 189 345
Smock, Audrey Chapman 213

Snare, Annika 348
Snerz, Peggy Ann 183
Snider, Herma L. 72
Snitow, Ann 175
Snow, Eliza R. 346
Snow, Kimberley 265
Snyder, Eloise C. 176
Snyder, Gary 3
Sobol, Marion Gross 370
Society to Cut Up Men 216 233
Södergran, Edith 150
Soeiro, Susan 121
Sogetsu-Ni, Imaizumi 31
Sojourner Truth, see Truth, Sojourner
Solanas, Valerie 132 216 233
Solberg, Don A. 155
Solé, Yolanda Russinovich 219
Solomon, Barbara 123
Solomon, David 2
Solomon, Robert 157
Solovyova, Poliksena 355
Somerville, Rose 70
Sonnett, Sherry 24 220
Sontag, Susan 173 288
Soon, Ching-Ling 307
Soper, Mary 143
Sophocles 339
Sorensen, Janet 61
Sorrells, Helen 109 137 245 345
Soule, John W. 163
Sousa, Noemia da, see da Sousa, Noemia
Souster, Raymond 305
Southerland, Ellease 222
Southgate, Eliza 104 187
Sowell, Thomas 180
Spacks, Barry 245
Spacks, Patricia Meyer 47 359
Spain, Amy 28
Spain, Jayne B. 6
Spake, Amanda 191
Spark, Muriel 273 279 356
Sparks, Elizabeth 12
Sparks, Richard F. 51
Spears, Betty 358
Spector, William D. 371
Speght, Rachel 242 345
Spence, Janet T. 172
Spencer, Anna Garlin 13 44 44 87 234
Spencer, Anne 374
Spencer, Carol 51
Spencer, Herbert 232
Spenser, Edmund 242
Speyer, Leonora 374
Spiegel, Don 200
Spiegel, Frances S. 204
Spiegelman, Robert G. 40
Spiel, Hilde 5
Spillers, Hortense J. 214 222
Spinellis, C.D. 206
Spinks, Sarah 271
Spitz, Rene A. 296
Spivack, Kathleen 109 147 224
Spock, Benjamin 284 292
Spofford, Harriet Prescott 10 119
Spottiswood, Alicia Anne, see Scott, Lady John
Sprafkin, Joyce N. 105
Spring, Anita 317
Springer, Beverly 329
Springer, Marlene 240
Spruill, Julia Cherry 151
Sprung, Barbara 156
Sreenivasan, M.A. 114
Stacey, Judith 35 251
Stack, Carol B. 249
Stadelman, Cate 74
Stadler, Quandra Prettyman 98
Stafford, Frank P. 202
Stafford, Jean 220 245 277
Staines, Graham L. 73 141 266 267 327
Stainton, Rita Tomasallo 137
Stallings, Jane 40
Stamp, Judy 143
Stanbrough, Jane 214
Stanford, Ann 109 111 240 242 245 292 345
Stanley, Julia P. 207 361
Stanley, Margaret P. 80
Stannard, Una 254
Stansell, Christine 360
Stanton, Domna C. 98
Stanton, Elizabeth Cady 9 44 72 74 87 104 153 234 237 257
Stanton, Helen 12
Stanwick, Kathy 344
Stanwyck, Douglas J. 196
Stapleton, Jean 280
Star, Susan Leigh 332
Starer, Ruana 243
Starhawk 263
Starobin, Robert 12
Starr, Rachel R. 327
Stavitsky, Gail 140
Stead, Bette Ann 314
Steady, Filomina Chioma 302
Stearns, Bertha Monica 336
Stearns, Jonathan F. 234
Stearns, Peter N. 223
Stecklein, John E. 166
Steckler, Jane Faggen 196

Stedman, Jane W. 223
Stedman, Louise A. 166
Steele, Zulma 128
Steene, Birgitta 212
Steeves, Edna L. 88
Steffa, Meredith 173
Stefflre, Buford 200 208 271
Stein, Aletha H. 22 266 267
Stein, Gertrude 147 374
Stein, Judy 237
Stein, Robert L. 252
Steinem, Gloria 3 9 127 256 284 362
Steinen, Karl von den 335
Steiner, Stan 233
Steinmann, Anne 196 250 330
Steinson, Barbara J. 183 349
Stembridge, Jane 147
Stendahl, Krister 210
Stent, Angela 341
Stenton, Doris 299
Stephens, Suzanne 303
Stephenson, Marylee 304
Stern, Bernard J. 252
Stern, Daniel N. 199
Stern, Edith M. 234
Stern, Elizabeth Gertrude 104
Stern, G.B. 373
Stern, Joan 76
Stern, Paula 139 233
Sternburg, Janet 224
Sternglanz, Sarah H. 22
Steslick, Gail 137
Stevens, Evelyn P. 71
Stevens, Mary Otis 303
Stevens, May 369
Stevens, Sarah Christie 72 72
Stevens, Wallace 242
Stevenson, Anne 147 357
Stevenson, Mary Huff 202 354
Stewart, Frances 165
Stewart, Joseph, Jr. 174
Stewart, Maria 27 28
Stewart, Mary 368
Stewart, Robert S. 198
Stewart, Vivien 201
Stewart, Walter A. 76
Sticca, Sandro 185
Stiehm, Judith 329
Stillman, Ronni Gordon 122
Stimpson, Catharine R. 90 254 276 278 341 369
Stites, Richard 318
Stivens, Maila 350
Stock, Irvin 192
Stocker, E.S. 77
Stoddard, Susan 40
Stoddart, Jennifer 304
Stoedefalke, Karl 286 286
Stoeltje, Beverly J. 274
Stokes, Gail 26
Stokes, Olivia 114
Stoler, Ann 281
Stoll, C.S. 209
Stoller, Robert J. 76 170 268
Stolte-Heiskanen, Veronica 91
Stone, Ann Gardner 215
Stone, Betsey 86
Stone, Francis 72
Stone, Huldah J. 69
Stone, Kay 274
Stone, Lucy 9 44 72 87 234 237 257
Stone, Luther 72
Stone, Merlin 263
Stone, Pauline Terrelonge 264
Stone, Ruth 147 345
Stone, Sarah 72
Stone, Shirley M. 62
Stone, Susan C. 68
Stone, Sylvia 15
Stoper, Emily 163
Storm, Theodor 279
Storni, Alfonsina 150 313
Storr, Anthony 89
Stowe, Harriet Beecher 72 153 292
Strainchamps, Ethel 254
Strathern, Marilyn 67
Strati, Joan 286
Straus, Murray A. 331
Streatfeild, Guy 289
Strete, Craig 16
Stricker, Frank 360
Strider, Marjorie 15
Strindberg, August 132 310 353
Strobel, Margaret 302
Strober, Myra H. 202 276 291 328
Strom, Sharon Hartman 116
Strommen, Ellen A. 269
Strong-Boag, Veronica 138 304
Strong, Ellen 216
Strongin, Lynn 109 147 216
Stuard, Susan Mosher 315
Stuart, Martha 62
Stuart, Richard B. 99
Stucker, John J. 163 326
Stuers, Vreede-de-, Cora, see Vreede-de-Stuers, Cora
Stupek, Sophie 12
Sturino, Franc 116
Stuyvesant, Elizabeth 226
Su-gil, An 95
Su, Hsiao-Hsaio 148
Sudarkasa, Niara 140 281

Suelzle, Marijean 209 342 362
Sueur, Meridel Le, see Le Sueur, Meridel
Sugnet, Charles J. 341
Suharu, Anryū 31
Sukenick, Lynn 17 147
Sullerot, Evelyne 352
Sumako, Fukao 31
Summerhayes, Martha 124
Summers, Anne 92
Sumner, Charles 44
Sumner, Helen 12
Sun, Tao-Hsüan 148
Sun, Yün-Feng 148
Sundberg, Norman D. 342
Suruma, Lynn 222
Susan, Barbara 127 237
Sute-Jo, Den 31
Suter, Larry E. 39
Sutheim, Susan 81 142 147 216
Sutherland, Elizabeth 127 216
Sutherland, Sandra 94
Sutiasumarga, Rusman 95
Sutton-Smith, Brian 18
Sutton, Constance 213 297
Suwo, Lady 31
Swacker, Marjorie 120 219
Swaminathan, Mina 114
Swanson, Cheryl 174
Swanson, Richard A. 358
Sweet, James A. 287 326
Sweet, Louise E. 131
Swensen, May 109
Swenson, Karen 239
Swenson, May 34 111 147 168 298 345 347
Swiderski, Marie Laure 255
Swidler, Leonard 283
Swift, Jonathan 81 228 242
Swift, Kate 280
Swinburne, Algernon Charles 233 242
Swisshelm, Jane 72
Syfers, Judy 175
Sykes, Barbara 230 297
Sylvis, William 12
Symonds, Alexandra 170 311
Symons, Arthur 373
Synge, John Millington 233 339
Szabady, Egon 91
Szalai, Alexander 289
Szécsi, Margit 150
T'ang, Wan 148
Taeko, Tomoika 31
Taeuber, Karl E. 287
Tafolla, Carmen 353
Taft, Margo 147
Taggard, Genevieve 226 374 346
Tait, G. Thomas 286
Takahashi, Nobuko 352
Takajo, Mitsuhashi 31
Takako, Hashimoto 31
Takamura, Hiroko 178
Talburtt, Margaret A. 140
Talmon, Yonina 252
Tambiah, S.J. 30
Tan, Ying 148
Tancer, Shoshana B. 71
Tangri, Sandra Schwartz 267 291
Tanner, Leslie B. 216 237
Tanner, Nancy 249
Tanzer, Deborah 73
Tappan, Benjamin 72
Tapper, Nancy 325
Tarkington, Booth 241
Tarlton, Hannah 69
Tarry, Ellen 28
Task Force on Family Law and Policy 260
Tatsuko, Hoshino 31
Tatum, Charles M. 122
Tavard, George H. 258
Tavris, Carol 73
Tax, Meredith 74 175
Tayler, Irene 240
Taylor, Anna Marie 212
Taylor, Barbara 225
Taylor, Elizabeth 33 356
Taylor, Lee 166
Taylor, Martin C. 122
Taylor, Paul W. 180
Taylor, Peter 277
Taylor, Rachel Annand 374
Taylor, Susie King 27 28 104
Taylor, Suzanne S. 196
Taylor, William R. 259
Taynor, Janet 266
Teasdale, Sara 34 374
Teather, Lynne 320
Teeples, Mrs. C.A. 124
Teffi, Nadezhda 355
Teijo, Nakamura 31
Temin, Carolyn Engel 51
Tenenbaum, Betsy 278
Tennyson, Alfred, Lord 81 242
Tentler, Leslie W. 140 278
Tentori, Tullio 324
Tepperman, Jean 142 147 216 242 245
Terborg-Penn, Rosalyn 7
Teresa of Avila 34
Terman, Lewis M. 198
Terrell, Mary Church 28
Terry, Megan 161 310

Tessler, Mark A. 325
Testoff, Arthur 166
Tewarson, Heidi 275
Thalberg, Irving 203 282
Thapar, Romila 114
Tharp, Mike 314
Thaxter, C. 103
Theano 231
Theodore, Athena 166
Thériault, Yves 305
Thomas Aquinas, see Aquinas, Thomas
Thomas, John L. 62
Thomas, Keith 299
Thomas, M. Carey 13 60 234 257
Thomas, M. Wynn 52
Thompson, Clara 9 169 170 268 280 296
Thompson, Dorothy 181
Thompson, Jacqueline 314
Thompson, Laura 322
Thompson, Mary Lou 238
Thomson, Judith Jarvis 157 158
Thorne, Barrie 120 183 269
Thornton, Alice 32
Thornton, Naomi 369
Thornton, Sandra 163
Thorpe, JoAnne 358
Thorsell, Siv 37
Throw, Lester C. 333
Thurley, E. 63
Thurley, K. 63
Ticho, Gertrude R. 76
Ticktin, Esther 117
Tidball, Elizabeth 341
Tiedt, Iris M. 13 208
Tieszen, Helen Rose 236
Tiffany, Sharon W. 285
Tiger, Lionel 89 132 149 209 362
Tiger, Virginia 361
Tiller, Per Olav 37
Tillinghast, Elizabeth Sheldon 237
Tillmon, Johnnie 12
Tilly, Louise A. 183
Tilton, Helga 80
Timur, Serim 367
Tinbergen, Niko 198
Ting Ling 245
Tinker, Irene 59 227 293 327
Tinkham, Caroline B. 211
Tiptree, James Jr. 16
Tishler, Sigrid Lemlein 211
Tittle, Carol 13
Tittle, Carol Kehr 196
Tixier y Vigil, Yvonne 219
Tizard, Jack 135
Tobach, Ethel 99 365
Tobias, Sheila 106 190 197 266 271
Tobin, Dianne 204
Tocqueville, Alexis de 187 292
Todd, Gail 224
Todd, John 261
Todorovich, Miro M. 180
Toer, Pramoedya 347
Toer, Pramoedya Ananta 95
Toffler, Alvin 256
Tolbert-Stroud, Sharon 6
Tolstoy, Leo 108 339
Tolstoy, Sophie 179
Tomiko, Yamakawa 31
Tomoko, Fukunaka 31
Toney, Glen O. 45 45
Toomer, Jean 111 112 233 242
Topley, Marjorie 308
Tormey, Judith 282
Torok, M. 78
Torre, Susana 143 303
Torres, Teresa 150
Torrey, Jane W. 314
Toshiko, Takada 31
Trahey, Jane 256
Travis, Toni-Michelle C. 174
Traxler, Patricia 224
Treadway, C. Richard 250
Trebilcot, Joyce 85 159 203
Trecker, Janice Law 13 196 208 271
Treichler, Paula 361
Tresemer, David 14 73 251 266
Trew, Marsha 342
Trible, Phyllis 117 263
Trilling, Diana 253 284
Tripp, Maggie 256
Trofimenkoff, Susan Mann 138
Tröger, Annemarie 12
Troll, Lillian E. 99 129
Tropman, John E. 166
Trotter, Robert J. 280
Trudgill, Peter 120
Trueblood, Mary 12
Trumbo, Sherry Sonnett 175
Truth, Sojourner 9 27 28 44 72 74 87 237 245
Ts'ai, Yen 148
tSaoi, Maire Mhac an, see Mhac an tSaoi, Maire
Tsui, Kity 347
Tsvetayeva, Marina 34 108 150
Tuathaigh, Gearoid Ó, see Ó Tuathaigh, Gearoid
Tubman, Harriet 27 28
Tuchman, Gaye 14 105 328

Tuck, Sarah 28
Tucker, Sylvia 278
Tudor, Jeannette F. 39
Tuéni, Nadia 150
Tuo, Ssu 148
Tuqan, Fadwa 150
Turbin, Carole 334
Turchaninova, Svetlana 352
Turner, Barbara F. 99
Turner, Eileen 166
Turner, Inez 256
Turner, Maureen Finnerty 211
Turner, Ralph H. 166
Tuska, Shirley A. 166
Tussman, Malka Heifetz 150
Tuttleton, James W. 240
Twain, Mark 242
Tweeten, Luther 251
Tyler, Alice Felt 259
Tyler, Anne 375
Tyler, Leona M. 198
Tzu, Yeh 148
U.N. Economic and Social Council/Commission on the Status of Women 266
Udry, J. Richard 266
Uhlman, Thomas M. 368
Uits, Carolee 146
Ukihashi 31
Ullian, Dorothy Z. 67
Ullman, Dorothy Z. 199
Ullmann, Liv 224
Ullrich, Helen E. 213 309
Ulmschneider, Loretta 123
Umansky, Ellen M. 337
Umstead, Elizabeth C. 208
Underwood, Osta 6
Undset, Sigrid 273 279
Unger, Rhoda Kesler 243 250 266
Üngör, Beraët Zeki 294
Union of Women for Association 187
United Nations 107
Updike, John 279
Upton, Harriet Taylor 12
Urdang, Constance 33 109
Uren, Marjorie B. 254
Uribe de Acosta, Ofelia 313
Useem, Betsey 13
Useem, Ruth H. 62
Vadja, Mihaly 252
Vaerting, Mathias 232
Vaerting, Mathilde 232
Vajda, Mihaly 251
Valdes-Cruz, Rosa 122
Valentine, Jean 108
Valian, Virginia 85 369
Vallin, Jacques 367
van Aaken, Ernst, see Aaken, Ernst van
Van Allen, Judith 285 302 316 329
Van De Warker, Ely 1
Van Den Haag, Ernest 363
Van Duyn, Mona 34 109 147 345
Van Etten, Ida M. 72 187
Van Ghent, Dorothy 192
Van Hightower, Nikki R. 368
Van Houten, Donald R. 314
Van Kleeck, Mary 12
Van Lew, Rita 237
van Ophuijsen, J.H.W., see Ophuijsen, J.H.W. van
Van Rensselaer, Gratz 128
van Rensselaer, Maria, see Rensselaer, Maria van
van Vorst, Bessie, see Vorst, Bessie van
Van Wert, William 288
Vanderberg, Steven G. 204
Vanek, Joann 354
Vanistendael, Stefan 54
Vann, Richard T. 19
Varjrathon, Mallica 293
Vasques de Miranda, Glaura 281
Vasquez, Enriqueta Longauex y, see Longauex y Vasquez, Enriqueta
Vassiliou, George 206
Vassiliou, Vasso 206
Vatsyayan, Kapila 114
Vatter, Ethel L. 59
Vatuk, Sylvia 309
Vaughan, Mary C. 44
Vaughn, Laura Lynn 137
Vaughter, Reesa M. 173
Veblen, Thorstein 87 195 234 260
Veevers, J.E. 304
Venning, Corey 329
Verbitskaya, Anastasiya 355
Verbrugge, Lois M. 141
Verdery, Emily 12
Verdier, Philippe 184
Verduin, Rena Rietveld 72
Verene, D.P. 157
Verlinger, Dale E. 122
Veroff, Joseph 267
Vesonder, Timothy G. 68
Vest, George G. 234
Vetterling-Braggin, Mary 282
Vice Commission of Minneapolis 167
Vice Commission of Philadelphia 167
Vickers, Jill 320
Vidal, Isabel Pica 194

Vidal, Mirta 86
Vidlákovâ, Olga 20
Vieille, Paul 325
Vilar, Esther 159
Vinck, Catherine de 108
Vinge, Joan D. 133 134
Vinograd, Julia 109
Vinokur, Diane Kaplan 140
Viorst, Judith 127
Vipond, Mary 138
Virgillo, Carmelo 122
Vives, Juan Luis 299
Vogel, Elaine 352
Vogel, Lise 41 110
Vogel, Susan R. 155 176 208 250 267
Vogel, William 171 250
Vogt, Sally Peters 68
Voigt, Ellen Bryant 353
von den Steinen, Karl, see Steinen, Karl von den
von Le Fort, Gertrud, see Le Fort, Gertrud von
von Raffler-Engel, Walburga, see Raffler-Engel, Walburga von
Vonnegut, Kurt, Jr. 81
Vorse, Mary Heaton 12
Vorst, Bessie van 319
Vreede-de-Stuers, Cora 324
Vroman, Mary Elizabeth 33 112
Vukovic, Isabelle 150
Waber, Deborah P. 172 204
Wadley, Susan S. 281
Wagatsuma, Hiroshi 206
Wagner, N.N. 155
Wagner, Nathaniel N. 155
Wahlstrom, Billie J. 140
Waight, Lavinia 72
Wakoski, Diane 3 34 108 109 111 168 224 245 248
Waldman, Anne 224
Waldman, Elizabeth 252
Waldman, Gloria Feiman 122
Walker, Alexander 288
Walker, Alice 26 29 109 111 112 118 147 239 245 248 279 347 353 369 375
Walker, Anabelle 271
Walker, Lenore E. 235
Walker, Margaret 32 34 109 118 147 222 242 347 353 374 375
Walker, Mary 323
Walker, Sue Sheridan 315
Walker, Tomannie T. 365
Walkowitz, Daniel J. 42
Walkowitz, Judith R. 42 244
Wallace, Cecelia 320
Wallace, Michele 118 239
Wallace, Phyllis A. 48 287 291 333 333
Wallace, Walter L. 166
Wallach, Aleta 290
Waller, Edmund 242
Wallin, Paul 155
Walsh, Ethel Bent 197
Walsh, Francis R. 278
Walsh, Mary Roth 278 332
Walshok, Mary Lindenstein 371
Walstedt, Joyce Jennings 278 364
Walster, Elaine 77 196 197
Walter, Beatrice 147
Walters, Audie Lee 72
Walters, Dorothy 109
Walters, Margaret 181
Walters, Richard H. 198
Walters, Winifred Fields 347
Wang, Bee-Lan Chan 43
Wang, Ch'ing-Hui 148
Wang, Wei 148
Ward, David A. 51
Ward, Ingeborg L. 199
Ward, Jerry D. 222
Ward, Lester Frank 232
Ward, Renee E. 51
Warder, Ann Head 187
Ware, Caroline 41
Ware, Celestine 175
Ware, Helen 91
Ware, Norma C. 264
Warker, Ely Van De, see Van De Warker, Ely
Warmond, Ellen 150
Warner, Lucy A. 12
Warner, Sylvia Townsend 34
Warren, Barbara 81
Warren, Mary Anne 158
Warren, Patricia A. 365
Warren, Rachelle 140
Warrick, Alan E. 163
Warrior, Betsy 175 237
Warshay, Diana Wortman 269
Washbourn, Penelope 263 283
Washington, Margaret Murray 28
Washington, Mary Helen 222
Wasserman, Marlie Parker 68
Wasserstrom, Richard 157 158 217
Water, Christine Croft 215
Waters, Elinor 129
Waters, Mary-Alice 86
Watkins, Bari 341
Watley, Donivan J. 166
Watson, Barbara Bellow 68
Watson, John B 226
Watson, John B. 96

Watt, Barbara Fluckiger 215
Watts, Alan 164
Wax, Ann 146
Way, Peggy Ann 228
W.B.A.I. Consciousness Raising 17
Weatherford, Elizabeth 230 297
Weathers, Mary Ann 237
Webb, Marilyn Salzman 13 142
Webb, Phyllis 136
Webster, Paula 77 230
Wechsberg, Joseph 5
Weddington, Mrs. Henry 28
Wedel, Cynthia C. 6
Weeks, Jeffrey 335
Weg, Ruth 129
Wei, Lady 148
Weidman, Hazel Hitson 322
Weil, Mildred W. 166
Weil, Simone 150
Weimer, Michael 68
Weinbaum, Batya 35
Weiner, Annette B. 270
Weiner, Debra 288
Weiner, Samuel 40
Weinraub, Marsha 199
Weinreich, Helen 205
Weintraub, Rodelle 68
Weintraub, Stanley 68
Weir, Hugh C. 50
Weis, Elisabeth 212
Weisner, Thomas S. 18 331
Weiss, Kay 141 191
Weiss, Michael 300
Weiss, Paul 152
Weissman, Deborah 117
Weissman, Hilda 77
Weissman, Myrna M. 4 99
Weisstein, Naomi 9 73 77 97 127 139 142 175 186 203 216 233 237 254 332 363 369
Weithorn, Corinne J. 250
Weitzman, Lenore J. 4 51 208 251 264 264 301
Wekerle, Gerda R. 143
Welch, Susan 174
Weld, Angelina Grimké, see Grimké, Angelina
Weldon, Fay 356
Weller, Robert H. 70
Welles, Marcia 80
Wellesley, Dorothy 374
Wells-Barnett, Ida 27
Wells, April 220
Wells, Audrey Siess 316
Wells, C. 103
Wells, Robert V. 334
Welsch, Janice 288
Welter, Barbara 9 42 151 292 360
Welty, Eudora 33 34 111 112 113 242 248 279
Wemple, Suzanne F. 19 42 315
Wendlinger, Robert M. 6
Wendt, Ingrid 147
Wenig, Maggie 263
Werle-Einhorn, Juanita L. 354
Werner, Emmy E. 316
Werner, Karla 143
Wert, William Van, see Van Wert, William
Wertheimer, Barbara 344
Wertheimer, Barbara M. 59 264
Wertheimer, Roger 2
West, Candace 120
West, Charlotte 358
West, Dorothy 242
West, Jackie 84
West, Jayne 216
West, Jessamyn 33 34
West, Ray B., Jr. 192
West, W.G. 241
Westchester Radical Feminists 175
Westerman, Marcine P. 146
Weston, Peter J. 176 267
Westphal, Milton 176
Whalen, Richard E. 199
Whaley, Betti S. 45
Whalley, George 305
Wharton, Edith 111 112 279
Wheatley, Phillis 189 345 34 242 374
Wheeler, Elizabeth Hunting 324
Wheeler, Martha 75
Whitbeck, Caroline 282
White, Barbara Ehrlich 247
White, Betty 129
White, Edith 124
White, Elizabeth H. 325
White, Isobel M. 366
White, James J. 166
White, Jean Bickmore 215
White, Josephine Thomas 28
White, Martha E.D. 257
White, Martha S. 264 265
White, Patrick 108
White, Paulette Childress 222
White, Rodney F. 166
White, Sue Shelton 226
White, Terrence H. 304
Whitehead, Ann 55
Whiting, Beatrice 22
Whiting, J.W.M. 198
Whitman, Narcissa 96 187
Whitman, Ruth 109 111 112
Whitman, Walt 81 242

Whitmore, George 8
Whitney, Isabella 345
Whyte, Martin King 140 141
Whyte, William H., Jr. 149
Wickham, Anna 374
Widmann, R.L. 88
Wieber, Wendy 147
Wiegers, Mary 284
Wiegner, Kathleen 136
Wier, Dara 224
Wieser, Nora Jacquez 43
Wiggins, Ella May 12 374
Wilbur, Richard 81
Wilcox, Ella Wheeler 374
Wilcox, Mary 40
Wilde, Oscar 242
Wilder, Cherry 133
Wilhelm, Kate 134 340
Wilkie, Frances 204
Wilkins, David 185
Willard, Charity Cannon 184
Willard, Emma Hart 72 234
Willard, Frances E. 72 152 234 262
Willard, Nancy 109 109
Willett, Roslyn S. 254
Williams, Barbara J. 88
Williams, Bernard 203
Williams, Constance 208
Williams, Delores S. 118
Williams, Drid 154
Williams, Emlyn 339
Williams, Fannie Barrier 27 28 96
Williams, Gurney, III 280
Williams, Helen 26
Williams, Joy 24 220
Williams, Juanita H. 22 266
Williams, Lorna V. 222
Williams, Martha 314
Williams, Marvin 222
Williams, Maxine 9 86
Williams, Raymond L. 122
Williams, Rose 319
Williams, S.A. 118
Williams, Shirley 26
Williams, William Carlos 108 111
Williamson, Nancy E. 173
Williamson, Robert C. 206
Willis, Ellen 237 288
Wilson, Anne 264 264
Wilson, Arthur M. 255
Wilson, Deirdre 348
Wilson, Emma J. 72
Wilson, Ethel 305
Wilson, Frances 320
Wilson, Holly 358
Wilson, Luzena Stanley 124
Wilson, Margo I. 199
Wilson, Patricia 246 283
Wilson, Prince E. 217
Wilson, Suzanne F. 20
Wilson, Victoria 327
Wilson, Woodrow 44
Winant, Fran 136 239
Windham, Donald 108
Winick, Charles 209
Winkel, Gary 143
Winslow, Helen M. 257
Winslow, Mary Bowes 272
Winston, Elizabeth 359
Winter, David 278
Winters, Carol Jean 61
Winthrop, John 234
Wister, Sally 187
W.I.T.C.H., see Women's International Terrorist Conspiracy From Hell
Witing, Beatrice 77
Witke, Roxane 307 308
Witryol, Sam L. 200
Witt, Shirley Hill 77
Witter, Jean 228
Wittig, Michele Andrisin 204
Wittlinger, Ellen 224
Wittstock, Laura Waterman 43
Wohmann, Gabriele 102
Wolcott, Robert W. 128
Wolf, Arthur P. 308
Wolf, Christa 102
Wolf, Margery 249 308
Wolf, Rose de, see de Wolf, Rose
Wolf, Thomas M. 266
Wolfe, Ann 57
Wolff, Robert Paul 282
Wolff, Ruth 144
Wolfgang, Marvin E. 51 94
Wolfgang, Myra 12
Wolfson, Alice 127
Wolfson, Sharon 13
Wolitzer, Hilma 3 24
Wolkoff, Regina L. 141
Wollstonecraft, Mary 32 74 87 107 159 188 228 237 363
Wolman, Benjamin B. 250
Wolowitz, Howard M. 176
Wolpe, AnnMarie 84
Woman, Benjamin B. 243
Women of the American Revolution 216
Women on Words and Images 208
Women Against Daddy Warbucks 216
Women Magazine, staff of 89
Women's Bureau, Dept. of Labor 12 166 251 314

Women's Caucus Within the Youth International Party 216
Women's Caucus, Political Science Dept., University of Chicago 216
Women's Collective, N.Y. High School Students Union 216
Women's International Terrorist Conspiracy From Hell 142 216
Women's Liberation Collective 132
Women's Majority Union, Seattle 216
Wong, Aline K. 91 131
Wong, Diane 77
Wood, Ann Douglas 42 360
Wood, M.R. 309
Wood, Marion M. 314
Wood, Myrna 74 97 132 228 237
Wood, Sally Medora 237
Woodard, Maurice C. 174
Woodhull, Victoria 44 72 87 187
Woodul, Jennifer 89
Woodward, Josephine 257
Woodward, Kenneth 362
Woolf, Virginia 33 34 81 87 113 127 179 233 242 245 248 363
Wordsworth, Dorothy 179 179
Wordsworth, William 81
Worsnop, Richard L. 284
Wortis, Rochelle Paul 296 365
Wright, Benjamin D. 166
Wright, Carroll D. 44
Wright, Celeste Turner 345
Wright, Fanny 72
Wright, Florence S. 12
Wright, Frances 9 87 187 237
Wright, Gwendolyn 143 303
Wright, Judith 345
Wright, Madeleine 140
Wright, Margaret 28
Wright, Marjorie Brown 342
Wright, Martha Coffin 72
Wright, Richard 279
Wright, Sarah E. 118
Wrigley, E.A. 162
Wroth, Mary Sidney 345
Wu, Tsao 148
Wu, Tsê-T'ien 148
Wyke, T.J. 223
Wylie, Elinor 34 147 168 189 245 374
Wylie, Philip 233
Wyman, Lillie B. Chace 262
Wyntjes, Sherrin Marshall 19
Xenophon 231 260
Yamauchi, Wakako 220
Yans-McLaughlin, Virginia 41
Yarbro, Chelsea Quinn 340
Yardley, Jonathan 363
Yarnall, Eliza Coffin 72
Yarshater, Latifeh 324
Yeats, William Butler 81 242
Yee, Carole Zonis 110
Yellis, Kenneth A. 360
Yezierska, Anzia 353
Yishai, Yael 174
Yohalem, Alice M. 48
Yokobue 31
Yolles, Stanley F. 311
Yoon, Soon Young S. 236
Yosami, Wife of Hitomaro 31
Yosano, Akiko 150
Young, Allen 8
Young, Kate 84
Young, Marguerite 273 345
Young, Marilyn 369
Young, Phyllis Brett 305
Young, Stark 288
Young, Virginia Heyer 25
Young, W.F. 69
Youngblood, Sarah 109
Youssef, Nadia H. 281 293 325 329
Yü, Ch'in-Tsêng 148
Yu, Connie Young 369
Yü, Hsüan-Chi 148
Yuan, Ying-Ying 20
Yvonne 224 239
Zacharias, Donald W. 314
Zaldivar, Gladys 122
Zamudio, Adela 313
Zapata, Celia de 122
Zaretsky, Eli 89 251
Zaretsky, Linda 342
Zaturenska, Marya 34 345
Zavala, Iris 122
Zborilova, Jitka 54
Zeiger, L. L. 224
Zellner, Harriet 202
Zelman, Elizabeth Crouch 140
Zelnick, Melvin 155
Zetkin, Clara 87 89
Ziegler, Harmon 166
Ziegler, Susan 286
Zigler, Edward 198
Zikmund, Barbara Brown 337
Zilboorg, Gregory 170
Zimmer, Catherine H. 219
Zimmerman, Don H. 120
Zimmerman, Mary 219
Zimmerman, Toni Ortner 137
Zinn, Maxine Baca 342
Zinnes, Harriet 220
Zinovyeva-Annibal, Lidiya 355
Zitkala-Sä, see Bonnin, Gertrude

5

EDITOR INDEX

This section lists editors of the 375 indexed anthologies. Numbers refer to the book titles in ANTHOLOGIES: TABLES OF CONTENTS.

Acton, Janice 295
Adams, Elsie 233
Adelstein, Michael E. 362
Adler, Freda 51
Agonito, Rosemary 107
Aken, Carol G., Van, see Van Aken, Carol G.
Allen, Sheila 55
Allman, James 367
Altbach, Edith Hoshino 97
Anderson, Scarvia B. 197
Anderson, Susan Janice 16
Anglo, Sydney 52
Archer, John 67
Ardener, Shirley 53 154
Astin, Helen S. 106
Atkinson, Dorothy 318
B. Bunster, Ximena 281
Babcox, Deborah 127
Baines, Barbara J. 229
Baker, Denys Val 356
Baker, Elizabeth C. 15
Baker, Robert 157
Bambara, Toni Cade, see also Cade, Toni
Bankier, Joanna 150
Banner, Lois W. 42
Bardwick, Judith M. 82 176
Barker, Diana Leonard 55
Bass, Ellen 147
Baxandall, Rosalyn 12
Bay, Edna G. 302
Bean, Joan P. 22
Beck, Lois 325
Belkin, Madeline 127
Bell, Roseann P. 222
Bell, Susan G. 299
Benet, James 105
Bereaud, Susan 13
Berg,Stephen 3
Berkin, Carol Ruth 349 334
Bernikow, Louise 374
Biklen, Sari Knopp 272
Bishop, Sharon 158
Blackstone, William T. 217
Blake, Kathryn A. 11
Blaxall, Martha 291
Bleiweis, Linda H. 301
Blum, Harold P. 76
Blumhagen, Kathleen O'Connor 368
Bogin, Ruth 27
Bornstein, Diane 58
Bosmajian, Haig 207 228
Bosmajian, Hamida 228
Bourguignon, Erika 372
Boxer, Marilyn J. 218
Bracey, John H., Jr. 25
Bramsen, Michèle Bo 293
Brannigan, Marilyn B. 272
Bridenthal, Renate 19
Briscoe, Mary Louise 233
Brodsky, Annette M. 75
Brown, Cheryl L. 88
Brown, Donald R. 182
Brownlee, Mary M. 319
Brownlee, W. Elliot' 319
Buhle, Mary Jo 44
Buhle, Paul 44
Bujra, Janet M. 350
Bunch-Weeks, Charlotte 142
Bunch-Weeks, Charlotte, see also Bunch, Charlotte
Bunch, Charlotte 123
Burgess-Olson, Vicky 215
Burghardt, Walter J. 258
Burke, N. Peggy 64
Burman, Sandra 92
Burtle, Vasanti 330
Butturff, Douglas 361
Cade, Toni 26
Cahill, Susan 273
Cahn, Ann Foote 328
Calderwood, Ann 4
Cantor, Milton 41
Caplan, Patricia 350
Caroli, Betty Boyd 116
Carone, Pasquale A. 311
Carroll, Berenice A. 126
Cassirer, Sidonie 80
Cater, Libby A. 276
Change Magazine, editors 341
Chapman, Jane Roberts 59 235 331
Chappell, Duncan 94
Chasseguet-Smirgel, Janine 78
Chetwynd, Jane 205
Christ, Carol P. 263
Cohart, Mary 232
Cooke, Joanne 142
Cooper, James L. 188
Cooper, Sheila McIsaac 188
Cornillon, Susan Koppelman 110
Corrain, Donncha Ò 312
Cott, Nancy F. 187
Cox, Sue 77
Crites, Laura 321 321
Cross, Barbara M. 60
Crouch, Isabel 219
Cummings, Bernice 344
Dahlström, Edmund 37
Dallin, Alexander 318
Daniels, Arlene Kaplan 105
Daniels, Joan 13
Daniels, Pamela 369
De Souza, Alfred 309

Dean, Nancy 113
Delamont, Sara 145
Denmark, Florence L. 243 250 266
DeLamater, John 327
Diamond, Arlyn 10 17
Donovan, Josephine 90
Dreifus, Claudia 191
Duberman, Lucile 100
Dubois, Betty Lou 219
Duffin, Lorna 145
Edwards, Lee R. 10 17
Eisenstein, Hester 98
Eisenstein, Zillah R. 35
Elliott, Carolyn M. 281
Elliston, Frederick A. 157 85
English, Jane 85 203
Epstein, Cynthia 149
Epstein, Laurily Keir 326
Erens, Patricia 212
Etienne, Mona 270
Exum, Pat Crutchfield 118
Fannin, Alice 245
Farber, Seymour 164
Farrer, Claire R. 274
Feinstein, Karen Wolk 371
Ferguson, Mary Anne 111 112
Fidell, Linda S. 327
Fischer, Christiane 124
Fishel, Andrew 196
Folsom, Marcia McClintock 34
Fonda, Michie 135
Foner, Philip S. 69
Fout, John C. 66
Franks, Violet 99 330
Freeman, Jo 264 265
Fremon, Suzanne 280
Fried, Barbara 332
Friedman, Jean E. 151
Friedman, Richard C. 199
Fritz, Paul 255
Gaillard, Dawson 279
Gale, Fay 366
Garskof, Michele Hoffnung 186
Gates, Margaret 235 331
Geadelmann, Patricia L. 64
Geis, Gilbert 94
Geis, Robley 94
George, Carol V.R. 178
Gershuny, H. Lee 207
Gersoni, Diane 208
Ghougassian, Joseph P. 231
Gilbert, Sandra M. 214
Gill, Elaine 136
Ginzberg, Eli 48
Githens, Marianne 163
Glazer-Malbin, Nona 251
Glazer, Nona 252
Golde, Peggy J. 322
Goldsmith, Penny 295
Gomberg, Edith S. 99
Goode, William J. 149
Goodman, Kay 275
Goody, Jack 30
Gordon, Linda 12
Gornick, Vivian 254
Gould, Carol C. 282
Goulianos, Joan 32
Grant, Christine 64
Gross, Barry R. 180
Grumman, Joan 248
Gubar, Susan 214
Gullahorn, Jeanne E. 172
Guy-Sheftall, Beverly 222
Hafkin, Nancy J. 302
Hageman, Alice L. 210
Hahner, June E. 313
Hall, James 347
Hamalian, Leo 220
Hamalian, Linda 220
Hammer, Signe 296
Hammond, Nancy 269
Harkess, Shirley 354
Harley, Sharon 7
Harney, Robert F. 116
Harris, Dorothy V. 286
Hart, Donn Vorhis 221
Hartman, Mary 42
Hartnett, Conagh 205
Harvard Divinity School, Women's Caucus of, see Women's Caucus of Harvard Divinity School
Hatch, James 161
Hatch, Victoria 161
Henifin, Mary Sue 332
Henley, Nancy 120
Hepperle, Winifred 321
Hermey, Carl W. 46
Heslep, Robert D. 217
Hess, Thomas B. 15 247
Hesse, Myra 305
Hiller, Dana V. 278
Hirsch, Werner Z. 106
Hoch-Smith, Judith 317
Hoepner, Barbara J. 358
Hoffman, Lois Wladis 267 370
Hoffman, Nancy 353
Hogeland, Ronald W. 292
Hottel, Althea K. 294
Howard, Maureen 192
Howe, Florence 147 290 353
Hubbard, Ruth 332
Huber, Joan 39
Iglitzin, Lynne B. 329
Israel, Joan 129

Israel, Kenneth 129
Iverson, Lucille 239
Jacobus, Mary 357
Jaggar, Alison M. 89
Jain, Devaki 114
Jaquette, Jane S. 316
Jardine, Alice 98
Jay, Karla 8
Jelinek, Estelle 359
Jenness, Linda 86
Johnson, Walter D. 368
Jones, Nancy J. 347
Jongeward, Dorothy 6
Kaminski, Margaret 137
Kanner, Barbara 335
Kanter, Rosabeth Moss 14
Kaplan, Alexandra G. 22
Kaplan, Cora 189
Katz, Esther 360
Katz, Naomi 95
Kay, Karyn 288
Keddie, Nikki 325
Kidd, Virginia 133
Kieffer, Sherman N. 311
Kirkpatrick, Martha 18
Kirschner, Linda Heinlein 34
Koedt, Anne 175
Koltun, Elizabeth 117
Konek, Carol 109
Koon, Helene 79
Koonz, Claudia 19
Kopp, Claire B. 18
Kostman, Samuel 339
Kraditor, Aileen S. 234
Kreps, Juanita 287
Kriegel, Harriet 310
Krinsky, Leonard W. 311
Kuhn, Annette 84
Kupinsky, Stanley 91
La Fontaine, J. S. 193
Labalme, Patricia H. 23
Lamphere, Louise 249
Lapidus, Gail Warshofsky 318
Laurie, Bruce 41
Lavin, Mildred H. 246
Lavrin, Asunción 121
LaMond, Annette M. 333
Leacock, Eleanor 270
Lebra, Joyce 306
Lee, Patrick 198
Leppaluoto, Jean Ramage 342
Lerner, Gerda 28 72
Levine, Ellen 175
Lewin, Arie Y. 301
Lewis, Gogo 103 119
Lifshin, Lyn 224
Lifton, Robert Jay 253
Lin Chung 148
Lindsay, Beverly 43
Lipshitz, Susan 225
Liu, William T. 2 62
Lloyd, Barbara 67
Lloyd, Cynthia B. 202
Loewenberg, Bert James 27
Lovett, Clara M. 349
Lukens, Rebecca 245
Lussier, Virginia Lee 364
Mac Curtain, Margaret 312
Maccia, Elizabeth Steiner 271
Maccoby, Eleanor E. 56
Mahl, Mary R. 79
Mahowald, Mary Briody 159
Malbin, Nona, see Glazer-Malbin, Nona and Glazer, Nona
Manier, Edward 2
Manley, Seon 103 119
Mann, Catherine 245
Marks, S.J. 3
Martin, Wendy 9
Matheson, Gwen 320
Matthiasson, Carolyn J. 131
Mattielli, Sandra 236
McAllester, Susan 36
McAlpin, Michelle 281
McBee, Mary Louise 11
McGuigan, Dorothy G. 140 141 183 190
McIntyre, Vonda N. 16
McLaughlin, Eleanor 337
Mednick, Martha Tamara Shuch 267
Meier, August 25
Merriam, Eve 104
Meyer, Annie Nathan 262
Michel, Andrée 70
Middleton, Lucy 323
Miller, Jean Baker 170
Miller, Sally M. 93
Miller, Yvette E. 122
Millman, Marcia 14
Milton, Nancy 95
Mitchell, Juliet 181
Moffat, Mary Jane 179
Moore, Honor 144
Moran, Barbara 254
Morewedge, Rosemarie Thee 184
Morgan, Robin 142 216
Morley, David 143
Morton, Richard 255
Mortyna, Wendy 276
Mosier, John 279
Moskowitz, Samuel 241
Moss, Peter 135
Mott, Frank L. 351
Murray, Michele 108

Myron, Nancy 123
Nadelson, Carol C. 211
Nanda, B.R. 115
Nash, June 194
Nilsen, Alleen Pace 207
Niphuis-Nell, Marry 54
Nochlin, Linda 247
Norton, Mary Beth 334
Notman, Malkah T. 211
Nye, F. Ivan 370
O'Barr, Jean 227
O'Neill, William L. 257
Oakley, Ann 181
Oleson, Clara H. 246
Olson, Karen 88
Osipow, Samuel 61
Pachmuss, Temira 355
Painter, Charlotte 179
Pala, Achola O. 281
Palley, Marian Lief 174
Papanek, Hanna 281
Parish, Margaret 245
Parker, Bettye J. 222
Parker, Gail 153
Parsons, Jacquelynne E. 171
Patai, Raphael 324
Paulme, Denise 338
Paulson, Joy 306
Pearson, Carol 242
Peary, Gerald 288
Pescatello, Ann 71
Peters, Barbara 57
Petersen, Anne C. 204
Peterson, Rebecca 143
Pettman, Barrie O. 63
Pival, Jean G. 362
Plaskow, Judith 263 283
Pope, Katherine 242
Pottker, Janice 196
Powers, Elizabeth 306
Prentice, Alison 138
Prestage, Jewel L. 163
Preston, Michael B. 174
Psychology Today, editors of 73
Quataert, Jean H. 218
Quennell, Peter 5
Rabinowitz, Clara 365
Radcliffe-Umstead, Douglas 185
Rainey, Carol 168
Ramaley, Judith A. 49
Ranum, Orest 162
Ranum, Patricia 162
Raphael, Dana 20
Rapone, Anita 175 360
Reagan, Barbara 291
Reeves, Nancy 260
Reische, Diana 284
Reit, Ann 373
Reiter, Rayna R. 230
Reverby, Susan 12
Rexroth, Kenneth 31 148
Richart, Ralph M. 199
Riemer, Eleanor S. 66
Roberts, Joan 21
Robins, Philip K. 40
Rohrlich-Leavitt, Ruby 297
Romero, Joan Arnold 283
Rosaldo, Michelle Zimbalist 249
Rosenberg, Charles 1 130
Rosoff, Betty 101
Ross, Ruth 329
Rossi, Alice S. 4 65
Roszak, Betty 132
Roszak, Theodore 132
Rotter, Pat 24
Ruby, Kathryn 239
Ruddick, Sara 369
Rudwick, Elliott 25
Ruether, Rosemary Radford 337 177
Ruitenbeek, Hendrick M. 169
Rutschi-Herrmann, E. 102
Safa, Helen Icken 194 281
Salper, Roberta 74
Samuels, Victoria 57
Sanders, Ruth H. 275
Sargent, Pamela 134 340
Schaeffer, Dirk L. 200
Schlegel, Alice 213
Schneiderman, Beth K. 33
Schneir, Miriam 87
Schuck, Victoria 344
Scott, Anne Firor 276
Scott, Dru 6
Segnitz, Barbara 168
Sellin, Thorsten 294
Seward, Georgene H. 206
Shade, William G. 151
Sheets, Robin Ann 278
Shepard, Bonnie 295
Showalter, Elaine 226 363
Simon, Rita James 51
Slatton, Yvonne 64
Slung, Michelle B. 50
Smart, Barry 348
Smart, Carol 348
Smart, William 277
Smith-Rosenberg, Carroll 1 130
Sochen, June 139
Solomon, David 2
Souza, Alfred De, see De Souza, Alfred
Spacks, Patricia Meyer 47
Spinner, Stephanie 83
Spitz, E. Huttenmaier 102

Spring, Anita 317
Springer, Marlene 240
Sprung, Barbara 156
Stacey, Judith 13
Stanford, Ann 345
Stanley, Julia P. 207
Stark, Myra 113
Stead, Bette Ann 314
Stein, Leon 96 128
Stephenson, Marylee 304
Stern, Lenore O. 199
Sternburg, Janet 375
Stewart, Robert Sussman 198
Stimpson, Catharine R. 281
Stoll, Clarice Stasz 209
Streatfeild, Guy 289
Stromberg, Ann H. 354
Strouse, Jean 268
Struhl, Paula Rothenberg 89
Stuard, Susan Mosher 315
Stuart, Martha 62
Sudarkasa, Niara 281
Sutherland, Janet R. 347
Tambiah, S.J. 30
Tangri, Sandra Schwartz 267
Tanner, Leslie B. 237
Tatum, Charles M. 122
Tavris, Carol 73
Teitelbaum, Michael S. 201
Terborg-Penn, Rosalyn 7
Theodore, Athena 166
Thompson, Mary Lou 238
Thorne, Barrie 120
Tiffany, Sharon W. 285
Tinker, Irene 293
Tobach, Ethel 101
Tomasi, Lydio F. 116
Torre, Susana 303
Tripp, Maggie 256
Trofimenkoff, Susan Mann 138
Troll, Lillian E. 129
Trusky, Thomas 346
Tuchman, Gaye 105
Twin, Stephanie L. 152
Unger, Rhoda Kesler 250
Vande Wiele, Raymond L. 199
Vetterling-Braggin, Mary 85
Vicinus, Martha 223 244
Waehrer, Helen Youngelson 251 252
Wagner, Nathaniel N. 155
Wallace, Phyllis A. 333
Walstedt, Joyce Jennings 364
Walters, Dorothy 109
Warren, Barbara 81
Wartofsky, Marx W. 282
Washington, Mary Helen 29
Wasserman, Elga 301
Webber, Jeanette 248
Weiner, Samuel 40
Weintraub, Rodelle 68
Weinzweig, Marjorie 158
Wekerle, Gerda R. 143
Wellesley Editorial Committee 281
Welter, Barbara 259
Wesner, Robert W. 266
West, Uta 300
Williams, Juanita H. 173
Williamson, Robert C. 206
Wilson, Roger L. 164
Witke, Roxane 281 308
Wittig, Michele A. 204
Wolf, Margery 308
Wolpe, AnnMarie 84
Women's Caucus of Harvard Divinity School 210
Wortis, Helen 365
Yohalem, Alice M. 48
Yokkes, Stanley F. 311
Young, Allen 8
Young, Marilyn B. 307
Zaremba, Eve 165

ABOUT THE COMPILER

SUSAN CARDINALE is a reference librarian at the University of Maryland, College Park. A specialist in Women's Studies, she currently is preparing a reference guide to materials by and about women of seventeenth-century England.